W9-DFR-611

THE WORLD BOOK
ATLAS

World Book, Inc.
a Scott Fetzer company
Chicago

THE WORLD BOOK ATLAS

Introductory Section

Index Map	iv-v
How to Use the Atlas	vi-vii
Time Zone Map	viii
Legend	1

Maps

World	**2-5**
World, Political	2-3
World, Physical	4-5
Europe	**6-29**
Europe, Political	6-7
Northern Europe and Scandinavia	8-9
Baltic Regions and Moscow	10-11
British Isles	12-13
Northern France, Belgium, and the Netherlands	14-15
Germany, Czech Republic, Slovakia, and Poland	16-17
Southern France and Switzerland	18-19
Spain and Portugal	20-21
Northern Italy, Austria, and the Balkans	22-23
Southern Italy	24-25
Hungary, Serbia and Montenegro, Romania, and Bulgaria	26-27
Greece and Western Turkey	28-29

Asia	**30-59**
Asia, Political	30-31
Northwestern Asia	32-33
Northeastern Asia	34-35
China, Korea, and Japan	36-37
Japan, Korea, and Northeastern China	38-39
Central and Southern Japan	40-41
Eastern China	42-43
Southeast Asia	44-45
Southern Asia	46-47
Myanmar, Thailand, and Singapore	48-49
Borneo, Java, and Sumatra	50-51
Philippines	52
Southern India	53
Northern India	54-55
Southwestern Asia	56-57
Israel, Lebanon, and Jordan	58-59
Africa	**60-71**
Africa, Political	60-61
Northeastern Africa	62-63
Northwestern Africa	64-65
Central Africa	66-67
Southern Africa	68-69
South Africa	70-71

The World Book Atlas
Published in 2006 by World Book, Inc.

World Book, Inc.
233 N. Michigan Avenue
Chicago, IL 60601

© 2006 by Rand McNally and Company

WORLD BOOK and the GLOBE DEVICE are registered trademarks or trademarks of World Book, Inc.

ISBN: 0-7166-2655-1
LC: 2005938030

3 4 5 6 7 10 09 08 07 06

For information about other World Book publications, visit our Web site **http://www.worldbook.com** or call **1-800-WORLDBK (967-5325).** For sales to schools and libraries call **1-800-975-3250 (United States); 1-800-837-5365 (Canada).**

This Atlas is also published under the title **The World Atlas**
© 2006 Rand McNally and Company

5.449

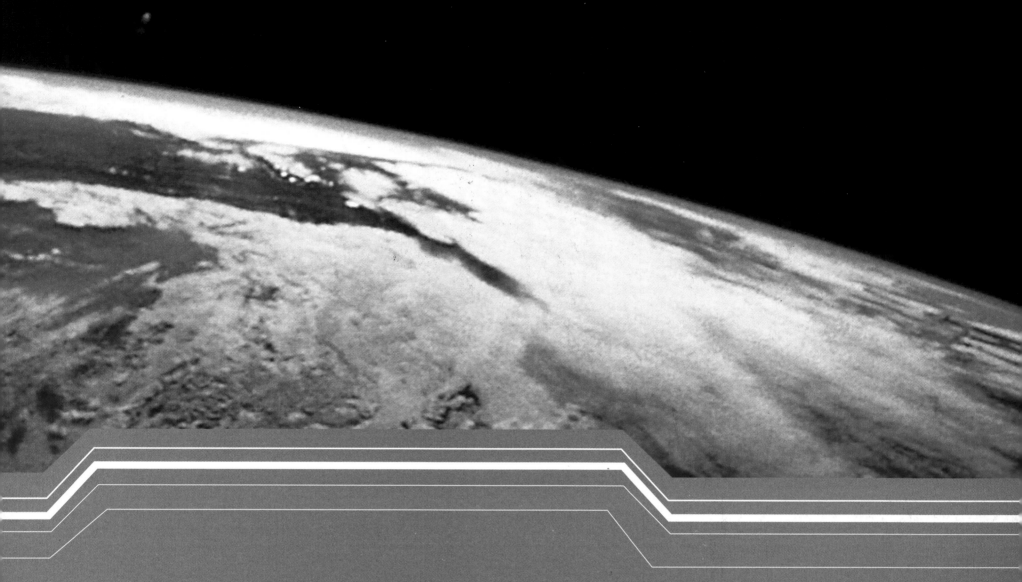

Australia and Oceania	**72-80**
Australia and Oceania, Political	72-73
Australia	74-75
Southeastern Australia	76-77
Islands of the Pacific	78-79
New Zealand	80
Antarctica	**81**
South America	**82-93**
South America, Political	82-83
Northern South America	84-85
Venezuela and Colombia	86-87
Eastern Brazil	88-89
Southern South America	90-91
Central Argentina and Chile	92-93
North America	**94-141**
North America, Political	94-95
Mexico, Central America, and the Caribbean	96-97
Northwestern Mexico and Southwestern United States	98-99
Central Mexico	100-101
Central America	102-103
Islands of the Caribbean	104-105
Canada	106-107

United States	108-109
Northeastern United States and Southeastern Canada	110-111
Great Lakes	112-113
Central Atlantic States	114-115
Southeastern United States	116-117
Northern Midwest	118-119
Midwest	120-121
Mississippi Delta	122-123
Northern Great Plains	124-125
Central Great Plains	126-127
Southern Great Plains	128-129
Southern Texas	130-131
Arizona and Utah	132-133
California, Nevada, and Hawaii	134-135
Northwestern United States	136-137
Southwestern Canada	138-139
Alaska and the Aleutians	140
Greenland	141
Oceans	**142-144**
Pacific and Indian Oceans	142-143
Atlantic Ocean	144
Index	
Index to the Reference Maps	I•1-I•64

Cover photo credits:
Jacques Descloitres, MODIS Land Rapid Response Team/NASA/GSF; © Art Wolfe, Getty Images; NASA/GSFC and U.S. Japan ASTER Science Team

Cover design:
Norman Baugher

About the cover

The large photograph on the cover of The World Book Atlas features one of Earth's most identifiable shapes—the boot-shaped peninsula occupied by Italy. This peninsula extends into the Mediterranean Sea from southern Europe.

Italy also includes two large islands, Sicily and Sardinia. Sicily, which lies to the west of the boot's tip, is home to Mount Etna, one of the most famous volcanoes in the world. Etna rises on the eastern coast of the island. The volcano's eruptions, which have

occurred periodically for thousands of years, are spectacular sights. As seen in the center inset photo, huge fiery clouds rise over the mountain, and glowing rivers of lava flow down its sides.

The inset photo on the bottom right is an ASTER (Advanced Spaceborne Thermal Emission and Reflection Radiometer) image of a sulfur dioxide plume that originated from Etna's summit. The plume, shown in reddish-purple in this view from space, drifts over the city of Catania and continues over the Ionian Sea.

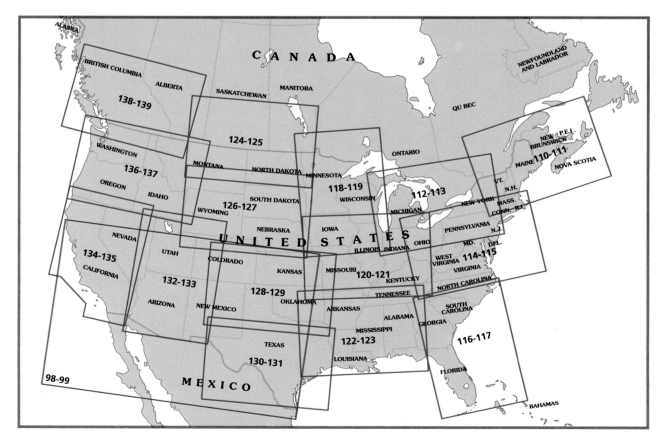

Index Map

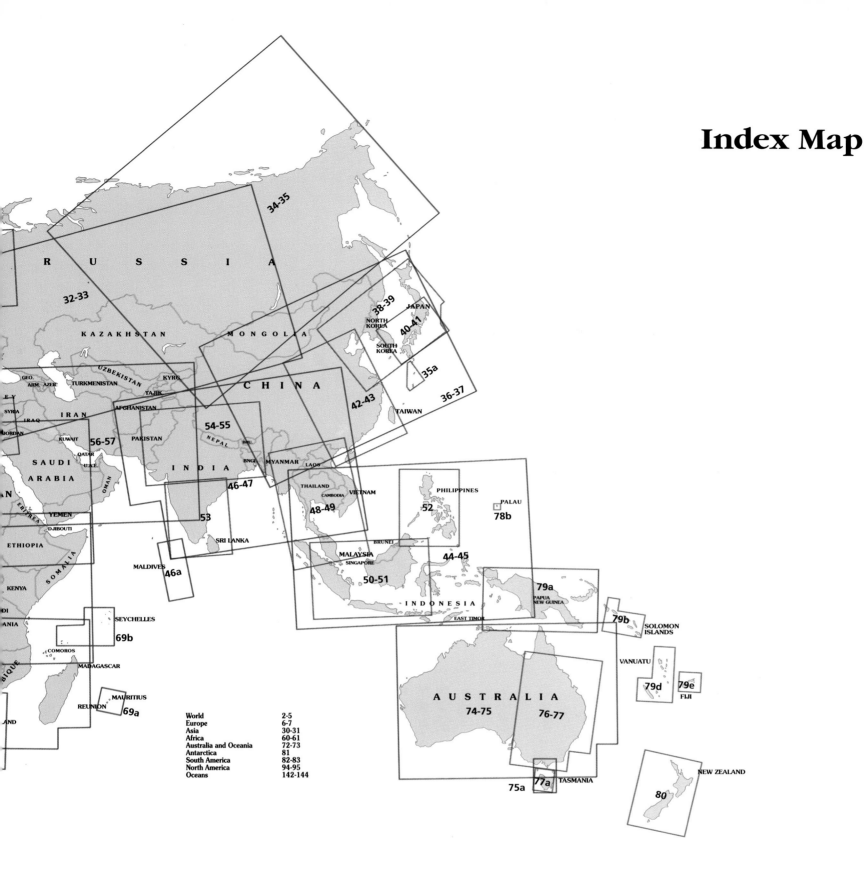

34-35

R   U   S   S   I   A

32-33

KAZAKHSTAN

MONGOLIA

38-39
NORTH KOREA
JAPAN
40-41
SOUTH KOREA

GEO.
ARM. AZER.
SYRIA
IRAQ
JORDAN
IRAN

UZBEKISTAN
TURKMENISTAN
TAJIK.
AFGHANISTAN

KYRG.

C   H   I   N   A

42-43

35a

TAIWAN

36-37

KUWAIT
QATAR
U.A.E.

56-57

PAKISTAN

54-55

NEPAL
BHU.

SAUDI ARABIA

OMAN

INDIA

46-47

BNG.
MYANMAR
LAOS

YEMEN
DJIBOUTI

53

THAILAND
CAMBODIA
VIETNAM

48-49

PHILIPPINES

52

PALAU

78b

ETHIOPIA

SRI LANKA

MALDIVES

46a

BRUNEI
MALAYSIA
SINGAPORE

44-45

SOMALIA

KENYA

SEYCHELLES

69b

COMOROS
MADAGASCAR

50-51

INDONESIA

EAST TIMOR

79a

PAPUA NEW GUINEA

79b

SOLOMON ISLANDS

MAURITIUS
REUNION

69a

VANUATU

79d

79e
FIJI

A   U   S   T   R   A   L   I   A

74-75

76-77

World	2-5
Europe	6-7
Asia	30-31
Africa	60-61
Australia and Oceania	72-73
Antarctica	81
South America	82-83
North America	94-95
Oceans	142-144

75a

77a
TASMANIA

NEW ZEALAND

80

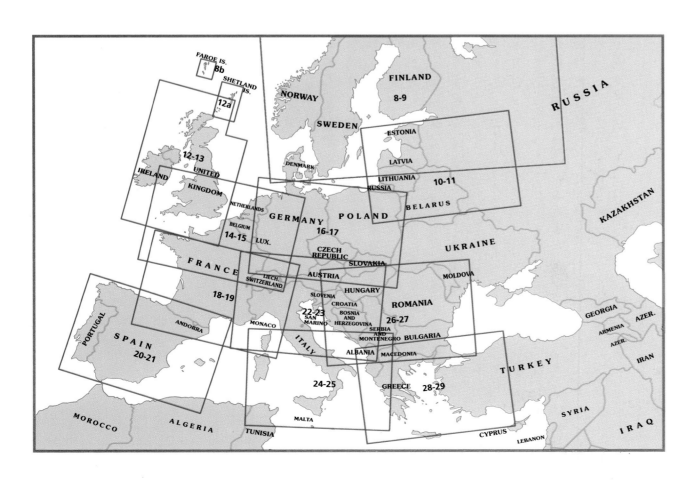

FAROE IS.
8b
SHETLAND IS.
12a

FINLAND

8-9

NORWAY

RUSSIA

SWEDEN

ESTONIA

12-13

IRELAND
UNITED KINGDOM

DENMARK

LATVIA

LITHUANIA
RUSSIA

10-11

NETHERLANDS
BELGIUM
LUX.

GERMANY

POLAND

BELARUS

16-17

14-15

CZECH REPUBLIC
SLOVAKIA

UKRAINE

FRANCE

LIECH.
SWITZERLAND

AUSTRIA

HUNGARY

MOLDOVA

18-19

SLOVENIA
CROATIA

ROMANIA

26-27

PORTUGAL

ANDORRA

MONACO

22-23
SAN MARINO

BOSNIA AND HERZEGOVINA

SERBIA AND MONTENEGRO

GEORGIA

ARMENIA
AZER.
AZER.

SPAIN

20-21

ITALY

ALBANIA

BULGARIA

MACEDONIA

TURKEY

IRAN

24-25

GREECE

28-29

MOROCCO

ALGERIA

TUNISIA

MALTA

CYPRUS

SYRIA

LEBANON

IRAQ

KAZAKHSTAN

How to use the atlas

What is an Atlas?

A set of maps bound together is called an atlas. Abraham Ortelius's *Theatrum orbis terrarum*, published in 1570, is considered to be the first modern "atlas," although it was not referred to as such for almost 20 years. In 1589, Gerardus Mercator coined the term when he named his collection of maps after Atlas, the mythological Titan who carried Earth on his shoulders as punishment for warring against Zeus. Since then, the definition of "atlas" has been expanded, and atlases often include additional geographic information in diagrams, tables, and text.

Latitude and Longitude

The terms "latitude" and "longitude" refer to the grid of horizontal and vertical lines found on most maps and globes. Any point on Earth can be located by its precise latitude and longitude coordinates.

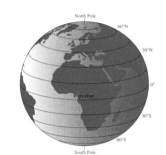

figure 1

The imaginary horizontal line that circles Earth halfway between the North and South poles is called the equator; it represents 0° latitude and lies 90° from either pole. The other lines of latitude, or parallels, measure distances north or south from the equator *(figure 1)*. The imaginary vertical line that measures 0° longitude runs through the Greenwich Observatory in the United Kingdom and is called the prime meridian. The other lines of longitude, or meridians, measure distances east or west from the prime meridian *(figure 2)*, up to a maximum of 180°. Lines of latitude and longitude cross each other, forming a grid *(figure 3)*.

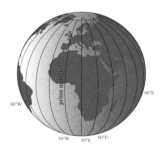

figure 2

figure 3

Map Projections

Every cartographer is faced with the problem of transforming the curved surface of Earth onto a flat plane with a minimum of distortion. The systematic transformation of locations on Earth (a spherical surface) to locations on a map (a flat surface) is called projection.

It is not possible to represent on a flat map the spatial relationships of angle, distance, direction, and area that only a globe can show faithfully. As a result, projections inevitably involve some distortion. On large-scale maps representing a few square miles, the distortion is generally negligible. But on maps depicting large countries, continents, or the entire world, the amount of distortion can be significant. On maps which use the Mercator projection *(figure 4)*, for example, distortion increases with distance from the equator. Thus the island of Greenland appears larger than the entire continent of South America, although South America is in fact nine time larger. In contrast, the Robinson projection *(figure 5)* renders the world's major land areas in generally correct proportion to one another, although distortion is still apparent in areas such as Antarctica, which is actually smaller than all of the continents except Europe and Australia.

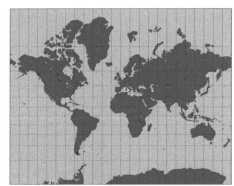

figure 4

figure 5

There are an infinite number of possible map projections, all of which distort one or more of the characteristics of the globe in varying degrees. The projection that a cartographer chooses depends on the size and location of the area being projected and the purpose of the map. In this atlas, most of the maps are drawn on projections that give a consistent or only slightly distorted area scale, good land and ocean shape, parallels that are parallel, and as consistent a linear scale as possible throughout the projection.

Map Scale

The scale of a map is the relationship between distances or areas shown on the map and the corresponding distances or areas on Earth's surface. Large-scale maps show relatively small areas in greater detail than do small-scale maps, such as those of individual continents or of the world.

There are three different ways to express scale. Most often scale is given as a fraction, such as 1:10,000,000, which means that the ratio of distances on the map to actual distances on Earth is 1 to

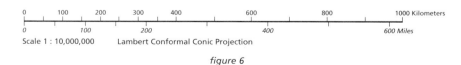

Scale 1 : 10,000,000 Lambert Conformal Conic Projection

figure 6

10,000,000. Scale can also be expressed as a phrase, such as "One inch represents approximately 10 million miles." Finally, scale can be illustrated via a bar scale on which various distances are labeled *(figure 6)*. Any of these three scale expressions can be used to calculate distances on a map.

Measuring Distances

Using a bar scale, it is possible to calculate the distance between any two points on a map. To find the approximate distance

between São Paulo and Rio de Janeiro, Brazil, for example, follow these steps:

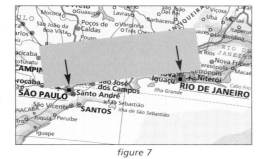

figure 7

1) Lay a piece of paper on the right-hand page of the "Eastern Brazil" map found on pages 88-89, lining up its edge with the city dots for São Paulo and Rio de Janeiro. Make a mark on the paper next to each dot (figure 7).

2) Place the paper along the scale bar found below the map, and position the first mark at 0. The second mark falls about a quarter of the way between the 200-mile tick and the 300-mile tick, indicating that the distance separating the two cities is approximately 225 miles (figure 8).

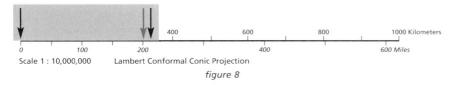

Scale 1 : 10,000,000   Lambert Conformal Conic Projection

figure 8

3) To confirm this measurement, make a third pencil mark (shown in red in figure 8) at the 200-mile tick. Slide the paper to the left so that this mark lines up with 0. The Rio de Janeiro mark now falls about halfway between the 0 tick and the 50-mile tick. Thus, São Paulo and Rio de Janeiro are indeed approximately 225 (200 + 25) miles apart.

Using the Index to Find Places

One of the most important purposes of an atlas is to help the reader locate cities, towns, and geographic features such as rivers, lakes, and mountains. This atlas uses a "bingo key" indexing system. In the index, found on pages I•1 through I•64, every entry is assigned an alpha-numeric code that consists of a letter and a number. This code relates to the red letters and numbers that run along the perimeter of each map. To locate places or features, follow the steps outlined in this example for the city of Bratsk, Russia.

1) Look up Bratsk in the index. The entry (figure 9) contains the following information: the place name (Bratsk), the name of the country (Russia) in which Bratsk is located, the map reference key

Brassey, Banjaran, mts.,		
Malay	A10	50
Brass Islands, is., V.I.U.S.	o7	104 b
Brasstown Bald, mtn., Ga.,		
U.S.	B2	116
Bratca, Rom.	C9	26
Bratislava, Slov.	H13	16
Bratislava, state, Slov.	H13	16
Bratsk, Russia	C18	32
Bratskoe vodohranilisce,		
res., Russia	C18	32

figure 9

(C18) that corresponds to Bratsk's location on the map, and the page number (32) of the map on which Bratsk can be found.

2) Turn to the Northwestern Asia map on pages 32-33. Look along either the

left- or right-hand margin for the red letter "C"—the letter code given for Bratsk. The "C" denotes a band that arcs horizontally across the map, between the grid lines representing 55° and 60° North latitude. Then, look along either the top or bottom margin for the red number "18"—the numerical part of the code given for Bratsk. The "18" denotes a widening vertical band, between the grid lines representing 100° and 105° East longitude, which angles from the top center of the map to right-hand edge.

3) Using your finger, follow the horizontal "C" band and the vertical "18" band to the area where they overlap. Bratsk lies within this overlap area.

Physical Maps and Political Maps

Most of the maps in the atlas are physical maps (figure 10) emphasizing terrain, landforms, and elevation. Political maps, as in figure 11, emphasize countries and other political units over topography. The atlas includes political maps of the world and each of the continents except Antarctica.

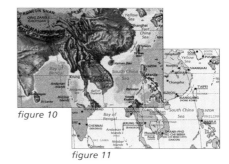

figure 10

figure 11

How Maps Show Topography

The physical maps in this atlas use two techniques to depict Earth's topography. Variations in elevation are shown through a series of colors called hypsometric tints. Areas below sea level appear as a dark green; as the elevation rises, the tints move successively through lighter green, yellow, and orange. Similarly, variations in ocean depth are represented by bathymetric tints. The shallowest areas appear as light blue; darker tints of blue indicate greater depths. The hypsometric/bathymetric scale that accompanies each map identifies, in feet and meters, all of the elevation and depth categories that appear on the map. Principal landforms, such as mountain ranges and valleys, are rendered

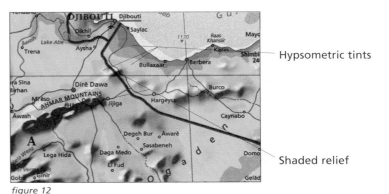

Hypsometric tints

Shaded relief

figure 12

in shades of gray, a technique known as shaded relief. The combination of hypsometric tints and shaded relief provides the map reader with a three-dimensional picture of Earth's surface (figure 12).

Time Zone Map

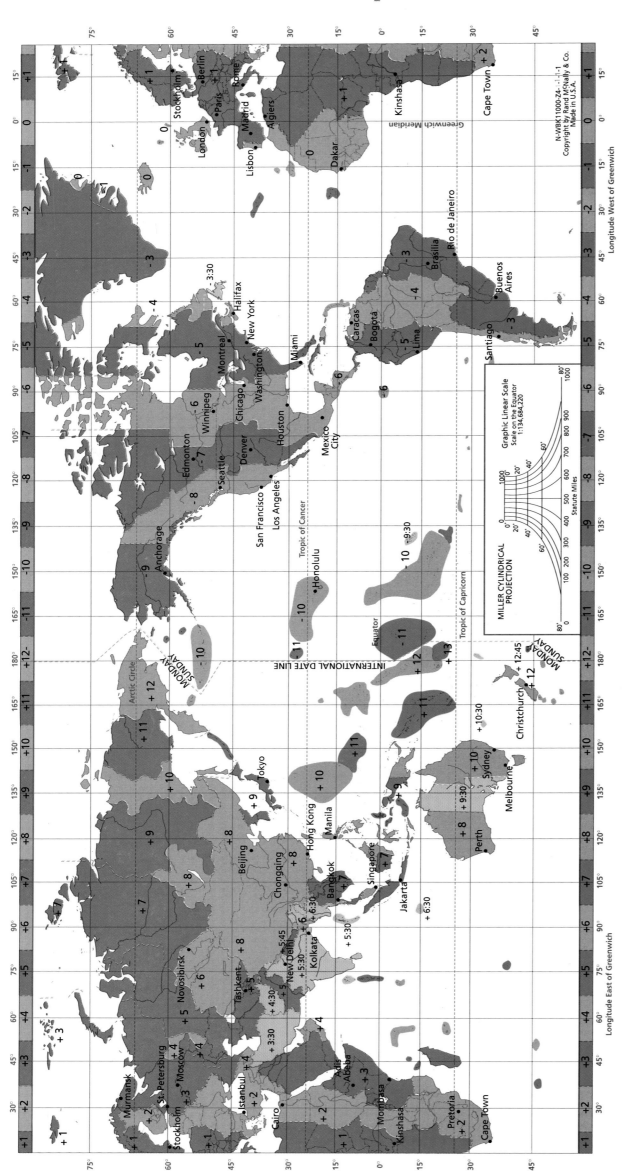

standard time differs from Greenwich mean time. These standard time zones are indicated by bands of blue and yellow. Areas which have a fractional deviation from standard time are shown in special colors. The irregularities in the zones and the fractional deviations are due to political and economic factors.

The surface of the earth is divided into 24 time zones. Each zone represents 15° of longitude or one hour of time. The time of the initial, or zero, zone is based on the Greenwich Meridian and extends eastward and westward for a distance of 7½° of longitude. Each of the zones is designated by a number representing the hours (+ or −) by which its

N-WBK11000-24-□-1-1-1
Copyright by Rand McNally & Co.
Made in U.S.A.

Time Zones

Standard time zone of even-numbered hours from Greenwich time

Standard time zone of odd-numbered hours from Greenwich time

Time varies from standard time zone by half an hour

Time varies from standard time zone by other than half an hour

Legend

Hydrographic Features

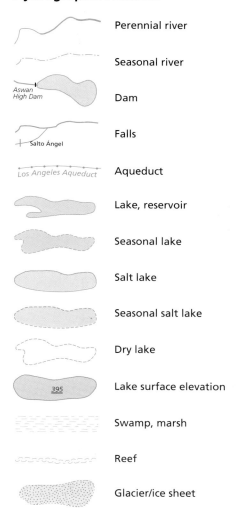

Perennial river

Seasonal river

Dam

Falls

Aqueduct

Lake, reservoir

Seasonal lake

Salt lake

Seasonal salt lake

Dry lake

Lake surface elevation

Swamp, marsh

Reef

Glacier/ice sheet

Topographic Features

764
▽   Depth of water

2278
▲   Elevation above sea level

1700
▼   Elevation below sea level

≍   Mountain pass

Huo Shan
1774   Mountain peak/elevation

The highest elevation on each continent is underlined.

The highest elevation in each country is shown in boldface.

Transportation Features

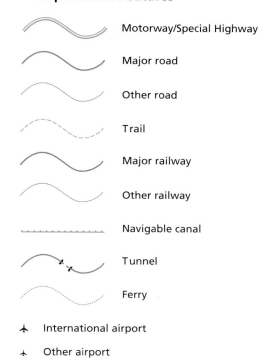

Motorway/Special Highway

Major road

Other road

Trail

Major railway

Other railway

Navigable canal

Tunnel

Ferry

✈   International airport

✦   Other airport

Political Features

International boundaries (First-order political unit)

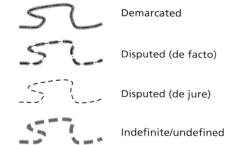

Demarcated

Disputed (de facto)

Disputed (de jure)

Indefinite/undefined

Demarcation line

Internal boundaries

State/province

Third-order (counties, oblasts, etc.)

NORMANDIE
(Denmark)

Cultural/historic region
Administering country

Cities and Towns

The size of symbol and type indicates the relative importance of the locality

■   **LONDON**

▣   **CHICAGO**

◉   **Milwaukee**

◎   Tacna

⊙   Iquitos

○   Old Crow

°   Mettawa

Urban area

Capitals

MEXICO CITY
Bratislava   Country, dependency

RIO DE JANEIRO
Perth   State, province

MANCHESTER
Chester   County

Cultural Features

or   ▪   National park, reservation

▪   Point of interest

⌐⌐⌐⌐⌐⌐   Wall

∴   Ruins

Military installation

•   Polar research station

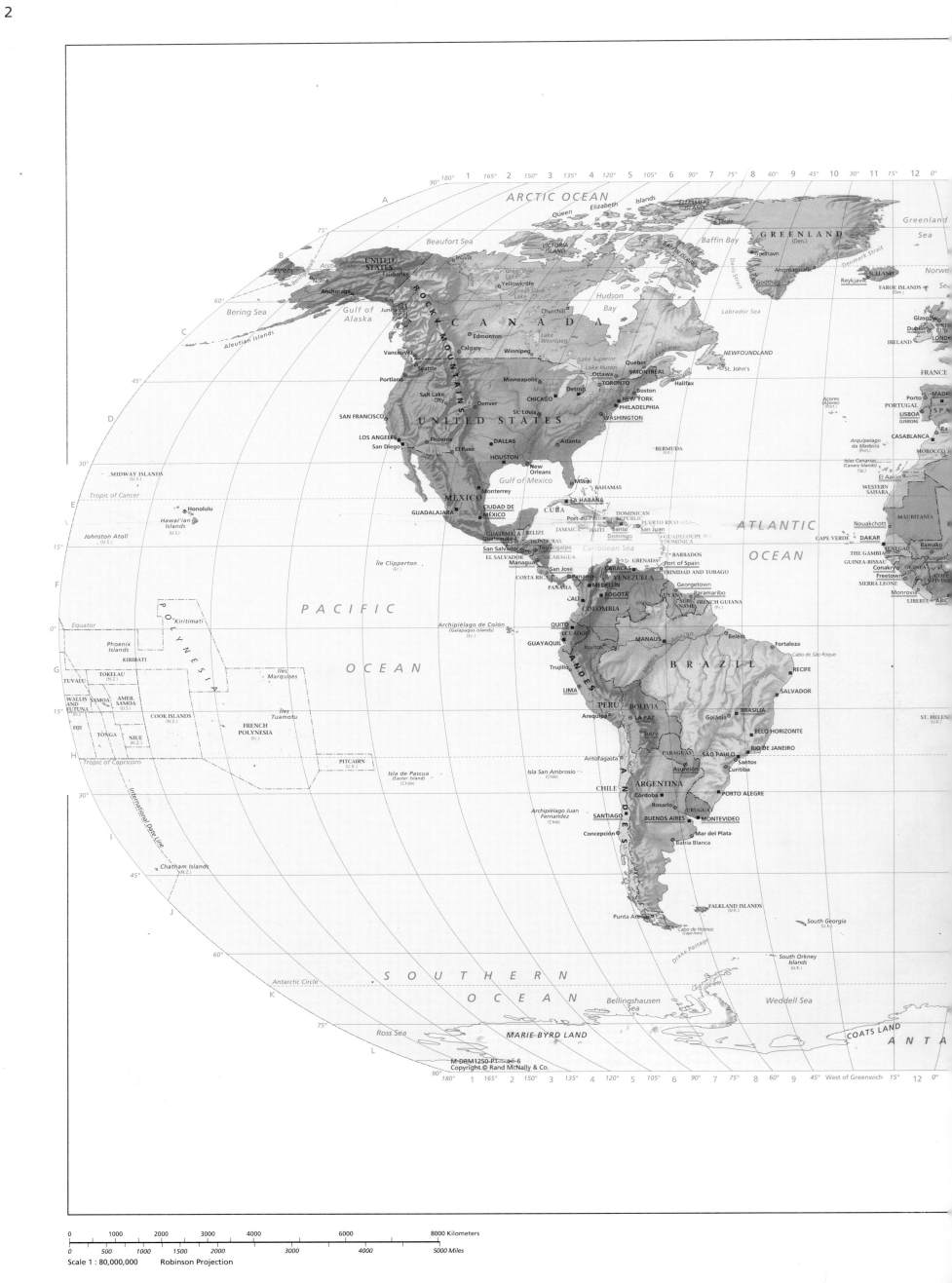

Scale 1 : 80,000,000   Robinson Projection

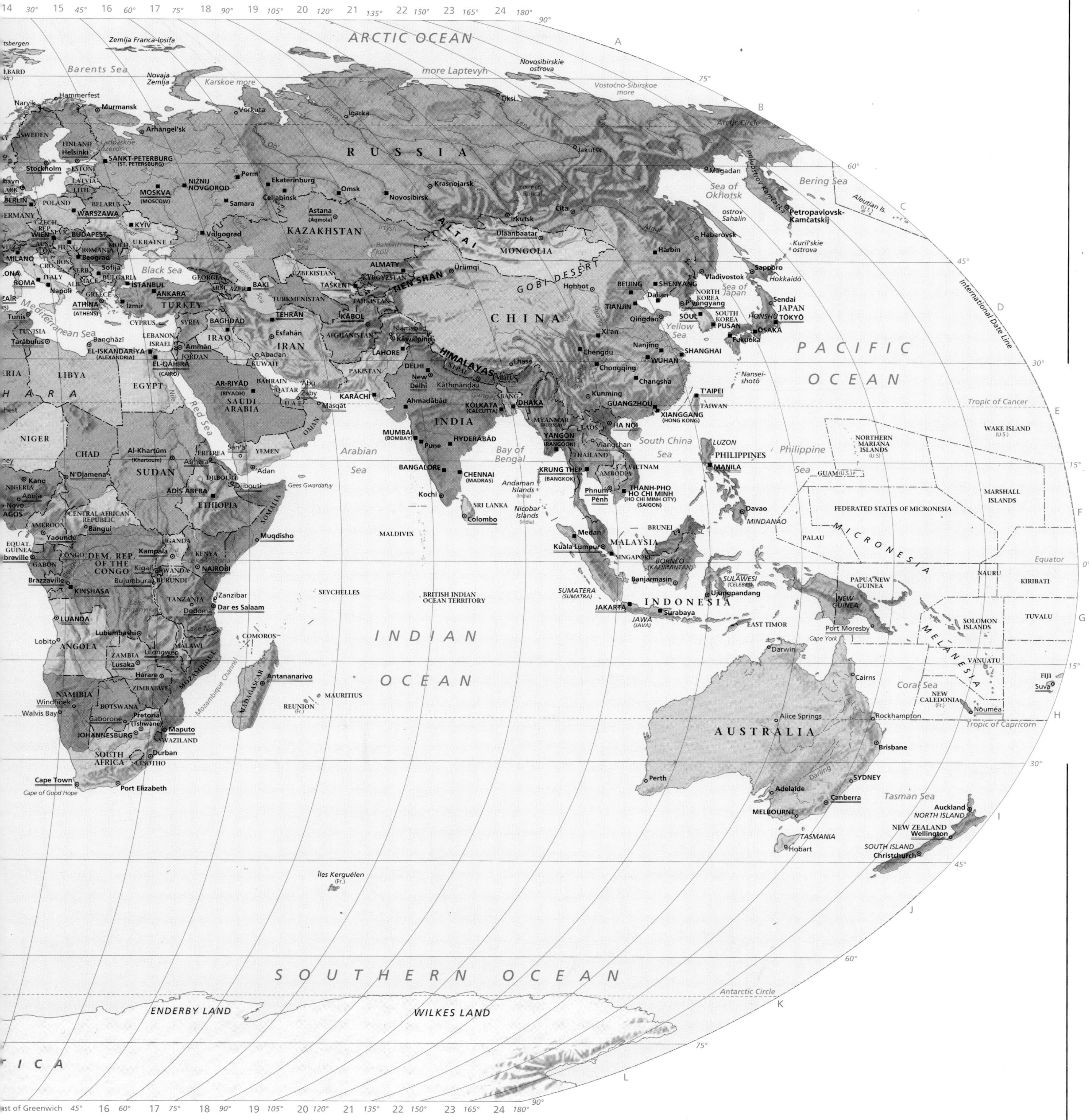

ARCTIC OCEAN
Zemlja Franca-Iosifa
Barents Sea
Novaja Zemlja
Karskoe more
more Laptevyh
Novosibirskie ostrova
Vostočno-Sibirskoe more
Arctic Circle
R U S S I A
Hammerfest
Narvik
Murmansk
Arhangel'sk
Vorkuta
Igarka
Tiksi
Jakutsk
SWEDEN
FINLAND
Helsinki
SANKT-PETERBURG (ST. PETERSBURG)
Stockholm
ESTONIA
LATVIA
LITH.
BELARUS
POLAND
BERLIN
WARSZAWA
MOSKVA (MOSCOW)
NIŽNIJ NOVGOROD
Perm'
Ekaterinburg
Čeljabinsk
Samara
Omsk
Novosibirsk
Krasnojarsk
Irkutsk
Čita
Magadan
Sea of Okhotsk
Bering Sea
Aleutian Is. (U.S.)
Petropavlovsk-Kamčatskij
ostrov Sahalin
Habarovsk
Kuril'skie ostrova
KYÏV
UKRAINE
Volgograd
Astana (Aqmola)
KAZAKHSTAN
Ulaanbaatar
MONGOLIA
ALTAI
Harbin
Sapporo
Hokkaidō
Vladivostok
BUDAPEST
WIEN
ROMANIA
Beograd
Sofija
BULGARIA
MILANO
ROMA
ITALY
Napoli
GREECE
ATHINA (ATHENS)
ISTANBUL
ANKARA
TURKEY
Black Sea
GEORGIA
BAKI
Caspian Sea
Aral Sea
UZBEKISTAN
TAŠKENT
KYRGYZSTAN
ALMATY
Ürümqi
TIEN SHAN
GOBI DESERT
Hohhot
BEIJING
SHENYANG
Dalian
P'yongyang
NORTH KOREA
SŎUL
SOUTH KOREA
PUSAN
Sea of Japan
Sendai
JAPAN
HONSHU
TŌKYŌ
OSAKA
Fukuoka
TIANJIN
Qingdao
Yellow Sea
TURKMENISTAN
TAJIKISTAN
TEHRAN
KABOL
AFGHANISTAN
Islamabad
Rawalpindi
LAHORE
C H I N A
Xi'an
Nanjing
SHANGHAI
WUHAN
Chengdu
Chongqing
Changsha
Lhasa
HIMALAYAS
NEPAL
Kāthmāndau
BHUTAN
DELHI
New Delhi
PAKISTAN
KARĀCHI
Ahmadābād
KOLKATA (CALCUTTA)
DHAKA
INDIA
MUMBAI (BOMBAY)
Pune
HYDERĀBĀD
BANGALORE
CHENNAI (MADRAS)
Kochi
SRI LANKA
Colombo
MALDIVES
Arabian Sea
Bay of Bengal
Andaman Islands (India)
Nicobar Islands (India)
MYANMAR (BURMA)
YANGON (RANGOON)
KRUNG THEP (BANGKOK)
THAILAND
LAOS
Viangchan
HA NOI
VIETNAM
CAMBODIA
Phnum Pénh
THANH-PHO HO CHI MINH (HO CHI MINH CITY) (SAIGON)
Kunming
GUANGZHOU
XIANGGANG (HONG KONG)
T'AIPEI
TAIWAN
South China Sea
LUZON
PHILIPPINES
MANILA
Philippine Sea
Davao
MINDANAO
Nansei-shotō
P A C I F I C
O C E A N
Tropic of Cancer
NORTHERN MARIANA ISLANDS (U.S.)
GUAM (U.S.)
WAKE ISLAND (U.S.)
MARSHALL ISLANDS
FEDERATED STATES OF MICRONESIA
PALAU
M I C R O N E S I A
International Date Line
Equator
NAURU
KIRIBATI
TUVALU
SOLOMON ISLANDS
M E L A N E S I A
VANUATU
FIJI
Suva
NEW CALEDONIA (Fr.)
Nouméa
Coral Sea
Tropic of Capricorn
PAPUA NEW GUINEA
NEW GUINEA
Port Moresby
Cape York
BRUNEI
MALAYSIA
Medan
Kuala Lumpur
SINGAPORE
BORNEO (KALIMANTAN)
Banjarmasin
SULAWESI (CELEBES)
Ujungpandang
SUMATERA (SUMATRA)
JAKARTA
INDONESIA
Surabaya
JAWA (JAVA)
EAST TIMOR
Darwin
Cairns
Alice Springs
Rockhampton
AUSTRALIA
Brisbane
Perth
Darling
Adelaide
SYDNEY
Canberra
MELBOURNE
TASMANIA
Hobart
Tasman Sea
Auckland
NORTH ISLAND
NEW ZEALAND
Wellington
SOUTH ISLAND
Christchurch
SYRIA
CYPRUS
LEBANON
ISRAEL
'Ammān
JORDAN
BAGHDĀD
IRAQ
Esfahān
IRAN
Abadan
KUWAIT
BAHRAIN
QATAR
Abū Zaby
U.A.E.
Masqat
OMAN
AR-RIYĀD (RIYADH)
SAUDI ARABIA
YEMEN
Ṣan'ā'
Adan
Gees Gwardafuy
Red Sea
EGYPT
EL-QÂHIRA (CAIRO)
EL-ISKANDARÎYA (ALEXANDRIA)
Nile
LIBYA
Banghāzī
Tarābulus
TUNISIA
Tunis
Mediterranean Sea
S A H A R A
NIGER
CHAD
SUDAN
Al-Kharṭūm (Khartoum)
ERITREA
Asmera
DJIBOUTI
Djibouti
ĀDĪS ĀBEBA
ETHIOPIA
SOMALIA
Muqdisho
N'Djamena
Kano
NIGERIA
Abuja
CAMEROON
Yaoundé
CENTRAL AFRICAN REPUBLIC
Bangui
EQUAT. GUINEA
GABON
CONGO
Brazzaville
DEM. REP. OF THE CONGO
KINSHASA
UGANDA
Kampala
KENYA
NAIROBI
Kigali
RWANDA
BURUNDI
Bujumbura
TANZANIA
Dodoma
Zanzibar
Dar es Salaam
SEYCHELLES
BRITISH INDIAN OCEAN TERRITORY
LUANDA
ANGOLA
Lobito
Lubumbashi
ZAMBIA
Lusaka
Lilongwe
MALAWI
MOZAMBIQUE
COMOROS
Mozambique Channel
MADAGASCAR
Antananarivo
REUNION (Fr.)
MAURITIUS
Harare
ZIMBABWE
NAMIBIA
Windhoek
Walvis Bay
BOTSWANA
Gaborone
Pretoria (Tshwane)
Maputo
JOHANNESBURG
SWAZILAND
SOUTH AFRICA
Durban
LESOTHO
Cape Town
Cape of Good Hope
Port Elizabeth
I N D I A N
O C E A N
Îles Kerguélen (Fr.)
S O U T H E R N   O C E A N
Antarctic Circle
ENDERBY LAND
WILKES LAND
East of Greenwich

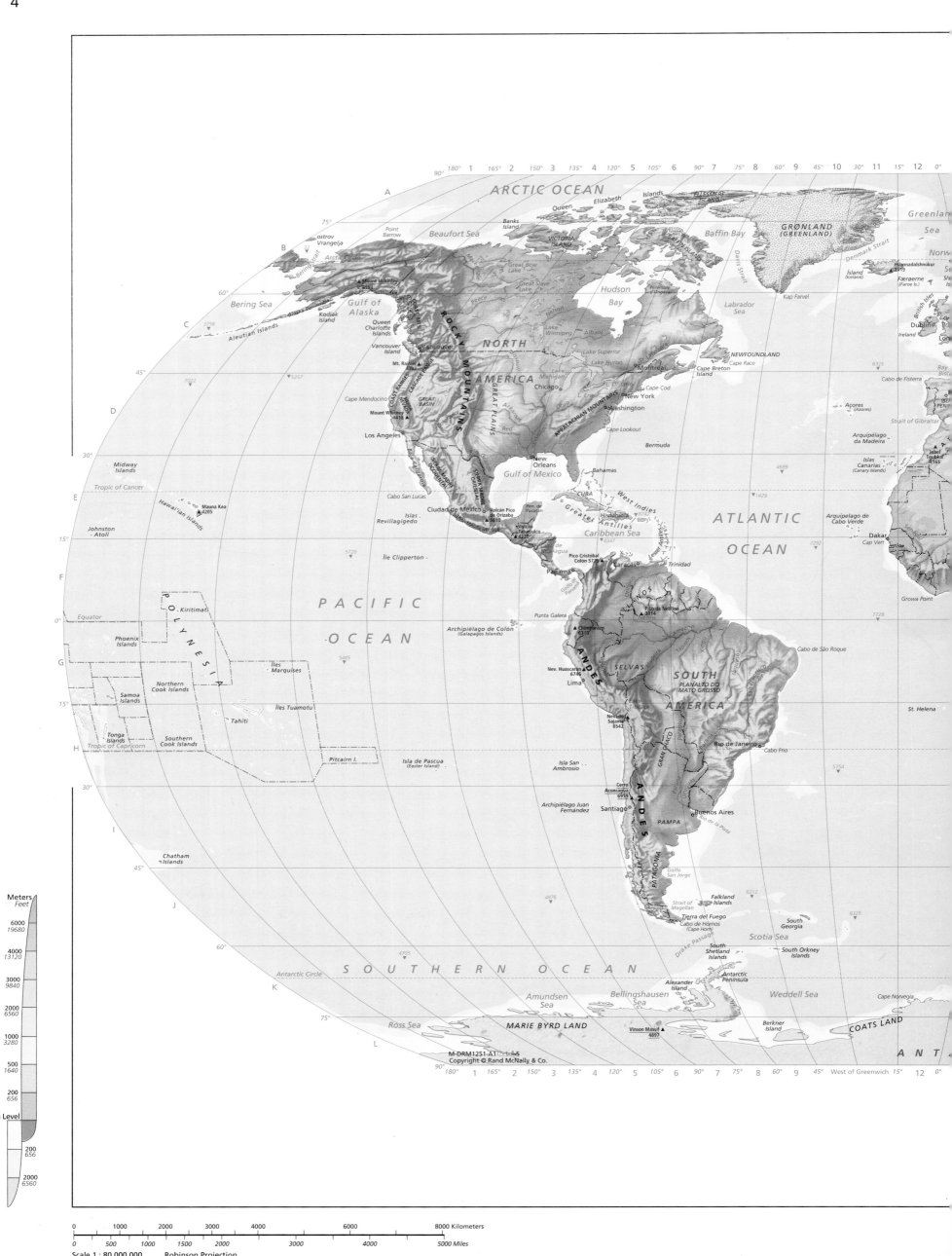

ARCTIC OCEAN

Queen Elizabeth Islands
ELLESMERE ISLAND
GRØNLAND (GREENLAND)
Greenland Sea

Banks Island
VICTORIA ISLAND
Baffin Bay
Bay
Norw

ostrov Vrangelja
Point Barrow
Beaufort Sea
Great Bear Lake
Denmark Strait
Ísland (Iceland)
Hvannadalshnúkur ▲ 2119
Sh

Bering Strait
Great Slave Lake
Hudson Bay
Peninsula d'Ungava
Davis Strait
Kap Farvel
Færøerne (Faroe Is.)
British Isles

Bering Sea
Gulf of Alaska
Kodiak Island
▲ Mount McKinley 6194
ROCKY MOUNTAINS
NORTH AMERICA
Lake Winnipeg
Albany
Nelson
Labrador Sea
6325
Dublin
Ireland
Lon

3758
Aleutian Islands
Queen Charlotte Islands
Vancouver Island
Vancouver
Lake Superior
Lake Michigan
Lake Huron
Montréal
Cape Breton Island
NEWFOUNDLAND
Cape Race
Bay of Bisc
Cabo de Fisterra

7022
5257
Mt. Rainier 4392
CASCADE RANGE
COAST RANGES
Chicago
Ohio
Cape Cod
New York
Washington
Acores (Azores)
Strait of Gibraltar
IBE PEN

Cape Mendocino
GREAT BASIN
GREAT PLAINS
APPALACHIAN MOUNTAINS
Cape Lookout
Arquipélago da Madeira

Mount Whitney ▲4418
Los Angeles
SIERRA MADRE OCCIDENTAL
Red
Arkansas
Bermuda
4699
Islas Canarias (Canary Islands)
Jebel Toubkal ▲4165

Tropic of Cancer
Midway Islands
Cabo San Lucas
New Orleans
Gulf of Mexico
Bahamas
CUBA
West Indies
1429
ATLANTIC
OCEAN

Johnston Atoll
Hawaiian Islands
Mauna Kea ▲4205
Islas Revillagigedo
Ciudad de México
Volcán Pico de Orizaba ▲5610
Pen. de Yucatán
Hispaniola
Greater Antilles
Caribbean Sea
Arquipélago de Cabo Verde
Dakar
Cap Vert

5720
Île Clipperton
Volcán Tajumulco ▲4220
4347
Pico Cristóbal Colón 5775 ▲
Caracas
Trinidad
7292

Equator
POLYNESIA
Kiritimati
PACIFIC
OCEAN
Archipiélago de Colón (Galápagos Islands)
Panamá
Golfo de Panamá
Punta Galera
LLANOS
Pico da Neblina ▲3014
Cabo de São Roque
7728
Growa Point

Phoenix Islands
Chimborazo ▲6310
ANDES
SELVAS
SOUTH
AMERICA

5485
Îles Marquises
Nev. Huascarán 6746
Lima
PLANALTO DO MATO GROSSO
St. Helena

Northern Cook Islands
Samoa Islands
Îles Tuamotu
Tahiti
Titicaca
Nevado Sajama 6542

Tonga Islands
Southern Cook Islands
Tropic of Capricorn
Pitcairn I.
Isla de Pascua (Easter Island)
Isla San Ambrosio
Río de Janeiro
Cabo Frio
5754

GRAN CHACO
Cerro Aconcagua ▲6959
Archipiélago Juan Fernández
Santiago
ANDES
PAMPA
Buenos Aires
Río de la Plata
6212

Chatham Islands
4876
Golfo San Jorge
PATAGONIA
Falkland Islands
8325

Strait of Magellan
Tierra del Fuego
Cabo de Hornos (Cape Horn)
South Georgia
Scotia Sea
Drake Passage

Antarctic Circle
SOUTHERN OCEAN
4705
South Shetland Islands
South Orkney Islands

Amundsen Sea
Bellingshausen Sea
Alexander Island
Antarctic Peninsula
Weddell Sea
Cape Norvegia

Ross Sea
MARIE BYRD LAND
Vinson Massif ▲4897
Berkner Island
COATS LAND
ANT

West of Greenwich

M-DRM1251-A1
Copyright © Rand McNally & Co.

Meters / Feet
6000 / 19680
4000 / 13120
3000 / 9840
2000 / 6560
1000 / 3280
500 / 1640
200 / 656
Sea Level
200 / 656
2000 / 6560

0   1000   2000   3000   4000   6000   8000 Kilometers
0   500   1000   1500   2000   3000   4000   5000 Miles
Scale 1 : 80,000,000   Robinson Projection

30° 15 45° 16 60° 17 75° 18 90° 19 105° 20 120° 21 135° 22 150° 23 165° 24 180° 90°

ARCTIC OCEAN

Zemlja Franca-Iosifa

Severnaja
Zemlja

Novosibirskie
ostrova

Barents Sea

more Laptevyh

Vostočno-Sibirskoe
more

75°

A

Nordkapp

Novaja
Zemlja

Karskoe more

Omoloj

gora
Pobeda
3147

Arctic Circle

B

Korsko
poluostrov

ZAPADNO-
SIBIRSKAJA

gora
Kamen
1701

SIBIR'
(SIBERIA)

Sea of
Okhotsk

Bering Sea

Galdhøpiggen
2469

RAVNINA
(WEST SIBERIAN PLAIN)

Nižnjaja Tunguska

Kolyma

poluostrov
Kamčatka

C

Ladozhskoe
ozero

Baltic Sea

URAL'SKIE GORY

Ekaterinberg

ASIA

Ob'

mys Lopatka

Moskva
(Moscow)

Ob'

Ishim

Irkutsk

ostrov
Sahalin

Kuril'skie
ostrova

45°

Berlin

Dnepr

Irtyš

ALTAI

Sea of
Japan

Hokkaido

D

EUROPE

CARPATHIANS

Danube

gora El'brus
5642

Aral
Sea

Balqash
köli

Pik Pobedy
7439

TIEN SHAN

SHOTKOTE

HONSHŪ

Tōkyō

ALPS

Roma

Black Sea

CAUCASUS

Syr Darya

Pik Ismail Samani
7495

Ulaanbaatar

Beijing

Fuji-san
3776

Shikoku

Istanbul

Caspian Sea

HINDU KUSH

KUNLUN SHAN

GOBI DESERT

Yellow
Sea

Kyūshū

9695

Sicilia
(Sicily)

Kriti

Tehran

Gollehyr
Damāvand
5604

DASHT-E
KAVIR

Jugai Feng
8611

QING ZANG
GAOYUAN

Shanghai

East
China
Sea

Nansei-shotō

PACIFIC

292

30°

Cyprus

KÜHHA-YE ZAGROS

HIMALAYAS

Gongga
Shan
7590

Taiwan

OCEAN

Mediterranean Sea

El Qahira
(Cairo)

Delhi

Mount
Everest
8848

Yu Shan
3997

Tropic of Cancer

Wake Island

E

TAGGAR

SAHARA

TIBESTI

Emi Koussi
3415

NUBIAN
DESERT

Red Sea

ARABIAN
PENINSULA

AR-RUB' AL-KHALI

Mumbai
(Bombay)

Godavari

WESTERN GHATS

EASTERN GHATS

Hainan Dao

South China
Sea

LUZON

Manila

Philippine

Sea

Guam

10915

Mariana Islands

Marshall
Islands

F

SUDAN

AFRICA

Ras Dashen
Terara
4620

Adis Abeba

Gulf of Aden

Gees Gwardafuy

Suqutrā

Arabian

Sea

Krung Thep

Andaman
Islands

Andaman
Sea

INDOCHINA

Palawan

Gulf of
Thailand

MINDANAO

Palau
Islands

MICRONESIA

Caroline Islands

Cape Comorin

Pidurutalagala
2524

Nicobar
Islands

Gunong
Kinabalu
4101

Celebes
Sea

Halmahera

Maldive
Islands

Sri Lanka

5423

Malay
Peninsula

BORNEO
(KALIMANTAN)

Equator

0°

Congo

Margherita
Peak
5109

Lake
Victoria

Kilimanjaro
5895

SUMATERA
(SUMATRA)

Greater Sunda Islands

Jakarta

SULAWESI
(CELEBES)

MALUKU

Seram
Laut
Banda

NEW
GUINEA

Mount Wilhelm
4509

New
Britain

Solomon
Islands

G

CONGO
BASIN

Kirinyaga
5199

Lake
Tanganyika

Zanzibar

Les
Amirantes

Seychelles

7125

JAWA
(JAVA)

Timor

Arafura Sea

Cape York

MELANESIA

New
Hebrides

Fiji
Islands

Tanjona
Bobaomby

Maromokotro
2876

INDIAN

6090

1706

Timor Sea

Kimberley
Plateau

Gulf of
Carpentaria

CAPE
YORK
PENINSULA

Coral Sea

15°

Cape Fria

KALAHARI
DESERT

Mozambique Channel

MADAGASCAR

Réunion

Mauritius

OCEAN

North West Cape

6658

Tanami
Desert

GREAT
SANDY
DESERT

Mount
Meharry
1253

AUSTRALIA

Nouvelle-
Caledonie

GREAT DIVIDING RANGE

Tropic of Capricorn

5304

H

Thabana-
Ntlenyana
3482

DRAKENSBERG

Tanjona
Vohimena

6400

Île Amsterdam

Cape Leeuwin

GREAT
VICTORIA
DESERT

Mount
Woodroffe
1435

Murray

Darling

Sydney

30°

Cape of
Good Hope

Cape Town

Great
Australian
Blight

Melbourne

Mount Kosciuszko
2229

Tasman
Sea

North Cape

NORTH ISLAND

Mount Ruapehu
2797

I

5536

Mount Ossa
1617

TASMANIA

SOUTH ISLAND

Aoraki
(Mount Cook)
3754

45°

Prince
Edward
Islands

3079

Îles de
Crozet

Îles
Kerguélen

2690

South East Cape

South West Cape

Heard
Island

6089

Macquarie
Island

J

4425

SOUTHERN OCEAN

60°

5124

Cape Poinsett

Antarctic Circle

K

ENDERBY LAND

WILKES LAND

Cape
Adare

75°

EN MAUD LAND

TICA

VICTORIA LAND

Ross
Sea

L

East of Greenwich 45° 16 60° 17 75° 18 90° 19 105° 20 120° 21 135° 22 150° 23 165° 24 180° 90°

6

40° 35° 30° 25° 20° 15° 10° 5° 0° 5° 10° 11 12

C B GREENLAND SEA A

Ísafjörður Horn

Akureyri

Reykjavík ICELAND Seyðisfjörður

Hvannadalshnúkur 2119 Arctic Circle NORWEGIAN SEA

VESTERÅLEN Tromsø

LOFOTEN

Narvik Kiru

Bodø

Mo i Rana

60°

55°

50°

45°

40°

35°

30°

NORWAY SWEDEN

Kristiansund Namsos

Ålesund Molde Trondheim Storuman

Østersund Umeå

Dombås Härnösand

FAROE ISLANDS Tórshavn (Den.) Galdhøpiggen 2469 Sundsvall Hudiksvall

Bergen Hamar

Haugesund Falun Gävle

SHETLAND ISLANDS (U.K.) Stavanger OSLO Västerås Uppsala

Rockall Kristiansand Drammen Karlstad

(U.K.) Skien Mäss Örebro STOCKHOLM

Thurso Lindesnes Norrköping

ORKNEY ISLANDS Göteborg Jönköping GOTLAND Linköping

HEBRIDES Inverness Frederikshavn Skagerrak Halmstad Kalmar

Aberdeen NORTH SEA DENMARK Aalborg Växjö ÖLAND

GLASGOW Dundee Holstebro Helsingborg Karlskrona

EDINBURGH København Bornholm Gdynia

ATLANTIC Londonderry UNITED Carlisle Esbjerg Odense (COPENHAGEN) (Den.) Gdańsk Kalini

Belfast KINGDOM NEWCASTLE Flensburg Kiel Lübeck Rostock Szczecin

Galway IRELAND Sligo UPON TYNE Bremerhaven Stralsund Rügen

DUBLIN Middlesbrough Groningen Bremen HAMBURG Bydgoszcz

Limerick LEEDS NETHERLANDS Hannover BERLIN Poznań

Waterford LIVERPOOL MANCHESTER 's-Gravenhage Münster Magdeburg POLA

Cork Sheffield AMSTERDAM Dortmund

Mizen BIRMINGHAM Nottingham (The Hague) ESSEN GERMANY Leipzig Dresden Wrocław

Head Swansea Leicester Norwich ROTTERDAM Bonn Erfurt Chemnitz Walbrzych Częstochowa

Cardiff Oxford Ipswich ANTWERPEN DÜSSELDORF Wiesbaden PRAHA Katowice

Bristol LONDON BRUXELLES KÖLN FRANKFURT Würzburg Plzeň Olomouc Ostrava

ISLES OF Penzance Southampton BELGIUM LILLE AM MAIN CZECH REP Brno

SCILLY Plymouth Brighton Dover Amiens Liège Luxembourg MANNHEIM Nürnberg SLOVAK

Land's End Strait of Dover Rouen Reims LUXEMBOURG Saarbrücken Regensburg Linz WIEN Bratislava Mo

English Channel Le Havre Metz Nancy STUTTGART Augsburg MÜNCHEN (VIENNA) Győr

GUERNSEY Cherbourg Caen Troyes Strasbourg Stuttgart (MUNICH) Salzburg AUSTRIA BUDAPEST

(U.K.) Pointe de Saint-Mathieu JERSEY Saint- PARIS Mulhouse Basel Zürich Bern Innsbruck Klagenfurt Graz HUNGA

Brest (U.K.) Malo Orléans Bourges LIECHT Vaduz SLOVENIA Balaton

Rennes Angers Tours Dijon Besançon Lausanne SWITZ Bolzano Ljubljana Zagreb Pécs

Nantes Le Mans Loire Geneva Mont Blanc Brescia Verona Trieste CROATIA

La Rochelle Poitiers Limoges FRANCE LYON 4807 TORINO MILANO Padova Venézia Rijeka

A Coruña Gijón Oviedo Santander Bordeaux Clermont- Saint- Grenoble GENOVA Parma (Venice) BOSNIA AND

Ferrand Étienne Nice Bologna Zadar HERZEGOVINA

Vigo Ourense León Bilbao Bayonne Nîmes Avignon Monaco La Spezia Firenze SAN Ancona

Porto Braga Burgos Donostia PYRENEES Montpellier MARSEILLE Toulon MARINO Split

Duero San Sebastián ANDORRA Perpignan Toulon LIGURIAN SEA Pisa Perugia Pescara

Salamanca Gasteiz Pamplona Andorra CORSE Livorno APPENNINO Dubrovnik

PORTUGAL Valladolid la Vella (CORSICA) L'Aquila ADRIATIC Podgorica

Coimbra Segovia Zaragoza Lleida (Fr.) VATICAN CITY Foggia

LISBOA Tagus MADRID Lérida BARCELONA Bastia ROMA Tirane

(LISBON) Toledo Castelló Tarragona SARDEGNA Olbia (ROME) ITALY Bari

Setúbal SPAIN de la Plana (SARDINIA) NAPOLI Salerno ALBA

Évora Badajoz Guadiana VALÈNCIA Sassari (It.) (NAPLES) Brindisi

Cabo de Albacete ILLES BALEARS Nuoro TYRRHENIAN Táranto Lecce

São Vicente Mérida (BALEARIC ISLANDS) Menorca SEA

Huelva Córdoba Jaén Eivissa Strait of Ota

Faro Sevilla Granada Elx Palma de MALLORCA Cagliari Cosenza

Murcia Mallorca Palermo Messina IONIAN

Cádiz Málaga Lorca Alacant Trapani Reggio SEA

Mulhacén Cartagena Catanzaro

GIBRALTAR 3478 MEDITERRANEAN Monte Etna di Calabria

(U.K.) Ceuta (Sp.) Isla de SICILIA 3323 Catania

Tanger Alborán Marsala (SICILY) Siracusa

CASABLANCA Salé Tetouan EL DJAZAÏR Isola di

Rabat Larache (ALGIERS) Tizi- Pantelleria

Al Hoceima El Boulaïd Ouzou Bejaïa Skikda La Galite (It.)

El-Jadida Melilla (Sp.) Wahran Mestghanem Annaba Bizerte Cap Bon

Meknès Fès Taza El Cheliff Qacentina Béja Nabeul Isola

Safi Sidi bel Bouira Sétif Batna TUNIS delle Correnti

Khouribga Abbès Tiaret Sousse (It.)

Essaouira Marrakech MOROCCO ATLAS MOUNTAINS Chott el Tbessa Kairouan MALTA Valletta

Jebel Toubkal Hodna TUNISIA

Agadir 4165 ALGERIA Beskra Sfax ISOLE

M-DRM3302-P1- -4- -6 Chott Chergui Chott PELAGIE

Copyright © Rand McNally & Co. Er-Rachidia Laghouat Gafsa Melrhir (It.)

West of Greenwich 0° East of Greenwich 9 5° 10° 15° 12

0 200 400 800 1200 Kilometers

0 100 200 400 600 800 Miles

Scale 1 : 12,500,000 Conic Equidistant Projection

BARENTS SEA

KANIN-KAMEN'

NENECKIJ
AVTONOMNYJ OKRUG

poluostrov Kanin

TIMANSKIJ

KRJAŽ

KOMI

Murmansk

Kola

Severomorsk

KEJVY

KOL'SKIJ
POLUOSTROV
(KOLA PENINSULA)

MURMANSKAJA
OBLAST

Kandalakša

Apatity
Kirovsk

BELOE MORE
(WHITE SEA)

Mezenskaja
guba

Češskaja guba
(Chesha Bay)

Dvinskaja
guba

Arhangel'sk

Severodvinsk
(Molotovsk)

Onega

ARHANGEL'SKAJA OBLAST

KARELIJA

OULU

ITÄ-SUOMI

Petrozavodsk

Onežskoe
ozero
(Lake Onega)

RUSSIA

KIROVSKAJA
OBLAST

Velikij Ustjug

Ladožskoe
ozero
(Lake Ladoga)

VOLOGODSKAJA OBLAST

KOSTROMSKAJA
OBLAST

**SANKT-PETERBURG
(ST. PETERSBURG)**

LENINGRADSKAJA OBLAST

Vologda

Narva

Pskov

NOVGORODSKAJA
OBLAST

Novgorod

Čerepovec

Rybinsk

Kostroma

JAROSLAVSKAJA
OBLAST

Jaroslavl'

Ivanovo

IVANOVSKAJA OBLAST

NIŽEGORODSKAJA
OBLAST

**NIŽNIJ
NOVGOROD
(GORKI)**

PSKOVSKAJA
OBLAST

VALDAJSKAJA

VOZVYŠENNOST'

TVERSKAJA
OBLAST

Tver

Vladimir

VLADIMIRSKAJA OBLAST

Murom

BELARUS

SMOLENSKAJA OBLAST

MOSKOVSKAJA
OBLAST

**MOSKVA
(MOSCOW)**

RJAZANSKAJA
OBLAST

Copyright © Rand McNally & Co.

Meters / Feet
2000 / 6560
1000 / 3280
500 / 1640
200 / 656
Sea Level
200 / 656
2000 / 6560

Scale 1 : 5,000,000   Lambert Conformal Conic Projection

0   50   100   150   200   300   400   500 Kilometers
0   50   100   200   300 Miles

Scale 1 : 2,500,000   Lambert Conformal Conic Projection

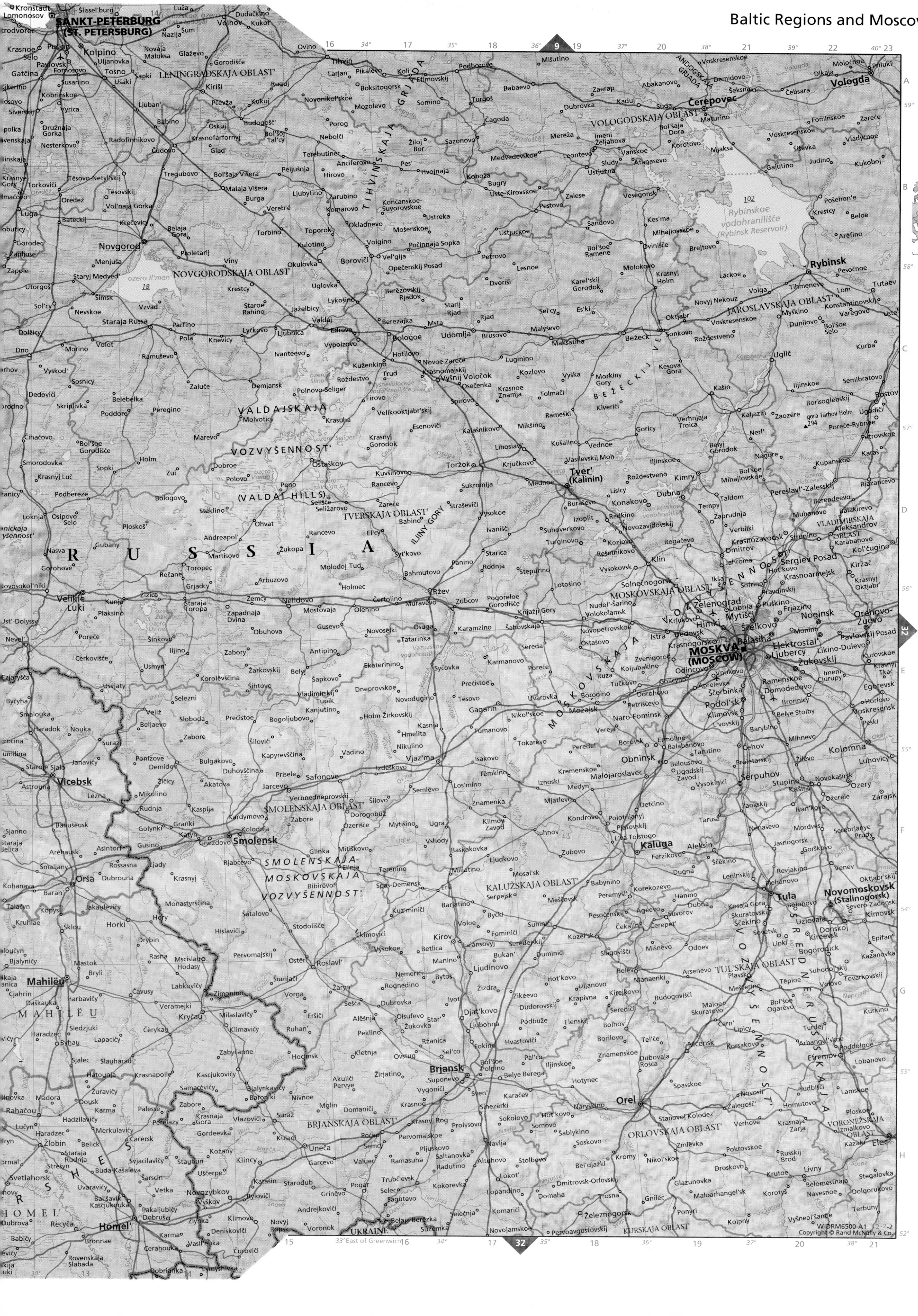

SANKT-PETERBURG (ST. PETERBURG)

LENINGRADSKAJA OBLAST'

Novgorod

NOVGORODSKAJA OBLAST'

ozero Il'men 18

VALDAJSKAJA VOZVYŠENNOST' (VALDAI HILLS)

R U S S I A

Vologda

Čerepovec

VOLOGODSKAJA OBLAST'

Rybinskoe vodohranilišče (Rybinsk Reservoir) 102

Rybinsk

JAROSLAVSKAJA OBLAST'

Rostov

Kašin

Uglič

TVERSKAJA OBLAST'

Tver' (Kalinin)

Dubna

VLADIMIRSKAJA OBLAST'

Sergiev Posad

Aleksandrov

MOSKOVSKAJA OBLAST'

Zelenograd

Himki

MOSKVA (MOSCOW)

Elektrostal'

Ljubercy

Noginsk

Orehovo-Zuevo

Podol'sk

Domodedovo

Kolomna

Serpuhov

Obninsk

Malojaroslavec

Kaluga

KALUŽSKAJA OBLAST'

Tula

Novomoskovsk (Stalinogorsk)

TUL'SKAJA OBLAST'

Mcensk

Orel

ORLOVSKAJA OBLAST'

VORONEŽSKAJA OBLAST'

Elec

Brjansk

BRJANSKAJA OBLAST'

KURSKAJA OBLAST'

SREDNERUSSKAJA VOZVYŠENNOST'

Smolensk

SMOLENSKAJA OBLAST'

SMOLENSKAJA-MOSKOVSKAJA VOZVYŠENNOST'

Vjaz'ma

Velikie Luki

Vicebsk

Mahilëu

MAHILËU

Orša

Homel'

HOMEL'

UKRAINE

TIHVINSKAJA GRJADA

W-DRM6500-A1   Copyright © Rand McNally & Co.

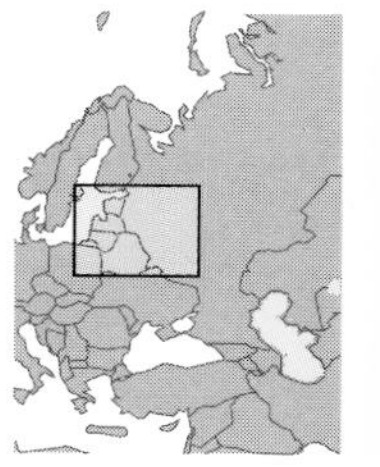

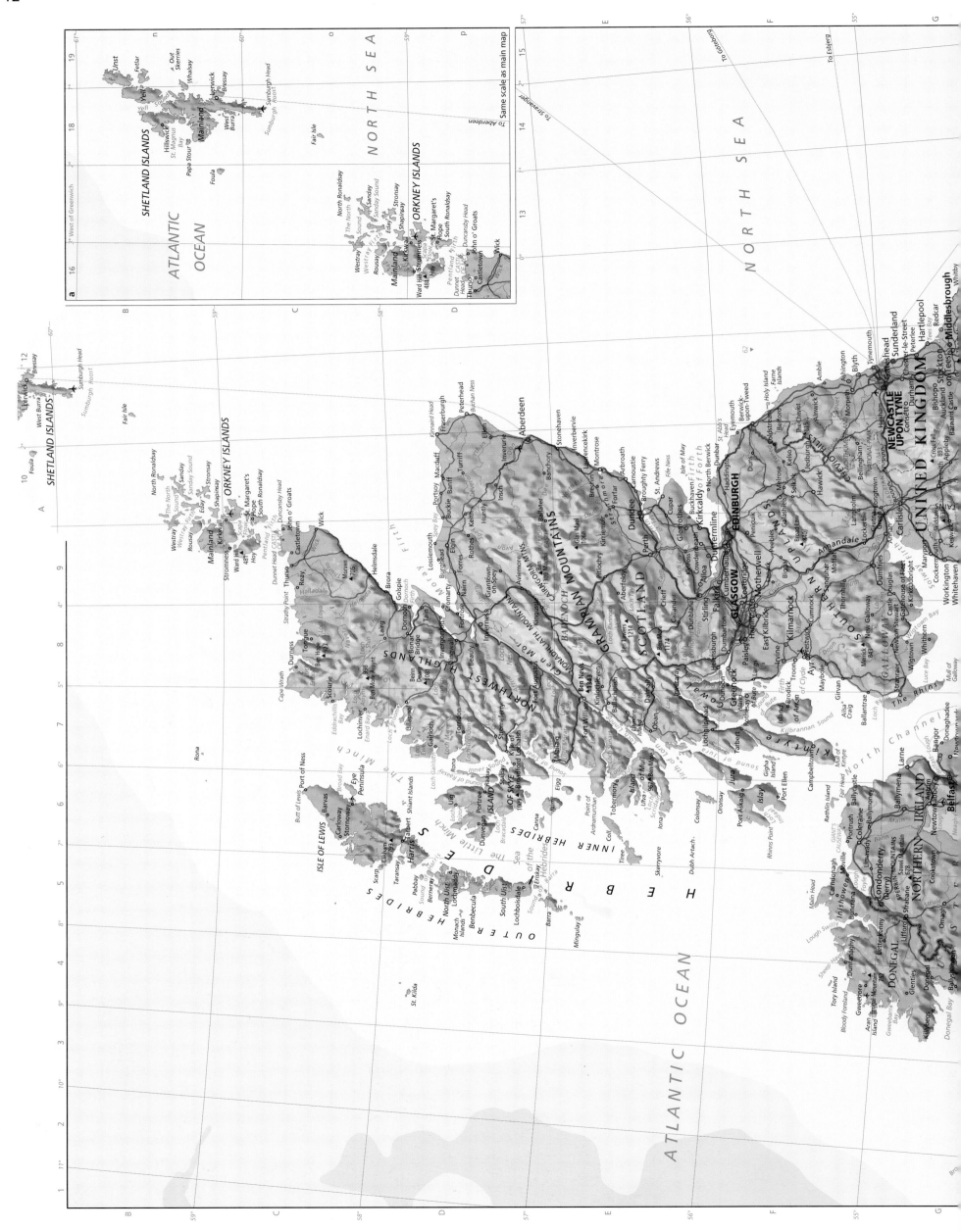

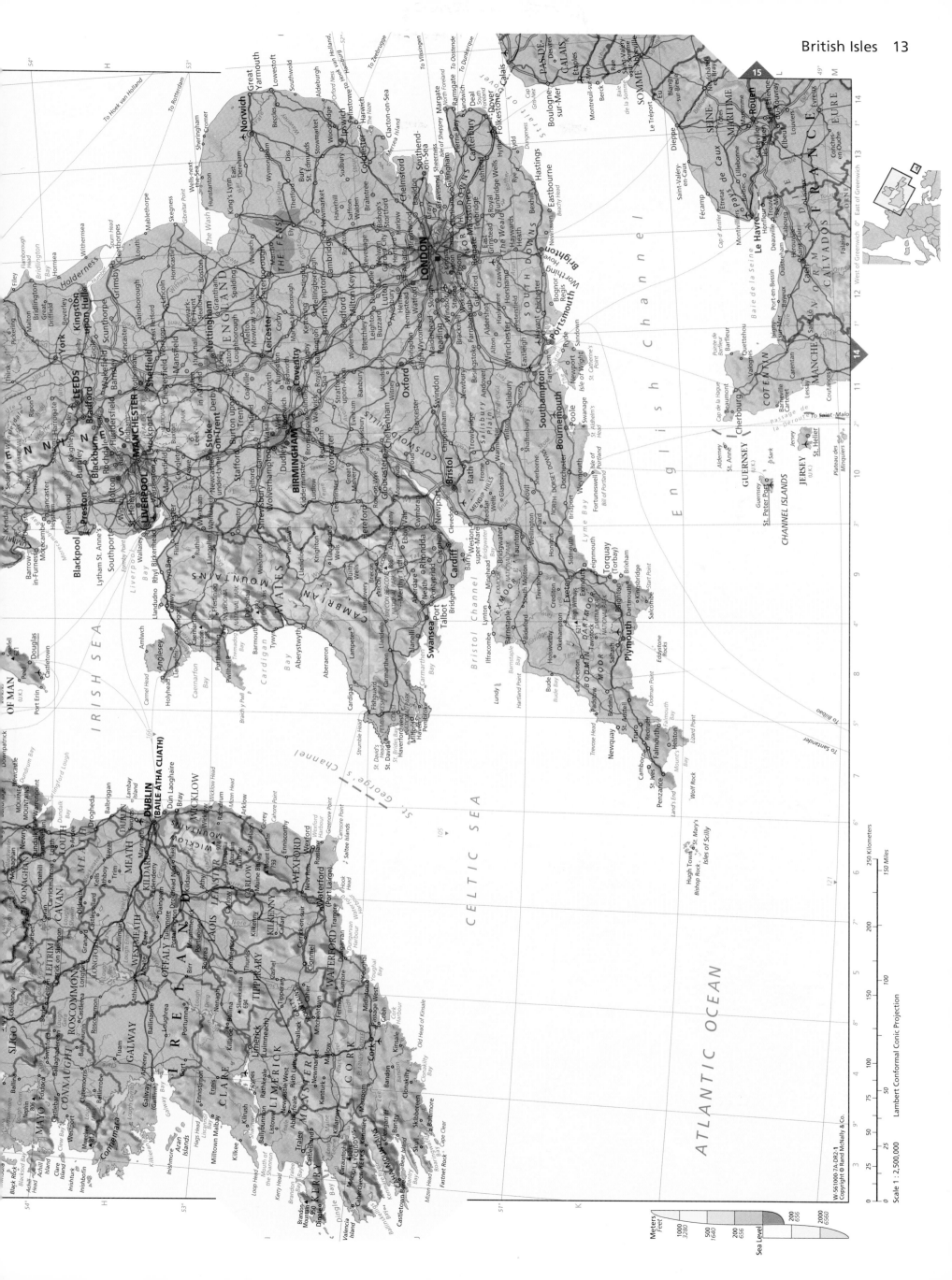

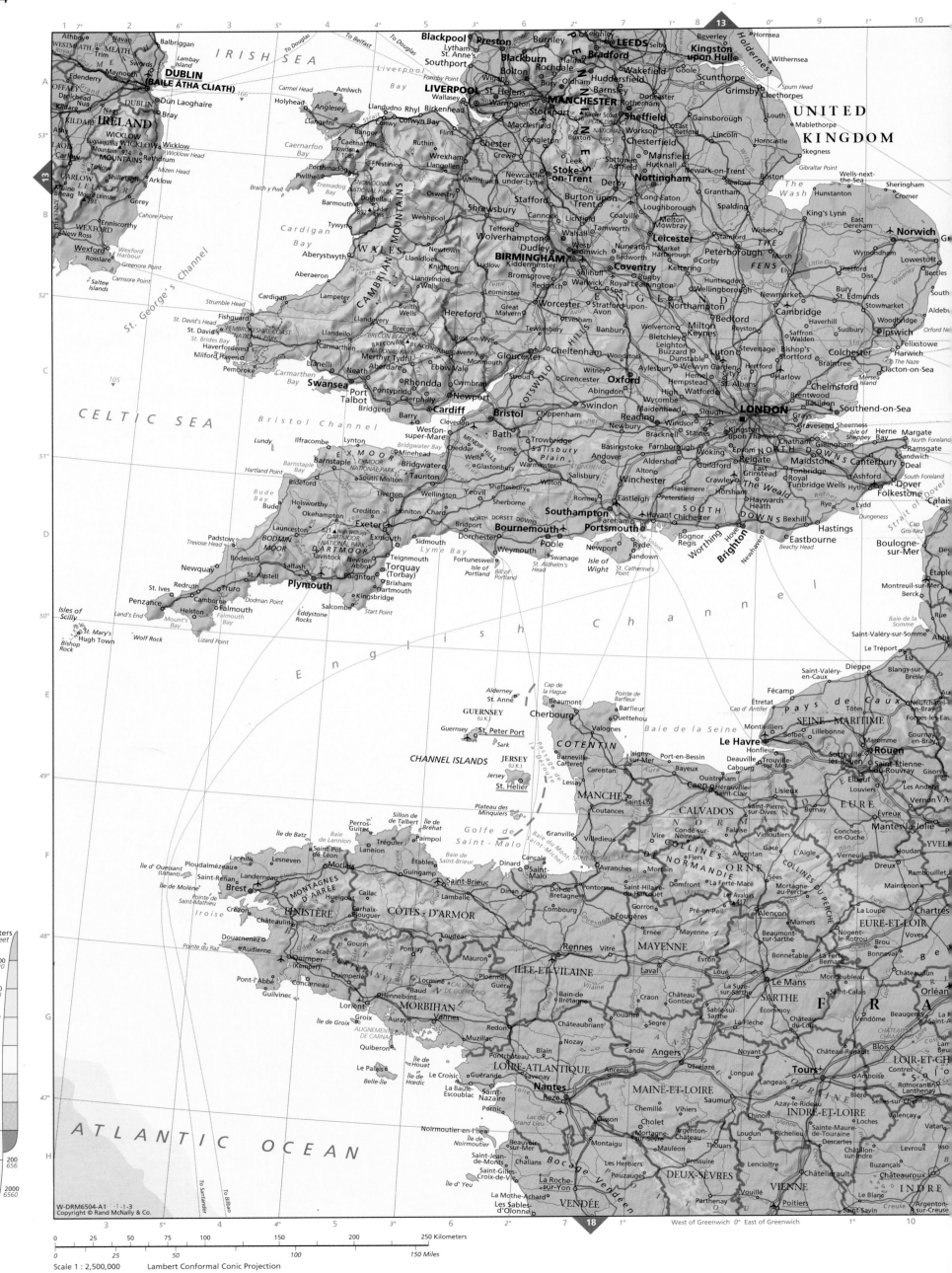

14

IRELAND

UNITED KINGDOM

WALES

IRISH SEA

CELTIC SEA

ENGLISH CHANNEL

ATLANTIC OCEAN

FRANCE

Scale 1 : 2,500,000   Lambert Conformal Conic Projection

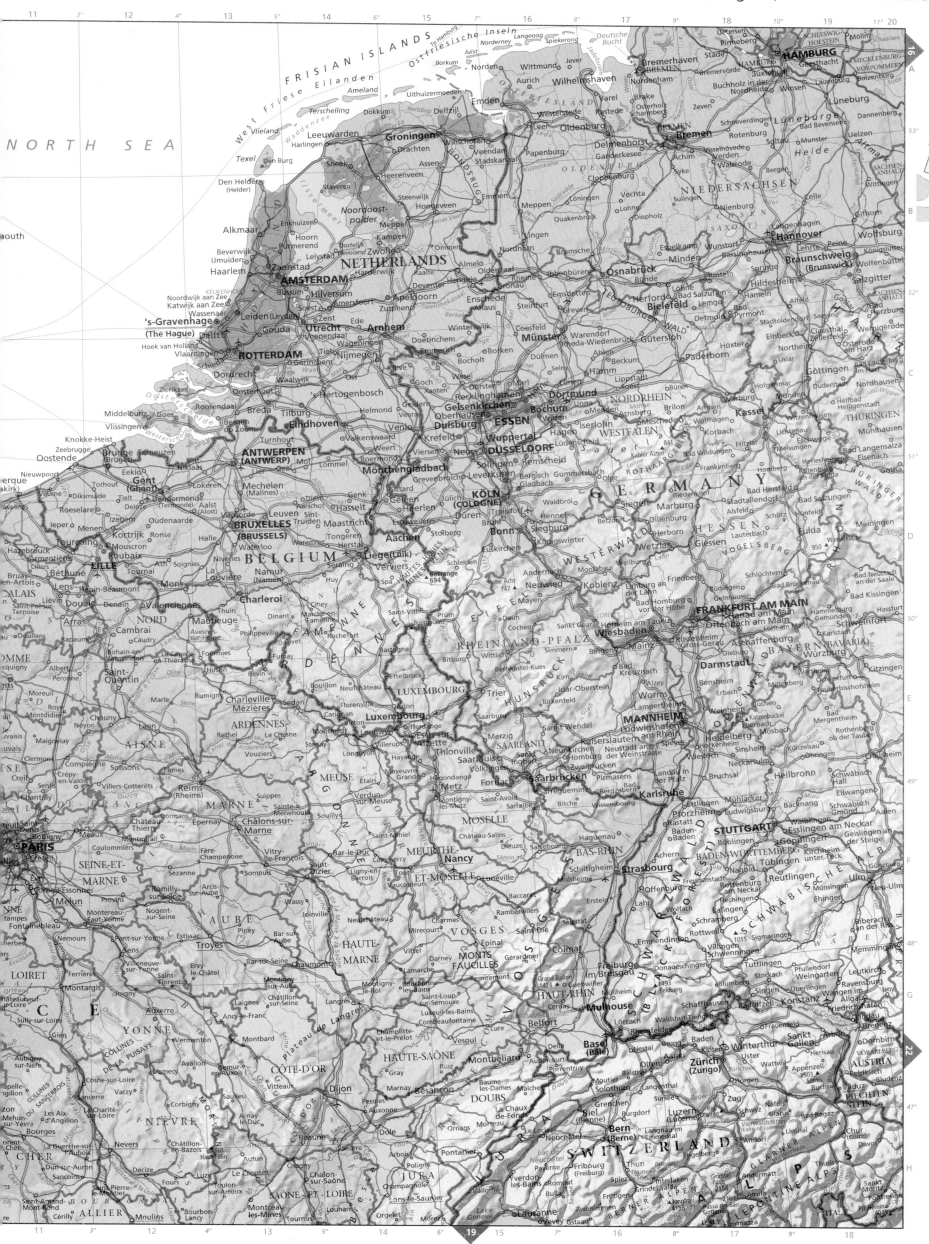

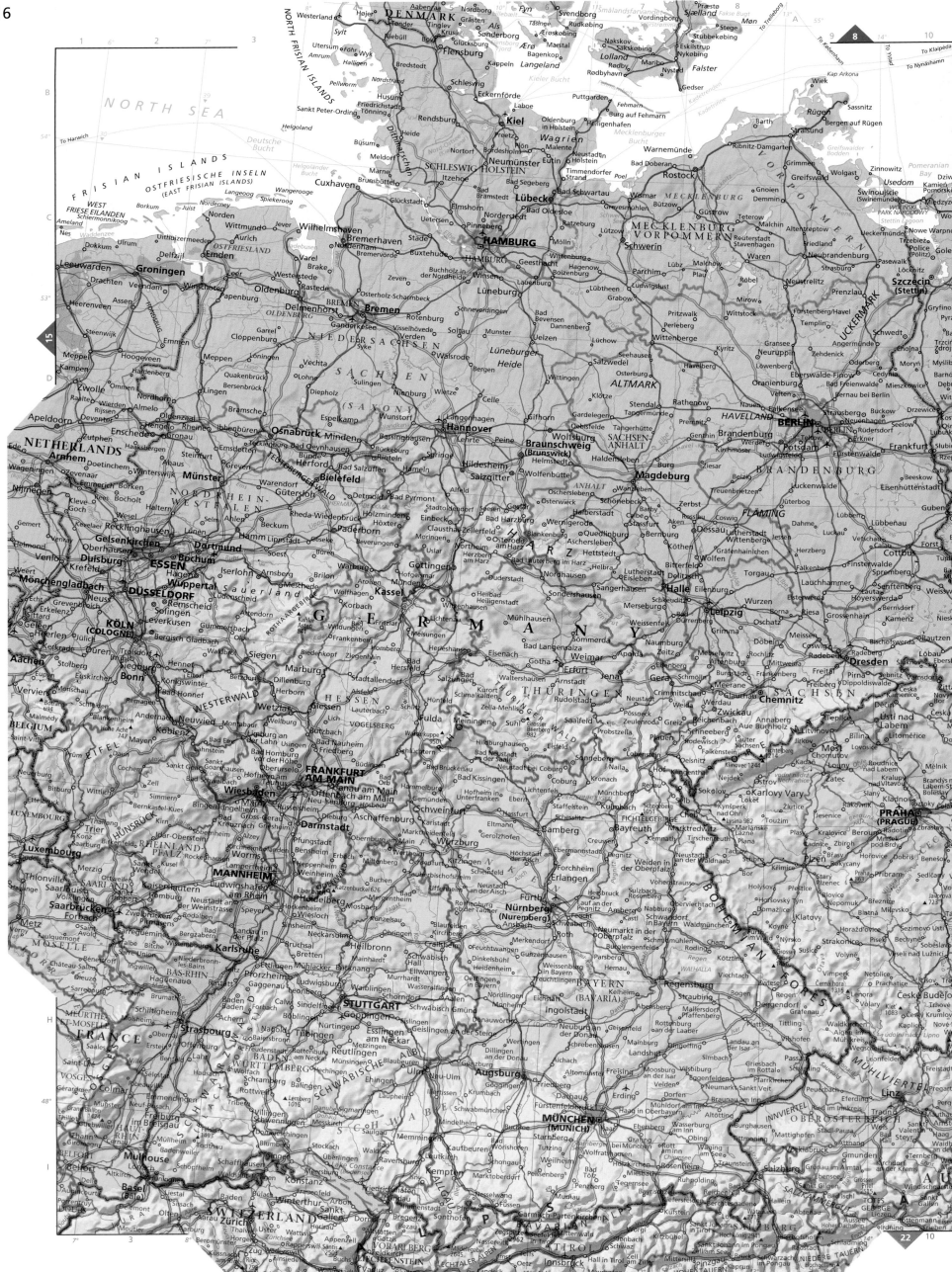

BALTIC SEA

POLAND

RUSSIA

LITHUANIA

BELARUS

UKRAINE

CZECH REPUBLIC

SLOVAKIA

HUNGARY

ROMANIA

CARPATHIAN MTS.

Meters	Feet
2000	6560
1000	3280
500	1640
200	656
Sea Level	
200	656
2000	6560

0   25   50   75   100   150   200   250 Kilometers

0   25   50   100   150 Miles

Scale 1 : 2,500,000   Lambert Conformal Conic Projection

Copyright by Rand McNally & Co.

18

Bay of Biscay
ATLANTIC OCEAN
ALBORAN SEA
Golfo de Cádiz
Costa del Sol
Strait of Gibraltar
MOROCCO
PORTUGAL
SPAIN
CORDILLERA CANTÁBRICA
SISTEMA CENTRAL
SIERRA MORENA
CORDILLERA
TIERRA DE CAMPOS
CASTILLA Y LEÓN
EXTREMADURA
ANDALUCÍA
GALICIA
ASTURIAS
CANTABRIA
ALENTEJO
ESTREMADURA
MADRID
LISBOA
(LISBON)
Porto
Sevilla
(Seville)
Córdoba
(Cordova)
Valladolid
Salamanca
Toledo
Granada
Málaga
Cádiz
Huelva
Badajoz
Mérida
Cáceres
León
Oviedo
Gijón
Santander
Bilbao
A Coruña
(Corunna)
Vigo
Ourense
Lugo
Burgos
Palencia
Zamora
Segovia
Ávila
Coimbra
Braga
Faro
Évora
Setúbal
Jerez de la Frontera
Algeciras
GIBRALTAR
(U.K.)
Meters
Feet
3000
9840
2000
6560
1000
3280
500
1640
200
656
Sea Level
200
656
2000
6560
W-DRM6503-A1
Copyright © Rand McNally & Co.
0 25 50 75 100 150 200 Kilometers
0 25 50 100 Miles
Scale 1 : 2,500,000
Lambert Conformal Conic Projection

FRANCE

PYRÉNÉES

NAVARRA

ARAGÓN

CATALUNYA

Golfe du Lion

Perpignan

BARCELONA
L'Hospitalet de Llobregat
Sabadell
Terrassa
Badalona

Zaragoza
(Saragossa)

Tarragona

Reus

Tortosa

Delta de l'Ebre

TERUEL

CASTELLÓ

Castelló de la Plana

VALÈNCIA

VALÈNCIA

Golf de València

(BALEARIC ISLANDS)

ILLES BALEARS

MENORCA
(Minorca)
Ciutadella de Menorca
Alaior
Maó

MALLORCA
(Majorca)
Palma de Mallorca
Manacor
Inca

Illa de
Cabrera

B A L E A R S

EIVISSA
(IBIZA)
Sant Antoni
de Portmany
Santa Eulària del Riu

FORMENTERA

CUENCA

MANCHA

Albacete

ALBACETE

MURCIA

Murcia

Cartagena

Lorca

ALMERÍA

M E D I T E R R A N E A N   S E A

Alacant
(Alicante)

Elx

Oriola

EL DJAZAÏR
(ALGIERS)

ATLAS

ALGERIA

MOUNTAINS

KABYLIE

MEDITERRANEAN SEA

TYRRHENIAN SEA

LIGURIAN SEA

Meters
Feet
4000
13120
3000
9840
2000
6560
1000
3280
500
1640
200
656
Sea Level
200
656
2000
6560

0   25   50   75   100   150 Kilometers
0   25   50   100 Miles
Scale 1 : 2,500,000   Lambert Conformal Conic Projection

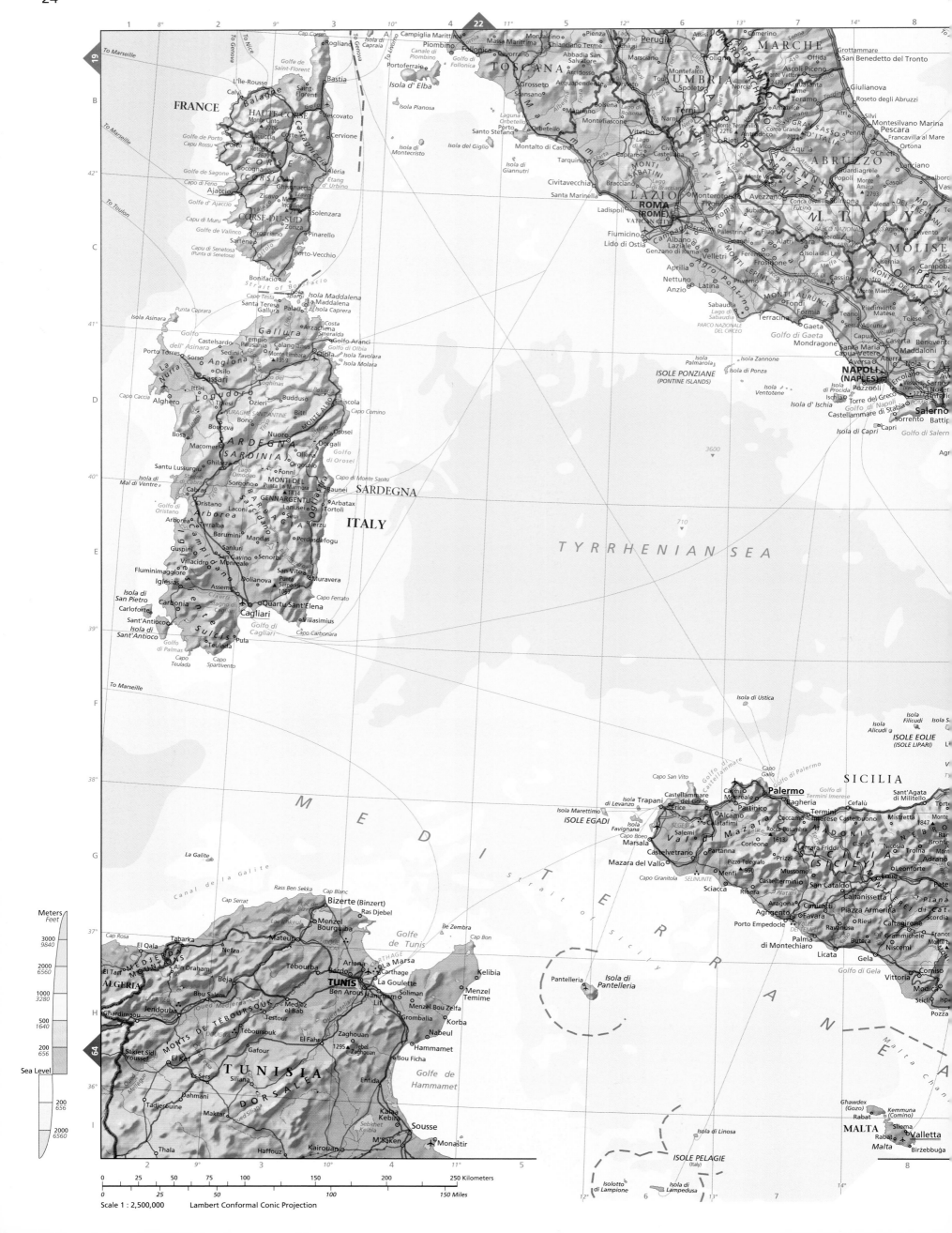

19

22

64

FRANCE

To Marseille
To Marseille
To Toulon

L'Ile-Rousse
Calvi
HAUTE-CORSE
Monte Cinto
2706

Rogliano
Cap Corse
Isola di Capraia
Isola di Gorgona

Campiglia Marittima
Piombino
Portoferraio
Isola d' Elba

Massa Marittima
Monzalino
Chianciano Terme
Pienza

MARCHE

Grottammare
San Benedetto del Tronto

CORSE
(CORSICA)

TOSCANA

UMBRIA

ABRUZZO

ITALY

MOLISE

SARDEGNA
(SARDINIA)

ITALY

ROMA
(ROME)

NAPOLI
(NAPLES)

LAZIO

Cagliari

Golfo di
Cagliari

T Y R R H E N I A N   S E A

3600

710

Isola di Ustica

Isola
Filicudi

ISOLE EOLIE
(ISOLE LIPARI)

SICILIA

Palermo

SICILI
(SICILY)

Capo San Vito
Golfo di
Castellammare
Golfo di Palermo
Capo
Gallo

ISOLE EGADI

M E D I T E R R A N E A N

La Galite
Canal de la Galite

Rass Ben Sekka
Cap Blanc
Cap Serrat
Cap Rosa
Tabarka
El Qala

Bizerte (Binzert)
Ras Djebel

Golfe
de Tunis
Ile Zembra
Cap Bon

ALGERIA

TUNISIA

TUNIS

Golfe de
Hammamet

Sousse
Monastir

Pantelleria
Isola di
Pantelleria

Golfo di Gela

Ghawdex
(Gozo)
Kemmuna
(Comino)
Rabat

MALTA

Valletta
Sliema
Birżebbuġa
Malta

ISOLE PELAGIE
(Italy)

Isolotto
di Lampione
Isola di
Lampedusa

Meters
Feet

3000
9840

2000
6560

1000
3280

500
1640

200
656

Sea Level

200
656

2000
6560

0   25   50   75   100   150   200   250 Kilometers

0   25   50   100   150 Miles

Scale 1 : 2,500,000   Lambert Conformal Conic Projection

CROATIA

BOSNIA AND HERZEGOVINA

SERBIA AND MONTENEGRO

CRNA GORA (MONTENEGRO)

SERBIA

KOSOVO-METOHIJA

MACEDONIA

Skopje

Priština

ALBANIA

Tiranë

Durrës

Elbasan

Berat

Vlorë

Gjirokastër

ADRIATIC SEA

ISOLE TREMITI

Otok Vis

Otok Korčula

Otok Lastovo

Otok Mljet

Dubrovnik

Cavtat

Herceg-Novi

Kotor

Podgorica

Cetinje

Bar

Ulcinj

Shkodër

PROMONTORIO DEL GARGANO

Monte Calvo

Manfredonia

Golfo di Manfredonia

San Severo

Foggia

Lucera

Cerignola

Barletta

Trani

Bisceglie

Molfetta

Andria

Canosa di Puglia

Corato

Bitonto

PUGLIA

Bari

Mola di Bari

Monopoli

Conversano

Castellana Grotte

Fasano

Alberobello

Ostuni

Martina Franca

Brindisi

Mesagne

Francavilla Fontana

Manduria

Lecce

Copertino

Galatina

Nardò

Gallipoli

Maglie

Òtranto

Santa Cesarea Terme

Tricase

Gagliano del Capo

Capo Santa Maria di Leuca

Salentina

Penisola

BASILICATA

Potenza

Matera

Altamura

Gravina in Puglia

Taranto

Massafra

Grottaglie

Golfo di Taranto

Metaponto

Castrovillari

Cassano allo Ionio

Rossano

Cariati

Cirò Marina

CALABRIA

SILA GRANDE

Cosenza

Rende

Paola

Amantea

Crotone

Capo Colonne

Isola di Capo Rizzuto

Catanzaro

Golfo di Squillace

Squillace

Soverato

Pizzo

Vibo Valentia

Tropea

Capo Vaticano

Nicotera

Gioia Tauro

Palmi

Cittanova

Polistena

Locri

Siderno

Marina di Gioiosa Ionica

Bovalino Marina

Reggio di Calabria

Villa San Giovanni

Melito di Porto Salvo

Capo Spartivento

Messina

Taormina

Giarre

Riposto

Acireale

Catania

Golfo di Catania

Augusta

Golfo di Augusta

Siracusa

Avola

Golfo di Noto

Pachino

Capo Passero

Isola delle Correnti

Isola Stromboli

Isola Panarea

Isola Lipari

GREECE

Kérkyra (Corfu)

Igoumenítsa

Párga

Préveza

Árta

Ioánnina

Lefkáda

Agrínio

IÓNIOI NÍSOI

Kefalloniá

Argostóli

Zákynthos

Pátra

Peloponnísos (Peloponnesus)

DYTIKÍ ELLÁDA

IONIAN SEA

Strait of Otranto

Sarandë

Delvinë

Othonoí

Paxoí

Kyparissiakós Kólpos

Kyparissía

Pýlos

Chóra

PELOPÓNNISOS

W-DRM6509-A1
Copyright © Rand McNally & Co.

ADRIATIC SEA

SERBIA AND MONT.
SRBIJA (SERBIA)

BALKAN PENINSULA

MACEDONIA

ALBANIA

BULGAR

SOFIJA

Plovdiv

PLOVDIV

RHODOPE MOUNTAINS

HASKO

ANATOLIKÍ MAKEDONÍA KAI THRÁKI

Thessaloníki
(Salónika)

KENTRIKÍ MAKEDONÍA

THRAKIKÓ
PÉLAGOS

ÁGIO ÓROS

DYTIKÍ MAKEDONÍA

Olympos
(Mount Olympus)
2917

ÍPEIROS

THESSALÍA

VÓREIO AIGAÍO

GREECE

Vóreioi Sporades

IÓNIOI
NÍSOI

DYTIKÍ ELLÁDA

STEREÁ ELLÁDA

AEGEAN
SEA

ATHÍNA
(ATHENS)

Peiraiás
(Piraeus)

ATTIKÍ

IONIAN SEA

PELOPÓNNISOS

PELOPÓNNISOS
(Peloponnesus)

MYRTÓON
PÉLAGOS

MEDITERRANEAN SEA

KRITIKÓN PÉLAGOS
(SEA OF CRETE)

KRÍTI

Irákleio

KRÍTI
(Crete)

Meters
Feet

3000
9840

2000
6560

1000
3280

500
1640

200
656

Sea Level

200
656

2000
6560

W-DRM6511-A1 -2-2-3
Copyright © Rand McNally & Co.

0   25   50   75   100   150   200   250 Kilometers

0   25   50   100   150 Miles

Scale 1 : 2,500,000   Lambert Conformal Conic Projection

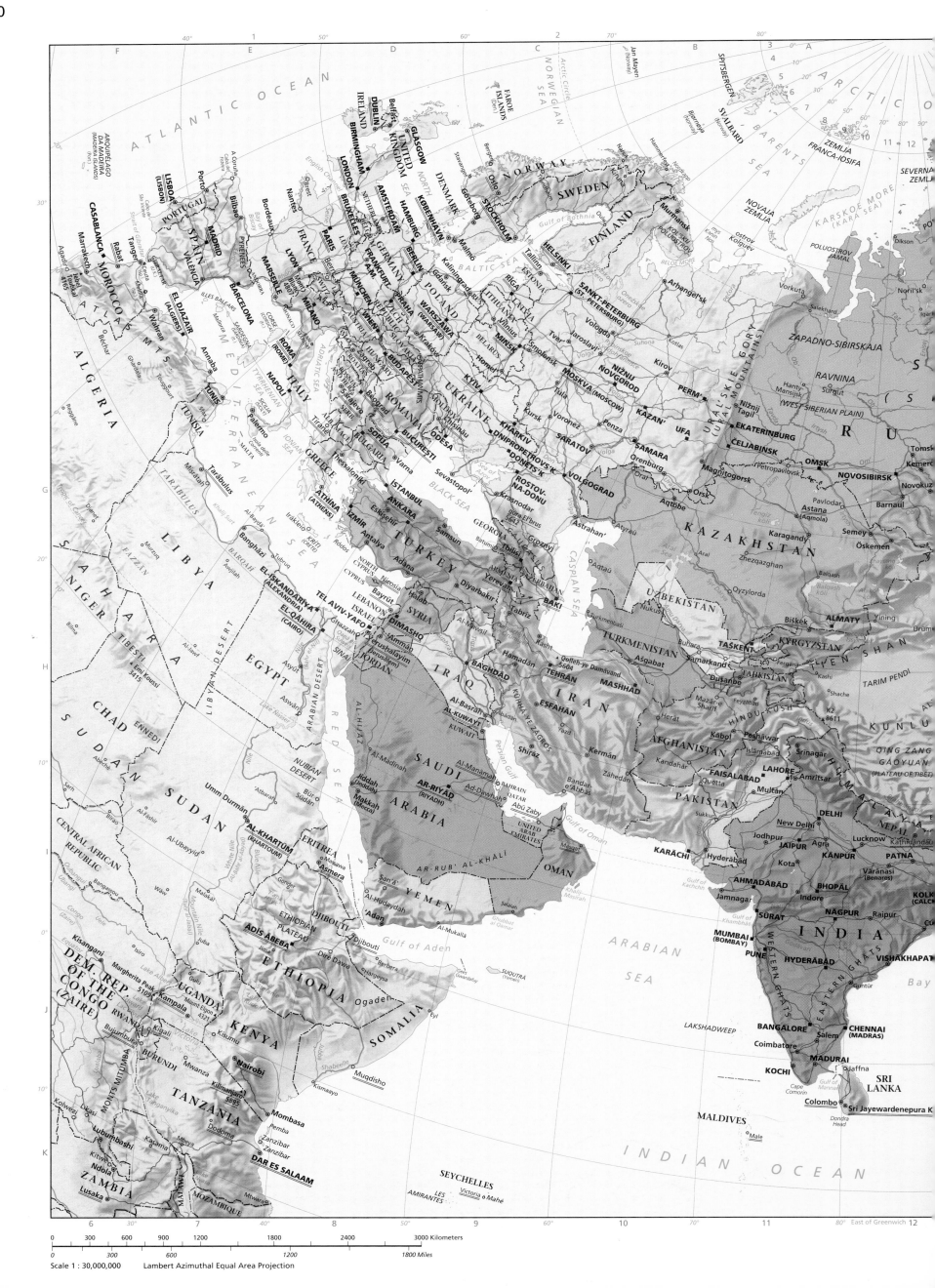

Scale 1 : 30,000,000   Lambert Azimuthal Equal Area Projection

A B C D E F G

ostrov Vrangelja

Bering Strait

St.Lawrence Island (U.S.)

BERING SEA

KOMANDORSKIE OSTROVA

ALEUTIAN ISLANDS (U.S.)

Attu Island

HAWAIIAN ISLANDS (U.S.)

MIDWAY ISLANDS (U.S.)

TAJMYR

MORE LAPTEVYH (LAPTEV SEA)

NOVOSIBIRSKIE OSTROVA

ozero Tajmyr

Hatanga

VOSTOČNO-SIBIRSKOE MORE

HREBET ČERSKOGO

SREDINNYJ HREBET

Petropavlovsk-Kamčatskij

PACIFIC OCEAN

SREDNESIBIRSKOE PLOSKOGOR'E (CENTRAL SIBERIAN PLATEAU)

SIBIR' (SIBERIA)

VERHOJANSKIJ HREBET

SEA OF OKHOTSK

POLUOSTROV KAMČATKA

Jakutsk

STANOVOJ HREBET

OSTROV SAHALIN

KURIL'SKIE OSTROVA (KURIL ISLANDS)

WAKE ISLAND (U.S.)

Bratsk

Irkutsk

Angarsk

Ulan-Ude

Komsomol'sk-na-Amure

Habarovsk

Blagoveščensk

SIHOTE-ALIN'

Južno-Sahalinsk

HOKKAIDŌ

Sapporo Asahikawa

Hakodate

Aomori

Sendai

HONSHŪ

Niigata

TŌKYŌ

YOKOHAMA

Minami-Tori-Shima (Japan)

Ulaanbaatar

HANGAYN NURUU

Choybalsan

Qiqihar

HARBIN

CHANGCHUN

Jilin

Vladivostok

Ch'ŏngjin

NORTH KOREA

P'yŏngyang

SEA OF JAPAN

Kanazawa

KYŌTO

NAGOYA

OSAKA

HIROSHIMA

JAPAN

IZU-SHOTŌ (Japan)

MONGOLIA

SHENYANG FUSHUN

Dandong

SŎUL (SEOUL)

SOUTH KOREA

PUSAN

Taegu

SHIKOKU

OGASAWARA-GUNTŌ (Japan)

GOBI DESERT

Hohhot

Zhangjiakou

BEIJING

DALIAN

Bo Hai

Mokp'o

FUKUOKA

KYŪSHŪ

Kagoshima

KAZAN-RETTŌ (Japan)

NORTHERN MARIANA ISLANDS (U.S.)

MARSHALL ISLANDS

Eneweták

Baotou

Yinchuan

TAIYUAN

Shijiazhuang

TIANJIN

JINAN

Qingdao

YELLOW SEA

Cheju-do

NANSEI-SHOTŌ (RYUKYU ISLANDS)

Amami-Ō-shima

Okinawa-jima

Naha

Farallon de Pajaros

Agrihan

Alamagan Pagan

Guguan

Anatahan Saipan

MARIANA ISLANDS

Tinian

Rota

Ujelang

Anxi

Xining

Lanzhou

Baoji

XI'AN

Zhengzhou

Xuzhou

Huainan

Nanjing

Hangzhou

SHANGHAI

Ningbo

EAST CHINA SEA

GUAM (U.S.)

MICRONESIA

Qinghai Hu

CHINA

CHENGDU

WUHAN

Nanchang

Wenzhou

Oroluk

Pohnpei Pakin

HALL ISLANDS

MORTLOCK ISLANDS

CHUUK

SENYAVIN ISLANDS

Lhasa

CHONGQING

CHANGSHA

Hengyang

Fuzhou

T'AIPEI

TAIWAN

Gaferut

Ulul

Puluwat

CAROLINE ISLANDS

FEDERATED STATES OF MICRONESIA

Kapingamarangi

Guiyang

Kunming

Liuzhou

GUANGZHOU

Xiamen

T'ainan

KAOHSIUNG

Luzon Strait

Woleai

Eauripik

Ifalik

Equator

GLADESH

DHAKA (DACCA)

HITTAGONG

MYANMAR (BURMA)

Mandalay

XIANGGANG (HONG KONG)

Nanning

Zhanjiang

Haikou

HAINAN DAO

Gulf of Tonkin

HA NOI (HANOI)

Hai Phong

LUZON

Baguio

Quezon City

MANILA

PHILIPPINES

Samar

YAP

Sorol

Ngulu

PALAU ISLANDS

Koror

PALAU

ADMIRALTY ISLANDS

Manus Island

NEW IRELAND

Kavieng

BISMARCK ARCHIPELAGO

Sittwe

YANGON (RANGOON)

THAILAND

VIETNAM

XISHA QUNDAO (PARACEL ISLANDS)

Da Nang

Mindoro

Panay

Iloilo

Cebu

Leyte

MINDANAO

SONSOROL ISLANDS

New Hanover

NEW BRITAIN

BISMARCK SEA

Rabaul

Chiang Mai

Udon Thani

Vientiane

Gulf of Martaban

COCO ISLANDS

KRUNG THEP (BANGKOK)

CAMBODIA

LAOS

SOUTH CHINA SEA

SULU SEA

Palawan

Zamboanga

Jolo Island

Moro Gulf

Mount Apo 2954

Davao

Tinaca Point

KEPULAUAN TALAUD

Morotai

Madang

Wewak

SOLOMON SEA

ANDAMAN ISLANDS (India)

Dawei

Phnum Pénh

Gulf of Thailand

Kâmpóng Saôm

THANH PHO HO CHI MINH (HO CHI MINH CITY) (SAIGON)

SPRATLY ISLANDS

Balabac Island

KEPULAUAN SANGIHE

Manado

HALMAHERA

KEPULAUAN OBI

Pulau Waigeo

Pulau Yapen

Biak

Jayapura

Puncak Jaya 5030

NEW GUINEA

PAPUA NEW GUINEA

Mount Wilhelm 4509

Lae

Gulf of Papua

Port Moresby

ANDAMAN SEA

Mui Ca Mau

Phuket

MALAY PENINSULA

Gunong Kinabalu 4101

Bandar Seri Begawan

BRUNEI

CELEBES SEA

SULAWESI (CELEBES)

LAUT MALUKU

KEPULAUAN SULA

Buru

MALUKU (MOLUCCAS)

LAUT SERAM

SERAM (CERAM)

KEPULAUAN ARU

Pulau Yos Sudarso

CAPE YORK

NICOBAR ISLANDS (India)

George Town (Penang)

MALAYSIA

KUALA LUMPUR

MEDAN

SINGAPORE

KEPULAUAN NATUNA BESAR

MALAYSIA

Kuching

BORNEO (KALIMANTAN)

Pontianak

Banjarmasin

Balikpapan

Teluk Tomini

LAUT BANDA

KEPULAUAN KAI

KEPULAUAN TANIMBAR

Cape Arnhem

ARAFURA SEA

CAPE YORK PENINSULA

Pulau Nias

KEPULAUAN MENTAWAI

Pulau Siberut

Padang

SUMATERA (SUMATRA)

Pulau Bangka

Belitung

Pulau Laut

Ujungpandang

Pulau Buton

Pulau Wetar

Melville Island

Gulf of Carpentaria

AUSTRALIA

Banda Aceh

Palembang

Bandar Lampung

JAKARTA

BANDUNG

JAWA (JAVA)

SURABAYA

Madura

Bali

Lombok

Sumbawa

LAUT FLORES

FLORES

LAUT SAWU

TIMOR

EAST TIMOR

Kupang

TIMOR SEA

INDONESIA

Sumba

Selat Makasar

CORAL SEA

Cairns

Great Barrier Reef

Torres Strait

Cape York

M-DRM2402-P1

Copyright © Rand McNally & Co.

BLACK SEA

FINLAND

HELSINKI

ESTONIA

RIGA LATVIA

LITHUANIA

MINSK

BELARUS

SANKT-PETERBURG
(ST. PETERSBURG)

MOSKVA
(MOSCOW)

UKRAINE

KYIV
(KIEV)

KHARKIV

DNIPROPETROVS'K

DONETS'K

ROSTOV-
NA-DONU

VOLGOGRAD

SARATOV

SAMARA

UFA

PERM'

EKATERINBURG

ČELJABINSK

NIŽNIJ
NOVGOROD (GORKI)

KAZAN'

R U S S

KOMI

UDMURTIJA

TATARIJA

BAŠKIRIJA

KALMYKIJA

CASPIAN DEPRESSION
(PRIKASPIJSKAJA NIZMENNOST')

Astrahan'

KAZAK

Aral
Sea

UST-URT
PLATEAU

TURKMENISTAN

UZBEKISTAN

BAKÍ
(BAKU)

AZERBAIJAN

ARMENIA
Yerevan
(Erevan)

GEORGIA
Tbilisi

CAUCASUS

TURKEY

SYRIA

IRAQ

IRAN

BELOE MORE
(WHITE SEA)

Arhangel'sk

KARELIJA

Meters
Feet

6000
19680

4000
13120

3000
9840

2000
6560

1000
3280

500
1640

200
656

Sea Level

200
656

2000
6560

W-DRM4711-A1- 3-4-5
Copyright © Rand McNally & Co.

0   100   200   300   400   600 Kilometers
0   100   200   400 Miles

Scale 1 : 10,000,000   Lambert Conformal Conic Projection

57

① ADYGEJA
② KARAČAEVO-ČERKESIJA
③ KABARDINO-BALKARIJA
④ SEVERNAJA OSETIJA
⑤ ČEČNJA
⑥ INGUŠETIJA

POLUOSTROV
JAMAL

Tazovskij
poluostrov

ZAPADNO-

SIBIR'

(SIBERIA)

SREDNESIBIRSKOE
PLOSKOGOR'E

(CENTRAL SIBERIAN PLATEAU)

CENTRALNO-
TUNGUSSKOE PLATO

WEST SIBERIAN PLAIN)

ENISEJSKIJ KRJAZ

VOSTOČNYJ SAJAN

SAYAN MOUNTAINS

ZAPADNYJ SAJAN

HAKASIJA

HREBET SANGILEN

TUVA

BURJATIJA

Surgut

Omsk

Novosibirsk

Krasnojarsk

Bratsk

Irkutsk

Angarsk

HANGAYN NURUU

MONGOLIA

Kemerovo

Tomsk

Novokuznezk

Barnaul

TANNU-OLA

ALTAI

Mount Belukha
4374

Mount
Kujtun
4374

MONGOL ALTAYN NURUU

Astana
(Aqmola)

Pavlodar

Semey
(Semipalatinsk)

Öskemen

Karagandy
(Karaganda)

QAZAQTYNG USAQSHOQYLYGHY

(KAZAKH HILLS)

KHREBET
TARBAGATAJ

JUNGGAR PENDI

Ürümqi

BOGDA SHAN

BEI SHAN

GANSU

DZHUNGARIAN ALATAU
MTS

BOROHORO SHAN

Turpan Pendi
(Turfan Depression)

Balqash
köli
(Lake Balkhash)

Betpaqdala

MOVYNQUM QUMY

Almaty

Biškek

HREBET KUNGEJ ALATOO

HREBET TERSKEJ ALATAU

ozero
Issyk-Kul'

TIEN SHAN

pik Pobedy
7439

KURUKTAG

XINJIANG

CHINA

ALTUN SHAN

 QAIDAM PENDI

Taškent

KIRGIZ RANGE

KYRGYZSTAN

Pamir

Taklimakan Shamo
(Takla Makan Desert)

KUNLUN SHAN

QINGHAI

TARIM PENDI

TAJIKISTAN

ALAJSKIJ HREBET

ZERAVŠANSKIJ HREBET

Dušanbe

PAMIR

AFG.

pik Ismail Samani
7495

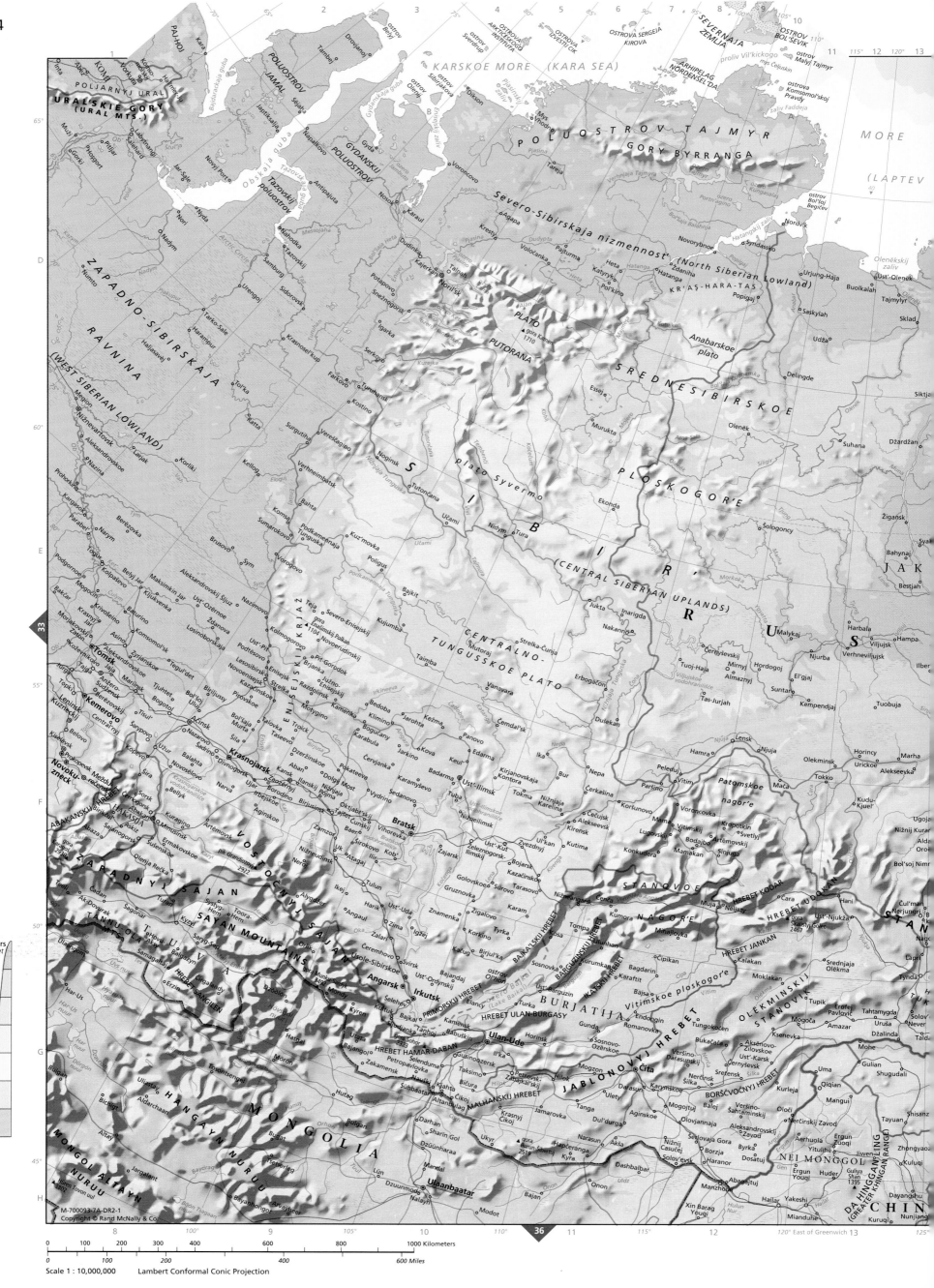

KARSKOE MORE   (KARA SEA)

MORE

(LAPTEV

POLUOSTROV TAJMYR
GORY BYRRANGA

Severo-Sibirskaja nizmennost' (North Siberian Lowland)

KOMI-JUL
POLJARNYJ URAL
URAL'SKIE GORY
(URAL MTS.)

ZAPADNO-SIBIRSKAJA
RAVNINA
(WEST SIBERIAN LOWLAND)

SREDNESIBIRSKOE

PLOSKOGORE'

JAK

S I B I R '   R U S S

(CENTRAL SIBERIAN UPLANDS)

PUTORANA

plato Syvermo

CENTRALNO-
TUNGUSSKOE PLATO

Tomsk
Kemerovo
Novoku-
zneck

Krasnojarsk

Bratsk

VOSTOČNIJ SAJAN

ZAPADNYJ SAJAN

SAYAN MOUNTAINS

HREBET

STANOVOE

NAGOR'E

HREBET KODAR

HREBET UDOKAN

STAN

Angarsk
Irkutsk

BURJATIJA

OLEKMINSKIJ
STANOVIK

TANNU-OLA MTS.

HANGAYN NURUU

TUVA

HREBET HAMAR-DABAN

Ulan-Ude

Čita

JABLONOVYJ HREBET

BORŠČOVOČNYJ HREBET

MONGOLIA

MONGOL ALTAYN
NURUU

Ulaanbaatar

NEI MONGGOL

DA HINGGAN LING
(GREATER KHINGAN RANGE)

CHIN

Meters / Feet
4000 / 13120
3000 / 9840
2000 / 6560
1000 / 3280
500 / 1640
200 / 656
Sea Level
200 / 656
2000 / 6560

0   100   200   300   400   600   800   1000 Kilometers
0   100   200   400   600 Miles
Scale 1 : 10,000,000   Lambert Conformal Conic Projection

RUSSIA

DA HING GAN LING (GREATER KHINGAN RAJ.)

HEILONGJIANG

DONG SAN SHE MANCHURIA

HARBIN

Qiqihar

CHANGCHUN

JILIN

SHENYANG FUSHUN

LIAONING

Anshan

NORTH KOREA

P'yŏngyang

SŎUL (SEOUL)

INCH'ŎN

SOUTH KOREA

Taejŏn

Taegu

PUSAN (FUSAN)

Kwangju

Mokp'o

Cheju-do (Quelpart Island) Halla-san 1950

SEA OF JAPAN (EAST SEA)

Vladivostok

Nahodka

HOKKAIDO

Sapporo

Hakodate

Aomori

Akita

HONSHŪ

Sendai

JAPAN

Niigata

TŌKYŌ KAWASAKI YOKOHAMA

KYŌTO OSAKA NAGOYA

KŌBE

HIROSHIMA

KITAKYŪSHŪ FUKUOKA

Nagasaki

KYŪSHŪ

SHIKOKU

Kagoshima

IZU-SHOTŌ (IZU ISLANDS)

PACIFIC OCEAN

YELLOW SEA

Bo Hai (Gulf of Chihli)

DALIAN (DAIREN)

Lüshun (Port Arthur)

Korea Bay

BEIJING (PEKING)

TIANJIN

HEBEI

JINAN

SHANDONG

Qingdao (Tsingtao)

Xuzhou

JIANGSU

NANJING

SHANGHAI

Wuxi Suzhou

Hefei

ANHUI

Hangzhou

ZHEJIANG

Ningbo

Wenzhou

Nanchang

JIANGXI

Fuzhou

FUJIAN

Xiamen

EAST CHINA SEA

NANSEI-SHOTŌ (RYUKYU ISLANDS)

AMAMI-SHOTŌ

Amami-Ō-shima

OKINAWA-SHOTŌ

Okinawa-jima

Naha

Tropic of Cancer

T'AIPEI Chilung

Hsinchu

T'aichung Hualien

T'ainan

Yü Shan 3997

KAOHSIUNG

TAIWAN

Taiwan Strait

SOUTH CHINA SEA

Bashi Channel

RUSSIA

SEA OF OKHOTSK

KURIL'SKIE OSTROVA (KURIL ISLANDS)

Habomai, Shikotan, Kunashiri and Etorofu, occupied since 1945, are claimed by Japan pending a final peace treaty.

RUSSIA

HOKKAIDŌ

Sapporo

S I H O T E   A L I N'

Vladivostok

Nahodka

S E A   O F   J A P A N

(E A S T   S E A)

J A P A N

SADO

Tok-to Take-shima
(claimed by S. Korea and Japan)

OKI-SHOTO

CHŪGOKU-SANCHI

HIROSHIMA

KYŌTO

NAGOYA

ŌSAKA

KŌBE

Himeji

Okayama

Kurashiki

Takamatsu

Wakayama

Tokushima

Matsuyama

Kōchi

SHIKOKU

HONSHŪ

TŌKYŌ

YOKOHAMA

KAWASAKI

Chiba

Numazu

Shizuoka

Hamamatsu

Toyohashi

PACIFIC OCEAN

KYŪSHŪ

Miyazaki

Beppu

Ōita

(IZU-SHOTO)

Inset map

a

Yaku-shima

TOKARA-RETTO

SATSUNAN-SHOTO

EAST CHINA SEA

N A N S E I - S H O T O

(R Y U K Y U   I S L A N D S)

JAPAN

PACIFIC OCEAN

Naha Okinawa

Okinawa-jima

Same scale as main map

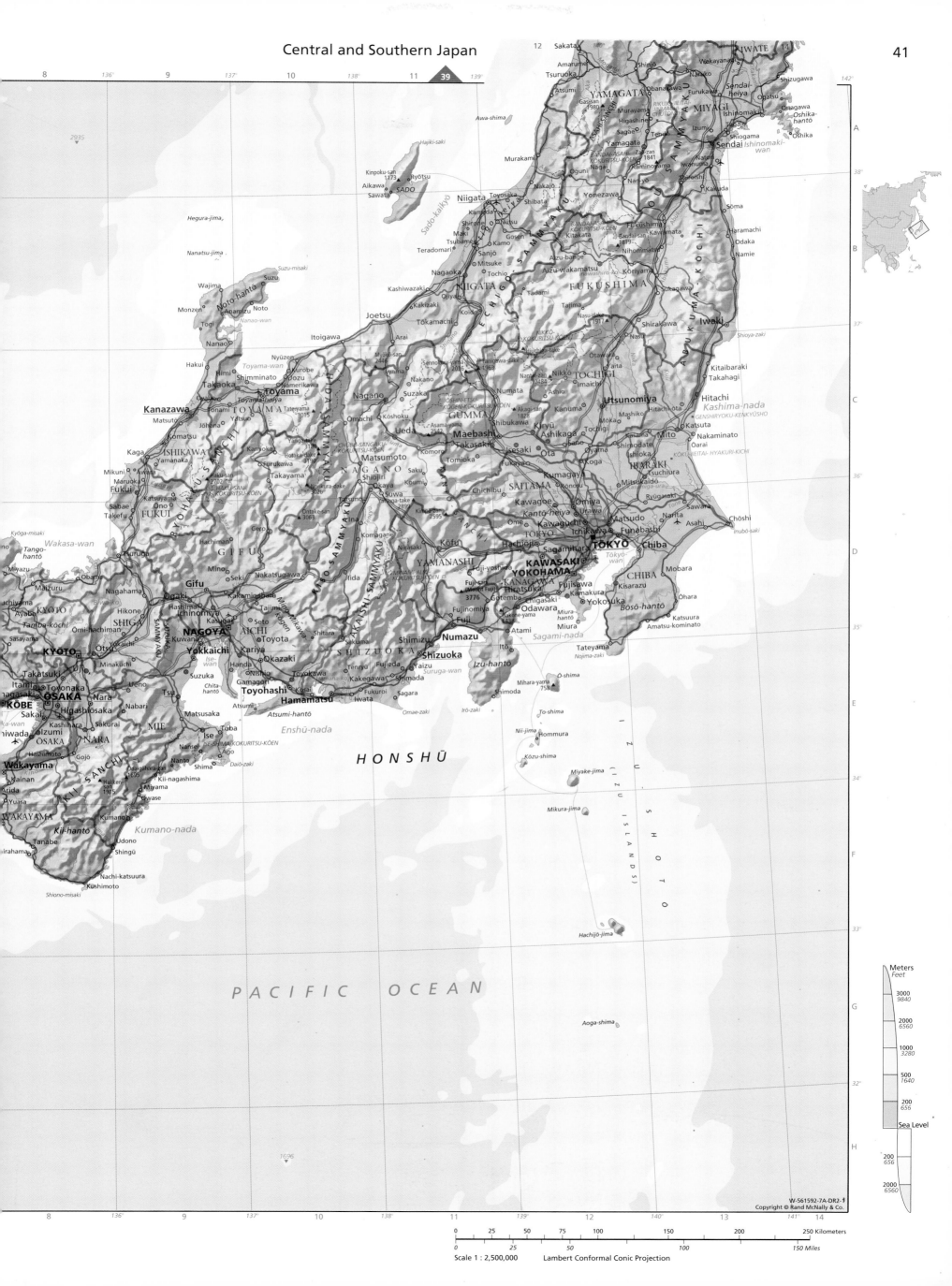

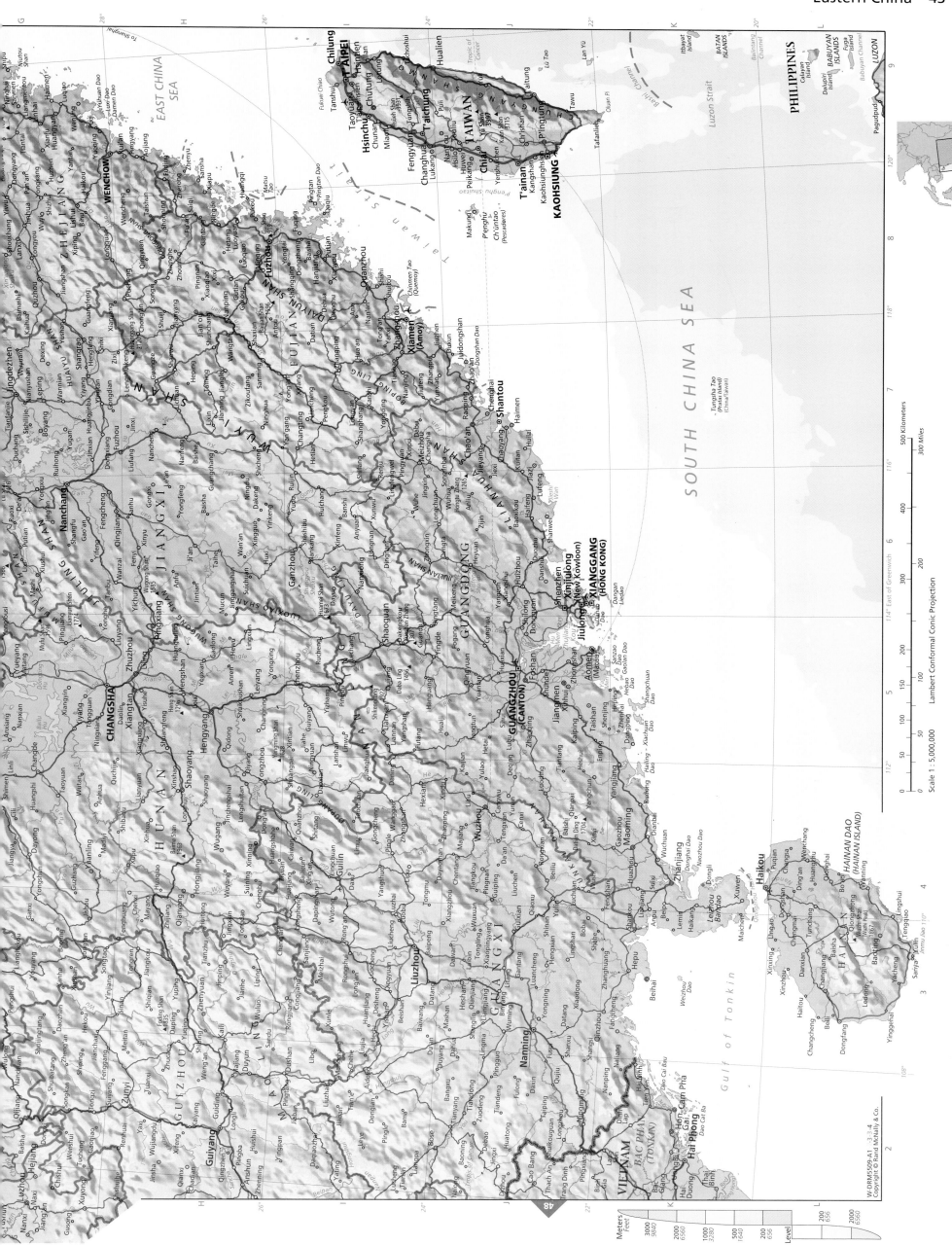

47 2 105 4 Gulf of Tonkin 110 5 A 36

HA NOI
Hai Phong
Ninh Binh Thai Binh
Nam Dinh
Thanh Hoa
Sam Son

Mông Cai
Móngcau Leizhou Bandao
Xuwen CHINA
Linga Qiongzhou Haixia 20°
Haikou
Changjiang Wenchang
Danxian
Dongfang Qionghai
Wuzhi Shan Baoting Wanning
Sanya Lingshui
HAINAN DAO
(HAINAN ISLAND)

Hsuhsuong
Ban Houayxay
Louangphrabang
Muang Ngoy
Xam Nua
Mông Hsat
Viangphoukha
Muang Thadua
Phayao
Chiang Rai
Mae Hong Son
Nan
Ban Napé Vangviang
Phou Bia 2819
LAOS
Khe Bo
Ky Son
Vinh
Ha Tinh
Ky Anh

Chiang Kham
Chiang Mai
Doi Inthanon 2600
Lamphun
Mae Sariang
Lampang
Phrae
Uttaradit

Muang Pakxan
Viangchan (Vientiane)
Nong Khai
Nakhon Phanom
Muang Khammouan
Bo Trach
Dong Hoi

VIETNAM
Vinh Ca Lo
Hue
Da Nang
Hoi An

XISHA QUNDAO
(PARACEL ISLANDS)
(Claimed by China, Taiwan and Vietnam)

MYANMAR
(BURMA)

THAILAND

Nakhon Sawan
Uthai Thani
Nakhon Si Ayutthaya
**KRUNG THEP
(BANGKOK)**
Samut Prakan
Chon Buri
Rayong
Chanthaburi

Ubon Ratchathani
Si Sa Ket
Surin
Nakhon Ratchasima

INDOCHINA

PHANOM DONGRAK RANGE

CAMBODIA

Phnum Aôral 1813
**Phnum Pénh
(Phnom Penh)**
Bătdâmbâng
ANGKOR WAT

Kâmpóng Cham
Stœng Trêng
Lumphăt

Buon Ma Thuot
Da Lat
Cam Ranh
Phan Rang
Phan Thiet
Nha Trang

SOUTH CHINA
SEA

Bien Hoa
**THANH PHO HO CHI MINH
(HO CHI MINH CITY)
(SAIGON)**
Long Xuyen
My Tho
Can Tho
Soc Trang
Bac Lieu

Ca Mau
Mui Ca Mau
Hon Khoai
Con Son

Nanshan Island

SPRATLY ISLANDS
(Claimed by Brunei, China, Malaysia, Philippines, Taiwan and Vietnam)

Andaman Sea
Gulf of Thailand

MERGUI ARCHIPELAGO

Ranong
Isthmus of Kra
Ko Samui
Surat Thani
Nakhon Si Thammarat

MALAY PENINSULA

Phuket
Trang
Songkhla
Hat Yai
Yala
Narathiwat
Kota Bharu
Pasir Mas
Kuala Krai
Kuala Terengganu

Pulau We
Banda Aceh
Lhokseumawe
Langsa

MEDAN
Tebingtinggi
Binjai
Gunung Leuser

KUALA LUMPUR
SEMENANJUNG MALAYSIA
Ipoh
MALAYSIA
Gunung Tahan 2187
Kuala Lipis
Gunung Benum 2107
Kuantan

KEPULAUAN NATUNA BESAR
Natuna Besar
Pulau Laut
KEPULAUAN ANAMBAS
Pulau Midai
Pulau Subi
KEPULAUAN NATUNA SELATAN
Pulau Serasan

BRUNEI
Bandar Seri Begawan
Miri
Gunung Mulu 2377
MALAYSIA
SARAWAK
Bintulu
Mukah
Sibu
Kuching

Kota Kinabalu
SABAH
Pulau Labuan
Labuan
Mount Mantalingajan

SUMATERA
(SUMATRA)
Pekanbaru
SINGAPORE
Johor Bahru
Pulau Batam
Pulau Bintan
Tanjungpinang
KEPULAUAN RIAU

Pematangsiantar
Padang
Bukittinggi
Jambi
Bangko
Palembang
PEGUNUNGAN BARISAN
Gunung Kerinci 3800

BORNEO
(KALIMANTAN)
Pontianak
Sambas
Singkawang
Putussibau
Semitau
Sintang
UPPER KAPUAS MTS.
IRAN MTS.
Gunung Menyapa 2000
Samarinda
Balikpapan
Bontang

KEPULAUAN MENTAWAI
Pulau Siberut

Lubuklinggau
Bengkulu
Gunung Dempo 3159

GREATER SUNDA

LAUT JAWA
(JAVA SEA)

Palangkaraya
Banjarmasin
Kumai
Sampit
Ketapang

Bandar Lampung
Serang
JAKARTA
Bogor
Purwakarta
Cirebon
Pekalongan
Kudus
Rembang
Tuban
Madura
Bangkalan
Sumenep
Pamekasan

BANDUNG
Sukabumi
Sumedang
Tegal
SEMARANG
SURABAYA
Surakarta
Yogyakarta
Magelang
Kediri
Malang
Jember
Banyuwangi
Probolinggo

INDIAN OCEAN

JAWA
(JAVA)
Denpasar
Bali
Gunung Rinjani 3726
Mataram
Lombok

Meters / Feet
4000 / 13120
3000 / 9840
2000 / 6560
1000 / 3280
500 / 1640
200 / 656
Sea Level
200 / 656
2000 / 6560

M-DRM4708-A1-1-2-2-4
Copyright © Rand McNally & Co.

0 100 200 300 400 600 800 1000 Kilometers
0 100 200 400 600 Miles
Scale 1 : 10,000,000   Sinusoidal Projection

Legend / Notes

The boundary between India and Pakistan through the disputed state of Jammu and Kashmir follows the "line of control" agreed upon by both countries in 1972.

(A) Area occupied by Pakistan and claimed by India.
(B) Area claimed and occupied by India; status disputed by Pakistan.
(C) Area occupied by China and claimed by India.
(D) Area occupied by India and claimed by China.

Scale 1 : 10,000,000   Lambert Conformal Conic Projection

Meters / Feet
6000 / 19680
4000 / 13120
3000 / 9840
2000 / 6560
1000 / 3280
500 / 1640
200 / 656
Sea Level
200 / 656
2000 / 6560

0 100 200 300 400 600 800 1000 Kilometers
0 100 200 400 600 Miles

Major labels

AFGHANISTAN
PAKISTAN
IRAN
BALUCHISTAN
INDIA
NEPAL
SRI LANKA
MALDIVES
XINJIANG
XIZANG (TIBET)
QING ZA (PLATE)

HINDU KUSH
KARAKORAM RANGE
KUNLUN
HIMALAYA
JAMMU AND KASHMIR
HIMACHAL PRADESH
PUNJAB
HARYANA
UTTARANCHAL
UTTAR PRADESH
RAJASTHAN
GUJARAT
MADHYA PRADESH
BIHAR
JHARKHAND
CHHATTISGARH
ORISSA
MAHARASHTRA
ANDHRA PRADESH
KARNATAKA
GOA
KERALA
TAMIL NADU
GREAT INDIAN DESERT
THAR DESERT
ARAVALLI RANGE
VINDHYA RA.
SATPURA RANGE
WESTERN GHATS
EASTERN GHATS
ARABIAN SEA
Bay of (Bengal)
INDIAN OCEAN
Lakshadweep Sea
Gulf of Kachchh
Gulf of Khambhat
Gulf of Mannar
Tropic of Cancer
Equator

DELHI, New Delhi, KARACHI, MUMBAI (BOMBAY), CHENNAI (MADRAS), KOLKATA, BANGALORE, HYDERABAD, AHMADABAD, SURAT, KANPUR (CAWNPORE), LUCKNOW, NAGPUR, BHOPAL, INDORE, JAIPUR, LAHORE, FAISALABAD, LUDHIANA, PATNA, VARANASI (BENARES), VISHAKHAPATNAM, KOCHI (COCHIN), MADURAI, Thiruvananthapuram (Trivandrum), Kozhikode (Calicut), Colombo, Kabol, Peshawar, Rawalpindi, Islamabad, Quetta, Kandahar, Herat, Zahedan, Kathmandu (Kathmandu)

Inset (a) — Maldives / Lakshadweep

a
MALDIVES
Male' Atoll, Ari Atoll, Mulaku Atoll, Suvadiva Atoll, Addu Atoll, Tiladummati Atoll, Miladummadulu Atoll, Fadiffolu Atoll, Male'
Minicoy Island (Ind.)
Nine Degree Channel
Eight Degree Channel
Lakshadweep Sea
INDIAN OCEAN
Same scale as main map
LAKSHADWEEP
Amindivi Islands
Chettlatt Island, Killtan Island, Kavaratti Island, Andrott Island
Kavaratti

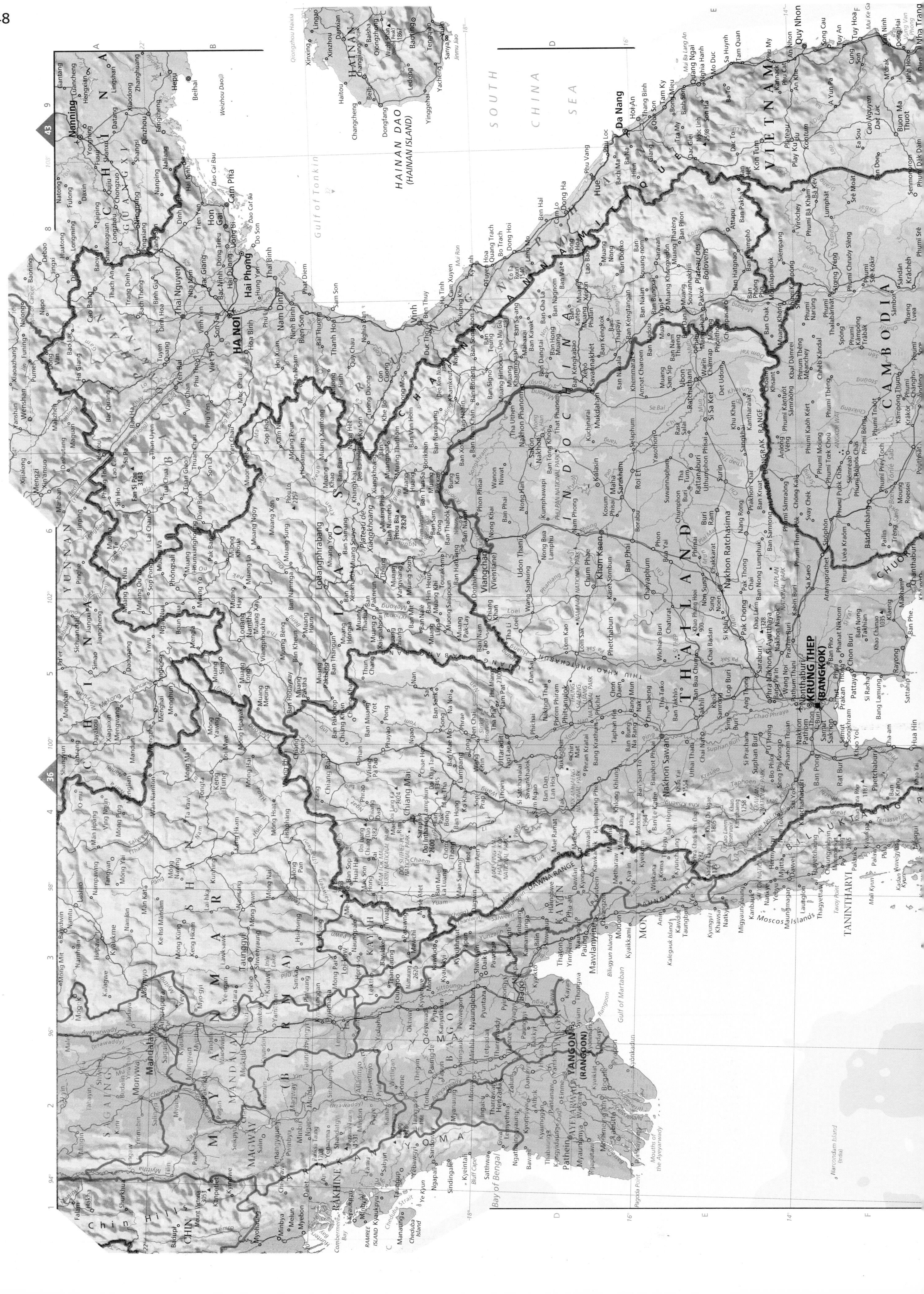
CHINA
GUANGXI
YUNNAN
HAINAN
HAINAN DAO
(HAINAN ISLAND)
Gulf of Tonkin
SOUTH CHINA SEA
VIETNAM
LAOS
THAILAND
CAMBODIA
MYANMAR (BURMA)
INDOCHINA
ANNAM
Nanning
HA NOI
Hai Phong
Vinh
Hue
Da Nang
Quy Nhon
Viangchan
(Vientiane)
Louangphrabang
Chiang Mai
Nakhon Ratchasima
Khon Kaen
Udon Thani
KRUNG THEP
(BANGKOK)
YANGON
(RANGOON)
Mandalay
Mawlamyine
Bago
Pathein
Taunggyi
Gulf of Martaban
Bay of Bengal
Mouths of the Ayeyarwady
SHAN
KAYAH
KAYIN
MON
BAGO
MAGWAY
MANDALAY
SAGAING
AYEYARWADY
RAKHINE
CHIN
TANINTHARYI
DAWNA RANGE
DANGRAK RANGE
Plateau des Bolovens
Plateau de Xiangkhoang
Moscos Islands
Mekong
Salween
Chao Phraya
Ayeyarwady

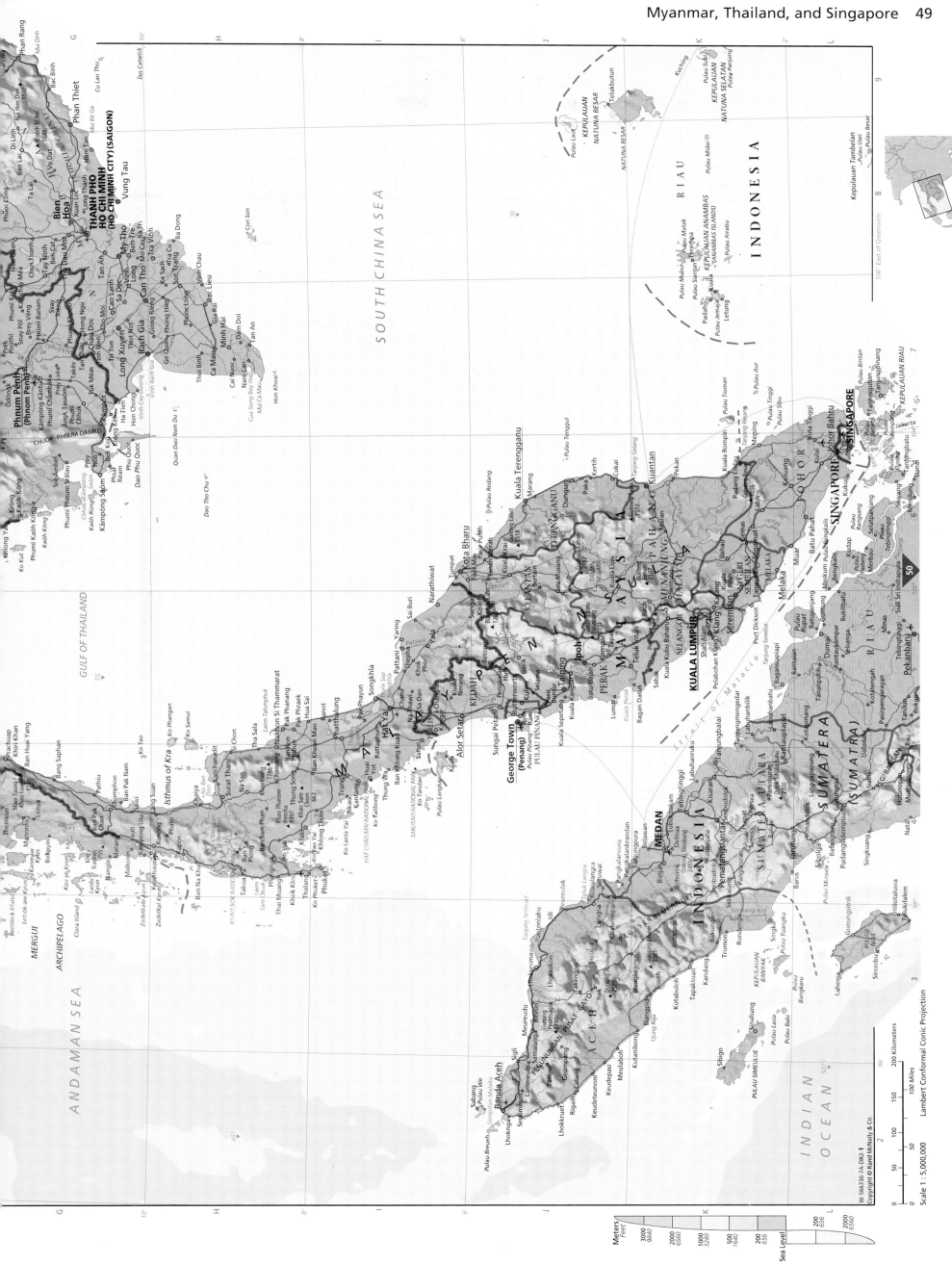

SOUTH CHINA SEA

INDONESIA

RIAU

KEPULAUAN
NATUNA BESAR

NATUNA BESAR

KEPULAUAN
NATUNA SELATAN

KEPULAUAN ANAMBAS
(ANAMBAS ISLANDS)

Kepulauan Tambelan

106° East of Greenwich

THANH PHO
HO CHI MINH
(HO CHI MINH CITY)(SAIGON)

Bien
Hoa

Phnum Penh
(Phnom Penh)

CHUOR PHNUM DAMREI

GULF OF THAILAND

MALAYSIA

TERENGGANU

PAHANG

KELANTAN

PERAK

SELANGOR

KUALA LUMPUR

NEGERI SEMBILAN

MELAKA

JOHOR

SINGAPORE
SINGAPORE

Kota Bharu

Ipoh

George Town
(Penang)
PULAU PINANG

KEDAH

PERLIS

Alor Setar

Songkhla

Phuket

Isthmus of Kra

HAT CHAO MAI NATIONAL PARK

TARUTAO NATIONAL PARK

KHAO SOK NATIONAL PARK

MERGUI
ARCHIPELAGO

ANDAMAN SEA

INDONESIA

MEDAN

SUMATERA UTARA

SUMATERA
(SUMATRA)

RIAU

Pekanbaru

ACEH

Banda Aceh

PEGUNUNGAN
PUSAT GAYO

BUKIT
BARISAN

PEGUNUNGAN

KEPULAUAN
BANYAK

PULAU SIMEULUE

PULAU NIAS

INDIAN
OCEAN

Strait of Malacca

Scale 1 : 5,000,000

200 Kilometers

100 Miles

Lambert Conformal Conic Projection

W 566730 7A DR2 1
Copyright © Rand McNally & Co.

Meters   Feet
3000   9840
2000   6560
1000   3280
500   1640
200   656
Sea Level

200   656
2000   6560

50

SOUTH CHINA SEA

MALAY PENINSULA

MEDAN

KUALA
LUMPUR

MALAYSIA

SINGAPORE
SINGAPORE

SUMATERA
UTARA

RIAU

SUMATERA
BARAT

Padang

JAMBI
Jambi

SUMATERA
(SUMATRA)

Palembang

BENGKULU

SUMATERA
SELATAN

Bengkulu

LAMPUNG

Bandar Lampung

INDIAN

OCEAN

GREATER S

IND

LAUT

PONTIANAK

KEPULAUAN
NATUNA BESAR

KEPULAUAN ANAMBAS
(ANAMBAS ISLANDS)

KEPULAUAN
NATUNA SELATAN

KEPULAUAN
RIAU

KEPULAUAN
KARIMATA

BANGKA

Pangkalpinang

Belitung

JAKARTA

BANDUNG

JAWA BARAT

JAWA (JAVA)

KEPULAUAN MENTAWAI
(MENTAWAI ISLANDS)

Meters
Feet

3000
9840

2000
6560

1000
3280

500
1640

200
656

Sea Level

200
656

2000
6560

W-DRM5521-A1
Copyright © Rand McNally & Co.

0   50   100   150   200   300   400   500 Kilometers
0   50   100   200   300 Miles

Scale 1 : 5,000,000   Sinusoidal Projection

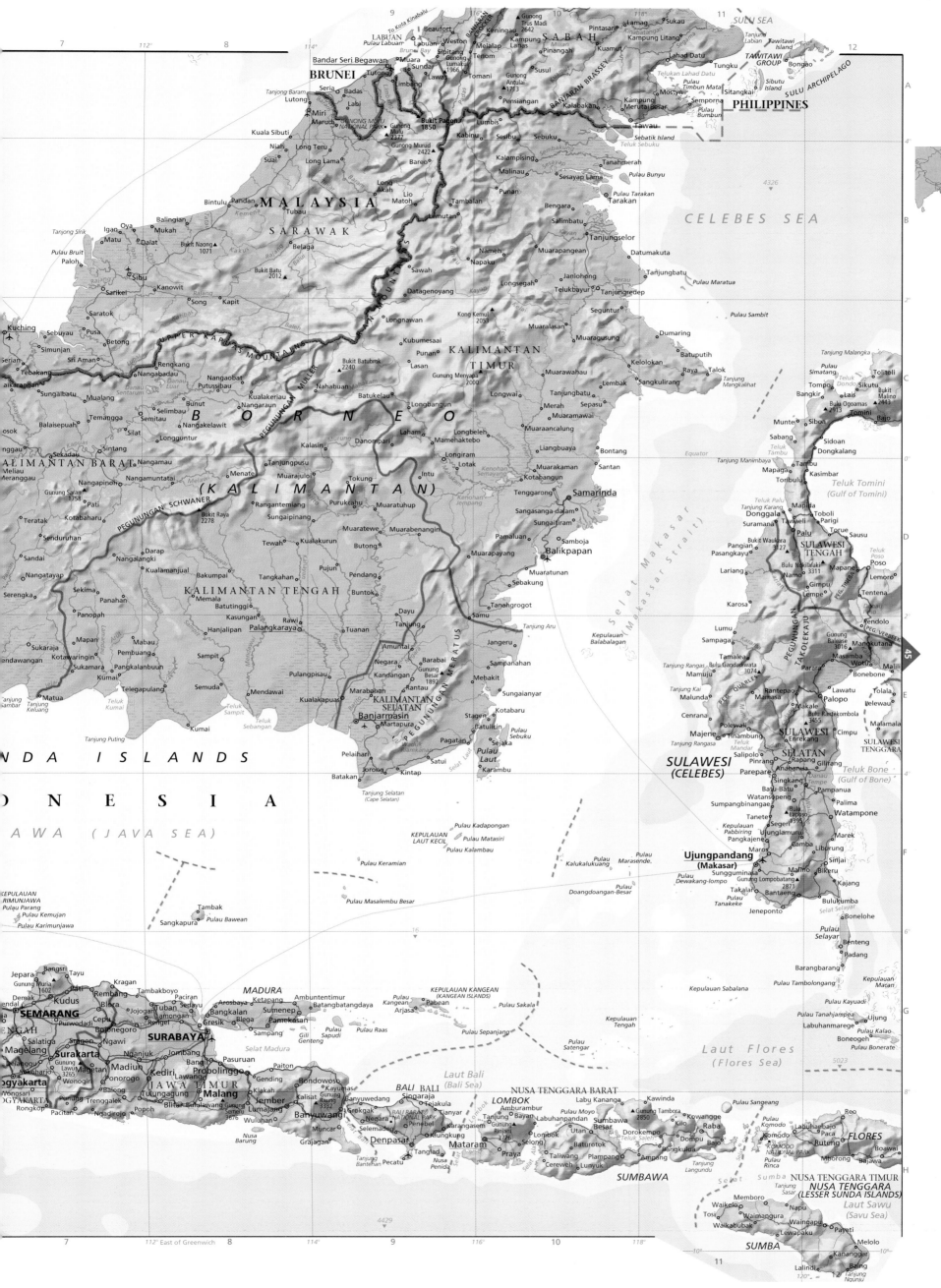

CELEBES SEA

SULU SEA

SULU ARCHIPELAGO

PHILIPPINES

BRUNEI

MALAYSIA

SABAH

SARAWAK

B O R N E O

(K A L I M A N T A N)

KALIMANTAN TIMUR

KALIMANTAN BARAT

KALIMANTAN TENGAH

KALIMANTAN SELATAN

Samarinda

Balikpapan

Banjarmasin

PEGUNUNGAN SCHWANER

PEGUNUNGAN MERATUS

UPPER KAPUAS MOUNTAINS

NDA ISLANDS

ONESIA

AWA (JAVA SEA)

KEPULAUAN KARIMUNJAWA

SEMARANG

SURABAYA

Surakarta

MADURA

KEPULAUAN KANGEAN (KANGEAN ISLANDS)

JAWA TIMUR

Malang

BALI

Bali

Denpasar

LOMBOK

Mataram

NUSA TENGGARA BARAT

SUMBAWA

Laut Flores (Flores Sea)

Laut Bali (Bali Sea)

NUSA TENGGARA TIMUR

NUSA TENGGARA (LESSER SUNDA ISLANDS)

FLORES

Laut Sawu (Savu Sea)

SUMBA

SULAWESI TENGAH

Palu

SULAWESI (CELEBES)

SULAWESI SELATAN

SULAWESI TENGGARA

Ujungpandang (Makasar)

Teluk Tomini (Gulf of Tomini)

Teluk Bone (Gulf of Bone)

PEGUNUNGAN TOKOLEKAJU

PEG. QUARLES

Selat Makasar (Makasar Strait)

Equator

PHILIPPINES

Seas and bodies of water: PHILIPPINE SEA, SOUTH CHINA SEA, SULU SEA, CELEBES SEA, VISAYAN SEA, SIBUYAN SEA, BOHOL SEA, Luzon Strait, Babuyan Channel, Lingayen Gulf, Dasol Bay, Manila Bay, Tayabas Bay, Ragay Gulf, Lagonoy Gulf, Lamon Bay, Leyte Gulf, Moro Gulf, Illana Bay, Davao Gulf, Sarangani Bay, Palawan Passage, Mindoro Strait, Tablas Strait, Balabac Strait, Basilan Strait, Sibutu Passage

Regions/Islands: LUZON, MINDORO, PALAWAN, CALAMIAN GROUP, PANAY, NEGROS, CEBU, BOHOL, LEYTE, SAMAR, MASBATE, VISAYAN ISLANDS, MINDANAO, Zamboanga Peninsula, SULU ARCHIPELAGO, JOLO GROUP, TAWITAWI GROUP, TAPUL GROUP, BABUYAN ISLANDS, POLILLO ISLANDS, CATANDUANES ISLAND, DINAGAT ISLAND, BORNEO, SABAH (MALAYSIA), INDONESIA

Mountains: CORDILLERA CENTRAL, SIERRA MADRE, Mount Sicapoo 2234, Mount Pulog 2931, Mount Palanan 212, Mount Pinatubo 1780, High Peak 2037, Mount Halcon 2585, Mount Baco 2487, Mount Isarog 1976, Mayon Volcano 2462, Mount Kaatoan 2896, Mount Apo 2954, Mount Busa 2083, Mount Mantalingajan 2085, Gunong Kinabalu (Mount Kinabalu) 4101, Trus Madi 2642, Gunong Meliau 1336

Cities (Luzon): Pagudpud, Laoag, San Nicolas, Batac, Vigan, Candon, Bangued, Aparri, Gonzaga, Alcala, Conner, Tuguegarao City, Tabuk, Lubuagan, Bontoc, Lagawe, Bangued, Ilagan, Echague, Cabarroguis, Maddela, San Fernando, La Trinidad, Baguio, Solano, Bayombong, Bira, Agno, Lingayen, Dagupan, Carranglan, Baler, San Carlos, Villasis, San Jose, Santa Cruz, Camiling, Cuyapo, Burgos, Gumba, Palayan, Iba, Tarlac, Cabanatuan, Palauig, Angeles, San Felipe, Mount Pinatubo, San Fernando, Olongapo, Orani, Balanga, Malolos, Meycauayan, Bataan Peninsula, Mariveles, Quezon City, Cavite, MANILA, Bacoor, Trece Martires, Tagaytay, Balayan, Santa Cruz, Lubang, Batangas, Lipa, San Pablo, Lucena, Lucban, Daet, Gumaca, Guinayangan, Naga, Pili, Iriga, Nabua, Goa, Bao, Legaspi, Ligao, Sorsogon, Bulan, Bulusan, Magallanes

Cities (Visayas): Nabas, Kalibo, Roxas, Panitan, Dumalag, Tibiao, Januiay, Iloilo, Silay, Talisay, Victorias, Sagay, Bogo, Toboso, La Carlota, San Carlos, Bacolod, Toledo, Mandaue, Cebu, Lapu-Lapu, Danao, Talibon, Hinigaran, Binalbagan, Kabankalan, Tagbilaran, Santander, Sipalay, Bayawan, Dumaguete, Bonawon, Siquijor, Catbalogan, Basey, Carigara, Tacloban, Ormoc, Baybay, Burauen, MacArthur, Hindang, Sogod, Maasin, Borongan, Llorente, Guiuan, Calbayog, Catarman, Gamay, Laoang, Roxas

Cities (Mindanao): Surigao, Dinagat, Siargao Island, Butuan, Cagayan de Oro, Gingoog, Balingasag, Jabonga, Tandag, Bislig, Mangagoy, Prosperidad, Ilinga, Dipolog, Katipunan, Sindangan, Oroquieta, Alubijid, Impasugong, Malaybalay, Ozamis, Tudela, Iligan, Marawi, Valencia, Bunawan, Zamboanga, Siraway, Vitali, Pagadian, Siocon, Buenavista, Margosatubig, Malabang, Tibal-og, Baganga, Panabo, Tagum, Babak, Cotabato, Sultan Kudarat, Parang, Datu Piang, Talayan, Midsayap, Kabacan, Kidapawan, Digos, Davao, Samal Island, Buluan, Lebak, Palimbang, Koronadal, Kiamba, Kling, General Santos, Malita, Lais, Tiblawan, Glan, Jose Abad Santos, Culaman

Cities (Palawan): Taytay, Caruray, Puerto Princesa, Marangas, Rio Tuba, Balabac

Malaysia/Borneo: Kota Belud, Tenghilan, Kota Kinabalu, Ranau, Beluran, Sandakan, Tambunan, Keningau, Pintasan, Lamag, Sukau, Kuamut, Lahad Datu, Tungku, Kunak, Semporna, Tawau, Kalabakan

Scale: Meters Feet — 3000/9840, 2000/6560, 1000/3280, 500/1640, 200/656, Sea Level, 200/656, 2000/6560

0 50 100 150 200 300 400 500 Kilometers
0 50 100 200 300 Miles

Scale 1 : 5,000,000   Lambert Conformal Conic Projection

W-562900-7A-DR2-1
Copyright © Rand McNally & Co.

GUJARĀT
Malegaon
Manmad
Chandvad
Nāshik
Yeola
Sinnar
Igatpuri
Kalyān
MUMBAI
(BOMBAY)
Pune
(Poona)
Mahābaleshwar
Harnai
Dābhol

MAHĀRĀSHTRA
Ahmadnagar
Solāpur
Belgaum

ARABIAN
SEA

GOA
Panaji
Mormugao
Madgaon
Cape
Ramas
Kārwār

KARNĀTAKA
Hubli-Dhārwār
Bhatkal
Udupi
Mangalore
Kāsaragod

DECCAN
Nānded
Warangal
HYDERĀBĀD
ANDHRA PRADESH
Nalgonda

INDIA

CHHATTISGARH
ORISSA
KHONDMĀL HILLS
Brahmapur

Vishākhapatnam

WESTERN GHATS
EASTERN GHATS

Nellore
Chennai
(MADRAS)
Bangalore
Mysore

COROMANDEL COAST

Bay of Bengal

KERALA
Kozhikode
(Calicut)
Coimbatore
(Koyambattur)
TAMIL NĀDU
Salem
PONDICHERRY
Pondicherry (Puducchéri)
Tiruchchirāppalli
KOCHI
(COCHIN)
MADURAI
Quilon
Tuticorin
Tirunelveli
Thiruvananthapuram
(Trivandrum)
Nāgercoil
Kanniyākumari Cape Comorin

LAKSHADWEEP
LAKSHADWEEP SEA

Jaffna
Rāmeswaram
Adam's Bridge
Gulf of Mannar
Trincomalee
SRI LANKA
Anurādhapura
Batticaloa
Kandy
COLOMBO
Sri Jayawardenepura Kotte
Moratuwa
Galle

INDIAN OCEAN

Scale 1 : 5,000,000   Lambert Conformal Conic Projection

Meters / Feet
2000 / 6560
1000 / 3280
500 / 1640
200 / 656
Sea Level
200 / 656
2000 / 6560

0 50 100 150 200 300 400 500 Kilometers
0 50 100 200 300 Miles

W-DRM5520-A1   1 - 2
Copyright © Rand McNally & Co.

Meters
Feet

6000
19680

4000
13120

3000
9840

2000
6560

1000
3280

500
1640

200
656

Sea Level

200
656

2000
6560

Scale 1 : 5,000,000   Lambert Conformal Conic Projection

0   50   100   150   200   300   400   500 Kilometers
0   50   100   200   300 Miles

A Area occupied by Pakistan and claimed by India.
B Area claimed and occupied by India; status disputed by Pakistan.
C Area occupied by China and claimed by India.
D Area occupied by India and claimed by China.

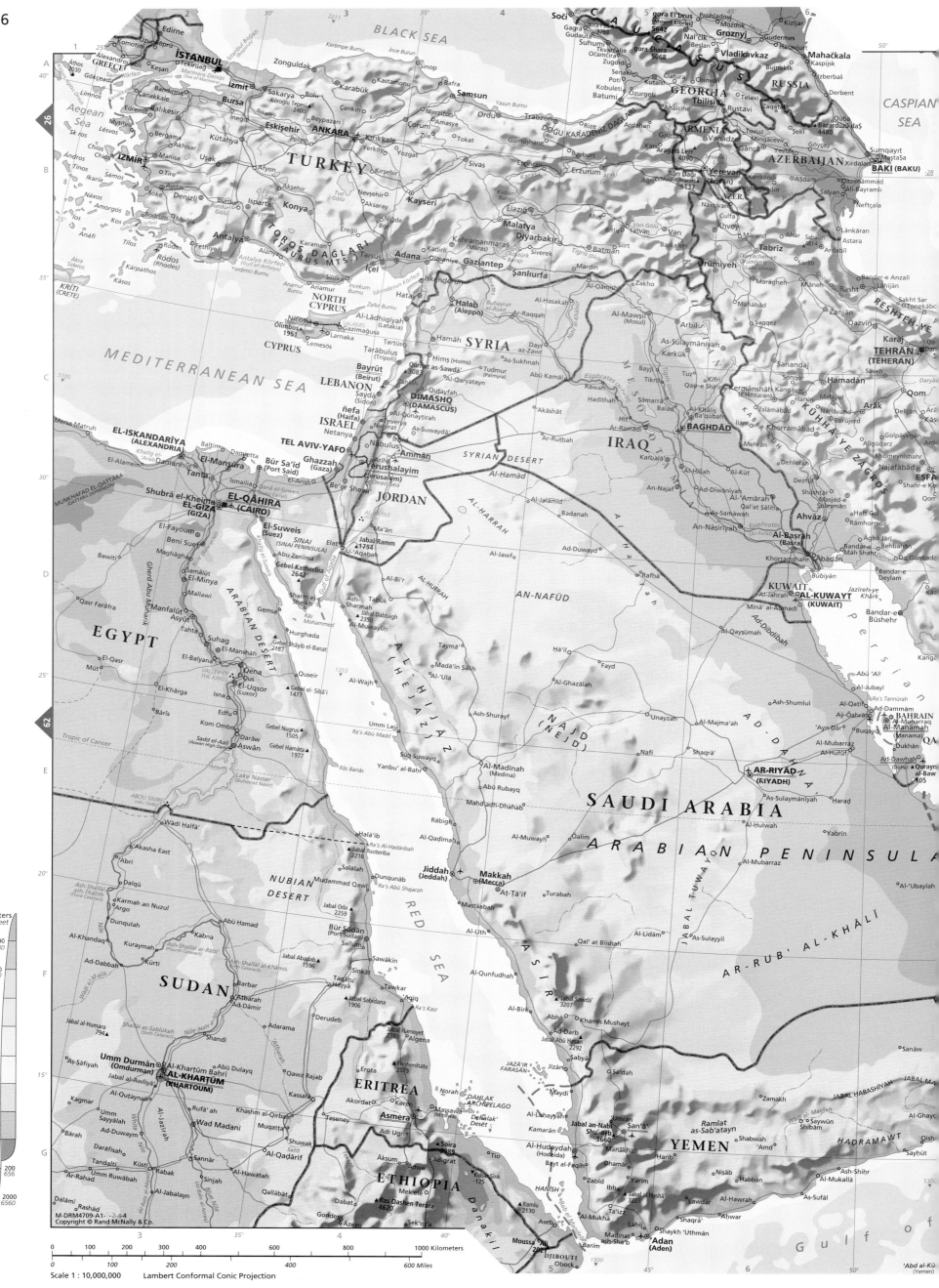

BLACK SEA

CAUCASUS

gora El'brus
(Mount Elbrus)
5642

Soči
Guaduta
Suhumi
Tkvarčelio
Zugdidi
Senaki
Kobuleti
Batumi

Prohladnyj
Mozdok
Nal'čik
Beslan
Clatura
Chinvali
Gori
Tbilisi

Groznyj
Gudermes
Hasavjurt
Mahačkala
Kaspijsk

GEORGIA
Telavi
Rustavi
Zaqatala
Šeki 4480

Bujnaksk
Derbent

RUSSIA

Izberbaš

CASPIAN
SEA

Edirne
Komotini
Alexandroúpoli
GREECE
Athos
2030
Gökçeada
Limnos
Lésvos
Aegean
Sea
Chíos
Sk ros
Andros
Náxos
Ikaria
Sámos
Tínos
Amorgós
Anáfi
Astipálaia
Kos
Ródos
(Rhodes)
Kárpathos
Kásos
KRÍTI
(CRETE)
Akra
Sídheros

İSTANBUL
Tekirdağ
İstanbul Boğazı
(Bosporus)
İzmit
Sakarya
Bursa
İnegöl
Bandırma
Balıkesir
Edremit
Akhisar
Bergama
İZMİR
Manisa
Uşak
Kütahya
ESKİŞEHIR
ANKARA
Bolu
Karabük
Çankırı
Zonguldak
Kastamonu
Bafra
Sinop
Samsun
Ordu
Trabzon
Rize
Artvin
Ardahan
Erzurum
ARMENIA
Gjumri
Aragats Lerr
4090
Vanadzor
YEREVAN
(Erevan)
AZERBAIJAN
Tovuz
Ganca
Mingacevir
Yevlax
Göyçay
Şamaxi
Sumqayit
BAKI (BAKU)

TURKEY

MEDITERRANEAN SEA

Scale 1 : 10,000,000   Lambert Conformal Conic Projection

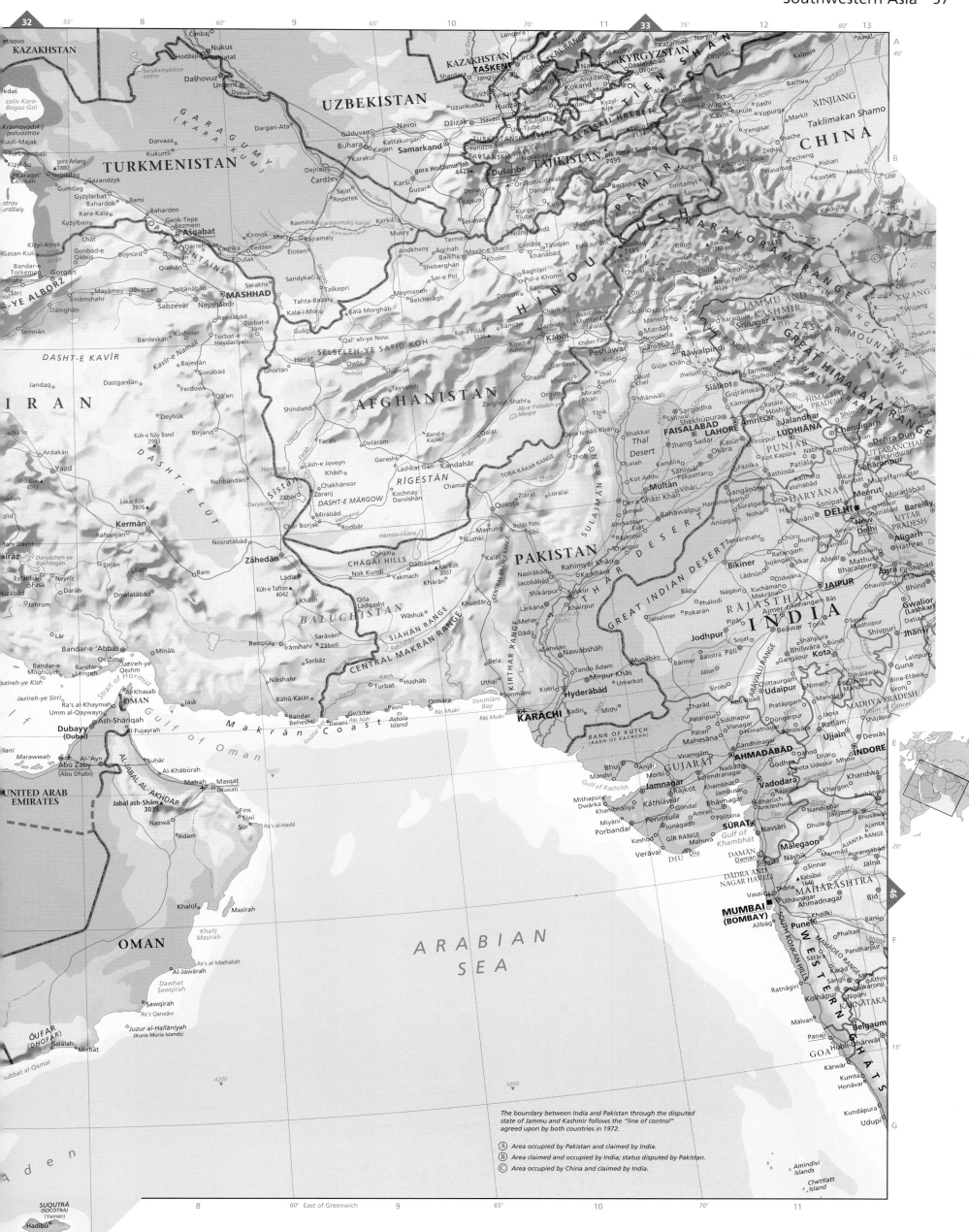

The boundary between India and Pakistan through the disputed
state of Jammu and Kashmir follows the "line of control"
agreed upon by both countries in 1972.

Ⓐ Area occupied by Pakistan and claimed by India.

Ⓑ Area claimed and occupied by India; status disputed by Pakistan.

Ⓒ Area occupied by China and claimed by India.

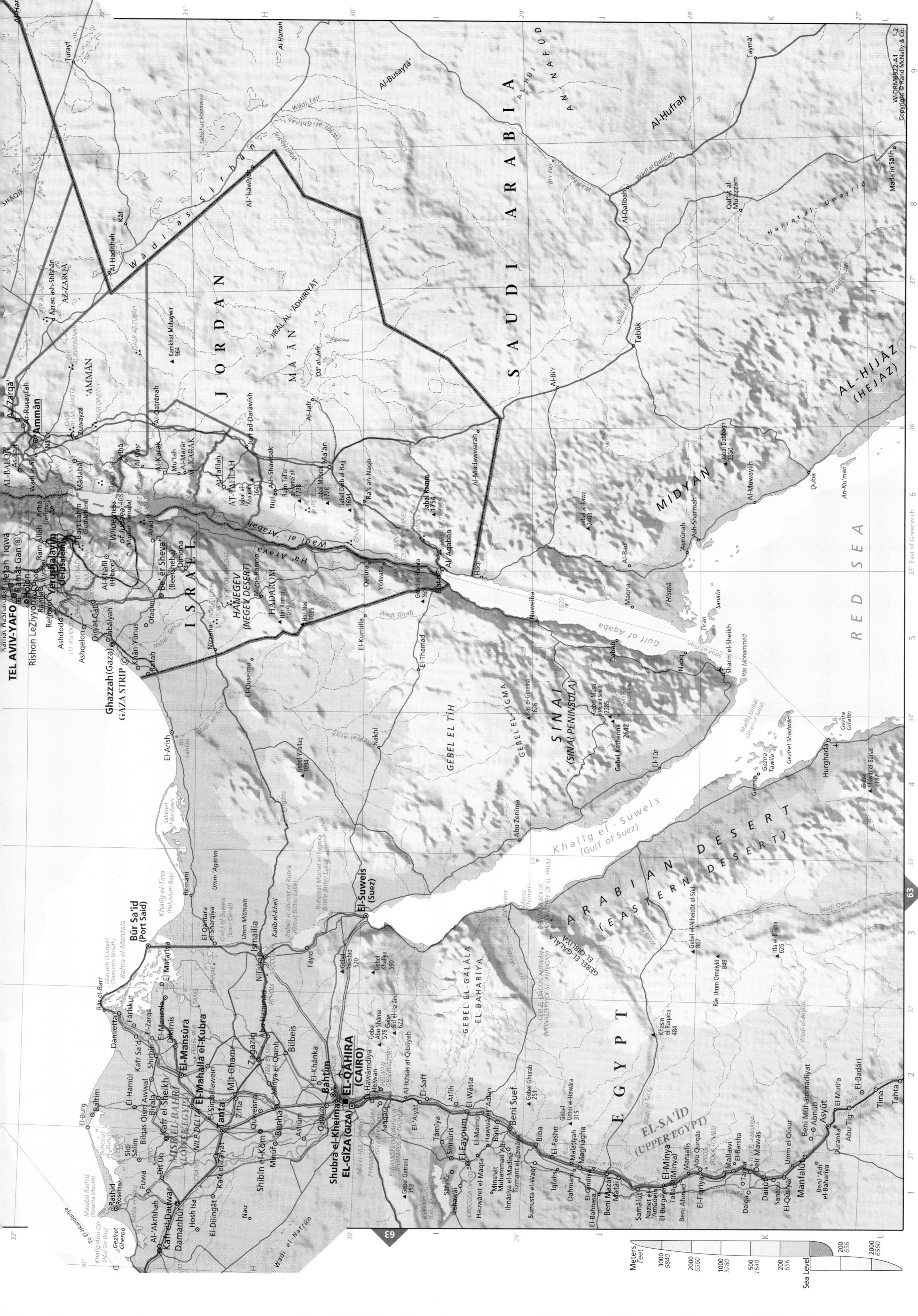

SAUDI ARABIA

JORDAN

ISRAEL

EGYPT

SINAI (SINAI PENINSULA)

AL-HIJÂZ (HEJAZ)

MIDYAN

RED SEA

Gulf of Aqaba

Khalîg el-'Suweis (Gulf of Suez)

ARABIAN DESERT (EASTERN DESERT)

AN NAFÛD

'AMMÂN

Ammân
Az-Zarqâ'
Madabâ
Al-Karak
Ma'ân
Al-'Aqabah
Tabûk
Taymâ'
Al-Hufrah

TEL AVIV-YAFO
Yerushalayim (Jerusalem)
Be'er Sheva (Beersheba)
Ashdod
Ashqelon
Ghazzah (Gaza)
GAZA STRIP
Rafah
El-'Arîsh

HANEGEV (NEGEV DESERT)

HADAROM

Wadi al-'Araba Ha-'Arava

EL-QAHIRA (CAIRO)
EL-GIZA (GIZA)
Shubrâ el-Kheima
El-Khanka
El-Matarîya
Ismâ'îlia
Bûr Sa'îd (Port Said)
El-Suweis (Suez)
El-Mansûra
El-Mahalla el-Kubra
Tanta
Damietta
Damanhûr
Kafr el-Dawwar

GEBEL EL TÎH

GEBEL EL JIGMA

Gebel Katherîna 2642
Gebel Mûsa 2285
El-Tûr
Sharm el-Sheikh
Râs Mohammed
Hurghada
Nuweiba
Dahab
Nabq

EL-SA'ÎD (UPPER EGYPT)

El-Minya
Mallawi
Asyût
El-Badâri
Beni Suef
El-Fayoum
El-Wâsta

Meters / Feet
3000 / 9840
2000 / 6560
1000 / 3280
200 / 656
Sea Level

Scale 1 : 2,500,000
Lambert Conformal Conic Projection

250 Kilometers
150 Miles

Copyright © Rand McNally & Co.

63

59

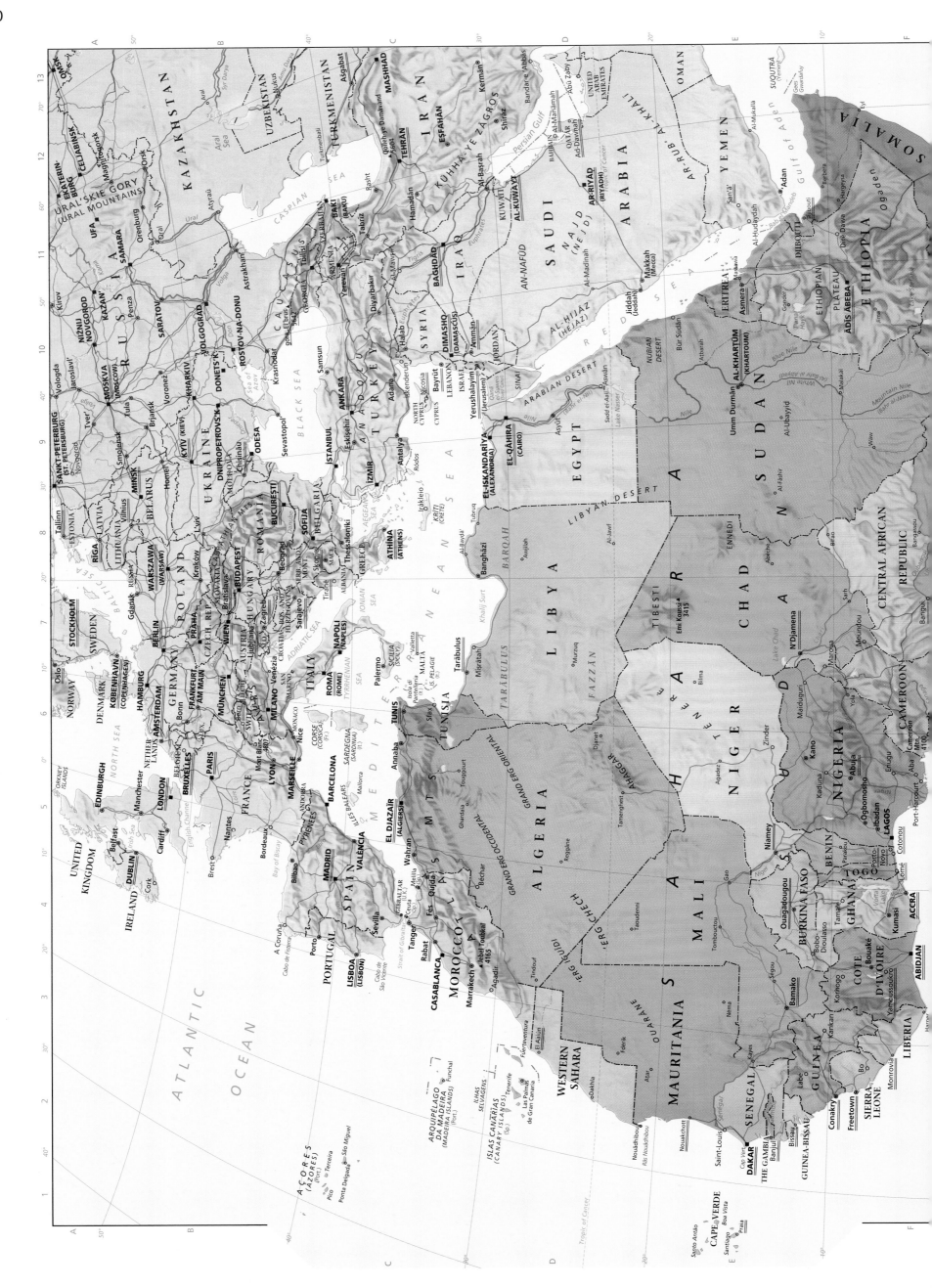

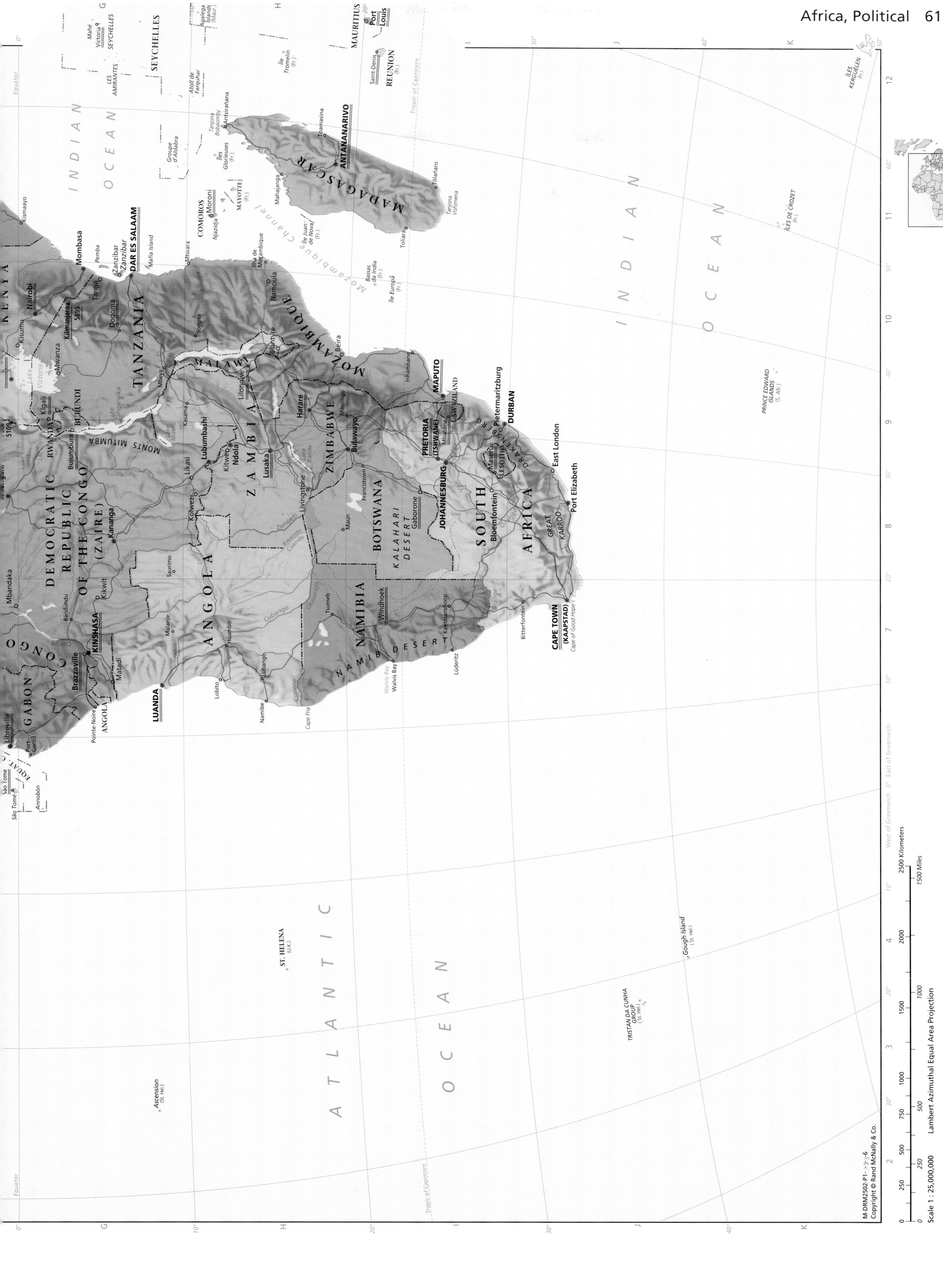

SEYCHELLES

G

Mahé
Victoria
SEYCHELLES

LES
AMIRANTES

Atoll de
Farquhar

Île
Tromelin
(Fr.)

Île
Tromelin
(Fr.)

MAURITIUS

Port
Louis

RÉUNION
(Fr.)

Saint-Denis

Equator

INDIAN

OCEAN

Agalega
Islands
(Maur.)

H

Groupe
d'Aldabra

Îles
Glorieuses
(Fr.)

Tanjona
Bobaomby

Antsiranana

Toamasina

MAYOTTE
(Fr.)

COMOROS
Moroni

Njazidja

Île Juan
de Nova
(Fr.)

MADAGASCAR

ANTANANARIVO

Mahajanga

Mahanoro

Tanjona
Vohimena

Toliara

Bassas
da India
(Fr.)

Île Europa
(Fr.)

Ilha de
Moçambique

Mozambique Channel

Kismaayo

KENYA

Mombasa

Zanzibar

Pemba
Zanzibar
Mafia Island

DAR ES SALAAM

Tanga

Nairobi

Kilimanjaro
5895

Kisumu

Lake
Victoria

Mwanza

Dodoma

TANZANIA

Mtwara

Songea

MALAWI

Mbeya

Lilongwe

Blantyre

Nampula

Beira

MOZAMBIQUE

Lake
Nyasa

INDIAN

OCEAN

PRINCE EDWARD
ISLANDS
(S. Afr.)

ÎLES DE CROZET
(Fr.)

ÎLES
KERGUÉLEN
(Fr.)

Harare

Bulawayo

ZIMBABWE

Mavingo

Inhambane

Francistown

Maun

BOTSWANA

Gaborone

KALAHARI
DESERT

MAPUTO

SWAZILAND

Mbabane

PRETORIA
(TSHWANE)

JOHANNESBURG

LESOTHO

Maseru

Pietermaritzburg

DURBAN

DRAKENSBERG

East London

Port Elizabeth

SOUTH

AFRICA

Bloemfontein

GREAT

KARROO

Orange

CAPE TOWN
(KAAPSTAD)

Cape of Good Hope

Bitterfontein

RWANDA
Kigali

BURUNDI
Bujumbura

Kasama

ZAMBIA

Lusaka

Livingstone

Kariba

Lake
Tanganyika

Lake
Kivu

MONTS MITUMBA

DEMOCRATIC

REPUBLIC

OF THE CONGO

(ZAÏRE)

Lubumbashi

Likasi

Kolwezi

Ndola

Kitwe

Kananga

Mbuji-Mayi

Lualaba

Zambezi

Kabwe

Kwando

Zambezi

NAMIBIA

Windhoek

Tsumeb

Rundu

Keetmanshoop

NAMIB DESERT

Walvis Bay
Walvis Bay

Lüderitz

Cape Frio

Namibe

Lobito

LUANDA

ANGOLA

Huambo

Lubango

Malanje

Saurimo

Cubango

Cuito

Cuanza

Cunene

KINSHASA

Brazzaville

CONGO

GABON

Libreville

Port-
Gentil

São Tomé

EQUAT.
GUINEA

Annobón

Pointe-Noire

Matadi

Bandundu

Kikwit

Mbandaka

Congo

ATLANTIC

OCEAN

ST. HELENA
(U.K.)

Ascension
(St. Hel.)

Gough Island
(St. Hel.)

TRISTAN DA CUNHA
GROUP
(St. Hel.)

West of Greenwich   0°   East of Greenwich

Tropic of Capricorn

Equator

0   250   500   750   1000   1500   2000   2500 Kilometers

0   250   500   1000   1500 Miles

Scale 1 : 25,000,000   Lambert Azimuthal Equal Area Projection

M-DRM2502-P1--3--6
Copyright © Rand McNally & Co.

J   K

G   H   J   K

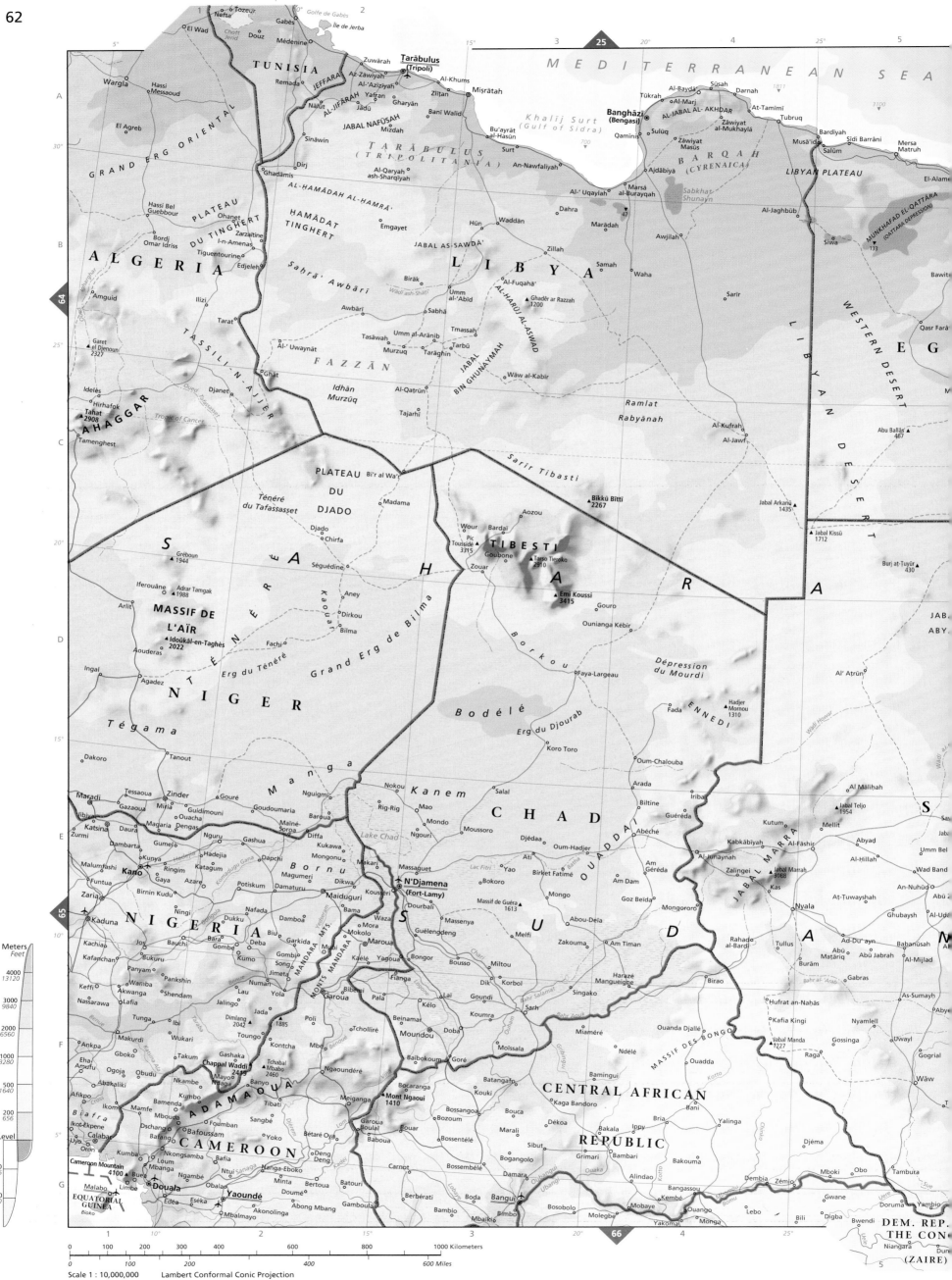

LEBANON
Saydā (Sidon)
Al-Qutayfah
DIMASHQ
(DAMASCUS)
SYRIA
Ḥefa (Haifa)
Nazeret
As-Suwaydā
Tavérya
An-Nabk
Ar-Ramādi
BAGHDAD
Najafābād
EṢFAHĀN
TEL AVIV-YAFO
Netanya
ISKANDARĪYA
(ALEXANDRIA)
Baltim
Damietta
-anhur
El-Mansūra
Tanta
Shubrā
l-Kheima
EL-QĀHIRA (CAIRO)
EL-GĪZA
(GIZA)
Fayoum
Beni Suef
ıhāga
-Minya
Mallawi
Manfalūt
Asyūt
Tahta
Suhag
El-Balyana
Qena
El-Khārga
Bārīs

IRBID
Irbid
Nabulus
Amman
JORDAN
Yerushalayim (Jerusalem)
Ghazzah (Gaza)
Be' er Sheva'
Ef-Arish
Ismailia
El-Suweis (Suez)
SINAI
(SINAI PENINSULA)
Elat
Al-'Aqabah
Jabal Ramm
1754
Al-Bi'r
Tabūk
Gebel
Katherina
2642
Sharm
el-Sheikh
Abu Zenima
Gemsa
Mohammed
Hurghada
Gebel Shāyib el-Banat
2187
Quseir
Gebel el-Sibā'i
1477
Gebel
Nugrus
1505
Gebel Hamāta
1977
Ra's Banās

IRAQ
SYRIAN DESERT
Ar-Rutbah
Baḥ al-milḥ
Karbalā'
Al-Hillah
Al-Kūt
Tigris
Euphrates
MESOPOTAMIA
An-Najaf
Ad-Dīwānīyah
As-Samāwah
An-Nāṣirīyah
Al-'Amārah
Qal'at Sālih
Al-Basrah (Basra)
Khorramshahr
Abādān
KUWAIT
AL-KUWAYT
(KUWAIT)
Al-Jahrah
Jazīreh-ye Khārk
Mīnā'
al-Ahmadī
Bandar-e Māh Shahr
Ahvāz
Masjed-e Soleymān
Behbahān
Aghā Jārī
Rāmhormoz

Dezfūl
Shahr-e Kord
IRAN
Ardakān
Yazd
Qomsheh
Shīr Kūh
4077
Ābādeh
Eqlīd

KŪHHĀ-YE ZAGROS

Al-Harrah
Al-Jalāmīd
Badanah
Ad-Duwayd
Al-Jawf
AN-NAFŪD
Ḥā'il
Al-Qaysūmah
Rafḥā'
Ar-Rutbah
Marv Dasht
Shīrāz
Kāzerūn
Do Gonbadān
Firūzābād
Bandar-e Deylam
Bandar-e Būshehr
Estahbān
Neyrīz
Dārāb
Fasā
Jahrom
Lār
Kangān
Jazīreh-ye Kīsh

Persian Gulf

AL-HUFRAH
Al-Qaysūmah
Ash-Shumlul
Al-Majma'ah
Al-Qatīf
Ad-Dammām
Az-Zahrān
BAHRAIN
Al-Muharraq
Al-Manāmah
(Manama)
QATAR
Ad-Dawhah
(Doha)
Dukhān
Qurayn Abā
al-Bawl
105
Abū 'Alī
Al-Jubayl
Jazīreh-ye
Kīsh
Şīr Banī
Yās
UNITED
ARAB
EMIRATES
Al-'Ubaylah

Ash-Sharmah
Al-Muwaylih
Taymā'
Fayd
Al-Ghazālah
'Unayzah
'Ayn Dār
Buqayq
Mīnā'
al-Ahmadī
Harad
Al-Hufūf
Al-Mubarraz
Yabrīn
Tropic of Cancer
Al-' Ubaylah

Aswān
Sadd el-'Alī
(Aswan High Dam)
First Cataract
VALLEY
OF THE KINGS
Isna
El-Uqsor (Luxor)
Edfu
Kom Ombo
Darāw
1353
Qena
Qus
Al-Wajh
Umm Lajj
Ra's
Abū Madd

ARABIAN DESERT

Ḥalā'ib
Ra's al-Hadāribah
Jabal Asoteriba
2216
Salālah
Dunqunāb
Ra's Abū
Shajarah
Muhammad Qawl
Jabal Oda
2259
Sallūm
Būr Sūdān
(Port Sudan)
Sawākin
2635
Al-Qadīmah
Rābigh
Zalim
Al-Muwayh
Mahd adh-Dhahab
Al-Ḥulwah
Al-Mubarraz

Al-'Ulā
Al-Madīnah
(Medina)
Abū Rubayq
Yanbu' al-Baḥr
Nafi
'Afīf
Turabah
Al-Qunfudhah
Al-Birk
Ad-Darb

OMAN

RED
SEA

NEJD

N
E
J
D

SAUDI
ARABIA

ARABIAN   PENINSULA

JABAL TUWAYQ

AR-RUB' AL-KHĀLI

AR-RUB' AL-KHĀLI

AS ĪR

Makkah
(Mecca)
Jiddah
(Jeddah)
Aṭ-Ṭā'if
Qal'at Bīshah
Al-Lidām
As-Sulayyil
Sanāw
JABAL MAHRĀT

AR-RIYĀD
(RIYADH)
As-Sulaymānīyah
Harad
Yabrīn

NUBIAN DESERT
Wādī Halfā'
Akasha East
Abri
Dalqū
Karmah an Nuzul
Kabna
Argo
Kuraymah
Kūrtī
Ash-Shallāl ar-Rabi'
(Fourth Cataract)
Ash-Shallāl al-Khāmis
(Fifth Cataract)
al-Humara
794

Abū Ḥamad
Mastāabah
Jabal Abadab
1596
Sinkāt
Taqatu'
Hayyā
Jabal
Sabidana
1906
Tawkar
'Aqīq
Algena
Jabal
Hamoyet
2780
Engershatu
2575
Erota

ERITREA

DAHLAK
ARCHIPELAGO
DAHLAK
Dehalak' Desēt
Norah
Ra's Kasr
JAZĀ'IR
FARASAN
Al-Lith
Al-Qunfudhah
Jabal Sawdā'
3207
Abhā
Khamis Mushayt
Jabal Abū
Hasan
2292
Sabyā
Jīzān
Sa'dah
Zamakh
Shibām
Saywūn
Tarīm
'Amd
JABAL
HABASHĪYAH
Al-Ghaydah
Ra's
Fartak
Qishn
Sayḥūt
5300

YEMEN

HADRAMAWT

JABAL MAHRĀT

Ramlat
as-Sab'atayn
Nişāb
Habbān
Al-Mukallā
As-Şufāl
Ash-Shihr
Shabwah
Ḥarīb
Ma'rib

Al-Luhayyah
Umrān
Jabal an-Nabi
Shu'ayb
3660
Şan'ā'
Kamarān
Al-Hudaydah
(Hodeida)
Bayt al-Faqīh
Zabīd
Dhamār
Yarīm
Ta'izz
Ibb
Jabal al Hashā'
3227
Lawdar
Al-Ḥawrah
Ahwar
Shaqrā'
Al-Mukhā
Madīnat
ash-Sha'b
Adan
(Aden)
Lahij
Shaykh 'Uthmān
Barīm
Bāb el Mandeb

Gulf of Aden

INDIAN

OCEAN

Calula
Gees
Gwardafuy
Ra's
'Abd al-Kūrī
(Yemen)

Raas Surud
Boosaaso
Qandala
Baxaya
3200
Raas
Xaafuun
Hurdiyo
Xaafuun
Meeladeen
Karin
Maydh
Raas
Khansīīr
Shimbiris
2407
Ceerigaabo
Bargaal

SOMALIA

Umm Durmān
(Omdurman)
Al-Khartūm Bahrī
AL-KHARTŪM
(KHARTOUM)
Jabal al-Awliyā'
Khashm
al-Qirbah
Kassalā
Asmera
Adi Ugri
Keren
Massawa
(Mitsiwa)
Akordat
Teseney
Muqatta'
Shuwak
Rufā' ah
Wad Madanī
Al-Ḥawātah
Al-Qadārif
Sinjah
Sannār
Soira
2989
Aksum
Adwa
Mek'elē
Adigrat
-125
Kobar
Sink
Ramlu
2130
Aseb
Tio

DAN

KORDOFĀN

AL-JAZĪRAH

KHAZZĀN
AR-RUŞAYRIŞ

AN-NŪBAH
JIBĀL

ETHIOPIAN

PLATEAU

CHOK'E

Kagmar
Umm Sayyālah
Ad-Duwaym
Kūstī
Rabak
Tandalti
Ar-Rahad
Rashād
Dalāmī
Dilling
1325
JIBĀL
Talawdī
Kadugli
Kaka
Paloich
Kodok
Malakāl
Fangak
Bentiu
Abwong
Nyerol

SUDD

Mongalla
Juba
Yei
Kajo Kaji
Nimule
UGANDA
Aruā
Atiak
Arua

Qawz Rajab
Adarama
Shandi
Ad-Dāmir
'Atbarah
Barbar
Derudeb
Togni
Kassalā
Khashm
al-Qirbah
Dabat
Gonder
Azezo
Debre Tabor
Bahir Dar
Dangila
Guba
Bambesi
Āsosa
Beigi
Gimbī
Tulu Welel
3001
Nek'emtē
Dembī Dolo
Gīdamī
Gambēla
Baro
Bedelē
Gorē
Dembī
Jīma
Mīzan Teferī
Maji
Bako
Tor
Waka
Guguftu
Negēlē
Guge
4200
Arba
Minch'
Ch'amo Hāyk'
Bako
Lake
Stefanie
Sabarei
Lokitaung
North
Horr

Adarama
Ras Dashen Terara
4620
Amba Farit
3975
Sek'ot'a
Mot'a
Lalibela
Weldiya
K'obo
Debre Mark'os
Debra Sīna
Debre Birhan
Āk'ak'ī Bēsek'a
Debre Zeyt
ĀDĪS ĀBEBA
(ADDIS ABABA)
Mojo
Nazrēt
Giyon
Welk'itē
Hosa'ina
Shashemenē
Yirga 'Alem
Sodo
Dila
Kibre Mengist
Ēl Kerē
Filtu

ETHIOPIA

RIFT   VALLEY

AHMAR MOUNTAINS

Danakil

Moussa 'Ali
2021
Serdo
Tendaho
Obock
Tadjoura
Djibouti
DJIBOUTI
Dikhil
Aysha
Mi'ēso
Awash
Dirē Dawa
Harer
Jijiga
Degeh Bur
Āwarē
Daga Medo
Ēl Fud
Imī
Wabera
El Kerē
Dhuusamarreeb
Hobyo

Saylac
Zeila
Lawya'ado
Bullaxaar
Berbera
Burco
Hargeysa
Caynaba
Laascaanood
Qardho
Xalin
Bandarbeyla
Garoowe
Eyl
Beyra
Werdēr
Gēladī
Denan
Mustahil
Beledweyne
Buulobarde
Ceelbuur
Xarardheere
Mereeg
Qooriga Neegro

OGADEN

MENDEBO

Awasa
Batu
4307
Goba
Ginir
Dodola
Adaba
Wabē Shebelē
Shala Hāyk'
Sasabeneh
Lega Hīda
Degeh Bur
K'ebrī Dehar
Dolow
Luuq
Baydhabo
Buulobarde
Waajid
Diinsoor

KENYA

Lake Rudolf
(Lake Turkana)
North
Horr
Moyale
Ēl Wak
Buna
Mandera
Mega
Ramu
Lodwar
Totiyas

M-DRM4713-A1-4-4-4
Copyright © Rand McNally & Co.

ITALY

TYRRHENIAN
SEA

SARDEGNA
(SARDINIA)

M E D I T E R R A N E A N   S E A

SICILIA
(SICILY)

MALTA

Valletta

Palermo
Catania
Messina

Cosenza
Catanzaro

ISOLE EOLIE
(ISOLE LIPARI)

Trapani
Agrigento

ISOLE
EGADI

ISOLE
PELAGIE

Isola di
Pantelleria (It.)

ATLANTIC OCEAN

PORTUGAL

SPAIN

MADRID

LISBOA
(LISBON)

VALÈNCIA

Sevilla
(Seville)

Córdoba

Málaga

Granada

SIERRA NEVADA

SIERRA MORENA

MALLORCA
(MAJORCA)

MENORCA

EIVISSA
(IBIZA)

I L E S   B A L E A R S
(BALEARIC ISLANDS)
(Sp.)

Palma
de Mallorca

Cartagena
Murcia
Alacant
Almería

Cádiz
Gibraltar
(U.K.)
Strait of Gibraltar
Tanger
(Tangier)

Ceuta (Sp.)

Melilla (Sp.)

TUNIS
TUNISIA

Tarābulus
(Tripoli)

L I B Y A

ÎLES KERKENNA

Île de Jerba

Sfax

Sousse
Monastir
Nabeul
Hammamet

Bizerte

Carthage

El Djazaïr
(ALGIERS)

A L G E R I A

Oran
(Wahran)

Constantine
(Qacentina)

Béjaïa

Annaba

Skikda

M O R O C C O

Rabat
Casablanca
(Dar-el-Beida)

Marrakech

Agadir

H A U T   A T L A S

Jbel Toubkal
4165

ANTI ATLAS

W E S T E R N   S A H A R A

Western Sahara has been
occupied by Morocco

M A U R I T A N I A

ARQUIPÉLAGO DA MADEIRA
(MADEIRA ISLANDS)
(Port.)

MADEIRA
Funchal

ISLAS CANARIAS
(CANARY ISLANDS)
(Sp.)

LANZAROTE
FUERTEVENTURA
GRAN CANARIA
Las Palmas
de Gran Canaria
TENERIFE
Santa Cruz
de Tenerife
LA PALMA
La Gomera
El Hierro

Tropic of Cancer

PLATEAU DU
DJADO

F A Z Z Ā N

H A G G A R

T A S S I L I - N - A J J E R

Tibesti

Sahra' Awbari

Murzuq

66

CHAD

NIGER

NIGERIA

MALI

BURKINA FASO

CÔTE D'IVOIRE

GHANA

TOGO

BENIN

GUINEA

SIERRA LEONE

LIBERIA

SENEGAL

THE GAMBIA

GUINEA-BISSAU

CAMEROON

EQUATORIAL GUINEA

GABON

CONGO

SAO TOME AND PRINCIPE

CAPE VERDE

Bornu

Adamaoua

Ténéré

Erg du Ténéré

Aïr

Talak

Ténéré

Azaouak

El 'Açâba

Fouta Djalon

Ashanti

Niger Delta

Gulf of Guinea

Bight of Biafra

Bight of Benin

Slave Coast

Gold Coast

Ivory Coast

Grain Coast

ATLANTIC OCEAN

N'Djamena

Maiduguri

Kano

Kaduna

Abuja

Zaria

Ilorin

Ogbomosho

Ibadan

Abeokuta

LAGOS

Porto-Novo

Cotonou

Lomé

ACCRA

Kumasi

ABIDJAN

Yamoussoukro

Ouagadougou

Bobo-Dioulasso

Niamey

Bamako

Conakry

Freetown

Monrovia

Banjul (Bathurst)

DAKAR

BISSAU

Yaoundé

Douala

Malabo

Santa Isabel

BIOKO

São Tomé

Libreville

Praia

SANTIAGO

Santa Isabel
Pico de Santa Isabel 3008

Camerôon Mt. 4100

Pico de São Tomé 2024

Annobón (Eq. Guinea)

Príncipe

Tombouctou (Timbuktu)

Lac Chad / Lake Chad

Niger

Benue

White Volta

Black Volta

Volta

Lake Volta

Pic de Tabé 1443

Mount Nimba 1752

Bintimani 1945

Hombori Tondo 1155

Idoukâl-en-Taghès 2022

Chappal Waddi 2419

M-DRM4714-A1-.-2-.-3
Copyright © Rand McNally & Co.

Scale 1 : 10,000,000

Lambert Conformal Conic Projection

0° East of Greenwich   West of Greenwich

Meters / Feet
4000 13120
3000 9840
2000 6560
1000 3280
500 1640
200 656
Sea Level
200 656
2000 6560

1000 Kilometers
600 Miles

a Same scale as main map

ATLANTIC OCEAN

CAPE VERDE
SANTO ANTÃO
SÃO NICOLAU
São Vicente
Mindelo
Sal
Boa Vista
Maio
SANTIAGO
Praia
Fogo
Brava
Pico 2829

Meters
Feet

4000
13120

3000
9840

2000
6560

1000
3280

500
1640

200
656

Sea Level

200
656

2000
6560

M-DRM4712-A1-?-3-?-3
Copyright © Rand McNally & Co.

0   100   200   300   400   600   800   1000 Kilometers

0   100   200   400   600 Miles

Scale 1 : 10,000,000   Sinusoidal Projection

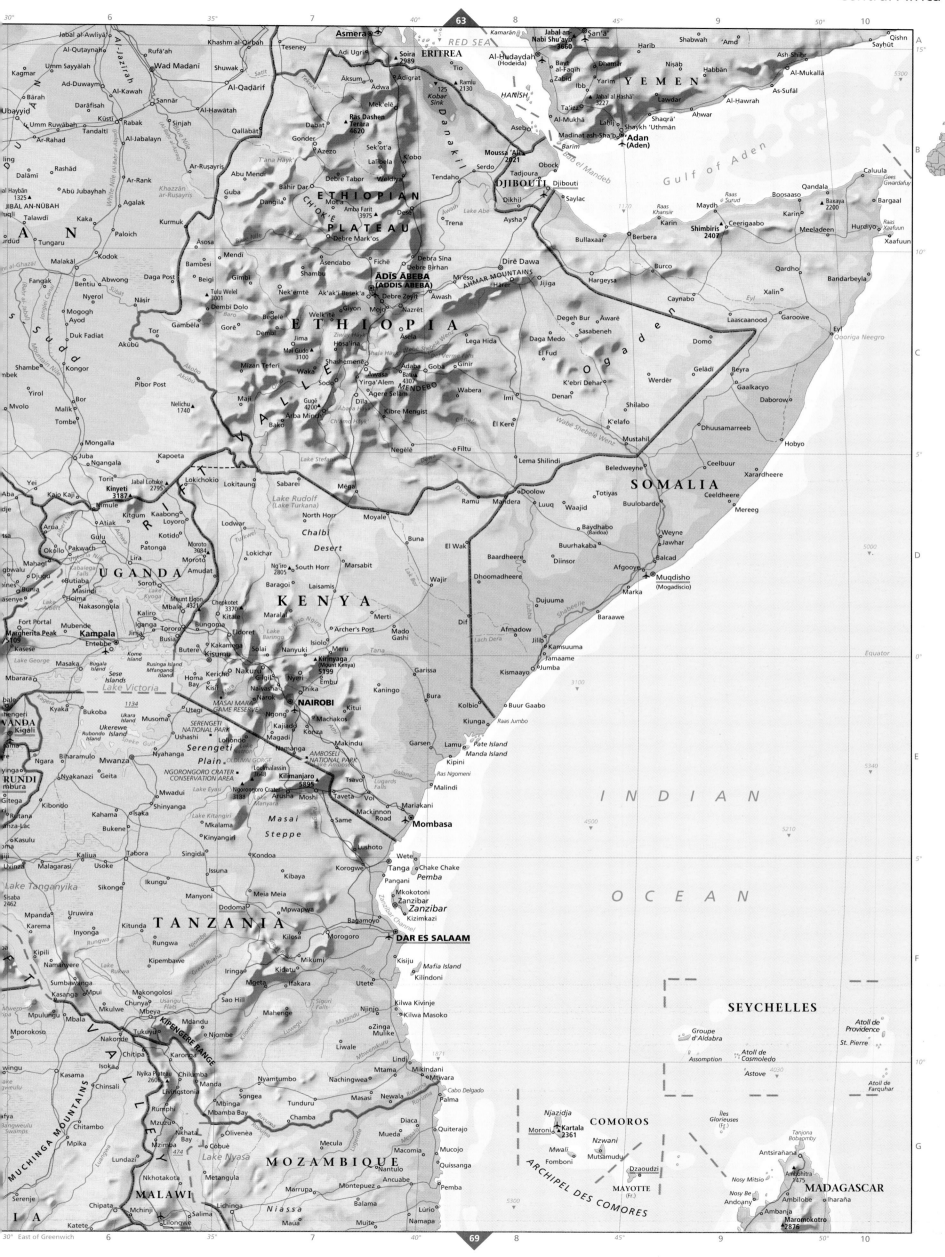

ATLANTIC OCEAN

Scale 1 : 10,000,000   Lambert Conformal Conic Projection

M-DRM4715-A1- - - -2
Copyright © Rand McNally & Co.

KAOKO VELD
Skeleton Coast
KUNENE
Fransfontein
Khorixas
Sorris-Sorris
Brandberg ▲ 2579   Uis
Cape Cross (Kaap Kruis)
Omaruru
Erongo 2305 ▲
Usakos   Karibib
Arandis
Hentiesbaai
Swakopmund
Walvis Bay (Walvisbaai)
Walvis Bay
Sandwich Bay   Ilhea Point
Conception Bay
Hollandsbird Island
Meobbaai
Diaz Point   Lüderitz
Possession Island

Outjo
Otjiwarongo
WATERBERG PLATOPARK
Kalkfeld
Omatako 2789
Etjo 2085
Ombotozo 1916
Okombahe
Sukses
Osire Süd
Hochfeld
Okahandja
Wilhelmstal
Otjimbingwe
Khomas Hochland
Windhoek
Dordabis
Rehoboth
Uhlenhorst

OTJOZONDJUPA
DAMARALAND
ERONGO
KHOMAS
NAMIBIA
HARDAP
GREAT NAMAQUALAND (GROOT NAMALAND)
Nomtsas
Maltahöhe
Schwarz-rand
Helmeringhausen
Bethanien
Seeheim
Aus
HUIB-HOCH PLATEAU
KARAS
Grünau
Kanus
Karasburg
Warmbad
Sendelingsdrif
Oranjemund (Oranje)
Alexander Bay
Noordoewer
Vioolsdrif
LITTLE NAMAQUALAND (KLEIN NAMALAND)
Goodhouse
Steinkopf
Aggeneys
Port Nolloth
Nababeep
Okiep
Springbok
Gamoep
Kamieskroon
Garies
Hondeklipbaai

NAMIB DESERT
NAMIB-NAUKLUFT PARK

Omitara
Witvlei
Seeis
Leonardville
Aminuis
Steinhausen
Gobabis
OMAHEKE
Otjinene
Epukiro
Epukiro
Rietfontein
Mamuno
Tshootsha

NGAMILAND
Mabeleapodi
Toteng
Lake Ngami
Sehithwa
MAKGADIKGADI PANS GAME RESERVE
Khasebake
Rakops
Xhumo
Mo
GHANZI
Ghanzi
Tswaane
Takachu
Kule
Khomodimo
CENTRAL KALAHARI GAME RESERVE
BOTSW

Kalkrand
Stampriet
Mariental
Gochas
Gibeon
Witbooisvlei
Berseba
Tses
Koës
Kalkfontein
Aroab
KALAHARI GEMSBOK NATIONAL PARK
GEMSBOK NATIONAL PARK
KGALAGADI DESERT
KALAHARI
Lehututu
Hukuntsi   Tshane
Kokong
Sekoma
Khakhea
Werda
MABUASEHUBE GAME RESERVE
Tshabong
Khuis
Van Zylsrus
Maralaleng
Pomfret
Morokweng
Tosca
Tshidilamolomo
Sonstraal
Hotazel
Dibeng
Olifantshoek
Sishen 1855 ▲
Gakarosa 1922 ▲
Reivilo
Jan Kempdor
Barkly Wes
BECHUANALAND
Askham
Twee Rivieren
Upington
Keimoes
Kakamas
Grootdrink
Onseepkans
Pofadder
Bladgrond-Noord
Namies
BUSHMAN LAND
Kenhardt
Marydale
Niekerkshoop
Griekwastad
Campbell
Douglas
Putsonderwater
GRIQUALAND WEST
KIMBERLEY
Postmasburg
Danielskuil
Ulco
Warrent
Delportshoop
SOUTH AF

KWENENG
KGWENENG
Kang
KUTSE GAME RESERVE
NORT
Stel
Ganyesa
Vryburg
Buxton

ALGRABIES FALLS NATIONAL PARK
Augrabiesvalle
Kuruman
Sishen
KURUMAN-ANTELKWELS

ATLANTIC OCEAN

Okiep
Springbok
Kamieskroon
Garies
Bitterfontein
Nuwerus
Nieuwoudtville
Calvinia
Williston
Loxton
Carnarvon
Victoria West
Richmond
Middel
Hopetown
Strydenburg
Britstown
Prieska
De Aar
Hanover
Noup
Petrusville
Philipstown
Vanderkl
Luckhof
Belmon
NORTHERN CAPE
Vanwyksvlei
Brandvlei
Sakrivier
Vosburg
Mynfontein
Grootvloer
Sak
Krom
Loeriesfontein

Lutzville
Vanrhynsdorp
Klawer
Vredendal
Lambert's Bay
Wupperthal
Clanwilliam
Elandsvlei
Sutherland
Fraserburg
Nelspoort
Murraysburg
Graaff-Reinet
Aberdeen
Kendrew
Nieu-Bethesda
Bastersberg 1596 ▲
Bontberg 1922 ▲
GREAT KARROO (GROOT KARROO)
Beaufort West
Merweville
Leeu-Gamka
Prince Albert
Willowmore
Steytlerville
Jansenville
Klipplaa
KAROO NATIONAL PARK
ROGGEVELDBERGE
NUWEVELDBERGE

Aurora
Velddrif
Vredenburg
Saldanha
Hopefield
Darling
Malmesbury
Cape Columbine
Helena baai
Piketberg
Porterville
Moorreesburg
Tulbagh
Ceres
Wolseley
Touwsrivier
Laingsburg
Matjiesfontein
Ladismith
Calitzdorp
Oudtshoorn
Uniondale
Avontuur
Joubertina
KOUGABERGE
GROOT-SWARTBERGE
LITTLE KARROO (KLEIN KARROO)
Zoar
Ladismith
Van Wyksdorp
Herbertsdale
George
Cape Seal
Plettenbergbaai
Knysna
Humansdo
St. Franc
Mosselbaai (Mossel Bay)

Wellington
Paarl
CAPE TOWN (KAAPSTAD)
Bellville
Stellenbosch
Somerset West
Simon's Town
Cape of Good Hope (Kaap die Goeie Hoop)
Worcester
De Doorns
Montagu
Ashton
Robertson
Bonnievale
Swellendam
Riversdale
Albertinia
Witsand
Stilbaai
BONTEBOK NATIONAL PARK
WESTERN CAPE
LANGEBERGE
Caledon
Klipdale
Protem
Bredasdorp
Elim
Gansbaai
Hermanus
False Bay
Walker Bay
Danger Point
Kaap Agulhas
Infanta
St. Sebastian Bay

Tropic of Capricorn

Meters / Feet
3000 / 9840
2000 / 6560
1000 / 3280
500 / 1640
200 / 656
Sea Level
200 / 656
2000 / 6560

0 100 200 300 400 500 600 700 800 900 1000 Kilometer
0 100 200 300 400 500 600 Miles
Scale 1 : 5,000,000   Lambert Conformal Conic Projection

East of Greenwich

A

69

12

13

ZIMBABWE

Nyamandlovu
Nkembesi
Shangani
MATABELELAND NORTH
Bulawayo
Fort Rixon
Matopos
Esigodini
Bannockburn
Chivi
MANICA-LAND
Chipinge
Gogoi
SOFALA
Beira
Goonda
Dondo

Ponte do Pungoe

Plumtree
Figtree
Marula
Mbalabala
Zvishavane
Ngomahuru
Zaka
Turwi
Selinda
Mount
Espungabera
Inhafenga
Dombe

NORTH EAST
Kezi
Gwanda
Colleen Bawn
Filabusi
Mnene
Mberengwa
MANICA
Machaze
Chibaba
Chingune

RHODES MATOPOS NATIONAL PARK
Mphoengs
Antelope Mine
West Nicholson
Mount Towla 1204
MASVINGO
Chiredzi
Runde
Mutanda
Divinhe
Machanga

Francistown
Tonotha
Legion
Rutenga
Mwenezi
GONAREZHOU NATIONAL PARK
Massangena
Covane
Jofane
Maave
Nova Mambone

Old Tate
MATABELELAND SOUTH
Tuli
Mazunga
Bubi
MATEKE HILLS
Malvérnia
Machaila
Mabote
Mapinhane
Macovane
Inhassoro

Serule
Mmadinare
Bobonong
Beitbridge
Limpopo
GREAT LIMPOPO TRANSFRONTIER PARK
Pafuri
Machaze
Cometela
Ilha do Bazaruto

CENTRAL
Serowe
Palapye
Messina
GAZA
Mapinhane
Pomene
Ponta São Sebastião

Mogapinyana
Alldays
Mopane
MOZAMBIQUE
Chigubo
Funhalouro
Ponta da Barra Falsa

Shoshong
Mahalapye
Machaneng
Tom Burke
Blouberg 2051
SOUTPANSBERG
Thohoyandou
Punda Milia
Quissico
Rio das Pedras

Lephephe
Dinokwe
Baltimore
Bochum
VENDA
Louis Trichardt
Shingwidzi
Mabalane
Mocodoene
Massinga

KGATLENG
Vaalwater
Potgietersrus
Pietersburg
Tzaneen
Duiwelskloof
KRUGER
Nalázi
Inharrime
Morrumbene
Tropic of Capricorn

Molepolole
Mochudi
Grootgeluk
Ellisras
NORTHERN PROVINCE
Haenertsburg
Gravelotte
Phalaborwa
Massingir
Chibuto
Mandlakazi
Inhambane
Maxixe
Miramar

Gaborone
Ramotswa
Thabazimbi
Naboomspruit
Zebediela
Penge
Mica
TIMBAVATI GAME RESERVE
Satara
Mapulanguene
Chókwè
Chicomo
Baía de Inhambane
Panda
Jangamo

Ramatlabama
Northam
Nylstroom
Settlers
Ohrigstad
Pilgrim's Rest
Graskop
Mabalane
Motaze
Magude
Xai Xai
Macia

Lobatse
Zeerust
Pilanesberg 1687
Warmbad
Marble Hall
Lydenburg
Die Berg 2331
Sabie
Skukuza
NATIONAL PARK
Xinavane

SOUTH EAST
Mmabatho
Mafikeng
GAME RESERVE PILANESBERG
Pienaarsrivier
Beestekraal
Groblersdal
Stoffberg
Nelspruit
Komatipoort
Moamba
Manhiça

Slurry
Lichtenburg
Ottoshoop
PRETORIA (TSHWANE)
GAUTENG
Middelburg
Belfast
Waterval Boven
Barberton
Namaacha
Matola Rio
MAPUTO

Bakerville
Koster
Rustenburg
Brits
Bronkhorstspruit
Witbank
MPUMALANGA
Carolina
Piet Retief
Piggs Peak
Marracuene
Baia de Maputo

Coligny
Ventersdorp
Krugersdorp
Benoni
Springs
Breyten
Ermelo
Mbabane
Manzini
SWAZILAND
Bela Vista

Sannieshof
JOHANNESBURG
Germiston
Nigel
Bethal
Lothair
Amsterdam
Mankayane
Big Bend
Catuane

Klerksdorp
Stilfontein
Soweto
Heidelberg
Morgenzon
Standerton
Amersfoort
SWAZILAND
Hlathikulu
Zitundo
Ponta do Ouro

Orkney
Wolmaransstad
Vredefort
Parys
Vereeniging
Vaal
Villiers
Wakkerstroom
Lavumisa
NDUMU GAME RESERVE

Makwassie
Bothaville
Koppies
Heilbron
Frankfort
Vrede
Volksrust
Charlestown
Paulpietersburg
Utrecht
Ubombo
Kosimeer

FREE STATE
Allanridge
Kroonstad
Edenville
Lindley
Reitz
Warden
Memel
Newcastle
Dannhauser
Vryheid
Louwsburg
Mkuze
SODWANA BAY NATIONAL PARK

Welkom
Virginia
Ventersburg
Arlington
Bethlehem
Harrismith
Van Reenen
Dundee
Glencoe
Hlobane
Nongoma
HLUHLUWE GAME RESERVE
Leven Point
Lake St. Lucia

Hertzogville
Bultfontein
Senekal
GOLDEN GATE HIGHLANDS NATIONAL PARK
Ladysmith
Wasbank
Kingsley
Mahlabatini
UMFOLOZI GAME RESERVE
ST. LUCIA GAME RESERVE

Boshof
Theunissen
Winburg
ROYAL NATAL NATIONAL PARK
Phofung
Colenso
Weenen
Estcourt
ZULULAND
Melmoth
Empangeni
Cape St. Lucia

Dealesville
Brandfort
Marquard
Ficksburg
Champagne Castle 3377
Mont-aux-Sources
eNjesuthi 3446
Mount Alida
Kranskop
Eshowe
Nkwalini
aMatikulu

Bloemfontein
Ladybrand
Butha-Buthe
Hlotse
GIANT'S CASTLE GAME RESERVE
Greytown
Richard's Bay
Felixton

Maseru
Teyateyaneng
Mokhotlong
Giant's Castle 3315
Mooi River
New Hanover
Stanger
1772

Dewetsdorp
Roma
CENTRAL RANGE
Thabana-Ntlenyana 3482
Howick
Pietermaritzburg
Tongaat
Verulam

Petrusburg
Reddersburg
Morija
Marakabei
LESOTHO
Underberg
Edendale
Richmond
Pinetown
DURBAN
Isipingo

Faurismith
Edenburg
Mafeteng
Matatiele
EASTERN CAPE
Ixopo
Donnybrook
Umkomaas

Trompsburg
Wepener
Quthing
Franklin
Kokstad
Umzinkulu
Scottburgh

Springfontein
Smithfield
Zastron
Herschel
Cedarville
Harding
Umzinto
Park Rynie
Sezela

Bethulie
Rouxville
Lady Grey
Ben Macdhui 3001
Mount Frere
Bizana
Margate
Port Edward

Aliwal North
Barkly East
Maclear
Qumbu
Flagstaff

Burgersdorp
Jamestown
Elliot
Dordrecht
Ugie
Tsolo
Libode
Lusikisiki
2999

Steynsburg
Molteno
Vaalkop 2107
DRAKENSBERG
TRANSKEI
Engcobo
Umtata
Mqanduli
Port St. Johns

Sterkstroom
Queenstown
EASTERN CAPE
Idutywa
Willowvale
Wild Coast

Cradock
Tarkastad
Whittlesea
2371
Cathcart
Stutterheim
Butterworth

MOUNTAIN ZEBRA NATIONAL PARK
WINTERBERG
Seymour
Alice
Komga

Bedford
Adelaide
King William's Town
Mdantsane
East London (Oos-Londen)

Somerset East
Cookhouse
Fort Beaufort
Peddie

Darlington Dam
Klipplaat
Kirkwood
Paterson
Grahamstown
Bathurst

ADDO ELEPHANT NATIONAL PARK
Port Alfred

Uitenhage
Despatch
Port Elizabeth
Algoa Bay
Francis Bay

INDIAN OCEAN

Mozambique Channel

1554
1132
2853

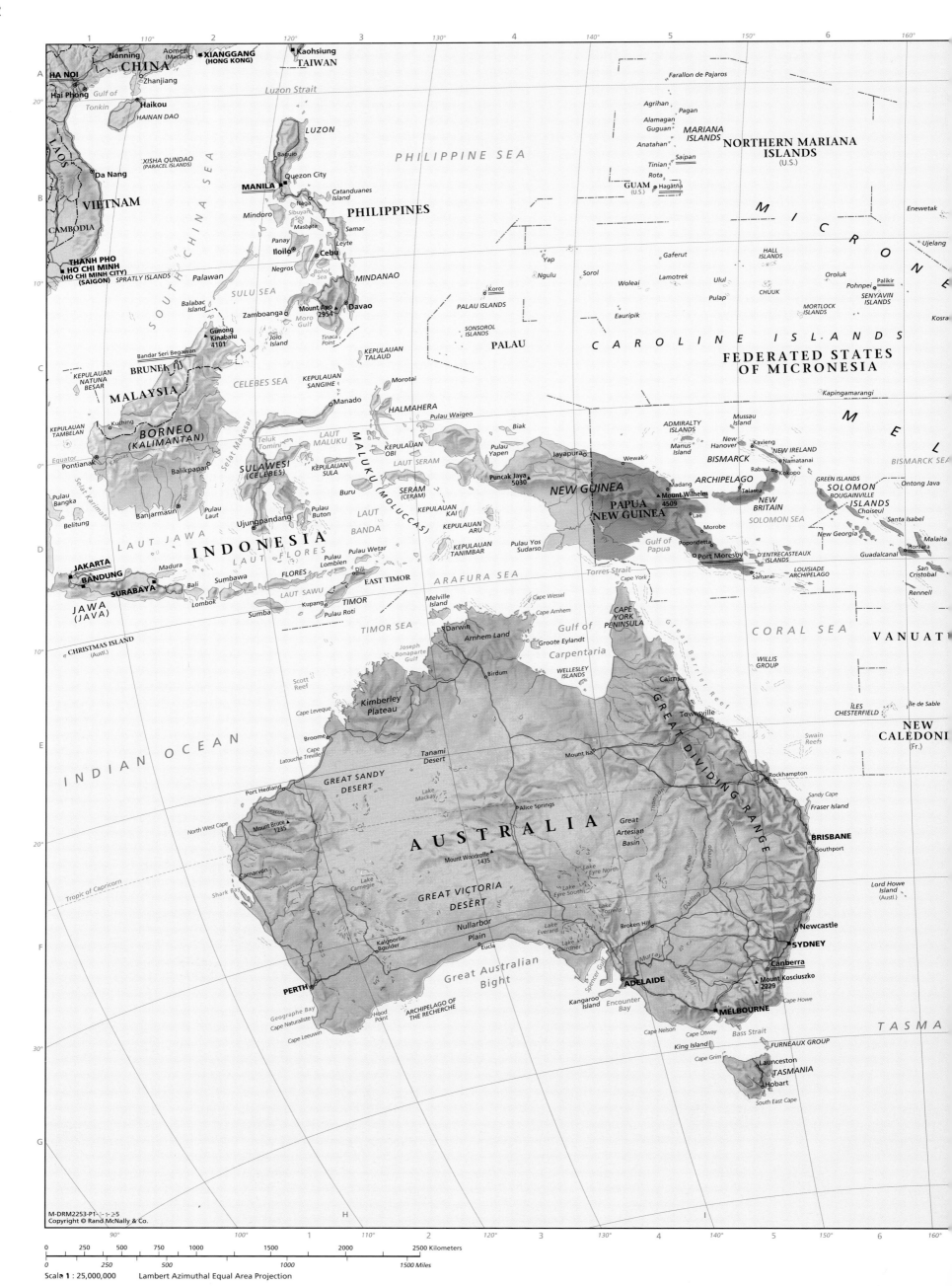

72

A

B

C

D

E

F

G

CHINA

HA NOI
Hai Phong
Gulf of
Tonkin

Nanning
Aomen
(Macau)
XIANGGANG
(HONG KONG)
Kaohsiung
TAIWAN

Zhanjiang
Haikou
HAINAN DAO

Luzon Strait

LUZON

XISHA QUNDAO
(PARACEL ISLANDS)

PHILIPPINE SEA

LAOS
VIETNAM

CAMBODIA

THANH PHO
HO CHI MINH
(HO CHI MINH CITY)
(SAIGON)

SPRATLY ISLANDS

Baguio

MANILA
Quezon City
Naga
Mindoro
Sibuyan
Sea
Masbate
Catanduanes
Island

PHILIPPINES

Panay
Samar
Leyte

Palawan

Iloilo
Cebu
Boho
Sea

Negros

Balabac
Island
MINDANAO

Zamboanga
Mount Apo
2954
Davao

KEPULAUAN
NATUNA
BESAR
Bandar Seri Begawan

BRUNEI

Gunong
Kinabalu
4101

Jolo
Island

Moro
Gulf

Tinaca
Point

KEPULAUAN
TALAUD

SULU SEA

Farallon de Pajaros

Agrihan
Pagan
Alamagan
Guguan
Anatahan
MARIANA
ISLANDS

Tinian
Rota
Saipan

GUAM
(U.S.)
Hagåtña

NORTHERN MARIANA
ISLANDS
(U.S.)

M I C R O

Enewetak

Ujelang

Yap
Ngulu
Sorol
Gaferut
HALL
ISLANDS

Woleai
Lamotrek
Ulul
Oroluk

Koror
PALAU ISLANDS
Pulap
CHUUK
Pohnpei
Palikir
SENYAVIN
ISLANDS

MORTLOCK
ISLANDS

Eauripik
SONSOROL
ISLANDS
PALAU

CAROLINE ISLANDS

Kapingamarangi

FEDERATED STATES
OF MICRONESIA

Kosra

CELEBES SEA

Manado

HALMAHERA

Morotai

KEPULAUAN
SANGIHE

Pulau Waigeo

MALAYSIA

KEPULAUAN
TAMBELAN

Kuching

BORNEO
(KALIMANTAN)

Pontianak

SULAWESI
(CELEBES)

Teluk
Tomini

LAUT
MALUKU

KEPULAUAN
SULA

Biak
Pulau
Yapen

Jayapura

Puncak Jaya
5030

NEW GUINEA

Wewak

ADMIRALTY
ISLANDS
Manus
Island

Madang
Mount Wilhelm
4509

Mussau
Island

New
Hanover
Kavieng
NEW IRELAND
Namatanai

BISMARCK
ARCHIPELAGO

Rabaul
Kokopo

NEW
BRITAIN

Talasea

M E L

L

GREEN ISLANDS
SOLOMON
BOUGAINVILLE
ISLANDS

BISMARCK SEA

Ontong Java

Equator

Kuala
Kapuas

Balikpapan

SELAT MAKASAR

Ujungpandang

Buru
SERAM (CERAM)

KEPULAUAN
KAI

LAUT SERAM

KEPULAUAN
ARU

Pulau Yos
Sudarso

PAPUA
NEW GUINEA

Lae
Morobe

Popondetta

SOLOMON SEA

New
Georgia

Choiseul

Santa Isabel

Malaita
Homara

Pulau
Bangka
Pulau
Laut

Banjarmasin

MALUKU
(MOLUCCAS)

LAUT
BANDA

Port Moresby
D'ENTRECASTEAUX
ISLANDS

Samarai

Gulf of
Papua

Guadalcanal

San
Cristobal

Rennell

Belitung

LAUT JAWA

Pulau
Buton

INDONESIA

LAUT FLORES

Pulau Wetar

KEPULAUAN
TANIMBAR

Torres Strait

Cape York

LOUISIADE
ARCHIPELAGO

VANUAT

JAKARTA
BANDUNG
SURABAYA

Madura

FLORES

Pulau
Lomblen

Dili

EAST TIMOR

ARAFURA SEA

CORAL SEA

JAWA
(JAVA)

Bali
Sumbawa

LAUT SAWU

TIMOR

Melville
Island
Cape Wessel

WILLIS
GROUP

NEW
CALEDONI
(Fr.)

Lombok
Sumba
Pulau Roti

Kupang

TIMOR SEA

Darwin
Arnhem Land
Groote Eylandt
Cape Arnhem

CHRISTMAS ISLAND
(Austl.)

Joseph
Bonaparte
Gulf

Gulf of
Carpentaria

CAPE
YORK
PENINSULA

ÎLES
CHESTERFIELD
Île de Sable

Cairns

Great Barrier Reef

Scott
Reef

Birdum

WELLESLEY
ISLANDS

INDIAN OCEAN

Kimberley
Plateau

Broome

Cape Leveque

Townsville

Swain
Reefs

Latouche Treville

Tanami
Desert

Mount Isa

Rockhampton

Sandy Cape
Fraser Island

Port Hedland

GREAT SANDY
DESERT

Lake
Mackay

Alice Springs

North West Cape
Mount Bruce
1235

AUSTRALIA

Great
Artesian
Basin

Tropic of Capricorn

Carnarvon

Mount Woodroffe
1435

Lake
Carnegie

GREAT VICTORIA
DESERT

Lake
Eyre North
Lake
Eyre South

BRISBANE
Southport

Lord Howe
Island
(Austl.)

Shark Bay

Lake
Everard

Lake
Torrens

Broken Hill

Newcastle

SYDNEY

Kalgoorlie-
Boulder

Nullarbor
Plain
Eucla

Lake
Gairdner

Canberra

Mount Kosciuszko
2229

PERTH

Great Australian
Bight

ADELAIDE

Cape Howe

Geographe Bay
Cape Naturaliste
Hood
Point

ARCHIPELAGO OF
THE RECHERCHE

Spencer Gulf

Kangaroo
Island
Encounter
Bay

MELBOURNE

Cape Nelson
Cape Otway
Bass Strait

TASMA

Cape Leeuwin

King Island

Cape Grim

FURNEAUX GROUP

Launceston

TASMANIA

Hobart

South East Cape

0 250 500 750 1000   1500   2000   2500 Kilometers

0   250   500   1000   1500 Miles

Scale 1 : 25,000,000   Lambert Azimuthal Equal Area Projection

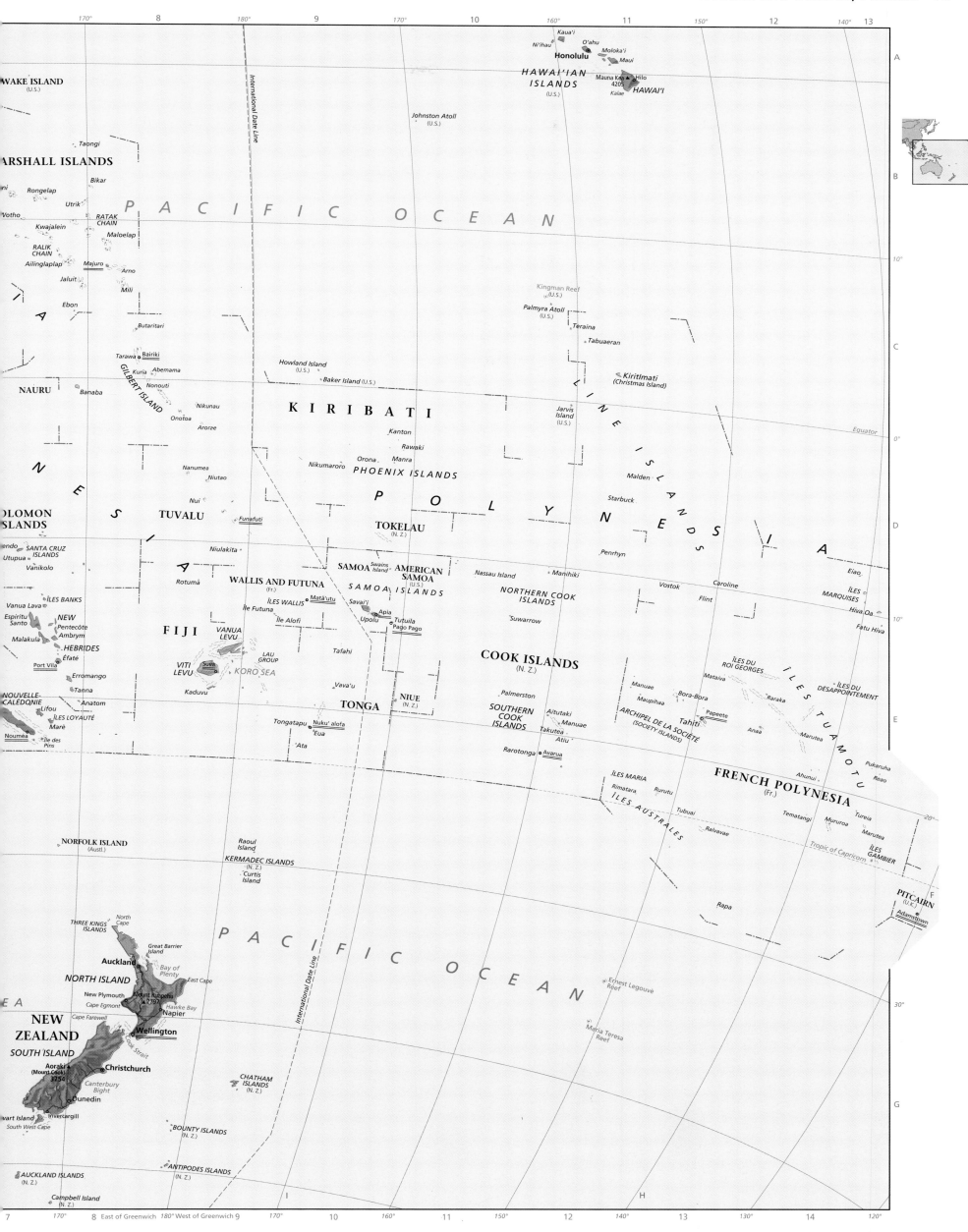

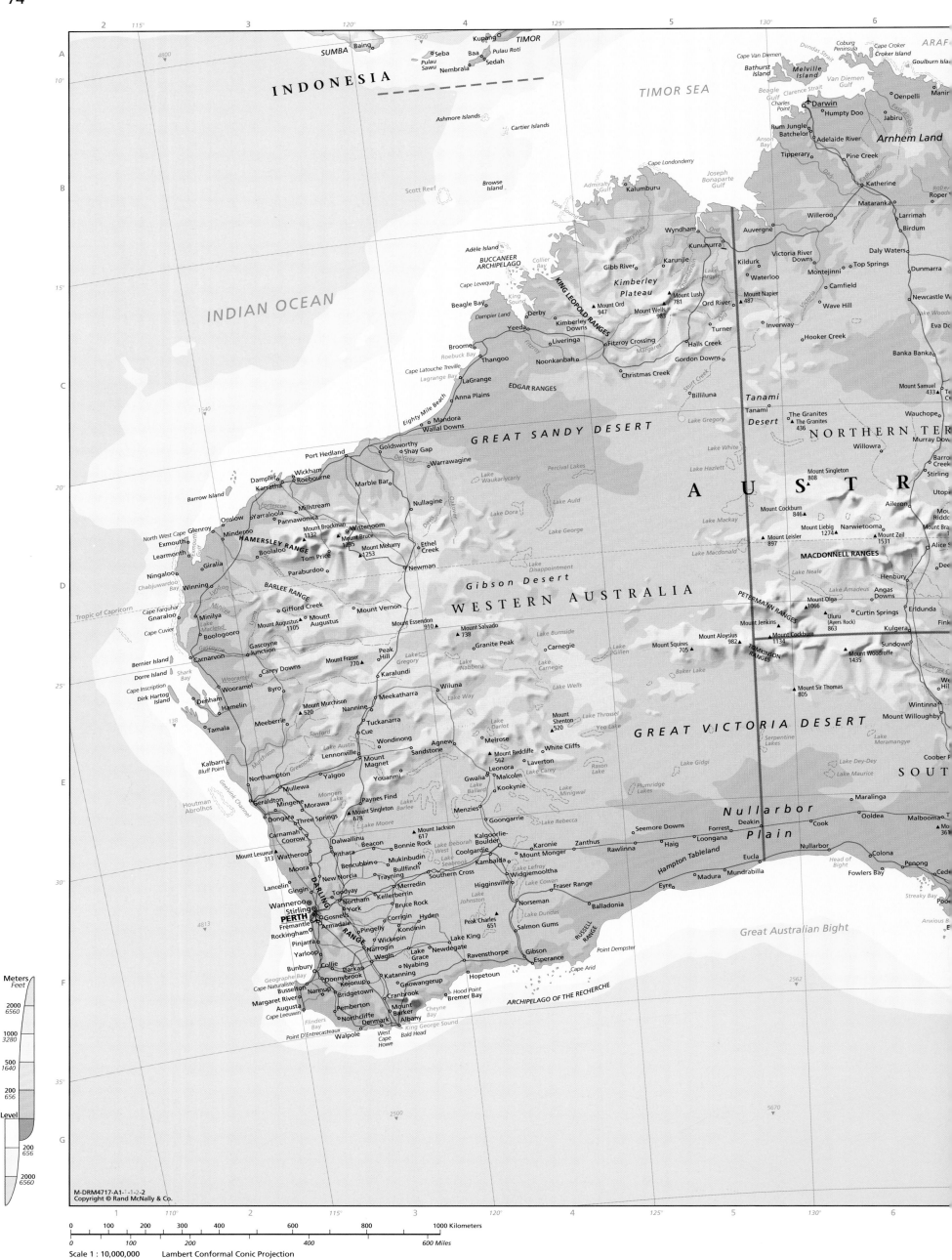

SUMBA   Baing   Kupang   TIMOR
Seba   Pulau Roti
Pulau   Baa   Sedah
Sawu   Nembrala

INDONESIA   TIMOR SEA

Ashmore Islands   Cartier Islands

INDIAN OCEAN

Scott Reef

Browse
Island

Cape Van Diemen   ARAF
Coburg   Cape Croker
Dundas Strait   Peninsula   Croker Island   Goulburn Isla
Bathurst   Melville
Island   Island   Van Diemen
Beagle   Clarence Strait   Gulf
Gulf   Oenpelli   Manir
Charles   Darwin
Point   Humpty Doo
Rum Jungle   Jabiru
Batchelor   Adelaide River
Anson   Arnhem Land
Bay   Tipperary   Pine Creek

Cape Londonderry   Willeroo   Katherine
Joseph   Mataranka   Roper
Bonaparte   Larrimah
Admiralty   Gulf   Wyndham   Auvergne   Birdum
Gulf   Kalumburu   Kununurra   Victoria River   Daly Waters
York Sound   Downs   Montejinni   Top Springs   Dunmarra
Gibb River   Karunjie   Kildurk   Camfield
Adèle Island   Waterloo   Wave Hill   Newcastle W
BUCCANEER   Kimberley   Mount Ord   Ord River   Mount Napier   Eva Do
ARCHIPELAGO   Collier   Plateau   947   Mount Lush   487
Cape Leveque   Bay   KING LEOPOLD RANGES   781   Hooker Creek   Banka Banka
Beagle Bay   King   Derby   Mount Wells   Inverway
Dampier Land   Sound   Kimberley   983   Turner
Downs   Fitzroy Crossing   Mount Samuel
Yeeda   Halls Creek   433
Broome   Liveringa   Christmas Creek   Gordon Downs   Wauchope
Roebuck Bay   Noonkanbah   Tanami   The Granites   Willowra   Barrow
Cape Latouche Treville   Thangoo   Billiluna   Tanami   436   Murray Dow
Lagrange Bay   LaGrange   Desert   The Granites   NORTHERN TER
EDGAR RANGES   Lake Gregory
Anna Plains   Lake White   AUSTR
Eighty Mile Beach   GREAT SANDY DESERT   Lake Hazlett   Mount Singleton   Stirling
Mandora   808   Utopia
Wallal Downs   Percival Lakes   Mount Cockburn   Aileron   Mou
Port Hedland   Goldsworthy   Lake Waukarlycarly   846   Riddo
Shay Gap   Lake White   Mount Liebig   Narwietooma   Mount Bra
Wickham   Warrawagine   1274   Mount Zeil
Dampier   Roebourne   Lake Auld   Mount Leisler   Alice S
Karratha   Marble Bar   Lake Dora   897   MACDONNELL RANGES
Barrow Island   Millstream   Lake Mackay   Henbury
Nullagine   Lake George   Lake Macdonald   Angas   Dee
North West Cape   Onslow   Yarraloola   Mount Brockman   Wittenoom   Lake   PETERMANN RANGES   Downs
Exmouth   Glenroy   Pannawonica   1132   Mount Bruce   Disappointment   Mount Olga   Uluru   Curtin Springs   Erldunda
Minderoo   HAMERSLEY RANGE   1235   1066   (Ayers Rock)   Kulgera
Learmonth   Boolaloo   Mount Meharry   WESTERN AUSTRALIA   863
Ningaloo   Tom Price   1253   Mount Jenkins   Mount Cockburn   TOMKINSON   Kugera
Giralia   Paraburdoo   Newman   Gibson Desert   1134   RANGES   Kulgera
Chabjuwardoo   BARLEE RANGE   Mount Aloysius   Mount Woodroffe
Bay   Winning   Gifford Creek   982   1435
Tropic of Capricorn   Mount Vernon   Mount Squires   Tomkinson
Cape Farquhar   Gnaraloo   Minilya   Mount Augustus   Mount Essendon   705
Cape Cuvier   Gascoyne   Mount Augustus   910   Mount Salvado   Mount Sir Thomas   Wintinna
Bernier Island   Junction   1105   738   805   Mount Willoughby
Dorre Island   Carnarvon   Mount Fraser   Granite Peak   Lake Burnside   GREAT VICTORIA DESERT
Cape Inscription   Carey Downs   770   Peak   Carnegie   Lake Gillen
Dirk Hartog   Hill   Karalundi   Mount Shenton   Serpentine
Island   Wooramel   520   Lakes   Lake Maurice   Coober P
Denham   Byro   Wiluna   Lake Carnegie   Baker Lake   Lake
Hamelin   Lake   Lake   Meramangye
138   Mount Murchison   Meekatharra   Nabberu   Lake Wells   Lake Dey-Dey   SOUT
Tamala   520   Darlot   Yeo Lake   Lake Throssel   Lake Dey-Dey
Meeberrie   Cue   Sandstone   Plumridge   Lake Meramangye
Kalbarri   Nannine   Wondinong   Melrose   Lakes   Serpentine
Bluff Point   Agnew   Mount Redcliffe   White Cliffs   Lakes   Cooper P
Northampton   Tuckanarra   562   Laverton   Rason   Lake Gidgi
Mullewa   Lennonville   Mount   Gwalia   Lake   Lake   Maralinga
Geraldton   Mingenew   Magnet   Leonora   Malcolm   Ballard   Minigwal
Houtman   Morawa   Youanmi   Kookynie   Nullarbor   Malboom
Abrolhos   Mount Singleton   Menzies   Lake Rebecca   Seemore Downs   Cook   Ooldea   36
Dongara   678   Paynes Find   Goongarrie   Plain   Forrest   Deakin
Three Springs   Lake   Kalgoorlie-   Haig   Loongana
Carnamah   Mount Jackson   Boulder   Karonie   Zanthus   Rawlinna   Eucla   Nullarbor   Penong   Ced
Coorow   617   Bonnie Rock   Coolgardie   Kambalda   Hampton Tableland   Madura   Colona
Mount Lesueur   Dalwallinu   Beacon   Widgiemooltha   Mundrabilla   Fowlers Bay
313   Watheroo   Bencubbin   Lake Deborah   Mount Monger   Eyre   Head of   Streaky Bay
Moora   Mukinbudin   West   Higginsville   Fraser Range   Bight
Bullfinch   Lake   Norseman   Anxious B
New Norcia   Trayning   Southern Cross   Seabrook   Balladonia   Great Australian Bight   E
Lancelin   Merredin   Johnston
Gingin   Kellerberrin   Peak Charles   Point Dempster   2562
Wanneroo   Toodyay   Bruce Rock   651   Salmon Gums   RUSSELL   Esperance
Stirling   York   Corrigin   Hyden   Gibson   Cape Arid   RANGE
PERTH   Gosnells   Kondinin   Lake King   Esperance
Fremantle   Armadale   Pingelly   Newdegate   Ravensthorpe   ARCHIPELAGO OF THE RECHERCHE
Rockingham   Wickepin   Lake   Hopetoun
Pinjarra   Narrogin   Grace   Hood Point
Yarloop   Wagin   Nyabing   Bremer Bay
Bunbury   Collie   Lake   Gnowangerup   5670
Darkan   Katanning   Mount   Cheyne
Cape Naturaliste   Donnybrook   Kojonup   Barker   Bay
Busselton   Bridgetown   Cranbrook   Albany
Margaret River   Nannup   Pemberton   King George Sound
Augusta   Northcliffe   Denmark
Cape Leeuwin   Flinders   Walpole   West   Bald Head
Bay   Point D'Entrecasteaux   Cape Howe

Meters
Feet

2000
6560

1000
3280

500
1640

200
656

Sea Level

200
656

2000
6560

M-DRM4717-A1-1-1-2-2
Copyright © Rand McNally & Co.

0   100   200   300   400   600   800   1000 Kilometers

0   100   200   400   600 Miles

Scale 1 : 10,000,000   Lambert Conformal Conic Projection

PAPUA NEW GUINEA

Wessel
Islands
Cape Wessel

Yirrkala
Nhulunbuy
Cape Arnhem

Frederick
Hills

Groote
Eylandt

Cape Beatrice

Maria Island
Limmen Bight

Sir Edward Pellew
Group
Vanderlin Island

Blue
Mud
Bay

Warwick Channel

Gulf of Carpentaria

OWEN STANLEY RANGE
Kupiano   Abau   Alotau   Samarai
Baniara   Esa'ala
Normanby
Island
Deboyne
Islands
Misima Island
Tagula Island
Yela Island

**SOLOMON
ISLANDS**

Louisiade Archipelago

Thursday Island
Prince of Wales
Island
Bamaga
Cape York
Endeavour   Newcastle Bay

Duifken Point
Albatross Bay
Weipa
Aurukun

Moreton

Mount Tozer
545

Iron Range

Wenlock

CAPE

YORK

PENINSULA

Cape Keer-Weer

Princess
Charlotte
Bay

Cape Melville

Cape Flattery

CORAL SEA

VANUATU

McArthur
River

Mornington
Island

Wellesley
Islands
Bentinct Island

Koolatah
Musgrave

Delta Downs
Highbury

Palmerville
Laura

Cooktown
Ayton

**CORAL SEA
ISLANDS TERRITORY
(Austl.)**

Mossman

Willis Group

Mellish Reef

**NEW
CALEDONIA**
(Fr.)

Corinda
Burketown
Karumba
Normanton

Mungana
Chillagoe
Almaden
Atherton
Mareeba
Babinda
Innisfail

Cairns
Battle Hero
1622
Ravenshoe

Lihov Reefs
and Cays

Lawn Hill
Croydon
Gilbert
River
Georgetown
Forsayth
Einasleigh

Tully
Cardwell
Hinchinbrook Island
Ingham
Halifax

Greenvale
Bambaroo

Flinders Reefs

1515

Iles Chesterfield

Riversleigh
Boomarra

Lyndhurst

Mount Elliot
1240
Giru
Home Hill

Townsville
Cape Bowling Green
Ayr

Great Barrier Reef

Camooweal

Cloncurry
Julia Creek
Richmond

Homestead
Pentland
Torrens Creek

Charters Towers
Collinsville
Bowen

Proserpine

Whitsunday Island

Marion Reef

Mount Isa
Malbon
McKinlay

Hughenden

CLARKE RANGE
Mackay
Sarina

Swain
Reefs

Duchess
Urandangi
Dajarra
Selwyn

SELWYN RANGE

Corfield
Middleton
Woodstock
Tower Hill

Mount Dalrymple 1259
Netherdale
Newlands

Koumala
Carmila

Annandale

Kenn Reef

Argadargada
Tobermorey

Hamilton
Hotel
Winton
Muttaburra

Blair Athol
DRUMMOND RANGE
Clermont

St. Lawrence
Ogmore

Saumarez Reef

Glenormiston
Boulia

Marion Downs
Brighton Downs

Old Cork

QUEENSLAND

Aramac
Jericho
Alpha
Bogantungan

Emerald
Comet
Duaringa

Yeppoon
Rockhampton
Mount Morgan

Capricorn
Group

Capricorn Channel

5000

Longreach
Ilfracombe
Barcaldine
Yalleroi

Springsure
Rolleston

Jambin
Biloela
Gladstone

Miriam Vale

Curtis Island

Tropic of Capricorn

Simpson
Desert

Birdsville

Great

Jundah
Yaraka
Emmet
Blackall

Tambo

Theodore

Thangool
Monto

Gin Gin
Childers
Howard

Sandy Cape

Fraser Island

Betoota

Artesian

Windorah
Adavale

Augathella
Morven
Mitchell

Mount Hutton
940
Injune
Taroom

Camboon
Gayndah
Murgon
Theebine

Maryborough
Pialba
Mungar Junction
Double Island Point

Hervey
Bay

Monkira

Basin

Thylungra
Quilpie

Charleville
Westgate
Boatman

Roma
Miles
Condamine

Wondai
Kingaroy
Nanango

Gympie
Cooroy
Nambour

Sturt
Stony
Desert

Bransby

Toompine

Wyandra

Surat
Glenmorgan

Mount Kiangara
1146
Chinchilla
Dalby
Yarraman

Moreton Island

Hungerford

Thargomindah
Cunnamulla

Bollon
Flinton
St. George

Darling

Oakey
Toowoomba

Redcliffe
Ipswich

BRISBANE

North Stradbroke Island

**PACIFIC
OCEAN**

Tibooburra

Dirranbandi

Goondiwindi

Downs
Allora
Warwick
Boonah

Southport (Gold Coast)

Milparinka
Wanaaring

Hebel
Goodooga

Thallon
Boggabilla

Inglewood
Stanthorpe
Texas

Murwillumbah
Mullumbimby
Cape Byron

Tibooburra
Benbonyathe Hill
1064

Tongo

Mungindi
Moree

Yetman
Ashford

Tenterfield
Casino
Lismore
Byron Bay
Ballina

St. Mary Peak
1168

BARRIER RANGE
White Cliffs
Tilpa

Pokataroo

Bourke
Louth

Narrabri

Warialda
Bingara

Mount Bajimba 1448
Maclean
Yamba

NORTH FLINDERS RANGES

Byrock

Carinda

Burren
Junction

Bellata
Barraba

Glen Innes
Dorrigo
Ulmarra
Grafton

Silverton

Broken Hill

Wilcannia
Stephens Creek

Coonamble

Gunnedah

Guyra
Armidale
Round Mt.
1586
Bellbrook

Coffs Harbour
Macksville

Cobar
Hermidale
Mount Kalumba 456
Nymagee

Nyngan
Warren

Gilgandra
Binnaway

Liverpool RANGE
Tamworth
Werris Creek

Kempsey

Port Macquarie

NEW SOUTH WALES

Ivanhoe
Matakana
Roto

Nymagee
Tottenham

Nevertire
Dubbo

Gulgong
Muswellbrook

Gloucester
Taree

Menindee

Hillston

Lake
Cargelligo
Condobolin
Parkes

Wellington
Mudgee
Dunedoo

Dungog
Maitland

5944

Wentworth

Booligal

Lake

Naradhan

Marsden
Forbes

Orange
Molong

Cessnock

Newcastle

Mildura
Euston
Maud

West Wyalong
Young

Bathurst
Cowra

Wyong
Gosford

11   160°

Meringur

Robinvale
Balranald

Hay

Griffith
Leeton
Narrandera

Cootamundra
Temora
Junee

Katoomba
Penrith
Parramatta

SYDNEY

St. Mary Peak

Pinnaroo

Swan Hill
Kerang

Deniliquin
Jerilderie

Wagga Wagga
The Rock

Gundagai
Yass

Campbelltown

Renmark
Barmera
Loxton

Hopetoun
Yanac
Nhill

Finley
Culcairn

Tumut
A.C.T.

Canberra
Queanbeyan

Wollongong
Shellharbour
Nowra
Ulladulla

Adelaide

Murray Bridge

Echuca
Shepparton

Albury
Wodonga
Tallangatta

Cooma
Nimmitabel

Jervis Bay Territory

Meningie

Pinnaroo
Ouyen

Donald
Inglewood

Benalla
Bright

Mount
Kosciuszko
2229

Bombala
Bega
Eden

Kingston Southeast
Bordertown

Dimboola
Horsham
St. Arnaud

Bendigo
Castlemaine
Euroa
Eildon

SNOWY MTS.
Omeo
Delegate

Cape Howe

Robe
Penola

Stawell
Ararat

VICTORIA

TASMAN SEA

Naracoorte

Millicent
Mount Gambier
Hamilton
Heywood
Portland
Cape Nelson

Mortlake

Ballarat

MELBOURNE
Sunshine
Werribee
Geelong

Healesville
Bairnsdale
Sale
Lakes
Entrance

Ninety Mile
Beach

Orbost
Cann River

Warrnambool
Cape Otway
Apollo Bay
Lorne

Colac
Warragul
Morwell
Yarram
Foster

Wonthaggi
Wilsons Promontory
South East Point

Cape Jaffa

Kingston Southeast

Cape Wickham
Egg Lagoon
King Island

Bass Strait
Kent
Group

Flinders
Island

Inset map (bottom right):

a
Ballarat
Sunshine
Werribee
Geelong
Colac

Healesville
MELBOURNE
Warragul
Morwell
Sale

Bairnsdale
Lakes
Entrance
Ninety Mile
Beach

Orbost
Cann
River

b

Lorne
Apollo
Bay
Wonthaggi
Foster
Yarram

Wilsons Promontory
South East Point

Cape
Otway

Cape
Wickham
Egg Lagoon

King Island

Bass Strait
Kent
Group

Flinders
Island
Whitemark

Hunter Island
Cape Grim

Three Hummock
Island

FURNEAUX
GROUP
Cape Barren
Island
Clarke Island

TASMANIA

Marrawah

Smithton
Stanley
Burnie
Ulverstone
Devonport
Beaconsfield

Cape Portland
George
Town
Scottsdale

St. Marys

Waratah
Mount Ossa
1617
Zeehan

Launceston
Campbell Town

Queenstown
Strahan

Oatlands
Triabunna

Freycinet
Peninsula

TASMANIA

Macquarie Harbour

New Norfolk
Huonville
Geeveston
Dover

Hobart

Port Arthur

Storm
Bay

South East Cape

Same scale
as main map

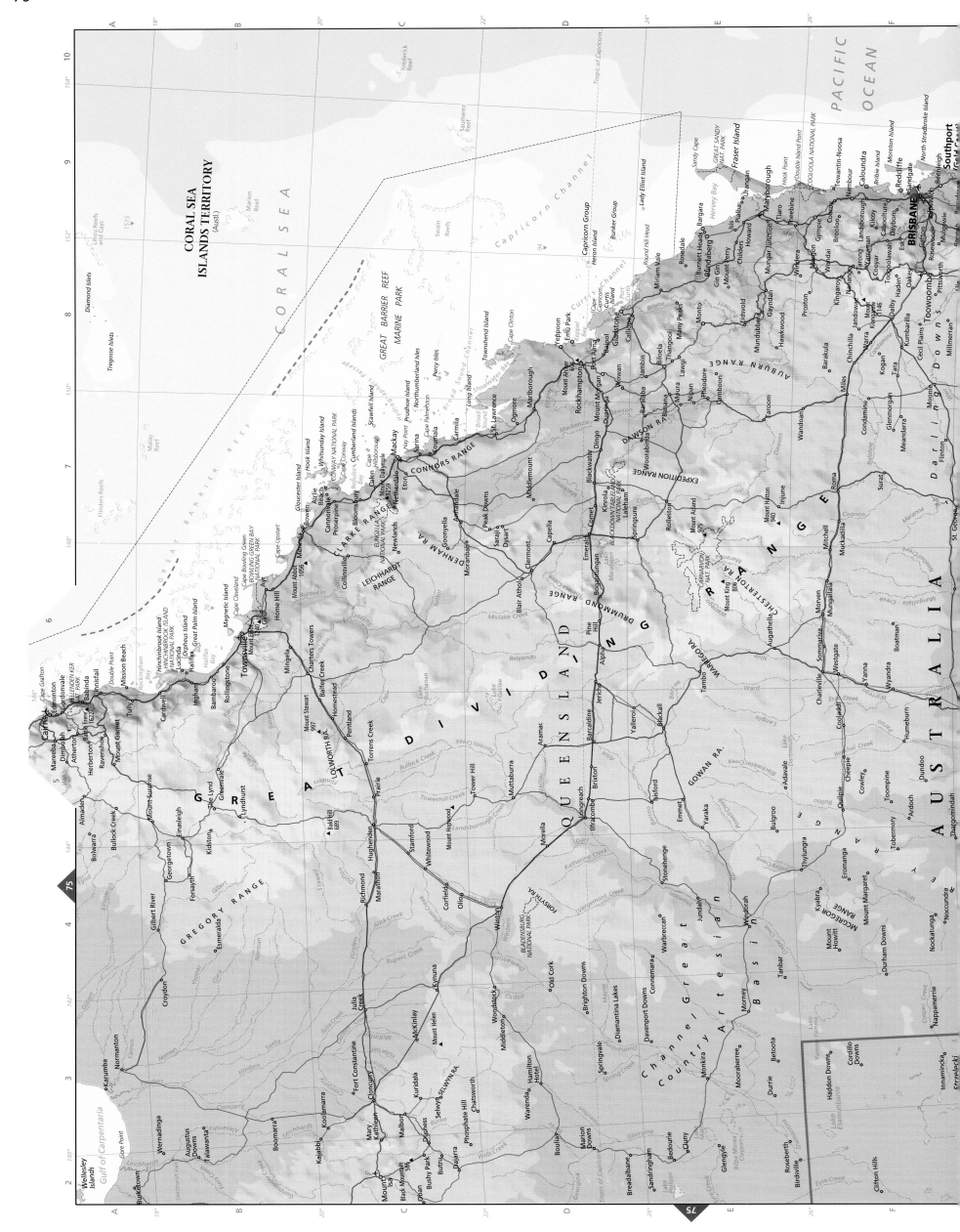

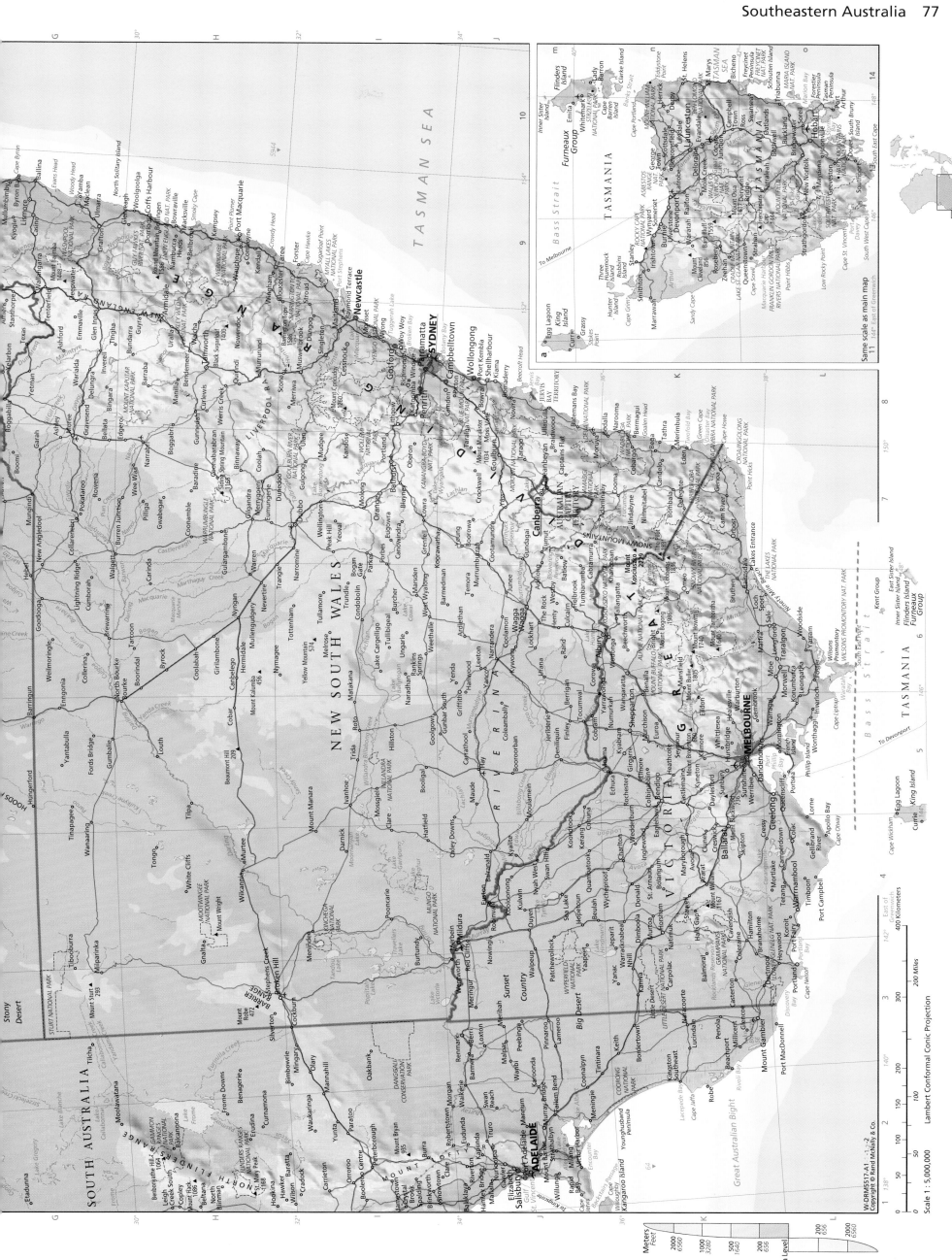

W-DRM5517-A1 -1,-2

Lambert Conformal Conic Projection

Scale 1 : 5,000,000

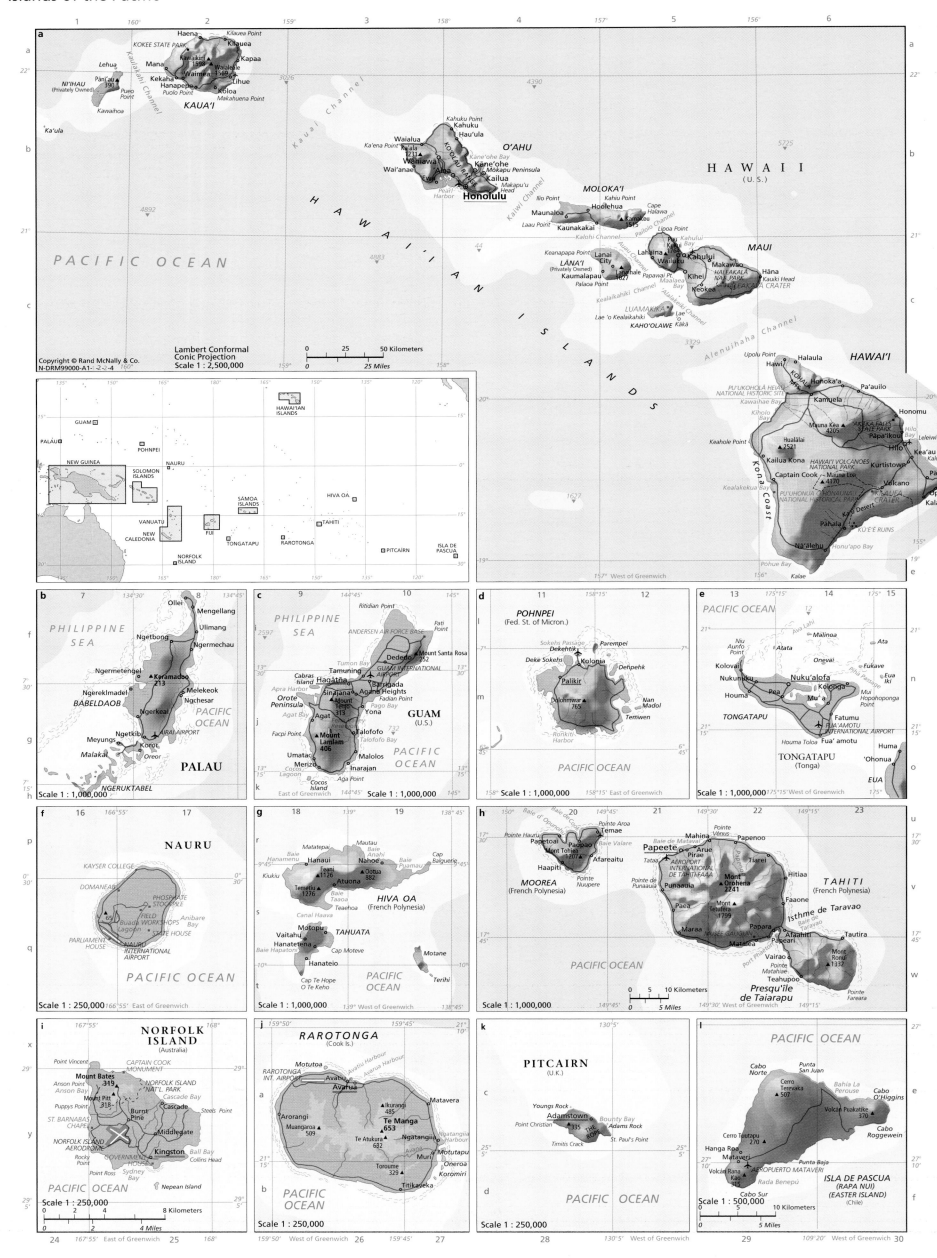

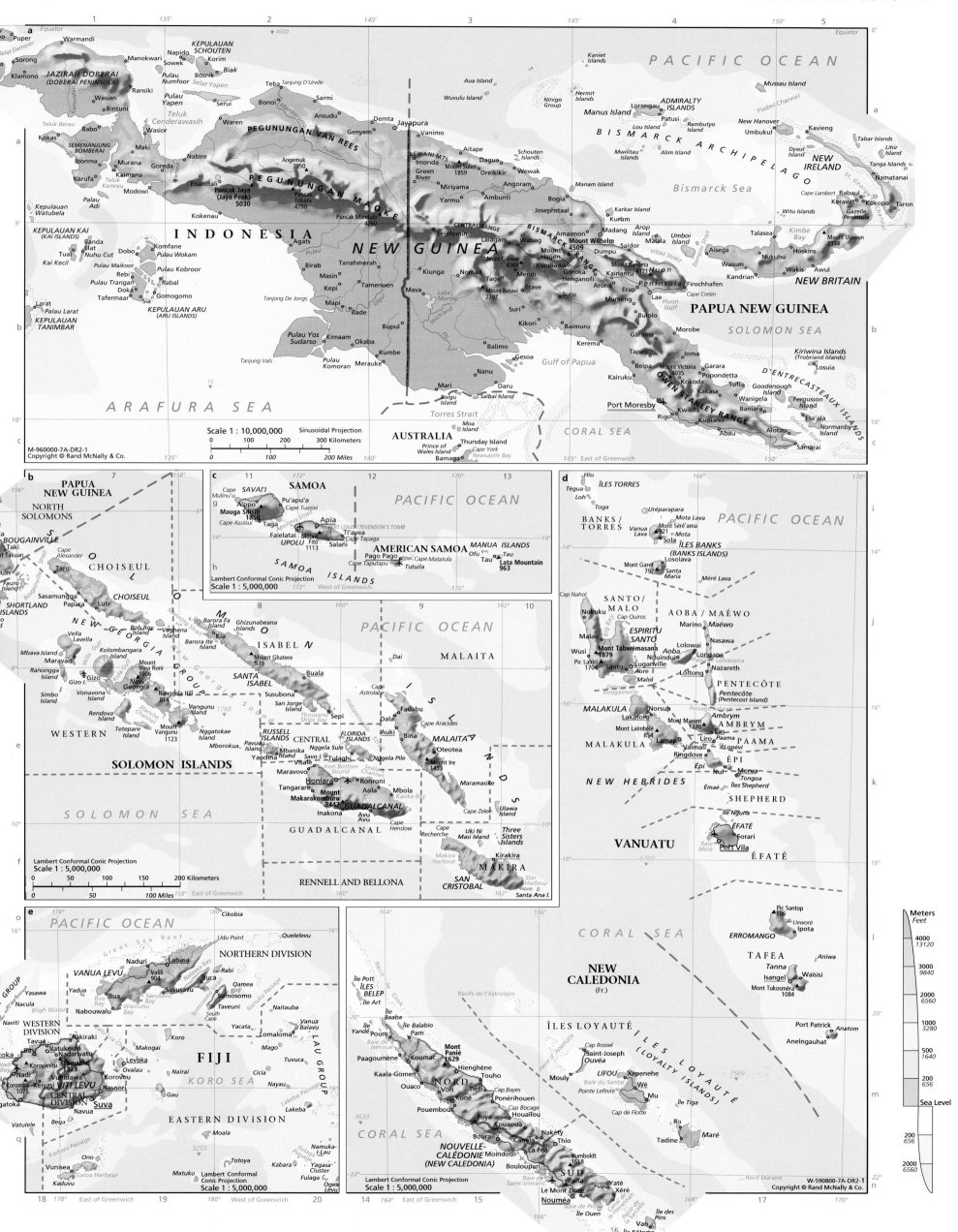

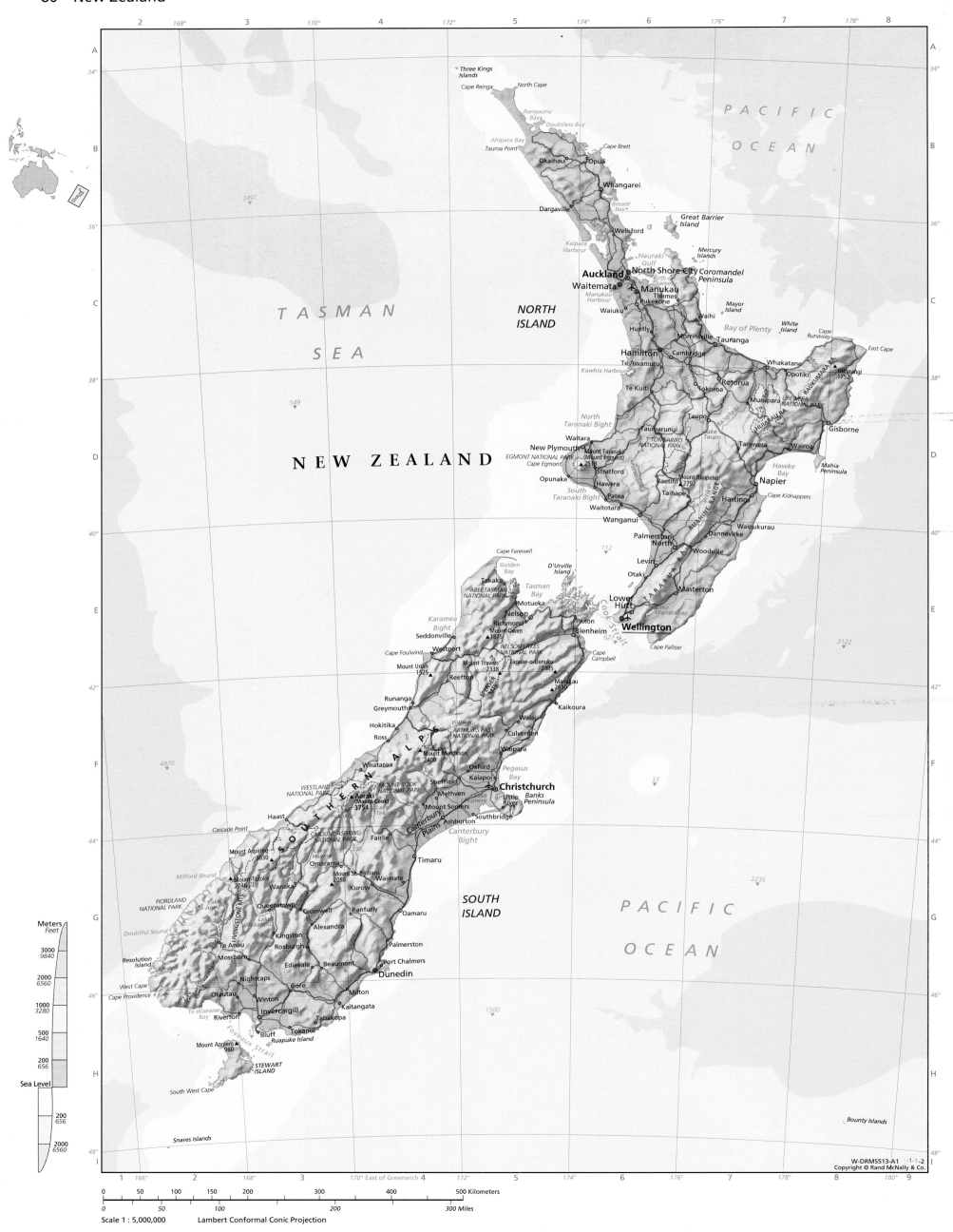

PACIFIC OCEAN

Three Kings Islands
Cape Reinga
North Cape
North Cape

Rangaunu Bay
Doubtless Bay
Ahipara Bay
Tauroa Point
Cape Brett
Okaihau
Opua
Whangarei

Dargaville
Bream Bay
Great Barrier Island

Wellsford
Hauraki Gulf
Mercury Islands
White Island
Cape Runaway

TASMAN
SEA

Kaipara Harbour
Auckland
North Shore City
Coromandel Peninsula
Waitemata
Manukau
Thames
Firth of Thames
NORTH ISLAND
Manukau Harbour
Pukekohe
Waiuku
Waihi
Bay of Plenty
Huntly
Morrinsville
Tauranga
Whakatane
Opotiki
Hikurangi 1752

Hamilton
Cambridge
Te Awamutu
Kawhia Harbour
Te Kuiti
Rotorua
RAUKUMARA RA.
UREWERA NATIONAL PARK
HUIARAU RA.
Tokoroa

NEW ZEALAND

North Taranaki Bight
Taumarunui
Lake Taupo
Taupo
Tarawera
Gisborne

549

Waitara
New Plymouth
Mount Taranaki (Mount Egmont)
EGMONT NATIONAL PARK
Cape Egmont
TONGARIRO NATIONAL PARK
Mount Ruapehu 2797
Wairoa
Mahia Peninsula

Stratford
2518
Hawera
Raetihi
Taihape
Napier
Hawke Bay

Opunake
Patea
Hastings
Cape Kidnappers

Waitotara
Wanganui
RUAHINE RANGE
Waipukurau
Waipawa

Palmerston North
Dannevirke

112
Levin
Woodville
Cape Farewell
Golden Bay
D'Urville Island
Otaki
Masterton
TARARUA RANGE

Takaka
ABEL TASMAN NATIONAL PARK
Tasman Bay
Motueka
Lower Hutt
Wellington
Karamea Bight
Nelson
Richmond
Picton
Cook Strait
677
Lake Wairarapa
Cape Palliser
3122

Seddonville
Mount Owen 1875
Blenheim
Cape Campbell

Cape Foulwind
Westport
NELSON LAKES NATIONAL PARK
Mount Uriah 1525
Mount Travers 2338
Tapuae-o-Uenuku 2885

Reefton
SPENCER MTS.
Manakau 2610

Runanga
Kaikoura
Greymouth
Waiau

Hokitika
ARTHUR'S PASS NATIONAL PARK
Ross
Culverden
Waipara

Whataroa
Mount Murchison 2400
Oxford
Pegasus Bay
Sheffield
Kaiapoi

WESTLAND NATIONAL PARK
MOUNT COOK NATIONAL PARK
Methven
Christchurch
Little River
Banks Peninsula

Aoraki (Mount Cook) 3754
Lake Tekapo
Mount Somers

Haast
Fairlie
Ashburton
Southbridge
Canterbury Plains
Canterbury Bight
MOUNT ASPIRING NATIONAL PARK

Mount Aspiring 3030
Lake Hawea
Omarama
Mount St. Bathans 2088
Waimate

33

Milford Sound
Mount Tutoko 2746
Wanaka
Kurow
Waitaki
2235

FIORDLAND NATIONAL PARK
Queenstown
Cromwell
Ranfurly
Oamaru
SOUTH ISLAND

Lake Wakatipu
Alexandra
Resolution Island
Kingston
Roxburgh
PACIFIC OCEAN

West Cape
Cape Providence
Mossburn
Edievale
Beaumont
Palmerston
Port Chalmers

Te Anau
Nightcaps
Gore
Milton
Dunedin

Otautau
Winton
Kaitangata
Te Waewae Bay
Riverton
Invercargill
Tahakopa
Tokanui
Foveaux Strait
Bluff
Ruapuke Island

Mount Anglem 980
STEWART ISLAND

South West Cape

Snares Islands

Bounty Islands

Meters Feet
3000 9840
2000 6560
1000 3280
500 1640
200 656
Sea Level
200 656
2000 6560

0 50 100 150 200 300 400 500 Kilometers
0 50 100 200 300 Miles

Scale 1 : 5,000,000   Lambert Conformal Conic Projection

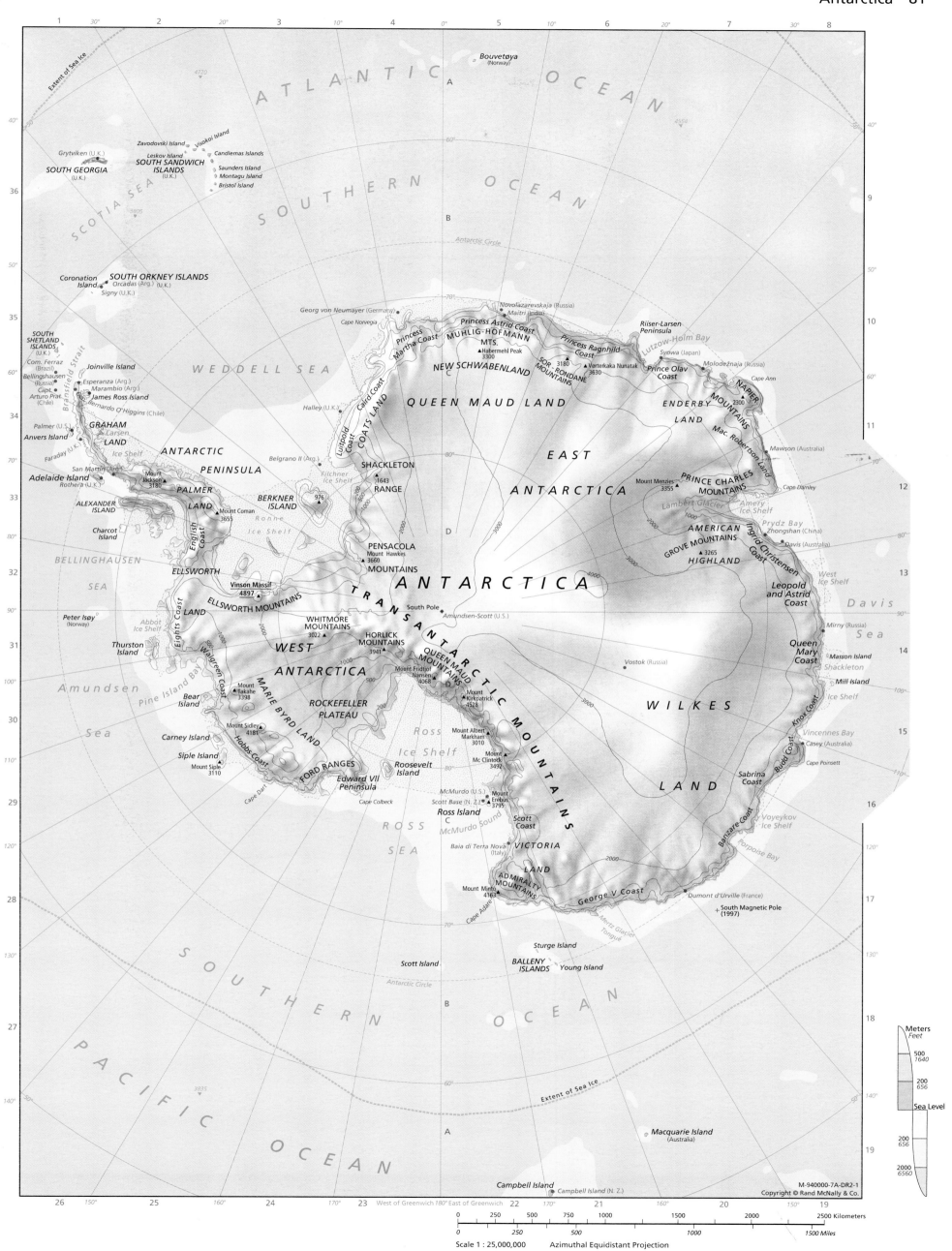

ATLANTIC   OCEAN

Bouvetøya
(Norway)

SOUTHERN   OCEAN

Antarctic Circle

Extent of Sea Ice

SCOTIA SEA

Grytviken (U.K.)
SOUTH GEORGIA
(U.K.)

Zavodovski Island
Leskov Island
SOUTH SANDWICH
ISLANDS
(U.K.)

Visokoi Island
Candlemas Islands
Saunders Island
Montagu Island
Bristol Island

Coronation
Island
SOUTH ORKNEY ISLANDS
Orcadas (Arg.)
(U.K.)
Signy (U.K.)

Georg von Neumayer (Germany)
Novolazarevskaja (Russia)
Maitri (India)

Cape Norvegia

Princess Astrid Coast
MUHLIG-HOFMANN
MTS.
Habermehl Peak
3300

Princess Ragnhild
Coast

Riiser-Larsen
Peninsula

Lutzow-Holm Bay
Syowa (Japan)
Molodežnaja (Russia)

SOUTH
SHETLAND
ISLANDS
(U.K.)
Com. Ferraz (Brazil)
Bellingshausen (Russia)
Capt. Arturo Prat (Chile)

Joinville Island
Esperanza (Arg.)
Marambio (Arg.)
James Ross Island
Bernardo O'Higgins (Chile)

Halley (U.K.)

Princess
Martha Coast

NEW SCHWABENLAND

SØR
RONDANE
MOUNTAINS
3180
Vorterkaka Nunatak
3630

Prince Olav
Coast

ENDERBY

NAPIER
2300

Cape Ann

GRAHAM
LAND

Larsen
Ice Shelf

ANTARCTIC
PENINSULA

Caird Coast

COATS LAND

QUEEN MAUD LAND

LAND

MOUNTAINS

Mac. Robertson Land

Mawson (Australia)

Palmer (U.S.)
Anvers Island

Faraday (U.K.)
San Martin (Arg.)

Adelaide Island
Rothera (U.K.)

PALMER
LAND

Mount
Jackson
3180

Belgrano II (Arg.)

Filchner
Ice Shelf

SHACKLETON
1643
RANGE

EAST
ANTARCTICA

PRINCE CHARLES
MOUNTAINS
Mount Menzies
3355

Lambert Glacier

Cape Darnley

Prydz Bay
Zhongshan (China)
Davis (Australia)

ALEXANDER
ISLAND

Charcot
Island

Mount Coman
3655

BERKNER
ISLAND

976

Ronne
Ice Shelf

PENSACOLA
Mount Hawkes
3660
MOUNTAINS

ANTARCTICA

Amery
Ice Shelf

GROVE
MOUNTAINS
3265

AMERICAN
HIGHLAND

Ingrid Christensen Coast

West
Ice Shelf

BELLINGHAUSEN

SEA

English Coast

ELLSWORTH
LAND

Vinson Massif
4897

ELLSWORTH MOUNTAINS

TRANSANTARCTIC

South Pole
Amundsen-Scott (U.S.)

Leopold
and Astrid
Coast

Davis

Sea

Peter Isøy
(Norway)

Abbot
Ice Shelf

Eights Coast

WHITMORE
MOUNTAINS
3022

HORLICK
MOUNTAINS
3941

WEST

QUEEN MAUD
MOUNTAINS

MOUNTAINS

Vostok (Russia)

Queen
Mary
Coast

Mirny (Russia)

Masson Island
Shackleton

Thurston
Island

Walgreen Coast

ANTARCTICA

Mount Fridtjof
Nansen
4068

WILKES

Mill Island
Ice Shelf

Amundsen

Sea

Pine Island Bay

Bear
Island

Mount
Takahe
3398

MARIE BYRD LAND

ROCKEFELLER
PLATEAU

Mount
Kirkpatrick
4528

LAND

Vincennes Bay
Casey (Australia)

Knox Coast

Budd Coast

Carney Island

Siple Island
Mount Siple
3110

Hobbs Coast

Mount Sidley
4181

FORD RANGES

Ross
Ice Shelf

Mount Albert
Markham
3010

Mount
Mc Clintock
3492

Sabrina
Coast

Cape Poinsett

Cape Dart

Edward VII
Peninsula

Roosevelt
Island

McMurdo (U.S.)

Banzare Coast

Voyeykov
Ice Shelf

Cape Colbeck

Scott Base (N.Z.)
Ross Island

Mount
Erebus
3795

Scott
Coast

Porpoise Bay

ROSS

SEA

McMurdo Sound

Baia di Terra Nova (Italy)

VICTORIA

George V Coast

Dumont d'Urville (France)
South Magnetic Pole
(1997)

ADMIRALTY
MOUNTAINS

LAND

Mount Minto
4163

Cape Adare

Mertz Glacier
Tongue

Sturge Island

Scott Island

BALLENY
ISLANDS
Young Island

SOUTHERN   OCEAN

Antarctic Circle

PACIFIC   OCEAN

Macquarie Island
(Australia)

Campbell Island
Campbell Island (N.Z.)

M-940000-7A-DR2-1
Copyright © Rand McNally & Co.

WEDDELL SEA

Bransfield Strait

Plopoid
Coast

Ludpoid
Coast

Meters
Feet
500
1640
200
656
Sea Level
200
656
2000
6560

0   250   500   750   1000   1500   2000   2500 Kilometers
0   250   500   1000   1500 Miles
Scale 1 : 25,000,000   Azimuthal Equidistant Projection

West of Greenwich 180° East of Greenwich

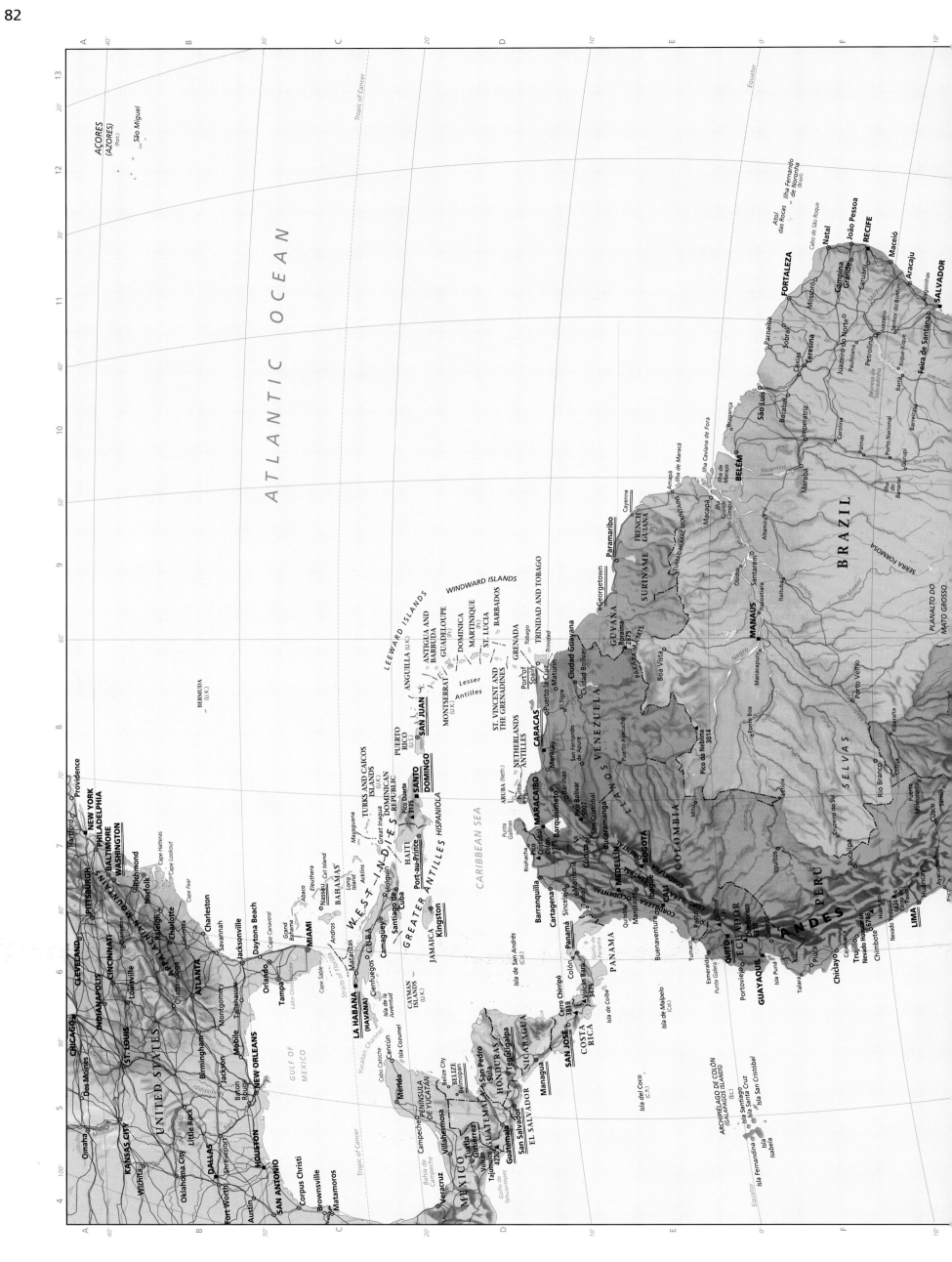

82

ATLANTIC OCEAN

AÇORES
(AZORES)
(Port.)

São Miguel

Tropic of Cancer

BERMUDA
(U.K.)

WINDWARD ISLANDS

LEEWARD ISLANDS

ANTIGUA AND
BARBUDA
(U.K.)

GUADELOUPE
(Fr.)

ANGUILLA
(U.K.)

MARTINIQUE
(Fr.)

DOMINICA

ST. LUCIA

BARBADOS

GRENADA

Lesser
Antilles

ST. VINCENT AND
THE GRENADINES

NETHERLANDS
ANTILLES

ARUBA (Neth.)

TRINIDAD AND TOBAGO

Tobago

Trinidad

MONTSERRAT
(U.K.)

PUERTO
RICO
(U.S.)

SAN JUAN

SANTO
DOMINGO

DOMINICAN
REPUBLIC

TURKS AND CAICOS
ISLANDS
(U.K.)

Great Inagua

Pico Duarte
3175

HAITI

Port-au-Prince

GREATER ANTILLES

HISPANIOLA

CARIBBEAN SEA

BAHAMAS

Nassau

Eleuthera

Cat Island

Long
Island

Acklins

Mayaguana

Abaco

Grand
Bahama

Andros

Cuba

Santiago de
Cuba

Holguín

Camagüey

Cienfuegos

JAMAICA

Kingston

CAYMAN
ISLANDS
(U.K.)

Isla de la
Juventud

LA HABANA
(HAVANA)

Matanzas

W E S T   I N D I E S

Isla de San Andrés
(Col.)

Isla de Malpelo
(Col.)

Isla del Coco
(C.R.)

ARCHIPIÉLAGO DE COLÓN
(GALÁPAGOS ISLANDS)
(Ec.)

Isla
Santiago

Isla Santa Cruz

Isla San Cristóbal

Isla
Isabela

Isla Fernandina

Equator

UNITED STATES

Providence

Hartford

NEW YORK

PHILADELPHIA

BALTIMORE

WASHINGTON

Richmond

Norfolk

Cape Hatteras

Cape Lookout

Cape Fear

PITTSBURGH

Raleigh

Charlotte

Charleston

Savannah

Jacksonville

Daytona Beach

Cape Canaveral

Orlando

Tampa

MIAMI

Lake Okeechobee

Cape Sable

Strait of Florida

CLEVELAND

CINCINNATI

CHICAGO

INDIANAPOLIS

Des Moines

Omaha

KANSAS CITY

ST. LOUIS

Louisville

Chattanooga

ATLANTA

Montgomery

Birmingham

Mobile

Tallahassee

Jackson

Baton
Rouge

Shreveport

NEW ORLEANS

Little Rock

Oklahoma City

DALLAS

Fort Worth

Wichita

Austin

SAN ANTONIO

HOUSTON

Corpus Christi

Brownsville

Matamoros

Veracruz

MÉXICO

Villahermosa

Tuxtla
Gutiérrez

Volcán
Tajumulco
4220

Mérida

Cancún

Isla Cozumel

Cabo Catoche

PENÍNSULA
DE YUCATÁN

Campeche

Bahía de
Campeche

Golfo de
Tehuantepec

Tropic of Cancer

Yucatán Channel

Belize City

Belmopan

BELIZE

GUATEMALA

Guatemala

San Salvador

EL SALVADOR

HONDURAS

San Pedro
Sula

Tegucigalpa

NICARAGUA

Managua

SAN JOSÉ

COSTA
RICA

Cerro Chirripó
3819

Volcán Barú
3475

Colón

Panamá

PANAMA

Golfo de
Panamá

Isla de Coiba

Buenaventura

QUITO

ECUADOR

GUAYAQUIL

Esmeraldas

Portoviejo

Punta Galera

Tumaco

Pasto

Isla Puná

Talara

Piura

Chiclayo

Chimbote

Trujillo

Cajamarca

Nevado Huascarán
6768

Nevado Huascarán
6745

LIMA

Huancayo

Cusco

PERÚ

A N D E S

Iquitos

Pucallpa

Cruzeiro do Sul

Rio Branco

BRAZIL

SELVAS

Pôrto Velho

Manacapuru

Pico da Neblina
3014

Manaus

MANAUS

Negro

Boa
Vista

Boa
Vista

Roraima
2875

PACARAIMA MTS.

TUMUC-HUMAC MOUNTAINS

GUYANA

Georgetown

SURINAME

Paramaribo

FRENCH
GUIANA
(Fr.)

Cayenne

Amapá

Ilha de
Marajó

BELÉM

Macapá

Óbidos

Santarém

Itaituba

Santarém

Ilha
Tupinambarana

PLANALTO DO
MATO GROSSO

SERRA FORMOSA

São Luís

BRAZIL

VENEZUELA

CARACAS

Ciudad Guayana

Ciudad Bolívar

El Tigre

Maturín

Barcelona

MARACAIBO

Barquisimeto

San Cristóbal

Bucaramanga

COLOMBIA

BOGOTÁ

MEDELLÍN

CALI

Barranquilla

Cartagena

Sincelejo

Montería

Manizales

Ibagué

Neiva

Quibdó

L L A N O S

Puerto Ayacucho

San Fernando
de Apure

Barinas

Orinoco

CORDILLERA CENTRAL

CORDILLERA OCCIDENTAL

CORDILLERA ORIENTAL

Cúcuta

Pico
Cristóbal
Colón
5775

Riohacha

Santa
Marta

Punta
Gallinas

Mérida

Pico Bolívar
5007

Maracaibo

Valencia

FORTALEZA

RECIFE

SALVADOR

Natal

João Pessoa

Maceió

Aracaju

Campina
Grande

Feira de
Santana

Mossoró

Sobral

Teresina

Caxias

Imperatriz

Carolina

Palmas

Marabá

Parnaíba

Juazeiro do Norte

Petrolina

Juazeiro

Barreiras

Pôrto Nacional

Gurupi

Tocantins

Ilha Fernando
de Noronha
(Brazil)

Atol
das Rocas

Cabo de São Roque

Cabo São Roque

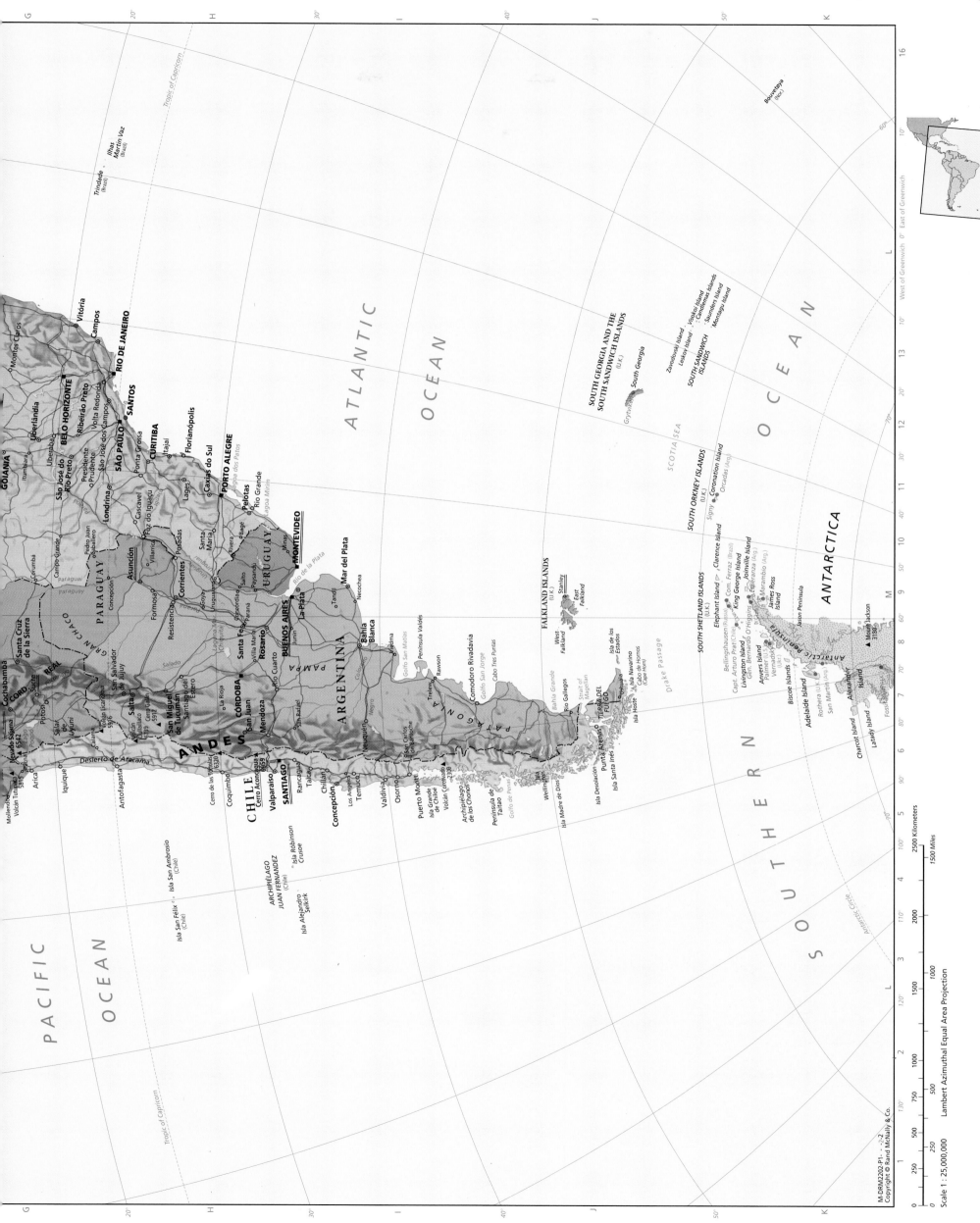

ATLANTIC

OCEAN

PACIFIC

OCEAN

S O U T H E R N

OCEAN

Drake Passage

SCOTIA SEA

ANTARCTICA

Antarctic Peninsula

ARGENTINA

PARAGUAY

CHILE

URUGUAY

PAMPA

PATAGONIA

GRAN CHACO

ANDES

CORD. REAL

Desierto de Atacama

Tropic of Capricorn

Antarctic Circle

SOUTH GEORGIA AND THE
SOUTH SANDWICH ISLANDS
(U.K.)

SOUTH SANDWICH
ISLANDS

SOUTH ORKNEY ISLANDS
(U.K.)

SOUTH SHETLAND ISLANDS
(U.K.)

FALKLAND ISLANDS
(U.K.)

TIERRA DEL
FUEGO

GOIÂNIA
Uberlândia
Itumbiara
Uberaba
BELO HORIZONTE
Ribeirão Preto
Volta Redonda
São José do
Rio Preto
Presidente
Prudente
SÃO PAULO
CURITIBA
Londrina
Ponta Grossa
Itajaí
Florianópolis
Cascavel
Lages
Caxias do Sul
Foz do Iguaçu
PORTO ALEGRE
Pelotas
Rio Grande
Bagé
Lagoa dos Patos
Lagoa Mirim
RIO DE JANEIRO
SANTOS
Campos
Vitória
Montes Claros
Ilhas
Martin Vaz
(Brazil)
Trindade
(Brazil)

Santa Cruz
de la Sierra
Cochabamba
Sucre
Potosí
Oruro
Salar de
Uyuni
Volcán Licancábur
5916
Volcán Ollagüe
5863
Nevado Sajama
6542
Arica
Iquique
Antofagasta
Mollendo
Volcán Tutupaca
5815
Corumbá

ASUNCIÓN
Concepción
Pedro Juan
Caballero
Campo Grande
Paraguay
Paraguay
Villarrica
Encarnación
Posadas
Corrientes
Resistencia
Formosa
Paraná

MONTEVIDEO
Minas
Rivera
Salto
Paysandú
Santa Maria
Rio Branco
Uruguay

BUENOS AIRES
La Plata
ROSARIO
Santa Fe
Villa María
CÓRDOBA
San Francisco
Río Cuarto
Junín
Tandil
Necochea
Mar del Plata
Bahía Blanca
Río Colorado
Salado
Laguna Mar Chiquita
San Salvador
de Jujuy
San Miguel
de Tucumán
Santiago del
Estero
La Rioja
San Juan
Mendoza
San Rafael
Cerro Galán
5912
Nevado Tres Cruces
6330
SANTIAGO
Valparaíso
Cerro Aconcagua
6959
Volcán Tupungato
6800
Rancagua
Talca
Chillán
Concepción
Los Ángeles
Temuco
Valdivia
Osorno
Puerto Montt
Isla Grande
de Chiloé
Volcán Corcovado
2300
Coquimbo
Cerro de las Tórtolas
6320
San Carlos
de Bariloche
Neuquén
Viedma
Trelew
Rawson
Península Valdés
Golfo San Matías
Golfo San Jorge
Cabo Tres Puntas
Comodoro Rivadavia
Río Gallegos
Bahía Grande
Puerto Aisén
Archipiélago
de los Chonos
Península de
Taitao
Golfo de Penas
Isla Madre de Dios
Wellington
Isla
Santa Inés
Isla Desolación
Isla Navarino
Cabo de Hornos
(Cape Horn)
Isla de los
Estados
Strait of
Magellan
Ushuaia
Punta Arenas
Río Grande

Isla San Félix
(Chile)
Isla San Ambrosio
(Chile)
ARCHIPIÉLAGO
JUAN FERNÁNDEZ
(Chile)
Isla Robinson
Crusoe
Isla Alejandro
Selkirk

West
Falkland
East
Falkland
Stanley

South Georgia
Grytviken

Zavodovski Island
Vostok Island
Leskov Island
Candlemas Islands
Saunders Island
Montagu Island

Bouvetøya
(Nor.)

Clarence Island
Elephant Island (U.K.)
King George Island
Joinville Island
Livingston Island
Anvers Island
Biscoe Islands
Adelaide Island
Charcot Island
Alexander
Island
Latady Island
Mount Jackson
3184

Bellingshausen (Russia)
Capt. Arturo Prat (Chile)
Com. Ferraz (Brazil)
Gen. Bernardo O'Higgins
(Chile)
Esperanza (Arg.)
Marambio (Arg.)
James Ross
Island
Jason Peninsula
Palmer (U.S.)
Vernadsky (Ukr.)
Rothera (U.K.)
San Martín (Arg.)
Fossil Bluff (U.K.)

Coronation Island
Signy
Orcadas (Arg.)

Scale 1 : 25,000,000

Lambert Azimuthal Equal Area Projection

2500 Kilometers
1500 Miles

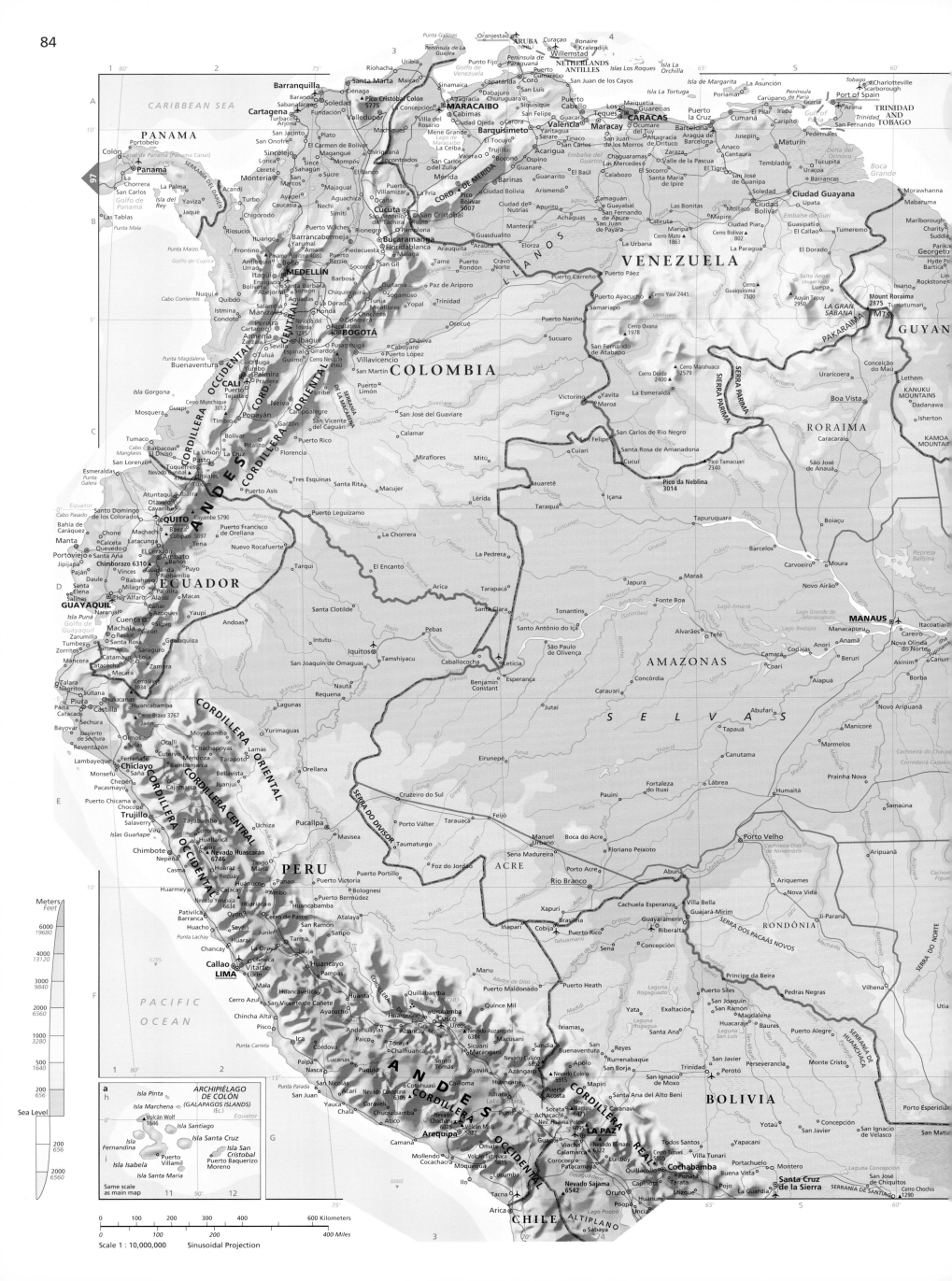

CARIBBEAN SEA

PACIFIC

OCEAN

PANAMA

ECUADOR

COLOMBIA

PERU

Meters
Feet

4000
13120

3000
9840

2000
6560

1000
3280

500
1640

200
656

Sea Level

200
656

2000
6560

0   50   100   150   200   300   400   500 Kilometers

0   50   100   200   300 Miles

Scale 1 : 5,000,000   Sinusoidal Projection

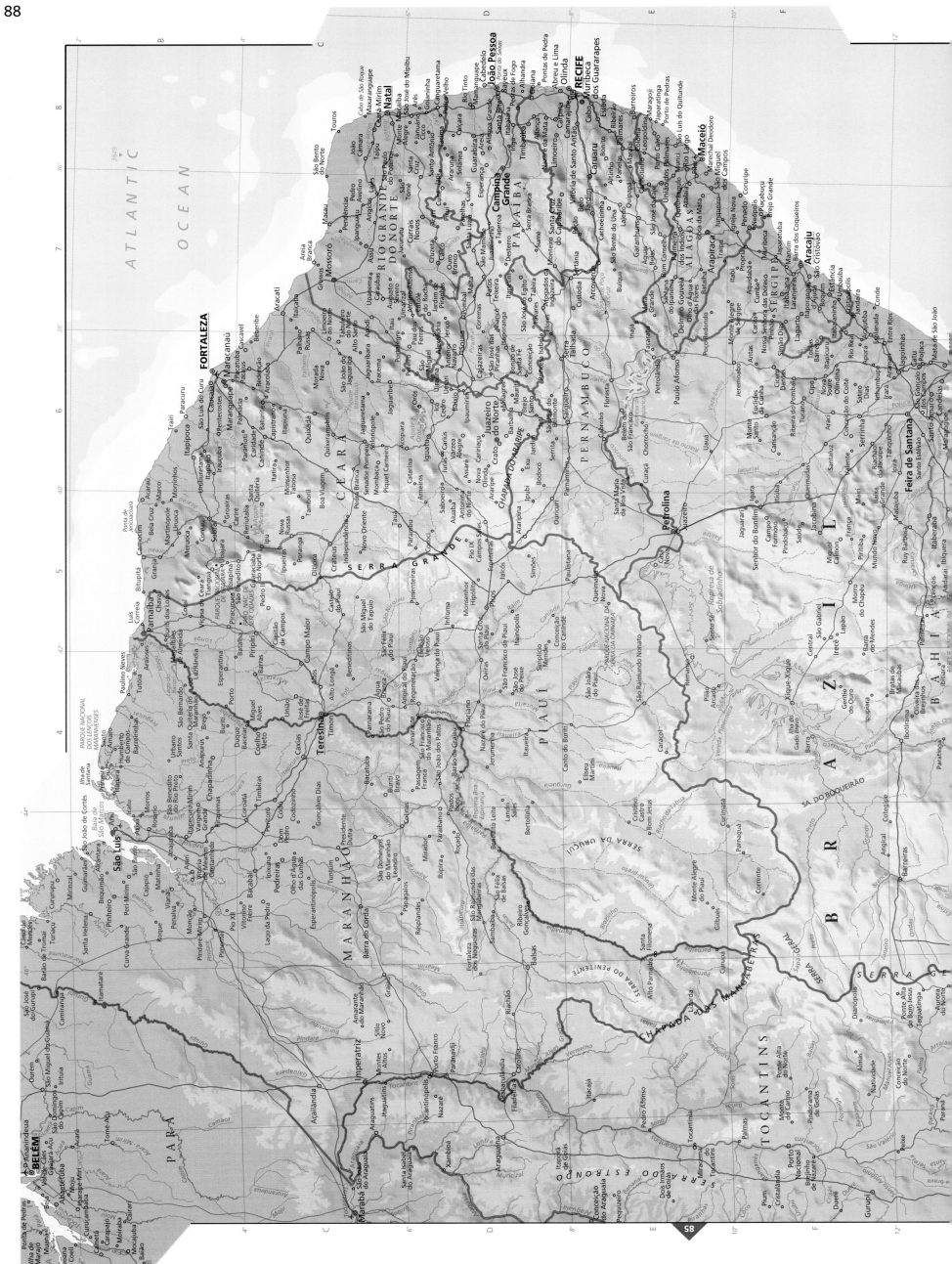

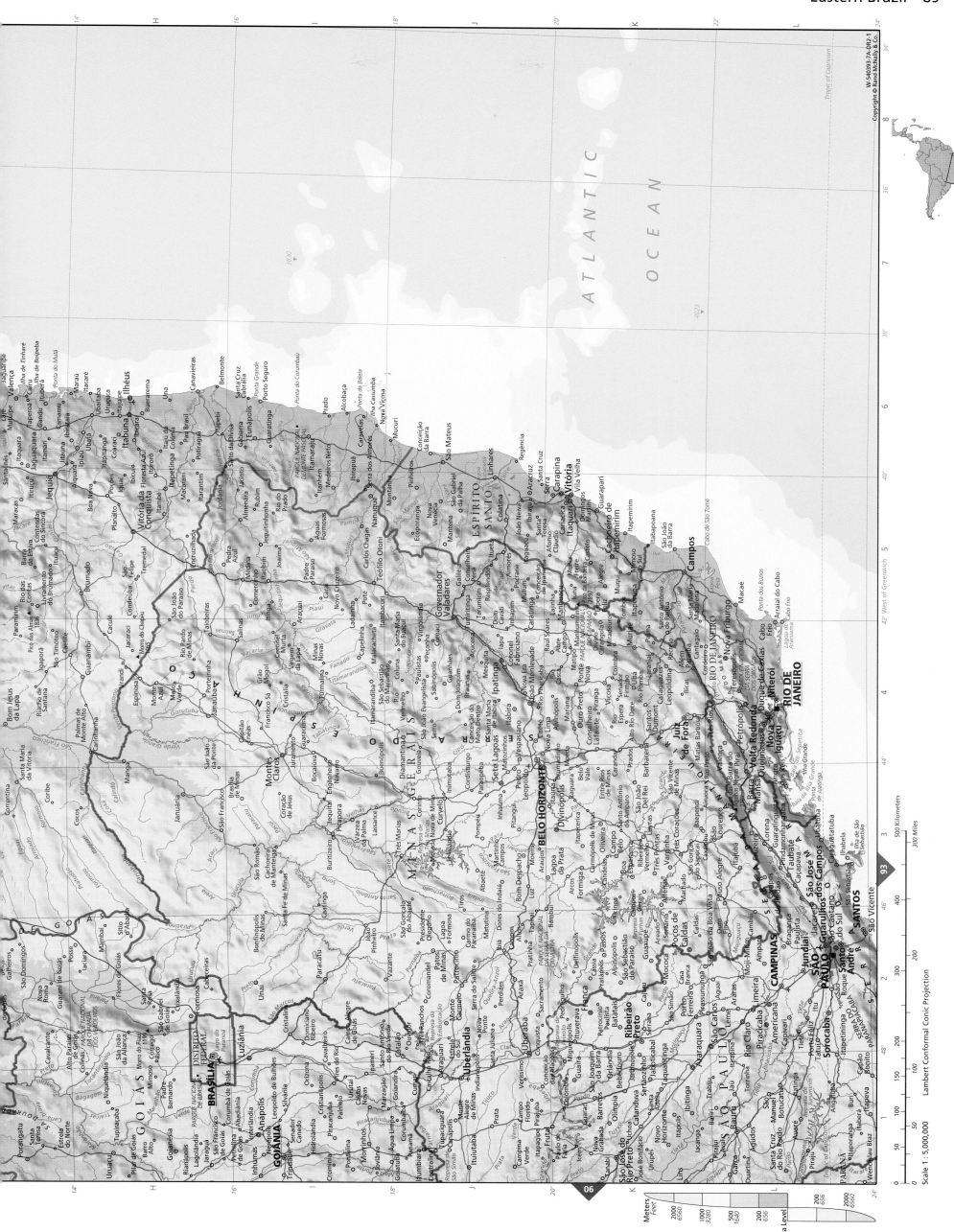

Scale 1 : 5,000,000

Lambert Conformal Conic Projection

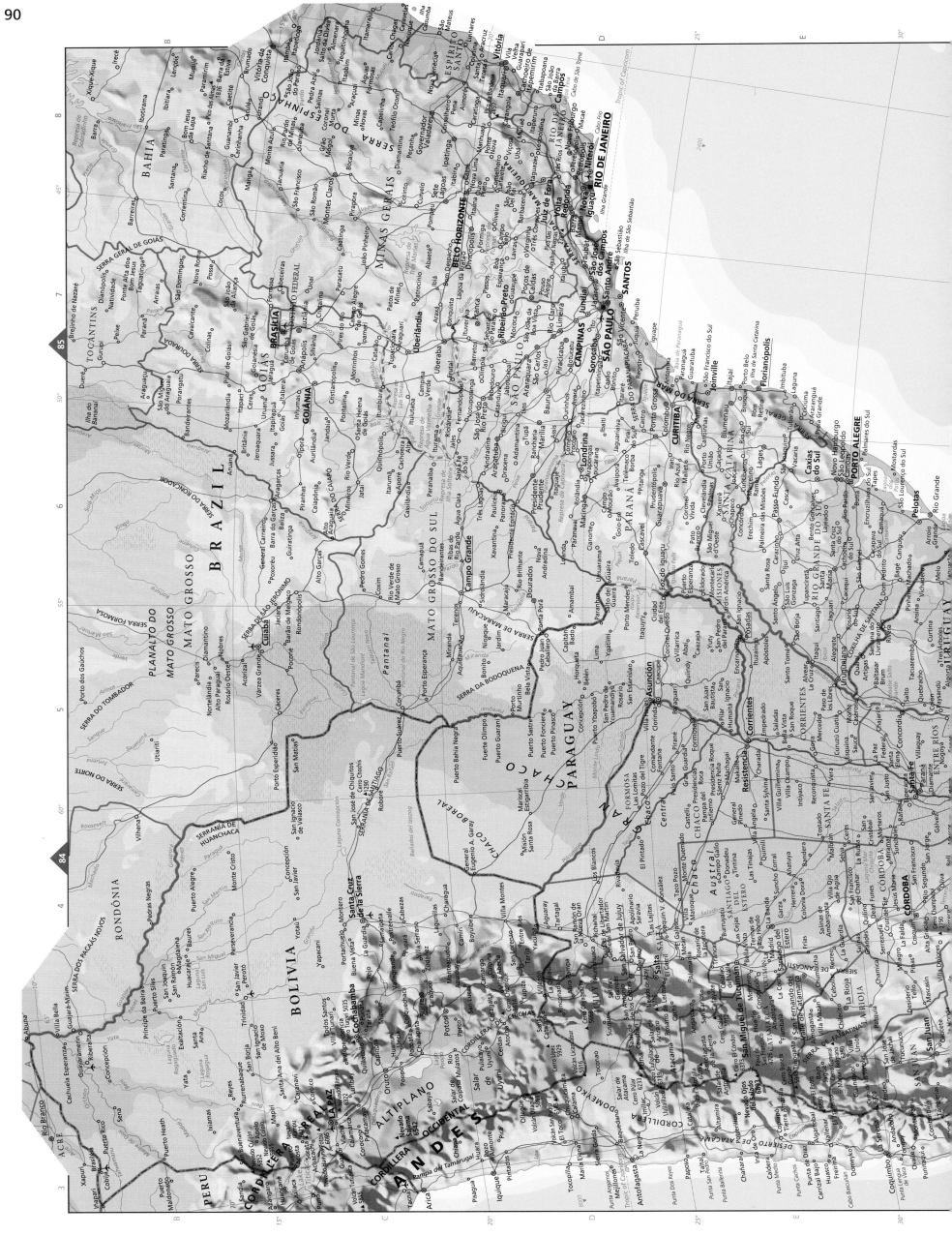

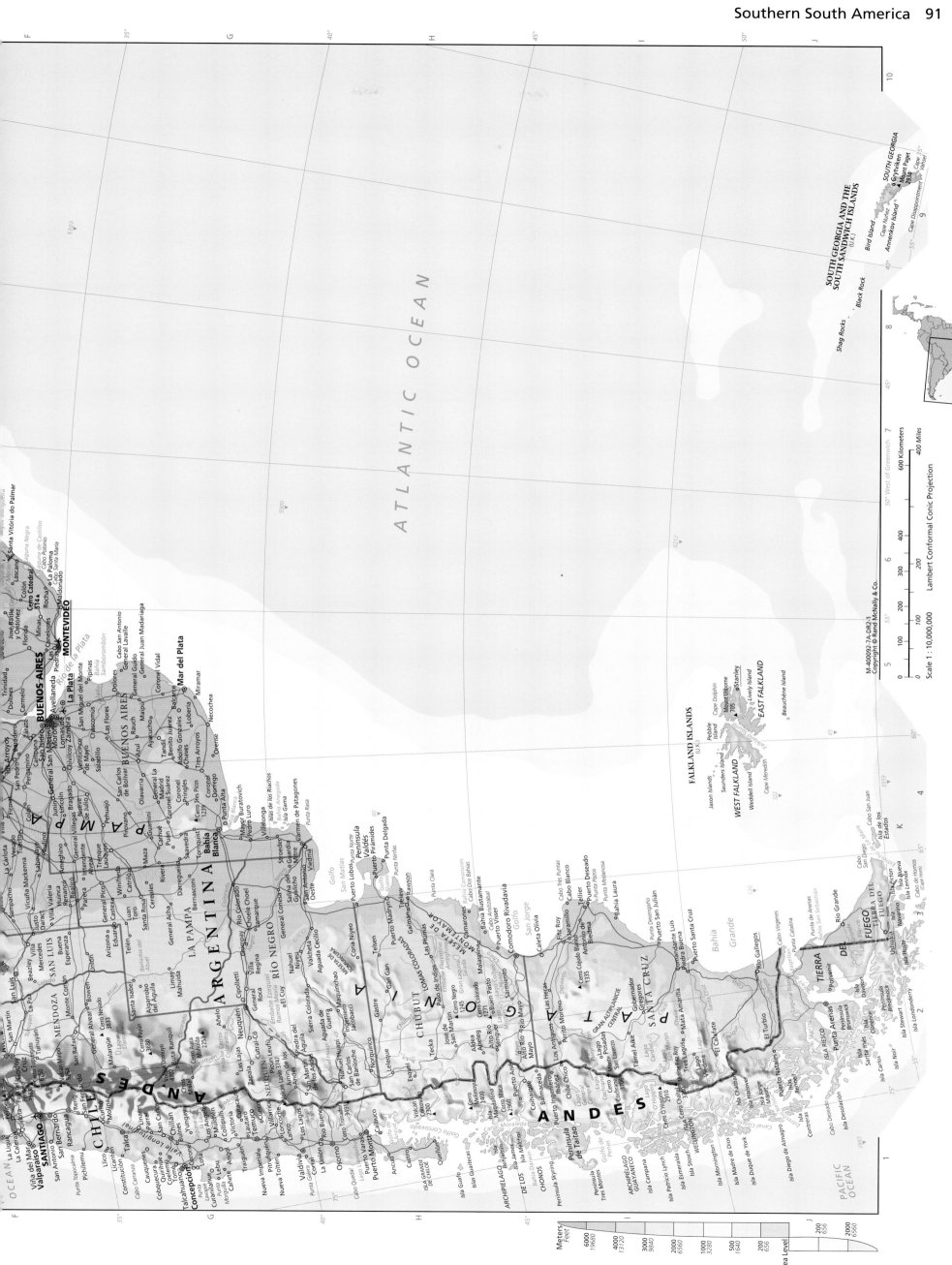

ATLANTIC OCEAN

PACIFIC OCEAN

ANDES

ARGENTINA

CHILE

PATAGONIA

LA PAMPA

BUENOS AIRES

PAMPA

MENDOZA

SAN LUIS

NEUQUÉN

RÍO NEGRO

CHUBUT

SANTA CRUZ

TIERRA DEL FUEGO

MESETA DE MONTEMAYOR

BUENOS AIRES
MONTEVIDEO
SANTIAGO
Valparaíso
Mar del Plata
La Plata
Concepción
Talcahuano

SOUTH GEORGIA AND THE
SOUTH SANDWICH ISLANDS
(U.K.)

SOUTH GEORGIA
Grytviken
Mount Paget
2934

Cape Nuñez
Annenkov Island
Cape Disappointment
Bird Island

Shag Rocks
Black Rock

FALKLAND ISLANDS
(U.K.)

WEST FALKLAND
EAST FALKLAND
Stanley
Mount Usborne
705

Jason Islands
Pebble Island
Saunders Island
Weddell Island
Beauchene Island
Lively Island
Cape Meredith
Cape Dolphin

M-400092-7A-DR2-1
Copyright © Rand McNally & Co.

Scale 1 : 10,000,000

Lambert Conformal Conic Projection

Meters/Feet
6000 19680
4000 13120
3000 9840
2000 6560
1000 3280
500   1640
200   656
Sea Level

200   656
2000 6560

ATLANTIC OCEAN

Meters
Feet
6000
19680

4000
13120

3000
9840

2000
6560

1000
3280

500
1640

200
656

Sea Level

200
656

2000
6560

W-S40195-7A-DR2-1
Copyright © Rand McNally & Co.

0 50 100 150 200 300 400 500 Kilometers

0 50 100 200 300 Miles

Scale 1 : 5,000,000   Lambert Conformal Conic Projection

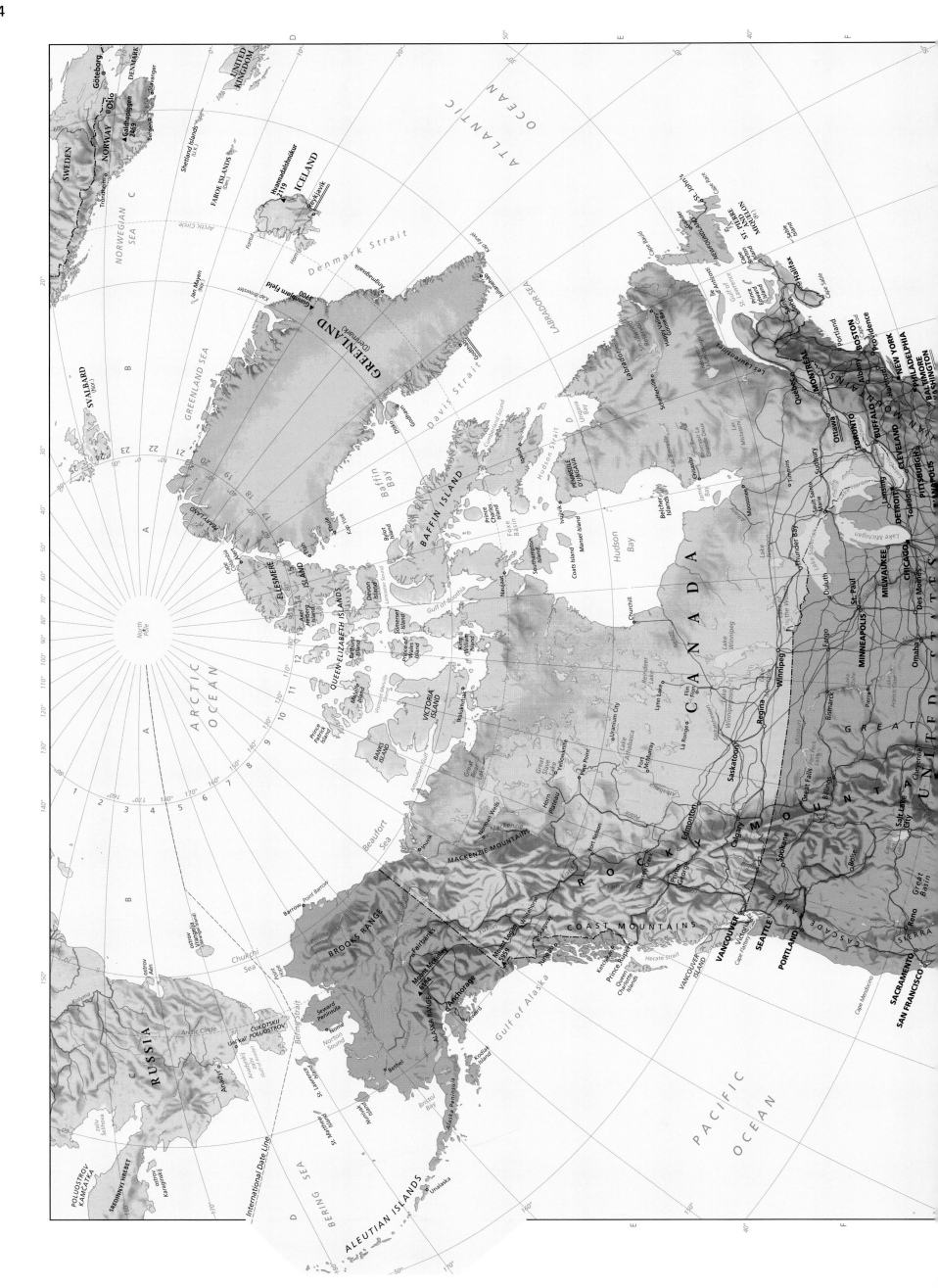

SWEDEN

Göteborg

NORWAY

Oslo

DENMARK

Stavanger

Bergen

Galdhøpiggen
2469

Trondheim

UNITED
KINGDOM

Shetland Islands
(U.K.)

FAROE ISLANDS

NORWEGIAN
SEA

Arctic Circle

Jan Mayen
(Nor.)

SVALBARD
(Nor.)

ICELAND

Hvannadalshnúkur
1119

Reykjavik

GREENLAND
SEA

Denmark Strait

Kangerlussuaq

Gunnbjørn Fjeld
3700

GREENLAND
(Denmark)

PEARYLAND

North Pole

ARCTIC
OCEAN

Kap York

Thule

Cape
Columbia

ELLESMERE
ISLAND

Axel
Heiberg
Island

QUEEN ELIZABETH ISLANDS

Devon
Island

Prince
Patrick
Island

Melville
Island

Bathurst
Island

Somerset
Island

King
William
Island

Prince of
Wales
Island

BANKS
ISLAND

VICTORIA
ISLAND

Amundsen Gulf

Great
Bear
Lake

Bylot
Island

Prince
Charles
Island

BAFFIN ISLAND

Baffin
Bay

Davis Strait

Godthåb

Nuuk

Ikaluktutiak

Iqaluit

Foxe
Basin

Southampton
Island

Coats Island

Mansel Island

LABRADOR SEA

Cape Farvel

Ungava
Bay

PENINSULE
D'UNGAVA

Belcher
Islands

Hudson
Bay

James
Bay

Naujaat

Hudson Strait

NEWFOUNDLAND

ST. PIERRE
AND
MIQUELON
(Fr.)

Cape Breton
Island

Prince Edward
Island

Sable Island

Cape Sable

Cape Cod

HALIFAX

Portland

BOSTON

Providence

NEW YORK

PHILADELPHIA

BALTIMORE

WASHINGTON

Quebec

Gulf of
St. Lawrence

Anticosti

Les Laurentides

MONTREAL

Ottawa

TORONTO

Albany

BUFFALO

CLEVELAND

PITTSBURGH

DETROIT

Toledo

Lansing

Labrador

Schefferville

Happy Valley
Goose Bay

Lac
Mistassini

Lac St-Jean

Réservoir La
Grande Deux

Kuujjuaq

Timmins

Sudbury

Sault Sainte
Marie

Lake Huron

Lake Erie

CANADA

Churchill

Lynn Lake

Reindeer
Lake

Lake
Winnipeg

Lake of
the Woods

Thunder Bay

Lake Superior

Lake Michigan

Duluth

MINNEAPOLIS

St. Paul

MILWAUKEE

CHICAGO

Des Moines

Omaha

Uranium City

Lake
Athabasca

Fort
McMurray

La Ronge

Flin
Flon

Saskatoon

Regina

Winnipeg

Brandon

Fargo

Bismarck

GREAT

Great Slave
Lake

Yellowknife

Hay River

Fort Smith

Peace Point

Fort Nelson

Fort
Providence

Edmonton

Calgary

ROCKY

Great Falls

Billings

Pierre

Missouri

Francis River

UNITED STATES

MONTANA

Spokane

Boise

Salt Lake
City

Reno

Great
Basin

SIERRA

CASCADE RANGE

SACRAMENTO

SAN FRANCISCO

Cape Mendocino

PORTLAND

SEATTLE

VANCOUVER

Cape Flattery

Victoria

VANCOUVER
ISLAND

Prince
George

COAST MOUNTAINS

Prince Rupert

Hecate Strait

Ketchikan

Queen Charlotte
Islands

Juneau

Mount Logan
5959

Whitehorse

Yukon

COAST MOUNTAINS

ROCKY
MOUNTAINS

MACKENZIE MOUNTAINS

Mackenzie

Norman Wells

Horn
Plateau

Fort Simpson

Inuvik

Beaufort
Sea

Point Barrow

Barrow

Colville

Point Hope

Chukchi
Sea

BROOKS RANGE

Fairbanks

Mount McKinley
6194

ALASKA RANGE

Anchorage

Gulf of Alaska

Seward

Kodiak
Island

Bristol
Bay

ALASKA RANGE

Seward
Peninsula

Nome

Norton
Sound

Bethel

Nunivak
Island

St. Matthew
Island

Bering Strait

St. Lawrence Island

ČUKOTSKIJ
POLUOSTROV

Uel'kal'

Arctic Circle

Anadyrskij
zaliv

Anadyr'

RUSSIA

Kolyma

ostrov
Ajon

ostrov
Vrangelja

SREDINNYJ HREBET

POLUOSTROV
KAMCATKA

ostrov
Karaginskij

zaliv
Šelihova

BERING
SEA

International Date Line

ALEUTIAN ISLANDS

Unalaska

PACIFIC
OCEAN

ATLANTIC
OCEAN

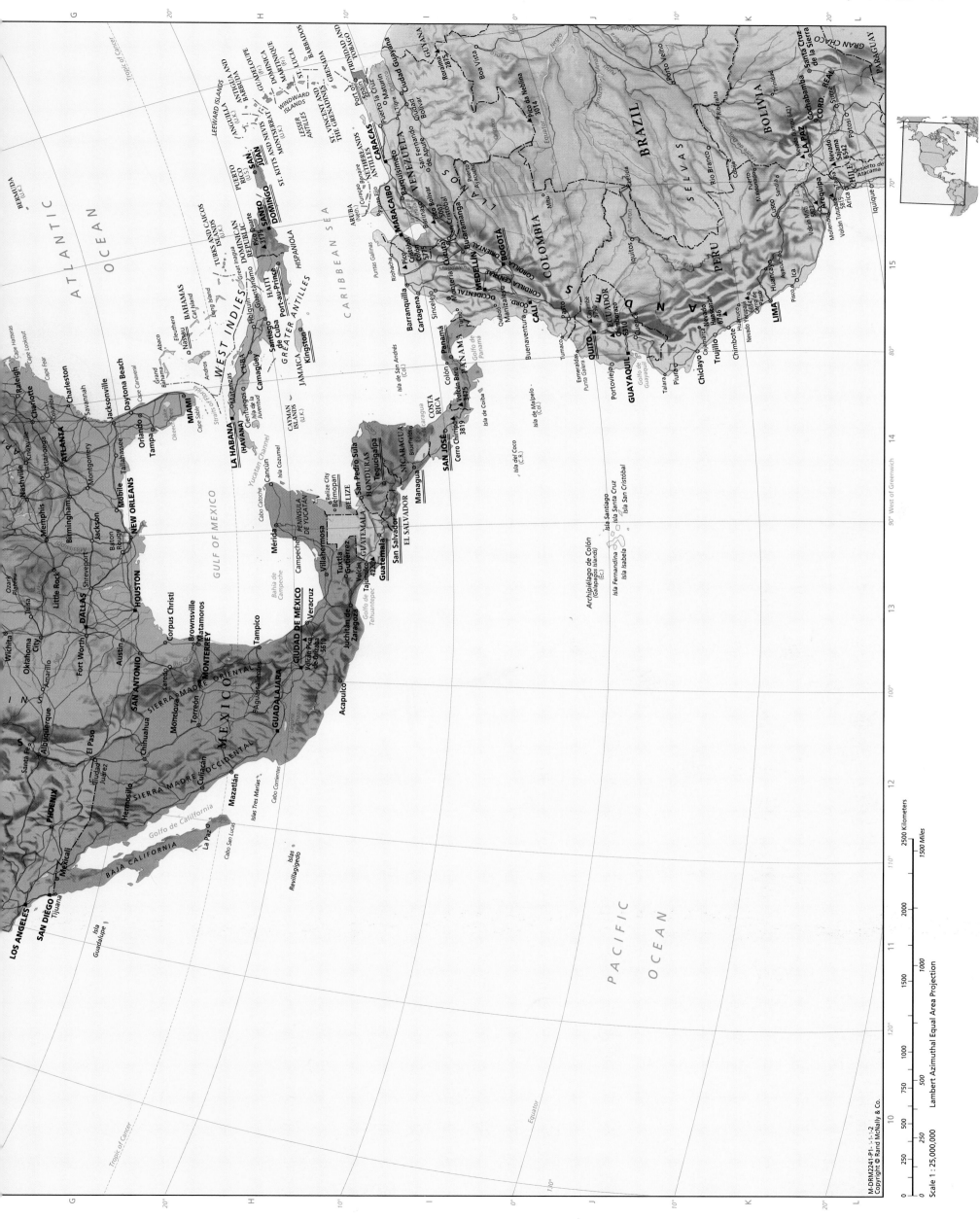

ATLANTIC

OCEAN

BERMUDA
(U.K.)

Tropic of Cancer

Cape Hatteras
Cape Lookout
Cape Fear

Raleigh
Charlotte
Columbia
Charleston
Savannah
Jacksonville
Daytona Beach
Cape Canaveral
Orlando
Tampa
MIAMI
Lake Okeechobee
Florida Keys
Straits of Florida

Knoxville
Chattanooga
ATLANTA
Montgomery
Tallahassee
Mobile

Nashville
Memphis
Birmingham
Jackson
Baton Rouge
NEW ORLEANS

Ozark Plateau
Little Rock
Shreveport
Mississippi

Wichita
Oklahoma City
Tulsa
Fort Smith
DALLAS
Fort Worth
Austin
HOUSTON
Corpus Christi
Brownsville
Matamoros

Amarillo
Lubbock
Santa Fe
Albuquerque
El Paso
Ciudad Juárez
Chihuahua

PHOENIX
Mexicali
Tijuana
SAN DIEGO
LOS ANGELES

Hermosillo
Culiacán

SIERRA MADRE OCCIDENTAL

BAJA CALIFORNIA

Golfo de California

La Paz
Cabo San Lucas
Islas Tres Marías
Mazatlán
Cabo Corrientes
GUADALAJARA
Aguascalientes
Torreón
MONTERREY
Saltillo
Monclova
Laredo
Nuevo Laredo
Reynosa

SIERRA MADRE ORIENTAL
San Luis Potosí
CIUDAD DE MÉXICO
Volcán Pico
de Orizaba
5610
MEXICO
Acapulco
Volcán 4392
Tampico
Veracruz
Juchitán de
Zaragoza
Golfo de Tehuantepec

Tuxtla
Gutiérrez
Villahermosa
Campeche
PENÍNSULA
DE YUCATÁN
Mérida
Bahía de
Campeche
Cabo Catoche
Cancún
Isla Cozumel

GULF OF MEXICO

Islas
Revillagigedo

Isla
Guadalupe

PACIFIC

OCEAN

Equator

BAHAMAS
Nassau
Eleuthera
Abaco
Grand Bahama
Andros
Great
Exuma

Isla de la
Juventud
Cienfuegos
Matanzas
LA HABANA
(HAVANA)
CUBA
Camagüey
Santiago
de Cuba
Guantánamo

WEST INDIES

Yucatán Channel

CAYMAN
ISLANDS
(U.K.)

JAMAICA
Kingston

GREATER ANTILLES

TURKS AND CAICOS
ISLANDS (U.K.)
Great
Inagua

HAITI
Port-au-Prince

DOMINICAN
REPUBLIC
SANTO
DOMINGO
Pico Duarte
3175
HISPANIOLA

PUERTO
RICO
(U.S.)
SAN
JUAN

LEEWARD ISLANDS
ANGUILLA (U.K.)
ANTIGUA AND
BARBUDA
ST. KITTS AND NEVIS
MONTSERRAT (U.K.)
GUADELOUPE
DOMINICA
MARTINIQUE
ST. LUCIA
BARBADOS
ST. VINCENT AND
THE GRENADINES
GRENADA
WINDWARD
ISLANDS
LESSER
ANTILLES

CARIBBEAN SEA

TRINIDAD AND
TOBAGO
Port of Spain

NETHERLANDS
ANTILLES
Curaçao Bonaire
(Neth.)
ARUBA
(Neth.)

BELIZE
Belize City
Belmopan
San Pedro Sula
HONDURAS
GUATEMALA
Guatemala
Volcán
Tajumulco
4220
San Salvador
EL SALVADOR
Tuxtla

NICARAGUA
Managua
Tegucigalpa
Bluefields
Isla de San Andrés
(Col.)

COSTA
RICA
SAN JOSÉ
Volcán Irazú
3819
Cerro Chirripó
3475

PANAMÁ
Colón
Panamá
Golfo de
Panamá
Isla de Coiba

Isla de Malpelo
(Col.)

Isla del Coco
(C.R.)

Archipiélago de Colón
(Galápagos Islands)
(Ec.)
Isla Fernandina
Isla Santiago
Isla Santa Cruz
Isla San Cristóbal
Isla Isabela

Puntas Gallinas
VENEZUELA
MARACAIBO
Maracaibo
Valencia
CARACAS
Barcelona
Ciudad Bolívar
Ciudad Guayana
GUYANA
Río Branco

Barranquilla
Cartagena
Sincelejo
PANAMÁ
Buenaventura
Tumaco
Esmeraldas
Punta Galera
Portoviejo
Talara
Piura
GUAYAQUIL
Golfo de
Guayaquil
ECUADOR
QUITO
Chimborazo
6310

Cúcuta
Bucaramanga
MEDELLÍN
Manizales
BOGOTÁ
CALI
Pasto
COLOMBIA
Quibdó
CORDILLERA OCCIDENTAL
CORD. CENTRAL
CORDILLERA ORIENTAL

A N D E S

PERU
LIMA
Chiclayo
Trujillo
Chimbote
Huánuco
Iquitos

BRAZIL

SELVAS

Boa Vista
Roraima
2875
Pico da Neblina
3014

Río Negro
Amazonas

Mitú

BOLIVIA
LA PAZ
Nevado Sajama
6542
Santa Cruz
de la Sierra
Cochabamba
CORD. REAL
Illampu
6421

Cuzco
Nevado
6746
Arequipa
Volcán Misti
5822
Volcán Sajama
6746
Potosí
GRAN CHACO
PARAGUAY

CHILE
Arica
Iquique
Desierto de
Atacama

Ica
Pisco
Pico
Puerto
Maldonado

Porto Velho

Cape Canaveral

WEST INDIES

Scale 1 : 25,000,000

Lambert Azimuthal Equal Area Projection

0   250   500   750   1000   1500   2000   2500 Kilometers
0   250   500   1000   1500 Miles

ATLANTIC OCEAN

BERMUDA (U.K.)

MISSISSIPPI
ALABAMA
GEORGIA
SOUTH CAROLINA
N.C.
FLORIDA

Jackson
Birmingham
Montgomery
ATLANTA
Macon
Augusta
Charleston
Savannah
Jacksonville
Orlando
Tampa
Melbourne
West Palm Beach
Fort Lauderdale
MIAMI
Key West

NEW ORLEANS
Baton Rouge
Mobile
Panama City
Tallahassee

BAHAMAS
Nassau
New Providence
San Salvador
Tropic of Cancer

MEXICO
YUCATÁN PENÍNSULA DE YUCATÁN
Mérida
Cancún
QUINTANA ROO
CAMPECHE
BELIZE
Belmopan
Belize City
Victoria Peak 1120

GUATEMALA
HONDURAS
Tegucigalpa
San Pedro Sula
EL SALVADOR
San Salvador
NICARAGUA
Managua
COSTA RICA
SAN JOSE
PANAMA
Panamá

LA HABANA (HAVANA)
Matanzas
Santa Clara
Cienfuegos
CUBA
Camagüey
Las Tunas
Holguín
Santiago de Cuba
Pico Turquino 1972
SIERRA MAESTRA
Guantánamo

CAYMAN ISLANDS (U.K.)
George Town

JAMAICA
Montego Bay
Kingston
Blue Mountain Peak 2256

HAITI
HISPANIOLA
Port-au-Prince
SANTO DOMINGO
DOMINICAN REPUBLIC
Pico Duarte 3175

PUERTO RICO (U.S.)
Mayagüez

GREATER ANTILLES
WEST INDIES
TURKS AND CAICOS ISLANDS (U.K.)
Grand Turk

CARIBBEAN SEA

ARUBA (Neth.)
NETH. ANT.
Oranjestad

VENEZUELA
MARACAIBO
CORD. DE MÉRIDA
Pico Bolívar 5007
Barquisimeto
Cúcuta
Bucaramanga

COLOMBIA
Cartagena
Barranquilla
Santa Marta
MEDELLÍN
BOGOTÁ
CORDILLERA OCCIDENTAL
CORDILLERA CENTRAL
LLANOS

PACIFIC OCEAN

NEVADA

GREAT BASIN

CALIFORNIA

ARIZONA

UTAH

BAJA CALIFORNIA

BAJA CALIFORNIA SUR

SONORA

Mojave Desert

Great Salt Lake Desert

Desierto de Altar

SAN FRANCISCO
OAKLAND
SAN JOSE
SACRAMENTO
Modesto
Stockton
Fresno
Visalia
Bakersfield
LOS ANGELES
ANAHEIM
Long Beach
RIVERSIDE
Santa Ana
SAN DIEGO
Chula Vista
Tijuana
Mexicali
Las Vegas
PHOENIX
Mesa
Tempe
Tucson
Nogales
Santa Rosa
Santa Barbara
Oxnard
Beverly Hills
Pasadena
San Bernardino

Meters
Feet

4000
13120

3000
9840

2000
6560

1000
3280

500
1640

200
656

Sea Level

200
656

2000
6560

0   50   100   150   200   300   400   500 Kilometers

0   50   100   200   300 Miles

Scale 1 : 5,000,000   Lambert Conformal Conic Projection

W-520599-7A-DR2-1
Copyright © Rand McNally & Co.

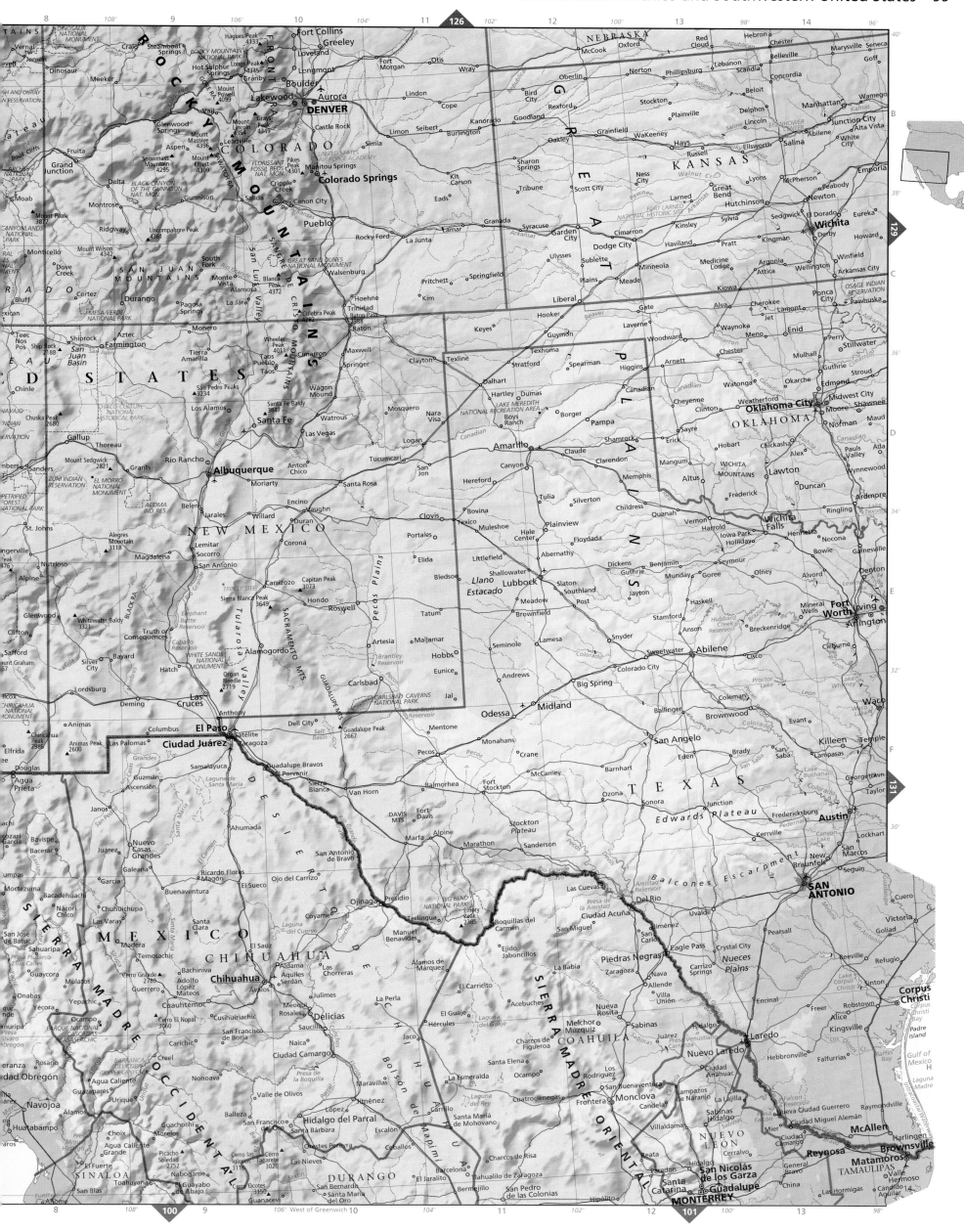

Map Labels

BAHAMAS

Deadman Cay, Clarence Town, Long Town, Cape Verde, Long Cay, Crooked Island, Samana Cay, North East Point, Bight of Acklins, Acklins, Ragged Island Range, Ragged Island, Salina Point, Mayaguana, Mayaguana Passage, Matthew Town, Great Inagua, Little Inagua, Seal Cays, Lake Rosa

TURKS AND CAICOS ISLANDS (U.K.)

Kew, Providenciales, Middle Caicos, North Caicos, West Caicos, East Caicos, CAICOS ISLANDS, Grand Turk, TURKS ISLANDS, Caicos Passage, Silver Bank Passage, Turks Island Passage, Mouchoir Passage

ATLANTIC OCEAN

CUBA

Canal de San Nicolás, Canal Viejo de Bahama, Cayo Coco, Cayo Romano, Cayo Lobos, Cayo Guajaba, Cayo Sabinal, Cayo Santa, Esmeralda, Archipiélago de los Jardines de la Reina, Caibarién, Yaguajay, Placetas, Morón, Ciego de Ávila, Florida, Camagüey, Vertientes, Minas, Nuevitas, Puerto Padre, Jesús Menéndez, Gibara, Holguín, Rafael Freyre, Punta de Mulas, Banes, Bahía de Nipe, Antilla, Cueto, Mayarí, Sagua de Tánamo, Baracoa, Manzanillo, Bayamo, Jiguaní, Palma Soriano, Alto Cedro, San Luis, Tiguabos, Guantánamo, Santiago de Cuba, Pico Turquino 1972, SIERRA MAESTRA, Marea del Portillo, Cabo Cruz, Golfo de Guacanayabo, Niquero, Campechuela, Las Tunas, Sancti Spíritus, Trinidad, Presa Zaza, Cabo Sabinal, Caimanera, GUANTANAMO BAY NAVAL STATION (U.S.), Punta de Quemado

Cayman Brac

GREATER ANTILLES

JAMAICA

Montego Bay, Falmouth, Saint Ann's Bay, Ocho Rios, Port Maria, Port Antonio, Mount Denham 986, Mandeville, Spanish Town, Kingston, Blue Mountain Peak 2256, Morant Bay, South Negril Point, Savanna-la-Mar, Portland Point, Portland Bight, Morant Point, Morant Cays, Pedro Cays, 2184

HISPANIOLA

HAITI

Port-de-Paix, Cap-Haïtien, Môle St-Nicolas, Cap du Môle, Gonaïves, Limbé, LA CITADELLE, SANS SOUCI, Desdunes, Saint-Marc, Golfe de la Gonâve, Île de la Gonâve, Jérémie, Anse-d'Hainault, Pointe Fanchon, Grande Cayemite, Pic Macaya 2347, Corail, Léogâne, Petit-Goâve, Port-au-Prince, Pétion-Ville, Morne La Selle 2674, Anse à Galets, Jacmel, Les Cayes, Coteaux, Île à Vache, Pointe Abacou, Navassa Island (U.S.), Windward Passage, Jamaica Channel, Canal du Sud, Baie de Port au Prince, Canal de Saint-Marc

DOMINICAN REPUBLIC

Monte Cristi, Cabo Isabela, Puerto Plata, Pico Diego de Ocampo 1249, Cabo Macorís, Cabo Francés Viejo, Dajabón, Mao, Moca, Nagua, Bahía Escocesa, Cabo Samaná, Santiago de los Caballeros, San Francisco de Macorís, Samaná, Bahía de Samaná, Pico Duarte 3175, La Vega, Bonao, Sabana de la Mar, Miches, Comendador, San Juan de la Maguana, Alto Bandera 2630, Hato Mayor del Rey, El Seibo, Higüey, Cabo Engaño, SANTO DOMINGO, San Cristóbal, Baní, San Pedro de Macorís, La Romana, Bahía de Yuma, Isla Saona, Azua, Neiba, Lago Enriquillo, Barahona, Pedernales, Enriquillo, Cabo Falso, Isla Beata, Cabo Beata, Morne Bonhomme 1788, Manzanillo Bay, Punta Palenque, Bahía de Ocoa, Mona Passage

CARIBBEAN SEA

Cayo de Serranilla (Col.), Bajo Nuevo (Col.)

5102

LESSER ANTILLES

ARUBA (Neth.)

Oranjestad

NETHERLANDS ANTILLES (Neth.)

Bonaire, Curaçao, Willemstad

VENEZUELA

Punta Gallinas, Bahía Honda, Puerto Bolívar, Cabo de la Vela, Bahía Portete, Punta Espada, Península de La Guajira, Cabo San Román, Punta Fijo, Punta Cardón, Península de Paraguaná, Pueblo Nuevo, Puerto Cumarebo, Punta Zamuro, Uribia, Los Taques, Golfo de Venezuela, Golfete de Coro, Coro, La Vela de Coro, Cabure, Maicao, Paraguaipoa, Sinamaica, San Rafael, Altagracia, Pedregal, San Luis, Dabajuro, FALCÓN, Churuguara, MARACAIBO, Mene de Mauroa, Siquisique, PARQUE NACIONAL YURUBI, YARACUY, San Felipe, La Concepción, Santa Rita, Cabimas, Cerro Cerrón, LARA, Barquisimeto, Quíbor, Tía Juana, Ciudad Ojeda, Machiques, Mene Grande, Bachaquero, La Ceiba, Carora, TRUJILLO, Sabana de Mendoza, Bobures, Valera, Carache, PORTUGUESA, Acarigua, Araure, La Villa del Rosario, Palmar, Lago de Maracaibo, ZULIA, San Carlos del Zulia, La Grita, El Vigía, Mérida, SIERRA NEVADA, Pico Bolívar (La Columna) 5007, Ospino, Guanare, Barinitas, PARQUE NAC. SIERRA NEVADA, BARINAS, Ciudad Bolivia, Libertad, Ciudad de Nutrias, CORDILLERA DE MÉRIDA, Tovar, Bailadores, Timotes, Mucuchíes, La Fría, Santa Bárbara, Barrancas, Guanarito, Ciudad de Nutrias, Caparo Viejo, LLANOS, Palmarito, Apure, APURE

COLOMBIA

Istmo de Panamá (Isthmus of Panama), Punta Manzanillo, Portobelo, Nombre de Dios, El Porvenir, SERRANÍA DE SAN BLAS, Golfo de San Blas, Punta Mosquito, Mansucum, Cabo Tiburón, Punta Caribana, Golfo de Urabá, Acandi, Turbo, Arboletes, Necoclí, Apartadó, San Pedro de Urabá, Santa Marta, Ciénaga, Barranquilla, Soledad, Baranoa, Malambo, Sabanalarga, Pivijay, Cartagena, Islas del Rosario, Arjona, Turbaco, Calamar, El Piñón, Islas de San Bernardo, María La Baja, El Guamo, Pedraza, Fundación, Aracataca, Valledupar, San Juan del Cesar, Albania, Fonseca, Barrancas, Villanueva, La Paz, San Juan, LA GUAJIRA, Pico Cristóbal Colón 5775, Sierra Nevada de Santa Marta, Riohacha, Ensenada de Calabozo, Ranchería, Guasare, Cabo de la Aguja, ATLÁNTICO, MAGDALENA, Golfo de Morrosquillo, Tolú, San Onofre, Ovejas, San Pedro, Corozal, Sincelejo, SUCRE, Ciénaga de Oro, Sahagún, Chinú, Cereté, Montería, Planeta Rica, San Marcos, Majagual, Achí, CÓRDOBA, ANTIOQUIA, Tierralta, Alto de Quimarí 2000, Ayapel, Montelíbano, Caucasia, Nechí, El Banco, Mompós, Guamal, BOLÍVAR, Magangué, San Benito Abad, Tamalameque, La Gloria, El Carmen, Pailitas, Chiriguaná, Chimichagua, Becerril, La Jagua de Ibirico, Codazzi, Villa del Rosario, Agustín Codazzi, NORTE DE SANTANDER, Cúcuta, San Cristóbal, San Antonio del Táchira, Rubio, TÁCHIRA, Ríonegro, Río de Oro, Ocaña, Aguachica, Gamarra, Río del Oro, Simití, Cerro Mu 2610, CESAR, Petrólea, Tibú, La Fría, Sardinata, San Calixto

Panamá

Paraíso, Chepo, Lago Bayano, Cañitas, Capira, Isla San Miguel, Isla del Rey, ARCHIPIÉLAGO DE LAS PERLAS, San José, Bahía de Panamá, Golfo de Panamá, Chimán, La Palma, Yaviza, El Real de Santa María, Garachiné, PARQUE NACIONAL DARIÉN, Punta Mala

86

87

78° West of Greenwich

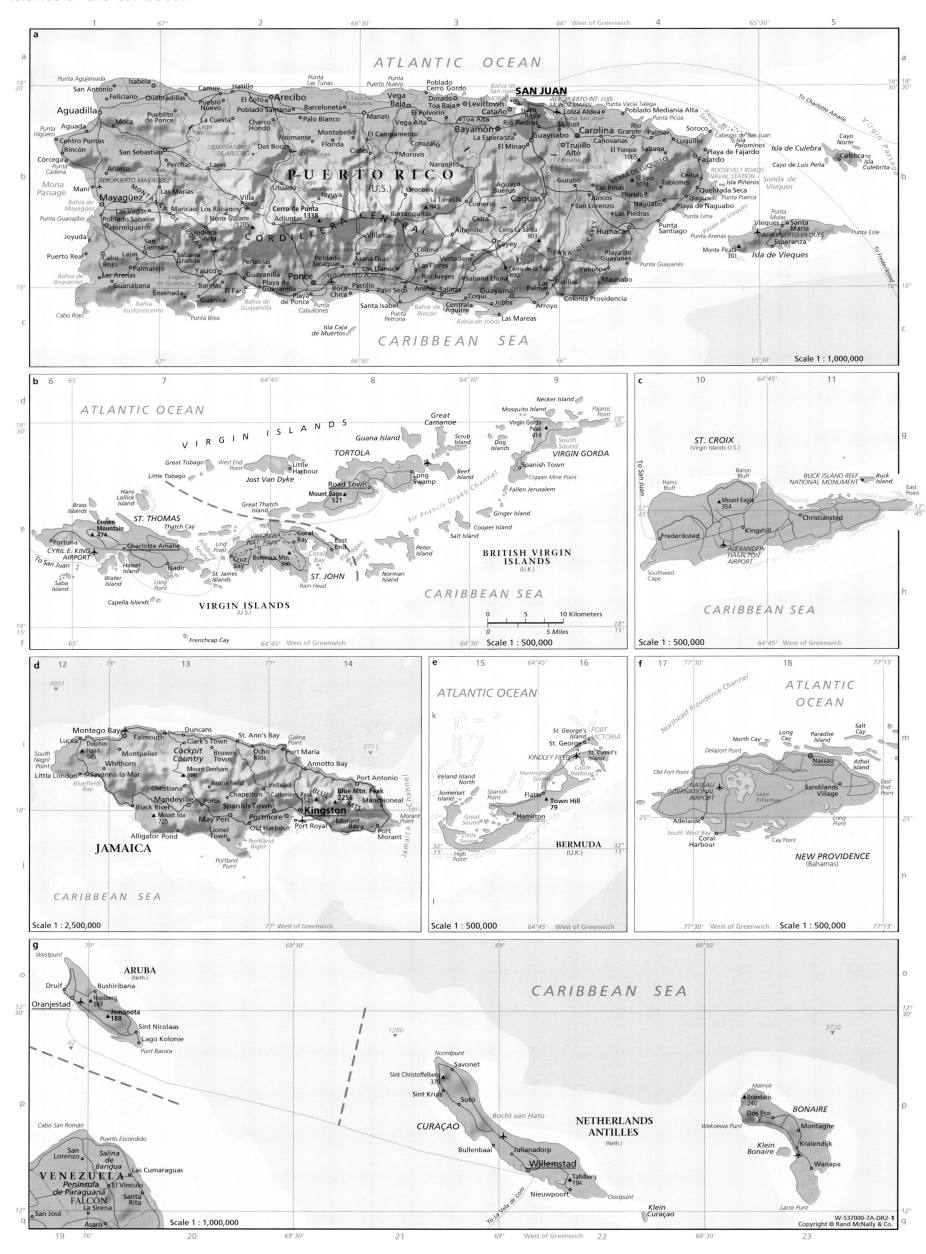

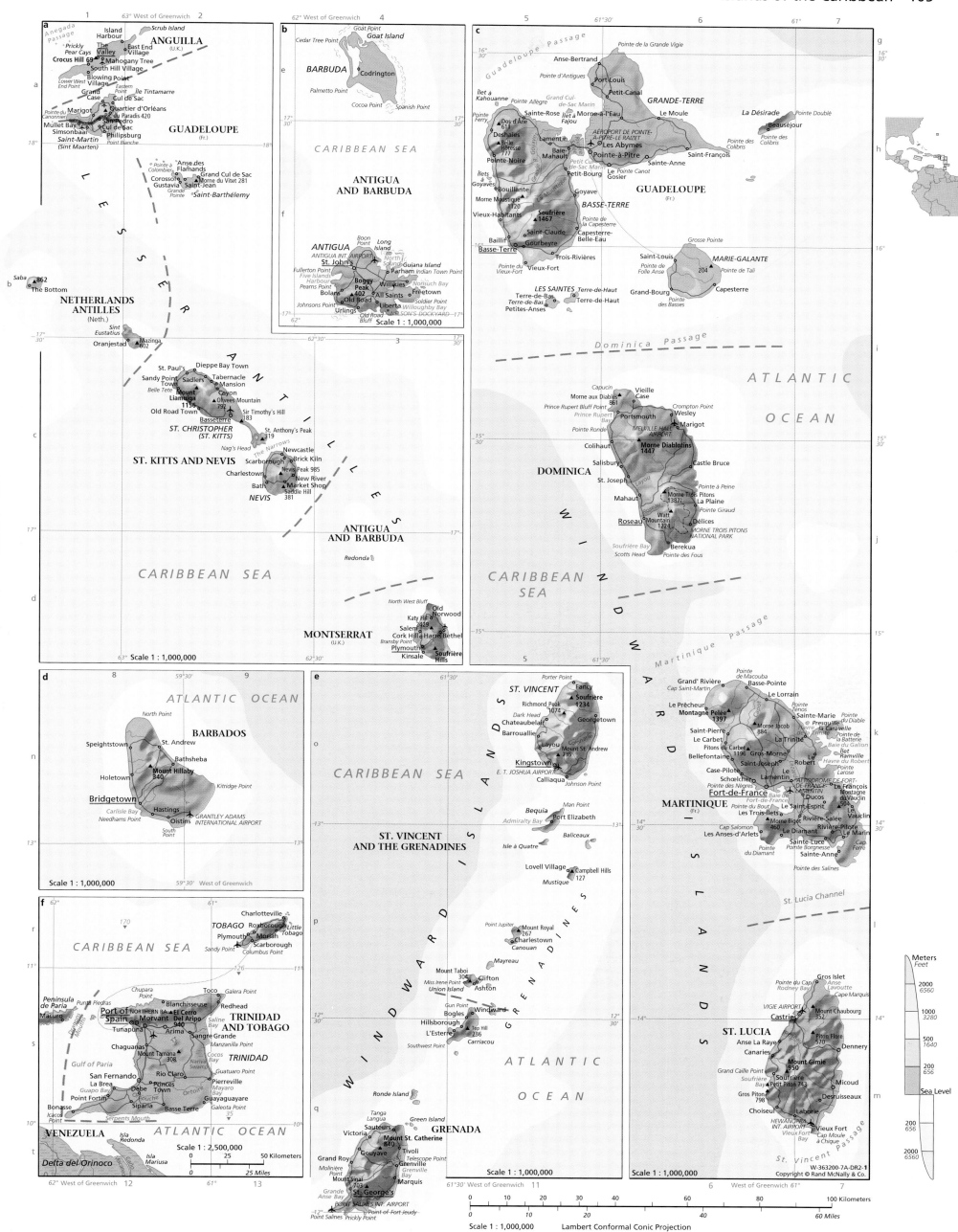

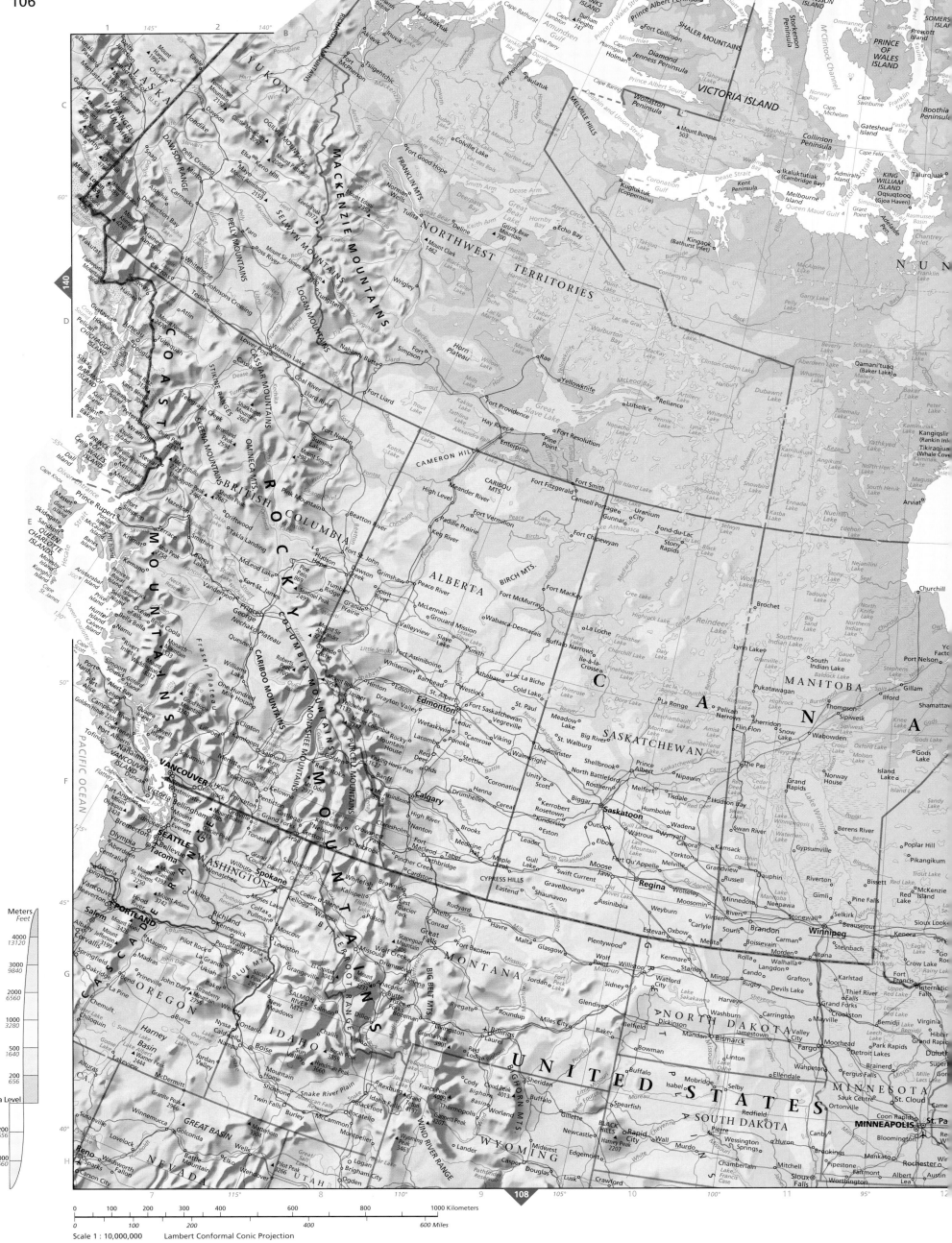

Meters
Feet
4000
13120
3000
9840
2000
6560
1000
3280
500
1640
200
656
Sea Level
200
656
2000
6560

0   100   200   300   400   600   800   1000 Kilometers

0   100   200   400   600 Miles

Scale 1 : 10,000,000   Lambert Conformal Conic Projection

PACIFIC
OCEAN

Meters
Feet

3000
9840

2000
6560

1000
3280

500
1640

200
656

Sea Level

200
656

2000
6560

M-205000-7A-DR2-1
Copyright © Rand McNally & Co.

0   100   200   300   400   600   800   1000 Kilometers

0   100   200   400   600 Miles

Scale 1 : 10,000,000   Lambert Conformal Conic Projection

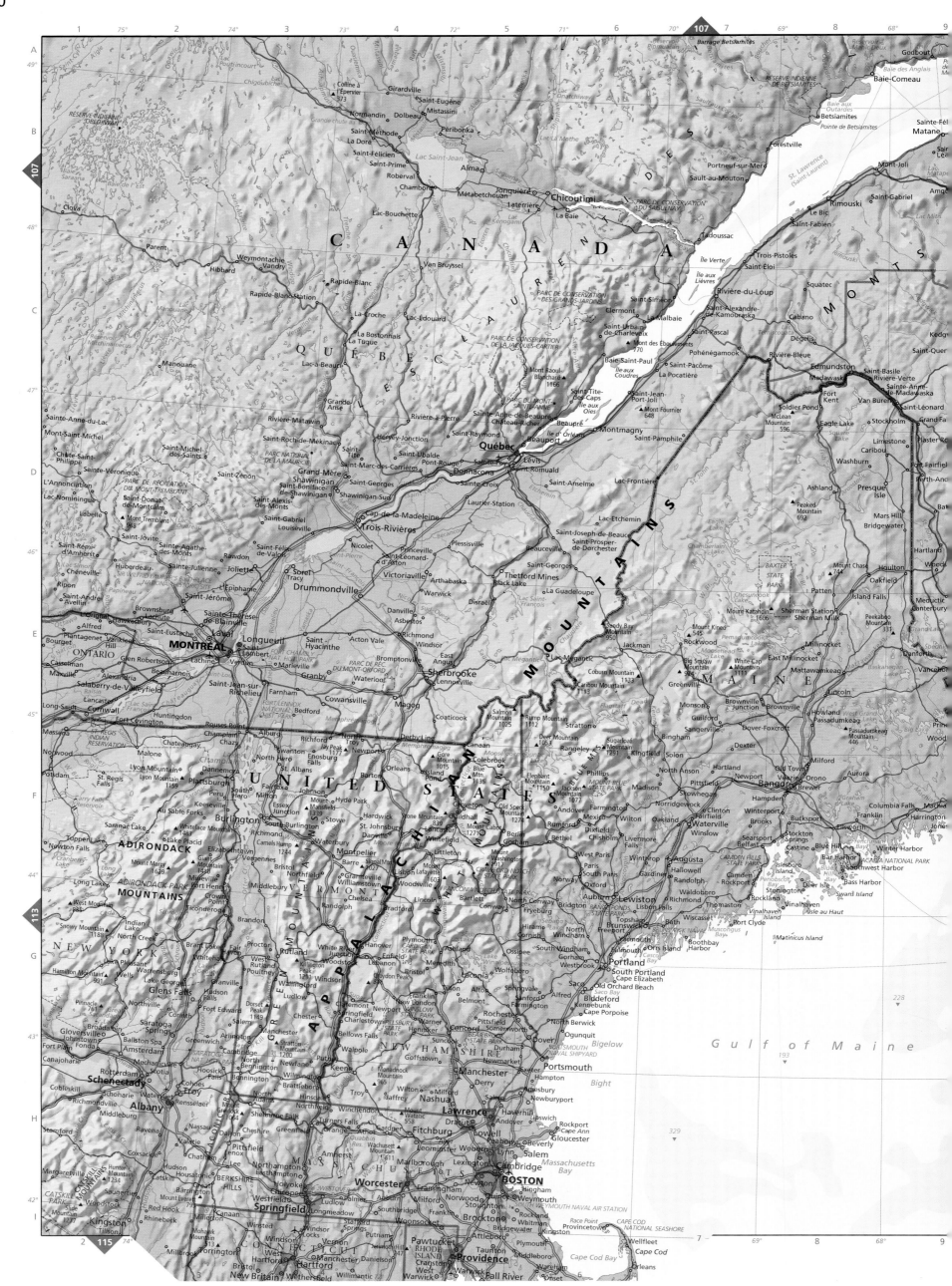

Meters | Feet
1000 / 3280
500 / 1640
200 / 656
Sea Level
200 / 656
2000 / 6560

0   25   50   75   100   150   200   250 Kilometers

0   25   50   100   150 Miles

Scale 1 : 2,500,000   Lambert Conformal Conic Projection

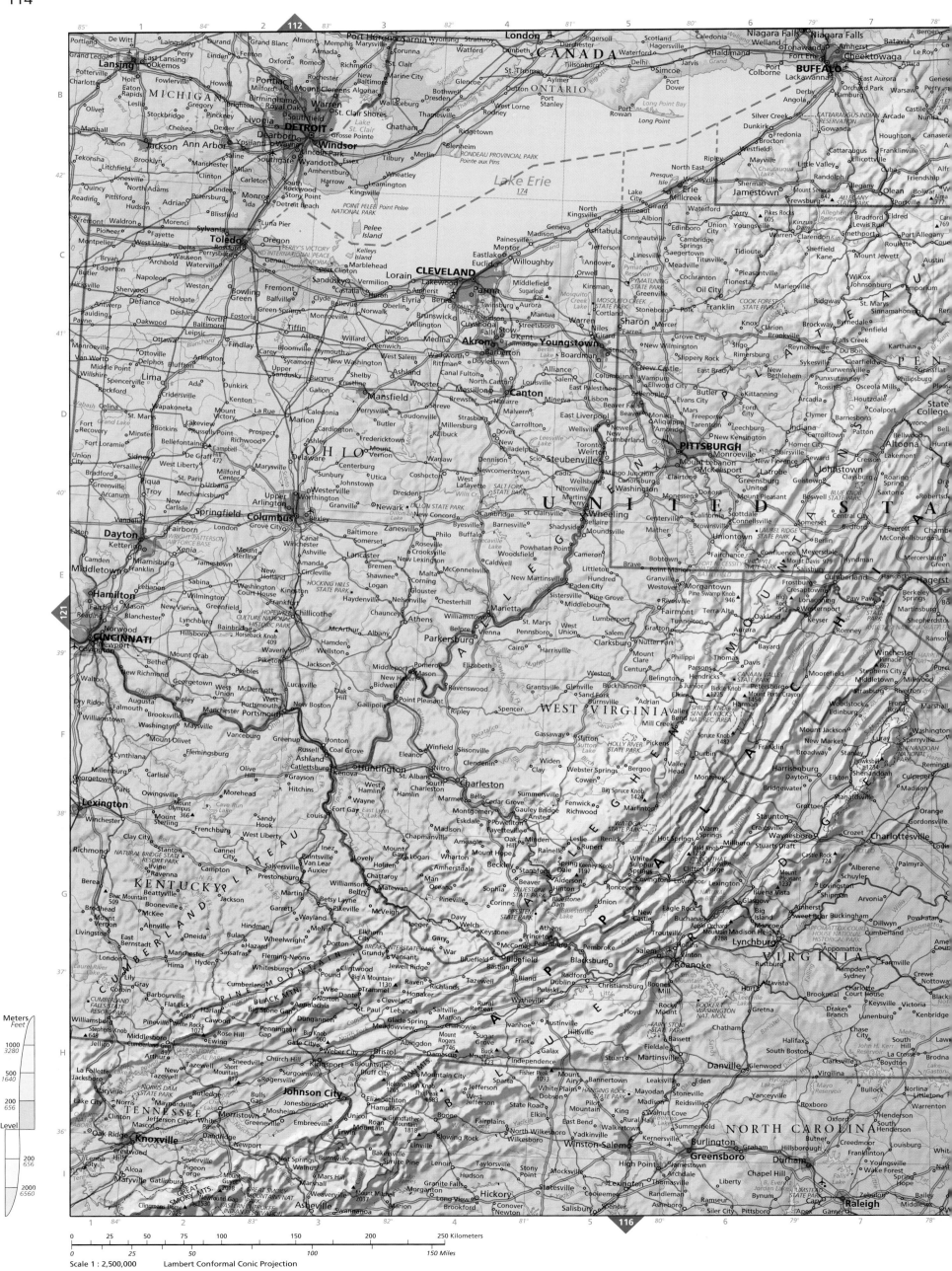

NEW YORK

VERMONT

NEW HAMPSHIRE

MASSACHUSETTS

CONNECTICUT

RHODE ISLAND

NEW JERSEY

DELAWARE

MARYLAND

Major cities: Syracuse, Albany, Schenectady, Springfield, Worcester, BOSTON, Providence, Hartford, New Haven, Bridgeport, NEWARK, NEW YORK, Jersey City, Trenton, PHILADELPHIA, Wilmington, BALTIMORE, WASHINGTON, Alexandria, Richmond, Norfolk, Virginia Beach, Portsmouth, Chesapeake, Suffolk

Scranton, Wilkes-Barre, Allentown, Bethlehem, Reading, Lancaster, Harrisburg, York, Binghamton, Elmira, Ithaca, Poughkeepsie, Atlantic City, Cape May

Long Island, Long Island Sound, Catskill Mountains, Catskill Park, Berkshire Hills, Delmarva Peninsula, Chesapeake Bay, Delaware Bay, Cape Cod, Cape Cod Bay, Nantucket Sound, Martha's Vineyard, Nantucket, Block Island

Gulf of Maine, Massachusetts Bay, ATLANTIC OCEAN, Albemarle Sound, Pamlico Sound, Currituck Sound, Great Dismal Swamp

Fire Island National Seashore, Assateague Island National Seashore, Cape Hatteras National Seashore, Wright Brothers National Memorial, Fort Raleigh National Historic Site, George Washington Birthplace National Monument

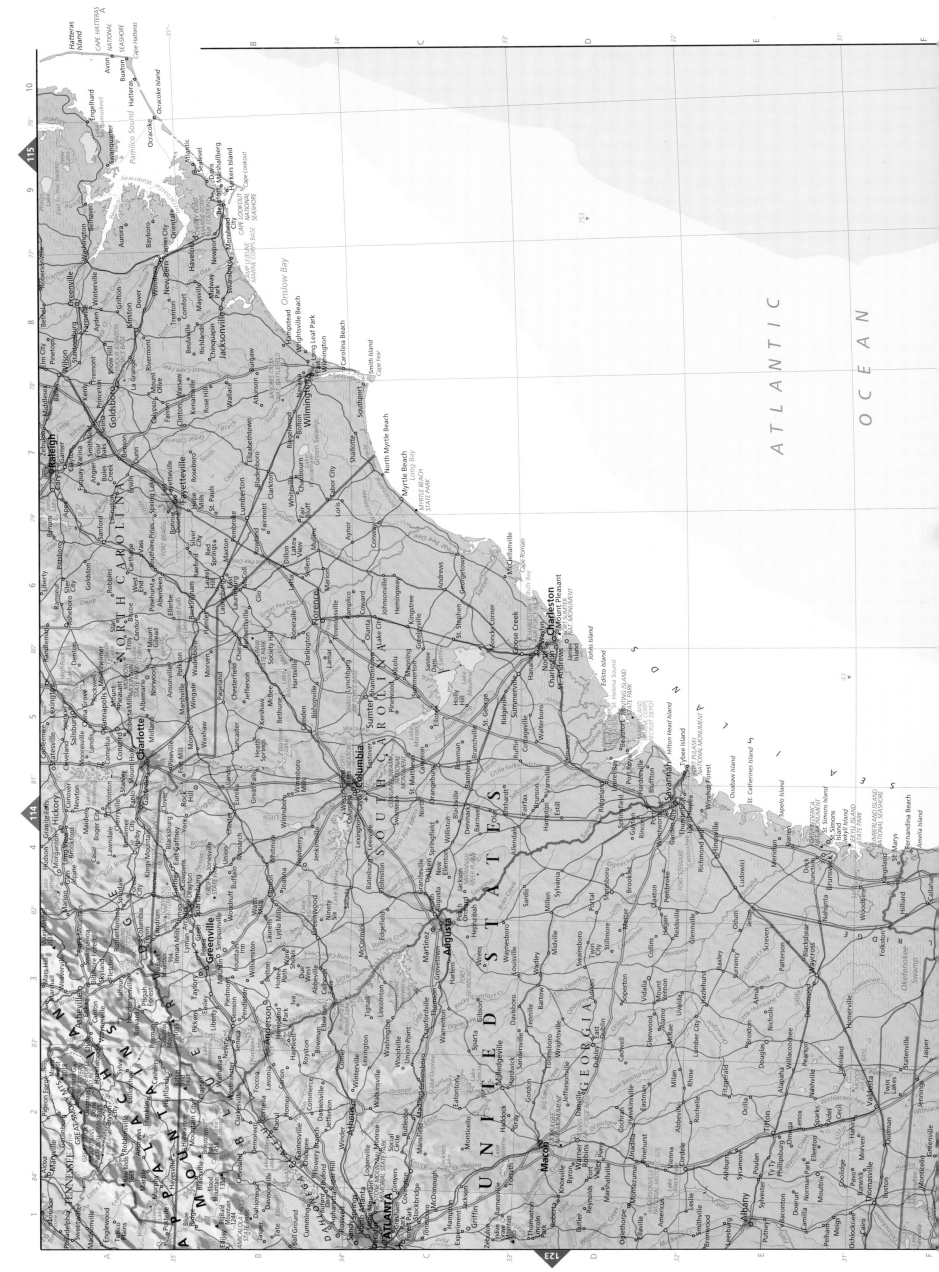

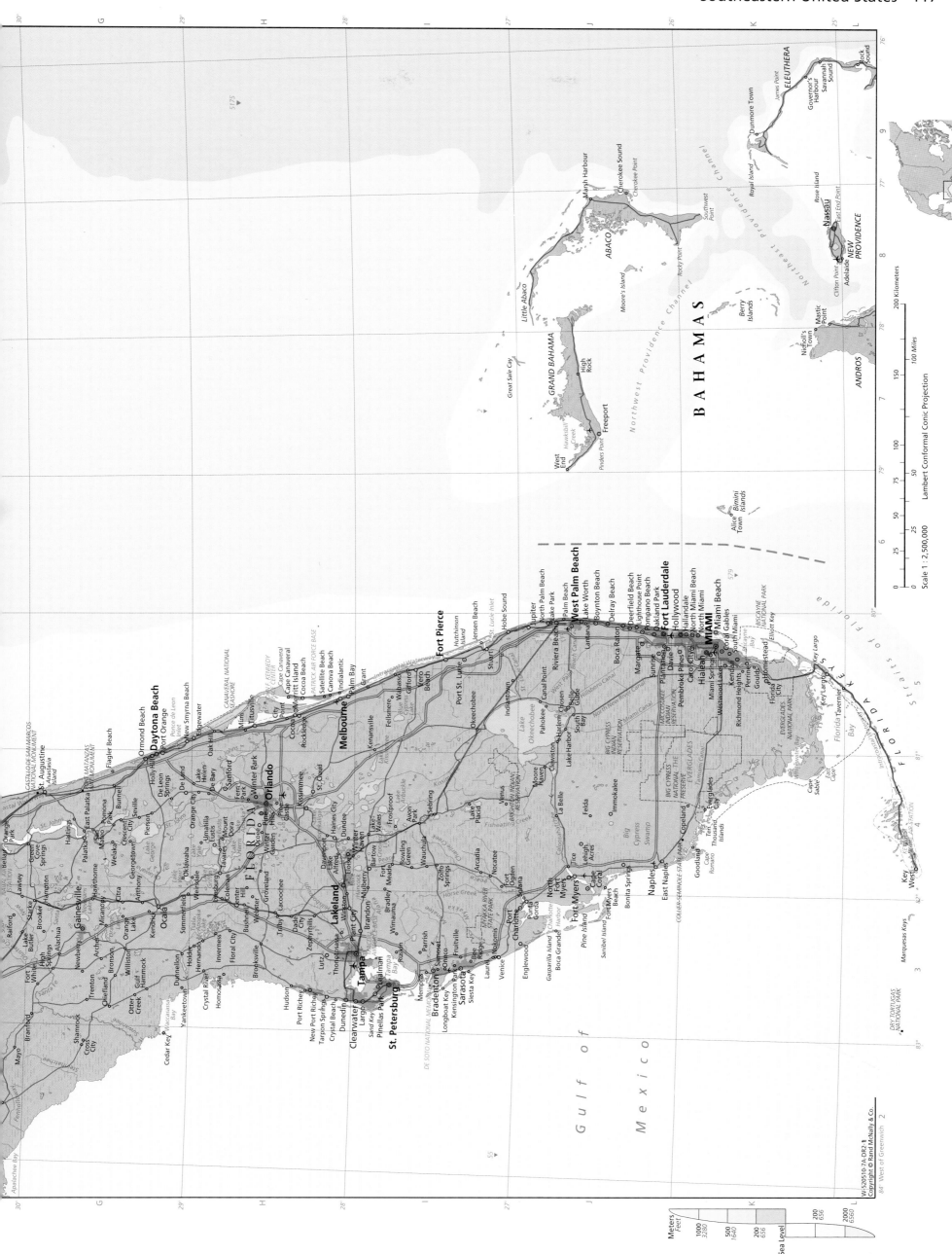

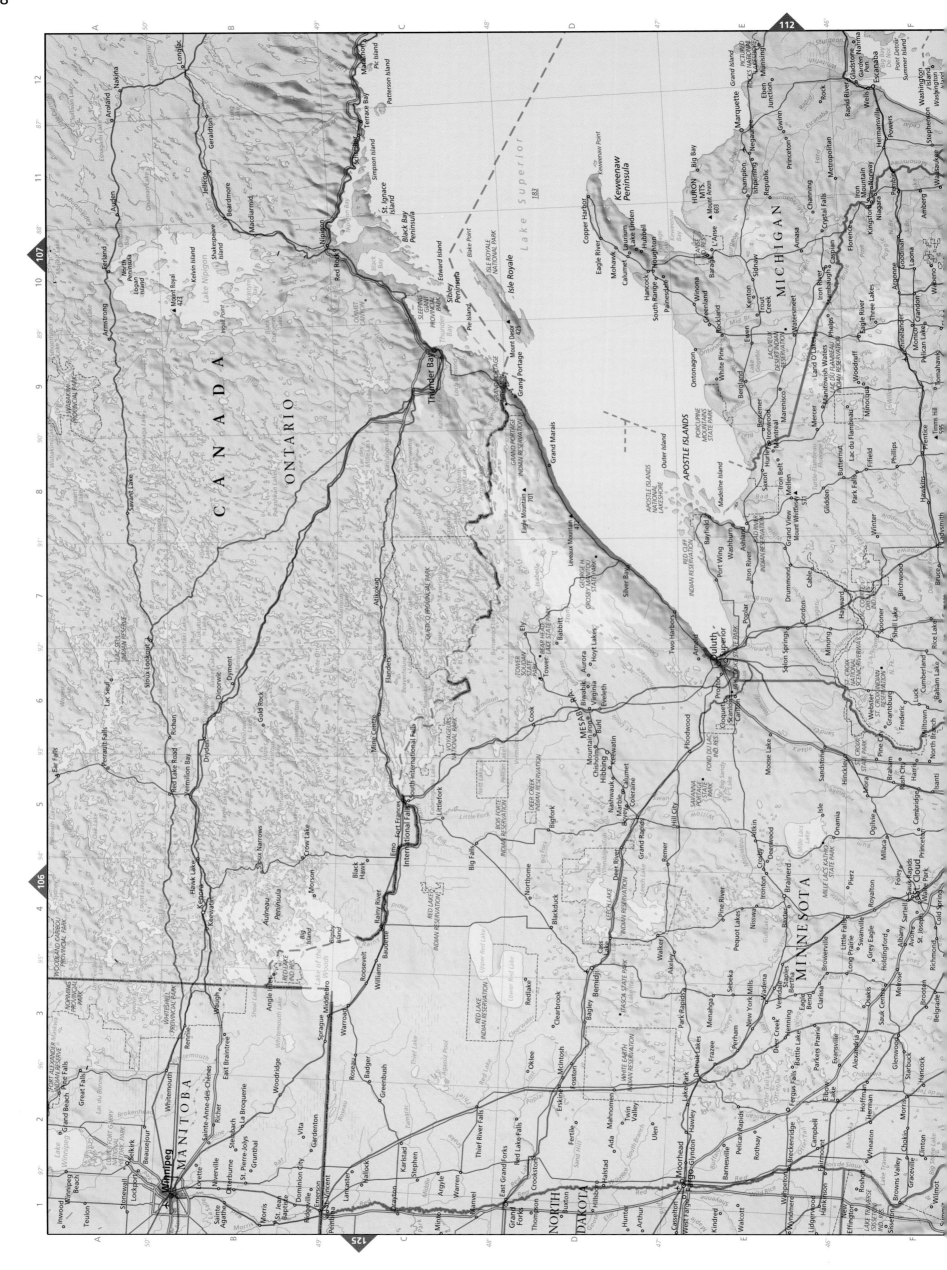

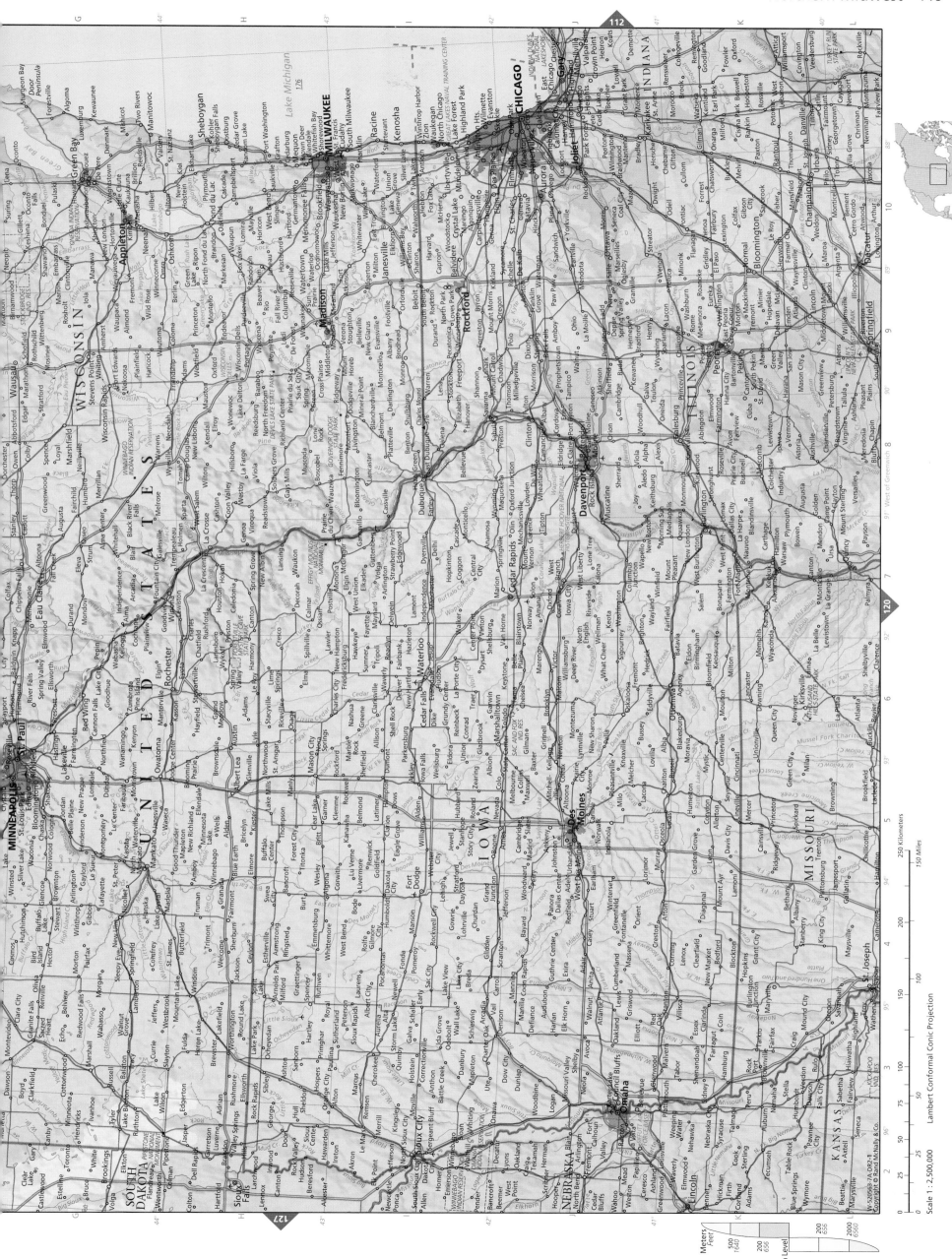

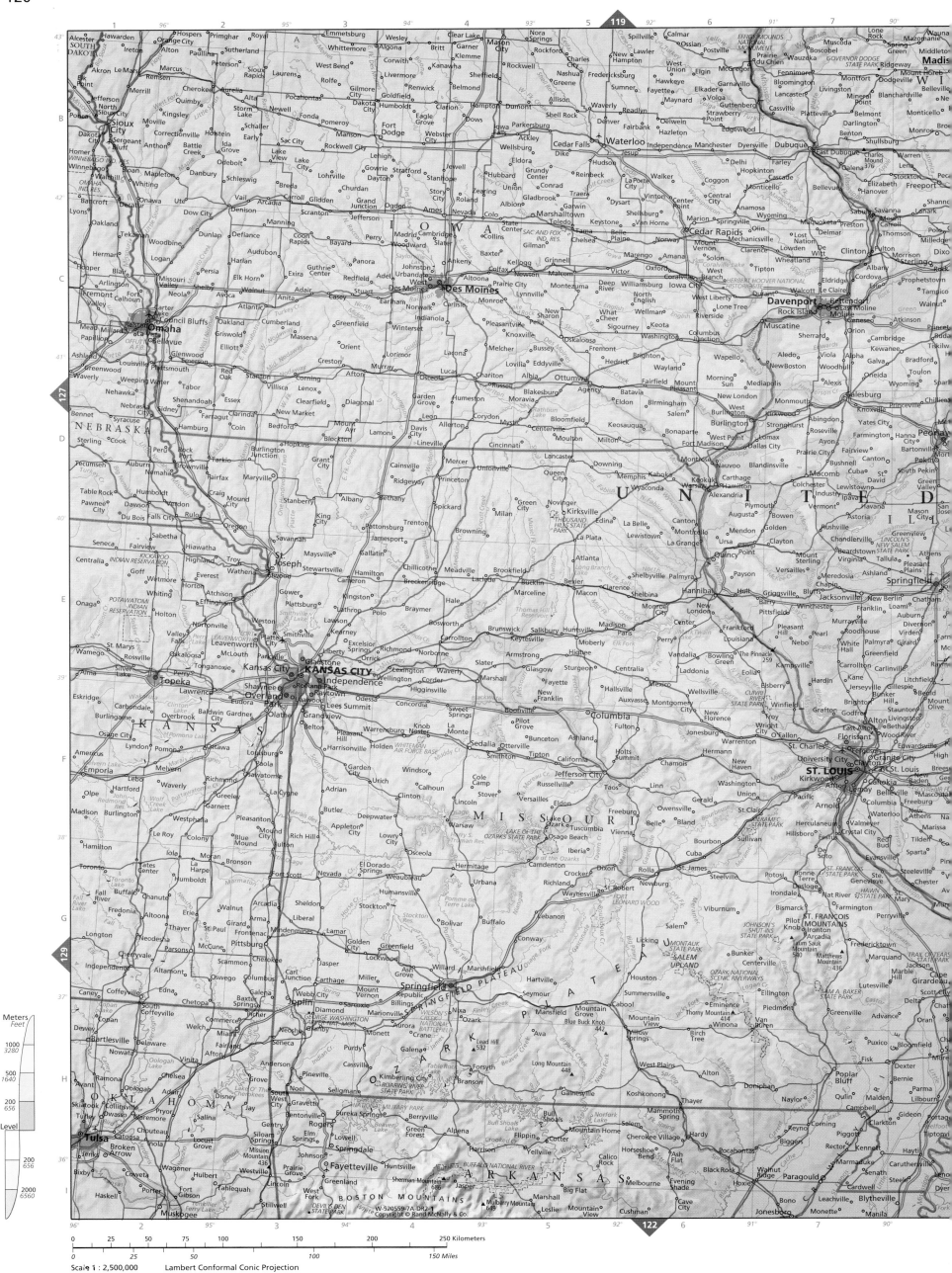

Meters
Feet

1000
3280

500
1640

200
656

Sea Level

200
656

2000
6560

0   25   50   75   100   150   200   250 Kilometers

0   25   50   100   150 Miles

Scale 1 : 2,500,000   Lambert Conformal Conic Projection

W-520599-7A-DR2
Copyright © by Rand McNally & Co.

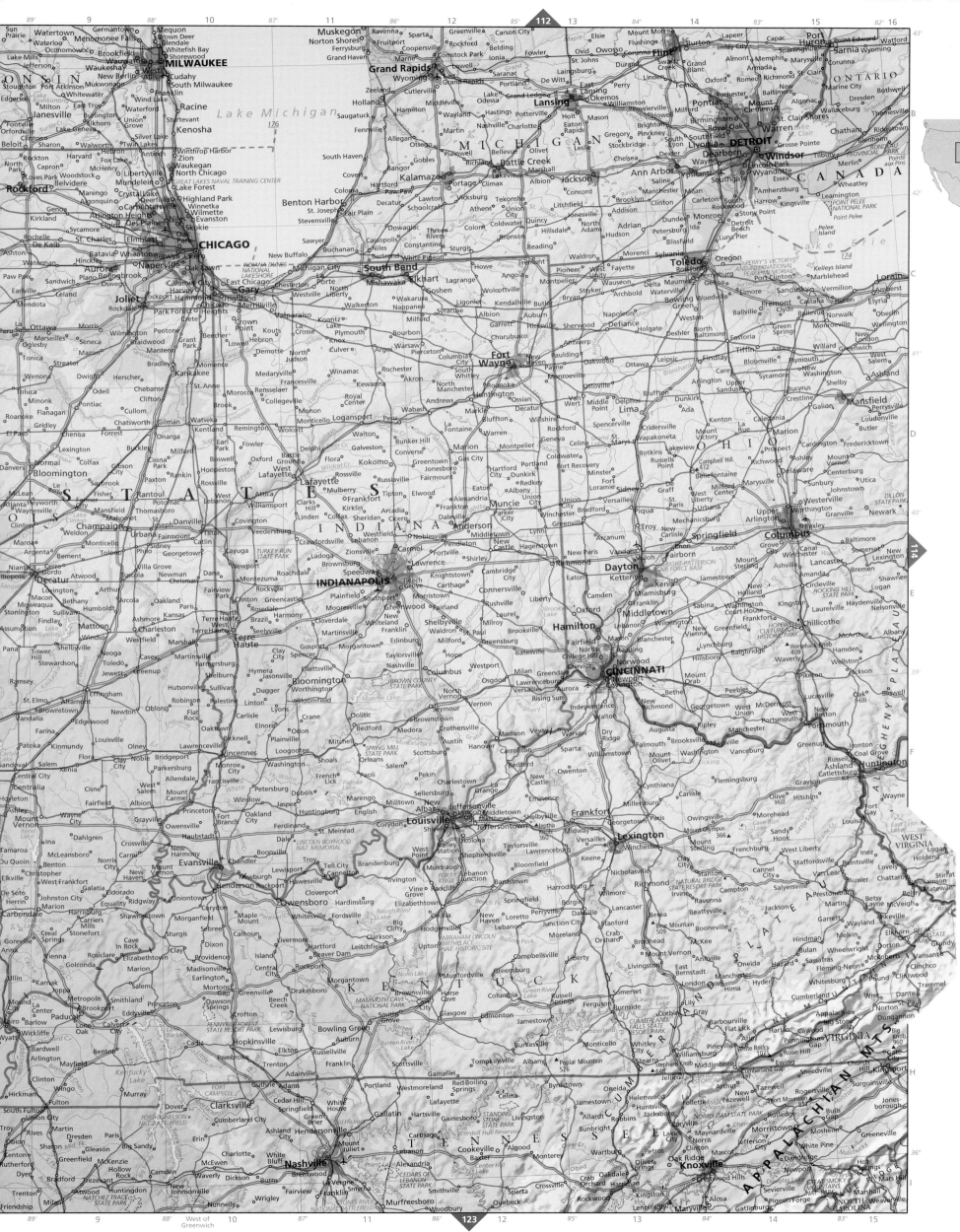

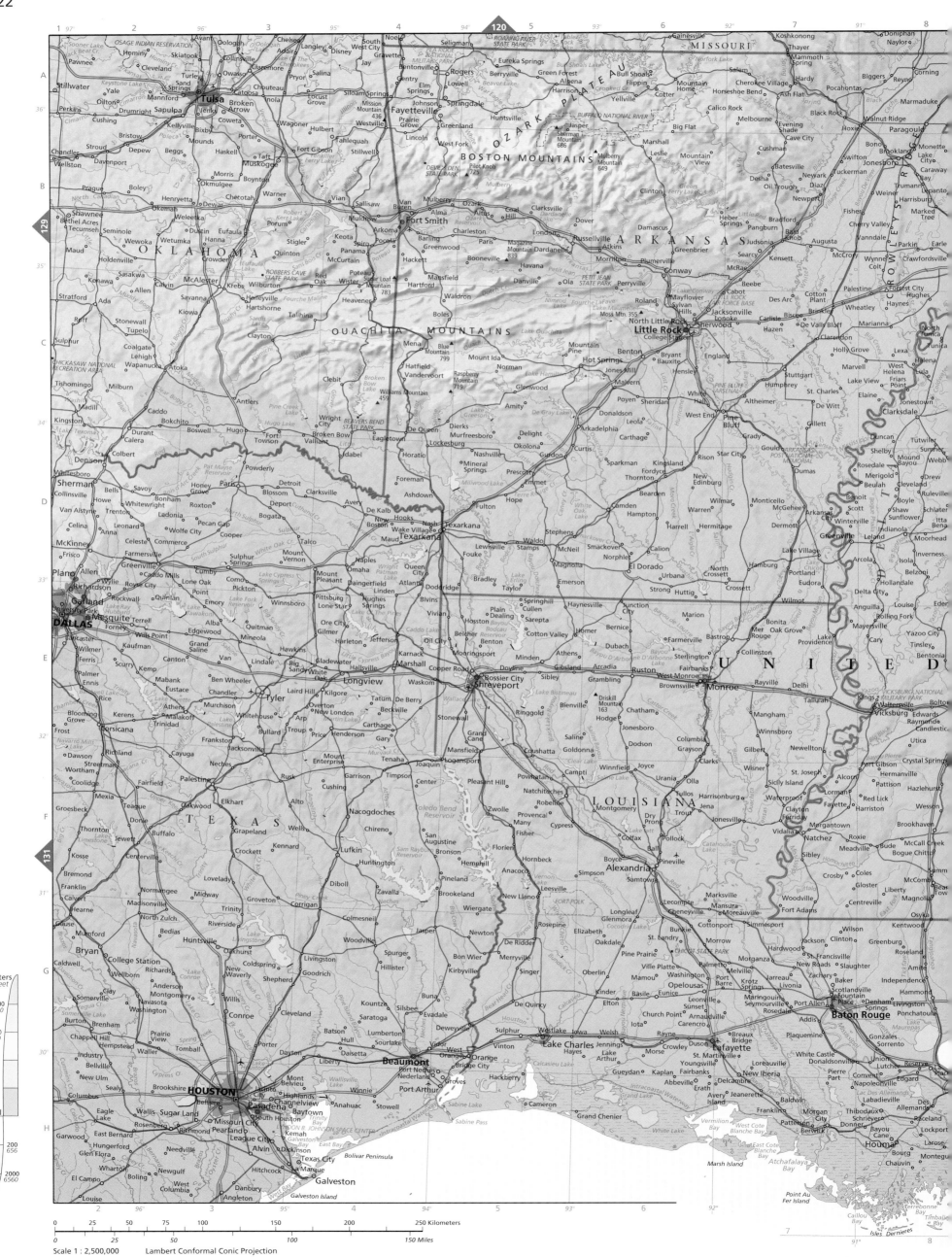

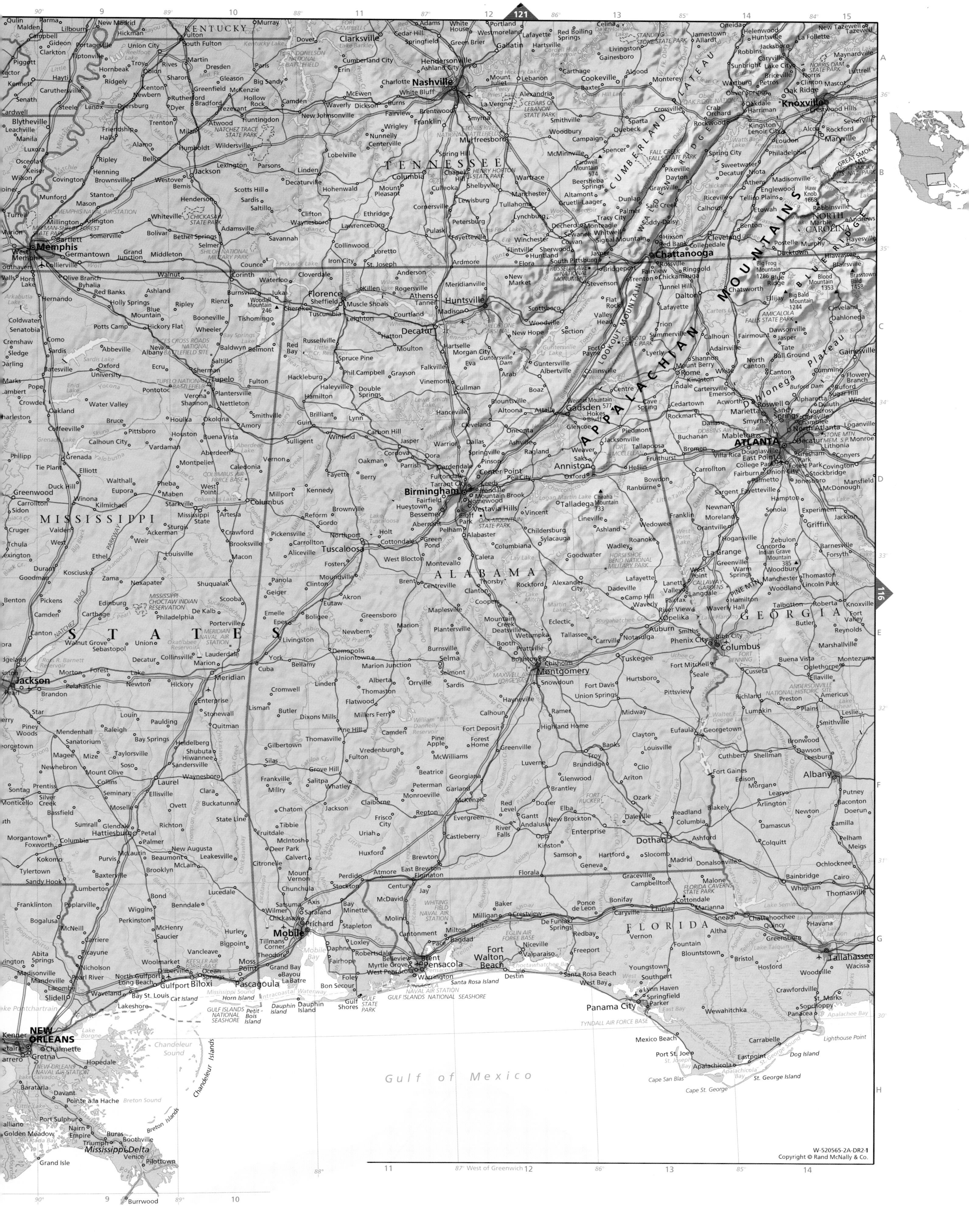

KENTUCKY
TENNESSEE
MISSISSIPPI
STATES
ALABAMA
GEORGIA
FLORIDA
NORTH CAROLINA
APPALACHIAN MOUNTAINS
CUMBERLAND PLATEAU
WALDEN RIDGE
LOOKOUT MOUNTAIN
BLUE RIDGE
Dahlonega Plateau
Gulf of Mexico
Nashville
Memphis
Knoxville
Chattanooga
Huntsville
Birmingham
ATLANTA
Montgomery
Columbus
Jackson
Mobile
Pensacola
Tallahassee
NEW ORLEANS
Gulfport
Biloxi
Pascagoula
Panama City
Tuscaloosa
Meridian
Hattiesburg
Tupelo
Florence
Decatur
Gadsden
Anniston
Dothan
Albany
Clarksville
Murfreesboro
Jackson
Auburn
Opelika
Selma
Laurel
Fort Walton Beach
Mississippi Delta
Chandeleur Islands
Chandeleur Sound
Breton Sound
Mississippi Sound
Mobile Bay
Choctawhatchee Bay
Apalachee Bay
Apalachicola Bay
Lake Pontchartrain
Cape San Blas
Cape St. George
St. George Island
Dog Island
Santa Rosa Island
GULF ISLANDS NATIONAL SEASHORE
TYNDALL AIR FORCE BASE
EGLIN AIR FORCE BASE
FORT RUCKER
FORT BENNING
NATCHEZ TRACE PARKWAY
GREAT SMOKY MTS. NAT. PARK
90°
89°
88°
87° West of Greenwich
86°
85°
84°
36°
35°
34°
33°
32°
31°
30°
9
10
11
12
13
14
15
A
B
C
D
E
F
G
H
121
116

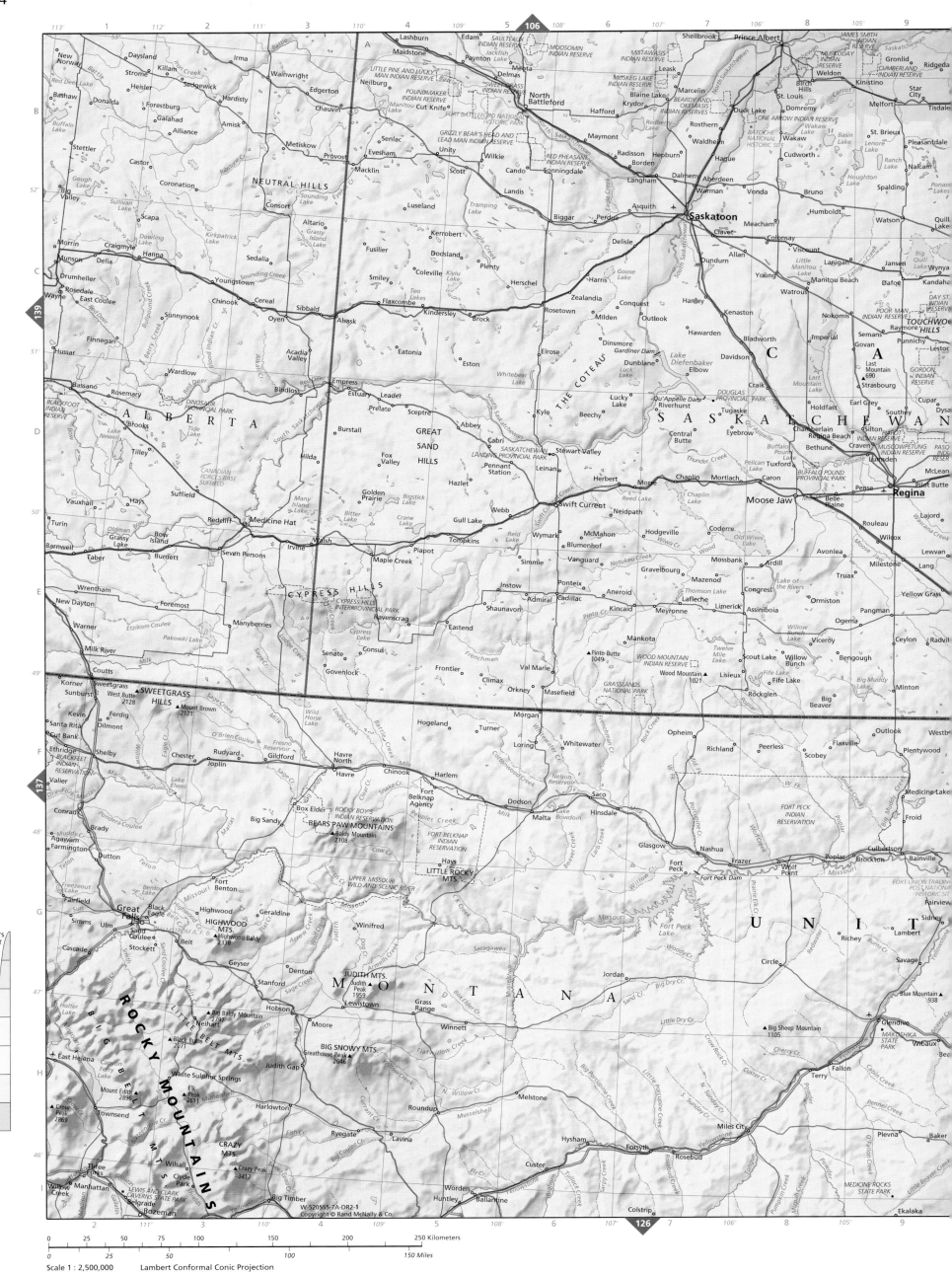

Meters / Feet

4000 / 13120
3000 / 9840
2000 / 6560
1000 / 3280
500 / 1640
200 / 656
Sea Level
200 / 656
2000 / 6560

0 25 50 75 100 150 200 250 Kilometers
0 25 50 100 150 Miles

Scale 1 : 2,500,000   Lambert Conformal Conic Projection

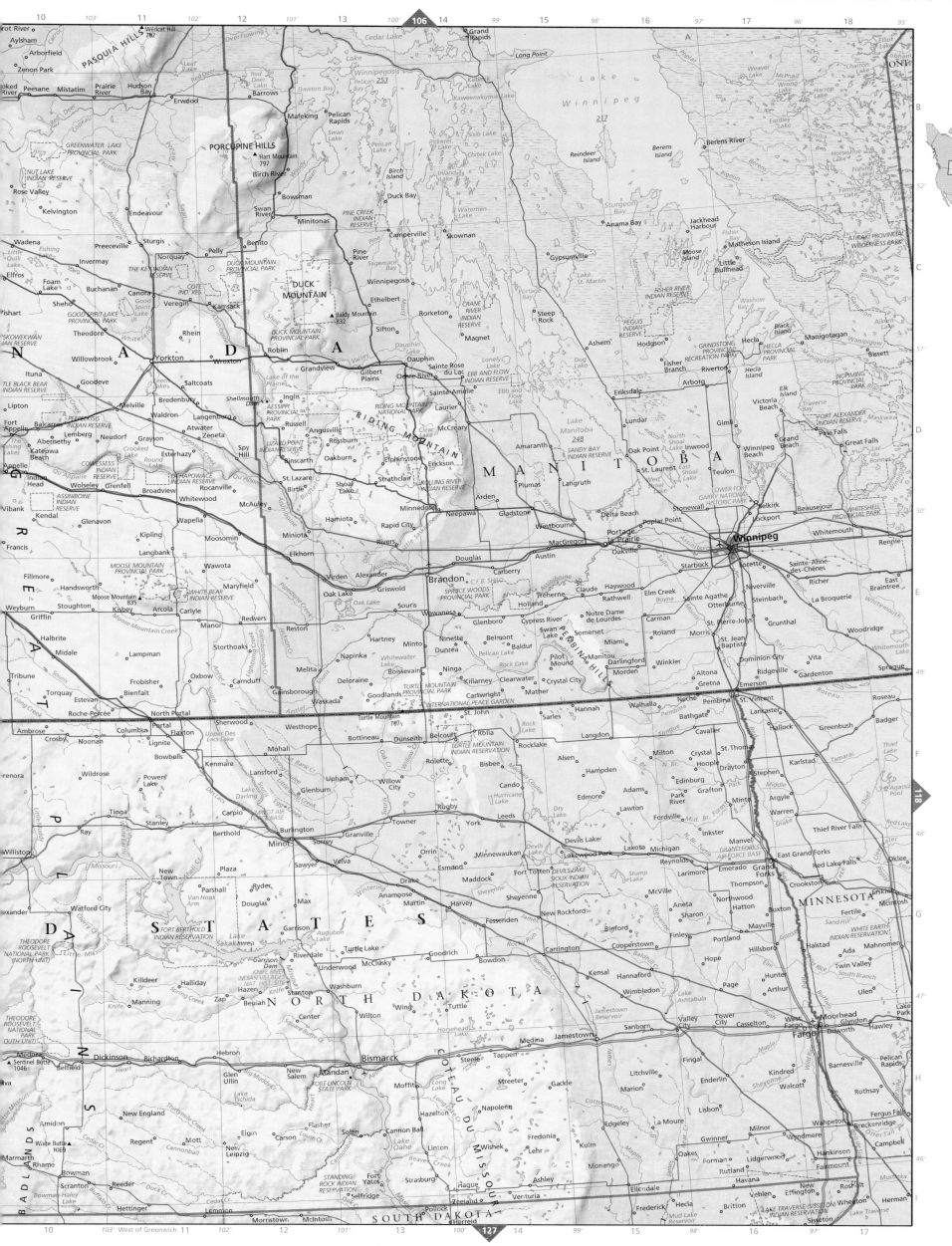

Meters / Feet
6000 / 19680
4000 / 13120
3000 / 9840
2000 / 6560
1000 / 3280
500 / 1640
200 / 656
Sea Level
200 / 656
2000 / 6560

Scale 1 : 2,500,000   Lambert Conformal Conic Projection

0 25 50 75 100 150 200 250 Kilometers

0 25 50 100 150 Miles

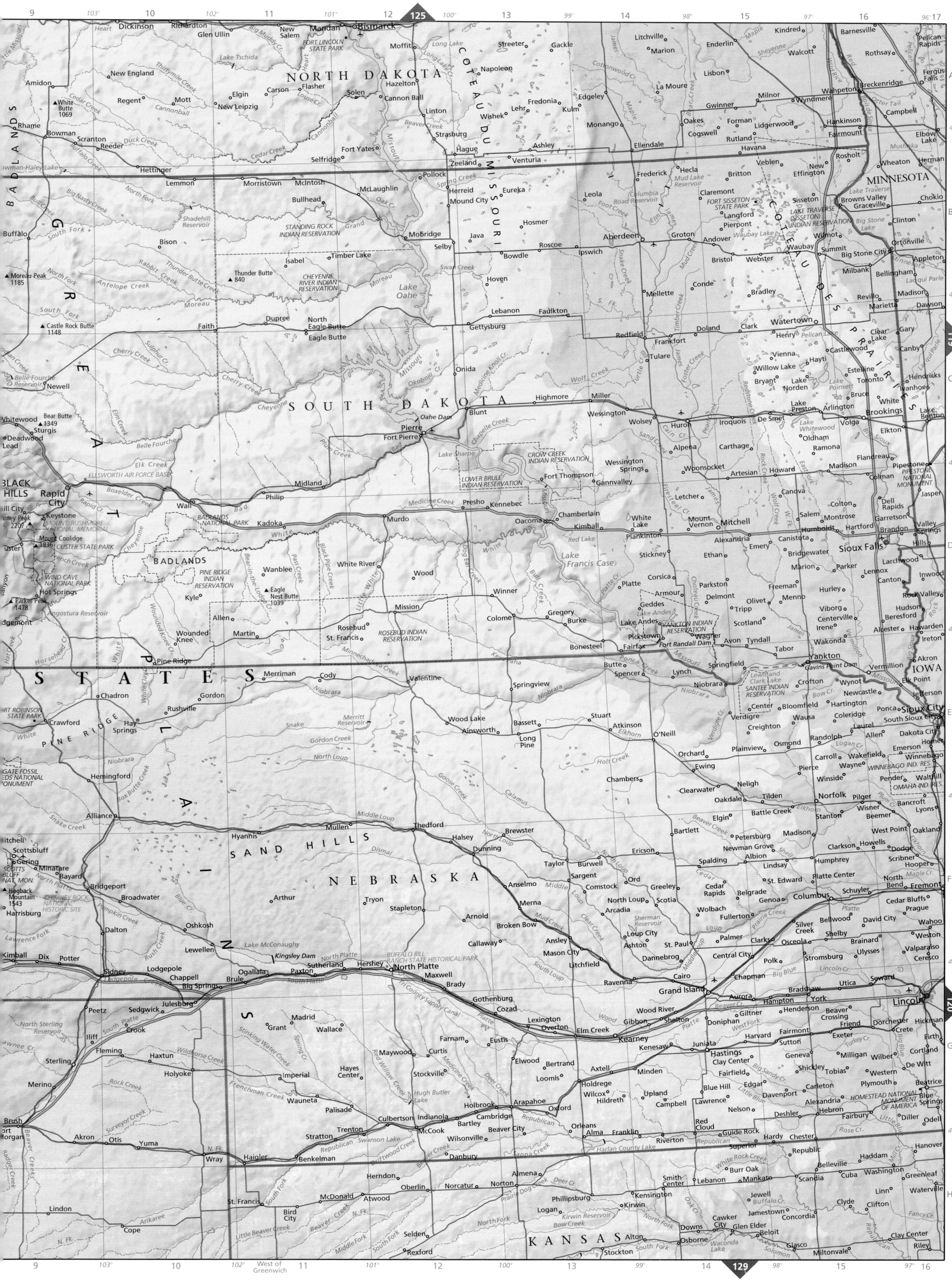
NORTH DAKOTA
SOUTH DAKOTA
NEBRASKA
KANSAS
MINNESOTA
IOWA
GREAT PLAINS
STATES
COTEAU DU MISSOURI
COTEAU DES PRAIRIES
SAND HILLS
BADLANDS
BLACK HILLS
PINE RIDGE
Bismarck
Mandan
Dickinson
Richardton
Glen Ullin
New Salem
FORT LINCOLN STATE PARK
Moffit
Streeter
Gackle
Litchville
Marion
Enderlin
Kindred
Barnesville
Pelican Rapids
Rothsay
Walcott
Fergus Falls
Lake Tschida
New England
Amidon
NORTH DAKOTA
Flasher
Hazelton
Napoleon
Lisbon
La Moure
Milnor
Wahpeton
Breckenridge
White Butte 1069
Regent
Mott
Elgin
New Leipzig
Carson
Solen
Cannon Ball
Linton
Wishek
Lehr
Fredonia
Kulm
Edgeley
Gwinner
Wyndmere
Campbell
Rhame
Bowman
Scranton
Reeder
Strasburg
Hague
Ashley
Monango
Oakes
Forman
Cogswell
Lidgerwood
Rutland
Hankinson
Fairmount
Elbow Lake
Fort Yates
Selfridge
Zeeland
Venturia
Ellendale
Havana
Veblen
Rosholt
Wheaton
Herman
Hettinger
Lemmon
Morristown
McIntosh
McLaughlin
Pollock
Herreid
Mound City
Eureka
Frederick
Hecla
Britton
New Effington
Bullhead
Leola
Claremont
FORT SISSETON STATE PARK
Langford
Pierpont
Sisseton
Browns Valley
Graceville
Chokio
Big Stone Lake
Clinton
Buffalo
Bison
Mobridge
Selby
Java
Hosmer
Roscoe
Ipswich
Aberdeen
Groton
Andover
Wilmot
Summit
Big Stone City
Ortonville
Isabel
Timber Lake
Bowdle
Bristol
Webster
Milbank
Appleton
Bellingham
Moreau Peak 1185
Thunder Butte 840
CHEYENNE RIVER INDIAN RESERVATION
STANDING ROCK INDIAN RESERVATION
Lake Oahe
Hoven
Mellette
Conde
Bradley
Revillo
Madison
Marietta
Dawson
Castle Rock Butte 1148
Faith
Dupree
North Eagle Butte
Eagle Butte
Lebanon
Gettysburg
Faulkton
Redfield
Frankfort
Doland
Clark
Watertown
Henry
Clear Lake
Gary
Tulare
Castlewood
Vienna
Hayti
Canby
Onida
Willow Lake
Bryant
Lake Norden
Estelline
Toronto
Hendricks
Ivanhoe
Bruce
White
Brookings
Newell
Highmore
Miller
Wessington
Lake Preston
Arlington
Lake Benton
Whitewood
Bear Butte 1349
Sturgis
Deadwood
Lead
Blunt
Oahe Dam
Pierre
Fort Pierre
Wolsey
Huron
Iroquois
De Smet
Volga
Elkton
Oldham
Ramona
Alpena
Carthage
Wessington Springs
Woonsocket
Artesian
Howard
Madison
Flandreau
Pipestone
PIPESTONE NATIONAL MONUMENT
Colman
Jasper
Lake Sharpe
CROW CREEK INDIAN RESERVATION
LOWER BRULE INDIAN RESERVATION
Fort Thompson
Gannvalley
ELLSWORTH AIR FORCE BASE
Rapid City
Midland
Philip
Wall
Presho
Kennebec
Letcher
Canova
Dell Rapids
Colton
Salem
Montrose
Garretson
Keystone
MOUNT RUSHMORE NATIONAL MEMORIAL
Mount Coolidge 1836
CUSTER STATE PARK
Custer
BADLANDS NATIONAL PARK
Kadoka
Murdo
Oacoma
Chamberlain
Kimball
White Lake
Plankinton
Mount Vernon
Mitchell
Humboldt
Hartford
Brandon
Valley Springs
Alexandria
Emery
Canistota
Sioux Falls
Hills
Lake Francis Case
Stickney
Ethan
Bridgewater
Marion
Parker
Lennox
Larchwood
Canton
Inwood
WIND CAVE NATIONAL PARK
Hot Springs
Parker Peak 1478
PINE RIDGE INDIAN RESERVATION
Wanblee
Eagle Nest Butte 1039
Kyle
White River
Wood
Winner
Corsica
Armour
Parkston
Delmont
Freeman
Menno
Hurley
Rock Valley
Hudson
Beresford
Platte
Geddes
Lake Andes
YANKTON INDIAN RESERVATION
Tripp
Olivet
Scotland
Viborg
Centerville
Irene
Hawarden
Alcester
Ireton
Angostura Reservoir
Edgemont
Allen
Wounded Knee
Martin
Mission
Rosebud
St. Francis
ROSEBUD INDIAN RESERVATION
Colome
Gregory
Burke
Pickstown
Fort Randall Dam
Wagner
Fairfax
Avon
Tyndall
Wakonda
Bonesteel
Tabor
Pine Ridge
Yankton
Gavins Point Dam
Vermillion
Akron
Elk Point
Merriman
Cody
Valentine
Butte
Spencer
Lynch
Springfield
Crofton
Wynot
Chadron
Gordon
Springview
Niobrara
Lewis and Clark Lake
SANTEE INDIAN RESERVATION
Newcastle
Jefferson
FORT ROBINSON STATE PARK
Crawford
Rushville
Hay Springs
Merritt Reservoir
Stuart
Atkinson
Center
Bloomfield
Hartington
Ponca
Sioux City
South Sioux City
Wood Lake
Ainsworth
Bassett
Long Pine
O'Neill
Verdigre
Creighton
Wausa
Coleridge
Laurel
Allen
Dakota City
Homer
Randolph
Osmond
Plainview
Orchard
Ewing
Carroll
Wakefield
Emerson
Winnebago
WINNEBAGO IND. RES.
Pierce
Wayne
Pender
Walthill
OMAHA IND. RES.
AGATE FOSSIL BEDS NATIONAL MONUMENT
Hemingford
Chambers
Clearwater
Neligh
Oakdale
Tilden
Winside
Norfolk
Pilger
Bancroft
Lyons
Wisner
Beemer
Stanton
Battle Creek
Alliance
Mullen
Thedford
Middle Loup
Elgin
Hyannis
Halsey
Brewster
Bartlett
Petersburg
Madison
West Point
Oakland
Scottsbluff
Mitchell
Gering
Minatare
SCOTTS BLUFF NAT. MON.
Bayard
Dunning
Taylor
Burwell
Ericson
Spalding
Newman Grove
Albion
Lindsay
Humphrey
Clarkson
Howells
Dodge
Scribner
Hooper
Bridgeport
Hogback Mountain 1543
CHIMNEY ROCK NATIONAL HISTORIC SITE
Broadwater
Arthur
Tryon
Stapleton
Anselmo
Sargent
Comstock
Ord
Greeley
Cedar Rapids
Belgrade
St. Edward
Platte Center
Columbus
Schuyler
North Bend
Fremont
Cedar Bluffs
Harrisburg
Merna
North Loup
Scotia
Genoa
Wolbach
Fullerton
Arcadia
Prague
Wahoo
Dalton
Oshkosh
Lewellen
Lake McConaughy
Kingsley Dam
Arnold
Broken Bow
Callaway
Ansley
Mason City
Loup City
Ashton
Sherman Reservoir
St. Paul
Dannebrog
Palmer
Silver Creek
Osceola
Shelby
Bellwood
David City
Brainard
Valparaiso
Weston
Ceresco
Ulysses
Stromsburg
Central City
Polk
Kimball
Dix
Potter
Sidney
Lodgepole
Chappell
Big Springs
Ogallala
Brule
Paxton
Sutherland
Hershey
North Platte
BUFFALO BILL RANCH STATE HISTORICAL PARK
Maxwell
Brady
Litchfield
Ravenna
Cairo
Chapman
Grand Island
Aurora
Hampton
Bradshaw
York
Utica
Seward
Lincoln
Julesburg
Sedgwick
Peetz
Crook
Iliff
Madrid
Grant
Wallace
Gothenburg
Cozad
Lexington
Overton
Elm Creek
Kearney
Gibbon
Shelton
Wood River
Doniphan
Giltner
Henderson
Beaver Crossing
Friend
Dorchester
Crete
Hickman
North Sterling Reservoir
Fleming
Haxtun
Holyoke
Sterling
Farnam
Eustis
Curtis
Maywood
Imperial
Hayes Center
Stockville
Elwood
Bertrand
Axtell
Minden
Kenesaw
Juniata
Hastings
Harvard
Clay Center
Fairfield
Fairmont
Sutton
Geneva
Exeter
Milligan
Wilber
Firth
Cortland
Shickley
Tobias
Western
De Witt
Merino
Wauneta
Palisade
Hugh Butler Lake
Holbrook
Arapahoe
Oxford
Loomis
Holdrege
Wilcox
Hildreth
Upland
Campbell
Blue Hill
Lawrence
Edgar
Davenport
Carleton
Alexandria
Plymouth
Beatrice
HOMESTEAD NATIONAL MONUMENT OF AMERICA
Blue Springs
Hebron
Deshler
Nelson
Fairbury
Diller
Odell
Brush
Fort Morgan
Akron
Otis
Yuma
Wray
Haigler
Benkelman
Stratton
Trenton
Swanson Lake
Culbertson
Indianola
McCook
Bartley
Cambridge
Wilsonville
Beaver City
Orleans
Alma
Franklin
Riverton
Red Cloud
Guide Rock
Superior
Hardy
Chester
Hanover
Harlan County Lake
Danbury
Republic
Haddam
Belleville
Cuba
Washington
Greenleaf
Herndon
Almena
Norton
Norcatur
Oberlin
Atwood
McDonald
St. Francis
Bird City
Phillipsburg
Kensington
Smith Center
Lebanon
Burr Oak
Mankato
Scandia
Jewell
Linn
Waterville
Kirwin
Kirwin Reservoir
Logan
Lindon
Cope
Selden
Rexford
Cawker City
Glen Elder
Downs
Osborne
Alton
Stockton
Beloit
Jamestown
Concordia
Clyde
Clifton
Clay Center
Glasco
Miltonvale
Riley
Waconda Lake
West of Greenwich
Missouri
Platte
North Platte
South Platte
Republican
Niobrara
Cheyenne
White
James
Big Sioux
Elkhorn
Loup
Little Blue
Big Blue
Red
Sheyenne
Maple
Moreau
Grand
Cannonball
Heart
Knife
Bad
Keya Paha
Snake
Dismal
Calamus
Solomon
Saline
Beaver Creek
Sappa Creek
Prairie Dog Creek
Frenchman Creek
Stinking Water Creek
Medicine Creek
Red Willow Creek
Lodgepole Creek
Pumpkin Creek
Blue Creek
Wood
Boxelder Creek
Elk Creek
Belle Fourche
Rapid Creek
9 10 11 12 13 14 15 16 17
103° 102° 101° 100° 99° 98° 97° 96°
46° 45° 44° 43° 42° 41° 40°
A B C D E F G H
125
119
120
129

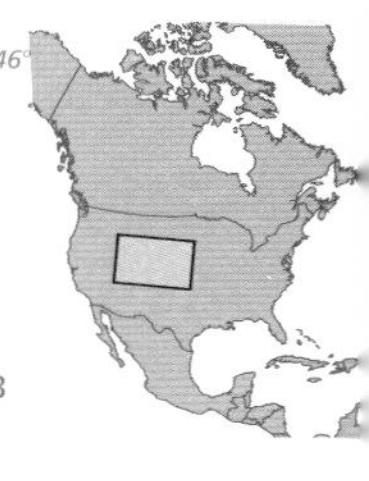

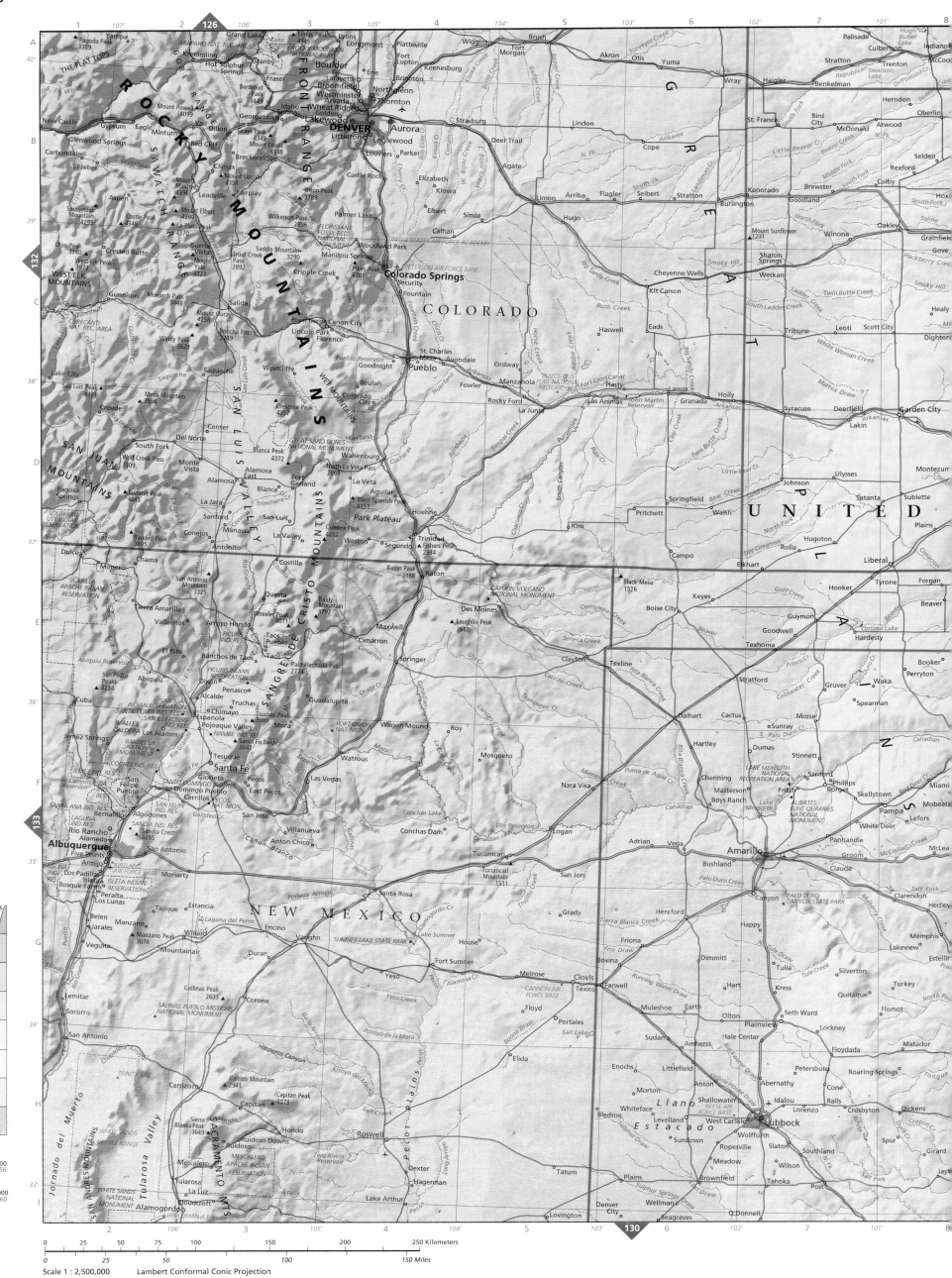

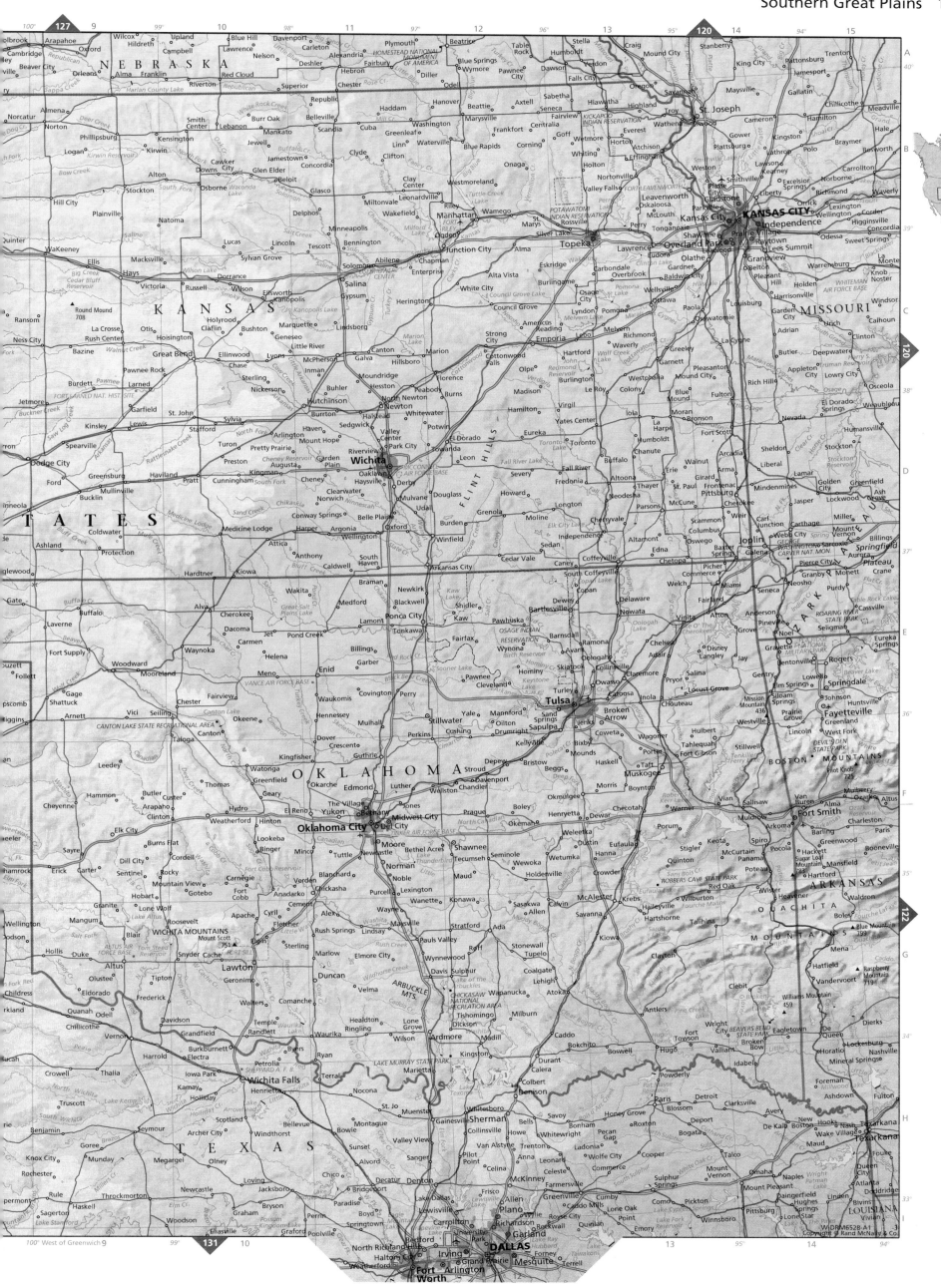

Meters / Feet

4000 / 13120
3000 / 9840
2000 / 6560
1000 / 3280
500 / 1640
200 / 656
Sea Level
200 / 656
2000 / 6560

0   25   50   75   100   150   250 Kilometers
0   25   50   100   150 Miles
Scale 1 : 2,500,000   Lambert Conformal Conic Projection

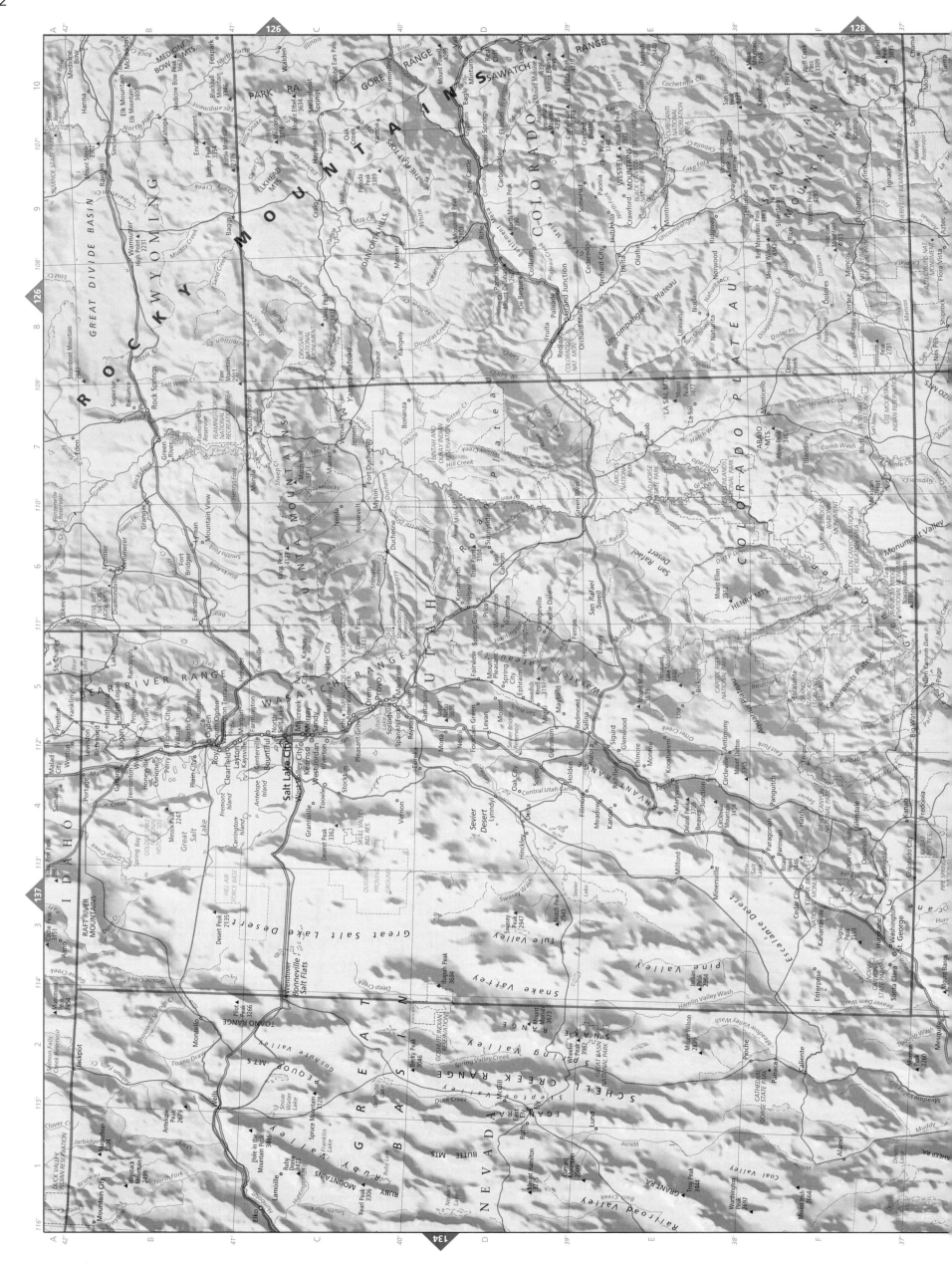

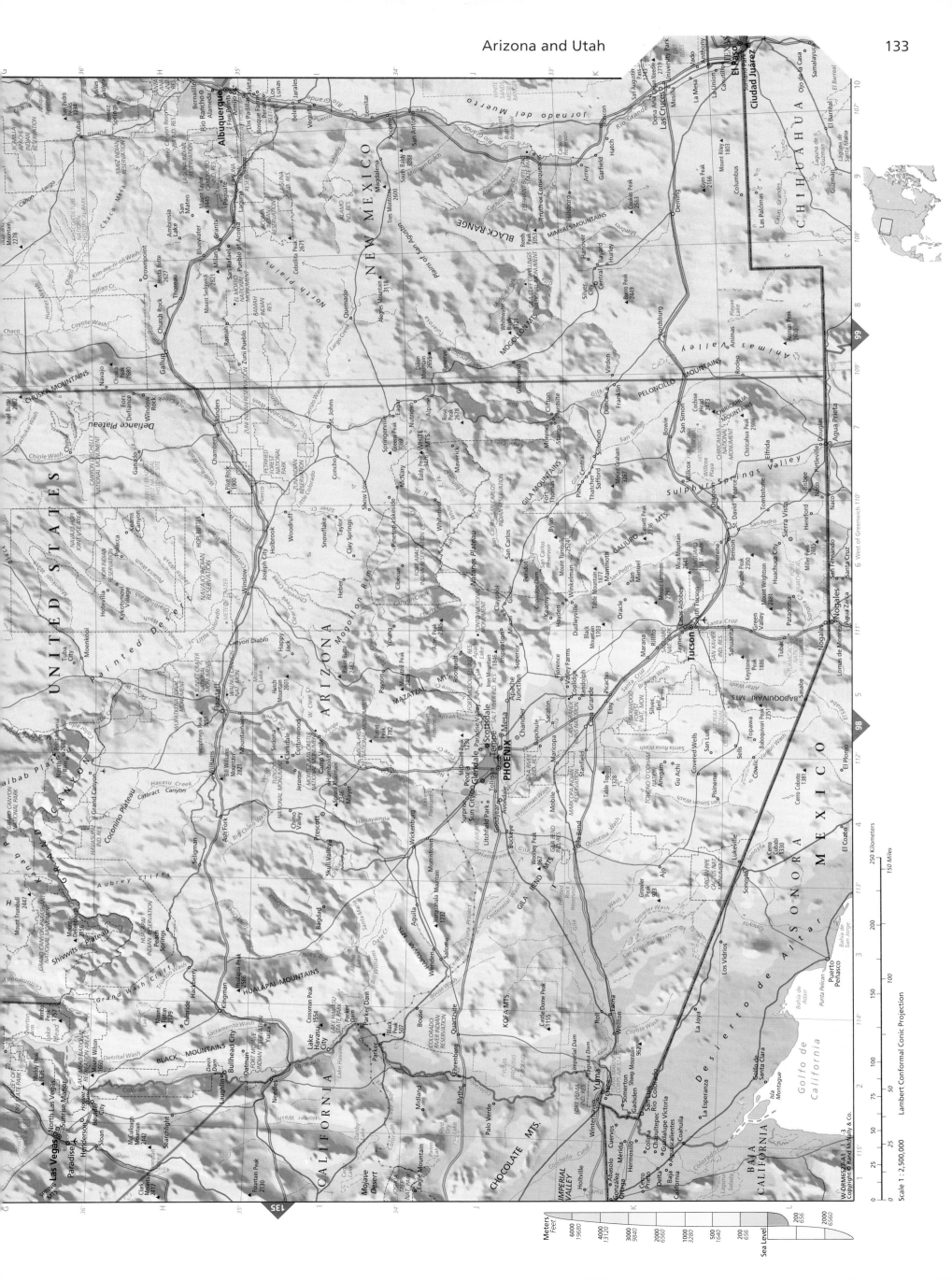

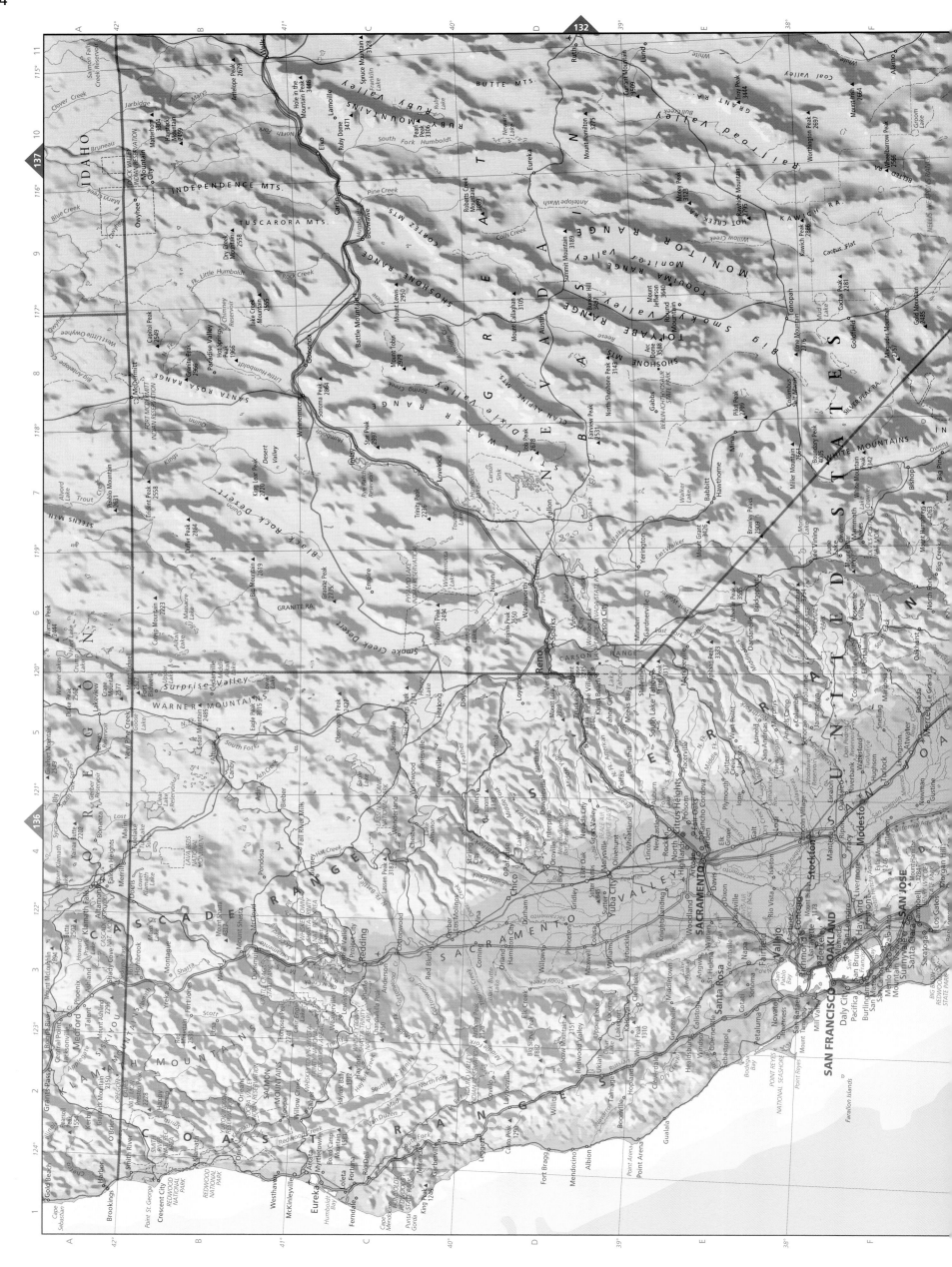

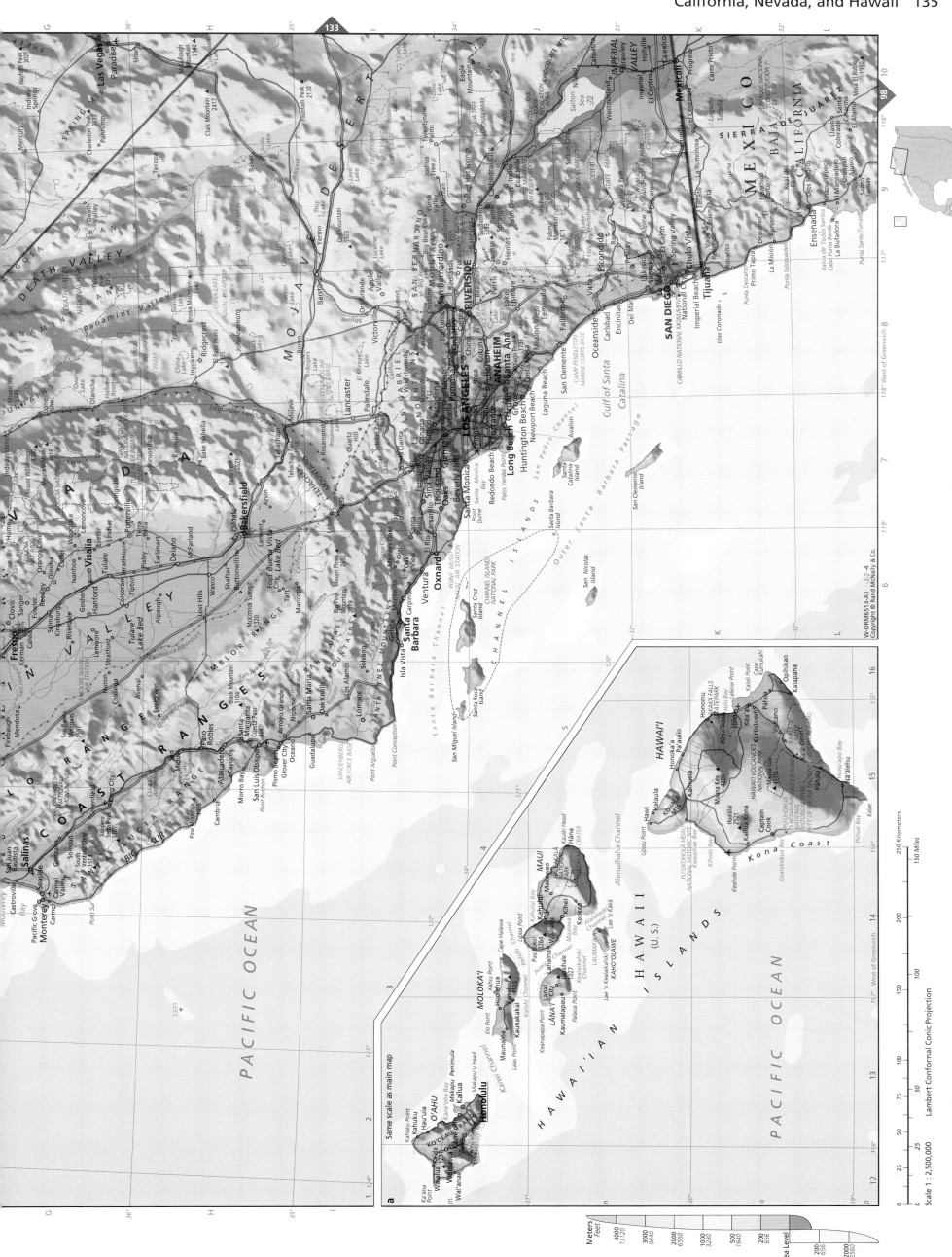

Meters
Feet

6000
19680

4000
13120

3000
9840

2000
6560

1000
3280

500
1640

200
656

Sea Level

200
656

2000
6560

0   25   50   75   100   150   200   250 Kilometers

0   25   50   100   150 Miles

Scale 1 : 2,500,000   Lambert Conformal Conic Projection

PACIFIC OCEAN

BRITISH COLUMBIA

VANCOUVER ISLAND

VANCOUVER

Scale 1 : 2,500,000   Lambert Conformal Conic Projection

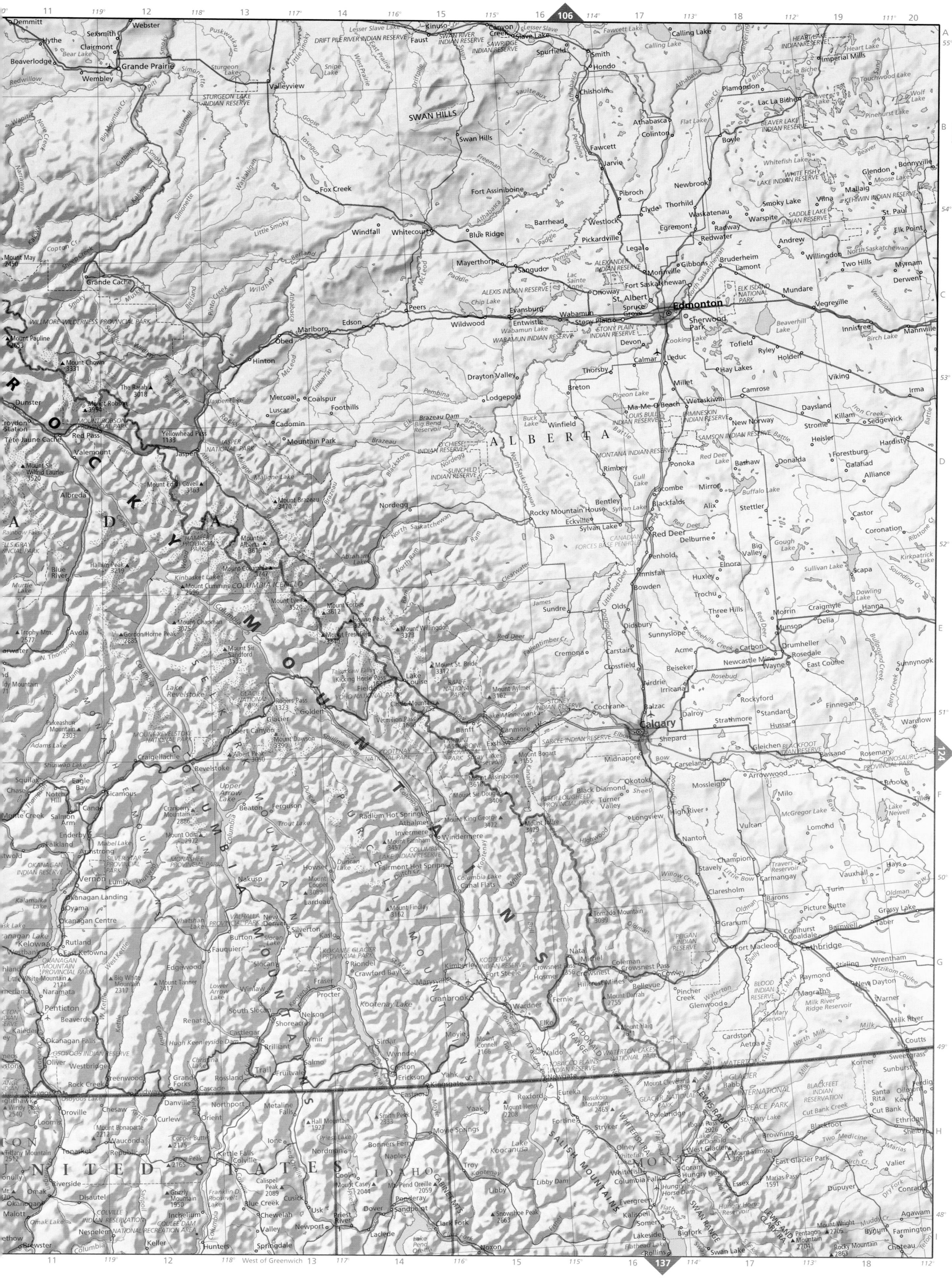

ALBERTA

ROCKY MOUNTAINS

COLUMBIA MOUNTAINS

UNITED STATES

IDAHO

MONTANA

SWAN HILLS

Edmonton

Calgary

Grande Prairie

Red Deer

Lethbridge

Jasper

Banff

Kelowna

Penticton

Grande Cache

Hinton

Edson

Whitecourt

Athabasca

Lac La Biche

St. Paul

Elk Point

Vegreville

Camrose

Wetaskiwin

Ponoka

Rocky Mountain House

Drumheller

Brooks

Medicine area

Fort Macleod

Cardston

Cranbrook

Fernie

Revelstoke

Nelson

Trail

Castlegar

Vernon

JASPER NATIONAL PARK

BANFF NATIONAL PARK

KOOTENAY NATIONAL PARK

COLUMBIA ICEFIELD

GLACIER NATIONAL PARK

MOUNT REVELSTOKE NATIONAL PARK

WELLS GRAY PROVINCIAL PARK

WILLMORE WILDERNESS PROVINCIAL PARK

ELK ISLAND NATIONAL PARK

WATERTON LAKES NATIONAL PARK

GLACIER NATIONAL PARK

BLACKFEET INDIAN RESERVATION

BLOOD INDIAN RESERVE

PEIGAN INDIAN RESERVE

SARCEE INDIAN RESERVE

STONEY INDIAN RESERVE

Lesser Slave Lake

Lac La Biche

Pigeon Lake

Gull Lake

Sullivan Lake

Okanagan Lake

Kootenay Lake

Columbia Lake

Upper Arrow Lake

Lower Arrow Lake

Mount Robson 3954

Mount Columbia 3747

Mount Assiniboine 3606

Mount Forbes 3612

Mount Sir Wilfrid Laurier 3520

Mount Chown 3331

Mount Bryce

West of Greenwich

ARCTIC OCEAN

GREENLAND SEA

SVALBARD

SPITSBERGEN

NORDGRØNLAND
(AVANERSUAQ)

Kong
Frederik VIII
Land

Peary Land

Knud Rasmussen Land

ELLESMERE ISLAND

Kong
Christian X
Land

NUNAVUT

BAFFIN BAY

BAFFIN ISLAND

CANADA

GREENLAND
(Den.)

ØSTGRØNLAND
(TUNU)

Gunnbjørn Field
3700

Kong Christian IX Land

DISKO

Davis Strait

Denmark Strait

ICELAND
Reykjavik
Keflavik

VESTGRØNLAND
(KITAA)

Godthåb
(Nuuk)

J.A.D. Jensens
Nunatakker
1680

Mont Forel
3360

Frederikshåb
(Paamiut)

Ivigtut

Natsaq

Julianehåb
(Qaqortoq)

Nanortalik

Frederiksdal

Kap Farvel

LABRADOR SEA

ATLANTIC
OCEAN

QUÉBEC

NEWFOUNDLAND
AND
LABRADOR

TORNGAT MTS.

Ungava
Bay

Hudson Strait

Meters	
Feet	
3000	*9840*
2000	*6560*
1000	*3280*
500	*1640*
200	*656*
Sea Level	
200	*656*
2000	*6560*

0   100   200   300   400   600   800   1000 Kilometers

0   100   200   400   600 Miles

Scale 1 : 10,000,000   Lambert Conformal Conic Projection

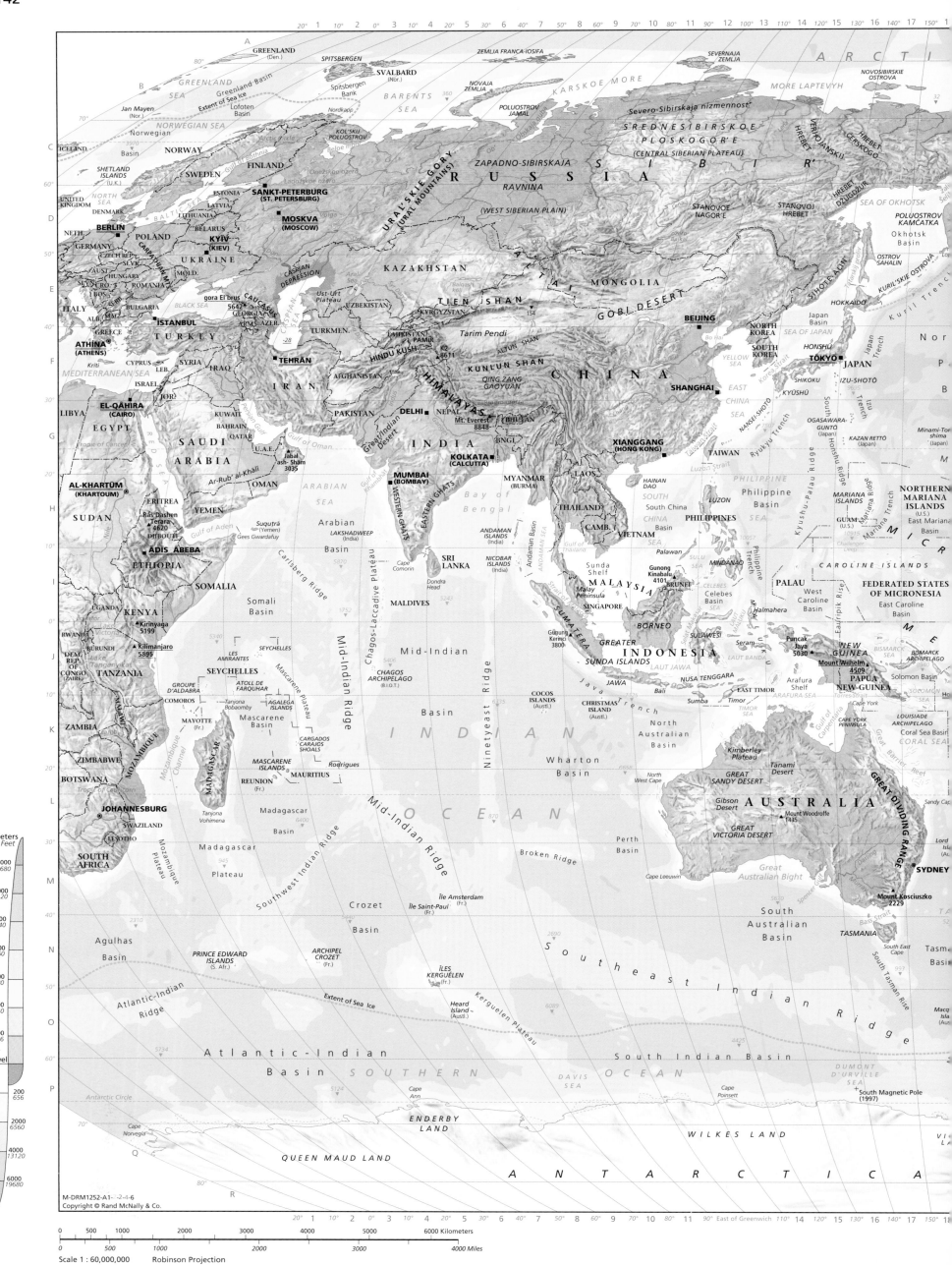

Scale 1 : 60,000,000   Robinson Projection

OCEAN

Canada Basin

OSTOČNO-SIBIRSKOE MORE

ostrov Vrangelja

CHUKCHI SEA

Point Barrow

BEAUFORT SEA

Banks Island

Amundsen Gulf

VICTORIA ISLAND

QUEEN ELIZABETH ISLANDS

ELLESMERE ISLAND

+ North Magnetic Pole (2001)

GREENLAND (Den.)

Baffin Bay

Baffin Basin

Gunnbjørn Fjeld 3700

Arctic Circle

BAFFIN ISLAND

Mackenzie

Great Bear Lake

Southampton Island

Hudson Strait

Foxe Basin

Péninsule d'Ungava

Davis Strait

Kap Farvel

Irminger Basin

Anadyrskij zaliv

BROOKS RANGE

ALASKA (U.S.)

Mount McKinley 6194

Bering Strait

RANGE

Mount Logan 5959

MACKENZIE MOUNTAINS

Great Slave Lake

CANADA

LABRADOR

LABRADOR SEA

Labrador Basin

Extent of Sea Ice

BERING SEA

Aleutian

Alaska Peninsula

Kodiak Island

Gulf of Alaska

COAST MTS.

ROCKY MOUNTAINS

Lake Athabasca

Nelson

Lake Winnipeg

NEW-FOUNDLAND

ST. PIERRE AND MIQUELON (Fr.)

KOMANDORSKIE OSTROVA

ALEUTIAN ISLANDS

Aleutian Trench

QUEEN CHARLOTTE ISLANDS

Mount Waddington 3994

Lake Superior

Lake Huron

Lake Michigan

GREAT PLAINS

Ottawa

Montreal

APPALACHIAN MTS.

Cape Cod

Emperor Seamounts

International Date Line

VANCOUVER ISLAND

Cape Mendocino

CASCADE RANGE

COAST RANGES

Missouri

CHICAGO

UNITED STATES

NEW YORK

Washington

ATLANTIC

North American

BERMUDA (U.K.)

Cape Lookout

Blake Plateau

PACIFIC OCEAN

Mendocino Fracture Zone

Murray Fracture Zone

Mount Whitney 4418

LOS ANGELES

GREAT BASIN

Arkansas

Red

HOUSTON

Gulf of Mexico

Mexico Basin

Tropic of Cancer

BAHAMAS

Basin

OCEAN

MIDWAY ISLANDS (U.S.)

Hawaiian Ridge

HAWAI'IAN ISLANDS (U.S.)

O'ahu

Molokai Fracture Zone

Isla Guadalupe (Mex.)

Baja California

Cabo San Lucas

SIERRA MADRE OCCIDENTAL

Golfo de California

SIERRA MADRE ORIENTAL

CIUDAD DE MÉXICO

MEXICO

Volcán Pico de Orizaba 5610

SIERRA MADRE DEL SUR

Pen. de Yucatán

CUBA

WEST INDIES

GREATER

HAITI

DOM. REP.

PUERTO RICO (U.S.)

pacific Mountains

Pacific Mountains

WAKE ISLAND (U.S.)

Central

Christmas Ridge

Johnston Atoll (U.S.)

Hawai'i

Clarion Fracture Zone

ISLAS REVILLAGIGEDO (Mex.)

Middle America Trench

BELIZE

GUAT.

HONDURAS

EL SALV.

NICARAGUA

JAMAICA

ANTILLES

CARIBBEAN SEA

MARSHALL ISLANDS

RATAK CHAIN

Pacific

Basin

Île Clipperton (Fr.)

Guatemala Basin

Lago de Nicaragua

COSTA RICA

PANAMA

Istmo de Panamá

Panama Basin

VENEZUELA

RALIK CHAIN

GILBERT ISLANDS

Howland Island (U.S.)

Baker Island (U.S.)

Kiritimati

Clipperton Fracture Zone

Cocos Ridge

Isla del Coco (C.R.)

ARCHIPIÉLAGO DE COLÓN (Ec.)

Chimborazo 6310

BOGOTÁ

COLOMBIA

ECUADOR

NAURU

PHOENIX ISLANDS

Jarvis Island (U.S.)

Punta Parinas

BRAZIL

SOLOMON ISLANDS

SANTA CRUZ ISLANDS

TUVALU

KIRIBATI

TOKELAU (N.Z.)

NORTHERN COOK ISLANDS

ÎLES MARQUISES

Nevado Huascarán 6746

PERU

LINE ISLANDS

POLYNESIA

FRENCH POLYNESIA

Lima

NUATU

North Fiji Basin

WALLIS AND FUTUNA (Fr.)

SAMOA

AMERICAN SAMOA (U.S.)

COOK ISLANDS (N.Z.)

ARCHIPEL DE LA SOCIÉTÉ

ÎLES TUAMOTU

Tuamotu Ridge

Tahiti

Peru Basin

NEW CALEDONIA (Fr.)

FIJI

Suva

TONGA

NIUE (N.Z.)

SOUTHERN COOK ISLANDS

ÎLES AUSTRALES

Austral Seamounts

ÎLES GAMBIER

PITCAIRN (U.K.)

Pitcairn Island

Isla Sala y Gómez (Chile)

Sala y Gomez Ridge

Isla de Pascua (Chile)

East Pacific Rise

Tropic of Capricorn

Nazca Ridge

Peru-Chile Trench

BOLIVIA

La Paz

NELLE-DONIE

New Hebrides Trench

South Fiji Basin

New Caledonia Ridge

Lau Ridge

Tonga Ridge

Tonga Trench

KERMADEC ISLANDS (N.Z.)

International Date Line

Southwest

PACIFIC OCEAN

Cerro Aconcagua 6959

SANTIAGO

ARGENTINA

CHILE

PAMPA

ANDES

Norfolk Basin

NORFOLK ISLAND (Austl.)

Kermadec Ridge

Kermadec Trench

Louisville Ridge

Pacific

Basin

Chile Rise

Isla Grande de Chiloé

Golfo San Matias

SEA

NEW ZEALAND

Cook Strait

NORTH ISLAND

Chatham Rise

CHATHAM ISLANDS (N.Z.)

PATAGONIA

ATLANTIC

Golfo San Jorge

Argentine Basin

KLAND ANDS

SOUTH ISLAND

Aoraki (Mount Cook) 3754

Bounty Trough

BOUNTY ISLANDS (N.Z.)

ANTIPODES ISLANDS (N.Z.)

Strait of Magellan

TIERRA DEL FUEGO

Cabo de Hornos (Cape Horn)

FALKLAND ISLANDS (U.K.)

OCEAN

SCOTIA SEA

Campbell Plateau

Campbell Island (N.Z.)

Pacific-Antarctic Ridge

Extent of Sea Ice

Drake Passage

SOUTH SHETLAND ISLANDS (U.K.)

SOUTH ORKNEY ISLANDS (U.K.)

Antarctic Circle

BALLENY ISLANDS

Scott Island

SOUTHERN

Southeast Pacific Basin

Pacific OCEAN

ALEXANDER ISLAND

ANTARCTIC PENINSULA

Atlantic-Indian Basin

Cape Adare

ROSS SEA

Roosevelt Island

Ross Ice Shelf

MARIE BYRD LAND

AMUNDSEN SEA

Thurston Island

BELLINGSHAUSEN SEA

Vinson Massif 5140

Ronne Ice Shelf

BERKNER ISLAND

WEDDELL SEA

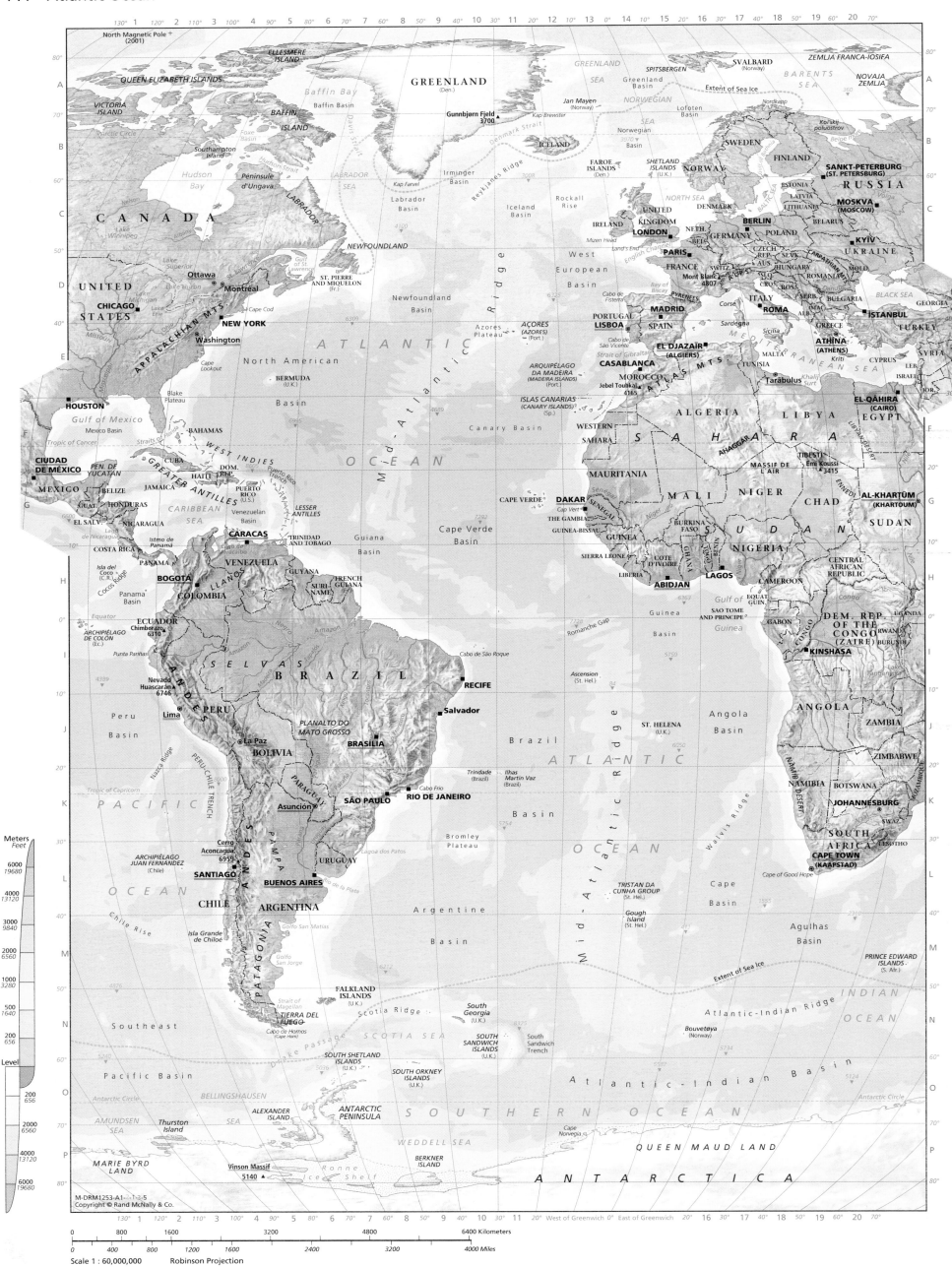

Meters
Feet

6000
19680

4000
13120

3000
9840

2000
6560

1000
3280

500
1640

200
656

Sea Level

200
656

2000
6560

4000
13120

6000
19680

0   800   1600   3200   4800   6400 Kilometers

0   400   800   1200   1600   2400   3200   4000 Miles

Scale 1 : 60,000,000   Robinson Projection

Index to World Reference Maps

Introduction to the Index

This index includes in a single alphabetical list approximately 54,000 names of places and geographical features that appear on the reference maps. Each name is followed by the name of the country or continent in which it is located, an alpha-numeric map reference key and a page reference.

Names The names of cities and towns appear in the index in regular type. The names of all other features appear in *italics*, followed by descriptive terms (hill, mtn., state) to indicate their nature.

Abbreviations of names on the maps have been standardized as much as possible. Names that are abbreviated on the maps are generally spelled out in full in the index.

Country names and names of features that extend beyond the boundaries of one country are followed by the name of the continent in which each is located. Country designations follow the names of all other places in the index. The locations of places in the United States, Canada, and the United Kingdom are further defined by abbreviations that indicate the state, province, or other political division in which each is located.

All abbreviations used in the index are defined in the List of Abbreviations to the right.

Alphabetization Names are alphabetized in the order of the letters of the English alphabet. Spanish *ll* and *ch*, for example, are not treated as distinct letters. Furthermore, diacritical marks are disregarded in alphabetization — German or Scandinavian *ä* or *ö* are treated as *a* or *o*.

The names of physical features may appear inverted, since they are always alphabetized under the proper, not the generic, part of the name, thus: "Gibraltar, Strait of". Otherwise every entry, whether consisting of one word or more, is alphabetized as a single continuous entity. "Lakeland," for example, appears after "La Crosse" and before "La Salle". Names beginning with articles (Le Havre, Den Helder, Al-Manāmah) are not inverted. Names beginning "St.", "Ste." and "Sainte" are alphabetized as though spelled "Saint".

In the case of identical names, towns are listed first, then political divisions, then physical features. Entries that are completely identical are listed alphabetically by country name.

Map Reference Keys and Page References The map reference keys and page references are found in the last two columns of each entry.

Each map reference key consists of a letter and number. The letters correspond to letters along the sides of the maps. Lowercase letters refer to inset maps. The numbers correspond to numbers that appear across the tops and bottoms of the maps.

Map reference keys for point features, such as cities and mountain peaks, indicate the locations of the symbols for these features. For other features, such as countries, mountain ranges, or rivers, the map reference keys indicate the locations of the names.

The page number generally refers to the main map for the country in which the feature is located. Page references for two-page maps always refer to the left-hand page.

List of Abbreviations

Ab., Can.	Alberta, Can.
Afg.	Afghanistan
Afr.	Africa
Ak., U.S.	Alaska, U.S.
Al., U.S.	Alabama, U.S.
Alb.	Albania
Alg.	Algeria
Am. Sam.	American Samoa
anch.	anchorage
And.	Andorra
Ang.	Angola
Ant.	Antarctica
Antig.	Antigua and Barbuda
aq.	aqueduct
Ar., U.S.	Arkansas, U.S.
Arg.	Argentina
Arm.	Armenia
at.	atoll
Aus.	Austria
Austl.	Australia
Az., U.S.	Arizona, U.S.
Azer.	Azerbaijan
b.	bay, gulf, inlet, lagoon
B.C., Can.	British Columbia, Can.
Bah.	Bahamas
Bahr.	Bahrain
Barb.	Barbados
bas.	basin
Bdi.	Burundi
Bel.	Belgium
Bela.	Belarus
Ber.	Bermuda
Bhu.	Bhutan
B.I.O.T.	British Indian Ocean Territory
Blg.	Bulgaria
Bngl.	Bangladesh
Bol.	Bolivia
Bos.	Bosnia and Hercegovina
Bots.	Botswana
Braz.	Brazil
Bru.	Brunei
Br. Vir. Is.	British Virgin Islands
Burkina	Burkina Faso
c.	cape, point
Ca., U.S.	California, U.S.
Cam.	Cameroon
Camb.	Cambodia
Can.	Canada
can.	canal
C.A.R.	Central African Republic
Cay. Is.	Cayman Islands
Christ. I.	Christmas Island
C. Iv.	Cote d'Ivoire
clf.	cliff, escarpment
Co., U.S.	Colorado, U.S.
co.	county, district, etc.
Cocos Is.	Cocos (Keeling) Islands
Col.	Colombia
Com.	Comoros
cont.	continent
Cook Is.	Cook Islands
C.R.	Costa Rica
crat.	crater
Cro.	Croatia
cst.	coast, beach
Ct., U.S.	Connecticut, U.S.
ctry.	independent country
C.V.	Cape Verde
cv.	cave
Cyp.	Cyprus
Czech Rep.	Czech Republic
D.C., U.S.	District of Columbia, U.S.
De., U.S.	Delaware, U.S.
Den.	Denmark
dep.	dependency, colony
depr.	depression
des.	desert
Dji.	Djibouti
Dom.	Dominica
Dom. Rep.	Dominican Republic
D.R.C.	Democratic Republic of the Congo
Ec.	Ecuador
El Sal.	El Salvador
Eng., U.K.	England, U.K.
Eq. Gui.	Equatorial Guinea
Erit.	Eritrea
Est.	Estonia
est.	estuary
Eth.	Ethiopia
E. Timor	East Timor
Eur.	Europe
Falk. Is.	Falkland Islands
Far. Is.	Faroe Islands
Fin.	Finland
Fl., U.S.	Florida, U.S.
for.	forest, moor
Fr.	France
Fr. Gu.	French Guiana
Fr. Poly.	French Polynesia
Ga., U.S.	Georgia, U.S.
Gam.	The Gambia
Gaza	Gaza Strip
Geor.	Georgia
Ger.	Germany
Gib.	Gibraltar
Golan	Golan Heights
Grc.	Greece

Gren.	Grenada
Grnld.	Greenland
Guad.	Guadeloupe
Guat.	Guatemala
Guern.	Guernsey
Gui.	Guinea
Gui.-B.	Guinea-Bissau
Guy.	Guyana
gysr.	geyser
Hi., U.S.	Hawaii, U.S.
hist.	historic site, ruins
hist. reg.	historic region
Hond.	Honduras
Hung.	Hungary
i.	island
Ia., U.S.	Iowa, U.S.
Ice.	Iceland
ice	ice feature, glacier
Id., U.S.	Idaho, U.S.
Il., U.S.	Illinois, U.S.
In., U.S.	Indiana, U.S.
Indon.	Indonesia
I. of Man	Isle of Man
Ire.	Ireland
is.	islands
Isr.	Israel
isth.	isthmus
Jam.	Jamaica
Jer.	Jericho Area
Jord.	Jordan
Kaz.	Kazakhstan
Kir.	Kiribati
Kor., N.	Korea, North
Kor., S.	Korea, South
Ks., U.S.	Kansas, U.S.
Kuw.	Kuwait
Ky., U.S.	Kentucky, U.S.
Kyrg.	Kyrgyzstan
l.	lake, pond
La., U.S.	Louisiana, U.S.
Lat.	Latvia
lav.	lava flow
Leb.	Lebanon
Leso.	Lesotho
Lib.	Liberia
Liech.	Liechtenstein
Lith.	Lithuania
Lux.	Luxembourg
Ma., U.S.	Massachusetts, U.S.
Mac.	Macedonia
Madag.	Madagascar
Malay.	Malaysia
Mald.	Maldives
Marsh. Is.	Marshall Islands
Mart.	Martinique
Maur.	Mauritania
May.	Mayotte
Mb., Can.	Manitoba, Can.
Md., U.S.	Maryland, U.S.
Me., U.S.	Maine, U.S.
Mex.	Mexico
Mi., U.S.	Michigan, U.S.
Micron.	Micronesia, Federated States of
Mid. Is.	Midway Islands
misc. cult.	miscellaneous cultural
Mn., U.S.	Minnesota, U.S.
Mo., U.S.	Missouri, U.S.
Mol.	Moldova
Mon.	Monaco
Mong.	Mongolia
Monts.	Montserrat
Mor.	Morocco
Moz.	Mozambique
Mrts.	Mauritius
Ms., U.S.	Mississippi, U.S.
Mt., U.S.	Montana, U.S.
mth.	river mouth or channel
mtn.	mountain
mts.	mountains
Mwi.	Malawi
Mya.	Myanmar
N.A.	North America
N.B., Can.	New Brunswick, Can.
N.C., U.S.	North Carolina, U.S.
N. Cal.	New Caledonia
N. Cyp.	North Cyprus
N.D., U.S.	North Dakota, U.S.
Ne., U.S.	Nebraska, U.S.
Neth.	Netherlands
Neth. Ant.	Netherlands Antilles
Nf., Can.	Newfoundland and Labrador, Can.
ngh.	neighborhood
N.H., U.S.	New Hampshire, U.S.
Nic.	Nicaragua
Nig.	Nigeria
N. Ire., U.K.	Northern Ireland, U.K.
N.J., U.S.	New Jersey, U.S.
N.M., U.S.	New Mexico, U.S.
N. Mar. Is.	Northern Mariana Islands
Nmb.	Namibia
Nor.	Norway
Norf. I.	Norfolk Island
N.S., Can.	Nova Scotia, Can.
N.T., Can.	Northwest Territories, Can.
Nu., Can.	Nunavut, Can.
Nv., U.S.	Nevada, U.S.
N.Y., U.S.	New York, U.S.
N.Z.	New Zealand
Oc.	Oceania

Oh., U.S.	Ohio, U.S.
Ok., U.S.	Oklahoma, U.S.
On., Can.	Ontario, Can.
Or., U.S.	Oregon, U.S.
p.	pass
Pa., U.S.	Pennsylvania, U.S.
Pak.	Pakistan
Pan.	Panama
Pap. N. Gui.	Papua New Guinea
Para.	Paraguay
P.E., Can.	Prince Edward Island, Can.
pen.	peninsula
Phil.	Philippines
Pit.	Pitcairn
pl.	plain, flat
plat.	plateau, highland
p.o.i.	point of interest
Pol.	Poland
Port.	Portugal
P.R.	Puerto Rico
Qc., Can.	Quebec, Can.
r.	rock, rocks
reg.	physical region
rel.	religious facility
res.	reservoir
Reu.	Reunion
rf.	reef, shoal
R.I., U.S.	Rhode Island, U.S.
Rom.	Romania
Rw.	Rwanda
s.	sea
S.A.	South America
S. Afr.	South Africa
sand	sand area
Sau. Ar.	Saudi Arabia
S.C., U.S.	South Carolina, U.S.
sci.	scientific station
Scot., U.K.	Scotland, U.K.
S.D., U.S.	South Dakota, U.S.
Sen.	Senegal
Serb.	Serbia and Montenegro
Sey.	Seychelles
S. Geor.	South Georgia
Sing.	Singapore
Sk., Can.	Saskatchewan, Can.
S.L.	Sierra Leone
Slov.	Slovakia
Slvn.	Slovenia
S. Mar.	San Marino
Sol. Is.	Solomon Islands
Som.	Somalia
Sp. N. Afr.	Spanish North Africa
Sri L.	Sri Lanka
state	state, province, etc.
St. Hel.	St. Helena
St. K./N.	St. Kitts and Nevis
St. Luc.	St. Lucia
stm.	stream (river, creek)
S. Tom./P.	Sao Tome and Principe
St. P./M.	St. Pierre and Miquelon
strt.	strait, channel, etc.
St. Vin.	St. Vincent and the Grenadines
Sur.	Suriname
sw.	swamp, marsh
Swaz.	Swaziland
Swe.	Sweden
Switz.	Switzerland
Tai.	Taiwan
Taj.	Tajikistan
Tan.	Tanzania
T./C. Is.	Turks and Caicos Islands
Thai.	Thailand
Tn., U.S.	Tennessee, U.S.
Tok.	Tokelau
Trin.	Trinidad and Tobago
Tun.	Tunisia
Tur.	Turkey
Turkmen.	Turkmenistan
Tx., U.S.	Texas, U.S.
U.A.E.	United Arab Emirates
Ug.	Uganda
U.K.	United Kingdom
Ukr.	Ukraine
unds.	undersea feature
Ur.	Uruguay
U.S.	United States
Ut., U.S.	Utah, U.S.
Uzb.	Uzbekistan
Va., U.S.	Virginia, U.S.
val.	valley, watercourse
Vat.	Vatican City
Ven.	Venezuela
Viet.	Vietnam
V.I.U.S.	Virgin Islands (U.S.)
vol.	volcano
Vt., U.S.	Vermont, U.S.
Wa., U.S.	Washington, U.S.
Wake I.	Wake Island
Wal./F.	Wallis and Futuna
W.B.	West Bank
well	well, spring, oasis
Wi., U.S.	Wisconsin, U.S.
W. Sah.	Western Sahara
wtfl.	waterfall, rapids
W.V., U.S.	West Virginia, U.S.
Wy., U.S.	Wyoming, U.S.
Yk., Can.	Yukon Territory, Can.
Zam.	Zambia
Zimb.	Zimbabwe

Index

A

Name | Map Ref. | Page

Å, Nor. — C5 8
Aabenraa, Den. — I3 8
Aachen, Ger. — F1 16
Aalborg, Den. — H4 8
Aalborg Bugt, b., Den. — H4 8
Aalen, Ger. — H6 16
Aali, Sadd el- (Aswan High Dam), dam, Egypt — C6 62
Aalst (Alost), Bel. — D13 14
Äänekoski, Fin. — E11 8
Aarau, Switz. — C4 22
Aare, stm., Switz. — C5 22
Aarlen see Arlon, Bel. — E14 14
Aarschot, Bel. — D14 14
Aasiaat see Egedesminde, Grnld. — D15 141
Aat see Ath, Bel. — D12 14
Aba, China — E5 36
Aba, D.R.C. — D6 66
Aba, Nig. — H6 64
Abā al-Bawl, Qurayn, hill, Qatar. — E7 56
Abacaxis, stm., Braz. — E6 84
Abaco, i., Bah. — B9 96
Abacou, Pointe, c., Haiti. — D10 102
Abadab, Jabal, mtn., Sudan — D7 62
Ābādān, Iran — C6 56
Ābādeh, Iran — C7 56
Abadla, Alg. — C4 64
Abaeté, Braz. — J3 88
Abaeté, stm., Braz. — J3 88
Abaetetuba, Braz. — A1 88
Abag Qi, China. — C7 36
Abaí, Para. — C10 92
Abaj see Abay, Kaz. — E12 32
Abakaliki, Nig. — H6 64
Abakan, Russia. — D16 32
Abakan, stm., Russia — D15 32
Abakanovo, Russia — A20 10
Abakanskij hrebet, mts., Russia — D15 32
Abala, Niger — G5 64
Abalak, Niger — F6 64
Aban, Russia — C17 32
Abancay, Peru — F3 84
Abashiri, Japan — B16 38
Abasolo, Mex. — C6 100
Abasolo, Mex. — H7 130
Abasolo, Mex. — G6 130
Abau, Pap. N. Gui. — c4 79a
Abay, Kaz. — E12 32
Abay see Blue Nile, stm., Afr. — E6 62
Abaya, Lake see Ābaya Hāyk', l., Eth. — F7 62
Ābaya Hāyk', l., Eth. — F7 62
Abaza, Russia — D15 32
Abbadia San Salvatore, Italy — H8 22
Abbé, Lac see Abe, Lake, l., Afr. — E8 62
Abbeville, Fr. — D10 14
Abbeville, Ga., U.S. — D2 116
Abbeville, La., U.S. — H6 122
Abbeville, S.C., U.S. — B3 116
Abbey, Sk., Can. — D5 124
Abbeyfeale, Ire. — I3 12
Abbiategrasso, Italy — E5 22
Abbot, Mount, mtn., Austl. — B6 76
Abbot Ice Shelf, ice, Ant. — C31 81
Abbotsford, B.C., Can. — G8 138
Abbottābād, Pak. — A4 54
'Abd al-Kūrī, i., Yemen — G7 56
Ābdira, sci., Grc. — B7 28
Abdulino, Russia — D8 32
Abe, Lake, l., Afr. — E8 62
Abéché, Chad. — E4 62
Abel Tasman National Park, p.o.i., N.Z. — E5 80
Abemama, at., Kir. — C8 72
Abengourou, C. Iv. — H4 64
Abenojar, Spain. — F6 20
Abensberg, Ger. — H7 16
Abeokuta, Nig. — H5 64
Aberdare, Wales, U.K. — J9 12
Aberdeen, S. Afr. — H7 70
Aberdeen, Scot., U.K. — D10 12
Aberdeen, Id., U.S. — H14 136
Aberdeen, Md., U.S. — E9 114
Aberdeen, Ms., U.S. — D10 122
Aberdeen, N.C., U.S. — A6 116
Aberdeen, S.D., U.S. — B14 126
Aberdeen, Wa., U.S. — D3 136
Aberdeen Lake, l., Nu., Can. — C10 106
Aberdeen Lake, res., Ms., U.S. — D10 122
Aberfeldy, Scot., U.K. — E9 12
Abergavenny, Wales, U.K. — J9 12
Abernant, Al., U.S. — D11 122
Abernathy, Tx., U.S. — H7 128
Abernethy, Sk., Can. — D10 124
Abert, Lake, l., Or., U.S. — H6 136
Aberystwyth, Wales, U.K. — I8 12
Abez', Russia — A10 32
Abhā, Sau. Ar. — F5 56
Abidjan, C. Iv. — H4 64
Abilene, Tx., U.S. — B8 130
Abingdon, Eng., U.K. — J11 12
Abingdon, Il., U.S. — D7 120
Abingdon, Va., U.S. — H4 114
Abiquiu, N.M., U.S. — E2 128
Abiquiu Reservoir, res., N.M., U.S. — E2 128
Abisko, Swe. — B8 8
Abitibi, stm., On., Can. — E14 106
Abitibi, Lake, l., Can. — F15 106
Abja-Paluoja, Est. — B8 10
Abnūb, Egypt. — K2 58
Åbo see Turku, Fin. — F9 8
Abohar, India — C5 54
Abomey, Benin. — H5 64
Abongabong, Gunung, mtn., Indon. — J3 48
Abong Mbang, Cam. — D2 66
Abony, Hung. — B6 26
Aborigen, pik, mtn., Russia — D18 34
Abou-Deïa, Chad. — E3 62
Abou Simbel (Abu Simbel), sci., Egypt. — C6 62
Abraham Lake, res., Ab., Can. — D14 138
Abra Pampa, Arg. — D3 90
Abre Campo, Braz. — K4 88
Abreu e Lima, Braz. — D8 88
Abring, India — B6 54
Abrud, Rom. — C10 26
Abruzzo, state, Italy — H10 22
Abruzzo, Parco Nazionale d', p.o.i., Italy — C7 24
Absaroka Range, mts., U.S. — C3 126
Absecon, N.J., U.S. — E11 114
Abū 'Alī, i., Sau. Ar. — D6 56
Abū Ballāş, mtn., Egypt. — C5 62
Abu Dhabi see Abū Ẓaby, U.A.E. — E7 56
Abū Dulayq, Sudan — D6 62
Abū al-Hul (Sphinx), hist., Egypt. — I1 58
Abufari, Braz. — E5 84
Abū Ḥammād, Egypt. — H2 58
Abuja, Nig. — H6 64
Abū Jubayhah, Sudan — E6 62

Abū Kamāl, Syria — C5 56
Abukuma, stm., Japan — B13 40
Abukuma-kōchi, plat., Japan — B13 40
Abū Madd, Ra's, c., Sau. Ar. — E4 56
Abu Mendi, Eth. — E7 62
Abunã, Braz. — E4 84
Abu Qīr, Khalīj, b., Egypt — G1 58
Abu Qurāṣ, Egypt — K1 58
Abu Road, India — F4 54
Abū Rubayq, Sau. Ar. — E4 56
Abū Shajarah Ra's, c., Sudan — C7 62
Abū Shāma, Gebel, mtn., Egypt — I2 58
Abu Simbel see Abou Simbel, sci., Egypt. — C6 62
Abu Tīg, Egypt. — K2 58
Abū Zabad, Sudan. — E5 62
Abū Zaby (Abu Dhabi), U.A.E. — E7 56
Abwong, Sudan — F6 62
Abyei, Sudan — F5 62
Abyssinia see Ethiopia, ctry., Afr. — F7 62
Acacias, Col. — E5 86
Acadia National Park, p.o.i., Me., U.S. — F8 110
Acadia Valley, Ab., Can. — C3 124
Açailândia, Braz. — C2 88
Acajutiba, Braz. — F7 88
Acámbaro, Mex. — E8 100
Acandí, Col. — C3 86
Acaponeta, Mex. — D6 100
Acaponeta, stm., Mex. — D6 100
Acapulco de Juárez, Mex. — G8 100
Acará, Braz. — A1 88
Acará, stm., Braz. — A1 88
Acaraí Mountains, mts., S.A. — C6 84
Acará-Mirim, stm., Braz. — B1 88
Acaraú, Braz. — B5 88
Acaraú, stm., Braz. — B5 88
Acaray, stm., Para. — B10 92
Acarí, Peru — G3 84
Acarí, stm., Braz. — B3 88
Acarigua, Ven. — C7 86
Acatlán de Osorio, Mex. — F9 100
Acay, Nevado de, mtn., Arg. — B4 92
Acayucan, Mex. — F11 100
Acceglio, Italy — F3 22
Accomac, Va., U.S. — G10 114
Accra, Ghana — H5 64
Acebuches, Mex. — A7 100
Acegua, Braz. — E10 92
Aceh, state, Indon. — J3 48
Acerra, Italy — D8 24
Achacachi, Bol. — C3 90
Achaguas, Ven. — D7 86
Achalpur, India. — H6 54
Achar, Ur. — F9 92
Acharnés, Grc. — E6 28
Acheloós, stm., Grc. — E4 28
Acheng, China — B7 38
Achern, Ger. — H4 16
Achill Head, c., Ire. — G2 12
Achill Island, i., Ire. — H2 12
Achiras, Arg. — F5 92
Achit nuur, l., Mong. — E16 32
Achwa, stm., Afr. — D6 66
Ata Göl, l., Tur. — F12 28
Ačinsk, Russia — C16 32
Acıpayam, Tur. — F12 28
Acireale, Italy — G9 24
Ackerly, Tx., U.S. — B6 130
Ackley, Ia., U.S. — B4 120
Acklins, i., Bah. — C10 96
Acklins, Bight of, b., Bah. — A10 102
Acme, Ab., Can. — E17 138
Aconcagua, Cerro, mtn., Arg. — F3 92
Aconchi, Mex. — G7 98
Acopiara, Braz. — D6 88
Açores (Azores), is., Port. — C3 60
Acorizal, Braz. — G6 84
A Coruña (Corunna), Spain — A2 20
A Coruña, co., Spain — A2 20
Acquasanta Terme, Italy — H10 22
Acqui Terme, Italy — F5 22
Acre see 'Akko, Isr. — F6 58
Acre, state, Braz. — E4 84
Acre, stm., S.A. — F4 84
Acri, Italy — E10 24
Acton Vale, Qc., Can. — E4 110
Actopan, Mex. — E9 100
Açucena, Braz. — J4 88
Acuña, Arg. — D8 92
Ada, Mn., U.S. — D2 118
Ada, Oh., U.S. — D2 114
Ada, Ok., U.S. — C2 122
Adaba, Eth. — F7 62
Adair, Ia., U.S. — C3 120
Adair, Bahía de, b., Mex. — F6 98
Adair, Cape, c., Nu., Can. — A16 106
Adairsville, Ga., U.S. — C14 122
Adairville, Ky., U.S. — H11 120
Adak Island, i., Ak., U.S. — g23 140a
Adam, Oman — E8 56
Adamantina, Braz. — D6 90
Adamaoua, mts., Afr. — C2 66
Adamclisi, Rom. — E14 26
Adamello, mts., Italy — D7 22
Adaminaby, Austl. — K7 76
Adams, Mn., U.S. — H6 118
Adams, N.D., U.S. — F15 124
Adams, N.Y., U.S. — E13 112
Adams, Tn., U.S. — H10 120
Adams, Mount, vol, Wa., U.S. — D5 136
Adam's Bridge, rf., Asia — G4 53
Adams Lake, l., B.C., Can. — E11 138
Adams Peak, mtn., Sri L. — H5 53
Adams Rock, r., Pit. — c28 78k
Adamstown, Pit. — c28 78k
Adamsville, Tn., U.S. — B10 122
'Adan (Aden), Yemen — G6 56
Adana, Tur. — A6 58
Adana, state, Tur. — A6 58
Adarama, Sudan — D6 62
Adare, Cape, c., Ant. — C22 81
Adavale, Austl. — E5 76
Adda, stm., Italy — E6 22
Ad-Dabbah, Sudan — D6 62
Ad-Dahnā', des., Sau. Ar. — D6 56
Ad-Dāmir, Sudan — D6 62
Ad-Dammām, Sau. Ar. — D7 58
Ad-Dānā, Syria — B7 58
Ad-Dawhah (Doha), Qatar — D7 56
Ad-Dibdibah, reg., Sau. Ar. — D6 56
Addis Ababa see Ādīs Ābeba, Eth. — F7 62
Addis Abeba see Ādīs Ābeba, Eth. — F7 62
Addison, N.Y., U.S. — F5 112
Ad-Dīwānīyah, Iraq — C6 56
Addo Elephant National Park, p.o.i., S. Afr. — H7 70
Ad-Du'ayn, Sudan — E5 62
Ad-Duwaym, Sudan — E6 62
Adel, Ga., U.S. — E2 116
Adelaide, Austl. — J2 76
Adelaide, Bah. — n18 104f
Adelaide Island, i., Ant. — B33 81
Adelaide Peninsula, pen., Nu., Can. — B11 106
Adelaide River, Austl. — B6 74
Adèle Island, i., Austl. — C4 74
Adélie, Terre, cst., Ant. — B18 81

Adelie Coast see Adélie, Terre, cst., Ant. — B18 81
Adelong, Austl. — J6 76
Aden see 'Adan, Yemen. — G6 56
Aden, Gulf of, b. — E9 62
Adendorp, S. Afr. — H7 70
Adi, Pulau, i., Indon. — F9 44
Adiaké, C. Iv. — H4 64
Adige (Etsch), stm., Italy — E8 22
Adigrat, Eth. — E7 62
Adıgüzel Baraji, res., Tur. — E12 28
Adilābād, India. — B4 53
Adimi, Russia. — G16 34
Adin, Ca., U.S. — B5 134
Adirondack Mountains, mts., N.Y., U.S. — E15 112
Ādīs Ābeba (Addis Abeba), Eth. — F7 62
Adi Ugri, Erit. — E7 62
Adıyaman, Tur. — A9 58
Adıyaman, state, Tur. — A9 58
Adjuntas, Presa de las see Vicente Guerrero, Presa, res., Mex. — D9 100
Admiral, Sk., Can. — E5 124
Admiralty Gulf, b., Austl. — B5 74
Admiralty Inlet, b., Nu., Can. — A13 106
Admiralty Island, i., Nu., Can. — B10 106
Admiralty Island, i., Ak., U.S. — E13 140
Admiralty Islands, is., Pap. N. Gui. — a4 79a
Ado, Nig. — H5 64
Ado-Ekiti, Nig. — H6 64
Adolfo Gonzales Chaves, Arg. — H7 92
Adolfo López Mateos, Mex. — A5 100
Adolfo López Mateos, Presa, res., Mex. — C5 100
Adolfo Rodríguez Sáa see Santa Rosa del Conlara, Arg. — F5 92
Ādoni, India — D3 53
Adour, stm., Fr. — F4 18
Adra, India — G11 54
Adra, Spain — H7 20
Adrano, Italy — G8 24
Adrar, Alg. — D4 64
Adrār, reg., Maur. — E2 64
Adria, Italy — E9 22
Adrian, Mi., U.S. — C1 114
Adrian, Mo., U.S. — F3 120
Adrian, Or., U.S. — G9 136
Adrian, Tx., U.S. — F6 128
Adrian, W.V., U.S. — F5 114
Adriatic Sea, s., Eur. — G11 22
A Dun, stm., Viet. — F9 48
Adutiškis, Lith. — E9 10
Advance, Mo., U.S. — G7 120
Advocate Harbour, N.S., Can. — E11 110
Ādwa, Eth. — E7 62
Adycha, stm., Russia — C16 34
Adygea see Adygeja, state, Russia — F6 32
Adygeja, state, Russia — F6 32
Adygheya see Adygeja, state, Russia — F6 32
Adzopé, C. Iv. — H4 64
Aegean Sea, s. — E7 28
Aegina see Aígina, i., Grc. — F6 28
Aegviidu, Est. — A8 10
Aên, ostrov, i., Russia — B22 34
Aerku hu, l., China. — C9 54
Ærø, i., Den. — I4 8
Ærøskøbing, Den. — I4 8
A Estrada, Spain — B2 20
Aetna, Ab., Can. — G17 138
Afaahiti, Fr. Poly. — v22 78h
Afadjoto, mtn., Ghana — H5 64
Afareaitu, Fr. Poly. — v20 78h
Afars and Issas see Djibouti, ctry., Afr. — E8 62
Affton, Mo., U.S. — F7 120
Afghanistan, ctry., Asia — C9 56
Afgooye, Som. — D8 66
Afikpo, Nig. — H6 64
Aflou, Alg. — C5 64
Afmadow, Som. — D8 66
Afogados da Ingazeira, Braz. — D7 88
Afognak Island, i., Ak., U.S. — E9 140
Afonina, Russia — B25 8
A Fonsagrada, Spain — A3 20
Africa, cont. — F14 4
'Afrīn, Syria — B7 58
Afton, N.Y., U.S. — B10 114
Afton, Ok., U.S. — H2 120
Afton, Wy., U.S. — H16 136
'Afula, Isr. — F6 58
Afyon, state, Tur. — E13 28
Afyon, state, Tur. — E13 28
Agadez, Niger — F6 64
Agadir, Mor. — C2 64
Agadīr, Ràs, c., Maur. — E1 64
Agadyr', Kaz. — E12 32
Agalak, Sudan — E6 62
Agalega Islands, is., Mrts. — K8 142
Agan, stm., Russia — B13 32
Agana see Hagåtña, Guam — j10 78c
Agana Heights, Guam — j10 78c
Agano, stm., Japan — B12 40
Agapa, Russia — B6 34
Aga Point, c., Guam — k10 78c
Agar, India — G5 54
Agartala, India — G13 54
Agassiz, B.C., Can. — G9 138
Agassiz Pool, res., Mn., U.S. — C3 118
Agate Fossil Beds National Monument, p.o.i., Ne., U.S. — G4 126
Agawa Bay, b., On., Can. — A5 112
Agawam, Mt., U.S. — B14 136
Agboville, C. Iv. — H4 64
Ağdam, Azer. — B6 56
Ageevo, Russia — F19 10
Agen, Fr. — E6 18
Agency Lake, l., Or., U.S. — H5 136
Aggeneys, S. Afr. — F4 70
Aggteleki Nemzeti Park, p.o.i., Hung. — A7 26
Āghā Jārī, Iran — C6 56
Agia Marina, Grc. — F9 28
Agiásos, Grc. — D10 28
Agio Óros, state, Grc. — C7 28
Agio Óros, pen., Grc. — C7 28
Agios Nikólaos, Grc. — H8 28
Agiou Órous, Kólpos (Singitic Gulf), b., Grc. — C6 28
Aglasun, Tur. — F13 28
Agnes Lake, l., On., Can. — C7 118
Agnibilékrou, C. Iv. — H4 64
Agnita, Rom. — D11 26
Agno, stm., Phil. — C3 52
Ago, Japan — E9 40
Agogna, stm., Italy — E5 22
Agou, Mont, mtn., Togo. — H5 64
Agout, stm., Fr. — F8 18
Agra, India — E6 54
Agraciada, Ur. — F9 92
Agreda, Spain — B8 20
Āgri, Tur. — B5 56
Agri, stm., Italy — D9 24
Ağri Daği (Ararat, Mount), mtn., Tur. — B5 56
Agrigento, Italy — G7 24
Agrihan, i., N. Mar. Is. — B5 72
Agrínio, Grc. — E4 28

Agrio, stm., Arg. — H2 92
Agrópoli, Italy — D9 24
Agro Pontino, reg., Italy — C6 24
Agto, Grnld. — D15 141
Agua Branca, Braz. — C4 88
Agua Caliente, Mex. — B4 100
Agua Caliente Grande, Mex. — B4 100
Aguachica, Col. — C5 86
Agua Clara, Braz. — D6 90
Aguada Cecilio, Arg. — H3 90
Aguada de Guerra, Arg. — H3 90
Aguada de Pasajeros, Cuba. — A7 102
Aguadas, Col. — E4 86
Aguadilla, P.R. — B1 104a
Agua Doce, Braz. — C12 92
Aguadulce, Pan. — H7 102
Agua Dulce, stm., Az., U.S. — I4 132
Agua Fria, stm., Az., U.S. — G9 130
Agua Fria National Monument, p.o.i., Az., U.S. — I5 132
Aguaí, Braz. — L2 88
Agualeguas, Mex. — H8 130
Aguán, stm., Hond. — E4 102
Aguanaval, stm., Mex. — C7 100
Aguapey, stm., Arg. — D9 92
Água Preta, Igarapé, stm., Braz. — H9 86
Agua Prieta, Mex. — F8 98
Aguaray Guazú, stm., Para. — A9 92
A Guarda, Spain. — C1 20
Aguaro-Guariquito, Parque Nacional, p.o.i., Ven. — C8 86
Aguaruto, Mex. — C5 100
Aguasabon, stm., On., Can. — C11 118
Águas Belas, Braz. — E7 88
Aguas Buenas, P.R. — B3 104a
Aguascalientes, Mex. — E7 100
Aguascalientes, state, Mex. — D7 100
Aguas Formosas, Braz. — I5 88
Água Vermelha, Represa de, res., Braz. — C6 90
Aguayo, Arg. — D7 92
Agu Bay, b., Nu., Can. — A13 106
Agudos, Braz. — L1 88
Águeda, stm., Eur. — D4 20
Aguelhok, Mali — F5 64
Aguilar, Co., U.S. — D4 128
Aguilar de la Frontera, Spain — G6 20
Aguilares, Arg. — C5 92
Águilas, Spain. — G9 20
Aguililla, Mex. — F7 100
Aguja, Punta, c., Peru — E1 84
Agujereada, Punta, c., P.R. — A1 104a
Aguita, Mex. — G6 130
Agulhas, Kaap, c., S. Afr. — I5 70
Agulhas Basin, unds. — M15 144
Agulhas Negras, Pico das, mtn., Braz. — L3 88
Agung, Gunung, vol., Indon. — G6 44
Agusan, stm., Phil. — F5 52
Agustín Codazzi, Col. — C5 86
Ağva, Tur. — B12 28
Ahaggar, mts., Alg. — E6 64
Ahaggar, Tassili ta-n-, plat., Alg. — E5 64
Ahanta, Gor. — F6 32
Ahar, Iran. — B6 56
Ahaus, Ger. — D2 16
Ahipara Bay, b., N.Z. — B5 80
Ahlen, Ger. — E3 16
Ahmadābād, India — G4 54
Ahmadnagar, India — B2 53
Ahmadpur East, Pak. — D3 54
Ahmadpur Siāl, Pak. — D3 54
Ahmar Mountains, mts., Eth. — F8 62
Ahmetli, Tur. — E10 28
Ahmic Lake, l., On., Can. — C10 112
Ahoskie, N.C., U.S. — H9 114
Ahousat, B.C., Can. — G4 138
Ahraura, India — F9 54
Ahtuba, stm., Russia — E7 32
Ahtubinsk, Russia — E7 32
Ahuacatlán, Mex. — E6 100
Ahumada, Mex. — D1 130
Ahunui, at., Fr. Poly. — E12 72
Ahvāz, Iran — C6 56
Ahvenanmaa see Åland, state, Fin. — F9 8
Ahvenanmaa see Åland, is., Fin. — F8 8
Ahwar, Yemen — G6 56
Ahwa-ri, Kor., S. — D2 40
Ä i Åfjord, Nor. — D4 8
Aibonito, P.R. — B3 104a
Aichi, state, Japan — D10 40
Aidong, China — I2 42
'Aiea, Hi., U.S. — b3 78a
Aigina, i., Grc. — F6 28
Aígina, i., Grc. — F6 28
Aigio, Grc. — E5 28
Aigle, Switz. — D3 22
Aigle, stm., Qc., Can. — A1 110
Aiguá, Ur. — G10 92
Aigüestortes i Estany Sant Maurici, Parque Nacional d', p.o.i., Spain — B11 20
Aigüestortes i Llac de Sant Maurici, Parc Nacional d' see Aigüestortes i Esta, p.o.i., Spain. — B11 20
Aikawa, Japan — A11 40
Aiken, S.C., U.S. — C4 116
Aikens Lake, l., Mb., Can. — C18 124
Ailao Shan, mts., China — G5 36
Aileron, Austl. — D6 74
Ailinglaplap, at., Marsh. Is. — C7 72
Ailsa Craig, On., Can. — E8 112
Ailsa Craig, i., Scot., U.K. — F7 12
Aim, Russia. — E15 34
Aimorés, Braz. — J5 88
Aín, stm., Fr. — D11 18
Aïn Benian, Alg. — H13 20
Aïn Defla, Alg. — H12 20
Aïn Draham, Tun. — H2 24
Aïn el Beïda, Alg. — B6 64
Ainslie Lake, l., N.S., Can. — D15 110
Aïn Temouchent, Alg. — C3 64
Aioi, Japan — E7 40
Aiora, Spain — E9 20
Aïr, Massif de l', mts., Niger — F6 64
Airai Airport, Palau — g8 78b
Airbangis, Indon. — C1 50
Airdrie, Ab., Can. — E16 138
Aire, stm., Fr. — F14 14
Aire, stm., Eng., U.K. — H11 12
Aire-sur-l'Adour, Fr. — F5 18
Air Force Island, i., Nu., Can. — B16 106
Airhaji, Indon. — D2 50
Airlie Beach, Austl. — C7 76
Airolo, Switz. — D5 22

Aitkin, Mn., U.S. — E5 118
Aitoliko, Grc. — E4 28
Aitutaki, at., Cook Is. — E11 72
Aiuaba, Braz. — D5 88
Aiud, Rom. — C10 26
Aix-en-Provence, Fr. — F11 18
Aix, Île d', i., Fr. — C4 18
Aix-la-Chapelle see Aachen, Ger. — F1 16
Aix-les-Bains, Fr. — D11 18
Āīzawl, India — G14 54
Aizkraukle, Lat. — D8 10
Aizu-bange, Japan — B12 40
Aizu-wakamatsu, Japan — B12 40
Ajaccio, Fr. — H14 18
Ajaccio, Golfe d', b., Fr. — H14 18
Ajaguz see Ayaköz, Kaz. — E13 32
Ajajú, stm., Col. — G5 86
Ajan, Russia — E16 34
Ajanta, India — H5 54
Ajanta Caves, hist., India — H5 54
Ajanta Range, mts., India — H5 54
Ajari, stm., Braz. — E10 112
Ajdābiyā, Libya — A4 62
Ajdyrlinskij, Russia — D9 32
Ajka, Hung. — B4 26
'Ajlūn, Jord. — F6 58
Ajmer, India — E5 54
Ajnāla, India — C5 54
Ajo, Az., U.S. — K4 132
Ajos, Blg. — G14 26
Ajusco, Mex. — L9 134
Akabira, Japan — C15 38
Akabli, Alg. — D5 64
Akademii, zaliv, b., Russia — F16 34
Akagi-san, vol., Japan — C12 40
Akaishi-sammyaku, mts., Japan — D11 40
Ak'ak'ī Besek'a, Eth. — F7 62
Akalkot, India — C2 53
Akamas, Akrotírion, c., Cyp. — C3 58
Akan-kokuritsu-kōen, p.o.i., Japan — C16 38
Akasha East, Sudan — C6 62
'Akāshāt, Iraq — C5 56
Akashi, Japan — E7 40
Akbarpur, India — E9 54
Akbulak, Russia — D9 32
Akçakale, Tur. — B9 58
Akçakoca, Tur. — B14 28
Akçakoyunlu, Tur. — B8 58
Akçay, Tur. — F11 28
Akçay, stm., Tur. — G12 28
Akçay, stm., Tur. — F11 28
Akchâr, reg., Maur. — E2 64
Ak-Dovurak, Russia — D15 32
Akeley, Mn., U.S. — D4 118
Aken, Ger. — E8 16
Akershus, state, Nor. — F4 8
Aketi, D.R.C. — D4 66
Akhaltsikhe see Ahalcihe, Geor. — F6 32
Akhisar see Ahisar, Tur. — E10 28
Akhmîm, Egypt — B7 62
Akhtubinsk see Ahtubinsk, Russia — E7 32
Aki, Japan — F6 40
Akimiski Island, i., Nu., Can. — E14 106
Akıncı Burun, c., Tur. — B6 58
Akita, Japan — E13 38
Akjoujt, Maur. — F2 64
Akkeshi, Japan — C16 38
'Akko, Isr. — F6 58
Akkoy, Tur. — F10 28
Aklavik, N.T., Can. — B4 106
'Aklé 'Aouâna, reg., Afr. — F3 64
Akmenrags, c., Lat. — D3 10
Akmolinsk see Astana, Kaz. — D12 32
Akō, Japan — E7 40
Akobo (Akūbū), stm., Afr. — F6 62
Akola, India — H6 54
Akonolinga, Cam. — D2 66
Akordat, Erit. — D7 62
Akören, Tur. — F15 28
Akot, India — H6 54
Akpatok Island, i., Nu., Can. — C17 106
Akranes, Ice. — k28 8a
Akrérèb, Niger — F6 64
Akritas, Ákra, c., Grc. — G4 28
Akron, Co., U.S. — A5 128
Akron, In., U.S. — G4 112
Akron, Oh., U.S. — C4 114
Akrotíri, Cyp. — D3 58
Akša, Russia — F11 34
Aksaray, Tur. — B3 56
Aksay, Kaz. — D8 32
Akşehir, Tur. — E14 28
Akşehir Gölü, l., Tur. — E14 28
Akseki, Tur. — F14 28
Aksu, China — F14 32
Aksu, stm., Tur. — F14 28
Aksu, stm., Tur. — A8 58
Aktau see Aqtaū, Kaz. — F8 32
Aktjubinsk see Aqtöbe, Kaz. — D9 32
Aktogaj, Kaz. — D12 32
Akūbū (Akobo), stm., Afr. — F6 62
Akune, Japan — G3 40
Akureyri, Ice. — k30 8a
Akutan Island, i., Ak., U.S. — F6 140
Akwanga, Nig. — H6 64
Akyazı, Tur. — C13 28
Å, Nor. — F3 8
Alabama, state, U.S. — E11 122
Alabama, stm., Al., U.S. — F11 122
Alabaster, Al., U.S. — D12 122

Alakol', ozero see Alaköl köli, l., Kaz. — E14 32
Alaköl köli, l., Kaz. — E14 32
Al-'Akrīshah, Egypt. — G1 58
Alaktara, India — H9 54
Alakurtti, Russia. — C13 8
'Alalakeiki Channel, strt., Hi., U.S. — c5 78a
Alalaú, stm., Braz. — H11 86
Alamagan, i., N. Mar. Is. — B5 72
Alameda, Ca., U.S. — F3 134
Alameda, Sk., Can. — E10 124
Alamo, Mex. — D9 100
Alamo, Ga., U.S. — D3 116
Alamo, Tn., U.S. — B9 122
Alamo, Nv., U.S. — K1 132
Alamogordo, N.M., U.S. — B2 130
Alamo Heights, Tx., U.S. — E9 130
Alamo Lake, res., Az., U.S. — I3 132
Álamos, Mex. — B4 100
Álamos, stm., Mex. — A8 100
Alamosa, Co., U.S. — D3 128
Alamosa, stm., Co., U.S. — D3 128
Álamos de Márquez, Mex. — A7 100
Åland, state, Fin. — F9 8
Åland (Ahvenanmaa), is., Fin. — F8 8
Åland Islands see Åland, is., Fin. — F8 8
Åland Sea, s., Eur. — G8 8
Alandur, India — E5 53
Alanya, Tur. — G15 28
Alaotra, Farihy, l., Madag. — D8 68
Alapaevsk, Russia — C10 32
Alapaha, Ga., U.S. — E2 116
Alapaha, stm., U.S. — E2 116
Alappuzha see Alleppey, India — G3 53
Al-'Aqabah, Jord. — I6 58
Alarcón, Embalse de, res., Spain — E8 20
Alas, Selat, strt., Indon. — H10 50
Alashankou, China — C5 36
Alashtar, Iran. — C6 56
Alaska, state, U.S. — D9 140
Alaska, Gulf of, b., Ak., U.S. — E10 140
Alaska Peninsula, pen., Ak., U.S. — E7 140
Alaska Range, mts., Ak., U.S. — D9 140
Alassio, Italy — F5 22
Alatan'aola see Xin Barag Youqi, China. — B8 36
Alatri, Italy — I10 22
Alatyr', Russia — D7 32
Alausí, Ec. — I2 86
Alava, Cape, c., Wa., U.S. — B2 136
Álava, co., see Araba/Álava, co., Spain — B8 20
Al-'Ayn, U.A.E. — E8 56
Alayor see Alaior, Spain — E15 20
Alazeja, stm., Russia — B19 34
Al-'Azīzīyah, Libya — A2 62
Alba, Mi., U.S. — D5 112
Alba, Tx., U.S. — E3 122
Alba, state, Rom. — C10 26
Alba, Italy — F5 22
Al-Bāb, Syria — B8 58
Albacete, Spain — E9 20
Albacete, co., Spain — F9 20
Al-Bad', Sau. Ar. — J6 58
Alba de Tormes, Spain — D5 20
Alba Iulia, Rom. — C10 26
Al-Balqā', state, Jord. — F6 58
Al-Bālū'ah, l., Syria — C7 58
Albanel, Lac, l., Qc., Can. — E16 106
Albania, ctry., Eur. — C14 24
Albano Laziale, Italy — I9 22
Albany, Austl. — F3 74
Albany, Ga., U.S. — E1 116
Albany, Ky., U.S. — H12 120
Albany, Mn., U.S. — F4 118
Albany, Mo., U.S. — D3 120
Albany, N.Y., U.S. — B12 114
Albany, Or., U.S. — F3 136
Albany, Tx., U.S. — B8 130
Albany, stm., On., Can. — E14 106
Albarracín, Spain — D9 20
Al-Başrah (Basra), Iraq — C6 56
Al-Batrā' (Petra), sci., Jord. — H6 58
Albatross Bay, b., Austl. — B8 74
Al-Baydā', Libya — A4 62
Al-Baydā', Yemen — G6 56
Albemarle, N.C., U.S. — A5 116
Albemarle Island see Isabela, Isla, i., Ec. — i11 84a
Albemarle Sound, strt., N.C., U.S. — H9 114
Albenga, Italy — F5 22
Alberche, stm., Spain — D6 20
Alberdi, Para. — C8 92
Alberga Creek, stm., Austl. — E6 74
Albergaria-a-Velha, Port. — D2 20
Alberni Inlet, b., B.C., Can. — G6 138
Alberobello, Italy — D11 24
Albert, Fr. — E11 14
Albert, Lake, l., Afr. — D6 66
Albert, Lake, l., Austl. — J2 76
Alberta, Al., U.S. — E11 122
Alberta, Mount, mtn., Ab., Can. — D13 138
Albert Canyon, B.C., Can. — E13 138
Albert City, Ia., U.S. — I3 118
Albert Edward Bay, b., Nu., Can. — B10 106
Alberti, Arg. — G7 92
Albertina, Hung. — B6 26
Albertkanaal, can., Bel. — D14 14
Albert Lea, Mn., U.S. — H5 118
Albert Nile, stm., Afr. — D6 66
Alberton, P.E., Can. — D12 110
Albertville, Al., U.S. — C12 122
Albi, Fr. — F8 18
Albia, Ia., U.S. — C5 120
Albin, Wy., U.S. — F8 126
Albina, Sur. — B7 84
Albina, Ponta, c., Ang. — D1 68
Albion, Ca., U.S. — D2 134
Albion, Il., U.S. — F9 120
Albion, In., U.S. — G4 112
Albion, Mi., U.S. — B1 114
Albion, N.Y., U.S. — E11 112
Albion, Ne., U.S. — F15 126
Albion, Wa., U.S. — D9 136
Al-Biqā' (Bekaa Valley), val., Leb. — D7 58
Al-Bi'r, Sau. Ar. — J7 58
Al-Bocascar, Spain — D10 20
Alborán Sea, s. — B4 64
Alborz, Reshteh-ye Kūhhā-ye, mts., Iran — B7 56
Albufeira, Port. — G2 20
Albuñol, Spain — H7 20
Albuquerque, Cayos de, is., Col. — F6 102
Alburquerque, Spain — E3 20
Albury, Austl. — J6 76
Alcains, Port. — D3 20
Alcalá de Guadaira, Spain — G5 20
Alcalá de Henares, Spain — D7 20
Alcalá la Real, Spain — G7 20
Alcalde, N.M., U.S. — E3 128

Alcamo – Angemuk I • 3

Name	Map Ref.	Page
Alcamo, Italy	G6	24
Alcanar, Spain	D11	20
Alcañices, Spain	C4	20
Alcañiz, Spain	C10	20
Alcântara, Braz.	B3	88
Alcántara, Spain	E3	20
Alcantarilla, Spain	G9	20
Alcaraz, Spain	F8	20
Alcaudete, Spain	G6	20
Alcázar de San Juan, Spain	E7	20
Alcester, S.D., U.S.	A1	120
Alcira, Arg.	F5	92
Alcira *see* Alzira, Spain	E10	20
Alcobaça, Braz.	I6	88
Alcobendas, Spain	D7	20
Alcoi, Spain	F10	20
Alcolea del Pinar, Spain	C8	20
Alcolu, S.C., U.S.	C5	116
Alcorn, Ms., U.S.	F7	122
Alcorta, Arg.	F7	92
Alcoutim, Port.	G3	20
Alcoy *see* Alcoi, Spain	F10	20
Alcúdia, Spain	E14	20
Alcúdia, Badia d', b., Spain	E14	20
Aldabra, Groupe d', is., Sey.	k11	69b
Aldama, Mex.	A5	100
Aldama, Mex.	D9	100
Aldan, Russia	E14	34
Aldan, stm., Russia	D15	34
Aldan Plateau see Aldanskoe nagor'e, plat., Russia	E14	34
Aldanskoe nagor'e (Aldan Plateau), plat., Russia	E14	34
Aldarchaan, Mong.	B4	36
Aldeia Nova de São Bento, Port.	G3	20
Alden, Mn., U.S.	H5	118
Alderney, i., Guern.	E6	14
Aldershot, Eng., U.K.	J12	12
Alderson, W.V., U.S.	G5	114
Aledo, Il., U.S.	C7	120
Aleg, Maur.	F2	64
Alegre, Braz.	K5	88
Alegrete, Braz.	D10	92
Alej, stm., Russia	D14	32
Alejandro Roca, Arg.	F5	92
Alejandro Selkirk, Isla, i., Chile	I6	82
Alejsk, Russia	D14	32
Aleksandrov, Russia	D21	10
Aleksandrovskij Zavod, Russia	F12	34
Aleksandrovskoe, Russia	B13	32
Aleksandrovsk-Sahalinskij, Russia	F17	34
Aleksandrów Kujawski, Pol.	D14	16
Alekseevka, Kaz.	D12	32
Alekseevka, Kaz.	E14	32
Alekseevka, Russia	D5	32
Alekseevsk, Russia	C19	32
Aleksejevka *see* Alekseevka, Kaz.	D12	32
Alekseyevka *see* Alekseevka, Kaz.	D12	32
Aleksin, Russia	F19	10
Aleksinac, Serb.	F8	26
Alemania, Arg.	B5	92
Além Paraíba, Braz.	K4	88
Alençon, Fr.	F9	14
Alenquer, Braz.	D7	84
Alentejo, hist. reg., Port.	F3	20
Alenuihaha Channel, strt., Hi., U.S.	c5	78a
Aleppo *see* Ḥalab, Syria	B8	58
Aléria, Fr.	G15	18
Alert, Nu., Can.	A13	141
Alert Bay, B.C., Can.	F4	138
Alert Point, c., Nu., Can.	A8	141
Alès, Fr.	E10	18
Alëšnja, Russia	G16	10
Alessándria, Italy	F5	22
Ålesund, Nor.	E1	8
Aleutian Basin, unds.	D20	142
Aleutian Islands, is., Ak., U.S.	g22	140a
Aleutian Range, mts., Ak., U.S.	E8	140
Aleutian Trench, unds.	E21	142
Aleutka, Russia	G19	34
Alevina, mys, c., Russia	E19	34
Alex, Ok., U.S.	G11	128
Alexander, Mb., Can.	E13	124
Alexander, N.D., U.S.	G10	124
Alexander, Kap, c., Grnld.	B11	141
Alexander Archipelago, is., Ak., U.S.	E12	140
Alexander Bay, S. Afr.	F3	70
Alexander City, Al., U.S.	E12	122
Alexander Island, i., Ant.	B33	81
Alexandra, N.Z.	G3	80
Alexandra, stm., Austl.	B3	76
Alexandra Falls, wtfl., N.T., Can.	C7	106
Alexandretta *see* İskenderun, Tur.	B6	58
Alexandretta, Gulf of see İskenderun Körfezi, b., Tur.	B6	58
Alexandria, Braz.	D6	88
Alexandria, B.C., Can.	D8	138
Alexandria, On., Can.	E2	110
Alexandria *see* El-Iskandarīya, Egypt	A6	62
Alexandria, Rom.	F12	26
Alexandria, La., U.S.	F6	122
Alexandria, Mn., U.S.	F3	118
Alexandria, Mo., U.S.	D6	120
Alexandria, S.D., U.S.	D15	126
Alexandria, Tn., U.S.	H11	120
Alexandria, Va., U.S.	F8	114
Alexandria Bay, N.Y., U.S.	D14	112
Alexandrina, Lake, l., Austl.	J2	76
Alexandroúpoli, Grc.	C8	28
Alexis, Il., U.S.	C7	120
Alfambra, Spain	D9	20
Alfaro, Spain	B9	20
Alfarràs, Spain	C11	20
Alfarrás *see* Alfarràs, Spain	C11	20
Al-Fāshir, Sudan	E5	62
Alfeiós, stm., Grc.	F4	28
Alfeld, Ger.	D5	16
Alfenas, Braz.	K3	88
Alföld, pl., Hung.	C7	26
Alfonsine, Italy	F9	22
Alfred, On., Can.	E2	110
Alfred, Me., U.S.	G6	110
Alfred, N.Y., U.S.	B8	114
Al-Fujayrah, U.A.E.	D8	56
Al-Fuqahā', Libya	B3	62
Al-Furāt see Euphrates, stm., Asia	C6	56
Ålgård, Nor.	G1	8
Algarrobal, Chile	D2	92
Algarrobo, Chile	F2	92
Algarrobo del Águila, Arg.	H4	92
Algarve, hist. reg., Port.	G2	20
Algeciras, Col.	F4	86
Algeciras, Spain	H5	20
Algemesí, Spain	E10	20
Algeria, ctry., Afr.	D5	64
Algha, Kaz.	E9	32
Al-Ghāb, sw., Syria	C7	58
Al-Ghayḍah, Yemen	F7	56
Al-Ghāzīyah, Leb.	E6	58
Alghero, Italy	D2	24
Algiers *see* El Djazaïr, Alg.	B5	64
Alginet, Spain	E10	20
Algoabaai, b., S. Afr.	H7	70
Algoa Bay see Algoabaai, b., S. Afr.	H7	70
Algodón, stm., Peru	I5	86
Algodones, N.M., U.S.	F2	128
Algoma Mills, On., Can.	B7	112
Algona, Ia., U.S.	A3	120
Algonac, Mi., U.S.	B3	114
Algonquin, Il., U.S.	B9	120
Algorta, Spain	A7	20
Algorta, Ur.	F9	92
Al-Ḥaffah, Syria	C7	58
Al-Ḥajarah, reg., Asia	C5	56
Al-Ḥamād, pl., Sau. Ar.	C4	56
Alhama de Murcia, Spain	G9	20
Alhandra, Braz.	D8	88
Al-Ḥarrah, lav., Sau. Ar.	C4	56
Al-Harūj al-Aswad, hills, Libya	B3	62
Al-Ḥasakah, Syria	B5	56
Alhaurín el Grande, Spain	H6	20
Al-Ḥawātah, Sudan	E7	62
Al-Ḥawrah, Yemen	G6	56
Al-Ḥijāz (Hejaz), reg., Sau. Ar.	D4	56
Al-Ḥillah, Iraq	C5	56
Al-Hirmil, Leb.	D7	58
Al-Hoceima, Mor.	B4	64
Al-Ḥudaydah (Hodeida), Yemen	G5	56
Al-Ḥufrah, reg., Sau. Ar.	J9	58
Al-Hufūf, Sau. Ar.	D6	56
Al Hūj, hills, Sau. Ar.	J9	58
Al-Ḥulwah, Sau. Ar.	E6	56
Alía, Spain	E5	20
Aliağa, Tur.	E9	28
Aliákmonas, stm., Grc.	C4	28
Aliança, Braz.	D8	88
Alībāg, India	B1	53
Alibates Flint Quarries National Monument, p.o.i., Tx., U.S.	F7	128
Äli Bayramlı, Azer.	B6	56
Alibei, ozero, l., Ukr.	D17	26
Alibey Adası, i., Tur.	D9	28
Alibunar, Serb.	D7	26
Alicante *see* Alacant, Spain	F10	20
Alicante see Alacant, co., Spain	F10	20
Alice, S. Afr.	H8	70
Alice, Tx., U.S.	G9	130
Alice, stm., Austl.	D5	76
Alice, Punta, c., Italy	E11	24
Alice Springs, Austl.	D6	74
Alice Town, Bah.	K6	116
Aliceville, Al., U.S.	D10	122
Alick Creek, stm., Austl.	C4	76
Alīgarh, India	E6	54
Alignements de Carnac, hist., Fr.	G5	14
Alīgūdarz, Iran	C6	56
'Alī Kheyl, Afg.	B2	54
Al-Ikhṣāṣ al-Qiblīyah, Egypt	I2	58
Alima, stm., Congo	E3	66
Alim Island, i., Pap. N. Gui.	a4	79a
Alindao, C.A.R.	C4	66
Alingsås, Swe.	G5	8
Alīpur, Pak.	D3	54
Ālīpur Duār, India	E12	54
Aliquippa, Pa., U.S.	D5	114
Alīrājpur, India	G5	54
Aliseda, Spain	E4	20
Alitak, Cape, c., Ak., U.S.	E9	140
Alivéri, Grc.	E7	28
Aliwal North, S. Afr.	G8	70
Alix, Ab., Can.	D17	138
Al-Jabalayn, Sudan	E6	62
Al-Jafr, Jord.	H7	58
Al-Jaghbūb, Libya	B4	62
Al-Jahrah, Kuw.	D6	56
Al-Jawārah, Oman	F8	56
Al-Jawf, Libya	C4	62
Al-Jawf, Sau. Ar.	D4	56
Al-Jazaïr *see* El Djazaïr, Alg.	B5	64
Al-Jazīrah, reg., Sudan	E6	62
Al-Jifārah (Jeffara), pl., Afr.	C7	64
Al-Jubayl, Sau. Ar.	D6	56
Al-Junaynah, Sudan	E4	62
Aljustrel, Port.	G2	20
Al-Kafr, Syria	F7	58
Al-Karak, Jord.	G6	58
Al-Karak, state, Jord.	G6	58
Al-Khalīl (Hebron), W.B.	G5	58
Al-Khāliṣ, Iraq	C5	56
Al-Khandaq, Sudan	D6	62
Al-Kharṭām Baḥrī, Sudan	D6	62
Al-Kharṭūm (Khartoum), Sudan	D6	62
Al-Khaṣab, Oman	D8	56
Al-Khums, Libya	A2	62
Alkmaar, Neth.	B13	14
Al-Kufrah, Libya	C4	62
Al-Kūt, Iraq	C6	56
Al-Kuwayt (Kuwait), Kuw.	D6	56
Al-Labwah, Leb.	D7	58
Al-Lādhiqīyah (Latakia), Syria	C6	58
Al-Lādhiqīyah, state, Syria	C6	58
Allagash, stm., Me., U.S.	D7	110
Allahābād, India	F8	54
Allah-Jun', Russia	D16	34
Allakaket, Ak., U.S.	C9	140
Allan, Sk., Can.	C7	124
Allanmyo, Mya.	C2	48
Allanridge, S. Afr.	E8	70
Allatoona Lake, res., Ga., U.S.	C14	122
Alldays, S. Afr.	C9	70
Allegan, Mi., U.S.	F4	112
Allegany, N.Y., U.S.	B7	114
Allegheny, stm., U.S.	D6	114
Allegheny Mountains, mts., U.S.	E6	114
Allegheny Plateau, plat., U.S.	D5	114
Allegheny Reservoir, res., U.S.	C7	114
Allemands, Lac des, l., La., U.S.	H8	122
Allen, Ne., U.S.	I2	118
Allen, Ok., U.S.	C2	122
Allen, Tx., U.S.	D2	122
Allen, Lough, l., Ire.	G4	12
Allendale, Il., U.S.	F10	120
Allendale, S.C., U.S.	C4	116
Allende, Mex.	A8	100
Allenstein *see* Olsztyn, Pol.	C16	16
Allentown, Pa., U.S.	D10	114
Alleppey, India	G3	53
Aller, stm., Ger.	D5	16
Allevard, Fr.	D12	18
Allgäu *see* Kempten, Ger.	I6	16
Allgäu, reg., Ger.	I6	16
Alliance, Ab., Can.	D19	138
Alliance, Ne., U.S.	E10	126
Alliance, Oh., U.S.	D4	114
Al-Lidām, Sau. Ar.	E5	56
Allier, state, Fr.	C9	18
Allier, stm., Fr.	C9	18
Alligator Pond, Jam.	j13	104d
Allinagaram, India	F3	53
Allison, Ia., U.S.	B5	120
Al-Līth, Sau. Ar.	E5	56
Alloa, Scot., U.K.	E9	12
Allos, Fr.	E12	18
Allouez, Wi., U.S.	G11	118
Allred Peak, mtn., Co., U.S.	C8	132
All Saints, Antig.	f4	105b
Al-Luḥayyah, Yemen	F5	56
Allumette Lake, l., Can.	C12	112
Allumettes, Île aux, i., Qc., Can.	C12	112
Alma, N.B., Can.	E12	110
Alma, Qc., Can.	B5	110
Alma, Ar., U.S.	B4	122
Alma, Ga., U.S.	E3	116
Alma, Ks., U.S.	E1	120
Alma, Mi., U.S.	E5	112
Alma, Wi., U.S.	G7	118
Almada, Port.	F1	20
Almaden, Austl.	A5	76
Almadén, Spain	F6	20
Al-Madīnah (Medina), Sau. Ar.	E4	56
Al-Mafraq, Jord.	F7	58
Al-Mafraq, state, Jord.	F8	58
Almafuerte, Arg.	F5	92
Almagro, Spain	F7	20
Alma Hill, hill, N.Y., U.S.	B8	114
Al Māliḥah, Sudan	D5	62
Almalyk, Uzb.	F11	32
Al-Manāmah (Manama), Bahr.	D7	56
Almanor, Lake, res., Ca., U.S.	C4	134
Almansa, Spain	F9	20
Almanza, Spain	B5	20
Almanzor, mtn., Spain	D5	20
Al-Marj, Libya	A4	62
Almas, Braz.	F2	88
Almas, Pico das, mtn., Braz.	G4	88
Al-Mashrafah, Syria	D7	58
Almaty, Kaz.	F13	32
Al-Mawṣil (Mosul), Iraq	B5	56
Almeida, Port.	D3	20
Almejas, Bahía, b., Mex.	C3	100
Almelo, Neth.	B15	14
Almena, Ks., U.S.	B9	128
Almenara, Braz.	I5	88
Almendra, Embalse de, res., Spain	C4	20
Almendralejo, Spain	F4	20
Almería, Spain	H8	20
Almería, co., Spain	G8	20
Almería, Golfo de, b., Spain	H8	20
Al'metevsk, Russia	D8	32
Al-Mijlad, Sudan	E5	62
Al-Mīnā', Leb.	D6	58
Almira, Wa., U.S.	C7	136
Almirante, Pan.	H6	102
Almirante Latorre, Chile	D2	92
Almo, Id., U.S.	A3	132
Almodóvar del Campo, Spain	F6	20
Almont, Mi., U.S.	B2	114
Almonte, On., Can.	C13	112
Almonte, Spain	G4	20
Almonte, stm., Spain	E4	20
Almora, India	D7	54
Al-Mubarraz, Sau. Ar.	E6	56
Al-Mubarraz, Sau. Ar.	D6	56
Al-Mudawwarah, Jord.	I6	58
Almudévar, Spain	B10	20
Al-Muḥarraq, Bahr.	D7	56
Al-Mukallā, Yemen	G6	56
Al-Mukhā, Yemen	G5	56
Almuñécar, Spain	H7	20
Al-Muwayliḥ, Sau. Ar.	K6	58
Almyrós, Grc.	D5	28
Almyroú, Órmos, b., Grc.	H7	28
Alnwick, Eng., U.K.	F11	12
Alofi, Île, i., Wal./F.	E9	72
Alónnisos, Grc.	D6	28
Alónnisos, i., Grc.	D6	28
Alor, Pulau, i., Indon.	G7	44
Alor, Selat, strt., Indon.	G7	44
Alor Setar, Malay.	I5	48
Alosno, Spain	G3	20
Alost *see* Aalst, Bel.	D13	14
Alotau, Pap. N. Gui.	c5	79a
Aloysius, Mount, mtn., Austl.	E5	74
Alpachiri, Arg.	H5	92
Alpaugh, Ca., U.S.	H6	134
Alpena, Mi., U.S.	C6	112
Alpena, S.D., U.S.	C14	126
Alpercatas, stm., Braz.	D3	88
Alpes-de-Haute-Provence, state, Fr.	E12	18
Alpes-Maritimes, state, Fr.	F13	18
Alpha, Austl.	D6	76
Alpha, Il., U.S.	C7	120
Alpha, Mi., U.S.	B1	112
Alpharetta, Ga., U.S.	B1	116
Alphonse, i., Sey.	k12	69b
Alpine, Ca., U.S.	K9	134
Alpine, Tx., U.S.	D4	130
Alpine National Park, p.o.i., Austl.	K6	76
Alpinópolis, Braz.	K2	88
Alps, mts., Eur.	D6	22
Al-Qaḍārif, Sudan	E7	62
Al-Qaḍīmah, Sau. Ar.	E4	56
Al-Qāmishlī, Syria	B5	56
Al-Qaryah ash-Sharqīyah, Libya	A2	62
Al-Qaryatayn, Syria	D8	58
Al-Qaṭīf, Sau. Ar.	D6	56
Al-Qaṭrānah, Jord.	G7	58
Al-Qaṭrūn, Libya	C2	62
Al-Qayṣūmah, Sau. Ar.	D6	56
Al-Qunayṭirah, Syria	E6	58
Al-Qunayṭirah, state, Syria	E6	58
Al-Qunfudhah, Sau. Ar.	F5	56
Al-Quṭayfah, Syria	E7	58
Al-Quṭaynah, Sudan	E6	62
Als, i., Den.	I3	8
Alsace, hist. reg., Fr.	F16	14
Al'šany, Bela.	H10	10
Alsask, Sk., Can.	C4	124
Alsasua, Spain	B8	20
Alsea, Or., U.S.	F3	136
Alsek, stm., N.A.	D3	106
Alsen, N.D., U.S.	F15	124
Alsfeld, Ger.	F5	16
Alta, Nor.	B10	8
Altaelva, stm., Nor.	B10	8
Alta Gracia, Arg.	E5	92
Altagracia, Ven.	B6	86
Altagracia de Orituco, Ven.	C8	86
Altai, mts., Asia	E15	32
Altaj, state, Russia	D15	32
Altajskij, Russia	D14	32
Altamaha, stm., Ga., U.S.	E4	116
Altamira, Braz.	D7	84
Altamira, Chile	B3	92
Altamirano, Mex.	I10	130
Altamont, Ks., U.S.	G2	120
Altamont, Or., U.S.	A4	134
Altamont, Tn., U.S.	B13	122
Altamura, Italy	D10	24
Altamura, Isla, i., Mex.	C4	100
Altanbulag, Mong.	A6	36
Altar, Mex.	F7	98
Altar, stm., Mex.	F7	98
Altar, Desierto de, des., Mex.	F6	98
Altar de Los Sacrificios, sci., Guat.	D2	102
Altario, Ab., Can.	C3	124
Altata, Mex.	C4	100
Alta Vista, Ks., U.S.	C12	128
Altay, China	E15	32
Altay, Mong.	B4	36
Altay see Altaj, state, Russia	D15	32
Altay Mountains see Altai, mts., Asia	E15	32
Altdorf, Switz.	D5	22
Altenburg, Ger.	E8	16
Altentreptow, Ger.	C9	16
Alter do Chão, Port.	E3	20
Altevatnet, l., Nor.	B8	8
Altha, Fl., U.S.	G13	122
Altheimer, Ar., U.S.	C7	122
Altınekin, Tur.	E15	28
Altinho, Braz.	E7	88
Altınova, Tur.	D9	28
Altintaş, Tur.	D13	28
Altiplano, plat., S.A.	G4	84
Altmark, reg., Ger.	D7	16
Altmühl, stm., Ger.	G6	16
Alto, Tx., U.S.	F3	122
Alto Araguaia, Braz.	G7	84
Alto Chicapa, Ang.	C2	68
Alto Garças, Braz.	G7	84
Alto Longá, Braz.	C4	88
Altomünster, Ger.	H7	16
Alton, Eng., U.K.	J11	12
Alton, Ia., U.S.	B1	120
Alton, Il., U.S.	F7	120
Alton, Ks., U.S.	B9	128
Alton, N.H., U.S.	G5	110
Altona, Mb., Can.	E16	124
Altoona, Al., U.S.	C12	122
Altoona, Ia., U.S.	C4	120
Altoona, Pa., U.S.	D7	114
Altoona, Wi., U.S.	G7	118
Alto Paraguai, Braz.	F6	84
Alto Paraíso de Goiás, Braz.	G2	88
Alto Paraná, state, Para.	B10	92
Alto Parnaíba, Braz.	E2	88
Alto Río Mayo, Arg.	I2	90
Alto Río Senguer, Arg.	I2	90
Altos, Braz.	C4	88
Alto Santo, Braz.	C6	88
Altötting, Ger.	H8	16
Altun Shan, mts., China	D2	36
Alturas, Ca., U.S.	B5	134
Altus, Ar., U.S.	B5	122
Altus, Ok., U.S.	G9	128
Alu see Shortland Island, i., Sol. Is.	d6	79b
Al-'Ubaylah, Sau. Ar.	E7	56
Al-Ubayyiḍ, Sudan	E6	62
Alubijid, Phil.	F5	52
Al-Uḍayyah, Sudan	E5	62
Alūksne, Lat.	C9	10
Al-'Ulā, Sau. Ar.	D4	56
Al-'Uqaylah, Libya	A3	62
Al-'Uwaynāt, Libya	B2	62
Alva, Ok., U.S.	E10	128
Alvaiázere, Port.	E2	20
Alvarado, Mex.	F11	100
Alvarado, Tx., U.S.	B10	130
Álvaro Obregón, Presa, res., Mex.	B4	100
Alvear, Arg.	D9	92
Alverca, Port.	F1	20
Alvernia, Mount, hill, Bah.	C10	96
Alvesta, Swe.	H6	8
Alvin, Tx., U.S.	H3	122
Alvinópolis, Braz.	K4	88
Älvkarleby, Swe.	F7	8
Alvord, Tx., U.S.	H11	128
Alvord Desert, des., Or., U.S.	H8	136
Al-Wajh, Sau. Ar.	D4	56
Alwar, India	E6	54
Alwaye, India	F3	53
Alxa Zuoqi, China	B1	42
Alytus, Lith.	F6	10
Alzey, Ger.	G4	16
Alzira, Spain	E10	20
Amacuro (Amakura), stm., S.A.	C11	86
Amadeus, Lake, l., Austl.	D6	74
Amadjuak Lake, l., Nu., Can.	B16	106
Amagasaki, Japan	E8	40
Amagi, Japan	F3	40
Amahai, Indon.	F8	44
Amaichá del Valle, Arg.	C4	92
Amaimon, Pap. N. Gui.	b4	79a
Amajac, stm., Mex.	E9	100
Amakura (Amacuro), stm., S.A.	D11	86
Amakusa-nada, s., Japan	G2	40
Amakusa-shotō, is., Japan	G2	40
Åmål, Swe.	G5	8
Amalāpuram, India	C6	53
Amalfi, Col.	B2	84
Amaliáda, Grc.	F4	28
Amalner, India	H5	54
Amambaí, Braz.	D5	90
Amami Islands see Amami-Ō-shima, i., Japan	k19	39a
Amami-Ō-shima, i., Japan	k19	39a
Amami-shotō, is., Japan	I19	39a
Amana, Ia., U.S.	C6	120
Amana, stm., Ven.	C10	86
Amanã, Lago, l., Braz.	I9	86
Amanda, Oh., U.S.	E3	114
Amangeldi, Kaz.	D10	32
Amantea, Italy	E9	24
Amapá, Braz.	C7	84
Amapá, state, Braz.	C7	84
Amarante, Braz.	D4	88
Amaranth, Mb., Can.	D15	124
Amarapura, Mya.	B3	48
Amărăștii de Jos, Rom.	F11	26
Amarāvati, stm., India	F3	53
Amares, Port.	C2	20
Amargosa, Braz.	G6	88
Amargosa, stm., U.S.	H9	134
Amarillo, Tx., U.S.	F7	128
Amarkantak, India	G8	54
Amaro, Monte, mtn., Italy	H11	22
Amasra, Tur.	B15	28
Amasya, Tur.	A4	56
aMatikulu, S. Afr.	F10	70
Amatsu-kominato, Japan	D13	40
Amawbia Awka, Nig.	H6	64
Amazar, Russia	F13	34
Amazon (Amazonas) (Solimões), stm., S.A.	D7	84
Amazonas, state, Braz.	D4	84
Amazonas, state, Col.	H6	86
Amazonas, state, Ven.	F8	86
Ambājogāi, India	B3	53
Ambāla, India	C6	54
Ambalangoda, Sri L.	H4	53
Ambalavao, Madag.	E8	68
Ambam, Cam.	D2	66
Ambanja, Madag.	C8	68
Ambarčik, Russia	C21	34
Ambargasta, Salinas de, pl., Arg.	D5	92
Ambato, Ec.	H2	86
Ambatolampy, Madag.	D8	68
Ambatondrazaka, Madag.	D8	68
Ambelau, Pulau, i., Indon.	F8	44
Amberg, Ger.	G7	16
Amberg, Wi., U.S.	C2	112
Ambergris Cay, i., Belize	C4	102
Ambérieu-en-Bugey, Fr.	D11	18
Ambert, Fr.	D9	18
Ambidédi, Mali	G2	64
Ambikāpur, India	G9	54
Ambilobe, Madag.	C8	68
Ambla, Est.	A8	10
Amble, Eng., U.K.	F11	12
Ambo, Peru	F2	84
Ambodifototra, Madag.	D8	68
Ambohimahasoa, Madag.	E8	68
Amboise, Fr.	G10	14
Ambon, Indon.	F8	44
Ambon, Pulau, i., Indon.	F8	44
Amboseli, Lake, l., Afr.	E7	66
Amboseli National Park, p.o.i., Kenya	E7	66
Ambositra, Madag.	E8	68
Ambovombe, Madag.	F8	68
Amboy, Il., U.S.	C8	120
Amboy, Mn., U.S.	H4	118
Ambridge, Pa., U.S.	D5	114
Ambriz, Ang.	B1	68
Ambrosia Lake, N.M., U.S.	H9	132
Ambrym, state, Vanuatu	k17	79d
Ambrym, i., Vanuatu	k17	79d
Ambuntentimur, Indon.	G8	50
Ambunti, Pap. N. Gui.	a3	79a
Āmbūr, India	E4	53
Amchitka Island, i., Ak., U.S.	g22	140a
Amchitka Pass, strt., Ak., U.S.	g22	140a
Am Dam, Chad	E4	62
Amdo, China	B13	54
Ameagle, W.V., U.S.	G4	114
Ameca, Mex.	E6	100
Ameca, stm., Mex.	E6	100
Ameghino, Arg.	G6	92
Ameland, i., Neth.	A14	14
Amelia Court House, Va., U.S.	G8	114
Amelia Island, i., Fl., U.S.	F4	116
Āmer, India	E5	54
American, North Fork, stm., Ca., U.S.	D5	134
American, South Fork, stm., Ca., U.S.	E5	134
Americana, Braz.	L2	88
American Falls Reservoir, res., Id., U.S.	H13	136
American Fork, Ut., U.S.	C5	132
American Highland, plat., Ant.	C12	81
Americanos, Barra de los, i., Mex.	C10	100
American Samoa, dep., Oc.	h12	79c
Americus, Ga., U.S.	D1	116
Americus, Ks., U.S.	F1	120
Amersfoort, Neth.	B14	14
Amery, Wi., U.S.	F6	118
Amery Ice Shelf, ice, Ant.	B12	81
Ames, Ia., U.S.	B4	120
Amesbury, Ma., U.S.	B14	114
Amfilochía, Grc.	E4	28
Ámfissa, Grc.	E5	28
Amga, Russia	D15	34
Amga, stm., Russia	D15	34
Amguema, stm., Russia	C24	34
Amguid, Alg.	D6	64
Amgun', stm., Russia	F16	34
Amherst, N.S., Can.	E12	110
Amherst, Ma., U.S.	B13	114
Amherst, N.Y., U.S.	A7	114
Amherst, Oh., U.S.	C3	114
Amherst, Tx., U.S.	G6	128
Amherst, Wi., U.S.	G9	118
Amherstburg, On., Can.	F6	112
Amherstdale, W.V., U.S.	G4	114
Amherst Island, i., On., Can.	D13	112
Amherstview, On., Can.	D13	112
Amiens, Austl.	G8	76
Amiens, Fr.	E11	14
Amīndīvi Islands, is., India	F3	46
Amino, Japan	D8	40
Aminuis, Nmb.	C4	70
Amirantes, Les, is., Sey.	k12	69b
Amisk, Ab., Can.	B2	124
Amisk Lake, l., Sk., Can.	E10	106
Amistad, Parque Internacional de la, p.o.i., C.R.	H6	102
Amistad, Presa de la (Amistad Reservoir), res., N.A.	E6	130
Amistad National Recreation Area, p.o.i., Tx., U.S.	E6	130
Amistad Reservoir (Amistad, Presa de la), res., N.A.	E6	130
Amite, La., U.S.	G8	122
Amite, stm., La., U.S.	G8	122
Amity, Ar., U.S.	C5	122
Amla, India	H7	54
Åmli, Nor.	G3	8
'Ammān, Jord.	G6	58
'Ammān, state, Jord.	G7	58
Ämmänsaari, Fin.	D13	8
'Ammār, Tall, hill, Syria	F7	58
Ammasalik *see* Angmagssalik, Grnld.	D18	141
Ammon, Id., U.S.	G15	136
Amnat Charoen, Thai.	E7	48
Amnok-kang (Yalu), stm., Asia	D7	38
Amo (Torsa), stm., Asia	E12	54
Amo, stm., China	A5	48
Āmol, Iran	B7	56
Amorgós, i., Grc.	G8	28
Amory, Ms., U.S.	D10	122
Amos, Qc., Can.	F15	106
Åmot, Nor.	G2	8
Amoy *see* Xiamen, China	I7	42
Ampanihy, Madag.	E7	68
Amparo, Braz.	L2	88
Ampasimanolotra, Madag.	D8	68
Amposta, Spain	D11	20
Amqui, Qc., Can.	B9	110
Amrāvati, India	H6	54
Amreli, India	H3	54
Amritsar, India	C5	54
Amroha, India	D7	54
Amrum, i., Ger.	B4	16
Amsterdam, Neth.	B13	14
Amsterdam, S. Afr.	E10	70
Amsterdam, N.Y., U.S.	B11	114
Amsterdam, Île, i., Afr.	M10	142
Amstetten, Aus.	B11	22
Am Timan, Chad	E4	62
Amu Darya, stm., Asia	F10	32
Amugulang *see* Xin Barag Zuoqi, China	B8	36
Amund Ringnes Island, i., Nu., Can.	B6	141
Amundsen Gulf, b., Can.	B14	140
Amundsen-Scott, sci., Ant.	D19	81
Amundsen Sea, s., Ant.	P27	142
Amuntai, Indon.	E9	50
Amur (Heilong), stm., Asia	F16	34
Amursk, Russia	F16	34
Amuzhong, China	C10	54
Amvrakikós Kólpos, b., Grc.	E3	28
An, Mya.	C2	48
Ana, Parque Nacional dedo see Doñana, Parque Nacional de, p.o.i., Spain	H4	20
Anaa, at., Fr. Poly.	E12	72
Anabar, stm., Russia	B11	34
Anaco, Ven.	C9	86
Anaconda, Mt., U.S.	D14	136
Anaconda Range, mts., Mt., U.S.	E13	136
Anacortes, Wa., U.S.	B4	136
Anadarko, Ok., U.S.	F10	128
Anadolu (Anatolia), hist. reg., Tur.	H15	6
Anadyr', Russia	D24	34
Anadyr, stm., Russia	C23	34
Anadyr, Gulf of see Anadyrskij zaliv, b., Russia	C21	142
Anadyr Mountains see Anadyrskoe ploskogor'e, plat., Russia	C23	34
Anadyrskij liman, b., Russia	D24	34
Anadyrskij zaliv, b., Russia	C21	142
Anadyrskoe ploskogor'e, plat., Russia	C23	34
Anáfi, i., Grc.	G8	28
Anagni, Italy	C7	24
Anaheim, Ca., U.S.	J8	134
Anahim Lake, B.C., Can.	D5	138
Anáhuac, Mex.	I10	130
Ānai Mudi, mtn., India	F3	53
Anajás, Braz.	D8	84
Anakāpalle, India	C6	53
Anaktuvuk Pass, Ak., U.S.	C9	140
Analalava, Madag.	C8	68
Anamã, Braz.	D5	84
Anama Bay, Mb., Can.	C15	124
Ana María, Golfo de, b., Cuba	B8	102
Anambas, Kepulauan (Anambas Islands), is., Indon.	B5	50
Anambas Islands see Anambas, Kepulauan, is., Indon.	B5	50
Anamizu, Japan	B9	40
Anamoose, N.D., U.S.	G13	124
Anamur, Tur.	B3	58
Anamur Burnu, c., Tur.	B3	58
Anan, Japan	F7	40
Ānand, India	G4	54
Ānandapur, India	H11	54
Ananindeua, Braz.	A1	88
Anan'ïv, Ukr.	B16	26
Anantapur, India	D3	53
Anantnāg, India	B5	54
Anápolis, Braz.	I1	88
Anapurus, Braz.	B4	88
Añasco, P.R.	B1	104a
Anastasia Island, i., Fl., U.S.	G4	116
Anatahan, i., N. Mar. Is.	B5	72
Anatolia see Anadolu, hist. reg., Tur.	H15	6
Anatolikí Makedonía kai Thráki, state, Grc.	B8	28
Anatom, i., Vanuatu	m17	79d
Añatuya, Arg.	D6	92
Anauá, stm., Braz.	G11	86
Anavilhanas, Arquipélago das, is., Braz.	I11	86
Anbei, China	F17	32
Anbianbu, China	C2	42
Anbyŏn-ŭp, Kor., N.	E7	38
Ancaster, On., Can.	E9	112
Ancasti, Sierra de, mts., Arg.	D5	92
Anchiang *see* Qianyang, China	H3	42
Anch'ing *see* Anqing, China	F7	42
Anchorage, Ak., U.S.	D10	140
Anchuras, Spain	E6	20
Ancona, Italy	G10	22
Ancón de Sardinas, Bahía de, b., S.A.	G2	86
Ancuabe, Moz.	C6	68
Ancud, Chile	H2	90
Ancy-le-Franc, Fr.	G13	14
Anda, China	B10	36
Andacollo, Arg.	H2	92
Andahuaylas, Peru	F3	84
Andalgalá, Arg.	C4	92
Andalucía, state, Spain	G6	20
Andalusia *see* Jan Kempdorp, S. Afr.	E7	70
Andalusia, Al., U.S.	F12	122
Andalusia see Andalucía, state, Spain	G6	20
Andaman and Nicobar Islands, state, India	F7	46
Andaman Basin, unds.	H12	142
Andaman Islands, is., India	F7	46
Andaman Sea, s., Asia	G8	46
Andamook, Austl.	F7	74
Andapa, Madag.	C8	68
Andenes, Nor.	B6	8
Andéramboukane, Mali	F5	64
Andernach, Ger.	F3	16
Anderson, Ca., U.S.	C3	134
Anderson, In., U.S.	H4	112
Anderson, Mo., U.S.	H3	120
Anderson, S.C., U.S.	B3	116
Anderson, Tx., U.S.	G3	122
Anderson, stm., N.T., Can.	B5	106
Anderson, Mount, mtn., Wa., U.S.	C3	136
Anderson Dam, Id., U.S.	G11	136
Andes, Col.	E4	86
Andes, mts., S.A.	F7	82
Andfjorden, strt., Nor.	B7	8
Andhra Lake, res., India	B1	53
Andhra Pradesh, state, India	C4	53
Andilamena, Madag.	D8	68
Andingpu, China	B2	42
Andirlang, China	A5	46
Andižan, Uzb.	F12	32
Andkhvoy, Afg.	B10	56
Andoany, Madag.	C8	68
Andoga, stm., Russia	A19	10
Andong, Kor., S.	C1	40
Andong-chŏsuji, res., Kor., S.	C1	40
Andorra, ctry., Eur.	B12	20
Andorra, ctry., Eur.	B12	20
Andorra-la-Vella, And.	B12	20
Andover, Eng., U.K.	J11	12
Andover, Ma., U.S.	H5	110
Andover, Me., U.S.	F6	110
Andover, Oh., U.S.	C5	114
Andover, S.D., U.S.	B15	126
Andøya, i., Nor.	B6	8
Andradina, Braz.	D6	90
Andranopasy, Madag.	E7	68
Andreanof Islands, is., Ak., U.S.	g23	140a
Andreapol', Russia	D15	10
Andrews, In., U.S.	H4	112
Andrews, N.C., U.S.	A2	116
Andrews, S.C., U.S.	C6	116
Andrews, Tx., U.S.	B5	130
Andria, Italy	C10	24
Andriamena, Madag.	D8	68
Andriievo-Ivanivka, Ukr.	B17	26
Androka, Madag.	F7	68
Andronovskoe, Russia	F16	8
Andros, i., Bah.	C9	96
Ándros, i., Grc.	F7	28
Androscoggin, stm., Me., U.S.	F6	110
Āndrott Island, i., India	F1	53
Andrupene, Lat.	D10	10
Andudu, D.R.C.	D5	66
Andújar, Spain	F6	20
Andulo, Ang.	C2	68
Anduze, Fr.	E9	18
Anegada, Bahía, b., Arg.	H4	90
Anegada Passage, strt., N.A.	h15	96a
Aného, Togo	H5	64
Añelo, Arg.	I3	92
Anemata, Passe d', strt., N. Cal.	m16	79d
Anenii Noi, Mol.	C16	26
Aneroid, Sk., Can.	E6	124
Aneta, N.D., U.S.	G16	124
Anétis, Mali	F5	64
Aneto, mtn., Spain	B11	20
Anfu, China	H6	42
Angamos, Punta, c., Chile	D2	90
Ang'angxi, China	B9	36
Angara, stm., Russia	E8	34
Angarsk, Russia	D18	32
Angas Downs, Austl.	D6	74
Angastaco, Arg.	B4	92
Angaul, Russia	D18	32
Ånge, Swe.	E6	8
Ángel, Salto (Angel Falls), wtfl., Ven.	E10	86
Ángel de la Guarda, Isla, i., Mex.	G6	98
Angeles, Phil.	C3	52
Angel Falls see Ángel, Salto, wtfl., Ven.	E10	86
Ängelholm, Swe.	H5	8
Angelina, stm., Tx., U.S.	F4	122
Angellala Creek, stm., Austl.	F6	76
Angels Camp, Ca., U.S.	E5	134
Angemuk, mtn., Indon.	F10	44

Name	Map Ref.	Page
Ångermanälven, stm., Swe.	E7	8
Angermünde, Ger.	C9	16
Angers, Fr.	G8	14
Angical, Braz.	F3	88
Angical do Piauí, Braz.	D4	88
Angicos, Braz.	C7	88
Angijak Island, i., Nu., Can.	D13	141
Angikuni Lake, l., Nu., Can.	C11	106
Angkor Wat, sci., Camb.	F6	48
Ǎng Tasaòm, Camb.	G7	48
Angle Inlet, Mn., U.S.	B3	118
Anglem, Mount, mtn., N.Z.	H2	80
Anglesey, i., Wales, U.K.	H8	12
Anglet, Fr.	F4	18
Angleton, Tx., U.S.	H3	122
Anglona, reg., Italy	D2	24
Angmagssalik (Ǎmmasalik), Grnld.	D18	141
Angoche, Moz.	D6	68
Angol, Chile	H1	92
Angola, In., U.S.	G5	112
Angola, N.Y., U.S.	B6	114
Angola, ctry., Afr.	C2	68
Angola Basin, unds.	J14	144
Angora see Ankara, Tur.	D15	28
Angoram, Pap. N. Gui.	a3	79a
Angostura, Presa de la, res., Mex.	H12	100
Angoulême, Fr.	D6	18
Angoumois, hist. reg., Fr.	D5	18
Angra dos Reis, Braz.	L3	88
Angren, Uzb.	F12	32
Angu, D.R.C.	D4	66
Angualasto, Arg.	D3	92
Anguilla, Ms., U.S.	E8	122
Anguilla, dep., N.A.	h15	96a
Anguille, Cape, c., Nf., Can.	C17	110
Angul Nui I., China	A6	42
Anguo, China	B6	42
Angus, On., Can.	D10	112
Angusville, Mb., Can.	D13	124
Anhalt, hist. reg., Ger.	D7	16
Anholt, i., Den.	H4	8
Anhua, China	G4	42
Anhui, state see Anhui, state, China	F7	42
Anhwei see Anhui, state, China	F7	42
Aniak, Ak., U.S.	D8	140
Anibare Bay, b., Nauru	q17	78f
Anie, Pic d', mtn., Fr.	F5	18
Anil, Braz.	B3	88
Animas, N.M., U.S.	L8	132
Animas Valley, val., N.A.	L8	132
Anina, Rom.	D8	26
Anita, Ia., U.S.	C3	120
Anıtkaya, Tur.	E13	28
Aniva, mys, c., Russia	B13	36
Aniva, zaliv, b., Russia	G17	34
Aniwa, i., Vanuatu	l17	79d
Anjangaon, India	H6	54
'Anjar, India	G4	54
Anjou, hist. reg., Fr.	G8	14
Anjouan see Nzwani, i., Com.	C7	68
Anjudin, Russia	B9	32
Anjujsk, Russia	C21	34
Anjujskij hrebet, mts., Russia	C21	34
Anju-Up, Kor., N.	E6	38
Anka, Nig.	G6	64
Ankaboa, Tanjona, c., Madag.	E7	68
Ankang, China	E3	42
Ankara, Tur.	D15	28
Ankara, state, Tur.	D15	28
Ankavandra, Madag.	D8	68
Ankazoabo, Madag.	E7	68
Ankazobe, Madag.	D8	68
Ankeny, Ia., U.S.	C4	120
Anking see Anqing, China	F7	42
Ankleshwar, India	H4	54
Ankoro, D.R.C.	F5	66
Anlong, China	F6	36
Ǎnlong Vêng, Camb.	F5	42
Anlu, China	F5	42
An Muileann gCearr see Mullingar, Ire.	H5	12
Ann, i., Swe.	E5	8
Ann, Cape, c., Ant.	B10	81
Ann, Cape, pen., Ma., U.S.	H6	110
Anna, Il., U.S.	G8	120
Anna, Lake, res., Va., U.S.	F8	114
Annaba, Alg.	B6	64
An-Nabaṭīyah, state, Leb.	E6	58
An-Nabaṭīyah at-Taḥtā, Leb.	E6	58
Annaberg-Buchholz, Ger.	F9	16
An-Nabk, Syria	D7	58
An-Nafūd, des., Sau. Ar.	D5	56
An-Najaf, Iraq	C5	56
Annam see Trung Phan, hist. reg., Viet.	D8	48
Annamitique, Chaîne, mts., Asia	D8	48
Annan, Scot., U.K.	G9	12
Annandale, Austl.	C7	76
Annandale, Mn., U.S.	F4	118
Annandale, val., Scot., U.K.	F9	12
Annapolis, Md., U.S.	F9	114
Annapolis Royal, N.S., Can.	F11	110
Annapūrna, mtn., Nepal	D9	54
Ann Arbor, Mi., U.S.	B2	114
An Nás see Naas, Ire.	H6	12
An-Nāṣirīyah, Iraq	C6	56
An-Nāṣirīyah, Syria	E7	58
An-Nawfalīyah, Libya	A3	62
Annecy, Fr.	D12	18
Annecy, Lac d', l., Fr.	D12	18
Annemasse, Fr.	C12	18
Annenkov Island, i., S. Geor.	J9	90
An Nhon, Viet.	F9	48
Anning, China	G5	36
Anniston, Al., U.S.	D13	122
Annobón, i., Eq. Gui.	J6	64
Annonay, Fr.	D10	18
Annville, Ky., U.S.	G2	114
Annville, Pa., U.S.	D9	114
Anoka, Mn., U.S.	F5	118
Anori, Braz.	D5	84
Anpu, China	K3	42
Anqing, China	F7	42
Anqiu, China	C8	42
Anren, China	H5	42
Ansai, China	C3	42
Ansbach, Ger.	G6	16
Anse d'Hainault, Haiti	C10	102
Anse La Raye, St. Luc.	m6	105c
Anselmo, Ne., U.S.	F13	126
Anserma, Col.	E4	86
Anshan, China	D5	38
Anshun, China	H1	42
Ansina, Ur.	E10	92
Ansley, Ne., U.S.	F13	126
Anson Bay, b., Austl.	B5	74
Anson Bay, b., Norf. I.	y24	78i
Ansongo, Mali	F5	64
Ansonville, N.C., U.S.	A5	116
Ansted, W.V., U.S.	F4	114
Antakya see Hatay, Tur.	B7	58
Antalaha, Madag.	C9	68
Antalieptė, Lith.	E8	10
Antalya, Tur.	G13	28
Antalya, state, Tur.	F14	28
Antalya, Gulf of see Antalya Körfezi, b., Tur.	G14	28
Antalya Körfezi (Antalya, Gulf of), b., Tur.	G14	28
Antananarivo, Madag.	D8	68
An tAonach see Nenagh, Ire.	I4	12
Antarctica, cont.	D11	81
Antarctic Peninsula, pen., Ant.	C35	81
Antas, Braz.	F6	88
Antas, stm., Braz.	D12	92
Antelope Island I., Ut., U.S.	C4	132
Antelope Mine, Zimb.	B9	70
Antelope Peak, mtn., Nv., U.S.	B1	132
Antenor Navarro, Braz.	D6	88
Antequera, Para.	A9	92
Antequera, Spain	H6	20
Anthon, Ia., U.S.	B2	120
Anthony, Ks., U.S.	D10	128
Anthony, N.M., U.S.	K10	132
Anthony, Tx., U.S.	E9	98
Anti-Atlas, mts., Mor.	D3	64
Antibes, Fr.	F13	18
Anticosti, Île d', i., Qc., Can.	F18	106
Antifer, Cap d', c., Fr.	E8	14
Antigonish, N.S., Can.	E14	110
Antigua, i., Antig.	f4	105b
Antigua and Barbuda, ctry., N.A.	h15	96a
Antigua International Airport, Antig.	f4	105b
Antiguo Morelos, Mex.	D9	100
Antikýthira, i., Grc.	H6	28
Anti-Lebanon (Sharqī, Al-Jabal ash-), mts., Asia	E7	58
Antilla, Cuba	B10	102
Antillen, Nederlandse see Netherlands Antilles, dep., N.A.	i14	96a
Antimony, Ut., U.S.	E5	132
Antioch see Hatay, Tur.	B7	58
Antioch, Il., U.S.	F1	112
Antioquia, Col.	D4	86
Antioquia, state, Col.	D4	86
Antipajuta, Russia	C4	34
Antipodes Islands, is., N.Z.	H9	72
Antisana, vol., Ec.	H2	86
Antler, stm., N.A.	E12	124
Antofagasta, Chile	A2	92
Antofagasta, state, Chile	B3	92
Antofagasta de la Sierra, Arg.	C4	92
Antofalla, Salar de, pl., Arg.	C3	92
Antofalla, Volcán, vol., Arg.	B4	92
Antón, Pan.	H7	102
Anton, Tx., U.S.	H6	128
Anton Chico, N.M., U.S.	F3	128
Antongila, Helodrano, b., Madag.	D8	68
Antonina, Braz.	B13	92
Antonina do Norte, Braz.	D5	88
Antônio Prado, Braz.	D12	92
Antonito, Co., U.S.	D2	128
Antón Lizardo, Punta, c., Mex.	F10	100
Antonovo, Kaz.	E8	32
Antopal', Bela.	H7	10
Antrim, N. Ire., U.K.	G6	12
Antropovo, Russia	G20	8
Antsalova, Madag.	D7	68
Antsirabe, Madag.	D8	68
Antsirañana, Madag.	C8	68
Antsohihy, Madag.	C8	68
Antulaj, Gunong, mtn., Malay.	A10	50
Antun', Russia	G16	34
Antung see Dandong, China	D5	38
Antwerp see Antwerpen, Bel.	C13	14
Antwerp, Oh., U.S.	C1	114
Antwerpen (Antwerp), Bel.	C13	14
An Uaimh see Navan, Ire.	H6	12
Anugul, India	H10	54
Anūpgarh, India	D4	54
Anuradhapura, Sri L.	G5	53
Anvers see Antwerpen, Bel.	C13	14
Anvers Island, i., Ant.	B34	81
Anvik, Ak., U.S.	D7	140
Anxi, China	I8	42
Anxi, China	C4	36
Anxiang, China	G5	42
Anxious Bay, b., Austl.	F6	74
Anyang, China	C6	42
Anyang, Kor., S.	F7	38
Anyêmaqên Shan, mts., China	D4	36
Anyer Kidul, Indon.	G4	50
Anykščiai, Lith.	E7	10
Anyuan, China	I6	42
Anyuanyi see Tianzhu, China	D5	36
Anyue, China	F1	42
Anze, China	C5	42
Anžero-Sudžensk, Russia	C15	32
Anzio, Italy	C6	24
Anzoátegui, state, Ven.	C9	86
Anžu, ostrova, is., Russia	A17	34
Aoba, i., Vanuatu	j16	79d
Aoba i Maéwo, state, Vanuatu	j17	79d
Aoga-shima, i., Japan	G12	40
Aohan Qi, China	C3	38
Aojiang, China	H9	42
Aoji-ri, Kor., N.	C9	38
Ao Luk, Thai.	H4	48
Aomar, Alg.	H14	20
Aomen (Macau), China	J5	42
Aomori, Japan	D14	38
Aomori, state, Japan	D14	38
Aonla, India	D7	54
Aöös (Vjosës), stm., Eur.	D13	24
A'opo, Samoa	g11	79c
Aoraki (Cook, Mount), mtn., N.Z.	F4	80
Aôral, Phnum, mtn., Camb.	F7	48
Aore, i., Vanuatu	j16	79d
Aosta (Aoste), Italy	E4	22
Aoste see Aosta, Italy	E4	22
Aouderas, Niger	F6	64
Aouk, Bahr, stm., Afr.	F3	62
Aoukâr, reg., Maur.	F3	64
Aoya, Japan	D7	40
Aozou, Chad	C3	62
Apache Junction, Az., U.S.	J5	132
Apache Peak, mtn., Az., U.S.	L6	132
Apalachee, stm., Ga., U.S.	C2	116
Apalachicola, Fl., U.S.	H13	122
Apalachicola, stm., Fl., U.S.	H14	122
Apalachicola Bay, b., Fl., U.S.	H13	122
Apaporis, stm., S.A.	H7	86
Aparados da Serra, Parque Nacional da, p.o.i., Braz.	D12	92
Aparri, Phil.	A3	52
Apartadó, Col.	D3	86
Apatin, Serb.	D5	26
Apatity, Russia	C15	8
Apatzingán de la Constitución, Mex.	F7	100
Apaxtla de Castrejón, Mex.	F8	100
Apeldoorn, Neth.	B15	14
Apennines see Appennino, mts., Italy	G11	6
Apex, N.C., U.S.	I7	114
Api, mtn., Nepal	D8	54
Apia, Samoa	g12	79c
Apiaí, Braz.	B13	92
Apiaú, stm., Braz.	F11	86
Apishapa, stm., Co., U.S.	D4	128
Apizaco, Mex.	F9	100
Apo, Mount, mtn., Phil.	G5	52
Apodi, Braz.	C7	88
Apodi, stm., Braz.	C7	88
Apolakkiá, Grc.	G10	28
Apolda, Ger.	E7	16
Apolinario Saravia, Arg.	B6	92
Apongas, Braz.	G6	92
Apolo, Bol.	B3	90
Apopka, Lake, l., Fl., U.S.	H4	116
Aporá, Braz.	F6	88
Aporé, Braz.	C6	90
Apostle Islands, is., Wi., U.S.	E8	118
Apostle Islands National Lakeshore, p.o.i., Wi., U.S.	C10	92
Apóstoles, Arg.	C10	92
Apostolove, Ukr.	E4	32
Appalaches, Les see Appalachian Mountains, mts., N.A.	D12	108
Appalachia, Va., U.S.	H3	114
Appalachian Mountains, mts., N.A.	D12	108
Appennines see Appennino, mts., Italy	G11	6
Appennino, Calabro, mts., Italy	E10	24
Appennino Abruzzese, mts., Italy	B7	24
Appennino Ligure, mts., Italy	F6	22
Appennino Lucano, mts., Italy	D9	24
Appennino Tosco-Emiliano, mts., Italy	F8	22
Appennino Umbro-Marchigiano, mts., Italy	G9	22
Appenzell, Switz.	C6	22
Apple Orchard Mountain, mtn., Va., U.S.	G6	114
Appleton, Mn., U.S.	F3	118
Appleton, Wi., U.S.	G10	118
Appleton City, Mo., U.S.	F3	120
Apple Valley, Ca., U.S.	I8	134
Appomattox, Va., U.S.	G7	114
Appomattox, stm., Va., U.S.	G7	114
Aprelevka, Russia	E20	10
Aprília, Italy	C6	24
Apšeronsk, Russia	F5	32
Apt, Fr.	F11	18
Apucarana, Braz.	A12	92
Apulia see Puglia, state, Italy	C10	24
Apure, state, Ven.	D7	86
Apure, stm., Ven.	D8	86
Apurímac, stm., Peru	F3	84
Apurito, Ven.	D7	86
Aqaba, Gulf of, b.	J5	58
Āqchah, Afg.	B10	56
'Aqīq, Sudan	D7	62
Aqköl, Kaz.	F12	32
Aqköl, Kaz.	D12	32
Aqmola see Astana, Kaz.	D12	32
Aqsū, Kaz.	D13	32
Aqsū, Kaz.	D12	32
Aqsū, stm., Kaz.	E13	32
Aqsūat, Kaz.	E14	32
Aqsūat, Kaz.	E14	32
Aqtaū, Kaz.	F8	32
Aqtöbe, Kaz.	D9	32
Aqtöbe, Kaz.	F8	32
Aquidabã, Braz.	F7	88
Aquidauana, Braz.	D5	90
Aquila, Mex.	F7	100
Aquiles Serdán, Mex.	A6	100
Aquiles Serdán, Mex.	C9	100
Aquin, Haiti	C11	102
Ara, India	F10	54
Ara, stm., Japan	D12	40
'Arab, Bahr al-, stm., Sudan	E5	62
'Araba, Wadi ('Arabah, Wādī), stm., Egypt	I3	58
'Arabah, Wādī al- (Ha'Arava), Wādī al-, Asia	H6	58
Arabako, co., Spain	B8	20
Araban, Tur.	A8	58
Arabian Basin, unds.	H9	142
Arabian Desert (Eastern Desert), des., Egypt	B6	62
Arabian Gulf see Persian Gulf, b., Asia	D7	56
Arabian Peninsula, pen., Asia	E6	56
Arabian Sea, s.	F9	56
Araçá, stm., Braz.	G10	86
Aracaju, Braz.	F7	88
Aracataca, Col.	B4	86
Aracati, Braz.	C7	88
Araçatuba, Braz.	D6	90
Aracena, Spain	G4	20
Araci, Braz.	F6	88
Aracides, Cape, c., Sol. Is.	e9	79b
Aracoiaba, Braz.	C6	88
Aracruz, Braz.	J5	88
Araçuaí, Braz.	I4	88
Araçuaí, stm., Braz.	I5	88
'Arad, Isr.	G6	58
Arad, state, Rom.	C8	26
Aradhippou, Cyp.	D4	58
Arafura Sea, s.	J16	142
Arafura Shelf, unds.	K16	142
Aragarças, Braz.	G7	84
Aragats Lerr, mtn., Arm.	A5	56
Aragón, state, Spain	C10	20
Aragón, stm., Spain	B9	20
Aragona, Italy	G7	24
Aragua, state, Ven.	B8	86
Araguacema, Braz.	E8	84
Araguaçu, Braz.	F8	84
Aragua de Barcelona, Ven.	C9	86
Araguaia, stm., Braz.	E8	84
Araguaína, Braz.	H3	88
Araguari, Braz.	J1	88
Araguari, stm., Braz.	J1	88
Araguari, stm., Braz.	C7	84
Araguatins, Braz.	C1	88
Arahal, Spain	G5	20
Arai, Japan	B11	40
Araioses, Braz.	B4	88
Árak, Alg.	D5	64
Arāk, Iran	C6	56
Arakan see Rakhine, state, Mya.	C1	48
Arakan Yoma, mts., Mya.	C2	48
Arakkonam, India	E4	53
Araks see Aras, stm., Asia	B6	56
Araks see Aras, stm., Asia	B6	56
Aral, stm., Kaz.	E10	32
Aralbaj, Kaz.	E10	32
Aral Sea, l., Asia	E9	32
Aral'sk see Aral, Kaz.	E10	32
Aramac, Austl.	D5	76
Aramac, stm., Austl.	D5	76
Ārāmbāg, India	G11	54
Ārān, Iran	C7	56
Aranda de Duero, Spain	C7	20
Arandas, Mex.	E7	100
Arandis, Nmb.	C2	70
Arang, India	H8	54
Arani, India	E4	53
Aran Islands, is., Ire.	H3	12
Aran Islands, is., Ire.	H3	12
Aranos, Nmb.	D4	70
Aransas, stm., Tx., U.S.	F10	130
Arantāngi, India	F4	53
Aranyaprathet, Thai.	F6	48
Arao, Japan	G3	40
Araouane, Mali	F4	64
Arapaho, Ok., U.S.	F9	128
Arapahoe, Ne., U.S.	A9	128
Arapey Grande, stm., Ur.	E9	92
Arapiraca, Braz.	D6	90
Arapongas, Braz.	B12	92
Arapoti, Braz.	B13	92
Araranguá, Braz.	D13	92
Araraquara, Braz.	K1	88
Araras, Braz.	L2	88
Araras, Açude, res., Braz.	C5	88
Ararat, Austl.	K4	76
Ararat, Mount see Ağrı Dağı, mtn., Tur.	B5	56
Araripe, Braz.	D5	88
Araripe, Chapada do, plat., Braz.	D6	88
Araripina, Braz.	D5	88
Ararirá, stm., Braz.	H10	86
Araruama, Lagoa de, b., Braz.	L4	88
Araruna, Braz.	D8	88
Aras (Araz), stm., Asia	B6	56
Aras, stm., Asia	B6	56
Aratupe, Braz.	G6	88
Arauca, Col.	D6	86
Arauca, stm., S.A.	D6	86
Arauca, state, Col.	D6	86
Araucária, Braz.	B13	92
Araucanía, state, Chile	D6	86
Araure, Ven.	C7	86
Arāvalli Range, mts., India	F4	54
Arawa, Pap. N. Gui.	d6	79b
Araxá, Braz.	J2	88
Araya, Ven.	B9	86
Araya, Punta de, c., Ven.	B9	86
Arba (Aras), stm., Asia	B6	56
Árba Minch', Eth.	F7	62
Arbatax, Italy	E3	24
Arbil, Iraq	B5	56
Arboga, Swe.	G6	8
Arboledas, Arg.	H7	92
Arbon, Switz.	C6	22
Arborea, Italy	E2	24
Arborea, reg., Italy	E2	24
Arborfield, Sk., Can.	A10	124
Arbroath, Scot., U.K.	E10	12
Arbuckle, Ca., U.S.	D3	134
Arc, stm., Fr.	D12	18
Arcachon, Fr.	E4	18
Arcachon, Bassin d', b., Fr.	E4	18
Arcade, Ca., U.S.	E4	134
Arcade, N.Y., U.S.	B7	114
Arcadia, Ca., U.S.	I7	134
Arcadia, Fl., U.S.	I4	116
Arcadia, Ks., U.S.	B2	120
Arcadia, La., U.S.	E6	122
Arcadia, Mi., U.S.	D3	112
Arcadia, Mo., U.S.	G7	120
Arcadia, S.C., U.S.	B3	116
Arcadia, Wi., U.S.	G7	118
Arcanum, Oh., U.S.	D1	114
Arcas, Cayos, is., Mex.	E12	100
Arc Dome, mtn., Nv., U.S.	E8	134
Arcelia, Mex.	F8	100
Arcevia, Italy	G9	22
Archangel see Arhangel'sk, Russia	D19	8
Archbold, Oh., U.S.	C1	114
Archer, Fl., U.S.	G3	116
Archer, stm., Austl.	B8	74
Archer, Mount, mtn., Austl.	D8	76
Archer City, Tx., U.S.	H10	128
Archer's Post, Kenya	D7	66
Arches National Park, p.o.i., Ut., U.S.	E7	132
Archiac, Fr.	D5	18
Archidona, Spain	G6	20
Arcis-sur-Aube, Fr.	F13	14
Arco, Id., U.S.	G13	136
Arcola, Il., U.S.	E9	120
Arcola, Ms., U.S.	D8	122
Arcos, Braz.	K3	88
Arcos de la Frontera, Spain	H5	20
Arcot, India	E4	53
Arcoverde, Braz.	E7	88
Arctic Bay see Tununirusiq, Nu., Can.	A14	106
Arctic Ocean	A21	4
Arctic Red, stm., N.T., Can.	B4	106
Arctic Village, Ak., U.S.	C10	140
Arda, stm., Eur.	H12	26
Ardabīl, Iran	B6	56
Ardahan, Tur.	A5	56
Ardakān, Iran	C7	56
Ardatov, Russia	I20	8
Ardèche, state, Fr.	E10	18
Arden, Ca., U.S.	E4	134
Ardennes, state, Fr.	E13	14
Ardennes, reg., Eur.	D14	14
Ardennes, Canal des, can., Fr.	E13	14
Ardestān, Iran	C7	56
Ardila, stm., Eur.	F3	20
Ardill, Sk., Can.	E8	124
Ardlethan, Austl.	J6	76
Ardmore, Al., U.S.	B12	122
Ardmore, Ok., U.S.	G11	128
Ardmore, Pa., U.S.	D10	114
Åre, Swe.	E5	8
Areado, Braz.	K2	88
Arecibo, P.R.	B2	104a
Arecibo, Observatorio see Arecibo, Observatorio de, sci., P.R.	B2	104a
Arecibo, Observatorio de, sci., P.R.	B2	104a
Arêhausk, Bela.	F13	10
Areia, Braz.	D8	88
Areia, Braz.	H3	88
Areia Branca, Braz.	C7	88
Areia, Point, c., Ca., U.S.	E2	134
Arena, Punta, c., Mex.	D4	100
Arena de la Ventana, Punta, c., Mex.	C4	100
Arenal, Braz.	C5	88
Arenas, Cayo, i., Mex.	D13	100
Arenas, Punta de, c., Arg.	J3	90
Arenas de San Pedro, Spain	D5	20
Arendal, Nor.	G3	8
Arenys de Mar, Spain	C13	20
Arequipa, Peru	G3	84
Arévalo, Spain	C6	20
Arezzo, Italy	G8	22
Arga, stm., Spain	B9	20
Argadargada, Austl.	D7	74
Arganda del Rey, Spain	D7	20
Arga-Sala, stm., Russia	C10	34
Argelès-Gazost, Fr.	F5	18
Argens, stm., Fr.	F12	18
Argent, Côte d', cst., Fr.	E4	18
Argenta, Italy	F8	22
Argentan, Fr.	F8	14
Argentat, Fr.	D7	18
Argenteuil, Fr.	F11	14
Arges, stm., Rom.	E12	26
Argentina, ctry., S.A.	G3	90
Argentine Basin, unds.	L10	144
Argentino, Lago, l., Arg.	J2	90
Argenton-sur-Creuse, Fr.	H10	14
Arges, state, Rom.	E11	26
Arghandāb, stm., Afg.	C10	56
Argolikós Kólpos (Argolís, Gulf of), b., Grc.	F6	28
Argolis, Gulf of see Argolikós Kólpos, b., Grc.	F6	28
Argonne, Wi., U.S.	F10	118
Argonne, reg., Fr.	E14	14
Árgos, Grc.	F5	28
Árgos, In., U.S.	G3	112
Argostóli, Grc.	E3	28
Arguello, Point, c., Ca., U.S.	I5	134
Argun' (Ergun), stm., Asia	F12	34
Argungu, Nig.	G5	64
Argyle, Lake, l., Austl.	C5	74
Arhangel'sk, Russia	D19	8
Arhangel'skoe, Russia	G20	10
Arhara, Russia	G15	34
Arhipovo, Russia	C21	8
Århus, Den.	H4	8
Århus, state, Den.	H4	8
Ariana, Tun.	H4	24
Ariano Irpino, Italy	C9	24
Ariari, stm., Col.	F5	86
Arias, Arg.	G7	92
Ari Atoll, at., Mald.	i12	46a
Arica, Chile	C2	90
Arica, Col.	I6	86
Arichat, N.S., Can.	E16	110
Arichuna, Ven.	D8	86
Arid, Cape, c., Austl.	F4	74
Aridaia, Grc.	C5	28
Ariège, state, Fr.	G7	18
Arifwāla, Pak.	C4	54
Ariguani, stm., Col.	C5	86
Arīḥā (Jericho), Gaza	G6	58
Arīḥā, Syria	C7	58
Arikaree, stm., U.S.	B6	128
Arima, Trin.	s12	105f
Arinos, stm., Braz.	F6	84
Ariogala, Lith.	E6	10
Ariporo, stm., Col.	D6	86
Aripuanã, Braz.	E5	84
Aripuanã, stm., Braz.	E5	84
Ariquemes, Braz.	E5	84
Arisa, stm., Ven.	D9	86
Ark, Île, i., N. Cal.	I14	79d
Arka, Russia	D17	34
Arkadelphia, Ar., U.S.	C5	122
Arkalyk see Arqalyq, Kaz.	D11	32
Arkansas, state, U.S.	B6	122
Arkansas, stm., U.S.	E9	108
Arkansas, Salt Fork, stm., U.S.	D7	122
Arkansas City, Ar., U.S.	D7	122
Arkansas City, Ks., U.S.	D11	128
Arklow, Ire.	I6	12
Arkoma, Ok., U.S.	B4	122
Arkona, Kap, c., Ger.	B9	16
Arktičeskogo Instituta, ostrova, is., Russia	A5	34
Arlanza, stm., Spain	B7	20
Arlanzón, stm., Spain	B7	20
Arles, Fr.	F10	18
Arlington, S. Afr.	E8	70
Arlington, Ga., U.S.	F14	122
Arlington, Ks., U.S.	D10	128
Arlington, Mn., U.S.	H9	120
Arlington, Ne., U.S.	C1	120
Arlington, Oh., U.S.	D2	114
Arlington, Or., U.S.	E6	136
Arlington, S.D., U.S.	C15	126
Arlington, Tn., U.S.	B9	122
Arlington, Tx., U.S.	B10	130
Arlington, Va., U.S.	F8	114
Arlington, Vt., U.S.	G3	110
Arlington, Wa., U.S.	B4	136
Arlington Heights, Il., U.S.	F2	112
Arlit, Niger	F6	64
Arlon, Bel.	E14	14
Arm, stm., Sk., Can.	D8	124
Arma, Ks., U.S.	G3	120
Armada, Mi., U.S.	B3	114
Armadale, Austl.	F3	74
Armagedon see Tel Megiddo, sci., Isr.	F6	58
Armagh, N. Ire., U.K.	G6	12
Armançon, stm., Fr.	G13	14
Armavir, Russia	E6	32
Armenia, ctry., Asia	A5	56
Armenia see Armenia, ctry., Asia	A5	56
Armenia, Mex.	F6	100
Armentières, Fr.	D11	14
Armería, Mex.	F6	100
Armero, Col.	E4	86
Armidale, Austl.	H8	76
Armijo, N.M., U.S.	H10	132
Armstrong, Arg.	F7	92
Armstrong, B.C., Can.	F11	138
Armstrong, Ia., U.S.	A3	120
Armstrong, Mo., U.S.	E5	120
Armstrong, Mount, mtn., Yk., Can.	C4	106
Ārmūr, India	B4	53
Armutlu, Tur.	C11	28
Arnaía, Grc.	C6	28
Arnaud, stm., Qc., Can.	D16	106
Arnaudville, La., U.S.	G6	122
Arnay-le-Duc, Fr.	G13	14
Arnedo, Spain	B8	20
Arneiros, Braz.	D5	88
Arnes, Nor.	F4	8
Arnett, Ok., U.S.	E9	128
Arnhem, Neth.	C14	14
Arnhem, Cape, c., Austl.	B7	74
Arnhem Bay, b., Austl.	B7	74
Arnhem Land, reg., Austl.	B6	74
Arno, atoll, Marsh. Is.	C8	72
Arno, stm., Italy	G7	22
Arnold, Ca., U.S.	E5	134
Arnold, Mo., U.S.	F7	120
Arnold, Ne., U.S.	F12	126
Arnolds Park, Ia., U.S.	H3	118
Arnon, stm., Fr.	G11	14
Arnøya, i., Nor.	A9	8
Arnprior, On., Can.	C13	112
Arnsberg, Ger.	E4	16
Arnstadt, Ger.	F6	16
Aroa, Ven.	B7	86
Aroab, Nmb.	E4	70
Aroland, On., Can.	A12	118
Arolsen, Ger.	E5	16
Arona, Italy	E5	22
Arona, Pap. N. Gui.	b4	79a
Aroostook, stm., N.A.	D8	110
Arop Island (Long Island), i., Pap. N. Gui.	b4	79a
Arorae, i., Kir.	D8	72
Aroroy, Phil.	D4	52
Arosa, Ria de see Arousa, Ria de, est., Spain	B1	20
Arousa, Ria de est., Spain	B1	20
Arp, Tx., U.S.	E3	122
Arqalyq, Kaz.	D11	32
Arquata Scrivia, Italy	F5	22
Arraga, Arg.	D5	92
Ar-Rahad, Sudan	E6	62
Arraial do Cabo, Braz.	L5	88
Arraias, Braz.	G2	88
Arraias, stm., Braz.	G2	88
Ar-Ramādī, Iraq	C5	56
Ar-Ramthā, Jord.	F7	58
Arran, Island of, i., Scot., U.K.	F7	12
Ar-Rank, Sudan	E6	62
Ar-Raqqah, Syria	B9	58
Ar-Raqqah, state, Syria	B9	58
Arras, Fr.	D11	14
Ar-Rastan, Syria	D7	58
Arrecifes, Arg.	G7	92
Arrey, N.M., U.S.	K9	132
Arriaga, Mex.	G11	100
Ar-Riyāḍ (Riyadh), Sau. Ar.	E6	56
Arroio Grande, Braz.	F11	92
Arronches, Port.	E3	20
Arros, stm., Fr.	F5	18
Arrowhead, Lake, res., Tx., U.S.	H10	128
Arrowwood, Ab., Can.	F17	138
Arroyito, Arg.	E6	92
Arroyo, P.R.	C3	104a
Arroyo de la Luz, Spain	E4	20
Arroyo Grande, Ca., U.S.	H5	134
Arroyo Hondo, N.M., U.S.	E3	128
Arroyo Seco, Arg.	F7	92
Arroyos y Esteros, Para.	B9	92
Ar-Rub' al-Khālī, des., Asia	E6	56
Ar-Ruqayyah, sci., Syria	F8	58
Ar-Rusāfah, sci., Syria	C9	58
Ar-Rusayfah, Jord.	F6	58
Ar-Rusayris, Sudan	E6	62
Ar-Rutbah, Iraq	C5	56
Arsenev, Russia	B10	38
Arsen'evka, stm., Russia	B10	38
Arsikere, India	E3	53
Arsos, Cyp.	D3	58
Art, Île, i., N. Cal.	I14	79d
Arta, Spain	E14	20
Artà see Artà, Spain	E14	20
Arteaga, Mex.	F7	100
Art'em, Russia	C9	38
Artemisa, Cuba	A6	102
Artëmovsk, Russia	D16	32
Artëmovskij, Russia	C10	38
Artesia, Ms., U.S.	D10	122
Artesia, N.M., U.S.	B3	130
Arthabaska, ngh., Qc., Can.	D5	110
Arthal, India	B6	54
Arthur, On., Can.	E9	112
Arthur, Il., U.S.	E9	120
Arthur, N.D., U.S.	D1	118
Arthur, Mount, mtn., Austl.	n12	77a
Arthur's Pass National Park, p.o.i., N.Z.	F5	80
Arthur's Town, Bah.	C9	96
Artibonite, stm., Haiti	C11	102
Artigas, Ur.	E9	92
Artillery Lake, l., N.T., Can.	C9	106
Artois, hist. reg., Fr.	D11	14
Artsyz, Ukr.	D16	26
Artyk, Russia	D18	34
Aru, Kepulauan (Aru Islands), is., Indon.	G10	44
Aru, Tanjung, c., Indon.	E10	50
Aru, Ug.	D6	66
Aruanã, Braz.	G7	84
Aruba, dep., N.A.	F12	102
Aru Islands see Aru, Kepulauan, is., Indon.	G10	44
Arunāchal Pradesh, state, India	C7	46
Arun Qi, China	B9	36
Aruppukkottai, India	G4	53
Arurandeua, stm., Braz.	C1	88
Arusha, Tan.	E7	66
Aruví, stm., Indon.	E7	50
Aruvimi, stm., D.R.C.	D4	66
Arvada, Co., U.S.	B3	128
Arvayheer, Mong.	B5	36
Arvi, India	H7	54
Arviat, Nu., Can.	C12	106
Arvidsjaur, Swe.	D8	8
Arvika, Swe.	G5	8
Arvin, Ca., U.S.	H7	134
Arvon, Mount, mtn., Mi., U.S.	B1	112
Arvorezinha, Braz.	D11	92
Arys, Kaz.	F11	32
Arys köli, l., Kaz.	E10	32
Arzamas, Russia	I20	8
Arzignano, Italy	E8	22
Arz Lubnān, for., Leb.	D7	58
Arzúa, Spain	B2	20
Aš, Czech Rep.	F8	16
Aša, Russia	D9	32
Asa, stm., Ven.	D9	86
Asaba, Nig.	H6	64
Asad, Buhayrat al- (Assad, Lake), res., Syria	B9	58
Asadābād, Afg.	C11	56
Asadābād, Iran	C6	56
Aşağıbostancı, N. Cyp.	C3	58
Asahan, stm., Indon.	B1	50
Asahi, Japan	D13	40
Asahi, stm., Japan	E6	40
Asahidake, vol., Japan	C15	38
Asahikawa, Japan	C15	38
Asama-yama, vol., Japan	C11	40
Asan-man, b., Kor., S.	F7	38
Āsānsol, India	F11	54
Asaro, stm., Pap. N. Gui.	b3	79a
Åsaro, Swe.	q20	104g
Asbest, Russia	C10	32
Asbestos, Qc., Can.	E4	110
Asbestos Range National Park, p.o.i., Austl.	n13	77a
Asbury Park, N.J., U.S.	D12	114
Ascensión, Mex.	F9	98
Ascension, i., St. Hel.	G4	60
Aschaffenburg, Ger.	G5	16
Aschersleben, Ger.	E7	16
Ascoli Piceno, Italy	H10	22
Ascoli Satriano, Italy	C9	24
Ascör (Astor), stm., Eur.	G14	10
Aseb, Erit.	F8	62
Åseda, Swe.	H6	8
Asela, Eth.	F7	62
Åsele, Swe.	D7	8
Asenovgrad, Blg.	G11	26
Aseri, Est.	A9	10
Aşgabat, Turkmen.	B8	56
Ash Grove, Mo., U.S.	G4	120
Ashburn, Ga., U.S.	E2	116
Ashburton, N.Z.	F4	80
Ashburton, stm., Austl.	D3	74
Ashchysu, stm., Kaz.	E13	32
Ashcroft, B.C., Can.	F9	138
Ashdod, Isr.	G5	58
Ashdod, Tel, sci., Isr.	G5	58
Ashdown, Ar., U.S.	D4	122
Asheboro, N.C., U.S.	I6	114
Ashern, Mb., Can.	C15	124
Asheville, N.C., U.S.	A3	116
Ashford, Eng., U.K.	J13	12
Ashford, Al., U.S.	F13	122
Ash Fork, Az., U.S.	H4	132
Ashgabat see Aşgabat, Turkmen.	B8	56
Ashibe, Japan	F2	40

Name	Map Ref.	Page
Ashikaga, Japan	C12	40
Ashington, Eng., U.K.	F11	12
Ashiya, Japan	C12	40
Ashizuri-misaki, c., Japan	G6	40
Ashland, Al., U.S.	D13	122
Ashland, Il., U.S.	E7	120
Ashland, Ks., U.S.	D9	128
Ashland, Ky., U.S.	F3	114
Ashland, Mo., U.S.	F5	120
Ashland, Mt., U.S.	B6	126
Ashland, Ne., U.S.	C1	120
Ashland, N.H., U.S.	G5	110
Ashland, Oh., U.S.	D3	114
Ashland, Or., U.S.	A3	134
Ashland, Va., U.S.	G8	114
Ashland, Wi., U.S.	E7	118
Ashland, Mount, mtn., Or., U.S.	A3	134
Ashley, Austl.	G7	76
Ashley, Il., U.S.	F8	120
Ashley, Mi., U.S.	E5	112
Ashley, Oh., U.S.	D3	114
Ashmore, Il., U.S.	E9	120
Ashmore Islands, is., Austl.	B4	74
Ashoknagar, India	F6	54
Ashqelon, Isr.	G5	58
Ash-Shamāl, state, Leb.	D7	58
Ash-Shaqrā' see Shaqrā', Sau. Ar.	D6	56
Ash-Shāriqah, U.A.E.	D8	56
Ash-Shawbak, Jord.	H6	58
Ash-Shihr, Yemen	G6	56
Ash-Shurayf, Sau. Ar.	D4	56
Ashta, India	C2	53
Ashta, India	G6	54
Ashtabula, Oh., U.S.	C5	114
Ashtabula, Lake, res., N.D., U.S.	G16	124
Ashton, S. Afr.	H5	70
Ashton, St. Vin.	p11	105e
Ashton, Id., U.S.	F15	136
Ashton, Il., U.S.	C8	120
Ashton, Ne., U.S.	F14	126
Ashuanipi Lake, l., Nf., Can.	E17	106
Ashuapmushuan, stm., Qc., Can.	B3	110
Ashūm, Egypt	H1	58
Ashville, Al., U.S.	D12	122
Ashwaubenon, Wi., U.S.	D1	112
Asi see Orontes, stm., Asia	B7	58
Asia, cont.	C19	4
Asia, Kepulauan, is., Indon.	E9	44
Asia Minor, hist. reg., Tur.	E13	28
Asika, India	I10	54
Asinara, Golfo dell', b., Italy	D2	24
Asinara, Isola, i., Italy	C2	24
Asíni, sci., Grc.	F5	28
Asino, Russia	C15	32
Asintorf, Bela.	F13	10
Asipovičy, Bela.	G11	10
'Asīr, reg., Sau. Ar.	F5	56
Askham, S. Afr.	E5	70
Askiz, Russia	D16	32
Askja, vol., Ice.	k31	8a
Aslanapa, Tur.	D12	28
Aslantaş Baraji, res., Tur.	A7	58
Asmara see Asmera, Erit.	D7	62
Asmera, Erit.	D7	62
Asmjany, Bela.	F8	10
Asola, Italy	E7	22
Asomante, P.R.	B2	104a
Asosa, Eth.	E6	62
Asoteriba, Jabal, mtn., Sudan	C7	62
Asotin, Wa., U.S.	D9	136
Asouf, Oued, stm., Alg.	D5	64
Aspe, Spain	F10	20
Aspe see Asp, Spain	F10	20
Aspen, Co., U.S.	D10	132
Aspendos, sci., Tur.	G14	28
Aspermont, Tx., U.S.	A7	130
Aspiring, Mount, mtn., N.Z.	G3	80
Assad, Lake see Asad, Buhayrat al-, res., Syria	B9	58
As-Safīrah, Syria	B9	58
As-Şāfiyah, Sudan	D6	62
As-Salt, Jord.	F6	58
Assam, state, India	C7	46
As-Samāwah, Iraq	C6	56
Aş-Şanamayn, Syria	E7	58
As-Sulaymānīyah, Iraq	B6	56
As-Sulaymānīyah, Sau. Ar.	E6	56
As-Sulayyil, Sau. Ar.	E6	56
Assumption, Il., U.S.	E8	120
As-Suwaydā', Syria	F7	58
As-Suwaydā', state, Syria	F7	58
Astakós, Grc.	E3	28
Astana (Aqmola), Kaz.	D12	32
Astara, Azer.	B6	56
Asti, Italy	F5	22
Astica, Arg.	E4	92
Astola Island, i., Pak.	D9	56
Astorga, Spain	B4	20
Astoria, Il., U.S.	D7	120
Astoria, Or., U.S.	D3	136
Astove, i., Sey.	I11	69b
Astrahan', Russia	E7	32
Astrakhan see Astrahan', Russia	E7	32
Astrašyckі Haradok, Bela.	F10	10
Astrolabe, Cape, c., Sol. Is.	e9	79b
Astrolabe, Récifs de l', rf., N. Cal.	I15	79d
Astrolabe Reefs see Astrolabe, Récifs de l', rf., N. Cal.	I15	79d
Astronja, Bela.	E12	10
Astudillo, Spain	B6	20
Asturias, state, Spain	A5	20
Astypálaia, i., Grc.	G9	28
Asunción, Para.	B9	92
Asunción, Bahía la, b., Mex.	B1	100
Asunción Nochixtlán, Mex.	G10	100
Asunden, l., Swe.	H5	8
Asveja, Bela.	E11	10
Asvejskae, vozero, l., Bela.	D10	10
Aswān, Egypt	C6	62
Aswan High Dam see Sadd el-, dam, Egypt	C6	62
Asyūt, Egypt	K2	58
Asyūtī, Wadi el- (Asyūtī, Wadi al-), stm., Egypt	K2	58
'Ata, i., Tonga	F9	72
Atabapo, stm., S.A.	F8	86
Atacama, state, Chile	C3	92
Atacama, Desierto de, des., Chile	E2	90
Atacama, Puna de, plat., S.A.	B4	92
Atacama, Salar de, pl., Chile	D3	90
Atacama Desert see Atacama, Desierto de, des., Chile	B3	92
Ataco, Col.	F4	86
Atagaj, Russia	C17	32

Name	Map Ref.	Page
Atakpamé, Togo	H5	64
Atalaia, Braz.	E7	88
Atambua, Indon.	G7	44
Atami, Japan	D12	40
Atangmik, Grnld.	E15	141
Ațar, Maur.	E2	64
Atascadero, Ca., U.S.	H5	134
Atascosa, stm., Tx., U.S.	F9	130
Atasū, Kaz.	E12	32
Atata, i., Tonga	n14	78e
Atauro, Pulau, i., E. Timor	G8	44
'Atbarah, Sudan	D6	62
'Atbarah, stm., Afr.	D7	62
Atbasar, Kaz.	D11	32
Atchafalaya, stm., La., U.S.	G7	122
Atchafalaya Bay, b., La., U.S.	H7	122
Atchison, Ks., U.S.	E2	120
Ateca, Spain	C9	20
Aterno, stm., Italy	H10	22
Atfih, Egypt	I2	58
Ath, Bel.	D12	14
Athabasca, Ab., Can.	B17	138
Athabasca, stm., Ab., Can.	D8	106
Athabasca, Lake, l., Can.	D9	106
Athalmer, B.C., Can.	F14	138
Athboy, Ire.	H6	12
Athens, Oh., U.S.	E8	136
Athens, On., Can.	D14	112
Athens see Athína, Grc.	E6	28
Athens, Al., U.S.	C11	122
Athens, Ga., U.S.	C2	116
Athens, Il., U.S.	E8	120
Athens, La., U.S.	E5	122
Athens, Mi., U.S.	F4	112
Athens, Oh., U.S.	E3	114
Athens, Pa., U.S.	C9	114
Athens, Tn., U.S.	B14	122
Athens, Tx., U.S.	E3	122
Athens, W.V., U.S.	G5	114
Atherton, Austl.	A5	76
Athi, stm., Kenya	E7	66
Athiainou, Cyp.	C4	58
Athína (Athens), Grc.	E6	28
Athlone, Ire.	H4	12
Athni, India	C2	53
Athok, Mya.	D2	48
Athol, Ma., U.S.	B13	114
Áthos, mtn., Grc.	C7	28
Athos, Mount see Áthos, mtn., Grc.	C7	28
Ati, Chad	E3	62
Atiak, Ug.	D6	66
Atico, Peru	G3	84
Atienza, Spain	C8	20
Atikokan, On., Can.	C7	118
Atirāmpattinam, India	F4	53
Atka, i., Cook Is.	F11	72
Atka, Russia	D19	34
Atka Island, i., Ak., U.S.	g24	140a
Atkarsk, Russia	D6	32
Atkins, Ar., U.S.	B6	122
Atkinson, Il., U.S.	C8	120
Atkinson, N.C., U.S.	B7	116
Atlanta, Ga., U.S.	C1	116
Atlanta, Il., U.S.	D8	120
Atlanta, Mi., U.S.	D5	112
Atlanta, Mo., U.S.	E5	120
Atlantic, Ia., U.S.	C2	120
Atlantic, N.C., U.S.	B9	116
Atlantic Beach, Fl., U.S.	F4	116
Atlantic City, N.J., U.S.	E11	114
Atlantic-Indian Basin, unds.	O5	142
Atlantic-Indian Ridge, unds.	N15	144
Atlantic Ocean	E9	144
Atlantic Peak, mtn., Wy., U.S.	E3	126
Atlas Mountains, mts., Afr.	C4	64
Atlasova, ostrov, i., Russia	F20	34
Atlas Saharien, mts., Alg.	C4	64
Atlin, B.C., Can.	D4	106
Atlin Lake, l., Can.	D4	106
'Atlit, Isr.	F5	58
Atmakur, India	D4	53
Atmore, Al., U.S.	F11	122
Atnarko, stm., B.C., Can.	D5	138
Atocha, Bol.	D3	90
Atoka, Ok., U.S.	C2	122
Atotonilco, Cerro, mtn., Mex.	H3	100
Atoyac, stm., Mex.	F9	100
Atoyac de Álvarez, Mex.	G8	100
Atrak (Atrek), stm., Asia	B7	56
Atran, stm., Swe.	H5	8
Atrato, stm., Col.	D3	86
Atrauli, India	D7	54
Atrek (Atrak), stm., Asia	B7	56
Atri, Italy	H10	22
Atsumi, Japan	E10	40
Atsumi-hantō, pen., Japan	E10	40
Aṭ-Ṭafīlah, Jord.	H6	58
Aṭ-Ṭafīlah, state, Jord.	H6	58
Aṭ-Ṭā'if, Sau. Ar.	E5	56
At-Tall, Syria	E7	58
Attalla, Al., U.S.	C12	122
Attapu, Laos	E8	48
Attawapiskat, On., Can.	E13	106
Attawapiskat Lake, l., On., Can.	E13	106
Aṭ-Ṭawīl, mts., Sau. Ar.	D4	56
Aṭ-Ṭayyibah, Syria	C9	58
Attersee, l., Aus.	C10	22
Attica, In., U.S.	H2	112
Attica, Ks., U.S.	D10	128
Attica, N.Y., U.S.	B7	114
Attica see Attikí, hist. reg., Grc.	E6	28
Attikí, state, Grc.	E6	28
Attikí, hist. reg., Grc.	E6	28
Attleboro, Ma., U.S.	C14	114
Attu, Ak., U.S.	g21	140a
Attu Island, i., Ak., U.S.	g21	140a
Āttūr, India	F4	53
Aṭ-Tuwayshah, Sudan	E5	62
Atuel, stm., Arg.	G3	92
Atuel, Bañados del, sw., Arg.	G2	86
Atuona, Fr. Poly.	s18	78j
Atwater, Ca., U.S.	F5	134
Atwater, Mn., U.S.	F4	118
Atwood, Il., U.S.	E9	120
Atwood, Tn., U.S.	I9	120
Atwood, On., Can.	B7	128
Atwood Lake, l., Pap. N. Gui.	a3	79a
Auari, stm., Braz.	F9	86
Auau Channel, strt., Hi., U.S.	c5	78a
Aubagne, Fr.	F11	18
Aube, stm., Fr.	F13	14
Aube, co., Fr.	F12	14
Aubigny-sur-Nère, Fr.	G11	14
Aubinadong, stm., On., Can.	A6	112
Aubrey Cliffs, clf., Az., U.S.	H4	132
Aubrey Lake, res., On., Can.	A6	112
Aubry Lake, l., N.T., Can.	B5	106
Auburn, Al., U.S.	E13	122
Auburn, Ca., U.S.	E4	134
Auburn, Il., U.S.	E8	120
Auburn, In., U.S.	G4	112
Auburn, Ky., U.S.	H11	120
Auburn, Ma., U.S.	B14	114
Auburn, Me., U.S.	F6	110
Auburn, Ne., U.S.	E1	120
Auburn, N.Y., U.S.	B9	114
Auburn, Wa., U.S.	C4	136
Auburn, stm., Austl.	E8	76
Aubusson, Fr.	D8	18

Name	Map Ref.	Page
Auca Mahuida, Cerro, mtn., Arg.	H3	92
Auce, Lat.	D5	10
Auch, Fr.	F6	18
Auchi, Nig.	H6	64
Aucilla, stm., U.S.	F2	116
Auckland, N.Z.	C6	80
Auckland Islands, is., N.Z.	I7	72
Aude, state, Fr.	F8	18
Aude, stm., Fr.	F9	18
Audenarde see Oudenaarde, Bel.	D12	14
Audierne, Fr.	F4	14
Audincourt, Fr.	G15	14
Audubon Lake, res., N.D., U.S.	G12	124
Aue, Ger.	F8	16
Augathella, Austl.	E6	76
Augrabies Falls National Park, p.o.i., S. Afr.	F4	70
Augrabiesvalle, wtfl., S. Afr.	F5	70
Augsburg, Ger.	H6	16
Augusta, Austl.	F2	74
Augusta, Italy	G9	24
Augusta, Ar., U.S.	B7	122
Augusta, Ga., U.S.	C3	116
Augusta, Il., U.S.	D6	120
Augusta, Ky., U.S.	F1	114
Augusta, Me., U.S.	F7	110
Augusta, Mt., U.S.	C14	136
Augusta, Wi., U.S.	G7	118
Augusto Severo, Braz.	C7	88
Augustów, Pol.	C18	16
Augustowski, Kanal, can., Eur.	C19	16
Augustus, Mount, mtn., Austl.	D3	74
Auki, Sol. Is.	e9	79b
Aukstaitijos nacionalnis parkas, p.o.i., Lith.	E8	10
Aulander, N.C., U.S.	H8	114
Auld, Lake, l., Austl.	D4	74
Aulla, Italy	F6	22
Aulne, stm., Fr.	F5	14
Aulnoye, Fr.	D13	14
Aulneau Peninsula, pen., On., Can.	B4	118
Aumale, Fr.	E10	14
Auna, Nig.	G5	64
Auob, stm., Afr.	E5	70
Auraiya, India	E7	54
Aurangābād, India	B2	53
Aurangābād, India	F10	54
Aure, Nor.	E3	8
Aurelia, Ia., U.S.	B2	120
Aurich, Ger.	C3	16
Aurilândia, Braz.	G7	84
Aurillac, Fr.	E8	18
Aurine, Alpi (Zillertaler Alpen), mts., Eur.	C8	22
Aurora, On., Can.	D10	112
Aurora, Co., U.S.	B4	128
Aurora, Il., U.S.	C9	120
Aurora, In., U.S.	E13	120
Aurora, Me., U.S.	F8	110
Aurora, Mn., U.S.	D6	118
Aurora, N.C., U.S.	A9	116
Aurora, N.Y., U.S.	B9	114
Aurora, Ut., U.S.	E4	132
Aurora, W.V., U.S.	E6	114
Aurora do Norte, Braz.	G2	88
Aursunden, l., Nor.	E4	8
Aurukun, Austl.	B8	74
Aus, Nmb.	E3	70
Ausa, stm., Italy	G9	24
Au Sable, stm., Mi., U.S.	D6	112
Au Sable Forks, N.Y., U.S.	F3	110
Au Sable Point, c., Mi., U.S.	D6	112
Auschwitz see Oświęcim, Pol.	F15	16
Aust-Agder, state, Nor.	G3	8
Austin, In., U.S.	F12	120
Austin, Mn., U.S.	H6	118
Austin, Nv., U.S.	D8	134
Austin, Tx., U.S.	D10	130
Austin, Lake, l., Austl.	E3	74
Australes, Îles, is., Fr. Poly.	F11	72
Australia, ctry., Oc.	D5	74
Australian Capital Territory, state, Austl.	J7	76
Austral Islands see Australes, Îles, is., Fr. Poly.	F11	72
Austral Seamounts, unds.	L24	142
Austria, ctry., Eur.	C11	22
Austvågøya, i., Nor.	B6	8
Autlán de Navarro, Mex.	F6	100
Auvergne, hist. reg., Fr.	D8	18
Auxerre, Fr.	G12	14
Auxier, Ky., U.S.	G3	114
Auxi-le-Château, Fr.	D11	14
Auxvasse, Mo., U.S.	E5	120
Auyán Tepuy, mtn., Ven.	E10	86
Auzances, Fr.	C8	18
Auzangate, Nevado, mtn., Peru	F3	84
Ava, Mo., U.S.	H5	120
Avaj, Iran	C7	56
Avala, hist., Serb.	E7	26
Avallon, Fr.	G12	14
Avalon, Ca., U.S.	J7	134
Ávalos, Mex.	A5	100
Avan, Côte d', cst., Fr.	F13	18
Avanos, Tur.	B3	58
Avaré, Braz.	L1	88
Avarua, Cook Is.	a26	78j
Avarua Harbour, b., Cook Is.	a26	78j
Avatiu Harbour, b., Cook Is.	a26	78j
'Avedat, Horvot, sci., Isr.	H5	58
Aveiro, Port.	D2	20
Aveiro, state, Port.	D2	20
Aveiro, Ria de, mth., Port.	D1	20
Avellaneda, Arg.	G8	92
Avellino, Italy	D8	24
Averøya, i., Nor.	E2	8
Aversa, Italy	D8	24
Avery, Id., U.S.	C11	136
Avery Island, La., U.S.	H6	122
Aves, Islas de, is., Ven.	B8	86
Avesnes-sur-Helpe, Fr.	D12	14
Avesta, Swe.	F6	8
Aveyron, state, Fr.	E8	18
Aveyron, stm., Fr.	E7	18
Avezzano, Italy	H10	22
Avgó, i., Grc.	D9	24
Avignon, Fr.	F10	18
Ávila, Spain	D6	20
Ávila, co., Spain	D6	20
Ávila, Sierra de, mts., Spain	D5	20
Avilés, Spain	A4	20
Avinurme, Est.	B9	10
Avispa, Cerro, mtn., Ven.	G9	86
Avoca, Ia., U.S.	C2	120
Avoca, Austl.	K4	76
Avoca, stm., Austl.	K4	76
Avola, B.C., Can.	E11	138
Avola, Italy	H9	24
Avon, Il., U.S.	D7	120
Avon, Mn., U.S.	E5	112
Avon, N.C., U.S.	A10	116
Avon, N.Y., U.S.	B8	114
Avon, stm., Eng., U.K.	I11	12
Avon, stm., Eng., U.K.	K11	12

Name	Map Ref.	Page
Avon, stm., Eng., U.K.	J10	12
Avondale, Az., U.S.	J4	132
Avondale, Co., U.S.	C4	128
Avon Downs, Austl.	D7	74
Avon Park, Fl., U.S.	I4	116
Avontuur, S. Afr.	H6	70
Avranches, Fr.	F7	14
Awaaso, Ghana	H4	64
Awaji, Japan	E8	40
Awaji-shima, i., Japan	E7	40
Awara, Japan	C9	40
Awarē, Eth.	F8	62
Awasa, Eth.	F7	62
Awash, Eth.	F8	62
Awash, stm., Eth.	E8	62
Awa-shima, i., Japan	A12	40
Awbārī, Libya	B2	62
Awbārī, Şaḥrā', reg., Libya	B2	62
Awe, Loch, l., Scot., U.K.	E7	12
Aweil, Sudan	F5	62
Awjilah, Libya	B4	62
Awled Djellal, Alg.	D5	64
Awul, Pap. N. Gui.	b5	79a
Axel Heiberg Island, i., Can.	A7	141
Axim, Ghana	I4	64
Axiós (Vardar), stm., Eur.	C5	28
Axis, Al., U.S.	G10	122
Axixá, Braz.	B3	88
Axtell, Ks., U.S.	L2	118
Axtell, Ne., U.S.	G13	126
Ayabe, Japan	D8	40
Ayacucho, Arg.	H8	92
Ayacucho, Peru	F3	84
Ayakkum Hu, l., China	D2	36
Ayaköz, stm., Kaz.	E13	32
Ayaköz, Kaz.	E13	32
Ayam, C. Iv.	H4	64
Ayamonte, Spain	G3	20
Ayapel, Col.	C4	86
Ayaş, Tur.	C15	28
Ayaviri, Peru	F3	84
Aydin, Tur.	F10	28
Aydin, state, Tur.	F11	28
Aydinkent, Tur.	F14	28
Ayer, Ma., U.S.	B14	114
Ayers Rock see Uluru, mtn., Austl.	E6	74
Ayeyarwady, state, Mya.	D2	48
Ayeyarwady (Irrawaddy), stm., Mya.	E8	46
Aylesbury, Eng., U.K.	J12	12
Aylmer, Qc., Can.	C14	112
Aylmer Lake, l., N.T., Can.	C9	106
Aylsham, Sk., Can.	A10	124
'Ayn Dār, Sau. Ar.	D6	56
Ayon, S.C., U.S.	B6	116
'Aynūnah, Sau. Ar.	J6	58
Ayon Island see Ajon, ostrov, i., Russia	B22	34
Ayora see Aiora, Spain	E9	20
Ayorou, Niger	G5	64
'Ayoûn el 'Atroûs, Maur.	F3	64
Ayr, Austl.	B6	76
Ayr, Scot., U.K.	F8	12
Ayranci, Tur.	A4	58
Ayre, Point of, c., I. of Man	G2	12
Aysha, Eth.	E8	62
Aytos see Ajtos, Blg.	G14	26
Ayutla, Austl.	D9	16
Ayutla de los Libres, Mex.	G9	100
Ayvacik, Tur.	D9	28
Ayvalik, Tur.	D9	28
Azaila, Spain	C10	20
Azamgarh, India	E9	54
Azángaro, Peru	F3	84
Azaouâd, reg., Mali	F4	64
Azare, Nig.	G6	64
Azaryčy, Bela.	H12	10
A'zāz, Syria	B8	58
Azdavay, Tur.	B16	28
Azerbaijan, ctry., Asia	A6	56
Azerî, sand, Afr.	E2	64
Āzezo, Eth.	E7	62
Azhikode, India	F2	53
Azilal, Mor.	C3	64
Azogues, Ec.	I2	86
Azores see Açores, is., Port.	C16	12
Azores Plateau, unds.	E10	144
Azov, Russia	E5	32
Azov, Sea of, s., Eur.	E5	32
Azovskoje more see Azov, Sea of, s., Eur.	E5	32
Azraq, Al-Baḥr al- see Blue Nile, stm., Afr.	E6	62
Aztec, N.M., U.S.	G9	132
Aztec Peak, mtn., Az., U.S.	J5	132
Aztec Ruins National Monument, p.o.i., N.M., U.S.	G8	132
Azua, Dom. Rep.	C12	102
Azuaga, Spain	F5	20
Azuay, state, Ec.	I2	86
Azuay, stm., Ec.	F7	20
Azuero, Península de, pen., Pan.	D1	86
Azul, Arg.	H7	92
Azul, Cordillera, mts., Peru	E2	84
Azul, Volcán, vol., S.A.	B3	92
Azurduy, Bol.	C4	90
Azure Lake, l., B.C., Can.	D10	138
Az-Zahrān, Sau. Ar.	D6	56
Az-Zarqā', Jord.	F7	58
Az-Zarqā', state, Jord.	F7	58
Az-Zāwiyah, Libya	A2	62
Azzel Matti, Sebkha, pl., Alg.	D5	64

B

Name	Map Ref.	Page
Ba, Fiji	p18	79e
Ba, stm., China	F6	42
Ba, stm., China	C7	42
Ba, stm., Viet.	D9	48
Ba, Cam.	G2	64
Baa, Indon.	H7	44
Baaba, Île, i., N. Cal.	l14	79d
Baao, Phil.	D4	52
Baardheere, Som.	D8	66
Baba Burnu, c., Tur.	D9	28
Babaeski, Tur.	B10	28
Babahoyo, Ec.	H2	86
Babana, Nig.	G5	64
Babati, Tan.	E7	66
Babayevo, Russia	A18	10
Babb, Mt., U.S.	B14	136
Babeldaob, i., Palau	g7	78b
Bab el Mandeb see Mandeb, Bab el, strt., Afr.	E8	62
Babia, Arroyo de la, stm., Mex.	F5	130
Babian, stm., China	A5	48
Babičy, Bela.	H12	10
Babīna, India	F7	54
Babine, stm., B.C., Can.	D5	138
Babine Lake, l., B.C., Can.	B5	138
Babino, Russia	A14	10
Babiogórski Park Narodowy, p.o.i., Pol.	G15	16
Babo, Indon.	F9	44

Name	Map Ref.	Page
Bābol, Iran	B7	56
Baboquivari Peak, mtn., Az., U.S.	L5	132
Baborów, Pol.	F13	16
Babrujsk, Bela.	G12	10
Babuškin, Russia	F10	34
Babuyan Channel, strt., Phil.	A3	52
Babuyan Island, i., Phil.	A4	52
Babuyan Islands, is., Phil.	A3	52
Bacabal, Braz.	C3	88
Bacadéhuachi, Mex.	G8	98
Bacatuba, Braz.	C4	88
Bacău, state, Rom.	C13	26
Bacău, Rom.	C13	26
Baccarat, Fr.	F15	14
Bac Giang, Viet.	B8	48
Bachaquero, Ven.	B6	86
Bachiniva, Mex.	A5	100
Bach Ma, Viet.	D8	48
Bac Thong, Viet.	A7	48
Bachu, China	B12	56
Back, stm., Nu., Can.	B11	106
Bačka, reg., Eur.	E6	22
Bačka Palanka, Serb.	D6	26
Bačka Topola, Serb.	D6	26
Backnang, Ger.	H5	16
Backstairs Passage, strt., Austl.	J1	76
Bac Lieu, Viet.	H7	48
Bac Ninh, Viet.	B8	48
Baco, Mount, mtn., Phil.	D3	52
Bacoachi, Mex.	F8	98
Bacolod, Phil.	E4	52
Baconton, Ga., U.S.	E1	116
Bac Phan, hist. reg., Viet.	A7	48
Bacuri, Lago do, l., Braz.	B4	88
Bad, stm., Mi., U.S.	E5	112
Bad, stm., S.D., U.S.	C12	126
Badagara, India	F2	53
Badajós, Lago, l., Braz.	D5	84
Badajoz, Spain	F4	20
Badajoz, co., Spain	F4	20
Badalona, Spain	C13	20
Bādāmi, India	D2	53
Badanah, Sau. Ar.	C5	56
Badarīnāth, India	C7	54
Badas, Kepulauan, is., Indon.	C5	50
Bad Axe, Mi., U.S.	E7	112
Bad Bergzabern, Ger.	G3	16
Bad Bevensen, Ger.	C6	16
Bad Bramstedt, Ger.	C5	16
Baddeck, N.S., Can.	D16	110
Bad Doberan, Ger.	B7	16
Bad Dürrenberg, Ger.	E8	16
Bad Ems, Ger.	F3	16
Baden, Switz.	C5	22
Baden-Baden, Ger.	H4	16
Badenoch, hist. reg., Scot., U.K.	E8	12
Badenweiler, Ger.	I3	16
Baden-Württemberg, state, Ger.	H4	16
Bad Freienwalde, Ger.	D9	16
Badgastein, Aus.	C10	22
Badger, Mn., U.S.	C3	118
Bad Hall, Aus.	B11	22
Bad Harzburg, Ger.	E6	16
Bad Hersfeld, Ger.	F5	16
Bad Homburg vor der Höhe, Ger.	F4	16
Bad Honnef, Ger.	E3	16
Badin Lake, res., N.C., U.S.	A5	116
Bad Ischl, Aus.	C10	22
Bad Kissingen, Ger.	F6	16
Bad Kreuznach, Ger.	G3	16
Badlands, hills, S.D., U.S.	D10	126
Badlands, hills, U.S.	C3	126
Badlands National Park, p.o.i., S.D., U.S.	D10	126
Bad Langensalza, Ger.	E6	16
Bad Lauterberg im Harz, Ger.	E6	16
Bad Mergentheim, Ger.	G5	16
Bad Nauheim, Ger.	F4	16
Bad Neustadt an der Saale, Ger.	F6	16
Bad Oeynhausen, Ger.	D4	16
Bad Oldesloe, Ger.	C6	16
Bad Orb, Ger.	F5	16
Bad Pyrmont, Ger.	E5	16
Bad Reichenhall, Ger.	I8	16
Bad Salzuflen, Ger.	D4	16
Bad Salzungen, Ger.	F6	16
Bad Schwalbach, Ger.	F4	16
Bad Schwartau, Ger.	C6	16
Bad Segeberg, Ger.	C6	16
Bad Tölz, Ger.	I7	16
Badulla, Sri L.	H5	53
Bad Vöslau, Aus.	C13	22
Bad Waldsee, Ger.	I5	16
Bad Wildungen, Ger.	E5	16
Bad Wörishofen, Ger.	I6	16
Badžalъskij hrebet, mts., Russia	F15	34
Baena, Spain	G6	20
Baependi, Braz.	K3	88
Baeza, Spain	C17	32
Bafang, Cam.	C1	66
Bafatá, Gui.-B.	G2	64
Baffin Bay, b., N.A.	C12	141
Baffin Bay, b., Tx., U.S.	G10	130
Baffin Island, i., Nu., Can.	B16	106
Bafia, Cam.	D2	66
Bafing, stm., Afr.	G2	64
Bafoulabé, Mali	G2	64
Bafoussam, Cam.	C1	66
Bafra, Tur.	A4	56
Bafwaboli, D.R.C.	D5	66
Bafwasende, D.R.C.	D5	66
Bagaces, C.R.	G5	102
Bagaha, India	E10	54
Bagalkot, India	C2	53
Bagamoyo, Tan.	F7	66
Bagan Datuk, Malay.	K5	48
Bagansiapiapi, Indon.	C2	50
Baganuur, Mong.	B6	36
Bagata, D.R.C.	E3	66
Bagdarin, Russia	F11	34
Bagé, Braz.	E10	92
Bageshwar, India	D8	54
Baggs, Wy., U.S.	B9	132
Baghdād, Iraq	C5	56
Bagheria, Italy	F7	24
Baghlān, Afg.	B10	56
Bagley, Mn., U.S.	D3	118
Bago (Pegu), Mya.	D3	48
Bagodar, India	F10	54
Bagoé, stm., Afr.	G3	64

Name	Map Ref.	Page
Bağpınar, Tur.	A9	58
Baguio, Phil.	B3	52
Bagzane, Monts, mtn., Niger	G6	64
Bāh, India	E7	54
Bahādurgarh, India	D6	54
Bahama, Canal Viejo de, strt., N.A.	A8	102
Bahamas, ctry., N.A.	C9	96
Baharampur, India	F11	54
Bahau, Malay.	K6	48
Bahau, stm., Indon.	B9	50
Bahawalnagar, Pak.	C4	54
Bahawalpur, Pak.	D3	54
Bahçe, Tur.	A7	58
Bahi, Phil.	D4	52
Bahía see Salvador, Braz.	G6	88
Bahia, state, Braz.	G4	88
Bahía, Islas de la, is., Hond.	D4	102
Bahía Blanca, Arg.	I6	92
Bahía Bustamante, Arg.	I3	90
Bahía de Caráquez, Ec.	H1	86
Bahía Kino, Mex.	A3	100
Bahir Dar, Eth.	E7	62
Bahraich, India	E8	54
Bahrain, ctry., Asia	D7	56
Bahraba, Russia	B15	32
Bahtīm, Egypt	H2	58
Bahušėusk, Bela.	F13	10
Bai, stm., China	A7	42
Baia de Aramă, Rom.	E9	26
Baia di Terra Nova, sci., Ant.	C21	81
Baia Mare, Rom.	B10	26
Baião, Braz.	B1	88
Baicheng, China	F14	32
Baicheng, China	B9	36
Baidoa see Baydhabo, Som.	D8	66
Baie-Comeau, Qc., Can.	A8	110
Baie-Saint-Paul, Qc., Can.	C6	110
Baie-Trinité, Qc., Can.	C15	110
Baie Verte, Nf., Can.	j22	107a
Baihe, China	B11	46
Baijnāth, India	D7	54
Baikal, Lake see Bajkal, ozero, l., Russia	F10	34
Baikal Mountains see Bajkal'skij hrebet, mts., Russia	F10	34
Baikonur see Bayqongyr, Kaz.	E11	32
Baile Átha Cliath see Dublin, Ire.	H6	12
Baile Átha Luain see Athlone, Ire.	H4	12
Bāile Govora, Rom.	D11	26
Bailén, Spain	F7	20
Băileşti, Rom.	F10	26
Bailey, N.C., U.S.	I7	114
Bail Hongal, India	D2	53
Bailicun, China	I4	42
Bailique, Ilha, i., Braz.	C8	84
Baillie Islands, is., N.T., Can.	B14	140
Baillif, Guad.	h5	105c
Bailong, stm., China	E1	42
Bailu Hu, l., China	G5	42
Bailundo, Ang.	C2	68
Baima see Baxoi, China	E4	36
Baimamiao, China	C2	42
Baimuru, Pap. N. Gui.	b3	79a
Bainbridge, Ga., U.S.	G14	122
Bainbridge, N.Y., U.S.	B10	114
Baing, Indon.	I12	50
Bainville, Mt., U.S.	F9	124
Baio Grande, Spain	A2	20
Baião, Spain	A2	20
Baipeng, China	I3	42
Baiquan, China	B10	36
Baird, Tx., U.S.	B8	130
Baird Mountains, mts., Ak., U.S.	C7	140
Baird Peninsula, pen., Nu., Can.	B15	106
Bairiki, Kir.	C8	72
Bairin Zuoqi, China	C8	38
Bairnsdale, Austl.	K6	76
Baïse, stm., Fr.	F6	18
Baisha, China	L3	42
Baisha, China	I8	42
Baishan, China	D7	38
Baishuijiang, China	E1	42
Baisogala, Lith.	E6	10
Baiwang, China	I3	42
Baixing, China	B10	36
Baixo, Braz.	C4	38
Baiyin, China	D5	36
Baja, Punta, c., Chile	e29	78l
Baja, Hung.	C5	26
Baja California, pen., Mex.	F5	98
Baja California, state, Mex.	A1	100
Baja California Sur, state, Mex.	C2	100
Bajada del Agrio, Arg.	I2	92
Bajan, Mong.	B7	36
Bajanaul, Kaz.	D13	32
Bajangol, Russia	C10	34
Bajánsenye, Hung.	C3	26
Bajawa, Indon.	H12	50
Bajdarackaja guba, b., Russia	A11	32
Bajestān, Iran	C8	56
Bajkal, ozero (Baikal, Lake), l., Russia	F10	34
Bajkal'skij hrebet, mts., Russia	F10	34
Bajkonur see Bayqongyr, Kaz.	E11	32
Bajmak, Russia	D9	32
Bajmok, Serb.	D6	26
Bajo Boquete, Pan.	H6	102
Bajool, Austl.	D8	76
Bajram Curri, Alb.	B14	24
Bakala, C.A.R.	C4	66
Bakel, Sen.	G2	64
Baker, La., U.S.	G7	122
Baker, Mt., U.S.	A9	126
Baker, Or., U.S.	F9	136
Baker, Mount, vol., Wa., U.S.	B5	136
Baker Butte, mtn., Az., U.S.	I5	132
Baker Island, i., Oc.	C9	72
Baker Lake see Qamani'tuaq, Nu., Can.	C11	106
Baker Lake, l., Nu., Can.	C11	106
Bakersfield, Ca., U.S.	H7	134
Bakharden, Turkmen.	B8	56
Bakhtegān, Daryācheh-ye, l., Iran	D7	56
Bakı (Baku), Azer.	A6	56
Bakkafjördur, Ice.	j32	8a
Bakkaflói, b., Ice.	j32	8a
Bako, Eth.	F7	62
Bako, Eth.	F7	64
Bakouma, C.A.R.	C4	66
Baku see Bakı, Azer.	A6	56

Name	Map Ref.	Page
Bakumpai, Indon.	D8	50
Bakung, Pulau, i., Indon.	G1	52
Bakungan, Indon.	K3	48
Bakwanga see Mbuji-Mayi, D.R.C.	F4	66
Balà, Tur.	D16	28
Balabac, Phil.	F1	52
Balabac Island, i., Phil.	G1	52
Balabac Strait, strt., Asia	G1	52
Ba'labakk, Leb.	D7	58
Balalagan, Kepulauan, is., Indon.	E10	50
Balabanovo, Russia	E19	10
Balabio, Île, i., N. Cal.	m15	79d
Balad, Iraq	C5	56
Baladëk, Russia	F15	34
Bālāghāt, India	H8	54
Bālāghāt Range, mts., India	B3	53
Balagne, reg., Fr.	G14	18
Balaguer, Spain	C11	20
Balahna, Russia	H20	8
Balaikarangan, Indon.	C7	50
Balaisepuah, Indon.	C7	50
Balakirevo, Russia	D21	10
Balakovo, Russia	D7	32
Balama, Moz.	C6	68
Balambangan, Pulau, i., Malay.	G1	52
Bālā Morghāb, Afg.	B9	56
Balanga, Phil.	C3	52
Balāngīr, India	H9	54
Balapulang, Indon.	G6	50
Balarāmpur, India	G11	54
Balašiha, Russia	E20	10
Balašov, Russia	D6	32
Balassagyarmat, Hung.	A6	26
Balatina, Mol.	B14	26
Balaton, Mn., U.S.	G3	118
Balaton, l., Hung.	C4	26
Balayan, Phil.	D3	52
Balbieriškis, Lith.	F6	10
Balbina, Represa, res., Braz.	H12	86
Balcanoona, Austl.	H2	76
Balcarce, Arg.	H8	92
Balcarres, Sk., Can.	D10	124
Bălcești, Rom.	E10	26
Balcones Escarpment, clf., Tx., U.S.	D9	130
Balde, Arg.	F4	92
Bald Knob, Ar., U.S.	B7	122
Bald Knob, mtn., Va., U.S.	G6	114
Bald Mountain, mtn., Or., U.S.	G5	136
Bald Mountain, mtn., Or., U.S.	F3	136
Baldock Lake, l., Mb., Can.	D11	106
Baldone, Lat.	D7	10
Baldwin, La., U.S.	H7	122
Baldwin, Mi., U.S.	E4	112
Baldwin, Wi., U.S.	G6	118
Baldwinsville, N.Y., U.S.	E13	112
Baldwyn, Ms., U.S.	C10	122
Baldy Mountain, mtn., Mb., Can.	C13	124
Baldy Mountain, mtn., N.M., U.S.	E3	128
Baldy Peak, mtn., Az., U.S.	J7	132
Bâle see Basel, Switz.	C4	22
Baleares see Balears, state, Spain	E13	20
Baleares, Islas see Balears, Illes, is., Spain	E12	20
Balearic Islands see Balears, Illes, is., Spain	E13	20
Balearic Islands see Balears, Illes, is., Spain	E12	20
Balears, state, Spain	E13	20
Balears, Illes (Balearic Islands), is., Spain	E12	20
Balease, Gunung, mtn., Indon.	E12	50
Baleh, stm., Malay.	C8	50
Baleia, Ponta da, c., Braz.	I6	88
Baleine, stm., Qc., Can.	D17	106
Baleine, Grande rivière de la, stm., Qc., Can.	D15	106
Baleine, Petite rivière de la, stm., Qc., Can.	D15	106
Balej, Russia	F12	34
Baler, Phil.	C3	52
Baler Bay, b., Phil.	C3	52
Bāleshwar, India	H11	54
Balezino, Russia	C8	32
Balfate, Hond.	E4	102
Balfour, N.C., U.S.	A3	116
Balgazyn, Russia	D17	32
Balhaš, ozero see Balqash köli, l., Kaz.	E13	32
Bāli, India	F4	54
Bali, state, Indon.	G9	50
Bali, i., Indon.	G9	50
Bali, Laut (Bali Sea), s., Indon.	G9	50
Bali, Selat, strt., Indon.	H9	50
Bali Barat National Park, p.o.i., Indon.	H9	50
Baliceaux, i., St. Vin.	p11	105e
Balige, Indon.	B1	50
Balıkesir, Tur.	D10	28
Balıkesir, state, Tur.	D10	28
Balikh, stm., Syria	B10	58
Balikpapan, Indon.	D10	50
Balimbing, Indon.	F4	50
Balimbing, Phil.	H2	52
Balimo, Pap. N. Gui.	b3	79a
Balingen, Ger.	H4	16
Balingian, Malay.	B8	50
Balintang Channel, strt., Phil.	K9	42
Bali Sea see Bali, Laut, s., Indon.	G9	50
Bali Strait see Bali, Selat, strt., Indon.	H9	50
Baliza, Braz.	G7	84
Balkan Mountains, mts., Eur.	G11	26
Balkan Peninsula, pen., Eur.	B6	28
Balkaria see Kabardino-Balkarija, state, Russia	F6	32
Balkh, Afg.	B10	56
Balkhash, Lake see Balqash köli, l., Kaz.	E13	32
Ballachulish, Scot., U.K.	E7	12
Balladonia, Austl.	F4	74
Ballālpur, India	B4	53
Ballangen, Nor.	B7	8
Ballantine, Mt., U.S.	B4	126
Ballarat, Austl.	K4	76
Ballard, Lake, l., Austl.	E4	74
Ballantrae, Scot., U.K.	D9	12
Ball Bay, b., Norf. I.	y25	78i
Ballenas, Bahía de, b., Mex.	B2	100
Ballenita, Punta, c., Chile	B2	92
Balleny Islands, is., Ant.	B21	81
Balleza, Mex.	B5	100
Balleza, stm., Mex.	B5	100
Ball Ground, Ga., U.S.	B1	116
Ballia, India	F10	54
Ballina, Austl.	G9	76
Ballina, Ire.	G3	12
Ballina, Ire.	I4	12
Ballinrobe, Ire.	H3	12
Ballston Spa, N.Y., U.S.	G2	110
Ballville, Oh., U.S.	C2	114
Ballybunnion, Ire.	I3	12
Ballyhaunis, Ire.	H4	12
Ballymena, N. Ire., U.K.	G6	12
Ballymena, N. Ire., U.K.	F6	12
Ballyrogan, Lake, l., Austl.	I6	76
Balmaceda, Chile	I2	90
Balmoral, Austl.	K3	76
Balmorhea, Tx., U.S.	C4	130
Balnearia, Arg.	E6	92
Baloda Bāzār, India	H9	54
Balombo, Ang.	C1	68
Balong, Indon.	G7	50
Balonne, stm., Austl.	G7	76
Bālotra, India	F4	54
Balphakram National Park, p.o.i., India	F13	54
Balqash köli (Balkhash Lake), l., Kaz.	E13	32
Balrāmpur, India	E8	54
Balranald, Austl.	J4	76
Balș, Rom.	E11	26
Balsam Lake, Wi., U.S.	F6	118
Balsam Lake, l., On., Can.	D11	112
Balsas, Braz.	D2	88
Balsas, stm., Braz.	F2	88
Balsas, stm., Braz.	D3	88
Balsas, stm., Mex.	F8	100
Balsas, stm., Pan.	C3	86
Balsthal, Switz.	C4	22
Balta, Ukr.	B16	26
Baltasar Brum, Ur.	E9	92
Bălți, Mol.	B14	26
Baltic Sea, s., Eur.	D12	6
Baltijsk, Russia	F2	10
Baltijskaja kosa, spit, Eur.	F2	10
Baltijskoje more see Baltic Sea, s., Eur.	D12	6
Baltim, Egypt	G2	58
Baltimore, Ire.	J3	12
Baltimore, Md., U.S.	E9	114
Baltimore, Oh., U.S.	E3	114
Ba Lu, stm., Viet.	B8	48
Baluchistan, state, Pak.	C2	54
Baluchistan, hist. reg., Asia	D9	56
Balui, stm., Malay.	B8	50
Bālurghāt, India	F12	54
Balvi, Lat.	C10	10
Balygyčan, Russia	D19	34
Balyqshy, Kaz.	E8	32
Balzac, Ab., Can.	E16	138
Balzar, Ec.	H2	86
Bam, Iran	D8	56
Bama, China	J2	42
Bama, Nig.	G7	64
Bamaga, Austl.	B8	74
Bamako, Mali	G3	64
Bamba, Mali	F4	64
Bambamarca, Peru	E2	84
Bambana, stm., Nic.	F6	102
Bambari, C.A.R.	C4	66
Bambaroo, Austl.	B6	76
Bamberg, Ger.	G6	16
Bamberg, S.C., U.S.	C4	116
Bambio, C.A.R.	D3	66
Bambui, Braz.	K2	88
Bam Co, l., China	C13	54
Bamenda, Cam.	C1	66
Bami, Turkmen.	B8	56
Bamian, Afg.	C10	56
Bamingui, C.A.R.	C4	66
Bampūr, Iran	D9	56
Bāmra Hills, hills, India	H10	54
Bamumo, China	B14	54
Banaba, i., Kir.	D7	72
Banabuiú, Braz.	C6	88
Banabuiú, Açude, l., Braz.	C6	88
Banai, D.R.C.	D5	66
Banalia, D.R.C.	D5	66
Banana, Mali	G3	64
Banana Islands, is., S.L.	H2	64
Bananal, stm., Braz.	E1	88
Bananal, Ilha do, i., Braz.	F7	84
Banarli, Tur.	B10	28
Banās, stm., India	E6	54
Banās, Rās, c., Egypt	C7	62
Banāt, hist. reg., Eur.	D7	26
Banaz, Tur.	E12	28
Ban Ban, Laos	C6	48
Ban Bouang-nom, Laos	E8	48
Banbridge, N. Ire., U.K.	G6	12
Ban Bung Na Rang, Thai.	D5	48
Banbury, Eng., U.K.	I11	12
Ban Cha La, Laos	D7	48
Bancroft, On., Can.	C12	112
Bancroft, Ia., U.S.	H4	118
Bancroft, Id., U.S.	H15	136
Bancroft, Ne., U.S.	C1	120
Bānda, India	F8	54
Banda, Kepulauan, is., Indon.	F9	44
Banda, Laut (Banda Sea), s., Indon.	G8	44
Banda Aceh, Indon.	J2	48
Bānda Dāūd Shāh, Pak.	B3	54
Banda del Río Salí, Arg.	C5	92
Bandai-Asahi-kokuritsu-kōen, p.o.i., Japan	B12	40
Bandai-san, vol., Japan	B13	40
Bandama, stm., C. Iv.	H3	64
Bandama Blanc, stm., C. Iv.	H3	64
Ban Dan, Thai.	E7	48
Ban Dangtai, Laos	D7	48
Bandar Behešti, Iran	D9	56
Bandarbeyla, Som.	C10	66
Bandar-e 'Abbās, Iran	D8	56
Bandar-e Anzali, Iran	B6	56
Bandar-e Büshehr, Iran	D7	56
Bandar-e Deylam, Iran	D7	56
Bandar-e Lengeh, Iran	D7	56
Bandar-e Māh Shahr, Iran	C6	56
Bandar-e Moghūyeh, Iran	D7	56
Bandar-e Torkeman, Iran	B7	56
Bandar Lampung, Indon.	F4	50
Bandar Seri Begawan, Bru.	A9	50
Banda Sea see Banda, Laut, s., Indon.	G8	44
Bandeira, Pico da, mtn., Braz.	K5	88
Bandeirantes, Braz.	F7	84
Bandelier National Monument, p.o.i., N.M., U.S.	F2	128
Bandera, Arg.	D6	92
Bandera, Alto, mtn., Dom. Rep.	C12	102
Banderas, Mex.	C2	130
Banderas, Bahía de, b., Mex.	E6	100
Bandhavgarh National Park, p.o.i., India	G8	54
Bāndhi, Pak.	E2	54
Bandiagara, Mali	G4	64
Bandiantaolehai, China	C5	36
Bāndīkūi, India	E6	54
Bandipura, India	A5	54
Bandipur Tiger Reserve, India	F3	53
Bandırma, Tur.	C11	28
Bandon, Or., U.S.	G2	136
Ban Don, Ao, b., Thai.	H4	48
Ban Donhiang, Laos	C5	48
Bandung, Indon.	G5	50
Banes, Cuba	B10	102
Banff, Ab., Can.	E15	138
Banff, Scot., U.K.	D10	12
Banff National Park, p.o.i., Ab., Can.	E15	138
Banfora, Burkina	G4	64
Banga, D.R.C.	F4	66
Banga, India	C6	54
Banga, Serb.	G6	26
Banga, stm., Phil.	G5	52
Bangaon, India	G12	54
Bangassou, C.A.R.	D4	66
Bangdag Co, l., China	A8	54
Banggai, Indon.	F7	44
Banggai, Kepulauan, is., Indon.	F7	44
Banggai, Pulau, i., Malay.	G1	52
Banggong Co, l., China	B7	54
Banghāzī (Bengasi), Libya	A3	62
Banghiang, stm., Laos	D7	48
Bangil, Indon.	G8	50
Bangka, Pulau, i., Indon.	E5	50
Bangka, Selat, strt., Indon.	E4	50
Bangkalan, Indon.	G8	50
Bangkaru, Pulau, i., Indon.	L3	48
Bangkinang, Indon.	C2	50
Bangkir, Indon.	C12	50
Bangko, Indon.	E3	50
Bangkog Co, l., China	C12	54
Bangkok see Krung Thep, Thai.	F5	48
Bangladesh, ctry., Asia	G13	54
Bang Lamung, Thai.	F5	48
Bang Mun Nak, Thai.	D5	48
Bangor, N. Ire., U.K.	G7	12
Bangor, Wales, U.K.	H8	12
Bangor, Me., U.S.	F8	110
Bangor, Pa., U.S.	D10	114
Bangriposi, India	G11	54
Bangs, Tx., U.S.	C8	130
Bangs, Mount, mtn., Az., U.S.	G3	132
Bang Saphan, Thai.	G4	48
Bangued, Phil.	B3	52
Bangui, C.A.R.	D3	66
Bangweulu, Lake, l., Zam.	C4	68
Bangweulu Swamps, sw., Zam.	C5	68
Bangxu, China	J2	42
Ban Hatgnao, Laos	E8	48
Ban Hét, Laos	E8	48
Ban Hom, Thai.	E4	48
Ban Hong Muang, Laos	D7	48
Ban Houayxay, Laos	B5	48
Bani, C.A.R.	C4	66
Bani, Dom. Rep.	C12	102
Bani, Jbel, mts., Mor.	D3	64
Baniara, Pap. N. Gui.	b4	79a
Bani Bangou, Niger	F5	64
Banihāl Pass, p., India	B4	46
Banī Walīd, Libya	A2	62
Banīyās, Golan	E6	58
Banīyās, Syria	C6	58
Banja Luka, Bos.	E4	26
Banjarmasin, Indon.	E9	50
Banjul (Bathurst), Gam.	G1	64
Bānka, India	F11	54
Banka Banka, Austl.	C6	74
Ban Katēp, Laos	D7	48
Ban Kèngkabao, Laos	D7	48
Ban Kèngtangan, Laos	D7	48
Ban Kheun, Laos	B5	48
Ban Khuam Mao, Thai.	I4	48
Ban Kruat, Thai.	E6	48
Banks, Al., U.S.	F13	122
Banks, Îles (Banks Islands), is., Vanuatu	i16	79d
Banks Island, i., B.C., Can.	E4	106
Banks Island, i., N.T., Can.	B15	140
Banks Islands see Banks, Îles, is., Vanuatu	i16	79d
Banks Lake, res., Wa., U.S.	C7	136
Banks Peninsula, pen., N.Z.	F5	80
Banks Strait, strt., Austl.	n13	77a
Banks I Torres, state, Vanuatu	i16	79d
Bānkura, India	G11	54
Ban Mae La Luang, Thai.	C3	48
Ban Mit, Laos	C5	48
Ban Muangngat, Laos	C6	48
Ban, stm., N. Ire., U.K.	F6	12
Ban Nadou, Laos	E7	48
Ban Nahin, Laos	C7	48
Ban Nalan, Laos	E7	48
Ban Nam Chan, Thai.	C6	48
Ban Namnga, Laos	B6	48
Ban Nam Thaeng, Thai.	A7	48
Ban Naxouang, Laos	C7	48
Bannertown, N.C., U.S.	H5	114
Banning, Ca., U.S.	J9	134
Ban Nong Lumphuk, Thai.	E6	48
Bannu, Pak.	B3	54
Bañolas see Banyoles, Spain	B13	20
Baños, Ec.	H2	86
Banow, Afg.	B10	56
Ban Pak Bong, Thai.	C4	48
Ban Pakkhop, Laos	C6	48
Ban Pak Nam, Thai.	G4	48
Ban Phai, Thai.	D6	48
Ban Phai, Thai.	D6	48
Ban Pho, Thai.	F5	48
Ban Phōng Pho, Laos	E7	48
Ban Pong, Thai.	F4	48
Ban Salik, Thai.	C5	48
Ban Sam Pong, Laos	C6	48
Ban Samrong, Thai.	E6	48
Bānsda, India	H4	54
Banshadhāra, stm., India	B6	53
Banská Bystrica, Slov.	H15	16
Banská Štiavnica, Slov.	H14	16
Bansko, Blg.	H10	26
Ban Songkhon, Laos	D7	48
Bānswāra, India	G5	54
Bantaeng, Indon.	F11	50
Ban Takhlo, Thai.	E5	48
Bantarkawung, Indon.	G6	50
Bantayan, Phil.	E4	52
Ban Thabōk, Laos	C6	48
Ban Thapayi, Laos	D7	48
Ban Tian Sa, Laos	C5	48
Bantry, Ire.	J3	12
Bantry Bay, b., Ire.	J3	12
Ban Van Hom, Laos	C7	48
Ban Xènhalôk, Laos	C5	48
Banya, Testa de la, c., Spain	D11	20
Banyak, Kepulauan, is., Indon.	K3	48
Ban Ya Plong, Thai.	H4	48
Banyo, Cam.	C2	66
Banyoles, Spain	B13	20
Banyuwangi, Indon.	H9	50
Banzare Coast, cst., Ant.	B17	81
Baode, China	B4	42
Baoding, China	B6	42
Baofeng, China	E5	42
Bao Ha, Viet.	A7	48
Baoji, China	D2	42
Baojing, China	G3	42
Bao Lac, Viet.	A7	48
Baolunyuan, China	E1	42
Baoqing, China	B11	36
Baoting, China	L3	42
Baotou, China	A4	42
Baoulé, stm., Mali	G3	64
Baowei, China	E7	42
Baoying, China	E8	42
Bāpatla, India	D5	53
Bapaume, Fr.	D11	14
Bāqa el Gharbiyya, Isr.	F6	58
Baqanas, Kaz.	F13	32
Baqing, China	B14	54
Ba'qūbah, Iraq	C5	56
Baquedano, Chile	A3	92
Bar, Serb.	G6	26
Barā, Nig.	G7	64
Bar Rural Area, Tur.	D8	66
Barabinsk, Russia	C13	32
Baraawe, Som.	D8	66
Baracoa, Cuba	B10	102
Baradero, Arg.	F8	92
Baradine, Austl.	H7	76
Baraga, Mi., U.S.	B1	112
Bārah, Sudan	E6	62
Barahona, Dom. Rep.	C12	102
Barak, Tur.	B8	58
Barāk, stm., India	F14	54
Barakaldo, Spain	A8	20
Baraki Barak, Afg.	B2	54
Barakula, Austl.	F8	76
Baralaba, Austl.	E7	76
Baram, stm., Malay.	A9	50
Barama, stm., Guy.	D12	86
Bangladesh, ctry., Asia	B2	53
Bārāmati, India	B3	53
Baran', Bela.	F13	10
Bārān, India	F6	54
Baranagar, India	G12	54
Baranavičy, Bela.	G9	10
Barangbarong, Indon.	G12	50
Baranoa, Col.	B4	86
Baranof Island, i., Ak., U.S.	E12	140
Baranya, Russia	C12	10
Baranya, state, Hung.	D5	26
Barão de Grajaú, Braz.	D4	88
Barão de Melgaço, Braz.	G6	84
Barão de Tromaí, Braz.	A3	88
Barataria, La., U.S.	H8	122
Barataria Bay, b., La., U.S.	H8	122
Barat Daya, Kepulauan (Barat Daya Islands), is., Indon.	G8	44
Barat Daya Islands see Barat Daya, Kepulauan, is., Indon.	G8	44
Barauana, stm., Braz.	G11	86
Barauni, India	F10	54
Baraut, India	D6	54
Baraya, Col.	F4	86
Barbacena, Braz.	K4	88
Barbacoas, Col.	G2	86
Barbadillo del Mercado, Spain	B7	20
Barbados, ctry., N.A.	h16	96a
Barbalha, Braz.	D6	88
Barbaria, Cap de, c., Spain	F12	20
Barbas, Cap, c., W. Sah.	E1	64
Barbaši, Russia	C11	10
Barbastro, Spain	B10	20
Barbate, Spain	H4	20
Barbeau Peak, mtn., Nu., Can.	A10	141
Barberena, Guat.	E2	102
Barberton, S. Afr.	D10	70
Barberton, Oh., U.S.	C4	114
Barbil, India	G10	54
Barbosa, Col.	E5	86
Barbuda, i., Antig.	e4	105b
Barby, Ger.	E7	16
Bárcala, Rom.	F10	26
Barcaldine, Austl.	D5	76
Barcãu (Berettyó), stm., Eur.	B8	26
Barcellona Pozzo di Gotto, Italy	F9	24
Barcelona, Mex.	B7	100
Barcelona, Spain	C13	20
Barcelona, Ven.	B9	86
Barcelona, co., Spain	C13	20
Barceloneta, P.R.	B2	104a
Barcelos, Braz.	H10	86
Barcelos, Port.	C2	20
Barcin, Pol.	D13	16
Barcoo, stm., Austl.	E4	76
Barczewo, Pol.	C16	16
Barda del Medio, Arg.	I3	92
Bardaï, Chad	C3	62
Bardawīl, Sabkhat el-, b., Egypt	G4	58
Barddhamān, India	G11	54
Bardejov, Slov.	G17	16
Bardeskan, Iran	B8	56
Bardīyah, Libya	A5	62
Bardo, Fr.	H4	24
Bārdoli, India	H4	54
Bardstown, Ky., U.S.	G12	120
Bardwell Lake, res., Tx., U.S.	C2	48
Bareilly, India	D7	54
Barentsburg, Nor.	B29	141
Barentsøya, i., Nor.	B30	141
Barents Sea, s., Eur.	B7	30
Bareta, India	D5	54
Barfleur, Fr.	E7	14
Bargaal, Som.	B10	66
Bargara, Austl.	E9	76
Bargarh, India	D5	46
Barguzin, stm., Russia	F11	34
Barguzinskij hrebet, mts., Russia	F11	34
Bar Harbor, Me., U.S.	F8	110
Barharwa, India	F11	54
Barhi, India	F10	54
Bāri, India	E6	54
Bari, Italy	C10	24
Bāri, stm., India	D3	54
Barī, Volcán, vol., Pan.	H6	102
Bārūl, Jabal al-, mtn., Leb.	E6	58
Barumini, Italy	E2	24
Barumun, stm., Indon.	L4	48
Barung, Nusa, i., Indon.	H8	50
Barus, Indon.	L3	48
Baruun-Urt, Mong.	B7	36
Barvas, Scot., U.K.	C6	12
Barwon, Or., U.S.	G2	136
Barwāh, India	H6	54
Barwāni, India	H5	54
Barwick, Ga., U.S.	F2	116
Barwon, stm., Austl.	H6	76
Barybino, Russia	E20	10
Barycz, stm., Pol.	E13	16
Barysaw, Bela.	F11	10
Bari Sadri, India	F5	54
Barisāl, Bngl.	G13	54
Barisāl, state, Bngl.	G13	54
Barisan, Pegunungan, mts., Indon.	E2	50
Barito, stm., Indon.	E9	50
Barjols, Fr.	F11	18
Barka, China	E5	36
Barkava, Lat.	D9	10
Barkerville, B.C., Can.	C9	132
Bark Lake, l., On., Can.	H10	120
Barkley, Lake, res., U.S.	B7	114
Barkley Sound, strt., B.C., Can.	H5	138
Barkly East, S. Afr.	G8	70
Barkly West, S. Afr.	F7	70
Barkol, China	C3	36
Bārləd, Rom.	C14	26
Bar-le-Duc, Fr.	F14	14
Barlee, Lake, l., Austl.	E3	74
Barletta, Italy	C10	24
Barlinek, Pol.	D11	16
Barling, Ar., U.S.	B4	122
Barlow, Ky., U.S.	H8	120
Barmedman, Austl.	J6	76
Bärmer, India	F3	54
Barmera, Austl.	J3	76
Barnagar, India	H6	54
Barnard Castle, Eng., U.K.	G11	12
Barn Bluff, mtn., Austl.	n12	77a
Barnegat, N.J., U.S.	E11	114
Barnegat Bay, b., N.J., U.S.	E11	114
Barnes Ice Cap, ice, Nu., Can.	A16	106
Barnesville, Ga., U.S.	C1	116
Barnesville, Oh., U.S.	E4	114
Barnesville-Carteret, Fr.	E7	14
Barnhart, Tx., U.S.	C7	130
Barnsdall, Ok., U.S.	E12	128
Barnsley, Eng., U.K.	H11	12
Barnstable, Ma., U.S.	C15	114
Barnstaple, Eng., U.K.	J8	12
Barnstaple Bay, b., Eng., U.K.	J8	12
Barnwell, Ab., Can.	G18	138
Barnwell, S.C., U.S.	C4	116
Baro, stm., Afr.	F7	62
Baron Bluff, clf., V.I.U.S.	g10	104c
Baron'ki, Bela.	G15	10
Borora Fa Island, i., Sol. Is.	d8	79b
Borora Ite Island, i., Sol. Is.	d8	79b
Baroua, Niger	G7	64
Barpeta, India	E13	54
Barqah (Cyrenaica), hist. reg., Libya	A4	62
Barques, Pointe aux, c., Mi., U.S.	D7	112
Barquisimeto, Ven.	B7	86
Barra, Braz.	F4	88
Barra, i., Scot., U.K.	D5	12
Barra, Ponta da, c., Moz.	C12	70
Barraba, Austl.	H8	76
Barra da Estiva, Braz.	G5	88
Barra del Colorado, C.R.	G6	102
Barra de Rio Grande, Nic.	F6	102
Barra do Corda, Braz.	C3	88
Barra do Cuanza, Ang.	B1	68
Barra do Garças, Braz.	G7	84
Barra do Mendes, Braz.	F4	88
Barra do Piraí, Braz.	L3	88
Barra do Ribeiro, Braz.	E12	92
Barra Falsa, Ponta da, c., Moz.	C12	70
Barra Mansa, Braz.	L3	88
Barranca, Peru	F2	84
Barrancabermeja, Col.	D4	86
Barrancas, Ven.	C7	86
Barrancas, Ven.	C10	86
Barrancas, stm., Arg.	H2	92
Barranco Azul, Mex.	E3	130
Barranco do Velho, Port.	G3	20
Barranqueras, Arg.	C8	92
Barranquilla, Col.	B4	86
Barranquitas, P.R.	B3	104a
Barras, Braz.	C4	88
Barre, Vt., U.S.	F4	110
Barreiras, Braz.	G3	88
Barreirinha, Braz.	D6	84
Barreiro, Port.	F1	20
Barreiros, Braz.	E8	88
Barren, stm., Ky., U.S.	H11	120
Barren, Nosy, is., Madag.	D7	68
Barren Islands, is., Ak., U.S.	E9	140
Barren River Lake, res., Ky., U.S.	H11	120
Barretos, Braz.	K1	88
Barrhead, Ab., Can.	B16	138
Barrie, On., Can.	D10	112
Barrie Island, i., On., Can.	C7	112
Barrière, B.C., Can.	E10	138
Barrier Range, mts., Austl.	H3	76
Barriga, Guam	j10	78c
Barrington, N.S., Can.	G11	110
Barrington Tops National Park, p.o.i., Austl.	I8	76
Barringun, Austl.	G5	76
Barrouallie, St. Vin.	o11	105e
Barrow, Ar., U.S.	D4	54
Barrow, Ak., U.S.	B8	140
Barrow, stm., Ire.	I5	12
Barrow, Point, c., Ak., U.S.	B8	140
Barrow Creek, Austl.	D6	74
Barrow-in-Furness, Eng., U.K.	G9	12
Barrow Island, i., Austl.	D2	74
Barrows, Mb., Can.	B12	124
Barrow Strait, strt., Nu., Can.	C6	141
Barry, Wales, U.K.	J9	12
Barry, Il., U.S.	E6	120
Barryton, Mi., U.S.	E4	112
Barsalpur, India	D4	54
Barsi, India	B2	53
Barsinghausen, Ger.	D5	16
Barstow, Ca., U.S.	I9	134
Barstow, Tx., U.S.	C4	130
Bar-sur-Seine, Fr.	F13	14
Bartang, Taj.	B11	56
Bartın, Tur.	B15	28
Bartın, state, Tur.	B15	28
Bartle Frere, mtn., Austl.	A5	76
Bartlesville, Ok., U.S.	H2	120
Bartlett, N.H., U.S.	F5	110
Bartlett, Tx., U.S.	C10	130
Bartlett, Tx., U.S.	D9	130
Bartlett, Tx., U.S.	D10	130
Bartley, Ne., U.S.	A8	128
Barton, Vt., U.S.	F4	110
Bartoszyce, Pol.	B16	16
Bartow, Fl., U.S.	I4	116
Bartow, Ga., U.S.	D3	116
Barumun, stm., Indon.	L4	48
Barú, Volcán see Barí, Volcán, vol., Pan.	H6	102
Barú, Jabal al-, mtn., Leb.	E6	58
Barus, Indon.	L3	48
Barysh, Russia	D7	32
Basankusu, D.R.C.	D3	66
Basarabeasca, Mol.	C15	26
Basatongwula Shan, mtn., China	B13	54
Basavakalyān, India	C3	53
Basavilbaso, Arg.	F8	92
Basāwul, Afg.	A3	54
Bascuñán, Cabo, c., Chile	C2	92
Basel (Bâle), Switz.	C4	22
Basella see Bassella, Spain	B12	20
Basey, Phil.	E5	52
Bashi Channel, strt., Asia	K9	42
Bashkortostan see Baškortostan, state, Russia	D9	32
Basilan, Island, i., Phil.	H4	52
Basilan Strait, strt., Phil.	G4	52
Basile, La., U.S.	G6	122
Basilicata, state, Italy	D10	24
Basin, Wy., U.S.	C4	126
Basin Lake, l., Sk., Can.	B8	124
Basīrhāt, India	G13	54
Baskahegan Lake, l., Me., U.S.	E8	110
Baskatong, Réservoir, res., Qc., Can.	B13	112
Baškirija, state, Russia	D9	32
Başköy, Tur.	B5	58
Baskunchak, ozero, l., Russia	E7	32
Basmat, India	B3	53
Basoko, D.R.C.	D4	66
Basora, Punt, c., Aruba	p20	104g
Basque Provinces see Euskal Herrika, state, Spain	A8	20
Basra see Al-Basrah, Iraq	C6	56
Bas-Rhin, state, Fr.	F16	14
Bassano, Ab., Can.	F18	138
Bassano del Grappa, Italy	E8	22
Bassari, Togo	H5	64
Bassas da India, rf., Reu.	E6	68
Bassein, stm., Mya.	D2	48
Bassett, Va., U.S.	B12	20
Basse Santa Su, Gam.	G2	64
Basse-Terre, Guad.	i5	105c
Basseterre, St. K./N.	C2	105a
Basse Terre, Trin.	s12	105f
Basse-Terre, i., Guad.	i5	105c
Bassett, Ne., U.S.	E13	126
Bassett, Va., U.S.	H6	114
Bassfield, Ms., U.S.	F9	122
Bassikounou, Maur.	F3	64
Bassila, Benin	H5	64
Bass River, N.S., Can.	E13	110
Bass Strait, strt., Austl.	L6	76
Basswood Lake, l., N.A.	C6	118
Båstad, Swe.	H5	8
Bastenaken see Bastogne, Bel.	D14	14
Bastersberge, hill, S. Afr.	G5	70
Basti, India	E9	54
Bastia, Fr.	G15	18
Bastogne, Bel.	D14	14
Bastrop, La., U.S.	E6	122
Bastrop, Tx., U.S.	D10	130
Basu, Pulau, i., Indon.	D3	50
Basutoland see Lesotho, ctry., Afr.	F9	70
Bata, Eq. Gui.	I6	64
Bataan Peninsula, pen., Phil.	C3	52
Batabanó, Golfo de, b., Cuba	A6	102
Batac, Phil.	A3	52
Batagai, Russia	C15	34
Batagai-Alyta, Russia	C15	34
Batak, Blg.	H11	26
Batala, India	C5	54
Batalha, Braz.	E7	88
Batam, Port.	E2	20
Batam, Pulau, i., Indon.	C3	50
Batamaj, Russia	D14	34
Batang, China	E4	36
Batangas, Phil.	D3	52
Batangtoru, Indon.	C1	50
Batan Islands, is., Phil.	K9	42
Batanta, Pulau, i., Indon.	F9	44
Batataís, Braz.	K2	88
Batavia, Arg.	G5	92
Batavia see Jakarta, Indon.	G5	50
Batavia, Ia., U.S.	D5	120
Batavia, Il., U.S.	C9	120
Batavia, N.Y., U.S.	A7	114
Batchelor, Austl.	B6	74
Bátdâmbâng, Camb.	F6	48
Bateckij, Russia	B13	10
Batemans Bay, Austl.	J7	76
Bates, Mount, mtn., Norf. I.	y24	78i
Batesburg, S.C., U.S.	C4	116
Batesville, Ar., U.S.	B7	122
Batesville, In., U.S.	E12	120
Batesville, Ms., U.S.	C9	122
Batesville, Tx., U.S.	F8	130
Bath, N.B., Can.	D9	110
Bath, Eng., U.K.	J10	12
Bath, Me., U.S.	G7	110
Bath, N.Y., U.S.	B8	114
Batha, stm., Chad	E3	62
Bathgate, N.D., U.S.	F16	124
Bathinda, India	C5	54
Bathsheba, Barb.	n8	105d
Bathurst, Austl.	I7	76
Bathurst, N.B., Can.	C11	110
Bathurst see Banjul, Gam.	G1	64
Bathurst, Cape, c., N.T., Can.	A5	106
Bathurst Inlet see Kingaok, Nu., Can.	B9	106
Bathurst Island, i., Austl.	B5	74
Bathurst Island, i., Nu., Can.	B5	141
Batlow, Austl.	J6	76
Batman, Tur.	B5	56
Batna, Alg.	B6	64
Ba To, Viet.	E9	48
Baton Rouge, La., U.S.	G7	122
Batouri, Cam.	D2	66
Batson, Tx., U.S.	G4	122
Batterie, Pointe de la, c., Mart.	k7	105c
Batticaloa, Sri L.	H5	53
Battipaglia, Italy	D8	24
Battle, stm., Can.	D19	138
Battle Creek, Mi., U.S.	F4	112
Battle Creek, Ne., U.S.	F15	126
Battle Creek, stm., N.A.	H3	112
Battle Ground, In., U.S.	H3	112
Battle Ground, Wa., U.S.	E4	136
Battle Harbour, Nf., Can.	i22	107a
Battle Mountain, Nv., U.S.	C8	134
Battle Mountain, mtn., Wy., U.S.	B9	132
Batu, Eth.	F7	62
Batu, Kepulauan, is., Indon.	F2	44
Batu-Batu, Indon.	F11	50
Batu Berincang, Gunong, mtn., Malay.	J5	48
Batu Gajah, Malay.	J5	48
Batukelau, Indon.	D9	50
Batumi, Geor.	F6	32
Batu Pahat, Malay.	L6	48
Baturaja, Indon.	E4	50
Baturité, Russia	C15	32
Baturusa, Indon.	D5	50
Batusangkar, Indon.	D2	50
Batz, Île de, i., Fr.	F4	14
Bau, Malay.	C7	50
Bauchi, Nig.	G6	64
Bauda, India	H10	54
Baudette, Mn., U.S.	C4	118
Baudó, stm., Col.	E3	86
Bauld, Cape, c., Nf., Can.	i22	107a
Bauman Fiord, b., Nu., Can.	B8	141
Baume-les-Dames, Fr.	G15	14
Baures, Bol.	B4	90
Bauska, Lat.	D7	10
Bautzen, Ger.	E10	16
Bauxite, Ar., U.S.	C6	122
Bavaria see Bayern, state, Ger.	H7	16
Bavarian Alps, mts., Eur.	I7	16
Båven, l., Swe.	G7	8
Bavispe, Mex.	F8	98
Bawang, Indon.	A3	48
Bawang, Tanjung, c., Indon.	A3	48
Bawean, Pulau, i., Indon.	F8	50
Bawiti, Egypt	I1	58
Bawku, Ghana	G4	64
Bawmi, Mya.	D6	48
Baxian, China	C7	42
Baxian, China	G2	42
Baxley, Ga., U.S.	E3	116
Baxoi, China	E4	36
Baxter, Mn., U.S.	E4	118
Baxter, Tn., U.S.	H12	120
Baxterville, Ms., U.S.	F9	122
Bay, Laguna de, l., Phil.	C3	52
Bayamo, Cuba	B9	102
Bayamón, P.R.	B3	104a
Bayamón, P.R.	B3	104a
Bayan, China	H2	42
Bayan Har Shan, mts., China	E4	36
Bayanhongor, Mong.	B5	36
Bayannaobao, China	B2	42
Bayano, Lago, res., Pan.	H8	102

Name	Map Ref.	Page
Bayan Obo, China	C7	36
Bayard, Ia., U.S.	C3	120
Bayard, N.M., U.S.	K8	132
Bayard, W.V., U.S.	E6	114
Bayawan, Phil.	F4	52
Baybay, Phil.	E5	52
Bayboro, N.C., U.S.	A9	116
Bayburt, Tur.	A5	56
Bay City, Mi., U.S.	E6	112
Bay City, Or., U.S.	E3	136
Bay City, Tx., U.S.	F12	130
Baydhabo (Baidoa), Som.	D8	66
Baydrag, stm., Mong.	B4	36
Bayern (Bavaria), state, Ger.	H7	16
Bayeux, Braz.	D8	88
Bayeux, Fr.	E8	14
Bayfield, Co., U.S.	F9	132
Bayfield, Wi., U.S.	E8	118
Bayındır, Tur.	E10	28
Bayjī, Iraq	C5	56
Baykonur see Bayqongyr, Kaz.	E11	32
Bay Minette, Al., U.S.	G11	122
Bayombong, Phil.	B3	52
Bayona see Baiona, Spain	B2	20
Bayonne, Fr.	F4	18
Bayou Bodcau Reservoir, res., La., U.S.	E5	122
Bayou Cane, La., U.S.	H8	122
Bayou D'Arbonne Lake, res., La., U.S.	E6	122
Bayovar, Peru	E1	84
Bay Port, Mi., U.S.	E6	112
Bayport, Mn., U.S.	F6	118
Bayqongyr, Kaz.	E11	32
Bayramiç, Tur.	D9	28
Bayreuth, Ger.	G7	16
Bayrūt (Beirut), Leb.	E6	58
Bays, Lake of, l., On., Can.	C10	112
Bay Saint Louis, Ms., U.S.	G9	122
Bay Shore, N.Y., U.S.	D12	114
Bayside, On., Can.	D12	112
Bay Springs Lake, res., Ms., U.S.	C10	122
Bayt ad-Dīn, Leb.	E6	58
Bayt al-Faqīh, Yemen	G5	56
Bayt Lahm (Bethlehem), W.B.	G6	58
Baytown, Tx., U.S.	H4	122
Bayyā'iyah al-Kabīrah, Syria	C8	58
Baza, Spain	G8	20
Bazardüzü dağ, mtn., Azer.	A6	56
Bazaruto, Ilha do, i., Moz.	B12	70
Bazhong, China	F2	42
Baziège, Fr.	F7	18
Bazine, Ks., U.S.	C9	128
Be, stm., Viet.	G8	48
Be, Nosy, i., Madag.	C8	68
Beach Haven, N.J., U.S.	E11	114
Beachport, Austl.	K3	76
Beachville, On., Can.	E9	112
Beachy Head, c., Eng., U.K.	K13	12
Beacon, Austl.	F3	74
Beacon, N.Y., U.S.	C12	114
Beacon Hill, Wa., U.S.	D3	136
Beaconsfield, Austl.	n13	77a
Beagle Gulf, b., Austl.	B5	74
Bealanana, Madag.	C8	68
Bealdoaivi see Peäldoajvi, mtn., Fin.	B12	8
Beale, Cape, c., B.C., Can.	H5	138
Beals Creek, stm., Tx., U.S.	B7	130
Bear, stm., Ca., U.S.	D4	134
Bear, stm., U.S.	I14	136
Bear Bay, b., Nu., Can.	B8	141
Bear Creek, stm., U.S.	C10	122
Bear Creek, stm., U.S.	D6	128
Bearden, Ar., U.S.	D6	122
Beardmore, On., Can.	B11	118
Bear Island, i., Ant.	C29	81
Bear Island, i., Ire.	J3	12
Bear Island see Bjørnøya, i., Nor.	B5	30
Bear Lake, l., Ab., Can.	A11	138
Bear Lake, l., U.S.	A5	132
Bear Mountain, mtn., Or., U.S.	G3	136
Béarn, hist. reg., Fr.	F5	18
Bear River, N.S., Can.	F11	110
Bear River Range, mts., U.S.	B5	132
Beartooth Pass, p., Wy., U.S.	C3	126
Bear Town, Ms., U.S.	F8	122
Beās, stm., India	C6	54
Beasain, Spain	A8	20
Beata, Cabo, c., Dom. Rep.	D12	102
Beata, Isla, i., Dom. Rep.	D12	102
Beaton, B.C., Can.	F13	138
Beatrice, Al., U.S.	F11	122
Beatrice, Ne., U.S.	A12	128
Beatrice, Cape, c., Austl.	B7	74
Beattie, Ks., U.S.	L2	118
Beatton, stm., B.C., Can.	D6	106
Beatty, Nv., U.S.	G9	134
Beattyville, Ky., U.S.	G2	114
Beaucaire, Fr.	F10	18
Beauce, reg., Fr.	F10	14
Beauceville, Qc., Can.	D6	110
Beauchêne, Lac l., Qc., Can.	B11	112
Beauchêne Island, i., Falk. Is.	J5	90
Beaudesert, Austl.	F9	76
Beaufort, Malay.	A9	50
Beaufort, S.C., U.S.	D5	116
Beaufort Castle see Qal'at ash-Shaqīf, sci., Leb.	E6	58
Beaufort Sea, N.A.	B12	140
Beaufort West, S. Afr.	H6	70
Beaugency, Fr.	G10	14
Beauharnois, Qc., Can.	E12	110
Beaumont, Fr.	E7	14
Beaumont, N.Z.	G3	80
Beaumont, Ca., U.S.	J8	134
Beaumont, Ms., U.S.	F9	122
Beaumont, Tx., U.S.	G4	122
Beaumont Hill, hill, Austl.	H5	76
Beaune, Fr.	G13	14
Beauport, Qc., Can.	C6	110
Beaupré, Qc., Can.	C6	110
Beauregard, stm., Fr.	D11	18
Beausejour, Mb., Can.	D17	124
Beauséjour, Guad.	h6	105c
Beauvais, Fr.	E11	14
Beauvoir-sur-Mer, Fr.	H6	14
Beaver, Ak., U.S.	C10	140
Beaver, Ok., U.S.	E8	128
Beaver, Pa., U.S.	D5	114
Beaver, Ut., U.S.	E4	132
Beaver, stm., Can.	C6	106
Beaver, stm., U.S.	D9	106
Beaver, stm., Ut., U.S.	E3	132
Beaver, stm., U.S.	E8	128
Beaver Creek, stm., Co., U.S.	G9	126
Beaver Creek, stm., Ne., U.S.	F6	124
Beaver Creek, stm., Ne., U.S.	G14	126
Beaver Creek, stm., U.S.	C6	128
Beaver Creek, stm., U.S.	G10	128
Beaver Creek, stm., Tx., U.S.	H9	128
Beaver Creek, stm., U.S.	A8	128
Beaver Creek, stm., U.S.	G9	124
Beaver Crossing, Ne., U.S.	G15	126
Beaver Dam, Ky., U.S.	G11	120
Beaver Dam, Wi., U.S.	H9	118
Beaverdell, B.C., Can.	G11	138
Beaver Falls, Pa., U.S.	D5	114
Beaverhead, stm., Mt., U.S.	E14	136
Beaverhead Mountains, mts., U.S.	E13	136
Beaverhill Lake, l., Ab., Can.	C18	138
Beaver Island, i., On., Can.	C6	118
Beaver Island, i., Mi., U.S.	C4	112
Beaver Lake, l., Ab., Can.	B19	138
Beaver Lake, res., Ar., U.S.	H4	120
Beaverlodge, Ab., Can.	A11	138
Beaverton, On., Can.	D10	112
Beaverton, Mi., U.S.	E5	112
Beaverton, Or., U.S.	E3	136
Beãwar, India	E5	54
Beazley, Arg.	F4	92
Bebedouro, Braz.	K1	88
Becal, Mex.	B2	102
Bécancour, stm., Qc., Can.	D5	110
Beccles, Eng., U.K.	I14	12
Bečej, Serb.	D6	26
Beceni, Rom.	D13	26
Bečevinka, Russia	G17	8
Béchar, Alg.	C4	64
Becharof Lake, l., Ak., U.S.	E8	140
Bechevin Bay, b., Ak., U.S.	E7	140
Bechuanaland see Botswana, ctry., Afr.	E3	68
Bechuanaland, hist. reg., S. Afr.	E5	70
Beckley, W.V., U.S.	G4	114
Beckum, Ger.	E4	16
Bedarieux, Fr.	F9	18
Bedford, Qc., Can.	E4	110
Bedford, S. Afr.	H8	70
Bedford, Eng., U.K.	I12	12
Bedford, In., U.S.	D3	120
Bedford, In., U.S.	F11	120
Bedford, Ky., U.S.	F12	120
Bedford, Oh., U.S.	D7	114
Bedford, Tx., U.S.	B10	130
Bedi, India	G3	54
Bedoba, Russia	C17	32
Bedourie, Austl.	E2	76
Bedworth, Eng., U.K.	I11	12
Beebe, Ar., U.S.	B7	122
Beech Creek, Ky., U.S.	G10	120
Beech Fork, stm., Ky., U.S.	G12	120
Beechal Creek, stm., Austl.	F5	76
Beechworth, Austl.	K6	76
Beechy, Sk., Can.	D6	124
Beecroft Head, c., Austl.	J8	76
Beemer, Ne., U.S.	J2	118
Beenleigh, Austl.	F9	76
Be'er Sheva', Isr.	G6	58
Beersheba Springs, Tn., U.S.	B13	122
Be'ér Sheva' (Beersheba), Isr.	G6	58
Beeskow, Ger.	D10	16
Beeville, Tx., U.S.	F10	130
Befandriana Avaratra, Madag.	D4	66
Bega, Austl.	K7	76
Bega, stm., Eur.	D9	26
Begamganj, India	G7	54
Begur, Cap de, c., Spain	C14	20
Begusarai, India	F11	54
Behbahān, Iran	C7	56
Behshahr, Iran	B7	56
Bei'an, China	B10	36
Beibei, China	G2	42
Beicheng, China	G5	36
Beigi, Eth.	F6	62
Beijing (Peking), China	B7	42
Beijing, state, China	B6	42
Beili, China	L3	42
Beiliu, China	J4	42
Beinamar, Chad	F3	62
Beipa, Pap. N. Gui.	b4	79a
Beipan, stm., China	I1	42
Beipiao, China	D4	38
Beira, Moz.	A12	70
Beira, hist. reg., Port.	E3	20
Beirut see Bayrūt, Leb.	E6	58
Beiseker, Ab., Can.	E17	138
Beishan, China	I3	42
Beitbridge, Zimb.	C10	70
Beizhen, China	D4	38
Beja, Port.	G3	20
Béja, Tun.	H3	24
Beja, state, Port.	G3	20
Bejaïa, Alg.	B6	64
Béjar, Spain	D5	20
Beji, stm., Pak.	D2	54
Bejuco, Pan.	H8	102
Bekaa Valley see Al-Biqā', val., Leb.	D7	58
Bekabad, Uzb.	F11	32
Bekdaš, Turkmen.	A7	56
Békés, Hung.	C8	26
Békés, state, Hung.	C7	26
Békéscsaba, Hung.	C7	26
Bekilli, Tur.	E12	28
Bekily, Madag.	E8	68
Bekokoka, Madag.	D7	68
Bekopaka, Madag.	D7	68
Bela, India	F9	54
Bela, Pak.	D10	56
Belaazërsk, Bela.	H8	10
Bela Crkva, Serb.	D8	26
Belaga, Malay.	B8	50
Bel Air, Md., U.S.	E9	114
Belaja Gora, Russia	B14	10
Belambangammu, Indon.	F4	50
Belampalli, India	B4	53
Bela Palanka, Serb.	F9	26
Belarus, ctry., Eur.	E14	6
Belaruskaja hrada, mts., Bela.	F10	10
Belau see Palau, ctry., Oc.	g8	78b
Bela Vista, Braz.	D5	90
Bela Vista, Moz.	E11	70
Belawan, Indon.	B1	50
Belaya, stm., Indon.	C10	50
Belchатów, Pol.	E15	16
Belcher, La., U.S.	E5	122
Belcherāgh, Afg.	B10	56
Belcher Channel, strt., Nu., Can.	B6	141
Belcher Islands, is., Nu., Can.	D14	106
Belding, Mi., U.S.	E4	112
Belebelka, Russia	C13	10
Beledweyne, Som.	D8	66
Belém, Braz.	A1	88
Belém, Moz.	C6	68
Belém de São Francisco, Braz.	E6	88
Belén, Arg.	C4	92
Belén, Nic.	G5	102
Belén, Para.	D5	90
Belén, Ur.	E9	92
Belén, N.M., U.S.	I10	132
Belén, Arg.	C4	92
Belén, Embalse de, res., Spain	B3	20
Belfast, S. Afr.	D9	70
Belfast, N. Ire., U.K.	G6	12
Belfast, Me., U.S.	F7	110
Belfield, N.D., U.S.	A10	124
Belford, Eng., U.K.	F11	12
Belgaum, India	D2	53
Belgern, Ger.	E8	16
Belgium, ctry., Eur.	D13	14
Belgorod, Russia	D5	32
Belgrade, Mt., U.S.	E15	136
Belgrade, Ne., U.S.	F14	126
Belgrade see Beograd, Serb.	E7	26
Belhaven, N.C., U.S.	A9	116
Belick, Bela.	H13	10
Beliliou, i., Palau	D9	44
Belin, Fr.	E5	18
Belin-Béliet see Belin, Fr.	E5	18
Belington, W.V., U.S.	E5	114
Belinyu, Indon.	D4	50
Belitung, i., Indon.	E5	50
Belize, ctry., N.A.	D3	102
Belize see Belize	D3	102
Belize City, Belize	D3	102
Belkovski, ostrov see Bel'kovskij, ostrov, i., Russia	A16	34
Bel'kovskij, ostrov, i., Russia	A16	34
Bella Bella, B.C., Can.	D2	138
Bellac, Fr.	C7	18
Bella Coola, B.C., Can.	D4	138
Bella Coola, stm., B.C., Can.	D4	138
Bellair, Fl., U.S.	F4	116
Bellaire, Tx., U.S.	H3	122
Bellamy, Al., U.S.	E10	122
Bellaria, Italy	F9	22
Bellary, India	D3	53
Bella Unión, Ur.	E9	92
Bella Vista, Arg.	D8	92
Bella Vista, Arg.	B5	92
Bellavista, Peru	E2	84
Bellbrook, Austl.	H9	76
Belle, W.V., U.S.	F4	114
Bellefontaine, Mart.	k6	105c
Bellefontaine, Oh., U.S.	D2	114
Bellefonte, Pa., U.S.	D8	114
Belle Fourche, S.D., U.S.	C9	126
Belle Fourche, stm., U.S.	C10	126
Bellegarde-sur-Valserine, Fr.	C11	18
Belle Glade, Fl., U.S.	J5	116
Belle Hôtesse, mtn., Guad.	h5	105c
Belle-Île, i., Fr.	G5	14
Belle Isle, l., Nf., Can.	i22	107a
Belle Isle, Strait of, strt., Nf., Can.	i22	107a
Bellefontaine Ker National Park, p.o.i., Austl.	A5	76
Belle Plaine, Ia., U.S.	C5	120
Belle Plaine, Ks., U.S.	D11	128
Belle Plaine, Mn., U.S.	G5	118
Belleview, Fl., U.S.	G11	122
Belleville, On., Can.	D12	112
Belleville, Il., U.S.	F8	120
Belleville, Ks., U.S.	B11	128
Belleville, Pa., U.S.	D8	114
Belleville-sur-Saône, Fr.	C10	18
Bellevue, Ab., Can.	G16	138
Bellevue, Ia., U.S.	B7	120
Bellevue, Id., U.S.	G12	136
Bellevue, Mi., U.S.	F4	112
Bellevue, Ne., U.S.	C2	120
Bellevue, Oh., U.S.	C3	114
Bellevue, Wa., U.S.	C4	136
Belley, Fr.	D11	18
Bellingham, Mn., U.S.	F2	118
Bellingham, Wa., U.S.	B4	136
Bellinghausen, sci., Ant.	B35	81
Bellinghausen Sea, s., Ant.	P29	142
Bellinzona, Switz.	D6	22
Bell Island, i., Nf., Can.	j22	107a
Bellmead, Tx., U.S.	C10	130
Bello, Col.	D4	86
Bellot Strait, strt., Nu., Can.	A12	106
Bell Peninsula, pen., Nu., Can.	C14	106
Bells, Tn., U.S.	B9	122
Bells, Tx., U.S.	D2	122
Bells Corners, On., Can.	C14	112
Belluno, Italy	D9	22
Bell Ville, Arg.	F6	92
Bellville, S. Afr.	H4	70
Bellwood, Ne., U.S.	F15	126
Bellwood, Pa., U.S.	D7	114
Belly, stm., N.A.	G17	138
Bellyk, Russia	D16	32
Belmond, Ia., U.S.	B4	120
Belmont, N.S., Can.	E13	110
Belmont, S. Afr.	F7	70
Belmont, N.H., U.S.	G5	110
Belmont, Wi., U.S.	B7	120
Belmonte, Braz.	H6	88
Belmonte, Spain	A4	20
Belmopan, Belize	D3	102
Beloe, ozero, l., Russia	F17	8
Beloe more (White Sea), s., Russia	D18	8
Belogorsk, Russia	F14	34
Belo Horizonte, Braz.	J3	88
Beloit, Ks., U.S.	B10	128
Beloit, Wi., U.S.	B8	120
Belo Jardim, Braz.	E7	88
Belomestnaja, Russia	H20	10
Belomorsk, Russia	D16	8
Belören, Tur.	F15	28
Belorussia see Belarus, ctry., Eur.	E14	6
Belovo, Russia	D22	8
Belo sur Mer, Madag.	E7	68
Belot, Lac, l., N.T., Can.	B5	106
Belo Tsiribihina, Madag.	D7	68
Belousovo, Russia	E19	10
Belovo, Russia	D15	32
Belpre, Oh., U.S.	E4	114
Belt, Mt., U.S.	C16	136
Beltana, Austl.	H2	76
Belt Creek, stm., Mt., U.S.	C16	136
Belton, Mo., U.S.	F3	120
Belton, Tx., U.S.	C10	130
Belton Lake, res., Tx., U.S.	C9	130
Beltrán, Arg.	C5	92
Belukha, Mount, mtn., Asia	E15	32
Belūr, India	E2	53
Beluran, Malay.	H1	52
Belvedere Marittimo, Italy	E9	24
Belvidere, Il., U.S.	B9	120
Belvidere, N.J., U.S.	D10	114
Belyando, stm., Austl.	D6	76
Belye Berega, Russia	G17	10
Belyj, ostrov, i., Russia	A3	34
Belyj Gorodok, Russia	C20	10
Belyj Jar, Russia	C15	32
Belzec, Pol.	F19	16
Belzig, Ger.	D8	16
Belzoni, Ms., U.S.	D8	122
Bembèréke, Benin	G5	64
Bemidji, Mn., U.S.	D3	118
Bena-Dibele, D.R.C.	E4	66
Benagerie, Austl.	H3	76
Benalla, Austl.	K6	76
Benares see Vārānasi, India	F9	54
Ben Arous, Tun.	H4	24
Benavente, Spain	B5	20
Benbecula, i., Scot., U.K.	D5	12
Ben Bolt, Tx., U.S.	G9	130
Ben Cat, Viet.	G8	48
Bencha, Khao Phanom, mtn., Thai.	H4	48
Ben-Chicago, Col de p., Alg.	H13	20
Bencubbin, Austl.	F3	74
Bend, Or., U.S.	F5	136
Bendemeer, Austl.	H8	76
Bender Cassim see Boosaaso, Som.	B9	66
Bendigo, Austl.	K5	76
Bēne, Lat.	D6	10
Benedito Leite, Braz.	D3	88
Benepú, Rada, anch., Chile	f29	78l
Benevento, Italy	C8	24
Bèng, stm., Laos.	B5	48
Bengal, Bay of, b., Asia	F6	46
Bengara, Indon.	B10	50
Bengasi see Banghāzī, Libya	A3	62
Bengbu, China	E7	42
Benghazi see Banghāzī, Libya	A3	62
Bengkalis, Indon.	C3	50
Bengkalis, Pulau, i., Indon.	C3	50
Bengkayang, Indon.	C6	50
Bengkulu, Indon.	E3	50
Bengkulu, state, Indon.	E3	50
Bengough, Sk., Can.	E8	124
Benguela, Ang.	C1	68
Benguerua, Ilha, i., Moz.	B12	70
Benha, Egypt	H2	58
Beni, D.R.C.	D5	66
Beni, stm., Bol.	B3	90
Bení Abbas, Alg.	C4	64
Beni 'Adi el-Bahariya, Egypt	K1	58
Beni Ahmad, Egypt	J1	58
Benicarló, Spain	D11	20
Benidorm, Spain	F10	20
Beni Mazâr, Egypt	J1	58
Beni Muhammadiyat, Egypt	K2	58
Benin, ctry., Afr.	G5	64
Benin, Bight of, b., Afr.	I5	64
Benin City, Nig.	H6	64
Benissa see Benissa, Spain	F11	20
Benissa, Spain	F11	20
Beni Suef, Egypt	I2	58
Benito, Mb., Can.	C12	124
Benito Juárez, Arg.	H8	92
Benito Juárez, Presa, res., Mex.	G10	100
Benjamin, Tx., U.S.	H9	128
Benjamín, Isla, i., Chile	H2	90
Benjamin Constant, Braz.	D3	84
Benkelman, Ne., U.S.	A7	128
Benkovac, Cro.	F12	22
Benld, Il., U.S.	E8	120
Ben Lomond, Ca., U.S.	F3	134
Ben Lomond National Park, p.o.i., Austl.	n13	77a
Bennetta, ostrov, i., Russia	A18	34
Bennett Island see Bennetta, ostrov, i., Russia	A18	34
Bennettsville, S.C., U.S.	B6	116
Bennington, Ks., U.S.	B11	128
Bennington, Vt., U.S.	B12	114
Benoit, Ms., U.S.	D7	122
Benoni, S. Afr.	E9	70
Ben Sekka, Rass, c., Tun.	G3	24
Bensheim, Ger.	G4	16
Benson, Az., U.S.	L6	132
Benson, Mn., U.S.	F3	118
Benson, N.C., U.S.	A7	116
Benteng, Indon.	G12	50
Ben Thuy, Viet.	C7	48
Bentinck Island, i., Nu., Can.	C7	74
Bentinck Island, i., Mya.	G3	48
Bentiu, Sudan	F6	62
Bento Gonçalves, Braz.	D12	92
Benton, Ar., U.S.	C6	122
Benton, Il., U.S.	F9	120
Benton, Ky., U.S.	H9	120
Benton, La., U.S.	E5	122
Benton, Mo., U.S.	G8	120
Benton, Tn., U.S.	B14	122
Benton, Wi., U.S.	B7	120
Benton Harbor, Mi., U.S.	F3	112
Bentonville, Ar., U.S.	H3	120
Ben Tre, Viet.	G8	48
Bentung, Malay.	K5	48
Benua, Pulau, i., Indon.	C5	50
Benue, stm., Afr.	H6	64
Ben Wheeler, Tx., U.S.	E3	122
Benxi, China	D5	38
Benxi, China	D5	38
Beograd (Belgrade), Serb.	E7	26
Beohāri, India	F8	54
Béoumi, C. Iv.	H3	64
Beowawe, Nv., U.S.	C9	134
Bequia, i., St. Vin.	o11	105e
Bequimão, Braz.	B3	88
Berat, Alb.	D13	24
Berати see Berat, Alb.	D13	24
Berau, Indon.	B10	50
Berau, stm., Indon.	F9	44
Berazino, Bela.	G11	10
Berberа, Som.	B9	66
Berbérati, C.A.R.	D3	66
Berchtesgaden, Ger.	I8	16
Berck, Fr.	D10	14
Berclair, Tx., U.S.	F10	130
Berdians'k, Ukr.	E5	32
Berdigestjah, Russia	D14	34
Berdsk, Russia	D14	32
Berea, Ky., U.S.	C14	114
Berea, S.C., U.S.	B3	116
Berehomet, Ukr.	A12	26
Berehove, Ukr.	A9	26
Berekua, Dom.	j6	105c
Berekum, Ghana	H4	64
Berens, stm., Can.	B17	124
Berens River, Mb., Can.	B16	124
Beresford, N.B., Can.	C11	110
Beresford, S.D., U.S.	E1	118
Berești, Rom.	C14	26
Berettyó (Barcău), stm., Eur.	B8	26
Berettyóújfalu, Hung.	B8	26
Berezivka, Ukr.	B17	26
Bereznik, Russia	E20	8
Berezniki, Russia	C9	32
Berëzovka, Russia	C6	32
Berëzovskij, Russia	C15	32
Berëzovskij Rjadok, Russia	B17	10
Berga, Spain	B12	20
Bergama, Tur.	D10	28
Bergamo, Italy	E6	22
Bergara, Spain	A8	20
Bergby, Swe.	F7	8
Bergen see Mons, Bel.	D12	14
Bergen, Ger.	B9	16
Bergen, Nor.	F1	8
Bergen, N.Y., U.S.	E12	112
Bergen auf Rügen, Ger.	B9	16
Bergen op Zoom, Neth.	C13	14
Bergerac, Fr.	E6	18
Bergisch Gladbach, Ger.	F3	16
Bergville, S. Afr.	F9	70
Berhala, selat, strt., Indon.	D3	50
Beringa, ostrov, i., Russia	F22	34
Beringen, Bel.	D14	14
Beringovskij, Russia	D24	34
Bering Sea, s.	C1	140
Bering Strait, strt.	C6	140
Berja, Spain	H8	20
Berkåk, Nor.	E4	8
Berkane, Mor.	C4	64
Berkeley, Ca., U.S.	F3	134
Berkeley Springs, W.V., U.S.	E7	114
Berkner Island, i., Ant.	C35	81
Berkovitsa, Blg.	G10	26
Berkshire Hills, hills, Ma., U.S.	B12	114
Berlevåg, Nor.	A13	8
Berlin, Ger.	D9	16
Berlin, N.H., U.S.	F5	110
Berlin, N.J., U.S.	E11	114
Berlin, Pa., U.S.	E7	114
Berlin, Wi., U.S.	H9	118
Berlin, state, Ger.	D9	16
Berlinguet Inlet, b., Nu., Can.	A14	106
Bermagui, Austl.	K8	76
Bermejillo, Mex.	C7	100
Bermejito, stm., Arg.	B7	92
Bermejo, stm., Arg.	B4	92
Bermejo, stm., Arg.	C8	92
Bermejo, Paso del, p., S.A.	F2	92
Bermen, Lac, l., Qc., Can.	E17	106
Bermeo, Spain	A8	20
Bermuda, dep., N.A.	k16	104e
Bern (Berne), Switz.	C4	22
Bernalda, Italy	D10	24
Bernasconi, Arg.	H5	92
Bernau bei Berlin, Ger.	D9	16
Bernay, Fr.	E9	14
Bernburg, Ger.	E7	16
Berne see Bern, Switz.	C4	22
Berner Alpen, mts., Switz.	D4	22
Berneray, i., Scot., U.K.	D5	12
Bernese Alps see Berner Alpen, mts., Switz.	D4	22
Bernice, La., U.S.	E6	122
Bernie, Mo., U.S.	H8	120
Bernier Bay, b., Nu., Can.	A12	106
Bernier Island, i., Austl.	D2	74
Bernina, Piz, mtn., Eur.	H18	14
Bernkastel-Kues, Ger.	G3	16
Bernsdorf, Ger.	E10	16
Berón de Astrada, Arg.	C9	92
Beroroha, Madag.	E8	68
Beroun, Czech Rep.	G9	16
Berounka, stm., Czech Rep.	F9	16
Berre, Étang de, l., Fr.	F11	18
Berri, Austl.	J3	76
Berriyane, Alg.	C5	64
Berry, Al., U.S.	D11	122
Berry, hist. reg., Fr.	H11	14
Berry, Canal du, can., Fr.	G10	14
Berryessa, Lake, res., Ca., U.S.	E3	134
Berry Islands, is., Bah.	B9	96
Berseba, Nmb.	D3	70
Bershad', Ukr.	A16	26
Berthold, N.D., U.S.	F12	124
Berthoud, Co., U.S.	G7	126
Berthoud Pass, p., Co., U.S.	B3	128
Bertoua, Cam.	D2	66
Bertrand, Mi., U.S.	G3	112
Bertrand, Ne., U.S.	G13	126
Beruri, Braz.	D5	84
Berwick, La., U.S.	H7	122
Berwick, Pa., U.S.	C9	114
Berwick-upon-Tweed, Eng., U.K.	F11	12
Berwyn, Il., U.S.	G2	112
Besalampy, Madag.	D7	68
Besançon, Fr.	G14	14
Bešankovičy, Bela.	E12	10
Besar, Gunung, mtn., Indon.	E9	50
Besar, Gunung, vol., Malay.	K6	48
Besed', stm., Eur.	H14	10
Beskid Mountains see Beskids, mts., Eur.	G15	16
Beskids, mts., Eur.	G15	16
Beskra, Alg.	C6	64
Beslan, Russia	F6	32
Besni, Tur.	A8	58
Bessarabia, hist. reg., Eur.	C15	26
Bessemer, Al., U.S.	D11	122
Bessemer, Mi., U.S.	E8	118
Bessemer City, N.C., U.S.	A4	116
Bestjah, Russia	D15	34
Bestöbe, Kaz.	D12	32
Besuki, India	B2	53
Bestuževo, Russia	F20	8
Betafo, Madag.	D8	68
Betanzos, Spain	A2	20
Bétaré Oya, Cam.	C2	66
Bétera, Spain	E10	20
Bethal, S. Afr.	E9	70
Bethalto, Il., U.S.	F7	120
Bethanien, Nmb.	E3	70
Bethany, Oc., U.S.	D3	120
Bethany, Ok., U.S.	F11	128
Bethel, Ak., U.S.	D7	140
Bethel, Me., U.S.	F6	110
Bethel, N.C., U.S.	I8	114
Bethel Acres, Ok., U.S.	B2	122
Bethel Springs, Tn., U.S.	B10	122
Bethlehem, S. Afr.	F9	70
Bethlehem, Pa., U.S.	D10	114
Bethlehem, W.V., U.S.	H9	112
Bethlehem see Bayt Lahm, W.B.	G6	58
Bethulie, S. Afr.	G8	70
Béthune, Fr.	D11	14
Béthune, S.C., U.S.	B5	116
Beting, Malay.	C7	50
Betioky, Madag.	E7	68
Betong, Thai.	I5	48
Betong, Malay.	C7	50
Betoota, Austl.	E3	76
Betpaqdala, des., Kaz.	E11	32
Betroka, Madag.	E8	68
Bet She'arim, Horbat, sci., Isr.	F6	58
Betsiamites, stm., Qc., Can.	A7	110
Betsiamites, Barrage, dam, Qc., Can.	A7	110
Betsiamites, Pointe de, c., Qc., Can.	B8	110
Betsiboka, stm., Madag.	D8	68
Betsie, Point, c., Mi., U.S.	D3	112
Betsy Layne, Ky., U.S.	G3	114
Bettendorf, Ia., U.S.	C7	120
Bettiah, India	E10	54
Bettles Field, Ak., U.S.	C9	140
Bettola, Italy	F6	22
Betul, India	H6	54
Betung, Indon.	E4	50
Betwa, stm., India	F7	54
Betzdorf, Ger.	F3	16
Beulah, Austl.	J4	76
Beulah, Mi., U.S.	D3	112
Beulah, N.D., U.S.	G12	124
Beulaville, N.C., U.S.	B8	116
Beuvron, stm., Fr.	G11	14
B. Everett Jordan Lake, res., N.C., U.S.	I6	114
Beverley, Eng., U.K.	H12	12
Beverly, Ma., U.S.	B15	114
Beverly Hills, Ca., U.S.	I7	134
Beverly Lake, l., Nu., Can.	C10	106
Beverungen, Ger.	E5	16
Beverwijk, Neth.	B13	14
Bewani, Mountains, mts., Pap. N. Gui.	a3	79a
Bexhill, Eng., U.K.	K13	12
Bexley, Oh., U.S.	E3	114
Bey Dağları, mtn., Tur.	G13	28
Beydağı Olimpos Milli Parkı, p.o.i., Tur.	G13	28
Beyla, Gui.	H3	64
Beyneü, Kaz.	E9	32
Beypazarı, Tur.	C14	28
Beyporе, India	F2	53
Beyra, Som.	C9	66
Beysehir, Tur.	F14	28
Beyşehir Gölü, l., Tur.	F14	28
Bežanickaja vozvyšennost', plat., Russia	D12	10
Bežeck, Russia	C19	10
Bezmein, Turkmen.	B8	56
Bezwada see Vijayawada, India	C5	53
Bhādra, India	D5	54
Bhadrāchalam, India	C5	53
Bhadrak, India	H11	54
Bhadra Reservoir, res., India.	E2	53
Bhadrāvati, India	E2	53
Bhāgalpur, India	F11	54
Bhainsa, India	B3	53
Bhai Pheru, Pak.	C4	54
Bhairab Bāzār, Bngl.	F13	54
Bhaironghāti, India	C7	54
Bhakkar, Pak.	C3	54
Bhaktapur (Bhādgāon), Nepal.	E10	54
Bhālki, India	C3	53
Bhalwāl, Pak.	B4	54
Bhamo, Mya.	D8	46
Bhandāra, India	H7	54
Bhanvad, India	H2	54
Bharatpur, India	E6	54
Bharatpur, Nepal	E10	54
Bharthana, India	E7	54
Bhārūch, India	H4	54
Bhātāpāra, India	H8	54
Bhātghar Lake, res., India.	B1	53
Bhatkal, India	E2	53
Bhātpāra, India	G12	54
Bhattiprolu, India	C5	53
Bhāvnagar, India	H3	53
Bhāvnagar, India	H4	54
Bhāwani Mandi, India	F5	54
Bhawānipatna, India	I9	54
Bhera, Pak.	B4	54
Bhīkangaon, India	H5	54
Bhilai, India	H8	54
Bhīlwāra, India	F5	54
Bhīma, stm., India	C3	53
Bhīmavaram, India	C5	53
Bhind, India	E7	54
Bhindar, India	F4	54
Bhiwandi, India	B1	53
Bhiwāni, India	D6	54
Bhojpur, Nepal	E11	54
Bhokardan, India	H5	54
Bhopāl, India	G6	54
Bhuban, India	H10	54
Bhubaneshwar, India.	H10	54
Bhuj, India	G2	54
Bhusāwal, India	H5	54
Bhutan, ctry., Asia	E13	54
Bia, Phou, mtn., Laos.	C6	48
Biafra, Bight of, b., Afr.	I6	64
Biak, i., Indon.	F10	44
Biała Piska, Pol.	C18	16
Biała Podlaska, Pol.	D19	16
Biała Podlaska, state, Pol.	E19	16
Białobrzegi, Pol.	E16	16
Białogard, Pol.	B12	16
Białowieski Park Narodowy, p.o.i., Pol.	D19	16
Białystok, Pol.	C19	16
Białystok, state, Pol.	C19	16
Bianco, Monte see Blanc, Mont, mts., Eur.	D12	18
Biankouma, C. Iv.	H3	64
Biao, India	F6	54
Biaora, India	F6	54
Biarritz, Fr.	F4	18
Biasca, Switz.	D5	22
Biba, Egypt	I1	58
Bibai, Japan	C14	38
Bibala, Ang.	C1	68
Bibb City, Ga., U.S.	E14	122
Bibbiena, Italy	G8	22
Bibémi, Cam.	C2	66
Bicas, Braz.	K4	88
Bicaz, Rom.	C13	26
Biche, Lac la la, l., Ab., Can.	B18	138
Bichigt, Mong.	B4	36
Bicknell, In., U.S.	F10	120
Bicknell, Ut., U.S.	E5	132
Bicudo, stm., Braz.	J3	88
Bičura, Russia	F10	34
Bid, India	B2	53
Bida, Nig.	H6	64
Bidar, India	C3	53
Biddeford, Me., U.S.	G6	110
Bideford, Eng., U.K.	J8	12
Bieber, Ca., U.S.	B4	134
Biebrza, stm., Pol.	C18	16
Biebrzański Park Narodowy, p.o.i., Pol.	C18	16
Biecz, Pol.	G17	16
Biedenkopf, Ger.	F4	16
Biel (Bienne), Switz.	C4	22
Bielawa, Pol.	F12	16
Bielefeld, Ger.	D4	16
Bieler Lake, l., Nu., Can.	A15	106
Biella, Italy	E4	22
Bielsko-Biała, Pol.	G15	16
Bielsko-Biała, state, Pol.	G15	16
Bielsk Podlaski, Pol.	D19	16
Bienfait, Sk., Can.	E11	124
Bien Hoa, Viet.	G8	48
Bienne see Biel, Switz.	C4	22
Bienne, stm., Fr.	C11	18
Bien Son, Viet.	B7	48
Bienville, Lac, l., Qc., Can.	D16	106
Bienville, La., U.S.	E6	122
Biesiesvlei, S. Afr.	E7	70
Bieszczadzki Park Narodowy, p.o.i., Pol.	G18	16
Bifoun, Gabon	E2	66
Big, stm., Mo., U.S.	F7	120
Biga, Tur.	C10	28
Bigadiç, Tur.	D11	28
Big A Mountain, mtn., Va., U.S.	G3	114
Big Bald Mountain, mtn., N.B., Can.	B11	110
Big Bay, Mi., U.S.	B2	112
Big Bay De Noc, b., Mi., U.S.	C3	112
Big Bear Lake, Ca., U.S.	I9	134
Big Beaver, Sk., Can.	E8	124
Big Belt Mountains, mts., Mt., U.S.	D15	136
Big Bend, Swaz.	E10	70
Big Bend National Park, p.o.i., Tx., U.S.	E4	130
Big Bend Reservoir, res., Ab., Can.	D15	138
Big Black, stm., Ms., U.S.	E8	122
Big Blue, stm., U.S.	G16	126
Big Blue, West Fork, stm., Ne., U.S.	G15	126
Big Bonito Creek, stm., Az., U.S.	J7	132
Big Canyon, p., Tx., U.S.	D5	130
Big Chino Wash, stm., Az., U.S.	H4	132
Big Creek, B.C., Can.	E6	138
Big Creek, Ca., U.S.	F6	134
Big Creek, stm., B.C., Can.	E6	138
Big Creek, stm., Ks., U.S.	C9	128
Big Cypress Swamp, sw., Fl., U.S.	J4	116
Big Delta, Ak., U.S.	D10	140
Big Desert, des., Austl.	J3	76
Big Diomede Island see Ratmanova, ostrov, i., Russia	C27	34
Big Dry Creek, stm., Mt., U.S.	G7	124
Bigelow Bight, b., U.S.	G6	110
Big Flat, Ar., U.S.	I5	120
Bigfork, Mn., U.S.	D5	118
Big Fork, stm., Mn., U.S.	C5	118
Big Frog Mountain, mtn., Tn., U.S.	C14	122
Biggar, Sk., Can.	B6	124
Biggar, Scot., U.K.	F9	12
Biggs, Ca., U.S.	D4	134
Big Gull Lake, l., On., Can.	D12	112

I·8 Big Hole – Boqueirão

Name	Map Ref.	Page
Big Hole, stm., Mt., U.S.	E14	136
Bighorn, stm., U.S.	A5	126
Bighorn Basin, bas., U.S.	C4	126
Bighorn Canyon National Recreation Area, p.o.i., U.S.	B4	126
Bighorn Lake, res., U.S.	B4	126
Bighorn Mountains, mts., U.S.	C5	126
Bight, Head of, b., Austl.	F6	74
Big Island, Va., U.S.	G6	114
Big Island, i., Nu., Can.	C17	106
Big Lake, Mn., U.S.	F5	118
Big Lake, l., Me., U.S.	E9	110
Big Lookout Mountain, mtn., Or., U.S.	F9	136
Big Lost, stm., Id., U.S.	G13	136
Big Muddy, stm., Il., U.S.	G8	120
Big Muddy Creek, stm., Mt., U.S.	F9	124
Big Nemaha, North Fork, stm., Ne., U.S.	K2	118
Bignona, Sen.	G1	64
Big Pine, Ca., U.S.	F7	134
Big Pine Mountain, mtn., Ca., U.S.	I6	134
Big Piney, Wy., U.S.	H16	136
Big Piney, stm., Mo., U.S.	G6	120
Bigpoint, Ms., U.S.	G10	122
Big Porcupine Creek, stm., Mt., U.S.	H6	124
Big Prairie Creek, stm., Al., U.S.	E11	122
Big Quill Lake, l., Sk., Can.	C9	124
Big Raccoon Creek, stm., In., U.S.	I2	112
Big Rapids, Mi., U.S.	E4	112
Big Rideau Lake, l., On., Can.	D13	112
Big River, Sk., Can.	E9	106
Big Sable Point, c., Mi., U.S.	D3	112
Big Sand Lake, l., Mb., Can.	D11	106
Big Sandy, Tn., U.S.	H9	120
Big Sandy, Tx., U.S.	E3	122
Big Sandy, stm., Wy., U.S.	F3	126
Big Sandy, stm., U.S.	F3	114
Big Sandy Creek, stm., Co., U.S.	C6	128
Bigsby Island, i., On., Can.	B4	118
Big Signal Peak, mtn., Ca., U.S.	D2	134
Big Sioux, stm., U.S.	E16	126
Big Sky, Mt., U.S.	E15	136
Big Smoky Valley, val., Nv., U.S.	E8	134
Big Spring, Tx., U.S.	B6	130
Big Spruce Knob, mtn., W.V., U.S.	F5	114
Big Stone City, S.D., U.S.	F2	118
Big Stone Gap, Va., U.S.	H3	114
Big Stone Lake, l., U.S.	F2	118
Big Sunflower, stm., Ms., U.S.	D8	122
Big Sur, reg., Ca., U.S.	H4	134
Big Timber, Mt., U.S.	E16	136
Big Trout Lake, l., On., Can.	E12	106
Biguaçu, Braz.	C13	92
Big Water, Ut., U.S.	F5	132
Big Wells, Tx., U.S.	F8	130
Big White Mountain, mtn., B.C., Can.	G12	138
Big Wood, stm., Id., U.S.	G12	136
Bihać, Bos.	E2	26
Bīhar, India	F10	54
Bihār, state, India	E10	54
Biharamulo, Tan.	E6	66
Bihor, state, Rom.	C9	26
Bihor, Vârful, mtn., Rom.	C9	26
Bihoro, Japan	C16	38
Bihosava, Bela.	E10	10
Bihu, China	G8	42
Bija, stm., Russia	D15	32
Bijagós, Arquipélago dos, is., Gui.-B.	G1	64
Bijainagar, India	F5	54
Bijaipur, India	E6	54
Bijāpur, India	C2	53
Bījāpur, India	B5	53
Bijeljina, Bos.	E6	26
Bijelo Polje, Serb.	F6	26
Bijie, China	F6	36
Bijnor, India	D7	54
Bijsk, Russia	D15	32
Bīkāner, India	D4	54
Bikar, at., Marsh. Is.	B8	72
Bikeqi, China	A4	42
Bikin, Russia	B11	36
Bikini, at., Marsh. Is.	B7	72
Bīkkū Bīttī, mtn., Libya	C3	62
Bikoro, D.R.C.	E3	66
Bilāra, India	E4	54
Bilāri, India	D7	54
Bilāsipāra, India	E13	54
Bilāspur, India	C6	54
Bilāspur, India	G9	54
Bila Tserkva, Ukr.	F15	6
Bilauktaung Range, mts., Asia	F4	48
Bilbao, Spain	A7	20
Bilbeis, Egypt	H2	58
Bilbilis, sci., Spain	C9	20
Bileća, Bos.	G5	26
Bilecik, Tur.	C12	28
Bilecik, state, Tur.	C13	28
Biłgoraj, Pol.	F18	16
Bilgrām, India	E8	54
Bilhorod-Dnistrovs'kyi, Ukr.	C17	26
Bili, D.R.C.	D5	66
Biliaïvka, Ukr.	C17	26
Bīliköl köli, l., Kaz.	F12	32
Bīlīmora, India	H4	54
Bilin, Mya.	D3	48
Bilin, stm., Mya.	D3	48
Bílina, Czech Rep.	F9	16
Biliran Island, i., Phil.	E5	52
Billabong Creek, stm., Austl.	J5	76
Billings, Mo., U.S.	G4	120
Billings, Mt., U.S.	B4	126
Billings Heights, Mt., U.S.	B4	126
Billiton see Belitung, i., Indon.	E5	50
Bill Williams, stm., Az., U.S.	I3	132
Billy Chinook, Lake, res., Or., U.S.	F5	136
Bilma, Niger	F7	64
Biloela, Austl.	E8	76
Biloxi, Ms., U.S.	G10	122
Bilpa Morea Claypan, l., Austl.	E2	76
Bilqas Qism Awwal, Egypt	G2	58
Biltine, Chad	E4	62
Biltmore Forest, N.C., U.S.	A3	116
Bilugyun Island, i., Mya.	D3	48
Bimbo, C.A.R.	D3	66
Bimbowrie, Austl.	H3	76
Bimini Islands, is., Bah.	B9	96
Bīna-Etāwa, India	F7	54
Binaiya, Gunung, mtn., Indon.	F9	44
Binalbagan, Phil.	E4	52
Bin'an, China	B7	38
Bindki, India	E8	54
Bindloss, Ab., Can.	D3	124
Bindura, Zimb.	D5	68
Binéfar, Spain	C11	20
Binford, N.D., U.S.	G15	124
Binga, D.R.C.	D4	66
Binga, Monte, mtn., Afr.	D5	68
Bingara, Austl.	G8	76
Bingen, Ger.	G3	16
Binger, Ok., U.S.	F10	128
Binghamton, N.Y., U.S.	B10	114
Bin Ghunaymah, Jabal, mts., Libya	B3	62
Binhai, China	D8	42
Binh Gia, Viet.	B8	48
Binjai, Indon.	K4	48
Binnaway, Austl.	H7	76
Binongko, Pulau, i., Indon.	G7	44
Binscarth, Mb., Can.	D12	124
Bintan, Pulau, i., Indon.	C4	50
Bintimani, mtn., S.L.	H2	64
Bintuhan, Indon.	F3	50
Bintulu, Malay.	B8	50
Bintuni, Indon.	F9	44
Binxian, China	D3	42
Binxian, China	C7	42
Binxian, China	B7	38
Binyang, China	J3	42
Bin-Yauri, Nig.	G5	64
Biobío, state, Chile	H1	92
Biobío, stm., Chile	G2	90
Biogradska Gora Nacionalni Park, p.o.i., Serb.	G6	26
Bioko, i., Eq. Gui.	I6	64
Bira, Russia	G15	34
Birac, Phil.	B3	52
Birāk, Libya	B2	62
Birakan, Russia	G15	34
Bi'r al Wa'r, Libya	C2	62
Birao, C.A.R.	B4	66
Birch, stm., Ab., Can.	D8	106
Birch Creek, stm., Mt., U.S.	B14	136
Birch Hills, Sk., Can.	B8	124
Birch Island, B.C., Can.	E10	138
Birch Island, i., Mb., Can.	B13	124
Birch Mountains, hills, Ab., Can.	D8	106
Birch Run, Mi., U.S.	E6	112
Birch Tree, Mo., U.S.	H6	120
Birchwood, Wi., U.S.	F7	118
Bird Creek, stm., Ok., U.S.	E13	128
Bird Island, Mn., U.S.	G4	118
Bird Island, sci., S. Geor.	J9	90
Birdsville, Austl.	E2	76
Birdtail Creek, stm., Mb., Can.	D13	124
Birdum, Austl.	C6	74
Birecik, Tur.	A9	58
Bireun, Indon.	J3	48
Bir Ghbalou, Alg.	H14	20
Birigui, Braz.	D6	90
Biriljussy, Russia	C16	32
Bīrjand, Iran	C8	56
Birjul'ka, Russia	D19	32
Birjusa, stm., Russia	C17	32
Birjusinsk, Russia	C17	32
Birken, B.C., Can.	F8	138
Birkenfeld, Ger.	G3	16
Birkenhead, Eng., U.K.	H9	12
Birmingham, Eng., U.K.	I10	12
Birmingham, Al., U.S.	D11	122
Birmingham, Ia., U.S.	D6	120
Birmingham, Mi., U.S.	B2	114
Birmitrapur, India	G10	54
Bîr Mogreïn, Maur.	D2	64
Birnin Gaouré, Niger	G5	64
Birnin-Kebbi, Nig.	G5	64
Birnin Konni, Niger	G5	64
Birnin Kudu, Nig.	G6	64
Birobidžan, Russia	G15	34
Birrie, stm., Austl.	G6	76
Birsk, Russia	C9	32
Birštonas, Lith.	F7	10
Birtle, Mb., Can.	D12	124
Birūr, India	E2	53
Biržai, Lith.	D7	10
Birżebbuġa, Malta	I8	24
Bisaccia, Italy	C9	24
Bīsalpur, India	D7	54
Bisbee, Az., U.S.	L7	132
Bisbee, N.D., U.S.	F14	124
Biscarrosse et de Parentis, Étang de, l., Fr.	E4	18
Biscay, Bay of, b., Eur.	E2	18
Biscayne Bay, b., Fl., U.S.	K5	116
Biscayne National Park, p.o.i., Fl., U.S.	K5	116
Bisceglie, Italy	C10	24
Bischofshofen, Aus.	C10	22
Bischofswerda, Ger.	E10	16
Biscoe, N.C., U.S.	A6	116
Bishnupur, India	G11	54
Bisho, S. Afr.	H8	70
Bishop, Ca., U.S.	F7	134
Bishop, Tx., U.S.	G10	130
Bishop Auckland, Eng., U.K.	G11	12
Bishop Rock, r., Eng., U.K.	L6	12
Bishop's Falls, Nf., Can.	j22	107a
Bishop's Stortford, Eng., U.K.	J13	12
Bishopville, S.C., U.S.	B5	116
Biškek, Kyrg.	F12	32
Biskupiec, Pol.	C16	16
Bislig, Phil.	F6	52
Bismarck, Mo., U.S.	G7	120
Bismarck, N.D., U.S.	A12	126
Bismarck Archipelago, is., Pap. N. Gui.	a4	79a
Bismarck Range, mts., Pap. N. Gui.	b3	79a
Bismarck Sea, s., Pap. N. Gui.	a4	79a
Bismark, Kap, c., Grnld.	B22	141
Bissa, Djebel, mtn., Alg.	H12	20
Bissau, Gui.-B.	G1	64
Bissett, Mb., Can.	C18	124
Bissikrima, Gui.	G2	64
Bistcho Lake, l., Ab., Can.	D7	106
Bistineau, Lake, res., La., U.S.	E5	122
Bistrica, Slvn.	D13	22
Bistriţa, Rom.	B11	26
Bistriţa, stm., Rom.	C13	26
Bistriţa-Năsăud, state, Rom.	B11	26
Biswān, India	E8	54
Bitam, Gabon	D2	66
Bitburg, Ger.	G2	16
Bitche, Fr.	E16	14
Bitlis, Tur.	B5	56
Bitola, Mac.	B4	28
Bitolj see Bitola, Mac.	B4	28
Bitonto, Italy	C10	24
Bitou, Burkina	G4	64
Bitter Creek, stm., Wy., U.S.	B8	132
Bitterfeld, Ger.	E8	16
Bitterfontein, S. Afr.	G4	70
Bitterroot, stm., Mt., U.S.	D13	136
Bitterroot, West Fork, stm., Mt., U.S.	E12	136
Bitterroot Range, mts., U.S.	C11	136
Bitung, Indon.	E8	44
Bitupitá, Braz.	B5	88
Biu, Nig.	G7	64
Bivins, Tx., U.S.	E4	122
Biwabik, Mn., U.S.	D6	118
Biwa-ko, l., Japan	D8	40
Bixby, Ok., U.S.	I2	120
Biyala, Egypt	G2	58
Biyang, China	E5	42
Bizana, S. Afr.	G9	70
Bizen, Japan	E7	40
Bizerte (Binzert), Tun.	G3	24
Bizerte, Lac de, l., Tun.	G3	24
Bizkaiko, co., Spain	A8	20
Bjahoml', Bela.	F10	10
Bjala, Blg.	G14	26
Bjala Slatina, Blg.	F10	26
Bjalyničy, Bela.	F12	10
Bjarèzina, stm., Bela.	H13	10
Bjarèzina, stm., Bela.	G9	10
Bjaroza, Bela.	H7	10
Bjarozauka, Bela.	G8	10
Bjelovar, Cro.	E13	22
Björna, Swe.	E8	8
Björneborg see Pori, Fin.	F9	8
Bjorne Peninsula, pen., Nu., Can.	B8	141
Bjørnøya, i., Nor.	B5	30
Bla, Mali	G3	64
Blace, Serb.	F8	26
Black (Da, Song) (Lixian), stm., Asia	D9	46
Black, stm., Mb., Can.	D18	124
Black, stm., Ak., U.S.	C11	140
Black, stm., Az., U.S.	J6	132
Black, stm., La., U.S.	F7	122
Black, stm., Mi., U.S.	E7	112
Black, stm., N.Y., U.S.	E14	112
Black, stm., Wi., U.S.	G7	118
Black, stm., U.S.	I6	120
Blackall, Austl.	E5	76
Black Bay, b., On., Can.	C10	118
Black Bay Peninsula, pen., On., Can.	C10	118
Black Bear Creek, stm., Ok., U.S.	E11	128
Blackburn, Eng., U.K.	H10	12
Blackburn, Mount, mtn., Ak., U.S.	D11	140
Black Butte, mtn., Mt., U.S.	D15	136
Black Canyon of the Gunnison National Park, p.o.i., Co., U.S.	E9	132
Black Creek, stm., Ms., U.S.	G9	122
Black Creek, stm., S.C., U.S.	B6	116
Black Diamond, Ab., Can.	F16	138
Black Diamond, Wa., U.S.	C5	136
Blackdown Tableland National Park, p.o.i., Austl.	D7	76
Blackduck, Mn., U.S.	D4	118
Black Eagle, Mt., U.S.	C15	136
Blackfoot, Id., U.S.	G14	136
Blackfoot, Mt., U.S.	B14	136
Blackfoot, stm., Id., U.S.	G15	136
Blackfoot, stm., Mt., U.S.	D13	136
Blackfoot Reservoir, res., Id., U.S.	H15	136
Black Forest see Schwarzwald, mts., Ger.	H4	16
Black Hills, mts., U.S.	C9	126
Black Island, i., Mb., Can.	C17	124
Black Lake, Qc., Can.	D5	110
Black Lake, l., Sk., Can.	D10	106
Black Lake, l., Mi., U.S.	C5	112
Black Lake, l., N.Y., U.S.	D14	112
Black Mesa, mtn., U.S.	E6	128
Blackmore, Mount, mtn., Mt., U.S.	E15	136
Black Mountain, N.C., U.S.	A3	116
Black Mountain, mtn., Az., U.S.	K5	132
Black Mountain, mtn., Ca., U.S.	H5	134
Black Mountain, mtn., Mt., U.S.	D14	136
Black Mountain, hill, Austl.	C2	76
Black Mountain, mts., U.S.	H2	114
Black Nossob, stm., Nmb.	C4	70
Black Pine Peak, mtn., Id., U.S.	A3	132
Blackpool, Eng., U.K.	H9	12
Black Range, mts., N.M., U.S.	J9	132
Black River, N.Y., U.S.	D14	112
Black River Falls, Wi., U.S.	G8	118
Black Rock, Ar., U.S.	H6	120
Black Rock, r., Ire.	G2	12
Black Rock, r., S. Geor.	J8	90
Black Rock Desert, des., Nv., U.S.	B7	134
Blacksburg, S.C., U.S.	A4	116
Blacksburg, Va., U.S.	G5	114
Black Sea, s.	G15	6
Blacks Fork, stm., U.S.	B7	132
Blackshear, Lake, res., Ga., U.S.	D2	116
Blackstone, Va., U.S.	G8	114
Black Sturgeon Lake, l., On., Can.	B9	118
Blackville, S.C., U.S.	C4	116
Black Volta (Volta Noire) (Mouhoun), stm., Afr.	H4	64
Blackwater, Austl.	D7	76
Blackwater, stm., Ire.	I4	12
Blackwater, stm., Mo., U.S.	E4	120
Blackwater Creek, stm., Austl.	E5	76
Blackwater Draw, stm., Tx., U.S.	H7	128
Blackwater Lake, l., N.T., Can.	C6	106
Blackwell, Tx., U.S.	B7	130
Bladenboro, N.C., U.S.	B7	116
Bladensburg National Park, p.o.i., Austl.	D4	76
Bladgrond-Noord, S. Afr.	F4	70
Bladworth, Sk., Can.	C7	124
Bláfell, mtn., Ice.	k30	8a
Blagoevgrad, Blg.	G10	26
Blagoveščensk, Russia	D16	34
Blaine, Mn., U.S.	F5	118
Blaine, Wa., U.S.	B4	136
Blair, Ne., U.S.	C1	120
Blair, Ok., U.S.	G9	128
Blair, Wi., U.S.	G7	118
Blair Athol, Austl.	D6	76
Blairsville, Ga., U.S.	B2	116
Blairsville, Pa., U.S.	D6	114
Blaj, Rom.	C10	26
Blakely, Ga., U.S.	F13	122
Blake Plateau, unds.	E6	144
Blake Point, c., Mi., U.S.	C10	118
Blalock Island, i., Wa., U.S.	E7	136
Blanc, Mont, mtn., Eur.	D12	18
Blanca, Co., U.S.	D3	128
Blanca, Bahía, b., Arg.	G4	90
Blanca, Laguna, l., Chile	J2	90
Blanca, Punta, c., Chile	B2	92
Blanca, Sierra, mtn., Tx., U.S.	C2	130
Blanca Peak, mtn., Co., U.S.	D3	128
Blanchard, Ok., U.S.	F11	128
Blanchard, stm., Oh., U.S.	D2	114
Blanche, Lake, l., Austl.	G2	76
Blanche Channel, strt., Sol. Is.	e7	79b
Blanchester, Oh., U.S.	E1	114
Blanchisseuse, Trin.	s12	105f
Blanco, Tx., U.S.	D9	130
Blanco, stm., Arg.	D3	92
Blanco, stm., Ec.	G2	86
Blanco, stm., Tx., U.S.	E9	130
Blanco, Cabo, c., C.R.	H5	102
Blanco, Cañon, p., N.M., U.S.	F3	128
Blanco, Cape, c., Or., U.S.	H2	136
Blanco, Lago, l., Chile	J3	90
Blanc-Sablon, Qc., Can.	i22	107a
Bland, Va., U.S.	G4	114
Blanda, stm., Ice.	k30	8a
Blanding, Ut., U.S.	F7	132
Blandinsville, Il., U.S.	D7	120
Blanes, Spain	C13	20
Blangkejeren, Indon.	K3	48
Blangy-sur-Bresle, Fr.	E10	14
Blankenburg, Ger.	E6	16
Blanquilla, Isla, i., Ven.	B9	86
Blansko, Czech Rep.	G12	16
Blantyre, Mwi.	D6	68
Blarney Castle, sci., Ire.	J4	12
Błaszki, Pol.	E14	16
Blaubeuren, Ger.	H5	16
Blaufelden, Ger.	G5	16
Błażowa, Pol.	G18	16
Bledsoe, Tx., U.S.	H5	128
Blega, Indon.	G8	50
Bleik see Andenes, Nor.	B6	8
Blekinge, state, Swe.	H6	8
Blenheim, On., Can.	F8	112
Blenheim, N.Z.	E5	80
Blessing, Tx., U.S.	F11	130
Bletchley, Eng., U.K.	J12	12
Bligh Water, strt., Fiji	p18	79e
Blind River, On., Can.	B6	112
Blissfield, Mi., U.S.	C2	114
Blitar, Indon.	H8	50
Block Island, i., R.I., U.S.	C14	114
Blockton, Ia., U.S.	D3	120
Bloedel, B.C., Can.	F5	138
Bloemfontein, S. Afr.	F8	70
Bloemhof, S. Afr.	E7	70
Bloemhofdam, res., S. Afr.	E7	70
Blois, Fr.	G10	14
Blönduós, Ice.	k29	8a
Bloodvein, stm., Can.	E11	106
Bloody Foreland, c., Ire.	F4	12
Bloomer, Wi., U.S.	F7	118
Bloomfield, On., Can.	E12	112
Bloomfield, Ky., U.S.	G12	120
Bloomfield, Mo., U.S.	H8	120
Bloomfield, Ne., U.S.	E15	126
Bloomfield, N.M., U.S.	G9	132
Blooming Grove, Tx., U.S.	E2	122
Blooming Prairie, Mn., U.S.	H5	118
Bloomington, Il., U.S.	D9	120
Bloomington, In., U.S.	E11	120
Bloomington, Mn., U.S.	G5	118
Bloomington, Tx., U.S.	F11	130
Bloomington, Wi., U.S.	B7	120
Bloomsburg, Pa., U.S.	C9	114
Bloomsbury, Austl.	C7	76
Bloomville, Oh., U.S.	C2	114
Blora, Indon.	G7	50
Blosseville Kyst, cst., Grnld.	D20	141
Blossom, Tx., U.S.	D3	122
Blouberg, mtn., S. Afr.	C9	70
Blountstown, Fl., U.S.	G13	122
Blountsville, Al., U.S.	C12	122
Blowering Reservoir, res., Austl.	J6	76
Blowing Point Village, Anguilla	A1	105a
Blowing Rock, N.C., U.S.	H4	114
Bludenz, Aus.	C6	22
Blue, stm., Az., U.S.	J7	132
Blue, stm., Ok., U.S.	C2	122
Blue Creek, Wa., U.S.	B8	136
Blue Cypress Lake, l., Fl., U.S.	I5	116
Blue Earth, Mn., U.S.	H4	118
Blue Earth, stm., U.S.	H4	118
Bluefield, Va., U.S.	G4	114
Bluefield, W.V., U.S.	G4	114
Bluefields, Nic.	F6	102
Blue Hill, Ne., U.S.	A10	128
Blue Hill Bay, b., Me., U.S.	F8	110
Blue Island, Il., U.S.	G2	112
Blue Mound, Ks., U.S.	F3	120
Blue Mountain, Ms., U.S.	C9	122
Blue Mountain, mtn., Ar., U.S.	C4	122
Blue Mountain, mtn., Mt., U.S.	G9	124
Blue Mountain, mts., Pa., U.S.	D8	114
Blue Mountain Peak, mtn., Jam.	i14	104d
Blue Mountains, mts., Jam.	i14	104d
Blue Mountains, mts., Me., U.S.	F6	110
Blue Mountains, mts., U.S.	E8	136
Blue Mountains National Park, p.o.i., Austl.	J8	76
Blue Mud Bay, b., Austl.	B7	74
Blue Nile (Azraq, Al-Baḥr al-) (Ābay), stm., Afr.	E6	62
Bluenose Lake, l., Nu., Can.	B6	106
Blue Ridge, Ab., Can.	B15	138
Blue Ridge, Ga., U.S.	B1	116
Blue Ridge, mts., U.S.	H4	114
Blue River, B.C., Can.	D11	138
Bluestone Dam, dam, W.V., U.S.	G5	114
Bluestone Lake, res., W.V., U.S.	G5	114
Bluewater, N.M., U.S.	H9	132
Bluff, N.Z.	H3	80
Bluff, Ut., U.S.	F7	132
Bluff Cape, c., Mya.	D2	48
Bluff Creek, stm., U.S.	D11	128
Bluff Dale, Tx., U.S.	B9	130
Bluff Park, Al., U.S.	D12	122
Bluffs, Il., U.S.	E7	120
Bluffton, In., U.S.	H4	112
Bluffton, S.C., U.S.	D5	116
Blumberg, Ger.	I4	16
Blumenau, Braz.	C13	92
Blumenhof, Sk., Can.	D6	124
Bly, Or., U.S.	A4	134
Blyth, On., Can.	E8	112
Blyth, Eng., U.K.	F11	12
Blythe, Ca., U.S.	J2	132
Blytheville, Ar., U.S.	I7	120
Bø, Nor.	G3	8
Bo, S.L.	H2	64
Boac, Phil.	D3	52
Boaco, Nic.	F5	102
Boa Esperança, Braz.	K3	88
Boa Esperança, Represa, res., Braz.	D3	88
Bo'ai, China	D5	42
Boane, Moz.	E11	70
Board Camp Mountain, mtn., Ca., U.S.	C2	134
Boardman, Oh., U.S.	C5	114
Boatman, Austl.	F6	76
Boa Viagem, Braz.	C5	88
Boa Vista, Braz.	F11	86
Boa Vista, i., C.V.	k10	65a
Boawai, Indon.	H12	50
Boaz, Al., U.S.	C12	122
Bobai, China	J3	42
Bobaomby, Tanjona, c., Madag.	C8	68
Bobbili, India	B6	53
Bobcaygeon, On., Can.	D11	112
Bobigny, Fr.	F11	14
Böblingen, Ger.	H4	16
Bobo-Dioulasso, Burkina	G4	64
Bobolice, Pol.	C12	16
Bobonaza, stm., Ec.	H3	86
Bobonong, Bots.	B9	70
Bobr, Bela.	F12	10
Bobtown, Pa., U.S.	E5	114
Bobures, Ven.	C6	86
Boby, mtn., Madag.	E8	68
Bôca da Mata, Braz.	E7	88
Boca do Acre, Braz.	E4	84
Boca do Jari, Braz.	D7	84
Bocage, Cap, c., N. Cal.	m15	79d
Boca Grande, Fl., U.S.	J3	116
Bocaiúva, Braz.	I3	88
Bocaranga, C.A.R.	C3	66
Boca Raton, Fl., U.S.	J5	116
Bocas del Toro, Pan.	H6	102
Bocay, Nic.	E5	102
Bochnia, Pol.	G16	16
Bocholt, Ger.	E2	16
Bochum, Ger.	E3	16
Bocón, Caño, stm., Col.	F7	86
Boconó, Ven.	C6	86
Bocşa, Rom.	D8	26
Boda, C.A.R.	D3	66
Bodajbo, Russia	E11	34
Bodalla, Austl.	K8	76
Bodcau Creek, stm., Ar., U.S.	D5	122
Bode, Ia., U.S.	I4	118
Bodélé, reg., Chad	D3	62
Boden, Swe.	D9	8
Bodensee see Constance, Lake, l., Eur.	I5	16
Bodhan, India	B3	53
Bodh Gaya, India	F10	54
Bodināyakkanūr, India	G3	53
Bodmin, Eng., U.K.	K8	12
Bodø, Nor.	C6	8
Bodoquena, Serra da, plat., Braz.	D5	90
Bodrum, Tur.	F10	28
Bodzentyn, Pol.	F16	16
Boende, D.R.C.	E4	66
Bœng Lvea, Camb.	F7	48
Boeo, Capo, c., Italy	G6	24
Boesmans, stm., S. Afr.	H7	70
Boeuf, stm., U.S.	E7	122
Boffa, Gui.	G2	64
Bogale, Mya.	D2	48
Bogalusa, La., U.S.	G9	122
Bogan, stm., Austl.	H6	76
Bogan Gate, Austl.	I6	76
Bogangolo, C.A.R.	C3	66
Bogata, Tx., U.S.	D3	122
Bogcang, stm., China	C11	54
Bogda Shan, mts., China	C2	36
Bogen, Ger.	H8	16
Boger City, N.C., U.S.	A4	116
Boggabilla, Austl.	G8	76
Boggabri, Austl.	H7	76
Boggy Peak, mtn., Antig.	f4	105b
Bogles, Gren.	p11	105e
Bognor Regis, Eng., U.K.	K12	12
Bogo, Phil.	E5	52
Bogoljubovo, Russia	E15	10
Bogong, Mount, mtn., Austl.	K6	76
Bogor, Indon.	G5	50
Bogorodick, Russia	G21	10
Bogorodsk, Russia	H20	8
Bogorodskoe, Russia	F17	34
Bogotá, Col.	E4	86
Bogotol, Russia	C15	32
Bogra, Bngl.	F12	54
Bogučany, Russia	C17	32
Bogué, Maur.	F2	64
Bogue Chitto, stm., U.S.	G8	122
Bogue Phalia, stm., Ms., U.S.	D8	122
Böğürtlen, Tur.	A8	58
Bo Hai (Chihli, Gulf of), b., China	B8	42
Bohai Haixia, strt., China	B9	42
Bohain-en-Vermandois, Fr.	D12	14
Bohai Wan, b., China	B8	42
Bohemian Forest, mts., Eur.	G8	16
Böhmer Wald see Bohemian Forest, mts., Eur.	G8	16
Bohol, i., Phil.	F4	52
Bohol Sea, s., Phil.	F5	52
Boiaçu, Braz.	H11	86
Boiano, Italy	C8	24
Boiestown, N.B., Can.	D10	110
Boipeba, Ilha de, i., Braz.	G6	88
Bois, stm., Braz.	C6	90
Bois, Lac des, l., N.T., Can.	B6	106
Bois Blanc Island, i., Mi., U.S.	C5	112
Bois de Sioux, stm., U.S.	F2	118
Boise, Id., U.S.	G10	136
Boise, stm., Id., U.S.	G10	136
Boise, Middle Fork, stm., Id., U.S.	G11	136
Boise, South Fork, stm., Id., U.S.	G11	136
Boise City, Ok., U.S.	E6	128
Boissevain, Mb., Can.	E13	124
Boistfort Peak, mtn., Wa., U.S.	D3	136
Boizenburg, Ger.	C6	16
Boja, Indon.	G7	50
Bojadła, Pol.	E11	16
Bojeador, Cape, c., Phil.	A3	52
Bojnūrd, Iran	B8	56
Bojonegoro, Indon.	G7	50
Bojuru, Braz.	E12	92
Bokāro Steel City, India	G10	54
Bokchito, Ok., U.S.	C2	122
Boké, Gui.	G2	64
Bokhara, stm., Austl.	G6	76
Bok Koŭ, Camb.	G6	48
Boknafjorden, strt., Nor.	G1	8
Boko, Congo	E2	66
Bokoro, Chad	E3	62
Bokote, D.R.C.	E4	66
Boksitogorsk, Russia	A16	10
Bokungu, D.R.C.	E4	66
Bol, Cro.	G13	22
Bolama, Gui.-B.	G1	64
Bolaños, stm., Mex.	E7	100
Bolaños de Calatrava, Spain	F7	20
Bolān Pass, p., Pak.	D10	56
Bolayır, Tur.	C9	28
Bolbec, Fr.	E9	14
Bole, China	F14	32
Bole, Ghana	H4	64
Boles, Ar., U.S.	C4	122
Bolesławiec, Pol.	E11	16
Boley, Ok., U.S.	B2	122
Bolgatanga, Ghana	G4	64
Bolhov, Russia	G18	10
Bolhrad, Ukr.	D15	26
Boli, China	B11	36
Boligee, Al., U.S.	E10	122
Bolingbrook, Il., U.S.	C9	120
Bolishan, China	C5	38
Bolívar, Col.	G3	86
Bolívar, Col.	G3	86
Bolivar, Mo., U.S.	G4	120
Bolivar, N.Y., U.S.	B7	114
Bolivar, Tn., U.S.	B9	122
Bolívar, state, Col.	C4	86
Bolívar, state, Ec.	H2	86
Bolívar, state, Ven.	D10	86
Bolívar, Cerro, mtn., Ven.	D10	86
Bolívar, Pico (La Columna), mtn., Ven.	C6	86
Bolivar Peninsula, pen., Tx., U.S.	H4	122
Bolivia, ctry., S.A.	G5	84
Bollnäs, Swe.	F7	8
Bollon, Austl.	G6	76
Bolmen, l., Swe.	H5	8
Bolobo, D.R.C.	E3	66
Bologna, Italy	F8	22
Bolognesi, Peru	F3	84
Bologoe, Russia	C17	10
Bologovo, Russia	D14	10
Bolohovo, Russia	F20	10
Bolomba, D.R.C.	D3	66
Bolon', ozero, l., Russia	G16	34
Bolotnoe, Russia	C14	32
Bolovens, Plateau des, plat., Laos	E8	48
Bol'šaja Balahnja, stm., Russia	B9	34
Bol'šaja Heta, stm., Russia	C5	34
Bol'šaja Kuonamka, stm., Russia	C10	34
Bol'šaja Murta, Russia	C16	32
Bol'šaja Ussurka, stm., Russia	B11	38
Bol'šaja Višera, Russia	B15	10
Bol'šakovo, Russia	F4	10
Bolsena, Italy	H8	22
Bolsena, Lago di, l., Italy	H9	22
Bol'šereče, Russia	C13	32
Bol'šereck, Russia	F20	34
Bol'ševik, Russia	D18	34
Bol'ševik, ostrov, i., Russia	A10	34
Bol'šezemel'skaja Tundra, reg., Russia	A9	32
Bolshevik see Bol'ševik, ostrov, i., Russia	A10	34
Bol'šie Uki, Russia	C12	32
Bol'šoe Mihajlovskoe, Russia	D20	10
Bol'šoe Polpino, Russia	G17	10
Bol'šoe Selo, Russia	C21	10
Bol'šoj Anjuj, stm., Russia	C21	34
Bol'šoj Begičev, ostrov, i., Russia	B11	34
Bol'šoj Jugan, stm., Russia	B12	32
Bol'šoj Kamen', Russia	C10	38
Bol'šoj Ljahovskij, ostrov, i., Russia	B17	34
Bol'šoj Tal'cy, Russia	A15	10
Bolton, On., Can.	E10	112
Bolton, Eng., U.K.	H10	12
Bolton, Ms., U.S.	E8	122
Bolton, N.C., U.S.	B7	116
Bolu, Tur.	C14	28
Bolu, state, Tur.	C14	28
Bolva, stm., Russia	G17	10
Bolvadin, Tur.	E13	28
Bóly, Hung.	C5	26
Bolzano (Bozen), Italy	D8	22
Boma, D.R.C.	F2	66
Bomaderry, Austl.	J8	76
Bombala, Austl.	K7	76
Bombay see Mumbai, India	B1	53
Bomberai, Semenanjung, pen., Indon.	F9	44
Bomboma, D.R.C.	D3	66
Bom Conselho, Braz.	E7	88
Bom Despacho, Braz.	J3	88
Bomdila, India	E14	54
Bom Jesus, Braz.	E3	88
Bom Jesus da Lapa, Braz.	G4	88
Bomnak, Russia	F14	34
Bomokandi, stm., D.R.C.	D5	66
Bomongo, D.R.C.	D3	66
Bom Retiro, Braz.	C13	92
Bomu, stm., Afr.	D4	66
Bon, Cap, c., Tun.	G5	24
Bon Air, Va., U.S.	G8	114
Bonaire, i., Neth. Ant.	p23	104g
Bonampak, sci., Mex.	D2	102
Bonandolok, Indon.	C1	50
Bonanza, Or., U.S.	A4	134
Bonanza, Ut., U.S.	C7	132
Bonanza Peak, mtn., Wa., U.S.	B5	136
Bonao, Dom. Rep.	C12	102
Bonaparte, Ia., U.S.	D6	120
Bonaparte, stm., B.C., Can.	F9	138
Bonaparte, Mount, mtn., Wa., U.S.	B7	136
Bonaparte Lake, l., B.C., Can.	E10	138
Bonar Bridge, Scot., U.K.	D8	12
Bonasse, Trin.	s12	105f
Bonaventure, Qc., Can.	B11	110
Bonaventure, stm., Qc., Can.	B11	110
Bonaventure, Île, i., Qc., Can.	B12	110
Bonavista, Nf., Can.	j23	107a
Bonavista Bay, b., Nf., Can.	j23	107a
Bondeno, Italy	F8	22
Bondo, D.R.C.	D4	66
Bondo, D.R.C.	E4	66
Bondoc Peninsula, pen., Phil.	D4	52
Bondoukou, C. Iv.	H4	64
Bondowoso, Indon.	G8	50
Bonduel, Wi., U.S.	G10	118
Bone, Teluk, b., Indon.	F7	44
Bonebone, Indon.	E12	50
Boneogeh, Indon.	G12	50
Bonerate, Pulau, i., Indon.	G12	50
Bonesteel, S.D., U.S.	D13	126
Bonete Chico, Cerro, mtn., Arg.	D3	92
Bonete Grande, Cerro, mtn., Arg.	C3	92
Bongabong, Phil.	D3	52
Bongaigaon, India	E13	54
Bongandanga, D.R.C.	D4	66
Bongka, Indon.	F7	44
Bongo, Gabon	E2	66
Bongo, Massif des, mts., C.A.R.	C4	66
Bongor, Chad	E3	62
Bonham, Tx., U.S.	D2	122
Bonhomme, Morne, mtn., Haiti	C11	102
Bonifacio, Fr.	H15	18
Bonifacio, Strait of, strt., Eur.	H15	18
Bonifati, Capo, c., Italy	E9	24
Bonin Islands see Ogasawara-guntō, is., Japan	G18	30
Bonita, La., U.S.	E7	122
Bonita Springs, Fl., U.S.	J4	116
Bonito, Braz.	D5	90
Bonito, Braz.	E8	88
Bonito de Santa Fé, Braz.	D6	88
Bonn, Ger.	F2	16
Bonners Ferry, Id., U.S.	B10	136
Bonnet, Lac du, res., Mb., Can.	D17	124
Bonnétable, Fr.	F9	14
Bonne Terre, Mo., U.S.	G7	120
Bonnet Plume, stm., Yk., Can.	B3	106
Bonneville, Fr.	C12	18
Bonneville Peak, mtn., Id., U.S.	H14	136
Bonneville Salt Flats, pl., Ut., U.S.	C2	132
Bonney SE, Lake, l., Austl.	K3	76
Bonnie Rock, Austl.	F3	74
Bonny, Nig.	I6	64
Bonnyville, Ab., Can.	B20	138
Bono, Ar., U.S.	I7	120
Bonoi, Indon.	F10	44
Bonshaw, P.E., Can.	D13	110
Bontang, Indon.	C10	50
Bontebok National Park, p.o.i., S. Afr.	I5	70
Bonthe, S.L.	H2	64
Bontoc, Phil.	B3	52
Bon Wier, Tx., U.S.	G5	122
Booker, Tx., U.S.	E8	128
Booker T. Washington National Monument, p.o.i., Va., U.S.	H6	114
Boola, Gui.	H3	64
Boolaloo, Austl.	D3	74
Booleroo Centre, Austl.	I2	76
Boologooro, Austl.	D2	74
Boomarra, Austl.	B3	76
Boonah, Austl.	F9	76
Boone, Ia., U.S.	I5	118
Boone, N.C., U.S.	H4	114
Boone, stm., Ia., U.S.	B4	120
Booneville, Ar., U.S.	B5	122
Booneville, Ky., U.S.	G2	114
Booneville, Ms., U.S.	C10	122
Böön Tsagaan nuur, l., Mong.	B4	36
Boonville, Ca., U.S.	D2	134
Boonville, Mo., U.S.	F5	120
Boonville, N.Y., U.S.	E14	112
Boorindal, Austl.	H6	76
Booroorban, Austl.	J5	76
Boosaaso, Som.	B9	66
Booth, Al., U.S.	E12	122
Boothbay Harbor, Me., U.S.	G7	110
Boothia, Gulf of, b., Nu., Can.	A12	106
Boothia Peninsula, pen., Nu., Can.	A12	106
Boothville, La., U.S.	H9	122
Booué, Gabon	E2	66
Bophuthatswana, hist. reg., S. Afr.	E7	70
Boping Ling, mts., China	I7	42
Bopolu, Lib.	H2	64
Boqueirão, Serra do, hills, Braz.	F4	88

Boquilla – Bulan I • 9

Name	Map Ref.	Page
Boquilla, Presa de la, res., Mex.	B6	100
Boquim, Braz.	F7	88
Bor, Russia	H20	8
Bor, Russia	E20	8
Bor, Sudan	F6	62
Bor, Tur.	B3	56
Bor, Serb.	E9	26
Bor, Lak, stm., Kenya	D7	66
Bora-Bora, i., Fr. Poly.	E11	72
Borabu, Thai.	E6	48
Borah Peak, mtn., Id., U.S.	F13	136
Borås, Swe.	H5	8
Borba, Braz.	D6	84
Bordeaux, Fr.	E5	18
Bordeaux Mountain, hill, V.I.U.S.	e8	104b
Borden, Sk., Can.	B6	124
Borden Peninsula, pen., Nu., Can.	A14	106
Bordertown, Austl.	K3	76
Bordesholm, Ger.	B6	16
Bordighera, Italy	G4	22
Bordj Menaïel, Alg.	H14	20
Bordj Omar Idriss, Alg.	D6	64
Bordoy, i., Far. Is.	m34	8b
Borgå see Porvoo, Fin.	F11	8
Borgarnes, Ice.	k28	8a
Børgefjell Nasjonalpark, p.o.i., Nor.	D5	8
Borger, Tx., U.S.	F7	128
Borgholm, Swe.	H7	8
Borgne, Lake, b., La., U.S.	G9	122
Borgnesse, Pointe, c., Mart.	I7	105c
Borgomanero, Italy	E5	22
Borgo San Dalmazzo, Italy	F4	22
Borgosesia, Italy	E5	22
Borgo Val di Taro, Italy	F6	22
Borgworm see Waremme, Bel.	D14	14
Borikhan, Laos	C6	48
Borisoglebsk, Russia	D6	32
Borisoglebskij, Russia	C21	10
Borjas Blancas see Les Borges Blanques, Spain	C11	20
Borkavičy, Bela.	E11	10
Borken, Ger.	E2	16
Borkou, reg., Chad.	D3	62
Borkum, i., Ger.	C2	16
Borlänge, Swe.	F6	8
Bormes, Fr.	F12	18
Borna, Ger.	E9	16
Borneo (Kalimantan), i., Asia	E5	44
Bornholm, state, Den.	I6	8
Bornholm, i., Den.	I6	8
Borocay Island, i., Phil.	E3	52
Borodino, Russia	C17	32
Borogoncy, Russia	D15	34
Borohoro Shan, mts., China	F14	32
Boromo, Burkina	G4	64
Boron, Ca., U.S.	H8	134
Boronga Islands, is., Mya.	I14	54
Borongan, Phil.	E5	52
Borovan, Blg.	F10	26
Boroviči, Russia	B16	10
Borovljanka, Russia	D14	32
Borovsk, Russia	E19	10
Borovskij, Russia	C11	32
Borovskoy, Kaz.	D10	32
Borrachudo, stm., Braz.	J3	88
Borrazópolis, Braz.	A12	92
Borriana, Spain	E10	20
Borroloola, Austl.	C7	74
Borş, Rom.	B8	26
Borşa, Rom.	B11	26
Borsad, India	G4	54
Borščovočnyj hrebet, mts., Russia	F12	34
Borsod-Abaúj-Zemplén, state, Hung.	A8	26
Bort-les-Orgues, Fr.	D8	18
Borūjerd, Iran	C6	56
Borzja, Russia	F12	34
Bosa, Italy	D2	24
Bosanska Dubica, Bos.	D3	26
Bosanska Gradiška, Bos.	D4	26
Bosanska Krupa, Bos.	E3	26
Bosanski Novi, Bos.	D3	26
Bosanski Šamac, Bos.	D5	26
Bosavi, Mount, mtn., Pap. N. Gui.	b3	79a
Boscobel, Wi., U.S.	A7	120
Bose, China	J2	42
Boshan, China	C7	42
Boshof, S. Afr.	F7	70
Bosilegrad, Serb.	G9	26
Bosna, stm., Bos.	E5	26
Bosnia and Herzegovina, ctry., Eur.	E3	26
Bosnik, Indon.	F10	44
Bošnjakovo, Russia	G17	34
Bosobolo, D.R.C.	D3	66
Bōsō-hantō, pen., Japan	D13	40
Bosporus see İstanbul Boğazı, strt., Tur.	B12	28
Bossangoa, C.A.R.	C3	66
Bossembélé, C.A.R.	C3	66
Bossey Bangou, Niger	G5	64
Bossier City, La., U.S.	E5	122
Bosten Hu, l., China	C2	36
Boston, Eng., U.K.	H12	12
Boston, Ga., U.S.	F2	116
Boston, Ma., U.S.	B14	114
Boston Bar, B.C., Can.	G9	138
Boston Mountains, mts., Ar., U.S.	B5	122
Boswell, In., U.S.	H2	112
Boswell, Ok., U.S.	C3	122
Bosworth, Mo., U.S.	E4	120
Botād, India	G3	54
Botany Bay, b., Austl.	J8	76
Boteti, stm., Bots.	E3	68
Bothaville, S. Afr.	E8	70
Bothnia, Gulf of, b., Eur.	E9	8
Bothwell, On., Can.	F8	112
Boticas, Port.	C3	20
Botna, stm., Mol.	C15	26
Botoşani, Rom.	B13	26
Botoşani, state, Rom.	B13	26
Bo Trach, Viet.	D8	48
Botrange, mtn., Bel.	D15	14
Botswana, ctry., Afr.	E3	68
Botte Donato, Monte, mtn., Italy	E10	24
Bottineau, N.D., U.S.	F13	124
Botucatu, Braz.	L1	88
Botwood, Nf., Can.	j22	107a
Bouaflé, C. Iv.	H3	64
Bouaké, C. Iv.	H3	64
Bouar, C.A.R.	C3	66
Bouârfa, Mor.	C4	64
Bouca, C.A.R.	C3	66
Boucher, stm., Qc., Can.	A7	110
Bouches-du-Rhône, state, Fr.	F11	18
Bouctouche, N.B., Can.	D12	110
Boufarik, Alg.	H13	20
Bou Ficha, Tun.	H4	24
Bougainville, i., Pap. N. Gui.	d7	79b
Bougainville, Détroit de, strt., Vanuatu	j16	79d
Bougainville Strait, strt., Oc.	d7	79b
Bougouni, Mali	G3	64
Bouillante, Guad.	h5	105c
Bouillon, Bel.	E14	14
Bouïra, Alg.	B5	64
Boujdour, Cap, c., W. Sah.	D2	64
Boularderie Island, i., N.S., Can.	D16	110
Boulder, Co., U.S.	A3	128
Boulder, Mt., U.S.	D14	136
Boulder, stm., Mt., U.S.	D15	136
Boulder City, Nv., U.S.	H2	132
Boulia, Austl.	D2	76
Boulogne-sur-Mer, Fr.	D10	14
Bouloupari, N. Cal.	m15	79d
Boulsa, Burkina	G4	64
Bou Medfaa, Alg.	H13	20
Bouna, C. Iv.	H4	64
Boundary Peak, mtn., Nv., U.S.	F7	134
Boundiali, C. Iv.	H3	64
Boun Nua, Laos	B5	48
Bountiful, Ut., U.S.	C4	132
Bounty Bay, b., Pit.	c28	78k
Bounty Islands, is., N.Z.	H8	80
Bounty Trough, unds.	N20	142
Bourail, N. Cal.	m15	79d
Bourbeuse, stm., Mo., U.S.	F6	120
Bourbon, In., U.S.	G3	112
Bourbonnais, hist. reg., Fr.	C9	18
Bourbonne-les-Bains, Fr.	G14	14
Bourem, Mali	F4	64
Bourg, La., U.S.	H8	122
Bourg-en-Bresse, Fr.	C11	18
Bourges, Fr.	G11	14
Bourget, On., Can.	E1	110
Bourget, Lac du, l., Fr.	D11	18
Bourgogne (Burgundy), hist. reg., Fr.	B10	18
Bourgogne, Canal de, can., Fr.	G13	14
Bourgoin-Jallieu, Fr.	D11	18
Bourke, Austl.	H5	76
Bournemouth, Eng., U.K.	K11	12
Bou Saâda, Alg.	B5	64
Bou Salem, Tun.	H2	24
Bouse Wash, stm., Az., U.S.	J3	132
Bou Smail, Alg.	H13	20
Boussac, Fr.	C8	18
Bousso, Chad	E3	62
Boutilimit, Maur.	F2	64
Bouvetøya, i., Ant.	A5	81
Bouza, Niger	G6	64
Bøvågen, Nor.	F1	8
Bovec, Slvn.	D10	22
Bovey, Mn., U.S.	D5	118
Bovill, Id., U.S.	D10	136
Bovina, Tx., U.S.	G6	128
Bow, stm., Ab., Can.	G19	138
Bo-Wadrif, S. Afr.	H4	70
Bowbells, N.D., U.S.	F11	124
Bow Creek, stm., Ks., U.S.	B9	128
Bowden, Ab., Can.	E16	138
Bowdle, S.D., U.S.	B13	126
Bowdon, N.D., U.S.	G14	124
Bowen, Arg.	G4	92
Bowen, Austl.	C7	76
Bowen, Il., U.S.	D7	120
Bowen, stm., Austl.	C6	76
Bowie, Az., U.S.	K7	132
Bowie, Md., U.S.	F9	114
Bowling Green, Fl., U.S.	I4	116
Bowling Green, Ky., U.S.	H11	120
Bowling Green, Mo., U.S.	E6	120
Bowling Green, Oh., U.S.	C2	114
Bowling Green, Va., U.S.	F8	114
Bowling Green, Cape, c., Austl.	B6	76
Bowling Green Bay National Park, p.o.i., Austl.	B6	76
Bowman, N.D., U.S.	A9	126
Bowman, S.C., U.S.	C5	116
Bowman, Mount, mtn., B.C., Can.	E9	138
Bowmanville, On., Can.	E11	112
Bowral, Austl.	J8	76
Bowraville, Austl.	H9	76
Bowron, stm., B.C., Can.	C9	138
Bowsman, Mb., Can.	B12	124
Box Elder Creek, stm., Mt., U.S.	G5	124
Boxelder Creek, stm., S.D., U.S.	C10	126
Boxelder Creek, stm., U.S.	B8	126
Boxing, China	C8	42
Boyacá, state, Col.	E5	86
Boyang, China	G7	42
Boyce, La., U.S.	F6	122
Boyceville, Wi., U.S.	F6	118
Boyd, Tx., U.S.	A10	130
Boyd, stm., Austl.	G9	76
Boydton, Va., U.S.	H7	114
Boyer, stm., Ia., U.S.	C2	120
Boyertown, Pa., U.S.	D10	114
Boykins, Va., U.S.	H8	114
Boyle, Ms., U.S.	D8	122
Boylston, Al., U.S.	E12	122
Boyne, stm., Austl.	E8	76
Boyne, stm., Mb., Can.	E16	124
Boyne, stm., Ire.	H5	12
Boyne City, Mi., U.S.	C5	112
Boynton Beach, Fl., U.S.	J5	116
Boysen Reservoir, res., Wy., U.S.	D4	126
Boys Ranch, Tx., U.S.	F6	128
Bozburun, Tur.	G11	28
Bozburun Yarımadası, pen., Tur.	G11	28
Boz Dağ, mtn., Tur.	E11	28
Boz Dağlar, mts., Tur.	E10	28
Bozdoğan, Tur.	F11	28
Bozeman, Mt., U.S.	E15	136
Bozen see Bolzano, Italy	D8	22
Bozhen, China	B7	42
Bozhou, China	E6	42
Bozkurt, Tur.	F12	28
Bozoum, C.A.R.	C3	66
Bozova, Tur.	A9	58
Bozovici, Rom.	E9	26
Bozshaköl, Kaz.	D12	32
Bozüyük, Tur.	D13	28
Bra, Italy	F4	22
Brač, Otok, i., Cro.	G13	22
Bracciano, Italy	H9	22
Bracciano, Lago di, l., Italy	H9	22
Bracebridge, On., Can.	C10	112
Brackendale, B.C., Can.	G7	138
Brackettville, Tx., U.S.	E7	130
Bracknell, Eng., U.K.	J12	12
Braço do Norte, Braz.	D13	92
Brad, Rom.	C9	26
Bradano, stm., Italy	D10	24
Bradenton, Fl., U.S.	I3	116
Bradford, Eng., U.K.	H11	12
Bradford, Ar., U.S.	B7	122
Bradford, Pa., U.S.	C7	114
Bradford, Tn., U.S.	H9	120
Bradford, Vt., U.S.	G4	110
Bradford West Gwillimbury, On., Can.	D10	112
Bradley, Ar., U.S.	D5	122
Bradley, Fl., U.S.	I3	116
Bradley, Il., U.S.	G2	112
Bradley, S.D., U.S.	B15	126
Brady, Mt., U.S.	B15	136
Brady, Ne., U.S.	F12	126
Brady, Tx., U.S.	C8	130
Brady Creek, stm., Tx., U.S.	C8	130
Braga, Port.	C2	20
Braga, state, Port.	C2	20
Bragado, Arg.	G7	92
Bragança, Braz.	D8	84
Bragança, Port.	C4	20
Bragança, state, Port.	C4	20
Bragança Paulista, Braz.	L2	88
Brāhmanbāria, Bngl.	F13	54
Brāhmani, stm., India	H10	54
Brahmapur, India	B7	53
Brahmaputra (Yarlung), stm., Asia	C7	46
Braich y Pwll, c., Wales, U.K.	I8	12
Braidwood, Austl.	J7	76
Braidwood, Il., U.S.	C9	120
Brăila, Rom.	D14	26
Brăila, state, Rom.	D14	26
Brainard, Ne., U.S.	F15	126
Brainerd, Mn., U.S.	E4	118
Braintree, Eng., U.K.	J13	12
Brak, stm., S. Afr.	G6	70
Brake, Ger.	C4	16
Bralorne, B.C., Can.	F8	138
Brampton, On., Can.	E10	112
Bramsche, Ger.	D3	16
Branchville, S.C., U.S.	C5	116
Branco, stm., Braz.	H11	86
Branco, stm., Braz.	F3	88
Brandaris, hill, Neth. Ant.	p23	104g
Brandberg, mtn., Nmb.	B2	70
Brandbu, Nor.	F4	8
Brandenburg, Ger.	D8	16
Brandenburg, Ky., U.S.	G11	120
Brandenburg, state, Ger.	D9	16
Brandfort, S. Afr.	F8	70
Brandon, Mb., Can.	E14	124
Brandon, Fl., U.S.	I3	116
Brandon, Ms., U.S.	E9	122
Brandon, S.D., U.S.	H2	118
Brandon, Vt., U.S.	G3	110
Brandsen, Arg.	G8	92
Brandvlei, S. Afr.	G5	70
Brandy Peak, mtn., Or., U.S.	H3	136
Brandýs nad Labem-Stará Boleslav, Czech Rep.	F10	16
Branford, Fl., U.S.	G2	116
Braniewo, Pol.	B15	16
Bransby, Austl.	G4	76
Bransby Point, c., Monts.	D3	105a
Bransfield Strait, strt., Ant.	B35	81
Branson, Mo., U.S.	H4	120
Brantford, On., Can.	E9	112
Brantley, Al., U.S.	F12	122
Brantley Tank, res., N.M., U.S.	B3	130
Brantôme, Fr.	D6	18
Brantville, N.B., Can.	C12	110
Bras d'Or Lake, l., N.S., Can.	E16	110
Brasiléia, Braz.	F4	84
Brasília, Braz.	H1	88
Brasília, Parque Nacional de, p.o.i., Braz.	H1	88
Brasília de Minas, Braz.	I3	88
Braslau, Bela.	E9	10
Braşov, Rom.	D12	26
Braşov, state, Rom.	D12	26
Brassey, Banjaran, mts., Malay.	A10	50
Brass Islands, is., V.I.U.S.	e7	104b
Brasstown Bald, mtn., Ga., U.S.	B2	116
Bratca, Rom.	C9	26
Bratislava, Slov.	H13	16
Bratislava, state, Slov.	H13	16
Bratsk, Russia	C18	32
Bratskoe vodohranilišče, res., Russia	C18	32
Bratsk Reservoir see Bratskoe vodohranilišče, res., Russia	C18	32
Brattleboro, Vt., U.S.	B13	114
Braulio Carrillo, Parque Nacional, p.o.i., C.R.	G5	102
Braúnas, Braz.	J4	88
Braunau am Inn, Aus.	B10	22
Braunschweig (Brunswick), Ger.	D6	16
Brava, i., C.V.	I10	65a
Brava, Costa, cst., Spain	C14	20
Brava, Laguna, l., Arg.	D3	92
Brava, Punta, c., Ur.	G9	92
Brave, Pa., U.S.	E5	114
Bravo (Rio Grande), stm., N.A.	H13	98
Bravo, Cerro, mtn., Peru	E2	84
Bravo del Norte see Bravo, stm., N.A.	H13	98
Brawley, Ca., U.S.	K10	134
Bray, Ire.	H6	12
Bray Island, i., Nu., Can.	B15	106
Brazeau, stm., Ab., Can.	D15	138
Brazeau, Mount, mtn., Ab., Can.	D13	138
Brazeau Dam, dam, Ab., Can.	C15	138
Brazil, In., U.S.	E10	120
Brazil, ctry., S.A.	F9	82
Brazil Basin, unds.	J11	144
Brazoria, Tx., U.S.	E12	130
Brazos, stm., Tx., U.S.	E8	108
Brazos, Clear Fork, stm., Tx., U.S.	B8	130
Brazos, Double Mountain Fork, stm., Tx., U.S.	H8	128
Brazos, North Fork, stm., Tx., U.S.	H3	122
Brazzaville, Congo	E2	66
Brčko, Bos.	E5	26
Brda, stm., Pol.	C13	16
Bré see Bray, Ire.	H6	12
Brea, Ca., U.S.	J8	134
Bream Bay, b., N.Z.	B6	80
Brea Pozo, Arg.	D6	92
Breaux Bridge, La., U.S.	G7	122
Brebes, Indon.	G6	50
Brechin, Scot., U.K.	E10	12
Breckenridge, Mi., U.S.	E5	112
Breckenridge, Mn., U.S.	E2	118
Breckenridge, Mo., U.S.	E4	120
Brecknock, Península, pen., Chile	J2	90
Břeclav, Czech Rep.	H12	16
Brecon, Wales, U.K.	J9	12
Brecon Beacons, hills, Wales, U.K.	J9	12
Brecon Beacons National Park, p.o.i., Wales, U.K.	J9	12
Breda, Neth.	C13	14
Breda, Ia., U.S.	B3	120
Bredasdorp, S. Afr.	I5	70
Bredenbury, Sk., Can.	D11	124
Bredy, Russia	D9	32
Breë, stm., S. Afr.	I5	70
Breese, Il., U.S.	F8	120
Bregalnica, stm., Mac.	A5	28
Bregenz, Aus.	C6	22
Bregovo, Blg.	E9	26
Bréhat, Île de, i., Fr.	F6	14
Breiðafjörður, b., Ice.	k28	8a
Brejinho de Nazaré, Braz.	F1	88
Brejo, Braz.	B4	88
Brejo Grande, Braz.	F7	88
Brejo Santo, Braz.	D6	88
Brekstad, Nor.	E3	8
Bremen, Ger.	C4	16
Bremen, Ga., U.S.	D13	122
Bremen, Oh., U.S.	E3	114
Bremen, state, Ger.	C4	16
Bremer Bay, Austl.	F3	74
Bremer Bay, b., Austl.	F3	74
Bremerhaven, Ger.	C4	16
Bremerton, Wa., U.S.	C4	136
Bremervörde, Ger.	C4	16
Bremond, Tx., U.S.	F2	122
Brenham, Tx., U.S.	G2	122
Brenner Pass, p., Eur.	C8	22
Brent, Fl., U.S.	G11	122
Brenta, stm., Italy	D8	22
Brentwood, Eng., U.K.	J13	12
Brentwood, N.Y., U.S.	D12	114
Brentwood, Tn., U.S.	H11	120
Breo, Italy	F4	22
Brescia, Italy	E7	22
Breslau see Wrocław, Pol.	E13	16
Bressanone, Italy	D8	22
Bressay, i., Scot., U.K.	n18	12a
Bresse, reg., Fr.	C11	18
Bressuire, Fr.	H8	14
Brèst, Bela.	H6	10
Brest, Fr.	F4	14
Brèst, state, Bela.	H8	10
Bretagne (Brittany), hist. reg., Fr.	F5	14
Bretenoux, Fr.	E7	18
Breton, Ab., Can.	C16	138
Breton Islands, is., La., U.S.	H9	122
Breton Sound, strt., La., U.S.	H9	122
Brett, Cape, c., N.Z.	B6	80
Bretten, Ger.	G4	16
Breueh, Pulau, i., Indon.	J2	48
Breuil-Cervinia, Italy	E4	22
Brevard, N.C., U.S.	A3	116
Breves, Braz.	D7	84
Brevoort Island, i., Nu., Can.	E13	141
Brewarrina, Austl.	G6	76
Brewer, Me., U.S.	F8	110
Brewster, Mn., U.S.	H3	118
Brewster, Ne., U.S.	F13	126
Brewster, Wa., U.S.	B7	136
Brewster, Kap, c., Grnld.	C21	141
Brewton, Al., U.S.	F11	122
Breyten, S. Afr.	E10	70
Březnice, Czech Rep.	G9	16
Brezno, Slov.	H15	16
Bria, C.A.R.	C4	66
Brian Boru Peak, mtn., B.C., Can.	A3	138
Briançon, Fr.	E12	18
Brian Head, mtn., Ut., U.S.	F4	132
Briare, Canal de, can., Fr.	G11	14
Bribie Island, i., Austl.	F9	76
Bricelyn, Mn., U.S.	H5	118
Briceni, Mol.	A14	26
Briceville, Tn., U.S.	A14	122
Bri Chuallan see Bray, Ire.	H6	12
Bridge, stm., B.C., Can.	F7	138
Bridge City, Tx., U.S.	G5	122
Bridge Lake, B.C., Can.	E10	138
Bridgend, Wales, U.K.	J9	12
Bridgeport, Ca., U.S.	E6	134
Bridgeport, Ct., U.S.	C12	114
Bridgeport, Mi., U.S.	E6	112
Bridgeport, Ne., U.S.	F9	126
Bridgeport, Tx., U.S.	H11	128
Bridgeport, Wa., U.S.	C7	136
Bridgeport, Lake, res., Tx., U.S.	H10	128
Bridger, Mt., U.S.	B4	126
Bridger Peak, mtn., Wy., U.S.	B9	132
Bridgeton, N.J., U.S.	E10	114
Bridgetown, Austl.	F3	74
Bridgetown, Barb.	n8	105d
Bridgetown, N.S., Can.	F11	110
Bridgeville, De., U.S.	F10	114
Bridgewater, N.S., Can.	F12	110
Bridgewater, Ma., U.S.	B15	114
Bridgewater, S.D., U.S.	D15	126
Bridgewater, Va., U.S.	F6	114
Bridgwater, Eng., U.K.	J9	12
Bridgwater Bay, b., Eng., U.K.	J9	12
Bridlington, Eng., U.K.	G12	12
Bridport, Eng., U.K.	K10	12
Brie, reg., Fr.	F12	14
Brier Creek, stm., Ga., U.S.	C4	116
Brig, Switz.	D5	22
Briggs, Tx., U.S.	D10	130
Brigham City, Ut., U.S.	B4	132
Bright, Austl.	K6	76
Brighton, On., Can.	D12	112
Brighton, Eng., U.K.	K12	12
Brighton, Co., U.S.	A4	128
Brighton, Ia., U.S.	C6	120
Brighton, Mi., U.S.	B2	114
Brighton, N.Y., U.S.	E12	112
Brighton Downs, Austl.	D3	76
Brignoles, Fr.	F11	18
Brijuni, i., Cro.	F10	22
Brilliant, B.C., Can.	G13	138
Brilliant, Al., U.S.	C11	122
Brillion, Wi., U.S.	D1	112
Brilon, Ger.	E4	16
Brindisi, Italy	D11	24
Brinkworth, Austl.	I2	76
Brion, Île, i., Qc., Can.	C15	110
Brioude, Fr.	D9	18
Brisbane, Austl.	F9	76
Brisighella, Italy	F8	22
Bristol, Eng., U.K.	J10	12
Bristol, Ct., U.S.	C12	114
Bristol, Fl., U.S.	G14	122
Bristol, N.H., U.S.	G5	110
Bristol, Pa., U.S.	D11	114
Bristol, R.I., U.S.	C14	114
Bristol, Tn., U.S.	H3	114
Bristol, Vt., U.S.	F3	110
Bristol Bay, b., Ak., U.S.	E7	140
Bristol Channel, strt., U.K.	J8	12
Bristol Island, i., S. Geor.	A2	81
Bristol Lake, l., Ca., U.S.	I10	134
Bristow, Ok., U.S.	B2	122
Britannia Beach, B.C., Can.	G7	138
British Columbia, state, Can.	E5	106
British Guiana see Guyana, ctry., S.A.	C6	84
British Honduras see Belize, ctry., N.A.	D3	102
British Indian Ocean Territory, dep., Afr.	G17	2
British Isles, is., Eur.	C12	4
British Mountains, mts., N.A.	C11	140
British Solomon Islands see Solomon Islands, ctry., Oc.	D7	72
British Virgin Islands, dep., N.A.	h15	96a
Brits, S. Afr.	D8	70
Britstown, S. Afr.	G6	70
Britt, Ia., U.S.	A4	120
Brittany see Bretagne, hist. reg., Fr.	F5	14
Britton, S.D., U.S.	B15	126
Brive-la-Gaillarde, Fr.	D7	18
Brixen see Bressanone, Italy	D8	22
Brixham, Eng., U.K.	K9	12
Brixton, Austl.	D5	76
Brjanka, Russia	C16	32
Brjansk, Russia	G17	10
Brjanskaja oblast', co., Russia	H16	10
Brno, Czech Rep.	G12	16
Broa, Ensenada de la, b., Cuba	A6	102
Broad, stm., Ga., U.S.	B2	116
Broad, stm., U.S.	B4	116
Broadalbin, N.Y., U.S.	G2	110
Broad Sound, b., Austl.	D7	76
Broad Sound Channel, strt., Austl.	C8	76
Broadus, Mt., U.S.	B7	126
Broadwater, Ne., U.S.	F10	126
Broadway, Va., U.S.	F7	114
Brocēni, Lat.	D5	10
Brochet, Mb., Can.	D10	106
Brock, Sk., Can.	C5	124
Brockman, Mount, mtn., Austl.	D3	74
Brockton, Ma., U.S.	B14	114
Brockton, Mt., U.S.	F9	124
Brockville, On., Can.	D14	112
Brockway, Pa., U.S.	C7	114
Brocton, N.Y., U.S.	B6	114
Brodeur Peninsula, pen., Nu., Can.	A13	106
Brodhead, Wi., U.S.	B8	120
Brodick, Scot., U.K.	F7	12
Brodnax, Va., U.S.	H7	114
Brodnica, Pol.	C15	16
Brogan, Or., U.S.	F9	136
Brok, Pol.	D17	16
Broken Arrow, Ok., U.S.	H2	120
Broken Bay, b., Austl.	I8	76
Broken Bow, Ok., U.S.	C4	122
Broken Bow Lake, res., Ok., U.S.	C4	122
Broken Hill, Austl.	H3	76
Broken Hill see Kabwe, Zam.	C4	68
Broken Ridge, unds.	M12	142
Brokopondo, Sur.	B6	84
Brokopondo Stuwmeer, res., Sur.	C6	84
Bromley Plateau, unds.	K10	144
Bromptonville, Qc., Can.	E4	110
Bromsgrove, Eng., U.K.	I10	12
Bronkhorstspruit, S. Afr.	D9	70
Bronlund Peak, mtn., B.C., Can.	D5	106
Bronnae, Bela.	H13	10
Bronnicy, Russia	E21	10
Bronson, Fl., U.S.	G3	116
Bronson, Ks., U.S.	G2	120
Bronson, Mi., U.S.	G4	112
Bronte, Italy	G8	24
Bronte, Tx., U.S.	C7	130
Brook, In., U.S.	H2	112
Brookeland, Tx., U.S.	F5	122
Brooker, Fl., U.S.	G3	116
Brookfield, N.S., Can.	E13	110
Brookfield, Wi., U.S.	E1	112
Brookford, N.C., U.S.	I4	114
Brookhaven, Ms., U.S.	F8	122
Brookings, Or., U.S.	A1	134
Brookings, S.D., U.S.	G2	118
Brookland, Ar., U.S.	B8	122
Brooklyn, N.S., Can.	F12	110
Brooklyn, Ia., U.S.	J6	118
Brooklyn, Mi., U.S.	B1	114
Brooklyn Center, Mn., U.S.	F5	118
Brookmere, B.C., Can.	G10	138
Brookneal, Va., U.S.	G7	114
Brookport, Il., U.S.	G9	120
Brooks, Ab., Can.	F19	138
Brooks Bay, b., B.C., Can.	F2	138
Brookshire, Tx., U.S.	H3	122
Brooks Range, mts., Ak., U.S.	C8	140
Brooksville, Fl., U.S.	H3	116
Brooksville, Ms., U.S.	D10	122
Brookville, In., U.S.	E12	120
Brookville, Pa., U.S.	C6	114
Brookville Lake, res., In., U.S.	E13	120
Broome, Austl.	C4	74
Broomfield, Co., U.S.	B3	128
Brooten, Mn., U.S.	F3	118
Brora, Scot., U.K.	C9	12
Brosna, stm., Ire.	H5	12
Brotas de Macaúbas, Braz.	G4	88
Brou, Fr.	F10	14
Broughton, Mount, mtn., Austl.	K5	76
Broughty Ferry, Scot., U.K.	E10	12
Browerville, Mn., U.S.	E4	118
Brown, Mount, mtn., Mt., U.S.	B15	136
Brown, Point, c., Wa., U.S.	D2	136
Brown Deer, Wi., U.S.	E2	112
Browne Bay, b., Nu., Can.	A11	106
Brownfield, Tx., U.S.	A5	130
Browning, Mo., U.S.	D4	120
Browning, Mt., U.S.	B13	136
Brownlee Reservoir, res., U.S.	F9	136
Brownsburg, Qc., Can.	E2	110
Brownsburg, In., U.S.	I3	112
Brownsdale, Mn., U.S.	H5	118
Browns Town, Jam.	i13	104d
Brownstown, In., U.S.	F11	120
Brownsville, Ky., U.S.	G11	120
Brownsville, La., U.S.	E6	122
Brownsville, Or., U.S.	F4	136
Brownsville, Tn., U.S.	B9	122
Brownsville, Tx., U.S.	I10	130
Brownton, Mn., U.S.	G4	118
Brownville, Me., U.S.	E7	110
Brownville, Ne., U.S.	D2	120
Brownville Junction, Me., U.S.	E7	110
Brownwood, Tx., U.S.	C8	130
Brownwood, Lake, res., Tx., U.S.	C9	130
Browse Island, i., Austl.	B4	74
Broxton, Ga., U.S.	E3	116
Brožа, Bela.	H12	10
Bruay-en-Artois, Fr.	D11	14
Bruce, S.D., U.S.	G2	118
Bruce, Wi., U.S.	F7	118
Bruce, Mount, mtn., Austl.	D3	74
Bruce Mines, On., Can.	B6	112
Bruce Peninsula, pen., On., Can.	C8	112
Bruce Peninsula National Park, p.o.i., On., Can.	C8	112
Bruce Rock, Austl.	F3	74
Bruchsal, Ger.	G4	16
Bruck an der Leitha, Aus.	B13	22
Bruck an der Mur, Aus.	C12	22
Bruges see Brugge, Bel.	C12	14
Brugg, Switz.	C5	22
Brugge (Bruges), Bel.	C12	14
Brühl, Ger.	F2	16
Bruit, Pulau, i., Malay.	B7	50
Brule, Ne., U.S.	F11	126
Brumado, Braz.	H5	88
Brundidge, Al., U.S.	F13	122
Bruneau, Id., U.S.	H11	136
Bruneau, stm., U.S.	H11	136
Bruneck see Brunico, Italy	D8	22
Brunei, ctry., Asia	A9	50
Brunico, Italy	D8	22
Brunsbüttel, Ger.	C4	16
Brunson, S.C., U.S.	D4	116
Brunswick see Braunschweig, Ger.	D6	16
Brunswick, Ga., U.S.	E4	116
Brunswick, Md., U.S.	E8	114
Brunswick, Me., U.S.	G6	110
Brunswick, Mo., U.S.	E4	120
Brunswick, Oh., U.S.	C4	114
Brunswick, Península, pen., Chile	J2	90
Bruntál, Czech Rep.	F13	16
Brus, Laguna de, b., Hond.	E5	102
Brush, Co., U.S.	A5	128
Brusovo, Russia	C18	10
Brusque, Braz.	C13	92
Brussel see Bruxelles, Bel.	D13	14
Brussels see Bruxelles, Bel.	D13	14
Brussels, On., Can.	E8	112
Bruthen, Austl.	K6	76
Bruxelles (Brussels), Bel.	D13	14
Bruzual, Ven.	D7	86
Bryan, Oh., U.S.	C1	114
Bryan, Tx., U.S.	G2	122
Bryan, Mount, mtn., Austl.	I2	76
Bryant, Ar., U.S.	C6	122
Bryce Canyon National Park, p.o.i., Ut., U.S.	F4	132
Bryli, Bela.	G13	10
Bryson, Qc., Can.	C13	112
Bryson, Tx., U.S.	A9	130
Brzeg, Pol.	F13	16
Brześć Kujawski, Pol.	D14	16
Brzesko, Pol.	F16	16
Brzeziny, Pol.	E15	16
Bsharrī, Leb.	D6	58
Bua, Fiji	p19	79e
Bua Bay, b., Fiji	p19	79e
Buada Lagoon, b., Nauru	q17	78f
Buala, Sol. Is.	e8	79b
Bua Yai, Thai.	E6	48
Bubanza, Bdi.	E5	66
Bubaque, Gui.-B.	G1	64
Bubi, stm., Zimb.	B10	70
Būbiyān, i., Kuw.	D6	56
Bubuduo, China	C10	54
Bucak, Tur.	F13	28
Bucaramanga, Col.	D5	86
Buccaneer Archipelago, is., Austl.	C4	74
Buchanan, Sk., Can.	C11	124
Buchanan, Lib.	H2	64
Buchanan, Ga., U.S.	D13	122
Buchanan, Mi., U.S.	G3	112
Buchanan, Lake, l., Austl.	C5	76
Buchanan, Lake, l., Tx., U.S.	D9	130
Buchan Ness, c., Scot., U.K.	D11	12
Buchans, Nf., Can.	j22	107a
Bucharest see București, Rom.	E13	26
Buchen, Ger.	G5	16
Buchholz in der Nordheide, Ger.	C5	16
Buchloe, Ger.	H6	16
Buchon, Point, c., Ca., U.S.	H4	134
Buchs, Switz.	C6	22
Buckatunna, Ms., U.S.	F10	122
Buckatunna Creek, stm., Ms., U.S.	F10	122
Bückeburg, Ger.	D5	16
Buckeye, Az., U.S.	J4	132
Buckeye Lake, Oh., U.S.	I7	112
Buckhaven, Scot., U.K.	E9	12
Buckholts, Tx., U.S.	D10	130
Buckhorn Draw, stm., Tx., U.S.	D7	130
Buckie, Scot., U.K.	D10	12
Buckingham, Qc., Can.	C14	112
Buckingham, Va., U.S.	G7	114
Buckingham Bay, b., Austl.	B7	74
Buck Island, i., V.I.U.S.	g11	104c
Buck Island Reef National Monument, p.o.i., V.I.U.S.	g11	104c
Buck Lake, l., Ab., Can.	D16	138
Buckland, Ak., U.S.	C7	140
Buckley, Wa., U.S.	C4	136
Bucklin, Ks., U.S.	D9	128
Bucklin, Mo., U.S.	E5	120
Buck Mountain, mtn., Wa., U.S.	B7	136
Bucovăţ, Mol.	B15	26
Buco Zau, Ang.	A1	68
București (Bucharest), Rom.	E13	26
București, state, Rom.	E13	26
Bucyrus, Oh., U.S.	D3	114
Buda, Il., U.S.	C8	120
Buda, Tx., U.S.	D10	130
Budalin, Mya.	A2	48
Budapest, Hung.	B6	26
Budapest, state, Hung.	B6	26
Budaun, India	D7	54
Budd Coast, cst., Ant.	B16	81
Buddh Gaya see Bodh Gaya, India	F10	54
Buddusò, Italy	D3	24
Bude, Ms., U.S.	F8	122
Bude Bay, b., Eng., U.K.	K8	12
Budënnovsk, Russia	F6	32
Budeşti, Rom.	E13	26
Büdingen, Ger.	F5	16
Budišov nad Budišovkou, Czech Rep.	G13	16
Budjala, D.R.C.	D3	66
Budogovišči, Russia	G19	10
Budrio, Italy	F8	22
Budweis see České Budějovice, Czech Rep.	H10	16
Buea, Cam.	D1	66
Buena Esperanza, Arg.	G5	92
Buenaventura, Col.	F3	86
Buenaventura, Mex.	G9	98
Buena Vista, Bol.	C4	90
Buena Vista, Mex.	K9	134
Buenavista, Phil.	G4	52
Buena Vista, Co., U.S.	C2	128
Buena Vista, Ga., U.S.	E14	122
Buena Vista, Va., U.S.	G6	114
Buena Vista Lake Bed, reg., Ca., U.S.	H6	134
Buendía, Embalse de, res., Spain	D8	20
Buenópolis, Braz.	I3	88
Buenos Aires, Arg.	G8	92
Buenos Aires, Col.	F3	86
Buenos Aires, C.R.	H6	102
Buenos Aires, state, Arg.	G5	90
Buenos Aires, Lago see General Carrera, Lago, l., S.A.	I2	90
Buen Pasto, Arg.	I3	90
Buerarema, Braz.	H6	88
Buffalo, Ks., U.S.	G2	120
Buffalo, Mn., U.S.	F5	118
Buffalo, Mo., U.S.	G4	120
Buffalo, N.Y., U.S.	B7	114
Buffalo, Oh., U.S.	E4	114
Buffalo, S.C., U.S.	B4	116
Buffalo, S.D., U.S.	B9	126
Buffalo, Tx., U.S.	F2	122
Buffalo, stm., Can.	C8	106
Buffalo, stm., Ar., U.S.	H4	120
Buffalo, stm., Tn., U.S.	B11	122
Buffalo Creek, stm., Mn., U.S.	G4	118
Buffalo Lake, Mn., U.S.	G4	118
Buffalo Lake, l., Ab., Can.	D18	138
Buffalo Lake, l., N.T., Can.	C7	106
Buffalo Narrows, Sk., Can.	D8	106
Buffalo Pound Lake, l., Sk., Can.	D8	124
Buffels, stm., S. Afr.	F3	70
Buffels, stm., S. Afr.	F10	70
Buford, Ga., U.S.	B2	116
Buford Dam, dam, Ga., U.S.	B1	116
Buftea, Rom.	E12	26
Bug (Buh) (Zakhidnyy Buh), stm., Eur.	D17	16
Buga, Col.	F3	86
Bugala Island, i., Ug.	E6	66
Bugeat, Fr.	D7	18
Bugojno, Bos.	E4	26
Bugrino, Russia	B23	8
Bugsuk Island, i., Phil.	F1	52
Bugt, China	C4	38
Bugul'ma, Russia	D8	32
Buguruslan, Russia	D8	32
Buh, stm., China	D4	36
Buh (Bug) (Zakhidnyy Buh), stm., Eur.	D19	16
Buhara, Uzb.	G10	32
Buhl, Mn., U.S.	D6	118
Buhler, Ks., U.S.	C11	128
Buhuşi, Rom.	C13	26
Buies Creek, N.C., U.S.	A7	116
Builth Wells, Wales, U.K.	I9	12
Buin, Chile	F2	92
Buin, Pap. N. Gui.	d6	79b
Buíque, Braz.	E7	88
Buitsivango (Rietfontein), stm., Afr.	B4	70
Buj, Russia	G19	8
Bujalance, Spain	G6	20
Buje, Cro.	E10	22
Bujnaksk, Russia	F7	32
Bujumbura, Bdi.	E5	66
Bukačača, Russia	F12	34
Bukama, D.R.C.	F5	66
Bukan', Russia	G17	10
Bukavu, D.R.C.	E5	66
Bukeya, D.R.C.	G5	66
Bukhara see Buhara, Uzb.	G10	32
Bukittinggi, Indon.	D2	50
Bükki Nemzeti Park, p.o.i., Hung.	A7	26
Bukoba, Tan.	E6	66
Bukovica, reg., Cro.	F12	22
Bukovina, hist. reg., Eur.	B12	26
Bukuru, Nig.	H6	64
Bula, Indon.	F9	44
Būlaevo, Kaz.	C12	32
Bulajevo see Būlaevo, Kaz.	C12	32
Bulan, Phil.	D4	52

I·10 Bulandshahr – Canicattì

Name	Map Ref.	Page
Bulandshahr, India	D6	54
Bulawayo, Zimb.	B9	70
Bulbul, Syria	B7	58
Buldan, Tur.	E11	28
Buldāna, India	H6	54
Buldir Island, i., Ak., U.S.	g22	140a
Bulgan, Mong.	B5	36
Bulgan, Mong.	B3	36
Bulgaria, ctry., Eur.	G12	26
Bulkley, stm., B.C., Can.	B3	138
Bullard, Tx., U.S.	E3	122
Bulla Regia, sci., Tun.	H2	24
Bullas, Spain	F9	20
Bullaxaar, Som.	B8	66
Bulle, Switz.	D4	22
Buller, stm., N.Z.	E5	80
Buller, Mount, mtn., Austl.	K6	76
Bullfinch, Austl.	F3	74
Bull Harbour, B.C., Can.	F2	138
Bullhead, S.D., U.S.	B11	126
Bullhead City, Az., U.S.	H2	132
Bullock, N.C., U.S.	H7	114
Bullock Creek, Austl.	A5	76
Bullock Creek, stm., Austl.	C5	76
Bulloo, stm., Austl.	G4	76
Bullpound Creek, stm., Ab., Can.	E19	138
Bulls Gap, Tn., U.S.	H2	114
Bull Shoals, Ar., U.S.	H5	120
Bull Shoals Lake, res., U.S.	H5	120
Bulnes, Chile	H1	92
Bulolo, Pap. N. Gui.	b4	79a
Bulsār, India	H4	54
Buluan, Phil.	G5	52
Bulukumba, Indon.	F12	50
Bululawang, Indon.	H8	50
Bumba, D.R.C.	D4	66
Bumpus, Mount, hill, Nu., Can.	B8	106
Bumu Hu, l., China	C13	54
Buna, Kenya	D7	66
Bunawan, Phil.	F5	52
Bunbury, Austl.	F3	74
Bunceton, Mo., U.S.	F5	120
Bundaberg, Austl.	E9	76
Bundarra, Austl.	H8	76
Bünde, Ger.	D4	16
Būndi, India	F5	54
Bundoran, Ire.	G4	12
Būndu, India	G10	54
Bungamas, Indon.	E3	50
Bungo-suidō, strt., Japan	G5	40
Bungo-takada, Japan	F4	40
Bungtlang, India	G14	54
Bunia, D.R.C.	D6	66
Bunker, Mo., U.S.	G6	120
Bunker Group, is., Austl.	D9	76
Bunker Hill, In., U.S.	H3	112
Bunker Hill, Or., U.S.	G2	136
Bunker Hill, mtn., Nv., U.S.	D8	134
Bunkie, La., U.S.	G6	122
Bunnell, Fl., U.S.	G4	116
Buñol see Bunyolo, Spain	E10	20
Buntok, Indon.	D9	50
Bunyolo, Spain	E10	20
Bunyu, Pulau, i., Indon.	B10	50
Buolkalah, Russia	B12	34
Buolkalakh see Buolkalah, Russia	B12	34
Buon Ma Thuot, Viet.	F9	48
Buor-Haja, guba, b., Russia	B15	34
Buor-Haja, mys, c., Russia	B15	34
Bupul, Indon.	G11	44
Buqayq, Sau. Ar.	D6	56
Bura, Kenya	E7	66
Burām, Sudan	E5	62
Burang, China	C8	54
Buranhém, stm., Braz.	I6	88
Burāq, Syria	E7	58
Burauen, Phil.	E5	52
Burbank, Wa., U.S.	D8	136
Burç, Tur.	A8	58
Burcher, Austl.	I6	76
Burco, Som.	C9	66
Burdekin, stm., Austl.	C6	76
Burdekin Falls, wtfl., Austl.	C6	76
Burden, Ks., U.S.	D12	128
Burdett, Ks., U.S.	C9	128
Burdur, Tur.	F13	28
Burdur, state, Tur.	F13	28
Burdur Gölü, l., Tur.	F12	28
Bureinskij hrebet, mts., Russia	G15	34
Bureja, Russia	G15	34
Bureja, stm., Russia	F15	34
Büren, Ger.	E4	16
Bürenhayrhan, Mong.	B3	36
Burford, On., Can.	E9	112
Burg, Ger.	D7	16
Burg, Den see Den Burg, Neth.	A13	14
Burgas, Blg.	G14	26
Burgas, state, Blg.	G13	26
Burgas, Gulf of see Burgaski Zaliv, b., Blg.	G14	26
Burgaski Zaliv, b., Blg.	G14	26
Burg auf Fehmarn, Ger.	B7	16
Burgaw, N.C., U.S.	B8	116
Burgdorf, Switz.	C4	22
Burgenland, state, Aus.	C13	22
Burgeo, Nf., Can.	j22	107a
Burgersdorp, S. Afr.	G8	70
Burghausen, Ger.	H8	16
Burghead, Scot., U.K.	D9	12
Burgin, Ky., U.S.	G13	120
Burgo de Osma, Spain	C7	20
Burgos, Mex.	C9	100
Burgos, Phil.	C3	52
Burgos, Spain	B7	20
Burgos, co., Spain	B7	20
Burgstädt, Ger.	F8	16
Burgundy see Bourgogne, hist. reg., Fr.	B10	18
Burhan Budai Shan, mts., China	D4	36
Burhaniye, Tur.	D9	28
Burhānpur, India	H5	54
Burias Island, i., Phil.	D4	52
Burica, Punta, c., N.A.	I6	102
Burien, Wa., U.S.	C4	136
Burila Mare, Rom.	E9	26
Buri Ram, Thai.	E6	48
Buriti, Braz.	B4	88
Buriti Bravo, Braz.	C4	88
Buriticupu, stm., Braz.	C2	88
Buriti dos Lopes, Braz.	B5	88
Buritizeiro, Braz.	I3	88
Burjasot see Burjassot, Spain	E10	20
Burjassot, Spain	E10	20
Burjatija, state, Russia	F11	34
Burkburnett, Tx., U.S.	G10	128
Burke, S.D., U.S.	D13	126
Burke, stm., Austl.	D2	76
Burketown, Austl.	A2	76
Burkina Faso, ctry., Afr.	G4	64
Burleson, Tx., U.S.	B10	130
Burley, Id., U.S.	H13	136
Burlingame, Ca., U.S.	F3	134
Burlingame, Ks., U.S.	F2	120
Burlington, On., Can.	E10	112
Burlington, Co., U.S.	B6	128
Burlington, Ia., U.S.	D6	120
Burlington, Ks., U.S.	F2	120
Burlington, N.C., U.S.	H6	114
Burlington, Vt., U.S.	F3	110
Burlington, Wa., U.S.	B4	136
Burlington, Wi., U.S.	B9	120
Burlington, Wy., U.S.	C4	126
Burlington Junction, Mo., U.S.	D2	120
Burma see Myanmar, ctry., Asia	D8	46
Burnaby, B.C., Can.	G7	138
Burnet, Tx., U.S.	D9	130
Burnett, stm., Austl.	E8	76
Burnett Bay, b., N.T., Can.	B14	140
Burney, Ca., U.S.	C4	134
Burnie, Austl.	n12	77a
Burnley, Eng., U.K.	H10	12
Burns, Ks., U.S.	C12	128
Burns, Or., U.S.	G7	136
Burns, Tn., U.S.	H10	120
Burns, Wy., U.S.	F8	126
Burnside, Ky., U.S.	G13	120
Burnside, stm., Nu., Can.	B8	106
Burnside, Lake, l., Austl.	E4	74
Burns Lake, B.C., Can.	B5	138
Burnsville, Ms., U.S.	C10	122
Burnsville, N.C., U.S.	I3	114
Burnsville, W.V., U.S.	F5	114
Burnt, stm., Or., U.S.	F9	136
Burnt Pine, Norf. I.	y25	78i
Burntwood, stm., Mb., Can.	D11	106
Burqin, China	B2	36
Burra, Austl.	I2	76
Burragorang, Lake, res., Austl.	J7	76
Burrel, Alb.	C13	24
Burreli see Burrel, Alb.	C13	24
Burrendong, Lake, res., Austl.	I7	76
Burren Junction, Austl.	H7	76
Burriana see Borriana, Spain	E10	20
Burrinjuck Reservoir, res., Austl.	J7	76
Burr Oak, Ks., U.S.	B10	128
Burrton, Ks., U.S.	C11	128
Burruyacú, Arg.	E4	90
Bursa, Tur.	C11	28
Bursa, state, Tur.	C11	28
Bûr Sa'îd (Port Said), Egypt	G3	58
Burstall, Sk., Can.	D4	124
Būr Sūdān (Port Sudan), Sudan	D7	62
Burt, Ia., U.S.	H4	118
Burt Lake, l., Mi., U.S.	C5	112
Burtnieks ezers, l., Lat.	C8	10
Burton, Mi., U.S.	E6	112
Burton, Tx., U.S.	G2	122
Burton upon Trent, Eng., U.K.	I11	12
Buru, i., Indon.	F8	44
Burullus, Buheirat el-, l., Egypt	G1	58
Burundi, ctry., Afr.	E6	66
Burun-Šibertuj, gora, mtn., Russia	G10	34
Bururi, Bdi.	E5	66
Burwash, On., Can.	B9	112
Burwell, Ne., U.S.	F13	126
Bury, Eng., U.K.	H10	12
Buryatia see Burjatija, state, Russia	F11	34
Bury Saint Edmunds, Eng., U.K.	I13	12
Burzil, Pak.	A5	54
Busa, Mount, mtn., Phil.	G5	52
Busan see Pusan-jikhalsi, state, Kor., S.	D2	40
Busanga, D.R.C.	E4	66
Busby, Mt., U.S.	B5	126
Bûsh, Egypt	I2	58
Bushire see Bandar-e Būshehr, Iran	D7	56
Bushland, Tx., U.S.	F6	128
Bushman Land, reg., S. Afr.	F4	70
Bushnell, Fl., U.S.	H3	116
Bushnell, Il., U.S.	D7	120
Bushtyna, Ukr.	A10	26
Busia, Ug.	D6	66
Businga, D.R.C.	D4	66
Busira, stm., D.R.C.	E3	66
Buskerud, state, Nor.	F3	8
Busko-Zdrój, Pol.	F16	16
Buṣrá ash-Shām, Syria	F7	58
Busselton, Austl.	F3	74
Bussey, Ia., U.S.	C5	120
Bussum, Neth.	B14	14
Bustamante, Mex.	B8	100
Busto Arsizio, Italy	E5	22
Busuanga Island, i., Phil.	D2	52
Busu-Djanoa, D.R.C.	D4	66
Büsum, Ger.	B4	16
Buta, D.R.C.	D4	66
Buta Ranquil, Arg.	H2	92
Butare, Rw.	E5	66
Butaritari, at., Kir.	C8	72
Bute, Island of, i., Scot., U.K.	F7	12
Bute Inlet, b., B.C., Can.	F5	138
Butembo, D.R.C.	D5	66
Butera, Italy	G8	24
Butere, Kenya	D6	66
Butha-Buthe, Leso.	F9	70
Buthidaung, Mya.	D7	46
Butiá, Braz.	E11	92
Butler, Ga., U.S.	D1	116
Butler, In., U.S.	C1	114
Butler, Mo., U.S.	F3	120
Butler, Oh., U.S.	D3	114
Butler, Pa., U.S.	D6	114
Butner, N.C., U.S.	H7	114
Buto, hist., Egypt	G1	58
Buton, Pulau, i., Indon.	F7	44
Butrint, sci., Alb.	E14	24
Butru, Austl.	C2	76
Butte, Mt., U.S.	D14	136
Butte, Ne., U.S.	E14	126
Butte Creek, stm., Ca., U.S.	D4	134
Butte Falls, Or., U.S.	H4	136
Butternut, Wi., U.S.	E8	118
Butterworth, Malay.	J5	48
Butterworth, S. Afr.	H9	70
Buttle Lake, l., B.C., Can.	G5	138
Button Islands, is., Nu., Can.	C17	106
Buttonwillow, Ca., U.S.	H6	134
Butuan, Phil.	F5	52
Buturlino, Russia	I21	8
Buṭwal, Nepal	E9	54
Butzbach, Ger.	F4	16
Bützow, Ger.	C7	16
Buulobarde, Som.	D9	66
Buur Gaabo, Som.	E8	66
Buurgplaatz, mtn., Lux.	D15	14
Buxtehude, Ger.	C5	16
Buxton, S. Afr.	E7	70
Buxton, Eng., U.K.	H11	12
Buxton, N.C., U.S.	A10	116
Buxton, Mount, mtn., B.C., Can.	E2	138
Buyant-Uhaa, Mong.	C7	36
Buyr nuur, l., Asia	B8	36
Büyükada, Tur.	C12	28
Büyükçekmece, Tur.	B11	28
Büyükkarıştıran, Tur.	B10	28
Büyükkemikli Burnu, c., Tur.	C9	28
Büyükmenderes, stm., Tur.	F10	28
Buzău, Rom.	D13	26
Buzău, state, Rom.	D13	26
Buzău, stm., Rom.	D13	26
Buzen, Japan	F4	40
Búzi, stm., Moz.	A12	70
Buziaș, Rom.	D8	26
Buzuluk, Russia	D8	32
Byādgi, India	D2	53
Byam Channel, strt., Nu., Can.	A19	140
Byam Martin Island, i., Nu., Can.	B19	140
Bycen', Bela.	H8	10
Byčki, Russia	F17	10
Byczyna, Pol.	E14	16
Bydgoszcz, Pol.	C13	16
Bydgoszcz, state, Pol.	C13	16
Byelorussia see Belarus, ctry., Eur.	E14	6
Byers, Tx., U.S.	G10	128
Byesville, Oh., U.S.	E4	114
Bygdin, l., Nor.	F3	8
Byhalia, Ms., U.S.	C9	122
Byhau, Bela.	G13	10
Bykle, Nor.	G2	8
Bylnice, Czech Rep.	G14	16
Bylot Island, i., Nu., Can.	A15	106
Byng Inlet, On., Can.	C9	112
Bynum, Mt., U.S.	C14	136
Bynum, N.C., U.S.	I6	114
Byrd, Lac, l., Qc., Can.	A13	112
Byrnedale, Pa., U.S.	C7	114
Byro, Austl.	E3	74
Byron, Ga., U.S.	D2	116
Byron, Il., U.S.	B8	120
Byron, Cape, c., Austl.	G9	76
Byron Bay, Austl.	G9	76
Byrranga, gory, mts., Russia	B8	34
Bystřice pod Hostýnem, Czech Rep.	G13	16
Bytantaj, stm., Russia	C15	34
Bytča, Slov.	G14	16
Bytom, Pol.	F14	16
Bytoš', Russia	G17	10
Bytów, Pol.	B13	16

C

Name	Map Ref.	Page
Ca, stm., Asia	C7	48
Caacupé, Para.	B9	92
Caaguazú, Para.	B9	92
Caaguazú, state, Para.	B10	92
Caála, Ang.	C2	68
Caapiranga, Braz.	I11	86
Caatinga, Braz.	I3	88
Caazapá, Para.	C9	92
Caazapá, state, Para.	C9	92
Cabaiguán, Cuba	A8	102
Cabaliana, Lago, l., Braz.	I11	86
Caballococha, Peru	D3	84
Caballo Reservoir, res., N.M., U.S.	K9	132
Cabanatuan, Phil.	C3	52
Cabano, Qc., Can.	C8	110
Cabarroguis, Phil.	B3	52
Cabedelo, Braz.	D8	88
Cabeza del Buey, Spain	F5	20
Cabezas, Bol.	C4	90
Cabildo, Arg.	I7	92
Cabimas, Ven.	B6	86
Cabinda, Ang.	B1	68
Cabinda, state, Ang.	B1	68
Cabinet Mountains, mts., U.S.	B10	136
Cable, Wi., U.S.	E7	118
Cabo, Braz.	E8	88
Cabo Blanco, Arg.	I3	90
Cabo Frio, Braz.	L4	88
Cabonga, Réservoir, res., Qc., Can.	F15	106
Cabool, Mo., U.S.	G5	120
Caboolture, Austl.	F9	76
Caborca, Mex.	F6	98
Cabo Rojo, P.R.	B1	104a
Cabot, Ar., U.S.	C7	122
Cabot Head, c., On., Can.	C8	112
Cabot Strait, strt., Can.	j21	107a
Cabourg, Fr.	E8	14
Cabra Corral, Embalse, res., Arg.	B5	92
Cabramurra, Austl.	J7	76
Cabrera, stm., Col.	F4	86
Cabrera, Illa de, i., Spain	E13	20
Cabri, Sk., Can.	D5	124
Cabriel, stm., Spain	E9	20
Cabrillo National Monument, p.o.i., Ca., U.S.	K8	134
Cabrobó, Braz.	E6	88
Cabruta, Ven.	D8	86
Cabullónes, Punta, c., P.R.	C2	104a
Čabusy, Bela.	H11	10
Cabuyaro, Col.	E5	86
Caçador, Braz.	C12	92
Čačak, Serb.	F7	26
Caçapava, Braz.	L3	88
Caçapava do Sul, Braz.	E11	92
Cacapon, stm., W.V., U.S.	E7	114
Cacequi, Braz.	D10	92
Cáceres, Braz.	G6	84
Cáceres, Col.	D4	86
Cáceres, Spain	E4	20
Cáceres, co., Spain	E4	20
Čačèrsk, Bela.	H13	10
Cache, stm., Ar., U.S.	B7	122
Cache, stm., Il., U.S.	G8	120
Cache Creek, B.C., Can.	F9	138
Cache Creek, stm., Ca., U.S.	E3	134
Cache la Poudre, stm., Co., U.S.	G7	126
Cache Peak, mtn., Id., U.S.	A3	132
Cachi, Arg.	B4	92
Cachimbo, Braz.	E7	84
Cachimbo, Serra do, mts., Braz.	E6	84
Cachoeira Alta, Braz.	C6	90
Cachoeira de Manteiga, Braz.	I3	88
Cachoeira do Sul, Braz.	E11	92
Cachoeiro de Itapemirim, Braz.	K5	88
Cachos, Punta, c., Chile	C2	92
Cachuela Esperanza, Bol.	B3	90
Căciulați, Rom.	E13	26
Cacolo, Ang.	C2	68
Caconda, Ang.	C2	68
Cactus, Tx., U.S.	E6	128
Cactus Flat, pl., Nv., U.S.	F9	134
Cacuaco, Ang.	B1	68
Caculé, Braz.	H4	88
Çacuri, Ven.	E9	86
Čadan, Russia	D16	32
Čadca, Slov.	G14	16
Caddo, Ok., U.S.	C2	122
Caddo, stm., Ar., U.S.	C5	122
Caddo Lake, res., U.S.	E4	122
Caddo Mills, Tx., U.S.	D2	122
Cadell, stm., Austl.	D3	76
Cadena, Cerro, mtn., Mex.	I3	130
Cadena, Punta, c., P.R.	B1	104a
Cadillac, Sk., Can.	E6	124
Cadillac, Fr.	E5	18
Cadillac, Mi., U.S.	D4	112
Cádiz, Spain	H4	20
Cadiz, Ky., U.S.	H10	120
Cádiz, co., Spain	H5	20
Cádiz, Bahía de, b., Spain	H4	20
Cadiz Lake, l., Ca., U.S.	I1	132
Čadobec, stm., Russia	C17	32
Cadomin, Ab., Can.	C13	138
Cadore, reg., Italy	D9	22
Cadott, Wi., U.S.	G7	118
Cadwell, Ga., U.S.	D2	116
Čaek, Kyrg.	F12	32
Caen, Fr.	E8	14
Caengo (Kwenge), stm., Afr.	B2	68
Caernarfon, Wales, U.K.	H8	12
Caernarfon Bay, b., Wales, U.K.	H8	12
Caerphilly, Wales, U.K.	J9	12
Caesarea see Qesari, Horbat, sci., Isr.	F5	58
Caeté, Braz.	J4	88
Caetité, Braz.	H4	88
Cafayate, Arg.	C4	92
Cagayan, stm., Phil.	A3	52
Cagayan de Oro, Phil.	F5	52
Cagayan Islands, is., Phil.	F3	52
Cagayan Sulu Island, i., Phil.	G2	52
Čagda, Russia	E15	34
Çağış, Tur.	D10	28
Cagliari, Italy	E3	24
Cagliari, Golfo di, b., Italy	E3	24
Cagliari, Stagno di, l., Italy	E2	24
Cagnes-sur-Mer, Fr.	F13	18
Čagoda, stm., Russia	A17	10
Čagodošča, stm., Russia	A18	10
Caguán, stm., Col.	G4	86
Caguas, P.R.	B3	104a
Cahaba, stm., Al., U.S.	E11	122
Cahama, Ang.	D1	68
Caher, Ire.	I4	12
Cahokia, Il., U.S.	F7	120
Cahora Bassa, Albufeira, res., Moz.	D5	68
Cahors, Fr.	E7	18
Cahto Peak, mtn., Ca., U.S.	D2	134
Cahuinari, stm., Col.	H6	86
Cahul, Mol.	D15	26
Caí, stm., Braz.	D12	92
Caianda, Ang.	C3	68
Caiapó, Serra do, mts., Braz.	G7	84
Caibarién, Cuba	A8	102
Cai Bau, Dao, i., Viet.	B8	48
Caiçara, Braz.	D8	88
Caicara, Caño, stm., Ven.	D7	86
Caicara de Maturín, Ven.	C10	86
Caicara de Orinoco, Ven.	D8	86
Caicedonia, Col.	E4	86
Caicó, Braz.	D7	88
Caicos Islands, is., T./C. Is.	B11	102
Caicos Passage, strt., N.A.	B11	102
Caijiapo, China	D2	42
Caima Bay, b., Phil.	D4	52
Caimanera, Cuba	C10	102
Caimanero, Laguna del, l., Mex.	D5	100
Cain Creek, stm., S.D., U.S.	C14	126
Cai Nuoc, Viet.	H7	48
Cairari, Braz.	B1	88
Caird Coast, cst., Ant.	C3	81
Cairns, Austl.	A5	76
Cairo see El-Qâhira, Egypt	H2	58
Cairo, Ga., U.S.	F1	116
Cairo, Il., U.S.	G8	120
Cairo, Ne., U.S.	F14	126
Cairo, W.V., U.S.	E4	114
Cairo Montenotte, Italy	F5	22
Cairu, Braz.	G6	88
Caisleán an Bharraigh see Castlebar, Ire.	H3	12
Caiundo, Ang.	D2	68
Caiwan, China	I4	42
Caizi Hu, l., China	F7	42
Caja de Muertos, Isla, i., P.R.	C2	104a
Cajamarca, Peru	E2	84
Cajapió, Braz.	B3	88
Cajazeiras, Braz.	D6	88
Cajon Summit, p., Ca., U.S.	I8	134
Cajuru, Braz.	K2	88
Caka, China	D4	36
Çakmak, Tur.	A5	58
Čakovec, Cro.	D13	22
Calabar, Nig.	H6	64
Calabozo, Ven.	C8	86
Calabozo, Ensenada de, b., Ven.	B6	86
Calabria, state, Italy	F10	24
Calafat, Rom.	F9	26
Calagua Islands, is., Phil.	C4	52
Calahorra, Spain	B8	20
Calais, Fr.	C10	14
Calalaste, Sierra de, mts., Arg.	B4	92
Calama, Chile	D3	90
Calamar, Col.	B4	86
Calamar, Col.	F5	86
Calamian Group, is., Phil.	E3	52
Calamus, stm., Ne., U.S.	E13	126
Calañas, Spain	G4	20
Calang, Indon.	J2	48
Calapan, Phil.	D3	52
Călărași, Mol.	B15	26
Călărași, Rom.	E14	26
Călărași, state, Rom.	E14	26
Calarcá, Col.	E4	86
Calatafimi, Italy	G6	24
Calatayud, Spain	C9	20
Calau, Ger.	E9	16
Calavite Passage, strt., Phil.	D3	52
Calayan Island, i., Phil.	A3	52
Calbayog, Phil.	D5	52
Calbe, Ger.	E7	16
Calbuco, Chile	H2	90
Calcasieu, stm., La., U.S.	G5	122
Calcasieu Lake, l., La., U.S.	G5	122
Calceta, Ec.	H1	86
Calchaquí, Arg.	D7	92
Calchaquí, stm., Arg.	B4	92
Calçoene, Braz.	C7	84
Calcutta see Kolkata, India	G12	54
Caldaro, Italy	D8	22
Caldas, Col.	D4	86
Caldas, state, Col.	E4	86
Caldas da Rainha, Port.	E1	20
Caldas de Reis, Spain	B2	20
Caldas de Reyes see Caldas de Reis, Spain	B2	20
Caldas Novas, Braz.	I1	88
Caldera, Chile	C2	92
Caldwell, Id., U.S.	G10	136
Caldwell, Ks., U.S.	D11	128
Caldwell, Oh., U.S.	E4	114
Caldwell, Tx., U.S.	G2	122
Caledon, S. Afr.	I4	70
Caledon (Mohokare), stm., Afr.	F8	70
Caledonia, Belize	C3	102
Caledonia, N.S., Can.	F11	110
Caledonia, Ms., U.S.	D10	122
Caledonia, N.Y., U.S.	A8	114
Caledonia, Oh., U.S.	D3	114
Calella, Spain	C13	20
Calen, Austl.	C7	76
Calera, Al., U.S.	D12	122
Caleta Olivia, Arg.	I3	90
Caleufú, Arg.	G5	92
Calexico, Ca., U.S.	K10	134
Calgary, Ab., Can.	E16	138
Calhan, Co., U.S.	B4	128
Calhoun, Al., U.S.	E12	122
Calhoun, Ga., U.S.	C14	122
Calhoun, Mo., U.S.	F4	120
Calhoun, Tn., U.S.	B14	122
Calhoun City, Ms., U.S.	D9	122
Cali, Col.	F3	86
Calico Rock, Ar., U.S.	H5	120
Calicut see Kozhikode, India	F2	53
Caliente, Nv., U.S.	F2	132
California, Mo., U.S.	F5	120
California, state, U.S.	D3	108
California, Golfo de (California, Gulf of), b., Mex.	B2	96
California, Gulf of see California, Golfo de, b., Mex.	B2	96
California Aqueduct, aq., Ca., U.S.	I8	134
Calilegua, Parque Nacional, p.o.i., Arg.	A5	92
Calimere, Point, c., India	F4	53
Calingasta, Arg.	E3	92
Calion, Ar., U.S.	D6	122
Calipatria, Ca., U.S.	J10	134
Calispell Peak, mtn., Wa., U.S.	B9	136
Calistoga, Ca., U.S.	E3	134
Calitri, Italy	D9	24
Calitzdorp, S. Afr.	H5	70
Callabonna, Lake, l., Austl.	G2	76
Callabonna Creek, stm., Austl.	G3	76
Callahan, Mount, mtn., Co., U.S.	D8	132
Callan, Ire.	I5	12
Callander, On., Can.	B10	112
Callao, Peru	F2	84
Callaquén, Volcán, vol., Chile	H2	92
Callaway, Ne., U.S.	F12	126
Calliaqua, St. Vin.	o11	105e
Calling Lake, Ab., Can.	A17	138
Calling Lake, l., Ab., Can.	A17	138
Callosa de Segura, Spain	F9	20
Calmar, Ab., Can.	C17	138
Calmar, Ia., U.S.	A6	120
Calm Lake, l., On., Can.	C6	118
Čal'mny-Varre, Russia	C17	8
Čalna, Russia	F15	8
Caloundra, Austl.	F9	76
Calp, Spain	F11	20
Calpe see Calp, Spain	F11	20
Caltagirone, Italy	G8	24
Caltanissetta, Italy	G8	24
Călugăreni, Rom.	E12	26
Calulo, Ang.	B2	68
Calumet, Mn., U.S.	D5	118
Calumet City, Il., U.S.	G2	112
Calunda, Ang.	C3	68
Caluula, Som.	B10	66
Calvados, state, Fr.	E8	14
Calvert, Al., U.S.	F10	122
Calvert, Tx., U.S.	G2	122
Calvert Island, i., B.C., Can.	E2	138
Calvillo, Mex.	E7	100
Calvin, Ok., U.S.	C2	122
Calvinia, S. Afr.	G4	70
Calw, Ger.	H4	16
Calwa, Ca., U.S.	G6	134
Calypso, N.C., U.S.	A7	116
Camabatela, Ang.	B2	68
Camaçari, Braz.	G6	88
Camacupa, Ang.	C2	68
Camaguán, Ven.	C8	86
Camagüey, Cuba	B9	102
Camaiore, Italy	G7	22
Camajuaní, Cuba	A8	102
Camaná, Peru	G3	84
Camaná, stm., Peru	G3	84
Camanaú, stm., Braz.	H11	86
Camanche Reservoir, res., Ca., U.S.	E4	134
Camapuã, Braz.	C6	90
Camaquã, Braz.	E12	92
Camaquã, stm., Braz.	E11	92
Camará, Braz.	D5	84
Camarajibe, Braz.	D8	88
Camararé, stm., Braz.	F6	84
Camarat, Cap, c., Fr.	F12	18
Camarès, Fr.	F8	18
Camargo, Bol.	D3	90
Camargue, reg., Fr.	F10	18
Camarillo, Ca., U.S.	I6	134
Camarón, Arroyo, stm., Mex.	G7	130
Camarón, Cabo, c., Hond.	D5	102
Camarones, Arg.	H3	90
Camarones, Bahía, b., Arg.	H3	90
Camas Creek, stm., Id., U.S.	F14	136
Camatagua, Embalse de, l., Ven.	C8	86
Ca Mau, Viet.	H7	48
Ca Mau, Mui, c., Viet.	H7	48
Camba, Indon.	F11	50
Cambodia, ctry., Asia	C3	48
Camboon, Austl.	E8	76
Camboriú, Braz.	C13	92
Camborne, Eng., U.K.	K7	12
Cambrai, Fr.	D12	14
Cambria, Ca., U.S.	H4	134
Cambrian Mountains, mts., Wales, U.K.	I9	12
Cambridge, On., Can.	E9	112
Cambridge, N.Z.	C6	80
Cambridge, Eng., U.K.	I12	12
Cambridge, Ia., U.S.	C4	120
Cambridge, Il., U.S.	C7	120
Cambridge, Ma., U.S.	B14	114
Cambridge, Md., U.S.	F9	114
Cambridge, Mn., U.S.	F5	118
Cambridge, Ne., U.S.	A8	128
Cambridge, N.Y., U.S.	G3	110
Cambridge, Oh., U.S.	D4	114
Cambridge Bay see Ikaluktutiak, Nu., Can.	B10	106
Cambridge Fiord, b., Nu., Can.	A15	106
Cambridge Springs, Pa., U.S.	C5	114
Cambrils, Spain	C11	20
Cambuí, Braz.	L2	88
Cambulo, Ang.	B3	68
Cambundi-Catembo, Ang.	C2	68
Camden, Austl.	J8	76
Camden, Al., U.S.	F11	122
Camden, Ar., U.S.	D6	122
Camden, Me., U.S.	F7	110
Camden, N.C., U.S.	H9	114
Camden, N.J., U.S.	E10	114
Camden, N.Y., U.S.	E14	112
Camden, Oh., U.S.	E1	114
Camden, S.C., U.S.	B5	116
Camden, Tn., U.S.	H9	120
Camden Bay, b., Ak., U.S.	B11	140
Camdenton, Mo., U.S.	G5	120
Camels Hump, mtn., Vt., U.S.	F3	110
Camenca, Mol.	A15	26
Camerino, Italy	G10	22
Cameron, Mo., U.S.	E3	120
Cameron, Tx., U.S.	D10	130
Cameron, Wi., U.S.	F7	118
Cameron, W.V., U.S.	E5	114
Cameron Hills, hills, Can.	D7	106
Cameroon, ctry., Afr.	C2	66
Cameroon Mountain, vol., Cam.	D1	66
Camerota, Italy	D9	24
Cametá, Braz.	B1	88
Çamiçi Gölü, l., Tur.	F10	28
Camiguin Island, i., Phil.	F5	52
Camiguin Island, i., Phil.	A3	52
Camiling, Phil.	C3	52
Camilla, Ga., U.S.	E1	116
Camino, Ca., U.S.	E5	134
Camiranga, Braz.	A2	88
Camiri, Bol.	D4	90
Camissombo, Ang.	B3	68
Çamlıdere, Tur.	C15	28
Çamlıdere, Tur.	A10	58
Cam Lo, Viet.	D8	48
Camocim, Braz.	B5	88
Camooweal, Austl.	C7	74
Camorta Island, i., India	G7	46
Camotes Islands, is., Phil.	E5	52
Camotes Sea, s., Phil.	E5	52
Campagna di Roma, reg., Italy	C6	24
Campaign, Tn., U.S.	B13	122
Campana, Arg.	G8	92
Campana, Isla, i., Chile	I1	90
Campanario, Spain	F5	20
Campania, state, Italy	D8	24
Campano, Appennino, mts., Italy	C8	24
Campaspe, stm., Austl.	C6	76
Campbell, S. Afr.	F6	70
Campbell, Ca., U.S.	F4	134
Campbell, Mo., U.S.	H7	120
Campbell, Ne., U.S.	A10	128
Campbell, Cape, c., N.Z.	E6	80
Campbellford, On., Can.	D12	112
Campbell Hill, hill, Oh., U.S.	D2	114
Campbell Hills, hill, St. Vin.	p11	105e
Campbell Island, B.C., Can.	D2	138
Campbell Island, i., N.Z.	I7	72
Campbell Lake, l., B.C., Can.	G5	138
Campbell Plateau, unds.	O20	142
Campbellpore, Pak.	B4	54
Campbell River, B.C., Can.	F5	138
Campbell's Bay, Qc., Can.	C13	112
Campbellsport, Wi., U.S.	E1	112
Campbellton, N.B., Can.	C10	110
Campbellton, P.E., Can.	D12	110
Campbellton, Fl., U.S.	G13	122
Campbelltown, Austl.	J8	76
Campbell Town, Austl.	n13	77a
Campbeltown, Scot., U.K.	F7	12
Campeche, Mex.	C2	102
Campeche, state, Mex.	C2	102
Campeche, Bahía de, b., Mex.	D6	96
Campeche, Gulf of see Campeche, Bahía de, b., Mex.	E13	100
Campechuela, Cuba	B9	102
Câmpeni, Rom.	C10	26
Camperdown, Austl.	L4	76
Camperville, Mb., Can.	C13	124
Cam Pha, Viet.	B8	48
Camp Hill, Al., U.S.	E13	122
Camp Hill, Pa., U.S.	H12	112
Câmpia Turzii, Rom.	C10	26
Campidano, val., Italy	E2	24
Campiglia Marittima, Italy	G7	22
Campillos, Spain	G6	20
Câmpina, Rom.	D12	26
Campina, reg., Spain	G5	20
Campina Grande, Braz.	D7	88
Campinas, Braz.	L2	88
Campina Verde, Braz.	J1	88
Campoalegre, Col.	F4	86
Campo Alegre de Goiás, Braz.	I2	88
Campobasso, Italy	C8	24
Campo Belo, Braz.	K3	88
Campo de Criptana, Spain	E7	20
Campo Erê, Braz.	C11	92
Campo Florido, Braz.	J1	88
Campo Formoso, Braz.	F5	88
Campo Gallo, Arg.	C6	92
Campo Grande, Braz.	D6	90
Campo Largo, Arg.	C7	92
Campo Largo, Braz.	B13	92
Campo Maior, Braz.	C4	88
Campo Maior, Port.	F3	20
Campo Mourão, Braz.	A11	92
Campo Novo, Braz.	C11	92
Campos, Braz.	K5	88
Campos Altos, Braz.	J2	88
Campo Santo, Arg.	B5	92
Campos Belos, Braz.	G2	88
Campos do Jordão, Braz.	L3	88
Campos Gerais, Braz.	K2	88
Campos Novos, Braz.	C12	92
Campos Sales, Braz.	D5	88
Camp Point, Il., U.S.	D6	120
Campti, La., U.S.	F5	122
Campton, Ky., U.S.	G2	114
Câmpulung, Rom.	D11	26
Câmpulung Moldovenesc, Rom.	B12	26
Campuya, stm., Peru	H4	86
Camp Verde, Az., U.S.	I4	132
Cam Ranh, Viet.	G9	48
Cam Ranh, Vinh, b., Viet.	G9	48
Cam Ranh Bay see Cam Ranh, Vinh, b., Viet.	G9	48
Camrose, Ab., Can.	C18	138
Camsell, stm., N.T., Can.	B7	106
Camuy, P.R.	B2	104a
Çan, Tur.	C10	28
Canaan, Vt., U.S.	E5	110
Cana-brava, stm., Braz.	G1	88
Cana-brava, stm., Braz.	G1	88
Canada, ctry., N.A.	D9	106
Canada Basin, unds.	A25	142
Cañada de Gómez, Arg.	F7	92
Cañada Honda, Arg.	F3	92
Canadian, Tx., U.S.	F8	128
Canadian, stm., U.S.	F13	128
Canadian, Deep Fork, stm., Ok., U.S.	F13	128
Canaguá, stm., Ven.	D7	86
Canaima, Parque Nacional, p.o.i., Ven.	E10	86
Canajoharie, N.Y., U.S.	B11	114
Çanakkale, Tur.	C9	28
Çanakkale, state, Tur.	D9	28
Çanakkale Boğazı (Dardanelles), strt., Tur.	C9	28
Canala, N. Cal.	m15	79d
Canal Fulton, Oh., U.S.	D4	114
Canal Point, Fl., U.S.	J5	116
Canals, Arg.	F6	92
Canal Winchester, Oh., U.S.	E3	114
Canandaigua, N.Y., U.S.	B8	114
Cananea, Mex.	F7	98
Canápolis, Braz.	J1	88
Cañar, Ec.	I2	86
Cañar, state, Ec.	I2	86
Canarias, Islas (Canary Islands), is., Spain	D1	64
Canarreos, Archipiélago de los, is., Cuba	B6	102
Canary Basin, unds.	F11	144
Canary Islands see Canarias, Islas, is., Spain	D1	64
Cañas, C.R.	G5	102
Canaseraga, N.Y., U.S.	B8	114
Canastota, N.Y., U.S.	E14	112
Canatlán, Mex.	C6	100
Canaveral, Cape, c., Fl., U.S.	H5	116
Canaveral National Seashore, p.o.i., Fl., U.S.	H5	116
Cañaveras, Spain	D8	20
Canavese, hist. reg., Italy	E4	22
Canavieiras, Braz.	H6	88
Canbelego, Austl.	H6	76
Canberra, Austl.	J7	76
Canby, Ca., U.S.	B5	134
Canby, Mn., U.S.	G2	118
Canby, Or., U.S.	E4	136
Cancon, Fr.	E6	18
Cancún, Mex.	B4	102
Cancún, Punta, c., Mex.	B4	102
Çandarlı Körfezi, b., Tur.	E9	28
Candé, Fr.	G7	14
Candeias, Braz.	G6	88
Candeias, Braz.	K3	88
Candela, stm., Mex.	B8	100
Candelaria, Arg.	C10	92
Candelária, Braz.	D11	92
Candelaria, stm., Mex.	C2	102
Candelo, Austl.	K7	76
Cándido Aguilar, Mex.	C9	100
Cândido Mendes, Braz.	A3	88
Candlemas Islands, is., S. Geor.	K12	82
Candlestick, Ms., U.S.	E8	122
Cando, N.D., U.S.	F14	124
Candon, Phil.	B3	52
Candor, N.C., U.S.	A6	116
Candor, N.Y., U.S.	B9	114
Canea see Chaniá, Grc.	H7	28
Canela, Braz.	D12	92
Canelas, Mex.	C5	100
Canelli, Italy	F5	22
Canelones, Ur.	G9	92
Cañete, Chile	H1	92
Caney, stm., U.S.	E13	128
Caney Creek, stm., Tx., U.S.	F12	130
Canfranc, Spain	B10	20
Cangas de Narcea, Spain	A4	20
Cangas de Onís, Spain	A5	20
Cangkuang, Tanjung, c., Indon.	G4	50
Cangombe, Ang.	C2	68
Canguaretama, Braz.	D8	88
Canguçu, Braz.	E11	92
Cangumbe, Ang.	C2	68
Cangxi, China	F1	42
Cangzhou, China	B7	42
Caniapiscau, stm., Qc., Can.	D17	106
Caniapiscau, Lac, res., Qc., Can.	E17	106
Canicattì, Italy	G7	24

Canim Lake – Centralina I•11

Name Map Ref. Page

Canim Lake, B.C., Can. E10 138
Canim Lake, l., B.C., Can. E9 138
Canindé, Braz. C6 88
Canindé, stm., Braz. D4 88
Canindeyú, state, Para. B10 92
Canisteo, N.Y., U.S. B8 114
Canistota, S.D., U.S. D15 126
Cañitas de Felipe Pescador, Mex. D7 100
Canjáyar, Spain G8 20
Çankırı, Tur. A3 56
Çankırı, state, Tur. C15 28
Canmore, Ab., Can. E15 138
Cannanore, India F2 53
Cannelton, In., U.S. G11 120
Cannes, Fr. F13 18
Canning, N.S., Can. E12 110
Cannington, On., Can. D10 112
Cannock, Eng., U.K. I10 12
Cannon, stm., Mn., U.S. G5 118
Cannonball, stm., N.D., U.S. A11 126
Cannon Beach, Or., U.S. E2 136
Cannon Falls, Mn., U.S. G6 118
Cannonvale, Austl. C7 76
Cann River, Austl. K7 76
Canoas, Braz. D12 92
Canoas, stm., Braz. C12 92
Canoe, B.C., Can. F11 138
Canoe, stm., B.C., Can. D12 138
Canoinhas, Braz. C12 92
Canon City, Co., U.S. C3 128
Cañon de Río Blanco, Parque Nacional, p.o.i., Mex. F10 100
Canonsburg, Pa., U.S. D5 114
Canoochee, stm., Ga., U.S. E4 116
Canora, Sk., Can. C11 124
Canosa di Púglia, Italy C10 24
Canossa, sci., Italy F7 22
Canouan, i., St. Vin. p11 105e
Canova, S.D., U.S. D15 126
Canova Beach, Fl., U.S. H5 116
Cañovanas, P.R. B4 104a
Canowindra, Austl. I7 76
Canso, N.S., Can. E16 110
Cantabria, state, Spain A6 20
Cantabrian Mountains see Cantábrica, Cordillera, mts., Spain A5 20
Cantábrica, Cordillera, mts., Spain A5 20
Cantagalo, Braz. K4 88
Cantal, state, Fr. D8 18
Cantalejo, Spain C7 20
Cantanhede, Braz. B3 88
Cantaura, Ven. C9 86
Canterbury, Eng., U.K. J14 12
Canterbury Bight, b., N.Z. G4 80
Canterbury Plains, pl., N.Z. G4 80
Can Tho, Viet. G7 48
Canton *see* Guangzhou, China J5 42
Canton, Il., U.S. D7 120
Canton, Ks., U.S. C11 128
Canton, Mn., U.S. H7 118
Canton, Mo., U.S. D6 120
Canton, Ms., U.S. E8 122
Canton, N.Y., U.S. D14 112
Canton, Oh., U.S. D4 114
Canton, Ok., U.S. E10 128
Canton, Pa., U.S. C9 114
Canton, S.D., U.S. H2 118
Canton, Tx., U.S. E3 122
Canton see Kanton, i., Kir. D9 72
Canton Lake, res., Ok., U.S. E10 128
Cantonment, Fl., U.S. G11 122
Cantù, Italy E6 22
Cantu, stm., Braz. B11 92
Cantwell, Ak., U.S. D10 140
Cañuelas, Arg. G8 92
Canumã, Braz. D6 84
Canutama, Braz. E5 84
Čany, Russia C13 32
Čany, ozero, l., Russia D13 32
Canyon, Tx., U.S. G7 128
Canyon City, Or., U.S. F8 136
Canyon Creek, Ab., Can. A15 138
Canyon de Chelly National Monument, p.o.i., Az., U.S. G7 132
Canyon Ferry Lake, res., Mt., U.S. D15 136
Canyon Lake, res., Tx., U.S. E9 130
Canyonlands National Park, p.o.i., Ut., U.S. E6 132
Canyonville, Or., U.S. H3 136
Cao, stm., China D5 38
Cao Bang, Viet. A7 48
Cao Lanh, Viet. G7 48
Caombo, Ang. B2 68
Caorle, Italy E9 22
Caoxian, China D6 42
Cap, Pointe du, c., St. Luc. I7 105c
Capac, Mi., U.S. E7 112
Capanaparo, stm., S.A. D8 86
Capanema, Braz. D8 84
Capão Bonito, Braz. L1 88
Capão Doce, Morro do, mtn., Braz. C12 92
Caparaó, Parque Nacional do, p.o.i., Braz. K4 88
Caparo Viejo, stm., Ven. D6 86
Capatárida, Ven. B6 86
Cap aux Meules, Île du, i., Qc., Can. C14 110
Cap-Chat, Qc., Can. A10 110
Cap-de-la-Madeleine, Qc., Can. D4 110
Cape, stm., Austl. C5 76
Cape Barren Island, i., Austl. n13 77a
Cape Basin, unds. L14 144
Cape Breton Highlands National Park, p.o.i., N.S., Can. D16 110
Cape Breton Island, i., N.S., Can. D16 110
Cape Charles, Va., U.S. G9 114
Cape Coast, Ghana H4 64
Cape Cod Bay, b., Ma., U.S. C15 114
Cape Cod National Seashore, p.o.i., Ma., U.S. B16 114
Cape Coral, Fl., U.S. J4 116
Cape Dorset *see* Kinngait, Nu., Can. C15 106
Cape Elizabeth, Me., U.S. G6 110
Cape Fear, stm., N.C., U.S. B8 116
Cape Girardeau, Mo., U.S. G8 120
Cape Hatteras National Seashore, p.o.i., N.C., U.S. A10 116
Capelinha, Braz. I4 88
Cape Lisburne, Ak., U.S. C6 140
Capel'ka, Russia B11 10
Capella, Austl. D7 76
Capelongo, Ang. C2 68
Cape Lookout National Seashore, p.o.i., N.C., U.S. B9 116
Cape May, N.J., U.S. F10 114
Cape May Court House, N.J., U.S. E11 114
Cape Porpoise, Me., U.S. G6 110
Capernaum see Kefar Nahum, sci., Isr. F6 58
Cape Sable Island, i., N.S., Can. G11 110
Capesterre, Guad. i6 105c
Capesterre, Pointe de la, c., Guad. h5 105c
Capesterre-Belle-Eau, Guad. h5 105c
Cape Tormentine, N.B., Can. D12 110
Cape Town (Kaapstad), S. Afr. H4 70
Cape Verde, ctry., Afr. k9 65a
Cape Verde Basin, unds. G10 144
Cape Vincent, N.Y., U.S. D13 112
Cape York Peninsula, pen., Austl. B8 74
Cap-Haïtien, Haiti C11 102

Capilla del Monte, Arg. E5 92
Capim, stm., Braz. A2 88
Capinota, Bol. C3 90
Capira, Pan. H8 102
Capitan, N.M., U.S. H3 128
Capitán Arturo Prat, sci., Ant. B34 81
Capitán Bado, Para. D5 90
Capitán Bermúdez, Arg. F7 92
Capitán Meza, Para. C10 92
Capitão Enéas, Braz. I4 88
Capitola, Ca., U.S. G4 134
Capitol Peak, mtn., Nv., U.S. B8 134
Capitol Reef National Park, p.o.i., Ut., U.S. E5 132
Capivara, Represa de, res., Braz. D6 90
Capivari, Braz. L2 88
Capivari, stm., Braz. G6 88
Cap-Pelé, N.B., Can. D12 110
Cappella Islands, is., V.I.U.S. e7 104b
Capraia, Italy G6 22
Capraia, Isola di, i., Italy G6 22
Caprara, Punta, c., Italy C2 24
Caprarola, Italy B6 24
Capreol, On., Can. B9 112
Caprera, Isola, i., Italy C3 24
Capri, Italy D8 24
Capri, Isola di, i., Italy D8 24
Capricorn Channel, strt., Austl. D9 76
Capricorn Group, is., Austl. D9 76
Caprivi Strip, hist. reg., Nmb. D3 68
Capron, Il., U.S. B9 120
Captain Cook, Hi., U.S. d6 78a
Captain Cook Monument, hist., Norf. I. x25 78i
Captains Flat, Austl. J7 76
Capua, Italy C8 24
Capucapu, stm., Braz. H12 86
Capucin, c., Dom. i5 105c
Capulin Volcano National Monument, p.o.i., N.M., U.S. E5 128
Caquetá, state, Col. G4 86
Caquetá (Japurá), stm., S.A. H7 86
Čara, Russia E12 34
Čara, stm., Russia E12 34
Carabinani, stm., Braz. I10 86
Carabobo, state, Ven. B7 86
Caracal, Rom. E11 26
Caracaraí, Braz. G11 86
Caracas, Ven. B8 86
Caracol, Braz. E4 88
Caraguatatuba, Braz. L3 88
Caraguatay, Para. B9 92
Carajás, Braz. E7 84
Carajás, Serra dos, hills, Braz. E7 84
Carakol, sci., Belize D3 102
Caranavi, Bol. C3 90
Carandaí, Braz. K4 88
Carangola, Braz. K4 88
Caransebeş, Rom. D9 26
Carapá, stm., Para. B10 92
Carapajó, Braz. B1 88
Cara-Paraná, stm., Col. H5 86
Carapina, Braz. K5 88
Caraquet, N.B., Can. C11 110
Caraş-Severin, state, Rom. D8 26
Caratasca, Laguna de, b., Hond. E5 102
Caratinga, Braz. J4 88
Carauari, Braz. D4 84
Caraúbas, Braz. C7 88
Caravaca de la Cruz, Spain F8 20
Caravelas, Braz. I6 88
Caravelí, Peru G3 84
Caravelle, Presqu'île la, pen., Mart. k7 105c
Caraway, Ar., U.S. B8 122
Carayaó, Para. B9 92
Carazinho, Braz. D11 92
Carballiño, Spain B2 20
Carballo, Spain A2 20
Carberry, Mb., Can. E14 124
Carbon, Ab., Can. E17 138
Carbon, Tx., U.S. B9 130
Carbonara, Capo, c., Italy E3 24
Carbondale, Co., U.S. D9 132
Carbondale, Il., U.S. G8 120
Carbondale, Pa., U.S. C10 114
Carbonear, Nf., Can. j23 107a
Carboneras de Guadazaón, Spain E9 20
Carbon Hill, Al., U.S. D11 122
Carbonia, Italy E2 24
Carcagente *see* Carcaixent, Spain E10 20
Carcaixent, Spain E10 20
Carcajou, stm., N.T., Can. B5 106
Carcans, Lac de, b., Fr. D4 18
Carcarañá, Arg. F7 92
Carcarañá, stm., Arg. F7 92
Carcassonne, Fr. F8 18
Carchi, state, Ec. G3 86
Carcross, Yk., Can. C3 106
Çardak, Tur. F12 28
Cárdenas, Cuba A7 102
Cárdenas, Mex. F12 100
Cárdenas, Mex. D9 100
Cárdenas, Bahía de, b., Cuba A7 102
Cardiel, Lago, l., Arg. I2 90
Cardiff, Wales, U.K. J9 12
Cardigan, P.E., Can. D14 110
Cardigan, Wales, U.K. I8 12
Cardigan Bay, b., Wales, U.K. I8 12
Cardinal, On., Can. D14 112
Cardona, Ur. F9 92
Cardonal, Punta, c., Mex. A3 100
Cardoso, Ur. F9 92
Cardston, Ab., Can. G17 138
Cardwell, Austl. B5 76
Cardwell, Mo., U.S. H7 120
Cardwell Mountain, mtn., Tn., U.S. B13 122
Čardžev, Turkmen. B9 56
Carei, Rom. B9 26
Careiro, Braz. I12 86
Careiro, Ilha do, i., Braz. I12 86
Carèja, Bela. F12 10
Carencro, La., U.S. G6 122
Carey, Oh., U.S. D2 114
Carey, Lake, l., Austl. E4 74
Carey Downs, Austl. E3 74
Cargados Carajos Shoals, is., Mrts. K9 142
Carhaix-Plouguer, Fr. F5 14
Carhué, Arg. H6 92
Cariacica, Braz. K5 88
Cariaco, Golfo de, b., Ven. B9 86
Caribbean Sea, s. D7 82
Cariboo, stm., B.C., Can. D9 138
Cariboo Mountains, mts., B.C., Can. D10 138
Caribou, Me., U.S. D8 110
Caribou Lake, l., On., Can. A9 118
Caribou Mountain, mtn., Me., U.S. E6 110
Caribou Mountains, mts., Ab., Can. D7 106
Carichic, Mex. B5 100
Caridade, Braz. C6 88
Carigara, Phil. E5 52
Carignan, Fr. E14 14
Carinda, Austl. H6 76
Carinhanha, Braz. H4 88
Carinhanha, stm., Braz. H3 88
Carini, Italy F7 24
Carinthia see Kärnten, state, Aus. D10 22
Caripito, Ven. B10 86
Carira, Braz. F7 88
Cariré, Braz. C5 88
Cariús, Braz. D6 88
Carleton, Mi., U.S. B2 114

Carleton, Mount, mtn., N.B., Can. C10 110
Carleton Place, On., Can. C13 112
Carletonville, S. Afr. E8 70
Cârlibaba, Rom. B12 26
Carlin, Nv., U.S. C9 134
Carlingford Lough, b., Eur. H7 12
Carlinville, Il., U.S. E8 120
Carlisle, Eng., U.K. G9 12
Carlisle, Ia., U.S. C4 120
Carlisle, In., U.S. F10 120
Carlisle, Ky., U.S. F1 114
Carlisle, Pa., U.S. D8 114
Carl Junction, Mo., U.S. G3 120
Carlos, Isla, i., Chile J2 90
Carlos Casares, Arg. G7 92
Carlos Chagas, Braz. I5 88
Carlos Pellegrini, Arg. E6 92
Carlow, Ire. I5 12
Carlow, state, Ire. I6 12
Carloway, Scot., U.K. C6 12
Carlsbad *see* Karlovy Vary, Czech Rep. F8 16
Carlsbad, Ca., U.S. J8 134
Carlsbad, N.M., U.S. B3 130
Carlsbad, Tx., U.S. C7 130
Carlsbad Caverns National Park, p.o.i., N.M., U.S. B3 130
Carlsberg Ridge, unds. I9 142
Carlton, Or., U.S. E3 136
Carlton, Tx., U.S. C9 130
Carlyle, Sk., Can. E11 124
Carlyle Lake, res., Il., U.S. F8 120
Carmacks, Yk., Can. C3 106
Carmagnola, Italy F4 22
Carman, Mb., Can. E16 124
Carmangay, Ab., Can. F17 138
Carmarthen, Wales, U.K. J8 12
Carmarthen Bay, b., Wales, U.K. J8 12
Carmel, Ca., U.S. G3 134
Carmel, In., U.S. I3 112
Carmel, N.Y., U.S. G16 112
Carmel Head, c., Wales, U.K. H8 12
Carmelo, Ur. F8 92
Carmel Valley, Ca., U.S. G4 134
Carmen *see* Ciudad del Carmen, Mex. F12 100
Carmen, stm., Chile D2 92
Carmen, Isla, i., Mex. C3 100
Carmen, Isla del, i., Mex. F13 100
Carmen de Areco, Arg. G8 92
Carmen de Patagones, Arg. H4 90
Carmi, Il., U.S. F9 120
Carmila, Austl. C7 76
Carmine, Tx., U.S. D11 130
Carmo do Paranaíba, Braz. J2 88
Carmona, Spain G5 20
Carmópolis de Minas, Braz. K3 88
Carnarvon, Austl. D2 74
Carnarvon, S. Afr. G5 70
Carnarvon National Park, p.o.i., Austl. E6 76
Čarnaučycy, Bela. H6 10
Carnduff, Sk., Can. E12 124
Carnegie, Austl. E4 74
Carnegie, Lake, l., Austl. E4 74
Carney Island, i., Ant. C29 81
Carnia, reg., Italy D9 22
Carnic Alps, mts., Eur. D9 22
Car Nicobar Island, i., India G7 46
Carnot, C.A.R. D3 66
Carnoustie, Scot., U.K. E10 12
Carnsore Point, c., Ire. I6 12
Carnwath, stm., N.T., Can. B5 106
Caro, Mi., U.S. E6 112
Carol City, Fl., U.S. K5 116
Carolina, Braz. D2 88
Carolina, P.R. B4 104a
Carolina, S. Afr. E10 70
Carolina Beach, N.C., U.S. B8 116
Caroline, at., Kir. D12 72
Caroline Islands, is., Oc. C5 72
Caron, Sk., Can. D8 124
Caroní, stm., Ven. C10 86
Carora, Ven. B6 86
Carpathian Mountains, mts., Eur. B13 26
Carpaţii Meridionali (Transylvanian Alps), mts., Rom. D11 26
Carpentaria, Gulf of, b., Austl. B7 74
Carpenter, Wy., U.S. F8 126
Carpenter Lake, res., B.C., Can. F8 138
Carpentersville, Il., U.S. B9 120
Carpentras, Fr. E11 18
Carpi, Italy F7 22
Carpina, Braz. D8 88
Cărpineni, Mol. C15 26
Carpinteria, Ca., U.S. I6 134
Carpio, N.D., U.S. F12 124
Carp Lake, l., B.C., Can. B7 138
Carpolac, Austl. K3 76
Carrabelle, Fl., U.S. H14 122
Carranza, Cabo, c., Chile G1 92
Carrara, Italy F7 22
Carrathool, Austl. J5 76
Carrauntoohil, mtn., Ire. I3 12
Carreta, Punta, c., Peru F2 84
Carriacou, i., Gren. q11 105e
Carrick on Shannon, Ire. H4 12
Carrick-on-suir, Ire. I5 12
Carrie, Mount, mtn., Wa., U.S. C3 136
Carriers Mills, Il., U.S. G9 120
Carrieton, Austl. I2 76
Carrillo, Mex. B6 100
Carrington, N.D., U.S. G14 124
Carrión, stm., Spain B6 20
Carrión de los Condes, Spain B6 20
Carrizal Bajo, Chile D2 92
Carrizo Creek, stm., U.S. E5 128
Carrizo Mountain, mtn., N.M., U.S. H3 128
Carrizo Springs, Tx., U.S. F7 130
Carroll, Ia., U.S. B3 120
Carroll, Ne., U.S. E15 126
Carrollton, Al., U.S. D10 122
Carrollton, Ga., U.S. D13 122
Carrollton, Mi., U.S. E5 112
Carrollton, Mo., U.S. E4 120
Carrollton, Ms., U.S. D8 122
Carrollton, Oh., U.S. D4 114
Carrollton, Tx., U.S. A10 130
Carrolltown, Pa., U.S. D7 114
Carron, stm., Austl. A3 76
Carrot, stm., Can. E10 106
Carrot River, Sk., Can. A10 124
Carry Falls Reservoir, res., N.Y., U.S. F2 110
Carseland, Ab., Can. F17 138
Carson, N.D., U.S. A11 126
Carson, Wa., U.S. E5 136
Carson, East Fork, stm., U.S. E6 134
Carson City, Nv., U.S. D6 134
Carson Lake, res., Nv., U.S. D7 134
Carson Range, mts., U.S. D6 134
Carson Sink, l., Nv., U.S. D7 134
Carstairs, Ab., Can. E16 138
Cartagena, Chile F2 92
Cartagena, Col. B4 86
Cartagena, Spain G9 20
Cartago, Col. E3 86
Cartago, C.R. H6 102
Cartaxo, Port. E2 20
Cartaya, Spain G3 20
Carter, Ok., U.S. F9 128
Carter Lake, Ia., U.S. C2 120
Cartersville, Ga., U.S. C14 122
Carthage, Tun. H4 24
Carthage, Ar., U.S. C6 122
Carthage, Mo., U.S. G3 120
Carthage, Ms., U.S. E9 122

Carthage, N.C., U.S. A6 116
Carthage, S.D., U.S. C15 126
Carthage, Tn., U.S. H11 120
Carthage, Tx., U.S. E4 122
Carthage, sci., Tun. H4 24
Cartier Islands, is., Austl. B4 74
Cartwright, Mb., Can. E14 124
Caruaru, Braz. E8 88
Carúpano, Ven. B10 86
Carutapera, Braz. D8 84
Caruthersville, Mo., U.S. H8 120
Carutu, stm., Ven. E10 86
Carvoeiro, Braz. H10 86
Carvoeiro, Cabo, c., Port. E1 20
Cary, Ms., U.S. E8 122
Cary, N.C., U.S. I7 114
Čaryškoe, Russia D14 32
Caryville, Fl., U.S. G13 122
Casablanca (Dar-el-Beida), Mor. C3 64
Casa Branca, Braz. K2 88
Casa de Piedra, Embalse, res., Arg. I4 92
Casa Grande, Az., U.S. K5 132
Casa Grande Ruins National Monument, p.o.i., Az., U.S. K5 132
Casale Monferrato, Italy E5 22
Casanare, state, Col. E6 86
Casanare, stm., Col. D6 86
Casa Nova, Braz. E5 88
Casar, N.C., U.S. A4 116
Casarano, Italy D12 24
Casar de Cáceres, Spain E4 20
Casas Adobes, Az., U.S. K6 132
Casas Grandes, stm., Mex. F9 98
Casavieja, Spain D6 20
Casca, Braz. D12 92
Cascadas Basaseachic, Parque Nacional, p.o.i., Mex. A4 100
Cascade, B.C., Can. G12 138
Cascade, Norf. I. y25 78i
Cascade, Ia., U.S. B6 120
Cascade, Mt., U.S. C15 136
Cascade, Wi., U.S. E1 112
Cascade Bay, b., Norf. I. y25 78i
Cascade Mountains see Cascade Range, mts., N.A. C3 108
Cascade Range, mts., N.A. C3 108
Cascade Reservoir, res., Id., U.S. F10 136
Cascade-Siskiyou National Monument, p.o.i., Or., U.S. H4 136
Cascais, Port. F1 20
Cascapédia, stm., Qc., Can. B10 110
Cascavel, Braz. B11 92
Cascavel, Braz. C6 88
Cascina, Italy G7 22
Case-Pilote, Mart. k6 105c
Caserta, Italy C8 24
Caseville, Mi., U.S. E6 112
Casey, Il., U.S. E9 120
Casey, sci., Ant. B16 81
Casey, Mount, mtn., Id., U.S. B10 136
Cashel, Ire. I5 12
Cashiers, N.C., U.S. A2 116
Cashmere, Wa., U.S. C6 136
Cashton, Wi., U.S. H8 118
Casigua, Ven. C5 86
Casilda, Arg. F7 92
Casino, Austl. G9 76
Casiquiare, stm., Ven. F8 86
Čáslav, Czech Rep. G11 16
Casma, Peru E2 84
Čašniki, Bela. F12 10
Casoli, Italy H11 22
Caspe, Spain C10 20
Casper, Wy., U.S. E6 126
Caspian Depression (Prikaspijskaja nizmennost'), pl. E7 32
Caspian Sea, s. F7 32
Cass, stm., Mi., U.S. E6 112
Cassano allo Ionio, Italy E10 24
Cass City, Mi., U.S. E6 112
Casselman, On., Can. E1 110
Cássia, Braz. K2 88
Cassiar, B.C., Can. D5 106
Cassiar Mountains, mts., Can. D5 106
Cassilândia, Braz. C6 90
Cassinga, Ang. D2 68
Cassino, Italy C7 24
Cass Lake, Mn., U.S. D4 118
Cass Lake, res., Mn., U.S. D4 118
Cassongue, Ang. C1 68
Cassopolis, Mi., U.S. G3 112
Cassumba, Ilha, i., Braz. I6 88
Cassville, Mo., U.S. H4 120
Cassville, Wi., U.S. B7 120
Castagniccia, reg., Fr. G15 18
Castaños, Mex. H6 130
Castelbuono, Italy G8 24
Castelfranco Veneto, Italy E8 22
Castellammare, Golfo di, b., Italy F6 24
Castellammare del Golfo, Italy F6 24
Castellammare di Stabia, Italy D8 24
Castellana Grotte, Italy D11 24
Castellane, Fr. F12 18
Castellaneta, Italy D10 24
Castelli, Arg. B7 92
Castelli, Arg. H9 92
Castelló, co., Spain D10 20
Castelló de la Plana, Spain E11 20
Castellón de la Plana *see* Castelló de la Plana, Spain E11 20
Castellón de la Plana see Castelló, co., Spain D10 20
Castelnaudary, Fr. F7 18
Castelnau-Montratier, Fr. E7 18
Castelo, Braz. K5 88
Castelo Branco, Port. E3 20
Castelo Branco, state, Port. E3 20
Castelo de Paiva, Port. C2 20
Castel San Giovanni, Italy E6 22
Castelsarrasin, Fr. E6 18
Casteltermini, Italy G7 24
Castelvetrano, Italy G6 24
Casterton, Austl. K3 76
Castets, Fr. F4 18
Castiglione del Lago, Italy G8 22
Castile, N.Y., U.S. B7 114
Castilla, Peru E1 84
Castilla, Playa de, cst., Spain G4 20
Castilla-La Mancha, state, Spain E9 20
Castilla la Nueva, hist. reg., Spain E7 20
Castilla la Vieja (Old Castille), hist. reg., Spain C7 20
Castilla y León, state, Spain C6 20
Castillo de San Marcos National Monument, p.o.i., Fl., U.S. F5 116
Castillo Incaico de Ingapirca, sci., Ec. I2 86
Castillon-la-Bataille, Fr. E5 18
Castillos, Ur. G11 92
Castillos, Laguna de, l., Ur. G11 92
Castine, Me., U.S. F8 110
Castlebar, Ire. H3 12
Castle Bruce, Dom. j6 105c
Castle Dome Peak, mtn., Az., U.S. J2 132
Castlegar, B.C., Can. G13 138
Castle Hills, Tx., U.S. E9 130
Castleisland, Ire. I3 12
Castlemaine, Austl. K5 76
Castle Mountain, mtn., Yk., Can. C3 106

Castle Peak, mtn., Co., U.S. D9 132
Castlerea, Ire. H4 12
Castlereagh, stm., Austl. H7 76
Castle Rock, Co., U.S. B3 128
Castle Rock, Wa., U.S. D3 136
Castle Rock, mtn., Or., U.S. F8 136
Castle Rock Butte, mtn., S.D., U.S. B9 126
Castle Rock Lake, res., Wi., U.S. H8 118
Castletown, I. of Man G8 12
Castlewood, S.D., U.S. G1 118
Castor, Ab., Can. D19 138
Castor, stm., Mo., U.S. G7 120
Castres, Fr. F8 18
Castries, St. Luc. I6 105c
Castro, Braz. B13 92
Castro, Chile H2 90
Castro Barros, Arg. E5 92
Castro Daire, Port. D3 20
Castro del Río, Spain G6 20
Castronuño, Spain C5 20
Castro Verde, Port. G2 20
Castrovillari, Italy E10 24
Castroville, Ca., U.S. G4 134
Catacamas, Hond. E5 102
Catacaos, Peru E1 84
Catacocha, Ec. D2 84
Cataguazes, Braz. K4 88
Catahoula Lake, l., La., U.S. F6 122
Çatalan, Tur. A6 58
Catalão, Braz. J2 88
Çatalca, Tur. B11 28
Catalina, Chile B3 92
Catalina see Santa Catalina Island, i., Ca., U.S. J7 134
Catalina, Punta, c., Chile J3 90
Catalonia see Catalunya, state, Spain C12 20
Cataluña see Catalunya, state, Spain C12 20
Catalunya, state, Spain C12 20
Catamarca, state, Arg. C4 92
Catamayo, Ec. D2 84
Catanauan, Phil. D4 52
Catanduanes Island, i., Phil. D5 52
Catanduva, Braz. K1 88
Catania, Italy G9 24
Catania, Golfo di, b., Italy G9 24
Cataño, P.R. B3 104a
Catanzaro, Italy F10 24
Cataract Canyon, p., Az., U.S. H4 132
Catarina, Braz. D6 88
Catarino Rodríguez, Mex. C8 100
Catarman, Phil. F5 52
Catarman, Phil. D5 52
Catarroja, Spain E10 20
Catatumbo, stm., Ven. C5 86
Catawba, stm., U.S. B5 116
Catawissa, Pa., U.S. D9 114
Cat Ba, Dao, i., Viet. B8 48
Catbalogan, Phil. E5 52
Catedral, Cerro, hill, Ur. G10 92
Catete, Ang. B1 68
Cathcart, S. Afr. H8 70
Cathedral City, Ca., U.S. J9 134
Catherine, Mount see Katherîna, Gebel, mtn., Egypt J4 58
Catherines Peak, mtn., Jam. i14 104d
Cat Island, i., Bah. C9 96
Cat Lake, l., On., Can. E12 106
Catlettsburg, Ky., U.S. F3 114
Catlin, Il., U.S. H2 112
Catoche, Cabo, c., Mex. B4 102
Catolé do Rocha, Braz. D7 88
Catoosa, Ok., U.S. H2 120
Catriló, Arg. H6 92
Catrimani, stm., Braz. G11 86
Catskill, N.Y., U.S. B12 114
Catskill Mountains, mts., N.Y., U.S. B11 114
Catt, Mount, mtn., B.C., Can. B2 138
Cattaraugus, N.Y., U.S. B7 114
Cattolica, Italy G9 22
Catu, Braz. G6 88
Catuane, Moz. E11 70
Catur, Moz. C6 68
Çatwick, Îles, is., Viet. G9 48
Čatyrtaš, Kyrg. F13 32
Cau, stm., Viet. A7 48
Cauaburi, stm., Braz. G8 86
Caubvick, Mount, mtn., Can. F13 141
Cauca, state, Col. F3 86
Cauca, stm., Col. D4 86
Caucaia, Braz. B6 88
Caucasia, Col. D4 86
Caucasus, mts. F6 32
Caucete, Arg. E3 92
Cauchari, Salar de, pl., Arg. D3 90
Caudry, Fr. D12 14
Caungula, Ang. B2 68
Čaunskaja guba, b., Russia C22 34
Cauquenes, Chile G1 92
Caura, stm., Ven. D9 86
Caurés, stm., Braz. H10 86
Căuşani, Mol. C16 26
Causapscal, Qc., Can. B9 110
Caussade, Fr. E7 18
Cauto, stm., Cuba B9 102
Caux, Pays de, reg., Fr. E9 14
Cávado, stm., Port. C3 20
Cavaillon, Fr. F11 18
Cavalcante, Braz. G2 88
Cavalese, Italy D8 22
Cavalier, N.D., U.S. F16 124
Cavalla (Cavally), stm., Afr. H3 64
Cavalleria, Cap de, c., Spain D15 20
Cavally (Cavalla), stm., Afr. H3 64
Cavan, Ire. G5 12
Cavan, state, Ire. H5 12
Cavarzere, Italy E9 22
Çavdır, Tur. F12 28
Cave City, Ky., U.S. G11 120
Cave In Rock, Il., U.S. G9 120
Caveiras, stm., Braz. C12 92
Cavendish, Austl. K4 76
Cave Run Lake, res., Ky., U.S. F2 114
Cave Spring, Ga., U.S. C13 122
Caviana de Fora, Ilha, i., Braz. C8 84
Cavite, Phil. C3 52
Cavour, Canale, can., Italy E5 22
Çavuş, Tur. A2 58
Čavusy, Bela. G14 10
Cawood, Ky., U.S. H2 114
Cawston, B.C., Can. G11 138
Caxambu, Braz. K3 88
Caxias, Braz. C4 88
Caxias do Sul, Braz. D12 92
Caxito, Ang. B1 68
Çay, Tur. E13 28
Cayambe, Ec. G2 86
Cayambe, vol., Ec. G3 86
Cayce, S.C., U.S. C4 116
Çaycuma, Tur. B15 28
Cay Duong, Vinh, b., Viet. G7 48
Cayenne, Fr. Gu. C7 84
Cayey, P.R. B3 104a
Caylus, Fr. E7 18
Cayman Brac, i., Cay. Is. C8 102
Cayman Islands, dep., N.A. C7 102
Caynaba, Som. C9 66
Cayon, St. K./N. C2 105a
Cayuga, In., U.S. I2 112
Cayuga, Tx., U.S. F3 122
Cayuga Heights, N.Y., U.S. B9 114
Cayuga Lake, res., N.Y., U.S. B9 114
Cazalla de la Sierra, Spain G5 20
Cazaux et de Sanguinet, Étang de, l., Fr. E4 18
Cazères, Fr. F6 18
Cazombo, Ang. C3 68

Cazorla, Spain G7 20
Cea, stm., Spain B5 20
Ceanannas *see* Kells, Ire. H6 12
Ceará, state, Braz. C6 88
Ceará-Mirim, Braz. C8 88
Ceará-Mirim, stm., Braz. C8 88
Ceatharlach *see* Carlow, Ire. I5 12
Cebaco, Isla de, i., Pan. I7 102
Ceballos, Mex. B6 100
Čeboksary, Russia C7 32
Cebollar, Arg. D4 92
Cebollas, Mex. D6 100
Cebollatí, Ur. F11 92
Cebollatí, stm., Ur. F10 92
Céboruco, Volcán, vol., Mex. E6 100
Cebu, Phil. E4 52
Cebu, i., Phil. E4 52
Cebu Strait, strt., Phil. F4 52
Ceceda, Mex. H4 130
Čechtice, Czech Rep. G11 16
Čechy, hist. reg., Czech Rep. G10 16
Cecilia, Ky., U.S. G12 120
Cecil Plains, Austl. F8 76
Cecina, Italy G7 22
Čečnja, state, Russia F7 32
Cedar, stm., Ne., U.S. F14 126
Cedar, stm., U.S. J7 118
Cedar Bluffs, Ne., U.S. J2 118
Cedar Breaks National Monument, p.o.i., Ut., U.S. F3 132
Cedarburg, Wi., U.S. E1 112
Cedar City, Ut., U.S. F3 132
Cedar Creek, stm., Ia., U.S. C5 120
Cedar Creek, stm., Id., U.S. B2 132
Cedar Creek, stm., N.D., U.S. A11 126
Cedar Falls, Ia., U.S. B5 120
Cedar Grove, Wi., U.S. E2 112
Cedar Hill, Tn., U.S. H10 120
Cedar Key, Fl., U.S. G2 116
Cedar Lake, In., U.S. J11 118
Cedar Lake, l., On., Can. B11 112
Cedar Lake, res., Mb., Can. E10 106
Cedar Mountain, mtn., Ca., U.S. B5 134
Cedar Rapids, Ia., U.S. C6 120
Cedars of Lebanon see Arz Lubnān, for., Leb. D7 58
Cedar Springs, Mi., U.S. E4 112
Cedartown, Ga., U.S. C13 122
Cedar Tree Point, c., Antig. e4 105b
Cedarvale, B.C., Can. A2 138
Cedar Vale, Ks., U.S. D12 128
Cedarville, Ca., U.S. B5 134
Cedarville, Mi., U.S. B5 112
Cedeira, Spain A2 20
Cedillo, Embalse de, res., Eur. E3 20
Cedro, Braz. D6 88
Cedros, Mex. C8 100
Cedros, Isla, i., Mex. A1 100
Ceduna, Austl. F6 74
Ceelbuur, Som. D9 66
Ceepeecee, B.C., Can. G4 138
Ceerigaabo, Som. B9 66
Cefalonia see Kefalloniá, i., Grc. E3 28
Cefalù, Italy F8 24
Çega, stm., Spain C6 20
Čegdomyn, Russia F15 34
Cegléd, Hung. B6 26
Ceglie Messapico, Italy D11 24
Cehegín, Spain F9 20
Čehov, Russia E20 10
Čehov, Russia G17 34
Čekalin, Russia F19 10
Čekuevo, Russia E18 8
Čelákovice, Czech Rep. F10 16
Celano, Italy H10 22
Celaya, Mex. E8 100
Celebes see Sulawesi, i., Indon. F7 44
Celebes Basin, unds. I15 142
Celebes Sea, s., Asia E7 44
Čeleken, Turkmen. B7 56
Celeste, Tx., U.S. D2 122
Celestún, Mex. B2 102
Celina, Tn., U.S. H12 120
Celina, Tx., U.S. D2 122
Čeljabinsk, Russia C10 32
Celjahany, Bela. H8 10
Celje, Slvn. D12 22
Čeljuskin, mys, c., Russia A9 34
Celle, Ger. D6 16
Čelmozero, Russia D14 8
Celtic Sea, s., Eur. J6 12
Çeltikçi, Tur. A1 58
Čemal, Russia D15 32
Cement, Ok., U.S. G10 128
Cenajo, Embalse del, res., Spain F9 20
Cenderawasih, Teluk, b., Indon. F10 44
Cenovo, Blg. F12 26
Centenario, Arg. I3 92
Center, Co., U.S. D2 128
Center, Mo., U.S. E6 120
Center, N.D., U.S. G12 124
Center, Tx., U.S. F4 122
Centerburg, Oh., U.S. D3 114
Center Hill, Fl., U.S. H3 116
Center Hill Lake, res., Tn., U.S. H12 120
Center Moriches, N.Y., U.S. D13 114
Center Point, Al., U.S. D12 122
Center Point, Ia., U.S. B6 120
Centerville, Ia., U.S. D5 120
Centerville, Mo., U.S. G7 120
Centerville, Pa., U.S. D5 114
Centerville, Tn., U.S. B11 122
Centerville, Tx., U.S. F2 122
Centerville, Ut., U.S. C4 132
Central, Braz. F4 88
Central, Phil. D3 52
Central, Az., U.S. K7 132
Central, N.M., U.S. K8 132
Central, state, Bots. C8 70
Central, state, Para. B9 92
Central, state, Sol. Is. e8 79b
Central, Cordillera, mts., Col. E4 86
Central, Cordillera, mts., Peru E2 84
Central, Cordillera, mts., Phil. B3 52
Central, Cordillera, mts., P.R. B2 104a
Central, Massif, mts., Fr. D8 18
Central, Sistema, mts., Spain D6 20
Central African Republic, ctry., Afr. C4 66
Central Aguirre, P.R. C3 104a
Central Arizona Project Aqueduct, aq., U.S. J3 132
Central Bohemia see Středočeský, state, Czech Rep. G10 16
Central Borneo see Kalimantan Tengah, state, Indon. D8 50
Central Brāhui Range, mts., Pak. D10 56
Central Celebes see Sulawesi Tengah, state, Indon. D12 50
Central City, Ia., U.S. B6 120
Central City, Il., U.S. F8 120
Central City, Ky., U.S. G10 120
Central City, Pa., U.S. D7 114
Central Division, state, Fiji q19 79e
Centralia, Il., U.S. F8 120
Centralia, Ks., U.S. E1 120
Centralia, Mo., U.S. E5 120
Centralia, Wa., U.S. D4 136
Centralina, Braz. J1 88

Name	Map Ref.	Page
Central Java see Jawa Tengah, state, Indon.		
Central Kalahari Game Reserve, Bots.	C6	70
Central Lake, Mi., U.S.	C4	112
Central Makrān Range, mts., Pak.	D9	56
Central'nyj, Russia	C15	32
Central Pacific Basin, unds.	I21	142
Central Point, Or., U.S.	A2	134
Central Range, mts., Pap. N. Gui.	a3	79a
Central Russian Upland see Srednerusskaja vozvyšennost', plat., Russia	H20	10
Central Siberian Plateau see Srednesibirskoe ploskogor'e, plat., Russia	C10	34
Central Siberian Uplands see Srednesibirskoe ploskogor'e, plat., Russia	C10	34
Central Slovakia see Stredoslovenský Kraj, state, Slov.	H15	16
Central Utah Canal, can., Ut., U.S.	D4	132
Central Valley, Ca., U.S.	C3	134
Central Valley see Longitudinal, Valle, val., Chile	H1	92
Centre, Canal du, can., Fr.	C10	18
Centreville, Al., U.S.	E11	122
Centreville, Md., U.S.	E9	114
Centreville, Mi., U.S.	F7	122
Centro Puntas, P.R.	B1	104a
Century, Fl., U.S.	G11	122
Ceos see Kéa, i., Grc.	F7	28
Cepelare, Blg.	H11	26
Cephalonia see Kefaloniá, i., Grc.	E3	28
Cepu, Indon.	G7	50
Ceram see Seram, i., Indon.	F8	44
Ceram Sea see Seram, Laut, s., Indon.	F8	44
Čerčany, Czech Rep.	G10	16
Cerdas, Bol.	D3	90
Cereal, Ab., Can.	C3	124
Čereha, stm., Russia	C11	10
Čeremhovo, Russia	D18	32
Čeremšany, Russia	B31	38
Čerepanovo, Russia	D14	32
Čerepet', Russia	F19	10
Čerepovec, Russia	A20	10
Ceres, Arg.	D7	92
Ceres, Braz.	G8	84
Ceres, S. Afr.	H4	70
Ceresco, Ne., U.S.	J2	118
Ceresio see Lugano, Lago di, l., Eur.	D14	18
Ceretè, Col.	C4	86
Čerevkovo, Russia	F21	8
Cerignola, Italy	C9	24
Čerilly, Fr.	H11	14
Çerkeş, Tur.	C15	28
Čerkessk, Russia	F6	32
Čerkezköy, Tur.	B10	28
Čerlak, Russia	D12	32
Cermei, Rom.	C8	26
Čermoz, Russia	C9	32
Černa, Rom.	D15	26
Černá hora, mtn., Czech Rep.	G9	16
Cernavodă, Rom.	E15	26
Cernay, Fr.	G16	14
Černigovka, Russia	B10	38
Černjahovsk, Russia	F4	10
Černogorsk, Russia	D16	32
Černuška, Russia	C9	32
Černyševsk, Russia	F12	34
Černyševskij, Russia	D11	34
Cerralvo, Isla, i., Mex.	C4	100
Cërrik, Alb.	C14	24
Čeriku see Cërrik, Alb.	C14	24
Cerrillos, Arg.	B5	92
Cerrillos, N.M, U.S.	F2	128
Cerritos, Mex.	D8	100
Cerro Azul, Mex.	C10	92
Cerro Azul, Mex.	E9	100
Cerro Azul, Peru	F2	84
Cerro Chato, Ur.	E4	92
Cerro de las Mesas, sci., Mex.	F10	100
Cerro de Pasco, Peru	F2	84
Cerro Gordo, Il., U.S.	E9	120
Cerro Largo, Braz.	D10	92
Cerro Moreno, Chile	A2	92
Cerrón, Cerro, mtn., Ven.	B6	86
Cerrón Grande, Embalse, res., El Sal.	E3	102
Cerro Prieto, Mex.	K10	134
Cerros Colorados, Embalse, res., El Sal.	I3	92
Cerro Tololo, Observatorio Astronómico, sci., Chile.	E2	92
Čerskij, Russia	C21	34
Čerskogo, hrebet (Cherskiy Mountains), mts., Russia	C17	34
Čertolino, Russia	D16	10
Červen', Bela.	G11	10
Červen Brjag, Blg.	F11	26
Cervera, Spain	C12	20
Cervera de Pisuerga, Spain	B6	20
Cervia, Italy	F9	22
Cerviato, Monte, Italy	D9	24
Cervino see Matterhorn, mtn., Eur.	D13	18
Cervione, Fr.	G15	18
Cervo, Spain	A3	20
Cesar, state, Col.	C5	86
Cesar, stm., Col.	B5	86
Cesena, Italy	F9	22
Cesenatico, Italy	F9	22
Cēsis, Lat.	C8	10
Česká Kamenice, Czech Rep.	F10	16
Česká Lípa, Czech Rep.	F10	16
Česká Třebová, Czech Rep.	G12	16
České Budějovice, Czech Rep.	H10	16
Český Brod, Czech Rep.	F10	16
Çeşme, Tur.	E9	28
Češskaja guba (Chesha Bay), b., Russia.	C21	8
Cessnock, Austl.	I8	76
Cesvaine, Lat.	D9	10
Cetina, stm., Cro.	G13	22
Cetinje, Serb.	G5	26
Ceuta, Sp. N. Afr.	E6	64
Cévennes, reg., Fr.	E9	18
Cévennes, Parc National des, p.o.i., Fr.	E9	18
Cevizli, Tur.	F14	28
Ceyhan, Tur.	A6	58
Ceyhan, stm., Tur.	B6	58
Ceylon, Mn., U.S.	H4	118
Ceylon see Sri Lanka, ctry., Asia	G5	53
Cēze, stm., Fr.	E10	18
Cha-am, Thai.	F5	48
Chabanais, Fr.	D6	18
Chabás, Arg.	F7	92
Chabjuwardoo Bay, b., Austl.	D2	74
Chablais, reg., Fr.	C12	18
Chacabuco, Arg.	G7	92
Chachani, Nevado, vol., Peru	G3	84
Chachapoyas, Peru	E2	84
Chāchra, India	F6	54
Chāchro, Pak.	F3	54
Chaco, state, Arg.	C7	92
Chaco, stm., N.M., U.S.	G8	132
Chaco, Parque Nacional, p.o.i., Arg.	C8	92
Chaco Austral, reg., Arg.	C7	92
Chaco Boreal, reg., Para.	D4	90
Chaco Central, reg., Arg.	D4	90
Chaco Mesa, mtn., N.M., U.S.	H9	132
Chad, ctry., Afr.	E3	62
Chad, Lake, l., Afr.	G7	64
Chadbourn, N.C., U.S.	B7	116
Chadian, China	H1	42
Chadron, Ne., U.S.	E10	126
Chadwick, Il., U.S.	I9	118
Chaem, stm., Thai.	C4	48
Chāgai, Pak.	D9	56
Chāgai Hills, hills, Asia	D9	56
Chagos Archipelago, is., B.I.O.T.	J10	142
Chagos-Lacadive Plateau, unds.	J10	142
Chaguanas, Trin.	s12	105f
Chaguaramas, Ven.	C8	86
Chahal, Guat.	E3	102
Chahanwusu see Dulan, China.	D4	36
Chahe, China	E4	36
Chāībāsa, India	G10	54
Chaihe, China	B8	38
Chai Nat, Thai.	E4	48
Chaiya, Thai.	H4	48
Chaiyaphum, Thai.	E6	48
Chajari, Arg.	E8	92
Chakaria, Bngl.	H14	54
Chakdaha, India	G12	54
Chake Chake, Tan.	F7	66
Chākia, India	E10	54
Chakkarat, Thai.	E6	48
Chakradharpur, India	G10	54
Chāksu, India	E5	54
Chakwāl, Pak.	B4	54
Chala, Peru	G3	84
Chalais, Fr.	D6	18
Chalatenango, El Sal.	F3	102
Chalaxung, China	E4	36
Chalbi Desert, des., Kenya	D7	66
Chalcidice see Chalkidiki, hist. reg., Grc.	C6	28
Chalcis see Chalkida, Grc.	E6	28
Chaleur Bay, b., Can.	C11	110
Chalía, stm., Arg.	I2	90
Chalisgaon, India	H5	54
Chalke see Chálki, i., Grc.	G10	28
Chálki, i., Grc.	G10	28
Chalkida, Grc.	E6	28
Chalkidikí, hist. reg., Grc.	C6	28
Chalk River, On., Can.	B12	112
Challakere, India	D3	53
Challapata, Bol.	C3	90
Challenger Deep, unds.	H17	142
Chalmette, La., U.S.	H9	122
Châlons-sur-Marne, Fr.	F13	14
Chalon-sur-Saône, Fr.	H13	14
Chalosse, reg., Fr.	F5	18
Chaltel, Cerro (Fitz Roy, Monte), mtn., S.A.	I2	90
Châlus, Fr.	D6	18
Cham, Ger.	G8	16
Chama, N.M., U.S.	G10	132
Chama, stm., U.S.	E2	128
Chama, stm., Ven.	C6	86
Chamaicó, Arg.	G5	92
Chaman, Pak.	C10	56
Chamba, India	B6	54
Chambal, stm., India	E6	54
Chamberlain, Sk., Can.	D8	124
Chamberlain, S.D., U.S.	D13	126
Chamberlain, stm., Austl.	C5	74
Chamberlain Lake, l., Me., U.S.	D7	110
Chambers, In., U.S.	E14	126
Chambersburg, Pa., U.S.	E8	114
Chambers Island, i., Wi., U.S.	C2	112
Chambéry, Fr.	D11	18
Chambi, Jebel, mtn., Tun.	B6	64
Chamblee, Ga., U.S.	D14	122
Chambord, Qc., Can.	B4	110
Chamdo see Qamdo, China.	E4	36
Chamical, Arg.	E4	92
Chamelecón, stm., Hond.	E3	102
Ch'amo Hāyk', l., Eth.	F7	62
Chamois, Mo., U.S.	F6	120
Chamoli, India	C7	54
Chamonix-Mont-Blanc, Fr.	D12	18
Chāmpa, India	G9	54
Champagne, hist. reg., Fr.	F13	14
Champagne Castle, mtn., S. Afr.	F9	70
Champagnole, Fr.	H14	14
Champaign, Il., U.S.	D9	120
Champaqui, Cerro, mtn., Arg.	F5	92
Champasak, Laos	E7	48
Champoré, Lac, l., Qc., Can.	D17	106
Champion, Ab., Can.	F17	138
Champion, Mi., U.S.	B1	112
Champlain, Lake, l., N.A.	D16	112
Champlitte-et-le-Prélot, Fr.	G14	14
Champotón, Mex.	C2	102
Chamrajnagar, Rāmasamudram, India	F3	53
Chana, Thai.	I5	48
Chañaral, Chile	E4	92
Chañaral, Chile	C2	92
Chañaral, Isla, i., Chile.	D2	92
Chancay, Peru	F2	84
Chanchiang see Zhanjiang, China	K4	42
Chanco, Chile	G1	92
Chandalar, Ak., U.S.	C10	140
Chandalar, stm., Ak., U.S.	C10	140
Chandannagar, India	G11	54
Chandausi, India	D7	54
Chāndbāli, India	H11	54
Chandeleur Islands, is., La., U.S.	H10	122
Chandeleur Sound, strt., La., U.S.	H9	122
Chandigarh, India	C6	54
Chandler, Qc., Can.	B12	110
Chandler, Az., U.S.	J5	132
Chandler, In., U.S.	F10	120
Chandler, Tx., U.S.	E3	122
Chandler, stm., Ak., U.S.	C9	140
Chāndpur, Bngl.	G13	54
Chāndpur, India	D7	54
Chandrapur, India	B4	53
Chang (Yangtze), stm., China	F8	36
Chang, stm., China	G1	42
Chang, Ko, i., Thai.	G6	48
Changan see Xi'an, China	D3	42
Changanācheri, India	G3	53
Changane, stm., Moz.	D11	70
Changcheng, China	L3	42
Chang Cheng (Great Wall), misc. cult., China	D6	36
Chang Chenmo, stm., Asia	A7	54
Changchiakow see Zhangjiakou, China	A6	42
Changchou see Changzhi, China	C5	42
Changchow see Changzhou, China	F8	42
Changchou see Zhangzhou, China	I7	42
Changchow see Changzhou, China.	F8	42
Changchow see Zhangzhou, China.	I7	42
Changchun, China	C6	38
Changde, China	G4	42
Chang Hu, l., China	F5	42
Changhua, Tai.	I9	42
Changhŭng, Kor., S.	G7	38
Changji, China	C2	36
Changjiang, China	L3	42
Changjiakow see Zhangjiakou, China	A6	42
Changli, China	B8	42
Changling, China	B5	38
Changlun, Malay.	I5	48
Changmar, China	A7	54
Changning, China	G4	36
Changning, China	H5	42
Ch'angnyŏng, Kor., S.	D1	40
Changping, China	A7	42
Changsa, China	L4	42
Changsha, China	G5	42
Changshan Qundao, is., China	B10	42
Changshu, China	G2	42
Changshu, China	F9	42
Ch'angte see Changde, China	G4	42
Changteh see Anyang, China	C6	42
Changtien see Zibo, China	C8	42
Changting, China	I7	42
Changting, China	B8	38
Changwon, Kor., S.	D1	40
Changwu, China	D2	42
Changxing, China	F8	42
Changxing Dao, i., China	B9	42
Changyi, China	C8	42
Changyŏn-ŭp, Kor., N.	E6	38
Changzhi, China	C5	42
Changzhou, China	F8	42
Chaniá, Grc.	H7	28
Chanión, Kólpos, b., Grc.	H6	28
Chankiang see Zhanjiang, China	K4	42
Channagiri, India	D2	53
Channapatna, India	E3	53
Channel Country, reg., Austl.	E3	76
Channel Islands, is., Eur.	L10	12
Channel Islands, is., Ca., U.S.	J6	134
Channel Islands National Park, p.o.i., Ca., U.S.	J6	134
Channel-Port aux Basques, Nf., Can.	j22	107a
Channelview, Tx., U.S.	H3	122
Channing, Mi., U.S.	B11	112
Chanute, Ks., U.S.	G2	120
Chao, stm., China	A7	42
Chao'an, China	J7	42
Ch'aochou see Chao'an, China	J7	42
Chaochow see Chao'an, China	J7	42
Chao Hu, l., China	F7	42
Chao Phraya, stm., Thai.	E5	48
Chaor, stm., China	B9	36
Chaoxian, China	F7	42
Chaoyang, China	J7	42
Chaoyang, China	B7	38
Chaoyang, China	D4	38
Chaoyangshan, China	C6	38
Chapada dos Veadeiros, Parque Nacional da, p.o.i., Braz.	H2	88
Chapadinha, Braz.	B4	88
Chapaev, Kaz.	D8	32
Chapala, Mex.	E7	100
Chapala, Laguna de, l., Mex.	E7	100
Chāparmukh, India	E14	54
Chaparral, Col.	F3	86
Chapecó, Braz.	C11	92
Chapel Hill, N.C., U.S.	I6	114
Chapelton, Jam.	i13	104d
Chapéu, Morro do, mtn., Braz.	H4	88
Chapicuy, Ur.	E9	92
Chapin, Il., U.S.	E7	120
Chapleau, On., Can.	F14	106
Chapman, Ne., U.S.	F15	126
Chapman, Cape, c., Nu., Can.	B13	106
Chapmanville, W.V., U.S.	G3	114
Chapo, Mex.	E3	100
Chappell, Waddi, mtn., Afr.	H7	64
Chappell Hill, Tx., U.S.	G2	122
Chapultepec, Mex.	L9	134
Chaquiago, Arg.	C4	92
Charadai, Arg.	C8	92
Charalá, Col.	D5	86
Charata, Arg.	C7	92
Chār Borjak, Afg.	D8	100
Charcas, Mex.	D8	100
Charco Hondo, P.R.	B2	104a
Charcos de Risa, Mex.	B7	100
Charcot Island, i., Ant.	B33	81
Chard, Eng., U.K.	K10	12
Charente, state, Fr.	D6	18
Charente, stm., Fr.	C6	18
Charente-Maritime, state, Fr.	C5	18
Chāri, stm., Afg.	C1	54
Chārīkār, Afg.	B10	56
Chariton, Ia., U.S.	C5	120
Chariton, stm., U.S.	E5	120
Chariton, Mussel Fork, stm., Mo., U.S.	E5	120
Charity, Guy.	B6	84
Charkhāri, India	F7	54
Charjew see Türkmenabat, Turkmen.	B9	56
Charleroi, Bel.	D13	14
Charles, Cape, c., Va., U.S.	G10	114
Charles, Peak, mtn., Austl.	F4	74
Charles City, Ia., U.S.	A5	120
Charles City, Va., U.S.	G8	114
Charles Island, i., Nu., Can.	D16	106
Charles Mound, hill, Il., U.S.	B7	120
Charles Point, c., Austl.	B6	74
Charleston, N.Z.	E4	80
Charleston, Il., U.S.	E9	120
Charleston, Mo., U.S.	H8	120
Charleston, Ms., U.S.	C8	122
Charleston, S.C., U.S.	C6	116
Charleston, W.V., U.S.	F4	114
Charleston Peak, mtn., Nv., U.S.	G10	134
Charlestown, S. Afr.	E9	70
Charlestown, St. K./N.	C2	105a
Charlestown, St. Vin.	p11	105e
Charlestown, In., U.S.	F12	120
Charleville, Austl.	F5	76
Charleville-Mézières, Fr.	E13	14
Charlevoix, Mi., U.S.	C5	112
Charlevoix, Lake, l., Mi., U.S.	C5	112
Charlotte, Mi., U.S.	B1	114
Charlotte, N.C., U.S.	A5	116
Charlotte, Tn., U.S.	H10	120
Charlotte, Tx., U.S.	F9	130
Charlotte Harbor, b., Fl., U.S.	J3	116
Charlotte Lake, l., B.C., Can.	D5	138
Charlottesville, Va., U.S.	F7	114
Charlottetown, P.E., Can.	D13	110
Charlotteville, Trin.	r13	105f
Charlton Island, i., Nu., Can.	E14	106
Charouine, Alg.	D4	64
Charron Lake, l., Mb., Can.	B18	124
Charroux, Fr.	C6	18
Chārsadda, Pak.	A3	54
Charter Oak, Ia., U.S.	I3	118
Charters Towers, Austl.	C6	76
Chartres, Fr.	F10	14
Chascomús, Arg.	G8	92
Chase, B.C., Can.	F11	138
Chase, Mount, mtn., Me., U.S.	D8	110
Chase City, Va., U.S.	H7	114
Chaska, Mn., U.S.	G5	118
Chateaubelair, St. Vin.	o11	105e
Château-Chinon, Fr.	G12	14
Chāteaubriant, Fr.	G7	14
Château-du-Loir, Fr.	G9	14
Châteaudun, Fr.	F10	14
Chateaugay (Châteauguay), stm., N.A.	D15	112
Châteauneuf-sur-Charente, Fr.	D5	18
Château-Renault, Fr.	G9	14
Château-Richer, Qc., Can.	C5	110
Châteauroux, Fr.	H10	14
Château-Thierry, Fr.	E12	14
Châtellerault, Fr.	H9	14
Chatfield, Mn., U.S.	H6	118
Chatham, N.B., Can.	C11	110
Chatham, On., Can.	F7	112
Chatham, Eng., U.K.	J13	12
Chatham, Il., U.S.	E8	120
Chatham, La., U.S.	E6	122
Chatham, Ma., U.S.	C15	114
Chatham, N.Y., U.S.	B12	114
Chatham, Isla, i., Chile	J2	90
Chatham Islands, is., N.Z.	H9	72
Chatham Rise, unds.	N20	142
Chatham Strait, strt., Ak., U.S.	E13	140
Châtillon-en-Bazois, Fr.	G12	14
Châtillon-sur-Seine, Fr.	G13	14
Chatkal Range, mts., Asia	F12	32
Chatom, Al., U.S.	F10	122
Chatra, India	F10	54
Chatsworth, Austl.	C3	76
Chatsworth, Ga., U.S.	C14	122
Chatsworth, Il., U.S.	D9	120
Chattahoochee, stm., U.S.	G14	122
Chattanooga, Tn., U.S.	B13	122
Chattaroy, W.V., U.S.	G3	114
Chaturat, Thai.	E5	48
Chaubourg, Mount, hill, St. Luc.	I7	105c
Chaudière, stm., Qc., Can.	D5	110
Chau Doc, Viet.	G7	48
Chauk, Mya.	B2	48
Chaumont, Fr.	F13	14
Chauncey, Oh., U.S.	E3	114
Chautauqua Lake, l., N.Y., U.S.	B6	114
Chauvin, La., U.S.	H8	122
Chāvakkad, India	F2	53
Chavarría, Arg.	D8	92
Chaves, Port.	C3	20
Chávita, Col.	D5	86
Chawa'nanke, stm., Can.	C12	54
Chay, stm., Viet.	A7	48
Chayuan, China	G9	42
Chazy, N.Y., U.S.	F3	110
Chbar, stm., Camb.	F8	48
Cheaha Mountain, mtn., Al., U.S.	D13	122
Cheat, stm., U.S.	E6	114
Cheat, Shavers Fork, stm., W.V., U.S.	E6	114
Cheb, Czech Rep.	F8	16
Chebanse, Il., U.S.	G2	112
Cheboygan, Mi., U.S.	C5	112
Chech, 'Erg, des., Afr.	E4	64
Chechnya see Čečnja, state, Russia	F7	32
Chech'on, Kor., S.	B1	40
Checiny, Pol.	F16	16
Checleset Bay, b., B.C., Can.	F3	138
Checotah, Ok., U.S.	B3	122
Chedabucto Bay, b., N.S.	E15	110
Cheduba Island, i., Mya.	C1	48
Cheduba Strait, strt., Mya.	C1	48
Cheektowaga, N.Y., U.S.	B7	114
Cheepie, Austl.	F5	76
Chef-Boutonne, Fr.	C5	18
Chefoo see Yantai, China	C9	42
Chehalis, Wa., U.S.	D4	136
Chehalis, stm., Wa., U.S.	D3	136
Cheju, Kor., S.	H7	38
Cheju-do (Quelpart Island), i., Kor., S.	H7	38
Chekiang see Zhejiang, state, China	G8	42
Chela, Serra da, mts., Ang.	D1	68
Chelan, Lake, res., Wa., U.S.	B5	136
Chelif, Oued, stm., Alg.	B5	64
Chełm, Pol.	E19	16
Chelm, state, Pol.	E19	16
Chełmno, Pol.	C14	16
Chelmsford, On., Can.	B8	112
Chelmsford, Eng., U.K.	J13	12
Chełmża, Pol.	C14	16
Chelsea, On., Can.	C14	112
Chelsea, Mi., U.S.	B1	114
Chelsea, Vt., U.S.	G4	110
Cheltenham, Eng., U.K.	J10	12
Chelva see Xelva, Spain	E9	20
Chelyuskin, Cape see Čeljuskin, mys, c., Russia	A9	34
Chemainus, B.C., Can.	H7	138
Chemba, Moz.	D5	68
Chemnitz, Ger.	F8	16
Chemult, Or., U.S.	H5	136
Chenāb, stm., Asia	D3	54
Chenango, stm., N.Y., U.S.	B10	114
Chenchiang see Zhenjiang, China		
Chenderoh, Tasik, l., Malay.	J5	48
Chénéville, Qc., Can.	C14	112
Cheney, Wa., U.S.	C9	136
Cheney Reservoir, res., Ks., U.S.	D10	128
Cheneyville, La., U.S.	F6	122
Chengbu, China	H4	42
Chengchou see Zhengzhou, China	D5	42
Chengchow see Zhengzhou, China	D5	42
Chengde, China	A7	42
Chengdu, China	E5	36
Chenghai, China	J7	42
Chengmai, China	L3	42
Chengshan Jiao, c., China	C10	42
Chengteh see Chengde, China	A7	42
Chengtu see Chengdu, China	E5	36
Chengxian, China	E1	42
Chengyang, China	C9	42
Chengzitan, China	B10	42
Chenhsien see Chenzhou, China	I5	42
Chen Hu, l., China	F5	42
Chennai (Madras), India	E5	53
Chenoa, Il., U.S.	D9	120
Chenteh see Chengde, China	A7	42
Chenxian, China	E1	36
Chen-si see Shaanxi, state, China	E3	42
Chentang, China	J4	42
Chenxi, China	H3	42
Chenyang see Shenyang, China	D5	38
Chenzhou, China	I5	42
Cheonan see Ch'ŏnan, Kor., S.	F7	38
Cheongju see Ch'ŏngju, Kor., S.	F7	38
Chepén, Peru	E2	84
Chepes, Arg.	E4	92
Chepkotet, mtn., Kenya	D7	66
Chepo, Pan.	H8	102
Cher, state, Fr.	B8	18
Cher, stm., Fr.	B7	18
Cheradi, Isole, i., Italy	D11	24
Cherbourg, Fr.	E7	14
Cherchell, Alg.	H13	20
Chergui, Chott ech, l., Alg.	C5	64
Cheriton, Va., U.S.	G10	114
Cheriyam Island, i., India	F1	53
Cherkasy see Cherkasy, Ukr.	E4	32
Cherkasy, Ukr.	E4	32
Cherkessia see Karačaevo-Cherkesija, state, Russia	F6	32
Chernihiv, Ukr.	D4	32
Chernivtsi, Ukr.	A12	26
Chernivtsi, co., Ukr.	A13	26
Chernobyl see Chornobyl', Ukr.	D4	32
Cherokee, Ia., U.S.	B2	120
Cherokee, Ks., U.S.	G3	120
Cherokee, Ok., U.S.	E10	128
Cherokee, Tx., U.S.	C9	130
Cherokee Lake, res., Tn., U.S.	H2	114
Cherokee Point, c., Bah.	J8	116
Cherokees, Lake O' The, res., Ok., U.S.	H2	120
Cherokee Sound, Bah.	J8	116
Cherrapunji, India	F13	54
Cherry Creek, stm., S.D., U.S.	C11	126
Cherry Hill, N.J., U.S.	E10	114
Cherryvale, Ks., U.S.	G2	120
Cherry Valley, Ar., U.S.	B8	122
Cherryville, N.C., U.S.	A4	116
Cherskiy Mountains see Čerskogo, hrebet, mts., Russia	C17	34
Chesapeake, Va., U.S.	H9	114
Chesapeake Bay, b., U.S.	F9	114
Chesapeake Bay Bridge-Tunnel, Va., U.S.	G9	114
Chesapeake Beach, Md., U.S.	F9	114
Chesaw, Wa., U.S.	B7	136
Chesha Bay see Češskaja guba, b., Russia	C21	8
Cheslatta Lake, l., B.C., Can.	C5	138
Chesnee, S.C., U.S.	A4	116
Chester, Eng., U.K.	H10	12
Chester, Ca., U.S.	C4	134
Chester, Il., U.S.	G8	120
Chester, Mt., U.S.	B15	136
Chester, Ne., U.S.	A11	128
Chester, Pa., U.S.	E10	114
Chester, S.C., U.S.	A4	116
Chester, Va., U.S.	G8	114
Chester Basin, N.S., Can.	F12	110
Chesterfield, Eng., U.K.	H11	12
Chesterfield, S.C., U.S.	B6	116
Chesterfield, Îles, is., N. Cal.	E6	72
Chesterfield Inlet see Igluligaarjuk, Nu., Can.	C12	106
Chesterfield Inlet, b., Can.	C12	106
Chesterfield Islands see Chesterfield, Îles, is., N. Cal.	E6	72
Chesterhill, Oh., U.S.	E4	114
Chester-le-Street, Eng., U.K.	G11	12
Chesterton, In., U.S.	G2	112
Chestertown, Md., U.S.	E9	114
Chesterville, On., Can.	C14	112
Chesuncook Lake, l., Me., U.S.	E7	110
Chetek, Wi., U.S.	F7	118
Chetumal, Mex.	C3	102
Chetumal, Bahía, b., N.A.	C3	102
Chevelon Creek, stm., Az., U.S.	I6	132
Cheviot, N.Z.	F5	80
Cheviot, Oh., U.S.	E13	120
Cheviot Hills, hills, U.K.	F10	12
Cheviot, The, mtn., Eng., U.K.	F10	12
Chew Bahir see Stefanie, Lake, l., Afr.	G7	62
Chewelah, Wa., U.S.	B9	136
Cheyenne, Ok., U.S.	F8	128
Cheyenne, Wy., U.S.	F8	126
Cheyenne, stm., U.S.	C12	126
Cheyenne Wells, Co., U.S.	C5	128
Cheyne Bay, b., Austl.	F3	74
Chhabra, India	F6	54
Chhapra, India	F10	54
Chhata, India	E6	54
Chhatak, Bngl.	F13	54
Chhatarpur, India	F7	54
Chhattisgarh, state, India	G8	54
Chhay Arèng, stm., Camb.	G6	48
Chhlong, Camb.	F8	48
Chhota-Chhindwāra, India	G7	54
Chhota Udepur, India	H5	54
Chhuka, Bhu.	E12	54
Chi, stm., Thai.	E7	48
Chiai, Tai.	J9	42
Chiamboni, stm., Afr.	E8	66
Chiamussu see Jiamusi, China	B11	36
Chiang Dao, Thai.	C4	48
Chiang Kham, Thai.	C5	48
Chiang Khan, Thai.	D6	48
Chiang Mai, Thai.	C4	48
Chiangmen see Jiangmen, China	J5	42
Chiang Rai, Thai.	B4	48
Chiang Saen, Thai.	B4	48
Chiangsu see Jiangsu, state, China	E8	42
Chiangyin see Jiangyin, China	F9	42
Chiaohsien see Jiaoxian, China	C8	42
Chiaotso see Jiaozuo, China	D5	42
Chiapas, state, Mex.	G12	100
Chiari, Italy	E6	22
Chiavari, Italy	F6	22
Chiavenna, Italy	D6	22
Chiba, Japan	D13	40
Chiba, state, Japan	D13	40
Chibabava, Moz.	B11	70
Chibemba, Ang.	D1	68
Chibougamau, Qc., Can.	F15	106
Chibuto, Moz.	D11	70
Chicago, Il., U.S.	G2	112
Chicago Heights, Il., U.S.	G2	112
Chicapa, stm., Afr.	B3	68
Chichagof Island, i., Ak., U.S.	E12	140
Chichén Itzá, sci., Mex.	B3	102
Chichester, Eng., U.K.	K12	12
Chichibu, Japan	D12	40
Chichiriviche, Ven.	B7	86
Chickamauga, Ga., U.S.	C13	122
Chickamauga Lake, res., Tn., U.S.	B14	122
Chickasaw, Al., U.S.	G10	122
Chickasawhay, stm., Ms., U.S.	F10	122
Chickasaw National Recreation Area, p.o.i., Ok., U.S.	G12	128
Chickasha, Ok., U.S.	F11	128
Chicken, Ak., U.S.	D11	140
Chiclana de la Frontera, Spain	H4	20
Chiclayo, Peru	E2	84
Chico, Ca., U.S.	D4	134
Chico, Tx., U.S.	H11	128
Chico, stm., Arg.	I2	90
Chico, stm., Arg.	I3	90
Chico, stm., Phil.	B3	52
Chicomba, Ang.	C2	68
Chicopee, Ga., U.S.	B2	116
Chicopee, Ma., U.S.	B13	114
Chicoutimi, Qc., Can.	B5	110
Chicoutimi, stm., Qc., Can.	B5	110
Chicuma, Ang.	C1	68
Chidambaram, India	H4	53
Chidenguele, Moz.	D12	70
Chiefland, Fl., U.S.	G3	116
Chiehyang see Jieyang, China	J7	42
Chiemsee, l., Ger.	I8	16
Chieo Lan Reservoir, res., Thai.	H4	48
Chieri, Italy	F4	22
Chiese, stm., Italy	E7	22
Chieti, Italy	H11	22
Chifeng, China	C3	38
Chigasaki, Japan	D12	40
Chignahuapan, Mex.	F9	100
Chignecto, Cape, c., N.S., Can.	E11	110
Chignecto Bay, b., Can.	E12	110
Chignik, Ak., U.S.	E8	140
Chigoubiche, Lac, l., Qc., Can.	A3	110
Chigubo, Moz.	C11	70
Chigu Co, l., China	D13	54
Ch'ihfeng see Chifeng, China	C3	38
Chihli, Gulf of see Bo Hai, b., China	B8	42
Chihsi see Jixi, China	B9	38
Chihuahua, Mex.	A5	100
Chihuahua, state, Mex.	B3	96
Chihuahua, Desierto de, des., N.A.	F6	108
Chihuahuan Desert see Chihuahua, Desierto de, des., N.A.	F6	108
Chii-san, mtn., Kor., S.	G7	38
Chikaskia, stm., U.S.	E11	128
Chik Ballāpur, India	E3	53
Chikhli, India	H6	54
Chikmagalūr, India	E2	53
Chiknāyakanhalli, India	E3	53
Chikodi, India	C2	53
Chikrēng, stm., Camb.	F7	48
Chi-kyaw, Mya.	B1	48
Chilakalūrupet, India	C4	53
Chilako, stm., B.C., Can.	C7	138
Chilanko Forks, B.C., Can.	D6	138
Chilapa de Álvarez, Mex.	G9	100
Chilās, Pak.	B11	56
Chilcotin, stm., B.C., Can.	E8	138
Childers, Austl.	E9	76
Childersburg, Al., U.S.	D12	122
Childress, Tx., U.S.	G8	128
Chile, ctry., S.A.	F2	90
Chile Chico, Chile	I2	90
Chilecito, Arg.	D4	92
Chilecito, Arg.	F3	92
Chile Rise, unds.	M5	144
Chilia, Brațul, stm., Eur.	D16	26
Chilika Lake, l., India	H10	54
Chililabombwe, Zam.	C4	68
Chilin see Jilin, China	C7	38
Chilko, stm., B.C., Can.	E6	138
Chilko Lake, l., B.C., Can.	E6	138
Chillagoe, Austl.	C8	74
Chillán, Chile	H1	92
Chillicothe, Mo., U.S.	E4	120
Chillicothe, Oh., U.S.	E3	114
Chillicothe, Tx., U.S.	G9	128
Chilliwack, B.C., Can.	G9	138
Chiloé, Isla Grande de, i., Chile	H2	90
Chilón, Mex.	G12	100
Chiloquin, Or., U.S.	H5	136
Chilpancingo de los Bravo, Mex.	G9	100
Chiluage, Ang.	B3	68
Chilumba, Mwi.	C5	68
Chilung, Tai.	I9	42
Chilwa, Lake, l., Afr.	D6	68
Chimaltenango, Guat.	E2	102
Chimán, Pan.	H8	102
Chimay, Bel.	D13	14
Chimayo, N.M., U.S.	E3	128
Chimbarongo, Chile	G2	92
Chimbay see Chimboy, Uzb.	E9	32
Chimborazo, vol., Ec.	H2	86
Chimbote, Peru	E2	84
Chimoio, Moz.	D5	68
Chimpay, Arg.	G3	92
Chin, state, Mya.	B1	48
Chin, stm., Mya.	B1	48
China, ctry., Asia	A5	36
China, Mex.	C9	100
Chinandega, Nic.	F4	102
Chinati Peak, mtn., Tx., U.S.	E3	130
Chincha Alta, Peru	F2	84
Chinchaga, stm., Can.	D7	106
Chinchilla, Austl.	F8	76
Chinchilla de Monte-Aragón, Spain	F9	20
Chinchiná, Col.	E4	86
Chinchou see Jinzhou, China	A9	42
Chinchow see Jinzhou, China	A9	42
Chincoteague, Va., U.S.	G10	114
Chinde, Moz.	D6	68
Chindwin, stm., Mya.	D7	46
Ch'ingchiang see Qingjiang, China	E8	42
Chingleput, India	E5	53
Chingola, Zam.	C4	68
Chingshih see Jinshi, China	G4	42
Ch'ingtao see Qingdao, China	C9	42
Chingtechen see Jingdezhen, China	G7	42
Chinguetti, Maur.	E2	64
Chin Hills, hills, Mya.	D7	46
Chinhoyi, Zimb.	D5	68
Chinhsien see Jinzhou, China	B9	42
Chinhua see Jinhua, China	G8	42
Chining see Jining, China	D7	42
Chining see Jining, China	A5	42
Chiniot, Pak.	C4	54
Chinít, stm., Camb.	F7	48

Name	Map Ref.	Page
Chinjan, Pak.	C1	54
Chinju, Kor., S.	G7	38
Chinkiang see Zhenjiang, China.	E8	42
Chinko, stm., C.A.R.	C4	66
Chinle, Az., U.S.	G7	132
Chinle Wash, stm., Az., U.S.	G7	132
Chinmen Tao (Quemoy), i., Tai.	I8	42
Chino, Ca., U.S.	J8	134
Chinon, Fr.	G9	14
Chinook, Ab., Can.	C2	124
Chinook Cove, B.C., Can.	E10	138
Chino Valley, Az., U.S.	I4	132
Chinquapin, N.C., U.S.	B8	116
Chinsali, Zam.	C5	68
Chintāmani, India	E4	53
Chinú, Col.	C4	86
Chinwangtao see Qinhuangdao, China.	B8	42
Chioco, Moz.	D5	68
Chioggia, Italy.	E9	22
Chios, Grc.	E9	28
Chios, i., Grc.	E8	28
Chios see Chíos, i., Grc.	E8	28
Chipata, Zam.	C5	68
Chip Lake, l., Ab., Can.	C15	138
Chiplún, India	C1	53
Chipman, N.B., Can.	D11	110
Chipola, stm., Fl., U.S.	G13	122
Chippenham, Eng., U.K.	J10	12
Chippewa, stm., Mn., U.S.	F3	118
Chippewa, stm., Wi., U.S.	G6	118
Chippewa, East Fork, stm., Wi., U.S.	F8	118
Chippewa Falls, Wi., U.S.	G7	118
Chiquimula, Guat.	E3	102
Chiquinquirá, Col.	E4	86
Chīrāla, India.	D5	53
Chirāva, India	D5	54
Chiredzi, Zimb.	B10	70
Chireno, Tx., U.S.	F4	122
Chirfa, Niger	E7	64
Chīrgaon, India	F7	54
Chiribiquete, Parque Nacional, p.o.i., Col.	G5	86
Chiricahua Mountains, mts., Az., U.S.	L7	132
Chiricahua National Monument, p.o.i., Az., U.S.	L7	132
Chiricahua Peak, mtn., Az., U.S.	L7	132
Chiriguaná, Col.	C5	86
Chirikof Island, i., Ak., U.S.	E8	140
Chiriquí, Golfo de, b., Pan.	H6	102
Chiriquí, Laguna de, b., Pan.	H6	102
Chiromo, Mwi.	D5	68
Chirpan see Čirpan, Blg.	G12	26
Chirripó, Cerro, mtn., C.R.	H6	102
Chirripó, Parque Nacional, p.o.i., C.R.	H6	102
Chisago City, Mn., U.S.	F5	118
Chisamba, Zam.	C4	68
Chisasibi, Qc., Can.	E15	106
Chisep'o, Kor., S.	E1	40
Ch'ishan, Tai.	J9	42
Chisholm, B.C., Can.	B16	138
Chisholm, Me., U.S.	F6	110
Chisholm, Mn., U.S.	D5	118
Chishtiān Mandi, Pak.	D4	54
Chishui, China.	G1	42
Chishui, stm., China	G1	42
Chisimayu see Kismaayo, Som.	E8	66
Chişinău, Mol.	B15	26
Chişineu-Criş, Rom.	C8	26
Chita, Col.	D5	86
Chitado, Ang.	D1	68
Chitagá, Col.	D5	86
Chita-hantō, pen., Japan	E9	40
Chitato, Ang.	B3	68
Chitek Lake, l., Mb., Can.	B14	124
Chitembo, Ang.	C2	68
Chitina, Ak., U.S.	D11	140
Chitina, stm., Ak., U.S.	D11	140
Chitipa, Mwi.	B5	68
Chitokoloki, Zam.	C3	68
Chitose, Japan.	C14	38
Chitradurga, India	D3	53
Chitrakūt Dhām, India	F8	54
Chitrāl, Pak.	B11	56
Chitrāvati, stm., India	D3	53
Chitré, Pan.	H7	102
Chittagong, Bngl.	G13	54
Chittagong, state, Bngl.	G13	54
Chittaŭr, India	F5	54
Chittaurgarh, India	F5	54
Chittoor, India.	E4	53
Chittūr, India.	F3	53
Chitungwiza, Zimb.	D5	68
Chiuchiang see Jiujiang, China.	G6	42
Chiumbe (Tshumbe), stm., Afr.	B3	68
Chiume, Ang.	D3	68
Chiusi, Italy	G8	22
Chiva see Xiva, Spain.	E10	20
Chivacoa, Ven.	B7	86
Chivasso, Italy	E4	22
Chivi, Zimb.	B10	70
Chivilcoy, Arg.	G7	92
Chivirira Falls, wtfl., Zimb.	B11	70
Chizu, Japan.	D7	40
Chkalov, Az., U.S.	H2	132
Chmielnik, Pol.	F16	16
Chôâm Khsant, Camb.	E7	48
Choapa, stm., Chile	E2	92
Choceň, Czech Rep.	F12	16
Chochis, Cerro, mtn., Bol.	C5	90
Choch'iwŏn, Kor., S.	F7	38
Chociwel, Pol.	C11	16
Chocó, state, Col.	E3	86
Chocolate Mountains, mts., U.S.	J1	132
Chocontá, Col.	E5	86
Chocope, Peru	E2	84
Choctawhatchee, West Fork, stm., Al., U.S.	G13	122
Choctawhatchee Bay, b., Fl., U.S.	G12	122
Chodzież, Pol.	D12	16
Choele Choel, Arg.	G3	90
Choiseul, St. Luc.	m6	105c
Choiseul, state, Sol. Is.	d7	79b
Choiseul, i., Sol. Is.	d7	79b
Chojna, Pol.	D10	16
Chojnice, Pol.	C13	16
Chojnów, Pol.	E11	16
Ch'ok'ē, mtn., Eth.	E7	62
Choke Canyon Reservoir, res., Tx., U.S.	F9	130
Chokio, Mn., U.S.	F2	118
Chokwe, Moz.	D11	70
Cholet, Fr.	G8	14
Choluteca, Hond.	F4	102
Choluteca, stm., Hond.	F4	102
Choma, Zam.	D4	68
Chomo Lhāri, mtn., Asia	E12	54
Chomūm, India.	E5	54
Chomutov, Czech Rep.	F9	16
Ch'ŏnan, Kor., S.	F7	38
Chon Buri, Thai.	F5	48
Chon Daen, Thai.	D5	48
Chone, Ec.	H1	86
Ch'ŏngan, China	H8	42
Ch'ŏngdo, Kor., S.	D1	40
Ch'ŏngjin, Kor., N.	D8	38
Ch'ŏngju, Kor., S.	F7	38
Chong Kal, Camb.	E6	48
Chongming, China.	G9	42
Chongming Dao, i., China	F9	42
Chongoroi, Ang.	C1	68
Chongqing (Chungking), China.	G2	42

Chongqing, state, China	F6	36
Chŏngsŏn, Kor., S.	B1	40
Chŏngŭp, Kor., S.	G7	38
Chongxin, China.	D2	42
Chongzuo, China	A8	48
Chŏnju, Kor., S.	G7	38
Chonos, Archipiélago de los, is., Chile.	I1	90
Ch'ŏnsu-ri, Kor., N.	D8	38
Chontaleña, Cordillera, mts., Nic.	G5	102
Cho Oyu see Chopu, mtn., Asia	D11	54
Cho Oyu see Qowowuyag, mtn., Asia	D11	54
Chopda, India	H5	54
Chopim, stm., Braz.	C11	92
Chopinzinho, Braz.	B11	92
Chopu (Qowowuyag), mtn., Asia	D11	54
Chorna, Ukr.	B16	26
Chornobyl', Ukr.	D4	32
Choros, Isla, i., Chile	D2	92
Ch'ŏrwŏn, Kor., S.	E7	38
Chorzele, Pol.	C16	16
Chosen, Fl., U.S.	J5	116
Chōshi, Japan	D13	40
Chosica, Peru	F2	84
Chos Malal, Arg.	H2	92
Choszczno, Pol.	C11	16
Chotila, India.	G3	54
Chouchak'ou see Shangshui, China.	E6	42
Chouk'ou see Shangshui, China.	E6	42
Choushan Islands see Zhoushan Qundao, is., China.	F10	42
Chowchilla, Ca., U.S.	F5	134
Chown, Mount, mtn., Ab., Can.	C11	138
Choya, Arg.	D5	92
Choybalsan, Mong.	B7	36
Choyr, Mong.	B6	36
Chrisman, Il., U.S.	I2	112
Christiansbåb (Qasigiannguit), Grnld.	D15	141
Christchurch, N.Z.	F5	80
Christian, Cape, c., Nu., Can.	A17	106
Christian, Point, c., Pit.	c28	78k
Christiana, Jam.	i13	104d
Christiana, S. Afr.	E7	70
Christian Island, i., On., Can.	D9	112
Christiansburg, Va., U.S.	G5	114
Christian Sound, strt., Ak., U.S.	E12	140
Christiansted, V.I.U.S.	h11	104c
Christmas Island, dep., Oc.	K13	142
Christmas Island, i., Christ. I.	E1	72
Christmas Island see Kiritimati, at., Kir.	C11	72
Christmas Ridge, unds.	J22	142
Christoval, Tx., U.S.	C7	130
Chrudim, Czech Rep.	G11	16
Chrzanów, Pol.	F15	16
Chu (Xam), stm., Asia.	B7	48
Chuàdanga, Bngl.	G12	54
Chuanchou see Quanzhou, China.	I8	42
Chubbuck, Id., U.S.	H14	136
Chūbu-Sangaku-kokuritsu-kōen, p.o.i., Japan.	C10	40
Chubut, state, Arg.	H3	90
Chubut, stm., Arg.	H3	90
Ch'üchiang see Shaoguan, China.	I5	42
Chuchi Lake, l., B.C., Can.	A6	138
Chuchou see Zhuzhou, China.	H5	42
Chuckow see Zhuzhou, China.	H5	42
Chu Chua, B.C., Can.	E10	138
Chucunaque, stm., Pan.	H9	102
Chugach Mountains, mts., Ak., U.S.	D10	140
Chuginadak Island, i., Ak., U.S.	g25	140a
Chūgoku-sanchi, mts., Japan	D6	40
Chugwater Creek, stm., Wy., U.S.	F8	126
Chuhuichupa, Mex.	G8	98
Chui, Braz.	F11	92
Chukchi Sea, s.	C5	94
Chuke Hu, l., China	C11	54
Chukotka Peninsula see Čukotskij poluostrov, pen., Russia.	C26	34
Chula Vista, Ca., U.S.	K8	134
Chulucanas, Peru	E1	84
Chumbicha, Arg.	D4	92
Chum Phae, Thai.	D6	48
Chumphon, Thai.	G4	48
Chumphon Buri, Thai.	E6	48
Chum Saeng, Thai.	E5	48
Chumunjin, Kor., S.	B1	40
Chun'an, China	G8	42
Chunan, Tai.	I9	42
Chuncheon see Ch'unch'ŏn, Kor., S.	F7	38
Chunchi, Ec.	I2	86
Ch'unch'ŏn, Kor., S.	F7	38
Chunchula, Al., U.S.	G10	122
Ch'ungch'ŏng-bukto, state, Kor., S.	B1	40
Ch'ungju, Kor., S.	F7	38
Chungking see Chongqing, China.	G2	42
Ch'ungmu, Kor., S.	E1	40
Chungsan see Zhongshan, China.	J5	42
Chungyang Shanmo, mts., Tai.	J9	42
Chunhua, China	D3	42
Chunhuhux, Mex.	C3	102
Chuquibamba, Peru	G3	84
Chuquicamata, Chile	D3	90
Chur (Coire), Switz.	D6	22
Church Hill, Tn., U.S.	H3	114
Churchill, Mb., Can.	D12	106
Churchill, stm., Nf., Can.	E18	106
Churchill, stm., Can.	D11	106
Churchill, Mount, mtn., B.C., Can.	G7	138
Churchill, Mount, vol., Ak., U.S.	D11	140
Churchill Falls, wtfl., Nf., Can.	E17	106
Churchill Lake, l., Sk., Can.	D9	106
Church Point, La., U.S.	G6	122
Church Rock, N.M., U.S.	H8	132
Chūru, India.	D5	54
Churuguara, In., U.S.	G4	112
Churuguara, Ven.	B7	86
Churuhul, India.	B7	54
Chute-Saint-Philippe, Qc., Can.	D1	110
Chutung, Tai.	I9	42
Chuuk, i., Micron.	C6	72
Chuvashia see Čuvašija, state, Russia.	C7	32
Chuxian, China	E8	42
Chuxiong, China	F5	36
Ci, stm., China	E6	42
Ci, stm., China	B6	42
Ciadâr Lunga, Mol.	C15	26
Ciales, P.R.	B3	104a
Ciamis, Indon.	G5	50
Cianjur, Indon.	G5	50
Cianorte, Braz.	A11	92
Ciatura, Geor.	F6	32
Ciawi, Indon.	G5	50
Cibaliung, Indon.	G4	50

Cibatu, Indon.	G6	50
Cibinong, Indon.	G5	50
Cibola Creek, stm., Tx., U.S.	E3	130
Cibolo Creek, stm., Tx., U.S.	E10	130
Cicero, Il., U.S.	G2	112
Cicero, In., U.S.	H3	112
Cicero Dantas, Braz.	F6	88
Cicurug, Indon.	G5	50
Cidra, P.R.	B3	104a
Ciechanów, Pol.	D16	16
Ciechanów, state, Pol.	C16	16
Ciechanowiec, Pol.	D18	16
Ciego de Ávila, Cuba	B8	102
Ciempozuelos, Spain	D7	20
Ciénaga, Col.	B4	86
Ciénega de Flores, Mex.	H7	130
Cienfuegos, Cuba	A7	102
Cíes, Islas see Cíes, Illas, is., Spain.	B1	20
Cíes, Illas, is., Spain.	B1	20
Cieszanów, Pol.	F19	16
Cieszyn, Pol.	G14	16
Cieza, Spain	F9	20
Çifteler, Tur.	D13	28
Cifuentes, Spain	D8	20
Ciğūela, stm., Spain	E7	20
Cihanbeyli, Tur.	E15	28
Cijara, Embalse de, res., Spain	E6	20
Cijulang, Uzb.	G6	50
Cikampek, Indon.	G5	50
Çikobia, i., Fiji	o20	79e
Čikoj, Russia	F10	34
Cilacap, Indon.	G6	50
Cilamaya, Indon.	G5	50
Cilento, reg., Italy	D9	24
Cili, China	G4	42
Cilician Gates see Gülek Boğazı, p., Tur.	A5	58
Çilik see Shelek, Kaz.	F13	32
Cill Chainnigh see Kilkenny, Ire.	I5	12
Cilleruelo de Bezana, Spain	B7	20
Ci'ma, stm., Russia	D24	8
Cimarron, N.M., U.S.	E4	128
Cimarron, stm., U.S.	F12	128
Cimarron, North Fork, stm., U.S.	D7	128
Cimișlia, Uzb.	D1	32
Cimișlia, Mol.	C15	26
Cimljanskoe vodohranilišče, res., Russia.	E6	32
Cimone, Monte, mtn., Italy.	F7	22
Cimpu, Indon.	E12	50
Cina, Tanjung, c., Indon.	G4	50
Cinaruco, stm., Ven.	D7	86
Cinaruco-Capanaparo Santos Luzardo, Parque Nacional, p.o.i., Ven.	D8	86
Cinca, stm., Spain.	C11	20
Cincinnati, Ia., U.S.	D4	120
Cincinnati, Oh., U.S.	E1	114
Cinco, Canal Numero, can., Arg.	H9	92
Cinco de Mayo, Mex.	F8	130
Cinco Saltos, Arg.	I3	92
Çine, Tur.	F10	28
Ciney, Bel.	D14	14
Cinfães, Port.	C2	20
Cinişeuţi, Mol.	B15	26
Cintalapa, Mex.	G12	100
Cinto, Monte, mtn., Fr.	G14	18
Cintra, Golfe de, b., W. Sah.	E1	64
Ciociaria, reg., Italy	I10	22
Cipa, stm., Russia	F11	34
Cipatujah, Indon.	G5	50
Cipó, Braz.	F6	88
Cipó, stm., Braz.	J4	88
Cipolletti, Arg.	G3	90
Circeo, Parco Nazionale del, p.o.i., Italy	C6	24
Cirčik, Uzb.	F11	32
Circle, Ak., U.S.	C11	140
Circle, Mt., U.S.	G8	124
Circleville, Oh., U.S.	E3	114
Circleville, Ut., U.S.	E4	132
Circleville Mountain, mtn., Ut., U.S.	E4	132
Cirebon, Indon.	G6	50
Ciremay, Gunung, vol., Indon.	G6	50
Cirencester, Eng., U.K.	J11	12
Ćirgalandy, Russia	D17	32
Ciriè, Italy	E4	22
Cirò Marina, Italy	E11	24
Çirpan, Blg.	G12	26
Ciskei, hist. reg., S. Afr.	H8	70
Cisnădie, Rom.	D11	26
Cisne, Il., U.S.	F9	120
Cisne, Islas del see Santanilla, Islas, is., Hond.	D6	102
Cisneros, Col.	D4	86
Cisolok, Indon.	G5	50
Cïstoozërnoe, Russia	D13	32
Čistopol', Russia	C8	32
Cita, Russia	F11	34
Citlaltépetl, Volcán see Pico de Orizaba, Volcán, vol., Mex.	F10	100
Citra, Fl., U.S.	G3	116
Citrus Heights, Ca., U.S.	E4	134
Citrus Park, Fl., U.S.	H2	112
Città del Castello, Italy	G9	22
Cittanova, Italy	F10	24
City of Sunrise see Sunrise, Fl., U.S.	J5	116
City Point, Fl., U.S.	H5	116
Ciudad Acuña, Mex.	A8	100
Ciudad Altamirano, Mex.	F8	100
Ciudad Anáhuac, Mex.	B8	100
Ciudad Bolívar, Ven.	C10	86
Ciudad Bolivia, Ven.	C6	86
Ciudad Camargo, Mex.	B6	100
Ciudad Camargo, Mex.	B9	100
Ciudad Constitución, Mex.	C3	100
Ciudad Cortés, C.R.	H6	102
Ciudad Darío, Nic.	F4	102
Ciudad del Carmen, Mex.	F12	100
Ciudad del Este, Para.	B10	92
Ciudad de Libertador General San Martín, Arg.	A5	92
Ciudad de México (Mexico City), Mex.	F9	100
Ciudad de Nutrias, Ven.	C7	86
Ciudadela see Ciutadella de Menorca, Spain.	D14	20
Ciudad Guayana, Ven.	C10	86
Ciudad Hidalgo, Mex.	F8	100
Ciudad Jiménez see Jiménez, Mex.	B6	100
Ciudad Juárez, Mex.	C1	100
Ciudad Lerdo see Lerdo, Mex.	C7	100
Ciudad Madero, Mex.	D10	100
Ciudad Mante, Mex.	E9	18
Ciudad Miguel Alemán, Mex.	B9	100
Ciudad Morelos, Mex.	E5	98
Ciudad Netzahualcóyotl, Mex.	F9	100
Ciudad Obregón, Mex.	B4	100
Ciudad Ojeda, Ven.	B6	86
Ciudad Piar, Ven.	D10	86
Ciudad Real, Spain	F7	20
Ciudad Rodrigo, Spain	D4	20
Ciudad Valles, Mex.	E9	100
Ciudad Victoria, Mex.	D9	100
Ciutadella de Menorca, Spain	D14	20
Civita Castellana, Italy	H9	22
Civitanova Marche, Italy	G10	22
Civitavecchia, Italy	H8	22
Çivril, Tur.	E12	28
Clifton, Az., U.S.	J7	132

Cixi, China.	F9	42
Clifton, Tn., U.S.	B11	122
Clifton, Tx., U.S.	C10	130
Çıjalua, Bela.	G12	10
Clifton Forge, Va., U.S.	G6	114
Čkalovsk, Russia	H20	8
Clifton Hills, Austl.	F2	76
Clackamas, stm., Or., U.S.	E4	136
Climax, Sk., Can.	E5	124
Claflin, Ks., U.S.	C10	128
Climax, co., U.S.	B2	128
Claiborne, Al., U.S.	F11	122
Clinch, stm., U.S.	H13	120
Clain, stm., Fr.	C6	18
Clinchco, Va., U.S.	G15	120
Claire, Lake, l., Ab., Can.	D8	106
Clingmans Dome, mtn., U.S.	I2	114
Clair Engle Lake, res., Ca., U.S.	C3	134
Clinton, B.C., Can.	E9	138
Clairton, Pa., U.S.	D6	114
Clinton, On., Can.	E8	112
Clallam Bay, Wa., U.S.	B2	136
Clinton, Al., U.S.	E11	122
Clanton, Al., U.S.	E12	122
Clinton, Ar., U.S.	B6	122
Clanwilliam, S. Afr.	H4	70
Clinton, Ia., U.S.	C7	120
Clinton, In., U.S.	I2	112
Clapperton Island, i., On., Can.	B7	112
Clinton, Ky., U.S.	H9	120
Clara, Ire.	H5	12
Clinton, La., U.S.	G7	122
Clara, Ms., U.S.	F10	122
Clinton, Mi., U.S.	B2	114
Clara, stm., Austl.	B4	76
Clinton, Mn., U.S.	F2	118
Clara, Punta, c., Arg.	H4	90
Clinton, Mo., U.S.	F4	120
Clare, Ire.	I4	76
Clinton, N.C., U.S.	A7	116
Clare, Mi., U.S.	E5	112
Clinton, Ok., U.S.	F9	128
Clare, state, Ire.	I3	12
Clinton, S.C., U.S.	B4	116
Clare Island, i., Ire.	H2	12
Clinton, Wi., U.S.	B9	120
Claremont, N.H., U.S.	G4	110
Clinton, Lake, res., Il., U.S.	D9	120
Claremont, S.D., U.S.	B15	126
Clinton-Colden Lake, l., N.T., Can.	C9	106
Claremore, Ok., U.S.	H2	120
Clinton Lake, res., Ks., U.S.	F2	120
Claremont, mtn., Ca., U.S.	D4	134
Clintonville, Wi., U.S.	G10	118
Clarence, stm., Austl.	G9	76
Clintwood, Va., U.S.	G3	114
Clarence, stm., N.Z.	F5	80
Clio, Al., U.S.	E12	122
Clarence, Cape, c., Nu.	A13	106
Clio, Mi., U.S.	E6	112
Clarence, Isla, i., Chile	J2	90
Clio, S.C., U.S.	B6	116
Clarence Strait, strt., Austl.	B6	74
Clipperton, Île, at., Oc.	H28	142
Clarence Strait, strt., Ak., U.S.	E13	140
Clipperton Fracture Zone, unds.	I25	142
Clarendon, Ar., U.S.	C7	122
Clipperton Island see Clipperton, Île, at., Oc.	H28	142
Clarendon, Tx., U.S.	G8	128
Clisson, Fr.	G7	14
Clarenville, Nf., Can.	j23	107a
Clodomira, Arg.	C5	92
Claresholm, Ab., Can.	F17	138
Cloete, Mex.	G6	130
Clarinda, Ia., U.S.	D2	120
Cloncurry, Austl.	C3	76
Clarines, Ven.	C9	86
Cloncurry, stm., Austl.	B3	76
Clarington, On., Can.	E11	112
Clonmel, Ire.	I5	12
Clarion, Ia., U.S.	B4	120
Cloppenburg, Ger.	D3	16
Clarion, Pa., U.S.	C6	114
Cloquet, Mn., U.S.	E6	118
Clarion, stm., Pa., U.S.	C6	114
Clorinda, Arg.	B9	92
Clarion Fracture Zone, unds.	H25	142
Cloud Peak, mtn., Wy., U.S.	C5	126
Clarissa, Mn., U.S.	E3	118
Clova, Qc., Can.	A11	110
Clark, Mount, mtn., N.T., Can.	C6	106
Clover, S.C., U.S.	A4	116
Clarke, stm., Austl.	B6	76
Cloverdale, Ca., U.S.	E2	134
Clarke Island, i., Austl.	n14	77a
Cloverdale, In., U.S.	E11	120
Clarkesville, Ga., U.S.	B2	116
Cloverport, Ky., U.S.	G11	120
Clark Fork, Id., U.S.	B10	136
Clovis, Ca., U.S.	G6	134
Clark Fork, stm., U.S.	C11	136
Clovis, N.M., U.S.	G5	128
Clarks, La., U.S.	E6	122
Cluain Meala see Clonmel, Ire.	I5	12
Clarksburg, W.V., U.S.	E5	114
Cohoes, N.Y., U.S.	B12	114
Clarksdale, Ms., U.S.	C8	122
Cluj, state, Rom.	C10	26
Cohuna, Austl.	J5	76
Clark's Harbour, N.S., Can.	G11	110
Cluj-Napoca, Rom.	C10	26
Coiba, Isla de, i., Pan.	I6	102
Clarks Hill, In., U.S.	H3	112
Clunes, Austl.	K4	76
Coihaique, Chile	I2	90
Clarkson, Ky., U.S.	G11	120
Cluny, Austl.	E2	76
Coimbatore (Koyambattūr), India	F3	53
Clarks Summit, Pa., U.S.	C10	114
Cluny, Fr.	C10	18
Clarkston, Wa., U.S.	D9	136
Clusone, Italy	E7	22
Coimbra, India	F3	53
Clark's Town, Jam.	i13	104d
Clute, Tx., U.S.	E12	130
Coimbra, Port.	D2	20
Clarksville, Ar., U.S.	B5	122
Clutha, stm., N.Z.	H3	80
Coimbra, state, Port.	D2	20
Clarksville, Ia., U.S.	I6	118
Clyde, Ks., U.S.	B11	128
Coin, Spain	H6	20
Clarksville, Tn., U.S.	H10	120
Clyde, N.C., U.S.	A3	116
Coipasa, Lago l., Bol.	C3	90
Clarksville, Va., U.S.	H7	114
Clyde, Oh., U.S.	C3	114
Coipasa, Salar de, pl., S.A.	C3	90
Clarkton, Mo., U.S.	H7	120
Clyde, Tx., U.S.	B8	130
Coire see Chur, Switz.	D6	22
Clarkton, N.C., U.S.	B7	116
Clyde, Firth of, b., Scot., U.K.	F7	12
Cojedes, state, Ven.	C7	86
Claro, stm., Braz.	G7	84
Clyde Inlet, b., Nu., Can.	A17	106
Cojudo Blanco, Cerro, mtn., Arg.	I3	90
Claude, Tx., U.S.	F7	128
Clyde Park, Mt., U.S.	E16	136
Cojutepeque, El Sal.	F3	102
Clausthal-Zellerfeld, Ger.	E5	16
Clyde River see Kangiqtugaapik, Nu., Can.	A16	106
Cokato, Mn., U.S.	F4	118
Claveria, Phil.	B7	44
Clymer, Pa., U.S.	D6	114
Cokeville, Wy., U.S.	A6	132
Clavet, Sk., Can.	B7	124
Ćmielów, Pol.	F17	16
Cokurdah, Russia	B18	34
Claxton, Ga., U.S.	D4	116
Cna, stm., Russia	C17	10
Colac, Austl.	L4	76
Clay, stm., Russia	G10	120
Cna, stm., Russia	D6	32
Colatina, Braz.	J5	88
Clay, Ky., U.S.	D4	116
Cnossus see Knosós, sci., Grc.	H8	28
Colbeck, Cape, c., Ant.	C25	81
Clay Center, Ne., U.S.	G14	126
Côa, stm., Port.	D3	20
Colbert, Ok., U.S.	D2	122
Clay City, Il., U.S.	F9	120
Coachella, Ca., U.S.	J9	134
Colbinabbin, Austl.	K5	76
Clay City, In., U.S.	E10	120
Coachella Canal, can., Ca., U.S.	K1	132
Colbún, Chile	G2	92
Clay City, Ky., U.S.	G1	114
Coahoma, Tx., U.S.	B6	130
Colbún, Embalse, res., Chile	G2	92
Claymont, De., U.S.	E10	114
Coahuila, state, Mex.	B7	100
Colby, Ks., U.S.	B7	128
Claypool, Az., U.S.	J6	132
Coal City, Il., U.S.	J10	118
Colby, Wi., U.S.	G8	118
Claysburg, Pa., U.S.	D7	114
Coalcomán de Matamoros, Mex.	F7	100
Colchester, Eng., U.K.	J13	12
Clayton, Ab., Can.	G18	138
Coal Creek, stm., Wy., U.S.	C6	126
Colchester, Il., U.S.	D7	120
Clayton, Ga., U.S.	B2	116
Coaldale, Ab., Can.	G18	138
Cold Bay, Ak., U.S.	E7	140
Clayton, Il., U.S.	D7	120
Coalgate, Ok., U.S.	C2	122
Cold Lake, Ab., Can.	E8	106
Clayton, Mo., U.S.	F7	120
Coal Grove, Oh., U.S.	F3	114
Cold Spring, Mn., U.S.	F4	118
Clayton, N.M., U.S.	E5	128
Coal Hill, Ar., U.S.	B5	122
Coldstream, Scot., U.K.	F10	12
Clayton, N.Y., U.S.	D13	112
Coalinga, Ca., U.S.	G5	134
Coldwater, On., Can.	D9	128
Clayton, Ok., U.S.	C3	122
Coalmont, B.C., Can.	G10	138
Coldwater, Mi., U.S.	G4	112
Clayton, Wa., U.S.	B9	136
Coalport, Pa., U.S.	D7	114
Coldwater, Oh., U.S.	H5	112
Clear, Cape, c., Ire.	J3	12
Coal River, B.C., Can.	D5	106
Coldwater, stm., Ms., U.S.	C8	122
Clear Boggy Creek, stm., Ok., U.S.	C2	122
Coal Valley, val., Nv., U.S.	F1	132
Coldwater Creek, stm., U.S.	E7	128
Clearbrook, Mn., U.S.	D3	118
Coalville, Eng., U.K.	I11	12
Coleambally, Austl.	J5	76
Clear Creek, stm., Wy., U.S.	C6	126
Coalville, Ut., U.S.	C5	132
Colebrook, N.H., U.S.	F5	110
Clearfield, Pa., U.S.	D7	114
Coamo, P.R.	B3	104a
Cole Camp, Mo., U.S.	F4	120
Clearfield, Ut., U.S.	B4	132
Coari, Braz.	H6	84
Coleman, Ab., Can.	G16	138
Clearlake, Ca., U.S.	E3	134
Coari, stm., Braz.	D5	84
Coleman, Fl., U.S.	H3	116
Clear Lake, Ia., U.S.	A4	120
Coast Mountains, mts., N.A.	D4	106
Coleman, Mi., U.S.	E5	112
Clear Lake, S.D., U.S.	G2	118
Coast Ranges, mts., U.S.	C2	134
Coleman, Wi., U.S.	C1	112
Clear Lake, Wi., U.S.	F6	118
Coatbridge, Scot., U.K.	F8	12
Coleman, stm., Austl.	B8	74
Clear Lake, l., Mb., Can.	D14	124
Coatesville, Pa., U.S.	E10	114
Coleraine, N. Ire., U.K.	F6	12
Clear Lake, l., Ca., U.S.	D3	134
Coaticook, Qc., Can.	E5	110
Coleridge, Ne., U.S.	E15	126
Clear Lake Reservoir, res., Ca., U.S.	B4	134
Coats Island, i., Nu., Can.	C14	106
Coles, Ms., U.S.	I3	112
Clearmont, Wy., U.S.	C6	126
Coats Land, reg., Ant.	C2	81
Colesberg, S. Afr.	G7	70
Clearwater, B.C., Can.	E10	138
Coatzacoalcos, Mex.	F11	100
Coleville, Sk., Can.	C4	124
Clearwater, Mb., Can.	E14	124
Cobá, sci., Mex.	B4	102
Colfax, Il., U.S.	D9	120
Clearwater, Fl., U.S.	I3	116
Cobalt, On., Can.	F14	106
Colfax, In., U.S.	H3	112
Clearwater, Ne., U.S.	E14	126
Cobán, Guat.	E2	102
Colfax, La., U.S.	F5	122
Clearwater, stm., B.C., Can.	D15	138
Cobar, Austl.	H5	76
Colfax, Wa., U.S.	D9	136
Clearwater, stm., Can.	D10	138
Cobberas, Mount, mtn., Austl.	K6	76
Colgong, India	F11	54
Clearwater, stm., Id., U.S.	D10	136
Cobden, On., Can.	C13	112
Colhué Huapi, Lago, l., Arg.	I3	90
Clearwater, stm., Mn., U.S.	D3	118
Cobequid Bay, b., N.S., Can.	E13	110
Colibris, Pointe des, c., Guad.	h6	105c
Clearwater, stm., Mt., U.S.	C13	136
Cobh, Ire.	J4	12
Colico, Italy	D6	22
Clearwater, Middle Fork, stm., Id., U.S.	D11	136
Cobham, stm., Can.	B18	124
Coligny, S. Afr.	E8	70
Clearwater, North Fork, stm., Id., U.S.	D11	136
Cobija, Bol.	B3	90
Colihaut, Dom.	j5	105c
Clearwater Lake, l., B.C., Can.	D10	138
Cobleskill, N.Y., U.S.	B11	114
Colima, Mex.	F7	100
Clearwater Mountains, mts., Id., U.S.	D11	136
Cobourg, On., Can.	E11	112
Colima, Nevado de, vol., Mex.	F7	100
Clebit, Ok., U.S.	C4	122
Cobram, Austl.	J5	76
Colinas, Braz.	D3	88
Cle Elum, stm., Wa., U.S.	C5	136
Côbue, Moz.	C6	68
Colinas, Braz.	H1	88
Cle Elum Lake, res., Wa., U.S.	C5	136
Coburg, Ger.	F6	16
Coll, i., Scot., U.K.	E6	12
Cleethorpes, Eng., U.K.	H12	12
Coburg Island, i., Nu., Can.	B10	141
Collarenebri, Austl.	G7	76
Clementsport, N.S., Can.	F11	110
Coburg Peninsula, pen., Austl.	B6	74
College, Ak., U.S.	D10	140
Clemson, S.C., U.S.	B3	116
Coca, stm., Ec.	H3	86
Collegedale, Tn., U.S.	B13	122
Cocentaina, Spain	F10	20
College Park, Ga., U.S.	D14	122
Clermont, Austl.	D6	76
Cocal, Braz.	B5	88
College Park, Md., U.S.	E9	114
Clermont, Qc., Can.	C6	110
Côch, stm., Asia	B6	36
College Station, Ar., U.S.	C6	122
Clermont, Fl., U.S.	H4	116
Coche, Isla, i., Ven.	B10	86
College Station, Tx., U.S.	G2	122
Clermont-Ferrand, Fr.	D9	18
Cochem, Ger.	F3	16
Collerina, Austl.	G6	76
Clevedon, Eng., U.K.	J10	12
Cochin see Kochi, India	G3	53
Colleymount, B.C., Can.	B4	138
Cleveland, Al., U.S.	D12	122
Cochin China see Nam Phan, hist. reg., Viet.	G8	48
Collie, Austl.	F3	74
Cleveland, Ms., U.S.	D8	122
Cochinos, Bahía de (Pigs, Bay of), b., Cuba	A7	102
Collier Bay, b., Austl.	C4	74
Cleveland, N.C., U.S.	A5	116
Cochise Head, mtn., Az., U.S.	K7	132
Collierville, Tn., U.S.	B9	122
Cleveland, Oh., U.S.	C4	114
Cochran, Ga., U.S.	D2	116
Collingwood, On., Can.	D9	112
Cleveland, Ok., U.S.	E16	138
Cochrane, Ab., Can.	E16	138
Collins, Ga., U.S.	D3	116
Cleveland, Tn., U.S.	B14	122
Cochrane, On., Can.	F14	106
Collins, Ms., U.S.	F9	122
Cleveland, Tx., U.S.	G3	122
Cochrane, Wi., U.S.	H7	118
Collinsville, Al., U.S.	C13	122
Cleveland, Wi., U.S.	E2	112
Cochrane, Lago (Pueyrredón, Lago), l., S.A.	I2	90
Collinsville, Austl.	C6	76
Cleveland, Cape, c., Austl.	B6	76
Cochranton, Pa., U.S.	C5	114
Collinsville, Ok., U.S.	H2	120
Cleveland, Mount, mtn., Mt., U.S.	B13	136
Cockburn, Austl.	I3	76
Collinwood, Tn., U.S.	B11	122
Cleves see Kleve, Ger.	E2	16
Cockburn, Mount, mtn., Austl.	E5	74
Collipulli, Chile	H1	92
Clewiston, Fl., U.S.	J5	116
Cockburn, Mount, mtn., Austl.	D5	74
Colman, S.D., U.S.	H2	118
Clifden, St. Vin.	p11	105e
Cockburn Island, i., On., Can.	C6	112
Colmar, Fr.	H6	20
Clifton, Az., U.S.	J7	132
Colmenar, Spain	H6	20
Cockermouth, Eng., U.K.	G9	12
Colmenar Viejo, Spain	D7	20
Cockpit Country, reg., Jam.	i13	104d
Colmeneros, Mex.	E7	100
Côco, stm., Braz.	F1	88
Colmesneil, Tx., U.S.	G4	122
Coco, stm., N.A.	E6	102
Colne, Eng., U.K.	H10	12
Coco, Cayo, i., Cuba	A8	102
Colnett, Punta, c., Mex.	F4	98
Coco, Isla del, i., C.R.	F7	96
Cocoa, Fl., U.S.	H5	116
Cocoa Beach, Fl., U.S.	H5	116
Coco Channel, strt., Asia.	F7	46
Cocodrie Lake, res., La., U.S.	G6	122
Coconino Plateau, plat., Az., U.S.	H4	132
Cocos, Braz.	H3	88
Cocos Islands, is., Mya.	F7	46
Cocos Islands, dep., Oc.	K12	142
Cocos Lagoon, b., Guam	k9	78c
Cocos Ridge, unds.	H5	144
Cocula, Mex.	E7	100
Cod, Cape, pen., Ma., U.S.	C15	114
Codajás, Braz.	D5	84
Codera, Cabo, c., Ven.	B8	86
Coderre, Sk., Can.	D7	124
Codigoro, Italy	F9	22
Cod Island, i., Nf., Can.	F13	141
Codlea, Rom.	D12	26
Codó, Braz.	C3	88
Codogno, Italy	E6	22
Codózinho, Braz.	C3	88
Codroy, Nf., Can.	C17	110
Cody, Ne., U.S.	E11	126
Cody, Wy., U.S.	C3	126
Coelho Neto, Braz.	C4	88
Coen, Austl.	B8	74
Coëtivy, i., Sey.	k13	69b
Coeur d'Alene, Id., U.S.	C10	136
Coeur d'Alene, stm., Id., U.S.	C10	136
Coeur d'Alene Lake, res., Id., U.S.	C10	136
Coffeeville, Ms., U.S.	D9	122
Coffeyville, Ks., U.S.	G2	120
Coffs Harbour, Austl.	H9	76
Cofre de Perote, Cerro, mtn., Mex.	F10	100
Cofre de Perote, Parque Nacional, p.o.i., Mex.	F10	100
Cofrentes see Cofrents, Spain	E9	20
Cofrents, Spain	E9	20
Cogălnic (Kohyl'nyk), stm., Eur.	C15	26
Coggon, Ia., U.S.	B6	120
Cognac, Fr.	D5	18
Cogolludo, Spain	D7	20
Cogoon, stm., Austl.	F7	76
Cogswell, N.D., U.S.	A15	126
Cohocton, stm., N.Y., U.S.	F12	112
Cohoes, N.Y., U.S.	B12	114
Cohuna, Austl.	J5	76
Coiba, Isla de, i., Pan.	I6	102
Coihaique, Chile	I2	90
Coimbatore (Koyambattūr), India	F3	53
Coimbra, Port.	D2	20
Coimbra, state, Port.	D2	20
Coin, Spain	H6	20
Coipasa, Lago, l., Bol.	C3	90
Coipasa, Salar de, pl., S.A.	C3	90
Coire see Chur, Switz.	D6	22
Cojedes, state, Ven.	C7	86
Cojudo Blanco, Cerro, mtn., Arg.	I3	90
Cojutepeque, El Sal.	F3	102
Cokato, Mn., U.S.	F4	118
Cokeville, Wy., U.S.	A6	132
Cokurdah, Russia	B18	34
Colac, Austl.	L4	76
Colatina, Braz.	J5	88
Colbeck, Cape, c., Ant.	C25	81
Colbert, Ok., U.S.	D2	122
Colbinabbin, Austl.	K5	76
Colbún, Chile	G2	92
Colbún, Embalse, res., Chile	G2	92
Colby, Ks., U.S.	B7	128
Colby, Wi., U.S.	G8	118
Colchester, Eng., U.K.	J13	12
Colchester, Il., U.S.	D7	120
Cold Bay, Ak., U.S.	E7	140
Cold Lake, Ab., Can.	E8	106
Cold Spring, Mn., U.S.	F4	118
Coldstream, Scot., U.K.	F10	12
Coldwater, On., Can.	D9	128
Coldwater, Mi., U.S.	G4	112
Coldwater, Oh., U.S.	H5	112
Coldwater, stm., Ms., U.S.	C8	122
Coldwater Creek, stm., U.S.	E7	128
Coleambally, Austl.	J5	76
Colebrook, N.H., U.S.	F5	110
Cole Camp, Mo., U.S.	F4	120
Coleman, Ab., Can.	G16	138
Coleman, Fl., U.S.	H3	116
Coleman, Mi., U.S.	E5	112
Coleman, Wi., U.S.	C1	112
Coleman, stm., Austl.	B8	74
Coleraine, N. Ire., U.K.	F6	12
Coleridge, Ne., U.S.	E15	126
Coles, Ms., U.S.	I3	112
Colesberg, S. Afr.	G7	70
Coleville, Sk., Can.	C4	124
Colfax, Il., U.S.	D9	120
Colfax, In., U.S.	H3	112
Colfax, La., U.S.	F5	122
Colfax, Wa., U.S.	D9	136
Colgong, India	F11	54
Colhué Huapi, Lago, l., Arg.	I3	90
Colibris, Pointe des, c., Guad.	h6	105c
Colico, Italy	D6	22
Coligny, S. Afr.	E8	70
Colihaut, Dom.	j5	105c
Colima, Mex.	F7	100
Colima, Nevado de, vol., Mex.	F7	100
Colinas, Braz.	D3	88
Colinas, Braz.	H1	88
Coll, i., Scot., U.K.	E6	12
Collarenebri, Austl.	G7	76
College, Ak., U.S.	D10	140
Collegedale, Tn., U.S.	B13	122
College Park, Ga., U.S.	D14	122
College Park, Md., U.S.	E9	114
College Station, Ar., U.S.	C6	122
College Station, Tx., U.S.	G2	122
Collerina, Austl.	G6	76
Colleymount, B.C., Can.	B4	138
Collie, Austl.	F3	74
Collier Bay, b., Austl.	C4	74
Collierville, Tn., U.S.	B9	122
Collingwood, On., Can.	D9	112
Collins, Ga., U.S.	D3	116
Collins, Ms., U.S.	F9	122
Collinsville, Al., U.S.	C13	122
Collinsville, Austl.	C6	76
Collinsville, Ok., U.S.	H2	120
Collinwood, Tn., U.S.	B11	122
Collipulli, Chile	H1	92
Colman, S.D., U.S.	H2	118
Colmar, Fr.	H6	20
Colmenar, Spain	H6	20
Colmenar Viejo, Spain	D7	20
Colmeneros, Mex.	E7	100
Colmesneil, Tx., U.S.	G4	122
Colne, Eng., U.K.	H10	12
Colnett, Punta, c., Mex.	F4	98

Name	Map Ref.	Page
Cologne see Köln, Ger.	F2	16
Cologne, Mn., U.S.	G5	118
Coloma, Mi., U.S.	F3	112
Coloma, Wi., U.S.	G9	118
Colomb-Béchar see Béchar, Alg.	C4	64
Colombia, Col.	F4	86
Colombia, ctry., S.A.	C3	84
Colombie-Britannique see British Columbia, state, Can.	E5	106
Colombo, Braz.	B13	92
Colombo, Sri L.	H4	53
Colome, S.D., U.S.	D13	126
Colomiers, Fr.	F7	18
Colón, Arg.	F8	92
Colón, Arg.	F7	92
Colón, Cuba	A7	102
Colón, Pan.	H7	102
Colón, Ur.	F10	92
Colón, Mi., U.S.	G4	112
Colón, Archipiélago de (Galapagos Islands), is., Ec.	h12	84a
Colona, Austl.	F6	74
Colonelganj, India	E8	54
Colônia, stm., Braz.	H6	88
Colonia Alvear Norte see General Alvear, Arg.	G3	92
Colonia Dora, Arg.	C8	92
Colonia Elisa, Arg.	E9	92
Colonia Lavalleja, Arg.	C8	92
Colonial Heights, Va., U.S.	G8	114
Colonia Providencia, P.R.	C4	104a
Colonia Suiza, Ur.	G9	92
Colonias Unidas, Arg.	C8	92
Colonne, Capo, c., Italy	E11	24
Colonsay, Sk., Can.	B8	124
Colonsay, i., Scot., U.K.	E6	12
Colony, Ks., U.S.	F2	120
Colorada Grande, Salina, pl., Arg.	I5	92
Colorado, Lomas, hills, Arg.	H3	90
Colorado, Hond.	E4	102
Colorado, state, U.S.	D6	108
Colorado, stm., Arg.	G4	90
Colorado, stm., N.A.	D6	98
Colorado, stm., Tx., U.S.	F11	130
Colorado, Cerro, mtn., Arg.	H3	90
Colorado City, Co., U.S.	C4	128
Colorado City, Tx., U.S.	B7	130
Colorado Kolonie see Lago Colorado Kolonie, Aruba	p20	104g
Colorado National Monument, p.o.i., Co., U.S.	D8	132
Colorado Plateau, plat., U.S.	E7	132
Colorado River Aqueduct, aq., Ca., U.S.	E5	98
Colorado Springs, Co., U.S.	C4	128
Colotlán, Mex.	D7	100
Colquechaca, Bol.	C3	90
Colstrip, Mt., U.S.	B8	122
Colt, Ar., U.S.	B7	122
Coltauco, Chile	G2	92
Colton, Ca., U.S.	I8	134
Colton, S.D., U.S.	H2	118
Columbia, Al., U.S.	E5	134
Columbia, Il., U.S.	F7	120
Columbia, Ky., U.S.	G12	120
Columbia, La., U.S.	E6	122
Columbia, Md., U.S.	E9	114
Columbia, Mo., U.S.	F5	120
Columbia, N.C., U.S.	I9	114
Columbia, Pa., U.S.	D9	114
Columbia, S.C., U.S.	C4	116
Columbia, Tn., U.S.	B11	122
Columbia, stm., N.A.	D3	136
Columbia, Cape, c., Nu., Can.	A11	141
Columbia, Mount, mtn., Ab., Can.	D13	138
Columbia Basin, bas., Wa., U.S.	C8	136
Columbia Falls, Me., U.S.	G4	112
Columbia Falls, Mt., U.S.	F9	110
Columbia Icefield, ice, Can.	D13	138
Columbia Mountains, mts., N.A.	G13	138
Columbiana, Al., U.S.	D12	122
Columbiana, Oh., U.S.	D5	114
Columbine, Cape, c., S. Afr.	H3	70
Columbretes, Illes, is., Spain	E11	20
Columbus, Ga., U.S.	E14	122
Columbus, In., U.S.	E12	120
Columbus, Ks., U.S.	G3	120
Columbus, Ms., U.S.	D10	122
Columbus, N.C., U.S.	A3	116
Columbus, N.D., U.S.	F11	124
Columbus, Ne., U.S.	F15	126
Columbus, N.M., U.S.	L9	132
Columbus, Oh., U.S.	E2	114
Columbus, Tx., U.S.	H2	122
Columbus, Wi., U.S.	H9	118
Columbus Point, c., Trin.	r13	105f
Columbus Salt Marsh, pl., Nv., U.S.	E8	134
Colusa, Ca., U.S.	D3	134
Colville, Wa., U.S.	B9	136
Colville, stm., Ak., U.S.	C9	140
Colville Lake, l., N.T., Can.	B5	106
Colwyn Bay, Wales, U.K.	H9	12
Comacchio, Italy	F9	22
Comacchio, Valli di, l., Italy	F9	22
Comala, Mex.	F7	100
Comalcalco, Mex.	F12	100
Comales, Mex.	H9	130
Coman, Mount, mtn., Ant.	C34	81
Comana, Rom.	F15	26
Comanche, Ok., U.S.	G10	128
Comandante Ferraz, sci., Ant.	B35	81
Comandante Fontana, Arg.	B7	92
Comandante Leal, Arg.	E5	92
Comandante Luis Piedra Buena, Arg.	I3	90
Comănești, Rom.	C13	26
Comayagua, Hond.	E4	102
Combarbalá, Chile	E2	92
Combermere Bay, b., Mya.	C1	48
Combourg, Fr.	F7	14
Comboyne, Austl.	H9	76
Comendador, Dom. Rep.	C12	102
Comer, Ga., U.S.	B2	116
Comercinho, Braz.	I5	88
Comet, stm., Austl.	E7	76
Comfort, N.C., U.S.	B8	116
Comfort, Tx., U.S.	E8	130
Comfort, Cape, c., Nu., Can.	B14	106
Comilla, Bngl.	G13	54
Comino see Kemmuna, i., Malta	H8	24
Comiso, Italy	H8	24
Comitán de Domínguez, Mex.	G12	100
Commerce, Ga., U.S.	B2	116
Commerce, Ok., U.S.	H3	120
Commerce, Tx., U.S.	D3	122
Commerce City, Co., U.S.	B4	128
Commercy, Fr.	F14	14
Commingers, reg., Fr.	F6	18
Committee Bay, b., Nu., Can.	B13	106
Communism Peak see Ismail Samani, pik, mtn., Taj.	B11	56
Como, Italy	E6	22
Como, Tx., U.S.	D3	122
Como, Lago di, l., Italy	D6	22
Comodoro Rivadavia, Arg.	I3	90
Comores, Archipel des, is., Afr.	C7	68
Comorin, Cape, c., India	G3	53
Comoros, ctry., Afr.	C7	68
Comox, B.C., Can.	G6	138
Compiègne, Fr.	E11	14
Compostela, Mex.	E6	100
Compton, Ca., U.S.	J7	134
Comrat, Mol.	C15	26
Comstock, Mn., U.S.	E2	118
Comstock, Tx., U.S.	E6	130
Comstock Park, Mi., U.S.	E4	112
Cona, stm., Russia	B19	32
Co Nag, l., China	B13	54
Conakry, Gui.	H2	64
Conambo, stm., Ec.	H3	86
Cona Niyeo, Arg.	H3	90
Concarán, Arg.	F5	92
Concarneau, Fr.	G5	14
Conceição, Braz.	D6	88
Conceição, Braz.	J6	88
Conceição da Barra, Braz.	J6	88
Conceição das Alagoas, Braz.	J1	88
Conceição do Araguaia, Braz.	E1	88
Conceição do Canindé, Braz.	D5	88
Conceição do Coité, Braz.	F6	88
Conceição do Mato Dentro, Braz.	J4	88
Conceição do Norte, Braz.	G2	88
Concepción, Arg.	C5	92
Concepción, Bol.	D9	92
Concepción, Chile	H1	92
Concepción, Col.	D5	86
Concepción, Para.	D5	90
Concepción, Bahía, b., Mex.	B2	100
Concepción, Canal, strt., Chile	J2	90
Concepción, Laguna, l., Bol.	C4	90
Concepción, Volcán, vol., Nic.	G5	102
Concepción de la Sierra, Arg.	D10	92
Concepción del Oro, Mex.	C8	100
Concepción del Uruguay, Arg.	F8	92
Conception, Point, c., Ca., U.S.	I5	134
Conception Bay, b., Nf., Can.	j23	107a
Conception Bay, b., Nmb.	C2	70
Conchas, stm., Arg.	B5	92
Conchas Dam, N.M., U.S.	F4	128
Conchas Lake, res., N.M., U.S.	F4	128
Concho, Az., U.S.	I7	132
Concho, stm., Tx., U.S.	C8	130
Conchos, stm., Mex.	A6	100
Conchos, stm., Mex.	C10	100
Conconully, Wa., U.S.	B7	136
Concord, Ca., U.S.	E4	134
Concord, Ga., U.S.	D14	122
Concord, N.C., U.S.	A5	116
Concord, N.H., U.S.	G5	110
Concordia, Arg.	E8	92
Concórdia, Braz.	C11	92
Concordia, Mex.	D5	100
Concordia, Mex.	I4	130
Concordia, Mo., U.S.	F4	120
Concrete, Wa., U.S.	B5	136
Con Cuong, Viet.	C7	48
Conda, Ang.	C1	68
Condamine, Austl.	F7	76
Condamine, stm., Austl.	F8	76
Condat, Fr.	D8	18
Conde, S.D., U.S.	B14	126
Condeúba, Braz.	H5	88
Condobolin, Austl.	I6	76
Condom, Fr.	F6	18
Condon, Or., U.S.	E6	136
Condoto, Col.	E3	86
Condroz, hist. reg., Bel.	D14	14
Cone, Tx., U.S.	H7	128
Conecuh, stm., U.S.	F12	122
Conegliano, Italy	E9	22
Conejos, Co., U.S.	D3	128
Conejos, stm., Co., U.S.	D3	128
Confuso, stm., Para.	B8	92
Congaree Swamp National Monument, p.o.i., S.C., U.S.	C5	116
Congaz, Mol.	C15	26
Conghua, China	J5	42
Congjiang, China	I3	42
Congleton, Eng., U.K.	H10	12
Congo, ctry., Afr.	E3	66
Congo (Zaire), stm., Afr.	F2	66
Congo, Democratic Republic of the (Zaire), ctry., Afr.	E4	66
Congo Basin, bas., Afr.	E4	66
Congonhinhas, Braz.	A12	92
Congress, Sk., Can.	E8	124
Conitaca, Mex.	C5	100
Conn, Lough, l., Ire.	G3	12
Connacht see Connaught, hist. reg., Ire.	H3	12
Connaught, hist. reg., Ire.	H3	12
Conneaut, Oh., U.S.	C5	114
Conneautville, Pa., U.S.	C5	114
Connecticut, state, U.S.	C13	114
Connecticut, stm., U.S.	H4	110
Connellsville, Pa., U.S.	D6	114
Connemara, reg., Ire.	H3	12
Connersville, In., U.S.	E2	114
Conn Lake, l., Nu., Can.	A15	106
Connors Range, mts., Austl.	C7	76
Conoco, stm., Ven.	H3	86
Conorochite, stm., Ven.	F8	86
Conover, N.C., U.S.	I4	114
Conquest, Sk., Can.	C6	124
Conquista, Braz.	J2	88
Conrad, Ia., U.S.	B5	120
Conrad, Mt., U.S.	B15	136
Conroe, Tx., U.S.	G3	122
Conroe, Lake, res., Tx., U.S.	G2	122
Consecon, On., Can.	D12	112
Conselheiro Lafaiete, Braz.	K4	88
Conselheiro Pena, Braz.	J5	88
Conselice, Italy	F8	22
Consett, Eng., U.K.	G10	12
Consolación del Sur, Cuba	A6	102
Con Son, is., Viet.	H8	48
Consort, Ab., Can.	B3	124
Constance see Konstanz, Ger.	I4	16
Constance, Lake (Bodensee), l., Eur.	I5	16
Constância, Port.	E2	20
Constanța, Rom.	E15	26
Constantina, Spain	G5	20
Constantine see Qacentina, Alg.	B6	64
Constantine, Mi., U.S.	G4	112
Constantine, Cape, c., Ak., U.S.	E8	140
Constantinople see Istanbul, Tur.	B12	28
Constitución, Chile	G1	92
Constitución, Ur.	E9	92
Constitución de 1857, Parque Nacional, p.o.i., Mex.	K10	134
Consuegra, Spain	E7	20
Contai, India	H11	54
Contamana, Peru	E2	84
Contas, Rio de, stm., Braz.	H6	88
Contao, Chile	H2	90
Contes, Fr.	F13	18
Continental Peak, mtn., Wy., U.S.	E4	126
Contoocook Creek, stm., N.C., U.S.	A8	116
Contratación, Col.	D5	86
Contreras, Embalse de, res., Spain	E9	20
Contreras, Isla, i., Chile	J1	90
Contursi, Italy	D9	24
Contwoyto Lake, l., Can.	B8	106
Convent, La., U.S.	G8	122
Conversano, Italy	D10	24
Converse, In., U.S.	H4	112
Conway, Ar., U.S.	B6	122
Conway, Mo., U.S.	G5	120
Conway, N.H., U.S.	F5	110
Conway, N.C., U.S.	H8	114
Conway, S.C., U.S.	C6	116
Conway, Lake, res., Ar., U.S.	C6	122
Conway National Park, p.o.i., Austl.	C7	76
Conway Springs, Ks., U.S.	D11	128
Conwy, Wales, U.K.	H9	12
Coober Pedy, Austl.	E6	74
Cook, Austl.	F6	74
Cook, Ne., U.S.	D1	120
Cook, Mount, mtn., N.Z.	F4	80
Cook, Cape, c., B.C., Can.	F2	138
Cook, Récif de, rf., N. Cal.	I14	79d
Cookeville, Tn., U.S.	H12	120
Cooking Lake, l., Ab., Can.	C17	138
Cook Inlet, b., Ak., U.S.	D9	140
Cook Islands, dep., Oc.	E10	72
Cook Strait, strt., N.Z.	E6	80
Cooktown, Austl.	C9	74
Coolabah, Austl.	H6	76
Cooladdi, Austl.	F5	76
Coolamon, Austl.	J6	76
Coolangatta, Austl.	G9	76
Cooleemee, N.C., U.S.	I5	114
Coolgardie, Austl.	F4	74
Coolidge, Ga., U.S.	E2	116
Coolidge, Tx., U.S.	E2	130
Coolidge, Mount, mtn., S.D., U.S.	D9	126
Coolidge Dam, dam, Az., U.S.	J6	132
Coolin, Id., U.S.	B10	136
Cooloola National Park, p.o.i., Austl.	F9	76
Cooma, Austl.	K7	76
Coonabarabran, Austl.	H7	76
Coonalpyn, Austl.	J2	76
Coonamble, Austl.	H7	76
Coonoor, India	F3	53
Coon Rapids, Mn., U.S.	F5	118
Coon Valley, Wi., U.S.	H8	118
Cooper, Tx., U.S.	D3	122
Cooper Creek, stm., Austl.	G2	76
Cooper Road, La., U.S.	E5	122
Coopers, Al., U.S.	E12	122
Cooperstown, N.Y., U.S.	B11	114
Coopersville, Mi., U.S.	E4	112
Coorabie, Austl.	F6	74
Coorong National Park, p.o.i., Austl.	K2	76
Coorow, Austl.	E3	74
Cooroy, Austl.	F9	76
Coosa, stm., U.S.	E12	122
Coos Bay, Or., U.S.	G2	136
Cootamundra, Austl.	J7	76
Cootehill, Ire.	H6	12
Copacabana, Arg.	D4	92
Copacabana, Col.	D4	86
Copainalá, Mex.	G12	100
Copan, Ok., U.S.	H2	120
Copán, sci., Hond.	E3	102
Copatana, Braz.	I8	86
Copeland, Fl., U.S.	K4	116
Copenhagen see København, Den.	I4	8
Copenhagen, N.Y., U.S.	E14	112
Copertino, Italy	D11	24
Copiapó, Chile	C2	92
Copiapó, stm., Chile	C2	92
Copley, Austl.	H2	76
Copparo, Italy	F8	22
Copper, stm., Ak., U.S.	D11	140
Copper Canyon see Cobre, Barranca del, misc. cult., Mex.	B5	100
Copper Center, Ak., U.S.	D10	140
Copper Harbor, Mi., U.S.	D10	118
Coppermine see Kugluktuk, Nu., Can.	B8	106
Coppermine, stm., Can.	B7	106
Copper Mine Point, c., Br. Vir. Is.	e9	104b
Copper Mountain, B.C., Can.	G10	138
Coqui, P.R.	C3	104a
Coquilhatville see Mbandaka, D.R.C.	D3	66
Coquimbo, Chile.	E2	92
Coquimbo, state, Chile	E2	92
Corabia, Rom.	F11	26
Coração de Jesus, Braz.	I3	88
Coradi, Isole see Cheradi, Isole, i., Italy	D11	24
Coral Gables, Fl., U.S.	K5	116
Coral Harbour, Bah.	n18	104f
Coral Harbour see Sallig, Nu., Can.	C14	106
Coral Sea, s., Oc.	B9	76
Coral Sea Basin, unds.	K18	142
Coral Sea Islands Territory, dep., Oc.	B9	76
Coralville, Ia., U.S.	C6	120
Coram, Mt., U.S.	B12	136
Corangamite, Lake, l., Austl.	K4	76
Corato, Italy	C10	24
Corbeil-Essonnes, Fr.	F11	14
Corbett National Park, p.o.i., India	D7	54
Corbigny, Fr.	G12	14
Corbin, Ky., U.S.	H1	114
Corbones, stm., Spain	G5	20
Corby, Eng., U.K.	I12	12
Corcaigh see Cork, Ire.	J4	12
Córcega, P.R.	B1	104a
Corcoran, Ca., U.S.	G6	134
Corcovado, Golfo, b., Chile	H2	90
Corcovado, Parque Nacional, p.o.i., C.R.	H6	102
Corcubión, Spain	B1	20
Cordeiro, Braz.	L4	88
Cordele, Ga., U.S.	E2	116
Cordell Hull Reservoir, res., Tn., U.S.	H12	120
Corder, Mo., U.S.	E4	120
Cordes-sur-Ciel, Fr.	E8	18
Cordillera, state, Para.	B9	92
Cordillo Downs, Austl.	F3	76
Córdoba, Arg.	E5	92
Córdoba, Mex.	F10	100
Córdoba (Cordova), Spain	G6	20
Córdoba, state, Arg.	E5	92
Córdoba, state, Col.	C4	86
Córdoba, co., Spain	F6	20
Córdoba, Sierras de, mts., Arg.	F5	92
Cordova see Córdoba, Spain	G6	20
Cordova, Ak., U.S.	D10	140
Cordova, Al., U.S.	D11	122
Cordova, Il., U.S.	C7	120
Cordova Peak, mtn., Ak., U.S.	D10	140
Coreaú, Braz.	B5	88
Coreaú, stm., Braz.	B5	88
Corentyne, stm., S.A.	C6	84
Corfield, Austl.	C4	76
Corfu see Kérkyra, i., Grc.	D2	28
Corfu see Kérkyra, Grc.	D2	28
Coria, Spain	D4	20
Coria del Río, Spain	G4	20
Coribe, Braz.	G3	88
Coricudgy, Mount, mtn., Austl.	I8	76
Corigliano Calabro, Italy	E10	24
Corinne, Ut., U.S.	B4	132
Corinne, W.V., U.S.	G4	114
Corinth see Kórinthos, Grc.	F5	28
Corinth, Ms., U.S.	C10	122
Corinth, N.Y., U.S.	G3	110
Corinth, Gulf of see Korinthiakós Kólpos, b., Grc.	E5	28
Corinto, Braz.	J3	88
Corinto, Nic.	G4	102
Corisco, Isla de i., Eq. Gui.	I6	64
Cork, Ire.	J4	12
Cork, state, Ire.	I4	12
Corleone, Italy	G7	24
Çorlu, Tur.	B10	28
Cornélia, stm., Braz.	B2	116
Cornélio Procópio, Braz.	D6	90
Cornelius Grinnell Bay, b., Nu., Can.	E13	141
Cornell, Wi., U.S.	F7	118
Corner Brook, Nf., Can.	j22	107a
Corneşti, Mol.	B14	26
Corneta, Punta, c., Mex.	H10	100
Corning, Ar., U.S.	H7	120
Corning, Ca., U.S.	D3	134
Corning, Ia., U.S.	D3	120
Corning, Ks., U.S.	B12	128
Corning, N.Y., U.S.	B9	114
Cornish, Me., U.S.	G6	110
Corno Grande, mtn., Italy	H10	22
Cornwall, On., Can.	E2	110
Cornwall Island, i., Nu., Can.	B7	141
Cornwallis Island, i., Nu., Can.	B6	141
Coro, Ven.	B7	86
Coro, Golfete de, b., Ven.	B6	86
Coroaci, Braz.	J4	88
Coroatá, Braz.	C3	88
Corocoro, Bol.	C3	90
Corocoro, Isla, i., S.A.	C11	86
Coroico, Bol.	C3	90
Coromandel, Braz.	J2	88
Coromandel, N.Z.	C6	80
Coromandel Coast, cst., India	E5	53
Coromandel Peninsula, pen., N.Z.	C6	80
Corona, Ca., U.S.	J8	134
Corona, N.M., U.S.	G3	128
Coronado, Mex.	D8	100
Coronado, Bahía de, b., C.R.	H6	102
Coronado, Islas, is., Mex.	K8	134
Coronation, Ab., Can.	D19	138
Coronation Gulf, b., Nu., Can.	B8	106
Coronation Island, i., Ant.	B36	81
Coronda, Arg.	E7	92
Coronel, Chile	H1	92
Coronel Bogado, Para.	C9	92
Coronel Dorrego, Arg.	I7	92
Coronel Fabriciano, Braz.	J4	88
Coronel Moldes, Arg.	B5	92
Coronel Moldes, Arg.	F5	92
Coronel Oviedo, Para.	B9	92
Coronel Pringles, Arg.	H7	92
Coronel Suárez, Arg.	H6	92
Coronel Vidal, Arg.	H9	92
Coronel Vivida, Braz.	C11	92
Coropuna, Nevado, vol., Peru	G3	84
Corossol, Guad.	B2	105a
Çorovodë, Alb.	D14	24
Corowa, Austl.	J6	76
Corozal, Belize	C3	102
Corozal, P.R.	B3	104a
Corpus Christi, Tx., U.S.	G10	130
Corpus Christi, Lake, res., Tx., U.S.	F9	130
Corpus Christi Bay, b., Tx., U.S.	G10	130
Corral, Chile	H2	90
Corral de Almaguer, Spain	E7	20
Corral de Bustos, Arg.	F6	92
Corrales, Cerro, mtn., Mex.	H2	130
Corralito, Arg.	F5	92
Correctionville, Ia., U.S.	B2	120
Corregidor Island, i., Phil.	C3	52
Corrente, Braz.	G3	88
Corrente, stm., Braz.	G4	88
Correntes, Cabo das, c., Moz.	D12	70
Correntina, Braz.	G3	88
Corrèze, state, Fr.	D7	18
Corrib, Lough, l., Ire.	H3	12
Corrientes, Arg.	C8	92
Corrientes, state, Arg.	D9	92
Corrientes, stm., Arg.	D8	92
Corrientes, stm., S.A.	D2	84
Corrientes, Bahía de, b., Cuba	B5	102
Corrientes, Cabo, c., Arg.	I9	92
Corrientes, Cabo, c., Col.	E3	86
Corrientes, Cabo, c., Mex.	E6	100
Corrigan, Tx., U.S.	F4	122
Corrigin, Austl.	F3	74
Corriverton, Guy.	C6	84
Corrumpa Creek, stm., U.S.	E5	128
Corry, Pa., U.S.	C6	114
Corse (Corsica), i., Fr.	G15	18
Corse, Cap, c., Fr.	F15	18
Corse-du-Sud, state, Fr.	H15	18
Corsica see Corse, i., Fr.	G15	18
Corsica, S.D., U.S.	D14	126
Corsicana, Tx., U.S.	E2	122
Cort Adelaer, Kap, c., Grnld.	E17	141
Cortazar, Mex.	E8	100
Corte, Fr.	G15	18
Cortés, Mar de see California, Golfo de, b., Mex.	B2	96
Cortez, Co., U.S.	F8	132
Cortez, Sea of see California, Sea of see California, Golfo de, b., Mex.	B2	96
Cortina d'Ampezzo, Italy	D8	22
Cortland, Ne., U.S.	K2	118
Cortland, N.Y., U.S.	B9	114
Cortland, Oh., U.S.	C5	114
Cortona, Italy	G8	22
Corubal, stm., Gui.-B.	G2	64
Coruche, Port.	F2	20
Çorum, Tur.	A4	56
Corumbá, Braz.	C5	90
Corumbá, stm., Braz.	I1	88
Corumbaíba, Braz.	J1	88
Corumbataí, stm., Braz.	B11	92
Coruña see A Coruña, Spain	A2	20
Coruripe, Braz.	F7	88
Corvallis, Mt., U.S.	D12	136
Corvallis, Or., U.S.	F3	136
Corwith, Ia., U.S.	B3	120
Corydon, Ia., U.S.	D4	120
Corydon, In., U.S.	F11	120
Corydon, Ky., U.S.	G10	120
Corzu, Rom.	E10	26
Cosalá, Mex.	C5	100
Cosamaloapan de Carpio, Mex.	F10	100
Coscomate, Mex.	I2	130
Cosenza, Italy	E10	24
Coshocton, Oh., U.S.	D4	114
Cosigüina, Punta, c., Nic.	F4	102
Cosigüina, Volcán, vol., Nic.	F4	102
Cosmoledo, Atoll de, i., Sey.	k11	69b
Cosmos, Mn., U.S.	G4	118
Cosne-sur-Loire, Fr.	G11	14
Cosquín, Arg.	E5	92
Cossato, Italy	E5	22
Cossatot, stm., Ar., U.S.	C4	122
Costa Mesa, Ca., U.S.	J8	134
Costa Rica, Mex.	H5	102
Costa Rica, ctry., N.A.	H5	102
Coswig, Ger.	E8	16
Cotabato, Phil.	G5	52
Cotahuasi, Peru	G3	84
Coteaux, Haiti	C10	102
Côte d'Ivoire, ctry., Afr.	H3	64
Côte-d'Or, state, Fr.	G13	14
Cotegipe, Braz.	F3	88
Cotentin, pen., Fr.	E7	14
Côtes-d'Armor, state, Fr.	F5	14
Cotiella, mtn., Spain	B10	20
Cotijuení, Mol.	B15	26
Cotonou, Benin	H5	64
Cotopaxi, state, Ec.	H2	86
Cotopaxi, Parque Nacional, p.o.i., Ec.	H2	86
Cotswold Hills, hills, Eng., U.K.	J10	12
Cottage Grove, Or., U.S.	G3	136
Cottbus, Ger.	E10	16
Cotter, Ar., U.S.	H5	120
Cottian Alps, mts., Eur.	G13	122
Cottondale, Fl., U.S.	G13	122
Cotton Plant, Ar., U.S.	C7	122
Cotton Valley, La., U.S.	E5	122
Cottonport, La., U.S.	G6	122
Cottonwood, Az., U.S.	I5	132
Cottonwood, Ca., U.S.	C3	134
Cottonwood, Id., U.S.	D10	136
Cottonwood, Mn., U.S.	G3	118
Cottonwood, stm., Ks., U.S.	C12	128
Cottonwood, stm., Mn., U.S.	G3	118
Cottonwood Creek, stm., Mt., U.S.	F5	124
Cottonwood Falls, Ks., U.S.	C12	128
Coubre, Pointe de la, c., Fr.	D4	18
Couchiching, Lake, l., On., Can.	D10	112
Coudersport, Pa., U.S.	C8	114
Coudres, Île aux, i., Qc., Can.	C6	110
Coulee City, Wa., U.S.	C7	136
Coulee Dam, Wa., U.S.	B8	136
Coulommiers, Fr.	F12	14
Coulonge, stm., Qc., Can.	C13	112
Coulterville, Il., U.S.	F8	120
Counce, Tn., U.S.	B10	122
Council, Id., U.S.	F10	136
Council Bluffs, Ia., U.S.	C2	120
Council Grove, Ks., U.S.	C12	128
Coupeville, Wa., U.S.	B4	136
Courantyne see Corentyne, stm., S.A.	C6	84
Courland (Kurzeme), hist. reg., Lat.	C5	10
Courland Lagoon, b., Eur.	E3	10
Courmayeur, Italy	E3	22
Courtenay, B.C., Can.	G5	138
Courtland, Al., U.S.	C11	122
Courtland, Va., U.S.	H8	114
Courtrai see Kortrijk, Bel.	D12	14
Coutras, Fr.	D5	18
Coutts, Ab., Can.	G19	138
Couture, Lac, l., Qc., Can.	C16	106
Covasna, state, Rom.	C12	26
Cove, Or., U.S.	E9	136
Cove Island, i., On., Can.	C8	112
Covelo, Ca., U.S.	D2	134
Coventry, Eng., U.K.	I11	12
Covert, Mi., U.S.	F3	112
Covilhã, Port.	D3	20
Covington, Ga., U.S.	C2	116
Covington, In., U.S.	H2	112
Covington, Ky., U.S.	E1	114
Covington, La., U.S.	G8	122
Covington, Oh., U.S.	D1	114
Covington, Tn., U.S.	B9	122
Covington, Va., U.S.	G5	114
Cowal, pen., Scot., U.K.	E7	12
Cowal, Lake, l., Austl.	I6	76
Cowan, Tn., U.S.	B13	122
Cowan, Lake, l., Austl.	F4	74
Cowansville, Qc., Can.	E4	110
Cowarie, Austl.	E7	74
Cow Creek, stm., Ks., U.S.	C10	128
Cowdenbeath, Scot., U.K.	E9	12
Cowell, Austl.	F7	74
Cowen, W.V., U.S.	F5	114
Coweta, Ok., U.S.	C10	128
Cowhouse Creek, stm., Tx., U.S.	C10	130
Cowichan Bay, B.C., Can.	H7	138
Cowichan Lake, l., B.C., Can.	H6	138
Cowley, Austl.	F5	76
Cowley, Wy., U.S.	C5	126
Cowlic, Az., U.S.	L4	132
Cowlitz, stm., Wa., U.S.	D4	136
Cowpasture, stm., Va., U.S.	A4	116
Cowpens, S.C., U.S.	A3	116
Cowra, Austl.	I7	76
Coxá, stm., Braz.	H3	88
Cox's Bāzār, Bngl.	H13	54
Coyaguaima, Cerro, mtn., Arg.	D3	90
Coyame, Mex.	A6	100
Coyle see Coig, stm., Arg.	J3	90
Coyote, stm., Mex.	F6	98
Coyote Wash, stm., N.M., U.S.	G8	132
Coyuca de Benítez, Mex.	G8	100
Coyuca de Catalán, Mex.	F8	100
Cozad, Ne., U.S.	G12	126
Cozumel, Mex.	B4	102
Cozumel, Isla, i., Mex.	B4	102
Crab Orchard, Tn., U.S.	I13	120
Crab Orchard Lake, res., Il., U.S.	G9	120
Cradle Mountain–Lake Saint Clair National Park, p.o.i., Austl.	n12	77a
Cradock, S. Afr.	H7	70
Craig, Co., U.S.	C9	132
Craig, Ne., U.S.	J2	118
Craigellachie, B.C., Can.	E12	138
Craigmont, Id., U.S.	D10	136
Craigsville, Va., U.S.	F6	114
Craik, Sk., Can.	C8	124
Crailsheim, Ger.	G6	16
Craiova, Rom.	E10	26
Cranberry Lake, l., N.Y., U.S.	F1	110
Cranbrook, Austl.	F3	74
Cranbrook, B.C., Can.	G15	138
Crandon, Wi., U.S.	F9	118
Crane, Az., U.S.	K2	132
Crane, Tx., U.S.	B5	130
Crane Lake, l., Sk., Can.	D4	124
Crane Mountain, mtn., Or., U.S.	A5	134
Crânǵeni, Rom.	E11	26
Cranston, R.I., U.S.	C14	114
Crasna, Rom.	D13	26
Crasna, stm., Eur.	B9	26
Crasnoe, Mol.	C16	26
Crater Lake, l., Or., U.S.	H4	136
Crater Lake National Park, p.o.i., Or., U.S.	H5	136
Craters of the Moon National Monument, p.o.i., Id., U.S.	G13	136
Crateús, Braz.	C5	88
Crato, Braz.	D6	88
Crauford, Cape, c., Nu., Can.	A14	106
Cravo Norte, Col.	D6	86
Cravo Norte, stm., Col.	D6	86
Cravo Sur, stm., Col.	E6	86
Crawford, Ne., U.S.	E9	132
Crawford, Tx., U.S.	C10	130
Crawford Bay, B.C., Can.	G14	138
Crawfordsville, Ar., U.S.	B8	122
Crawfordsville, In., U.S.	H2	112
Crawfordville, Fl., U.S.	G14	122
Crawley, Eng., U.K.	J12	12
Crazy Woman Creek, stm., Wy., U.S.	C6	126
Creal Springs, Il., U.S.	G9	120
Cree, stm., Sk., Can.	D9	106
Creede, Co., U.S.	F10	132
Cree Lake, l., Sk., Can.	D9	106
Creemore, On., Can.	D9	112
Creighton, Ne., U.S.	E15	126
Creighton Mine, On., Can.	B8	112
Creil, Fr.	E11	14
Crema, Italy	E6	22
Cremona, Italy	E7	22
Crenshaw, Ms., U.S.	C8	122
Crepori, stm., Braz.	E6	84
Crépy-en-Valois, Fr.	E11	14
Cres, Cro.	F11	22
Cres, Otok, i., Cro.	F11	22
Cresaptown, Md., U.S.	E7	114
Crescent, Or., U.S.	G5	136
Crescent City, Ca., U.S.	B1	134
Crescent City, Fl., U.S.	G4	116
Crescent Spur, B.C., Can.	C10	138
Cresco, Ia., U.S.	H6	118
Crespo, Arg.	F7	92
Cresson, Tx., U.S.	B10	130
Cressy, Austl.	K4	76
Crested Butte, Co., U.S.	E9	132
Crestline, Ca., U.S.	I8	134
Creston, B.C., Can.	G14	138
Creston, Ia., U.S.	C3	120
Crestone Peak, mtn., Co., U.S.	D3	128
Crestview, Fl., U.S.	G12	122
Crestwood Hills, Tn., U.S.	I1	114
Creswell, Or., U.S.	G3	136
Creswell Bay, b., Nu., Can.	A12	106
Crete, Il., U.S.	G2	112
Crete, Ne., U.S.	G16	126
Crete see Kriti, i., Grc.	H7	28
Crete, Sea of see Kritikón Pélagos, s., Grc.	H8	28
Créteil, Fr.	F11	14
Cretin, Cape, c., Pap. N. Gui.	b4	79a
Creus, Cap de, c., Spain	B14	20
Creuse, state, Fr.	C8	18
Creuse, stm., Fr.	C8	18
Creussen, Ger.	G7	16
Creve Coeur, Il., U.S.	K9	118
Crevillent, Spain	F10	20
Crevillente see Crevillent, Spain	F10	20
Crewe, Eng., U.K.	H10	12
Crewe, Va., U.S.	G7	114
Cricaré, stm., Braz.	J5	88
Criciúma, Braz.	D13	92
Crikvenica, Cro.	E11	22
Crimea see Kryms'kyi pivostriv, pen., Ukr.	E4	32
Crimean Peninsula see Kryms'kyi pivostriv, pen., Ukr.	E4	32
Crimmitschau, Ger.	F8	16
Cripple Creek, Co., U.S.	C3	128
Crisfield, Md., U.S.	F10	114
Criss Creek, B.C., Can.	E10	138
Crissiumal, Braz.	C10	92
Cristal, Monts de, mts., Afr.	I7	64
Cristalândia, Braz.	F1	88
Cristália, Braz.	I4	88
Cristalina, Braz.	I2	88
Cristinápolis, Braz.	F7	88
Cristino Castro, Braz.	E3	88
Cristóbal Colón, Pico, mtn., Col.	B5	86
Crişul Alb, stm., Eur.	C8	26
Crişul Negru, stm., Eur.	C8	26
Crişul Repede (Sebes Körös), stm., Eur.	B8	26
Crivitz, Wi., U.S.	C1	112
Crna, stm., Mac.	B4	28
Crna Gora (Montenegro), state, Serb.	G6	26
Crni Drim (Drinit tě Zi), stm., Eur.	C14	24
Črnomelj, Slvn.	E12	22
Croajingolong National Park, p.o.i., Austl.	K7	76
Croatia, ctry., Eur.	E13	22
Croche, stm., Qc., Can.	C4	110
Crocker, Mo., U.S.	G5	120
Crocker, Banjaran, mts., Malay.	H1	52
Crockett, Tx., U.S.	F3	122
Crocodillopolis, hist., Egypt	I1	58
Crocus Hill, hill, Anguilla	A1	105a
Crofton, Ky., U.S.	G10	120
Croghan, N.Y., U.S.	E14	112
Croix, Lac la, l., N.A.	C6	118
Croker, Cape, c., Austl.	B6	74
Croker, Cape, c., On., Can.	D9	112
Croker Island, i., Austl.	B6	74
Cromer, Eng., U.K.	I14	12
Cromínia, Braz.	I1	88
Crompton Point, c., Dom.	i6	105c
Cromwell, N.Z.	G3	80
Cromwell, Al., U.S.	E10	122
Crooked Creek, Ak., U.S.	D7	140
Crooked Creek, stm., U.S.	D8	140
Crooked Island, i., Bah.	A10	102
Crooked Island Passage, strt., Bah.	A10	102
Crooked River, Sk., Can.	B10	124
Crookston, Mn., U.S.	D2	118
Crookston, Ne., U.S.	E12	126
Crooksville, Oh., U.S.	E4	114
Crosby, Mn., U.S.	E5	118
Crosby, Mount, mtn., Wy., U.S.	D3	126
Crosbyton, Tx., U.S.	H7	128
Cross, stm., Afr.	H6	64
Crossett, Ar., U.S.	D7	122
Cross Lake, res., Mb., Can.	E11	106
Crossman Peak, mtn., Az., U.S.	I2	132
Cross Plains, Wi., U.S.	H9	118
Cross Sound, strt., Ak., U.S.	E12	140
Crossville, Il., U.S.	F9	120
Crossville, Tn., U.S.	I12	120
Croswell, Mi., U.S.	E7	112
Crotone, Italy	E11	24
Crow, North Fork, stm., Mn., U.S.	F4	118
Crow, South Fork, stm., Mn., U.S.	G4	118
Crow Agency, Mt., U.S.	B5	126
Crow Creek, stm., U.S.	C8	126
Crowder, Ms., U.S.	C8	122
Crowduck Lake, l., Mb., Can.	A3	118
Crowdy Head, c., Austl.	H9	76

Name / Map Ref. / Page

Crowell, Tx., U.S. H9 128
Crow Lake, On., Can. B5 118
Crowley, La., U.S. G6 122
Crowleys Ridge, mts., U.S. B8 122
Crown Mountain, mtn., V.I.U.S. e7 104b
Crown Point, In., U.S. G2 112
Crownpoint, N.M., U.S. H8 132
Crown Point, N.Y., U.S. G3 110
Crown Prince Frederik Island, i., Nu., Can. A13 106
Crowsnest Pass, Ab., Can. G16 138
Crowsnest Pass, p., Can. G16 138
Crows Nest Peak, mtn., S.D., U.S. C8 126
Crow Wing, stm., Mn., U.S. E4 118
Croydon, Austl. B4 76
Croydon Station, B.C., Can. C11 138
Crozet, Va., U.S. F7 114
Crozet, Îles, is., Afr. J16 4
Crozet Basin, unds. M9 142
Crucea, Rom. E15 26
Cruces, Cuba A7 102
Cruger, Ms., U.S. D8 122
Crump Lake, l., Or., U.S. A6 134
Cruz, Cabo, c., Cuba. C9 102
Cruz Alta, Arg. F6 92
Cruz Alta, Braz. D11 92
Cruz Bay, V.I.U.S. e7 104b
Cruz del Eje, Arg. E5 92
Cruzeiro, Braz. L3 88
Cruzeiro do Oeste, Braz. A11 92
Cruzeiro do Sul, Braz. E3 84
Cruzeta, Braz. D7 88
Cruz Grande, Chile. D2 92
Crysler, On., Can. C14 112
Crystal, Mn., U.S. F5 118
Crystal, N.D., U.S. F16 124
Crystal Brook, Austl. I2 76
Crystal City, Mb., Can. E15 124
Crystal City, Mo., U.S. F7 120
Crystal City, Tx., U.S. F8 130
Crystal Falls, Mi., U.S. B1 112
Crystal Lake, l., Mi., U.S. B9 120
Crystal Lake, l., Mi., U.S. D3 112
Crystal Springs, Ms., U.S. E8 122
Csongrád, Hung. C7 26
Csongrád, state, Hung. C7 26
Csorna, Hung. B4 26
Cu see Shù, stm., Asia F12 32
Cúa, Ven. B8 86
Cuajinicuilapa, Mex. G9 100
Cuamba, Moz. C6 68
Cuando (Kwando), stm., Afr. D3 68
Cuangar, Ang. D2 68
Cuango, Ang. B2 68
Cuango see Kwango, stm., Afr. F3 66
Cuanza, stm., Ang. C2 68
Cuao, stm., Ven. E8 86
Cuareim (Quaraí), stm., S.A. E9 92
Cuaró, Ur. E9 92
Cuarto, stm., Arg. F5 92
Cuatrociénegas, Mex. B7 100
Cuauhtémoc, Mex. A5 100
Cuautitlán, Mex. F6 100
Cuba, Port. F3 20
Cuba, Al., U.S. E10 122
Cuba, Il., U.S. D7 120
Cuba, Mo., U.S. F6 120
Cuba, N.M., U.S. G10 132
Cuba, ctry., N.A. C9 96
Cubagua, Isla, i., Ven. B9 86
Cubal, Ang. C1 68
Cubango (Okavango), stm., Afr. D2 68
Cubatí, Braz. D7 88
Cubuk, Russia D21 8
Çubuk, Tur. C15 28
Cuchi, stm., Ang. C2 68
Cuchillo Co, Arg. I5 92
Cuchivero, stm., Ven. D9 86
Cucurpe, Mex. F7 98
Cúcuta, Col. D5 86
Cucuy, Piedra de, hill, Ven. G8 86
Cudahy, Wi., U.S. F2 112
Cuddalore, India. F4 53
Cuddapah, India. D4 53
Čudovo, Russia A14 10
Cudworth, Sk., Can. B8 124
Cudzin, Bela. H9 10
Cue, Austl. E3 74
Cuemba, Ang. C2 68
Cuenca, Ec. I2 86
Cuenca, Spain D8 20
Cuenca, co., Spain E9 20
Cuencamé de Ceniceros, Mex. C7 100
Cuernavaca, Mex. F9 100
Cuero, Tx., U.S. E10 130
Cuers, Fr. F12 18
Cuervo, Laguna del, l., Mex. A6 100
Cuesta Pass, p., Ca., U.S. H5 134
Cueto, Cuba B9 102
Cugir, Rom. D10 26
Čuguevka, Russia. B10 38
Čuhlomskoe, ozero, l., Russia G19 8
Cuiabá, Braz. G6 84
Cuiabá, stm., Braz. G6 84
Cuiari, Braz. G7 86
Cuicatlán, Mex. G10 100
Cuilapa, Guat. E2 102
Cuilco see Grijalva, stm., N.A. G12 100
Cuilo (Kwilu), stm., Afr. F3 66
Cuité, Braz. D7 88
Cuíto, stm., Ang. D2 68
Cuito Cuanavale, Ang. D2 68
Cuitzeo, Lago de, l., Mex. F8 100
Cuiuni, stm., Braz. H10 86
Cukai, Malay. J6 48
Cukas, Indon. D4 50
Čukotskij, mys, c., Russia. D26 34
Čukotskij poluostrov (Chukotsk Peninsula), pen., Russia C26 34
Culbertson, Mt., U.S. F9 124
Cul de Sac, Guad. A1 105a
Cul de Sac, Neth. Ant. A1 105a
Culebra, P.R. B5 104a
Culebra, Isla de, i., P.R. B5 104a
Culebra Peak, mtn., Co., U.S. D3 128
Culfa, Azer. B6 56
Culgoa, stm., Austl. G6 76
Culiacán, Mex. C5 100
Culiacán, stm., Mex. C5 100
Culion Island, i., Phil. D2 52
Cúllar, Spain G8 20
Cullen, La., U.S. E5 122
Culleoka, Tn., U.S. B12 122
Cullera, Spain E10 20
Cullman, Al., U.S. D9 120
Cul'man, Russia E13 34
Culpeper, Va., U.S. F7 114
Culpina, Bol. D4 90
Culuene, stm., Braz. F7 84
Culver, In., U.S. G3 112
Culver, Or., U.S. F5 136
Culverden, N.Z. F5 80
Culym, Russia C14 32
Culym, stm., Russia C14 32
Cumaná, Ven. B9 86
Cumare, Cerro, hill, Col. G5 86
Cumari, Braz. J1 88
Cumbal, Nevado, vol., Col. G2 86
Cumbe, Braz. F7 88
Cumberland, B.C., Can. G5 138
Cumberland, Ky., U.S. G2 114

Cumberland, Md., U.S. E7 114
Cumberland, Va., U.S. G7 114
Cumberland, Wi., U.S. F6 118
Cumberland, stm., U.S. H2 114
Cumberland Lake, res., Ky., U.S. H13 120
Cumberland, South Fork, stm., U.S. H13 120
Cumberland Gap, p., U.S. H2 114
Cumberland Island National Seashore, p.o.i., Ga., U.S. F4 116
Cumberland Islands, is., Austl. C7 76
Cumberland Lake, l., Sk., Can. E10 106
Cumberland Peninsula, pen., Nu., Can. B17 106
Cumberland Plateau, plat., U.S. G14 120
Cumberland Sound, strt., Nu., Can. B17 106
Cumbernauld, Scot., U.K. F9 12
Cumbrian Mountains, mts., Eng., U.K. G9 12
Cumby, Tx., U.S. D3 122
Čumikan, Russia F16 34
Cumming, Ga., U.S. B1 116
Cummins, Austl. F7 74
Cumnock, Scot., U.K. F8 12
Cumpas, Mex. F8 98
Çumra, Tur. F15 28
Čumyš, stm., Russia D15 32
Čuna, stm., Russia. C17 32
Cunani, Braz. C7 84
Cunaviche, Ven. D8 86
Cunco, Chile. G2 90
Cundinamarca, state, Col. E4 86
Cunene (Kunene), stm., Afr. D1 68
Cuneo (Coni), Italy F4 22
Cunha Porã, Braz. C11 92
Čunja, stm., Russia B17 32
Cunnamulla, Austl. G6 76
Cunningham, Ks., U.S. D10 128
Čunskij, Russia C17 32
Čunucunuma, stm., Ven. F9 86
Čuny, Russia. G17 8
Cuorgnè, Italy E4 22
Cupar, Sk., Can. D9 124
Cupar, Scot., U.K. E9 12
Cúpica, Golfo de, b., Col. D3 86
Čuprovo, Russia D22 8
Cuquenán, stm., Ven. E11 86
Curaçá, Braz. E6 88
Curaçao, i., Neth. Ant. p21 104g
Curacautín, Chile I2 92
Curanilahue, Chile H1 92
Curanipe, Chile G1 92
Čurapča, Russia D15 34
Curaray, stm., S.A. H4 86
Curdimurka, Austl. i10 69a
Curepto, Chile G1 92
Curicó, Chile G2 92
Curicuriari, stm., Braz. H8 86
Curimatá, Braz. E3 88
Curitiba, Braz. B13 92
Curitibanos, Braz. C12 92
Curiuaú, stm., Braz. H11 86
Curlew, Wa., U.S. B8 136
Curnamona, Austl. H2 76
Currais Novos, Braz. D7 88
Curralinho, Braz. D8 84
Currant Mountain, mtn., Nv., U.S. E1 132
Current, stm., U.S. H7 120
Currie, Austl. m12 77a
Currituck, N.C., U.S. H9 114
Currituck Sound, strt., N.C., U.S. H10 114
Curtea de Argeş, Rom. D11 26
Curtina, Ur. F9 92
Curtis, Ar., U.S. D5 122
Curtis, Ne., U.S. G12 126
Curtis, Port, b., Austl. D8 76
Curtis Channel, strt., Austl. D8 76
Curtis Island, i., Austl. D8 76
Curtis Island, i., N.Z. G9 72
Curu, stm., Braz. B6 88
Curuá, stm., Braz. D7 84
Curuá, stm., Braz. E7 84
Curuá, Ilha do, i., Braz. C7 84
Curuá-Una, stm., Braz. D7 84
Curuçá, Braz. D8 84
Curumu, Braz. D7 84
Curup, Indon. E3 50
Curupá, Braz. E2 88
Cururupu, Braz. A3 88
Curuzú Cuatiá, Arg. D8 92
Curvelo, Braz. J3 88
Cusco, Peru F3 84
Cushing, Ok., U.S. B2 122
Cushing, Tx., U.S. F4 122
Cushman, Ar., U.S. I6 120
Cusiana, stm., Col. E5 86
Čusovaja, stm., Russia C9 32
Čusovoj, Russia C9 32
Cusset, Fr. C9 18
Cusseta, Ga., U.S. E14 122
Čust, Uzb. F12 32
Custer, Mi., U.S. E3 112
Custer, Mt., U.S. A5 126
Custer, S.D., U.S. D9 126
Custódia, Braz. E7 88
Cut, Nuhu u, Indon. G9 44
Cut Bank, Mt., U.S. B14 136
Cut Bank, Ab., Can. B12 138
Cut Bank Creek, stm., Mt., U.S. B14 136
Cut Bank Creek, stm., U.S. F12 124
Cutervo, Peru E2 84
Cutler, Ca., U.S. G6 134
Cutler, Me., U.S. F9 110
Cutlerville, Mi., U.S. F4 112
Cutral-Có, Arg. G3 90
Cutro, Italy E10 24
Cuttack, India H10 54
Cuttamalá, stm., Mex. F8 100
Čuvašija, state, Russia C7 32
Cuvier, Cape, c., Austl. D2 74
Cuvo, stm., Ang. C1 68
Cuxhaven, Ger. C4 16
Cuyahoga Falls, Oh., U.S. C4 114
Cuyahoga Valley National Park, p.o.i., Oh., U.S. C4 114
Cuyama, stm., Ca., U.S. I6 134
Cuyamaca Peak, mtn., Ca., U.S. J9 134
Cuyarí, stm., S.A. G7 86
Cuyo, Phil. E3 52
Cuyo East Pass, strt., Phil. E3 52
Cuyo Islands, is., Phil. E3 52
Cuyo West Pass, strt., Phil. E3 52
Cuyubini, stm., Ven. D11 86
Cuyuni-Mazaruni, state, Guy. D11 86
Cwmbran, Wales, U.K. J10 12
Cyclades see Kikládes, is., Grc. F7 28
Cypress, La., U.S. F5 122
Cypress Hills, hills, Can. E4 124
Cypress River, Mb., Can. E14 124
Cypress Springs, Lake, res., Tx., U.S. D3 122
Cyprus, ctry., Asia C4 58
Cyprus, i., Asia D15 4
Cyprus, North, ctry., Asia. C4 58
Cyrenaica see Barqah, hist. reg., Libya A4 62
Cyril, Ok., U.S. G10 128

Cyril E. King Airport, V.I.U.S. e7 104b
Cyrus Field Bay, b., Nu., Can. E13 141
Çyrvonae, vozero, l., Bela. H10 10
Cythera see Kýthira, i., Grc. G5 28
Czaplinek, Pol. C12 16
Czarna Woda, Pol. C14 16
Czarnków, Pol. D12 16
Czechoslovakia see Czech Republic, ctry., Eur. G11 16
Czechowice-Dziedzice, Pol. G15 16
Czech Republic, ctry., Eur. G11 16
Czerniejewo, Pol. D13 16
Czersk, Pol. C13 16
Czerwieńsk, Pol. D11 16
Częstochowa, Pol. F15 16
Częstochowa, state, Pol. F15 16
Człuchów, Pol. C13 16

D

Da, stm., China G8 42
Da, Song see Black, stm., Asia D9 46
Da'an, China J4 42
Dabajuro, Ven. B6 86
Daba Ling, mtn., China I5 42
Daba Shan, mts., China E3 42
Dabat, Eth. E7 62
Dabeiba, Col. D3 86
Dabhoi, India. G4 54
Dabie, Pol. D14 16
Dabie Shan, mts., China. F6 42
Dabnou, Niger G5 64
Dabola, Gui. G2 64
Dabou, C. Iv. H4 64
Daboya, Ghana H4 64
Dabra, India F7 54
Dąbrowa Białostocka, Pol. C19 16
Dabu, China I7 42
Dacca see Dhaka, Bngl. G13 54
Dac Glei, Viet. E8 48
Dachau, Ger. H7 16
Dačice, Czech Rep. G11 16
Dacoma, Ok., U.S. E10 128
Dadanawa, Guy. F12 86
Dade City, Fl., U.S. H3 116
Dadeldhurā, Nepal. D8 54
Dadeville, Al., U.S. E13 122
Dādra and Nagar Haveli, state, India. I4 54
Dādu, Pak. D10 56
Daegu see Taegu, Kor., S. D1 40
Daejeon see Taejŏn, Kor., S. F7 38
Daet, Phil. C4 52
Dafang, China F6 36
Dafeng, China E9 42
Dafni, Grc. F5 28
Dafoe, Sk., Can. C9 124
Dafu, stm., China F5 42
Dagâ, stm., Mya. D2 48
Dagana, Sen. F1 64
Dagana, Port. F6 62
Dagda, Lat. D10 10
Dagestan, state, Russia F7 32
Daglung, China D13 54
Dagu, China E8 42
Dagua, Pap. N. Gui. a3 79a
Daguan Hu, l., China F7 42
Daguao, P.R. B4 104a
Daguipa, China C6 38
Dagupan, Phil. B3 52
Dagzê Co, l., China B11 54
Dahab, Egypt J5 58
Dahei, India H4 54
Daheiding Shan, mtn., China B10 36
Da Hinggan Ling (Greater Khingan Range), mts., China B9 36
Dahlak Archipelago, is., Erit. D8 62
Dahlonega, Ga., U.S. B1 116
Dahlonega Plateau, plat., U.S. C14 122
Dahmani, Tun. I2 24
Dahme, Ger. E9 16
Dāhod, India G5 54
Dahomey see Benin, ctry., Afr. G5 64
Dahra, Alg. B3 62
Dahra, mts., Alg. H11 20
Dahshur, Pyramides de (Dashur, Pyramids of), hist., Egypt I1 58
Dai, i., Sol. Is. d9 79b
Daia, Rom. E12 26
Daik-Hu, China A5 42
Daik-u, Mya. D3 48
Da'il, Syria F7 58
Daimiel, Spain E7 20
Daingean, Ire. H5 12
Daingerfield, Tx., U.S. D4 122
Dainkog, China E4 36
Daireaux, Arg. H7 92
Dairen see Dalian, China B9 42
Dairût, Egypt K1 58
Dai-sen, vol., Japan D6 40
Daisetta, Tx., U.S. G4 122
Dajarra, Austl. C2 76
Dajian Shan, mtn., China. F5 36
Dakar, Sen. G1 64
Dakeng, China H6 42
Dakhin Shāhbāzpur Island, i., Bngl. H13 54
Dakhla, W. Sah. E1 64
Dākoānk, India F7 46
Dakoro, Niger G6 64
Dakota City, Ia., U.S. B3 120
Dakota City, Ne., U.S. B1 120
Dakovica, Serb. G7 26
Đakovo, Cro. E15 22
Dala, Sol. Is. e9 79b
Dalaba, Gui. G2 64
Dalad Qi, China A4 42
Dalälven, stm., Swe. F7 8
Dalaman, Tur. G11 28
Dalaman, stm., Tur. G12 28
Dalandzadgad, Mong. C5 36
Dalarna, state, Swe. F6 8
Da Lat, Viet. F9 48
Dālbandin, Pak. D9 56
Dalby, Austl. F8 76
Dale, Nor. F1 8
Dale Hollow Lake, res., U.S. H12 120
Dalet, Mya. B1 48
Daleville, In., U.S. H4 112
Dalga, Egypt K1 58
Dalhart, Tx., U.S. E6 128
Dalhousie, India B5 54
Dalhousie, Cape, c., N.T., Can. B14 140
Dali, China. G5 36
Dali, China. D5 42
Dalian (Dairen), China B9 42
Daliang Shan, mts., China F5 36
Dalian Wan, b., China B9 42
Daling, stm., China D4 38
Dalizi, China D7 38
Dalkeith, Scot., U.K. F9 12
Dalkola, India F11 54
Dallas, Or., U.S. F3 136
Dallas, Tx., U.S. E2 122
Dallas, Wi., U.S. F7 118

Dallas Center, Ia., U.S. J4 118
Dallas City, Il., U.S. D6 120
Dalli Rājhara, India H8 54
Dall Island, i., Ak., U.S. F13 140
Dall Lake, l., Ak., U.S. D7 140
Dalmacija see Dalmatia, hist. reg., Eur. G12 22
Dalmatia, hist. reg., Eur. G12 22
Dalmau, India E8 54
Dalmellington, Scot., U.K. F8 12
Dal'negorsk, Russia B11 38
Dal'nerečensk, Russia B11 36
Dal'nyk, Ukr. C17 26
Daloa, C. Iv. H3 64
Dalqū, Sudan C6 62
Dalroy, Ab., Can. E17 138
Dalrymple, Mount, mtn., Austl. C7 76
Dalsing Saraī, India F10 54
Dāltenganj, India F10 54
Dalton, Ga., U.S. C13 122
Dalton, Ma., U.S. B12 114
Dalton, Ne., U.S. F10 126
Daludalu, Indon. C2 50
Daluguti Island, i., Phil. A3 52
Dalwallinu, Austl. F3 74
Daly, stm., Austl. B6 74
Daly Bay, b., Nu., Can. C13 106
Daly City, Ca., U.S. F3 134
Daly Lake, l., Sk., Can. D9 106
Daly Waters, Austl. C6 74
Dam, stm., China B14 54
Damanar, Port. F1 20
Damān, India H4 54
Damān and Diu, state, India. H4 54
Damanhûr, Egypt G1 58
Damar, Pulau, i., Indon. G8 44
Damaraland, hist. reg., Nmb. B3 70
Damascus see Dimashq, Syria E7 58
Damascus, Ar., U.S. B6 122
Damascus, Ga., U.S. F14 122
Damascus, Md., U.S. E8 114
Damaturu, Nig. G7 64
Damāvand, Qolleh-ye, vol., Iran. B7 56
Damba, Ang. B2 68
Dambacha, Eth. E7 62
Damboa, Nig. G7 64
Dâmbovița, state, Rom. E12 26
Dâmbovița, stm., Rom. D12 26
Dam Doi, Viet. H7 48
Damen Dao, i., China H9 42
Dāmghān, Iran B7 56
Damiao, China C1 42
Damietta, Egypt G2 58
Damietta Mouth see Dumyāt, mth., Egypt G3 58
Daming, China C6 42
Damodar, stm., India G11 54
Damoh, India G7 54
Damongo, Ghana H4 64
Dampier, Austl. D3 74
Dampier, Selat, strt., Indon. F9 44
Dampier Land, pen., Austl. C4 74
Dampier Strait, strt., Pap. N. Gui. b4 79a
Dāmrei, Chuŏr Phnum, mts., Camb. G7 48
Damxung, China C13 54
Dan, stm., U.S. H6 114
Dan, In., U.S. I2 112
Danai, Indon. C3 50
Danakil, reg., Afr. E8 62
Danané, C. Iv. H3 64
Da Nang, Viet. D9 48
Danao, Phil. E5 52
Danba, China E5 36
Danbury, Ct., U.S. C12 114
Danbury, Ia., U.S. B2 120
Danbury, Ne., U.S. A8 128
Danby Lake, l., Ca., U.S. I1 132
Dandeli, India C2 53
Dandenong, Austl. K5 76
Dandong, China D5 38
Dandridge, Tn., U.S. H2 114
Danfeng, China E4 42
Danforth, Me., U.S. E9 110
Dangan, Taj. B10 56
Danger Point, c., S. Afr. I4 70
Danggali Conservation Park, p.o.i., Austl. I3 76
Dangila, Eth. E7 62
Dangriga, Belize D3 102
Dangshan, China D7 42
Dangtu, China F8 42
Dan-Gulbi, Nig. G6 64
Dangyang, China F4 42
Daniel, Wy., U.S. H16 136
Daniel-Johnson, Barrage, dam, Qc., Can. E17 106
Danielskuil, S. Afr. F6 70
Danielson, Ct., U.S. C13 114
Daniels Pass, p., Ut., U.S. C5 132
Danielsville, Ga., U.S. B2 116
Danilov, Russia G18 8
Danilovka, Kaz. D12 32
Danja, Nig. G6 64
Danjiangkou Shuiku, res., China E4 42
Danjo-guntō, is., Japan G1 40
Dankov, Russia D5 32
Danli, Hond. E4 102
Danmark Fjord, b., Grnld. A22 141
Dannebrog, Ne., U.S. F14 126
Dannenberg, Ger. C6 16
Dannevirke, N.Z. E7 80
Danshui, China J6 42
Dansville, N.Y., U.S. B8 114
Dantan, India H11 54
Dante, S.D., U.S. D14 126
Dantewāra, India B5 53
Danube, stm., Eur. E16 26
Danube, Mouths of the, mth., Eur. E16 26
Danubyu, Mya. D2 48
Danvers, Il., U.S. D8 120
Danville, Ar., U.S. B6 122
Danville, Qc., Can. E4 110
Danville, Ca., U.S. F4 134
Danville, Il., U.S. D2 112
Danville, In., U.S. I3 112
Danville, Ky., U.S. G13 120
Danville, Pa., U.S. D9 114
Danville, Va., U.S. H6 114
Danville, Vt., U.S. F4 110
Dānxian, China L3 42
Danyang, China F8 42
Danzig, Gulf of see Gdańsk, Gulf of, b., Eur. B15 16
Daocheng, China F5 36
Daosa, India E6 54
Daotiandi, China B10 36
Daoukro, C. Iv. H4 64
Dapango see Dapaong, Togo G5 64
Dapaong, Togo G5 64
Dapchi, Nig. G7 64
Daphne, Al., U.S. G11 122
Daphne, hist., Egypt G3 58
Dapitan, Phil. F4 52
Da Qaidam, China D4 36
Daqing, China B10 36
Daqu Dao, i., China F9 42
Dar'ā, Syria F7 58
Dar'ā, state, Syria F7 58
Dārāb, Iran D7 56
Dāraban, Pak. C3 54

Darabani, Rom. A13 26
Darasun, Russia F11 34
Daravica, mtn., Serb. G7 26
Darāw, Egypt C6 62
Dārayyā, Syria E7 58
Darb al-Ḥajj, Jabal, mtn., Jord. H6 58
Darbhanga, India. E10 54
D'Arbonne, Bayou, stm., La., U.S. E6 122
Darby, Mt., U.S. D12 136
Dardanelle, Ar., U.S. B5 122
Dardanelle Lake, res., Ar., U.S. B5 122
Dardanelles see Çanakkale Boğazı, strt., Tur. C9 28
Dar-el-Beida see Casablanca, Mor. C3 64
Dar es Salaam, Tan. F7 66
Darfo, Italy E7 22
Dargai, Pak. A3 54
Dargan-Ata, Turkmen. A9 56
Dargaville, N.Z. B5 80
Dargol, Niger G5 64
Darhan, Mong. B6 36
Darıca, Tur. C12 28
Darién, Col. F3 86
Darien, Ga., U.S. E4 116
Darién, Parque Nacional, p.o.i., Pan. D2 86
Darién, Serranía del, mts. C3 86
Dārjiling, India E12 54
Dark Head, c., St. Vin. o11 105e
Darling, S. Afr. H4 70
Darling, stm., Austl. I4 76
Darling, Ms., U.S. C8 122
Darling Downs, reg., Austl. F8 76
Darlingford, Mb., Can. E15 124
Darling Range, mts., Austl. F3 74
Darlington, Eng., U.K. G11 12
Darlington, Wi., U.S. B7 120
Darlington Dam, res., S. Afr. H7 70
Darlot, Lake, l., Austl. E4 74
Darłowo, Pol. B12 16
Darmstadt, Ger. G4 16
Darnah, Libya A4 62
Darnall, S. Afr. F10 70
Darney, Fr. F15 14
Darnley, Cape, c., Ant. B11 81
Darnley Bay, b., N.T., Can. B6 106
Darr, stm., Austl. D4 76
Darregueira, Arg. H6 92
Darreh Gaz, Iran B8 56
Darrington, Wa., U.S. B5 136
Darrouzett, Tx., U.S. E8 128
Dart, Cape, c., Ant. C27 81
Dartmoor, Austl. K3 76
Dartmoor National Park, p.o.i., Eng., U.K. K9 12
Dartmouth, Austl. K3 76
Dartmouth, N.S., Can. F13 110
Dartmouth, Eng., U.K. K9 12
Dartmouth, Lake, l., Austl. E5 76
Dartmouth Reservoir, res., Austl. K6 76
Daru, Pap. N. Gui. b3 79a
Daruvar, Cro. E14 22
Darvaza, Turkmen. A8 56
Därwha, India H6 54
Darwin, Austl. B6 74
Darwin, Bahía, b., Chile I1 90
Darya Khān, Pak. C3 54
Dashbalbar, Mong. B7 36
Dashitou, China C8 38
Dashoūz, Turkmen. A8 56
Dasht, stm., Pak. D9 56
Dashur, Pyramids of see Dahshur, Pyramides de, hist., Egypt I1 58
Dashuqiao, China A6 48
Dasol Bay, b., Phil. C2 52
Dassel, Mn., U.S. F4 118
Datça, Tur. G10 28
Date, Japan C14 38
Datia, India F7 54
Datian, China I7 42
Datian Ding, mtn., China J4 42
Datong, China A5 42
Datong, China D5 36
Datong, China B9 36
Datong Shan, mts., China D4 36
Datu, Cape, c., Asia E4 44
Datu Piang, Phil. G5 52
Daua (Dawa), stm., Afr. G8 62
Daudnagar, India F10 54
Daugai, Lith. F7 10
Daugavpils, Bela. E9 10
Daule, stm., Ec. H1 86
Daund, India B1 53
Daung Kyun, i., Mya. F3 48
Dauphin, Mb., Can. C13 124
Dauphin Island, i., Al., U.S. G10 122
Dauphin Island, i., Al., U.S. G10 122
Dauphiné, hist. reg., Fr. E11 18
Dauphin Lake, l., Mb., Can. C14 124
Davant, La., U.S. H9 122
Dāvangere, India D2 53
Davao, Phil. G5 52
Davao Gulf, b., Phil. G5 52
Dāvarzan, Iran B8 56
Davenport, Ia., U.S. C7 120
Davenport, Ok., U.S. B2 122
Davenport, Wa., U.S. C8 136
Davenport Downs, Austl. E3 76
Davey, Port, b., Austl. o12 77a
David, Pan. H6 102
David City, Ne., U.S. F15 126
Davidson, Sk., Can. C7 124
Davidson Mountains, mts., Ak., U.S. C11 140
Davis, Ca., U.S. E4 134
Davis, N.C., U.S. B9 116
Davis, Ok., U.S. C2 122
Davis, W.V., U.S. E6 114
Davis, sci., Ant. B12 81
Davis, Mount, mtn., Pa., U.S. E6 114
Davis Dam, dam, U.S. H2 132
Davis Inlet, Nf., Can. D18 106
Davis Mountains, mts., Tx., U.S. D3 130
Davis Sea, s., Ant. B14 81
Davis Strait, strt., N.A. C15 94
Davos, Switz. D6 22
Davy, W.V., U.S. G4 114
Davyd-Haradok, Bela. H9 10
Dawa (Daua), stm., Afr. G8 62
Dawei (Tavoy), Mya. E4 48
Dawen, stm., China D7 42
Dawlish, Eng., U.K. K9 12
Dawna Range, mts., Mya. D4 48
Dawson, Ga., U.S. F14 122
Dawson, Mn., U.S. G2 118
Dawson, Ne., U.S. D1 120
Dawson, stm., Austl. D7 76
Dawson, Isla, i., Chile J2 90
Dawson Bay, b., Mb., Can. B13 124
Dawson Creek, B.C., Can. C12 106
Dawson Inlet, b., Micron. m11 78c
Dawson Range, mts., Yk., Can. C3 106
Dawsonville, Ga., U.S. B1 116
Dax, Fr. F4 18

Daxian, China F2 42
Daxing, China B7 42
Daxue Shan, mts., China. I4 42
Daxue Shan, mts., China. F5 36
Dayangshu, China D5 38
Dayangshu, China B9 36
Dayao, China F5 36
Daye, China F6 42
Daying, China B5 42
Daylesford, Austl. K5 76
Dayman, stm., Ur. E9 92
Dayong, China G4 42
Dayr az-Zawr, Syria B4 56
Dayr Ḥāfir, Syria B8 58
Daysland, Ab., Can. D18 138
Dayton, Oh., U.S. E1 114
Dayton, Or., U.S. E3 136
Dayton, Tn., U.S. B13 122
Dayton, Tx., U.S. G4 122
Dayton, Wa., U.S. D9 136
Dayton, Wy., U.S. C5 126
Daytona Beach, Fl., U.S. G5 116
Dayu, China I6 42
Dayu Ling, mts., China I6 42
Da Yunhe (Grand Canal), can., China E8 42
Dayville, Or., U.S. F7 136
Dazhu, China F2 42
Dazkırı, Tur. F12 28
De Aar, S. Afr. G7 70
Deadhorse, Ak., U.S. B10 140
Deadman's Cay, Bah. A10 102
Dead Sea, l., Asia G6 58
Deadwood, S.D., U.S. C9 126
Deakin, Austl. F5 74
Deal, Eng., U.K. J14 12
Dealesville, S. Afr. F7 70
Deal Island, Md., U.S. F10 114
De'an, China G6 42
Dean, stm., B.C., Can. D4 138
Deán Funes, Arg. E5 92
Deans Dundas Bay, b., N.T., Can. B16 140
Dearborn, Mi., U.S. B2 114
Dearg, Beinn, mtn., Scot., U.K. D8 12
Dease, stm., B.C., Can. D5 106
Dease Arm, b., N.T., Can. B6 106
Dease Lake, B.C., Can. D5 106
Dease Strait, strt., Nu., Can. B9 106
Death Valley, Ca., U.S. G9 134
Death Valley, val., Ca., U.S. G9 134
Death Valley National Park, p.o.i., U.S. G8 134
Deatsville, Al., U.S. E12 122
Deauville, Fr. E8 14
Deba, Nig. G7 64
Debao, China J2 42
Debar, Mac. B3 28
De Bary, Fl., U.S. H4 116
Debe, Trin. s12 105f
De Berry, Tx., U.S. F4 122
Dębica, Pol. F17 16
Dęblin, Pol. E17 16
Débo, Lac, l., Mali F4 64
Deborah West, Lake, l., Austl. F3 74
Debrecen, Hung. B8 26
Debre Birhan, Eth. F7 62
Debre Mark'os, Eth. E7 62
Debre Tabor, Eth. E7 62
Debre Zeyit, Eth. F7 62
Debrzno, Pol. C13 16
Decatur, Al., U.S. C11 122
Decatur, Ga., U.S. C1 116
Decatur, Il., U.S. E9 120
Decatur, In., U.S. H4 112
Decatur, Mi., U.S. F3 112
Decatur, Ms., U.S. E9 122
Decatur, Tn., U.S. B14 122
Decaturville, Tn., U.S. B10 122
Decazeville, Fr. E8 18
Deccan, plat., India B4 53
Decelles, Réservoir, res., Qc., Can. F15 106
Deception, stm., Bots. B6 70
Dechang, China F5 36
Decherd, Tn., U.S. B12 122
Dechu, India E4 54
Děčín, Czech Rep. F10 16
Decize, Fr. H12 14
Decker Lake, B.C., Can. B5 138
Decorah, Ia., U.S. H7 118
Dedaye, Mya. D2 48
Dedegöl Tepesi, mtn., Tur. F14 28
De Doorns, S. Afr. H4 70
Dédougou, Burkina G4 64
Dedovsk, Russia C12 10
Dee, stm., Scot., U.K. D10 12
Dee, stm., Wales, U.K. I9 12
Deenwood, Ga., U.S. E3 116
Deep, stm., N.C., U.S. A6 116
Deep Creek, stm., Wa., U.S. B12 136
Deep River, On., Can. B12 112
Deep River, Ia., U.S. C5 120
Deepwater, Mo., U.S. F4 120
Deep Well, Austl. D6 74
Deer Creek, stm., Ms., U.S. D8 122
Deerfield, Il., U.S. F2 112
Deerfield, Ks., U.S. C7 128
Deerfield Beach, Fl., U.S. J5 116
Deering, Ak., U.S. C7 140
Deer Island, i., N.B., Can. F10 110
Deer Isle, Me., U.S. F8 110
Deer Lake, Nf., Can. j22 107a
Deer Lodge, Mt., U.S. D14 136
Deer Park, Al., U.S. F10 122
Deer Park, Wa., U.S. C9 136
Deer Trail, Co., U.S. B4 128
Defiance, Ia., U.S. C2 120
Defiance, Oh., U.S. C1 114
Defiance, Mount, mtn., Or., U.S. E5 136
De Forest, Wi., U.S. H9 118
De Funiak Springs, Fl., U.S. G12 122
Degê, China E4 36
Degeh Bur, Eth. F8 62
Dégelis, Qc., Can. C8 110
Deggendorf, Ger. H8 16
Değh, stm., Asia B5 54
De Gray Lake, res., Ar., U.S. C5 122
Dehalak Desēt, i., Erit. D8 62
Dehiwala-Mount Lavinia, Sri L. H4 53
Dehra Dūn, India C6 54
Dehri, India F10 54
Dehua, China I8 42
Dehui, China B6 38
Deim Zubeir, Sudan F5 62
Deir Mawās, Egypt K1 58
Dej, Rom. B10 26
Dejnau, Turkmen. A9 56
De Kalb, Ms., U.S. E10 122
De Kalb, Tx., U.S. D4 122
Dekese, D.R.C. E4 66
Dékoa, C.A.R. C3 66
De Land, Fl., U.S. G4 116
Delano, Ca., U.S. H6 134
Delano, Mn., U.S. F5 118

Name	Map Ref.	Page

Delaport Point, c., Bah. — m18 104f
Delapu, China — C13 54
Delarof Islands, is., Ak., U.S. — g23 140a
Delaware, Oh., U.S. — D2 114
Delaware, Ok., U.S. — H2 120
Delaware, state, U.S. — F10 114
Delaware, stm., Ks., U.S. — E2 120
Delaware, stm., U.S. — D10 114
Delaware, East Branch, stm., N.Y., U.S. — B10 114
Delaware, West Branch, stm., U.S. — B11 114
Delaware Bay, b., U.S. — E10 114
Delaware City, De., U.S. — E10 114
Delburne, Ab., Can. — D17 138
Del Campillo, Arg. — G5 92
Del City, Ok., U.S. — F11 128
Delegate, Austl. — K7 76
De Leon, Tx., U.S. — B9 130
Delfinópolis, Braz. — K2 88
Délfoi, sci., Grc. — E5 28
Delft, Neth. — B13 14
Delft Island, i., Sri L. — G4 53
Delfzijl, Neth. — A15 14
Delgado, Cabo, c., Moz. — C7 68
Delger, stm., Mong. — G8 34
Delgerhet, Mong. — B7 36
Delhi, On., Can. — F9 112
Delhi, India — D6 54
Delhi, La., U.S. — B6 120
Delhi, La., U.S. — E7 122
Delhi, N.Y., U.S. — B11 114
Delhi, state, India — D6 54
Delia, Ab., Can. — E18 138
Deliblato, Serb. — D8 26
Delicias, Mex. — A6 100
Delight, Ar., U.S. — C5 122
Delijân, Iran — C7 56
Deline, N.T., Can. — B6 106
Delingde, Russia — B11 34
Delingha, China — D4 36
Dèlinkalns, hill, Lat. — C9 10
Delisle, Sk., Can. — C6 124
Delitzsch, Ger. — E8 16
Dell City, Tx., U.S. — C2 130
Delle, Fr. — G16 14
Dellys, Alg. — H14 20
Del Mar, Ca., U.S. — K8 134
Delmar, Ia., U.S. — C7 120
Delmar, Md., U.S. — F10 114
Delmarva Peninsula, pen., U.S. — F10 114
Delmas, Sk., Can. — B5 124
Delmenhorst, Ger. — C4 16
Delmiro Gouveia, Braz. — E7 88
Delnice, Cro. — E11 22
Del Norte, Co., U.S. — D2 128
De-Longa, ostrova, is., Russia — A19 34
De Long Mountains, mts., Ak., U.S. — C7 140
Deloraine, Mb., Can. — E13 124
Delorme, Lac, l., Qc., Can. — E16 106
Delos see Dílos, sci., Grc. — F8 28
Delphi, In., U.S. — H3 112
Delphi see Délfoi, sci., Grc. — E5 28
Delphos, Ks., U.S. — B11 128
Delportshoop, S. Afr. — F7 70
Delray Beach, Fl., U.S. — J5 116
Del Rio, Tx., U.S. — E7 130
Delta, Co., U.S. — E8 132
Delta, Mo., U.S. — G8 120
Delta, Ut., U.S. — D4 132
Delta Amacuro, state, Ven. — C11 86
Delta Beach, Mb., Can. — D15 124
Delta City, Ms., U.S. — D8 122
Delta Downs, Austl. — C8 74
Delta Junction, Ak., U.S. — D10 140
Delta Peak, mtn., B.C., Can. — D4 106
Del Valle, Tx., U.S. — D10 130
Del Verme Falls, wtfl., Eth. — F8 62
Delvinë, Alb. — E14 24
Demak, Indon. — G7 50
Demarcation Point, c., Ak., U.S. — C11 140
Demavend, Mount see Damâvand, Qolleh-ye, vol., Iran — B7 56
Demba, D.R.C. — F4 66
Dembî, Eth. — F7 62
Dembia, C.A.R. — C4 66
Dembi Dolo, Eth. — F6 62
Demidov, Russia — E14 10
Deming, N.M., U.S. — K9 132
Demini, stm., Braz. — H10 86
Demirci, Tur. — D11 28
Demirköprü Baraji, res., Tur. — E11 28
Demirköy, Tur. — B10 28
Demjanka, stm., Russia — C12 32
Demjanovo, Russia — F22 8
Demjanskoe, Russia — C11 32
Demmin, Ger. — C8 16
Demmitt, Ab., Can. — A11 138
Demopolis, Al., U.S. — E11 122
Demorest, Ga., U.S. — B2 116
Dempo, Gunung, vol., Indon. — F3 50
Demta, Indon. — F11 44
Denain, Fr. — D12 14
Denali, Ak., U.S. — D10 140
Denali National Park, Ak., U.S. — D10 140
Denan, Eth. — F8 62
Denau, Uzb. — G11 32
Den Burg, Neth. — A13 14
Dendang, Indon. — E5 50
Dendermonde (Termonde), Bel. — C12 14
Deng Deng, Cam. — C2 66
Dengkou, China — A2 42
Dengqên, China — E4 36
Dengxian, China — E5 42
Denham, Austl. — E2 74
Denham, Mount, mtn., Jam. — i13 104d
Denham Range, mts., Austl. — C6 76
Denham Springs, La., U.S. — G8 122
Den Helder (Helder), Neth. — B13 14
Dénia, Spain — F11 20
Deniliquin, Austl. — J5 76
Daniskovičí, Russia — H14 10
Denison, Tx., U.S. — D2 122
Denison, Mount, vol., Ak., U.S. — E9 140
Denizli, Tur. — F12 28
Denizli, state, Tur. — F12 28
Denkanikota, India — E3 53
Denmark, Austl. — F3 74
Denmark, S.C., U.S. — C4 116
Denmark, Wi., U.S. — D2 112
Denmark, ctry., Eur. — D10 6
Denmark Strait, strt. — C20 141
Dennery, St. Luc. — m7 105c
Denpasar, Indon. — H9 50
Denton, Md., U.S. — F10 114
Denton, Mt., U.S. — C17 136
Denton, N.C., U.S. — A5 116
Denton, Tx., U.S. — H11 128
Denton Creek, stm., Tx., U.S. — H11 128
D'Entrecasteaux, Point, c., Austl. — F3 74
D'Entrecasteaux Islands, is., Pap. N. Gui. — D6 72
Denver, Co., U.S. — B3 128
Denver, Ia., U.S. — D9 114
Denver, Pa., U.S. — D9 114
Denver City, Tx., U.S. — A5 130
Deoband, India — D6 54
Deogarh, India — F4 54
Deogarh, India — F7 54
Deogarh, India — G9 54
Deogarh Hills, hills, India — G9 54
Deoghar, India — F11 54
Deori, India — G7 54
Deoria, India — E9 54

De Pere, Wi., U.S. — D1 112
Depew, Ok., U.S. — B2 122
Depoe Bay, Or., U.S. — F2 136
Depok, Indon. — G5 50
Deposit, N.Y., U.S. — B10 114
Depue, Il., U.S. — C8 120
Dêqên, China — F4 36
Deqing, China — J4 42
De Quincy, La., U.S. — G5 122
Dera, Lach, stm., Afr. — D8 66
Dera Bugti, Pak. — D2 54
Dera Ghâzi Khân, Pak. — C3 54
Dera Ismâîl Khân, Pak. — C3 54
Derâwar Fort, Pak. — D3 54
Derbent, Russia — F7 32
Derby, Austl. — C4 74
Derby, Eng., U.K. — I11 12
Derby, Ks., U.S. — D11 128
Derby, N.Y., U.S. — B6 114
Dereköy, Tur. — B10 28
Derg, Lough, l., Ire. — I4 12
Dergači, Russia — D7 32
De Ridder, La., U.S. — G5 122
Dermott, Ar., U.S. — D7 122
Dernieres, Isles, is., La., U.S. — H8 122
Dérrame, Mex. — H3 130
Derry see Londonderry, N. Ire., U.K. — F6 12
Derry, N.H., U.S. — B14 114
Derudeb, Sudan — D7 62
Derventa, Bos. — E4 26
Derwent, Ab., Can. — C19 138
Derwent, stm., Austl. — o13 77a
Derwent, stm., Eng., U.K. — G12 12
Derwent Water, l., Eng., U.K. — G9 12
Derzhavinsk, Kaz. — D11 32
Desaguadero, stm., Arg. — F4 92
Desaguadero, stm., S.A. — G4 84
Désappointement, Îles du, is., Fr. Poly. — E12 72
Des Arc, Ar., U.S. — C7 122
Descabezado Grande, Volcán, vol., Chile — G2 92
Descanso, Braz. — C11 92
Descanso, Ca., U.S. — K9 134
Descanso, Punta, c., Mex. — K8 134
Descartes, Fr. — G9 14
Deschambault Lake, l., Sk., Can. — E10 106
Deschutes, stm., Or., U.S. — E6 136
Desdunes, Haiti — C11 102
Desê, Eth. — E7 62
Deseado, stm., Arg. — I3 90
Desengaño, Punta, c., Arg. — I3 90
Desenzano del Garda, Italy — E7 22
Deseret Peak, mtn., Ut., U.S. — C4 132
Deseronto, On., Can. — D12 112
Désert, stm., Qc., Can. — B13 112
Désert, Lac, l., Qc., Can. — B13 112
Desert Hot Springs, Ca., U.S. — J9 134
Desert Lake, l., Nv., U.S. — F1 132
Desert Peak, mtn., Ut., U.S. — B3 132
Desert Valley, val., Nv., U.S. — B7 134
Desha, Ar., U.S. — B7 122
Deshaies, Guad. — h5 105c
Deshler, Oh., U.S. — C1 114
Deshnok, India — E4 54
Desiderio Tello, Arg. — E4 92
Deskáti, Grc. — D4 28
Desloge, Mo., U.S. — G7 120
Des Moines, Ia., U.S. — C4 120
Des Moines, N.M., U.S. — E5 128
Des Moines, stm., U.S. — K7 118
Des Moines, East Fork, stm., U.S. — H4 118
Desna, stm., Eur. — D4 32
Desolación, Isla, i., Chile — J2 90
De Soto, Il., U.S. — G8 120
De Soto, Mo., U.S. — F7 120
Despatch, S. Afr. — H7 70
Despeñaperros, Desfiladero de, p., Spain — F7 20
Des Plaines, Il., U.S. — F1 112
Des Plaines, stm., U.S. — C9 120
Desroches, i., Sey. — k12 69b
Desruisseaux, St. Luc. — m7 105c
Dessau, Ger. — E8 16
Destruction Bay, Yk., Can. — C3 106
Desvres, Fr. — D10 14
Detčino, Russia — F19 10
Dete, Zimb. — D4 68
Detmold, Ger. — E4 16
Detour, Point, c., Mi., U.S. — C3 112
De Tour Village, Mi., U.S. — C5 112
Detrital Wash, stm., Az., U.S. — H2 132
Detroit, Mi., U.S. — B2 114
Detroit, Or., U.S. — F4 136
Detroit, Tx., U.S. — D3 122
Detroit Beach, Mi., U.S. — B2 114
Dettifoss, wtfl., Ice. — k31 8a
Det Udom, Thai. — E7 48
Detva, Slov. — H15 16
Deua National Park, p.o.i., Austl. — J7 76
Deulgaon Râja, India — H5 54
Deutsche Bucht, b., Ger. — C4 16
Deutschlandsberg, Aus. — D12 22
Deux-Sèvres, state, Fr. — C5 18
Deva, Rom. — D9 26
Devakottai, India — G4 53
Dévaványa, Hung. — B7 26
Deventer, Neth. — B15 14
Deveron, stm., Scot., U.K. — D10 12
Devgadh Bâriya, India — G4 54
De View, Bayou, stm., Ar, U.S. — B8 122
Devils, stm., Tx., U.S. — E6 130
Devils Island see Diable, Île du, i., Fr. Gu. — B7 84
Devils Lake, N.D., U.S. — F15 124
Devils Lake, l., N.D., U.S. — F14 124
Devils Postpile National Monument, p.o.i., Ca., U.S. — F6 134
Devils Tower National Monument, p.o.i., Wy., U.S. — C8 126
Devine, Tx., U.S. — E9 130
Devli, India — F5 54
Devoll, stm., Alb. — D14 24
Devon, Ab., Can. — C17 138
Devon Island, i., Nu., Can. — B8 141
Devonport, Austl. — n13 77a
Devoto, Arg. — E6 92
Devrek, Tur. — B14 28
Dewakang-lompo, Pulau, i., Indon. — F11 50
Dewar, Ok., U.S. — B3 122
Dewas, India — G6 54
Dewey, Ok., U.S. — H2 120
Deweyville, Tx., U.S. — G5 122
De Witt, Ar., U.S. — C7 122
De Witt, Ia., U.S. — C7 120
De Witt, N.Y., U.S. — A9 114
Dexing, China — G7 42
Dexter, Me., U.S. — E7 110
Dexter, Mi., U.S. — B2 114
Dexter, Mo., U.S. — H8 120
Dexter, N.M., U.S. — H4 128
Dexter, N.Y., U.S. — D13 112
Dexterity Fiord, b., Nu., Can. — A16 106
Deyang, China — E5 36
Dey-Dey, Lake, l., Austl. — E6 74
Dezfûl, Iran — C6 56
Dezhou, China — C7 42
Dežneva, mys, c., Russia — C27 34
Dezong, China — B13 54

Dhahran see Az-Zahrân, Sau. Ar. — D6 56
Dhaka (Dacca), Bngl. — G13 54
Dhaka, state, Bngl. — F13 54
Dhamâr, Yemen — G5 56
Dhampur, India — D7 54
Dhamtari, India — H8 54
Dhanbâd, India — G11 54
Dhandhuka, India — G3 54
Dhangadhi, Nepal — D8 54
D'Hanis, Tx., U.S. — E8 130
Dhankuta, Nepal — E11 54
Dhâr, India — G5 54
Dharân, Nepal — E11 54
Dhârâpuram, India — F3 53
Dharmâbâd, India — B3 53
Dharmapuri, India — E4 53
Dharmavaram, India — D3 53
Dharmshâla, India — B6 54
Dhaulpur, India — E6 54
Dhawalâgiri, mtn., Nepal — D9 54
Dhenkânâl, India — H10 54
Dherinia, Cyp. — C4 58
Dhofar see Zufar, reg., Oman — F7 56
Dholka, India — G4 54
Dhone, India — D3 53
Dhoomadheere, Som. — D8 66
Dhorâji, India — H3 54
Dhrângadhra, India — G3 54
Dhrol, India — G3 54
Dhuburi, India — E13 54
Dhule, India — H5 54
Dhuliân, India — F12 54
Dhupgâri, India — E12 54
Dhuusamareeb, Som. — C9 66
Diable, Île du (Devils Island), i., Fr. Gu. — B7 84
Diable, Pointe du, c., Mart. — k7 105c
Diables, Morne aux, vol., Dom. — i5 105c
Diablo, Canyon, p., Az., U.S. — H5 132
Diablo, Mount, mtn., Ca., U.S. — F4 134
Diablo, Pico del, mtn., Mex. — F4 98
Diablo Range, mts., Ca., U.S. — G4 134
Diablotins, Morne, vol., Dom. — j6 105c
Diaca, Moz. — C6 68
Dialakoto, Sen. — G2 64
Diamante, Arg. — F7 92
Diamante, stm., Arg. — G4 92
Diamantina, Braz. — J4 88
Diamantina, stm., Austl. — E2 76
Diamantina Lakes, Austl. — D3 76
Diamantino, Braz. — F6 84
Diamond, Mo., U.S. — G3 120
Diamond Harbour, India — G12 54
Diamond Islets, is., Austl. — A8 76
Diamond Peak, mtn., Id., U.S. — F13 136
Diamond Peak, mtn., Wa., U.S. — D9 136
Diamondville, Wy., U.S. — B6 132
Diana Bay, b., Can. — C16 106
Dianbai, China — K4 42
Dian Chi, l., China — G5 36
Dianjiang, China — F2 42
Dianópolis, Braz. — F2 88
Diapaga, Burkina — G5 64
Diaz, Ar., U.S. — B7 122
Díaz Point, c., Nmb. — E2 70
Dibai, India — D7 54
Dibaya, D.R.C. — F4 66
Diberg, S. Afr. — E6 70
D'Iberville, Ms., U.S. — G9 122
Dibete, Bots. — C8 70
Dibrugarh, India — C7 46
Dickens, Tx., U.S. — H8 128
Dickinson, N.D., U.S. — A10 126
Dickinson, Tx., U.S. — H3 122
Dickson, Tn., U.S. — H10 120
Didao, China — B9 38
Didsbury, Ab., Can. — E16 138
Didwâna, India — E5 54
Didymóteicho, Grc. — B9 28
Dieburg, Ger. — G4 16
Dieciocho de Julio, Ur. — F11 92
Diefenbaker, Lake, res., Sk., Can. — C7 124
Diego de Almagro, Chile — C2 92
Diego de Almagro, Isla, i., Chile — J1 90
Diego de Ocampo, Pico, mtn., Dom. Rep. — C12 102
Diégo-Suarez see Antsiranana, Madag. — C8 68
Diemuchuoke, China — B7 54
Dien Bien, Viet. — B6 48
Dien Bien Phu see Dien Bien, Viet. — B6 48
Diepholz, Ger. — D4 16
Dieppe, N.B., Can. — D12 110
Dieppe, Fr. — E9 14
Dieppe Bay Town, St. K./N. — C2 105a
Dierks, Ar., U.S. — C4 122
Di'er Songhua, stm., China — B6 38
Diest, Bel. — D14 14
Dieulefit, Fr. — E10 18
Dieveniškės, Lith. — F8 10
Diez de Octubre, Mex. — C6 100
Diffa, Niger — G7 64
Differdange, Lux. — E14 14
Dig, India — E6 54
Digba, D.R.C. — D5 66
Digboi, India — C8 46
Digby, N.S., Can. — F11 110
Digby Neck, pen., N.S., Can. — F10 110
Digges Islands, is., Nu., Can. — C8 128
Dighton, Ks., U.S. — C8 128
Digôr, India — B3 53
Digne-les-Bains, Fr. — E12 18
Digoin, Fr. — C9 18
Digos, Phil. — G5 52
Digras, India — H6 54
Digul, stm., Indon. — G10 44
Diinsoor, Som. — D8 66
Dijlah (Tigris), stm., Asia — C5 56
Dijon, Fr. — G14 14
Dikanäs, Swe. — D6 8
Dikaya, Russia — A22 10
Dike, Ia., U.S. — B5 120
Dikhil, Dji. — E8 62
Dikili, Tur. — D9 28
Dikirnis, Egypt — G2 58
Dikodougou, C. Iv. — H3 64
Diksmuide, Bel. — C11 14
Dikwa, Nig. — G7 64
Díla, Eth. — F7 62
Dilek Yarımadası Milli Parkı, p.o.i., Tur. — F10 28
Dili, E. Timor — G8 44
Dillenburg, Ger. — F4 16
Diller, Ne., U.S. — A12 128
Dilley, Tx., U.S. — E8 130
Dilling, Sudan — E5 62
Dillingen an der Donau, Ger. — H6 16
Dillingham, Ak., U.S. — E8 140
Dillon, Mt., U.S. — E14 136
Dillon, S.C., U.S. — B6 116
Dillon Mountain, mtn., N.M., U.S. — J8 132
Dillwyn, Va., U.S. — G7 114
Dilolo, D.R.C. — G4 66
Dílos, sci., Grc. — F8 28
Dilworth, Mn., U.S. — H17 124
Dimâpur, India — C7 46
Dimashq (Damascus), Syria — E7 58
Dimashq, state, Syria — E7 58
Dimbelenge, D.R.C. — F4 66
Dimbokro, C. Iv. — H4 64
Dimbulah, Austl. — A5 76
Dimitrovgrad, Blg. — G12 26

Dimitrovgrad, Russia — D8 32
Dimitsána, Grc. — F4 28
Dimlang, mtn., Nig. — H7 64
Dimmitt, Tx., U.S. — G6 128
Dimona, Isr. — G6 58
Dinagat Island, i., Phil. — E5 52
Dinajpur, Bngl. — F12 54
Dinan, Fr. — F6 14
Dinant, Bel. — D13 14
Dinar, Tur. — E13 28
Dinard, Fr. — F6 14
Dinaric Alps (Dinara), mts., Eur. — G13 22
Dindi, stm., India — C4 53
Dindigul, India — F4 53
Dindori, India — G8 54
Dingalan Bay, b., Phil. — C3 52
Ding'an, China — L4 42
Dingbian, China — C2 42
Dingelstädt, Ger. — E6 16
Dinggyê, China — D11 54
Dinghai, China — F9 42
Dingle, Ire. — I2 12
Dingle Bay, b., Ire. — I2 12
Dingnan, China — I6 42
Dingo, Austl. — D7 76
Dingolfing, Ger. — H8 16
Dingshuzhen, China — F8 42
Dingtao, China — D6 42
Dinguiraye, Gui. — G2 64
Dingwall, N.S., Can. — D16 110
Dingxian, China — B6 42
Dingxiang, China — B5 42
Dingyuan, China — E7 42
Dinhâta, India — E12 54
Dinh Hoa, Viet. — B7 48
Dinh Lap, Viet. — B8 48
Dinkelsbühl, Ger. — G6 16
Dinnebito Wash, stm., Az., U.S. — H5 132
Dinorwic, On., Can. — B6 118
Dinosaur, Co., U.S. — C8 132
Dinosaur National Monument, p.o.i., U.S. — C8 132
Dinsmore, Sk., Can. — C6 124
Dinuba, Ca., U.S. — G6 134
Dinwiddie, Va., U.S. — G8 114
Dionisio Cerqueira, Braz. — C11 92
Dioulouloulou, Sen. — G1 64
Diourbel, Sen. — G1 64
Dipalpur, Pak. — C4 54
Diplo, Pak. — F2 54
Dipolog, Phil. — F4 52
Dippoldiswalde, Ger. — F9 16
Dir, Pak. — B11 56
Dirê, Mali — F4 64
Dirê Dawa, Eth. — F8 62
Dirico, Ang. — D3 68
Dirj, Libya — A2 62
Dirk Hartog Island, i., Austl. — E2 74
Dirkou, Niger — F7 64
Dirranbandi, Austl. — G7 76
Dîsa, India — F4 54
Disappointment, Cape, c., S. Geor. — J9 90
Disappointment, Cape, c., Wa., U.S. — D2 136
Disappointment, Lake, l., Austl. — D4 74
Disaster Bay, b., Austl. — K8 76
Discovery Bay, b., Austl. — L3 76
Dishman, Wa., U.S. — B7 136
Disko, i., Grnld. — D15 141
Disko Bugt, b., Grnld. — D15 141
Dismal, stm., Ne., U.S. — F12 126
Dispur, India — E13 54
Disraéli, Qc., Can. — E5 110
Distrito Capital, state, Col. — E4 86
Distrito Federal, state, Braz. — H2 88
Distrito Federal, state, Ven. — B8 86
Dis Uq, Egypt. — G1 58
Dithâmarschen, reg., Ger. — B5 16
Diu, India — H3 54
Dive, can., Fr. — H8 14
Divenskaja, Russia — A12 10
Divernon, Il., U.S. — E8 120
Divinhe, Moz. — B12 70
Divi Point, c., India — D5 53
Divisor, Serra do, plat., S.A. — E3 84
Divnoe, Russia — E6 32
Divnogorsk, Russia — C16 32
Divo, C. Iv. — H3 64
Diwâl Qol, Afg. — A1 54
Dixie Valley, val., Nv., U.S. — D8 134
Dixon, Ca., U.S. — E4 134
Dixon, Il., U.S. — C8 120
Dixon, Ky., U.S. — G10 120
Dixon, N.M., U.S. — E3 128
Dixon Entrance, strt., N.A. — E4 106
Diyarbakir, Tur. — B4 56
Djado, Niger — E7 64
Djado, Plateau du, plat., Niger — E7 64
Djakarta see Jakarta, Indon. — G5 50
Djamâa, Alg. — C6 64
Djambala, Congo — E2 66
Djanet, Alg. — E6 64
Djaret, Oued, stm., Alg. — D5 64
Djat'kovo, Russia — G17 10
Djedi, Oued, stm., Alg. — C5 64
Djéma, C.A.R. — C4 66
Djenné, Mali — G4 64
Djenoun, Garet el, mtn., Alg. — D6 64
Djérem, stm., Cam. — C2 66
Djibo, Burkina — G4 64
Djibouti, Dji. — E8 62
Djibouti, ctry., Afr. — E8 62
Djoku-Punda, D.R.C. — F4 66
Djolu, D.R.C. — D4 66
Djougou, Benin — H5 64
Djourab, Erg du, sand, Chad — D3 62
Djûpivogur, Ice. — k32 8a
Djurâs, Sen. — F6 8
Djurtjuli, Russia — C8 32
Dmitrija Lapteva, proliv, strt., Russia — B16 34
Dmitrov, Russia — D20 10
Dneprovskoe, Russia — E16 10
Dnieper (Dnepr), stm., Eur. — G19 16
Dniester (Dnister), stm., Eur. — A17 26
Dno, Russia — C12 10
Doaktown, N.B., Can. — D10 110
Doangdoangan-Besar, Pulau, i., Indon. — F10 50
Doba, Chad — F3 62
Dobczyce, Pol. — G15 16
Dobele, Lat. — D6 10
Doberai, Jazirah (Doberai Peninsula), pen., Indon. — F9 44
Doberai Peninsula see Doberai, Jazirah, pen., Indon. — F9 44
Dobo, Indon. — G9 44
Doboj, Bos. — E5 26
Dobre Miasto, Pol. — C16 16
Dobrič, Blg. — F14 26

Dobříš, Czech Rep. — G10 16
Dobrjanka, Russia — C9 32
Dobroe, Russia — C15 10
Dobroteasa, Rom. — E11 26
Dobruja, hist. reg., Eur. — E15 26
Dobruš, Bela. — H14 10
Dobruška, Czech Rep. — F12 16
Dobson, N.C., U.S. — H5 114
Dobzha, China — D12 54
Dock Junction, Ga., U.S. — E4 116
Doctor Cecilio Báez, Para. — B9 92
Doctor Coss, Mex. — I8 130
Doctor González, Mex. — I8 130
Dod Ballâpur, India — E3 53
Doddridge, Ar., U.S. — D4 122
Dodecanese see Dodekánisoy, is., Grc. — G10 28
Dodekánisoy (Dodecanese), is., Grc. — G10 28
Dodge Center, Mn., U.S. — G5 118
Dodge City, Ks., U.S. — D9 128
Dodgeville, Wi., U.S. — B7 120
Dodoma, Tan. — F7 66
Dodoni, sci., Grc. — D3 28
Dodsland, Sk., Can. — C5 124
Dodson, Mt., U.S. — F5 124
Dodson, Tx., U.S. — G8 128
Doerun, Ga., U.S. — E1 116
Doetinchem, Neth. — C15 14
Dogai Coring, l., China. — A12 54
Doğanbey, Tur. — E9 28
Doğanhisar, Tur. — E14 28
Dog Island, i., Fl., U.S. — H14 122
Dog Islands, is., Br. Vir. Is. — e9 104b
Dog Lake, l., On., Can. — C15 124
Dog Lake, l., On., Can. — C9 118
Dogliani, Italy — F4 22
Dôgo, i., Japan — C6 40
Dogondoutchi, Niger — G5 64
Doğu Karadeniz Dağları, mts., Tur. — A5 56
Doha see Ad-Dawhah, Qatar — D7 56
Dohrighât, India — E9 54
Dois Irmãos de Goiás, Braz. — E1 88
Doka, Indon. — G9 44
Dokkum, Neth. — A14 14
Doksy, Czech Rep. — F10 16
Doland, S.D., U.S. — C14 126
Dolbeau, Qc., Can. — B4 110
Dol-de-Bretagne, Fr. — F6 14
Dole, Fr. — G14 14
Dolega, Pan. — H6 102
Dolgeville, N.Y., U.S. — E15 112
Dolgij Most, Russia — C17 32
Dolgoščele, Russia — C20 8
Dolinsk, Russia — G17 34
Dolj, state, Rom. — E10 26
Dolný Kubín, Slov. — G15 16
Dolomites see Dolomiti, mts., Italy — D8 22
Dolomiti, mts., Italy — D8 22
Dolores, Arg. — H9 92
Dolores, Col. — F4 86
Dolores, Guat. — D3 102
Dolores, Mex. — H6 130
Dolores, stm., U.S. — E7 132
Dolores Hidalgo, Mex. — E8 100
Dolphin, Cape, c., Falk. Is. — J5 90
Dolphin and Union Strait, strt., Nu., Can. — B7 106
Dolphin Head, mtn., Jam. — i12 104d
Dolsk, Pol. — D13 16
Dolžicy, Russia — C11 10
Domaniči, Russia — G16 10
Domažlice, Czech Rep. — G8 16
Dombås, Nor. — E3 8
Dombes, reg., Fr. — D11 18
Dombóvár, Hung. — C4 26
Dôme, Puy de, mtn., Fr. — D8 18
Dome Creek, B.C., Can. — C9 138
Domeyko, Chile — D2 92
Domeyko, Cordillera, mts., Chile — D3 90
Domfront, Fr. — F8 14
Domiciano Ribeiro, Braz. — I2 88
Domingo M. Irala, Para. — B10 92
Dominica, ctry., N.A. — j5 105c
Dominica Channel see Martinique Passage, strt., N.A. — k6 105c
Dominicana, República see Dominican Republic, ctry., N.A. — D10 96
Dominican Republic, ctry., N.A. — D10 96
Dominica Passage, strt., N.A. — i6 105c
Dominion, Cape, c., Nu., Can. — B15 106
Dominion City, Mb., Can. — E16 124
Dom Joaquim, Braz. — J4 88
Domo, Eth. — F9 62
Domodedovo, Russia — E20 10
Domodossola, Italy — D5 22
Dom Pedrito, Braz. — E10 92
Dom Pedro, Braz. — C3 88
Dompu, Indon. — H11 50
Domremy, Sk., Can. — B8 124
Dom Yai, stm., Thai. — E7 48
Domuyo, Volcán, vol., Arg. — H2 92
Don, stm., India — C2 53
Don, stm., Russia — E6 32
Don, stm., Scot., U.K. — D10 12
Donadeu, Arg. — C6 92
Donaghadee, N. Ire., U.K. — G7 12
Donald, Austl. — K4 76
Donalda, Ab., Can. — D18 138
Donaldson, Ar., U.S. — C6 122
Donaldsonville, La., U.S. — G7 122
Doñana, Parque Nacional de, p.o.i., Spain — H4 20
Donau see Danube, stm., Eur. — F11 6
Donaueschingen, Ger. — I4 16
Donauwörth, Ger. — H6 16
Don Benito, Spain — F5 20
Doncaster, Eng., U.K. — H11 12
Dondaicha, India — H5 54
Dondo, Ang. — B1 68
Dondo, Moz. — A12 70
Dondo, Teluk, b., Indon. — C12 50
Dondra Head, c., Sri L. — I5 53
Donduşeni, Mol. — A14 26
Donegal, Ire. — G4 12
Donegal, state, Ire. — G5 12
Donegal Bay, b., Ire. — G4 12
Donets'k, Ukr. — E5 32
Donga, stm., Nig. — H7 64
Dong'an, China — H4 42
Dongara, Austl. — E2 74
Dongargarh, India — H8 54
Dong Ha, Viet. — D8 48
Dông Hải Dăo, i., China — K4 42
Dong Hene, Laos — D8 48
Dong Hoi, Viet. — D8 48
Dong Hu, l., China — B10 54
Dongjiang, China — F6 42

Dongjingcheng, China — B8 38
Donglan, China — I2 42
Dongliao, stm., China — C5 38
Dong Nai, stm., Viet. — G8 48
Dongning, China — B9 38
Dongo, D.R.C. — D3 66
Dongou, Congo — D3 66
Dongping, China — D7 42
Dongping, China — K5 42
Dong San Shen (Manchuria), hist. reg., China — L4 42
Dongshan, China — L4 42
Dongshan Dao, i., China — J7 42
Dongsheng, China — B4 42
Dongtai, China — E9 42
Dongting Hu, l., China — G5 42
Dong Trieu, Viet. — B8 48
Dongwe, stm., Zam. — C3 68
Dongxi, China — G2 42
Dongxiang, China — G7 42
Dongyang, China — G9 42
Dongzhi, China — F7 42
Donie, Tx., U.S. — F2 122
Doniphan, Ne., U.S. — G14 126
Donja Stubica, Cro. — E12 22
Donjek, stm., Yk., Can. — C3 106
Don Martín, Mex. — G7 130
Donna, Tx., U.S. — H9 130
Donnacona, Qc., Can. — D5 110
Donnelly, Id., U.S. — F10 136
Donner, La., U.S. — H7 122
Donner Pass, p., Ca., U.S. — D5 134
Donner und Blitzen, stm., Or., U.S. — G8 136
Donnybrook, Austl. — F3 74
Donora, Pa., U.S. — D6 114
Donostia see Donostia-San Sebastián, Spain — A9 20
Donostia-San Sebastián, Spain — A9 20
Don Pedro Reservoir, res., Ca., U.S. — F5 134
Don Peninsula, pen., B.C., Can. — D2 138
Donskoj, Russia — G21 10
Doolow, Som. — D8 66
Doonerak, Mount, mtn., Ak., U.S. — C9 140
Doornik see Tournai, Bel. — D12 14
Door Peninsula, pen., Wi., U.S. — D2 112
Dor, Isr. — F5 58
Dora, Al., U.S. — D11 122
Dora, Lake, l., Austl. — D4 74
Dora Baltea, stm., Italy — E4 22
Dorado, P.R. — B3 104a
Doraville, Ga., U.S. — D14 122
Dorcheat, Bayou, stm., U.S. — D5 122
Dorchester, N.B., Can. — E12 110
Dorchester, On., Can. — F8 112
Dorchester, Eng., U.K. — K10 12
Dorchester, Ne., U.S. — G15 126
Dorchester, Cape, c., Nu., Can. — B15 106
Dordabis, Nmb. — C3 70
Dordogne, state, Fr. — D6 18
Dordogne, stm., Fr. — D8 18
Dordrecht, Neth. — C13 14
Dordrecht, S. Afr. — G8 70
Dore Lake, l., Sk., Can. — E9 106
Dorena, Or., U.S. — G4 136
Dores do Indaiá, Braz. — J3 88
Dorgali, Italy — D3 24
Dörgön nuur, l., Mong. — B3 36
Dori, Burkina — G4 64
Doring, stm., S. Afr. — H4 70
Dornbirn, Aus. — C6 22
Dornoch, Scot., U.K. — D8 12
Dorog, Hung. — B5 26
Dorogobuž, Russia — F16 10
Dorohoi, Russia — A13 26
Dorokempo, Indon. — H11 50
Dorre Island, i., Austl. — E2 74
Dorrigo, Austl. — H9 76
Dorris, Ca., U.S. — B4 134
Dorsale, mts., Tun. — I3 24
Dorset see Dordrecht, Neth. — C13 14
Dortan, Fr. — B11 18
Dorton, Ky., U.S. — G3 114
Dörtyol, Tur. — B7 58
Doruma, D.R.C. — D5 66
Dos, Canal Numero, can., Arg. — H9 92
Dosatuj, Russia — A8 36
Dos Bahías, Cabo, c., Arg. — H3 90
Dos Bocas, P.R. — B1 104a
Dösemealtı, Tur. — F13 28
Dos Hermanas, Spain — G4 20
Dos Pos, Neth. Ant. — p23 104g
Dos Quebradas, Col. — E4 86
Dosso, Niger — G5 64
Dossor, Kaz. — E8 32
Dothan, Al., U.S. — F13 122
Dotnuva, Lith. — E6 10
Dou, China — B8 42
Douai, Fr. — D11 14
Douala, Cam. — D1 66
Douarnenez, Fr. — F4 14
Double Island Point, c., Austl. — E9 76
Double Springs, Al., U.S. — C11 122
Doubletop Peak, mtn., Wy., U.S. — G16 136
Doubs, state, Fr. — G15 14
Doubs, stm., Eur. — H14 14
Doubtful Sound, strt., N.Z. — G2 80
Doubtless Bay, b., N.Z. — B5 80
Douentza, Mali — F4 64
Douglas, I. of Man — G8 12
Douglas, S. Afr. — F6 70
Douglas, Az., U.S. — L7 132
Douglas, Ga., U.S. — E3 116
Douglas, Wy., U.S. — E7 126
Douglas Channel, strt., B.C., Can. — C1 138
Douglas Lake, B.C., Can. — F10 138
Douglas Lake, res., Tn., U.S. — H2 114
Douglasville, Ga., U.S. — D14 122
Doullens, Fr. — D11 14
Doumé, Cam. — E8 66
Dourada, Serra, plat., Braz. — G8 84
Dourados, Braz. — D6 90
Dourbali, Chad — E3 62
Douro (Duero), stm., Eur. — C2 20
Douz, Tun. — C6 64
Douze, stm., Fr. — F5 18
Dove Bugt, strt., Grnld. — B21 141
Dove Creek, Co., U.S. — F7 132
Dover, Austl. — o13 77a
Dover, Eng., U.K. — J14 12
Dover, De., U.S. — D10 114
Dover, N.H., U.S. — G6 110
Dover, N.J., U.S. — C11 114
Dover, Oh., U.S. — D4 114
Dover, Tn., U.S. — H10 120
Dover, Strait of, strt., Eur. — K14 12
Dover-Foxcroft, Me., U.S. — E7 110
Dovrefjell Nasjonalpark, p.o.i., Nor. — E3 8
Dow City, Ia., U.S. — C2 120
Dowlatâbâd, Iran — D7 56
Downey, Id., U.S. — H14 136
Downieville, Ca., U.S. — D5 134
Downing, Mo., U.S. — D5 120
Downingtown, Pa., U.S. — D10 114

Downpatrick – Elektrostal' I • 17

Name	Map Ref.	Page
Downpatrick, N. Ire., U.K.	G7	12
Downs, Ks., U.S.	B10	128
Downton, Mount, mtn., B.C., Can.	D6	138
Dows, Ia., U.S.	B4	120
Dowshī, Afg.	B10	56
Doyle, Ca., U.S.	C5	134
Doyles, Nf., Can.	C17	110
Doylestown, Pa., U.S.	D10	114
Doyline, La., U.S.	E5	122
Dōzen, is., Japan	C5	40
Dozier, Al., U.S.	F12	122
Dra, Cap, c., Mor.	D2	64
Dra'a, Hamada du, des., Alg.	D3	64
Drâa, Oued, stm., Afr.	D2	64
Drac, stm., Fr.	E2	22
Dracena, Braz.	D6	90
Drachten, Neth.	A15	14
Dracut, Ma., U.S.	B14	114
Dragalina, Rom.	E14	26
Drăgăneşti-Vlaşca, Rom.	E12	26
Drăgăşani, Rom.	E11	26
Dragonera, Sa, i., Spain	E13	20
Dragons Mouths, strt.	s12	105f
Dragoon, Az., U.S.	K6	132
Draguignan, Fr.	F12	18
Drahičyn, Bela.	H8	10
Drake, N.D., U.S.	G13	124
Drakensberg, mts., Afr.	F9	70
Drake Passage, strt.	K8	82
Drakesboro, Ky., U.S.	G10	120
Drakes Branch, Va., U.S.	H7	114
Dráma, Grc.	B7	28
Drammen, Nor.	G3	8
Drang, stm., Asia	F8	48
Drangajökull, ice, Ice.	j28	8a
Dranov, Ostrovul, i., Rom.	E16	26
Drau (Dráva), stm., Eur.	D11	22
Dráva (Drau), stm., Eur.	D14	22
Dravograd, Slvn.	D12	22
Drawsko Pomorskie, Pol.	C11	16
Drayton, N.D., U.S.	C1	118
Drayton, S.C., U.S.	B4	116
Drayton Valley, Ab., Can.	C15	138
Dresden, On., Can.	F7	112
Dresden, Ger.	E9	16
Dresden, Oh., U.S.	D3	114
Drètun', Bela.	E12	10
Dreux, Fr.	F10	14
Drew, Ms., U.S.	D8	122
Drienov, Slov.	H17	16
Driftwood, B.C., Can.	D5	106
Driftwood, stm., In., U.S.	E12	120
Driggs, Id., U.S.	G15	136
Drin, stm., Alb.	C13	24
Drina, stm., Eur.	F16	22
Drinit, Gjiri i, b., Alb.	C13	24
Drinit të Zi (Crni Drim), stm., Eur.	C14	24
Driskill Mountain, hill, La., U.S.	E6	122
Drissa (Drysa), stm., Eur.	E11	10
Drniš, Cro.	G13	22
Drobeta-Turnu Severin, Rom.	E9	26
Drochia, Mol.	A14	26
Drogheda, Ire.	H6	12
Droichead Átha *see* Drogheda, Ire.	H6	12
Droichead Nua, Ire.	H6	12
Drôme, state, Fr.	E11	18
Dronero, Italy	F4	22
Dronne, stm., Fr.	D6	18
Dronning Louise Land, reg., Grnld.	B20	141
Druc', stm., Bela.	G12	10
Druif, Aruba	o19	104g
Druja, Bela.	E10	10
Drūkšiai, l., Eur.	E9	10
Drumheller, Ab., Can.	E18	138
Drummond, Mt., U.S.	D13	136
Drummond, Wi., U.S.	E7	118
Drummond Island, i., Mi., U.S.	C6	112
Drummondville, Qc., Can.	E4	110
Druskininkai, Lith.	F7	10
Družba *see* Dostyq, Kaz.	E14	32
Druzhba *see* Dostyq, Kaz.	E14	32
Družina, Russia	C18	34
Drvar, Bos.	E3	26
Dry Arm, b., Mt., U.S.	G7	124
Dry Bay, b., Ak., U.S.	E12	140
Dryberry Lake, l., On., Can.	B4	118
Dry Cimarron, stm., U.S.	B2	122
Dry Creek Mountain, mtn., Nv., U.S.	B9	134
Dryden, On., Can.	B6	118
Dry Devils, stm., Tx., U.S.	D7	130
Dry Prong, La., U.S.	F6	122
Dry Ridge, Ky., U.S.	F1	114
Drysdale, stm., Austl.	C5	74
Dry Tortugas, is., Fl., U.S.	G11	108
Dry Tortugas National Park, p.o.i., Fl., U.S.	L3	116
Drzewica, Pol.	E16	16
Dschang, Cam.	C1	66
Du, stm., China	E4	42
Du'an, China	I3	42
Duaringa, Austl.	D7	76
Duarte, Pico, mtn., Dom. Rep.	C12	102
Duartina, Braz.	L1	88
Ḍubā, Sau. Ar.	K6	58
Dubach, La., U.S.	E6	122
Dubai *see* Dubayy, U.A.E.	D8	56
Dubăsari, Mol.	B16	26
Dubăsari, Lacul, res., Mol.	B15	26
Dubawnt, stm., Can.	C10	106
Dubawnt Lake, l., Can.	C10	106
Dubayy (Dubai), U.A.E.	D8	56
Dubbo, Austl.	I7	76
Dubh Artach, r., Scot., U.K.	E6	12
Dublin (Baile Átha Cliath), Ire.	H6	12
Dublin, Ga., U.S.	D3	116
Dublin, Tx., U.S.	B9	130
Dublin, Va., U.S.	G5	114
Dublin, state, Ire.	H6	12
Dubna, Russia	D20	10
Dubna, Russia	F19	10
Dubna, stm., Russia	D21	10
Dubnica nad Váhom, Slov.	H14	16
Dubois, In., U.S.	F11	120
Du Bois, Ne., U.S.	D1	120
Du Bois, Pa., U.S.	C7	114
Dubois, Wy., U.S.	D3	126
Dubossary Reservoir see Dubăsari, Lacul, res., Mol.	B15	26
Dubovka, Russia	E6	32
Dubrājpur, India	G11	54
Dubréka, Gui.	H2	64
Dubrouna, Bela.	F13	10
Dubrovka, Russia	G16	10
Dubrovnik, Cro.	H15	22
Dubrovnoe, Russia	C11	32
Dubuque, Ia., U.S.	B7	120
Dubysa, stm., Lith.	E6	10
Duchang, China	G7	42
Duchesne, Ut., U.S.	C6	132
Duchesne, stm., Ut., U.S.	C7	132
Duchess, Austl.	C2	76
Duck, stm., Tn., U.S.	B11	122
Duck Creek, stm., Nv., U.S.	D2	132
Duck Hill, Ms., U.S.	D9	122
Duck Lake, Sk., Can.	B7	124
Ducktown, Tn., U.S.	B14	122
Duda, stm., Col.	F4	86
Dudačkino, Russia	A15	10
Duderstadt, Ger.	E6	16
Dudinka, Russia	C6	34
Dudley, Eng., U.K.	I10	12
Dudleyville, Az., U.S.	K6	132
Dudna, stm., India	B2	53
Dudorovskij, Russia	G18	10
Dudwa National Park, p.o.i., India	D8	54
Dueré, stm., Braz.	F1	88
Duero (Douro), stm., Eur.	C2	20
Due West, S.C., U.S.	B3	116
Dufourspitze, mtn., Eur.	D13	18
Dufur, Or., U.S.	E5	136
Duga-Zapadnaja, mys, c., Russia	E18	34
Dugdemona, stm., La., U.S.	F6	122
Dugi Otok, i., Cro.	F11	22
Dugna, Russia	F19	10
Du Gué, stm., Qc., Can.	D16	106
Duhovščina, Russia	E15	10
Duida, Cerro, mtn., Ven.	F9	86
Duisburg, Ger.	E2	16
Duitama, Col.	E5	86
Duiwelskloof, S. Afr.	C10	70
Dujuuma, Som.	D8	66
Duke, Ok., U.S.	G9	128
Duke of York Bay, b., Nu., Can.	B13	106
Duk Fadiat, Sudan	F6	62
Dukhān, Qatar	D7	56
Duki, Pak.	C2	54
Dukla Pass, p., Eur.	G17	16
Dukou, China	F5	36
Dūkštas, Lith.	E9	10
Dulan, China	D4	36
Dulce, N.M., U.S.	G9	132
Dulce, stm., Arg.	D6	92
Dulce, Golfo, b., C.R.	H6	102
Dul'durga, Russia	F11	34
Dulgalah, stm., Russia	C15	34
Dullstroom, S. Afr.	D10	70
Dulovka, Russia	C11	10
Dulq Maghār, Syria	B9	58
Duluth, Ga., U.S.	C14	122
Duluth, Mn., U.S.	E6	118
Dūmā, Syria	E7	58
Dumaguete, Phil.	F4	52
Dumai, Indon.	C2	50
Dumalag, Phil.	E4	52
Dumali Point, c., Phil.	D3	52
Dumaran Island, i., Phil.	E2	52
Dumaresq, stm., Austl.	G8	76
Dumaring, Indon.	C11	50
Dumas, Tx., U.S.	F7	128
Dumbarton, Scot., U.K.	F8	12
Dumbrăveni, Rom.	C11	26
Dume, Point, c., Ca., U.S.	J7	134
Dumfries, Scot., U.K.	F9	12
Dumka, India	F11	54
Dumlupınar, Tur.	E12	28
Dummar, Syria	E7	58
Dumoine, Lac, l., Qc., Can.	B12	112
Dumont, Ia., U.S.	B4	120
Dumont d'Urville, sci., Ant.	B18	81
Dumpu, Pap. N. Gui.	b4	79a
Dumraon, India	F10	54
Dumyâṭ, Masabb (Damietta Mouth), mth., Egypt	G3	58
Duna see Danube, stm., Eur.	F11	6
Dunaharaszti, Hung.	B6	26
Dunaj see Danube, stm., Eur.	F11	6
Dunajec, stm., Eur.	F16	16
Dunajská Streda, Slov.	H13	16
Dunakeszi, Hung.	B6	26
Dunărea Veche, Braţul, stm., Rom.	E15	26
Dunaújváros, Hung.	C5	26
Dunavăţu de Sus, Rom.	E16	26
Duna-völgyi-főcsatorna, can., Hung.	C6	26
Dunav-Tisa-Dunav, Kanal, can., Serb.	D6	26
Dunbar, Scot., U.K.	E10	12
Dunblane, Sk., Can.	C6	124
Duncan, B.C., Can.	H7	138
Duncan, Az., U.S.	K7	132
Duncan, Ok., U.S.	G11	128
Duncan, stm., B.C., Can.	F13	138
Duncan Lake, res., B.C., Can.	F14	138
Duncannon, Pa., U.S.	D8	114
Duncan Passage, strt., India	F7	46
Duncans, Jam.	i13	104d
Duncansby Head, c., Scot., U.K.	C9	12
Dundaga, Lat.	C5	10
Dundalk, On., Can.	D9	112
Dundalk (Dún Dealgan), Ire.	G6	12
Dundalk, Md., U.S.	E9	114
Dundalk Bay, b., Ire.	H6	12
Dundas, On., Can.	E9	112
Dundas, Lake, l., Austl.	F4	74
Dundas Peninsula, pen., Can.	B17	140
Dundas Strait, strt., Austl.	B6	74
Dún Dealgan *see* Dundalk, Ire.	G6	12
Dundee, S. Afr.	F10	70
Dundee, Scot., U.K.	E10	12
Dundee, Fl., U.S.	H4	116
Dundee, Mi., U.S.	C2	114
Dundurn, Sk., Can.	C7	124
Dund-Us, Mong.	B3	36
Dunedin, N.Z.	G4	80
Dunedin, Fl., U.S.	H3	116
Dunedoo, Austl.	I7	76
Dunfermline, Scot., U.K.	E9	12
Dungannon, N. Ire., U.K.	G6	12
Dūngarpur, India	G4	54
Dungarvan, Ire.	I5	12
Dungeness, c., Eng., U.K.	K13	12
Dungog, Austl.	I8	76
Dungu, D.R.C.	D5	66
Dungun, Malay.	J6	48
Dunhua, China	C8	38
Dunhuang, China	C3	36
Dunilovo, Russia	C21	10
Dunkerque (Dunkirk), Fr.	C11	14
Dunkirk *see* Dunkerque, Fr.	C11	14
Dunkirk, In., U.S.	H4	112
Dunkirk, N.Y., U.S.	B6	114
Dunkirk, Oh., U.S.	D2	114
Dunkwa, Ghana	H4	64
Dún Laoghaire, Ire.	H6	12
Dunlap, Tn., U.S.	B13	122
Dunmore, Pa., U.S.	C10	114
Dunmore Town, Bah.	K9	116
Dunn, N.C., U.S.	A7	116
Dunnellon, Fl., U.S.	G3	116
Dunnet Head, c., Scot., U.K.	C9	12
Dunning, Ne., U.S.	F12	126
Dunnville, On., Can.	F10	112
Dunoon, Scot., U.K.	F8	12
Dunqulah, Sudan	D5	62
Dunqunāb, Sudan	C7	62
Duns, Scot., U.K.	F10	12
Dunseith, N.D., U.S.	F13	124
Dunsmuir, Ca., U.S.	B3	134
Dunstable, Eng., U.K.	J12	12
Dunster, B.C., Can.	C11	138
Dunyāpur, Pak.	D3	54
Duolun, China	C2	38
Duolundabohuer, China	B14	54
Duomula, China	A9	54
Duozhu, China	J6	42
Dupang Ling, mts., China	I4	42
Dupnica, Blg.	G10	26
Dupnitsa *see* Dupnica, Blg.	G10	26
Dupuyer, Mt., U.S.	B14	136
Duque Bacelar, Braz.	C4	88
Duque de Caxias, Braz.	L4	88
Duque de York, Isla, i., Chile	J1	90
Duran, N.M., U.S.	G3	128
Durance, stm., Fr.	F11	18
Durand, Il., U.S.	B8	120
Durand, Wi., U.S.	G7	118
Durand, Récif, rf., N. Cal.	n17	79d
Durand Reef see Durand, Récif, rf., N. Cal.	n17	79d
Durango, Mex.	C6	100
Durango, Spain	A8	20
Durango, Co., U.S.	F9	132
Durango, state, Mex.	C6	100
Durant, Ia., U.S.	C6	120
Durant, Ms., U.S.	D9	122
Durant, Ok., U.S.	D2	122
Duras, Fr.	E6	18
Durazno, Ur.	F9	92
Durban, S. Afr.	F10	70
Đurđevac, Cro.	D14	22
Düren, Ger.	F2	16
Durg, India	H8	54
Durgāpur, India	G11	54
Durham, On., Can.	D9	112
Durham, Eng., U.K.	G11	12
Durham, Ca., U.S.	D4	134
Durham, N.C., U.S.	H6	114
Durham, N.H., U.S.	G5	110
Durham Downs, Austl.	F3	76
Durham Heights, mtn., N.T., Can.	A6	106
Durlas éile *see* Thurles, Ire.	I5	12
Durleşti, Mol.	B15	26
Durmitor, mtn., Serb.	F5	26
Durmitor Nacionalni Park, p.o.i., Serb.	F6	26
Dürnkrut, Aus.	B13	22
Durrës, Alb.	C13	24
Durrësi *see* Durrës, Alb.	C13	24
Durrie, Austl.	E3	76
Dursunbey, Tur.	D11	28
Duru Gölü, l., Tur.	B11	28
Durūz, Jabal ad-, mtn., Syria	F7	58
D'Urville, Tanjung, c., Indon.	F10	44
D'Urville Island, i., N.Z.	E5	80
Dušak, Turkmen.	B9	56
Dusa Marreb *see* Dhuusamarreeb, Som.	C9	66
Dušanbe, Taj.	B10	56
Dušekan, Russia	B19	32
Dusetos, Lith.	E8	10
Dushan, China	I2	42
Du Shan, mtn., China	A8	42
Dushanzi, China	C1	36
Duson, La., U.S.	G6	122
Düsseldorf, Ger.	E2	16
Dustin, Ok., U.S.	B2	122
Dutch John, Ut., U.S.	C7	132
Dutton, Mt., U.S.	C15	136
Dutton, stm., Austl.	C4	76
Duvno, Bos.	F4	26
Duxun, China	J7	42
Duyfken Point, c., Austl.	B8	74
Duyun, China	H2	42
Düzce, Tur.	C14	28
Dve Mogili, Blg.	F12	26
Dvine, ozero, l., Russia	D14	10
Dvinskaja guba, b., Russia	D17	8
Dvuh Cirkov, gora, mtn., Russia	C22	34
Dvůr Králové nad Labem, Czech Rep.	F11	16
Dwārka, India	G2	54
Dwight, Il., U.S.	C9	120
Dworshak Reservoir, res., Id., U.S.	D11	136
Dwyka, stm., S. Afr.	H5	70
Dyer, Tn., U.S.	H8	120
Dyer, Cape, c., Nu., Can.	D13	141
Dyer Bay, b., On., Can.	C8	112
Dyersburg, Tn., U.S.	H8	120
Dyje (Thaya), stm., Eur.	H12	16
Dyment, On., Can.	B6	118
Dynów, Pol.	G18	16
Dysart, Sk., Can.	D9	124
Dysart, Ia., U.S.	B5	120
Dysna (Dzisna), stm., Eur.	E9	10
Dytikí Elláda, state, Grc.	E4	28
Dytikí Makedonía, state, Grc.	C4	28
Džagdy, hrebet, mts., Russia	F15	34
Džalal-Abad, Kyrg.	F12	32
Džalinda, Russia	F13	34
Dzaoudzi, May.	C8	68
Džardžan, Russia	C13	34
Dzavhan, stm., Mong.	B3	36
Dzeržinsk, Russia	H20	8
Dzeržinskoe, Russia	C16	32
Džetygara *see* Zhetiqara, Kaz.	D10	32
Dzhankoi, Ukr.	E4	32
Dzhugdzhur Mountains see Džugdžur, hrebet, mts., Russia	E16	34
Dzhungarian Alatau Mountains, mts., Asia	E14	32
Działoszyce, Pol.	F16	16
Dzibilchaltún, sci., Mex.	B3	102
Dzierżoniów, Pol.	F12	16
Dzilam González, Mex.	B3	102
Dzisna, Bela.	E11	10
Dzisna (Dysna), stm., Eur.	E9	10
Dzitbalché, Mex.	B2	102
Dziwnów, Pol.	B10	16
Džizak, Uzb.	F11	32
Dzjarèčyn, Bela.	G7	10
Dzjaršynskaja, hara, hill, Bela.	G9	10
Dzjaržynsk, Bela.	G9	10
Dzjatlavičy, Bela.	H9	10
Dzöölön, Mong.	F8	34
Džugdžur, hrebet, mts., Russia	E16	34
Dzūkijos nacionalinis parkas, p.o.i., Lith.	F7	10
Dzungarian Basin see Junggar Pendi, bas., China	B2	36
Dzungarian Gate, p., Asia	E14	32
Dzüünharaa, Mong.	B6	36
Dzuunmod, Mong.	B6	36
Dzyhivka, Ukr.	A15	26

E

Name	Map Ref.	Page
Eads, Co., U.S.	C6	128
Eagle, Ak., U.S.	D11	140
Eagle, Co., U.S.	D10	132
Eagle, stm., Co., U.S.	B2	128
Eagle Bay, B.C., Can.	F11	138
Eagle Butte, S.D., U.S.	C11	126
Eagle Creek, stm., Sk., Can.	B6	124
Eagle Grove, Ia., U.S.	B4	120
Eaglehawk, Austl.	K4	76
Eagle Lake, Tx., U.S.	H2	122
Eagle Lake, l., On., Can.	B5	118
Eagle Lake, l., Ca., U.S.	C5	134
Eagle Lake, l., Me., U.S.	D7	110
Eagle Mountain, Ca., U.S.	J1	132
Eagle Mountain, mtn., Id., U.S.	D11	136
Eagle Mountain, mtn., Mn., U.S.	D8	118
Eagle Mountain Lake, res., Tx., U.S.	A10	130
Eagle Pass, Tx., U.S.	F7	130
Eagle Peak, mtn., Ca., U.S.	B5	134
Eagle River, Mi., U.S.	D10	118
Eagle River, Wi., U.S.	F9	118
Eagletown, Ok., U.S.	C4	122
Ear Falls, On., Can.	A5	118
Earle, Ar., U.S.	B8	122
Earl Grey, Sk., Can.	D9	124
Earlham, Ia., U.S.	C3	120
Earlimart, Ca., U.S.	H6	134
Earlville, Il., U.S.	C8	120
Early, Ia., U.S.	B2	120
Early, Tx., U.S.	C9	130
Eas, Vanuatu	k17	79d
Easley, S.C., U.S.	B3	116
East Alton, Il., U.S.	F7	120
East Angus, Qc., Can.	E5	110
East Antarctica, reg., Ant.	C8	81
East Aurora, N.Y., U.S.	B7	114
East Bay, b., Tx., U.S.	H4	122
East Bend, N.C., U.S.	H5	114
East Bernard, Tx., U.S.	H2	122
East Bernstadt, Ky., U.S.	G1	114
East Borneo see Kalimantan Timur, state, Indon.	C10	50
Eastbourne, Eng., U.K.	K13	12
East Brady, Pa., U.S.	D6	114
East Brewton, Al., U.S.	F11	122
East Cache Creek, stm., Ok., U.S.	G10	128
East Caicos, i., T./C. Is.	B12	102
East Cape, c., N.Z.	C8	80
East Cape, c., Fl., U.S.	K4	116
East Carbon, Ut., U.S.	D6	132
East Caroline Basin, unds.	I17	142
East Chicago, In., U.S.	G2	112
East China Sea, s., Asia	F9	36
East Cote Blanche Bay, b., La., U.S.	H7	122
East Coulee, Ab., Can.	E18	138
East Dereham, Eng., U.K.	I13	12
East Dismal Swamp, sw., N.C., U.S.	A9	116
East Dubuque, Il., U.S.	B7	120
East Ely, Nv., U.S.	D2	132
East End, V.I.U.S.	e8	104b
Easter Island see Pascua, Isla de, i., Chile	f30	78l
Eastern Cape, state, S. Afr.	G8	70
Eastern Channel see Tsushima-kaikyō, strt., Japan	F2	40
Eastern Creek, stm., Austl.	C3	76
Eastern Desert see Arabian Desert, des., Egypt	B6	62
Eastern Division, state, Fiji	q20	79e
Eastern Ghāts, mts., India	E4	53
Eastern Point, c., Guad.	A1	105a
Eastern Sayans see Vostočnyj Sajan, mts., Russia	D17	32
East Falkland, i., Falk. Is.	J5	90
East Fayetteville, N.C., U.S.	A7	116
East Frisian Islands see Ostfriesische Inseln, is., Ger.	C3	16
East Gaffney, S.C., U.S.	A4	116
East Germany see Germany, ctry., Eur.	E6	16
East Glacier Park, Mt., U.S.	B13	136
East Grand Forks, Mn., U.S.	D2	118
East Grand Rapids, Mi., U.S.	F4	112
East Grinstead, Eng., U.K.	J12	12
Easthampton, Ma., U.S.	B13	114
East Java see Jawa Timur, state, Indon.	G8	50
East Jordan, Mi., U.S.	C4	112
East Kelowna, B.C., Can.	G11	138
East Kilbride, Scot., U.K.	F8	12
Eastlake, Mi., U.S.	D3	112
Eastlake, Oh., U.S.	C4	114
Eastland, Tx., U.S.	B9	130
East Lansing, Mi., U.S.	B1	114
East Laurinburg, N.C., U.S.	B6	116
Eastleigh, Eng., U.K.	K11	12
East Liverpool, Oh., U.S.	D5	114
East London (Oos-Londen), S. Afr.	H9	70
Eastmain, Qc., Can.	E15	106
Eastmain, stm., Qc., Can.	E15	106
Eastmain-Opinaca, Réservoir, res., Qc., Can.	E15	106
Eastman, Ga., U.S.	D2	116
East Mariana Basin, unds.	H18	142
East Matagorda Bay, b., Tx., U.S.	F11	130
East Missoula, Mt., U.S.	D13	136
East Moline, Il., U.S.	C7	120
East Naples, Fl., U.S.	J4	116
East Nishnabotna, stm., Ia., U.S.	C2	120
East Nusa Tenggara see Nusa Tenggara Timur, state, Indon.	H12	50
East Olympia, Wa., U.S.	D3	136
Easton, Md., U.S.	F9	114
Easton, Pa., U.S.	D10	114
East Pacific Rise, unds.	N27	142
East Palatka, Fl., U.S.	G4	116
East Pecos, N.M., U.S.	F3	128
East Peoria, Il., U.S.	D8	120
Eastpoint, Fl., U.S.	H14	122
East Point, Ga., U.S.	D14	122
East Point, c., P.E., Can.	D15	110
East Point, c., V.I.U.S.	g11	104c
Eastport, Id., U.S.	B10	136
Eastport, Me., U.S.	F9	110
East Prairie, Mo., U.S.	H8	120
East Prairie, stm., Ab., Can.	A14	138
East Pryor Mountain, mtn., Mt., U.S.	B4	126
East Retford, Eng., U.K.	H12	12
East Saint Louis, Il., U.S.	F7	120
East Sea (Japan, Sea of), s., Asia	D11	38
East Shoal Lake, l., Mb., Can.	D16	124
East Siberian Sea see Vostočno-Sibirskoe more, s., Russia	B20	34
East Sister Island, i., Austl.	L6	76
East Slovakia see Východoslovenský Kraj, state, Slov.	H17	16
East Stroudsburg, Pa., U.S.	D11	114
East Timor, ctry., Asia	G8	44
East Troy, Wi., U.S.	B9	120
Eastville, Va., U.S.	G10	114
East Wenatchee, Wa., U.S.	C6	136
East Wilmington, N.C., U.S.	B8	116
Eaton, In., U.S.	H4	112
Eaton, Oh., U.S.	E1	114
Eaton Rapids, Mi., U.S.	B1	114
Eatonton, Ga., U.S.	C2	116
Eatonville, Wa., U.S.	D4	136
Eau Claire, Wi., U.S.	G7	118
Eau Claire, Lac à l', l., Qc., Can.	D16	106
Eauripik, at., Micron.	C5	72
Eauripik Rise, unds.	I17	142
Eauze, Fr.	F6	18
Ebano, Mex.	D9	100
Ebb and Flow Lake, l., Mb., Can.	D14	124
Ebbw Vale, Wales, U.K.	J9	12
Ebebiyín, Eq. Gui.	I7	64
Eben Junction, Mi., U.S.	B2	112
Ebensee, Aus.	C10	22
Eberbach, Ger.	G4	16
Eber Gölü, l., Tur.	E14	28
Ebern, Ger.	F6	16
Ebersbach, Ger.	E10	16
Eberswalde-Finow, Ger.	D9	16
Ebetsu, Japan	C14	38
Ebino, Japan	G3	40
Ebinur Hu, l., China	F14	32
Eboli, Italy	D9	24
Ebolowa, Cam.	D2	66
Ebon, at., Marsh. Is.	C7	72
Ebre see Ebro, stm., Spain	C11	20
Ebre, Delta de l', Spain	D11	20
Ebro (Ebre), stm., Spain	C11	20
Ebro, Delta del see Ebre, Delta de l', Spain	D11	20
Ebro, Embalse del, res., Spain	B7	20
Eceabat, Tur.	C9	28
Ech Cheliff, Alg.	B5	64
Echeng, China	E7	36
Echínos, Grc.	B7	28
Echt, Neth.	E1	16
Echuca, Austl.	K5	76
Écija, Spain	G5	20
Eckernförde, Ger.	B5	16
Eckerö, i., Fin.	F8	8
Eckville, Ab., Can.	D16	138
Eclectic, Al., U.S.	E12	122
Eclipse Sound, strt., Nu., Can.	A14	106
Ecoporanga, Braz.	J5	88
Écorce, Lac de l', res., Qc., Can.	B13	112
Écrins, Barre des, mtn., Fr.	E12	18
Écrins, Massif des, plat., Fr.	E12	18
Ecru, Ms., U.S.	C9	122
Ecuador, ctry., S.A.	D2	84
Ed, Swe.	G4	8
Edam, Sk., Can.	A5	124
Eddrachillis Bay, b., Scot., U.K.	C7	12
Eddystone Rocks, r., Eng., U.K.	K8	12
Eddyville, Ia., U.S.	C5	120
Eddyville, Ky., U.S.	G9	120
Ede, Neth.	B14	14
Ede, Nig.	H5	64
Edéa, Cam.	D2	66
Edehon Lake, l., Nu., Can.	C11	106
Edelény, Hung.	A7	26
Eden, Austl.	K7	76
Eden, Ms., U.S.	D8	122
Eden, N.C., U.S.	H6	114
Eden, Wy., U.S.	A7	132
Eden, stm., Eng., U.K.	G10	12
Edendale, S. Afr.	F10	70
Eden Valley, Mn., U.S.	F4	118
Edenville, S. Afr.	E8	70
Eder, stm., Ger.	E4	16
Édessa, Grc.	C4	28
Edfu, Egypt	C6	62
Edgar, Ne., U.S.	G14	126
Edgar, Wi., U.S.	G8	118
Edgard, La., U.S.	H8	122
Edgartown, Ma., U.S.	C15	114
Edgeley, N.D., U.S.	A14	126
Edgell Island, i., Grnld.	E13	141
Edgemont, S.D., U.S.	D9	126
Edgeøya, i., Nor.	B30	141
Edgeroi, Austl.	H7	76
Edgerton, Ab., Can.	B3	124
Edgerton, Mn., U.S.	H2	118
Edgerton, Oh., U.S.	C1	114
Edgerton, Wi., U.S.	B8	120
Edgewater, Fl., U.S.	H5	116
Edgewood, Ia., U.S.	B6	120
Edgewood, Il., U.S.	F9	120
Edgewood, Md., U.S.	E9	114
Edgewood, Tx., U.S.	E3	122
Edina, Mn., U.S.	G5	118
Edina, Mo., U.S.	D5	120
Edinburg, Il., U.S.	E8	120
Edinburg, In., U.S.	E11	120
Edinburg, Ms., U.S.	E9	122
Edinburg, Tx., U.S.	H9	130
Edinburg, Va., U.S.	F7	114
Edinburgh, Scot., U.K.	F9	12
Edincik, Tur.	C10	28
Edineţ, Mol.	A14	26
Edirne, Tur.	B9	28
Edirne, state, Tur.	B9	28
Edison, Ga., U.S.	F14	122
Edisto, stm., S.C., U.S.	D5	116
Edisto, North Fork, stm., S.C., U.S.	C4	116
Edisto Island, i., S.C., U.S.	D5	116
Edith, Mount, mtn., Mt., U.S.	D15	136
Edith Cavell, Mount, mtn., Ab., Can.	D12	138
Edjeleh, Alg.	D6	64
Edmond, Ok., U.S.	F11	128
Edmonds, Wa., U.S.	C4	136
Edmonton, Austl.	A5	76
Edmonton, Ab., Can.	C17	138
Edmonton, Ky., U.S.	G12	120
Edmore, N.D., U.S.	F15	124
Edmundston, N.B., Can.	C8	110
Edna, Ks., U.S.	G2	120
Edna, Tx., U.S.	E11	130
Edremit, Tur.	D10	28
Edremit Körfezi, b., Tur.	D9	28
Edrovo, Russia	C16	10
Edson, Ab., Can.	C14	138
Eduardo Castex, Arg.	G5	92
Eduni, Mount, mtn., N.T., Can.	C5	106
Edward, stm., Austl.	J5	76
Edward, Lake, l., Afr.	E5	66
Edward Island, i., On., Can.	C10	118
Edwards, Ms., U.S.	E8	122
Edwards Air Force Base, Ca., U.S.	I8	134
Edwards Plateau, plat., Tx., U.S.	D7	130
Edwardsville, Il., U.S.	F8	120
Edward VII Peninsula, pen., Ant.	C25	81
Eek, Ak., U.S.	D7	140
Eeklo, Bel.	C12	14
Eel, stm., Ca., U.S.	D2	134
Eel, stm., In., U.S.	E10	120
Eel, stm., In., U.S.	G4	112
Eems (Ems), stm., Eur.	A16	14
Éfaté, state, Vanuatu	k17	79d
Éfaté, i., Vanuatu	k17	79d
Eferding, Aus.	B10	22
Efes (Ephesus), sci., Tur.	F10	28
Effigy Mounds National Monument, p.o.i., Ia., U.S.	A6	120
Effingham, Il., U.S.	E9	120
Effingham, Ks., U.S.	E2	120
Eflâni, Tur.	B15	28
Eforie Nord, Rom.	E15	26
Eforie Sud, Rom.	F15	26
Efremov, Russia	G20	10
Eg, stm., Mong.	F9	34
Egadi, Isole, is., Italy	G5	24
Egaña, Arg.	H8	92
Egan Range, mts., Nv., U.S.	D2	132
Egedesminde (Aasiaat), Grnld.	D15	141
Egegik, Ak., U.S.	E8	140
Eger, Hung.	B7	26
Egersund, Nor.	G1	8
Eggenfelden, Ger.	H8	16
Egg Harbor City, N.J., U.S.	E11	114
Égletons, Fr.	D7	18
Egmont, Cape, c., N.Z.	D5	80
Egmont, Mount see Taranaki, Mount, vol., N.Z.	D6	80
Egmont Bay, b., P.E., Can.	D12	110
Egmont National Park, p.o.i., N.Z.	D5	80
Egorevsk, Russia	E22	10
Egremont, Ab., Can.	B17	138
Eğridir, Tur.	F13	28
Eğridir Gölü, l., Tur.	E13	28
Éguas, stm., Braz.	G3	88
Egvekinot, Russia	C25	34
Egypt, ctry., Afr.	B5	62
Eha-Amufu, Nig.	H6	64
Ehime, state, Japan	F5	40
Ehingen, Ger.	H5	16
Ehrhardt, S.C., U.S.	C4	116
Eibar, Spain	A8	20
Eibiswald, Aus.	D12	22
Eichstätt, Ger.	H7	16
Eidsvold, Austl.	E8	76
Eifel, mts., Ger.	F2	16
Eigg, i., Scot., U.K.	E6	12
Eight Degree Channel, strt., Asia	h12	46a
Eights Coast, cst., Ant.	C31	81
Eighty Mile Beach, cst., Austl.	C4	74
Eildon, Austl.	K5	76
Eildon, Lake, res., Austl.	K5	76
Eilenburg, Ger.	E8	16
Eiler Rasmussen, Kap, c., Grnld.	A21	141
Einasleigh, Austl.	B5	76
Einasleigh, stm., Austl.	A4	76
Einbeck, Ger.	E5	16
Eindhoven, Neth.	C14	14
Einme, Mya.	D2	48
Eirunepé, Braz.	E4	84
Eiseb, stm., Afr.	B4	70
Eisenach, Ger.	E6	16
Eisenberg, Ger.	F7	16
Eisenerz, Aus.	C11	22
Eisenhüttenstadt, Ger.	D10	16
Eisenstadt, Aus.	C13	22
Eisfeld, Ger.	F6	16
Eišiškės, Lith.	F7	10
Eislingen, Ger.	H5	16
Eitorf, Ger.	F3	16
Eivissa (Iviza), Spain	F12	20
Eivissa (Ibiza), i., Spain	F12	20
Ejea de los Caballeros, Spain	B9	20
Ejeda, Madag.	E7	68
Ejido Jaboncillos, Mex.	A7	100
Ejin Horo Qi, China	B3	42
Ejin Qi, China	C5	36
Ejsk, Russia	E5	32
Ejura, Ghana	H4	64
Ejutla de Crespo, Mex.	G10	100
Ekaterinburg, Russia	C10	32
Ekaterinino, Russia	E16	10
Ekateriny, proliv, strt., Russia	B17	38
Ekenäs *see* Tammisaari, Fin.	G10	8
Ekibastuz, Kaz.	D13	32
Ekimčan, Russia	F15	34
Ekonda, Russia	C10	34
Ekwan, stm., On., Can.	E14	106
Ela, Mya.	C3	48
El Aaiún (Laayoune), W. Sah.	D2	64
El 'Açâba, plat., Maur.	F2	64
El Affroun, Alg.	H13	20
El Agreb, Alg.	C6	64
El Ahijadero, Cerro, mtn., Mex.	E1	130
Elaine, Ar., U.S.	C8	122
El-'Aiyât, Egypt	I2	58
El-Alamein, Egypt	A5	62
El Álamo, Mex.	G7	130
El Álamo, Mex.	L9	134
El Álamo, Mex.	H8	130
El Alto, Arg.	D5	92
Elan', Russia	D6	32
Elancy, Russia	F10	34
El Ángel, Ec.	G2	86
El-Arish, Egypt	G4	58
Elat, Isr.	I5	58
Elat, Gulf of see Aqaba, Gulf of, b.	J5	58
El Ávila, Parque Nacional, p.o.i., Ven.	B8	86
Elazığ, Tur.	B4	56
Elba, Isola d', i., Italy	H7	22
El-Badâri, Egypt	K2	58
El-Bahnasa, Egypt	J1	58
El-Balyana, Egypt	B6	62
El'ban, Russia	F16	34
El Banco, Col.	C4	86
El Barco de Ávila, Spain	D5	20
Elbasan, Alb.	C13	24
Elbasani *see* Elbasan, Alb.	C13	24
El Baúl, Ven.	C7	86
El Baúl, Cerro, mtn., Mex.	G11	100
Elbe (Labe), stm., Eur.	C5	16
Elbe-Havel-Kanal, can., Ger.	D8	16
Elbert, Co., U.S.	B4	128
Elbert, Mount, mtn., Co., U.S.	D10	132
Elberta, Mi., U.S.	D3	112
Elberton, Ga., U.S.	B3	116
Elbeuf, Fr.	E10	14
Elbeyli, Tur.	B8	58
El Beyyadh, Alg.	C5	64
Elbląg, Pol.	B15	16
Elbląg, state, Pol.	B15	16
El Bluff, Nic.	G6	102
El Bonillo, Spain	F8	20
El Boulaïda, Alg.	B5	64
Elbow, stm., Ab., Can.	E16	138
Elbow Lake, Mn., U.S.	E3	118
El'brus, gora, mtn., Russia	F6	32
Elbrus, Mount see El'brus, gora, mtn., Russia	F6	32
El-Burg, Egypt	G1	58
El-Burgâya, Egypt	J1	58
Elburs see Alborz, Reshteh-ye Kūhhā-ye, mts., Iran	B7	56
Elburz Mountains see Alborz, Reshteh-ye Kūhhā-ye, mts., Iran	B7	56
El Cadilla, Embalse, res., Arg.	C5	92
El Cajon, Ca., U.S.	K9	134
El Calafate, Arg.	J2	90
El Callao, Ven.	D11	86
El Calvario, Ven.	C8	86
El Campamento, P.R.	B3	104a
El Campo, Tx., U.S.	H2	122
El Capitan, mtn., Mt., U.S.	D12	136
El Carmen, Arg.	B5	92
El Carmen, Col.	C5	86
El Carmen, stm., Mex.	F9	98
El Carmen de Bolívar, Col.	C4	86
El Carricito, Mex.	A7	100
El Carril, Arg.	B5	92
El Centinela, Mex.	K10	134
El Centro, Ca., U.S.	K10	134
El Cerrito, Col.	F3	86
El Cerro Del Aripo, mtn., Trin.	s12	105f
Elche *see* Elx, Spain	F10	20
El Chile, Montaña, mtn., Nic.	E4	102
Elcho, Wi., U.S.	F9	118
Elcho Island, i., Austl.	B7	74
El Cocuy, Col.	D5	86
El Colorado, Arg.	C8	92
El Cóndor, Cerro, vol., Arg.	C3	92
El Corazón, Ec.	H2	86
El Corpus, Hond.	F4	102
El Coto, P.R.	B2	104a
El'cy, Russia	D16	10
Elda, Spain	F10	20
El Desemboque, Mex.	G6	98
El Desemboque, Mex.	F6	98
El'dikan, Russia	D16	34
El-Dilingât, Egypt	H1	58
El Diviso, Col.	G2	86
El Djazaïr (Algiers), Alg.	B5	64
El Djelfa, Alg.	C5	64
Eldon, Ia., U.S.	D5	120
Eldora, Ia., U.S.	B4	120
Eldorado, Arg.	C10	92
Eldorado, Braz.	B13	92
El Dorado, Ar., U.S.	D6	122
Eldorado, Il., U.S.	G9	120
El Dorado, Ks., U.S.	D12	128
Eldorado, Ok., U.S.	G9	128
El Dorado, Ven.	D11	86
El Dorado Springs, Mo., U.S.	G3	120
Eldoret, Kenya	D7	66
Eldred, Pa., U.S.	C7	114
Eldridge, Ia., U.S.	C7	120
Eleanor, W.V., U.S.	F3	114
Elec, Russia	H21	10
Electric City, Wa., U.S.	C7	136
Elefantes (Olifants), stm., Afr.	D10	70
Elefsína, Grc.	E6	28
Eleftheroúpoli, Grc.	C7	28
Elektrostal', Russia	E21	10

Name	Map Ref.	Page
Elena, Blg.	G12	26
El Encanto, Col.	H5	86
Elephant Butte Reservoir, res., N.M., U.S.	J9	132
Elephant Mountain, mtn., Me., U.S.	F6	110
Elesbão Veloso, Braz.	D4	88
El Estor, Guat.	I3	102
Eleuthera, i., Bah.	B9	96
Elewa, Wi., U.S.	G7	118
Eleven Point, stm., U.S.	H6	120
El Fahs, Tun.	H3	24
El Faro, P.R.	C2	104a
El-Fiqriya, Egypt	K1	58
Elfrida, Az., U.S.	L7	132
El Fuerte, Mex.	B4	100
El Galpón, Arg.	B5	92
Elgin, Scot., U.K.	D9	12
Elgin, Ia., U.S.	B6	120
Elgin, Il., U.S.	B9	120
Elgin, Mn., U.S.	G6	118
Elgin, N.D., U.S.	A11	126
Elgin, Ne., U.S.	F14	126
Elgin, Ok., U.S.	G10	128
Elgin, Or., U.S.	E8	136
El-Gindiya, Egypt	J1	58
El-Gîza (Giza), Egypt	H1	58
Elgon, Mount, mtn., Afr.	D6	66
El Grara, Alg.	C5	64
El Grove see El Grove, Spain	B2	20
El Guaje, Mex.	A7	100
El Guamo, Col.	B4	86
El Guapo, Ven.	B9	86
El Hachero, Cerro, mtn., Mex.	H2	130
El Hammâmi, reg., Maur.	E2	64
El-Hamûl, Egypt	G2	58
El Hank, clf., Afr.	E3	64
El-Hawâmdîya, Egypt	I2	58
Elhovo, Blg.	G13	26
El Huisache, Mex.	D8	100
Eliase, Indon.	G9	44
Elida, N.M., U.S.	H5	128
Elila, stm., D.R.C.	E5	66
Elim, Ak., U.S.	D7	140
Elisenvaara, Russia	F13	8
Eliseu Martins, Braz.	E4	88
El-Iskandarîya (Alexandria), Egypt	A6	62
Elista, Russia	E6	32
Elizabeth, Austl.	J2	76
Elizabeth, Co., U.S.	B4	128
Elizabeth, Il., U.S.	B7	120
Elizabeth, N.J., U.S.	D11	114
Elizabeth, W.V., U.S.	E4	114
Elizabeth City, N.C., U.S.	H9	114
Elizabethton, Tn., U.S.	H3	114
Elizabethtown, Il., U.S.	G9	120
Elizabethtown, Ky., U.S.	G11	120
Elizabethtown, N.Y., U.S.	F3	110
Elizabethtown, Pa., U.S.	D9	114
Elizavety, mys, c., Russia	F17	34
Elizovo, Russia	F20	34
El-Jadida, Mor.	C3	64
El Jaralito, Mex.	B6	100
El Jebel, Co., U.S.	D9	132
Elk, Pol.	C18	16
Elk, stm., B.C., Can.	F16	138
Elk, stm., Ks., U.S.	D12	128
Elk, stm., W.V., U.S.	F4	114
Elk, stm., U.S.	C12	122
Elkader, Ia., U.S.	B6	120
Elk City, Ok., U.S.	F9	128
Elk Creek, Ca., U.S.	D3	134
Elk Creek, stm., S.D., U.S.	C10	126
El Kef, Tun.	H2	24
El-Kelaa-Srarhna, Mor.	C3	64
El Kerè, Eth.	F8	62
Elk Grove, Ca., U.S.	E4	134
El-Khânka, Egypt	H2	58
El-Khârga, Egypt	B6	62
Elkhart, In., U.S.	G4	112
Elkhart, Ks., U.S.	D7	128
Elkhart, Tx., U.S.	F3	122
El Khnâchîch, clf., Mali	E4	64
Elk Horn, Ia., U.S.	C2	120
Elk Horn, Wi., U.S.	B9	120
Elkhorn, stm., Ne., U.S.	F16	126
Elkhorn City, Ky., U.S.	G3	114
Elkhorn Mountains, B.C., Can.	G4	138
Elkhovo see Elhovo, Blg.	G13	26
Elkins, W.V., U.S.	F6	114
Elk Island, i., Mb., Can.	D17	124
Elk Island National Park, p.o.i., Ab., Can.	C18	138
Elkland, Pa., U.S.	C8	114
Elk Mountain, mtn., Wy., U.S.	B10	132
Elko, B.C., Can.	G15	138
Elko, Nv., U.S.	C1	132
Elk Point, Ab., Can.	C19	138
Elk Point, S.D., U.S.	B1	120
Elk Rapids, Mi., U.S.	D4	112
Elk River, Mn., U.S.	F5	118
Elkton, Md., U.S.	E10	114
Elkton, Mi., U.S.	E6	112
Elkton, S.D., U.S.	G2	118
Elkton, Va., U.S.	F7	114
Ellaville, Ga., U.S.	D1	116
Ellef Ringnes Island, i., Nu., Can.	B5	141
Ellen, Mount, mtn., Ut., U.S.	E6	132
Ellendale, Mn., U.S.	H5	118
Ellendale, N.D., U.S.	A14	126
Ellensburg, Wa., U.S.	C6	136
Ellenton, Ga., U.S.	E2	116
Ellesmere, Lake, l., N.Z.	F5	80
Ellesmere Island, i., Nu., Can.	B9	141
Ellettsville, In., U.S.	E11	120
Ellice, stm., Nu., Can.	B10	106
Ellice Islands see Tuvalu, ctry., Oc.	D8	72
Ellicottville, N.Y., U.S.	B7	114
Ellijay, Ga., U.S.	B1	116
Ellinwood, Ks., U.S.	C10	128
Elliot, S. Afr.	G8	70
Elliot, Mount, mtn., Austl.	B6	76
Elliot Lake, On., Can.	B7	112
Elliot Lake, l., Mb., Can.	B18	124
Elliott, Ia., U.S.	C2	120
Elliott, Ms., U.S.	D9	122
Ellisras, S. Afr.	C8	70
Elliston, Austl.	F6	74
Ellisville, Ms., U.S.	F9	122
Ellon, Scot., U.K.	D10	12
Ellora Caves, hist., India	A2	53
Elloree, S.C., U.S.	C5	116
Ellsworth, Ks., U.S.	C10	128
Ellsworth, Me., U.S.	F8	110
Ellsworth, Mi., U.S.	C4	112
Ellsworth, Mi., U.S.	H3	118
Ellsworth, Wi., U.S.	G8	118
Ellsworth Land, reg., Ant.	C32	81
Ellsworth Mountains, mts., Ant.	C32	81
El Lucero, Mex.	I4	130
Ellwangen, Ger.	H5	16
Elwood City, Pa., U.S.	D5	114
Elm, stm., U.S.	B14	126
Elma, Wa., U.S.	D3	136
El-Mahalla el-Kubra, Egypt	H2	58
El-Maimûn, Egypt	I2	58
Elmali, Tur.	G12	28
El Maneadero, Mex.	L9	134
El-Mansûra, Egypt	G2	58
El Manteco, Ven.	D10	86
El-Manzala, Egypt	G2	58
El-Matarîya, Egypt	G3	58
Elm Creek, Ne., U.S.	G13	126
El Médano, Mex.	C3	100
El Menia, Alg.	C5	64
Elmer, N.J., U.S.	E10	114
Elmhurst, Il., U.S.	G2	112
El-Minya (Minya), Egypt	J1	58
Elmira, On., Can.	E9	112
Elmira, P.E., Can.	D14	110
Elmira, N.Y., U.S.	B9	114
El Moral, Mex.	F7	130
Elmore, Austl.	K5	76
Elmore, Mn., U.S.	H4	118
Elmore, Oh., U.S.	C2	114
Elmore City, Ok., U.S.	G11	128
El Morro, hist., P.R.	B3	104a
El Morro National Monument, p.o.i., N.M., U.S.	H8	132
El Mreyyé, reg., Maur.	F3	64
Elmshorn, Ger.	C5	16
Elm Springs, Ar., U.S.	H3	120
El Mulato, Mex.	E3	130
El-Mutî'a, Egypt	K2	58
Elmvale, On., Can.	D10	112
Elmwood, Il., U.S.	K8	118
Elmwood, Ne., U.S.	K2	118
Elmwood, On., Can.	E4	102
Elnora, Ab., Can.	D17	138
Elnora, In., U.S.	F10	120
Eloguj, stm., Russia	B15	32
Eloise, Fl., U.S.	H4	116
Elora, On., Can.	E9	112
Elorza, Ven.	D7	86
Éloten, Turkmen.	B9	56
Eloy, Az., U.S.	K5	132
Eloy Alfaro, Ec.	I2	86
El Palmar, Ven.	D10	86
El Palmar de los Sepúlveda, Mex.	C5	100
El Palmito, Mex.	C6	100
El Palqui, Chile	E2	92
El Paso, Il., U.S.	C7	86
El Paso, Tx., U.S.	D8	120
El Paso, Tx., U.S.	L10	132
El Paso de Robles see Paso Robles, Ca., U.S.	H5	134
El Paso Peaks, mtn., Ca., U.S.	H8	134
El Perú, Arg.	D11	86
El Piñón, Col.	B4	86
El Pintado, Arg.	B7	92
El Pital, Cerro, mtn., N.A.	E3	102
El Planchón, Volcán (Planchón, Cerro del), vol., S.A.	G2	92
El Polvorín, P.R.	B3	104a
El Portal, Ca., U.S.	F6	134
El Porvenir, Mex.	F6	130
El Porvenir, Mex.	K9	134
El Porvenir, Pan.	H8	102
El Potrero, Mex.	H7	130
El Potro, Cerro (Potro, Cerro del), mtn., S.A.	D3	92
El Prat de Llobregat, Spain	C12	20
El Progreso, Hond.	E4	102
El Puerto de Santa María, Spain	H4	20
El Puesto, Arg.	C4	92
El-Qâhira (Cairo), Egypt	H2	58
El-Qantara el-Sharqîya, Egypt	H3	58
El-Qasr, Egypt	B5	62
El Quebrachal, Arg.	B5	92
El Quelite, Mex.	D5	100
Elqui, stm., Chile	D2	92
El-Qûsîya, Egypt	K1	58
El Real de Santa María, Pan.	H9	102
El Remolino, Mex.	F6	130
El Reno, Ok., U.S.	F10	128
El Rio, Ca., U.S.	I6	134
El Roble, Mesa, mtn., Mex.	H8	118
Elroy, Wi., U.S.	H8	118
Elsa, Yk., Can.	C3	106
Elsa, Tx., U.S.	H9	130
El-Saff, Egypt	I2	58
El-Sa'îd (Upper Egypt), hist. reg., Egypt	J2	58
El Salado, Chile	C2	92
El Salado, Parque Nacional, p.o.i., Ec.	I1	86
El Salto, Mex.	D6	100
El Salvador, Chile	C3	92
El Salvador, ctry., N.A.	F3	102
El Samán de Apure, Ven.	D7	86
El Sauz, Mex.	A5	100
El Sauzal, Mex.	L9	134
El Seíbo, Dom. Rep.	C13	102
Elsen Nur, l., China	D3	36
El-Simbillawein, Egypt	H2	58
Elsinore see Helsingør, Den.	H5	8
Elsinore, Ut., U.S.	E4	132
El Sombrero, Ven.	C8	86
Elsterwerda, Ger.	E9	16
El Sueco, Mex.	E1	130
El-Suweis (Suez), Egypt	I3	58
El Tajín, sci., Mex.	E10	100
El Tala, Arg.	C5	92
El Tanque, Mex.	H8	130
El Tecuán, Mex.	F5	100
El-Thamad, Egypt	I3	58
El Tigre, Ven.	C9	86
Eltmann, Ger.	G6	16
El Toco, Chile	D3	90
El Tocuyo, Ven.	C7	86
Elton, La., U.S.	G6	122
El Tránsito, Chile	D2	92
El Trébol, Arg.	F7	92
El Tule, Mex.	G1	130
El Tuparro, Parque Nacional, p.o.i., Col.	E7	86
El-Tûr, Egypt	J4	58
El Turbio, Arg.	J2	90
El-Uqsor (Luxor), Egypt	B6	62
Elúru, India	C5	53
El Valle, Pan.	H7	102
El Vendrell, Spain	C12	20
Elverum, Nor.	F4	8
El Viejo, Nic.	F4	102
El Vigía, Ven.	C6	86
El Volcán, Chile	p20	104g
Elvira, Arg.	G8	92
El Volcán, Chile	F2	92
El Wad, Alg.	C6	64
El-Wâsta, Egypt	I1	58
Elwell, Lake, res., Mt., U.S.	B15	136
Elwood, In., U.S.	H4	112
Elwood, Ne., U.S.	G13	126
Elx, Spain	F10	20
Ely, Eng., U.K.	I13	12
Ely, Mn., U.S.	D7	118
Ely, Nv., U.S.	D2	132
El Yagual, Ven.	D7	86
Elyria, Oh., U.S.	C3	114
El Yunque, mtn., P.R.	B4	104a
El-Zarqa, Egypt	G2	58
Émaé, i., Vanuatu	k17	79d
Emajõgi, stm., Est.	B9	10
Emâmshahr, Iran	B8	56
Emba see Embi, stm., Kaz.	E9	32
Embarras, stm., Il., U.S.	G10	118
Embarcación, Arg.	B5	92
Embi, Kaz.	E9	32
Embi, stm., Kaz.	E9	32
Emborcação, Represa da, res., Braz.	J2	88
Embreeville, Tn., U.S.	H3	114
Embrun, Fr.	E12	18
Embu, Kenya	E7	66
Emca, stm., Russia	E19	8
Emden, Ger.	C3	16
Emden, Il., U.S.	K9	118
Emelle, Al., U.S.	E10	122
Emerado, N.D., U.S.	G16	124
Emerald, Austl.	D6	76
Emerson, Mb., Can.	E16	124
Emerson, Ar., U.S.	D5	122
Emerson, Ia., U.S.	C2	120
Emery, Ut., U.S.	D15	126
Emery, Ut., U.S.	E5	132
Emet, Tur.	D12	28
Emiliano Zapata, Mex.	G13	100
Emilia-Romagna, state, Italy	F8	22
Emin, China	B1	36
Emine, nos, c., Blg.	G14	26
Eminence, Mo., U.S.	G6	120
Emirdağ, Tur.	D14	28
Emir Dağları, mts., Tur.	m13	73a
Emita, Austl.	n13	77a
Emlembe, mtn., Afr.	D10	70
Emlenton, Pa., U.S.	G10	112
Emmaste, Est.	B5	10
Emmaus, Pa., U.S.	D10	114
Emmaville, Austl.	G8	76
Emmen, Neth.	B15	14
Emmendingen, Ger.	H3	16
Emmerich, Ger.	E2	16
Emmet, Ar., U.S.	D5	122
Emmetsburg, Ia., U.S.	A3	120
Emmiganüru, India	D3	53
Emmitsburg, Md., U.S.	E8	114
Emmonak, Ak., U.S.	D7	140
Emo, On., Can.	C5	118
Emory Peak, mtn., Tx., U.S.	A3	100
Empalme, S. Afr.	F10	70
Empangeni, S. Afr.	F10	70
Empedrado, Arg.	C8	92
Emperor Seamounts, unds.	E19	142
Empire, La., U.S.	H9	122
Empire, Nv., U.S.	C6	134
Empoli, Italy	G7	22
Emporia, Ks., U.S.	F1	120
Emporia, Va., U.S.	H8	114
Emporium, Pa., U.S.	C7	114
Empty Quarter see Ar-Rub' al-Khâlî, des., Asia	E6	56
Ems, stm., Eur.	C3	16
Emsdetten, Ger.	D3	16
Emu, China	C8	38
Emu Park, Austl.	D8	76
Enarotali, Indon.	F10	44
Enašimskij Polkan, gora, mtn., Russia	C16	32
Encampment, Wy., U.S.	B10	132
Encantado, Braz.	D11	92
Encarnación, Para.	C9	92
Enchi, Ghana	H4	64
Enchilayas, Mex.	C9	100
Encinal, Tx., U.S.	F8	130
Encinitas, Ca., U.S.	J8	134
Encino, N.M., U.S.	G3	128
Encontrados, Ven.	C5	86
Encounter Bay, b., Austl.	J2	76
Encruzilhada, Braz.	H5	88
Encruzilhada do Sul, Braz.	E12	92
Encs, Hung.	A8	26
Endako, B.C., Can.	B5	138
Ende, Indon.	G7	44
Endeavor, Wi., U.S.	H9	118
Endeavour Strait, strt., Austl.	B8	74
Enderby, B.C., Can.	F11	138
Enderby Land, reg., Ant.	B10	81
Enderlin, N.D., U.S.	A15	126
Endicott, N.Y., U.S.	B9	114
Endicott, Wa., U.S.	C9	136
Endicott Mountains, mts., Ak., U.S.	C9	140
Ene, stm., Peru	F3	84
Enewetak, at., Marsh. Is.	B7	72
Enez, Tur.	C9	28
Enfield, N.C., U.S.	H8	114
Engaño, Cabo, c., Dom. Rep.	C13	102
Engcobo, S. Afr.	G9	70
Engelhard, N.C., U.S.	A10	116
Engel's, Russia	D7	32
Engen, B.C., Can.	B6	138
Engenheiro Navarro, Braz.	I3	88
Enggano, Pulau, i., Indon.	F2	50
England, state, U.K.	I12	12
Englefield, Cape, c., Nu., Can.	B13	106
Englehart, On., Can.	F15	106
Englewood, B.C., Can.	F4	138
Englewood, Co., U.S.	B4	128
Englewood, Fl., U.S.	J3	116
Englewood, Ks., U.S.	D8	128
Englewood, Tn., U.S.	A1	116
English, In., U.S.	F11	120
English, stm., On., Can.	A4	118
English Channel, strt., Eur.	D7	14
English Coast, cst., Ant.	C33	81
Engure, Lat.	C6	10
Engure ezers, l., Lat.	C6	10
Enid, Ok., U.S.	E11	128
Enid Lake, res., Ms., U.S.	C9	122
Enisej, stm., Russia	C6	34
Enisejsk, Russia	C16	32
Enisejskij krjaž, mts., Russia	C16	32
Enisejskij zaliv, b., Russia	B5	34
Eniwetok see Enewetak, at., Marsh. Is.	B7	72
eNjesuthi, mtn., Afr.	F9	70
Enkhuizen, Neth.	B14	14
Enköping, Swe.	G7	8
Enmedio, Mex.	E4	130
Enmedio, Cerro de, mtn., Mex.	F8	100
Enna, Italy	G8	24
Ennadai, Lake, l., Nu., Can.	C10	106
Ennedi, plat., Chad	D4	62
Ennis, Ire.	I3	12
Ennis, Mt., U.S.	E15	136
Ennis, Tx., U.S.	E2	122
Enniscorthy, Ire.	I6	12
Enniskillen, N. Ire., U.K.	G5	12
Enns, Aus.	B11	22
Enns, stm., Aus.	B11	22
Enontekiö, Fin.	B10	8
Enoree, stm., S.C., U.S.	B3	116
Enoree, S.C., U.S.	B3	116
Enosburg Falls, Vt., U.S.	F4	110
Enping, China	J5	42
Enrekang, Indon.	E11	50
Enrique Urién, Arg.	C7	92
Enriquillo, Dom. Rep.	D12	102
Enriquillo, Lago, l.,	C12	102
Enschede, Neth.	B15	14
Ensenada, Arg.	G9	92
Ensenada, Mex.	L9	134
Enshi, China	F3	42
Enshū-nada, b., Japan	E10	40
Entebbe, Ug.	D6	66
Enterprise, N.T., Can.	C7	106
Enterprise, Al., U.S.	F13	122
Enterprise, Or., U.S.	E9	136
Enterprise, Ut., U.S.	F3	132
Entre-Ríos, Bol.	D4	90
Entre Ríos, state, Arg.	E8	92
Entrevaux, Fr.	F12	18
Entroncamento, Port.	E2	20
Entwistle, Ab., Can.	C16	138
Enugu, Nig.	H6	64
Enurmino, Russia	C26	34
Envalira, Port d', p., And.	B12	20
Envigado, Col.	D4	86
Envira, stm., Braz.	E3	84
Enyamba, D.R.C.	E5	66
Enying, Hung.	C5	26
Eólia, Mo., U.S.	E6	120
Eólie, Ísole (Lipari, Ísole), is., Italy	F8	24
Epanomi, Grc.	C5	28
Epecuén, Lago, l., Arg.	H6	92
Epernay, Fr.	E12	14
Epes, Al., U.S.	E10	122
Ephesus see Efes, sci., Tur.	F10	28
Ephraim, Ut., U.S.	D5	132
Ephrata, Pa., U.S.	D9	114
Ephrata, Wa., U.S.	C7	136
Épi, i., Vanuatu	k17	79d
Épi, state, Vanuatu	k17	79d
Épidavros, sci., Grc.	F6	28
Épila, Spain	C9	20
Épinal, Fr.	F15	14
Epírus, hist. reg., Grc.	D3	28
Epsom, Eng., U.K.	J12	12
Epukiro, Nmb.	B4	70
Epukiro, stm., Nmb.	B4	70
Eqlid, Iran	C7	56
Equatorial Guinea, ctry., Afr.	I6	64
Erap, Pap. N. Gui.	b4	79a
Erath, La., U.S.	H6	122
Erave, Pap. N. Gui.	b3	79a
Erawan National Park, p.o.i., Thai.	E4	48
Erbach, Ger.	G5	16
Erbogačon, Russia	B19	32
Ercevo, Russia	F18	8
Ercolano, Italy	D8	24
Érd, Hung.	B5	26
Erdao, stm., China	C8	38
Erdaohezi, China	B8	38
Erdek, Tur.	C10	28
Erdemli, Tur.	B5	58
Erding, Ger.	H7	16
Erebato, stm., Ven.	E9	86
Erebus, Mount, mtn., Ant.	C21	81
Erechim, Braz.	C11	92
Ereğli, Tur.	A4	58
Ereğli, Tur.	B14	28
Erenhot, China	C7	36
Erepecuru, Lago do, l., Braz.	D6	84
Ereymentaü, Kaz.	D12	32
Erfoud, Mor.	C4	64
Erft, stm., Ger.	E2	16
Erfurt, Ger.	F7	16
Ergene, stm., Tur.	B10	28
Ergeni, hills, Russia	E6	32
Ergli, Lat.	D8	10
Ergun Youqi, China	F13	34
Ergun Zuoqi, China	F13	34
Er Hai, l., China	F5	36
Erice, Italy	F6	24
Ericeira, Port.	F1	20
Erichsen Lake, l., Nu., Can.	A14	106
Erick, Ok., U.S.	F9	128
Erickson, Mb., Can.	D14	124
Ericson, Ne., U.S.	F14	126
Erie, Co., U.S.	A3	128
Erie, Il., U.S.	C8	120
Erie, Pa., U.S.	B5	114
Erie, Lake, l., N.A.	B4	114
Erie Canal see New York State Barge Canal, can., N.Y., U.S.	E12	112
Eriksdale, Mb., Can.	D15	124
Erimo-misaki, c., Japan	D15	38
Erin, On., Can.	E9	112
Erin, Tn., U.S.	H10	120
Eriskay, i., Scot., U.K.	D5	12
Eritrea, ctry., Afr.	D7	62
Erivan see Yerevan, Arm.	A5	56
Erkelenz, Ger.	E2	16
Erkner, Ger.	D9	16
Erlangen, Ger.	G7	16
Erlenbach, S. Afr.	E10	70
Ermenek, Tur.	B3	58
Ermenek, stm., Tur.	B3	58
Ermica, Russia	C25	8
Ermolaevo, Russia	D9	32
Ermolino, Russia	E19	10
Ermoúpoli, Grc.	F7	28
Erne, Lower Lough, l., U.K.	G4	12
Erne, Upper Lough, l., Eur.	G5	12
Ernée, Fr.	F8	14
Erode, India	F3	53
Erofej Pavlovič, Russia	F13	34
Eromanga, Austl.	F4	76
Erongo, state, Nmb.	C2	70
Erongo, stm., Nmb.	C2	70
Eropol, Russia	C22	34
Erota, Erit.	D7	62
Er-Rachidia, Mor.	C4	64
Errego, Moz.	D6	68
Errigal Mountain, mtn., Ire.	F4	12
Errinundra National Park, p.o.i., Austl.	K7	76
Erris Head, c., Ire.	G2	12
Errol Heights, Or., U.S.	E4	136
Erromango, i., Vanuatu	l17	79d
Erši, Russia	F17	10
Erstein, Fr.	F16	14
Ertai, China	C4	36
Ertis, Kaz.	D12	32
Ertis see Irtysh, stm., Asia	D13	32
Ertis see Irtysh, stm., Asia	E15	32
Ertoma, Russia	E22	8
Erval, Braz.	F11	92
Erval-le-Châtel, Fr.	F12	14
Erwin, N.C., U.S.	A7	116
Erwin, Tn., U.S.	H3	114
Erymanthos, mtn., Grc.	F4	28
Eryuan, China	A5	48
Erzhan, China	B8	38
Erzin, Russia	D17	32
Erzincan, Tur.	B4	56
Erzurum, Tur.	B5	56
Esa'ala, Pap. N. Gui.	b5	79a
Esashi, Japan	D13	38
Esashi, Japan	D14	38
Esbjerg, Den.	I3	8
Esbo see Espoo, Fin.	F11	8
Escada, Braz.	E8	88
Escalante, Ut., U.S.	F5	132
Escalante, stm., Ut., U.S.	F5	132
Escalón, Mex.	B6	100
Escanaba, Mi., U.S.	C2	112
Escanaba, stm., Mi., U.S.	B2	112
Escandón, prto., Spain	D9	20
Escárcega, Mex.	C2	102
Escatawpa, stm., U.S.	G10	122
Esch-sur-Alzette, Lux.	E14	14
Escobedo, Mex.	G6	130
Escocesa, Bahía, b., Dom. Rep.	C13	102
Escondido, Ca., U.S.	J8	134
Escondido, stm., Nic.	F6	102
Escuinapa de Hidalgo, Mex.	D5	100
Escuintla, Guat.	E2	102
Escuintla, Mex.	H12	100
Eséka, Cam.	D2	66
Ese-Haja, Russia	C16	34
Eséka, Cam.	D2	66
Esenguly, Turkmen.	B7	56
Eşfahân, Iran	C7	56
Esguevas, stm., Spain	C6	20
Eshkâshem, Afg.	B11	56
Eshowe, S. Afr.	F10	70
Esil see Ishim, stm., Asia	D11	32
Esil, stm., Asia	D11	32
Esk, Austl.	F9	76
Eškar-Ola, Russia	C7	32
Eskdale, W.V., U.S.	F4	114
Eski, Russia	C19	10
Eskilstuna, Swe.	G7	8
Eskimo Lakes, l., N.T., Can.	B4	106
Eskimo Point see Arviat, Nu., Can.	C12	106
Eskişehir, Tur.	D13	28
Eskişehir, state, Tur.	D13	28
Eskridge, Ks., U.S.	F1	120
Eslâmâbâd, Iran	C6	56
Eşme, Tur.	E11	28
Esmeralda, Cuba	B8	102
Esmeralda, Isla, i., Chile	I1	90
Esmeraldas, Ec.	G2	86
Esmeraldas, state, Ec.	G2	86
Esmeraldas, stm., Ec.	G2	86
Espada, Punta, c., Col.	A6	86
Espalion, Fr.	E8	18
Espanola, On., Can.	B8	112
Española, N.M., U.S.	F2	128
Espejo, Spain	G6	20
Espelkamp, Ger.	D4	16
Espera Feliz, Braz.	K5	88
Esperança, Braz.	D7	88
Esperance, Braz.	D4	84
Esperance, Austl.	F4	74
Esperantina, Braz.	B4	88
Esperantinópolis, Braz.	B4	88
Esperanza, Arg.	E7	92
Esperanza, Mex.	B4	100
Esperanza, sci., Ant.	B35	81
Esperanza, P.R.	h10	104a
Espichel, Cabo, c., Port.	F1	20
Espinal, Col.	E4	86
Espinhaço, Serra do, mts., Braz.	I4	88
Espinho, Port.	D2	20
Espino, Ven.	C9	86
Espinosa, Braz.	H4	88
Espírito Santo, state, Braz.	J5	88
Espíritu Santo, i., Vanuatu	j16	79d
Espíritu Santo, Isla del, i., Mex.	C3	100
Espita, Mex.	B3	102
Esplanada, Braz.	F7	88
Espoo, Fin.	F11	8
Espungabera, Moz.	B11	70
Esquel, Arg.	H2	90
Esquimalt, B.C., Can.	H7	138
Esquina, Arg.	D8	92
Esquiú, Arg.	D5	92
Essaouira, Mor.	C3	64
Essej, Russia	C9	34
Essen, Ger.	E3	16
Essendon, Mount, mtn., Austl.	D3	74
Essequibo, stm., Guy.	C6	84
Es Sers, Tun.	H2	24
Essex, On., Can.	F7	112
Essex, Md., U.S.	E9	114
Essex, Mt., U.S.	B13	136
Essex Junction, Vt., U.S.	F3	110
Essexville, Mi., U.S.	E6	112
Esslingen am Neckar, Ger.	H5	16
Essonne, state, Fr.	F11	14
Est, Pointe de l', c., Qc., Can.	A15	110
Estaca de Bares, Punta de la see Estaca de Bares, Punta da, c., Spain	A3	20
Estaca de Bares, Punta da, c., Spain	A3	20
Estacado, Llano, pl., U.S.	H6	128
Estação Adolfo Rodríguez Sáa see Santa Rosa del Conlara, Arg.	F5	92
Estação Colônia Alvear Norte see General Alvear, Arg.	G4	92
Estação Foguista J. F. Juárez see El Galpón, Arg.	B5	92
Estação Gobernador Vera see Vera, Arg.	D7	92
Estación J. J. Castelli see Castelli, Arg.	B7	92
Estación Manuel F. Mantilla see Pedro R. Fernández, Arg.	D8	92
Estación Vela see María Ignacia, Arg.	H8	92
Estados, Isla de los, i., Arg.	J4	90
Eştahbân, Iran	D7	56
Estância, Braz.	F7	88
Estancia, N.M., U.S.	G2	128
Estanislao del Campo, Arg.	B7	92
Estarreja, Port.	D2	20
Estats, Pique d' (Estats, Pic d'), mtn., Eur.	G7	18
Estats, Pic d', mtn., Eur.	G7	18
Estats, Pique d' (Estats, Pic d'), mtn., Eur.	G7	18
Estcourt, S. Afr.	F9	70
Este, Italy	E8	22
Esteio, Braz.	D12	92
Esteli, Nic.	F4	102
Estella, Spain	B8	20
Estelline, S.D., U.S.	C1	118
Estelline, Tx., U.S.	G8	128
Estepa, Spain	G5	20
Estepona, Spain	H5	20
Esterhazy, Sk., Can.	D11	124
Estero Bay, b., Ca., U.S.	H5	134
Esteros, Para.	D4	90
Estevan, Sk., Can.	E10	124
Estevan Point, B.C., Can.	G4	138
Estherville, Ia., U.S.	H4	118
Estill, S.C., U.S.	D4	116
Estissac, Fr.	F12	14
Estiva, stm., Braz.	G3	88
Eston, Sk., Can.	C4	124
Estonia, ctry., Eur.	G11	8
Estrela, Braz.	D11	92
Estrela, mtn., Port.	D3	20
Estrela do Sul, Braz.	J2	88
Estremadura, hist. reg., Port.	E1	20
Estremoz, Port.	F3	20
Estrondo, Serra do, plat., Braz.	E1	88
Esztergom, Hung.	B5	26
Étah, Grnld.	B11	141
Étah, India	E14	54
Étain, Fr.	E14	14
Étampes, Fr.	F11	14
Étaples, Fr.	D10	14
Etâwah, India	E7	54
Etelä-Suomi, state, Fin.	F11	8
Ethan, S.D., U.S.	D15	126
Ethel, Ms., U.S.	D9	122
Ethel, Mount, mtn., Co., U.S.	C10	132
Ethelbert, Mb., Can.	C13	124
Ethiopia, ctry., Afr.	F7	62
Ethiopian Plateau, plat., Afr.	F7	62
Ethridge, Mt., U.S.	B14	136
Etigo-heiya, pl., Japan	B12	40
Etihe, stm., China	B8	38
Étive, Loch, b., Scot., U.K.	E7	12
E. T. Joshua Airport, St. Vin.	o11	105e
Etna, Ca., U.S.	B3	134
Etna, Monte, vol., Italy	G8	24
Etobicoke, ngh., On., Can.	E10	112
Etolin Island, i., Ak., U.S.	E13	140
Etolin Strait, strt., Ak., U.S.	D6	140
Etomami, stm., Sk., Can.	B11	124
Eton, Austl.	C7	76
Etorofu-tō (Iturup, ostrov), i., Russia	B17	38
Etosha Pan, pl., Nmb.	D2	68
Etoumbi, Congo	D2	66
Etowah, Tn., U.S.	B14	122
Etowah, stm., Ga., U.S.	C14	122
Étretat, Fr.	E9	14
Etsch see Adige, stm., Italy	E9	22
Et Tîdra, i., Maur.	F1	64
Ettlingen, Ger.	H4	16
Etzikom Coulee, stm., Ab., Can.	E2	124
Etzná, sci., Mex.	C2	102
Eu, Fr.	D10	14
Euabalong, Austl.	I6	76
Euboea, Gulf of see Vóreios Evvoïkós, b., Grc.	E5	28
Eucla, Austl.	F5	74
Euclid, Oh., U.S.	C4	114
Euclides da Cunha, Braz.	F6	88
Eucumbene, Lake, res.,	K7	76
Eudora, Ar., U.S.	D7	122
Eudora, Ks., U.S.	F2	120
Eufaula, Al., U.S.	F13	122
Eufaula Lake, res., Ok., U.S.	B3	122
Eugene, Or., U.S.	F3	136
Eugênia, Punta, c., Mex.	B1	100
Eugenio Bustos, Arg.	F3	92
Eugowra, Austl.	I7	76
Eumungere, Austl.	H6	76
Eunápolis, Braz.	I6	88
Eungella National Park, p.o.i., Austl.	C7	76
Eunice, La., U.S.	G6	122
Eunice, N.M., U.S.	B4	130
Euphrates (Al-Furât), stm., Asia	C6	56
Eupora, Ms., U.S.	D9	122
Eure, state, Fr.	E9	14
Eure, stm., Fr.	E10	14
Eure-et-Loir, state, Fr.	F10	14
Eureka, Ca., U.S.	C1	134
Eureka, Ks., U.S.	D12	128
Eureka, Mt., U.S.	B11	136
Eureka, Nv., U.S.	D10	134
Eureka, S.D., U.S.	B14	126
Eureka Springs, Ar., U.S.	H4	120
Eurinilla Creek, stm., Austl.	K5	76
Euroa, Austl.	K5	76
Europa, Île, i., Reu.	E7	68
Europa, Picos de, mts., Spain	A6	20
Europa Island see Europa, Île, i., Reu.	E7	68
Europa Point, c., Gib.	H5	20
Europe, cont.	C13	4
Euskal Herriko, state, Spain	A8	20
Euskirchen, Ger.	F2	16
Eustace, Tx., U.S.	E2	122
Eustis, Fl., U.S.	H4	116
Eustis, Lake, l., Fl., U.S.	H4	116
Euston, Austl.	J4	76
Eutin, Ger.	B6	16
Eutsuk Lake, l., B.C., Can.	C4	138
Eva, Al., U.S.	C12	122
Evadale, Tx., U.S.	G4	122
Evandale, Austl.	n13	77a
Evans, Lac, l., Qc., Can.	E15	106
Evans, Mount, mtn., Co., U.S.	B3	128
Evansburg, Ab., Can.	C15	138
Evansdale, Ia., U.S.	B5	120
Evans Strait, strt., Nu., Can.	C14	106
Evanston, Il., U.S.	F2	112
Evanston, Wy., U.S.	B6	132
Evansville, Mn., U.S.	F3	118
Evansville, Wi., U.S.	B8	120
Evansville, In., U.S.	G10	120
Evart, Mi., U.S.	E4	112
Eveleth, Mn., U.S.	D6	118
Evening Shade, Ar., U.S.	H6	120
Evensk, Russia	D20	34
Everard, Lake, l., Austl.	F6	74
Everest, Mount (Qomolangma Feng), mtn., Asia	E11	54
Everett, Pa., U.S.	D7	114
Everett, Mount, mtn., Ma., U.S.	B12	114
Everett, Wa., U.S.	C4	136
Everglades, The, sw., Fl., U.S.	K4	116
Everglades City, Fl., U.S.	K4	116
Everglades National Park, p.o.i., Fl., U.S.	K5	116
Evergreen, Al., U.S.	F12	122
Evergreen, Mt., U.S.	B12	136
Evermann, Cerro, vol., Mex.	F3	100
Evesham, Sk., Can.	B4	124
Evesham, Eng., U.K.	I11	12
Évian-les-Bains, Fr.	C12	18
Evje, Nor.	G2	8
Évora, Port.	F3	20
Évora, state, Port.	F3	20
Evoron, ozero, l., Russia	F16	34
Évreux, Fr.	E10	14
Évry, Fr.	F11	14
E. V. Spence Reservoir, res., Tx., U.S.	C7	130
'Ewa, Hi., U.S.	b3	78a
Ewing, Ne., U.S.	E14	126
Ewing, Va., U.S.	H2	114
Ewo, Congo	E2	66
Excelsior Mountain, mtn., Ca., U.S.	E6	134
Excelsior Springs, Mo., U.S.	E3	120
Exeter, On., Can.	E8	112
Exeter, Eng., U.K.	K9	12
Exeter, Ca., U.S.	G7	134
Exeter, Ne., U.S.	G15	126
Exeter Sound, strt., Nu., Can.	D13	141
Exira, Ia., U.S.	C3	120
Exmoor, plat., Eng., U.K.	J9	12
Exmoor National Park, p.o.i., Eng., U.K.	J9	12
Exmore, Va., U.S.	G10	114
Exmouth, Austl.	D2	74
Exmouth, Eng., U.K.	K9	12
Exmouth Gulf, b., Austl.	D2	74
Extremadura, state, Spain	E4	20
Exuma Cays, is., Bah.	C9	96
Exuma Sound, strt., Bah.	C9	96
Eyasi, Lake, l., Tan.	E6	66
Eyebrow, Sk., Can.	D7	124
Eyemouth, Scot., U.K.	F10	12
Eye Peninsula, pen., Scot., U.K.	C6	12
Eyjafjörður, b., Ice.	j30	8a
Eyl, Som.	C9	66
Eyl, val., Som.	C9	66
Eylar Mountain, mtn., Ca., U.S.	F4	134
Eyota, Mn., U.S.	H6	118
Eyrarbakki, Ice.	I29	8a
Eyre, Austl.	F5	74

Name	Map Ref.	Page
Eyre Creek, stm., Austl.	F2	76
Eyre North, Lake, l., Austl.	E7	74
Eyre Peninsula, pen., Austl.	F7	74
Eyre South, Lake, l., Austl.	E7	74
Ezequiel Ramos Mexía, Embalse, res., Arg.	G3	90
Ežerėlis, Lith.	F6	10
Ezine, Tur.	D9	28

F

Name	Map Ref.	Page
Faaone, Fr. Poly.	v22	78h
Faber Lake, l., N.T., Can.	C7	106
Fabriano, Italy	G9	22
Facatativá, Col.	E4	86
Fachi, Niger	F7	64
Facpi Point, c., Guam.	j9	78c
Factoryville, Pa., U.S.	C10	114
Fada, Chad	D4	62
Fada-Ngourma, Burkina	G5	64
Faddeevskij, ostrov, i., Russia	A18	34
Faddeja, zaliv, b., Russia	A10	34
Fadiffolu Atoll, at., Mald.	h12	46a
Faenza, Italy	F8	22
Fafe, Port.	C2	20
Făgăraş, Rom.	D11	26
Fagernes, Nor.	F3	8
Fagersta, Swe.	F6	8
Faguibine, Lac, l., Mali	F4	64
Fagurhólsmýri, Ice.	I31	8a
Fairbank, Ia., U.S.	B5	120
Fairbanks, Ak., U.S.	D10	140
Fairbanks, Ia., U.S.	E6	122
Fair Bluff, N.C., U.S.	B6	116
Fairborn, Oh., U.S.	E1	114
Fairbury, Il., U.S.	K10	118
Fairbury, Ne., U.S.	A11	128
Fairchance, Pa., U.S.	E6	114
Fairchild, Wi., U.S.	G8	118
Fairfax, Ca., U.S.	C4	118
Fairfax, Mo., U.S.	D2	120
Fairfax, S.C., U.S.	D4	116
Fairfax, S.D., U.S.	D14	126
Fairfax, Va., U.S.	F8	114
Fairfax, Vt., U.S.	F3	110
Fairfield, Al., U.S.	D11	122
Fairfield, Ca., U.S.	E3	134
Fairfield, Id., U.S.	G12	136
Fairfield, Il., U.S.	F9	118
Fairfield, Il., U.S.	F7	110
Fairfield, Ne., U.S.	G14	126
Fairfield, Oh., U.S.	E1	114
Fairfield, Tx., U.S.	F2	122
Fairgrove, Mi., U.S.	E6	112
Fairhaven, Ma., U.S.	C15	114
Fair Haven, N.Y., U.S.	E13	112
Fair Head, c., N. Ire., U.K.	F6	12
Fairhope, Al., U.S.	G11	122
Fairlie, N.Z.	G4	80
Fairmont, Mn., U.S.	H4	118
Fairmont, N.C., U.S.	B6	116
Fairmont, Ne., U.S.	G15	126
Fairmont, W.V., U.S.	E5	114
Fairmount Hot Springs, B.C., Can.	F14	138
Fairmount, Il., U.S.	H2	112
Fairmount, In., U.S.	H4	112
Fairmount, N.D., U.S.	E2	118
Fair Ness, c., Nu., Can.	C16	106
Fair Oaks, Ca., U.S.	E4	134
Fair Plain, Mi., U.S.	F3	112
Fairplay, Co., U.S.	B3	128
Fairview, Ga., U.S.	C13	122
Fairview, Il., U.S.	D7	120
Fairview, Mi., U.S.	D5	112
Fairview, Mt., U.S.	G9	124
Fairview, Tn., U.S.	I10	120
Fairview, Ut., U.S.	D5	132
Fairview Park, In., U.S.	I2	112
Fairview Peak, mtn., Nv., U.S.	D7	134
Fairweather Mountain, mtn., N.A.	D3	106
Faisalabad (Lyallpur), Pak.	C4	54
Faison, N.C., U.S.	A7	116
Faistós, sci., Grc.	H7	28
Faith, S.D., U.S.	B10	126
Faizābād, India	E9	54
Fajardo, P.R.	B4	104a
Fajou, Îlet à, i., Guad.	h5	105c
Fajr, Bi'r, well, Sau. Ar.	J8	58
Fajr, Wādī, stm., Sau. Ar.	H9	58
Fajr, Wādī, stm., Sau. Ar.	J8	58
Fakse Bugt, b., Den.	A8	16
Faku, China	C5	38
Falaba, S.L.	H2	64
Falaise, Fr.	F8	14
Fālākāta, India	E12	54
Falcón, state, Ven.	B7	86
Falcón, Presa (Falcon Reservoir), res., N.A.	H8	130
Falconara Marittima, Italy	G10	22
Falcon Reservoir (Falcón, Presa), res., N.A.	H8	130
Falelatai, Samoa	g11	79c
Falémé, stm., Afr.	G2	64
Fălești, Mol.	B14	26
Falfurrias, Tx., U.S.	G9	130
Falkenberg, Ger.	E9	16
Falkenberg, Swe.	H5	8
Falkensee, Ger.	D9	16
Falkenstein, Ger.	F8	16
Falkirk, Scot., U.K.	E9	12
Falkland, Scot., U.K.	F11	138
Falkland Islands, dep., S.A.	J4	90
Falkland Sound, strt., Falk. Is.	J5	90
Falköping, Swe.	G5	8
Falkville, Al., U.S.	C11	122
Fall, stm., Ks., U.S.	D13	128
Fallbrook, Ca., U.S.	J8	134
Fallon, Nv., U.S.	D7	134
Fall River, Ma., U.S.	C14	114
Fall River, Wi., U.S.	H9	118
Fall River Mills, Ca., U.S.	C4	134
Falls City, Ne., U.S.	D2	120
Falls City, Or., U.S.	F3	136
Falls Creek, Pa., U.S.	C7	114
Falls Lake, res., N.C., U.S.	I7	114
Falmouth, Jam.	i13	104d
Falmouth, Eng., U.K.	K7	12
Falmouth, Ma., U.S.	C15	114
Falmouth, Me., U.S.	G6	110
False Bay, b., S. Afr.	I4	70
False Divi Point, c., India	D5	53
False Pass, Ak., U.S.	F7	140
Falset, Spain	C11	20
Falso, Cabo, c., Dom. Rep.	D12	102
Falster, i., Den.	I4	8
Fălticeni, Rom.	B13	26
Falun, Swe.	F6	8
Famagusta see Gazimağusa, N. Cyp.	C4	58
Famaillá, Arg.	C5	92
Famatina, Sierra de, mts., Arg.	D4	92
Famenne, reg., Bel.	D14	14
Family Lake, l., Mb., Can.	B18	124
Fanchang, China	F8	42
Fanch'eng see Xiangfan, China	F4	42
Fanchon, Pointe, c., Haiti	C10	102
Fancy, St. Vin.	o11	105e
Fang, Thai.	C4	48
Fangak, Sudan	F6	62
Fangcheng, China	E5	42
Fangxian, China	E4	42
Fangzheng, China	B10	36
Fanipal', Bela.	G10	10
Fanjiatun, China	C6	38
Fanny Bay, B.C., Can.	G6	138
Fano, Italy	G10	22
Fan Si Pan, mtn., Viet.	A6	48
Faraday, sci., Ant.	B34	81
Faradje, D.R.C.	D5	66
Farafangana, Madag.	E8	68
Farāh, Afg.	C9	56
Farāh, stm., Afg.	C9	56
Farallon de Pajaros, i., N. Mar. Is.	A5	72
Farallon Islands, is., Ca., U.S.	F2	134
Faranah, Gui.	G2	64
Farāsān, Jazā'ir, is., Sau. Ar.	F5	56
Fareham, Eng., U.K.	K11	12
Farewell, Ak., U.S.	D9	140
Farewell, Cape, c., N.Z.	E5	80
Fargo, N.D., U.S.	E2	118
Faribault, Mn., U.S.	G5	118
Faribault, Lac, l., Qc., Can.	D16	106
Faridabad, India	D6	54
Faridkot, India	C5	54
Faridpur, Bngl.	G12	54
Faridpur, India	D7	54
Farilhões, is., Port.	E1	20
Farim, Gui.-B.	G2	64
Farina, Il., U.S.	F9	120
Farinha, stm., Braz.	D2	88
Fāriskūr, Egypt	G2	58
Färjestaden, Swe.	H7	8
Farley, Ia., U.S.	B7	120
Farmer City, Il., U.S.	D9	120
Farmersville, Il., U.S.	E8	120
Farmersville, Tx., U.S.	D2	122
Farmerville, La., U.S.	E6	122
Farmington, Il., U.S.	D7	120
Farmington, Me., U.S.	F6	110
Farmington, Mn., U.S.	G5	118
Farmington, Mo., U.S.	G7	120
Farmington, Mt., U.S.	C14	136
Farmington, N.H., U.S.	G5	110
Farmington, N.M., U.S.	G8	132
Farmington, Ut., U.S.	C5	132
Far Mountain, mtn., B.C., Can.	D5	138
Farmville, N.C., U.S.	A8	116
Farmville, Va., U.S.	G7	114
Farnborough, Eng., U.K.	J12	12
Farne Islands, is., Eng., U.K.	F11	12
Farnham, Qc., Can.	E3	110
Farnmoselle, Spain	C4	20
Faro, Braz.	D6	84
Faro, Yk., Can.	C4	106
Faro, Port.	H3	20
Faro, state, Port.	H2	20
Faroe Islands, dep., Eur.	n34	8b
Fårön, i., Swe.	H8	8
Farquhar, Atoll de, i., Sey.	l12	69b
Farquhar, Cape, c., Austl.	D2	74
Farrars Creek, stm., Austl.	E3	76
Farrell, Pa., U.S.	D5	114
Farrukhābād, India	E7	54
Fārsala, Grc.	D5	28
Fartak, Ra's, c., Yemen	F7	56
Farvel, Kap, c., Grnld.	F17	141
Farwell, Mi., U.S.	E5	112
Fasā, Iran	D7	56
Fasano, Italy	D11	24
Fastnet Rock, r., Ire.	J3	12
Fatehābād, India	D5	54
Fatehjang, Pak.	B4	54
Fatehpur, India	F8	54
Fatehpur, India	E5	54
Fatehpur Sikri, India	E6	54
Fathom Five National Marine Park, p.o.i., On., Can.	C8	112
Fatick, Sen.	G1	64
Fátima, Port.	E2	20
Fatu Hiva, i., Fr. Poly.	E13	72
Fatumu, Tonga	n14	78e
Fatwā, India	F10	54
Fauabu, Sol. Is.	e9	79b
Faucilles, Monts, mts., Fr.	F15	14
Faulkton, S.D., U.S.	B13	126
Fauquier, B.C., Can.	G12	138
Făurei, Rom.	D14	26
Fauresmith, S. Afr.	F7	70
Fauro Island, i., Sol. Is.	d6	79b
Fauske, Nor.	C6	8
Faust, Ab., Can.	A15	138
Favara, Italy	G7	24
Fawcett Lake, l., Ab., Can.	A17	138
Fawn, stm., On., Can.	E13	106
Fawnie Nose, mtn., B.C., Can.	C5	138
Faxaflói, b., Ice.	k28	8a
Faxinal do Soturno, Braz.	D11	92
Faya-Largeau, Chad	D3	62
Fayette, Al., U.S.	D11	122
Fayette, Ia., U.S.	B6	120
Fayette, Mo., U.S.	E5	120
Fayette, Ms., U.S.	F7	122
Fayette, Lake, l., Tx., U.S.	E2	122
Fayetteville, Ar., U.S.	H3	120
Fayetteville, Ga., U.S.	D14	122
Fayetteville, N.C., U.S.	A7	116
Fayetteville, Tn., U.S.	B12	122
Fayetteville, W.V., U.S.	F4	114
Fāyid, Egypt	H3	58
Fāzilka, India	C5	54
Fāzilpur, Pak.	D3	54
Fazzān (Fezzan), hist. reg., Libya	B2	62
Féderik, Maur.	E2	64
Fear, Cape, c., N.C., U.S.	C8	116
Feather, stm., Ca., U.S.	D4	134
Feather, Middle Fork, stm., Ca., U.S.	D5	134
Feather, North Fork, East Branch, stm., Ca., U.S.	C4	134
Fécamp, Fr.	E9	14
Federación, Arg.	E8	92
Federal, Arg.	E8	92
Federally Administered Tribal Areas, state, Pak.	B2	54
Federal Republic of Germany see Germany, ctry., Eur.	E6	16
Federalsburg, Md., U.S.	F10	114
Federated States of Micronesia see Micronesia, Federated States of, ctry., Oc.	C6	72
Fehérgyarmat, Hung.	A9	26
Fehmarn, i., Ger.	B7	16
Feia, Lagoa, b., Braz.	L5	88
Fei Huang, stm., China	D8	42
Feijó, Braz.	E3	84
Feiketu, China	B7	38
Feira de Santana, Braz.	G6	88
Feixi, China	F8	42
Feixian, China	D7	42
Fejér, state, Hung.	B5	26
Felanitx, Spain	E14	20
Felda, Fl., U.S.	J4	116
Feldbach, Aus.	D12	22
Feldberg, mtn., Ger.	I4	16
Feldkirch, Aus.	C6	22
Feliciano, P.R.	B1	104a
Feliciano, Arroyo, stm., Arg.	E8	92
Felipe Carrillo Puerto, Mex.	C4	102
Felix, Cape, c., Nu., Can.	B11	106
Felixlândia, Braz.	J3	88
Felixstowe, Eng., U.K.	I14	12
Felletin, Fr.	D8	18
Fellsmere, Fl., U.S.	I5	116
Feltre, Italy	E8	22
Femunden, l., Nor.	E4	8
Femundsmarka Nasjonalpark, p.o.i., Nor.	E4	8
Fen, stm., China	D4	42
Fenelon Falls, On., Can.	D11	112
Fengcheng, China	G6	42
Fengcheng, China	D6	38
Fengdu, China	G2	42
Fengfeng, China	C6	42
Fenggang, China	G2	42
Fenghuang, China	H3	42
Fengjiabao, China	C1	42
Fengning, China	A7	42
Fengqing, China	G4	36
Fengqiu, China	D6	42
Fengtai, China	B7	42
Fengtai, China	E7	42
Fengtian see Shenyang, China	D5	38
Fengxi, China	F3	42
Fengxian, China	D7	42
Fengyang, China	E7	42
Fengyuan, Tai.	I9	42
Fengzhen, China	A5	42
Feni, Bngl.	G13	54
Fennimore, Wi., U.S.	B7	120
Fenoarivo Atsinanana, Madag.	D8	68
Fenton, Mi., U.S.	F5	112
Fentress, Tx., U.S.	E10	130
Fenwick, W.V., U.S.	F5	114
Fenyang, China	C4	42
Fenyi, China	H6	42
Fer, Cap de, c., Alg.	B6	64
Ferdinand, In., U.S.	F10	120
Ferdows, Iran	C8	56
Ferentino, Italy	I10	22
Fergana, Uzb.	F12	32
Fergana Mountains see Ferganskij hrebet, mts., Kyrg.	F12	32
Ferganskij hrebet, mts., Kyrg.	F12	32
Fergus, On., Can.	E9	112
Fergus Falls, Mn., U.S.	E2	118
Ferguson, B.C., Can.	F13	138
Ferguson, Ky., U.S.	G13	120
Ferguson, Mo., U.S.	F7	120
Fergusson Island, i., Pap. N. Gui.	b5	79a
Ferkéssédougou, C. Iv.	H4	64
Ferlo, reg., Sen.	F2	64
Ferme-Neuve, Qc., Can.	B14	112
Fermo, Italy	G10	22
Fermont, Qc., Can.	E17	106
Fermoselle, Spain	C4	20
Fernández, Arg.	C6	92
Ferndale, Ca., U.S.	C1	134
Ferndale, Wa., U.S.	B4	136
Ferney, B.C., Can.	G15	138
Fernley, Nv., U.S.	D6	134
Fern Park, Fl., U.S.	H4	116
Fernwood, Id., U.S.	C10	136
Ferokh, India	F2	53
Ferrandina, Italy	D10	24
Ferrara, Italy	F8	22
Ferrato, Capo, c., Italy	E3	24
Ferreira Gomes, Braz.	C7	84
Ferreñafe, Peru	E2	84
Ferret, Cap, c., Fr.	E4	18
Ferrières, Fr.	F11	14
Ferris, Tx., U.S.	E2	122
Ferrol, Spain	A2	20
Ferron, Ut., U.S.	D5	132
Ferrysburg, Mi., U.S.	E3	112
Fertő-tavi Nemzeti Park, p.o.i., Hung.	B3	26
Fès, Mor.	C3	64
Feshi, D.R.C.	F3	66
Fessenden, N.D., U.S.	G14	124
Festus, Mo., U.S.	F7	120
Feteşti, Rom.	E14	26
Fethiye, Tur.	G12	28
Fetisovo, Kaz.	F8	32
Fetlar, i., Scot., U.K.	n19	12a
Feucht, Ger.	G7	16
Feuchtwangen, Ger.	G6	16
Feuilles, stm., Qc., Can.	D16	106
Feuilles, Baie aux, b., Can.	D16	106
Feurs, Fr.	D10	18
Feyzābād, Afg.	B11	56
Fez see Fès, Mor.	C3	64
Fezzan see Fazzān, hist. reg., Libya	B2	62
Ffestiniog, Wales, U.K.	I9	12
Fianarantsoa, Madag.	E8	68
Fianga, Chad	E3	62
Fiché, Eth.	F7	62
Fichtelgebirge, mts., Eur.	F7	16
Ficksburg, S. Afr.	F8	70
Fidalgo, stm., Braz.	E5	88
Fidenza, Italy	F7	22
Field, B.C., Can.	E14	138
Fier, Alb.	D13	24
Fier see Fier, Alb.	D13	24
Fiery Creek, stm., Austl.	B2	76
Fierzës, Liqeni i, res., Alb.	B14	24
Fife Lake, Sk., Can.	E8	124
Fife Lake, Mi., U.S.	D4	112
Fife Lake, l., Sk., Can.	E8	124
Fife Ness, c., Scot., U.K.	E10	12
Fifield, Wi., U.S.	F8	118
Fifth Cataract see Khamis, Ash-Shallāl al-, wtfl., Sudan	D6	62
Figeac, Fr.	E7	18
Figtree, Zimb.	B9	70
Figueira da Foz, Port.	D1	20
Figueras see Figueres, Spain	B13	20
Figueres, Spain	B13	20
Figuig, Mor.	C4	64
Fiji, ctry., Oc.	E8	72
Filabusi, Zimb.	B9	70
Filadélfia, Braz.	F2	88
Filadelfia, Italy	F10	24
Filchner Ice Shelf, ice, Ant.	C1	81
Filey, Eng., U.K.	G12	12
Filiatrá, Grc.	F4	28
Filiaşi, Rom.	E10	26
Filingué, Niger	G5	64
Filippoi, sci., Grc.	B7	28
Fillmore, Ca., U.S.	I7	134
Fillmore, Ut., U.S.	E4	132
Filottrano, Italy	G10	22
Filtu, Eth.	F8	62
Fimbul Ice Shelf see Fimbulisen, ice, Ant.	C5	81
Fimi, stm., D.R.C.	E3	66
Finale Emilia, Italy	F8	22
Finale Ligure, Italy	F5	22
Finca El Rey, Parque Nacional, p.o.i., Arg.	B5	92
Finch, On., Can.	C14	112
Findik, Tur.	B5	58
Findlay, Il., U.S.	E9	120
Findlay, Oh., U.S.	C2	114
Findlay, Mount, mtn., B.C., Can.	F14	138
Fingal, N.D., U.S.	H16	124
Fingoè, Moz.	D5	68
Finike, Tur.	G13	28
Finisterre, Cabo de, c., Spain	B1	20
Finke, Austl.	E6	74
Finke, stm., Austl.	D6	74
Finland, Gulf of, b., Eur.	G11	8
Finland, state, Eur.	D11	8
Finlay, stm., B.C., Can.	D5	106
Finley, N.D., U.S.	G16	124
Finmoore, B.C., Can.	C7	138
Finnegan, Ab., Can.	E18	138
Finnis, Cape, c., Austl.	F6	74
Finnmark, state, Nor.	B11	8
Finnsnes, Nor.	B8	8
Finschhafen, Pap. N. Gui.	b4	79a
Finse, Nor.	F2	8
Finspång, Swe.	G6	8
Finsterwalde, Ger.	E9	16
Fiordland National Park, p.o.i., N.Z.	G2	80
Fiorenzuola d'Arda, Italy	F6	22
Fire Island National Seashore, p.o.i., N.Y., U.S.	D12	114
Firenze (Florence), Italy	G8	22
Firmat, Arg.	F7	92
Firminy, Fr.	D10	18
Firovo, Russia	C16	10
Firozābād, India	E7	54
Firozpur, India	C5	54
Firozpur Jhirka, India	E6	54
First Cataract, wtfl., Egypt.	C6	62
Firth, Ne., U.S.	K2	118
Firth, stm., N.A.	C11	140
Firūzābād, Iran	D7	56
Fisher, Ar., U.S.	B7	122
Fisher, Il., U.S.	D9	120
Fisher Bay, b., Mb., Can.	C17	124
Fisher Branch, Mb., Can.	C16	124
Fisher Peak, mtn., Va., U.S.	H5	114
Fishers Island, i., N.Y., U.S.	C14	114
Fisher Strait, strt., Nu., Can.	C14	106
Fishing Creek, Md., U.S.	F9	114
Fishing Creek, stm., N.C., U.S.	H8	114
Fishing Lake, l., Mb., Can.	B18	124
Fisk, Mo., U.S.	H7	120
Fiskárdo, Grc.	E3	28
Fisterra, Cabo de, c., Spain	B1	20
Fitchburg, Ma., U.S.	B14	114
Fito, Mount, vol., Samoa	g12	79c
Fitri, Lac, l., Chad	E3	62
Fitzgerald, Ga., U.S.	E2	116
Fitz Roy, Arg.	I3	90
Fitzroy, stm., Austl.	D8	76
Fitzroy, stm., Austl.	C4	74
Fitz Roy, Monte (Chaltel, Cerro), mtn., S.A.	I2	90
Fitzroy Crossing, Austl.	C5	74
Fitzwilliam Island, i., On., Can.	C8	112
Fiuggi, Italy	I10	22
Fiume see Rijeka, Cro.	E11	22
Fiumicino, Italy	I9	22
Five Islands, N.S., Can.	E12	110
Five Islands Harbour, b., Antig.	f4	105b
Five Points, N.M., U.S.	H10	132
Fizi, D.R.C.	E5	66
Fjällåsen, Swe.	C8	8
Flagler, Co., U.S.	B5	128
Flagstaff, Az., U.S.	H5	132
Flagstaff Lake, res., Me., U.S.	E6	110
Flamands, Anse des, Guad.	B2	105a
Flambeau, stm., Wi., U.S.	F8	118
Flamborough, On., Can.	E9	112
Flamborough Head, c., Eng., U.K.	G12	12
Fläming, reg., Ger.	E8	16
Flaming Gorge National Recreation Area, p.o.i., U.S.	B7	132
Flaming Gorge Reservoir, res., U.S.	B7	132
Flanagan, Il., U.S.	D9	120
Flanders, On., Can.	C6	118
Flasher, N.D., U.S.	A11	126
Flåsjön, l., Swe.	D6	8
Flat, Ak., U.S.	D8	140
Flat, stm., Can.	C10	130
Flat Creek, stm., N.T., Can.	C5	106
Flat Rock, Mi., U.S.	C12	112
Flat River, stm., In., U.S.	E4	112
Flatey, Ice.	k28	8a
Flathead (Flathead, North Fork), stm., N.A.	H16	138
Flathead, stm., Mt., U.S.	C12	136
Flathead, Middle Fork, stm., Mt., U.S.	B13	136
Flathead, North Fork (Flathead), stm., N.A.	H16	138
Flathead, South Fork, stm., Mt., U.S.	B13	136
Flathead Lake, l., Mt., U.S.	C12	136
Flat Lake, l., Ab., Can.	B17	138
Flatonia, Tx., U.S.	E10	130
Flat River, P.E., Can.	D13	110
Flat River, Mo., U.S.	G7	120
Flat Rock, stm., In., U.S.	E4	112
Flattery, Cape, c., Wa., U.S.	B2	136
Flatts, Ber.	k15	104e
Flatwillow Creek, stm., Mt., U.S.	H5	124
Flatwood, U.S.	D11	122
Flaxton, N.D., U.S.	F11	124
Flaxville, Mt., U.S.	F8	124
Fleetwood, Eng., U.K.	H10	12
Fleetwood, Pa., U.S.	D10	114
Flekkefjord, Nor.	G2	8
Fleming-Neon, Ky., U.S.	G3	114
Flemingsburg, Ky., U.S.	F2	114
Flen, Swe.	G7	8
Flensburg, Ger.	B5	16
Fletcher, N.C., U.S.	A3	116
Fletcher Pond, l., Mi., U.S.	D5	112
Fleurance, Fr.	F6	18
Flers, Fr.	F8	14
Flin Flon, Mb., Can.	E10	106
Flint, Wales, U.K.	H9	12
Flint, Mi., U.S.	E6	112
Flint, i., Kir.	E11	72
Flint, stm., Ga., U.S.	G14	122
Flinton, Austl.	F7	76
Flintstone, Md., U.S.	E7	114
Flippin, Ar., U.S.	H5	120
Flisa, Nor.	F4	8
Flix, Pantà de, res., Spain	C11	20
Flomaton, Al., U.S.	F11	122
Floodwood, Mn., U.S.	E6	118
Flora, Il., U.S.	F9	120
Flora, In., U.S.	H3	112
Floral City, Fl., U.S.	H3	116
Floral Park, Mt., U.S.	E14	136
Flora Vista, N.M., U.S.	G8	132
Flore, Piton, mtn., St. Luc.	m7	105c
Florence see Firenze, Italy	G8	22
Florence, Al., U.S.	C11	122
Florence, Az., U.S.	J5	132
Florence, Co., U.S.	C3	128
Florence, Ks., U.S.	C12	128
Florence, S.C., U.S.	B6	116
Florence, Wi., U.S.	C1	112
Florencia, Col.	G4	86
Florentino Ameghino, Embalse, res., Arg.	H3	90
Flores, Braz.	D7	88
Flores, i., Indon.	G7	44
Flores, Laut (Flores Sea), s., Indon.	G11	50
Flores, Selat, strt., Indon.	G7	44
Flores de Goiás, Braz.	H2	88
Flores Island, i., B.C., Can.	G4	138
Flores Sea see Flores, Laut s., Indon.	G11	50
Floresta, Braz.	E6	88
Floreşti, Mol.	B15	26
Floresville, Tx., U.S.	E9	130
Floriano, Braz.	D4	88
Floriano Peixoto, Braz.	E4	84
Florianópolis, Braz.	C13	92
Florida, Col.	F3	86
Florida, Cuba	B8	102
Florida, P.R.	B4	104a
Florida, Ur.	G9	92
Florida, state, U.S.	F11	108
Florida, Straits of, strt., N.A.	G11	108
Florida Bay, b., Fl., U.S.	K5	116
Florida City, Fl., U.S.	K5	116
Floridablanca, Col.	D5	86
Florida Islands, is., Sol. Is.	e9	79b
Florida Keys, is., Fl., U.S.	L4	116
Floridia, Italy	G9	24
Florido, stm., Mex.	B6	100
Flórina, Grc.	C4	28
Florien, La., U.S.	F5	122
Florissant, Mo., U.S.	F7	120
Florissant Fossil Beds National Monument, p.o.i., Co., U.S.	B3	128
Flørø, Nor.	F1	8
Flotte, Cap de c., N. Cal.	m16	79d
Floyd, N.M., U.S.	G5	128
Floyd, Va., U.S.	H5	114
Floyd, stm., Ia., U.S.	I2	118
Floydada, Tx., U.S.	G7	128
Flumendosa, stm., Italy	E3	24
Fluminimaggiore, Italy	E2	24
Flushing see Vlissingen, Neth.	C12	14
Fluvanna, Tx., U.S.	B5	130
Fly, stm.	b3	79a
Foča, Bos.	F5	26
Foça, Tur.	E9	28
Focşani, Rom.	D14	26
Fogang, China	J5	42
Foggaret ez Zoua, Alg.	D5	64
Foggia, Italy	C9	24
Fogo, i., C.V.	k10	65a
Fogo, stm., Austl.	C4	74
Fogo Island, i., Nf., Can.	j23	107a
Foix, Fr.	G7	18
Foix, hist. reg., Fr.	F7	18
Fojnica, Bos.	F4	26
Fokino, Russia	G17	10
Foláidl, Koh-e, mtn., Afg.	C10	56
Folda, b., Nor.	C6	8
Foley, Al., U.S.	G11	122
Foleyet, On., Can.	F14	106
Foley Island, i., Nu., Can.	B15	106
Folgefonni, ice, Nor.	G2	8
Foligno, Italy	H9	22
Folkestone, Eng., U.K.	J14	12
Folkston, Ga., U.S.	F3	116
Follett, Tx., U.S.	E8	128
Fölinge, Swe.	E6	8
Follonica, Italy	H7	22
Follonica, Golfo di, b., Italy	H7	22
Folsom, Ca., U.S.	E4	134
Folsom Lake, res., Ca., U.S.	E4	134
Fomboni, Com.	C7	68
Fominič, Russia	F17	10
Fominskoe, Russia	A22	10
Fonda, N.Y., U.S.	B11	114
Fond-du-Lac, Sk., Can.	D9	106
Fond du Lac, Wi., U.S.	H10	118
Fond du Lac, stm., Sk., Can.	D9	106
Fondi, Italy	C7	24
Fonni, Italy	D3	24
Fonseca, Col.	B5	86
Fonseca, Golfo de, b., N.A.	F4	102
Fontainebleau, Fr.	F11	14
Fontana, Ca., U.S.	I8	134
Fontana Lake, res., N.C., U.S.	A2	116
Fontanelle, Ia., U.S.	J4	118
Fonte Boa, Braz.	I8	86
Fontenay-le-Comte, Fr.	C5	18
Fontenelle, Qc., Can.	B12	110
Fontenelle Reservoir, res., Wy., U.S.	A6	132
Fonyód, Hung.	C4	26
Foochow see Fuzhou, China	H8	42
Foothills, Ab., Can.	C14	138
Forari, Vanuatu	k17	79d
Forbach, Ger.	H4	16
Forbach, Fr.	E14	14
Forbes, Austl.	I7	76
Forbes, Mount, mtn., Ab., Can.	E14	138
Forbesganj, India	E11	54
Forchheim, Ger.	G7	16
Ford, Ks., U.S.	D9	128
Ford, stm., Mi., U.S.	B2	112
Ford City, Ca., U.S.	H6	134
Ford City, Pa., U.S.	D6	114
Førde, Nor.	F1	8
Ford Ranges, mts., Ant.	C26	81
Fords Bridge, Austl.	G5	76
Fordville, N.D., U.S.	F16	124
Fordyce, Ar., U.S.	D6	122
Forécariah, Gui.	H2	64
Foreman, Ar., U.S.	D4	122
Forest, On., Can.	E8	112
Forest, Ms., U.S.	E9	122
Forest Acres, S.C., U.S.	B4	116
Forestburg, Ab., Can.	D18	138
Forest City, N.C., U.S.	A4	116
Forest City, Pa., U.S.	C10	114
Forest Grove, B.C., Can.	E9	138
Foresthill, Ca., U.S.	D5	134
Forestier Peninsula, pen., Austl.	o14	77a
Forest Lake, Mn., U.S.	F5	118
Forest Park, Ga., U.S.	C1	116
Forestville, Qc., Can.	B7	110
Forez, Monts du, mts., Fr.	D10	18
Forgan, Ok., U.S.	E7	128
Forillon, Parc national de, p.o.i., Qc., Can.	B12	110
Forked Deer, stm., Tn., U.S.	I8	120
Forks, Wa., U.S.	C2	136
Forlì, Italy	F9	22
Formby Point, c., Eng., U.K.	H9	12
Formentera, i., Spain	F12	20
Formentor, Cap de c., Spain	E14	20
Formia, Italy	C7	24
Formiga, Braz.	K3	88
Formosa, Arg.	B8	92
Formosa see Taiwan, ctry., Asia	I9	42
Formosa, Braz.	H2	88
Formosa, Serra, plat., Braz.	F6	84
Formosa Strait see Taiwan Strait, strt., Asia	I8	42
Formoso, stm., Braz.	G3	88
Forney, Tx., U.S.	E2	122
Fornosovo, Russia	A13	10
Forres, Scot., U.K.	D9	12
Forrest, Austl.	F6	74
Forrest City, Ar., U.S.	B8	122
Forreston, Il., U.S.	B8	120
Forsayth, Austl.	B5	76
Forst, Ger.	E10	16
Forster, Austl.	I8	76
Forsyth, Ga., U.S.	C2	116
Forsyth, Mo., U.S.	H4	120
Forsyth, Mt., U.S.	A5	126
Fort Abbās, Pak.	D4	54
Fort Albany, On., Can.	E14	106
Fortaleza, Braz.	B6	88
Fortaleza do Ituxi, Braz.	E4	84
Fort Assiniboine, Ab., Can.	B15	138
Fort Atkinson, Wi., U.S.	B9	120
Fort Bayard see Zhanjiang, China	K4	42
Fort Beaufort, S. Afr.	H8	70
Fort Belknap Agency, Mt., U.S.	F5	124
Fort Benton, Mt., U.S.	C16	136
Fort Bragg, Ca., U.S.	D2	134
Fort Branch, In., U.S.	F10	120
Fort Bridger, Wy., U.S.	B6	132
Fort Calhoun, Ne., U.S.	C1	120
Fort Chipewyan, Ab., Can.	D8	106
Fort Collins, Co., U.S.	G7	126
Fort-Coulonge, Qc., Can.	C13	112
Fort Davis, Al., U.S.	E13	122
Fort Davis, Tx., U.S.	D4	130
Fort-de-France, Mart.	k6	105c
Fort-de-France-Lamentin, Aérodrome de, Mart.	k7	105c
Fort Deposit, Al., U.S.	F12	122
Fort Dodge, Ia., U.S.	B3	120
Fort Duchesne, Ut., U.S.	C7	132
Forte dei Marmi, Italy	G7	22
Fort Edward, N.Y., U.S.	G3	110
Forte Erie, On., Can.	F10	112
Fortescue, stm., Austl.	D3	74
Fortezza, Italy	D8	22
Fort Frances, On., Can.	C5	118
Fort Fraser, B.C., Can.	B6	138
Fort Frederica National Monument, p.o.i., Ga., U.S.	E4	116
Fort Gaines, Ga., U.S.	F13	122
Fort Garland, Co., U.S.	D3	128
Fort Gibson, Ok., U.S.	I2	120
Fort Good Hope, N.T., Can.	B5	106
Forth, Firth of, b., Scot., U.K.	E10	12
Fort Hall, Id., U.S.	G14	136
Fortine, Mt., U.S.	B12	136
Fortín Uno, Arg.	I5	92
Fort Jones, Ca., U.S.	B3	134
Fort Klamath, Or., U.S.	H4	136
Fort Knox, Ky., U.S.	G12	120
Fort-Lamy see N'Djamena, Chad	E3	62
Fort Laramie, Wy., U.S.	G17	126
Fort Lauderdale, Fl., U.S.	J5	116
Fort Liard, N.T., Can.	C6	106
Fort Loramie, Oh., U.S.	D1	114
Fort Loudoun Lake, res., Tn., U.S.	B15	122
Fort Lyon Canal, can., Co., U.S.	C5	128
Fort MacKay, Ab., Can.	D8	106
Fort Macleod, Ab., Can.	G17	138
Fort Madison, Ia., U.S.	D6	120
Fort Matanzas National Monument, p.o.i., Fl., U.S.	G4	116
Fort McMurray, Ab., Can.	D8	106
Fort McPherson, N.T., Can.	B4	106
Fort Meade, Fl., U.S.	I4	116
Fort Mill, S.C., U.S.	A5	116
Fort Morgan, Co., U.S.	A5	128
Fort Myers, Fl., U.S.	J3	116
Fort Myers Beach, Fl., U.S.	J3	116
Fort Nelson, B.C., Can.	D6	106
Fort Nelson, stm., B.C., Can.	D6	106
Fort Ogden, Fl., U.S.	I4	116
Fort Payne, Al., U.S.	C13	122
Fort Peck, Mt., U.S.	F7	124
Fort Peck, dam, Mt., U.S.	G7	124
Fort Peck Lake, res., Mt., U.S.	F5	124
Fort Pierce, Fl., U.S.	I5	116
Fort Plain, N.Y., U.S.	B11	114
Fort Providence, N.T., Can.	C7	106
Fort Portal, Ug.	D6	66
Fort Pulaski National Monument, p.o.i., Ga., U.S.	E5	116
Fort Qu'Appelle, Sk., Can.	D10	124
Fort Randall Dam, dam, S.D., U.S.	D14	126
Fort Recovery, Oh., U.S.	D1	114
Fort Resolution, N.T., Can.	C8	106
Fort Rixon, Zimb.	B9	70
Fort Saint James, B.C., Can.	B6	138
Fort Saint John, B.C., Can.	D6	106
Fort Saskatchewan, Ab., Can.	C17	138
Fort Scott, Ks., U.S.	G3	120
Fort Severn, On., Can.	D13	106
Fort-Shevchenko, Kaz.	F7	32
Fort Simpson, N.T., Can.	C6	106
Fort Smith, N.T., Can.	C8	106
Fort Smith, Ar., U.S.	B4	122
Fort Stockton, Tx., U.S.	D4	130
Fort Sumner, N.M., U.S.	G4	128
Fort Sumter National Monument, p.o.i., S.C., U.S.	D6	116
Fort Supply, Ok., U.S.	E9	128
Fort Thomas, Az., U.S.	J7	132
Fort Totten, N.D., U.S.	G15	124
Fort Towson, Ok., U.S.	D3	122
Fortuna, Ca., U.S.	C1	134
Fortuna, C.R.	G5	102
Fortune, Bay, b., Nf., Can.	j22	107a
Fortuneswell, Eng., U.K.	K10	12
Fort Union National Monument, p.o.i., N.M., U.S.	F3	128
Fort Valley, Ga., U.S.	D2	116
Fort Vermilion, Ab., Can.	D7	106
Fort Victoria, sci., Ber.	k16	104e
Fort Walton Beach, Fl., U.S.	G12	122
Fort Wayne, In., U.S.	G4	112
Fort White, Fl., U.S.	G3	116
Fort William, Scot., U.K.	E7	12
Fort Worth, Tx., U.S.	B10	130
Fort Yates, N.D., U.S.	A12	126
Fort Yukon, Ak., U.S.	C10	140
Foshan, China	J5	42
Fosheim Peninsula, pen., Nu., Can.	B9	141
Foso, Ghana	H4	64
Fossano, Italy	F4	22
Fossil, Or., U.S.	F6	136
Fossil Butte National Monument, p.o.i., Wy., U.S.	B6	132
Fossil Lake, l., Or., U.S.	G6	136
Fossombrone, Italy	G9	22
Fosston, Mn., U.S.	D3	118
Foster Bugt, strt., Grnld.	C21	141
Fostoria, Oh., U.S.	C2	114
Fougamou, Gabon	E2	66
Fouhsin see Fuxin, China	C4	38
Fou-nien see Fujian, state, China	I7	42
Foula, i., Scot., U.K.	n17	12a
Fouling see Fuling, China	G2	42
Foumban, Cam.	C2	66
Foum-el-Hassan, Mor.	D3	64
Foum-Zguid, Mor.	C3	64
Foundiougne, Sen.	G1	64
Fountain, Co., U.S.	C4	128
Fountain City, Wi., U.S.	G7	118
Fountain Green, Ut., U.S.	D5	132
Fountain Peak, mtn., Ca., U.S.	I1	132

I·20 Fountain Place – Gemsbok National Park

Name	Map Ref.	Page
Fountain Place, La., U.S.	G7	122
Fourche LaFave, stm., Ar., U.S.	C6	122
Fourchu, N.S., Can.	E16	110
Four Corners, Or., U.S.	F4	136
Fourmies, Fr.	D13	14
Four Mountains, Islands of, is., Ak., U.S.	g24	140a
Four Oaks, N.C., U.S.	A7	116
Fourth Cataract see Rābi', Ash-Shallāl ar-, wtfl., Sudan	D6	62
Fous, Pointe des, c., Dom.	j6	105c
Fouta Djalon, reg., Gui.	G2	64
Foux, Cap à, c., Haiti	C11	102
Fouyang see Fuyang, China	E6	42
Foveaux Strait, strt., N.Z.	H3	80
Fowler, Co., U.S.	C4	128
Fowler, In., U.S.	H2	112
Fowler, Mi., U.S.	E5	112
Fowlers Bay, Austl.	F6	74
Fowlerville, Mi., U.S.	B1	114
Fox, stm., Wi., U.S.	H10	118
Fox, stm., U.S.	D5	120
Fox, stm., U.S.	C9	120
Fox Creek, Ab., Can.	B14	138
Foxe Basin, b., Nu., Can.	B15	106
Foxe Channel, strt., Nu., Can.	C15	106
Foxe Peninsula, pen., Nu., Can.	C15	106
Foxford, Ire.	H3	12
Fox Islands, is., Ak., U.S.	g25	140a
Fox Lake, Il., U.S.	B9	120
Foxpark, Wy., U.S.	B10	132
Fox Valley, Sk., Can.	D4	124
Foxworth, Ms., U.S.	F9	122
Foyle, Lough, b., Eur.	F5	12
Foz do Areia, Represa de, res., Braz.	B12	92
Foz do Cunene, Ang.	D1	68
Foz do Iguaçu, Braz.	B10	92
Foz do Jordão, Braz.	E3	84
Foz Giraldo, Port.	E3	20
Fraga, Spain	C11	20
Fraile Muerto, Ur.	F10	92
Framingham, Ma., U.S.	B14	114
Franca, Braz.	K2	88
França, Braz.	F5	88
Franca-Iosifa, Zemlja, is., Russia	B9	30
Francavilla al Mare, Italy	H11	22
Francavilla Fontana, Italy	D11	24
France, ctry., Eur.	C8	18
Frances, stm., Yk., Can.	C5	106
Frances Lake, l., Yk., Can.	C4	106
Francés Viejo, Cabo, c., Dom. Rep.	C13	102
Franceville, Gabon	E2	66
Franche-Comté, hist. reg., Fr.	B12	18
Francis, Sk., Can.	D10	124
Francis Case, Lake, res., S.D., U.S.	D13	126
Francisco Beltrão, Braz.	B11	92
Francisco I. Madero, Mex.	I4	130
Francisco I. Madero, Mex.	C6	100
Francisco Murguía, Mex.	C7	100
Francisco Sá, Braz.	I4	88
Francistown, Bots.	B8	70
Francofonte, Italy	G8	24
François Lake, B.C., Can.	B5	138
Francois Lake, l., B.C., Can.	C5	138
Francs Peak, mtn., Wy., U.S.	C3	126
Frankel City, Tx., U.S.	B5	130
Franken, hist. reg., Ger.	G6	16
Frankenberg, Ger.	F9	16
Frankenberg, Ger.	E4	16
Frankenmuth, Mi., U.S.	E6	112
Frankford, On., Can.	D12	112
Frankford, Mo., U.S.	E6	120
Frankfort, S. Afr.	E9	70
Frankfort, In., U.S.	H3	112
Frankfort, Ks., U.S.	B12	128
Frankfort, Ky., U.S.	F13	120
Frankfort, N.Y., U.S.	A10	114
Frankfort, Oh., U.S.	E2	114
Frankfort, S.D., U.S.	C14	126
Frankfurt, Ger.	D10	16
Frankfurt am Main, Ger.	F4	16
Franklin, Az., U.S.	K7	132
Franklin, Ga., U.S.	D13	122
Franklin, Id., U.S.	A5	132
Franklin, Il., U.S.	E7	120
Franklin, In., U.S.	E11	120
Franklin, Ma., U.S.	B14	114
Franklin, N.C., U.S.	A2	116
Franklin, Ne., U.S.	A9	128
Franklin, N.H., U.S.	G5	110
Franklin, N.J., U.S.	C11	114
Franklin, Oh., U.S.	E1	114
Franklin, Pa., U.S.	C6	114
Franklin, Tn., U.S.	I11	120
Franklin, Tx., U.S.	F2	122
Franklin, Va., U.S.	H9	114
Franklin, Wi., U.S.	F2	112
Franklin Bay, b., N.T., Can.	B5	106
Franklin D. Roosevelt Lake, res., Wa., U.S.	B4	108
Franklin Gordon Wild Rivers National Park, p.o.i., Austl.	o12	77a
Franklin Grove, Il., U.S.	C8	120
Franklin Lake, l., Nu., Can.	B12	106
Franklin Mountains, mts., N.T., Can.	B5	106
Franklin Strait, strt., Nu., Can.	A11	106
Franklinton, La., U.S.	G8	122
Franklinville, N.Y., U.S.	B7	114
Frankston, Tx., U.S.	E3	122
Frankton, In., U.S.	H4	112
Fransfontein, Nmb.	B2	70
Franzensfeste see Fortezza, Italy	D8	22
Franz Josef Land see Franca-Iosifa, Zemlja, is., Russia	B9	30
Frascati, Italy	I9	22
Fraser, B.C., Can.	G13	138
Fraser, Co., U.S.	B3	128
Fraser, stm., B.C., Can.	G9	138
Fraser, Mount, mtn., Austl.	E3	74
Fraserburgh, Scot., U.K.	D11	12
Fraser Island, i., Austl.	E9	76
Fraser Lake, B.C., Can.	B6	138
Fraser Lake, l., B.C., Can.	B6	138
Fraser Plateau, plat., B.C., Can.	E8	138
Fraser Range, Austl.	F4	74
Frauenfeld, Switz.	C5	22
Fray Bentos, Ur.	F8	92
Fray Jorge, Parque Nacional, p.o.i., Chile	E2	92
Fray Marcos, Ur.	G10	92
Frazer, Mt., U.S.	F7	124
Frederic, Wi., U.S.	F6	118
Frederica, De., U.S.	E10	114
Fredericia, Den.	I3	8
Frederick, Md., U.S.	E8	114
Frederick, S.D., U.S.	B14	126
Frederick Hills, hills, Austl.	B7	74
Frederick Reef, rf., Austl.	C10	76
Fredericksburg, Ia., U.S.	B5	120
Fredericksburg, Tx., U.S.	D9	130
Fredericksburg, Va., U.S.	F8	114
Fredericktown, Oh., U.S.	D3	114
Frederico Westphalen, Braz.	C11	92
Fredericton, N.B., Can.	E10	110
Fredericton Junction, N.B., Can.	E10	110
Frederiksborg, state, Den.	H5	8
Frederiksdal, Grnld.	E17	141
Frederikshåb (Paamiut), Grnld.	E15	141
Frederikshavn, Den.	H4	8
Frederiksted, V.I.U.S.	h10	104c
Fredonia, Ks., U.S.	G2	120
Fredonia, N.D., U.S.	A13	126
Fredonia, N.Y., U.S.	B6	114
Fredrika, Swe.	D8	8
Fredrikstad, Nor.	G4	8
Freeburg, Il., U.S.	F8	120
Freeland, Mi., U.S.	E5	112
Freeland, Pa., U.S.	C9	114
Freel Peak, mtn., Ca., U.S.	E5	134
Freels, Cape, c., Nf., Can.	j23	107a
Freeman, S.D., U.S.	D15	126
Freeport, Bah.	B9	96
Freeport, N.S., Can.	F10	110
Freeport, Fl., U.S.	G12	122
Freeport, Il., U.S.	B8	120
Freeport, N.Y., U.S.	H16	112
Freeport, Pa., U.S.	D6	114
Freeport, Tx., U.S.	F12	130
Free State, state, S. Afr.	F8	70
Freetown, Antig.	f4	105b
Freetown, S.L.	H2	64
Fregenal de la Sierra, Spain	F4	20
Freiberg, Ger.	F9	16
Freiburg see Fribourg, Switz.	D4	22
Freiburg im Breisgau, Ger.	I3	16
Freirina, Chile	D2	92
Freising, Ger.	H7	16
Freistadt, Aus.	B11	22
Freital, Ger.	F9	16
Fréjus, Fr.	F12	18
Fremantle, Austl.	F3	74
Fremont, Ca., U.S.	F4	134
Fremont, Ia., U.S.	C5	120
Fremont, In., U.S.	C1	114
Fremont, Mi., U.S.	E4	112
Fremont, Ne., U.S.	C1	120
Fremont, Oh., U.S.	C2	114
Fremont, Wi., U.S.	G10	118
Fremont, stm., Ut., U.S.	E6	132
French, stm., On., Can.	B9	112
French Broad, stm., U.S.	I3	114
Frenchcap Cay, i., V.I.U.S.	f7	104b
French Guiana, dep., S.A.	C7	84
French Island, i., Austl.	L5	76
French Lick, In., U.S.	F11	120
Frenchman (Frenchman Creek), stm., N.A.	E5	124
Frenchman Creek (Frenchman), stm., N.A.	E5	124
Frenchman Creek, stm., U.S.	G11	126
Frenchmans Cap, mtn., Austl.	o12	77a
French Polynesia, dep., Oc.	K24	142
French Somaliland see Djibouti, ctry., Afr.	E8	62
Fresco, C. Iv.	H3	64
Fresco, stm., Braz.	E7	84
Fresnillo, Mex.	D7	100
Fresno, Ca., U.S.	G6	134
Fresno, stm., Ca., U.S.	F6	134
Fresno Reservoir, res., Mt., U.S.	B16	136
Freu, Cap des, c., Spain	E14	20
Freudenstadt, Ger.	H4	16
Frewena, Austl.	C7	74
Frewsburg, N.Y., U.S.	B6	114
Freycinet National Park, p.o.i., Austl.	o14	77a
Freycinet Peninsula, pen., Austl.	o14	77a
Freyre, Arg.	E6	92
Fria, Gui.	G2	64
Fria, Cape, c., Nmb.	D1	68
Friant, Ca., U.S.	G6	134
Friars Point, Ms., U.S.	C8	122
Frías, Arg.	D5	92
Fribourg (Freiburg), Switz.	D4	22
Fridley, Mn., U.S.	F5	118
Fridtjof Nansen, Mount, mtn., Ant.	D25	81
Friedberg, Aus.	C12	22
Friedberg, Ger.	H7	16
Friedberg, Ger.	F4	16
Friedland, Ger.	C9	16
Friedrichshafen, Ger.	I5	16
Friend, Ne., U.S.	G15	126
Friendship, N.Y., U.S.	B7	114
Friendship, Tn., U.S.	I8	120
Fries, Va., U.S.	H4	114
Friesach, Aus.	D11	22
Frio, stm., Tx., U.S.	F9	130
Frio, Cabo, c., Braz.	L5	88
Frio Draw, stm., U.S.	G6	128
Friona, Tx., U.S.	G6	128
Frisco, Tx., U.S.	D2	122
Frisian Islands, is., Eur.	A14	14
Fritch, Tx., U.S.	F7	128
Fritzlar, Ger.	E5	16
Friuli, hist. reg., Italy	E9	22
Friuli-Venezia Giulia, state, Italy	D9	22
Frjazino, Russia	E21	10
Frobisher, Sk., Can.	E11	124
Frobisher Bay, b., Nu., Can.	C17	106
Frobisher Lake, l., Sk., Can.	D9	106
Froid, Mt., U.S.	F9	124
Frolovo, Russia	E6	32
Frome, Eng., U.K.	J10	12
Frome, stm., Austl.	G2	76
Frome, Lake, l., Austl.	H2	76
Fronteiras, Braz.	D5	88
Frontenac, Ks., U.S.	G3	120
Frontera, Mex.	F12	100
Frontera, Mex.	B8	100
Frontier, Sk., Can.	E5	124
Frontier, Wy., U.S.	B6	132
Frontino, Col.	B2	84
Frontino, Páramo, mtn., Col.	D3	86
Front Range, mts., Co., U.S.	H7	126
Front Royal, Va., U.S.	F7	114
Frosinone, Italy	C7	24
Frostburg, Md., U.S.	E6	114
Frostproof, Fl., U.S.	I4	116
Frøya, i., Nor.	E3	8
Fruges, Fr.	D11	14
Fruita, Co., U.S.	D8	132
Fruitdale, Or., U.S.	H3	136
Fruithurst, Al., U.S.	D13	122
Fruitland, Id., U.S.	F10	136
Fruitport, Mi., U.S.	E3	112
Fruitvale, B.C., Can.	G13	138
Fruitvale, Wa., U.S.	D6	136
Frunzivka, Ukr.	B16	26
Frutal, Braz.	J1	88
Frutigen, Switz.	D4	22
Frýdek-Místek, Czech Rep.	G14	16
Fryeburg, Me., U.S.	G6	110
Fu, stm., China	G7	42
Fu, stm., China	F2	42
Fu, stm., China	G6	42
Fua'amotu International Airport, Tonga	n14	78e
Fu'an, China	H8	42
Fuchou see Fuzhou, China	H8	42
Fuchow see Fuzhou, China	G7	42
Fuchū, Japan	E6	40
Fuchun, stm., China	G8	42
Fuding, China	H9	42
Fuego, Volcán de, vol., Guat.	E2	102
Fuencaliente, Spain	F6	20
Fuengirola, Spain	H6	20
Fuensalida, Spain	D6	20
Fuente, Mex.	F7	130
Fuente de Cantos, Spain	F4	20
Fuente de Oro, Col.	F5	86
Fuentes de Ebro, Spain	C10	20
Fuerte, stm., Mex.	B4	100
Fuerte Olimpo, Para.	D5	90
Fuga Island, i., Phil.	A3	52
Fugou, China	D6	42
Fuhai, China	B2	36
Fuhsien see Wafangdian, China	B9	42
Fuji, Japan	D11	40
Fuji, Mount see Fuji-san, vol., Japan	D11	40
Fujian, state, China	I7	42
Fujieda, Japan	E11	40
Fujin, China	B11	36
Fujinomiya, Japan	D11	40
Fuji-san (Fuji, Mount), vol., Japan	D11	40
Fujisawa, Japan	D12	40
Fujiyama see Fuji-san, vol., Japan	D11	40
Fuji-yoshida, Japan	D11	40
Fukagawa, Japan	C14	38
Fukang, China	C2	36
Fukave, i., Tonga	n14	78e
Fukaya, Japan	C12	40
Fukien see Fujian, state, China	I7	42
Fukuchiyama, Japan	D8	40
Fukue, Japan	G1	40
Fukue-jima, i., Japan	G1	40
Fukui, Japan	C9	40
Fukui, state, Japan	D9	40
Fukuoka, Japan	F3	40
Fukuoka, state, Japan	F3	40
Fukuroi, Japan	E10	40
Fukushima, Japan	B13	40
Fukushima, state, Japan	B12	40
Fukuyama, Japan	E6	40
Fulaga Passage, strt., Fiji	q20	79e
Fulda, Ger.	F5	16
Fulda, Mn., U.S.	H3	118
Fulda, stm., Ger.	E5	16
Fuling, China	G2	42
Fullarton, stm., Austl.	C3	76
Fullerton, Ca., U.S.	J8	134
Fullerton Point, c., Antig.	f4	105b
Fulong, China	J2	42
Fulton, Al., U.S.	F11	122
Fulton, Ar., U.S.	D5	122
Fulton, Il., U.S.	C7	120
Fulton, Ks., U.S.	F3	120
Fulton, Ky., U.S.	H9	120
Fulton, Mo., U.S.	F5	120
Fulton, N.Y., U.S.	E13	112
Fulton, Tx., U.S.	F10	130
Fumay, Fr.	D13	14
Funabashi, Japan	D12	40
Funafuti, i., Tuvalu	D8	72
Funan, China	E6	42
Funchal, Port.	C1	64
Fundación, Col.	B4	86
Fundão, Port.	D3	20
Fundy, Bay of, b., Can.	F10	110
Fundy National Park, p.o.i., N.B., Can.	E11	110
Funhalouro, Moz.	C12	70
Funing, China	E8	42
Funiu Shan, mts., China	E5	42
Funsi, Ghana	G4	64
Funtua, Nig.	G6	64
Fuping, China	D3	42
Fuqing, China	I8	42
Fuquay-Varina, N.C., U.S.	A7	116
Furculești, Rom.	F12	26
Furmanov, Russia	H19	8
Furnas, Represa de, res., Braz.	K2	88
Furneaux Group, is., Austl.	m13	77a
Furnes see Veurne, Bel.	C11	14
Fürstenberg / Havel, Ger.	C9	16
Fürstenfeld, Aus.	C12	22
Fürstenfeldbruck, Ger.	H7	16
Fürstenwalde, Ger.	D9	16
Fürth, Ger.	G6	16
Furth im Wald, Ger.	G8	16
Furukawa, Japan	C10	40
Furukawa, Japan	A13	40
Fury and Hecla Strait, strt., Nu., Can.	B14	106
Fusagasugá, Col.	E4	86
Fusan see Pusan, Kor., S.	D2	40
Fushan, China	C9	42
Fushan, China	D4	42
Fushih see Yan'an, China	C3	42
Fushun, China	G1	42
Fushun, China	D5	38
Fusilier, Sk., Can.	C4	124
Fusong, China	C7	38
Füssen, Ger.	I6	16
Fuste, Picacho del, mtn., Mex.	G5	130
Fusui, China	J2	42
Futun, stm., China	H7	42
Futuna, Île, i., Wal./F.	E9	72
Futuyu, China	B6	42
Fuwa, Egypt	G1	58
Fuxian Hu, l., China	G5	36
Fuxin, China	C4	38
Fuyang, China	E6	42
Fuyang, stm., China	C6	42
Fuyu, China	B6	38
Fuyu, China	B9	36
Fuyuan, China	F5	36
Fuyuan see Tongjiang, China	B11	36
Fuyuan, China	B11	36
Fuzhou, China	G7	42
Fuzhou, China	H8	42
Fylí, sci., Grc.	E6	28
Fyn, state, Den.	I4	8
Fyn, i., Den.	I4	8
Fyne, Loch, b., Scot., U.K.	E7	12
Fyresvatnet, l., Nor.	G2	8
G		
Gaalkacyo, Som.	C9	66
Gabare, Blg.	F10	26
Gabarus, N.S., Can.	E16	110
Gabela, Ang.	C1	68
Gaberones see Gaborone, Bots.	D7	70
Gabès, Tun.	C7	64
Gabiarra, Braz.	I6	88
Gabon, ctry., Afr.	E2	66
Gaborone, Bots.	D7	70
Gabras, Sudan	E5	62
Gabriel Strait, strt., Nu., Can.	C17	106
Gabriel y Galán, Embalse de, res., Spain	D4	20
Gabrovo, Blg.	G12	26
Gacé, Fr.	F9	14
Gackle, N.D., U.S.	A13	126
Gadag, India	D2	53
Gādarwāra, India	G7	54
Gäddede, Swe.	D6	8
Gado Bravo, Ilha do, i., Braz.	F4	88
Gádor, Spain	H8	20
Gadsden, Al., U.S.	C12	122
Gadsden, Az., U.S.	K2	132
Gadwāl, India	C3	53
Gael Hamke Bugt, b., Grnld.	C22	141
Găești, Rom.	E12	26
Gaeta, Italy	C7	24
Gaeta, Golfo di, b., Italy	C7	24
Gaferut, i., Micron.	C5	72
Gaffney, S.C., U.S.	A4	116
Gafour, Tun.	H3	24
Gafsa, Tun.	C6	64
Gag, Pulau, i., Indon.	F8	44
Gagarin, Russia	E17	10
Gage, Ok., U.S.	E9	128
Gaggenau, Ger.	H4	16
Gagliano del Capo, Italy	E12	24
Gagnoa, C. Iv.	H3	64
Gagra, Geor.	F5	32
Gaibandha, Bngl.	F12	54
Gail, Tx., U.S.	B6	130
Gaillac, Fr.	F7	18
Gaillimh see Galway, Ire.	H3	12
Gaimán, Arg.	H3	90
Gainesboro, Tn., U.S.	H12	120
Gainesville, Fl., U.S.	G3	116
Gainesville, Ga., U.S.	B2	116
Gainesville, Mo., U.S.	H5	120
Gainesville, Tx., U.S.	H11	128
Gainsborough, Eng., U.K.	H12	12
Gainsborough Creek, stm., Can.	E12	124
Gairdner, Lake, l., Austl.	F7	74
Gaithersburg, Md., U.S.	E8	114
Gaixian, China	A10	42
Gaizina Kalns, hill, Lat.	D8	10
Gajendragarh, India	D2	53
Gajny, Russia	B8	32
Gajuapara, stm., Braz.	C2	88
Gajutino, Russia	B21	10
Gakarosa, mtn., S. Afr.	E6	70
Gakona, Ak., U.S.	D10	140
Galahad, Ab., Can.	D19	138
Galâla el Baharîya, Gebel el-, mts., Egypt	I3	58
Galâla el-Qiblîya, Gebel el-, mts., Egypt	J3	58
Galán, Cerro, mtn., Arg.	C4	92
Galana, stm., Kenya	E7	66
Galanta, Slov.	H13	16
Galapagos Islands see Colón, Archipiélago de, is., Ec.	h12	84a
Galashiels, Scot., U.K.	F9	12
Galați, Rom.	D14	26
Galați, state, Rom.	D14	26
Galatia, Il., U.S.	G9	120
Galatina, Italy	D12	24
Galaxídi, Grc.	E5	28
Galdhøpiggen, mtn., Nor.	F2	8
Galeana, Mex.	C8	100
Galeana, Mex.	F9	98
Galela, Indon.	E8	44
Galena, Ak., U.S.	D8	140
Galena, Il., U.S.	B7	120
Galena, Mo., U.S.	H4	120
Galena Park, Tx., U.S.	E12	130
Galeota Point, c., Trin.	s13	105f
Galera, Punta, c., Chile	G2	90
Galera, Punta, c., Ec.	G1	86
Galera Point, c., Trin.	s13	105f
Galeras, Volcán, vol., Col.	G3	86
Galesburg, Il., U.S.	D7	120
Galesville, Wi., U.S.	G7	118
Galeton, Pa., U.S.	C8	114
Galiano Island, i., B.C., Can.	H7	138
Galič, Russia	G20	8
Galicia, state, Spain	B3	20
Galicia, hist. reg., Eur.	G18	16
Galičica Nacionalni Park, p.o.i., Mac.	C3	28
Galičskaja vozvyšennost', hills, Russia	G20	8
Galičskoe, ozero, l., Russia	G20	8
Galilee, Lake, l., Austl.	D5	76
Galilee, Sea of see Kinneret, Yam, l., Isr.	F6	58
Galiléia, Braz.	J5	88
Galina Point, c., Jam.	i14	104d
Galion, Oh., U.S.	D3	114
Galite, Canal de la, strt., Tun.	G3	24
Gallarate, Italy	E5	22
Gallatin, Tn., U.S.	H11	120
Gallatin, stm., U.S.	E15	136
Galle, Sri L.	H5	53
Gállego, stm., Spain	B10	20
Gallegos, stm., Arg.	J3	90
Galliano, La., U.S.	H8	122
Gallinas, stm., N.M., U.S.	F4	128
Gallinas, Punta, c., Col.	A6	86
Gallipoli, Italy	D11	24
Gallipoli see Gelibolu, Tur.	C9	28
Gallipoli Peninsula see Gelibolu Yarımadası, pen., Tur.	C9	28
Gallipolis, Oh., U.S.	F3	114
Gällivare, Swe.	C9	8
Gallo, Capo, c., Italy	F7	24
Gallo Arroyo, stm., N.M., U.S.	G3	128
Galloo Island, i., N.Y., U.S.	E13	112
Galloway, hist. reg., Scot., U.K.	G8	12
Galloway, Mull of, c., Scot., U.K.	G8	12
Gallup, N.M., U.S.	H8	132
Gallura, reg., Italy	C3	24
Galoa Harbour, b., Fiji	q19	79e
Galt, Ca., U.S.	E4	134
Galtat Zemmour, W. Sah.	D2	64
Galty Mountains, mts., Ire.	I4	12
Galva, Il., U.S.	C7	120
Galva, Ks., U.S.	C11	128
Galveston, In., U.S.	H3	112
Galveston, Tx., U.S.	H4	122
Galveston Bay, b., Tx., U.S.	H4	122
Galveston Island, i., Tx., U.S.	E13	130
Gálvez, Arg.	F7	92
Galway (Gaillimh), Ire.	H3	12
Galway, state, Ire.	H4	12
Galway Bay, b., Ire.	H3	12
Gam (Jin), stm., Asia	A7	48
Gama, Isla, i., Arg.	H4	90
Gamagōri, Japan	E10	40
Gamarra, Col.	C5	86
Gamay, Phil.	D5	52
Gamba, China	D12	54
Gambaga, Ghana	G4	64
Gambēla, Eth.	F6	62
Gambell, Ak., U.S.	D5	140
Gambia (Gambie), stm., Afr.	G1	64
Gambia, The, ctry., Afr.	G1	64
Gambie (Gambia), stm., Afr.	G2	64
Gambier, Îles, is., Fr. Poly.	F13	72
Gamboa, Pan.	C2	86
Gamboma, Congo	E3	66
Gamboula, C.A.R.	D2	66
Gamka, stm., S. Afr.	H5	70
Gamlakarleby see Kokkola, Fin.	E10	8
Gamleby, Swe.	H7	8
Gammon Ranges National Park, p.o.i., Austl.	H2	76
Ga-Mogara, stm., S. Afr.	E6	70
Gan, stm., China	B10	36
Gan, stm., China	G6	42
Ganado, Az., U.S.	H7	132
Ganado, Tx., U.S.	E11	130
Gananoque, On., Can.	D13	112
Gäncä, Azer.	A6	56
Gand see Gent, Bel.	C12	14
Ganda, Ang.	C1	68
Gandadiwata, Bulu, mtn., Indon.	E11	50
Gandajika, D.R.C.	F4	66
Gandak (Nārāyani), stm., Asia	E10	54
Gándara, Spain	A2	20
Gander, Nf., Can.	j23	107a
Ganderkesee, Ger.	C4	16
Gandesa, Spain	C11	20
Gandevi, India	H4	54
Gāndhinagar, India	G4	54
Gandhi Reservoir see Gāndhi Sāgar, res., India	F5	54
Gāndhi Sāgar, res., India	F5	54
Gandia, Spain	F10	20
Gandu, Braz.	G6	88
Ganga see Ganges, stm., Asia	F11	54
Gan Gan, Arg.	H3	90
Gangānagar, India	D4	54
Gangāpur, India	B2	53
Gangāpur, India	E6	54
Gangāpur, India	F5	54
Gangārāmpur, India	F12	54
Gangaw, Mya.	A2	48
Gangāwati, India	D3	53
Gangdhār, India	G5	54
Gangdisê Shan, mts., China	C9	54
Ganges, B.C., Can.	H7	138
Ganges (Ganga) (Padma), stm., Asia	G13	54
Ganges, Mouths of the, mth., Asia	H12	54
Ganghu, China	B11	54
Gangmar Co, l., China	B10	54
Gangneung see Kangnŭng, Kor., S.	B1	40
Gangoa, China	D5	36
Gangotri, India	C7	54
Gangotri, India	C7	54
Gangoumen, China	D2	38
Gangtok, India	E12	54
Gangu, China	D1	42
Gangweon see Kangwŏn-do, state, Kor., S.	B1	40
Gannan, China	B9	36
Gannett Peak, mtn., Wy., U.S.	D3	126
Gannvalley, S.D., U.S.	C14	126
Ganquan, China	C3	42
Gansbaai, S. Afr.	I4	70
Gansu, state, China	D5	36
Gantang, China	H8	42
Gantt, Al., U.S.	F12	122
Gantung, Indon.	E6	50
Ganyanchi, China	C1	42
Ganyesa, S. Afr.	E7	70
Ganzê, China	E4	36
Ganzhou, China	I6	42
Gao, Mali	F4	64
Gao'an, China	G6	42
Gaochun, China	F8	42
Gaohebu, China	F7	42
Gaojian, China	F9	36
Gaolan, China	D5	36
Gaolong, China	H5	42
Gaona, Arg.	B5	92
Gaoping, China	D5	42
Gaotan, China	E3	42
Gaotang, China	C7	42
Gaoua, Burkina	G4	64
Gaoual, Gui.	G2	64
Gaoxian, China	F5	36
Gaoyi, China	C6	42
Gaoyou, China	E8	42
Gaoyou Hu, l., China	E8	42
Gaozhou, China	K4	42
Gap, Fr.	E12	18
Gar, China	B8	54
Gar, stm., China	C8	54
Gara, Lough, l., Ire.	H4	12
Garagumskij kanal (Kara-Kum Canal), can., Turkmen.	B9	56
Garagumy (Kara-Kum), des., Turkmen.	A8	56
Garaina, Pap. N. Gui.	b4	79a
Garanhuns, Braz.	E7	88
Garapan, N. Mar. Is.	B5	72
Garara, Pap. N. Gui.	b4	79a
Garber, Ok., U.S.	E11	128
Garberville, Ca., U.S.	C2	134
Gârbovu, Rom.	E10	26
Garça, Braz.	L1	88
García, Mex.	G8	98
García de Sola, Embalse de, res., Spain	E5	20
Gard, state, Fr.	F10	18
Garda, Italy	E7	22
Garda, Lago di, l., Italy	E7	22
Gardelegen, Ger.	D7	16
Garden City, Ks., U.S.	C8	128
Garden City, Mo., U.S.	F3	120
Garden City, Tx., U.S.	C6	130
Gardendale, Al., U.S.	D12	122
Garden Grove, Ca., U.S.	J7	134
Garden Grove, Ia., U.S.	D4	120
Garden Island, i., Mi., U.S.	C4	112
Garden Peninsula, pen., Mi., U.S.	C3	112
Garden Reach, India	G11	54
Gardenton, Mb., Can.	E17	124
Gardey, Arg.	H8	92
Gardeyz, Afg.	C10	56
Gardiner, Mt., U.S.	E16	136
Gardiner, Or., U.S.	G2	136
Gardiner Dam, dam, Sk., Can.	C6	124
Gardner, Ks., U.S.	F2	120
Gardner, Ma., U.S.	B13	114
Gardner Canal, b., B.C., Can.	C2	138
Gardnerville, Nv., U.S.	E6	134
Garessio, Italy	F5	22
Garet, Mont, vol., Vanuatu	j16	79d
Garfield, Ks., U.S.	C9	128
Garfield, N.M., U.S.	K9	132
Garfield Mountain, mtn., Mt., U.S.	F14	136
Gargano, Promontorio del, mts., Italy	I12	22
Gargano, Testa del, c., Italy	I13	22
Gargždai, Lith.	E4	10
Garhākota, India	G7	54
Garibaldi, Braz.	D12	92
Garibaldi, B.C., Can.	G7	138
Garibaldi, Or., U.S.	E2	136
Garibaldi, Mount, vol., B.C., Can.	G8	138
Gariep Dam, res., S. Afr.	G7	70
Garies, S. Afr.	G4	70
Garigliano, stm., Italy	C7	24
Gariglione, Monte, mtn., Italy	E10	24
Garissa, Kenya	E7	66
Garland, Tx., U.S.	E2	122
Garland, Ut., U.S.	B4	132
Garlasco, Italy	E5	22
Garlin, Fr.	F5	18
Garm, Taj.	B11	56
Garmisch-Partenkirchen, Ger.	I7	16
Garnavillo, Ia., U.S.	B6	120
Garner, Ia., U.S.	A4	120
Garner, N.C., U.S.	I7	114
Garnpung Lake, l., Austl.	I4	76
Garona (Garonne), stm., Eur.	E5	18
Garonne (Garona), stm., Eur.	E5	18
Garoowe, Som.	C9	66
Garoua, Cam.	C2	66
Garoua Boulaï, Cam.	C2	66
Garqu Yan, China	B14	54
Garqu Yan, China	A14	54
Garrel, Ger.	D3	16
Garretson, S.D., U.S.	H2	118
Garrett, In., U.S.	G4	112
Garrett, Ky., U.S.	G3	114
Garrison, N.D., U.S.	G12	124
Garrison, Tx., U.S.	F4	122
Garrison Dam, dam, N.D., U.S.	G12	124
Garry Bay, b., Nu., Can.	B13	106
Garry Lake, l., Nu., Can.	B10	106
Garsen, Kenya	E7	66
Garson, On., Can.	B9	112
Garut, Indon.	G5	50
Garwolin, Pol.	E17	16
Garwood, Tx., U.S.	H2	122
Gary, In., U.S.	G2	112
Gary, Tx., U.S.	E4	122
Gary, W.V., U.S.	G4	114
Garyarsa, China	C8	54
Garza, Arg.	D6	92
Garza Ayala, Mex.	H7	130
Garzón, Col.	F4	86
Garzón, Ur.	G10	92
Gasan-Kuli, Turkmen.	B7	56
Gas City, In., U.S.	H4	112
Gascogne (Gascony), hist. reg., Fr.	F6	18
Gasconade, stm., Mo., U.S.	F6	120
Gasconade, Osage Fork, stm., Mo., U.S.	G5	120
Gascony see Gascogne, hist. reg., Fr.	F6	18
Gascoyne, stm., Austl.	D2	74
Gashaka, Nig.	H7	64
Gashua, Nig.	G7	64
Gaspar, Braz.	C13	92
Gasparilla Island, i., Fl., U.S.	J3	116
Gaspé, Qc., Can.	B12	110
Gaspé, Baie de, b., Qc., Can.	B12	110
Gaspé, Cap, c., Qc., Can.	B12	110
Gaspe Peninsula see Gaspésie, Péninsule de la, pen., Qc., Can.	B11	110
Gaspésie, Péninsule de la (Gaspe Peninsula), pen., Qc., Can.	B11	110
Gassaway, W.V., U.S.	F5	114
Gasteiz (Vitoria), Spain	B8	20
Gaston, Lake, res., U.S.	H7	114
Gastonia, N.C., U.S.	A4	116
Gastre, Arg.	H3	90
Gata, Cabo de, c., Spain	H8	20
Gata, Sierra de, mts., Spain	D4	20
Gătaia, Rom.	D8	26
Gátas, Akrotírion, c., Cyp.	D4	58
Gatčina, Russia	A12	10
Gate City, Va., U.S.	H3	114
Gateshead, Eng., U.K.	G11	12
Gateshead Island, i., Nu., Can.	A11	106
Gatesville, N.C., U.S.	H9	114
Gatesville, Tx., U.S.	C10	130
Gateway, Co., U.S.	E8	132
Gatineau, Qc., Can.	C14	112
Gatineau, stm., Qc., Can.	C14	112
Gatineau, Parc de la, p.o.i., Qc., Can.	C13	112
Gatlinburg, Tn., U.S.	I2	114
Gattinara, Italy	E5	22
Gatton, Austl.	F9	76
Gatún, Lago, res., Pan.	H7	102
Gatun Lake see Gatún, Lago, res., Pan.	H7	102
Gauer Lake, l., Mb., Can.	D11	106
Gauja (Koiva), stm., Eur.	C7	10
Gaujiena, Lat.	C9	10
Gauley, stm., W.V., U.S.	F4	114
Gauley Bridge, W.V., U.S.	F4	114
Gaurela, India	G8	54
Gauribidanūr, India	E3	53
Gause, Tx., U.S.	G2	122
Gaustatoppen, mtn., Nor.	G3	8
Gauteng, state, S. Afr.	D9	70
Gavà, Spain	C12	20
Gávdos, i., Grc.	I7	28
Gavião, stm., Braz.	H5	88
Gavins Point Dam, dam, U.S.	E15	126
Gävle, Swe.	F7	8
Gävleborg, state, Swe.	F7	8
Gavorrano, Italy	H7	22
Gavrilov-Jam, Russia	H18	8
Gawachab, Nmb.	E3	70
Gāwān, India	F10	54
Gawler, Austl.	J2	76
Gawler Ranges, mts., Austl.	F7	74
Gaya, India	F10	54
Gaya, Nig.	G6	64
Gaya, Niger	G5	64
Gaylord, Mn., U.S.	G4	118
Gayndah, Austl.	E8	76
Gays Mills, Wi., U.S.	H8	118
Gaza see Ghazzah, Gaza	G5	58
Gaza, state, Moz.	C11	70
Gazandzhyk see Gazandzyk, Turkmen.	B8	56
Gazandzyk, Turkmen.	B8	56
Gazaoua, Niger	G6	64
Gaza Strip, dep., Asia	G5	58
Gazelle Peninsula, pen., Pap. N. Gui.	a5	79a
Gaziantep, Tur.	A8	58
Gaziantep, state, Tur.	B8	58
Gazimağusa (Famagusta), N. Cyp.	C4	58
Gazimağusa Körfezi, b., N. Cyp.	C4	58
Gazipaşa, Tur.	G15	28
Gazivoda Jezero, res., Serb.	G7	26
Gbanga, Lib.	H3	64
Gboko, Nig.	H6	64
Gdańsk (Danzig), Pol.	B14	16
Gdańsk, state, Pol.	B14	16
Gdansk, Gulf of, b., Eur.	B15	16
Gdov, Russia	B10	10
Gdynia, Pol.	B14	16
Gearhart Mountain, mtn., Or., U.S.	A5	134
Geary, N.B., Can.	E10	110
Geary, Ok., U.S.	F10	128
Gebe, Pulau, i., Indon.	E8	44
Gebze, Tur.	C12	28
Geçitkale, N. Cyp.	C4	58
Gediz, Tur.	D12	28
Gediz (Hermus), stm., Tur.	E10	28
Gedser, Den.	B7	16
Geel, Bel.	C13	14
Geelong, Austl.	L5	76
Geelvink Channel, strt., Austl.	E2	74
Geesthacht, Ger.	C6	16
Geeveston, Austl.	o13	77a
Ge Hu, l., China	F8	42
Geiger, Al., U.S.	E10	122
Geikie, stm., Sk., Can.	D9	106
Geisenfeld, Ger.	H7	16
Geislingen an der Steige, Ger.	H5	16
Geistown, Pa., U.S.	D7	114
Geita, Tan.	E6	66
Gejiu, China	G5	36
Gela, Italy	G8	24
Gela, Golfo di, b., Italy	H7	24
Gelādī, Eth.	F9	62
Gelang, Tanjong, c., Malay.	K6	48
Gelasa, Selat, strt., Indon.	E5	50
Geleen, Neth.	D14	14
Gelembe, Tur.	D10	28
Gelendžik, Russia	F5	32
Gelgaudiškis, Lith.	E6	10
Gelibolu, Tur.	C9	28
Gelibolu Yarımadası (Gallipoli Peninsula), pen., Tur.	C9	28
Gellibrand River, Austl.	L4	76
Gelsenkirchen, Ger.	E2	16
Gemas, Malay.	K6	48
Gemena, D.R.C.	D3	66
Gemert, Neth.	E1	16
Gemlik, Tur.	C12	28
Gemlik Körfezi, b., Tur.	C11	28
Gemona del Friuli, Italy	D10	22
Gemsa, Egypt	K4	58
Gemsbok National Park, p.o.i., Bots.	D5	70

Gemünden – Grand I • 21

Name Map Ref. Page

Gemünden, Ger. F5 16
Gen, stm., China A9 36
Genalē (Jubba), stm., Afr. C8 66
Gending, Indon. G8 50
General Acha, Arg. H5 92
General Alvear, Arg. G3 92
General Alvear, Arg. H8 92
General Belgrano, Arg. G8 92
General Bernardo O'Higgins, sci., Ant. B35 81
General Bravo, Mex. C9 100
General Cabrera, Arg. F6 92
General Campos, Arg. E8 92
General Carrera, Lago, l., S.A. I2 90
General Conesa, Arg. H4 90
General Conesa, Arg. H9 92
General Daniel Cerri, Arg. I6 92
General Elizardo Aquino, Para. C9 92
General Enrique Martínez, Ur. F10 92
General Escobedo, Mex. I7 130
General Eugenio A. Garay, Para. D4 90
General Galarza, Arg. F8 92
General Güemes, Arg. B5 92
General Guido, Arg. H8 92
General José de San Martín, Arg. C8 92
General Juan José Ríos, Mex. C4 100
General Juan Madariaga, Arg. H9 92
General La Madrid, Arg. H7 92
General Lavalle, Arg. H9 92
General Levalle, Arg. G5 92
General Manuel Belgrano, Cerro, mtn., Arg. D4 92
General Pico, Arg. G6 92
General Pinedo, Arg. C7 92
General Pizarro, Arg. B6 92
General Ramírez, Arg. F7 92
General Roca, Arg. G3 90
General San Martín, Arg. G8 92
General Santos, Phil. G5 52
General Terán, Mex. C9 100
General Toševo, Blg. F14 26
General Toshevo see General Toševo, Blg. F14 26
General Treviño, Mex. H8 130
General Trias, Mex. F1 130
General Viamonte, Arg. G7 92
General Villegas, Arg. G6 92
Genesee, Id., U.S. D9 136
Genesee, stm., U.S. F12 112
Geneseo, Il., U.S. C7 120
Geneseo, Ks., U.S. C10 128
Geneseo, N.Y., U.S. B8 114
Geneva see Genève, Switz. D3 22
Geneva, Il., U.S. J10 118
Geneva, In., U.S. H5 112
Geneva, Ne., U.S. G15 126
Geneva, N.Y., U.S. B8 114
Geneva, Oh., U.S. C4 114
Geneva, Lake, l., Eur. C12 18
Genève (Geneva), Switz. D3 22
Genève, Lac de see Geneva, Lake, l., Eur. C12 18
Genf see Genève, Switz. D3 22
Gengma, China G4 36
Genil, stm., Spain G5 20
Genk, Bel. C14 14
Genkai-nada, s., Japan F2 40
Genoa, Austl. K7 76
Genoa see Genova, Italy F5 22
Genoa, Ne., U.S. F15 126
Genoa, Oh., U.S. C2 114
Genoa, Wi., U.S. H7 118
Genova (Genoa), Italy F5 22
Genova, Golfo di, b., Italy G5 22
Genrietty, ostrov, i., Russia A20 34
Gens de Terre, stm., Qc., Can. B13 112
Genshiryoku-kenkyūsho, sci., Japan C13 40
Gent (Ghent), Bel. C12 14
Genteng, Gili, i., Indon. G8 50
Genthin, Ger. D8 16
Gentio do Ouro, Braz. F4 88
Genzano di Roma, Italy I9 22
Geographe Bay, b., Austl. F3 74
Geographical Society Ø, i., Grnld. C21 141
Geok-Tepe, Turkmen. B8 56
George, S. Afr. H6 70
George, Ia., U.S. H2 118
George, stm., Qc., Can. D17 106
George, Lake, l., Austl. J7 76
George, Lake, l., Austl. D4 74
George, Lake, l., Ug. E6 66
George, Lake, l., Fl., U.S. G4 116
George, Lake, res., N.Y., U.S. G3 110
George Town, Austl. n13 77a
Georgetown, Austl. B4 76
Georgetown, On., Can. E9 112
Georgetown, P.E., Can. D14 110
George Town, Cay. Is. C7 102
Georgetown, Gam. G2 64
Georgetown, Guy. B6 84
George Town (Penang), Malay. J4 48
Georgetown, St. Vin. o11 105e
Georgetown, Co., U.S. B3 128
Georgetown, De., U.S. F10 114
Georgetown, Fl., U.S. G4 116
Georgetown, Id., U.S. H15 136
Georgetown, Ky., U.S. F1 114
Georgetown, Ms., U.S. F8 122
Georgetown, Oh., U.S. F2 114
Georgetown, S.C., U.S. C6 116
Georgetown, Tx., U.S. D10 130
George V Coast, cst., Ant. B19 81
George Washington Birthplace National Monument, p.o.i., Va., U.S. F9 114
George Washington Carver National Monument, p.o.i., Mo., U.S. H3 120
George West, Tx., U.S. F9 130
Georgia, ctry., Asia F6 32
Georgia, state, U.S. E11 108
Georgia, Strait of, strt., N.A. G7 138
Georgian Bay, b., On., Can. C8 112
Georgian Bay Islands National Park, p.o.i., On., Can. D9 112
Georgievka, Kaz. E14 32
Georgina, stm., Austl. D2 76
Georg von Neumayer, sci., Ant. B3 81
Gera, Ger. F7 16
Geral, Serra, mts., Braz. C12 92
Geral, Serra, clf., Braz. F2 88
Gerald, Mo., U.S. F6 120
Geral de Goiás, Serra, clf., Braz. G2 88
Geraldine, Mt., U.S. C16 136
Geraldton, Austl. E2 74
Geraldton, On., Can. B11 118
Gérardmer, Fr. F15 14
Gerber, Ca., U.S. C3 134
Gerdine, Mount, mtn., Ak., U.S. D9 140
Gerede, Tur. C15 28
Gereshk, Afg. C9 56
Gérgal, Spain G8 20
Gerik, Malay. J5 48
Gerlachovský štít, mtn., Slov. G16 16
German Democratic Republic see Germany, ctry., Eur. E6 16
Germania Land, reg., Grnld. B21 141
Germantown, Il., U.S. F8 120
Germantown, Tn., U.S. B9 122
Germantown, Wi., U.S. E1 112
Germany, ctry., Eur. E6 16
Germany, Federal Republic of see Germany, ctry., Eur. E6 16
Germencik, Tur. F10 28
Germfask, Mi., U.S. B4 112
Germiston, S. Afr. E9 70
Gernika, Spain A8 20
Gero, Japan D10 40
Gerolimenas, Grc. G5 28
Gerona see Girona, Spain B13 20
Geronimo, Ok., U.S. G10 128
Gers, state, Fr. F6 18
Gers, stm., Fr. F6 18
Gêrzê, China B10 54
Geseke, Ger. E4 16
Geser, Indon. F9 44
Getafe, Spain D7 20
Gettysburg, Pa., U.S. E8 114
Getúlio Vargas, Braz. C11 92
Geumpang, Indon. J2 48
Gevgelija, Mac. B5 28
Geyikli, Tur. D9 28
Geyser, Mt., U.S. C16 136
Geyserville, Ca., U.S. E3 134
Geyve, Tur. C13 28
Ghaapplato, plat., S. Afr. E7 70
Ghadāmis, Libya B1 62
Ghaggar, stm., India D5 54
Ghāghara (Karnāli), stm., Asia E9 54
Ghāghra see Ghāghara, stm., Asia E9 54
Ghakhar, Pak. B4 54
Ghana, ctry., Afr. H4 64
Ghanzi, Bots. B5 70
Ghanzi, state, Bots. C6 70
Gharandal, sci., Jord. H6 58
Gharaunda, India D6 54
Ghardaïa, Alg. C5 64
Ghardimaou, Tun. H2 24
Gharyān, Libya A2 62
Ghāt, Libya C2 62
Ghatere, Mount, mtn., Sol. Is. d8 79b
Ghātprabha, stm., India C2 53
Ghātsila, India G11 54
Ghawdex (Gozo), i., Malta H8 24
Ghazāl, Bahr al-, stm., Sudan F6 62
Ghāziābād, India D6 54
Ghāzīpur, India F9 54
Ghazlūna, Pak. C1 54
Ghazni, Afg. C10 56
Ghazni, state, Afg. B1 54
Ghazni, stm., Afg. B2 54
Ghazzah (Gaza), Gaza G5 58
Ghazzah, Leb. E6 58
Ghent see Gent, Bel. C12 14
Gheorgheni, Rom. C12 26
Gherla, Rom. C10 26
Gheroo, Geziret, i., Egypt G1 58
Ghīnah, Wādī al-, stm., Sau. Ar. H9 58
Ghisonaccia, Fr. H15 18
Ghizo see Gizo Island, i., Sol. Is. e7 79b
Ghizunabeana Islands, is., Sol. Is. d8 79b
Ghoriān, Afg. C9 56
Ghotki, Pak. E2 54
Ghubaysh, Sudan E5 62
Gianh, stm., Viet. C7 48
Giannitsá, Grc. C5 28
Giant Mountain, mtn., N.Y., U.S. F3 110
Giant's Castle, mtn., S. Afr. F9 70
Giant's Castle Game Reserve, S. Afr. F9 70
Giant Sequoia National Monument, p.o.i., Ca., U.S. G7 134
Gia Rai, Viet. H7 48
Giarre, Italy G9 24
Gibara, Cuba B9 102
Gibbon, Mn., U.S. G4 118
Gibbon, Ne., U.S. G14 126
Gibbons, Ab., Can. C17 138
Gibbonsville, Id., U.S. E13 136
Gibb River, Austl. C5 74
Gibeon, Nmb. D3 70
Gibraleón, Spain G3 20
Gibraltar, Gib. H5 20
Gibraltar, dep., Eur. H5 20
Gibraltar, Strait of, strt. B3 64
Gibraltar Point, c., Eng., U.K. H13 12
Gibsland, La., U.S. E5 122
Gibson City, Il., U.S. D9 120
Gibson Desert, des., Austl. D4 74
Gibsons, B.C., Can. G7 138
Giddalūr, India D4 53
Giddings, Tx., U.S. D11 130
Gidgi, Lake, l., Austl. E5 74
Giedraičiai, Lith. E8 10
Gien, Fr. G11 14
Giessen, Ger. F4 16
Gifatîn, Gezira, is., Egypt K4 58
Gifford, Fl., U.S. I5 116
Gifford, stm., Nu., Can. A14 106
Gifford Creek, Austl. D3 74
Gifgâfa, Bîr, well, Egypt H4 58
Gifhorn, Ger. D6 16
Gifu, Japan D9 40
Gifu, state, Japan D10 40
Giganta, Sierra de la, mts., Mex. C3 100
Gigena see Alcira, Arg. F5 92
Gigha Island, i., Scot., U.K. F7 12
Giglio, Isola del, i., Italy H7 22
Gihu see Gifu, Japan D9 40
Gijón, Spain A5 20
Gila, stm., U.S. K2 132
Gila Bend, Az., U.S. K4 132
Gila Cliff Dwellings National Monument, p.o.i., N.M., U.S. J8 132
Gilbert, La., U.S. E7 122
Gilbert, stm., Austl. C8 74
Gilbert Islands see Kiribati, ctry., Oc. D9 72
Gilbert Islands, is., Kir. D8 72
Gilbert Peak, mtn., Wa., U.S. D5 136
Gilbert Plains, Mb., Can. C13 124
Gilbués, Braz. E3 88
Gildford, Mt., U.S. B16 136
Gilford Island, i., B.C., Can. F4 138
Gilgandra, Austl. H7 76
Gilgil, Kenya E7 66
Gil Gil Creek, stm., Austl. G8 76
Gilgit, Pak. B11 56
Gilirang, Indon. E12 50
Gil Island, i., B.C., Can. C1 138
Giljuj, stm., Russia F14 34
Gillam, Mb., Can. D12 106
Gillen, Lake, l., Austl. E5 74
Gillespie, Il., U.S. E8 120
Gillett, Ar., U.S. C7 122
Gillette, Wy., U.S. C7 126
Gillian, Lake, l., Nu., Can. B16 106
Gillingham, Eng., U.K. J13 12
Gills Rock, Wi., U.S. C3 112
Gilman, Il., U.S. D10 120
Gilman, Wi., U.S. F8 118
Gilmer, Tx., U.S. E4 122
Gilmore City, Ia., U.S. B3 120
Gilroy, Ca., U.S. F4 134
Giltner, Ne., U.S. G14 126
Giluwe, Mount, mtn., Pap. N. Gui. b3 79a
Gīmbī, Eth. F7 62
Gimcheon see Kimch'ŏn, Kor., S. F8 38
Gimie, Mount, vol., St. Luc. m6 105c
Gimli, Mb., Can. D16 124
Gimpu, Indon. D12 50
Gineina, Râs el-, mtn., Egypt I4 58
Gin Gin, Austl. E8 76
Gingoog, Phil. F5 52
Ginir, Eth. F8 62
Ginosa, Italy D10 24
Gioia, Golfo di, b., Italy F9 24
Gioia del Colle, Italy D10 24
Gioia Tauro, Italy F9 24
Giong Rieng, Viet. H7 48
Gipuzkoako, co., Spain A8 20
Girafi, Wadi (Paran, Nahal), stm. I5 58
Giralia, Austl. D2 74
Girard, Il., U.S. E8 120
Girard, Ks., U.S. G3 120
Girard, Oh., U.S. C5 114
Girard, Pa., U.S. C5 114
Girardot, Col. E4 86
Giraud, Pointe, c., Dom. j6 105c
Girgarre, Austl. K5 76
Giridih, India F11 54
Girna, stm., India H5 54
Gir National Park, p.o.i., India H3 54
Girne (Kyrenia), N. Cyp. C4 58
Girón, Ec. D2 84
Girona, Spain B13 20
Girona, co., Spain B13 20
Gironde, state, Fr. E5 18
Gironde, est., Fr. D5 18
Gir Range, mts., India H3 54
Giru, Austl. B6 76
Giruá, Braz. D10 92
Girvan, Scot., U.K. F8 12
Gisborne, N.Z. D8 80
Giscome, B.C., Can. B8 138
Gislaved, Swe. H5 8
Gisors, Fr. E10 14
Gitarama, Rw. E5 66
Gitega, Bdi. E5 66
Giulianova, Italy H10 22
Giurgiu, Rom. F12 26
Giurgiu, state, Rom. E13 26
Giuvala, Pasul, p., Rom. D12 26
Givet, Fr. D13 14
Givors, Fr. D10 18
Giyon, Eth. F7 62
Giza see El-Gîza, Egypt H1 58
Gižduvan, Uzb. F10 32
Gižiga, Russia D21 34
Gižiginskaja guba, b., Russia D20 34
Gizo, Sol. Is. e7 79b
Gizo Island, i., Sol. Is. e7 79b
Giżycko, Pol. B17 16
Gjirokastër, Alb. D14 24
Gjirokastra see Gjirokastër, Alb. D14 24
Gjoa Haven see Oqsuqtooq, Nu., Can. B11 106
Gjøvik, Nor. F4 8
Gjuhëzës, Kepi i, c., Alb. D13 24
Gjumri, Arm. A5 56
Glace Bay, N.S., Can. D17 110
Glacier, B.C., Can. E13 138
Glacier Bay, b., Ak., U.S. E12 140
Glacier National Park, p.o.i., B.C., Can. E13 138
Glacier National Park, p.o.i., Mt., U.S. B12 136
Glacier Peak, vol., Wa., U.S. B5 136
Glacier Strait, strt., Nu., Can. B10 141
Glad', Russia A15 10
Gladbrook, Ia., U.S. B5 120
Gladewater, Tx., U.S. E4 122
Gladstone, Austl. D8 76
Gladstone, Mb., Can. D14 124
Gladstone, Mi., U.S. C2 112
Gladstone, Mo., U.S. E3 120
Glåma, stm., Nor. F4 8
Glan, Phil. H5 52
Glaris see Glarus, Switz. C5 22
Glarner Alpen, mts., Switz. D6 22
Glarus, Switz. C5 22
Glarus Alps see Glarner Alpen, mts., Switz. D6 22
Glasco, Ks., U.S. B11 128
Glasgow, Scot., U.K. F8 12
Glasgow, Ky., U.S. G12 120
Glasgow, Mo., U.S. E5 120
Glasgow, Mt., U.S. F7 124
Glasgow, Va., U.S. G6 114
Glassboro, N.J., U.S. E10 114
Glastonbury, Eng., U.K. J10 12
Glauchau, Ger. F8 16
Glazov, Russia C8 32
Glazunovka, Russia H19 10
Gleichen, Ab., Can. F17 138
Glen Alpine, N.C., U.S. A4 116
Glenavon, Sk., Can. D10 124
Glenboro, Mb., Can. E14 124
Glenburn, N.D., U.S. F12 124
Glen Burnie, Md., U.S. E9 114
Glen Canyon, p., U.S. F6 132
Glen Canyon Dam, dam, Az., U.S. G5 132
Glen Canyon National Recreation Area, p.o.i., U.S. F6 132
Glencoe, On., Can. F8 112
Glencoe, S. Afr. F9 70
Glencoe, Mn., U.S. G4 118
Glen Cove, N.Y., U.S. D12 114
Glendale, Az., U.S. J4 132
Glendale, Ca., U.S. I7 134
Glendale, Ms., U.S. F9 122
Glendale, Ut., U.S. F4 132
Glendale, Wi., U.S. A10 120
Glendive, Mt., U.S. G9 124
Glendo, Wy., U.S. E7 126
Glendon, Ab., Can. B19 138
Glendo Reservoir, res., Wy., U.S. E8 126
Glen Elder, Ks., U.S. B10 128
Glenelg, stm., Austl. K3 76
Glengarriff, Ire. J3 12
Glengyle, Austl. E2 76
Glen Innes, Austl. G8 76
Glenmora, La., U.S. G6 122
Glennallen, Ak., U.S. D10 140
Glenns Ferry, Id., U.S. H11 136
Glenoma, Wa., U.S. D4 136
Glenormiston, Austl. D7 74
Glenreagh, Austl. G9 76
Glen Robertson, On., Can. E2 110
Glen Rock, Pa., U.S. E9 114
Glenrock, Wy., U.S. E7 126
Glen Rose, Tx., U.S. B10 130
Glenrothes, Scot., U.K. E9 12
Glens Falls, N.Y., U.S. G3 110
Glenville, Mn., U.S. H5 118
Glenwood, Ab., Can. G17 138
Glenwood, Al., U.S. F12 122
Glenwood, Ar., U.S. C5 122
Glenwood, Ga., U.S. D3 116
Glenwood, Ia., U.S. C2 120
Glenwood, Mn., U.S. F3 118
Glenwood, Va., U.S. H6 114
Glenwood City, Wi., U.S. F6 118
Glenwood Springs, Co., U.S. D9 132
Glidden, Wi., U.S. E8 118
Glide, Or., U.S. G3 136
Glina, Cro. E13 22
Glittertind see Glittertinden, mtn., Nor. F3 8
Glittertinden, mtn., Nor. F3 8
Gliwice, Pol. F14 16
Gljadjanskoe, Russia D10 32
Globe, Az., U.S. J6 132
Glodeni, Mol. B14 26
Głogów, Pol. E11 16
Głogów Małopolski, Pol. F17 16
Glomma see Glåma, stm., Nor. F4 8
Glommersträsk, Swe. D8 8
Glorieta, N.M., U.S. F3 128
Glorieuses. Îles, is., Reu. C8 68
Glorioso Islands see Glorieuses. Îles, is., Reu. C8 68
Gloucester, Austl. H9 76
Gloucester, Eng., U.K. J10 12
Gloucester, Ma., U.S. B15 114
Gloucester, Va., U.S. G9 114
Gloucester Island, i., Austl. B7 76
Glouster, Oh., U.S. E3 114
Gloversville, N.Y., U.S. A11 114
Głowno, Pol. E15 16
Głubczyce, Pol. F13 16
Glūbokoe, Kaz. D14 32
Glubokoje see Glūbokoe, Kaz. D14 32
Głuchołazy, Pol. F13 16
Glücksburg, Ger. B5 16
Glückstadt, Ger. C5 16
Glucomanka, gora, mtn., Russia B11 38
Glyndon, Mn., U.S. E2 118
Gmünd, Aus. B12 22
Gmünd, Aus. D10 22
Gmunden, Aus. C10 22
Gnalta, Austl. H4 76
Gnezdovo, Russia F14 10
Gniew, Pol. C14 16
Gniezno, Pol. D13 16
Gnilec, Russia H19 10
Gnjilane, Serb. G8 26
Gnowangerup, Austl. F3 74
Gō, stm., Japan E5 40
Goa, state, India D2 53
Goālpāra, India E13 54
Goaso, Ghana H4 64
Goat Island, i., Antig. e4 105b
Goat Point, c., Antig. e4 105b
Goba, Eth. F8 62
Gobabis, Nmb. C4 70
Göbel, Tur. D11 28
Gobernador Gregores, Arg. I2 90
Gobernador Ingeniero Valentín Virasoro, Arg. D9 92
Gobernador Juan E. Martínez, Arg. D8 92
Gobernador Vera see Vera, Arg. D7 92
Gobi Desert, des., Asia C5 36
Gobō, Japan F8 40
Goce Delčev, Blg. H10 26
Goch, Ger. E2 16
Goďafoss, wtfl., Ice. k31 8a
Godāvari, stm., India C5 53
Godāvari, Mouths of the, mth., India C5 53
Godbout, Qc., Can. A9 110
Goderich, On., Can. E8 112
Godfrey, Il., U.S. F7 120
Godhavn (Qeqertarsuaq), Grnld. D15 141
Godhra, India G4 54
Gödöllő, Hung. B6 26
Godoy Cruz, Arg. F3 92
Gods, stm., Mb., Can. D12 106
Gods Lake, Mb., Can. E12 106
Gods Lake, l., Mb., Can. E12 106
Gods Mercy, Bay of, b., Nu., Can. C13 106
Godthåb (Nuuk), Grnld. E15 141
Godwin Austen see K2, mtn., Asia B12 56
Goeie Hoop, Kaap die see Good Hope, Cape of, c., S. Afr. I4 70
Goéland, Lac au, l., Qc., Can. E15 106
Goes, Neth. C12 14
Goffstown, N.H., U.S. G5 110
Gogebic, Lake, res., Mi., U.S. E9 118
Gogoi, Moz. B11 70
Gogrial, Sudan F5 62
Gohad, India E7 54
Gohpur, India E14 54
Goiana, Braz. D8 88
Goianésia, Braz. H1 88
Goiânia, Braz. I1 88
Goianinha, Braz. D8 88
Goiás, Braz. G7 84
Goiás, state, Braz. C7 90
Goiatuba, Braz. J1 88
Goio-Erê, Braz. B11 92
Gôio-Erê, stm., Braz. B11 92
Góis, Port. D2 20
Gojō, Japan E8 40
Gojra, Pak. C4 54
Gokāk, India C2 53
Gökçeada, i., Tur. C8 28
Gökova Körfezi (Kerme, Gulf of), b., Tur. G10 28
Göksu, stm., Tur. B4 58
Göksu, stm., Tur. A6 58
Göktepe, Tur. F11 28
Gokwe, Zimb. D4 68
Golāghāt, India C7 46
Gola Gokarannāth, India D8 54
Gołańcz, Pol. D13 16
Gölbaşı, Tur. D15 28
Gölbası, Tur. A8 58
Golcanda, sci., India C4 53
Golconda, Il., U.S. G9 120
Golconda, Nv., U.S. C8 134
Gölcük, Tur. C12 28
Gołdap, Pol. B18 16
Gold Bridge, B.C., Can. F8 138
Gold Coast see Southport, Austl. F9 76
Gold Coast, cst., Ghana I4 64
Golden, B.C., Can. E13 138
Golden, Co., U.S. B3 128
Golden, Il., U.S. D7 120
Golden Bay, b., N.Z. E5 80
Golden City, Mo., U.S. G3 120
Goldendale, Wa., U.S. E6 136
Golden Gate Highlands National Park, p.o.i., S. Afr. F9 70
Golden Hinde, mtn., B.C., Can. G5 138
Golden Lake, l., On., Can. C12 112
Golden Meadow, La., U.S. H8 122
Goldfield, Ia., U.S. B3 120
Goldfield, Nv., U.S. F8 134
Gold Mountain, mtn., Nv., U.S. F8 134
Goldonna, La., U.S. E5 122
Gold River, B.C., Can. G4 138
Gold Rock, On., Can. B6 118
Goldsboro, N.C., U.S. A7 116
Goldston, N.C., U.S. A6 116
Goldsworthy, Austl. D3 74
Goldthwaite, Tx., U.S. C9 130
Goleniów, Pol. C10 16
Goleta, Ca., U.S. I6 134
Golfito, C.R. H6 102
Golfo de Santa Clara, Mex. F5 98
Gölhisar, Tur. F12 28
Goliad, Tx., U.S. F10 130
Golicyno, Russia E19 10
Golina, Pol. D13 16
Golin Baixing, China B4 38
Gölmarmara, Tur. E10 28
Golmud, China D3 36
Golmud, stm., China A7 46
Golodnaja Guba, ozero, l., Russia C24 8
Golovin, Ak., U.S. D7 140
Golpāyegān, Iran C7 56
Gölpazarı, Tur. C13 28
Golub-Dobrzyń, Pol. C14 16
Golva, N.D., U.S. A8 126
Golyšmanovo, Russia C11 32
Goma, D.R.C. E5 66
Gomang Co, l., China C12 54
Gomati, stm., India E8 54
Gombe, Nig. G7 64
Gombi, Nig. G7 64
Gómez Farías, Mex. A5 100
Gómez Palacio, Mex. C7 100
Gómez Plata, Col. D4 86
Gomo Co, l., China B10 54
Gomogomo, Indon. b1 79a
Gomoh, India G10 54
Gonābād, Iran C8 56
Gonaïves, Haiti C11 102
Gonam, Russia E15 34
Gonam, stm., Russia E14 34
Gonarezhou National Park, p.o.i., Zimb. B10 70
Gonâve, Golfe de la, b., Haiti C11 102
Gonâve, Île de la, i., Haiti C11 102
Gonbad-e Qābūs, Iran B8 56
Gonda, India E8 54
Gondal, India G3 54
Gondar see Gonder, Eth. E7 62
Gondarbal, India A5 54
Gonder, Eth. E7 62
Gondia, India H8 54
Gönen, Tur. C10 28
Gong, stm., China I6 42
Gong'an, China F4 42
Gongcheng, China I4 42
Gongchenqiao, China F8 42
Gonggar, China D13 54
Gongga Shan, mtn., China F5 36
Gonghe, China D5 36
Gongliu, China F14 32
Gongola, stm., Nig. G7 64
Gongshiya, China C10 54
Gongxi, China H6 42
Gongxian, China D5 42
Gongzhuling, China C6 38
Goñi, Ur. F9 92
Goniądz, Pol. C18 16
Gōnoura, Japan F2 40
Gonzales, Ca., U.S. G4 134
Gonzales, La., U.S. G8 122
González, Mex. D9 100
González Moreno, Arg. G6 92
Goochland, Va., U.S. G8 114
Goodenough Island, i., Pap. N. Gui. b5 79a
Gooderham, On., Can. D11 112
Goodeve, Sk., Can. C10 124
Good Hope, Cape of (Goeie Hoop, Kaap die), c., S. Afr. I4 70
Good Hope Mountain, mtn., B.C., Can. E6 138
Goodhue, Mn., U.S. G6 118
Goodland, Fl., U.S. K4 116
Goodland, In., U.S. K11 118
Goodland, Ks., U.S. B7 128
Goodlands, Mb., Can. E13 124
Goodman, Wi., U.S. C1 112
Goodnews Bay, Ak., U.S. E7 140
Goodnight, Co., U.S. C4 128
Goodooga, Austl. G6 76
Goodrich, N.D., U.S. G13 124
Good Spirit Lake, l., Sk., Can. C11 124
Goodview, Mn., U.S. G7 118
Goodwater, Al., U.S. D12 122
Goodyear, Az., U.S. J4 132
Goole, Eng., U.K. H12 12
Goolgowi, Austl. I5 76
Goonda, Moz. A11 70
Goondiwindi, Austl. G8 76
Goongarrie, Austl. F4 74
Goose, stm., N.D., U.S. G17 124
Goose Creek, S.C., U.S. C6 116
Goose Island, i., B.C., Can. E2 138
Goose Lake, l., Sk., Can. C6 124
Goose Lake, l., U.S. B5 134
Gooty, India D3 53
Gopālganj, Bngl. G12 54
Gopālganj, India E10 54
Gopichettipālaiyam, India F3 53
Göppingen, Ger. H5 16
Goqên, China F4 36
Go Quao, Viet. H7 48
Góra Kalwaria, Pol. E17 16
Gorakhpur, India E9 54
Goražde, Bos. F5 26
Gorda, Punta, c., Cuba A6 102
Gorda, Punta, c., Nic. E6 102
Gordeevka, Russia H14 10
Gordion, sci., Tur. D15 28
Gordo, Al., U.S. D11 122
Gordon, Ga., U.S. D2 116
Gordon, Wi., U.S. E7 118
Gordon, Lake, res., Austl. o13 77a
Gordon Creek, stm., Ne., U.S. E11 126
Gordon Downs, Austl. C5 74
Gordon Horne Peak, mtn., B.C., Can. E12 138
Gordonsville, Va., U.S. F7 114
Gordonvale, Austl. A5 76
Gore, N.S., Can. E13 110
Goré, Chad F3 62
Gorē, Eth. F7 62
Gore, N.Z. H3 80
Goreda, Indon. F9 44
Goree, Tx., U.S. H9 128
Gore Range, mts., Co., U.S. H6 126
Goreville, Il., U.S. G8 120
Gorgān, Iran B7 56
Gorgona, Isla, i., Col. F2 86
Gorgota, Rom. E13 26
Gorham, Me., U.S. G6 110
Gori, Geor. F6 32
Gorica see Gorizia, Italy E10 22
Goricy, Russia C19 10
Gorinchem, Neth. C14 14
Gorizia (Gorica), Italy E10 22
Gorj, state, Rom. E10 26
Gorkhā, Nepal E10 54
Gorki see Nižnij Novgorod, Russia H21 8
Gorki, Russia A11 32
Gorkiy Reservoir see Gor'kovskoe vodohranilišče, res., Russia H20 8
Gor'kovskoe vodohranilišče (Gorkiy Reservoir), res., Russia H20 8
Gorlice, Pol. G17 16
Görlitz, Ger. E10 16
Gorman, Tx., U.S. B9 130
Gorna Orjahovica, Blg. F12 26
Gornjak, Russia D14 32
Gornji Vakuf, Bos. F4 26
Gorno-Altajsk, Russia D15 32
Gornozavodsk, Russia B13 36
Gornye Ključi, Russia B10 38
Gorodec, Russia H20 8
Gorodec, Russia B12 10
Gorodno, Russia C12 10
Goroka, Pap. N. Gui. b4 79a
Gorong, Pulau, i., Indon. F9 44
Gorongosa, stm., Moz. B12 70
Gorongosa, Serra da, mtn., Moz. D5 68
Gorontalo, Indon. E7 44
Górowo Iławeckie, Pol. B16 16
Gorškovo, Russia F20 10
Görükle, Tur. C11 28
Gorutuba, stm., Braz. H4 88
Gorzów, state, Pol. D11 16
Gorzów Śląski, Pol. E14 16
Gorzów Wielkopolski (Landsberg), Pol. D11 16
Goschen Strait, strt., Pap. N. Gui. c5 79a
Gosen, Japan B12 40
Gosford, Austl. I8 76
Goshen, N.S., Can. E15 110
Goshen, Ca., U.S. G6 134
Goshen, In., U.S. G4 112
Goshen, N.Y., U.S. C11 114
Goshute Lake, l., Nv., U.S. C2 132
Goshute Valley, val., Nv., U.S. C2 132
Goslar, Ger. E6 16
Gosnells, Austl. F3 74
Gossinga, Sudan F5 62
Gostivar, Mac. B3 28
Gostynin, Pol. D15 16
Göta, stm., Swe. G5 8
Gotebo, Ok., U.S. F10 128
Göteborg (Gothenburg), Swe. H4 8
Gotemba, Japan D11 40
Gotești, Mol. C15 26
Gotha, Ger. F6 16
Gothenburg see Göteborg, Swe. H4 8
Gothenburg, Ne., U.S. G12 126
Gothèye, Niger G5 64
Gotland, state, Swe. G8 8
Gotland, i., Swe. H8 8
Gotō-rettō, is., Japan F1 40
Gotska Sandön, i., Swe. G8 8
Gōtsu, Japan D5 40
Göttingen, Ger. E5 16
Goubangzi, China D4 38
Gouda, Neth. B13 14
Goudge, Arg. G3 92
Goudiri, Sen. G2 64
Gough Island, i., St. Hel. K5 60
Gough Lake, l., Ab., Can. D18 138
Gouin, Réservoir, res., Qc., Can. B1 110
Goulais, stm., On., Can. B6 112
Goulburn, Austl. J7 76
Goulburn Islands, is., Austl. B6 74
Goulburn River National Park, p.o.i., Austl. I7 76
Gould, Ar., U.S. D7 122
Goulds, Fl., U.S. K5 116
Goumbou, Mali G3 64
Goundam, Mali F4 64
Goundi, Chad F3 62
Gourbeyre, Guad. h5 105c
Gourdon, Fr. E7 18
Gouré, Niger G7 64
Gourma-Rharous, Mali F4 64
Gournay-en-Bray, Fr. E10 14
Gouro, Chad D3 62
Gouverneur, N.Y., U.S. D14 112
Govan, Sk., Can. C9 124
Gove, Ks., U.S. C8 128
Govena, mys, c., Russia E22 34
Govenlock, Sk., Can. E4 124
Governador Valadares, Braz. J5 88
Govind Ballabh Pant Reservoir see Govind Ballabh Pant Sāgar, res., India F9 54
Govind Ballabh Pant Sāgar, res., India F9 54
Govind Reservoir see Govind Sāgar, res., India C6 54
Govind Sāgar, res., India C6 54
Gowanda, N.Y., U.S. B7 114
Gower, Mo., U.S. E3 120
Gowmal, Afg. B2 54
Gowmal (Gumal), stm., Asia B2 54
Gowrie, Ia., U.S. B3 120
Goya, Arg. D8 92
Goyaves, Îlets à, is., Guad. h5 105c
Göyçay, Azer. A6 56
Goz Beïda, Chad E4 62
Gozdnica, Pol. E11 16
Gozha Co, l., China A5 46
Gozo see Għawdex, i., Malta H8 24
Graaff-Reinet, S. Afr. H7 70
Grabo, C. Iv. I3 64
Grabow, Ger. C7 16
Grabów nad Prosną, Pol. E13 16
Gračac, Cro. F12 22
Gračanica, Bos. E5 26
Grace, Id., U.S. H15 136
Gracefield, Qc., Can. B13 112
Graceville, Fl., U.S. G13 122
Gracias a Dios, Cabo, c., N.A. E6 102
Gradaús, Braz. E7 84
Grado, Italy E10 22
Grado, Spain A4 20
Grad Sofija, state, Blg. G10 26
Grady, Ar., U.S. C7 122
Grady, N.M., U.S. G5 128
Graettinger, Ia., U.S. H4 118
Grafenau, Ger. H9 16
Gräfenhainichen, Ger. E8 16
Grafing bei München, Ger. H7 16
Grafton, Austl. G9 76
Grafton, Il., U.S. F7 120
Grafton, N.D., U.S. F16 124
Grafton, Wi., U.S. E2 112
Grafton, W.V., U.S. E5 114
Grafton, Cape, c., Austl. A5 76
Graham, N.C., U.S. H6 114
Graham, Mount, mtn., Az., U.S. K7 132
Graham Island, i., B.C., Can. E4 106
Graham Island, i., Nu., Can. B7 141
Graham Lake, res., Me., U.S. F8 110
Graham Land, reg., Ant. B34 81
Graham Moore, Cape, c., Nu., Can. A15 106
Grahamstad see Grahamstown, S. Afr. H8 70
Grahamstown, S. Afr. H8 70
Graian Alps, mts., Eur. E3 22
Grain Coast, cst., Lib. I3 64
Grainfield, Ks., U.S. B8 128
Grajaú, Braz. C2 88
Grajaú, stm., Braz. B3 88
Grajewo, Pol. C18 16
Gramada, Blg. F9 26
Grambling, La., U.S. E6 122
Gramilla, Arg. C5 92
Grammichele, Italy G8 24
Grampian Mountains, mts., Scot., U.K. E9 12
Grampians National Park, p.o.i., Austl. K3 76
Gramsh, Alb. D14 24
Granada, Col. F5 86
Granada, Nic. G5 102
Granada, Spain G7 20
Granada, Co., U.S. C6 128
Granada, co., Spain G7 20
Granadella see La Granadella, Spain C11 20
Granbury, Tx., U.S. B10 130
Granbury, Lake, res., Tx., U.S. B10 130
Granby, Qc., Can. E4 110
Granby, Co., U.S. A3 128
Granby, Mo., U.S. H3 120
Granby, stm., B.C., Can. G12 138
Granby, Lake, res., Co., U.S. A2 128
Gran Chaco, reg., S.A. D5 90
Grand, stm., On., Can. E9 112
Grand, stm., Mi., U.S. E3 112
Grand, stm., Oh., U.S. C4 114
Grand, stm., S.D., U.S. B12 126
Grand, stm., U.S. E4 120
Grand, East Fork, stm., U.S. D3 120
Grand, Lac, l., Qc., Can. A12 112
Grand, North Fork, stm., U.S. B10 126
Grand, South Fork, stm., S.D., U.S. B9 126

I·22 Grandas – Gunnison

Name | Map Ref. | Page

Grandas, Spain A4 20
Grand Bahama, i., Bah. B9 96
Grand Ballon, mtn., Fr. G16 14
Grand Bank, Nf., Can. j22 107a
Grand-Bassam, C. Iv. H4 64
Grand Bay, Al., U.S. G10 122
Grand Beach, Mb., Can. D17 124
Grand Bend, On., Can. E8 112
Grand-Bourg, Guad. i6 105c
Grand Caille Point, c., St. Luc. m6 105c
Grand Calumet, Île du, i., Qc., Can. C13 112
Grand Canal see Da Yunhe, can., China E8 42
Grand Canal, can., Ire. H6 12
Grand Cane, La., U.S. E5 122
Grand Canyon, Az., U.S. G4 132
Grand Canyon, p., Az., U.S. G4 132
Grand Canyon National Park, p.o.i., Az., U.S. G4 132
Grand Canyon-Parashant National Monument, p.o.i., Az., U.S. G3 132
Grand Case, Guad. A1 105a
Grand Cayman, i., Cay. Is. C7 102
Grand Cess, Lib. I3 64
Grand Chenier, La., U.S. H6 122
Grand Coulee Dam, dam, Wa., U.S. C8 136
Grand Cul de Sac, Guad. B2 105a
Grande, stm., Arg. A5 92
Grande, stm., Arg. H3 92
Grande, stm., Bol. C4 90
Grande, stm., Braz. F4 88
Grande, stm., Braz. C7 90
Grande, stm., S.A. J3 90
Grande, stm., Ven. C11 86
Grande, Arroyo, stm., Ur. F9 92
Grande, Bahía, b., Arg. J3 90
Grande, Boca, mth., Ven. C11 86
Grande, Cerro, mtn., Mex. G2 130
Grande, Cerro, mtn., Mex. E7 100
Grande, Ilha, i., Braz. L3 88
Grande, Ilha, i., Braz. A11 92
Grande, Ponta, c., Braz. I6 88
Grande, Rio see Rio Grande, stm., N.A. H13 98
Grande, Serra, mts., Braz. D5 88
Grande-Anse, Qc., Can. C4 110
Grande Cache, Ab., Can. C11 138
Grande Cayemite, i., Haiti C11 102
Grande de Manacapuru, Lago, l., Braz. I11 86
Grande de Matagalpa, stm., Nic. F6 102
Grande de Santiago, stm., Mex. E6 100
Grande do Gurupá, Ilha, i., Braz. D7 84
Grande-Entrée, Qc., Can. C15 110
Grande Prairie, Ab., Can. A12 138
Grand Erg de Bilma, des., Niger F7 64
Grand Erg Occidental, des., Alg. C5 64
Grand Erg Oriental, des., Alg. C6 64
Grande-Rivière, Qc., Can. B12 110
Grande Rivière, La, stm., Qc., Can. E15 106
Grande Ronde, stm., U.S. E9 136
Grandes, Salinas, pl., Arg. A4 92
Grandes, Salinas, pl., Arg. D5 92
Grand-Étang, N.S., Can. D15 110
Grande-Terre, i., Guad. h6 105c
Grande Vigie, Pointe de la, c., Guad. g6 105c
Grand Falls, N.B., Can. C9 110
Grandfather Mountain, mtn., N.C., U.S. H4 114
Grandfield, Ok., U.S. G10 128
Grand Forks, B.C., Can. G12 138
Grand Forks, N.D., U.S. D1 118
Grand Haven, Mi., U.S. E3 112
Grandin, Lac, l., N.T., Can. C7 106
Grand Island, Ne., U.S. G14 126
Grand Island, i., Mi., U.S. B3 112
Grand Isle, La., U.S. H9 122
Grand Junction, Co., U.S. D8 132
Grand Junction, Ia., U.S. B3 120
Grand Lake, Co., U.S. A3 128
Grand Lake, l., N.B., Can. D11 110
Grand Lake, l., N.A. E9 110
Grand Lake, l., La., U.S. H6 122
Grand Lake, l., Mi., U.S. C6 112
Grand Lake, res., Oh., U.S. D1 114
Grand Ledge, Mi., U.S. B1 114
Grand Manan, N.B., Can. F10 110
Grand Manan Island, i., N.B., Can. F10 110
Grand Marais, Mi., U.S. B4 112
Grand Meadow, Mn., U.S. H6 118
Grand-Mère, Qc., Can. D4 110
Grand Morin, stm., Fr. F12 14
Grand Portage, Mn., U.S. D9 118
Grand Portage National Monument, p.o.i., Mn., U.S. C9 118
Grand Prairie, Tx., U.S. B11 130
Grand Rapids, Mb., Can. A14 124
Grand Rapids, Mi., U.S. F4 112
Grand Rapids, Mn., U.S. D5 118
Grand Rhône, stm., Fr. F10 18
Grand Saline, Tx., U.S. E3 122
Grand Staircase – Escalante National Monument, p.o.i., Ut., U.S. F5 132
Grand Teton, mtn., Wy., U.S. G16 136
Grand Teton National Park, p.o.i., Wy., U.S. F16 136
Grand Tower, Il., U.S. G8 120
Grand Traverse Bay, b., Mi., U.S. C4 112
Grand Turk, T./C. Is. B12 102
Grandview, Mb., Can. C13 124
Grandview, Mo., U.S. F3 120
Grandview, Tx., U.S. B10 130
Grandview, Wa., U.S. D6 136
Grand View, Wi., U.S. E7 118
Grand Wash Cliffs, clf., Az., U.S. H3 132
Grañén, Spain C10 20
Graneros, Chile G2 92
Granger, Wa., U.S. D6 136
Granger, Wy., U.S. B6 132
Granger Draw, stm., Tx., U.S. D7 130
Granger Lake, res., Tx., U.S. D10 130
Granges see Grenchen, Switz. C4 22
Grangeville, Id., U.S. E10 136
Granite City, Il., U.S. F7 120
Granite Falls, Mn., U.S. G3 118
Granite Falls, N.C., U.S. I4 114
Granite Falls, Wa., U.S. B5 136
Granite Pass, p., Wy., U.S. C5 126
Granite Peak, Austl. E4 74
Granite Peak, mtn., Mt., U.S. E17 136
Granite Peak, mtn., Mt., U.S. E14 136
Granite Peak, mtn., Nv., U.S. C6 134
Graniteville, S.C., U.S. C4 116
Granitola, Capo, c., Italy G6 24
Granja, Braz. B5 88
Gran Laguna Salada, l., Arg. H3 90
Gränna, Swe. G6 8
Granollers, Spain C13 20
Gran Paradiso, mtn., Italy E4 22
Gran Paradiso, Parco Nazionale del, p.o.i., Italy E4 22
Gran Rio, stm., Sur. C6 84
Gran Sasso d'Italia, mts., Italy H10 22
Gransee, Ger. C9 16
Grant, Fl., U.S. I5 116
Grant, Mi., U.S. E4 112
Grant City, Mo., U.S. D3 120
Grantham, Eng., U.K. I12 12
Grantley Adams International Airport, Barb. n9 105d
Grant Park, Il., U.S. C10 120
Grant Point, c., Nu., Can. B11 106
Grants, N.M., U.S. H9 132
Grantsburg, Wi., U.S. F6 118
Grants Pass, Or., U.S. A2 134
Grant-Suttie Bay, b., Nu., Can. B15 106
Grantsville, W.V., U.S. F4 114
Grantville, Ga., U.S. D14 122
Granum, Ab., Can. G17 138
Granville, Fr. F7 14
Granville, Il., U.S. J9 118
Granville, N.D., U.S. F13 124
Granville, W.V., U.S. E5 114
Granville Lake, l., Mb., Can. D10 106
Granvin, Nor. F2 8
Grão Mogol, Braz. I4 88
Grapeland, Tx., U.S. F3 122
Grapevine Lake, res., Tx., U.S. B10 130
Grapevine Peak, mtn., Nv., U.S. G8 134
Gras, Lac de, l., N.T., Can. C8 106
Gräsö, i., Swe. F8 8
Grasonville, Md., U.S. F9 114
Grass, stm., N.Y., U.S. D15 112
Grass Creek, Wy., U.S. D4 126
Grasse, Fr. F12 18
Grassflat, Pa., U.S. D7 114
Grasslands National Park, p.o.i., Sk., Can. E6 124
Grass Valley, Ca., U.S. D4 134
Grass Valley, Or., U.S. E6 136
Grassy, Austl. n12 77a
Grassy Plains, B.C., Can. C4 138
Graulhet, Fr. F7 18
Gravelbourg, Sk., Can. E7 124
Gravelines, Fr. D11 14
Gravelotte, S. Afr. C10 70
Gravenhage, 's- see 's-Gravenhage, Neth. B12 14
Gravenhurst, On., Can. D10 112
Gravesend, Eng., U.K. J13 12
Gravette, Ar., U.S. H3 120
Gravina in Puglia, Italy D10 24
Gray, Fr. G14 14
Gray, Ga., U.S. D2 116
Grayback Mountain, mtn., Or., U.S. A2 134
Grayling, Mi., U.S. D5 112
Grays, Eng., U.K. J13 12
Grays Harbor, b., Wa., U.S. D2 136
Grays Lake, sw., Id., U.S. G15 136
Grayson, Sk., Can. D11 124
Grayson, Al., U.S. C11 122
Grayson, La., U.S. E6 122
Grays Peak, mtn., Co., U.S. B3 128
Graysville, Tn., U.S. B13 122
Grayville, Il., U.S. F9 120
Graz, Aus. C12 22
Grdelica, Serb. G9 26
Great Artesian Basin, bas., Austl. E3 76
Great Australian Bight, b., Austl. F5 74
Great Barrier Island, i., N.Z. C6 80
Great Barrier Reef, rf., Austl. C9 74
Great Basin, bas., U.S. C4 108
Great Basin National Park, p.o.i., Nv., U.S. E2 132
Great Bear, stm., N.T., Can. B6 106
Great Bear Lake, l., N.T., Can. B6 106
Great Beaver Lake, l., B.C., Can. B7 138
Great Belt see Storebælt, strt., Den. I4 8
Great Bend, Ks., U.S. C10 128
Great Bitter Lake see Murrat el-Kubra, Buheirat, l., Egypt H3 58
Great Britain see United Kingdom, ctry., Eur. D8 6
Great Camanoe, i., Br. Vir. Is. e8 104b
Great Central, B.C., Can. G6 138
Great Channel, strt., Asia G7 46
Great Dismal Swamp, sw., U.S. H9 114
Great Divide Basin, bas., Wy., U.S. F4 126
Great Dividing Range, mts., Austl. C8 74
Great Driffield, Eng., U.K. G12 12
Greater Antilles, is., N.A. H15 94
Greater Khingan Range see Da Hinggan Ling, mts., China B9 36
Greater Sunda Islands, is., Asia F4 44
Great Exuma, i., Bah. C9 96
Great Falls, Mb., Can. D18 124
Great Falls, Mt., U.S. C15 136
Great Falls, S.C., U.S. B4 116
Great Himalayan National Park, p.o.i., India C6 54
Great Inagua, i., Bah. B11 102
Great Indian Desert (Thar Desert), des., Asia D3 54
Great Karroo (Groot Karroo), plat., S. Afr. H6 70
Great La Cloche Island, i., On., Can. B8 112
Great Lake, res., Austl. n13 77a
Great Limpopo Transfrontier Park, p.o.i., Afr. C10 70
Great Malvern, Eng., U.K. I10 12
Great Miami, stm., U.S. E13 120
Great Namaqualand (Groot Namaland), hist. reg., Nmb. D3 70
Great Nicobar, i., India G7 46
Great Ouse, stm., Eng., U.K. I13 12
Great Palm Island, i., Austl. B6 76
Great Pee Dee, stm., S.C., U.S. C6 116
Great Plain of the Koukdjuak, pl., Nu., Can. B16 106
Great Plains, pl., N.A. C4 108
Great Point, c., Ma., U.S. C15 114
Great Ruaha, stm., Tan. F7 66
Great Sacandaga Lake, res., N.Y., U.S. G2 110
Great Sale Cay, i., Bah. I7 116
Great Salt Lake, l., Ut., U.S. B4 132
Great Salt Lake Desert, des., Ut., U.S. C3 132
Great Salt Plains Lake, res., Ok., U.S. E10 128
Great Sand Dunes National Monument, p.o.i., Co., U.S. D3 128
Great Sand Hills, hills, Sk., Can. D4 124
Great Sandy Desert, des., Austl. D4 74
Great Sandy National Park, p.o.i., Austl. E9 76
Great Scarcies, stm., Afr. H2 64
Great Sea Reef, rf., Fiji p19 79e
Great Slave Lake, l., N.T., Can. C8 106
Great Smoky Mountains, mts., U.S. A2 116
Great Smoky Mountains National Park, p.o.i., U.S. A2 116
Great Tenasserim, stm., Mya. F4 48
Great Thatch Island, i., Br. Vir. Is. e7 104b
Great Tobago, i., Br. Vir. Is. e7 104b
Great Victoria Desert, des., Austl. E5 74
Great Wall see Chang Cheng, misc. cult., China D6 36
Great Yarmouth, Eng., U.K. I14 12
Gréboun, mtn., Niger F6 64
Grecco, Ur. F9 92
Gredos, Sierra de, mts., Spain D5 20
Greece, N.Y., U.S. E12 112
Greece, ctry., Eur. H13 6
Greeley, Co., U.S. G8 126
Greeley, Ks., U.S. F2 120
Greeleyville, S.C., U.S. C6 116
Greely Fiord, b., Nu., Can. A9 141
Green, stm., Il., U.S. C8 120
Green, stm., Ky., U.S. G10 120
Green, stm., N.D., U.S. G17 136
Green, stm., Wa., U.S. C5 136
Green, stm., U.S. E7 132
Green Bay, Wi., U.S. D1 112
Green Bay, b., U.S. D2 112
Greenbrier, Ar., U.S. B6 122
Green Brier, Tn., U.S. H11 120
Greenbrier, stm., W.V., U.S. F5 114
Greenburg, La., U.S. G8 122
Greenbush, Mn., U.S. C2 118
Greencastle, In., U.S. E10 120
Greencastle, Pa., U.S. E8 114
Green Cove Springs, Fl., U.S. G4 116
Greendale, In., U.S. E13 120
Greene, Ia., U.S. B5 120
Greeneville, Tn., U.S. H3 114
Greenfield, Ca., U.S. B13 114
Greenfield, Ia., U.S. C3 120
Greenfield, Il., U.S. E7 120
Greenfield, Ma., U.S. H4 110
Greenfield, Mo., U.S. G4 120
Greenfield, Oh., U.S. E2 114
Greenfield, Ok., U.S. F10 128
Green Forest, Ar., U.S. H4 120
Green Island Bay, b., Phil. E2 52
Green Islands, is., Pap. N. Gui. D6 72
Green Lake, Wi., U.S. H10 118
Green Lake, l., B.C., Can. E9 138
Green Lake, l., Wi., U.S. H9 118
Greenland, Ar., U.S. I3 120
Greenland, dep., N.A. B19 94
Greenland Basin, unds. A14 144
Greenland Sea, s. B21 94
Greenleaf, Ks., U.S. B11 128
Green Lookout Mountain, mtn., Wa., U.S. E4 136
Green Mountains, mts., N.A. G4 110
Greenock, Scot., U.K. F8 12
Greenore Point, c., Ire. I6 12
Greenough, stm., Austl. E3 74
Greenport, N.Y., U.S. C13 114
Green River, Pap. N. Gui. a3 79a
Green River, Ut., U.S. D7 132
Green River, Wy., U.S. B7 132
Green River Lake, res., Ky., U.S. G12 120
Greensboro, Fl., U.S. G14 122
Greensboro, Ga., U.S. C2 116
Greensboro, N.C., U.S. H6 114
Greensburg, In., U.S. E12 120
Greensburg, Ks., U.S. D9 128
Greensburg, Pa., U.S. D6 114
Green Springs, Oh., U.S. C2 114
Green Swamp, sw., N.C., U.S. B7 116
Greentown, In., U.S. H4 112
Greenup, Il., U.S. E9 120
Greenup, Ky., U.S. F3 114
Greenvale, Austl. B5 76
Green Valley, Az., U.S. L6 132
Greenville, Lib. H3 64
Greenville, Al., U.S. F12 122
Greenville, Ga., U.S. D14 122
Greenville, Il., U.S. F8 120
Greenville, Ky., U.S. G10 120
Greenville, Me., U.S. E7 110
Greenville, Mi., U.S. E4 112
Greenville, Mo., U.S. G7 120
Greenville, Ms., U.S. D7 122
Greenville, N.C., U.S. A8 116
Greenville, Oh., U.S. D1 114
Greenville, Pa., U.S. C5 114
Greenville, S.C., U.S. B3 116
Greenville, Tx., U.S. D2 122
Greenwater Lake, l., On., Can. C8 118
Greenwich, Ct., U.S. C12 114
Greenwich, Oh., U.S. C3 114
Greenwood, B.C., Can. G12 138
Greenwood, Ar., U.S. B4 122
Greenwood, In., U.S. E11 120
Greenwood, Ms., U.S. D8 122
Greenwood, S.C., U.S. B3 116
Greenwood, Wi., U.S. G8 118
Greenwood, Lake, res., S.C., U.S. B4 116
Greer, S.C., U.S. B3 116
Greers Ferry Lake, res., Ar., U.S. B6 122
Greeson, Lake, res., Ar., U.S. C5 122
Gregório, stm., Braz. E3 84
Gregory, Mi., U.S. B1 114
Gregory, S.D., U.S. D13 126
Gregory, Tx., U.S. G10 130
Gregory, stm., Austl. C7 74
Gregory, Lake, l., Austl. E3 74
Gregory, Lake, l., Austl. G2 76
Gregory, Lake, l., Austl. D5 74
Gregory Range, mts., Austl. B4 76
Greifswald, Ger. B9 16
Greifswalder Bodden, b., Ger. B9 16
Greiz, Ger. F8 16
Gremiha, Russia B18 8
Grenaa, Den. H4 8
Grenada, Ms., U.S. D9 122
Grenada, ctry., N.A. q11 105e
Grenada Lake, res., Ms., U.S. D9 122
Grenadines, is., N.A. p11 105e
Grenchen, Switz. C4 22
Grenen, c., Den. H4 8
Grenfell, Austl. I7 76
Grenoble, Fr. D11 18
Grenola, Ks., U.S. D12 128
Grenora, N.D., U.S. F10 124
Grenville, Gren. q10 105e
Gresham, Or., U.S. E4 136
Gresik, Indon. G8 50
Gresik, Indon. E3 50
Gressåmoen Nasjonalpark, p.o.i., Nor. D5 8
Gretna, Mb., Can. E16 124
Gretna, La., U.S. H8 122
Gretna, Va., U.S. H6 114
Gretna Green, Scot., U.K. F9 12
Greven, Ger. D3 16
Grevená, Grc. C4 28
Grevenbroich, Ger. E2 16
Grevesmühlen, Ger. C7 16
Greybull, stm., Wy., U.S. C4 126
Grey Eagle, Mn., U.S. F4 118
Grey Islands, is., Nf., Can. i22 107a
Greylock, Mount, mtn., Ma., U.S. B12 114
Greymouth, N.Z. F4 80
Grey Range, mts., Austl. F4 76
Greytown, S. Afr. F10 70
Gribbel Island, i., B.C., Can. C1 138
Gribingui, stm., C.A.R. C3 66
Gridley, Ca., U.S. D4 134
Gridley, Il., U.S. D9 120
Griesheim, Ger. G4 16
Griffin, Sk., Can. E10 124
Griffin, Ga., U.S. C1 116
Griffin, Lake, l., Fl., U.S. H4 116
Griffith, Austl. J5 76
Griggsville, Il., U.S. E7 120
Grignols, Fr. E5 18
Grigoriopol, Mol. B16 26
Grijalva (Cuilco), stm., N.A. G12 100
Grim, Cape, c., Austl. n12 77a
Grimari, C.A.R. C3 66
Grimma, Ger. E8 16
Grimmen, Ger. B9 16
Grimsby, On., Can. E10 112
Grimsby, Eng., U.K. H12 12
Grimsel Pass, p., Switz. D5 22
Grímsey, i., Ice. j30 8a
Grimshaw, Ab., Can. D7 106
Grimstad, Nor. G3 8
Grímsvötn, vol., Ice. k31 8a
Grindelwald, Switz. D5 22
Grinnell, Ia., U.S. C5 120
Grinnell Peninsula, pen., Nu., Can. B7 141
Grintavec, mtn., Slvn. D11 22
Griqualand East, hist. reg., S. Afr. G9 70
Griqualand West, hist. reg., S. Afr. F6 70
Grise Fiord see Ausuittuq, Nu., Can. B9 141
Gris-Nez, Cap, c., Fr. D10 14
Griswold, Mb., Can. E13 124
Griswold, Ia., U.S. C2 120
Grizzly Bear Mountain, mtn., N.T., Can. B6 106
Grizzly Mountain, mtn., Id., U.S. C10 136
Grjadcy, Russia D14 10
Grjazovec, Russia G18 8
Groaíras, Braz. B5 88
Groblersdal, S. Afr. D9 70
Grodków, Pol. F13 16
Grodzisk Mazowiecki, Pol. D16 16
Groen, stm., S. Afr. G6 70
Groesbeck, Tx., U.S. F2 122
Grofa, hora, mtn., Ukr. A10 26
Groix, Fr. G5 14
Groix, Île de, i., Fr. G5 14
Grójec, Pol. E16 16
Grombalia, Tun. H4 24
Gronau, Ger. D3 16
Grong, Nor. D5 8
Groningen, Neth. A15 14
Groningen, Sur. B6 84
Groom, Tx., U.S. F7 128
Groot, stm., S. Afr. H7 70
Groot-Berg, stm., S. Afr. H4 70
Groot-Brakrivier, S. Afr. I6 70
Grootdraaidam, res., S. Afr. E9 70
Groote Eylandt, i., Austl. B7 74
Grootfontein, Nmb. D2 68
Grootgeluk, S. Afr. C8 70
Groot Karasberge, mts., Nmb. E4 70
Groot Karroo see Great Karroo, plat., S. Afr. H6 70
Groot-Kei, stm., S. Afr. H9 70
Groot Laagte, stm., Afr. B5 70
Groot Namaland see Great Namaqualand, hist. reg., Nmb. D3 70
Groot-Swartberge, mts., S. Afr. H6 70
Groot-Vis, stm., S. Afr. H8 70
Grootvloer, pl., S. Afr. F5 70
Gros Islet, St. Luc. I7 105c
Gros-Morne, Mart. k6 105c
Gros Morne, mtn., Nf., Can. j22 107a
Gros Piton, vol., St. Luc. m6 105c
Grossenhain, Ger. E9 16
Grosse Pointe, Mi., U.S. B3 114
Grosse Pointe, c., Guad. h6 105c
Grosser Beerberg, mtn., Ger. F6 16
Grosseto, Italy H7 22
Gross-Gerau, Ger. G4 16
Grossglockner, mtn., Aus. C9 22
Grossos, Braz. C7 88
Grossvenediger, mtn., Aus. C9 22
Groton, N.Y., U.S. F13 112
Groton, S.D., U.S. B14 126
Grottaglie, Italy D11 24
Grottammare, Italy G11 22
Grottoes, Va., U.S. F7 114
Grouard Mission, Ab., Can. D7 106
Groundhog, stm., On., Can. F14 106
Grove City, Mn., U.S. F4 118
Grove City, Oh., U.S. E2 114
Grove City, Pa., U.S. C5 114
Grove Hill, Al., U.S. F11 122
Grove Mountains, mts., Ant. C12 81
Grover City, Ca., U.S. H5 134
Groves, Tx., U.S. H5 122
Groveton, N.H., U.S. F5 110
Groveton, Tx., U.S. F3 122
Grovetown, Ga., U.S. C3 116
Growa Point, c., Lib. I3 64
Growler Peak, mtn., Az., U.S. K3 132
Groznyj, Russia F7 32
Grubišno Polje, Cro. E14 22
Grudziądz, Pol. C14 16
Grulla, Tx., U.S. H9 130
Grumo Appula, Italy D10 24
Grundy, Va., U.S. G3 114
Grundy Center, Ia., U.S. B5 120
Grušino, Russia G21 8
Gruver, Tx., U.S. E7 128
Gruznovka, Russia E10 34
Gryfice, Pol. C11 16
Gryfino, Pol. C10 16
Grytviken, S. Geor. J9 90
Guacanayabo, Golfo de, b., Cuba B9 102
Guacara, Ven. B7 86
Guacarí, Col. F3 86
Gu Achi, Az., U.S. K4 132
Guachiría, stm., Col. E6 86
Guachochi, Mex. B5 100
Guadajoz, stm., Spain G6 20
Guadalajara, Mex. E7 100
Guadalajara, Spain D7 20
Guadalajara, co., Spain D8 20
Guadalcanal, state, Sol. Is. f8 79b
Guadalcanal, i., Sol. Is. e9 79b
Guadalete, stm., Spain H4 20
Guadalhorce, stm., Spain G6 20
Guadalimar, stm., Spain F7 20
Guadalmena, stm., Spain F8 20
Guadalope, stm., Spain D10 20
Guadalquivir, stm., Spain H4 20
Guadalquivir, Marismas del, sw., Spain G4 20
Guadalupe, Mex. D7 100
Guadalupe, Mex. C8 100
Guadalupe, Ca., U.S. I5 134
Guadalupe, stm., Tx., U.S. F11 130
Guadalupe, Isla, i., Mex. G3 98
Guadalupe Bravos, Mex. C1 130
Guadalupe Mountains, mts., U.S. B3 130
Guadalupe Mountains National Park, p.o.i., Tx., U.S. C3 130
Guadalupe Peak, mtn., Tx., U.S. C3 130
Guadalupe Victoria, Mex. C6 100
Guadalupe Victoria, Mex. G6 130
Guadarrama, Puerto de, p., Spain D6 20
Guadarrama, Sierra de, mts., Spain D6 20
Guadeloupe, dep., N.A. h15 96a
Guadeloupe Passage, strt., N.A. g5 105c
Guadiana, stm., Eur. G3 20
Guadiana Menor, stm., Spain G7 20
Guadiato, stm., Spain F5 20
Guadiela, stm., Spain D8 20
Guadix, Spain G7 20
Guafo, Isla, i., Chile H1 90
Guaíba, Braz. E12 92
Guaíba, est., Braz. E12 92
Guaimaca, Hond. E4 102
Guainía, state, Col. F7 86
Guainía, stm., S.A. F8 86
Guaiquinima, Cerro, mtn., Ven. E10 86
Guaíra, Braz. B10 92
Guaíra, Braz. K1 88
Guairá, state, Para. B9 92
Guairá, Salto del (Sete Quedas, Salto das), wtfl., S.A. B10 92
Guáitara, stm., Col. G3 86
Guaitecas, Islas, is., Chile H2 90
Guajaba, Cayo, i., Cuba B9 102
Guajará-Açu, Braz. A1 88
Guajará-Mirim, Braz. F4 84
Guaje, Laguna del, l., Mex. B7 100
Gualaca, Pan. H6 102
Gualaceo, Ec. I2 86
Gualala, Ca., U.S. E2 134
Gualdo Tadino, Italy G9 22
Gualeguay, Arg. F8 92
Gualeguay, stm., Arg. F8 92
Gualeguaychú, Arg. F8 92
Gualicho, Salina del, pl., Arg. H4 90
Guam, dep., Oc. j10 78c
Guamá, stm., Braz. A1 88
Guamal, Col. F5 86
Guamal, Col. C4 86
Guaminí, Arg. H6 92
Guam International Airport, Guam i10 78c
Guamote, Ec. H2 86
Guamúchil, Mex. C4 100
Guamués, stm., Col. G3 86
Gua Musang, Malay. J5 48
Guanacaste, Cordillera de, mts., C.R. G5 102
Guanaceví, Mex. C6 100
Guanahacabibes, Golfo de, b., Cuba A5 102
Guana Island, i., Br. Vir. Is. e8 104b
Guanaja, Hond. D5 102
Guanaja, Isla de, i., Hond. D5 102
Guanajuato, Mex. E8 100
Guanajuato, state, Mex. E8 100
Guanambi, Braz. H4 88
Guanaparo, Caño, stm., Ven. C7 86
Guañape, Islas, is., Peru E2 84
Guanare, Ven. C7 86
Guanare, stm., Ven. C7 86
Guanarito, Ven. C7 86
Guandacol, Arg. D3 92
Guandu, China I5 42
Guane, Cuba A5 102
Guang'an, China F2 42
Guangchang, China H7 42
Guangde, China F8 42
Guangdong, state, China J6 42
Guangfeng, China G8 42
Guangji, China G6 42
Guangling, China B6 42
Guangming Ding, mtn., China F7 42
Guangnan, China G5 36
Guangxi, state, China G6 36
Guangxi Zhuangzu Zizhiqu see Guangxi, state, China G6 36
Guangyuan, China E1 42
Guangze, China H7 42
Guangzhou (Canton), China J5 42
Guanhães, Braz. J4 88
Guánica, P.R. C2 104a
Guanipa, stm., Ven. C10 86
Guanta, Ven. B9 86
Guantánamo, Cuba B10 102
Guantao, China C6 42
Guanting Shuiku, res., China A6 42
Guanxian, China E5 36
Guanxian, China C6 42
Guanyun, China D8 42
Guapí, Col. F3 86
Guapiara, Braz. B13 92
Guápiles, C.R. G6 102
Guaporé, Braz. D11 92
Guaporé (Iténez), stm., S.A. F5 84
Guaqui, Bol. C3 90
Guará, stm., Braz. G3 88
Guarabira, Braz. D8 88
Guaraciaba do Norte, Braz. C5 88
Guaraciana, Braz. I4 88
Guaranda, Ec. H2 86
Guaraniaçu, Braz. B11 92
Guarapari, Braz. K5 88
Guarapuava, Braz. B12 92
Guaraqueçaba, Braz. B13 92
Guaratinguetá, Braz. L3 88
Guaratuba, Braz. B13 92
Guarda, Port. D3 20
Guarda, state, Port. D3 20
Guardafui, Cape see Gwardafuy, Gees, c., Som. B10 66
Guardia Escolta, Arg. D6 92
Guardiagrele, Italy H11 22
Guardia Mitre, Arg. H4 90
Guardo, Spain B6 20
Guareña, Spain F4 20
Guarenas, Ven. B8 86
Guárico, state, Ven. C8 86
Guárico, stm., Ven. C8 86
Guárico, Embalse del, l., Ven. C8 86
Guariquito, stm., Ven. C8 86
Guarulhos, Braz. L2 88
Guasare, stm., Ven. B5 86
Guasave, Mex. C4 100
Guasdualito, Ven. D6 86
Guasipati, Ven. D11 86
Guastalla, Italy F7 22
Guatemala, Guat. E2 102
Guatemala, ctry., N.A. E2 102
Guatemala Basin, unds. H29 142
Guateque, Col. E5 86
Guatimozín, Arg. F6 92
Guatopo, Parque Nacional, p.o.i., Ven. B8 86
Guatuaro Point, c., Trin. s13 105f
Guaviare, state, Col. G5 86
Guaviare, stm., Col. E8 86
Guaxupé, Braz. K2 88
Guayabal, Cuba B9 102
Guayabal, Ven. D8 86
Guayabero, stm., Col. F5 86
Guayacán, Chile D2 92
Guayaguayare, Trin. s12 105f
Guayama, P.R. C3 104a
Guayana see Guyana, ctry., S.A. C6 84
Guayana, Macizo de (Guiana Highlands), mts., S.A. E10 86
Guayaneco, Archipiélago, is., Chile I1 90
Guayanilla, P.R. B2 104a
Guayape, stm., Hond. E4 102
Guayapo, stm., Ven. E8 86
Guayaquil, Ec. I1 86
Guayaquil, Golfo de, b., S.A. D1 84
Guayaramerín, Bol. B3 90
Guayas, state, Ec. H1 86
Guayas, stm., Ec. I2 86
Guaymallén, Arg. F3 92
Guaymas, Mex. B3 100
Guaynabo, P.R. B3 104a
Guayquiraró, stm., Arg. E8 92
Guazapares, Mex. B4 100
Guazárachi, Mex. B5 100
Guba, D.R.C. G5 66
Gubaha, Russia C9 32
Gûbâl, Madîq (Jubal, Strait of), strt., Egypt K4 58
Gubavica, wtfl., Cro. G13 22
Gubbi, India E3 53
Gubbio, Italy G9 22
Guben, Ger. E10 16
Gubin, Pol. E10 16
Gucheng, China E4 42
Gūdalūr, India G3 53
Gúdar, Sierra de, mts., Spain D10 20
Gudauta, Geor. F6 32
Gudermes, Russia F7 32
Gudivāda, India C5 53
Gudiyāttam, India E4 53
Güdül, Tur. C15 28
Gūdūr, India D4 53
Guebwiller, Fr. G16 14
Güejar, stm., Col. F5 86
Guékédou, Gui. H2 64
Guélengdeng, Chad E3 62
Guelma, Alg. B6 64
Guelmime, Mor. D2 64
Guelph, On., Can. E9 112
Guérande, Fr. G6 14
Guercif, Mor. C4 64
Guerdjoumane, Djebel, mtn., Alg. H13 20
Güere, stm., Ven. C9 86
Guéréda, Chad E4 62
Guéret, Fr. C7 18
Guerla Mandata Shan, mtn., China C8 54
Guernesey see Guernsey, dep., Eur. L10 12
Guerneville, Ca., U.S. E3 134
Guernica see Gernika, Spain A8 20
Guernica y Luno see Gernika, Spain A8 20
Guernsey, dep., Eur. E6 14
Guernsey, i., Guern. E6 14
Guerrero, Mex. A5 100
Guerrero, Mex. F7 130
Guerrero, state, Mex. G8 100
Guerrero Negro, Mex. B1 100
Gueydan, La., U.S. G6 122
Guga, Russia F16 34
Gugē, mtn., Eth. F7 62
Guguan, i., N. Mar. Is. B5 72
Gui, stm., China I4 42
Guiana Basin, unds. G9 144
Guiana Highlands (Guayana, Macizo de), mts., S.A. E10 86
Güicán, Col. D5 86
Guichi, China F7 42
Guide, China D5 36
Guidimouni, Niger G6 64
Guiding, China H2 42
Guier, Lac de, l., Sen. F1 64
Guijuelo, Spain D5 20
Guilarte, Monte, mtn., P.R. B2 104a
Guildford, Eng., U.K. J12 12
Guildhall, Vt., U.S. F5 110
Guilford, Me., U.S. E7 110
Guilin, China I4 42
Guillaume-Delisle, Lac, l., Qc., Can. D15 106
Guillestre, Fr. E12 18
Guimarães, Braz. B3 88
Guimaras Island, i., Phil. E4 52
Guimba, Phil. C3 52
Guin, Al., U.S. D11 122
Guinan, China D5 36
Guindulman, Phil. F5 52
Guinea, ctry., Afr. G2 64
Guinea, Gulf of, b., Afr. I6 64
Guinea Basin, unds. H13 144
Guinea-Bissau, ctry., Afr. G1 64
Güines, Cuba A7 102
Guingamp, Fr. F5 14
Güinope, Hond. F4 102
Guiping, China J4 42
Guipúzcoa see Gipuzkoako, co., Spain A8 20
Guiratinga, Braz. G7 84
Güiria, Ven. B10 86
Guitry, C. Iv. H3 64
Guiuan, Phil. E5 52
Guixian, China J3 42
Guiyang, China I5 42
Guiyang, China H2 42
Güiza, stm., Col. G2 86
Guizhou, state, China F6 36
Gujarāt, state, India G3 54
Gūjar Khān, Pak. B4 54
Gujrānwāla, Pak. B4 54
Gujrāt, Pak. B4 54
Gukou, China H8 42
Gulargambone, Austl. H7 76
Gulbarga, India C3 53
Gulbene, Lat. C9 10
Güldüzü, Tur. B8 58
Guledagudda, India C2 53
Gülek Boğazı, p., Tur. A5 58
Gulf Islands National Seashore, p.o.i., U.S. G10 122
Gulfport, Ms., U.S. G9 122
Gulf Shores, Al., U.S. G11 122
Gulgong, Austl. I7 76
Gulian, China F13 34
Gulistan, Uzb. F11 32
Gulkana, Ak., U.S. D10 140
Gull, stm., On., Can. B9 118
Gullfoss, wtfl., Ice. k29 8a
Gull Lake, Sk., Can. D5 124
Gull Lake, l., Ab., Can. D17 138
Gull Lake, l., Mn., U.S. E4 118
Güllük, Tur. F10 28
Güllük Körfezi, b., Tur. F10 28
Gülpınar, Tur. D9 28
Gulu, Ug. D6 66
Guluogongba, China A10 54
Gumaca, Phil. D4 52
Gumal (Gowmal), stm., Asia B2 54
Gumbalie, Austl. G5 76
Gumdag, Turkmen. B7 56
Gumel, Nig. G6 64
Gumla, India G10 54
Gumma, state, Japan C11 40
Gummersbach, Ger. E3 16
Gümüşhane, Tur. A4 56
Gümüşsu, Tur. E12 28
Guna, India F6 54
Gundagai, Austl. J7 76
Gundji, D.R.C. D4 66
Gundlupet, India F3 53
Gündoğdu, Tur. C9 28
Güney, Tur. E12 28
Gungu, D.R.C. F3 66
Gunmi, Nig. G6 64
Gunnar, Sk., Can. D9 106
Gunnarn, Swe. D7 8
Gunnbjørn Fjeld, mtn., Grnld. D19 141
Gunnedah, Austl. H7 76
Gunnison, Ut., U.S. D5 132
Gunnison, stm., Co., U.S. E8 132

Name	Map Ref.	Page

Gunong Mulu National Park, p.o.i., Malay. A9 50
Gun Point, c., Gren. p11 105e
Gunpowder Creek, stm., Austl. B2 76
Gunsan see Kunsan, Kor., S. F7 38
Guntakal, India. D3 53
Guntersville, Al., U.S. C12 122
Guntersville Dam, dam, Al., U.S. C12 122
Guntersville Lake, res., Al., U.S. C12 122
Guntür, India C5 53
Gunungkencana, Indon. G4 50
Gunungsahilan, Indon. C2 50
Gunungsitoli, Indon. L3 48
Gunupur, India B6 53
Günzburg, Ger. H6 16
Gunzenhausen, Ger. G6 16
Guo, stm., China. E7 42
Guoyangzhen, China. E7 42
Gupis, Pak. B11 56
Gurabo, P.R. B4 104a
Gura Humorului, Rom. B12 26
Gurais, India A5 54
Gurdãspur, India B5 54
Gurdon, Ar., U.S. D5 122
Güre, Tur. E12 28
Gurevsk, Russia. D15 32
Gurgueia, stm., Braz. D4 88
Gurha, India F3 54
Guri, Embalse de, res., Ven. . D10 86
Gurskoe, Russia. F16 34
Gurskøya, i., Nor. E1 8
Gürsu, Tur. C12 28
Gurupá, Braz. D7 84
Gurupi, Braz. F1 88
Gurupi, stm., Braz. D8 84
Guru Sikhar, mtn., India ... F4 54
Gurvan Sayhan uul, mts., Mong. C5 36
Gusau, Nig. G6 64
Gusev, Russia. F5 10
Gušgy, Turkmen. B9 56
Gushan, China B10 42
Gushi, China E6 42
Gus'-Hrustal'nyj, Russia I19 8
Gusino, Russia F14 10
Gusinoozersk, Russia F10 34
Gus'-Hrustal'nyy see Gus'-Hrustal'nyj, Russia .. I19 8
Guspini, Italy E2 24
Güssing, Aus. C13 22
Gustav Holm, Kap, c., Grnld. . D19 141
Gustavus, Ak., U.S. E12 140
Gustine, Ca., U.S. F5 134
Gustine, Tx., U.S. C9 130
Güstrow, Ger. C8 16
Gütersloh, Ger. E4 16
Guthrie, Ok., U.S. F11 128
Guthrie, Tx., U.S. H8 128
Guthrie Center, Ia., U.S. ... C3 120
Gutian, China H8 42
Gutiérrez Zamora, Mex. E10 100
Guttenberg, Ia., U.S. B6 120
Guwähäti, India E13 54
Guxian, China E5 42
Guyana, ctry., S.A. C6 84
Guyang, China A4 42
Guye, China B8 42
Guy Fawkes River National Park, p.o.i., Austl. H9 76
Guymon, Ok., U.S. E7 128
Guyot, Mount, mtn., U.S. ... I2 114
Guyra, Austl. H8 76
Guyton, Ga., U.S. D4 116
Guyuan, China D2 42
Guzar, Uzb. G11 32
Güzelyurt, N. Cyp. C3 58
Güzelyurt Körfezi, b., N. Cyp. C3 58
Guzhen, China E7 42
Guzmán, Mex. F7 100
Guzmán, Mex. F9 98
Gvardejsk, Russia F4 10
Gwa, Mya. D2 48
Gwaai, Zimb. D4 68
Gwädar, Pak. D9 56
Gwalia, Austl. E4 74
Gwalior (Lashkar), India E7 54
Gwanda, Zimb. B9 70
Gwane, D.R.C. D5 66
Gwangju see Kwangju, Kor., S. G7 38
Gwardafuy, Gees, c., Som. . B10 66
Gwätar Bay, b., Asia. D9 56
Gwayi, stm., Zimb. D4 68
Gwda, stm., Pol. C12 16
Gweedore, Ire. F4 12
Gweru, Zimb. D4 68
Gwinn, Mi., U.S. B2 112
Gwydir, stm., Austl. H7 76
Gyangtse see Gyangzê, China D12 54
Gyangzê, China D12 54
Gyaring Co, l., China C12 54
Gyaring Hu, l., China E4 36
Gyda, Russia B4 34
Gydanskaja guba, b., Russia B4 34
Gydanskij poluostrov, pen., Russia B4 34
Gyeongsu see Kyŏngju, Kor., S. D2 40
Gyirong, China D10 54
Gyldenløves Fjord, b., Grnld. E17 141
Gym Peak, mtn., N.M., U.S. . K9 132
Gympie, Austl. F9 76
Gyobingauk, Mya. C2 48
Gyoma, Hung. C7 26
Gyöngyös, Hung. B6 26
Győr (Raab), Hung. B4 26
Győr-Moson-Sopron, state, Hung. B4 26
Gypsum, Co., U.S. D10 132
Gypsum, Ks., U.S. C11 128
Gypsumville, Mb., Can. C15 124
Gyula, Hung. C8 26
Gyulafehérvár see Alba Iulia, Rom. C10 26
Gyzylarbat, Turkmen. B8 56

H

Haag in Oberbayern, Ger. ... H8 16
Haaksbergen, Neth. D2 16
Haapiti, Fr. Poly. v20 78h
Haapsalu, Est. G10 8
Haar, Ger. H7 16
Ha'Arava ('Arabah, Wädi al-), val., Asia. H6 58
Ha'Arava (Jayb, Wädi al-), stm., Asia ... H6 58
Haarlem, Neth. B13 14
Habaqila, China C6 36
Habarovsk, Russia G16 34
Habary, Russia D13 32
Habashiyah, Jabal, mts., Yemen. F7 56
Habbān, Yemen. G6 56
Habermehl Peak, mtn., Ant. . C6 81
Habiganj, Bngl. F13 54
Habomai Islands see Malaja Kuril'skaja Grjada, is., Russia C17 38
Hachijō-jima, i., Japan. F12 40
Hachiman, Japan D9 40
Hachinohe, Japan D14 38
Hachiōji, Japan. D12 40
Hackberry, La., U.S. H5 122

Hackberry Creek, stm., Ks., U.S. C8 128
Hackett, Ar., U.S. B4 122
Hackettstown, N.J., U.S. ... D11 114
Hadali, Pak. B4 54
HaDarom, state, Isr. H5 58
Hadd, Ra's al-, c., Oman ... E8 56
Haddam, Ks., U.S. B11 128
Haddington, Scot., U.K. F10 12
Haddock, Ga., U.S. C2 116
Haddon Downs, Austl. F3 76
Hadejia, Nig. G7 64
Hadejia, stm., Nig. G6 64
Haden, Austl. F8 76
Hadera, Isr. F5 58
Haderslev, Den. I3 8
Hadibu, Yemen. G7 56
Hadïthah, Iraq. C5 56
Hadley Bay, b., Nu., Can. ... A9 106
Hadlock, Wa., U.S. B4 136
Ha Dong, Viet. B7 48
Hadramawt, reg., Yemen ... F6 56
Hadrian's Wall, misc. cult., Eng., U.K. ... G10 12
Hadzilavičy, Bela. G13 10
Haeju, Kor., N. E6 38
Haenam, Kor., S. G7 38
Haerhpin see Harbin, China . . B7 38
Haffner Bjerg, mtn., Grnld. B13 141
Hafford, Sk., Can. B6 124
Haffouz, Tun. I3 24
Häfïzäbäd, Pak. B4 54
Häflong, India. F14 54
Hafnarfjördur, Ice. k28 8a
Haft Gel, Iran. C6 56
Hagan, Ga., U.S. D3 116
Hagari, stm., India D3 53
Hagåtña (Agana), Guam ... j10 78c
Hagemeister Island, i., Ak., U.S. E7 140
Hagen, Ger. E3 16
Hagenow, Ger. C7 16
Hagensborg, B.C., Can. D4 138
Hagerman, N.M., U.S. A3 130
Hagerstown, In., U.S. I4 112
Hagerstown, Md., U.S. E8 114
Hagerstown, Oc., Can. F9 112
Hagtors, Swe. F7 8
Haggin, Mount, mtn., Mt., U.S. D13 136
Hagi, Japan E4 40
Ha Giang, Viet. A7 48
Hagondange, Fr. E15 14
Hags Head, c., Ire. I3 12
Hague, Sk., Can. B7 124
Hague, Cap de la, c., Fr. ... E7 14
Hagueneau, Fr. F16 14
Hagues Peak, mtn., Co., U.S. . G7 126
Hahira, Ga., U.S. F2 116
Hai'an, China E9 42
Haibei, China B10 36
Haicheng, China A10 42
Haichow Bay see Haizhou Wan, b., China D8 42
Haidargarh, India E8 54
Hai Duong, Viet. B8 48
Haifa see Hefa, Isr. F5 58
Haifa see Hefa, state, Isr. ... F5 58
Haifeng, China J6 42
Haig, Austl. F5 74
Haigler, Ne., U.S. A7 128
Haikang, China K3 42
Haikou, China K4 42
Haikou, China G9 42
Hā'il, Sau. Ar. D5 56
Hailäkändi, India F14 54
Hailar, China B8 36
Hailar, stm., China B8 36
Haileybury, Ok., U.S. C3 122
Hailin, China B8 38
Hailun, China B10 36
Hailuoto, i., Fin. D11 8
Haimen, China J7 42
Haimen, China G9 42
Hainan, state, China. L3 42
Hainan Dao (Hainan Island), i., China L4 42
Hainan Island see Hainan Dao, i., China L4 42
Hainan Strait see Qiongzhou Haixia, strt., China K4 42
Haines, Ak., U.S. E12 140
Haines, Or., U.S. F8 136
Haines City, Fl., U.S. H4 116
Haines Junction, Yk., Can. .. C3 106
Haining, China F9 42
Hai Ninh, Viet. B8 48
Hai Phong, Viet. B8 48
Haiphong see Hai Phong, Viet. B8 48
Haiti, ctry., N.A. C11 102
Haitun, China D4 36
Haivoron, Ukr. A16 26
Haiyuan, China C1 42
Haizhou, China D8 42
Haizhou Wan, b., China ... D8 42
Hajdú-Bihar, state, Hung. ... B8 26
Hajdúböszörmény, Hung. ... B8 26
Hajdúnánás, Hung. B8 26
Hajdúszoboszló, Hung. B8 26
Hájípur, India F10 54
Hajnówka, Pol. D19 16
Hakasija, state, Russia D16 32
Hakha, Mya. A1 48
Hakken-san, mtn., Japan ... E8 40
Hakodate, Japan. D14 38
Hakone-yama, vol., Japan .. D12 40
Hakui, Japan C9 40
Haku-san, vol., Japan. C9 40
Haku-san-kokuritsu-kōen, p.o.i., Japan C9 40
Halab see Halle, Bel. D13 14
Halab (Aleppo), Syria B8 58
Halab, state, Syria. B8 58
Halachó, Mex. B2 102
Halahai, China B6 38
Hala'ib, Sudan. C7 62
Halawa, Cape, c., Hi., U.S. .. b5 78a
Halberstadt, Ger. E7 16
Halbrite, Sk., Can. E10 124
Halcon, Mount, mtn., Phil. .. D3 52
Halden, Nor. G4 8
Haldensleben, Ger. D7 16
Haldimand, On., Can. F10 112
Haldwäni, India D7 54
Haleakalā Crater, crat., Hi., U.S. c5 78a
Haleakalā National Park, p.o.i., Hi., U.S. c5 78a
Hale Center, Tx., U.S. G7 128
Halenkov, Czech Rep. G14 16
Halfmoon Bay, B.C., Can. ... G6 138
Halfway, Md., U.S. E8 114
Halfway, Or., U.S. F9 136
Halianassus, sci., Tur. F10 28
Halifax, Austl. B6 76
Halifax, N.S., Can. F13 110
Halifax, Eng., U.K. H11 12
Halifax, Va., U.S. H6 114
Halifax Bay, b., Austl. B6 76
Haliyäl, India D2 53
Haljala, Est. A9 10
Halkapınar, Tur. A5 58
Halladale, Stat., Swe. H5 8
Hallandale, Fl., U.S. K5 116
Hallanïyah, Juzur al- (Kuria Muria Islands), is., Oman. F8 56
Halla-san, mtn., Kor., S. H7 38
Hall Basin, b., N.A. A13 141
Halle, Bel. D13 14

Halle, Ger. E7 16
Hällefors, Swe. G6 8
Hallein, Aus. C10 22
Hallettsville, Tx., U.S. E11 130
Halley, sci., Ant. C2 81
Halligen, is., Ger. B4 16
Hall in Tirol, Aus. C8 22
Hall Islands, is., Micron. C6 72
Hall Lake, l., Nu., Can. B14 106
Hall Land, reg., Grnld. A14 141
Hall Mountain, mtn., Wa., U.S. B9 136
Hallock, Mn., U.S. C2 118
Hallowell, Me., U.S. F7 110
Hall Peninsula, pen., Nu., Can. C17 106
Halls, Tn., U.S. I8 120
Hallsberg, Swe. G6 8
Halls Creek, Austl. C5 74
Hallstahammar, Swe. G7 8
Hallstavik, Swe. F8 8
Hallstead, Pa., U.S. C10 114
Hallsville, Mo., U.S. E5 120
Halmahera, i., Indon. E8 44
Halmahera, Laut (Halmahera Sea), s., Indon. F8 44
Halmahera Sea see Halmahera, Laut, s., Indon. F8 44
Hal'mer-Ju, Russia A10 32
Halmstad, Swe. H5 8
Haloučyn, Bela. F12 10
Hal'šany, Bela. F9 10
Halsey, Ne., U.S. F12 126
Halsey, Or., U.S. F3 136
Halstead, Ks., U.S. D11 128
Haltern, Ger. E3 16
Haltiatunturi, mtn., Eur. ... B9 8
Haltom City, Tx., U.S. B10 130
Halton Hills see Georgetown, On., Can. ... E9 112
Halvorson, Mount, mtn., B.C., Can. C10 138
Ham, stm., Nmb. F4 70
Hamada, Japan E4 40
Hamadän, Iran C6 56
Hamäh, Syria C7 58
Hamäh, state, Syria. C8 58
Hamamatsu, Japan. E10 40
Haman, Kor., S. D1 40
Hamana-ko, l., Japan E10 40
Hamar, Nor. F4 8
Ha Marakabei, Leso. F9 70
Hamar-Daban, hrebet, mts., Russia F9 34
Hamáta, Gebel, mtn., Egypt C6 62
Hamburg, Ger. C6 16
Hamburg, Ar., U.S. D7 122
Hamburg, Ia., U.S. D2 120
Hamburg, N.J., U.S. C11 114
Hamburg, N.Y., U.S. B7 114
Hamburg, state, Ger. C6 16
Hamden, Ct., U.S. C13 114
Hamden, Oh., U.S. E3 114
Hämeenlinna (Tavastehus), Fin. F10 8
Hamelin, Austl. E2 74
Hameln, Ger. D5 16
HaMerkaz, state, Isr. F5 58
Hamersley Range, mts., Austl. D3 74
Hamgyŏng-sanjulgi, mts., Kor., N. D8 38
Hamhŭng, Kor., N. E7 38
Hami, China C3 36
Hamilton, Austl. K4 76
Hamilton, Ber. k15 104e
Hamilton, On., Can. E10 112
Hamilton, N.Z. C6 80
Hamilton, Scot., U.K. F8 12
Hamilton, Al., U.S. C11 122
Hamilton, Ga., U.S. E14 122
Hamilton, Il., U.S. D6 120
Hamilton, Mi., U.S. F4 112
Hamilton, Mo., U.S. E3 120
Hamilton, Mt., U.S. D12 136
Hamilton, N.Y., U.S. B10 114
Hamilton, Oh., U.S. E1 114
Hamilton, stm., Austl. D3 76
Hamilton, Lake, res., Ar., U.S. C5 122
Hamilton, Mount, mtn., Ca., U.S. F4 134
Hamilton City, Ca., U.S. ... D3 134
Hamilton Dome, Wy., U.S. .. D4 126
Hamilton Hotel, Austl. D3 76
Hamilton Mountain, mtn., U.S. G2 110
Hamina, Fin. F12 8
Hamiota, Mb., Can. D13 124
Hamirpur, India. F7 54
Hamlin, Tx., U.S. B7 130
Hamlin, W.V., U.S. F3 114
Hamlin Valley Wash, stm., U.S. E3 132
Hamm, Ger. E3 16
Hammamet, Tun. H4 24
Hammamet, Golfe de, b., Tun. H4 24
Hammam Lif, Tun. H4 24
Hammelburg, Ger. F5 16
Hammerdal, Swe. E6 8
Hammerfest, Nor. A10 8
Hammon, Ok., U.S. F9 128
Hammond, In., U.S. G2 112
Hammond, La., U.S. G8 122
Hammondsport, N.Y., U.S. .. F12 112
Hampden, Me., U.S. F8 110
Hampden, N.D., U.S. F15 124
Hampi, India D3 53
Hampshire, Il., U.S. I10 118
Hampstead, N.C., U.S. B8 116
Hampton, N.B., Can. E11 110
Hampton, Ar., U.S. D6 122
Hampton, Fl., U.S. G3 116
Hampton, Ga., U.S. C1 116
Hampton, Ia., U.S. B4 120
Hampton, Ne., U.S. G15 126
Hampton, N.H., U.S. H5 110
Hampton, Tn., U.S. H3 114
Hampton, Va., U.S. G9 114
Hampton Butte, mtn., Or., U.S. G6 136
Hampton Tableland, plat., Austl. F5 74
Hamra, Swe. F6 8
Hamra', Al-Hamädah al-, des., Libya B2 62
Hamra, As Saquia al, stm., W. Sah. D2 64
Hamrä, Tur. B8 58
Hams Fork, stm., Wy., U.S. .. B7 132
Ham Tan, Viet. G8 48
Hämün, Daryächeh-ye, l., Iran. C9 56
Han, stm., China F6 42
Han, stm., China I7 42
Han, Nong, l., Thai. D7 48
Hanak, Tur. A5 58
Hanamaki, Japan E14 38
Hananui see Anglem, Mount, mtn., N.Z. ... H2 80
Hanapepe, Hi., U.S. b2 78a
Hanateio, Fr. Poly. s18 78g
Hanatetena, Fr. Poly. s18 78g
Hanau am Main, Ger. F4 16
Hanburg, stm., Nu., Can. .. C9 106
Hancavičy, Bela. H9 10
Hăncesti, Mol. C15 26
Hanceville, Al., U.S. C12 122
Hancheng, China D7 36
Hancheng, China D4 42

Hanchung see Hanzhong, China E2 42
Hancock, Md., U.S. E7 114
Hancock, Mi., U.S. D10 118
Hancock, Mn., U.S. F3 118
Hancock, N.Y., U.S. C10 114
Handa, Japan E9 40
Handan, China C6 42
Handlová, Slov. H14 16
Handsworth, Sk., Can. E10 124
Handyga, Russia D16 34
HaNegev (Negev Desert), reg., Isr. H5 58
Hanford, Ca., U.S. G7 134
Hanga Roa, Chile. e29 78l
Hangayn nuruu, mts., Mong. B4 36
Hangchow see Hangzhou, China F9 42
Hangchow Bay see Hangzhou Wan, b., China . . F9 42
Hanggin Houqi, China A2 42
Hanggin Qi, China B3 42
Hangman Creek, stm., U.S. .. C9 136
Hangö see Hanko, Fin. G10 8
Hangokurt, Russia. B10 32
Hangu, China B7 42
Hangu, Pak. B3 54
Hanguang, China I5 42
Hangzhou, China F9 42
Hangzhou Wan, b., China . . F9 42
Hanino, Russia F19 10
Hanish, is., Yemen G5 56
Hanish Islands see Hanish, is., Yemen G5 56
Hanjiang, China I8 42
Hankinson, N.D., U.S. E1 118
Hanko, Fin. G10 8
Hankow see Wuhan, China . . F6 42
Hanksville, Ut., U.S. E6 132
Hanle, India B7 54
Hanley, Sk., Can. C7 124
Hanna, Ab., Can. E19 138
Hanna, Ok., U.S. B3 122
Hanna, Wy., U.S. B10 132
Hanna City, Il., U.S. D8 120
Hannah, N.D., U.S. F15 124
Hannah Bay, b., On., Can. .. E14 106
Hannibal, Mo., U.S. E6 120
Hannover, Ger. D5 16
Ha Noi (Hanoi), Viet. B7 48
Hanoi see Ha Noi, Viet. B7 48
Hanover, On., Can. D8 112
Hanover, S. Afr. G7 70
Hanover, i., B.C., U.S. B7 120
Hanover, In., U.S. F12 120
Hanover, N.H., U.S. G4 110
Hanover, N.M., U.S. K8 132
Hanover, Pa., U.S. E9 114
Hanover, Va., U.S. G8 114
Hanover, Isla, i., Chile J2 90
Hanshan, China F11 54
Hansi, India D5 54
Hanska, Mn., U.S. G4 118
Hantajskoe, ozero, l., Russia C6 34
Hantan see Handan, China . . C6 42
Hantsport, N.S., Can. E12 110
Hanty-Mansijsk, Russia. ... B11 32
Hantzsch, stm., Nu., Can. .. B16 106
Hanumangarh, India C3 46
Hanuy, stm., Mong. B5 36
Hanyin, China E3 42
Hanzhong, China E2 42
Hanzhuang, China D7 42
Haojiadian, China F5 42
Haoli see Hegang, China ... B11 36
Häora, India G12 54
Haparanda, Swe. D10 8
Hapčeranga, Russia G11 34
Happy Jack, Az., U.S. I5 132
Happy Valley-Goose Bay, Nf., Can. E18 106
Hapur, India D6 54
Haql, Sau. Ar. I5 58
Harad, Sau. Ar. E6 56
Haradok, Bela. E13 10
Haradzec, Bela. H7 10
Haradzišča, Bela. G9 10
Haramachi, Japan B13 40
Haranor, Russia F8 62
Hararit see Härer, Eth. F8 62
Harare, Zimb. D5 68
Harazé Mangueigne, Chad. . E4 62
Harbala, Russia D13 34
Harbavičy, Bela. G13 10
Harbin, China B7 38
Harbiye, Tur. B7 58
Harbor, Or., U.S. A1 134
Harbor Beach, Mi., U.S. ... E7 112
Harbour Breton, Nf., Can. .. j22 107a
Harbourville, N.S., Can. ... E12 110
Harda, India G6 54
Hardangerfjorden, b., Nor. . . F2 8
Hardangerjøkulen, ice, Nor. F2 8
Hardangervidda Nasjonalpark, p.o.i., Nor. . . F2 8
Hardap, state, Nmb. D3 70
Hardeeville, S.C., U.S. D4 116
Harderwijk, Neth. B14 14
Hardin, Il., U.S. E7 120
Hardin, Mt., U.S. B5 126
Harding, S. Afr. G9 70
Harding, Lake, res., U.S. ... E13 122
Hardinsburg, Ky., U.S. G11 120
Hardoi, India E7 54
Hardtner, Ks., U.S. D10 128
Hardwick, Ga., U.S. C2 116
Hardwick, Vt., U.S. F4 110
Hardy, Ar., U.S. H6 120
Hardy, Ne., U.S. G15 126
Hardy Bay, b., N.T., Can. ... B16 140
Hare Bay, b., Nf., Can. i22 107a
Hare Indian, stm., N.T., Can. B5 106
Hareøen, i., Grnld. C14 141
Härer, Eth. F8 62
Hargeysa, Som. C8 66
Harghita, state, Rom. C12 26
Har Hu, l., China D4 36
Hari, i., Indon. D3 50
Haridwär, India D7 54
Harihar, India D2 53
Härim, Syria B7 58
Haripäd, India G5 53
Harirüd (Tedžen), stm., Asia C9 56
Harischandra Range, mts., India B1 53
Haritonovo, Russia F22 8
Harkers Island, N.C., U.S. .. B9 116
Harlan County Lake, res., Ne., U.S. A9 128
Harlem, Fl., U.S. J5 116
Harlem, Mt., U.S. F18 136
Harleton, Tx., U.S. E4 122
Harlingen, Neth. A14 14
Harlingen, Tx., U.S. H10 130
Harlovka, Russia B17 8
Harlow, Eng., U.K. J13 12
Harlowton, Mt., U.S. D17 136
Harman, W.V., U.S. F6 114
Harmanck, Tur. D12 28
Harmanlı, Blg. H12 26
Harmony, In., U.S. E10 120

Harnai, India C1 53
Harney Basin, bas., Or., U.S. . G8 136
Harney Lake, l., Or., U.S. ... G7 136
Harney Peak, mtn., S.D., U.S. D9 126
Härnösand, Swe. E8 8
Har nuur, l., Mong. B3 36
Haro, Spain. B8 20
Haro, Cabo, c., Mex. B3 100
Hârot, stm., Afg. C9 56
Harovsk, Russia. F18 8
Harpanahalli, India D3 53
Harper, Lib. I3 64
Harper, Ks., U.S. D10 128
Harper, Tx., U.S. D8 130
Harper, Mount, mtn., Ak., U.S. D11 140
Harqin Qi, China D3 38
Harrai, India G7 54
Harricana, stm., Can. E15 106
Harriman, Tn., U.S. I13 120
Harrington, De., U.S. F10 114
Harrington, Me., U.S. F9 110
Harris, Sk., Can. C6 124
Harris, Monts. D3 105a
Harris, reg., Scot., U.K. ... F5 118
Harris, Lake, l., Fl., U.S. ... H4 116
Harrisburg, Ar., U.S. B8 122
Harrisburg, Il., U.S. F9 126
Harrisburg, Or., U.S. F3 136
Harrisburg, Pa., U.S. D8 114
Harrismith, S. Afr. F9 70
Harrison, Ar., U.S. H4 120
Harrison, Mi., U.S. D5 112
Harrison, Ne., U.S. E9 126
Harrison Bay, b., Ak., U.S. .. B9 140
Harrisonburg, La., U.S. ... F7 122
Harrisonburg, Va., U.S. ... F6 114
Harrison Islands, is., Nu., Can. B13 106
Harrison, On., Can. D8 112
Harriston, Ms., U.S. F7 122
Harrisville, N.Y., U.S. D14 112
Harrisville, W.V., U.S. E4 114
Harrodsburg, Ky., U.S. ... G13 120
Harrogate, Eng., U.K. H11 12
Harrold, Tx., U.S. G9 128
Harrowsmith, On., Can. ... D13 112
Harry Aubert, Île du, i., Qc., Can. ... C14 110
Harry S. Truman Reservoir, res., Mo., U.S. . . F4 120
Har Sai Shan, mtn., China .. D4 36
Harsin, Iran C6 56
Hârşova, Rom. E14 26
Harstad, Nor. B7 8
Harsüd, India G6 54
Hart, Mi., U.S. E3 112
Hart, stm., Yk., Can. G6 128
Hart, stm., Yk., Can. B3 106
Hartbees, stm., S. Afr. F5 70
Hartberg, Aus. C12 22
Hartford, Ar., U.S. C4 122
Hartford, Ct., U.S. C13 114
Hartford, Ia., U.S. F2 120
Hartford, Ky., U.S. G11 120
Hartford, Mi., U.S. F3 112
Hartford, S.D., U.S. H2 118
Hartford, Wi., U.S. H10 118
Hartford City, In., U.S. H4 112
Hartland, N.B., Can. D9 110
Hartland, Me., U.S. E6 110
Hartlepool, Eng., U.K. G11 12
Hartley, Ia., U.S. H3 118
Hartley Bay, B.C., Can. ... C1 138
Hart Mountain, mtn., Mb., Can. B12 124
Hartney, Mb., Can. E13 124
Hartselle, Al., U.S. C12 122
Hartshorne, Ok., U.S. C3 122
Hartsville, S.C., U.S. B5 116
Hartville, Oh., U.S. B4 114
Hartwell, Ga., U.S. B3 116
Hartwell Lake, res., U.S. ... B3 116
Hartz Mountains National Park, p.o.i., Austl. o13 77a
Haruniye, Tur. A7 58
Har-Us nuur, l., Mong. ... B3 36
Harvard, Il., U.S. B9 120
Harvard, Ne., U.S. G14 126
Harvey, Il., U.S. G2 112
Harvey, N.B., Can. E12 110
Harwich, Eng., U.K. J14 12
Haryana, state, India D6 54
Haryn', stm., Eur. H10 10
Harz, mts., Ger. E6 16
Hasanpur, India D7 54
Hasavjurt, Russia F7 32
Hase, stm., Ger. D3 16
Hasenkamp, Arg. E8 92
Hashima, Japan D9 40
Hashimoto, Japan E8 40
Häsilpur, Pak. D4 54
Haskell, Tx., U.S. A8 130
Haskell, Ok., U.S. B3 122
Haskovo, state, Blg. H12 26
Hasle, Den. I6 8
Haslemere, Eng., U.K. J12 12
Hasperos Canyon, p., N.M., U.S. H3 128
Hass, Jabal al-, hill, Syria ... B8 58
Hassa, Tur. B7 58
Hassberge, mts., Ger. E6 16
Hassela, Swe. E8 8
Hasselt, Bel. D14 14
Hassfurt, Ger. F6 16
Hassi Messaoud, Alg. C6 64
Hässleholm, Swe. H5 8
Hastings, Barb. n8 105d
Hastings, N.Z. D7 80
Hastings, Eng., U.K. K13 12
Hastings, Mi., U.S. F4 112
Hastings, Mn., U.S. G6 118
Hastings, Ne., U.S. A10 128
Hastings Heath, Eng., U.K. .. J6 12
Hazadâr, India G10 54
Hazafon, state, Isr. F6 58
Hazard, Ky., U.S. G5 114
Hazârïbâg, India G10 54
Hazawza, Sabkhat, l., Sau. Ar. H9 58
Hazelbrouck, Fr. D11 14
Hazel Green, Wi., U.S. ... B7 120
Hazelton, B.C., Can. A3 138
Hazelton, N.D., U.S. A12 126
Hazelton Mountains, mts., B.C., Can. B3 138
Hazelwood, N.C., U.S. ... A3 116
Hazen, Ar., U.S. C7 122
Hazen, N.D., U.S. G12 124
Hazen, Lake, l., Nu., Can. .. A11 141
Hazlehurst, Ms., U.S. D5 124
Hazlehurst, Ga., U.S. E3 116
Hazlet, Sk., Can. D5 124
Hazleton, Pa., U.S. D10 114
Hazor HaGelilit, Isr. F6 58
He, stm., China I4 42
He Tien, Viet. H7 48
Ha Tinh, Viet. C7 48
Hatip, Tur. A4 58
Healdsburg, Ca., U.S. E2 134
Heard Island, i., Austl. O10 142
Hearst, On., Can. F14 106
Hearst, stm., N.D., U.S. ... H12 124
Heart Lake, l., Ab., Can. ... A19 138
Heath, Pointe, c., Qc., Can. . I15 110
Heathcote, Austl. K5 76
Heath Springs, S.C., U.S. .. B5 116
Heathsville, Va., U.S. G9 114
Hebei, state, China B7 42
Hebel, Austl. G6 76
Heber, Az., U.S. I6 132
Heber City, Ut., U.S. C5 132
Heber Springs, Ar., U.S. ... B6 122

I·24 Hebgen Lake – Hoxie

Name	Map Ref.	Page
Hebgen Lake, res., Mt., U.S.	F15	136
Hebi, China	D6	42
Hebrides, is., Scot., U.K.	D5	12
Hebrides, Sea of the, s., Scot., U.K.	D6	12
Hebron, Nf., Can.	F13	141
Hebron, Il., U.S.	B9	120
Hebron, N.D., U.S.	H11	124
Hebron, Ne., U.S.	A11	128
Hebron *see* Al-Khalīl, W.B.	G5	58
Hecate Strait, strt., B.C., Can.	E4	106
Hecelchakán, Mex.	B2	102
Hechi, China	I3	42
Hechiceros, Mex.	F4	130
Hechingen, Ger.	H4	16
Hechuan, China	G2	42
Hecla, Mb., Can.	C17	124
Hecla, Cape, c., Nu., Can.	A13	141
Hecla Island, i., Mb., Can.	D17	124
Hectanooga, N.S., Can.	F10	110
Hector, Mn., U.S.	G4	118
Hede, Swe.	E5	8
Hedemora, Swe.	F6	8
He Devil, mtn., Id., U.S.	E10	136
Hedley, Tx., U.S.	G8	128
Hedmark, state, Nor.	F4	8
Hedrick, Ia., U.S.	C5	120
Heerenveen, Neth.	B14	14
Heerlen, Neth.	D15	14
Ḥefa (Haifa), Isr.	F5	58
Ḥefa, state, Isr.	F5	58
Hefei, China	F7	42
Heflin, Al., U.S.	D13	122
Hegang, China	B11	36
Heho, Mya.	B3	48
Hei, stm., China	A7	42
Heide, Ger.	B5	16
Heidelberg, Ger.	G4	16
Heidelberg, S. Afr.	E9	70
Heidelberg, Ms., U.S.	F10	122
Heidenheim, Ger.	G6	16
Heihe, China	A10	36
Heilbad Heiligenstadt, Ger.	E6	16
Heilbron, S. Afr.	E8	70
Heilbronn, Ger.	G5	16
Heiligenhafen, Ger.	B6	16
Heilong (Amur), stm., Asia	F14	34
Heilongguan, China	C4	42
Heilongjiang, state, China	B10	36
Heilungkiang see Heilongjiang, state, China	B8	38
Heimaey, i., Ice.	I29	8a
Heinola, Fin.	F12	8
Heishan, China	D4	38
Heishuisi, China	C3	42
Hejaz see Al-Ḥijāz, reg., Sau. Ar.	D4	56
Hejian, China	B7	42
Hejiang, China	G1	42
Hejing, China	C2	36
Hekla, vol., Ice.	k30	8a
Hekou, China	A6	48
Hekou, China	G4	42
Helagsfjället, mtn., Swe.	E5	8
Helan Mountains see Helan Shan, mts., China	B1	42
Helan Shan, mts., China	B1	42
Helbra, Ger.	E7	16
Helder *see* Den Helder, Neth.	B13	14
Helder, Den *see* Den Helder, Neth.	B13	14
Helen, Mount, hill, Austl.	C3	76
Helena, Ar., U.S.	C8	122
Helena, Mt., U.S.	D14	136
Helena, Ok., U.S.	E10	128
Helensburgh, Scot., U.K.	E8	12
Helenwood, Tn., U.S.	H13	120
Helgoland, i., Ger.	B3	16
Helgoländer Bucht, b., Ger.	C4	16
Heli, China	B11	36
Heliopolis, sci., Egypt	H2	58
Helixi, China	F8	42
Hellesylt, Nor.	E2	8
Hellín, Spain	F9	20
Hells Canyon, p., U.S.	E10	136
Hells Canyon National Recreation Area, p.o.i., Or., U.S.	E10	136
Hells Gate, p., B.C., Can.	G9	138
Helmand, stm., Asia	C9	56
Helmcken Falls, wtfl., B.C., Can.	E10	138
Helmond, Neth.	C14	14
Helmstedt, Ger.	D6	16
Helong, China	C8	38
Helper, Ut., U.S.	D6	132
Helsingborg, Swe.	H5	8
Helsingfors *see* Helsinki, Fin.	F11	8
Helsingør, Den.	H5	8
Helsinki (Helsingfors), Fin.	F11	8
Helska, Mierzeja, pen., Pol.	B14	16
Helston, Eng., U.K.	K7	12
Helvecia, Arg.	E7	92
Helwan, Egypt	I2	58
Helwan Observatory, sci., Egypt	I2	58
Hemau, Ger.	G7	16
Hemāvati, stm., India	E2	53
Hemel Hempstead, Eng., U.K.	J12	12
Hemet, Ca., U.S.	J9	134
Hemingford, Ne., U.S.	E9	126
Hemingway, S.C., U.S.	C6	116
Hemphill, Tx., U.S.	F5	122
Hemsön, i., Swe.	E8	8
Henan, state, China	E5	42
Henares, stm., Spain	D7	20
Henbury, Austl.	D6	74
Hendek, Tur.	C13	28
Henderson, Ky., U.S.	G10	120
Henderson, Mn., U.S.	G5	118
Henderson, N.C., U.S.	H7	114
Henderson, Ne., U.S.	G15	126
Henderson, Nv., U.S.	G1	132
Henderson, Tn., U.S.	B10	122
Henderson, Tx., U.S.	E4	122
Hendersonville, Tn., U.S.	H11	120
Hendricks, Mn., U.S.	G2	118
Hendricks, W.V., U.S.	E6	114
Henefer, Ut., U.S.	B5	132
Henganofi, Pap. N. Gui.	b4	79a
Hengchow *see* Hengyang, China	H5	42
Hengdaozi, China	C7	38
Hengelo, Neth.	B15	14
Hengfeng, China	G7	42
Henglu, China	D7	38
Hengshan, China	C3	42
Hengshan, China	H5	42
Heng Shan, mts., China	B5	42
Hengshui, China	C6	42
Hengxian, China	J3	42
Hengyang, China	H5	42
Hénin-Beaumont, Fr.	D11	14
Henlopen, Cape, c., De., U.S.	F10	114
Hennebont, Fr.	G5	14
Hennef, Ger.	F3	16
Hennessey, Ok., U.S.	E11	128
Henniker, N.H., U.S.	G5	110
Henning, Mn., U.S.	E3	118
Henrietta, N.Y., U.S.	A8	114
Henrietta, Tx., U.S.	H10	128
Henrietta Island see Genrietty, ostrov, i., Russia	A20	34
Henrietta Maria, Cape, c., On., Can.	D14	106
Henri Pittier, Parque Nacional, p.o.i., Ven.	B8	86
Henry, Il., U.S.	C8	120
Henry, Cape, c., Va., U.S.	H10	114
Henry, Mount, mtn., Mt., U.S.	B11	136
Henryetta, Ok., U.S.	B2	122
Henry Kater, Cape, c., Nu., Can.	B17	106
Henrys Fork, stm., Id., U.S.	F15	136
Hensall, On., Can.	E8	112
Hensley, Ar., U.S.	C6	122
Henslow, Cape, c., Sol. Is.	e9	79b
Hentiesbaai, Nmb.	C2	70
Hentiyn nuruu, mts., Mong.	G10	34
Henzada, Mya.	D2	48
Hephzibah, Ga., U.S.	C3	116
Heping, China	H7	42
Heppenheim, Ger.	G4	16
Heppner, Or., U.S.	E7	136
Hepu, China	K3	42
Hequ, China	B4	42
Héraðsflói, b., Ice.	k32	8a
Herāt, Afg.	C9	56
Hérault, state, Fr.	F9	18
Hérault, stm., Fr.	F9	18
Herbert, Sk., Can.	D6	124
Herberton, Austl.	A5	76
Herbertsdale, S. Afr.	H5	70
Herborn, Ger.	F4	16
Herceg-Novi, Serb.	G5	26
Hércules, Mex.	A7	100
Herðubreið, vol., Ice.	k31	8a
Heredia, C.R.	G5	102
Hereford, Eng., U.K.	I10	12
Hereford, Az., U.S.	L6	132
Hereford, Tx., U.S.	G6	128
Hereke, Tur.	C12	28
Herencia, Spain	E7	20
Herford, Ger.	D4	16
Herington, Ks., U.S.	C11	128
Herisau, Switz.	C6	22
Herkimer, N.Y., U.S.	E15	112
Hermagor, Aus.	D10	22
Herman, Mn., U.S.	F2	118
Herman, Ne., U.S.	C1	120
Hermanas, Mex.	G6	130
Hermanns-Denkmal, hist., Ger.	E4	16
Hermansverk, Nor.	F2	8
Hermansville, Mi., U.S.	C2	112
Hermanus, S. Afr.	I4	70
Hermanville, Ms., U.S.	F8	122
Hermiston, Or., U.S.	E7	136
Hermitage, Ar., U.S.	D6	122
Hermit Islands, is., Pap. N. Gui.	a4	79a
Hermleigh, Tx., U.S.	B7	130
Hermon, Mount (Shaykh, Jabal ash-), mtn., Asia	E6	58
Hermosillo, Mex.	A3	100
Hermyingyi, Mya.	E4	48
Hernád (Hornad), stm., Eur.	H17	16
Hernandarias, Arg.	E8	92
Hernandarias, Para.	B10	92
Hernando, Arg.	F6	92
Hernando, Fl., U.S.	H3	116
Hernando, Ms., U.S.	C9	122
Herndon, Pa., U.S.	D9	114
Herne Bay, Eng., U.K.	J14	12
Herning, Den.	H3	8
Heroica Zitácuaro, Mex.	F8	100
Heron Island, i., Austl.	D8	76
Heron Lake, Mn., U.S.	H3	118
Hérouville-Saint-Clair, Fr.	E8	14
Herradura, Arg.	C8	92
Herreid, S.D., U.S.	B12	126
Herrera de Pisuerga, Spain	B6	20
Herrick, Austl.	n13	77a
Herrin, Il., U.S.	G8	120
Hersbruck, Ger.	G7	16
Herschel, Sk., Can.	C5	124
Herschel, S. Afr.	G8	70
Herschel Island, i., Yk., Can.	C12	140
Herscher, Il., U.S.	C9	120
Hershey, Ne., U.S.	F11	126
Hershey, Pa., U.S.	D9	114
Herstal, Bel.	D14	14
Hertford, Eng., U.K.	J12	12
Hertogenbosch, 's- *see* 's-Hertogenbosch, Neth.	C14	14
Herval d'Oeste, Braz.	C12	92
Hervás, Spain	D5	20
Hervey Bay, b., Austl.	E9	76
Hervey-Jonction, Qc., Can.	D4	110
Herzberg, Ger.	E9	16
Herzberg am Harz, Ger.	E6	16
Heshan, China	J3	42
Heshui, China	J4	42
Heshun, China	C5	42
Hesperia, Mi., U.S.	E3	112
Hesperus Mountain, mtn., Co., U.S.	F8	132
Hess, stm., Yk., Can.	C4	106
Hessen, state, Ger.	F5	16
Hesston, Ks., U.S.	C11	128
Het, stm., Laos	B6	48
Heta, stm., Russia	B8	34
Hetang, China	H8	42
Heṭauṇḍā, Nepal	E10	54
Hetch Hetchy Aqueduct, aq., Ca., U.S.	F4	134
Hetögeln, l., Swe.	D6	8
Hettstedt, Ger.	E7	16
Heuvelton, N.Y., U.S.	D14	112
Heves, Hung.	B7	26
Heves, state, Hung.	A7	26
Hewanorra International Airport, St. Luc.	m6	105c
Hewu, China	H5	42
Hexham, Eng., U.K.	F11	12
Hexian, China	I4	42
Heyang, China	D3	42
Heyburn, Id., U.S.	H13	136
Heysham, Eng., U.K.	G10	12
Heyuan, China	J6	42
Heywood, Austl.	L3	76
Heyworth, Il., U.S.	D9	120
Heze, China	D6	42
Hezheng, China	D5	36
Hialeah, Fl., U.S.	K5	116
Hiawatha, Ks., U.S.	E2	120
Hiawatha, Ut., U.S.	D6	132
Hibbard, Qc., Can.	C2	110
Hibbing, Mn., U.S.	D5	118
Hickman, Ky., U.S.	H8	120
Hickory, Ms., U.S.	E9	122
Hickory, N.C., U.S.	I4	114
Hickory Flat, Ms., U.S.	C9	122
Hicks, Point, c., Austl.	K7	76
Hico, Tx., U.S.	C9	130
Hida *see* Hita, Japan	F3	40
Hidalgo, Mex.	C9	100
Hidalgo, Mex.	B8	100
Hidalgo, Mex.	B9	100
Hidalgo, state, Mex.	E9	100
Hidalgo del Parral, Mex.	B6	100
Hida-sammyaku, mts., Japan	C10	40
Hidrolândia, Braz.	I1	88
Hieflau, Aus.	C11	22
Hienghène, N. Cal.	m15	79d
Hierapolis see Pamukkale, sci., Tur.	F12	28
Higashīhiroshima, Japan	E5	40
Higashiichiki, Japan	H3	40
Higashine, Japan	A13	40
Higashiōsaka, Japan	E8	40
Higgins, Tx., U.S.	E8	128
Higgins Lake, l., Mi., U.S.	D5	112
Higginsville, Mo., U.S.	E4	120
Highbury, Austl.	C8	74
Highland, Il., U.S.	F8	120
Highland, In., U.S.	G2	112
Highland, Ks., U.S.	E2	120
Highland Park, Il., U.S.	F2	112
Highlands, N.C., U.S.	A2	116
Highlands, N.J., U.S.	D12	114
Highlands, Tx., U.S.	H3	122
High Level, Ab., Can.	D7	106
High Point, N.C., U.S.	I5	114
High Point, mtn., N.J., U.S.	C11	114
High Point, mtn., Wy., U.S.	B9	132
High Point, c., Ber.	I15	104e
High River, Ab., Can.	F17	138
Highrock Lake, l., Mb., Can.	D10	106
Highrock Lake, l., Sk., Can.	D9	106
High Rock Lake, res., N.C., U.S.	A5	116
High Springs, Fl., U.S.	G3	116
Hightstown, N.J., U.S.	D11	114
High Willhays, mtn., Eng., U.K.	K9	12
Highwood, Mt., U.S.	C16	136
Highwood, stm., Ab., Can.	F17	138
Highwood Baldy, mtn., Mt., U.S.	C16	136
High Wycombe, Eng., U.K.	J11	12
Higuera de Abuya, Mex.	C5	100
Higueras, Mex.	I8	130
Higüero, Punta, c., P.R.	B1	104a
Higüey, Dom. Rep.	C13	102
Hiiumaa, i., Est.	G10	8
Hikari, Japan	F4	40
Hikone, Japan	D9	40
Hilbert, Wi., U.S.	D1	112
Hilda, Ab., Can.	D3	124
Hildburghausen, Ger.	F6	16
Hildesheim, Ger.	D5	16
Hiliotaluwa, Indon.	L3	48
Hillaby, Mount, mtn., Barb.	n8	105d
Hill Bank, Belize	D3	102
Hill City, Ks., U.S.	B9	128
Hill City, S.D., U.S.	D9	126
Hillcrest Mines, Ab., Can.	G16	138
Hillerød, Den.	I4	8
Hilliard, Fl., U.S.	F4	116
Hill Island Lake, l., N.T., Can.	C9	106
Hillister, Tx., U.S.	G4	122
Hills, Mn., U.S.	H2	118
Hillsboro, Il., U.S.	E8	120
Hillsboro, Ks., U.S.	C11	128
Hillsboro, Mo., U.S.	F7	120
Hillsboro, N.D., U.S.	D1	118
Hillsboro, Oh., U.S.	E2	114
Hillsboro, Or., U.S.	E3	136
Hillsboro, Wi., U.S.	H8	118
Hillsboro Canal, can., Fl., U.S.	J5	116
Hillsborough, Gren.	q10	105e
Hillsborough, N.C., U.S.	H6	114
Hillsborough, stm., Fl., U.S.	H3	116
Hillsborough, Cape, c., Austl.	C7	76
Hillsborough Bay, b., P.E., Can.	D13	110
Hillsdale, Mi., U.S.	G5	112
Hillston, Austl.	I5	76
Hillsville, Va., U.S.	H5	114
Hillswick, Scot., U.K.	n18	12a
Hilo, Hi., U.S.	d6	78a
Hilok, Russia	F11	34
Hilok, stm., Russia	F10	34
Hilton, N.Y., U.S.	E12	112
Hilton Head Island, i., S.C., U.S.	D5	116
Hilvan, Tur.	A9	58
Hilversum, Neth.	B14	14
Himāchal Pradesh, state, India	B6	54
Himalayas, mts., Asia	F10	142
Himarë, Alb.	D13	24
Himatnagar, India	G4	54
Himeji, Japan	E7	40
Himi, Japan	C9	40
Himki, Russia	E20	10
Ḥimṣ (Homs), Syria	D7	58
Ḥimṣ, state, Syria	D8	58
Hinchinbrook Island, i., Austl.	B6	76
Hinchinbrook Island, i., Ak., U.S.	D10	140
Hinchinbrook Island National Park, p.o.i., Austl.	B6	76
Hinckley, Il., U.S.	C9	120
Hinckley, Mn., U.S.	E5	118
Hinckley, Ut., U.S.	D4	132
Hindang, Phil.	E5	52
Hindaun, India	E6	54
Hindmarsh, Lake, l., Austl.	J3	76
Hindu Kush, mts., Asia	B10	56
Hindupur, India	E3	53
Hines, Or., U.S.	G7	136
Hinesville, Ga., U.S.	E4	116
Hinganghāt, India	H7	54
Hingham, Ma., U.S.	B15	114
Hingol, stm., Pak.	D10	56
Hingoli, India	B3	53
Hinigaran, Phil.	E4	52
Hinnøya, i., Nor.	B6	8
Hinojosa del Duque, Spain	F5	20
Hinokage, Japan	G4	40
Hinsdale, Mt., U.S.	F6	124
Hinterrhein, stm., Switz.	D6	22
Hinton, Ab., Can.	C13	138
Hinton, Ok., U.S.	F10	128
Hinton, W.V., U.S.	G5	114
Hipólito, Mex.	C8	100
Hipólito Yrigoyen, Arg.	F4	92
Hirado, Japan	F2	40
Hirado-shima, i., Japan	F2	40
Hīrākud, India	H9	54
Hīrākud Reservoir, res., India	H10	54
Hirara, Japan	G10	36
Hirata, Japan	D5	40
Hiratsuka, Japan	D12	40
Hiriyūr, India	E3	53
Hirosaki, Japan	D14	38
Hiroshima, Japan	E5	40
Hiroshima, state, Japan	E5	40
Hirosima *see* Hiroshima, Japan	E5	40
Hirovo, Russia	B16	10
Hirson, Fr.	E13	14
Hisār, India	D5	54
Hisarönü, Tur.	B14	28
Hispaniola, i., N.A.	D10	96
Hisua, India	F10	54
Ḥisyah, Syria	D7	58
Hita, Japan	F3	40
Hitachi, Japan	C13	40
Hitachi-ōta, Japan	C13	40
Hitchcock, Tx., U.S.	H3	122
Hitchins, Ky., U.S.	F3	114
Hitiaa, Fr. Poly.	v22	78h
Hitoyoshi, Japan	G3	40
Hitra, i., Nor.	E3	8
Hiuchiga-take, vol., Japan	C12	40
Hiuchi-nada, s., Japan	E6	40
Hiva, Uzb.	F10	32
Hiva Oa, i., Fr. Poly.	s19	78g
Hiwannee, Ms., U.S.	F10	122
Hiwasa, Japan	F7	40
Hiwassee, stm., U.S.	B14	122
Hiwassee Lake, res., N.C., U.S.	A1	116
Hixson, Tn., U.S.	B13	122
Hjälmaren, l., Swe.	G6	8
Hjo, Swe.	G6	8
Hjørring, Den.	H3	8
Hkakabo Razi, mtn., Mya.	C8	46
Hkok (Kok), stm., Asia	B4	48
Hlaingbwe, Mya.	D3	48
Hlathikulu, Swaz.	E10	70
Hlinsko, Czech Rep.	G11	16
Hlohovec, Slov.	H13	16
Hlotse, Leso.	F9	70
Hluhluwe, S. Afr.	F11	70
Hluhluwe Game Reserve, S. Afr.	F10	70
Hluša, Bela.	G11	10
Hlyboka, Ukr.	A12	26
Hlybokae, Bela.	E10	10
Hmelita, Russia	E16	10
H. Neely Henry Lake, res., Al., U.S.	D12	122
Ho, Ghana	H5	64
Hoa Binh, Viet.	B7	48
Hoare Bay, b., Nu., Can.	D13	141
Hobart, Austl.	o13	77a
Hobart, Ok., U.S.	F9	128
Hobbs, N.M., U.S.	B4	130
Hobbs Coast, cst., Ant.	C28	81
Hobe Sound, Fl., U.S.	I5	116
Hobgood, N.C., U.S.	H8	114
Hobq Shamo, des., China	A2	42
Hobson Lake, l., B.C., Can.	D10	138
Hobyo, Som.	C9	66
Hochalmspitze, mtn., Aus.	C10	22
Hochfeld, Nmb.	B3	70
Ho Chi Minh City *see* Thanh Pho Ho Chi Minh, Viet.	G8	48
Hochkönig, mtn., Aus.	C10	22
Höchstadt an der Aisch, Ger.	G6	16
Hochstetter Forland, pen.	B21	141
Hoch'uan *see* Hechuan, China	G2	42
Ḥocimsk, Bela.	G15	10
Hockenheim, Ger.	G4	16
Hocking, stm., Oh., U.S.	E15	120
Ḥôḍ, reg., Maur.	F3	64
Hodal, India	E6	54
Hodeida *see* Al-Ḥudaydah, Yemen	G5	56
Hodge, La., U.S.	E6	122
Hodgenville, Ky., U.S.	G12	120
Hodgeville, Sk., Can.	D7	124
Hódmezővásárhely, Hung.	C7	26
Hodna, Chott el, l., Alg.	B6	64
Hodonín, Czech Rep.	H12	16
Hodžanur'jah, gora, mtn., Uzb.	G11	32
Hodžejli, Uzb.	F9	32
Hœdic, Île de, i., Fr.	G6	14
Hoehne, Co., U.S.	D4	128
Hoei *see* Huy, Bel.	D14	14
Hoek van Holland, Neth.	C12	14
Hoeryŏng-ŭp, Kor., N.	C8	38
Hoeyang-ŭp, Kor., N.	E7	38
Hof, Ger.	F7	16
Hof, Ice.	k32	8a
Hofei *see* Hefei, China	F7	42
Hoffman, Mn., U.S.	F3	118
Hofgeismar, Ger.	E5	16
Hofheim am Taunus, Ger.	F4	16
Hofheim in Unterfranken, Ger.	F6	16
Hofors, Swe.	F7	8
Hofsjökull, ice, Ice.	k30	8a
Hōfu, Japan	E4	40
Hofuf *see* Al-Hufūf, Sau. Ar.	D6	56
Hogansville, Ga., U.S.	D14	122
Hogback Mountain, mtn., Ne., U.S.	F9	126
Hogback Mountain, mtn., S.C., U.S.	A3	116
Högsby, Swe.	H6	8
Hohenwald, Tn., U.S.	B11	122
Hoher Dachstein, mtn., Aus.	C10	22
Hohe Tauern, mts., Aus.	C9	22
Hohhot, China	A4	42
Hohoe, Ghana	H5	64
Hōhoku, Japan	E3	40
Hoh Xil Hu, l., China	D3	36
Hoh Xil Shan, mts., China	D2	36
Hoi An, Viet.	E9	48
Hoihong *see* Haikang, China	K3	42
Hoihow *see* Haikou, China	K4	42
Hoima, Ug.	D6	66
Hoisington, Ks., U.S.	C10	128
Hojāi, India	E14	54
Højer, Den.	B4	16
Hōjō, Japan	F5	40
Hokah, Mn., U.S.	H7	118
Hokang *see* Hegang, China	B11	36
Hokitika, N.Z.	F4	80
Hokkaidō, i., Japan	C15	38
Holalkere, India	D3	53
Holberg, B.C., Can.	F2	138
Holbrook, Austl.	J6	76
Holbrook, Az., U.S.	I6	132
Holbrook, Ne., U.S.	A8	128
Holden, Ab., Can.	C18	138
Holden, Mo., U.S.	F4	120
Holden, W.V., U.S.	G3	114
Holden Village, Wa., U.S.	B6	136
Holder, Fl., U.S.	H3	116
Holderness, pen., Eng., U.K.	H12	12
Holdfast, Sk., Can.	D8	124
Holdingford, Mn., U.S.	F4	118
Hold With Hope, reg., Grnld.	C22	141
Hole in the Mountain Peak, mtn., Nv., U.S.	C1	132
Hole Narsipur, India	E2	53
Holetown, Barb.	n8	105d
Holgate, Oh., U.S.	C1	114
Holguín, Cuba	B9	102
Holíč, Slov.	H13	16
Hollabrunn, Aus.	B13	22
Holland, Mi., U.S.	F3	112
Holland, Tx., U.S.	D10	130
Holland see Netherlands, ctry., Eur.	B15	14
Holland, hist. reg., Neth.	B13	14
Hollandale, Ms., U.S.	D8	122
Hollandia *see* Jayapura, Indon.	F11	44
Hollandsbird Island, i., Nmb.	D2	70
Holley, N.Y., U.S.	E11	112
Holliday, Tx., U.S.	H10	128
Hollins, Va., U.S.	G6	114
Hollister, Ca., U.S.	G4	134
Hollow Rock, Tn., U.S.	H9	120
Holly, Co., U.S.	C6	128
Holly Grove, Ar., U.S.	C7	122
Holly Hill, Fl., U.S.	G4	116
Holly Springs, Ms., U.S.	C9	122
Hollywood, Fl., U.S.	J5	116
Holm, Russia	C14	10
Holman, N.T., Can.	A7	106
Hólmavík, Ice.	k28	8a
Holmen, Wi., U.S.	H7	118
Holmes, Mount, mtn., Wy., U.S.	F16	136
Holm Land, pen., Grnld.	A22	141
Holm Ø, i., Grnld.	C14	141
Holmogorskaja, Russia	E19	8
Holmsk, Russia	G17	34
Holmsund, Swe.	E9	8
Ḥolon, Isr.	F5	58
Holoog, Nmb.	E4	70
Holovanivs'k, Ukr.	A17	26
Holstebro, Den.	H3	8
Holstein, Ia., U.S.	B2	120
Holsteinsborg (Sisimiut), Grnld.	D15	141
Holston, stm., Tn., U.S.	H2	114
Holston, North Fork, stm., U.S.	H3	114
Holsworthy, Eng., U.K.	K8	12
Holt, Fl., U.S.	G12	122
Holt, Mi., U.S.	B1	114
Holton, Ks., U.S.	E2	120
Holts Summit, Mo., U.S.	F5	120
Holy Cross, Ak., U.S.	D8	140
Holy Cross Mountain, mtn., B.C., Can.	C10	138
Holyhead, Wales, U.K.	H8	12
Holy Island, i., Eng., U.K.	F11	12
Holyoke, Co., U.S.	G10	126
Holyoke, Ma., U.S.	B13	114
Holyrood, Ks., U.S.	C10	128
Holzkirchen, Ger.	I7	16
Holzminden, Ger.	E5	16
Hom, stm., Nmb.	F4	70
Homa Bay, Kenya	E6	66
Homalin, Mya.	D7	46
Homathko, stm., B.C., Can.	E6	138
Homathko Icefield, ice, B.C., Can.	E6	138
Homberg, Ger.	E5	16
Hombori Tondo, mtn., Mali	F4	64
Hombre Muerto, Salar del, pl., Arg.	B4	92
Homburg, Ger.	G3	16
Home Bay, b., Nu., Can.	B17	106
Home Hill, Austl.	B6	76
Homel', Bela.	H13	10
Homel', state, Bela.	H12	10
Homeland Park, S.C., U.S.	B3	116
Homer, Ak., U.S.	E9	140
Homer, Ga., U.S.	B2	116
Homer, La., U.S.	E5	122
Homer, Ne., U.S.	B1	120
Homer City, Pa., U.S.	D6	114
Homerville, Ga., U.S.	E3	116
Homestead, Fl., U.S.	K5	116
Homestead National Monument of America, p.o.i., Ne., U.S.	A11	128
Homewood, Al., U.S.	D12	122
Hommura, Japan	E12	40
Homnābād, India	C3	53
Homochitto, stm., Ms., U.S.	F7	122
Homoíne, Moz.	C12	70
Homosassa, Fl., U.S.	H3	116
Homs *see* Al-Khums, Libya	A2	62
Homs *see* Ḥimṣ, Syria	D7	58
Honaker, Va., U.S.	H4	114
Honan *see* Luoyang, China	D5	42
Honan see Henan, state, China	E5	42
Honāvar, India	D2	53
Hon Chong, Viet.	G7	48
Honda, Col.	E4	86
Honda, Bahía, b., Col.	A5	86
Honda Bay, b., Phil.	F2	52
Hondeklipbaai, S. Afr.	G3	70
Hon Dien, Nui, mtn., Viet.	G9	48
Hondo, Ab., Can.	A16	138
Hondo, Japan	G3	40
Hondo, N.M., U.S.	H3	128
Hondo, stm., N.A.	C3	102
Hondo Creek, stm., Tx., U.S.	E8	130
Honduras, ctry., N.A.	E4	102
Honduras, Cabo de, c., Hond.	D5	102
Honduras, Gulf of, b., N.A.	D4	102
Honea Path, S.C., U.S.	B3	116
Hønefoss, Nor.	F4	8
Honesdale, Pa., U.S.	C10	114
Honey Grove, Tx., U.S.	D3	122
Honey Lake, l., Ca., U.S.	C5	134
Honeyville, Ut., U.S.	B4	132
Honfleur, Fr.	E9	14
Hong, stm., China	E6	42
Hong, Song see Red, stm., Asia	D9	46
Hon Gai, Viet.	B8	48
Hong Hu, l., China	F5	42
Hongjiang, China	H4	42
Hong Kong *see* Xianggang, China	J6	42
Hongliuyuan, China	F17	32
Hong Ngu, Viet.	G7	48
Hongqi, China	B7	38
Hongshi, China	C7	38
Hongshui, stm., China	J3	42
Hongtong, China	C4	42
Honguedo, Détroit d', strt., Qc., Can.	A12	110
Hongze, China	E8	42
Hongze Hu, l., China	E8	42
Honiara, Sol. Is.	e8	79b
Honjō, Japan	E13	38
Honningsvåg, Nor.	A11	8
Honoka'a, Hi., U.S.	c6	78a
Honolulu, Hi., U.S.	b4	78a
Honomu, Hi., U.S.	d6	78a
Hon Quan, Viet.	G8	48
Honshū, i., Japan	G12	38
Honuu, Russia	C17	34
Hood, stm., Nu., Can.	B9	106
Hood, Mount, vol., Or., U.S.	E5	136
Hood Canal, b., Wa., U.S.	C4	136
Hoodoo Peak, mtn., Wa., U.S.	B6	136
Hood Point, c., Austl.	F3	74
Hoodsport, Wa., U.S.	C3	136
Hoogeveen, Neth.	B15	14
Hoogeveense Vaart, can., Neth.	B15	14
Hooker, Ok., U.S.	E7	128
Hook Head, c., Ire.	I6	12
Hookina, Austl.	H2	76
Hook Island, i., Austl.	C7	76
Hook Point, c., Austl.	E9	76
Hooks, Tx., U.S.	D4	122
Hoonah, Ak., U.S.	E12	140
Hoopa, Ca., U.S.	B2	134
Hooper, Ne., U.S.	C1	120
Hooper Bay, Ak., U.S.	D6	140
Hoople, N.D., U.S.	F16	124
Hoopstad, S. Afr.	E7	70
Hoorn, Neth.	B14	14
Hoosick Falls, N.Y., U.S.	H3	110
Hoover Dam, dam, U.S.	G2	132
Hooversville, Pa., U.S.	H11	112
Hopatcong, N.J., U.S.	D11	114
Hope, B.C., Can.	G9	138
Hope, Ar., U.S.	D5	122
Hope, In., U.S.	E12	120
Hope, Ben, mtn., Scot., U.K.	C8	12
Hope, Point, c., Ak., U.S.	C6	140
Hopedale, La., U.S.	H9	122
Hopeh see Hebei, state, China	D8	36
Ho-pei see Hebei, state, China	D8	36
Hopelchén, Mex.	C3	102
Hope Mills, N.C., U.S.	B7	116
Hopër, stm., Russia	E17	6
Hopes Advance, Cap, c., Qc., Can.	C17	106
Hopetoun, Austl.	F4	74
Hopetoun, Austl.	J4	76
Hopetown, S. Afr.	F6	70
Hope Valley, R.I., U.S.	C14	114
Hopewell, Va., U.S.	G8	114
Hopewell Culture National Historic Park, p.o.i., Oh., U.S.	E2	114
Hopewell Islands, is., Nu., Can.	D14	106
Hopi *see* Hebi, China	D6	42
Hopkins, Mo., U.S.	D3	120
Hopkins, stm., Austl.	K4	76
Hopkinsville, Ky., U.S.	H10	120
Hopkinton, Ia., U.S.	B6	120
Hopólite Bouchard, Arg.	G6	92
Hoppo *see* Hepu, China	K3	42
Hopwood, Mount, hill, Austl.	C5	76
Hoquiam, Wa., U.S.	C2	136
Hor, Russia	G16	34
Hor, stm., Russia	B12	36
Hor, stm., Russia	G16	34
Horatio, Ar., U.S.	D4	122
Hordaland, state, Nor.	F2	8
Horezu, Rom.	D10	26
Horicon, Wi., U.S.	H10	118
Horinger, China	A4	42
Horinsk, Russia	F10	34
Horizontina, Braz.	C10	92
Horlick Mountains, mts., Ant.	D29	81
Horlivka, Ukr.	E5	32
Horlovo, Russia	E21	10
Hormigueros, P.R.	B1	104a
Hormuz, Strait of, strt., Asia	D8	56
Horn, Aus.	B12	22
Horn, c., Ice.	j28	8a
Horn, stm., N.T., Can.	C7	106
Horn, Cape see Hornos, Cabo de, c., Chile	K3	90
Hornad (Hernád), stm., Eur.	H17	16
Hornaday, stm., Can.	B6	106
Hornafjörður, b., Ice.	k32	8a
Hornavan, l., Swe.	C7	8
Hornbeck, La., U.S.	F5	122
Hornbrook, Ca., U.S.	B3	134
Hornby Bay, b., N.T., Can.	B7	106
Hornell, N.Y., U.S.	B8	114
Hornepayne, On., Can.	F13	106
Horn Island, i., Ms., U.S.	G10	122
Horn Lake, Ms., U.S.	C8	122
Hornos, Cabo de (Horn, Cape), c., Chile	K3	90
Horn Plateau, plat., N.T., Can.	C6	106
Hornsea, Eng., U.K.	H12	12
Horodkivka, Ukr.	A15	26
Horodok, Ukr.	G19	16
Horog, Taj.	B11	56
Horol', Russia	B10	38
Horqin Youyi Zhongqi, China	B4	38
Horqin Zuoyi Houqi, China	C4	38
Horqin Zuoyi Zhongqi, China	B5	38
Horqueta, Para.	D5	90
Horse Cave, Ky., U.S.	G12	120
Horse Creek, stm., Co., U.S.	C5	128
Horse Creek, stm., U.S.	F8	126
Horsefly, B.C., Can.	D9	138
Horsefly Lake, l., B.C., Can.	D10	138
Horseheads, N.Y., U.S.	B9	114
Horse Islands, is., Nf., Can.	i22	107a
Horsens, Den.	I3	8
Horseshoe Bend, Id., U.S.	G10	136
Horsham, Austl.	K4	76
Horsham, Eng., U.K.	J12	12
Horšovský Týn, Czech Rep.	G8	16
Horten, Nor.	G4	8
Hortobágy, reg., Hung.	B8	26
Hortobágyi Nemzeti Park, p.o.i., Hung.	B8	26
Horton, Ks., U.S.	E2	120
Horton, stm., N.T., Can.	B6	106
Horton Lake, l., N.T., Can.	B6	106
Hortonville, Wi., U.S.	G10	118
Hory, Bela.	F14	10
Hosa'ina, Eth.	F7	62
Hösbach, Ger.	F5	16
Hosedahard, Russia	A9	32
Hosford, Fl., U.S.	G14	122
Hoshāb, Pak.	D9	56
Hoshangābād, India	G6	54
Hoshiārpur, India	C5	54
Hosh Isa, Egypt	H1	58
Hosmer, B.C., Can.	G15	138
Hospers, Ia., U.S.	A2	120
Hospet, India	D3	53
Hospitalet *see* L'Hospitalet de Llobregat, Spain	C13	20
Hossegor, Fr.	F4	18
Hosston, La., U.S.	E5	122
Hosta Butte, mtn., N.M., U.S.	H8	132
Hoste, Isla, i., Chile	K3	90
Hosūr, India	E3	53
Hotagen, l., Swe.	E5	8
Hotaka-dake, mtn., Japan	C10	40
Hotamış, Tur.	A4	58
Hotan, China	A5	46
Hotazel, S. Afr.	E6	70
Hotevilla, Az., U.S.	H6	132
Hotilovo, Russia	C17	10
Hot'kovo, Russia	D21	10
Hot'kovo, Russia	G18	10
Hot Springs, Ar., U.S.	C5	122
Hot Springs, N.C., U.S.	I3	114
Hot Springs, S.D., U.S.	D9	126
Hot Springs, Va., U.S.	F6	114
Hot Springs National Park *see* Hot Springs, Ar., U.S.	C5	122
Hot Springs Peak, mtn., Nv., U.S.	B8	134
Hot Sulphur Springs, Co., U.S.	A2	128
Hottah Lake, l., N.T., Can.	B7	106
Hottentotsbaai, b., Nmb.	E2	70
Hotynec, Russia	G18	10
Houaïlou, N. Cal.	m15	79d
Houat, Île de, i., Fr.	G6	14
Houdan, Fr.	F10	14
Houghton, Mi., U.S.	D10	118
Houghton, N.Y., U.S.	B7	114
Houghton Lake, l., Mi., U.S.	D4	112
Houlka, Ms., U.S.	C10	122
Houlton, Me., U.S.	D9	110
Houma, China	D4	42
Houma, Tonga	n13	78e
Houma, La., U.S.	H8	122
Hou-pei see Hubei, state, China	F5	42
Hourtin, Étang d', l., Fr.	D4	18
Housatonic, Ma., U.S.	B12	114
House, N.M., U.S.	G5	128
Houston, B.C., Can.	B4	138
Houston, Mn., U.S.	H7	118
Houston, Mo., U.S.	G6	120
Houston, Tx., U.S.	H3	122
Houston, Lake, res., Tx., U.S.	H3	122
Hout, stm., S. Afr.	C9	70
Houtman Abrolhos, is., Austl.	E2	74
Houxinqiu, China	C5	38
Hovd, Mong.	C5	36
Hovd, stm., Mong.	E16	32
Hove, Eng., U.K.	K12	12
Hoven, S.D., U.S.	B13	126
Hovenweep National Monument, p.o.i., U.S.	F7	132
Hoverla, hora, mtn., Ukr.	A11	26
Hovgaard Ø, i., Grnld.	A22	141
Hövsgöl nuur, l., Mong.	F9	34
Hovu-Aksy, Russia	D16	32
Howar, Wādī, val., Afr.	D5	62
Howard, Austl.	E9	76
Howard, Ks., U.S.	D12	128
Howard, Pa., U.S.	D8	114
Howard, S.D., U.S.	C15	126
Howard City, Mi., U.S.	E4	112
Howard Draw, stm., Tx., U.S.	D6	130
Howard Lake, Mn., U.S.	F4	118
Howe, In., U.S.	G4	112
Howe, Cape, c., Austl.	K7	76
Howe Island, i., On., Can.	D13	112
Howell, Mi., U.S.	B2	114
Howells, Ne., U.S.	F15	126
Howick, S. Afr.	F10	70
Howitt, Mount, mtn., Austl.	K6	76
Howland Island, i., Oc.	C9	72
Howser, B.C., Can.	F13	138
Howson Peak, mtn., B.C., Can.	B3	138
Hoxie, Ar., U.S.	H6	120
Hoxie, Ks., U.S.	B8	128

Name	Map Ref.	Page
Höxter, Ger.	E5	16
Hoxtolgay, China	B2	36
Hoy, i., Scot., U.K.	C9	12
Hoyerswerda, Ger.	E10	16
Hoyos, Spain	D4	20
Höytiäinen, l., Fin.	E13	8
Hoyt Lakes, Mn., U.S.	D6	118
Hradec Králové, Czech Rep.	F11	16
Hradzjanka, Bela.	G11	10
Hranice, Czech Rep.	G13	16
Hřesk, Bela.	G10	10
Hristoforovo, Russia	F22	8
Hrodna, Bela.	G6	10
Hrodna, state, Bela.	G7	10
Hroma, stm., Russia	B17	34
Hron, stm., Slov.	H14	16
Hronov, Czech Rep.	F12	16
Hrubieszów, Pol.	F19	16
Hrustal'nyj, Russia	B11	38
Hsiakuan see Dali, China	F5	36
Hsiamen see Xiamen, China	I7	42
Hsian see Xi'an, China	D3	42
Hsiang't'an see Xiangtan, China	H5	42
Hsianyang see Xiangfan, China	F4	42
Hsienyang see Xianyang, China	D3	42
Hsi-hseng, Mya.	B3	48
Hsilo, Tai.	J9	42
Hsim, stm., Mya.	B4	48
Hsinchu, Tai.	I9	42
Hsinghua see Xinghua, China	E8	42
Hsingt'ai see Xingtai, China	C6	42
Hsinhailien see Lianyungang, China	D8	42
Hsinhsiang see Xinxiang, China	D5	42
Hsining see Xining, China	D5	36
Hsinking see Changchun, China	C6	38
Hsinp'u see Lianyungang, China	D8	42
Hsintien, Tai.	I9	42
Hsinyang see Xinyang, China	E6	42
Hsipaw, Mya.	A3	48
Hsüanhua see Xuanhua, China	A6	42
Hsüch'ang see Xuchang, China	D5	42
Hsüchou see Xuzhou, China	D7	42
Hua'an, China	I7	42
Huab, stm., Nmb.	B2	70
Huacaraje, Bol.	B4	90
Huacho, Peru	F2	84
Huachuca City, Az., U.S.	L6	132
Huadian, China	C7	38
Huading Shan, mtn., China	G9	42
Hua Hin, Thai.	F4	48
Huai, stm., China	E8	42
Huai'an, China	E8	42
Huai'an, China	B8	42
Huai'an, China	A6	42
Huaibin, China	E6	42
Huaicheng see Huai'an, China	E8	42
Huaidezhen, China	C6	38
Huaiji, China	I5	42
Huailai, China	A6	42
Huainan, China	E7	42
Huairou, China	A7	42
Huaite see Gongzhuling, China	C6	38
Huaiyang, China	E6	42
Huai Yot, Thai.	I4	48
Huaiyuan, China	E7	42
Huajuapan de León, Mex.	G10	100
Hualahuises, Mex.	C9	100
Hualālai, vol., Hi., U.S.	d6	78a
Hualañé, Chile	G2	92
Hualfín, Arg.	C4	92
Hualien, Tai.	J9	42
Huallaga, stm., Peru	E2	84
Huallanca, Peru	E2	84
Hualong, China	D6	36
Huambo, Ang.	C2	68
Huamei Shan, mtn., China	I5	42
Huan, stm., China	F6	42
Huanan, China	B11	36
Huancabamba, Peru	E2	84
Huancané, Peru	G4	84
Huancavelica, Peru	F2	84
Huancayo, Peru	F2	84
Huang (Yellow), stm., China	D8	36
Huangchuan, China	E6	42
Huanggang Hu, l., China	G5	42
Huanggang, China	F6	42
Huanggangliang, mtn., China	C2	38
Huanghua, China	B7	42
Huangjinbu, China	G7	42
Huangling, China	D3	42
Huanglong, China	D3	42
Huangnihe, China	C7	38
Huangpi, China	F6	42
Huangqi, China	H8	42
Huangshane, China	H4	42
Huangshan, China	G8	42
Huangshan see Guangming Ding, mtn., China	F7	42
Huangshi, China	G4	42
Huangshi, China	F6	42
Huangtang Hu, l., China	G6	42
Huangtuliangzi, China	A8	42
Huanguelen, Arg.	H6	92
Huangyan, China	C9	42
Huangyan, China	G9	42
Huangyuan, China	D5	36
Huangzhong, China	D5	36
Huangzhu, China	L4	42
Huanjiang, China	I3	42
Huanren, China	D6	38
Huánuco, Peru	E2	84
Huanuni, Bol.	C3	90
Huanxian, China	C2	42
Huara, Chile	C3	90
Huaral, Peru	F2	84
Huaraz, Peru	E2	84
Huariaca, Peru	F2	84
Huarmey, Peru	F2	84
Huarong, China	G5	42
Huasaga, stm., S.A.	I3	86
Hua Sai, Thai.	H5	48
Huascarán, Nevado, mtn., Peru	E2	84
Huasco, Chile	D2	92
Huasco, stm., Chile	D2	92
Huatabampo, Mex.	B4	100
Huating, China	D2	42
Huatusco, Mex.	A9	42
Huauchinango, Mex.	E9	100
Huaxi, China	J5	42
Huaxian, China	D6	42
Huaxian, China	D3	42
Huaynamota, stm., Mex.	D6	100
Huazamota, Mex.	D6	100
Huazhou, China	K4	42
Hubbard, Ia., U.S.	B4	120
Hubbard Creek Reservoir, l., Tx., U.S.	B8	130
Hubbards, N.S., Can.	F12	110
Hubbell, Mi., U.S.	D10	118
Hubei, state, China	F5	42
Huberdeau, Qc., Can.	E2	110
Hubli-Dhārwār, India	C2	53
Hubuleng, China	A4	42
Huchow see Huzhou, China	F9	42
Huckleberry Mountain, mtn., Or., U.S.	G4	136
Hucknall, Eng., U.K.	H11	12
Huddersfield, Eng., U.K.	H11	12
Huddinge, Swe.	G8	8
Huder, China	A9	36
Hudiksvall, Swe.	F7	8
Hudson, Fl., U.S.	H3	116
Hudson, Ia., U.S.	B5	120
Hudson, N.C., U.S.	I4	114
Hudson, N.Y., U.S.	B13	110
Hudson, Oh., U.S.	C4	114
Hudson, S.D., U.S.	H2	118
Hudson, Wy., U.S.	E4	126
Hudson, stm., U.S.	G16	112
Hudson, Baie d' see Hudson Bay, b., Can.	C13	106
Hudson Bay, Sk., Can.	B11	124
Hudson Bay, b., Can.	C13	106
Hudson Falls, N.Y., U.S.	G3	110
Hudson's Hope, B.C., Can.	D6	106
Hudson Strait, strt., Can.	C16	106
Hudžand, Taj.	A10	56
Hue, Viet.	D8	48
Huebra, stm., Spain	D4	20
Huehuetenango, Guat.	E2	102
Huejutla de Reyes, Mex.	E9	100
Huelgoat, Fr.	F5	14
Huelva, Spain	G3	20
Huelva, co., Spain	G4	20
Huentelauquén, Chile	E2	92
Huércal-Overa, Spain	G8	20
Huerfano, stm., Co., U.S.	C4	128
Huerlumada, China	B13	54
Huerva, stm., Spain	C9	20
Huesca, Spain	B10	20
Huesca, co., Spain	B10	20
Huéscar, Spain	G8	20
Huetamo de Núñez, Mex.	F8	100
Hueytown, Al., U.S.	D11	122
Hufrat an-Nahās, Sudan	F4	62
Hughenden, Austl.	C4	76
Hughes, Ak., U.S.	C9	140
Hughes, Ar., U.S.	C8	122
Hughes Springs, Tx., U.S.	E4	122
Hugh Keenleyside Dam, dam, B.C., Can.	G12	138
Hughson, Ca., U.S.	F5	134
Hugh Town, Eng., U.K.	L6	12
Huglí, stm., India	G12	54
Hugo, Co., U.S.	B5	128
Hugo, Ok., U.S.	C3	122
Hugoton, Ks., U.S.	D7	128
Huhar, stm., China	B4	38
Huhehaote see Hohhot, China	A4	42
Huhehot see Hohhot, China	A4	42
Huichang, China	I6	42
Huicheng see Huilai, China	J7	42
Hŭich'ŏn, Kor., N.	D7	38
Huichou see Huizhou, China	J6	42
Huila, state, Col.	F4	86
Huila, Nevado del, vol., Col.	F3	86
Huili, China	J7	42
Huili, China	F5	36
Huillapima, Arg.	D4	92
Huimin, China	C7	42
Huinan, China	C7	38
Huisachal, Mex.	H6	130
Huishui, China	H2	42
Huisne, stm., Fr.	F9	14
Huitong, China	H3	42
Huitzo, Mex.	G10	100
Huitzuco de los Figueroa, Mex.	F9	100
Huixian, China	E2	42
Huixian, China	D5	42
Huixtla, Mex.	H12	100
Huize, China	F5	36
Huizhou, China	J6	42
Hŭksan-chedo, is., Kor., S.	G6	38
Hukuntsi, Bots.	D5	70
Hulan, China	B7	38
Hulan Ergi, China	B9	36
Hulbert, Mi., U.S.	B4	112
Hulett, Wy., U.S.	C8	126
Hulga, stm., Russia	B10	32
Hulin, China	B11	36
Hulin, stm., China	B4	38
Huliu, stm., China	A6	42
Hull, Ia., U.S.	H2	118
Hull, Il., U.S.	E6	120
Hull, ngh., Qc., Can.	C14	112
Hullo, Est.	A6	10
Hulun Nur see Hailar, China	B8	36
Hulun Nur, l., China	B8	36
Huma, China	F14	34
Huma, Tonga	o15	78e
Humacao, P.R.	B4	104a
Humahuaca, Arg.	D3	90
Humaitá, Braz.	E5	84
Humaitá, Para.	C8	92
Humansdorp, S. Afr.	I7	70
Humansville, Mo., U.S.	G4	120
Humara, Jabal al, hill, Sudan	D6	62
Humbe, Ang.	D1	68
Humber, stm., Eng., U.K.	H12	12
Humbird, Wi., U.S.	G8	118
Humboldt, Sk., Can.	B8	124
Humboldt, Az., U.S.	I4	132
Humboldt, Il., U.S.	B3	120
Humboldt, Ne., U.S.	E9	120
Humboldt, S.D., U.S.	D2	120
Humboldt, stm., Nv., U.S.	D15	126
Humboldt, stm., Nv., U.S.	C7	134
Humboldt, North Fork, stm., Nv., U.S.	B1	132
Humboldt, South Fork, stm., Nv., U.S.	C1	132
Humboldt Gletscher, ice, Grnld.	B13	141
Humboldt Lake, l., Nv., U.S.	D7	134
Hume, Ca., U.S.	G7	134
Hume, Lake, res., Austl.	J6	76
Humeburn, Austl.	F5	76
Humeston, Ia., U.S.	D4	120
Hummi, ozero, l., Russia	F16	34
Humphrey, Ne., U.S.	F15	126
Humphreys, Mount, mtn., Ca., U.S.	F7	134
Humphreys Peak, mtn., Az., U.S.	H5	132
Humpolec, Czech Rep.	G11	16
Humpty Doo, Austl.	B6	74
Hūn, Libya	B3	62
Hun, stm., China	D5	38
Hun, stm., China	D5	38
Húnaflói, b., Ice.	j29	8a
Hunan, state, China	H4	42
Hunchun, China	C9	38
Hundested, Den.	A9	42
Hundred, W.V., U.S.	F4	114
Hunedoara, Rom.	D9	26
Hunedoara, state, Rom.	C9	26
Hünfeld, Ger.	F5	16
Hungary, ctry., Eur.	B6	26
Hungchiang see Hongjiang, China	H4	42
Hüngdök-dong, Kor., N.	E7	38
Hungerford, Austl.	G5	76
Hungerford, Eng., U.K.	H2	122
Hungry Horse Dam, dam, Mt., U.S.	B13	136
Hungry Horse Reservoir, res., Mt., U.S.	B12	136
Hung Yen, Viet.	B8	48
Hunjiang, China	C7	38
Hunsberge, mts., Nmb.	E3	70
Hunsrück, mts., Ger.	G3	16
Hunsür, India	E3	53
Hunte, stm., Ger.	D4	16
Hunter, N.D., U.S.	D1	118
Hunter, stm., Austl.	I8	76
Hunter Island i., Austl.	n12	77a
Hunter Island, i., B.C., Can.	E2	138
Hunter Mountain, mtn., N.Y., U.S.	B11	114
Hunter River, P.E., Can.	D13	110
Hunters, Wa., U.S.	B8	136
Hunters Bay, b., Mya.	C1	48
Huntingdon, Qc., Can.	E2	110
Huntingdon, Eng., U.K.	I12	12
Huntingdon, Pa., U.S.	D7	114
Huntington, In., U.S.	I9	120
Huntington, Tn., U.S.	H4	112
Huntington, Tx., U.S.	F4	122
Huntington, Ut., U.S.	D5	132
Huntington, W.V., U.S.	F3	114
Huntington Beach, Ca., U.S.	J7	134
Huntland, Tn., U.S.	B12	122
Huntley, Mt., U.S.	B4	126
Huntly, N.Z.	C6	80
Huntly, Scot., U.K.	D10	12
Huntsville, On., Can.	C10	112
Huntsville, Al., U.S.	C12	122
Huntsville, Mo., U.S.	E5	120
Huntsville, Tn., U.S.	H13	120
Huntsville, Tx., U.S.	G3	122
Huntsville, Ut., U.S.	B5	132
Hunyuan, China	B5	42
Huong Hoa, Viet.	D8	48
Huon Gulf, b., Pap. N. Gui.	b4	79a
Huon Peninsula, pen., Pap. N. Gui.	b4	79a
Huoqiu, China	E7	42
Huoshan, China	E7	42
Huoxian, China	C4	42
Hurd, Cape, c., On., Can.	C8	112
Hüren Tovon uul, mtn., Mong.	C4	36
Hure Qi, China	B9	36
Hurghada, Egypt	K4	58
Hurley, N.M., U.S.	K8	132
Hurley, S.D., U.S.	D15	126
Hurley, Wi., U.S.	E8	118
Huron, Ca., U.S.	G5	134
Huron, Oh., U.S.	C3	114
Huron, S.D., U.S.	C14	126
Huron, stm., Mi., U.S.	B2	114
Huron, Lake, l., N.A.	D7	112
Huron Mountains, hills, Mi., U.S.	B2	112
Hurricane, Ut., U.S.	F3	132
Hurstbridge, Austl.	K5	76
Hurtado, Chile	E2	92
Hurtsboro, Al., U.S.	E13	122
Hurunui, stm., N.Z.	F5	80
Húsavík, Ice.	n34	8b
Húsavík, Ice.	j31	8a
Hushtai, China	C5	38
Huşi, Rom.	C15	26
Huslia, Ak., U.S.	C8	140
Hussar, Ab., Can.	E18	138
Husum, Ger.	B4	16
Hutag, Mong.	B5	36
Hutanopan, Indon.	C1	50
Hutchinson, Ks., U.S.	C6	70
Hutchinson, Ks., U.S.	C11	128
Hutchinson, Mn., U.S.	G4	118
Hutch Mountain, mtn., Az., U.S.	I5	132
Hutsonville, Il., U.S.	E10	120
Huttig, Ar., U.S.	D6	122
Hutto, Tx., U.S.	D10	130
Hutuo, stm., China	B5	42
Huwei, Tai.	J9	42
Huxi, China	H6	42
Huxian, China	D3	42
Huxley, Ab., Can.	E17	138
Huy, Bel.	D14	14
Huzhen, China	G9	42
Huzhou, China	F9	42
Hvannadalshnúkur, mtn., Ice.	k31	8a
Hvar, Cro.	G13	22
Hvar, Otok i., Cro.	G13	22
Hveragerði, Ice.	k29	8a
Hvolsvöllur, Ice.	l29	8a
Hwainan see Huainan, China	E7	42
Hwange, Zimb.	D4	68
Hwang Ho see Huang, stm., China	D8	36
Hwangju-ŭp, Kor., N.	E6	38
Hwangshih see Huangshi, China	F6	42
Hyannis, Ma., U.S.	C15	114
Hyannis, Ne., U.S.	F11	126
Hyargas nuur, l., Mong.	B3	36
Hyattville, Wy., U.S.	C5	126
Hyden, Austl.	F3	74
Hyden, Ky., U.S.	G2	114
Hyde Park, Guy.	B6	84
Hyde Park, N.Y., U.S.	C12	114
Hyde Park, Vt., U.S.	F4	110
Hyderābād, India	C4	53
Hyderābād, Pak.	F2	54
Hydra see Ýdra, i., Grc.	F6	28
Hydraulic, B.C., Can.	D9	138
Hydro, Ok., U.S.	F10	128
Hyères, Fr.	F12	18
Hyères, Iles d', is., Fr.	G12	18
Hyesan, Kor., N.	D8	38
Hyland, stm., Can.	C5	106
Hyndman, Pa., U.S.	E7	114
Hyndman Peak, mtn., Id., U.S.	G12	136
Hyōgo, state, Japan	D7	40
Hyrum, Ut., U.S.	B5	132
Hysham, Mt., U.S.	A5	126
Hythe, Eng., U.K.	J13	12
Hyūga, Japan	G4	40
Hyūga-nada, s., Japan	G4	40
Hyvinge see Hyvinkää, Fin.	F11	8
Hyvinkää, Fin.	F11	8

I

Name	Map Ref.	Page
Iaciara, Braz.	H2	88
Iaco (Yaco), stm., S.A.	F4	84
Iapeba, Braz.	G5	88
Iaeger, W.V., U.S.	G4	114
Ialomiţa, state, Rom.	E14	26
Ialomiţa, stm., Rom.	E13	26
Iamonia, Lake, l., Fl., U.S.	F1	116
Iapu, Braz.	J4	88
Iargara, Mol.	C15	26
Iaşi, Rom.	B14	26
Iaşi, state, Rom.	B14	26
Iatt, Lake, res., La., U.S.	F6	122
Ib, stm., India	G10	54
Iba, Phil.	C2	52
Ibadan, Nig.	H5	64
Ibagué, Col.	E4	86
Ibaiti, Braz.	A13	92
Ibáneşti, Rom.	C12	26
Ibapah Peak, mtn., Ut., U.S.	D3	132
Ibar, stm., Serb.	F7	26
Ibaraki, state, Japan	C13	40
Ibarra, Ec.	G2	86
Ibb, Yemen	G5	56
Ibbenbüren, Ger.	D3	16
Iberá, Esteros del, sw., Arg.	D8	92
Iberia, Mo., U.S.	F5	120
Iberian Mountains see Ibérico, Sistema, mts., Spain	D8	20
Iberian Peninsula, pen., Eur.	D12	4
Ibérico, Sistema (Iberian Mountains), mts., Spain	D8	20
Ibiá, Braz.	J2	88
Ibiapina, Braz.	B5	88
Ibicaraí, Braz.	H6	88
Ibicuí, Braz.	H5	88
Ibicuí, stm., Braz.	D9	92
Ibiquera, Braz.	G5	88
Ibiraçu, Braz.	J5	88
Ibirapuã, Braz.	J5	88
Ibirapuitã, stm., Braz.	D10	92
Ibirataia, Braz.	H6	88
Ibirubá, Braz.	D11	92
Ibitiara, Braz.	G4	88
Ibitinga, Braz.	K1	88
Ibiza see Eivissa, Spain	F12	20
Ibiza see Eivissa, i., Spain	F12	20
Ibotirama, Braz.	G4	88
Ibriktepe, Tur.	B9	28
Ibshawāi, Egypt	I1	58
Ibusuki, Japan	H3	40
Içá (Putumayo), stm., S.A.	D4	84
Içabarú, stm., Ven.	E10	86
Icacos Point, c, Trin.	s11	105f
Icamaquã, stm., Braz.	D10	92
Icamole, Mex.	I7	130
Içana, Braz.	G8	86
Içana (Isana), stm., S.A.	G7	86
Icaño, Arg.	D5	92
Iceberg Pass, p., Co., U.S.	B3	128
Iceland, ctry., Eur.	k30	8a
Iceland Basin, unds.	C11	144
Ice Mountain, mtn., B.C., Can.	C4	36
Ichalkaranji, India	C2	53
Ichchāpuram, India	B7	53
Ichikawa, Japan	D12	40
Ichinomiya, Japan	D9	40
Ichkeul, Lac, l., Tun.	G3	24
Ichnia, Ukr.	D4	32
Ich'un see Yichun, China	B10	36
Ico, Braz.	D6	88
Icy Cape, c., Ak., U.S.	B7	140
Ida, Mount see Idi Óros, mtn., Grc.	H7	28
Idabel, Ok., U.S.	D4	122
Ida Grove, Ia., U.S.	B2	120
Idah, Nig.	H6	64
Idaho, state, U.S.	G12	136
Idaho City, Id., U.S.	G11	136
Idaho Falls, Id., U.S.	G14	136
Idaho National Engineering Laboratory, sci., Id., U.S.	G14	136
Idalou, Tx., U.S.	H7	128
Idanha-a-Nova, Port.	E3	20
Idāppādi, India	F3	53
Idar, India	G4	54
Idar-Oberstein, Ger.	G3	16
Idelès, Alg.	E6	64
Idi, Indon.	J3	48
Idiofa, D.R.C.	F3	66
Idi Oros, mtn., Grc.	H7	28
Idku, Bahra el-, l., Egypt	G1	58
Idlib, Syria	C7	58
Idlib, state, Syria	C7	58
Idolo, Isla del, i., Mex.	E10	100
Idoukâl-en-Taghès, mtn., Niger	F6	64
Idre, Swe.	F5	8
Idrija, Slvn.	D11	22
Idutywa, S. Afr.	H9	70
Ieper, Bel.	D11	14
Ierápetra, Grc.	H8	28
Ierzu, Italy	E3	24
Iesolo, Italy	E9	22
Ifakara, Tan.	F7	66
Ife, Nig.	H5	64
Iferouâne, Niger	F6	64
Iferten see Yverdon-les-Bains, Switz.	D3	22
Ifôghas, Adrar des, mts., Afr.	F5	64
Igan, Malay.	B7	50
Igan, stm., Malay.	B7	50
Iganga, Ug.	D6	66
Igara, Braz.	F5	88
Igara Paraná, stm., Col.	H5	86
Igarapé-Açu, Braz.	D8	84
Igarapé-Miri, Braz.	B1	88
Igarka, Russia	A15	32
Igatpuri, India	B1	53
Igboho, Nig.	H5	64
Igharghar, Oued, stm., Alg.	D6	64
Igiugig, Ak., U.S.	E8	140
Iglesia, Italy	E2	24
Iglesias, Cerro las, mtn., Mex.	B5	100
Iglesiente, reg., Italy	E2	24
Igluligaarjuk (Chesterfield Inlet), Nu., Can.	C12	106
Iglulik, Nu., Can.	B14	106
'Igma, Gebel el-, mts., Egypt	I4	58
Ignacio, Co., U.S.	F9	132
Ignalina, Lith.	E9	10
Ignatei, Mol.	B15	26
Igoumenitsa, Grc.	D3	28
Igra, Russia	C8	32
Iguaçu (Iguazú), stm., S.A.	B10	92
Iguaçu, Parque Nacional do, p.o.i., Braz.	B11	92
Iguaí, Braz.	H5	88
Iguala, Mex.	F9	100
Igualada, Spain	C12	20
Iguana, stm., Ven.	D9	86
Iguape, Braz.	B14	92
Iguatemi, stm., Braz.	A10	92
Iguatu, Braz.	D6	88
Iguazú (Iguaçu), stm., S.A.	B10	92
Iguazú, Parque Nacional, p.o.i., S.A.	B10	92
Iguéla, Gabon	E1	66
Iguéla, Lagune b., Gabon	E1	66
Iguidi, 'Erg, sand, Afr.	D3	64
Iharaña, Madag.	C9	68
Iheya-shima, i., Japan	I18	39a
Ihnāsiya el-Madina, Egypt	I1	58
Ihosy, Madag.	E8	68
Ihtiman, Blg.	G10	26
Iida, Japan	D10	40
Iide-san, mtn., Japan	B12	40
Iijoki, stm., Fin.	D12	8
Iisalmi, Fin.	E12	8
Iiyama, Japan	C11	40
Iizuka, Japan	F3	40
Ijebu-Ode, Nig.	H5	64
IJmuiden, Neth.	B13	14
IJssel, stm., Neth.	B15	14
IJsselmeer, l., Neth.	B14	14
Ijuí, Braz.	D10	92
Ijuí, stm., Braz.	D10	92
Ika, Russia	C19	32
Ikali, D.R.C.	E4	66
Ikalukutiak (Cambridge Bay), Nu., Can.	B10	106
Ikaría, i., Grc.	F9	28
Ikatskij hrebet, mts., Russia	F11	34
Ikeda, Japan	E6	40
Ikeja, Nig.	H5	64
Ikej, Russia	C18	32
Ikela, D.R.C.	E4	66
Ikerre, Nig.	H6	64
Ikizce, Tur.	D15	28
Ikom, Nig.	H6	64
Ikot-Ekpene, Nig.	H6	64
Ikuno, Japan	D8	40
Ikurangi, hill, Cook Is.	a26	78j
Ila, Nig.	H6	64
Ilagan, Phil.	B3	52
Ilaiýänkudi, India	G4	53
Ilām, Iran	C6	56
Ilām, Nepal	E11	54
Ilan, Tai.	I9	42
Ilanskij, Russia	C17	32
Ilaro, Nig.	H5	64
Iława, Pol.	C15	16
Ilbenge, Russia	D13	34
Île-à-la-Crosse, Sk., Can.	D9	106
Ilebo, D.R.C.	E4	66
Île-de-France, hist. reg., Fr.	E11	14
Île de France, i., Grnld.	B22	141
Île-du-Prince-Édouard see Prince Edward Island, state, Can.	D13	110
Ilek, stm., Asia	D8	32
Ilesha, Nig.	H5	64
Îles Loyauté, state, N. Cal.	m16	79d
Île Tintamarre, i., Anguilla	A2	105a
Ilesvkij Pogost, Russia	F20	8
Ileza, Russia	F20	8
Ilfracombe, Austl.	D5	76
Ilfracombe, Eng., U.K.	J8	12
Ilhabela, Braz.	L3	88
Ilha Grande, Baía da, b., Braz.	L3	88
Ilha Solteira, Represa de, res., Braz.	D6	90
Ilha Point, c., Nmb.	C2	70
Ilhéus, Braz.	H6	88
Ilia, Rom.	D9	26
Iliamna, Ak., U.S.	E8	140
Iliamna Lake, l., Ak., U.S.	D9	140
Ilicinea, Braz.	K3	88
Iligan, Phil.	F5	52
Iligan Bay, b., Phil.	F4	52
Iliniza, vol., Ec.	H2	86
Ilion, N.Y., U.S.	A10	114
Ilir, Russia	C18	32
Ilizi, Alg.	D6	64
Il'ja, Bela.	F10	10
Ilo, Peru	G3	84
Iloilo, Phil.	E4	52
Ilomantsi, Fin.	E14	8
Ilorin, Nig.	H5	64
Il'pyrskij, Russia	D21	34
Ilūkste, Lat.	E9	10
Ilullissat see Jakobshavn, Grnld.	D15	141
Ilwaki, Indon.	G8	44
Ilwól-san, mtn., Kor., S.	C1	40
Ilyich, Kaz.	F11	32
Imabari, Japan	E5	40
Imaichi, Japan	C12	40
Imambane, Moz.	C12	70
Imamoğlu, Tur.	A6	58
Imari, Japan	F2	40
Imaruí, Braz.	D13	92
Imaruí, Lagoa do, l., Braz.	D13	92
Imatra, Fin.	F13	8
Imavere, Est.	G11	8
Imbabura, state, Ec.	G2	86
Imbituba, Braz.	D13	92
Imeni Cjurupy, Russia	E21	10
Imeni Kirova, Russia	E14	34
Imeni Poliny Osipenko, Russia	F16	34
Imeni Stepana Razina, Russia	I21	8
Imeni Željabova, Russia	A19	10
Imi, Eth.	F8	62
Imias, Cuba	B10	102
Imilac, Chile	B3	92
Imlay, Nv., U.S.	C7	134
Imlay City, Mi., U.S.	E6	112
Immenstadt, Ger.	I6	16
Immokalee, Fl., U.S.	J4	116
Imnaha, stm., Or., U.S.	E10	136
Imola, Italy	F8	22
Imonda, Pap. N. Gui.	a3	79a
Imotski, Cro.	G13	22
Impasugong, Phil.	F5	52
Imperatriz, Braz.	C2	88
Imperia, Italy	G5	22
Imperial, Sk., Can.	G8	124
Imperial, Ca., U.S.	K10	134
Imperial, Ne., U.S.	G9	126
Imperial, Tx., U.S.	D4	130
Imperial Beach, Ca., U.S.	K8	134
Imperial Dam, dam, U.S.	K2	132
Imperial de Aragón, Canal, can., Spain	C9	20
Imperial Valley, val., Ca., U.S.	J9	134
Impfondo, Congo	D3	66
Imphāl, India	D7	46
Imroz, Tur.	C7	22
Imst, Aus.	C7	22
Imuris, Mex.	F7	98
Ina, Il., U.S.	F9	120
Inaja, Braz.	D6	88
I-n-Amenas, Alg.	D6	64
Iñapari, Peru	F4	84
Inari, Fin.	B12	8
Inarigda, Russia	B19	32
Inarijärvi, l., Fin.	B12	8
Inawashiro-ko, l., Japan	B13	40
Inca, Spain	E13	20
Inca de Oro, Chile	C3	92
Incahuasi, Cerro de, mtn., S.A.	C3	92
İnce Burun, c., Tur.	C10	28
İncekum Burnu, c., Tur.	B4	58
Incesu, Tur.	B3	58
Inch'ŏn, Kor., S.	F7	38
Incirliova, Tur.	F10	28
Incomáti (Komati), stm., Afr.	E10	70
Incudine, Monte, mtn., Fr.	H15	18
Incy, Russia	D19	8
Indaiá, stm., Braz.	J3	88
Indalsälven, stm., Swe.	E6	8
Indaw, Mya.	D8	46
Indé, Mex.	C6	100
Independence, Ca., U.S.	G7	134
Independence, Ia., U.S.	B6	120
Independence, Ks., U.S.	G1	120
Independence, Ky., U.S.	F13	120
Independence, La., U.S.	G8	122
Independence, Mo., U.S.	E3	120
Independence, Or., U.S.	F3	136
Independence, Va., U.S.	H4	114
Independence, Wi., U.S.	G7	118
Independence Mountains, mts., Nv., U.S.	B1	134
Independence Rock, Grnld.	A20	141
Independencia, Bol.	C3	90
Independência, Braz.	C5	88
Inderbor, Kaz.	E8	32
Indi, India	C2	53
India, ctry., Asia	D4	46
Indialantic, Fl., U.S.	H5	116
Indiana, Pa., U.S.	D6	114
Indiana, state, U.S.	D11	120
Indiana Dunes National Lakeshore, p.o.i., In., U.S.	G2	112
Indianapolis, In., U.S.	I3	112
Indian Bayou, stm., Ar., U.S.	C7	122
Indian Church, Belize	D3	102
Indian Head, Sk., Can.	D10	124
Indian Lake, N.Y., U.S.	G2	110
Indian Lake, l., On., Can.	A17	112
Indian Lake, l., Mi., U.S.	B3	112
Indian Ocean	K11	142
Indianola, Ia., U.S.	C4	120
Indianola, Ms., U.S.	D8	122
Indianola, Ne., U.S.	A8	128
Indian Peak, mtn., Ut., U.S.	E3	132
Indian River, Mi., U.S.	C5	112
Indian Rock, mtn., Wa., U.S.	E6	136
Indiantown, Fl., U.S.	I5	116
Indiera Alta, P.R.	B2	104a
Indiga, Russia	C23	8
Indigirka, stm., Russia	C18	34
Indin, Mya.	H14	54
Indio, Ca., U.S.	J9	134
Indira Gandhi Canal, can., India	E4	54
Indispensable Strait, strt., Sol. Is.	e9	79b
Indochina, reg., Asia	D7	48
Indonesia, ctry., Asia	J16	30
Indore, India	G5	54
Indragiri, stm., Indon.	D2	50
Indramayu, Indon.	G6	50
Indrāvati, stm., India	B5	53
Indravati Tiger Reserve, p.o.i., India	B5	53
Indre, state, Fr.	C7	18
Indre, stm., Fr.	G10	14
Indre-et-Loire, state, Fr.	G9	14
Indus, stm., Asia	D2	46
Industry, Tx., U.S.	H2	122
Iñez, stm., Ec.	B10	28
In Ecker, Alg.	E6	64
Inegöl, Tur.	C12	28
Ineu, Rom.	C8	26
Inez, Ky., U.S.	G3	114
Inez, Tx., U.S.	F11	130
Inferior, Laguna, b., Mex.	G11	100
Infiernillo, Canal del, strt., Mex.	G6	98
Infiernillo, Presa del, res., Mex.	F7	100
Ing, stm., Thai.	C5	48
Ingá, Braz.	D8	88
Ingabu, Mya.	D2	48
Ingal, Niger	F6	64
Ingall Point, c., On., Can.	B10	118
Ingelheim, Ger.	G4	16
Ingende, D.R.C.	E3	66
Ingeniero Jacobacci, Arg.	H3	90
Ingeniero Luiggi, Arg.	G5	92
Ingham, Austl.	B6	76
Inglefield Land, reg., Grnld.	B12	141
Ingleside, Tx., U.S.	G10	130
Inglewood, Austl.	G8	76
Inglewood, Austl.	K4	76
Inglewood, Ca., U.S.	J7	134
Ingolf Fjord, b., Grnld.	A22	141
Ingolstadt, Ger.	H7	16
Ingonish, N.S., Can.	D16	110
Ingrāj Bāzār, India	F12	54
Ingrid Christensen Coast, cst., Ant.	B12	81
In Guezzam, Alg.	F6	64
Ingušetija, state, Russia	F6	32
Ingushetia see Ingušetija, state, Russia	F6	32
Inhaca, Ilha da, i., Moz.	E11	70
Inhambane, Moz.	C12	70
Inhambane, state, Moz.	C12	70
Inhambupe, Braz.	F6	88
Inhaminga, Moz.	D5	68
Inhapim, Braz.	J4	88
Inharrime, Moz.	D12	70
Inhassoro, Moz.	B12	70
Inhuma, Braz.	D5	88
Inhumas, Braz.	I1	88
Ining see Yining, China	F14	32
Inírida, stm., Col.	F7	86
Inis see Ennis, Ire.	I3	12
Inis Córthaidh see Enniscorthy, Ire.	I6	12
Inishbofin, i., Ire.	H2	12
Inishmore, i., Ire.	H3	12
Inishowen, pen., Ire.	F5	12
Inishturk, i., Ire.	H2	12
Inja, Russia	E17	34
Inja, stm., Russia	D18	34
Injune, Austl.	E7	76
Inkom, Id., U.S.	H14	136
Inkster, N.D., U.S.	F16	124
Inland Lake, l., Mb., Can.	B14	124
Inland Sea see Seto-naikai, s., Japan	E5	40
Inle Lake, l., Mya.	B3	48
Inman, Ks., U.S.	C11	128
Inman Mills, S.C., U.S.	A3	116
Inn, stm., Eur.	B10	22
Innamincka, Austl.	F3	76
Inner Channel, strt., Belize	D3	102
Inner Hebrides, is., Scot., U.K.	E6	12
Inner Mongolia see Nei Monggol, state, China	C7	36
Inner Sister Island, i., Austl.	m13	77a
Innisfail, Austl.	A6	76
Innisfail, Ab., Can.	D17	138
Innisfree, Ab., Can.	C19	134
Innokentevka, Russia	C16	34
Innoko, stm., Ak., U.S.	D8	140
Innoshima, Japan	E6	40
Innsbruck, Aus.	C8	22
Innviertel, reg., Aus.	B10	22
Inola, Ok., U.S.	H2	120
Inongo, D.R.C.	E3	66
Inönü, Tur.	D13	28
İnözü, Tur.	B14	28
İnquka, Qc., Can.	D15	106
Inuvik, N.T., Can.	B4	106
Inverbervie, Scot., U.K.	E10	12
Invercargill, N.Z.	H3	80
Inverell, Austl.	G8	76
Inverleigh, Austl.	L5	76
Inverness, N.S., Can.	D15	110
Inverness, Scot., U.K.	D8	12
Inverness, Ca., U.S.	E2	134
Inverness, Fl., U.S.	H3	116

Name	Map Ref.	Page
Inverurie, Scot., U.K.	D10	12
Inverway, Austl.	C5	74
Investigator Strait, strt., Austl.	G7	74
Inwood, Mb., Can.	D16	124
Inyangani, mtn., Zimb.	D5	68
Inyathi, Zimb.	D4	68
Inyo, Mount, mtn., Ca., U.S.	G8	134
Inyokern, Ca., U.S.	H8	134
Inyo Mountains, mts., Ca., U.S.	G7	134
Inzana Lake, l., B.C., Can.	B6	138
Ioánnina, Grc.	D3	28
Iokanga, stm., Russia	C18	8
Iola, Ks., U.S.	G2	120
Iola, Ang.	b4	79a
Iona, N.S., Can.	D16	110
Iona, Id., U.S.	G15	136
Iona, i., Scot., U.K.	E6	12
Ione, Ca., U.S.	E5	134
Ione, Wa., U.S.	B9	136
Ionia, Mi., U.S.	E4	112
Ionian Islands see Iónioi Nísoi, is., Grc.	E3	28
Ionian Sea, s., Eur.	F11	24
Iónioi Nísoi (Ionian Islands), is., Grc.	E3	28
Iony, ostrov, i., Russia	E17	34
Íos, i., Grc.	G8	28
Iosegun Lake see Fox Creek, Ab., Can.	B14	138
Iowa, La., U.S.	G5	122
Iowa, state, U.S.	I5	118
Iowa, stm., Ia., U.S.	C6	120
Iowa City, Ia., U.S.	C6	120
Iowa Falls, Ia., U.S.	B4	120
Iowa Park, Tx., U.S.	H10	128
Ipameri, Braz.	I1	88
Ipanema, stm., Braz.	E7	88
Ipanguaçu, Braz.	C7	88
Ipatinga, Braz.	J4	88
Ipatovo, Russia	E6	32
Ipaumirim, Braz.	D6	88
Ipeiros, state, Grc.	D3	28
Ipeiros, hist. reg., Grc.	D3	28
Ipel' (Ipoly), stm., Eur.	I14	16
Ipiales, Col.	G3	86
Ipiaú, Braz.	H6	88
Ipin see Yibin, China	F5	36
Ipirá, Braz.	G5	88
Ipixuna, Braz.	C3	88
Ipoh, Malay.	J5	48
Ipojuca, stm., Braz.	E7	88
Iporã, Braz.	G7	84
Iporá, Braz.	A11	92
Ipota, Vanuatu	I17	79d
Ipsala, Tur.	C9	28
Ipswich, Austl.	F9	76
Ipswich, Eng., U.K.	I14	12
Ipswich, S.D., U.S.	B15	114
Ipswich, S.D., U.S.	B13	126
Ipu, Braz.	C5	88
Ipubi, Braz.	D5	88
Ipuc' (Iput'), stm., Eur.	H14	10
Ipueiras, Braz.	C5	88
Iput' (Ipuc'), stm., Eur.	H14	10
Iqaluit, Nu., Can.	C17	106
Iqfahs, Egypt	J1	58
Iquique, Chile	D2	90
Iquitos, Peru	D3	84
Ira, Tx., U.S.	B7	130
Iracema, Braz.	C6	88
Irákleia, i., Grc.	G8	28
Iráklefo, Grc.	H8	28
Iran, ctry., Asia	C7	56
Iran Mountains, mts., Asia	C9	50
Iránshahr, Iran	D9	56
Irapa, Ven.	B10	86
Irapuato, Mex.	E8	100
Iraq, ctry., Asia	C5	56
Irará, Braz.	F6	88
Irati, Braz.	B12	92
Irazú, Volcán, vol., C.R.	G6	102
Irbejskoe, Russia	C17	32
Irbid, Jord.	F6	58
Irbid, state, Jord.	F6	58
Irbit, Russia	C10	32
Irdning, Aus.	C11	22
Irebu, D.R.C.	E3	66
Irecê, Braz.	F5	88
Ireland, ctry., Eur.	H4	12
Ireland Island North, i., Ber.	k15	104e
Irene, S.D., U.S.	D15	126
Ireng (Maú), stm., S.A.	F12	86
Ireton, Ia., U.S.	B1	120
Iri, Kor., S.	G7	38
Iriba, Chad	E4	62
Iriga, Phil.	D4	52
Irígui, reg., Afr.	F3	64
Iringa, Tan.	F7	66
Irinjálakuda, India	F3	53
Iriomote-jima, i., Japan	G9	36
Iriri, stm., Braz.	D7	84
Irish, Mount, mtn., Nv., U.S.	F1	132
Irish Sea, s., Eur.	H7	12
Iritula, Braz.	A2	88
Irkutsk, Russia	D18	32
Irma, Ab., Can.	D19	138
Irminger Basin, unds.	B10	144
Irnijärvi, l., Fin.	D13	8
Iroise, b., Fr.	F4	14
Iron Bottom Sound, strt., Sol. Is.	e8	79b
Iron Bridge, On., Can.	B6	112
Iron City, Tn., U.S.	B11	122
Irondale, Al., U.S.	D12	122
Irondale, Mo., U.S.	G7	120
Irondequoit, N.Y., U.S.	E12	112
Iron Gate, p., Eur.	E9	26
Iron Knob, Austl.	F7	74
Iron Mountain, Mi., U.S.	C1	112
Iron Range, Austl.	B8	74
Iron River, Mi., U.S.	E10	118
Ironton, Mn., U.S.	E5	118
Ironton, Mo., U.S.	G7	120
Ironton, Oh., U.S.	F3	114
Ironwood, Mi., U.S.	E8	118
Ironwood Forest National Monument, p.o.i., Az., U.S.	K5	132
Iroquois, On., Can.	D14	112
Iroquois, stm., U.S.	H2	112
Iroquois Falls, On., Can.	F14	106
Irō-zaki, c., Japan	E11	40
Irrawaddy see Ayeyarwady, stm., Mya.	E8	46
Irricana, Ab., Can.	E17	138
Irrigon, Or., U.S.	E7	136
Irshava, Ukr.	A10	26
Irsina, Italy	D10	24
Irtyš see Irtysh, stm., Asia	C11	32
Irtysh (Irtyš) (Ertis) (Ertix), stm., Asia	C11	32
Irún, Spain	A9	20
Iruña see Pamplona, Spain	B9	20
Irurzun, Spain	B9	20
Irú Tepuy, mtn., Ven.	E11	86
Irvine, Ab., Can.	E3	124
Irvine, Scot., U.K.	F8	12
Irvines Landing, B.C., Can.	G6	138
Irving, Tx., U.S.	B10	130
Irvington, Ky., U.S.	G11	120
Isa, Nig.	G6	64
Isaac, stm., Austl.	D7	76
Isaac Lake, l., B.C., Can.	C10	138
Isabel, state, Sol. Is.	d8	79b
Isabela, Phil.	G3	52
Isabela, P.R.	A1	104a
Isabela, Cabo, c., Dom. Rep.	C12	102
Isabela, Isla, i., Ec.	i11	84a
Isabelia, Cordillera, mts., Nic.	F5	102
Isaccea, Rom.	D15	26
Isachsen, Cape, c., Nu., Can.	B4	141
Isafjarðardjúp, b., Ice.	j28	8a
Isafjörður, Ice.	j28	8a
Isahaya, Japan	G3	40
Isak, Indon.	J3	48
Isaka, Tan.	E6	66
Ísa Khel, Pak.	B3	54
Işalnița, Rom.	E10	26
Isana (Içana), stm., S.A.	G7	86
Isangel, Vanuatu	l17	79d
Isanti, Mn., U.S.	F5	118
Isar, stm., Eur.	H8	16
Iscehisar, Tur.	E13	28
Ischia, Italy	D7	24
Ischia, Isola d', i., Italy	D7	24
Ise, Japan	E9	40
Iseo, Lago d', l., Italy	E6	22
Isère, state, Fr.	D11	18
Isère, stm., Fr.	D11	18
Iserlohn, Ger.	E3	16
Isernia, Italy	C8	24
Isesaki, Japan	C12	40
Ise-shima-kokuritsu-kōen, p.o.i., Japan	E9	40
Isetan, Japan	E9	40
Ise-wan, b., Japan	E9	40
Iseyin, Nig.	H5	64
Isezaki see Isesaki, Japan	C12	40
Isfahan see Eşfahān, Iran	C7	56
Isfara, Taj.	A11	56
Isherton, Guy.	F12	86
Ishigaki, Japan	G9	36
Ishikari, Japan	C14	38
Ishikari-wan, b., Japan	C14	38
Ishikawa, state, Japan	C9	40
Ishim (Esil) (Išim), stm., Asia	C12	32
Ishinomaki, Japan	A14	40
Ishioka, Japan	C13	40
Ishizuchi-san, mtn., Japan	F5	40
Ishpeming, Mi., U.S.	B2	112
Ishurdi, Bngl.	F12	54
Isigny-sur-Mer, Fr.	E7	14
Işıklı, Tur.	E12	28
Isil'kul', Russia	C12	32
Isil'kul', Russia	C12	32
Išim, Russia	C11	32
Išimskaja ravnina, pl., Asia	C11	32
Isiolo, Kenya	D7	66
Isiro, D.R.C.	D5	66
Isis, Austl.	E9	76
Iskăr, stm., Blg.	F11	26
Iskăr, Jazovir, res., Blg.	G10	26
Iskenderun (Alexandretta), Tur.	B6	58
Iskenderun Körfezi, b., Tur.	B6	58
Iskitim, Russia	D14	32
Iskut, stm., B.C., Can.	D4	106
Isla, Mex.	G11	100
Isla, Salar de la, pl., Chile	B3	92
Islāhīye, Tur.	A7	58
Islāmābād, Pak.	B4	54
Islāmkot, Pak.	F3	54
Islāmpur, India	F10	54
Islāmpur, India	E12	54
Island, Ky., U.S.	C2	53
Island Falls, Me., U.S.	E8	110
Island Harbour, Anguilla	A1	105a
Island Lake, l., Mb., Can.	E12	106
Island Park, Id., U.S.	F15	136
Island Pond, Vt., U.S.	F5	110
Islands, Bay of, b., Nf., Can.	j22	107a
Isla Patrulla, Ur.	F10	92
Isla Vista, Ca., U.S.	I5	134
Islay, i., Scot., U.K.	F6	12
Isle, stm., Fr.	E5	118
Isle, Mn., U.S.	E5	118
Isle of Man, dep., Eur.	G8	12
Isle of Wight, U.S.	H9	114
Isle Royale National Park, p.o.i., Mi., U.S.	C10	118
Islesboro Island, i., Me., U.S.	F8	110
Isleta, N.M., U.S.	I10	132
Isleton, Ca., U.S.	E4	134
Islón, Chile	D2	92
Ismailia (Al-Ismā'īlīyah), Egypt	H3	58
Ismail Samani, pik, mtn., Taj.	B11	56
Isna, Egypt	B6	62
Isny, Ger.	I5	16
Isoka, Zam.	C5	68
Isola del Liri, Italy	I10	22
Isola di Capo Rizzuto, Italy	F11	24
Isonzo, stm., Eur.	E10	22
Isparta, Tur.	F13	28
Isparta, state, Tur.	F13	28
Ispica, Italy	H8	24
Israel, ctry., Asia	G5	58
Isrā'īl see Israel, ctry., Asia	G5	58
Issa, stm., Russia	D11	10
Isser, Oued, stm., Alg.	H14	20
Issia, C. Iv.	H3	64
Issoire, Fr.	D9	18
Issoudun, Fr.	H10	14
Issuna, Tan.	F6	66
Issyk-Kul', Kyrg.	F13	32
Issyk-Kul, Lake see Issyk-Kul', ozero, l., Kyrg.	F13	32
Issyk-Kul', ozero, l., Kyrg.	F13	32
İstanbul, Tur.	B12	28
İstanbul, state, Tur.	B11	28
İstanbul Boğazı (Bosporus), strt., Tur.	B12	28
Istmina, Col.	E3	86
Isto, Mount, mtn., Ak., U.S.	C11	140
Istra, Russia	E19	10
Istria, pen., Eur.	E10	22
Itá, Para.	B9	92
Itabaiana, Braz.	D8	88
Itabaiana, Braz.	F7	88
Itabaianinha, Braz.	F7	88
Itabapoana, Braz.	K5	88
Itaberaba, Braz.	G5	88
Itaberaí, Braz.	I1	88
Itabi, Braz.	F7	88
Itabira, Braz.	J4	88
Itabuna, Braz.	H6	88
Itacajá, Braz.	E2	88
Itacambiruçu, stm., Braz.	I4	88
Itacoatiara, Braz.	D6	84
Itacurubí del Rosario, Para.	B9	92
Itaeté, Braz.	G5	88
Itaguaçu, Braz.	J5	88
Itaguaí, stm., Braz.	K3	88
Itaguari, stm., Braz.	G2	88
Itagüí, Col.	D4	86
Itaí, Braz.	A13	92
Itaim, stm., Braz.	D5	88
Itaiópolis, Braz.	C13	92
Itaipu, Braz.	L3	88
Itaituba, Braz.	D6	84
Itajaí, Braz.	C13	92
Itajubá, Braz.	L3	88
Itajuípe, Braz.	H6	88
Itália de Colônia, Braz.	H6	88
Itala Game Reserve, S. Afr.	E10	70
Itália, sci., Braz.	G4	20
Italy, Tx., U.S.	B11	130
Italy, ctry., Eur.	G11	6
Itamaraju, Braz.	I6	88
Itamarandiba, Braz.	I4	88
Itamarandiba, stm., Braz.	I4	88
Itamari, Braz.	G6	88
Itambacuri, Braz.	I5	88
Itambé, Braz.	H5	88
Itami, Japan	E8	40
Itampolo, Madag.	E7	68
Itanagar, India	E14	54
Itanhaém, Braz.	B14	92
Itanhém, Braz.	I5	88
Itaobim, Braz.	I5	88
Itapagipe, Braz.	J1	88
Itapajé, Braz.	B6	88
Itaparica, Ilha de, i., Braz.	G6	88
Itaparica, Represa de, res., Braz.	E6	88
Itapebi, Braz.	H6	88
Itapecerica, Braz.	K3	88
Itapecuru-Mirim, Braz.	B3	88
Itapemirim, Braz.	K5	88
Itaperuna, Braz.	K5	88
Itapetinga, Braz.	D7	88
Itapetininga, Braz.	H5	88
Itapeva, Braz.	L1	88
Itapetininga, stm., Braz.	A14	92
Itapeva, Braz.	L1	88
Itapicuru, Braz.	F6	88
Itapicuru, stm., Braz.	F6	88
Itapicuru, stm., Braz.	B3	88
Itapipoca, Braz.	B6	88
Itapiranga, Braz.	D6	84
Itapiúna, Braz.	C6	88
Itápolis, Braz.	K1	88
Itaporã de Goiás, Braz.	D1	88
Itaporanga, Braz.	D6	88
Itaporanga d'Ajuda, Braz.	F7	88
Itapúa, state, Para.	C10	92
Itapura, Braz.	G6	88
Itaquara, Braz.	K5	88
Itaquari, Braz.	K5	88
Itaqui, Braz.	D9	92
Itarantim, Braz.	H5	88
Itararé, Braz.	B13	92
Itararé, stm., Braz.	A13	92
Itärsi, India	G6	54
Itarumã, Braz.	C6	88
Itasca, Tx., U.S.	B10	130
Itasca, Lake, l., Mn., U.S.	D3	118
Itä-Suomi, state, Fin.	E12	8
Itata, stm., Chile	H1	92
Itatiaia, Braz.	L1	88
Itatinga, Braz.	C6	88
Itatupã, Braz.	D7	84
Itaueira, Braz.	D4	88
Itaueira, stm., Braz.	D4	88
Itaúna, Braz.	K3	88
Itaqui, Braz.	D9	92
Itbayat Island, i., Phil.	K9	42
Itéa, Grc.	E5	28
Iténez (Guaporé), stm., S.A.	F5	84
Ithaca, Mi., U.S.	E5	112
Ithaca, N.Y., U.S.	B9	114
Ithaca see Itháki, i., Grc.	E3	28
Itháki, i., Grc.	E3	28
Itimbiri, stm., D.R.C.	D4	66
Itiquira, stm., Braz.	G6	84
Itiruçu, Braz.	G5	88
Itiúba, Braz.	F5	88
Ito, Japan	E12	40
Itoigawa, Japan	B10	40
Iton, stm., Fr.	F9	14
Itororó, Braz.	H5	88
Itsuki, Japan	G3	40
Ittiri, Italy	D2	24
Ittoqqortoormiit see Scoresbysund, Grnld.	C21	141
Itu, Braz.	L2	88
Itu, stm., Braz.	D10	92
Ituaçu, Braz.	G5	88
Ituango, Col.	D4	86
Ituberá, Braz.	G6	88
Ituí, stm., Braz.	E3	84
Ituiutaba, Braz.	J1	88
Itumbiara, Braz.	J1	88
Ituna, Sk., Can.	C10	124
Itupiranga, Braz.	E8	84
Ituporanga, Braz.	C13	92
Iturama, Braz.	C6	90
Iturbide, Mex.	C3	102
Iturup, ostrov (Etorofu-tō), i., Russia	B12	38
Ituverava, Braz.	K2	88
Ituxi, stm., Braz.	E4	84
Ituzaingó, Arg.	C9	92
Itzehoe, Ger.	C5	16
Iuka, Ms., U.S.	C10	122
Iul'tin, Russia	C25	34
Iúna, Braz.	K5	88
Ivacevičy, Bela.	H8	10
Ivačovo, Russia	F17	8
Ivai, stm., Braz.	D6	90
Ivaiporã, Braz.	B12	92
Ivalo, Fin.	B12	8
Ivalojoki, stm., Fin.	B12	8
Ivanava, Bela.	H7	10
Ivančice, Czech Rep.	G12	16
Ivangorod, Russia	A11	10
Ivangrad, Serb.	G6	26
Ivanhoe, Austl.	I5	76
Ivanhoe, Ca., U.S.	G6	134
Ivanhoe, Mn., U.S.	G2	118
Ivanhoe, Va., U.S.	H4	114
Ivanišči, Russia	D18	10
Ivanjica, Serb.	F7	26
Ivan'kovo, Russia	F20	10
Ivan'kovskoe vodohranilišče, res., Russia	D19	10
Ivano-Frankivs'k, Ukr.	F13	6
Ivano-Frankivs'k, co., Ukr.	A11	26
Ivanovka, Russia	F14	34
Ivanovo, Russia	H19	8
Ivanovo oblast', co., Russia	H19	8
Ivanpah Lake, l., Ca., U.S.	H1	132
Ivatsevichi see Ivacevičy, Bela.	H8	10
Ivdel', Russia	B9	32
Ivigtut, Grnld.	E16	141
Iviza see Eivissa, Spain	F11	20
Ivohibe, Madag.	E8	68
Ivory Coast see Cote d'Ivoire, ctry., Afr.	H3	64
Ivory Coast, cst., C. Iv.	I3	64
Ivrea, Italy	E4	22
Ivrindi, Tur.	D10	28
Ivujivik, Qc., Can.	C15	106
Iwaki, Japan	B13	40
Iwaki, stm., vol., Japan	D13	38
Iwakuni, Japan	E5	40
Iwamizawa, Japan	C14	38
Iwanai, Japan	C14	38
Iwanuma, Japan	A13	40
Iwase, Japan	C13	40
Iwate, state, Japan	E14	38
Iwate-san, vol., Japan	E14	38
Iwo, Nig.	H5	64
Ixmiquilpan, Mex.	E9	100
Ixopo, S. Afr.	G10	70
Ixtapa, Mex.	G8	100
Ixtlán del Río, Mex.	E6	100
Iyang see Yiyang, China	G5	42
Iyo, Japan	F5	40
Iyo-mishima, Japan	F6	40
Iyo-nada, s., Japan	F4	40
Izabal, Lago de, l., Guat.	E3	102
Izamal, Mex.	B3	102
Izapa, sci., Mex.	H12	100
Izberbaš, Russia	F7	32
Izbica, Pol.	F19	16
Izegem, Bel.	D12	14
Iževsk, Russia	C8	32
Izium, Ukr.	E5	32
Izma, stm., Russia	B8	32
Izmail, Ukr.	D15	26
Izmalkovo, Russia	H21	10
Izmayil see Izmail, Ukr.	D15	26
Izmir (Smyrna), Tur.	E10	28
Izmir, state, Tur.	E10	28
İzmit (Kocaeli), Tur.	C12	28
İzmit Körfezi, b., Tur.	C12	28
Iznik, Tur.	C12	28
İznik Gölü, l., Tur.	C12	28
Iznoski, Russia	E18	10
Izozog, Bañados del, sw., Bol.	C4	90
Izra', Syria	F7	58
Izsák, Hung.	C6	26
Iztaccíhuatl, Volcán, vol., Mex.	F9	100
Iztaccíhuatl y Popocatéptl, Parques Nacionales, p.o.i., Mex.	F9	100
Izucar de Matamoros, Mex.	F9	100
Izu-hantō, pen., Japan	E11	40
Izuhara, Japan	E2	40
Izu Islands see Izu-shotō, is., Japan	E12	40
Izumi, Japan	G3	40
Izumi, Japan	A13	40
Izumi, Japan	E8	40
Izumo, Japan	D5	40
Izu-shotō (Izu Islands), is., Japan	E12	40
Izu Trench, unds.	G17	142
Izvestij CIK, ostrova, is., Russia	A5	34
Izvorul Muntelui, Lacul, l., Rom.	C12	26

J

Name	Map Ref.	Page
Jabal, Bahr al- see Mountain Nile, stm., Afr.	F6	62
Jabal al-Awlīyā', Sudan	D6	62
Jabal Lubnān, state, Leb.	D6	58
Jabalón, stm., Spain	F7	20
Jabalpur, India	G7	54
Jabbūl, Sabkhat al-, l., Syria	B8	58
Jabiru, Austl.	B6	74
Jablah, Syria	C6	58
Jablanica, Bos.	F4	26
Jablaničko jezero, res., Bos.	F4	26
Jablonec nad Nisou, Czech Rep.	F11	16
Jablonka, Pol.	G15	16
Jablonovyj hrebet, mts., Russia	F11	34
Jablunkov, Czech Rep.	G14	16
Jaboticabal, Braz.	K1	88
Jaca, Spain	B10	20
Jacala, Mex.	E9	100
Jacaré, stm., Braz.	F5	88
Jacarei, Braz.	L2	88
Jacarezinho, Braz.	D7	90
Jáchal, stm., Arg.	E4	92
Jaciara, Braz.	G6	84
Jacinto, Braz.	I5	88
Jacinto Aráuz, Arg.	I6	92
Jacinto City, Tx., U.S.	H3	122
Jackfish Lake, l., Sk., Can.	A5	124
Jackhead Harbour, Mb., Can.	C16	124
Jack Mountain, mtn., Mt., U.S.	D14	136
Jackpot, Nv., U.S.	B2	132
Jacksboro, Tn., U.S.	H1	114
Jacksboro, Tx., U.S.	H10	128
Jackson, Ca., U.S.	E5	134
Jackson, Ky., U.S.	G2	114
Jackson, La., U.S.	G7	122
Jackson, Mi., U.S.	B4	114
Jackson, Mn., U.S.	H4	118
Jackson, Ms., U.S.	E8	122
Jackson, N.C., U.S.	H8	114
Jackson, Oh., U.S.	E3	114
Jackson, S.C., U.S.	C4	116
Jackson, Tn., U.S.	B10	122
Jackson, Wy., U.S.	G16	136
Jackson, stm., Va., U.S.	G6	114
Jackson, Mount, mtn., Ant.	C34	81
Jackson, Mount, mtn., Austl.	F3	74
Jackson Creek, stm., Can.	E12	124
Jackson Lake, l., Wy., U.S.	G16	136
Jacksonville, Al., U.S.	D13	122
Jacksonville, Ar., U.S.	C7	122
Jacksonville, Fl., U.S.	F4	116
Jacksonville, Il., U.S.	E7	120
Jacksonville, N.C., U.S.	B8	116
Jacksonville, Or., U.S.	A2	134
Jacksonville, Tx., U.S.	F3	122
Jacksonville Beach, Fl., U.S.	F4	116
Jacmel, Haiti	C11	102
Jaco, Mex.	B5	100
Jacobābād, Pak.	D2	54
Jacobina, Braz.	F5	88
Jacobsdal, S. Afr.	F7	70
Jacques-Cartier, Mont, mtn., Qc., Can.	A11	110
Jacui, stm., Braz.	D11	92
Jacuí, stm., Braz.	D8	88
Jacuipe, stm., Braz.	F6	88
Jacundá, Braz.	D8	84
Jacupiranga, Braz.	B13	92
Jacurici, stm., Braz.	F6	88
Jadebusen, b., Ger.	C4	16
J.A.D. Jensens Nunatakker, mtn., Grnld.	E16	141
Jadraque, Spain	D8	20
Jādū, Libya	A2	62
Jaén, Peru	E2	84
Jaén, Spain	G7	20
Jaffa see Tel Aviv-Yafo, Israel	F5	58
Jaffa, Cape, c., Austl.	K2	76
Jaffna, Sri L.	G4	53
Jaffna Lagoon, b., Sri L.	G4	53
Jaffrey, N.H., U.S.	B13	114
Jafr, Qā' al-, depr., Jord.	H7	58
Jagadhri, India	C6	54
Jagannāthganj Ghāt, Bngl.	F12	54
Jagdalpur, India	B5	53
Jagdaqi, China	F14	34
Jagersfontein, S. Afr.	F7	70
Jaghīn, stm., Iran	D8	56
Jagodnoe, Russia	D18	34
Jagtiāl, India	B4	53
Jaguaquara, Braz.	G5	88
Jaguarão, Braz.	F11	92
Jaguarari, Braz.	F5	88
Jaguaretama, Braz.	C6	88
Jaguari, stm., Braz.	D10	92
Jaguariaíva, Braz.	B13	92
Jaguaribara, Braz.	C6	88
Jaguaribe, Braz.	C6	88
Jaguaribe, stm., Braz.	C6	88
Jaguaruana, Braz.	B7	88
Jaguey Grande, Cuba	A7	102
Jagüé, stm., Arg.	D3	92
Jahān, stm., Iran	D8	56
Jahrom, Iran	D7	56
Jaicós, Braz.	D5	88
Jailolo, Indon.	E8	44
Jaintiāpur, Bngl.	F14	54
Jaipur, India	E5	54
Jaipur Hāt, Bngl.	F12	54
Jais, India	E8	54
Jaisalmer, India	E3	54
Jaito, India	C5	54
Jaja, Russia	C15	32
Jājapur, India	H11	54
Jajce, Bos.	E4	26
Jakarta, Indon.	G5	50
Jakarta, Teluk, b., Indon.	F5	50
Jakalevičy, Bela.	F13	10
Jakhāu, India	G2	54
Jakin, Mol.	F5	50
Jakobstad see Pietarsaari, Fin.	E10	8
Jakovlevka, Russia	B10	38
Jaksa, Russia	C8	72
Jakutija, state, Russia	C14	34
Jakutsk, Russia	D14	34
Jal, N.M., U.S.	B4	130
Jalaid Qi, China	B9	36
Jalālābād, Afg.	C11	56
Jalalpur, India	E9	54
Jalandhar, India	C5	54
Jalapa, Guat.	E3	102
Jalapa see Xalapa, Mex.	F10	100
Jālaun, India	E7	54
Jales, Braz.	D6	90
Jalesar, India	E7	54
Jaleshwar, India	H11	54
Jālgaon, India	H5	54
Jālgaon, India	H6	54
Jalīngo, Nig.	H7	64
Jalisco, state, Mex.	E6	100
Jālna, India	B2	53
Jalón, stm., Spain	C9	20
Jalor, India	F4	54
Jalostotitlán, Mex.	E7	100
Jalpa, Mex.	E7	100
Jalpāiguri, India	E12	54
Jalpan, Mex.	E9	100
Jaluit, at., Marsh. Is.	C7	72
Jalutorovsk, Russia	C11	32
Jamaame, Som.	G3	54
Jamaica, ctry., N.A.	D8	102
Jamaica Channel, strt., N.A.	D9	102
Jamal, poluostrov, pen., Russia	B2	34
Jam-Alin', hrebet, mts., Russia	F15	34
Jamalpur, Bngl.	F12	54
Jamalpur, India	F11	54
Jamanota, hill, Aruba	o20	104g
Jamantau, gora, mtn., Russia	D9	32
Jamanxim, stm., Braz.	E6	84
Jamari, stm., Braz.	E5	84
Jamarovka, Russia	F11	34
Jambeli, Canal de, strt., Ec.	I2	86
Jambes, Bela.	D3	50
Jambi, state, Indon.	D3	50
Jamboaye, stm., Indon.	J3	48
Jamböl, Blg.	G13	26
Jambongan, Pulau, i., Malay.	G1	52
Jambuair, Tanjung, c., Indon.	J3	48
Jambusar, India	G4	54
James, stm., Mo., U.S.	H4	120
James, stm., Va., U.S.	G9	114
James, stm., U.S.	C8	108
James, Isla, i., Chile	H2	90
James Bay, b., Can.	E14	106
James City, N.C., U.S.	A8	116
James Craik, Arg.	F5	92
James Island, S.C., U.S.	D5	116
James Point, c., Bah.	K9	116
James Ross, Cape, c., N.T., Can.	B17	140
James Ross Island, i., Ant.	B35	81
James Ross Strait, strt., Nu., Can.	A11	106
Jamestown, Austl.	I2	76
Jamestown, S. Afr.	H8	70
Jamestown, Ca., U.S.	F5	134
Jamestown, Ky., U.S.	H12	120
Jamestown, N.C., U.S.	I6	114
Jamestown, N.D., U.S.	H15	124
Jamestown, N.Y., U.S.	B6	114
Jamestown, Tn., U.S.	H13	120
Jamestown, misc. cult., Va., U.S.	G9	114
Jäm Jodhpur, India	H3	54
Jamkhandi, India	C2	53
Jamm, Russia	B10	10
Jammerbugten, b., Den.	H3	8
Jammu, India	B5	54
Jammu and Kashmir see Kashmir, hist. reg., Asia	B4	46
Jamnagar (Navanagar), India	G3	54
Jämpang-kulon, Indon.	G5	50
Jāmpur, Pak.	D3	54
Jämsä, Fin.	F11	8
Jamshedpur, India	G11	54
Jamsk, Russia	E19	34
Jämtland, state, Swe.	E6	8
Jamūi, India	F11	54
Jamuna, stm., Bngl.	F12	54
Jämnagar see Jamnagar, India	G3	54
Jan, stm., Russia	C15	34
Janaúba, Braz.	H4	88
Janaucu, Ilha, i., Braz.	D8	84
Jand, Pak.	B4	54
Jandaia, Braz.	C1	88
Jandiála, India	C5	54
Jandowae, Austl.	F8	76
Janesville, Ca., U.S.	C5	134
Janesville, Mn., U.S.	G5	118
Janesville, Wi., U.S.	B8	120
Jangamo, Moz.	D12	70
Jangeru, Indon.	D10	50
Jangijul', Uzb.	F11	32
Jangipur, India	F11	54
Janīn, W.B.	F6	58
Janjira, India	B1	53
Janisjarvi, ozero, l., Russia	E14	8
Januay, Phil.	E4	52
Jan Kempdorp, S. Afr.	E7	70
Jan Mayen, i., Nor.	B22	94
Janos, Mex.	F7	98
Jánoshalma, Hung.	C6	26
Jánosháza, Hung.	B4	26
Janowiec Wielkopolski, Pol.	D13	16
Jansenville, S. Afr.	H7	70
Januária, Braz.	H3	88
Januário Cicco, Braz.	D8	88
Japan, ctry., Asia	e12	38
Japan, Sea of (East Sea), s., Asia	E16	142
Japan Basin, unds.	F17	142
Japan Trench, unds.	F17	142
Japaratinga, Braz.	E8	88
Japi, Braz.	D7	88
Japonskoje more see East Sea, s., Asia	D11	38
Japonskoje more see Japan, Sea of, s., Asia	D11	38
Japurá, Braz.	I9	86
Japurá (Caquetá), stm., S.A.	D4	84
Jaqué, Pan.	H8	102
Jarābulus, Syria	B8	58
Jaraguá, Braz.	H1	88
Jaraguá do Sul, Braz.	C13	92
Jaraíz de la Vera, Spain	D5	20
Jarales, N.M., U.S.	I10	132
Jarama, stm., Spain	D7	20
Jaramānah, Syria	E7	58
Jaransk, Russia	C7	32
Jarānwāla, Pak.	C4	54
Jarash, Jord.	F6	58
Jarash, sci., Jord.	F6	58
Jarcevo, Russia	E15	10
Jardim, Braz.	D6	88
Jardim, Braz.	D5	90
Jardim de Piranhas, Braz.	D7	88
Jardim América, Arg.	C10	92
Jardines de la Reina, Archipiélago de los, is., Cuba	B8	102
Jardinópolis, Braz.	K1	88
Jarej-Uliga-Delap, Marsh. Is.	C8	72
Jarenga, Russia	E23	8
Jarensk, Russia	E23	8
Jargalant, Mong.	B4	36
Jari, stm., Braz.	C7	84
Jaridih, India	G11	54
Jarkand see Shache, China	B12	56
Jarkino, Russia	C17	32
Jarocin, Pol.	C17	32
Jarohta, Russia	C17	32
Jaroměř, Czech Rep.	F11	16
Jarosław, Pol.	H19	8
Jaroslavskaja oblast', co., Russia	H18	8
Jarosław, Pol.	F18	16
Jarratt, Va., U.S.	H8	114
Jar-Sale, Russia	A12	32
Jartai Yanchi, l., China	B1	42
Jarud Qi, China	B4	38
Järvakandi, Est.	G11	8
Järvenpää, Fin.	F11	8
Jarvie, Ab., Can.	B17	138
Jarvis, On., Can.	F9	112
Jarvis, i., Oc.	D10	72
Jarvis Island, i., Oc.	D10	72
Jasaan, Som.	G3	54
Jaseľda, stm., Bela.	H8	10
Jashpurnagar, India	D5	46
Jasień, Pol.	D8	56
Jāsk, Iran	D8	56
Jaškuľ', Russia	F17	8
Jasło, Pol.	G17	16
Jasnogorsk, Russia	F20	10
Jasnyj, Russia	D8	32
Jasper, Ab., Can.	D12	138
Jasper, Al., U.S.	D11	122
Jasper, Ar., U.S.	I4	120
Jasper, Fl., U.S.	F3	116
Jasper, Ga., U.S.	B1	116
Jasper, In., U.S.	F10	120
Jasper, Mn., U.S.	H2	118
Jasper, Mo., U.S.	G3	120
Jasper, Tn., U.S.	B13	122
Jasper Lake, l., Ab., Can.	C13	138
Jasper National Park, p.o.i., Ab., Can.	D13	138
Jastarnia, Pol.	B14	16
Jászapáti, Hung.	B7	26
Jászberény, Hung.	B6	26
Jász-Nagykun-Szolnok, state, Hung.	B7	26
Jatai, Braz.	G7	84
Jatapu, stm., Braz.	D6	84
Jataté, stm., Mex.	G13	100
Jati, Braz.	D6	88
Jāti, Pak.	F2	54
Játiva see Xàtiva, Spain	F10	20
Jatni, India	H10	54
Jaú, Braz.	L1	88
Jaú, Parque Nacional do, p.o.i., Braz.	I10	86
Jauaperi, stm., Braz.	H11	86
Jauá Sarisariñama, Parque Nacional, p.o.i., Ven.	E9	86
Jauja, Peru	F2	84
Jaunjelgava, Lat.	D7	10
Jaunpiebalga, Lat.	C9	10
Jaunpur, India	F9	54
Javalambre, stm., Spain	D9	20
Java Sea see Jawa, Laut, s., Indon.	F6	50
Java Trench, unds.	J13	142
Jávea see Xàbia, Spain	F11	20
Javornik, Czech Rep.	F13	16
Javorová skála, mtn., Czech Rep.	G10	16
Jawa (Java), i., Indon.	H6	50
Jawa, Laut (Java Sea), s., Indon.	F6	50
Jawa Barat, state, Indon.	G5	50
Jawa Tengah, state, Indon.	G7	50
Jawa Timur, state, Indon.	G8	50
Jawhar, Som.	D9	66
Jawi, Indon.	D6	50
Jawor, Pol.	E12	16
Jaworzno, Pol.	F15	16
Jay, Fl., U.S.	G11	122
Jay, Ok., U.S.	H3	120
Jaya, Puncak (Jaya Peak), mtn., Indon.	F10	44
Jaya Peak see Jaya, Puncak, mtn., Indon.	F10	44
Jayapura, Indon.	F11	44
Jayb, Wādī al- (Ha'Arava), stm., Asia	H6	58
Jaynes, Az., U.S.	K5	132
Jaypur, India	B6	53
Jayuya, P.R.	B2	104a
Jäzelbicy, Russia	B15	10
Jažma, Russia	C21	8
Jean, Nv., U.S.	H1	132
Jeanerette, La., U.S.	H7	122
Jeannette Island see Žannetty, ostrov, i., Russia	A20	34
Jebba, Nig.	H5	64
Jebel, Rom.	D8	26
Jedburgh, Scot., U.K.	F10	12
Jeddah see Jiddah, Sau. Ar.	E4	56
Jędrzejów, Pol.	F16	16
Jeffara (Al-Jifārah), pl., Afr.	C7	64
Jeffers, Mn., U.S.	G3	118
Jefferson, Ga., U.S.	B2	116
Jefferson, Ia., U.S.	B3	120
Jefferson, Or., U.S.	F3	136
Jefferson, S.C., U.S.	B5	116
Jefferson, Tx., U.S.	E4	122
Jefferson, Wi., U.S.	A9	120
Jefferson, Mount, mtn., Nv., U.S.	E1	134
Jefferson, Mount, vol., Or., U.S.	F5	136
Jefferson City, Mo., U.S.	F5	120
Jefferson City, Tn., U.S.	H2	114
Jeffersontown, Ky., U.S.	F12	120
Jeffersonville, Ga., U.S.	D2	116
Jeffersonville, In., U.S.	F12	120
Jeffrey City, Wy., U.S.	E5	126
Jehol see Chengde, China	A7	42
Jejsk see Ejsk, Russia	E5	32
Jejui Guazú, stm., Para.	B9	92
Jēkabpils, Lat.	D8	10
Jekyll Island, i., Ga., U.S.	E4	116
Jelai, stm., Indon.	E7	50
Jelcz, Pol.	E13	16
Jelenia Góra, Pol.	F11	16
Jelenia Góra, state, Pol.	E11	16
Jelgava, Lat.	D6	10
Jelgavkrasti, Lat.	C7	10
Jellicoe, On., Can.	B11	118

Jelm Mountain – Kamieńsk I • 27

Name	Map Ref.	Page
Jelm Mountain, mtn., Wy., U.S.	F7	126
Jemaja, Pulau, i., Indon.	B4	50
Jember, Indon.	H8	50
Jemez Canyon Reservoir, res., N.M., U.S.	H9	132
Jemez Springs, N.M., U.S.	H10	132
Jemnice, Czech Rep.	H11	16
Jempang, Kenohan, l., Indon.	D9	50
Jena, Ger.	F7	16
Jena, La., U.S.	F6	122
Jendouba, Tun.	H2	24
Jeneponto, Indon.	F11	50
Jenks, Ok., U.S.	H2	120
Jennings, Fl., U.S.	F2	116
Jennings, La., U.S.	G6	122
Jensen, Ut., U.S.	C7	132
Jens Munk Island, i., Nu., Can.	B14	106
Jens Munks Ø, i., Grnld.	E17	141
Jenu, Indon.	D6	50
Jeonju see Chŏnju, Kor., S.	G7	38
Jepara, Indon.	G7	50
Jeparit, Austl.	K4	76
Jeptha Knob, hill, Ky., U.S.	F12	120
Jequié, Braz.	G5	88
Jequitinhonha, Braz.	I5	88
Jequitinhonha, stm., Braz.	H5	88
Jerada, Mor.	C4	64
Jerba, Île de, i., Tun.	C7	64
Jerécuaro, Mex.	E8	100
Jérémie, Haiti	C10	102
Jeremoabo, Braz.	F6	88
Jerevan see Yerevan, Arm.	A5	56
Jerez de García Salinas, Mex.	D7	100
Jerez de la Frontera, Spain	H4	20
Jerez de los Caballeros, Spain	F4	20
Jericho, Austl.	D5	76
Jericho see Arīḥā, Gaza	G6	58
Jericó, Braz.	D7	88
Jerid, Chott, l., Tun.	C6	64
Jerimoth Hill, hill, R.I., U.S.	C14	114
Jeroaquara, Braz.	G7	84
Jerome, Az., U.S.	I4	132
Jerome, Id., U.S.	H12	136
Jersey, dep., Eur.	E6	14
Jersey, i., Jersey	E6	14
Jersey City, N.J., U.S.	D11	114
Jerseyville, Il., U.S.	E7	120
Jerumenha, Braz.	D4	88
Jerusalem see Yerushalayim, Isr.	G6	58
Jervis, Cape, c., Austl.	J1	76
Jervis Bay, b., Austl.	J8	76
Jervis Bay Territory, co., Austl.	J8	76
Jervis Inlet, b., B.C., Can.	F7	138
Jesenice, Czech Rep.	F9	16
Jeseník, Czech Rep.	F13	16
Jesi (Iesi), Italy	G10	22
Jessen, Ger.	E9	16
Jessore, Bngl.	G12	54
Jesup, Ga., U.S.	E4	116
Jesup, Ia., U.S.	B5	120
Jesús Carranza, Mex.	G11	100
Jesús María, Arg.	E5	92
Jesús Menéndez, Cuba	B9	102
Jet, Ok., U.S.	E10	128
Jetmore, Ks., U.S.	C9	128
Jetpur, India	H3	54
Jeune Landing, B.C., Can.	F3	138
Jever, Ger.	C3	16
Jewel Cave National Monument, p.o.i., S.D., U.S.	D8	126
Jewell, Ks., U.S.	B10	128
Jewell Ridge, Va., U.S.	G4	114
Jewett, Il., U.S.	E9	120
Jewett City, Ct., U.S.	C13	114
Jezercës, maja e, mtn., Alb.	B13	24
Jeziorany, Pol.	B16	16
Jhābua, India	G5	54
Jha Jha, India	F11	54
Jhālakāti, Bngl.	G13	54
Jhālāwār, India	F6	54
Jhang Sadar, Pak.	C4	54
Jhānsi, India	F7	54
Jhārgrām, India	G11	54
Jharia, India	G11	54
Jharkhand, state, India	G10	54
Jhārsuguda, India	H10	54
Jhelum, Pak.	B4	54
Jhelum, stm., Asia	C4	54
Jhinkpāni, India	G10	54
Jhok Rind, Pak.	C3	54
Jhunjhunūn, India	D5	54
Jiaban, China	I2	42
Jiading, China	F9	42
Jiāganj, India	F12	54
Jiahe, China	I5	42
Jiali, China	C14	54
Jialing, stm., China	G2	42
Jialu, stm., China	E5	42
Jiamusi, China	B11	36
Ji'an, China	D7	38
Ji'an, China	H6	42
Jian, stm., China	H8	42
Jianchang, China	A8	42
Jianchang, China	B10	42
Jianchuan, China	F4	36
Jiande, China	G8	42
Jiang'an, China	G1	42
Jiangcheng, China	A5	48
Jiangdu, China	E8	42
Jiange, China	E1	42
Jianghua, China	I4	42
Jiangjin, China	G2	42
Jiangkou, China	J4	42
Jiangkou, China	H3	42
Jiangkou, China	F4	42
Jiangle, China	H7	42
Jiangling, China	F4	42
Jiangmen, China	J5	42
Jiangmifeng, China	B7	38
Jiangshan, China	G8	42
Jiangsu, state, China	E8	42
Jiangtun, China	J5	42
Jiangxi, state, China	H6	42
Jiangya, China	G4	42
Jiangyin, China	F9	42
Jiangyou, China	F1	42
Jiangzhong, China	D14	54
Jianli, China	G5	42
Jianning, China	H7	42
Jian'ou, China	H8	42
Jianping, China	D3	38
Jianshi, China	F3	42
Jianshui, China	G5	36
Jianyang, China	E5	36
Jianyang, China	H8	42
Jiaocheng, China	C4	42
Jiaohe, China	C7	38
Jiaolai, stm., China	C4	38
Jiaonan, China	D8	42
Jiaoxian, China	C8	42
Jiaozhou Wan, b., China	C9	42
Jiaozuo, China	D5	42
Jiashan, China	E7	42
Jiashi, China	B12	56
Jiashun Hu, l., China	A10	54
Jiawang, China	D7	42
Jiaxian, China	D5	42
Jiaxian, China	B4	42
Jiaxing, China	F9	42
Jiazi, China	J6	42
Jibuti see Djibouti, Dji.	E8	62
Jicarón, Isla, i., Pan.	I7	102
Jičín, Czech Rep.	F11	16
Jiddah (Jeddah), Sau. Ar.	E4	56
Jidingxilin, China	B14	54
Jieshi Wan, b., China	J6	42
Jieshou, China	E6	42
Jiexi, China	J6	42
Jiexiu, China	C4	42
Jieyang, China	J7	42
Jieznas, Lith.	F7	10
Jiguaní, Cuba	B9	102
Jigüey, Bahía de, strt., Cuba	A8	102
Jigzhi, China	E5	36
Jihlava, Czech Rep.	G11	16
Jihlava, stm., Czech Rep.	G12	16
Jihočeský kraj, state, Czech Rep.	G10	16
Jihomoravský kraj, state, Czech Rep.	G12	16
Jijia, stm., Rom.	B14	26
Jijiga, Eth.	F8	62
Jilantai, China	B1	42
Jilib, Som.	D8	66
Jili Hu, l., China	B2	36
Jilin, China	C7	38
Jilin, state, China	C10	36
Jill, Kediet ej, mtn., Maur.	E2	64
Jiloca, stm., Spain	C9	20
Jīma, Eth.	F7	62
Jimbolia, Rom.	D7	26
Jimena de la Frontera, Spain	H5	20
Jiménez, Mex.	B6	100
Jiménez, Mex.	A8	100
Jiménez del Téul, Mex.	D7	100
Jimeta, Nig.	H7	64
Jim Ned Creek, stm., Tx., U.S.	C8	130
Jimo, China	C9	42
Jimsar, China	C2	36
Jim Thorpe, Pa., U.S.	D10	114
Jin (Gam), stm., Asia	A7	48
Jin, stm., China	H7	42
Jinan (Tsinan), China	C7	42
Jincang, China	C9	38
Jincheng, China	D5	42
Jīnd, India	D6	54
Jindabyne, Austl.	K7	76
Jindřichův Hradec, Czech Rep.	G11	16
Jing, stm., China	D3	42
Jing'an, China	G6	42
Jingbian, China	C3	42
Jingbohu, res., China	C8	38
Jingde, China	F8	42
Jingdezhen, China	G7	42
Jinggangshan, China	H6	42
Jinghai, China	B7	42
Jinghe, China	F14	32
Jinghong, China	B5	48
Jingle, China	B4	42
Jingmen, China	F5	42
Jingning, China	D1	42
Jingxi, China	J2	42
Jingxian, China	F8	42
Jingxian, China	C7	42
Jingxian, China	H3	42
Jingxin, China	I6	42
Jingyu, China	C7	38
Jingzhi, China	C8	42
Jinhae see Chinhae, Kor., S.	D1	40
Jinhua, China	G8	42
Jining, China	D7	42
Jining, China	A5	42
Jinja, Ug.	D6	66
Jinjiazhen, China	C5	38
Jinju see Chinju, Kor., S.	G7	38
Jinmu Jiao, c., China	L3	42
Jinning, China	G5	36
Jinotega, Nic.	F5	102
Jinotepe, Nic.	G4	102
Jinping, China	H3	42
Jinqian, stm., China	E3	42
Jinsha, China	H1	42
Jinsha (Yangtze), stm., China	F5	36
Jinshi, China	G4	42
Jintian, China	H6	42
Jintotolo Channel, strt., Phil.	E4	52
Jinxi, China	A9	42
Jinxi, China	H7	42
Jinxian, China	G7	42
Jinxian, China	B6	42
Jinzhou, China	B9	42
Jinzhou, China	A9	42
Ji-Paraná, Braz.	F5	84
Jipijapa, Ec.	H1	86
Jiquiriçá, stm., Braz.	G6	88
Jiri, stm., India	F14	54
Jirkov, Czech Rep.	F9	16
Jishou, China	G3	42
Jisr ash-Shughūr, Syria	C7	58
Jitaúna, Braz.	G6	88
Jiu, stm., Rom.	F10	26
Jiudaoliang, China	F4	42
Jiufeng, China	I7	42
Jiujiang, China	G6	42
Jiulian Shan, mts., China	I6	42
Jiuliguan, China	F6	42
Jiuling Shan, mts., China	G6	42
Jiulong, China	J5	42
Jiulong, stm., China	I7	42
Jiuquan, China	D4	36
Jiutai, China	B6	38
Jiuyuanqu, China	D4	42
Jiuzhan, China	C7	38
Jiuzhen, China	I7	42
Jiwen, China	A9	36
Jixi, China	B9	38
Jixi, China	F8	42
Jixian, China	A7	42
Jixian, China	D6	42
Jiyi, China	D4	42
Jiyuan, China	D5	42
Jiyun, stm., China	B7	42
Jīzān, Sau. Ar.	F5	56
Jizl, Wādī al-, stm., Sau. Ar.	K8	58
J. J. Castelli see Castelli, Arg.	B7	92
J.M. Lencinas see Las Catitas, Arg.	F3	92
Joaçaba, Braz.	C12	92
Joana Coeli, Braz.	A1	88
Joanes, Braz.	D8	84
João Câmara, Braz.	C8	88
João Monlevade, Braz.	J4	88
João Pessoa, Braz.	D8	88
João Pinheiro, Braz.	I2	88
Joaquim Távora, Braz.	A12	92
Joaquin, Tx., U.S.	F4	122
Joaquín V. González, Arg.	B5	92
Jobos, P.R.	C3	104a
Job Peak, mtn., Nv., U.S.	D7	134
Jocolí, Arg.	F3	92
Jódar, Spain	G7	20
Jodhpur, India	E4	54
Jodiya, India	G3	54
Joensuu, Fin.	E13	8
Joetsu, Japan	B11	40
Jõgeva, Est.	G12	8
Jog Falls, wtfl., India	D2	53
Joggins, N.S., Can.	E12	110
Jogjakarta see Yogyakarta, Indon.	G7	50
Jōhana, Japan	C9	40
Johannesburg, S. Afr.	E8	70
John Day, Or., U.S.	F8	136
John Day, stm., Or., U.S.	E6	136
John Day, Middle Fork, stm., Or., U.S.	F8	136
John Day, North Fork, stm., Or., U.S.	F8	136
John Day Fossil Beds National Monument, p.o.i., Or., U.S.	F7	136
John F. Kennedy Space Center, sci., Fl., U.S.	H5	116
John H. Kerr Reservoir, res., U.S.	H7	114
John Martin Reservoir, res., Co., U.S.	C6	128
John o' Groats, Scot., U.K.	C9	12
John Redmond Reservoir, res., Ks., U.S.	F1	120
Johns Island, i., S.C., U.S.	D5	116
Johnson, Ar., U.S.	H3	120
Johnson, Ks., U.S.	D7	128
Johnsonburg, Pa., U.S.	C7	114
Johnson City, N.Y., U.S.	B10	114
Johnson City, Tn., U.S.	H3	114
Johnson City, Tx., U.S.	D9	130
Johnsondale, Ca., U.S.	H7	134
Johnson Draw, stm., Tx., U.S.	D6	130
Johnson Point, c., St. Vin.	o11	105e
Johnsonville, S.C., U.S.	C6	116
Johnston, Ia., U.S.	C4	120
Johnston, S.C., U.S.	C4	116
Johnston, Lake, l., Austl.	F4	74
Johnston Atoll, at., Oc.	B10	72
Johnstown, Co., U.S.	G8	126
Johnstown, N.Y., U.S.	G2	110
Johnstown, Oh., U.S.	D3	114
Johnstown, Pa., U.S.	D7	114
Johor, state, Malay.	L6	48
Johor Bahru, Malay.	L6	48
Joigny, Fr.	G12	14
Joiner, Ar., U.S.	B8	122
Joinville, Braz.	C13	92
Joinville Island, i., Ant.	B35	81
Jojogan, Indon.	G7	50
Jokkmokk, Swe.	C8	8
Jökulsá á Brú, stm., Ice.	k32	8a
Jökulsárgljúfur Nasjonalpark, p.o.i., Ice.	k32	8a
Joliet, Il., U.S.	C9	120
Joliette, Qc., Can.	D3	110
Jolo, Phil.	G3	52
Jolo Group, is., Phil.	G3	52
Jolo Island, i., Phil.	H3	52
Jombang, Indon.	G8	50
Jomda, China	E4	36
Jonava, Lith.	E7	10
Jones, Ok., U.S.	F11	128
Jonesboro, Ar., U.S.	I7	120
Jonesboro, Ga., U.S.	C1	116
Jonesboro, Il., U.S.	G8	120
Jonesboro, La., U.S.	E6	122
Jonesborough, Tn., U.S.	H3	114
Jones Mill, Ar., U.S.	C6	122
Jonesport, Me., U.S.	F9	110
Jones Sound, strt., Nu., Can.	B8	141
Jonestown, Ms., U.S.	C8	122
Jonesville, La., U.S.	F7	122
Jonesville, Mi., U.S.	B1	114
Jonglei Canal, can., Sudan	F6	62
Joniškėlis, Lith.	D6	10
Joniškis, Lith.	D6	10
Jönköping, Swe.	H6	8
Jönköping, state, Swe.	H6	8
Jonquière, Qc., Can.	B5	110
Jonuta, Mex.	F12	100
Jonzac, Fr.	D5	18
Joplin, Mo., U.S.	G3	120
Joplin, Mt., U.S.	B16	136
Joppa, Il., U.S.	G9	120
Jora, India	E6	54
Jordan, Mn., U.S.	G5	118
Jordan, Mt., U.S.	G6	124
Jordan, ctry., Asia	H7	58
Jordan (Al-Urdunn) (HaYarden), stm., Asia	F6	58
Jordan, stm., Ut., U.S.	C5	132
Jordan Creek, stm., U.S.	H10	136
Jordânia, Braz.	H5	88
Jordan Valley, Or., U.S.	G10	136
Jordão, stm., Braz.	B12	92
Jorge Montt, Isla, i., Chile	J2	90
Jorhāt, India	C7	46
Jornado del Muerto, des., N.M., U.S.	J10	132
Joroinen, Fin.	E12	8
Jos, Nig.	G6	64
Jose Abad Santos, Phil.	H5	52
José Batlle y Ordóñez, Ur.	F10	92
José Bonifácio, Braz.	K1	88
José de Freitas, Braz.	C4	88
José de San Martín, Arg.	H2	90
José Pedro Varela, Ur.	F10	92
Joseph, Or., U.S.	E9	136
Joseph, Lac, l., Nf., Can.	E17	106
Joseph Bonaparte Gulf, b., Austl.	B5	74
Joshīmath, India	C7	54
Jōshin-Etsu-kōgen-kokuritsu-kōen, p.o.i., Japan	C11	40
Joshua, Tx., U.S.	B10	130
Joshua Tree, Ca., U.S.	I9	134
Joshua Tree National Park, p.o.i., Ca., U.S.	J10	134
Jostedalsbreen, ice, Nor.	F2	8
Jostedalsbreen Nasjonalpark, p.o.i., Nor.	F2	8
Jotunheimen Nasjonalpark, p.o.i., Nor.	F2	8
Joubertina, S. Afr.	H6	70
Jourdanton, Tx., U.S.	F9	130
Joutsijärvi, Fin.	C13	8
Joviânia, Braz.	I1	88
Jowai, India	F14	54
Joya, Mex.	H6	130
Joyce, La., U.S.	F6	122
Joyuda, P.R.	B1	104a
J. Percy Priest Lake, res., Tn., U.S.	H11	120
J. Strom Thurmond Reservoir, res., U.S.	C3	116
Juami, stm., Braz.	I7	86
Juana Díaz, P.R.	B2	104a
Juan Aldama, Mex.	C7	100
Juan Bautista Alberdi, Arg.	C5	92
Juan de Fuca, Strait of, strt., N.A.	B2	136
Juan de Garay, Arg.	I5	92
Juan de Nova, Île, i., Reu.	D7	68
Juan E. Barra, Arg.	H7	92
Juan Fernández, Archipiélago, is., Chile	I6	82
Juanjuí, Peru	E2	84
Juan N. Fernández, Arg.	I8	92
Juan Viñas, C.R.	H6	102
Juárez see Benito Juárez, Arg.	H8	92
Juárez, Mex.	B8	100
Juárez, Mex.	F8	98
Juatinga, Ponta de, c., Braz.	L3	88
Juazeirinho, Braz.	D7	88
Juazeiro, Braz.	E5	88
Juazeiro do Norte, Braz.	D6	88
Juba, Sudan	G6	62
Juba see Jubba, stm., Afr.	D8	66
Juba see Genalē, stm., Afr.	C8	66
Jubal, Strait of see Gûbâi, Madîq, strt., Egypt	K4	58
Jubayl, Leb.	D6	58
Jubba (Genalē), stm., Afr.	D8	66
Juby, Cap, c., Mor.	D2	64
Júcar (Xúquer), stm., Spain	E10	20
Juchipila, Mex.	E7	100
Juchitán de Zaragoza, Mex.	G11	100
Jucurucu, stm., Braz.	I5	88
Jucurutu, Braz.	C7	88
Judenburg, Aus.	C11	22
Judino, Russia	B22	10
Judique, N.S., Can.	E15	110
Judith, stm., Mt., U.S.	C17	136
Judith Gap, Mt., U.S.	D17	136
Judith Peak, mtn., Mt., U.S.	C17	136
Judoma, stm., Russia	E16	34
Jufari, stm., Braz.	H10	86
Jug, stm., Russia	G21	8
Jugorskij poluostrov, pen., Russia	A10	32
Juhnov, Russia	F18	10
Juidongshan, China	J7	42
Juigalpa, Nic.	F5	102
Juist, i., Ger.	C2	16
Juiz de Fora, Braz.	K4	88
Jujuy, state, Arg.	D3	90
Jukagirskoe ploskogor'e, plat., Russia	C19	34
Jukta, Russia	B19	32
Jula, stm., Russia	E21	8
Julesburg, Co., U.S.	G10	126
Juliaca, Peru	G3	84
Julia Creek, Austl.	C3	76
Julia Creek, stm., Austl.	C3	76
Julianadorp, Neth. Ant.	p22	104g
Julian Alps, mts., Eur.	D10	22
Juliana Top, mtn., Sur.	C6	84
Julianehåb (Qaqortoq), Grnld.	E16	141
Jülich, Ger.	F2	16
Juliette, Lake, res., Ga., U.S.	D2	116
Julimes, Mex.	A6	100
Júlio de Castilhos, Braz.	D11	92
Juma, Russia	D15	8
Juma, stm., China	B6	42
Jumba, Som.	E8	66
Jumilla, Spain	F9	20
Jumlā, Nepal	D9	54
Jūnāgadh, India	H3	54
Juncos, P.R.	B4	104a
Junction, Tx., U.S.	D8	130
Junction City, Ar., U.S.	E6	122
Junction City, Ks., U.S.	B12	128
Junction City, Ky., U.S.	G13	120
Jundah, Austl.	E4	76
Jundiaí, Braz.	L2	88
Juneau, Ak., U.S.	E13	140
Juneau, Wi., U.S.	H10	118
Junee, Austl.	J6	76
June Lake, Ca., U.S.	F6	134
Jungar Qi, China	B4	42
Jungfrau, mtn., Switz.	D4	22
Junggar Pendi, bas., China	B2	36
Juniata, Ne., U.S.	G14	126
Juniata, stm., Pa., U.S.	D8	114
Junín, Arg.	G7	92
Junín, Ec.	H1	86
Junín de los Andes, Arg.	G2	90
Juniper, N.B., Can.	D9	110
Junipero Serra Peak, mtn., Ca., U.S.	G4	134
Jūniyah, Leb.	E6	58
Junlian, China	F5	36
Junnar, India	B1	53
Junqueiro, Braz.	E7	88
Junxian, China	E4	42
Juodkrantė, Lith.	E3	10
Juozapinės kalnas, hill, Lith.	F8	10
Juparanã, Lagoa, l., Braz.	J5	88
Jupiter, Fl., U.S.	J5	116
Juquiá, Braz.	B14	92
Juquiá, Ponta do, c., Braz.	B14	92
Jur, Russia	E16	34
Jur, stm., Sudan	F5	62
Jura, Mol.	B16	26
Jura, state, Fr.	C11	18
Jura, mts., Eur.	B12	18
Jura, i., Scot., U.K.	F7	12
Jūra, stm., Lith.	E5	10
Jurbarkas, Lith.	E5	10
Jurenino, Russia	G20	8
Jurevec, Russia	H20	8
Jurga, Russia	C15	32
Juriti, Braz.	D6	84
Jūrmala, Lat.	C6	10
Jurong, China	F8	42
Juruá, stm., S.A.	D4	84
Juruena, stm., Braz.	E6	84
Jurumirim, Represa de, res., Braz.	L1	88
Jusepín, Ven.	C10	86
Juškovo, Russia	G21	8
Justiniano Posse, Arg.	F6	92
Justino Solari see Mariano I. Loza, Arg.	D8	92
Justo Daract, Arg.	F5	92
Jutaí, stm., Braz.	D4	84
Jüterbog, Ger.	D9	16
Jutiapa, Guat.	E3	102
Juticalpa, Hond.	E4	102
Jutland see Jylland, reg., Den.	H3	8
Jutrosin, Pol.	E13	16
Juventud, Isla de la (Pines, Isle of), i., Cuba	B6	102
Juxian, China	D8	42
Juye, China	D6	42
Juža, Russia	H20	8
Južna Morava, stm., Serb.	F8	26
Južno-Enisejskij, Russia	C17	32
Južno-Sahalinsk, Russia	G17	34
Južno-Ural'sk, Russia	D10	32
Južnyj, mys, c., Russia	E20	34
Južnyj Ural, mts., Russia	D9	32
Jwayyā, Leb.	E6	58
Jyekundo see Yushu, China	E4	36
Jylland (Jutland), reg., Den.	H3	8
Jyväskylä, Fin.	E11	8

K

Name	Map Ref.	Page
K2, mtn., Asia	B12	56
Kaabong, Ug.	D6	66
Kaahka, Turkmen.	B8	56
Ka'ala, mtn., Hi., U.S.	b3	78a
Kaala-Gomen, N. Cal.	m15	79d
Kaapstad see Cape Town, S. Afr.	H4	70
Kaarli, Est.	A9	10
Kaatoan, Mount, mtn., Phil.	F5	52
Kabacan, Phil.	G5	52
Kabaena, Pulau, i., Indon.	G7	44
Kabah, sci., Mex.	B3	102
Kabala, S.L.	H2	64
Kabale, Ug.	E5	66
Kabalega Falls, wtfl., Ug.	D6	66
Kabalo, D.R.C.	F5	66
Kabambare, D.R.C.	E5	66
Kabanjahe, Indon.	K4	48
Kabankalan, Phil.	F4	52
Kabardin-Balkaria see Kabardino-Balkarija, state, Russia	F6	32
Kabardino-Balkarija, state, Russia	F6	32
Kabba, Nig.	H6	64
Kabbani, stm., India	F3	53
Kåbdalis, Swe.	C8	8
Kabetogama Lake, l., Mn., U.S.	C5	118
Kab-hegy, mtn., Hung.	B4	26
Kabinda, D.R.C.	F4	66
Kabinu, Indon.	A9	50
Kabīr Kūh, mts., Iran	C6	56
Kabna, Sudan	D6	62
Kābol, Afg.	C10	56
Kābol, state, Afg.	A2	54
Kabompo, Zam.	C3	68
Kabompo, stm., Zam.	C3	68
Kabongo, D.R.C.	F5	66
Kābul see Kābol, Afg.	C10	56
Kabul (Kābol), stm., Asia	A4	54
Kabwe, Zam.	C4	68
Kabylie, reg., Alg.	H14	20
Kačanik, Serb.	G8	26
Kačerginė, Lith.	F6	10
Kachchh, Gulf of, b., India	G2	54
Kachīry, Kaz.	D13	32
Kačkanar, Russia	C10	32
Kačug, Russia	D19	32
Kadaiyanallūr, India	G3	53
Kadaň, Czech Rep.	F9	16
Kadan Kyun, i., Mya.	F4	48
Kadapongan, Pulau, i., Indon.	F9	50
Kaddam, res., India	B4	53
Kade, Ghana	H4	64
Kadéï, stm., Afr.	G2	62
Kadi, India	G4	54
Kadina, Austl.	F7	74
Kading, stm., Laos	C7	48
Kadınhanı, Tur.	E15	28
Kadiolo, Mali	G3	64
Kādīpur, India	E9	54
Kadiri, India	D4	53
Kadirli, Tur.	A7	58
Kadoka, S.D., U.S.	D11	126
Kadoma, Zimb.	D4	68
Kaduj, Russia	A20	10
Kaduna, Nig.	G6	64
Kaduna, stm., Nig.	G6	64
Kāduqlī, Sudan	E5	62
Kadūr, India	E3	53
Kaduvu, i., Fiji	q19	79e
Kaduvu Passage, strt., Fiji	q18	79e
Kadyj, Russia	H20	8
Kadžerom, Russia	B9	32
Kaédi, Maur.	F2	64
Kaélé, Cam.	B2	66
Ka'ena Point, c., Hi., U.S.	b3	78a
Kaesŏng, Kor., N.	F7	38
Kafanchan, Nig.	H6	64
Kaffrine, Sen.	G1	64
Kafia Kingi, Sudan	F4	62
Kafr el-Dauwar, Egypt	G1	58
Kafr el-Sheikh, Egypt	G1	58
Kafr el-Zaiyât, Egypt	H1	58
Kafr Sa'd, Egypt	G2	58
Kafue, Zam.	D4	68
Kafue, stm., Zam.	D4	68
Kaga, Japan	C9	40
Kaga Bandoro, C.A.R.	C3	66
Kāgān, Pak.	A4	54
Kagan, Uzb.	G10	32
Kagawa, state, Japan	E6	40
Kagawong, Lake, l., On., Can.	C7	112
Kagaznagar, India	B4	53
Kagera, stm., Afr.	E6	66
Kagmar, Sudan	E6	62
Kagoshima, Japan	H3	40
Kagoshima, state, Japan	H3	40
Kagoshima-wan, b., Japan	H3	40
Kahama, Tan.	E6	66
Kahayan, stm., Indon.	D8	50
Ka-Hem see Malyj Enisej, stm., Russia	F8	34
Kahemba, D.R.C.	F3	66
Kahiu Point, c., Hi., U.S.	b5	78a
Kahoka, Mo., U.S.	D6	120
Kaho'olawe, i., Hi., U.S.	c5	78a
Kahouanne, Îlet à, i., Guad.	h5	105c
Kahramanmaraş (Maraş), Tur.	A7	58
Kahraman Maraş, state, Tur.	A7	58
Kahuku Point, c., Hi., U.S.	b4	78a
Kahului, Hi., U.S.	c5	78a
Kai, Kepulauan (Kai Islands), is., Indon.	G9	44
Kaiapoi, N.Z.	F5	80
Kaibab Plateau, plat., Az., U.S.	G4	132
Kaidu, stm., China	F15	32
Kaieteur Fall, wtfl., Guy.	E12	86
Kaieteur National Park, p.o.i., Guy.	E12	86
Kaifeng, China	D6	42
Kaihua, China	G8	42
Kai Islands see Kai, Kepulauan, is., Indon.	G9	44
Kaijian, China	J4	42
Kaijiang, China	F2	42
Kai Kecil, i., Indon.	G9	44
Kaikoura, N.Z.	F5	80
Kailahun, S.L.	H2	64
Kailas see Kangrinboqê Feng, mtn., China	C8	54
Kailāshahar, India	F14	54
Kailas Range see Gangdisê Shan, mts., China	C9	54
Kaili, China	H2	42
Kailu, China	C4	38
Kailua, Hi., U.S.	b4	78a
Kailua Kona, Hi., U.S.	d6	78a
Kaïmaktsalán (Kajmakčalan), mtn., Eur.	C15	24
Kaimana, Indon.	F9	44
Kaimon-dake, vol., Japan	H3	40
Kainabrivier, stm., Nmb.	E4	70
Kainan, Japan	E8	40
Kainantu, Pap. N. Gui.	b4	79a
Kainji Reservoir, res., Nig.	G5	64
Kaipara Harbour, b., N.Z.	C5	80
Kaiparowits Plateau, plat., Ut., U.S.	F5	132
Kaiping, China	J5	42
Kairouan, Tun.	I3	24
Kairuku, Pap. N. Gui.	b4	79a
Kaiserslautern, Ger.	G3	16
Kaišiadorys, Lith.	F7	10
Kait, Tanjung, c., Indon.	E5	50
Kaitangata, N.Z.	H3	80
Kaithal, India	D6	54
Kaituma, stm., Guy.	D12	86
Kaiwi Channel, strt., Hi., U.S.	b4	78a
Kaixian, China	F3	42
Kaiyang, China	H2	42
Kaiyuan, China	G5	36
Kaiyuan, China	C6	38
Kaiyuancheng, China	C6	38
Kaiyuh Mountains, mts., Ak., U.S.	D8	140
Kajaani, Fin.	D12	8
Kajabbi, Austl.	B2	76
Kajakī, Band-e, res., Afg.	C10	56
Kajang, Malay.	K5	48
Kajmysovy, Russia	C13	32
Kajo Kaji, Sudan	G6	62
Kaka, Sudan	E6	62
Kakabeka Falls, wtfl., On., Can.	C9	118
Kakagi Lake, l., On., Can.	B5	118
Kakamas, S. Afr.	F5	70
Kakamega, Kenya	D6	66
Kakamigahara, Japan	D9	40
Kakata, Lib.	H2	64
Kākdwīp, India	H12	54
Kakegawa, Japan	E10	40
Kakhonak, Ak., U.S.	E9	140
Kakhovka Reservoir see Kakhovs'ke vodoskhovyshche, res., Ukr.	E4	32
Kakhovs'ke vodoskhovyshche, res., Ukr.	E4	32
Kākināda (Cocanada), India	C6	53
Kakisa Lake, l., N.T., Can.	C7	106
Kakizaki, Japan	B11	40
Kakogawa, Japan	E7	40
Kakšaal-Too, hrebet, mts., Asia	F13	32
Kaktovik, Ak., U.S.	B11	140
Kakuda, Japan	B13	40
Kakus, stm., Malay.	B8	50
Kakwa, stm., Ab., Can.	B12	138
Kala, stm., Sri L.	G4	53
Kalaa Kebira, Tun.	I4	24
Kalabahi, Indon.	G7	44
Kalabakan, Malay.	A10	50
Kalabo, Zam.	D3	68
Kalač, Russia	D6	32
Kalačinsk, Russia	D12	32
Kalač-na-Donu, Russia	E6	32
Kaladan, stm., Asia	G14	54
Kalae, c., Hi., U.S.	e6	78a
Kalahari Desert, des., Afr.	C5	70
Kalahari Gemsbok National Park, p.o.i., S. Afr.	D5	70
Kalajoki, Fin.	D10	8
Kalakan, Russia	E12	34
Kalām, Pak.	B11	56
Kalama, Wa., U.S.	D4	136
Kalamalka Lake, l., B.C., Can.	F11	138
Kalamáta, Grc.	F5	28
Kalamazoo, Mi., U.S.	F4	112
Kalamazoo, stm., Mi., U.S.	F4	112
Kalamb, India	B1	53
Kalampising, Indon.	B10	50
Kalao, Pulau, i., Indon.	G12	50
Kalaotoa, Pulau, i., Indon.	G7	44
Kalar, stm., Russia	E12	34
Kalasin, Thai.	D6	48
Kalašnikovo, Russia	C18	10
Kalāt, Pak.	D10	56
Kalávryta, Grc.	E5	28
Kalaw, Mya.	B3	48
Kalbarri, Austl.	E2	74
Kale, Tur.	G12	28
Kale, Tur.	F11	28
Kaleden, B.C., Can.	G11	138
Kalegauk Island, i., Mya.	E3	48
Kalehe, D.R.C.	E5	66
Kalemie, D.R.C.	F5	66
Kalemyo, Mya.	D7	46
Kaletwa, Mya.	H14	54
Kalevala, Russia	D14	8
Kalewa, Mya.	D7	46
Kálfafell, Ice.	k31	8a
Kalgan see Zhangjiakou, China	A6	42
Kalgoorlie-Boulder, Austl.	F4	74
Kaliakra, nos, c., Blg.	F15	26
Kalianda, Indon.	F4	50
Kalibo, Phil.	E4	52
Kalima, D.R.C.	E5	66
Kalimantan (Borneo), i., Asia	F5	44
Kalimantan Barat, state, Indon.	D7	50
Kalimantan Selatan, state, Indon.	E9	50
Kalimantan Tengah, state, Indon.	D8	50
Kalimantan Timur, state, Indon.	C10	50
Kālimpang, India	E12	54
Kālīnadi, stm., India	D2	53
Kalinin see Tver', Russia	D18	10
Kaliningrad (Königsberg), Russia	F3	10
Kaliningradskaja oblast', co., Russia	F4	10
Kalinkavičy, Bela.	H12	10
Kaliro, Ug.	D6	66
Kalisat, Indon.	H8	50
Kāli Sindh, stm., India	F6	54
Kalispell, Mt., U.S.	B12	136
Kalisz, Pol.	E14	16
Kalisz, state, Pol.	E13	16
Kalisz Pomorski, Pol.	C11	16
Kaliua, Tan.	E6	66
Kaliveli Tank, l., India	E4	53
Kalixälven, stm., Swe.	C9	8
Kaljazin, Russia	C20	10
Kālka, India	C6	54
Kalkaska, Mi., U.S.	D4	112
Kalkfonteindam, res., S. Afr.	F7	70
Kalkım, Tur.	D10	28
Kalkrand, Nmb.	D3	70
Kallar Kahār, Pak.	B4	54
Kallavesi, l., Fin.	E12	8
Kallsjön, l., Swe.	E5	8
Kalmar, Swe.	H6	8
Kalmar, state, Swe.	H7	8
Kalmarsund, strt., Swe.	H7	8
Kalmykia see Kalmykija, state, Russia	E7	32
Kalmykija, state, Russia	E7	32
Kālna, India	G12	54
Kalocsa, Hung.	C5	26
Kalofer, Blg.	G12	26
Kalohi Channel, strt., Hi., U.S.	b4	78a
Kalol, India	G4	54
Kālol, India	G4	54
Kalomo, Zam.	D4	68
Kalona, Ia., U.S.	J7	118
Kalone Peak, mtn., B.C., Can.	D4	138
Kalpeni Island, i., India	F1	53
Kālpi, India	E7	54
Kalpin, China	A12	56
Kalsūbai, mtn., India	B1	53
Kaltag, Ak., U.S.	D8	140
Kaluga, Russia	F19	10
Kalukalukuang, Pulau, i., Indon.	F10	50
Kalumburu, Austl.	B5	74
Kałuszyn, Pol.	D17	16
Kalutara, Sri L.	H4	53
Kalužskaja oblast', co., Russia	F18	10
Kalyān, India	B1	53
Kalyāndurg, India	D3	53
Kálymnos, Grc.	G9	28
Kálymnos, i., Grc.	F9	28
Kama, stm., Russia	C8	32
Kamae, Japan	G4	40
Kamaishi, Japan	E14	38
Kamakou, mtn., Hi., U.S.	b5	78a
Kamakura, Japan	D12	40
Kamālia, Pak.	C4	54
Kamamaung, Mya.	D3	48
Kaman, stm., Laos	E8	48
Kamanjab, Nmb.	D1	68
Kamarān, i., Yemen	F5	56
Kāmāreddi, India	B4	53
Kama Reservoir see Kamskoe vodohranilišče, res., Russia	C9	32
Kamas, Ut., U.S.	C5	132
Kamay, Tx., U.S.	H10	128
Kambalda, Austl.	F4	74
Kambam, India	G3	53
Kambarka, Russia	C8	32
Kambja, Est.	B9	10
Kambove, D.R.C.	G5	66
Kamčatka, stm., Russia	E21	34
Kamčatka, poluostrov, pen., Russia	E19	34
Kamčatskij poluostrov, pen., Russia	E21	34
Kamčatskij zaliv, b., Russia	E21	34
Kamchatka Peninsula see Kamčatka, poluostrov, pen., Russia	E20	34
Kameda, Japan	B12	40
Kámeiros, sci., Grc.	G10	28
Kamen', gora, mtn., Russia	C8	34
Kameng, stm., India	E14	54
Kamenjak, Rt, c., Cro.	F10	22
Kamenka, Kaz.	D11	32
Kamenka, Russia	D6	32
Kamenka, Russia	D21	8
Kamen'-na-Obi, Russia	D14	32
Kameno, Blg.	G14	26
Kamen-Rybolov, Russia	B9	38
Kamenskoe, Russia	D22	34
Kamensk-Ural'skij, Russia	C10	32
Kamenz, Ger.	E10	16
Kāmet, mtn., Asia	C7	54
Kam'ians'ke, Ukr.	D16	26
Kamień Krajeński, Pol.	C13	16
Kamienna Góra, Pol.	F12	16
Kamieńsk, Pol.	E15	16

Name	Map Ref.	Page
Kamieskroon, S. Afr.	G3	70
Kamiiso, Japan	D14	38
Kamilukuak Lake, l., Can.	C10	106
Kamina, D.R.C.	F4	66
Kaminak Lake, l., Nu., Can.	C12	106
Kaminoyama, Japan	A13	40
Kaminuriak Lake, l., Nu., Can.	C12	106
Kamioka, Japan	C10	40
Kamjanec, Bela.	H6	10
Kamkhat Muḩaywir, hill, Jord.	G7	58
Kamloops, B.C., Can.	F10	138
Kamnik, Slvn.	D11	22
Kamo, Japan	B12	40
Kamoa Mountains, mts., Guy.	C6	84
Kamojima, Japan	E7	40
Kāmoke, Pak.	B5	54
Kampala, Ug.	D6	66
Kampar, Malay.	J5	48
Kampar, stm., Indon.	C3	50
Kamparkalns, hill, Lat.	C5	10
Kampar Kanan, stm., Indon.	C2	50
Kampen, Neth.	B14	14
Kamphaeng Phet, Thai.	D4	48
Kampinoski Park Narodowy, p.o.i., Pol.	D16	16
Kâmpóng Cham, Camb.	F7	48
Kâmpóng Chhnăng, Camb.	F7	48
Kâmpóng Kântuŏt, Camb.	G7	48
Kâmpóng Saôm, Camb.	G6	48
Kâmpóng Saôm, Chhâk, b., Camb.	G6	48
Kâmpóng Thum, Camb.	F7	48
Kampong Ulu, Mya.	G4	48
Kâmpôt, Camb.	G7	48
Kampsville, Il., U.S.	E7	120
Kampti, Burkina	G4	64
Kampuchea see Cambodia, ctry., Asia	C3	48
Kampungbaru, Indon.	D3	50
Kampung Litang, Malay.	A11	50
Kamrau, Teluk, b., Indon.	F9	44
Kamsack, Sk., Can.	C12	124
Kamskoe vodohranilišče, res., Russia	C9	32
Kāmthi, India	H7	54
Kamuela, Hi., U.S.	d6	78a
Kámuk, Cerro, mtn., C.R.	H6	102
Kamundan, stm., Indon.	F9	44
Kamyšin, Russia	D7	32
Kamyšlov, Russia	C10	32
Kan, stm., Russia	C17	32
Kanaaupscow, stm., Qc., Can.	E15	106
Kanab, Ut., U.S.	F4	132
Kanab Creek, stm., U.S.	G4	132
Kanaga Island, i., Ak., U.S.	g23	140a
Kanagawa, state, Japan	D12	40
Kanakapura, India	E3	53
Kananga (Luluabourg), D.R.C.	F4	66
Kananggar, Indon.	I12	50
Kanangra-Boyd National Park, p.o.i., Austl.	I7	76
Kanaš, Russia	C7	32
Kanawha, Ia., U.S.	B4	120
Kanawha, stm., W.V., U.S.	F4	114
Kanazawa, Japan	C9	40
Kanbauk, Mya.	E3	48
Kanchanaburi, Thai.	F4	48
Kanchanjanggā (Kānchenjunga), mtn., Asia	E11	54
Kānchenjunga (Kanchanjanggā), mtn., Asia	E11	54
Kānchipuram, India	E4	53
Kanchow see Ganzhou, China	I6	42
Kańczuga, Pol.	F18	16
Kanda, Japan	F3	40
Kandahār, Afg.	C10	56
Kandahar, Sk., Can.	C9	124
Kandalakša, Russia	C15	8
Kandalakšskaja guba, b., Russia	C15	8
Kandale, D.R.C.	F3	66
Kandang, Indon.	K3	48
Kandangan, Indon.	E9	50
Kandanghaur, Indon.	G6	50
Kandé, Togo	H5	64
Kandhkot, Pak.	D2	54
Kandi, India	G12	54
Kandi, Tanjung, c., Indon.	E7	44
Kandıra, Tur.	B13	28
Kandla, India	G3	54
Kandos, Austl.	I7	76
Kandreho, Madag.	D8	68
Kandy, Sri L.	H5	53
Kane, Pa., U.S.	C7	114
Kane Basin, b., N.A.	B12	141
Kanem, state, Chad	E3	62
Kāne'ohe, Hi., U.S.	b4	78a
Kanëvka, Russia	C18	8
Kang, Bots.	C6	70
Kangaba, Mali	G3	64
Kangalassy, Russia	D15	34
Kangâmiut, Grnld.	D15	141
Kangān, Iran	D7	56
Kangar, Malay.	I5	48
Kangaroo Island, i., Austl.	G7	74
Kangāvar, Iran	C6	56
Kangbao, China	C7	36
Kangding, China	C9	46
Kangean, Kepulauan (Kangean Islands), is., Indon.	G9	50
Kangean, Pulau, i., Indon.	G9	50
Kangean Islands see Kangean, Kepulauan, is., Indon.	G9	50
Kangeeak Point, c., Nu., Can.	B18	106
Kangerlussuaq, b., Grnld.	D19	141
Kangersuatsiaq see Prøven, Grnld.	C14	141
Kanger Valley National Park, p.o.i., India	B6	53
Kanggye, Kor., N.	D7	38
Kanghwa-do, i., Kor., S.	F7	38
Kangiqsliniq (Rankin Inlet), Nu., Can.	C12	106
Kangiqsualujjuaq, Qc., Can.	D17	106
Kangiqsujuaq, Qc., Can.	C16	106
Kangiqtugaapik (Clyde River), Nu., Can.	A16	106
Kangirsuk, Qc., Can.	C17	106
Kangmar, China	D12	54
Kangnŭng, Kor., S.	B1	40
Kango, Gabon	D2	66
Kangping, China	C5	38
Kangpu, China	F4	36
Kangrinboqê Feng, mtn., China	C8	54
Kangshan, Tai.	J9	42
Kangsŏ, Kor., N.	E6	38
Kangto, mtn., Asia	D14	54
Kangwŏn-do, state, Kor., S.	B1	40
Kanha National Park, p.o.i., India	G8	54
Kanhar, stm., India	F9	54
Kanhsien see Ganzhou, China	I6	42
Kani, Mya.	A2	48
Kaniama, D.R.C.	F4	66
Kanibadam, Taj.	A11	56
Kaniet Islands, is., Pap. N. Gui.	a4	79a
Kanigiri, India	D4	53
Kanin, poluostrov, pen., Russia	C21	8
Kanin-Kamen', mts., Russia	B21	8
Kanin Nos, Russia	B20	8
Kanin Nos, mys, c., Russia	B20	8
Kaniva, Austl.	K3	76
Kanjiža, Serb.	C7	26
Kankaanpää, Fin.	F10	8
Kankakee, Il., U.S.	G2	112
Kankan, Gui.	G3	64
Kānker, India	H8	54
Kankunskij, Russia	E14	34
Kanmaw Kyun, i., Mya.	G4	48
Kannack, Viet.	E9	48
Kannad, India	H5	54
Kannapolis, N.C., U.S.	A5	116
Kannauj, India	E7	54
Kanniyākumari, India	G3	53
Kannod, India	G6	54
Kannur see Cannanore, India	F2	53
Kannus, Fin.	E10	8
Kano, Nig.	G6	64
Kanonji, Japan	E6	40
Kanopolis, Ks., U.S.	C10	128
Kanorado, Ks., U.S.	B6	128
Kanosh, Ut., U.S.	E4	132
Kanoya, Japan	H3	40
Kanpetlet, Mya.	B1	48
Kānpur (Cawnpore), India	E7	54
Kansas, state, U.S.	C10	128
Kansas, stm., Ks., U.S.	B13	128
Kansas City, Ks., U.S.	E3	120
Kansas City, Mo., U.S.	E3	120
Kansk, Russia	C17	32
Kansŏng, Kor., S.	A1	40
Kan-sou see Gansu, state, China	D5	36
Kansu see Gansu, state, China	D5	36
Kantang, Thai.	I4	48
Kantchari, Burkina	G5	64
Kānth, India	D7	54
Kantishna, stm., Ak., U.S.	D9	140
Kantō-heiya, pl., Japan	D12	40
Kanton, i., Kir.	D9	72
Kantō-sanchi, mts., Japan	D11	40
Kantu-long, Mya.	C3	48
Kantunilkin, Mex.	B4	102
Kanuku Mountains, mts., Guy.	F12	86
Kanuma, Japan	C12	40
Kanye, Bots.	D7	70
Kanyutkwin, Mya.	C3	48
Kaohiung see Kaohsiung, Tai.	J8	42
Kaohsiung, Tai.	J8	42
Kaohsiunghsien, Tai.	J9	42
Kaoka Bay, b., Sol. Is.	e9	79b
Kaoko Veld, plat., Nmb.	D1	68
Kaolack, Sen.	G1	64
Kaolinovo, Blg.	F14	26
Kaoma, Zam.	C3	68
Kaouar, reg., Niger	F7	64
Kapaa, Hi., U.S.	a2	78a
Kapadvanj, India	G4	54
Kapanga, D.R.C.	F4	66
Kapaonik, mts., Serb.	G8	26
Kapatkevičy, Bela.	H11	10
Kapčagajskoe vodohranilišče see Kapshaghay bögeni, res., Kaz.	F13	32
Kapchagay Reservoir see Kapshaghay bögeni, res., Kaz.	F13	32
Kapfenberg, Aus.	C12	22
Kapıdağ Yarımadası, pen., Tur.	C10	28
Kapikotongwa, stm., On., Can.	A11	118
Kapingamarangi, at., Micron.	C6	72
Kapiri Mposhi, Zam.	C4	68
Kapisigdlit, Grnld.	E16	141
Kapiskau, stm., On., Can.	E14	106
Kapit, Malay.	C8	50
Kaplan, La., U.S.	G6	122
Kaplice, Czech Rep.	H10	16
Kapoeta, Sudan	G6	62
Kapona, D.R.C.	F5	66
Kapos, stm., Hung.	C5	26
Kaposvár, Hung.	C4	26
Kaposvar Creek, stm., Sk., Can.	D11	124
Kappeln, Ger.	B5	16
Kapshaghay bögeni, res., Kaz.	F13	32
Kaptai, Bngl.	G14	54
Kaptai Lake see Karnaphuli Reservoir, res., Bngl.	G14	54
Kapuas, stm., Indon.	D6	50
Kapuas, stm., Indon.	E9	50
Kapunda, Austl.	J2	76
Kapūrthala, India	C5	54
Kapuskasing, On., Can.	F14	106
Kapuvár, Hung.	B4	26
Kapyl', Bela.	G9	10
Kara, Russia	C1	34
Kara-Balta, Kyrg.	F12	32
Karabanovo, Russia	D21	10
Karabaš, Russia	C9	32
Kara-Bogaz-Gol, zaliv, b., Turkmen.	A7	56
Kara-Bogaz-Gol Gulf see Kara-Bogaz-Gol, zaliv, b., Turkmen.	A7	56
Karabük, Tur.	B15	28
Karabula, Russia	C17	32
Karaburun, Tur.	E9	28
Karacabey, Tur.	C11	28
Karačaevo-Čerkesija, state, Russia	F6	32
Karacasu, Tur.	F11	28
Karačev, Russia	G17	10
Karachay see Karačaevo-Čerkesija, state, Russia	F6	32
Karachay-Cherkessia see Karačaevo-Čerkesija, state, Russia	F6	32
Karāchi, Pak.	E10	56
Karād, India	C2	53
Karaftit, Russia	F11	34
Karaganda see Karagandy, Kaz.	E12	32
Karagandy (Karaganda), Kaz.	E12	32
Karagayly see Qarqaraly, Kaz.	E13	32
Karaginskij, ostrov, i., Russia	E21	34
Karaginskij zaliv, b., Russia	E21	34
Karagoš, gora, mtn., Russia	D15	32
Karahallı, Tur.	E12	28
Kāraikkudi, India	F4	53
Karaisalı, Tur.	A6	58
Karaj, Iran	B7	56
Kara-Kala, Turkmen.	B8	56
Karakaralong, Pulau, is., Indon.	E8	44
Karakax, stm., China	A7	54
Karakol, Kyrg.	F13	32
Karakoram Pass, p., Asia	A6	54
Karakoram Range, mts., Asia	A4	46
Karakul', Uzb.	G10	32
Kara-Kum Canal see Garagumskij kanal, can., Turkmen.	B9	56
Karama, stm., Indon.	E11	50
Karamai see Karamay, China	B1	36
Karaman, Tur.	A4	58
Karaman, state, Tur.	A4	58
Karamanlı, Tur.	F12	28
Karamay, China	B1	36
Karamea Bight, b., N.Z.	E4	80
Karamürsel, Tur.	C12	28
Karamyševo, Russia	C18	32
Karamzino, Russia	D17	10
Karangasem, Indon.	H9	50
Karangnunggal, Indon.	G6	50
Kāranja, India	H6	54
Karanjia, India	H10	54
Karapınar, Tur.	A4	58
Karaqoyyn köli, l., Kaz.	E11	32
Karas, state, Nmb.	E3	70
Karaşar, Tur.	C14	28
Karasburg, Nmb.	F4	70
Kara Sea see Karskoe more, s., Russia	B10	30
Karasjok, Nor.	B11	8
Karasu, Tur.	B13	28
Karasu, stm., Tur.	B4	56
Karasuk, Russia	D13	32
Karatal, Kaz.	E15	32
Karataş Burun, c., Tur.	B6	58
Karatau, hrebet see Qarataū zhotasy, mts., Kaz.	F11	32
Karatau Range see Qarataū zhotasy, mts., Kaz.	F11	32
Karatöbe, Kaz.	E8	32
Karatsu, Japan	F2	40
Karaul, Russia	B5	34
Karauli, India	E6	54
Karawa, D.R.C.	D4	66
Karawang, Indon.	G5	50
Karawang, Tanjung, c., Indon.	F5	50
Karawanken, mts., Eur.	D11	22
Karažal see Qarazhal, Kaz.	E12	32
Karbalā', Iraq	C5	56
Kårböle, Swe.	E6	8
Karcag, Hung.	B7	26
Kardámaina, Grc.	G9	28
Kardeljevo, Cro.	G14	22
Kárditsa, Grc.	D4	28
Kärdla, Est.	G10	8
Kărdžali, Blg.	H12	26
Karelia see Karelija, state, Russia	D15	8
Karelia, hist. reg., Eur.	E14	8
Karelija, state, Russia	D15	8
Karelija see Karelia, hist. reg., Eur.	E14	8
Karel'skij Gorodok, Russia	B19	10
Karema, Tan.	F6	66
Karen, India	F7	46
Karesuando, Swe.	B9	8
Kärevere, Est.	B9	10
Kargasok, Russia	C14	32
Kargat, Russia	C14	32
Kargil, India	A5	54
Kargopol', Russia	F18	8
Kariba, Zimb.	D4	68
Kariba, Lake, res., Afr.	D4	68
Karibib, Nmb.	B2	70
Kariega, stm., S. Afr.	H6	70
Karimata, Kepulauan, is., Indon.	D6	50
Karimata, Selat, strt., Indon.	E6	50
Karīmganj, India	F14	54
Karīmnagar, India	B4	53
Karimunjawa, Kepulauan, is., Indon.	F7	50
Karimunjawa, Pulau, i., Indon.	F7	50
Karisimbi, vol., Afr.	E5	66
Káristos, Grc.	E7	28
Kariya, Japan	D10	40
Kārkal, India	E2	53
Karkaralinsk see Qarqaraly, Kaz.	E13	32
Karkar Island, i., Pap. N. Gui.	a4	79a
Karkonoski Park Narodowy, p.o.i., Pol.	F11	16
Karkūk, Iraq	B5	56
Karleby see Kokkola, Fin.	E10	8
Karlino, Pol.	B11	16
Karl-Marx-Stadt see Chemnitz, Ger.	F8	16
Karlovac, Cro.	E12	22
Karlovo, Blg.	G11	26
Karlovy Vary, Czech Rep.	F8	16
Karlsborg, Swe.	D10	8
Karlsburg see Alba Iulia, Rom.	C10	26
Karlshamn, Swe.	H6	8
Karlskoga, Swe.	G6	8
Karlskrona, Swe.	H6	8
Karlsruhe, Ger.	G4	16
Karlstad, Swe.	G5	8
Karlstadt, Ger.	G5	16
Karluk, Ak., U.S.	E9	140
Karma, Bela.	H14	10
Karma, Niger	G5	64
Karmah an Nuzul, Sudan	D6	62
Karmāla, India	B2	53
Karmøy, i., Nor.	G1	8
Karnack, Tx., U.S.	E4	122
Karnak, Il., U.S.	G9	120
Karnāl, India	D6	54
Karṇāli, stm., Asia	D8	54
Karnāli, stm., Nepal	D8	54
Karnaphuli Reservoir, res., Bngl.	G14	54
Karnātaka, state, India	D2	53
Karnobat, Blg.	G13	26
Kärnten, state, Aus.	D10	22
Karoli, India	G7	54
Karonga, Mwi.	B5	68
Karoo National Park, p.o.i., S. Afr.	H6	70
Karoonda, Austl.	J2	76
Karor, Pak.	C3	54
Kárpathos, Grc.	H10	28
Kárpathos, i., Grc.	H10	28
Karpats'kyi Pryrodnyi Natsional'nyi Park, p.o.i., Ukr.	A11	26
Karpenísi, Grc.	E4	28
Karpogory, Russia	D21	8
Karpuzlu, Tur.	F10	28
Karratha, Austl.	D3	74
Karrats Fjord, b., Grnld.	C14	141
Kars, Tur.	A5	56
Karsantı, Tur.	A6	58
Karši, Uzb.	G11	32
Karsin, Pol.	C13	16
Karskoe more (Kara Sea), s., Russia	B10	30
Kartala, vol., Com.	C7	68
Kartaly, Russia	D10	32
Kartārpur, India	C5	54
Karthaus, Pa., U.S.	C7	114
Kartuzy, Pol.	B14	16
Karufa, Indon.	F9	44
Karumba, Austl.	A3	76
Karungi, Swe.	C10	8
Karunjie, Austl.	C5	74
Karūr, India	F4	53
Karviná, Czech Rep.	G14	16
Kārwār, India	D1	53
Karyés, Grc.	C7	28
Karymskoe, Russia	F11	34
Kasai (Cassai), stm., Afr.	E3	66
Kasaji, D.R.C.	G4	66
Kasama, Japan	C13	40
Kasama, Zam.	C5	68
Kasane, Bots.	D3	68
Kasanga, Tan.	F6	66
Kasangulu, D.R.C.	E3	66
Kasaoka, Japan	E6	40
Kāsaragod, India	E2	53
Kasba, India	F11	54
Kasba Lake, l., Can.	C10	106
Kascjukouka, Bela.	H13	10
Kascjukovičy, Bela.	G14	10
Kaseda, Japan	H3	40
Kasempa, Zam.	C4	68
Kasenga, D.R.C.	G5	66
Kasenye, D.R.C.	D6	66
Kasese, D.R.C.	E5	66
Kasese, Ug.	D6	66
Kaset Sombun, Thai.	D5	48
Kāsganj, India	E7	54
Kāshān, Iran	C7	56
Kashgar see Kashi, China	B12	56
Kashi, China	B12	56
Kashihara, Japan	E8	40
Kashima, Japan	F3	40
Kashima-nada, s., Japan	C13	40
Kashing see Jiaxing, China	F9	42
Kāshīpur, India	D7	54
Kashiwazaki, Japan	B11	40
Kāshmar, Iran	B8	56
Kashmir, hist. reg., Asia	A3	46
Kasia, India	E9	54
Kasimbar, Indon.	D12	50
Kasimov, Russia	I19	8
Kašin, Russia	C20	10
Kašira, Russia	F21	10
Kasiruta, Pulau, i., Indon.	F8	44
Kaskaskia, stm., Il., U.S.	E9	120
Kaskinen, Fin.	E9	8
Kaslo, B.C., Can.	G13	138
Kasnja, Russia	E17	10
Kasongo, D.R.C.	E5	66
Kasongo-Lunda, D.R.C.	F3	66
Kásos, i., Grc.	H9	28
Kasota, Mn., U.S.	G5	118
Kaspijsk, Russia	F7	32
Kaspijskij, Russia	E7	32
Kaspijskoje more see Caspian Sea, s.	F7	32
Kasplja, stm., Eur.	E13	10
Kasr, Ra's, c., Afr.	D7	62
Kassab, Syria	C6	58
Kassalā, Sudan	D7	62
Kassándra, pen., Grc.	C6	28
Kassandra, Gulf of see Kassándras, Kólpos, b., Grc.	C6	28
Kassándras, Kólpos, b., Grc.	C6	28
Kassel, Ger.	E5	16
Kasserine, Tun.	B6	64
Kastamonu, Tur.	A3	56
Kastamonu, state, Tur.	B16	28
Kastélli, Grc.	H6	28
Kastoría, Grc.	C4	28
Kastorías, Límni, l., Grc.	C4	28
Kastrakíou, Technití Límni, res., Grc.	E4	28
Kasugai, Japan	D9	40
Kasulu, Tan.	E6	66
Kasumi, Japan	D7	40
Kasumiga-ura, l., Japan	C13	40
Kasungan, Indon.	E8	50
Kasūr, Pak.	C5	54
Kaszuby, hist. reg., Pol.	B13	16
Kataba, Zam.	D4	68
Katahdin, Mount, mtn., Me., U.S.	E7	110
Katako-Kombe, D.R.C.	E4	66
Katanga, hist. reg., D.R.C.	F4	66
Katanga, stm., Russia	C18	32
Katangi, India	G7	54
Katangli, Russia	F17	34
Katanning, Austl.	F3	74
Katchall Island, i., India	G7	46
Katepwa Beach, Sk., Can.	D10	124
Kateríni, Grc.	C5	28
Kates Needle, mtn., N.A.	D4	106
Katete, Zam.	C5	68
Katha, Mya.	D8	46
Katherîna, Gebel, mtn., Egypt	J4	58
Katherine, Austl.	B6	74
Katherine, stm., Austl.	B6	74
Katherine Creek, stm., Austl.	D4	76
Kāthiāwār Peninsula, pen., India	H3	54
Kathla, India	C6	54
Kāṭhmāṇḍāū (Kathmandu), Nepal	E10	54
Kathmandu see Kāṭhmāṇḍāū, Nepal	E10	54
Kathor, India	H4	54
Kathua, India	B5	54
Kati, Mali	G3	64
Katibas, stm., Malay.	C8	50
Katihār, India	F11	54
Katimik Lake, l., Mb., Can.	B14	124
Katiola, C. Iv.	H4	64
Katipunan, Phil.	F4	52
Ka Tiritiri o te Moana see Southern Alps, mts., N.Z.	F4	80
Katmai, Mount, vol., Ak., U.S.	E8	140
Káto Achaïa, Grc.	E4	28
Kātol, India	H7	54
Katoomba, Austl.	I8	76
Katowice, Pol.	F14	16
Katowice, state, Pol.	F15	16
Katrineholm, Swe.	G7	8
Katsina, Nig.	G6	64
Katsina Ala, stm., Afr.	H6	64
Katsuta, Japan	C13	40
Katsuura, Japan	D13	40
Katsuyama, Japan	C9	40
Katsuyama, Japan	D6	40
Kattakurgan, Uzb.	G11	32
Kattegat, strt., Eur.	H4	8
Katul, Jabal, mtn., Sudan	E5	62
Katun', stm., Russia	D15	32
Katunino, Russia	G21	8
Kātwa, India	G11	54
Katwijk aan Zee, Neth.	B13	14
Katyn, Russia	F14	10
Katzenbuckel, mtn., Ger.	G5	16
Kaua'i, i., Hi., U.S.	b2	78a
Kauai Channel, strt., Hi., U.S.	b3	78a
Kaufbeuren, Ger.	I6	16
Kaufman, Tx., U.S.	E2	122
Kaukauna, Wi., U.S.	D1	112
Kaukau Veld, plat., Afr.	D3	68
Kaulakahi Channel, strt., Hi., U.S.	b2	78a
Kaumalapau, Hi., U.S.	c4	78a
Kaunas, Lith.	F6	10
Kaura-Namoda, Nig.	G6	64
Kauriālā (Ghāghara), stm., Asia	D8	54
Kautokeino, Nor.	B10	8
Kau-ye Kyun, i., Mya.	G4	48
Kavača, Russia	D23	34
Kavadarci, Mac.	B5	28
Kavaja see Kavajë, Alb.	C13	24
Kavajë, Alb.	C13	24
Kavaklıdere, Tur.	F11	28
Kavála, Grc.	C7	28
Kavalerovo, Russia	B11	38
Kāvali, India	D4	53
Kavaratti, India	F3	46
Kavaratti Island, i., India	F3	46
Kāveri (Cauvery), stm., India	F4	53
Kāveri Falls, wtfl., India	E3	53
Kavieng, Pap. N. Gui.	a5	79a
Kavīr, Dasht-e, des., Iran	C8	56
Kaw, Ok., U.S.	E12	128
Kawa, Mya.	D3	48
Kawagama Lake, l., On., Can.	C10	112
Kawagoe, Japan	D12	40
Kawaguchi, Japan	D12	40
Kawaihoa, c., Hi., U.S.	b1	78a
Kawaikini, mtn., Hi., U.S.	a2	78a
Kawambwa, Zam.	B4	68
Kawanoe, Japan	E6	40
Kawardha, India	H8	54
Kawasaki, Japan	D12	40
Kawatana, Japan	F2	40
Kawdut, Mya.	E3	48
Kaweenakumik Lake, l., Mb., Can.	B14	124
Kawhia Harbour, b., N.Z.	D6	80
Kawich Peak, mtn., Nv., U.S.	F9	134
Kawkareik, Mya.	D4	48
Kaw Lake, res., Ok., U.S.	E12	128
Kawludo, Mya.	C3	48
Kawnipi Lake, l., On., Can.	C7	118
Kawthaung, Mya.	H4	48
Kaxgar, stm., China	B12	56
Kaya, Burkina	G4	64
Kayah, state, Mya.	C3	48
Kayak Island, i., Ak., U.S.	E11	140
Kāyalpattinam, India	G4	53
Kayan, Mya.	D3	48
Kayan, stm., Indon.	B10	50
Kāyankulam, India	G3	53
Kaycee, Wy., U.S.	D6	126
Kayenta, Az., U.S.	G6	132
Kayes, Mali	G2	64
Kayin, state, Mya.	D3	48
Kaymaz, Tur.	D14	28
Kayseri, Tur.	B4	56
Kaysville, Ut., U.S.	B4	132
Kayuadi, Pulau, i., Indon.	G12	50
Kayuagung, Indon.	E4	50
Kayumas, Indon.	G9	50
Kazače, Russia	B16	34
Kazačinskoe, Russia	E7	34
Kazačinskoe, Russia	C19	32
Kazahskij melkosopočnik see Qazaqtyng usaqshoqylyghy, hills, Kaz.	D12	32
Kazakh Hills see Qazaqtyng usaqshoqylyghy, hills, Kaz.	E12	32
Kazakhstan, ctry., Asia	E10	32
Kazaki, Russia	H21	10
Kazan', Russia	C7	32
Kazan, stm., Can.	C11	106
Kazanlăk, Blg.	G12	26
Kazanlı, Tur.	B5	58
Kazan-rettō, is., Japan	G18	30
Kazanskoe, Russia	C11	32
Kāzerūn, Iran	D7	56
Kazimierza Wielka, Pol.	F16	16
Kazincbarcika, Hung.	A7	26
Kaziranga National Park, p.o.i., India	E14	54
Kazlų Rūda, Lith.	F6	10
Kaztalovka, Kaz.	E7	32
Kazula, Moz.	D5	68
Kazym, Russia	B11	32
Kazym, stm., Russia	B11	32
Kazyr, stm., Russia	D16	32
Kbal Dâmrei, Camb.	E7	48
Kdyně, Czech Rep.	G9	16
Kéa, Grc.	F7	28
Kéa, i., Grc.	F7	28
Keahole Point, c., Hi., U.S.	d5	78a
Kealaikahiki Channel, strt., Hi., U.S.	c5	78a
Keams Canyon, Az., U.S.	H6	132
Keanapapa Point, c., Hi., U.S.	c4	78a
Kearney, Mo., U.S.	E3	120
Kearney, Ne., U.S.	G13	126
Kearns, Ut., U.S.	C4	132
Kearny, Az., U.S.	J6	132
Keban Barajı, res., Tur.	B4	56
Keban Reservoir see Keban Barajı, res., Tur.	B4	56
Kébèmer, Sen.	F1	64
Kebnekaise, mtn., Swe.	B8	8
K'ebrī Dehar, Eth.	F8	62
Kech, stm., Pak.	D9	56
Kechika, stm., B.C., Can.	D5	106
Keçiborlu, Tur.	F13	28
Kecskemét, Hung.	C6	26
Kedah, state, Malay.	J5	48
Kėdainiai, Lith.	E6	10
Kediri, Indon.	G8	50
Kedon, Russia	D20	34
Kédougou, Sen.	G2	64
Kędzierzyn-Koźle, Pol.	F14	16
Keefers, B.C., Can.	F9	138
Keele, stm., N.T., Can.	C5	106
Keele Peak, mtn., Yk., Can.	C4	106
Keeling Islands see Cocos Islands, dep., Oc.	K12	142
Keelung see Chilung, Tai.	I9	42
Keene, Ky., U.S.	G13	120
Keene, N.H., U.S.	B13	114
Keene, Tx., U.S.	B10	130
Keeney Knob, mtn., W.V., U.S.	G5	114
Keer-Weer, Cape, c., Austl.	B8	74
Keeseville, N.Y., U.S.	F3	110
Keetmanshoop, Nmb.	E3	70
Keewatin, On., Can.	B4	118
Keewatin, Mn., U.S.	D5	118
Kefalloniá, i., Grc.	E3	28
Kefamenanu, Indon.	G7	44
Kefar Naḥum (Capernaum), sci., Isr.	F6	58
Kefar Sava, Isr.	F5	58
Keffi, Nig.	H6	64
Keflavík, Ice.	k28	8a
Ke Ga, Mui, c., Viet.	F9	48
Kegalla, Sri L.	H5	53
Keg River, Ab., Can.	D7	106
Kegums, Lat.	D7	10
Ke-hsi Mānsām, Mya.	B3	48
Keighley, Eng., U.K.	H10	12
Keila, Est.	G11	8
Keimoes, S. Afr.	F5	70
Keith, Scot., U.K.	D9	12
Keith Arm, b., N.T., Can.	B6	106
Keithley Creek, B.C., Can.	D9	138
Keithsburg, Il., U.S.	J8	118
Keiyasi, Fiji	p18	79e
Keizer, Or., U.S.	F3	136
Kejimkujik National Park, p.o.i., N.S., Can.	F11	110
Kejvy, mts., Russia	C17	8
Kekaha, Hi., U.S.	b2	78a
Kékes, mtn., Hung.	B7	26
Kekri, India	E5	54
K'elafo, Eth.	F8	62
Kelai, stm., Indon.	C10	50
Kelani, stm., Sri L.	H5	53
Kelantan, state, Malay.	J6	48
Kelantan, stm., Malay.	J6	48
Kelapa, Indon.	D4	50
Kelbia, Sebkhet, l., Tun.	I4	24
Kelheim, Ger.	H7	16
Kelibia, Tun.	H5	24
Kéllé, Congo	E2	66
Kellerberrin, Austl.	F3	74
Keller Lake, l., N.T., Can.	C6	106
Kellett, Cape, c., N.T., Can.	B14	140
Kelleys Island, i., Oh., U.S.	C3	114
Kellogg, Ia., U.S.	C5	120
Kellogg, Id., U.S.	C10	136
Kellogg, Mn., U.S.	G6	118
Kelloselkä, Fin.	C13	8
Kells, Ire.	H6	12
Kelmė, Lith.	E5	10
Kélo, Chad	F3	62
Kelolokan, Indon.	C10	50
Kelowna, B.C., Can.	G11	138
Kelsey Bay, B.C., Can.	F5	138
Kelseyville, Ca., U.S.	D3	134
Kelso, Scot., U.K.	F10	12
Kelso, Wa., U.S.	D4	136
Keluang, Malay.	K6	48
Kelvington, Sk., Can.	B10	124
Kelvin Island, i., On., Can.	B10	118
Kem', Russia	D16	8
Kem', stm., Russia	D15	8
Kemano, B.C., Can.	C2	138
Kemena, stm., Malay.	B8	50
Kemer, Tur.	F13	28
Kemer Barajı, res., Tur.	F11	28
Kemerhisar, Tur.	A5	58
Kemerovo, Russia	C15	32
Kemi, Fin.	D11	8
Kemijärvi, Fin.	C12	8
Kemijärvi, l., Fin.	C12	8
Kemijoki, stm., Fin.	C12	8
Kemmerer, Wy., U.S.	B6	132
Kemmuna (Comino), i., Malta	H8	24
Kemnath, Ger.	G7	16
Kemp, Tx., U.S.	E2	122
Kemp, Lake, res., Tx., U.S.	H9	128
Kempner, Tx., U.S.	C9	130
Kempsey, Austl.	H9	76
Kempt, Lac, l., Qc., Can.	F16	106
Kempten, Ger.	I6	16
Kemptville, On., Can.	C14	112
Kemujan, Pulau, i., Indon.	F7	50
Kemul, Kong, mtn., Indon.	C9	50
Ken, stm., India	F8	54
Kenai, Ak., U.S.	D9	140
Kenai Mountains, mts., Ak., U.S.	E9	140
Kenai Peninsula, pen., Ak., U.S.	E9	140
Kenansville, Fl., U.S.	I5	116
Kenansville, N.C., U.S.	B7	116
Kenbridge, Va., U.S.	H7	114
Kendal, Sk., Can.	D10	124
Kendal, Indon.	G7	50
Kendal, Eng., U.K.	G10	12
Kendall, Austl.	H9	76
Kendall, Fl., U.S.	K5	116
Kendall, Wi., U.S.	H8	118
Kendall, Cape, c., Nu., Can.	C13	106
Kendari, Indon.	F7	44
Kendawangan, Indon.	E7	50
Kendrāparha, India	H11	54
Kendrew, S. Afr.	H7	70
Kendrick, Fl., U.S.	G3	116
Kendrick, Id., U.S.	D10	136
Kendujhargarh, India	H10	54
Kenedy, Tx., U.S.	F10	130
Kenema, S.L.	H2	64
Kenga, Russia	C14	32
Kenge, D.R.C.	E3	66
Keng Hkam, Mya.	B3	48
Kēng Tung, Mya.	B4	48
Kenhardt, S. Afr.	F5	70
Kenilworth, Ut., U.S.	D6	132
Kénitra, Mor.	C3	64
Kenly, N.C., U.S.	A7	116
Kenmare, Ire.	J3	12
Kenmare, N.D., U.S.	F11	124
Kennard, Tx., U.S.	F3	122
Kennebec, stm., Me., U.S.	F7	110
Kennebecasis Bay, b., N.B., Can.	E11	110
Kennebunk, Me., U.S.	G6	110
Kennedy, Al., U.S.	D11	122
Kennedy, Cape see Canaveral, Cape, c., Fl., U.S.	H5	116
Kennedy, Mount, mtn., B.C., Can.	F5	138
Kennedy, Mount, mtn., Yk., Can.	C3	106
Kennedy Lake, l., B.C., Can.	G5	138
Kenner, La., U.S.	G8	122
Kennetcook, N.S., Can.	E13	110
Kennett, Mo., U.S.	H7	120
Kennewick, Wa., U.S.	D7	136
Kenney Dam, dam, B.C., Can.	C6	138
Kenogami, stm., On., Can.	E13	106
Kénogami, Lac, res., Qc., Can.	B5	110
Keno Hill, Yk., Can.	C3	106
Kenora, On., Can.	B4	118
Kenosha, Wi., U.S.	F2	112
Kenozero, ozero, l., Russia	E18	8
Kensal, N.D., U.S.	G15	124
Kensett, Ar., U.S.	B7	122
Kensington, Ks., U.S.	B9	128
Kensington Park, Fl., U.S.	I3	116
Kent, Oh., U.S.	C4	114
Kent, Wa., U.S.	C4	136
Kentaū, Kaz.	F11	32
Kent Group, is., Austl.	L6	76
Kentland, In., U.S.	H2	112
Kenton, Mi., U.S.	E10	118
Kenton, Tn., U.S.	H8	120
Kent Peninsula, pen., Nu., Can.	B9	106
Kentrikí Makedonía, state, Grc.	C6	28
Kentucky, state, U.S.	G12	120
Kentucky, stm., Ky., U.S.	F13	120
Kentucky, Middle Fork, stm., Ky., U.S.	G2	114
Kentucky, North Fork, stm., Ky., U.S.	G2	114
Kentucky Lake, res., U.S.	H9	120
Kentville, N.S., Can.	E12	110
Kentwood, La., U.S.	G8	122
Kenya, ctry., Afr.	D7	66
Kenya, Mount see Kirinyaga, mtn., Kenya	E7	66
Kenyon, Mn., U.S.	G6	118
Keokuk, Ia., U.S.	D6	120
Keoladeo National Park, p.o.i., India	E6	54
Keo Nua, Deo, p., Asia	C7	48
Keosauqua, Ia., U.S.	D5	120
Keota, Ia., U.S.	C6	120
Keota, Ok., U.S.	B4	122
Keowee, Lake, res., S.C., U.S.	B2	116
Kepi, Indon.	G10	44
Kepina, Russia	D19	8
Kępno, Pol.	E13	16
Keppel Bay, b., Austl.	D8	76
Kepsut, Tur.	D11	28
Kerala, state, India	F3	53
Keramadoo, mtn., Palau	f8	78b
Keramian, Pulau, i., Indon.	F9	50
Kerang, Austl.	J4	76
Keratéa, Grc.	F6	28
Keravat, Pap. N. Gui.	a5	79a
Kerch, Ukr.	E5	32
Kerec, mys, c., Russia	D18	8
Kerema, Pap. N. Gui.	b4	79a
Keremeos, B.C., Can.	G11	138
Keren, Erit.	D7	62
Kerens, Tx., U.S.	E2	122
Keret', Russia	C15	8
Keret', ozero, l., Russia	D15	8
Kerewan, Gam.	G1	64
Kerguélen, Îles, is., Afr.	J17	4
Kerguelen Plateau, unds.	O10	142
Kerí, Grc.	F3	28
Kericho, Kenya	E7	66
Kerinci, Gunung, vol., Indon.	D2	50
Kerkenna, Îles, is., Tun.	C7	64
Kerkhoven, Mn., U.S.	F3	118
Kerkiči, Turkmen.	B10	56
Kerkrade, Neth.	F2	16
Kérkyra (Corfu), Grc.	D2	28
Kérkyra (Corfu), i., Grc.	D2	28
Kermadec Islands, is., N.Z.	F9	72
Kermadec Ridge, unds.	M20	142
Kermadec Trench, unds.	M21	142
Kermān, Iran	C8	56
Kermānshāh (Bākhtarān), Iran	C6	56
Kerme, Gulf of see Gökova Körfezi, b., Tur.	G10	28
Kermit, Tx., U.S.	C4	130
Kern, stm., Ca., U.S.	H7	134

Name	Map Ref.	Page
Kern, South Fork, stm., Ca., U.S.	H7	134
Kernersville, N.C., U.S.	H5	114
Kernville, Ca., U.S.	H7	134
Kérouané, Gui.	H3	64
Kerrobert, Sk., Can.	C4	124
Kerrville, Tx., U.S.	D8	130
Kerry, state, Ire.	I2	12
Kerry Head, c., Ire.	I2	12
Kershaw, S.C., U.S.	B5	116
Kersley, B.C., Can.	D8	138
Kertamulia, Indon.	D6	50
Kerulen, stm., Asia	B7	36
Kesagami Lake, l., On., Can.	E14	106
Keşan, Tur.	C9	28
Kesennuma, Japan	E14	38
Keshan, China	B10	36
Keshod, India	H3	54
Kes'ma, Russia	B20	10
Kesova Gora, Russia	C20	10
Kestell, S. Afr.	F9	70
Keswick, Eng., U.K.	G9	12
Keszthely, Hung.	C4	26
Ket', stm., Russia	C14	32
Keta, Ghana	H5	64
Keta, ozero, l., Russia	C6	34
Ketapang, Indon.	D6	50
Ketapang, Indon.	F4	50
Ketchikan, Ak., U.S.	E13	140
Ketchum, Id., U.S.	G12	136
Kete-Krachi, Ghana	H4	64
Ketoj, ostrov, i., Russia	G19	34
Kętrzyn, Pol.	B17	16
Kettering, Eng., U.K.	I12	12
Kettering, Oh., U.S.	E1	114
Kettle, stm., N.A.	H12	138
Kettle Falls, Wa., U.S.	B8	136
Kety, Pol.	G15	16
Keudetsunom, Indon.	J2	48
Keuka Lake, l., N.Y., U.S.	B8	114
Keukenhof, misc. cult., Neth.	B13	14
Keul', Russia	C18	32
Kevelaer, Ger.	E2	16
Kevin, Mt., U.S.	B14	136
Kew, T./C. Is.	A12	102
Kewanee, Il., U.S.	C7	120
Kewaunee, Wi., U.S.	D2	112
Keweenaw Bay, b., Mi., U.S.	E10	118
Keweenaw Peninsula, pen., Mi., U.S.	D11	118
Keweenaw Point, c., Mi., U.S.	D11	118
Key, Lough, l., Ire.	G4	12
Keya Paha, stm., U.S.	E13	126
Keyes, Ok., U.S.	E6	128
Keyhole Reservoir, res., Wy., U.S.	C8	126
Key Largo, Fl., U.S.	K5	116
Key Largo, i., Fl., U.S.	K5	116
Keyser, W.V., U.S.	E7	114
Keystone, S.D., U.S.	D9	126
Keystone, W.V., U.S.	G4	114
Keystone Lake, res., Ok., U.S.	A2	122
Keystone Peak, mtn., Az., U.S.	L5	132
Keysville, Va., U.S.	G7	114
Keytesville, Mo., U.S.	E5	120
Key West, Fl., U.S.	L4	116
Kezi, Zimb.	B9	70
Kežma, Russia	C18	32
Kežmarok, Slov.	G16	16
Kgalagadi, state, Bots.	D5	70
Kgatleng, state, Bots.	D8	70
Khadki, India	B1	53
Khadzhybeis'kyi lyman, l., Ukr.	C17	26
Khagaria, India	F11	54
Khairāgarh, India	H8	54
Khairpur, Pak.	E2	54
Khairpur, Pak.	D4	54
Khajrāho, India	F8	54
Khakassia see Hakasija, state, Russia	D16	32
Kha Khaeng, stm., Thai.	E4	48
Khakhea, Bots.	D6	70
Khalatse, India	A6	54
Khālidī, Khirbat al-, sci., Jord.	I6	58
Khaliya, Gebel, mtn., Egypt	I3	58
Khaluf, Oman	E8	56
Khambhāliya, India	G2	54
Khambhāt, India	G4	54
Khambhāt, Gulf of, b., India	H3	54
Khamgaon, India	H6	54
Khāmis, Ash-Shallāl al- (Fifth Cataract), wtfl., Sudan	D6	62
Khamis Mushayt, Sau. Ar.	F5	56
Khammam, India	C5	53
Khan, stm., Laos	C6	48
Khan, stm., Nmb.	C2	70
Khānābād, Afg.	B10	56
Khān Abū Shāmāt, Syria	E7	58
Khancoban, Austl.	K7	76
Khandela, India	E5	54
Khandwa, India	H6	54
Khanewāl, Pak.	C3	54
Khāngarh, Pak.	D3	54
Khangchendzonga National Park, p.o.i., India	E12	54
Khangkhai, Laos	C6	48
Khania, Gulf of see Chanión, Kólpos, b., Grc.	H6	28
Khanka, Lake, l., Asia	B10	38
Khanna, India	C6	54
Khānpur, Pak.	D3	54
Khansiir, Raas, c., Som.	B9	66
Khantaū, Kaz.	F12	32
Khān Yūnus, Gaza	G5	58
Khao Laem Reservoir, res., Thai.	E4	48
Khao Sok National Park, p.o.i., Thai.	H4	48
Khao Yoi, Thai.	F4	48
Kharagpur, India	G11	54
Kharān, Pak.	D10	56
Kharāyij, Sabkhat al-, l., Syria	C8	58
Kharg Island see Khārk, Jazīreh-ye, i., Iran	D7	56
Khargon, India	H5	54
Khariān Cantonment, Pak.	B4	54
Khārk, Jazīreh-ye, i., Iran	D7	56
Kharkiv, Ukr.	D5	32
Kharmanli see Harmanli, Blg.	H12	26
Khartoum see Al-Khartūm, Sudan	D6	62
Khartoum North see Al-Khartūm Bahrī, Sudan	D6	62
Khasebake, Bots.	B7	70
Khāsh, Afg.	C9	56
Khāsh, Iran	D9	56
Khashm al-Qirbah, Sudan	D7	62
Khaskovo see Haskovo, Blg.	H12	26
Khatanga see Hatanga, Russia	B9	34
Khatanga see Hatanga, stm., Russia	B9	34
Khatauli, India	D6	54
Khāvast see Havast, Uzb.	F11	32
Khawsa, Mya.	E3	48
Khayung, stm., Thai.	E7	48
Khed, India	C1	53
Kheil, Katib el-, sand, Egypt	H3	58
Khemis el Khechna, Alg.	H14	20
Khemis Melyana, Alg.	H13	20
Khemmarat, Thai.	D7	48
Khenchla, Alg.	B6	64
Khenifra, Mor.	C3	64
Kherson, Ukr.	F15	6
Kheta see Heta, stm., Russia	B8	34
Khetia, India	H5	54
Khimki see Himki, Russia	E20	10
Khipro, Pak.	F2	54
Khisfin, Golan	F6	58
Khiva see Hiva, Uzb.	F10	32
Khlong Thom, Thai.	I4	48
Khlung, Thai.	F6	48
Khok Kloi, Thai.	H4	48
Khok Samrong, Thai.	E5	48
Kholm, Afg.	B10	56
Khomas, state, Nmb.	C3	70
Khomeynishahr, Iran	C7	56
Khondmāl Hills, hills, India	H10	54
Khong see Mekong, stm., Asia	E10	46
Khon Kaen, Thai.	D6	48
Khordha, India	H10	54
Khorixas, Nmb.	B2	70
Khorog see Horog, Taj.	B11	56
Khorramābād, Iran	C6	56
Khorramshahr, Iran	C6	56
Khotyn, Ukr.	A13	26
Khouribga, Mor.	C3	64
Khowai, India	F13	54
Khovrost, Afg.	C10	56
Khrisokhous, Kólpos, b., Cyp.	C3	58
Khuis, Bots.	E5	70
Khuīyāla, India	E3	54
Khulna, Bngl.	G12	54
Khulna, state, Bngl.	G12	54
Khun Tan, Doi, mtn., Thai.	C4	48
Khunti, India	G10	54
Khurai, India	F7	54
Khurja, India	D6	54
Khushāb, Pak.	B4	54
Khust, Ukr.	A10	26
Khuzdār, Pak.	D10	56
Khvoy, Iran	B6	56
Khwae Noi, stm., Thai.	E4	48
Khyber Pass, p., Asia	A3	54
Khyriv, Ukr.	G18	16
Kiama, Austl.	J8	76
Kiama, D.R.C.	F3	66
Kiamba, Phil.	H5	52
Kiambi, D.R.C.	F5	66
Kiamichi, stm., Ok., U.S.	C3	122
Kiamusze see Jiamusi, China	B11	36
Kian see Ji'an, China	H6	42
Kiangarow, Mount, mtn., Austl.	F8	76
Kiang-si see Jiangxi, state, China	H6	42
Kiangsi see Jiangxi, state, China	H6	42
Kiang-sou see Jiangsu, state, China	E8	42
Kiangsu see Jiangsu, state, China	E8	42
Kiaohsien see Jiaoxian, China	C8	42
Kibangou, Congo	E2	66
Kibombo, D.R.C.	E5	66
Kibondo, Tan.	E6	66
Kibre Mengist, Eth.	F7	62
Kibris see Cyprus, ctry., Asia	C4	58
Kibrīşcik, Tur.	C14	28
Kibuye, Rw.	E5	66
Kićevo, Mac.	B3	28
Kickapoo, stm., Wi., U.S.	H8	118
Kicking Horse Pass, p., Can.	E14	138
Kidal, Mali	F5	64
Kidapawan, Phil.	G5	52
Kidatu, Tan.	F7	66
Kidderminster, Eng., U.K.	I10	12
Kidira, Sen.	G2	64
Kidnappers, Cape, c., N.Z.	D7	80
Kidston, Austl.	B5	76
Kiefersfelden, Ger.	I8	16
Kiel, Ger.	B6	16
Kiel, Wi., U.S.	H10	118
Kiel Bay see Kieler Bucht, b., Ger.	B6	16
Kiel Canal see Nord-Ostsee-Kanal, can., Ger.	B5	16
Kielce, Pol.	F16	16
Kielce, state, Pol.	F16	16
Kieler Bucht, b., Ger.	B6	16
Kiester, Mn., U.S.	H5	118
Kiev see Kyïv, Ukr.	D4	32
Kievka, Russia	D12	32
Kiev Reservoir see Kyïvs'ke vodoskhovyshche, Ukr.	D4	32
Kiffa, Maur.	F2	64
Kifisiá, Grc.	E6	28
Kigali, Rw.	E6	66
Kigoma, Tan.	E5	66
Kihčik, Russia	F20	34
Kīhei, Hi., U.S.	c5	78a
Kihnu, Fin.	B10	8
Kihnu, i., Est.	G10	8
Kii-hantō, pen., Japan	F8	40
Kiik, Kaz.	E12	32
Kii-suidō, strt., Japan	F7	40
Kikerino, Russia	A12	10
Kikinda, Serb.	D7	26
Kikládes (Cyclades), is., Grc.	F7	28
Kikori, Pap. N. Gui.	b3	79a
Kikori, stm., Pap. N. Gui.	b3	79a
Kikuchi, Japan	G3	40
Kikwit, D.R.C.	F3	66
Kilakkarai, India	G4	53
Kilauea, Hi., U.S.	a2	78a
Kīlauea Crater, crat., Hi., U.S.	d6	78a
Kılbasan, Tur.	A4	58
Kilbuck Mountains, mts., Ak., U.S.	D8	140
Kilchu-ŭp, Kor., N.	D8	38
Kilcoy, Austl.	F9	76
Kildare, state, Ire.	H6	12
Kildare, Cape, c., P.E., Can.	D13	110
Kildonan, Austl.	C5	74
Kildurk, Austl.	C5	74
Kilembe, D.R.C.	F3	66
Kilian Island, i., Nu., Can.	B18	140
Kilic, Tur.	C12	28
Kiliia, Ukr.	D16	26
Kilikollūr, India	G3	53
Kilimanjaro, mtn., Tan.	E7	66
Kilimli, Tur.	B14	28
Kilindoni, Tan.	F7	66
Kilis, Tur.	B8	58
Kilkenny, Ire.	I5	12
Kilkenny, state, Ire.	I5	12
Kilkís, Grc.	C5	28
Killaloe, Ire.	I4	12
Killaloe Station, On., Can.	C12	112
Killam, Ab., U.S.	D19	138
Killarney, Austl.	E14	124
Killarney, On., Can.	C8	112
Killarney, Ire.	I3	12
Kildeer, N.D., U.S.	G11	124
Killeen, Tx., U.S.	C10	130
Killen, Al., U.S.	C11	122
Killington Peak, mtn., Vt., U.S.	G4	110
Killiniq Island, i., Can.	E13	141
Killybegs, Ire.	G4	12
Kilmarnock, Scot., U.K.	F8	12
Kilmarnock, Va., U.S.	G9	114
Kilmore, Austl.	K5	76
Kilo, Indon.	H11	50
Kilombero, stm., Tan.	F7	66
Kilomines, D.R.C.	D5	66
Kilosa, Tan.	F7	66
Kilrush, Ire.	I3	12
Kilttān Island, i., India	F3	46
Kilwa, D.R.C.	F5	66
Kilwa Kivinje, Tan.	F7	66
Kim, Co., U.S.	D5	128
Kimba, Austl.	F7	74
Kimball, Ne., U.S.	F9	126
Kimball, S.D., U.S.	D13	126
Kimbe Bay, b., Pap. N. Gui.	b5	79a
Kimberley, B.C., Can.	G15	138
Kimberley, S. Afr.	F7	70
Kimberley Downs, Austl.	C4	74
Kimberley Plateau, plat., Austl.	C5	74
Kimberling City, Mo., U.S.	H4	120
Kimberly, Id., U.S.	H12	136
Kimberly, Wi., U.S.	G10	118
Kimch'aek, Kor., N.	D8	38
Kimch'ŏn, Kor., S.	F8	38
Kimhae, Kor., S.	D1	40
Kimito, Fin.	F10	8
Kim-me-ni-oli Wash, stm., N.M., U.S.	H8	132
Kimmirut, Nu., Can.	C17	106
Kímolos, i., Grc.	G7	28
Kimovsk, Russia	F21	10
Kimpō-zan, mtn., Japan	D11	40
Kimry, Russia	D20	10
Kinabalu, Gunung (Kinabalu, Mount), mtn., Malay.	G1	52
Kinabalu National Park, p.o.i., Malay.	H1	52
Kinabatangan, stm., Malay.	H2	52
Kinbasket Lake, res., B.C., Can.	D12	138
Kincaid, Sk., Can.	E6	124
Kincardine, On., Can.	D8	112
Kinchafoonee Creek, stm., Ga., U.S.	F14	122
Kinchega National Park, p.o.i., Austl.	I4	76
Kinda, D.R.C.	F4	66
Kinde, Mi., U.S.	E7	112
Kinder, La., U.S.	G6	122
Kindersley, Sk., Can.	C4	124
Kindia, Gui.	G2	64
Kindu, D.R.C.	E5	66
Kinešma, Russia	H19	8
King, N.C., U.S.	H5	114
King and Queen Court House, Va., U.S.	G9	114
Kingaok (Bathurst Inlet), Nu., Can.	B9	106
Kingaroy, Austl.	F8	76
King City, On., Can.	E10	112
King City, Ca., U.S.	G4	134
Kingfield, Me., U.S.	F6	110
Kingfisher, Ok., U.S.	F10	128
King George, Va., U.S.	F8	114
King George, Mount, mtn., B.C., Can.	F15	138
King George Islands, is., Nu., Can.	D14	106
King George Sound, strt., Austl.	H2	74
King Hill, Id., U.S.	G11	136
Kingisepp, Russia	A11	10
King Island, i., Austl.	m12	77a
King Island, i., B.C., Can.	D3	138
King Leopold Ranges, mts., Austl.	C4	74
Kingman, Az., U.S.	H2	132
Kingman, Ks., U.S.	D10	128
Kingman Reef, rf., Oc.	C10	72
King Mountain, mtn., Or., U.S.	H3	136
Kingombe, D.R.C.	E5	66
Kingoonya, Austl.	F7	74
King Peak, mtn., Ca., U.S.	C1	134
Kings, stm., Ca., U.S.	G6	134
Kings Beach, Ca., U.S.	D5	134
Kingsbridge, Eng., U.K.	K9	12
Kingsburg, Ca., U.S.	G6	134
Kings Canyon National Park, p.o.i., Ca., U.S.	G7	134
Kingsford, Mi., U.S.	C1	112
Kingshill, V.I.U.S.	h10	104c
Kingsland, Ar., U.S.	D6	122
Kingsland, Ga., U.S.	F4	116
Kingsley, S. Afr.	E10	70
Kingsley, Mi., U.S.	D4	112
Kingsley Dam, dam, Ne., U.S.	F11	126
King's Lynn, Eng., U.K.	I13	12
Kings Mountain, N.C., U.S.	A4	116
King Sound, strt., Austl.	C4	74
Kings Peak, mtn., Ut., U.S.	C5	132
Kingsport, Tn., U.S.	H3	114
Kingston, On., Can.	C13	112
Kingston, Jam.	i14	104d
Kingston, N.Z.	G3	80
Kingston, Norf. I.	y25	78l
Kingston, Ga., U.S.	C14	122
Kingston, Mo., U.S.	E3	120
Kingston, N.Y., U.S.	C11	114
Kingston, Oh., U.S.	E3	114
Kingston, Ok., U.S.	C2	122
Kingston, Pa., U.S.	C9	114
Kingston, R.I., U.S.	C14	114
Kingston, Tn., U.S.	I13	120
Kingston Southeast, Austl.	K2	76
Kingston upon Hull, Eng., U.K.	H12	12
Kingston upon Thames, Eng., U.K.	J12	12
Kingstown, St. Vin.	o11	105e
Kingstree, S.C., U.S.	C6	116
Kingsville, On., Can.	G7	112
Kingsville, Tx., U.S.	G10	130
Kingtechen see Jingdezhen, China	G7	42
King William Island, i., Nu., Can.	B11	106
King William's Town, S. Afr.	H8	70
Kinhwa see Jinhua, China	G8	42
Kınık, Tur.	D10	28
Kinira, stm., S. Afr.	G9	70
Kinistino, Sk., Can.	B9	124
Kinkala, Congo	E2	66
Kinlochleven, Scot., U.K.	E8	12
Kinnaird Head, c., Scot., U.K.	D10	12
Kinneret, Yam (Galilee, Sea of), l., Isr.	F6	58
Kinngait (Cape Dorset), Nu., Can.	C15	106
Kinosaki, Japan	D7	40
Kinoosao, Sk., Can.	D10	106
Kinross, Scot., U.K.	E9	12
Kinsale, Monts.	D3	105a
Kinsale, Old Head of, c., Ire.	J4	12
Kinsarvik, Nor.	F2	8
Kinshasa (Léopoldville), D.R.C.	E3	66
Kinsley, Ks., U.S.	D9	128
Kinsman, Oh., U.S.	C5	114
Kinston, N.C., U.S.	A8	116
Kintampo, Ghana	H4	64
Kintinian, Gui.	G3	64
Kintyre, pen., Scot., U.K.	F7	12
Kintyre, Mull of, c., Scot., U.K.	F7	12
Kinuseo Falls, wtfl., B.C., Can.	B9	138
Kinyinya, Tan.	E6	66
Kinyeti, mtn., Sudan	G6	62
Kinzia, D.R.C.	F3	66
Kinzua, Or., U.S.	E7	136
Kinzua Dam, dam, Pa., U.S.	C6	114
Kiowa see Jieyang, China	J7	42
Kiowa, Ok., U.S.	C3	122
Kiowa Creek, stm., Co., U.S.	A4	128
Kipawa, stm., Qc., Can.	B11	112
Kipawa, Lac, res., Qc., Can.	A10	112
Kipembawe, Tan.	F6	66
Kipengere Range, mts., Tan.	F6	66
Kipili, Tan.	F6	66
Kipini, Kenya	E8	66
Kipling, Sk., Can.	D11	124
Kipnuk, Ak., U.S.	E7	140
Kipushi, D.R.C.	G5	66
Kirakira, Sol. Is.	f9	79b
Kirandul, India	B5	53
Kirauskas, Bela.	G12	10
Kirazlı, Tur.	C9	28
Kirbla, Est.	B6	10
Kirchberg, Ger.	G5	16
Kirchmöser, Ger.	D8	16
Kireevsk, Russia	G20	10
Kirejkovo, Russia	G18	10
Kirenga, stm., Russia	C19	32
Kirensk, Russia	C19	32
Kirghizia see Kyrgyzstan, ctry., Asia	F12	32
Kirgiz Range, mts., Asia	F12	32
Kirgiz Soviet Socialist Republic see Kyrgyzstan, ctry., Asia	F12	32
Kiri, D.R.C.	E3	66
Kiribati, ctry., Oc.	D9	72
Kirikhan, Tur.	B7	58
Kirikkale, Tur.	B3	56
Kirillovo, Russia	H21	8
Kirin see Jilin, China	C7	38
Kirin see Jilin, state, China	C10	36
Kirinyaga (Kenya, Mount), mtn., Kenya	E7	66
Kirishima-kokuritsu-kōen, p.o.i., Japan	H3	40
Kirishima-yama, vol., Japan	H3	40
Kirişli, Russia	A15	10
Kiritimati (Christmas Island), at., Kir.	C11	72
Kiriwina Islands (Trobriand Islands), is., Pap. N. Gui.	b5	79a
Kirka, Tur.	D13	28
Kirkağaç, Tur.	D10	28
Kirkcaldy, Scot., U.K.	E9	12
Kirkcudbright, Scot., U.K.	G8	12
Kirkenes, Nor.	B14	8
Kirkland, Il., U.S.	B9	120
Kirkland, Tx., U.S.	G8	128
Kirkland, Wa., U.S.	C4	136
Kirkland Lake, On., Can.	F14	106
Kirklareli, Tur.	B10	28
Kırklareli, state, Tur.	B10	28
Kirklin, In., U.S.	H3	112
Kirkpatrick, Mount, mtn., Ant.	D21	81
Kirksville, Mo., U.S.	D5	120
Kirkwall, Scot., U.K.	B9	12
Kirksdorp, S. Afr.	E8	70
Kirkwood, Mo., U.S.	F7	120
Kirmir, stm., Tur.	C15	28
Kirov, Russia	G3	16
Kirov, Russia	C7	32
Kirovakan see Vanadzor, Arm.	A5	56
Kirovohrad, Ukr.	E4	32
Kirovohrad, co., Ukr.	A17	26
Kirovsk, Russia	C15	8
Kirovsk, Turkmen.	B9	56
Kirovskaja oblast', co., Russia	F22	8
Kirovskiy, Russia	F20	34
Kirovskiy, Kaz.	F13	32
Kirriemuir, Scot., U.K.	E9	12
Kirs, Russia	C8	32
Kirsanov, Russia	D6	32
Kırşehir, Tur.	B3	56
Kirthar Range, mts., Pak.	D10	56
Kirtland, N.M., U.S.	G8	132
Kiruna, Swe.	C8	8
Kirundu, D.R.C.	D5	66
Kirwin, Ks., U.S.	B9	128
Kiryū, Japan	C12	40
Kirżač, Russia	D21	10
Kisa, Swe.	G6	8
Kisangani (Stanleyville), D.R.C.	D5	66
Kisar, Pulau, i., Indon.	G8	44
Kisaran, Indon.	B1	50
Kisarazu, Japan	D12	40
Kisbey, Sk., Can.	E11	124
Kiselëvsk, Russia	D15	32
Kish, Jazireh-ye, i., Iran	D7	56
Kishanganj, India	E11	54
Kishangarh, India	E3	54
Kishangarh Bās, India	E5	54
Kishi, Nig.	H5	64
Kishinev see Chişinău, Mol.	B15	26
Kishiwada, Japan	E8	40
Kishorganj, Bngl.	F13	54
Kishtwār, India	B5	54
Kisii, Kenya	E6	66
Kisiju, Tan.	F7	66
Kisiwada see Kishiwada, Japan	E8	40
Kiska Island, i., Ak., U.S.	g22	140a
Kiskatinaw, stm., B.C., Can.	A10	138
Kiska Volcano, vol., Ak., U.S.	g22	140a
Kiskőrei-víztároló, res., Hung.	B7	26
Kiskőrös, Hung.	C6	26
Kiskunfélegyháza, Hung.	C6	26
Kiskunhalas, Hung.	C6	26
Kiskunmajsa, Hung.	C6	26
Kiskunsági Nemzeti Park, p.o.i., Hung.	C6	26
Kislovodsk, Russia	F6	32
Kismaayo, Som.	E8	66
Kiso-sammyaku, mts., Japan	D10	40
Kissidougou, Gui.	H2	64
Kissimmee, Fl., U.S.	H4	116
Kissimmee, stm., Fl., U.S.	I4	116
Kissimmee, Lake, l., Fl., U.S.	I4	116
Kississing Lake, l., Mb., Can.	D10	106
Kisújszállás, Hung.	B7	26
Kisumu, Kenya	E6	66
Kisvárda, Hung.	A9	26
Kita, Mali	G3	64
Kitaa, state, Grnld.	D16	141
Kitaibaraki, Japan	C13	40
Kitakami, stm., Japan	E14	38
Kitakyūshū, Japan	F3	40
Kitale, Kenya	D7	66
Kitami, Japan	C15	38
Kitangiri, Lake, l., Tan.	E6	66
Kitchener, On., Can.	E9	112
Kitee, Fin.	E13	8
Kitgum, Ug.	D6	66
Kithārah, Khirbat, sci., Jord.	I6	58
Kitimat, B.C., Can.	B2	138
Kitinen, stm., Fin.	C12	8
Kitreli, Tur.	D4	58
Kitsuki, Japan	F4	40
Kittanning, Pa., U.S.	D6	114
Kittatinny Mountain, mtn., U.S.	C2	138
Kittery, Me., U.S.	G6	110
Kitt Peak National Observatory, sci., Az., U.S.	K5	132
Kittilä, Fin.	C11	8
Kitunda, Tan.	F6	66
Kitwe, Zimb.	C4	68
Kityang see Jieyang, China	J7	42
Kitzbühel, Aus.	C9	22
Kitzingen, Ger.	G6	16
Kiukiang see Jiujiang, China	G6	42
Kiunga, Pap. N. Gui.	b3	79a
Kiuruvesi, Fin.	E12	8
Kivalina, Ak., U.S.	C7	140
Kivijärvi, l., Fin.	E11	8
Kivik, Swe.	I6	8
Kivu, Lake, l., Afr.	E5	66
Kıyıköy, Tur.	B11	28
Kiyiu Lake, l., Sk., Can.	C5	124
Kızıl Adalar, is., Tur.	C11	28
Kızılcabölük, Tur.	F11	28
Kızılcahamam, Tur.	C15	28
Kizil, Est.	B6	10
Kızıldağ Milli Parkı, p.o.i., Tur.	F14	28
Kızılırmak, stm., Tur.	A4	56
Kızılören, Tur.	F15	28
Kızkalesi, sci., Tur.	B4	58
Kızıl Su, Turkmen.	B7	56
Kjahta, Russia	F10	34
Kjungej-Ala-Too, hrebet, mts., Asia	F13	32
Kjustendil, Blg.	G9	26
Klabat, Gunung, vol., Indon.	E8	44
Kladno, Czech Rep.	F9	16
Kladovo, Serb.	E9	26
Klagan, Malay.	G1	52
Klagenfurt, Aus.	D11	22
Klaipėda (Memel), Lith.	E3	10
Klakah, Indon.	G8	50
Klamath, stm., U.S.	B2	134
Klamath Falls, Or., U.S.	A3	134
Klamath Marsh, sw., Or., U.S.	H5	136
Klamath Mountains, mts., U.S.	B2	134
Klamono, Indon.	F9	44
Klang, Malay.	K5	48
Klangenan, Indon.	G6	50
Klangenang, Indon.	G6	50
Klangpi, Mya.	G14	54
Klarälven, stm., Swe.	E5	8
Klatovy, Czech Rep.	G9	16
Klawer, S. Afr.	G4	70
Kleck, Bela.	G9	10
Kleczew, Pol.	D14	16
Kleena Kleene, B.C., Can.	E5	138
Klein Curaçao, i., Neth. Ant.	q22	104g
Klein Karroo see Little Karroo, plat., S. Afr.	H5	70
Klein Namaland see Little Namaqualand, hist. reg., S. Afr.	F3	70
Klekovača, mtn., Bos.	E3	26
Klemme, Ia., U.S.	A4	120
Klenak, Indon.	F5	44
Klerksdorp, S. Afr.	E8	70
Kletnja, Russia	G16	10
Kleve, Ger.	E2	16
Klickitat, stm., Wa., U.S.	D5	136
Klimaviçy, Bela.	G14	10
Klimino, Russia	C17	32
Klimovo, Russia	H15	10
Klimovsk, Russia	E20	10
Klimpfjäll, Swe.	D6	8
Klin, Russia	D19	10
Klinaklini, stm., B.C., Can.	E5	138
Klincy, Russia	H15	10
Klingenthal, Ger.	F8	16
Klinovec, mtn., Czech Rep.	F8	16
Klintehamn, Swe.	H8	8
Klip, stm., S. Afr.	F9	70
Klipdale, S. Afr.	I4	70
Klipplaat, S. Afr.	H7	70
Klisura, Blg.	G11	26
Kljazma, stm., Russia	E21	10
Ključ, Bos.	E3	26
Ključevskaja Sopka, vulkan, vol., Russia	E21	34
Ključi, Russia	E21	34
Kljukvenka, Russia	C15	32
Klobuck, Pol.	F14	16
Kłodawa, Pol.	D14	16
Kłodzko, Pol.	F12	16
Klondike, hist. reg., Yk., Can.	C3	106
Klooga, Est.	A7	10
Klosterneuburg, Aus.	B13	22
Kloten, Switz.	C5	22
Klotz, Lac, l., Qc., Can.	C16	106
Klötze, Ger.	D7	16
Kluane Lake, l., Yk., Can.	C3	106
Kluczbork, Pol.	F14	16
Klungkung, Indon.	H9	50
Knaddah, Syria	C7	58
Knapp, Wi., U.S.	G6	118
Kneehills Creek, stm., Ab., Can.	E17	138
Knee Lake, l., Mb., Can.	D12	106
Kneža, Blg.	F11	26
Knić, Serb.	F7	26
Knickerbocker, Tx., U.S.	C7	130
Knife, stm., N.D., U.S.	G12	124
Knight Inlet, b., B.C., Can.	F4	138
Knights Landing, Ca., U.S.	E4	134
Knin, Cro.	F13	22
Knippa, Tx., U.S.	E8	130
Knittelfeld, Aus.	C11	22
Knjaževac, Serb.	F9	26
Knob Noster, Mo., U.S.	F4	120
Knokke-Heist, Bel.	C12	14
Knosós, sci., Grc.	H8	28
Knox, Pa., U.S.	C6	114
Knox, Cape, c., B.C., Can.	E4	106
Knox City, Tx., U.S.	H9	128
Knox Coast, cst., Ant.	B15	81
Knoxville, Ga., U.S.	D2	116
Knoxville, Ia., U.S.	C4	120
Knoxville, Il., U.S.	D7	120
Knoxville, Tn., U.S.	I2	114
Knud Rasmussen Land, reg., Grnld.	A14	141
Knysna, S. Afr.	I6	70
Ko'au Channel, strt., Hi., U.S.	b8	78a
Kobar Sink, depr., Eth.	E8	62
Kobayashi, Japan	H3	40
Kōbe, Japan	E8	40
Kōbi, Japan	D10	40
København (Copenhagen), Den.	I5	8
Kobja, Russia	D14	34
Koboža, stm., Russia	B18	10
K'obo, Eth.	E7	62
Kobrin, Bela.	G10	10
Kobryn, Bela.	H7	10
Kobuk, stm., Ak., U.S.	C8	140
Kobuleti, Geor.	F6	32
Kočani, Mac.	B5	28
Koçarlı, Tur.	F10	28
Kočeljevo, Serb.	E7	26
Kočevje, Slvn.	E12	22
Kōch, Japan	F6	40
Koch Bihār, India	E12	54
Kochi (Cochin), India	G3	53
Kōchi, state, Japan	F6	40
Kōchi Island, i., Nu., Can.	B15	106
Kochiu see Gejiu, China	G5	36
Kodaikānal, India	F3	53
Kodar, hrebet, mts., Russia	E12	34
Kodāri, Nepal	E10	54
Kodarma, India	F10	54
Kodiak, Ak., U.S.	E9	140
Kodiak Island, i., Ak., U.S.	E9	140
Kodinār, India	H3	54
Kodok, Sudan	F6	62
Kodyma, Ukr.	A16	26
Kodyma, stm., Ukr.	B17	26
Koës, Nmb.	D4	70
Köflach, Aus.	C11	22
Koforidua, Ghana	H4	64
Kōfu, Japan	D11	40
Koga, Japan	C12	40
Kogaluc, stm., Qc., Can.	D15	106
Kogaluc, Baie, b., Qc., Can.	D15	106
Kogan, Austl.	F8	76
Køge, Den.	I5	8
Kogon, stm., Gui.	G2	64
Kohanava, Bela.	F12	10
Kohāt, Pak.	B3	54
Kohīma, India	C7	46
Kohtla-Järve, Est.	G12	8
Kohyl'nyk (Cogâlnic), stm., Eur.	C15	26
Koide, Japan	B11	40
Koigi, Est.	B8	10
Koindu, S.L.	H2	64
Koiva (Gauja), stm., Eur.	C7	10
Kojda, Russia	C20	8
Kóje-do, i., Kor., S.	E1	40
Kojgorodok, Russia	B8	32
Kojonup, Austl.	F3	74
Kok (Hkok), stm., Asia	B4	48
Kokand, Uzb.	F12	32
Kokas, Indon.	F9	44
Kokemäki, Fin.	F9	8
Kokkilai Lagoon, b., Sri L.	G5	53
Kokkola, Fin.	E10	8
Kokoda, Pap. N. Gui.	b4	79a
Kokomo, In., U.S.	H3	112
Kokomo, Ms., U.S.	F8	122
Kokong, Bots.	D6	70
Kokopo, Pap. N. Gui.	a5	79a
Kokorevka, Russia	H17	10
Koksan-ŭp, Kor., N.	E7	38
Kokshetaū, Kaz.	D12	32
Kökshetaü see Kokčetav, Kaz.	D12	32
Koksoak, stm., Qc., Can.	D17	106
Kokstad, S. Afr.	G9	70
Kokubu, Japan	H3	40
Kola, Indon.	B15	8
Kolachel, India	G3	53
Kolahun, Indon.	H2	64
Kolangār, Afg.	A2	54
Kola Peninsula see Kol'skij poluostrov, pen., Russia	C17	8
Kolār, India	E4	53
Kolāras, India	F6	54
Kolar Gold Fields, India	E4	53
Kolari, Fin.	C10	8
Kolašin, Serb.	G6	26
Kolbio, Kenya	E8	66
Kolbuszowa, Pol.	F17	16
Kol'čugino, Russia	D22	10
Kolda, Sen.	G2	64
Kolding, Den.	I3	8
Kole, D.R.C.	E4	66
Kolea, Alg.	H13	20
Kolguev, ostrov, i., Russia	B18	8
Kolhāpur, India	C4	53
Kolhāpur, India	C1	53
Koli, Russia	A17	10
Kolin, Czech Rep.	F11	16
Koljubakino, Russia	E19	10
Kolkata (Calcutta), India	G12	54
Kollam see Quilon, India	G3	53
Kollegāl, India	E3	53
Kolleru Lake, l., India	C5	53
Kolmogorovo, Russia	C16	32
Köln (Cologne), Ger.	E2	16
Kolno, Pol.	C17	16
Kolo, Pol.	D14	16
Koloa, Hi., U.S.	b2	78a
Kolobrzeg, Pol.	B11	16
Kologriv, Russia	F15	10
Kolokani, Mali	G3	64
Kolombangara Island, i., Sol. Is.	d7	79b
Kolomna, Russia	E21	10
Kolomyia, Ukr.	A12	26
Kolonga, Tonga	n14	78e
Kolonia, Micron.	m11	78d
Kolosib, India	F14	54
Kolosovka, Russia	C12	32
Kolozsvár see Cluj-Napoca, Rom.	C10	26
Kolp', stm., Russia	A19	10
Kolpino, Russia	A13	10
Kolpny, Russia	H19	10
Kol'skij poluostrov (Kola Peninsula), pen., Russia	C17	8
Kolwezi, D.R.C.	G5	66
Kolyma see Kolymskaja nizmennost', pl., Russia	C19	34
Kolymskaja, Russia	C19	34
Kolymskaja nizmennost' (Kolyma Plain), pl., Russia	C19	34
Kom, mtn., Blg.	F10	26
Koma, Mya.		
Komadugu Gana, stm., Nig.	G7	64
Komagane, Japan	D10	40
Komandorskie ostrova, is., Russia	D20	30
Komandorski Islands see Komandorskie ostrova, is., Russia	D20	30
Komárno, Slov.	I13	16
Komárom, Hung.	G19	16
Komárom-Esztergom, state, Hung.	B5	26
Komati (Incomati), stm., Afr.	D10	70
Komatipoort, S. Afr.	D10	70
Komatsu, Japan	C9	40
Komatsushima, Japan	E7	40
Kome Island, i., Ug.	E6	66
Komering, stm., Indon.	E3	50
Komfane, Indon.	G9	44
Komi, state, Russia	B8	32
Komissarovo, Russia	B9	38
Kommunizma, pik see Ismail Samani, pik, mtn., Taj.	B11	56
Komodo, Pulau, i., Indon.	H11	50
Komodo National Park, p.o.i., Indon.	H11	50
Komoé, stm., Afr.	H4	64
Komono, Congo	E2	66
Komoran, Pulau, i., Indon.	G10	44
Komoro, Japan	C11	40
Komotiní, Grc.	B8	28
Kompasberg, mtn., S. Afr.	G7	70
Komsomolec, Kaz.	D10	32
Komsomolets shyghanaghy, b., Kaz.	E8	32
Komsomol'sk, Russia	H18	8
Komsomol'sk, Russia	C15	32

I·30 Komsomol'sk-na-Amure – La Algaba

Name	Map Ref.	Page
Komsomol'sk-na-Amure, Russia	F16	34
Komsomol'skoj Pravdy, ostrova, is., Russia	A10	34
Konakovo, Russia	D19	10
Konakpınar, Tur.	D10	28
Konar, stm., Asia	A3	54
Konārak, India	I11	54
Konawa, Ok., U.S.	C2	122
Konch, India	F7	54
Konda, stm., Russia	B10	32
Kondagaon, India	B5	53
Kondega, Russia	F15	8
Kondinin, Austl.	F3	74
Kondoa, Tan.	E7	66
Kondopoga, Russia	E16	8
Kondoz, Afg.	B10	56
Kondrovo, Russia	F18	10
Kondukūr, India	D4	53
Koné, N. Cal.	m15	79d
Kong, stm., Asia	F8	48
Kŏng, Kaôh, i., Camb.	G6	48
Kongcheng, China	F7	42
Kong Christian IX Land, reg., Grnld.	D18	141
Kong Christian X Land, reg., Grnld.	C19	141
Kong Frederik VIII Land, reg., Grnld.	B19	141
Kong Frederik VI Kyst, cst., Grnld.	E17	141
Kongjiawopeng, China	B5	38
Kongju, Kor., S.	F7	38
Kongmoon see Jiangmen, China	J5	42
Kongolo, D.R.C.	F5	66
Kongor, Sudan	F6	62
Kong Oscar Fjord, strt., Grnld.	C21	141
Kongsvinger, Nor.	F5	8
Kongur Shan, mtn., China	G13	32
Kong Wilhelms Land, reg., Grnld.	B21	141
Konice, Czech Rep.	G12	16
Königsberg see Kaliningrad, Russia	F3	10
Königswinter, Ger.	F3	16
Konin, Pol.	D14	16
Konin, state, Pol.	D14	16
Konispol, Alb.	E14	24
Kónitsa, Grc.	C3	28
Konjic, Bos.	F4	26
Konkiep, stm., Nmb.	E3	70
Konkouré, stm., Gui.	G2	64
Konna, Mali	G4	64
Konnevesi, l., Fin.	E12	8
Konnur, India	C2	53
Konoša, Russia	F18	8
Kōnosu, Japan	C12	40
Konotop, Ukr.	E15	6
Końskie, Pol.	E16	16
Konstantinovskij, Russia	C22	10
Konstanz, Ger.	I4	16
Kontagora, Nig.	G5	64
Kontcha, Cam.	C2	66
Kontha, Mya.	C3	48
Kontseba, Ukr.	A16	26
Kon Tum, Viet.	E8	48
Konya, Tur.	F15	28
Konya, state, Tur.	E15	28
Konz, Ger.	G2	16
Konza, Kenya	E7	66
Konžakovskij Kamen', gora, mtn., Russia	C9	32
Koocanusa, Lake, res., N.A.	B11	136
Kookynie, Austl.	E4	74
Koolatah, Austl.	C8	74
Kooloonong, Austl.	J4	76
Koontz Lake, In., U.S.	G3	112
Koorawatha, Austl.	J7	76
Koosa, Est.	B9	10
Kooskia, Id., U.S.	D11	136
Kootenai (Kootenay), stm., N.A.	G13	138
Kootenay (Kootenai), stm., N.A.	G13	138
Kootenay Lake, l., B.C., Can.	G14	138
Kootenay National Park, p.o.i., B.C., Can.	F14	138
Kopāganj, India	E9	54
Kopargaon, India	B2	53
Kópavogur, Ice.	k29	8a
Kopejsk, Russia	C10	32
Koper, Slvn.	E10	22
Kopervik, Nor.	G1	8
Kopet Mountains, mts., Asia	B8	56
Köping, Swe.	G6	8
Koplik, Alb.	B13	24
Koppal, India	D3	53
Koppang, Nor.	F4	8
Koppies, S. Afr.	E8	70
Koprivnica, Cro.	D13	22
Köprü, stm., Tur.	F14	28
Köprülü Kanyon Milli Parkı, p.o.i., Tur.	F14	28
Kopylovo, Russia	F21	8
Korab (Korabit, Maja e), mtn., Eur.	C14	24
Korabit, Maja e (Korab), mtn., Eur.	C14	24
Korāput, India	B6	53
Korarou, Lac, l., Mali	F4	64
Koratla, India	B4	53
Korba, India	G9	54
Korba, Tun.	H4	24
Korbach, Ger.	E4	16
Korça see Korçë, Alb.	D14	24
Korçë, Alb.	D14	24
Korčula, Cro.	H14	22
Korčula, Otok, i., Cro.	H13	22
Korea, North, ctry., Asia	D7	38
Korea, South, ctry., Asia	G8	38
Korea Bay, b., Asia	E5	38
Korea Strait, strt., Asia	E2	40
Korelakša, Russia	D15	8
Korenovsk, Russia	E5	32
Korf, Russia	D22	34
Korhogo, C. Iv.	H3	64
Korientzé, Mali	F4	64
Korim, Indon.	F10	44
Korinthiakós Kólpos (Corinth, Gulf of), b., Grc.	E5	28
Kórinthos, Grc.	F5	28
Kōriyama, Japan	B13	40
Korjakskaja Sopka, vulkan, vol., Russia	F20	34
Korjakskoe nagor'e, mts., Russia	D22	34
Korjažma, Russia	F22	8
Korkino, Russia	D10	32
Korkuteli, Tur.	F13	28
Korla, China	C2	36
Korliki, Russia	B14	32
Körmend, Hung.	C3	26
Kornat, Otok, i., Cro.	G12	22
Kornati, Nacionalni Park, p.o.i., Cro.	G12	22
Korner, Mt., U.S.	A14	136
Korneuburg, Aus.	B13	22
Koro, i., Fiji	p19	79e
Köroğlu Tepesi, mtn., Tur.	C14	28
Korogwe, Tan.	F7	66
Koroleve, Ukr.	H19	16
Koromere see East Cape, c., N.Z.	C8	80
Koronadal, Phil.	G5	52
Koróni, Grc.	G4	28
Korónia, Límni, l., Grc.	C6	28
Korópi, Grc.	F6	28
Koror, Palau	g8	78b
Körös, stm., Hung.	C7	26
Koro Sea, s., Fiji	p20	79e
Korosten', Ukr.	E14	6
Koro Toro, Chad	D3	62
Korotyš, Russia	H20	10
Korovin Volcano, vol., Ak., U.S.	g24	140a
Korovou, Fiji	p19	79e
Koroyanitu, mtn., Fiji	p18	79e
Korsakov, Russia	G17	34
Korsakovo, Russia	G20	10
Korsør, Den.	I4	8
Koršunovo, Russia	C20	32
Kortrijk, Bel.	D12	14
Korucam, Cape see Koruçam Burnu, c., N. Cyp.	C3	58
Koruçam Burnu, c., N. Cyp.	C3	58
Korucu, Tur.	D10	28
Korumburra, Austl.	L5	76
Koryak Mountains see Korjakskoe nagor'e, mts., Russia	D22	34
Koryŏng, Kor., S.	D1	40
Kos (Cos), i., Grc.	G10	28
Kosa, Russia	C8	32
Kosa, Russia	F10	34
Kosai, Japan	E10	40
Kosaja Gora, Russia	F20	10
Kościan, Pol.	D12	16
Kościerzyna, Pol.	B14	16
Kosciusko, Ms., U.S.	D9	122
Kosciuszko, Mount, mtn., Austl.	K6	76
Kosciuszko National Park, p.o.i., Austl.	K6	76
Kose, Est.	A8	10
Koshikijima-rettō, is., Japan	H2	40
Koshkonong, Lake, l., Wi., U.S.	B9	120
Kōshoku, Japan	C11	40
Košice, Slov.	H17	16
Kosi Kalan, India	E6	54
Kosimeer, l., S. Afr.	E11	70
Kosiv, Ukr.	A12	26
Köşk, Tur.	F11	28
Koslan, Russia	E23	8
Kosŏng, Kor., S.	E1	40
Kosŏng-ŭp, Kor., N.	E8	38
Kosovo-Metohija, co., Serb.	G7	26
Kosovska Mitrovica, Serb.	G7	26
Kosrae, i., Micron.	C7	72
Kösreli, Tur.	A6	58
Kosse, Tx., U.S.	F2	122
Kossou, Lac de, res., C. Iv.	H3	64
Kostenec, Blg.	G10	26
Koster, S. Afr.	D8	70
Kostomukša, Russia	D14	8
Kostonjärvi, l., Fin.	D12	8
Kostroma, Russia	H19	8
Kostroma, stm., Russia	G19	8
Kostromskaja oblast', co., Russia	G20	8
Kostrzyn, Pol.	D10	16
Kosum Phisai, Thai.	D6	48
Koszalin, Pol.	B12	16
Koszalin, state, Pol.	C12	16
Kőszeg, Hung.	B3	26
Kota, India	G9	54
Kota, India	F5	54
Kotaagung, Indon.	F4	50
Kotabangun, Indon.	D10	50
Kotabaru, Indon.	E10	50
Kota Belud, Malay.	G1	52
Kota Bharu, Malay.	I6	48
Kotabumi, Indon.	F4	50
Kotadabok, Indon.	D4	50
Kot Addu, Pak.	C3	54
Kota Kinabalu, Malay.	G1	52
Kotamobagu, Indon.	E7	44
Kotapinang, Indon.	C1	50
Kota Tinggi, Malay.	L6	48
Kotawaringin, Indon.	E7	50
Kotcho Lake, l., B.C., Can.	D6	106
Kot Chutta, Pak.	D3	54
Kotel'nič, Russia	C7	32
Kotel'nikovo, Russia	E6	32
Kotel'nyj, ostrov, i., Russia	A16	34
Kotelnyj, ostrov, i., Russia	B3	34
Köthen, Ger.	E7	16
Kotikovo, Russia	G17	34
Kotka, Fin.	F12	8
Kot Kapūra, India	C5	54
Kotlas, Russia	F22	8
Kotli, Pak.	B4	54
Kotlik, Ak., U.S.	D7	140
Kôtomo, Île, i., N. Cal.	n16	79d
Kotor, Serb.	G5	26
Kotoriba, Cro.	D13	22
Kotovs'k, Ukr.	B16	26
Kot Pūtli, India	E6	54
Kotri, Pak.	F2	54
Kottagūdem, India	C5	53
Kottayam, India	G3	53
Kotto, stm., C.A.R.	C4	66
Kottūru, India	D3	53
Kotuj, stm., Russia	B9	34
Kotzebue, Ak., U.S.	C7	140
Kotzebue Sound, strt., Ak., U.S.	C7	140
Kötzting, Ger.	G8	16
Kouang-si see Guangxi, state, China	G6	36
Kouang-tong see Guangdong, state, China	J6	42
Kouaoua, N. Cal.	m15	79d
Kouchibouguac National Park, p.o.i., N.B., Can.	D11	110
Koudougou, Burkina	G4	64
Kouei-tcheou see Guizhou, state, China	H2	42
Kouga, stm., S. Afr.	H7	70
Kougaberge, mts., S. Afr.	H6	70
Koukdjuak, stm., Nu., Can.	B16	106
Kouki, C.A.R.	C3	66
Koúklia, Cyp.	D3	58
Koulamoutou, Gabon	E2	66
Koulikoro, Mali	G3	64
Koumala, Austl.	C7	76
Koumbia, Gui.	G2	64
Koumpentoum, Sen.	G2	64
Koumra, Chad	F3	62
Koundâra, Gui.	G2	64
Kourou, Fr. Gu.	B7	84
Kouroussa, Gui.	G3	64
Kousséri, Cam.	B2	66
Koussi, Emi, mtn., Chad	D3	62
Koutiala, Mali	G3	64
Kouts, In., U.S.	G2	112
Kouvola, Fin.	F12	8
Kova, Russia	C18	32
Kovada Milli Parkı, p.o.i., Tur.	F13	28
Kovarskas, Lith.	E7	10
Kovdor, Russia	C14	8
Kovdozero, ozero, res., Russia	C14	8
Kovilpatti, India	G3	53
Kovrov, Russia	H19	8
Kovūr, India	D5	53
Kovža, Russia	F18	8
Kowalewo Pomorskie, Pol.	C14	16
Kowloon see Jiulong, China	J5	42
Kowŏn-ŭp, Kor., N.	E7	38
Kowt-e 'Ashrow, Afg.	C10	56
Koxtag, China	A4	46
Köyceğiz Gölü, l., Tur.	G11	28
Koyna Reservoir, res., India	C1	53
Koyuk, Ak., U.S.	D7	140
Koyukuk, Ak., U.S.	D8	140
Koyukuk, stm., Ak., U.S.	C8	140
Kō-zaki, c., Japan	E2	40
Kozan, Tur.	A6	58
Kozáni, Grc.	C4	28
Kožany, Russia	H14	10
Kozel'sk, Russia	F18	10
Koževnikovo, Russia	C14	32
Kozhikode (Calicut), India	F2	53
Kozienice, Pol.	E17	16
Kozlov Bereg, Russia	B10	10
Kozlovo, Russia	D19	10
Kozlu, Tur.	B14	28
Koz'mino, Russia	F22	8
Kožposëlok, Russia	E17	8
Kōzu-shima, i., Japan	E12	40
Kpalimé, Togo	H5	64
Kra, Isthmus of, isth., Asia	H4	48
Kraai, stm., S. Afr.	G8	70
Krabi, Thai.	H4	48
Krâchéh, Camb.	F8	48
Kraeva, Russia	B9	38
Kragan, Indon.	G7	50
Kragujevac, Serb.	F7	26
Krajenka, Pol.	C13	16
Krakatoa see Rakata, Pulau, i., Indon.	G4	50
Krakovets', Ukr.	G19	16
Kraków, Pol.	F15	16
Kraków, state, Pol.	G15	16
Kralendijk, Neth. Ant.	p23	104g
Kraljevo, Serb.	F7	26
Kralovice, Czech Rep.	G9	16
Kralupy nad Vltavou, Czech Rep.	F10	16
Kramators'k, Ukr.	E5	32
Kramfors, Swe.	E7	8
Kranídi, Grc.	F6	28
Kranj (Krainburg), Slvn.	D11	22
Kranskop, S. Afr.	F10	70
Krapivna, Russia	G18	10
Krasavino, Russia	F22	8
Krasieo, stm., Thai.	E4	48
Krasivaja Meča, stm., Russia	G20	10
Krāslava, Lat.	E10	10
Krasnae, Bela.	F10	10
Krasnaja Gorbatka, Russia	I19	8
Krasnaja Slabada, Bela.	H9	10
Krasnaluki, Bela.	F11	10
Krasneno, Russia	D23	34
Kraśnik, Pol.	F18	16
Kraśnik Fabryczny, Pol.	F18	16
Krasni Okny, Ukr.	B16	26
Krasnoarmejsk, Russia	D21	10
Krasnoarmejskij, Russia	C23	34
Krasnobród, Pol.	F19	16
Krasnodar, Russia	E5	32
Krasnoe, ozero, l., Russia	D23	34
Krasnoe Selo, Russia	A12	10
Krasnoe Znamja, Russia	C18	10
Krasnogorodskoe, Russia	D11	10
Krasnogorsk, Russia	E20	10
Krasnogorsk, Russia	G17	34
Krasnojarovo, Russia	F14	34
Krasnojarsk, Russia	C16	32
Krasnojarskoe vodohranilišče, res., Russia	D16	32
Krasnokamsk, Russia	C8	32
Krasnomajskij, Russia	C17	10
Krasnoščele, Russia	C17	8
Krasnosel'kup, Russia	A14	32
Krasnoturjinsk, Russia	C10	32
Krasnoufimsk, Russia	C9	32
Krasnoural'sk, Russia	C10	32
Krasnovišersk, Russia	B9	32
Krasnovodskij poluostrov, pen., Turkmen.	A7	56
Krasnozavodsk, Russia	D20	10
Krasnozërskoe, Russia	D14	32
Krasnoznamensk, Russia	F5	10
Krasnoznamenskoe, Kaz.	D11	32
Krasnye Gory, Russia	B12	10
Krasnyj Čikoj, Russia	F10	34
Krasnyj Gorodok, Russia	C16	10
Krasnyj Jar, Russia	C12	32
Krasnyj Luč, Russia	C13	10
Krasnyj Oktjabr', Russia	D21	10
Krasnyj Tkač, Russia	E22	10
Krasnystaw, Pol.	E19	16
Kratovo, Mac.	A5	28
Krâvanh, Chuŏr Phnum, mts., Camb.	F6	48
Krbava, reg., Cro.	F12	22
Krečetovo, Russia	F18	8
Krefeld, Ger.	E2	16
Kremastón, Technití Límni, res., Grc.	E4	28
Kremenchug Reservoir see Kremenchuts'ke vodoskhovyshche, res., Ukr.	E4	32
Kremenchuk, Ukr.	E4	32
Kremenchuts'ke vodoskhovyshche, res., Ukr.	E4	32
Kremenskoe, Russia	E18	10
Kremmling, Co., U.S.	C10	132
Krems an der Donau, Aus.	B12	22
Kress, Tx., U.S.	G7	128
Kresta, zaliv, b., Russia	C25	34
Krestcy, Russia	B15	10
Krestcy, Russia	B22	10
Krest-Maër, Russia	C17	34
Kretinga, Lith.	E4	10
Kribi, Cam.	D1	66
Křimice, Czech Rep.	G9	16
Krishna, stm., India	C5	53
Krishna, Mouths of the, mth., India	D5	53
Krishnagiri, India	E4	53
Krishnanagar, India	G12	54
Krishnarāja Sāgara, res., India	E3	53
Krishnarājpet, India	E3	53
Kristiansand, Nor.	G3	8
Kristianstad, Swe.	I6	8
Kristiansund, Nor.	E2	8
Kristiinankaupunki (Kristinestad), Fin.	E9	8
Kristinehamn, Swe.	G6	8
Kristinestad see Kristiinankaupunki, Fin.	E9	8
Kríti, state, Grc.	H7	28
Kríti (Crete), i., Grc.	H7	28
Kritikón Pélagos (Crete, Sea of), s., Grc.	H8	28
Kriva Palanka, Mac.	A5	28
Krivodol, Blg.	F10	26
Križevci, Cro.	D13	22
Krjukovo, Russia	E20	10
Krjukovo, Russia	C20	34
Krk, Otok, i., Cro.	E11	22
Krnov, Czech Rep.	F13	16
Krobia, Pol.	E12	16
Krøderen, l., Nor.	F3	8
Krokodil, stm., S. Afr.	D8	70
Krom, stm., S. Afr.	G4	70
Kroměříž, Czech Rep.	G13	16
Kromy, Russia	H18	10
Kronach, Ger.	F7	16
Krŏng Kaôh Kŏng, Camb.	G6	48
Krŏng Kêb, Camb.	G7	48
Kronoberg, state, Swe.	H6	8
Kronockaja Sopka, vulkan, vol., Russia	F21	34
Kronockij zaliv, b., Russia	F21	34
Kronoki, Russia	F21	34
Kronprins Christian Land, reg., Grnld.	A22	141
Kronštadt, Russia	A12	10
Kroonstad, S. Afr.	E8	70
Kropotkin, Russia	E12	34
Kropotkin, Russia	E6	32
Krośniewice, Pol.	D14	16
Krosno, Pol.	G17	16
Krosno, state, Pol.	G17	16
Krotoszyn, Pol.	E13	16
Krotz Springs, La., U.S.	G7	122
Kroya, Indon.	G6	50
Krško, Slvn.	E12	22
Kruger National Park, p.o.i., S. Afr.	C10	70
Krugersdorp, S. Afr.	E8	70
Kruhlae, Bela.	F12	10
Krui, Indon.	F3	50
Kruisfontein, S. Afr.	H7	70
Kruja see Krujë, Alb.	C13	24
Krujë, Alb.	C13	24
Krumbach, Ger.	H6	16
Krumovgrad, Blg.	H12	26
Krung Thep (Bangkok), Thai.	F5	48
Kruså, Den.	B5	16
Kruševac, Serb.	F8	26
Krušinovka, Bela.	G12	10
Krutcy, Russia	C12	10
Krutoe, Russia	H20	10
Kruzenšterna, proliv, strt., Russia	G19	34
Kruzof Island, i., Ak., U.S.	E12	140
Kryčaŭ, Bela.	G14	10
Kryms'kyi pivostriv (Crimean Peninsula), pen., Ukr.	E4	32
Krynica, Pol.	G16	16
Krynychne, Ukr.	D15	26
Kryve Ozero, Ukr.	B17	26
Kryvošyn, Bela.	H8	10
Kryvyj Rih, Ukr.	E4	32
Kryzhopil', Ukr.	A15	26
Krzeszowice, Pol.	F15	16
Krzyż, Pol.	D11	16
Ksenevka, Russia	F12	34
Kstovo, Russia	H20	8
Kuah, Malay.	I4	48
Kuai, stm., China	E7	42
Kualacenako, Indon.	D3	50
Kuala Kangsar, Malay.	J5	48
Kualakapuas, Indon.	E9	50
Kuala Krai, Malay.	J6	48
Kuala Kubu Baharu, Malay.	K5	48
Kualakurun, Indon.	D8	50
Kualalangsa, Indon.	J4	48
Kuala Lipis, Malay.	J5	48
Kuala Lumpur, Malay.	K5	48
Kuala Nerang, Malay.	I5	48
Kualapesaguan, Indon.	E6	50
Kuala Pilah, Malay.	K6	48
Kuala Rompin, Malay.	K6	48
Kuala Sepetang, Malay.	J5	48
Kualasimpang, Indon.	J3	48
Kuala Terengganu, Malay.	J6	48
Kualu, stm., Indon.	B1	50
Kuamut, stm., Malay.	A10	50
Kuancheng, China	A8	42
Kuandian, China	D6	38
Kuan Shan, mtn., Tai.	J9	42
Kuantan, Malay.	K6	48
Kuanyün see Guanyun, China	D8	42
Kuban', stm., Russia	E6	32
Kubenskoe, ozero, l., Russia	G18	8
Kubokawa, Japan	F6	40
Kubrat, Blg.	F13	26
Kučema, Russia	D20	8
Kuchaiburi, India	G11	54
Kuchāman, India	E5	54
Kuching, Malay.	C7	50
Kuchurhan, stm., Eur.	B16	26
Kuçova see Kuçovë, Alb.	D13	24
Kuçovë, Alb.	D13	24
Kūd, India	B5	54
Kudamatsu, Japan	F4	40
Kudat, Malay.	G1	52
Kudever', Russia	D12	10
Kudirkos Naumiestis, Lith.	F5	10
Kudus, Indon.	G7	50
Kudymkar, Russia	C8	32
Kū'ē'ē Ruins, sci., Hi., U.S.	d6	78a
Kueisui see Hohhot, China	A4	42
Kueiyang see Guiyang, China	H2	42
K'uerhlo see Korla, China	C2	36
Kufstein, Aus.	C9	22
Kugluktuk (Coppermine), Nu., Can.	B8	106
Kugmallit Bay, b., N.T., Can.	C13	140
Kuhësi see Kukës, Alb.	B14	24
Kuhmoinen, Fin.	F11	8
Kuhn Ø, i., Grnld.	C22	141
Kuial'nyts'kyi lyman, l., Ukr.	C17	26
Kuiseb, stm., S. Afr.	C2	70
Kuitan, China	J7	42
Kuito, Ang.	C2	68
Kuiu Island, i., Ak., U.S.	E13	140
Kuivastu, Est.	G10	8
Kuja, Russia	D18	8
Kujang-ŭp, Kor., N.	E7	38
Kujawy, reg., Pol.	D14	16
Kujbyšev, Russia	C13	32
Kujbyševskoe vodohranilišče, res., Russia	D7	32
Kujū-san, vol., Japan	F4	40
Kukalaya, stm., Nic.	F6	102
Kukawa, Nig.	G7	64
Kukës, Alb.	B14	24
Kukoboj, Russia	B22	10
Kükong see Shaoguan, China	I5	42
Kukshi, India	G5	54
Kukuj, Russia	A15	10
Kukukus Lake, l., On., Can.	B7	118
Kukurtli, Turkmen.	B8	56
Kula, Blg.	F9	26
Kula, Tur.	E11	28
Kula, Serb.	D6	26
Kulagi, Russia	H15	10
Kula Gulf, strt., Sol. Is.	e7	79b
Kulai, Malay.	L6	48
Kula Kangri, mtn., Bhu.	E13	54
Kular, Russia	B15	34
Kulaura, Bngl.	F13	54
Kuldīga, Lat.	D5	10
Kuldja see Yining, China	F14	32
Kule, Bots.	C5	70
Kulebaki, Russia	I20	8
Kulen Vakuf, Bos.	E3	26
Kulim, Malay.	J5	48
Kuljab, Taj.	B10	56
Kulkyne Creek, stm., Austl.	H5	76
Kullu, India	B6	54
Kulm, N.D., U.S.	A13	126
Kulmbach, Ger.	F7	16
Kuloj, Russia	F20	8
Kuloj, Russia	D20	8
Kuloj, stm., Russia	D20	8
Kulsary, Kaz.	E8	32
Kulti, India	G11	54
Kultuk, Russia	D18	32
Kulu, Tur.	D16	28
Kulunda, Russia	D13	32
Kulundinskaja ravnina, pl., Asia	D13	32
Kulundinskoe, ozero, l., Russia	D13	32
Kulwin, Austl.	J4	76
Kumagaya, Japan	C12	40
Kumai, Indon.	E8	50
Kumai, Teluk, b., Indon.	E7	50
Kumajri see Gjumri, Arm.	A5	56
Kumamoto, Japan	G3	40
Kumamoto, state, Japan	G3	40
Kumano, Japan	F9	40
Kumano-nada, s., Japan	F9	40
Kumanovo, Mac.	A4	28
Kumara, Russia	F14	34
Kumārghāt, India	F14	54
Kumasi, Ghana	H4	64
Kumba, Cam.	D1	66
Kumbakonam, India	F4	53
Kumbarilla, Austl.	F8	76
Kumdanlı, Tur.	E13	28
Kume-jima, i., Japan	I18	39a
Kŭm-gang, stm., Kor., S.	F7	38
Kumla, Swe.	G6	8
Kumluca, Tur.	G13	28
Kumluca, Tur.	B15	28
Kumo, Nig.	H7	64
Kumon Range, mts., Mya.	C8	46
Kumora, Russia	E11	34
Kumta, India	D2	53
Kumu, D.R.C.	D5	66
Kumukahi, Cape, c., Hi., U.S.	o16	135a
Kümüx, China	C2	36
Kŭmya-ŭp, Kor., N.	E7	38
Kuna, Id., U.S.	G10	136
Kunašir, ostrov (Kunashiri-tō), i., Russia	C16	38
Kunda, Est.	G12	8
Kunda Hills, hills, India	F3	53
Kundāpura, India	E2	53
Kundar, stm., Asia	C2	54
Kunderu, stm., India	D4	53
Kundiān, Pak.	B3	54
Kundiawa, Pap. N. Gui.	b3	79a
Kundla, India	H3	54
Kundur, Pulau, i., Indon.	C3	50
Kunene, state, Nmb.	B2	70
Kunene (Cunene), stm., Afr.	D1	68
Kunes, Nor.	A12	8
Kungchuling see Gongzhuling, China	C6	38
Kunggyü Yumco, l., China	C9	54
Kunghit Island, i., B.C., Can.	E4	106
Kungrad, Uzb.	F9	32
Kungsbacka, Swe.	H4	8
Kungur, Russia	C9	32
Kunhegyes, Hung.	B7	26
Kuningan, Indon.	G6	50
Kunisaki, Japan	F4	40
Kunisaki-hantō, pen., Japan	F4	40
Kunja, Russia	D13	10
Kunja, stm., Russia	D13	10
Kunlong, Mya.	D8	46
Kunlun Mountains see Kunlun Shan, mts., China	A5	46
Kunlun Shan, mts., China	A5	46
Kunming, China	F5	36
Kunnamkulam, India	F2	53
Kunsan, Kor., S.	F7	38
Kunshan, China	F9	42
Kunting, China	G9	42
Kununurra, Austl.	C5	74
Kunwi, Kor., S.	C1	40
Kunya, Nig.	G6	64
Künzelsau, Ger.	G5	16
Kuopio, Fin.	E12	8
Kupa, stm., Eur.	E12	22
Kupang, Indon.	H7	44
Kupanskoe, Russia	D21	10
Kup'ians'k, Ukr.	E5	32
Kupino, Russia	D13	32
Kupiškis, Lith.	E7	10
Kupreanof Island, i., Ak., U.S.	E13	140
Kuqa, China	F14	32
Kuqa, China	F14	32
Kuragino, Russia	D16	32
Kuranec, Bela.	F9	10
Kurashiki, Japan	E6	40
Kurasiki see Kurashiki, Japan	E6	40
Kurauli, India	E7	54
Kuraymah, Sudan	D6	62
Kurayoshi, Japan	D6	40
Kurčatov, Russia	D5	32
Kŭrchatov, Kaz.	D13	32
Kurdistan, hist. reg., Asia	B5	56
Kurdistān see Kurdistan, hist. reg., Asia	B5	56
Kurdufān, state, Sudan	E6	62
Kurduvādi, India	B2	53
Kure, Japan	E5	40
Kurejka, stm., Russia	C7	34
Kuresaare, Est.	G10	8
Kurgan, Russia	C11	32
Kurgan-Tjube, Taj.	B10	56
Kuria, i., Kir.	C8	72
Kuria Muria Islands see Ḩallānīyah, Juzur al-, is., Oman	F8	56
Kuridala, Austl.	C3	76
Kurīgrām, Bngl.	F12	54
Kurikka, Fin.	E10	8
Kuril Islands see Kuril'skie ostrova, is., Russia	E19	30
Kuril'sk, Russia	B14	36
Kuril'skie ostrova (Kuril Islands), is., Russia	E19	30
Kuril Strait see Pervyj Kuril'skij proliv, strt., Russia	F20	34
Kuril Trench, unds.	E18	142
Kurinjippadi, India	F4	53
Kurinwás, stm., Nic.	F5	102
Kurjanovskaja, Russia	F19	8
Kurkliai, Lith.	E8	10
Kurmuk, Sudan	E6	62
Kurnool, India	D3	53
Kurobe, Japan	C10	40
Kurort Schmalkalden, Ger.	F6	16
Kurovskoe, Russia	E21	10
Kurow, N.Z.	G4	80
Kuršėnai, Lith.	D6	10
Kurseong, India	E12	54
Kürshim, Kaz.	E14	32
Kuršiu nerija (Kuršškaja kosa), spit, Eur.	E3	10
Kursk, Russia	D5	32
Kurskaja oblast', co., Russia	H19	10
Kuršškaja kosa (Kuršiu nerija), spit, Eur.	E3	10
Kuršumlija, Serb.	F8	26
Kurşunlu, Tur.	C16	28
Kūrtī, Sudan	D6	62
Kurtistown, Hi., U.S.	d6	78a
Kurtoğlu Burnu, c., Tur.	G11	28
Kuruktag, mts., China	C2	36
Kuruman, S. Afr.	E6	70
Kuruman, stm., S. Afr.	E5	70
Kurumanheuwels, mts., S. Afr.	E6	70
Kurume, Japan	F3	40
Kurumkan, Russia	F11	34
Kurunegala, Sri L.	H5	53
Kuruqi, China	B9	36
Kuryongp'o, Kor., S.	C2	40
Kuşadası, Tur.	F10	28
Kuşadası Körfezi, b., Tur.	F9	28
Kusan-ni, Kor., S.	B1	40
Kusawa Lake, l., Yk., Can.	D12	140
Kuş Gölü, l., Tur.	C10	28
Kuş Gölü Milli Parkı, p.o.i., Tur.	C10	28
Kushālgarh, India	G5	54
Kusheriki, Nig.	G6	64
Kushikino, Japan	H3	40
Kushima, Japan	H4	40
Kushiro, Japan	C16	38
Kushnytsia, Ukr.	A10	26
Kushtia, Bngl.	G12	54
Kushui, China	C3	36
Kusiro see Kushiro, Japan	C16	38
Kusiyāra, stm., Bngl.	F13	54
Kuskokwim, stm., Ak., U.S.	D7	140
Kuskokwim Bay, b., Ak., U.S.	E7	140
Kuskokwim Mountains, mts., Ak., U.S.	D8	140
Kuśmā, Nepal	D9	54
Kusmuryn, Kaz.	D10	32
Kusmuryn köli, l., Kaz.	D10	32
Kustanaj see Qostanay, Kaz.	D10	32
Kūstī, Sudan	E6	62
Kusu, Japan	F4	40
Kut, Ko, i., Thai.	G6	48
Kutabaru, Indon.	D3	50
Kutacane, Indon.	K3	48
Kütahya, Tur.	D13	28
Kütahya, state, Tur.	D12	28
Kutaisi, Geor.	F6	32
Kutch, Rann of (Kachchh, Rann of), reg., Asia	D2	46
Kutima, Russia	C19	32
Kutina, Cro.	E13	22
Kutiyāna, India	H3	54
Kutná Hora, Czech Rep.	G11	16
Kutno, Pol.	D15	16
Kutse Game Reserve, Bots.	C7	70
Kutu, D.R.C.	E3	66
Kutubdia Island, i., Bngl.	H13	54
Kutum, Sudan	E4	62
Kúty, Slov.	H13	16
Kuujjuaq, Qc., Can.	D17	106
Kuuli-Majak, Turkmen.	A7	56
Kuusamo, Fin.	D13	8
Kuusankoski, Fin.	F12	8
Kuvango, Ang.	C2	68
Kuvšinovo, Russia	C16	10
Kuwait see Al-Kuwayt, Kuw.	D6	56
Kuwait, ctry., Asia	D6	56
Kuwana, Japan	D9	40
Kuybyshev Reservoir see Kujbyševskoe vodohranilišče, res., Russia	D7	32
Kuye, stm., China	B4	42
Kuytun, Mount, mtn., Asia	E15	32
Kuženkino, Russia	C16	10
Kuz'miniči, Russia	F16	10
Kuz'movka, Russia	B16	32
Kuzneck, Russia	D7	32
Kuzneckij Alatau, mts., Russia	D15	32
Kuznecovka, Russia	D11	10
Kuznetsk see Kuzneck, Russia	D7	32
Kuzomen', Russia	C17	8
Kvænangen, b., Nor.	A9	8
Kvaløya, i., Nor.	B8	8
Kvaløya, i., Nor.	A10	8
Kvam, Nor.	F3	8
Kvarnbergsvattnet, l., Swe.	D5	8
Kvarner, b., Cro.	F11	22
Kvarnerić, b., Cro.	F11	22
Kverkfjöll, vol., Ice.	k31	8a
Kvichak Bay, b., Ak., U.S.	E8	140
Kwa, stm., D.R.C.	E3	66
Kwai see Khwae Noi, stm., Thai.	E4	48
Kwajalein, at., Marsh. Is.	C7	72
Kwakoegron, Sur.	B6	84
Kwamisa, mtn., Ghana	H4	64
Kwamouth, D.R.C.	E3	66
Kwando (Cuando), stm., Afr.	D3	68
Kwangchow see Guangzhou, China	J5	42
Kwangju, Kor., S.	G7	38
Kwango (Cuango), stm., Afr.	E3	66
Kwangsi Chuang see Guangxi, state, China	G6	36
Kwangtung see Guangdong, state, China	J6	42
KwaZulu-Natal, state, S. Afr.	F10	70
Kweichow see Guizhou, state, China	F6	36
Kweihwa see Hohhot, China	A4	42
Kweilin see Guilin, China	I4	42
Kweisui see Hohhot, China	A4	42
Kweiyang see Guiyang, China	H2	42
Kwekwe, Zimb.	D4	68
Kweneng, state, Bots.	C7	70
Kwenge (Caengo), stm., Afr.	B2	68
Kwethluk, Ak., U.S.	D7	140
Kwidzyn, Pol.	C14	16
Kwigillingok, Ak., U.S.	E7	140
Kwilu (Cuilo), stm., Afr.	F3	66
Kyabra, Austl.	F4	76
Kyabra Creek, stm., Austl.	E4	76
Kyabram, Austl.	K5	76
Kyaikkami, Mya.	D3	48
Kyaiklat, Mya.	D2	48
Kyaikto, Mya.	D3	48
Kya-in, Mya.	D4	48
Kyalite, Austl.	J4	76
Kyancutta, Austl.	F7	74
Ky Anh, Viet.	C8	48
Kyaukhnyat, Mya.	C3	48
Kyaukme, Mya.	A3	48
Kyaukpa, Mya.	F4	48
Kyaukpyu, Mya.	C1	48
Kyaukse, Mya.	B2	48
Kyauktaw, Mya.	D7	46
Kyaunggon, Mya.	D2	48
Kybartai, Lith.	F5	10
Kyebang-san, mtn., Kor., S.	B1	40
Kyeikdon, Mya.	E4	48
Kyidaunggan, Mya.	C3	48
Kyïv (Kiev), Ukr.	D4	32
Kyïvs'ke vodoskhovyshche, res., Ukr.	D4	32
Kyjov, Czech Rep.	G13	16
Kykotsmovi Village, Az., U.S.	H6	132
Kyle, Sk., Can.	D5	124
Kyle, S.D., U.S.	D10	126
Kyle, Lake, res., Zimb.	B10	70
Kyllíni, Grc.	F4	28
Kyneton, Austl.	K5	76
Kynšperk nad Ohří, Czech Rep.	F8	16
Kyoga, Lake, l., Ug.	D6	66
Kyogle, Austl.	G9	76
Kyŏngju, Kor., S.	D2	40
Kyŏngsan, Kor., S.	D1	40
Kyŏngsang-bukto, state, Kor., S.	C1	40
Kyŏngsang-namdo, state, Kor., S.	D1	40
Kyŏngsŏng-ŭp, Kor., N.	D8	38
Kyônkadun, Mya.	D2	48
Kyonpyaw, Mya.	D2	48
Kyōto, Japan	D8	40
Kyōto, state, Japan	D8	40
Kyparissía, Grc.	F4	28
Kyparissiakós Kólpos, b., Grc.	F4	28
Kyra, Russia	G11	34
Kyren, Russia	D18	32
Kyrgyzstan, ctry., Asia	F12	32
Kyritz, Ger.	D8	16
Kyrönjoki, stm., Fin.	E10	8
Kyrösjärvi, l., Fin.	F10	8
Kyštym, Russia	C10	32
Kýthira, Grc.	G5	28
Kýthira, i., Grc.	G5	28
Kýthnos, i., Grc.	F7	28
Kyundon, Mya.	B2	48
Kyungyi, i., Mya.	E3	48
Kyuquot, B.C., Can.	F3	138
Kyūshū, i., Japan	G2	40
Kyushu-Palau Ridge, unds.	H16	142
Kyūshū-sanchi, mts., Japan	G4	40
Kywong, Austl.	J6	76
Kyyjärvi, Fin.	E11	8
Kyyvesi, l., Fin.	E12	8
Kyzyl, Russia	D16	32
Kyzylbair, Turkmen.	B8	56
Kyzyl-Kija, Kyrg.	F12	32
Kyzylkum, des., Asia	F10	32
Kzyl-Orda see Qyzylorda, Kaz.	F11	32

L

Name	Map Ref.	Page
La Aguja, Cabo de, c., Col.	B4	86
La Albuera, Spain	F4	20
La Alcarria, reg., Spain	D8	20
La Algaba, Spain	G4	20

Name	Map Ref.	Page
La Almunia de Doña Godina, Spain	C9	20
La Antigua, Salina, pl., Arg.	D4	92
La Araucanía, region, Chile	I1	92
Laascaanood, Som.	C8	100
La Ascensión, hill, Mex.	C8	100
La Asunción, Ven.	B10	86
Laau Point, c., Hi., U.S.	b4	78a
Laayoune see El Aaiún, W. Sah.	D2	64
La Azufosa, Mex.	F7	130
La Babia, Mex.	A7	100
Labadieville, La., U.S.	H8	122
La Baie, Qc., Can.	B6	110
La Banda, Arg.	C5	92
La Bandera, Cerro, mtn., Mex.	C6	100
La Bañeza, Spain	B4	20
La Barca, Mex.	E7	100
La Barge, Wy., U.S.	H16	136
Labasa, Fiji	p19	79e
La Baule-Escoublac, Fr.	G6	14
Labé, Gui.	G2	64
Labe (Elbe), stm., Eur.	C5	16
Labelle, Mo., U.S.	D2	110
La Belle, Mo., U.S.	D5	120
Laberge, Lake, l., Yk., Can.	C4	106
Labi, Bru.	A9	50
Labian, Tanjong, c., Malay.	A11	50
La Biche, stm., Ab., Can.	B18	138
Labis, Malay.	K6	48
La Bisbal d'Empordà, Spain	C13	20
Łabiszyn, Pol.	D13	16
La Blanca Grande, Laguna, l., Arg.	I5	92
Labná, sci., Mex.	B3	102
Laboe, Ger.	B6	16
Laborde, Arg.	F6	92
Laborie, St. Luc.	m7	105c
La Bostonnais, Qc., Can.	C4	110
Laboulaye, Arg.	G6	92
Labrador, reg., Nf., Can.	E18	106
Labrador Basin, unds.	C9	144
Labrador City, Nf., Can.	E17	106
Labrador Sea, s., N.A.	D17	94
Lábrea, Braz.	E5	84
La Brea, Trin.	s12	105f
Labuan, Malay.	A9	50
Labuan, state, Malay.	A9	50
Labuan, Pulau, i., Malay.	A9	50
Labuchongshan, mts., China	C10	54
La Bufadora, Mex.	L9	134
Labuhan, Indon.	G4	50
Labuhanbajo, Indon.	H11	50
Labuhanbilik, Indon.	B2	50
Labuhanpandan, Indon.	H10	50
Labuhanruku, Indon.	B1	50
Labuk, stm., Malay.	H1	52
Labuk, Telukan, b., Malay.	G1	52
Labu Kananga, Indon.	H10	50
Labutta, Mya.	D2	48
Labytnangi, Russia	A11	32
Laç, Alb.	C13	24
Lača, ozero, l., Russia	F18	8
Lac-à-Beauce, Qc., Can.	C4	110
La Cadena, Mex.	I3	130
La Calera, Chile	F2	92
La Campana, Spain	G5	20
La Canada Flintridge, Ca., U.S.	I7	134
La Candelaria, Arg.	C5	92
La Candelaria, Mex.	C1	130
Lacantum, stm., Mex.	D2	102
La Capelle-en-Thiérache, Fr.	D12	14
La Carlota, Arg.	F6	92
La Carlota, Phil.	E4	52
La Carolina, Spain	F7	20
Lacaune, Fr.	I8	18
Laccadive Islands see Lakshadweep, is., India	F3	46
Lac-Édouard, Qc., Can.	C4	110
La Ceiba, Hond.	E4	102
Lacepede Bay, b., Austl.	K2	76
Lac-Étchemin, Qc., Can.	D6	110
Lacey, Wa., U.S.	C4	136
Lac-Frontière, Qc., Can.	D6	110
La Chapelle-d'Angillon, Fr.	G11	14
La Châtaigneraie, Fr.	C5	18
La Chaux-de-Fonds, Switz.	C3	22
Lachhmangarh Sikar, India	E5	54
La Chorrera, Col.	H5	86
La Chorrera, Pan.	H8	102
Lachute, Qc., Can.	E2	110
Laçi see Laç, Alb.	C13	24
La Ciénaga, Arg.	C4	92
La Ciotat, Fr.	F11	18
La Citadelle, hist., Haiti	C11	102
La Ciudad, Mex.	D6	100
Lackawanna, N.Y., U.S.	B6	114
Lac la Biche, Ab., Can.	B18	138
Lac la Hache, B.C., Can.	E9	138
Laclede, Id., U.S.	B10	136
Laclede, Mo., U.S.	E4	120
La Clotilde, Arg.	C7	92
Lac-Mégantic, Qc., Can.	D5	110
La Colorada, Mex.	A3	100
La Coma, Mex.	C9	100
Lacombe, Ab., Can.	D17	138
Lacombe, La., U.S.	G9	122
Lacona, Ia., U.S.	C4	120
La Concepción, Pan.	H6	102
La Concepción, Ven.	B5	86
Laconi, Italy	E2	24
Laconia, N.H., U.S.	G5	110
Laconia, Gulf of see Lakonikós Kólpos, b., Grc.	G5	28
La Consulta, Arg.	F3	92
Lacoochee, Fl., U.S.	H3	116
La Coruña see A Coruña, Spain	A2	20
La Coruña see A Coruña, co., Spain	A2	20
La Coste, Tx., U.S.	E9	130
La Courtine, Fr.	D8	18
La Crescent, Mn., U.S.	H7	118
La Crosse, Ks., U.S.	C9	128
La Crosse, Va., U.S.	H7	114
La Crosse, Wa., U.S.	D9	136
La Crosse, Wi., U.S.	H7	118
La Cruz, Arg.	D9	92
La Cruz, Col.	G3	86
La Cruz, Mex.	G2	130
La Cruz de Río Grande, Nic.	F5	102
Lac Seul, On., Can.	A6	118
La Cuesta, P.R.	B2	104a
La Cumbre, Arg.	E5	92
La Cygne, Ks., U.S.	F3	120
Ladákh, India	A6	54
Ladakh Range, mts., Asia	A6	54
Ladder Creek, stm., Ks., U.S.	C7	128
Laddonia, Mo., U.S.	E6	120
La Désirade, i., Guad.	h6	105c
La Digue, i., Sey.	j13	69b
Ladismith, S. Afr.	H5	70
Làdispoli, Italy	I8	22
Lädíz, Iran	D9	56
Lädnün, India	E5	54
Ladoga, In., U.S.	I3	112
Ladoga, Lake see Ladožskoe ozero, l., Russia	F14	8
La Dorada, Col.	E4	86
La Dormida, Arg.	F4	92
Ladožskoe ozero (Ladoga, Lake), l., Russia	F14	8
Ladva-Vetka, Russia	F15	8
Lady Ann Strait, strt., Nu., Can.	B10	141
Lady Barron, Austl.	n14	77a
Ladybrand, S. Afr.	F8	70
Lady Elliot Island, i., Austl.	E9	76
Ladysmith, B.C., Can.	H7	138
Ladysmith, S. Afr.	F9	70
Ladysmith, Wi., U.S.	F7	118
La Encantada, Mex.	C8	100
La Escondida, Mex.	H8	130
La Esmeralda, Mex.	B7	100
Læsø, i., Den.	H4	8
La Esperanza, Cuba	A5	102
La Esperanza, Hond.	E3	102
La Esperanza, Mex.	H4	130
La Esperanza, P.R.	B3	104a
La Estrada see A Estrada, Spain	B2	20
Lafa, China	C7	38
La Falda, Arg.	E5	92
La Farge, Wi., U.S.	H8	118
Lafayette, Al., U.S.	E13	122
Lafayette, Ca., U.S.	F3	134
Lafayette, Co., U.S.	A3	128
Lafayette, Ga., U.S.	C13	122
Lafayette, In., U.S.	H3	112
Lafayette, La., U.S.	G6	122
Lafayette, Tn., U.S.	H11	120
Lafayette, Mount, mtn., N.H., U.S.	F5	110
La Feria, Tx., U.S.	H10	130
La Ferté-Bernard, Fr.	F9	14
La Ferté-Saint-Aubin, Fr.	G10	14
Laflèche, Sk., Can.	E7	124
La Flèche, Fr.	G8	14
La Florida, Guat.	D2	102
La Foa, N. Cal.	m15	79d
La Follette, Tn., U.S.	H1	114
Lafourche, Bayou, stm., La., U.S.	H8	122
La Fragua, Arg.	C5	92
La Fría, Ven.	C5	86
La Fuente de San Esteban, Spain	D4	20
La Galite, i., Tun.	G2	24
La Gallareta, Arg.	D7	92
Lagan, stm., Swe.	E3	8
Lagarto, Braz.	F7	88
Lagawe, Phil.	B3	52
Lage, China	D10	54
Lågen, stm., Nor.	F4	8
Lages, Braz.	C12	92
Laghmān, state, Afg.	A3	54
Laghouat, Alg.	C5	64
Lagkadás, Grc.	C5	28
Lagoa da Prata, Braz.	K3	88
Lagoa Vermelha, Braz.	D12	92
Lago da Pedra, Braz.	C3	88
Lago Kolonie, Aruba	p20	104g
Lagolândia, Braz.	H1	88
Lagonegro, Italy	D9	24
Lagonoy Gulf, b., Phil.	D4	52
Lago Posadas, Arg.	I2	90
Lagos, Nig.	H5	64
Lagos, Port.	G2	20
Lagos de Moreno, Mex.	E8	100
La Gouéra, W. Sah.	E1	64
La Goulette, Tun.	H4	24
Lago Viedma, Arg.	I2	90
La Granadella, Spain	C11	20
La Grande, Or., U.S.	E8	136
La Grande Réservoir, res., Qc., Can.	E15	106
La Grande Quatre, Réservoir 4, res., Qc., Can.	E16	106
LaGrange, Austl.	C4	74
La Grange, Ga., U.S.	D13	122
La Grange, Ky., U.S.	F12	120
La Grange, Mo., U.S.	D6	120
La Grange, N.C., U.S.	E11	130
Lagrange, Wy., U.S.	F8	126
La Gran Sabana, pl., Ven.	E10	86
La Guadeloupe, Qc., Can.	E6	110
La Guajira, state, Col.	A1	102
La Guajira, Península de, pen., S.A.	A6	86
La Guardia, Arg.	D5	92
La Guardia, Bol.	C4	90
La Guardia see A Guardia, Spain	C1	20
La Guerche-sur-l'Aubois, Fr.	G11	14
Laguiole, Fr.	E8	18
Laguna, Arg.	D13	92
Laguna, Braz.	D7	92
Laguna, Ilha da, i., Braz.	D7	84
Laguna Beach, Ca., U.S.	J8	134
Laguna Dam, dam, U.S.	K2	132
Laguna de Jaco, Mex.	G4	130
Laguna Larga, Arg.	E6	92
Laguna Paiva, Arg.	E7	92
Laguna Peru, Arg.	E2	84
Lagunas de Chacagua, Parque Nacional, p.o.i., Mex.	H9	100
Lagunillas, Bol.	C4	90
Laha, China	B9	36
La Habana (Havana), Cuba	A6	102
Lahad Datu, Malay.	A11	50
Lahad Datu, Telukan, b., Malay.	A11	50
La Harpe, Il., U.S.	K7	118
La Harpe, Ks., U.S.	G2	120
Lahat, Indon.	E3	50
Lahdenpohja, Russia	F14	8
Lahemaa rahvus, p.o.i., Est.	G11	8
Lahfán, Bi'r, well, Egypt	H3	58
Lahij, Yemen	G5	56
Lähijän, Iran	B7	56
Lahnstein, Ger.	F3	16
Laholm, Swe.	H5	8
Lahontan Reservoir, res., Nv., U.S.	D6	134
Lahore, Pak.	C5	54
La Horqueta, Col.	F5	86
Lahr, Ger.	H3	16
Lahti, Fin.	F11	8
La Huerta, N.M., U.S.	H7	118
Lahva, Bela.	H10	10
Lai, Chad	F3	62
Laiagam, Pap. N. Gui.	b3	79a
Laibin, China	J3	42
Lai Chau, Viet.	A6	48
Laichow Bay see Laizhou Wan, b., China	C8	42
Laifeng, China	G3	42
L'Aigle, Fr.	F9	14
Laihia, Fin.	E9	8
Laïmbélé, Mont, mtn., Vanuatu	k16	79d
Laingsburg, S. Afr.	H5	70
Laingsburg, Mi., U.S.	B1	114
Lainioälven, stm., Swe.	C10	8
Lainsitz see Lužnice, stm., Eur.	G10	16
Laird Hill, Tx., U.S.	E3	122
Lais, Indon.	E3	50
Lais, Phil.	G5	52
Laitila, Fin.	F9	8
Laiwu, China	C7	42
Laixi, China	C9	42
Laiyang, China	C9	42
Laizhou Bay see Laizhou Wan, b., China	C8	42
Laizhou Wan (Laizhou Bay), b., China	C8	42
Laja, stm., Mex.	E8	100
Laja, Laguna de la, l., Chile	H2	92
Lajas, Salto del, wtfl., Chile	H2	92
La Jara, Co., U.S.	D2	128
La Jara, stm., Spain	E5	20
La Jara Canyon, p., N.M., U.S.	G9	132
La Jarita, Mex.	F4	130
Lajas, Peru	E2	84
Lajas, P.R.	B1	104a
Laje, Braz.	G6	88
Lajeado, Braz.	D11	92
Lajedo, Braz.	E7	88
Lajes, Braz.	C7	88
Lajinha, Braz.	K5	88
Laji Shan, mts., China	D5	36
Lajosmizse, Hung.	B6	26
Lajta (Leitha), stm., Eur.	H12	16
La Junta, Co., U.S.	D5	128
Lakar Küh, mtn., Iran	C8	56
Lakatoro, Vanuatu	k16	79d
Lake, Ms., U.S.	E9	122
Lake Alfred, Fl., U.S.	H4	116
Lake Andes, S.D., U.S.	D14	126
Lake Arthur, La., U.S.	G6	122
Lakeba, i., Fiji	q20	79e
Lakeba Passage, strt., Fiji	q20	79e
Lake Benton, Mn., U.S.	G2	118
Lake Brownwood, Tx., U.S.	C8	130
Lake Butler, Fl., U.S.	G3	116
Lake Cargelligo, Austl.	I6	76
Lake Charles, La., U.S.	G5	122
Lake Chelan National Recreation Area, p.o.i., Wa., U.S.	B6	136
Lake City, Ar., U.S.	B8	122
Lake City, Co., U.S.	E9	132
Lake City, Fl., U.S.	F3	116
Lake City, Ia., U.S.	B3	120
Lake City, Mi., U.S.	D4	112
Lake City, Mn., U.S.	G6	118
Lake City, Pa., U.S.	B5	114
Lake City, S.C., U.S.	C6	116
Lake City, Tn., U.S.	H1	114
Lake Cowichan, B.C., Can.	H6	138
Lake Crystal, Mn., U.S.	G4	118
Lake Dallas, Tx., U.S.	A10	130
Lake Delton, Wi., U.S.	H9	118
Lake District National Park, p.o.i., Eng., U.K.	G9	12
Lake Elsinore, Ca., U.S.	J8	134
Lakefield, On., Can.	D11	112
Lakefield, Mn., U.S.	H3	118
Lake Forest, Il., U.S.	F2	112
Lake Fork Reservoir, res., Tx., U.S.	E3	122
Lake Geneva, Wi., U.S.	B9	120
Lake George, N.Y., U.S.	G3	110
Lake Harbor, Fl., U.S.	J5	116
Lake Havasu City, Az., U.S.	I2	132
Lake Helen, Fl., U.S.	H4	116
Lakehurst, N.J., U.S.	D11	114
Lake Jackson, Tx., U.S.	E12	130
Lake King, Austl.	F3	74
Lakeland, Fl., U.S.	H3	116
Lakeland, Ga., U.S.	E2	116
Lake Linden, Mi., U.S.	D10	118
Lake Louise, Ab., Can.	E14	138
Lake Mead National Recreation Area, p.o.i., U.S.	G2	132
Lake Mills, Wi., U.S.	A8	120
Lake Minchumina, Ak., U.S.	D9	140
Lake Mohawk see Sparta, N.J., U.S.	C11	114
Lake Nash, Austl.	D7	74
Lake Norden, S.D., U.S.	C15	126
Lake Oswego, Or., U.S.	E4	136
Lake Ozark, Mo., U.S.	F5	120
Lake Park, Fl., U.S.	J5	116
Lake Park, Ia., U.S.	H3	118
Lake Placid, Fl., U.S.	I4	116
Lake Placid, N.Y., U.S.	F3	110
Lake Pleasant, N.Y., U.S.	G2	110
Lakeport, Ca., U.S.	D3	134
Lakeport, Mi., U.S.	E7	112
Lake Preston, S.D., U.S.	C15	126
Lakes Entrance, Austl.	K7	76
Lakeshore, Ms., U.S.	G9	122
Lakeside, Az., U.S.	I6	132
Lakeside, Ca., U.S.	K8	134
Lakeside, Mt., U.S.	B12	136
Lake Stevens, Wa., U.S.	B4	136
Laketown, Ut., U.S.	B5	132
Lake View, Ar., U.S.	C8	122
Lake View, Ia., U.S.	B2	120
Lakeview, Mi., U.S.	E4	112
Lakeview, Oh., U.S.	D2	114
Lakeview, Or., U.S.	A5	134
Lakeview, Oh., U.S.	D7	122
Lakeville, Mn., U.S.	G5	118
Lake Wales, Fl., U.S.	I4	116
Lake Wilson, Mn., U.S.	H3	118
Lakewood, Co., U.S.	B3	128
Lakewood, N.J., U.S.	D11	114
Lakewood, Oh., U.S.	C4	114
Lakewood, Wa., U.S.	C4	136
Lakewood, Wi., U.S.	C1	118
Lakewood Park, N.D., U.S.	F15	124
Lake Worth, Fl., U.S.	J5	116
Lakhdaria, Alg.	H14	20
Lakheri, India	D6	54
Lakhimpur, India	D8	54
Lakhīsarai, India	F11	54
Lakhnādon, India	G7	54
Lakinsk, Russia	H18	8
Lakonikós Kólpos (Laconia, Gulf of), b., Grc.	G5	28
Lakota, N.D., U.S.	F15	124
Laksefjorden, b., Nor.	A12	8
Lakshadweep, state, India	F3	46
Lakshadweep Sea, s., Asia	G3	46
Lakshām, Bngl.	G13	54
Lakshmeshwar, India	D2	53
La Laja, Chile	H1	92
Lāla Mūsa, Pak.	B4	54
Lālapaşa, Tur.	B9	28
L'Albufera, l., Spain	D10	20
Laleham, Austl.	D7	76
La Leona, Mex.	I6	130
La Leonesa, Arg.	C8	92
Lālganj, India	E10	54
Lalibela, Eth.	E7	62
La Libertad, Guat.	D2	102
La Ligua, Chile	F2	92
La Lima, Hond.	E3	102
Lalin, stm., China	B7	38
Lalín, Spain	B2	20
Lalindu, Indon.	I12	50
La Línea de la Concepción, Spain	H5	20
Lalitpur, India	F7	54
Lalitpur, Nepal	E10	54
Lalla Khedidja, Tamgout de, mtn., Alg.	H14	20
Lālmanir Hāt, Bngl.	F12	54
La Loche, Sk., Can.	D9	106
La Lora, plat., Spain	B7	20
Lalpur, India	G2	54
L'Alpe-d'Huez, Fr.	D12	18
Lālsot, India	E6	54
Lama, ozero, l., Russia	C7	34
La Macarena, Parque Nacional, p.o.i., Col.	F5	86
La Macarena, Serranía de, mts., Col.	F5	86
La Maddalena, Italy	D3	24
La Madrid, Arg.	C5	92
Lamadrid, Mex.	B8	100
La Magdalena, Mex.	H5	130
Lama-Kara, Togo	H5	64
La Malbaie, Qc., Can.	C6	110
La Mancha, reg., Spain	E8	20
Lamandau, stm., Indon.	D7	50
Lamap, Vanuatu	k16	79d
Lamar, Co., U.S.	C6	128
Lamar, Mo., U.S.	G3	120
Lamarche, Fr.	F14	14
La Marmora, Punta, mtn., Italy	D3	24
La Maroma, Mex.	H2	130
La Marque, Tx., U.S.	H4	122
La Marsa, Tun.	H4	24
La Martre, Lac, l., Can.	A10	110
Lamas, Peru	E2	84
Lamballe, Fr.	F6	14
Lambaréné, Gabon	E1	66
Lambari, stm., Braz.	J3	88
Lambayeque, Peru	E2	84
Lambert, Ms., U.S.	C8	122
Lambert, Cape, c., Pap. N. Gui.	a5	79a
Lambert Glacier, ice, Ant.	C11	81
Lambert Land, reg., Grnld.	B21	141
Lamberton, Mn., U.S.	G3	118
Lambertsbaai see Lambert's Bay, S. Afr.	H3	70
Lambert's Bay, S. Afr.	H3	70
Lambton, Cape, c., N.T., Can.	A6	106
Lame Deer, Mt., U.S.	B6	126
La Media Luna, Arrecifes de, rf., Hond.	E6	102
Lamentin, Guad.	h5	105c
Lamèque, N.B., Can.	C12	110
Lamèque, Île, i., N.B., Can.	C12	110
La Merced, Arg.	B5	92
La Merced, Arg.	D5	92
Lameroo, Austl.	J3	76
La Mesa, Ca., U.S.	K8	134
Lamesa, Tx., U.S.	B6	130
Lamia, Grc.	E5	28
Lamine, stm., Mo., U.S.	F5	120
La Misión, Mex.	K9	134
Lamitan, Phil.	G4	52
La Moille, Il., U.S.	C8	120
Lamoille, Nv., U.S.	C1	132
Lamon Bay, b., Phil.	C4	52
Lamone, stm., Italy	F9	22
Lamongan, Indon.	G8	50
Lamoni, Ia., U.S.	D3	120
Lamont, Ca., U.S.	H6	134
Lamont, Fl., U.S.	I7	118
Lamont, Ok., U.S.	E11	128
La Monte, Mo., U.S.	F4	120
La Mothe, Lac, l., Qc., Can.	B5	110
La Mothe-Achard, Fr.	H7	14
Lamotrek, at., Micron.	C5	72
Lamotte-Beuvron, Fr.	G11	14
Lampang, Thai.	C4	48
Lampasas, Tx., U.S.	C9	130
Lampasas, stm., Tx., U.S.	C9	130
Lampedusa, Isola di, i., Italy	I6	24
Lampertheim, Ger.	G4	16
Lamphun, Thai.	C4	48
Lampman, Sk., Can.	E11	124
Lampung, state, Indon.	F4	50
Lamskoe, Russia	H21	10
Lamu, Kenya	E8	66
La Mure, Fr.	E11	18
Lan', stm., Bela.	H10	10
Lana, Italy	D8	22
Lāna'i, i., Hi., U.S.	c4	78a
Lanai City, Hi., U.S.	c5	78a
Lanaihale, mtn., Hi., U.S.	c5	78a
Lanalhue, Lago, l., Chile	H1	92
Lanark, On., Can.	C13	112
Lanark, Scot., U.K.	F9	12
Landi Kyun, i., Mya.	G4	48
Lancang, China	A4	48
Lancang Jiang see Mekong, stm., Asia	D9	46
Lancashire, co., Eng., U.K.	G10	12
Lancaster, Ca., U.S.	I7	134
Lancaster, Mo., U.S.	D5	120
Lancaster, N.H., U.S.	F5	110
Lancaster, Oh., U.S.	E3	114
Lancaster, Pa., U.S.	D9	114
Lancaster, S.C., U.S.	B5	116
Lancaster, Tx., U.S.	E2	122
Lancaster, Wi., U.S.	B7	120
Lancaster Sound, strt., Nu., Can.	C8	141
Lance Creek, Wy., U.S.	D8	126
Lancelin, Austl.	F2	74
Lanchou see Lanzhou, China	D5	36
Lanchow see Lanzhou, China	D5	36
Lanciano, Italy	H11	22
Lanco, Chile	G2	90
Łańcut, Pol.	F18	16
Lândana, Ang.	B1	68
Landau an der Isar, Ger.	H8	16
Landeck, Aus.	C7	22
Lander, Wy., U.S.	E4	126
Landerneau, Fr.	F4	14
Landes, reg., Fr.	E5	18
Landete, Spain	E9	20
Landis, Sk., Can.	B5	124
Land O'Lakes, Wi., U.S.	E9	118
Landsberg am Lech, Ger.	H6	16
Landsborough Creek, stm., Austl.	D5	76
Land's End, c., Eng., U.K.	K7	12
Landshut, Ger.	H8	16
Landskrona, Swe.	I5	8
Lanesboro, Mn., U.S.	H6	118
Lanett, Al., U.S.	E13	122
Lanezi Lake, l., B.C., Can.	C10	138
La'nga Co, l., China	C8	54
Langang, Sk., Can.	D11	124
Langdale, Al., U.S.	E13	122
Langdon, N.D., U.S.	F15	124
Langeac, Fr.	D9	18
Langeland, i., Den.	I4	8
Langenhagen, Ger.	D5	16
Langenthal, Switz.	C4	22
Langfang, China	B7	42
Langford, S.D., U.S.	B15	126
Langgam, Indon.	D2	50
Langgapayung, Indon.	C1	50
Langhe, hist. reg., Italy	F5	22
Langholm, Scot., U.K.	F9	12
Langjökull, ice, Ice.	k29	8a
Langkawi, Pulau, i., Malay.	I4	48
Langley, B.C., Can.	G8	138
Langnau im Emmental, Switz.	D4	22
Langogne, Fr.	E9	18
Langøya, i., Nor.	B5	8
Langping, China	E4	42
Langres, Fr.	G13	14
Langruth, Mb., Can.	D15	124
Langsa, Indon.	J3	48
Langsa, Teluk, b., Indon.	J4	48
Langshan, China	A2	42
Lang Son, Viet.	B8	48
Langtang, Nig.	H6	64
Languedoc, hist. reg., Fr.	F9	18
Langzhong, China	F1	42
Lanigan, Sk., Can.	C8	124
Lanigan Creek, stm., Sk., Can.	B8	124
Lanín, Volcán, vol., S.A.	G2	90
Länkäran, Azer.	B6	56
Länkipohja, Fin.	F11	8
Lannemezan, Fr.	F6	18
Lannion, Fr.	F5	14
Lanping, China	F4	36
Lansdowne, India	D7	54
Lansdowne House, On., Can.	E13	106
L'Anse, Mi., U.S.	B1	112
Lansing, Ia., U.S.	H7	118
Lansing, Mi., U.S.	B1	114
Lānsi-Suomi, state, Fin.	E10	8
Lantana, Fl., U.S.	J5	116
Lantau Island, i., China	J6	42
Lanta Yai, Ko, i., Thai.	I4	48
Lantian, China	D3	42
Lanús, Arg.	G8	92
Lanusei, Italy	E3	24
Lanzhou, China	D5	36
Lanzo Torinese, Italy	E4	22
Lao, stm., Thai.	C4	48
Laoag, Phil.	A3	52
Laoang, Phil.	D5	52
Lao Cai, Viet.	A6	48
Laobao, stm., China	G5	42
Laofu, China	C3	38
Laohekou, China	E4	42
Laohokow see Laohekou, China	E4	42
Laois, state, Ire.	I5	12
Lao Ling, mtn., China	C9	38
Laon, Fr.	E12	14
Laona, Wi., U.S.	F10	118
La Orchila, Isla, i., Ven.	B8	86
La Oroya, Peru	C2	84
Laos, ctry., Asia	C6	48
Laoushan Wan, b., China	C9	42
Lapa, Braz.	B13	92
Lapai, Nig.	H6	64
Lapalisse, Fr.	C9	18
La Palma, Col.	E4	86
La Palma, Pan.	H8	102
La Palma, Pan.	I7	102
La Palma del Condado, Spain	G4	20
La Paloma, Ur.	G10	92
La Pampa, state, Arg.	G3	90
La Paragua, Ven.	D10	86
La Pasión, stm., Guat.	D2	102
La Paya, Parque Nacional, p.o.i., Col.	G4	86
La Paz, Arg.	E8	92
La Paz, Arg.	F4	92
La Paz, Bol.	C3	90
La Paz, Hond.	E4	102
La Paz, Mex.	C3	100
La Paz, Mex.	D8	100
La Paz, Ur.	G9	92
La Paz, Bahía de, b., Mex.	C3	100
La Paz, Mex.	A6	100
La Perla, Mex.	A6	100
La Perouse Strait, strt., Asia	B13	36
La Pesca, Mex.	D10	100
La Piedad de Cabadas, Mex.	E7	100
La Pine, Or., U.S.	G5	136
La Place, La., U.S.	G8	122
La Plant, S.D., U.S.	B12	126
La Plata, Arg.	G8	92
La Plata, Col.	F3	86
La Plata, Md., U.S.	F9	114
La Plata, Mo., U.S.	D5	120
La Plata Peak, mtn., Co., U.S.	D10	132
La Pobla de Segur, Spain	B11	20
La Pocatière, Qc., Can.	C6	110
Lapominka, Russia	D19	8
Laporte, Co., U.S.	G7	126
La Porte, In., U.S.	G3	112
Laporte, Pa., U.S.	C9	114
La Porte City, Ia., U.S.	B5	120
La Potherie, Lac, l., Qc., Can.	D16	106
La Poza Grande, Mex.	C2	100
Lappajärvi, l., Fin.	E10	8
Lappeenranta, Fin.	F12	8
Lappi, state, Fin.	C12	8
Laprida, Arg.	H7	92
Laprida, Arg.	C6	92
La Pryor, Tx., U.S.	E8	130
Lapta, N. Cyp.	C4	58
Laptev Sea see Laptevyh, more, s., Russia	B14	34
Laptevyh, more, s., Russia	B4	32
La Puebla de Montalbán, Spain	E6	20
La Puerta, Arg.	D5	92
La Puerta de Cabrera, Mex.	E4	52
Lapu-Lapu, Phil.	E4	52
La Purísima, Mex.	B2	100
Lāpwai, Id., U.S.	D10	136
L'Aquila, Italy	H10	22
Lär, Iran	D7	56
Lara, state, Ven.	B7	86
Laracha, Spain	A2	20
Larache, Mor.	B3	64
Laramie, stm., U.S.	E8	126
Laramie, Wy., U.S.	F7	126
Laramie Mountains, mts., Wy., U.S.	F7	126
Laramie Peak, mtn., Wy., U.S.	E7	126
Laranjal, Braz.	K4	88
Laranjeiras, Braz.	F7	88
Laranjeiras do Sul, Braz.	B11	92
Larantuka, Indon.	G7	44
Larap, Phil.	C4	52
Larat, Pulau, i., Indon.	G9	44
Larche Pass, p., Eur.	E12	18
Larchwood, Ia., U.S.	H2	118
Larde, Moz.	D6	68
L'Ardoise, N.S., Can.	E16	110
Laredo, Spain	A7	20
Laredo, Tx., U.S.	F8	130
La Reforma, Mex.	B2	100
Largo, Fl., U.S.	I3	116
Largo, Cañon, p., N.M., U.S.	G9	132
Largo, Cayo, i., Cuba	B7	102
Largs, Scot., U.K.	F8	12
Lario see Como, Lago di, l., Italy	E6	22
La Rioja, Arg.	D4	92
La Rioja, state, Arg.	E4	92
La Rioja, state, Spain	B8	20
La Robla, Spain	B5	20
La Rochefoucauld, Fr.	D6	18
La Rochelle, Fr.	C5	18
La Roche-sur-Yon, Fr.	H7	14
La Roda, Spain	E8	20
La Romaine, Qc., Can.	i21	107a
La Romana, Dom. Rep.	C13	102
La Ronge, Sk., Can.	D10	106
La Rosita, Mex.	F6	130
Larose, La., U.S.	H8	122
Larose, Pointe, c., Mart.	k7	105c
Larrys River, N.S., Can.	E15	110
Larsen Ice Shelf, ice, Ant.	B34	81
La Rubia, Arg.	E7	92
La Rue, Oh., U.S.	D2	114
Larvik, Nor.	G3	8
Larzac, Causse du, plat., Fr.	F9	18
La Sabanilla, Mex.	C8	100
La Sal, Ut., U.S.	E7	132
La Salle, Co., U.S.	G8	126
La Salle, Il., U.S.	C8	120
La Salle, stm., Mb., Can.	E16	124
Lasan, Indon.	C9	50
Las Animas, Co., U.S.	C5	128
Las Arenas, P.R.	B1	104a
La Sarre, Qc., Can.	F15	106
Las Arrias, Arg.	E6	92
Las Ballenas, Canal de, strt., Mex.	G6	98
Las Breñas, Arg.	C7	92
Las Cabezas de San Juan, Spain	G5	20
Las Cabras, Chile	G2	92
Lascano, Ur.	F10	92
Las Casitas, mtn., Mex.	D4	100
Las Cattitas, Arg.	F3	92
Las Choapas, Mex.	G11	100
Las Chorreras, Mex.	A6	100
Las Cruces, N.M., U.S.	K10	132
Las Cuatas, Mex.	D1	130
Las Cuevas, Mex.	A8	100
Las Cumaraguas, Ven.	p20	104g
La Selle, Morne, mtn., Haiti	C11	102
La Serena, Chile	D2	92
La Serena, reg., Spain	F5	20
La Seu d'Urgell, Spain	B12	20
La Seyne, Fr.	F11	18
La Seyne, Fr.	F11	18
Las Flores, Arg.	H7	92
Las Flores, P.R.	B3	104a
Las Flores, Arroyo, stm., Arg.	H7	92
Las Garcitas, Arg.	C7	92
Las Guayabas, Mex.	C10	100
Lashburn, Sk., Can.	A4	124
Las Heras, Arg.	I3	90
Las Heras, Arg.	F3	92
Lashkar Gāh, Afg.	C9	56
Las Hormigas, Mex.	C3	100
Lasia, Pulau, i., Indon.	K3	48
Łasin, Pol.	C15	16
La Sirena, Ven.	p20	104g
Łaskarzew, Pol.	E17	16
Las Lajas, Arg.	I2	92
Las Lajas, Pan.	H7	102
Las Lomitas, Arg.	B7	92
Las Malvinas, Arg.	G3	92
Las Mareas, P.R.	C3	104a
Las Margaritas, Mex.	G13	100
Las Marianas, Arg.	G8	92
Las Marías, P.R.	B1	104a
Las Minas, Cerro, mtn., Hond.	E3	102
Las Nopaleras, Cerro, mtn., Mex.	C7	100
La Solana, Spain	F7	20
Las Ovejas, Arg.	H2	92
Las Palmas, Arg.	C8	92
Las Palmas, P.R.	C3	104a
Las Palomas, Mex.	F9	98
La Spezia, Italy	F6	22
Las Piedras, P.R.	B4	104a
Las Piedras, Ur.	G9	92
Las Piedras, stm., Peru	F3	84
Las Plumas, Arg.	H3	90
Lasqueti Island, i., B.C., Can.	G6	138
Las Rosas, Arg.	F7	92
Las Rosas, Mex.	G12	100
Lassance, Braz.	I3	88
Lassen Peak, vol., Ca., U.S.	C4	134
Lassen Volcanic National Park, p.o.i., Ca., U.S.	C4	134
L'Assomption, stm., Qc., Can.	D3	110
Las Tablas, Pan.	I7	102
Las Tinajas, Arg.	C5	92
Last Mountain Lake, l., Sk., Can.	C8	124
Las Tórtolas, Cerro (Tórtolas, Cerro de las), mtn., S.A.	D2	92
Lastoursville, Gabon	E2	66
Las Tunas, Cuba	B9	102
Las Tunas Grandes, Laguna, l., Arg.	H6	92
Las Varas, Mex.	E6	100
Las Varas, Mex.	G8	98
Las Varillas, Arg.	E6	92
Las Vegas, N.M., U.S.	F3	128
Las Vegas, Nv., U.S.	H1	132
La Tagua, Col.	H4	86
Latacunga, Ec.	H2	86
La Tagua, Col.	H4	86
Latakia see Al-Lādhiqiyah, Syria	C6	58
Lata Mountain, vol., Am. Sam.	h13	79c
Latehar, India	G10	54
Le Teste-de-Buch, Fr.	E4	18
Lāthi, India	H3	54
Lathrop, Mo., U.S.	E3	120
Latimer, Ia., U.S.	B4	120
Latina, Italy	C6	24
Latisana, Italy	E10	22
Latium see Lazio, state, Italy	B6	24
Latjuga, Russia	D23	8
La Torrecilla, mtn., P.R.	B3	104a
La Tortuga, Isla, i., Ven.	B9	86
Latouche Treville, Cape, c., Austl.	C4	74
La Tour-d'Auvergne, Fr.	D8	18
La Trimouille, Fr.	C7	18
La Trinidad, Nic.	F4	102
La Trinidad, Phil.	B3	52
La Trinidad de Orichuna, Ven.	D7	86
La Trinité, Mart.	k6	105c
Latrobe, Pa., U.S.	D6	114
Latta, S.C., U.S.	B6	116
La Tuque, Qc., Can.	B3	53
Lātür, India	B3	53
Latvia, ctry., Eur.	D7	10
Lau, Nig.	H7	64
Lauchhammer, Ger.	E9	16
Lauenburg, Ger.	C6	16
Lauf an der Pegnitz, Ger.	G7	16
Lauge Koch Kyst, cst., Grnld.	B13	141
Laughlin, Nv., U.S.	H2	132
Laughlin Peak, mtn., N.M., U.S.	E4	128
Lau Group, is., Fiji	p20	79e
Laukaa, Fin.	E11	8
Laun, ...	G4	48
Launceston, Austl.	n13	77a
Launceston, Eng., U.K.	K8	12
Laupheim, Ger.	H5	16
La Unión, El Sal.	F4	102
La Unión, Mex.	G8	100
La Unión, Spain	G10	20
La Urbana, Ven.	D8	86
Laurel, Fl., U.S.	I3	116
Laurel, In., U.S.	E12	120
Laurel, Md., U.S.	E9	114
Laurel, Ms., U.S.	F9	122
Laurel, Mt., U.S.	B4	126
Laurel, Ne., U.S.	E15	126
Laurel Bay, S.C., U.S.	D5	116

Name	Map Ref.	Page
Laureldale, Pa., U.S.	D10	114
Laureles, Ur.	E9	92
Laurel River Lake, res., Ky., U.S.	G1	114
Laurelville, Oh., U.S.	E15	120
Laurencekirk, Scot., U.K.	E10	12
Laurens, S.C., U.S.	B3	116
Laurentides, Les, plat., Qc., Can.	F16	106
Lau Ridge, unds.	L21	142
Laurier, Mb., Can.	D14	124
Laurier-Station, Qc., Can.	D5	110
Laurinburg, N.C., U.S.	B6	116
Laurium, Mi., U.S.	D10	118
Lausanne, Switz.	D3	22
Lausitzer Neisse (Nysa Łużycka), stm., Eur.	F10	16
Laut, Pulau, i., Indon.	A5	50
Laut, Pulau, i., Indon.	E10	50
Laut, Selat, strt., Indon.	E9	50
Lauta, Ger.	E9	16
Lautaro, Chile	I1	92
Lauterbach, Ger.	F5	16
Lauter Sachsen, Ger.	F8	16
Laut Kecil, Kepulauan, is., Indon.	F9	50
Lautoka, Fiji	p18	79e
Lauzerte, Fr.	E7	18
Lava (tyna), stm., Eur.	B16	16
Lava Beds National Monument, p.o.i., Ca., U.S.	B4	134
Lavaca, stm., Tx., U.S.	E11	130
Laval, Qc., Can.	E3	110
Laval, Fr.	F8	14
La Vall d'Uixó, Spain	E10	20
Lavalle, Arg.	D5	92
Lavalle, Arg.	D8	92
Lavapié, Punta, c., Chile	H1	92
Lavassaare, Est.	G11	8
La Vega, Dom. Rep.	C12	102
La Vela de Coro, Ven.	B7	86
Lavelanet, Fr.	G7	18
Lavello, Italy	C9	24
La Venada, Mex.	H10	130
La Venta, sci., Mex.	F11	100
La Ventura, Mex.	C8	100
La Vera, reg., Spain	D5	20
La Vergne, Tn., U.S.	H11	120
Laverne, Ok., U.S.	E9	128
Laverton, Austl.	E4	74
La Veta, Co., U.S.	D4	128
Lavieille, Lake, l., On., Can.	C11	112
La Vila Joiosa, Spain	F10	20
Lavillette, N.B., Can.	C11	110
La Viña, Arg.	B5	92
Lavina, Mt., U.S.	A4	126
La Vista, Ne., U.S.	C1	120
La Voulte-sur-Rhône, Fr.	E10	18
Lavras, Braz.	K3	88
Lávrio, Grc.	F7	28
Lavumisa, Swaz.	E10	70
Lawang, Indon.	G8	50
Lawas, Malay.	A9	50
Lawdar, Yemen	G6	56
Lawers, Ben, mtn., Scot., U.K.	E8	12
Lawgi, Austl.	E8	76
Lawksawk, Mya.	B3	48
Lawler, Ia., U.S.	A5	120
Lawn, Tx., U.S.	B8	130
Lawndale, N.C., U.S.	A4	116
Lawn Hill, Austl.	C7	74
Lawn Hill Creek, stm., Austl.	C7	74
Lawrence, In., U.S.	I3	112
Lawrence, Ks., U.S.	F2	120
Lawrence, Ma., U.S.	B14	114
Lawrenceburg, In., U.S.	E12	120
Lawrenceburg, Ky., U.S.	F12	120
Lawrenceburg, Tn., U.S.	B11	122
Lawrenceville, Il., U.S.	F10	120
Lawrenceville, N.J., U.S.	D11	114
Lawson, Mo., U.S.	E3	120
Lawtey, Fl., U.S.	F3	116
Lawton, N.D., U.S.	F15	124
Lawton, Ok., U.S.	G10	128
Lawu, Gunung, vol., Indon.	G7	50
Lawz, Jabal al-, mtn., Sau. Ar.	J6	58
Laxå, Swe.	G6	8
Laxe, Spain	A1	20
Lay Lake, res., Al., U.S.	D12	122
Layou, St. Vin.	o11	105e
Layton, Ut., U.S.	B4	132
Laytonville, Ca., U.S.	D2	134
La Zarca, Mex.	C6	100
Lázaro Cárdenas, Mex.	F17	34
Lázaro Cárdenas, Presa, res., Mex.	C6	100
Lazdijai, Lith.	F6	10
Lazio, state, Italy	B6	24
Léach, Camb.	F6	48
Leachville, Ar., U.S.	I7	120
Lead, S.D., U.S.	C9	126
Leadbetter Point, c., Wa., U.S.	D2	136
Leader, Sk., Can.	D4	124
Lead Hill, hill, Mo., U.S.	H4	120
Leadore, Id., U.S.	F13	136
Leadville, Co., U.S.	D10	132
Leaf, stm., Ms., U.S.	F10	122
Leaf Lake, s., Sk., Can.	A11	124
Leaghur, Lake, l., Austl.	I4	76
League City, Tx., U.S.	H3	122
Leakey, Tx., U.S.	E8	130
Leaksville, N.C., U.S.	H5	114
Lealman, Fl., U.S.	I3	116
Leamington, On., Can.	F7	112
Le'an, China	H6	42
Leandro, Braz.	C3	88
Leandro N. Alem, Arg.	C10	92
Leary, Ga., U.S.	F14	122
Leatherman Peak, mtn., Id., U.S.	F13	136
Leavenworth, Ks., U.S.	E2	120
Leavenworth, Wa., U.S.	C6	136
Leawood, Ks., U.S.	F3	120
Lebak, Phil.	G5	52
Lebam, Wa., U.S.	D3	136
Lebanon, In., U.S.	H3	112
Lebanon, Ks., U.S.	B10	128
Lebanon, Ky., U.S.	G12	120
Lebanon, N.H., U.S.	G4	110
Lebanon, Oh., U.S.	E1	114
Lebanon, Or., U.S.	F3	136
Lebanon, Pa., U.S.	D9	114
Lebanon, S.D., U.S.	B13	126
Lebanon, Tn., U.S.	H11	120
Lebanon, Va., U.S.	H3	114
Lebanon, ctry., Asia	E6	58
Lebesby, Nor.	A12	8
Le Bic, Qc., Can.	B9	110
Le Blanc, Fr.	H10	14
Lebo, D.R.C.	D4	66
Lebo, Ks., U.S.	F2	120
Lebork, Pol.	B13	16
Lebrija, stm., Col.	D5	86
Lebrija, Spain	H4	20
Łebsko, Jezioro, l., Pol.	B13	16
Lebu, Chile	H1	92
Lebyazh'e, Kaz.	D12	32
Le Carbet, Mart.	k6	105c
Lecce, Italy	D12	24
Lecco, Italy	E6	22
Le Center, Mn., U.S.	G5	118
Lech, stm., Eur.	H6	16
Lechainá, Grc.	F4	28
Lechang, Fr.	I5	14
Lechang, China	E13	14
Lechiguanas, Islas de las, is., Arg.	F8	92
Lechuguilla, Cerro, mtn., Mex.	D6	100
Lecompte, La., U.S.	F6	122
Le Creusot, Fr.	H13	14
Le Croisic, Fr.	G6	14
Łęczyca, Pol.	D15	16
Ledesma, Spain	C4	20
Le Diamant, Mart.	I6	105c
Ledjanaja, gora, mtn., Russia	D23	34
Ledo, India	C8	46
Ledo, Indon.	C6	50
Ledong, China	L3	42
Le Dorat, Fr.	C7	18
Ledu, China	D5	36
Leduc, Ab., Can.	C17	138
Leechburg, Pa., U.S.	D6	114
Leech Lake, l., Mn., U.S.	D4	118
Leedey, Ok., U.S.	F9	128
Leeds, Eng., U.K.	H11	12
Leeds, Al., U.S.	D12	122
Leek, Eng., U.K.	H10	12
Leesville, La., U.S.	D4	112
Leelanau Peninsula, pen., Mi., U.S.	C4	112
Leer, Ger.	C3	16
Leesburg, Fl., U.S.	H4	116
Leesburg, Ga., U.S.	E1	116
Leesburg, Va., U.S.	E8	114
Leesville, La., U.S.	F3	120
Leesville, La., U.S.	F5	122
Leesville, Tx., U.S.	E10	130
Leeton, Austl.	J6	76
Leeu-Gamka, S. Afr.	H6	70
Leeuwarden, Neth.	A14	14
Leeuwin, Cape, c., Austl.	F2	74
Lee Vining, Ca., U.S.	F6	134
Leeward Islands, is., N.A.	h15	96a
Lefkáda, Grc.	E3	28
Lefkáda, i., Grc.	E3	28
Lefke, N. Cyp.	C3	58
Lefkosia see Nicosia, Cyp.	C4	58
Lefors, Tx., U.S.	F8	128
Le François, Mart.	k7	105c
Lefroy, Lake, l., Austl.	F4	74
Legal, Ab., Can.	C17	138
Leganés, Spain	D7	20
Legaspi, Phil.	D4	52
Leggett, Ca., U.S.	D2	134
Leghorn see Livorno, Italy	G7	22
Legion, Zimb.	B9	70
Legionowo, Pol.	D16	16
Legnago, Italy	E8	22
Legnano, Italy	E5	22
Legnica, state, Pol.	E12	16
Legnica, state, Pol.	E12	16
Le Gosier, Guad.	h6	105c
Le Grand, Ca., U.S.	F5	134
Le Guelta, Alg.	H11	20
Legume, Austl.	G9	76
Leh, India	A6	54
Le Havre, Fr.	E8	14
Lehčevo, Blg.	F10	26
Lehigh, Ia., U.S.	B3	120
Lehigh, Ok., U.S.	C2	122
Lehigh Acres, Fl., U.S.	J4	116
Lehighton, Pa., U.S.	D10	114
Lehrte, Ger.	D5	16
Lehtse, Est.	A8	10
Lehua, i., Hi., U.S.	a1	78a
Lehututu, Bots.	C5	70
Lei, stm., China	H5	42
Leiah, Pak.	C3	54
Leibnitz, Aus.	D12	22
Leicester, Eng., U.K.	I11	12
Leichhardt, stm., Austl.	A2	76
Leichhardt Falls, wtfl., Austl.	B2	76
Leiden (Leyden), Neth.	B13	14
Leigh Creek South, Austl.	H2	76
Leighton, Al., U.S.	C11	122
Leighton Buzzard, Eng., U.K.	J12	12
Leinan, Sk., Can.	D6	124
Leine, stm., Ger.	D5	16
Leinster, hist. reg., Ire.	I6	12
Leinster, Mount, mtn., Ire.	I6	12
Leipalingis, Lith.	F6	10
Leipsic, Oh., U.S.	C2	114
Leipsoí, i., Grc.	F9	28
Leipzig, Ger.	E8	16
Leiria, Port.	E2	20
Leiria, state, Port.	E2	20
Leisler, Mount, mtn., Austl.	D6	74
Leitariegos, Puerto de, p., Spain	A4	20
Leitha (Lajta), stm., Eur.	H12	16
Leitrim, Ire.	H4	12
Leitrim, state, Ire.	H5	12
Leivádia, Grc.	E5	28
Leiyang, China	H5	42
Leizhou Bandao, pen., China	K3	42
Lejasciems, Lat.	C9	10
Leketiio, Spain	A8	20
Leksozero, ozero, l., Russia	E14	8
Le Lamentin, Mart.	k6	105c
Leland, Il., U.S.	C9	120
Leland, Mi., U.S.	C4	112
Leland, Ms., U.S.	D8	122
Leleivi Point, c., Hi., U.S.	d7	78a
Leleque, Arg.	H2	90
Leles, Indon.	G5	50
Leli Shan, mtn., China	B8	54
Le Locle, Switz.	C3	22
Lelystad, Neth.	B14	14
Le Maire, Estrecho de, strt., Arg.	J4	90
Le Mans, Fr.	G9	14
Le Marin, Mart.	l7	105c
Le Mars, Ia., U.S.	B1	120
Lema Shilindi, Eth.	G8	62
Lemay, Mo., U.S.	F7	120
Lembak, Indon.	C10	50
Lemdiyya, Alg.	H13	20
Leme, Braz.	L2	88
Lemesos (Limassol), Cyp.	D4	58
Lemhi, stm., Id., U.S.	F13	136
Lemhi Pass, p., U.S.	F13	136
Lemhi Range, mts., Id., U.S.	F13	136
Lemieux Islands, is., Nu., Can.	E13	141
Leming, Tx., U.S.	E9	130
Lemitar, N.M., U.S.	I10	132
Lemmatsi, Est.	B9	10
Lemmenjoen kansallispuisto, p.o.i., Fin.	B11	8
Lemmon, S.D., U.S.	B10	126
Lemmon, Mount, mtn., Az., U.S.	K6	132
Lemnos see Limnos, i., Grc.	D8	28
Lemoncove, Ca., U.S.	G7	134
Le Mont-Dore, N. Cal.	n16	79d
Lemoore, Ca., U.S.	G6	134
Le Moule, Guad.	h6	105c
Lempa, stm., N.A.	F3	102
Lempe, Indon.	D12	50
Lemro, stm., Mya.	B1	48
Le Murge, hills, Italy	D10	24
Le Muy, Fr.	F12	18
Lemyethna, Mya.	D2	48
Lena, Wi., U.S.	D11	112
Lena, stm., Russia	B14	34
Lenart, Slvn.	D12	22
Lençóis, Braz.	G5	88
Lençóis Maranhenses, Parque Nacional dos, p.o.i., Braz.	B4	88
Lendinara, Italy	E8	22
Lenger, Kaz.	F12	32
Lenggor, stm., Malay.	K6	48
Lenghu, China	D3	36
Lengshuitan, China	H4	42
Lenhovda, Swe.	H6	8
Leningrad see Sankt-Peterburg, Russia	A13	10
Leningradskaja oblast', co., Russia	G15	8
Leninogor see Leninogorsk, Kaz.	D14	32
Leninogorsk, Kaz.	D14	32
Lenin Peak, mtn., Asia	B11	56
Leninsk, Kaz.	E10	32
Leninsk, Uzb.	F12	32
Leninskij, Russia	F20	10
Leninsk-Kuzneckij, Russia	D15	32
Leninskoe, Russia	G15	34
Lennonville, Austl.	E3	74
Lennox, S.D., U.S.	H2	118
Lennox, Isla, i., Chile	K3	90
Lennoxville, Qc., Can.	E5	110
Lenoir, N.C., U.S.	I4	114
Lenora, Czech Rep.	H9	16
Lenore Lake, l., Sk., Can.	B9	124
Lenox, Ga., U.S.	E2	116
Lenox, Ia., U.S.	D3	120
Lenox, Tn., U.S.	H8	120
Lens, Fr.	D11	14
Lensk, Russia	B20	32
Lenti, Hung.	C3	26
Lentini, Italy	G9	24
Lentua, l., Fin.	D13	8
Lentvaris, Lith.	F8	10
Lenya, stm., Mya.	G4	48
Léo, Burkina	G4	64
Leoben, Aus.	C12	22
Léogâne, Haiti	C11	102
Leola, Ar., U.S.	C6	122
Leola, S.D., U.S.	B14	126
Leominster, Eng., U.K.	I10	12
Leominster, Ma., U.S.	B14	114
Léon, Fr.	F4	18
León, Mex.	E8	100
León, Nic.	F4	102
León, Spain	B5	20
León, Ks., U.S.	D12	128
León, stm., Tx., U.S.	C10	130
León, Montes de, mts., Spain	B4	20
Leona, stm., Tx., U.S.	F8	130
Leonard, Tx., U.S.	D2	122
Leonardtown, Md., U.S.	F9	114
Leonardville, Ks., U.S.	B12	128
Leonberg, Ger.	H4	16
Leones, Arg.	F6	92
Leonforte, Italy	G8	24
Leongatha, Austl.	L5	76
Leoniha, Russia	G18	8
Leonora, Austl.	E4	74
Leopold and Astrid Coast, cst., Ant.	B13	81
Leopoldina, Braz.	K4	88
Leopoldo de Bulhões, Braz.	I1	88
Léopoldville see Kinshasa, D.R.C.	E3	66
Leoti, Ks., U.S.	C7	128
Leova, Mol.	C15	26
Lepanto see Náfpaktos, Grc.	E4	28
Lepanto, Ar., U.S.	B8	122
Lepar, Pulau, i., Indon.	E5	50
Lepe, Spain	G3	20
Lepel', Bela.	F11	10
Lepontine Alps, mts., Eur.	C14	18
Lepreau, Point, c., N.B., Can.	E10	110
Le Prêcheur, Mart.	k6	105c
Lepsi, Kaz.	E13	32
Lepsy see Lepsi, Kaz.	E13	32
Le Puy, Fr.	D9	18
Lequeitio see Lekeitio, Spain	A8	20
Lercara Friddi, Italy	G7	24
Lerdo, Mex.	C7	100
Lérida, Col.	G6	86
Lérida see Lleida, Spain	C11	20
Lerma, stm., Mex.	E8	100
Le Roy, Il., U.S.	D9	120
Le Roy, Ks., U.S.	F2	120
Le Roy, N.Y., U.S.	B7	114
Lerum, Swe.	H5	8
Lerwick, Scot., U.K.	n18	12a
Les Abymes, Guad.	h5	105c
Le Saint-Esprit, Mart.	k7	105c
Les Andelys, Fr.	E10	14
Les Anses-d'Arlets, Mart.	l6	105c
Les Borges Blanques, Spain	C11	20
Lesbos see Lésvos, i., Grc.	D9	28
Les Cayes, Haiti	C11	102
Les Herbiers, Fr.	H7	14
Lésina, Lago di, b., Italy	H12	22
Lesko, Pol.	G18	16
Leskovac, Serb.	F8	26
Leskov Island, i., S. Geor.	K12	82
Les Laurentides see Laurentides, Les, plat., Qc., Can.	F16	106
Leslie, Ar., U.S.	I5	120
Leslie, Mi., U.S.	B1	114
Leslie, W.V., U.S.	F5	114
Lesneven, Fr.	F4	14
Lesnoe, Russia	B18	10
Lesogorsk, Russia	G17	34
Lesosibirsk, Russia	E7	34
Lesotho, ctry., Afr.	F9	70
Lesozavodsk, Russia	B10	38
Lesozavodskij, Russia	C15	8
Les Sables-d'Olonne, Fr.	H7	14
Les Saintes, is., Guad.	i5	105c
Lesser Antilles, is.	D8	82
Lesser Khingan Range see Xiao Hinggan Ling, mts., China	B10	36
Lesser Slave, stm., Ab., Can.	A16	138
Lesser Slave Lake, l., Ab., Can.	D8	106
Lesser Sunda Islands see Tenggara, Nusa, is., Indon.	G6	44
L'Esterre, Gren.	q10	105e
Lestock, Sk., Can.	C9	124
Le Sueur, Mn., U.S.	G5	118
Le Sueur, stm., Mn., U.S.	G5	118
Lešukonskoe, Russia	D21	8
Lésvos (Lesbos), i., Grc.	D9	28
Leszno, Pol.	E12	16
Leszno, state, Pol.	E12	16
Letaba, stm., S. Afr.	C10	70
Letea, Ostrovul, i., Rom.	D16	26
Lethbridge, Ab., Can.	G18	138
Letham, Guy.	F12	86
Le Thillot, Fr.	G15	14
Leti, Kepulauan, is., Indon.	G8	44
Leticia, Col.	D4	84
Letlhakane, Bots.	B7	70
Letlhakeng, Bots.	D7	70
Letnjaja Zolotica, Russia	D17	8
Letohrad, Czech Rep.	F12	16
Letong, Indon.	B4	50
Letpadan, Mya.	D2	48
Letsôk-aw Kyun, i., Mya.	G3	48
Letung, Indon.	B4	50
Leucas see Lefkáda, i., Grc.	E3	28
Leucate, Étang de, l., Fr.	G9	18
Leuk, Switz.	D4	22
Leuser, Gunung, mtn., Indon.	K3	48
Leutkirch, Ger.	I6	16
Leuven, Bel.	D13	14
Levack, On., Can.	B8	112
Levan, Ut., U.S.	D5	132
Levanger, Nor.	D4	8
Levante, Riviera di, cst., Italy	F6	22
Levanzo, Isola di, i., Italy	F6	24
Le Vauclin, Mart.	k7	105c
Levelland, Tx., U.S.	H6	128
Leveque, Cape, c., Austl.	C4	74
Leverkusen, Ger.	E3	16
Levice, Slov.	H14	16
Levin, N.Z.	E6	80
Lévis, Qc., Can.	D5	110
Levisa Fork, stm., U.S.	G3	114
Levittown, P.R.	b3	104a
Levittown, N.Y., U.S.	D12	114
Levittown, Pa., U.S.	D11	114
Levkosia see Nicosia, Cyp.	C4	58
Levoča, Slov.	H16	16
Levuka, Fiji	p19	79e
Lévuo, stm., Lith.	E7	10
Lewe, Mya.	C2	48
Lewellen, Ne., U.S.	F10	126
Lewer, stm., Nmb.	D3	70
Lewes, De., U.S.	F10	114
Lewin Brzeski, Pol.	F13	16
Lewis, Ia., U.S.	C3	120
Lewis, Butt of, c., Scot., U.K.	C6	12
Lewis, Isle of, i., Scot., U.K.	C6	12
Lewis, Mount, mtn., Nv., U.S.	C8	134
Lewis and Clark Lake, res., U.S.	E15	126
Lewis and Clark Range, mts., Mt., U.S.	C13	136
Lewisburg, Ky., U.S.	H10	120
Lewisburg, Pa., U.S.	D8	114
Lewisburg, Tn., U.S.	B12	122
Lewis Range, mts., N.A.	B13	136
Lewis Run, Pa., U.S.	C7	114
Lewis Smith Lake, res., Al., U.S.	C11	122
Lewiston, Ca., U.S.	C3	134
Lewiston, Id., U.S.	D10	136
Lewiston, Me., U.S.	F6	110
Lewiston, Mi., U.S.	D5	112
Lewiston, Mn., U.S.	H7	118
Lewiston, Ut., U.S.	B5	132
Lewiston Orchards, Id., U.S.	D10	136
Lewistown, Il., U.S.	D7	120
Lewistown, Mt., U.S.	C17	136
Lewistown, Pa., U.S.	D8	114
Lewisville, N.B., Can.	D12	110
Lewisville, Ar., U.S.	D5	122
Lewisville, Tx., U.S.	A10	130
Lewisville Lake, res., Tx., U.S.	H12	128
Lewvan, Sk., Can.	D9	124
Lexa, Ar., U.S.	C8	122
Lexington, Ga., U.S.	C2	116
Lexington, Il., U.S.	D9	120
Lexington, Ky., U.S.	F1	114
Lexington, Ma., U.S.	B14	114
Lexington, Mi., U.S.	E7	112
Lexington, Ms., U.S.	D8	122
Lexington, N.C., U.S.	I5	114
Lexington, Ne., U.S.	G13	126
Lexington, Ok., U.S.	F11	128
Lexington, Or., U.S.	E7	136
Lexington, S.C., U.S.	C4	116
Lexington, Tx., U.S.	D10	130
Lexington, Va., U.S.	G6	114
Lexington Park, Md., U.S.	F9	114
Leyden see Leiden, Neth.	B13	14
Leye, China	I2	42
Leyte, i., Phil.	E5	52
Leyte Gulf, b., Phil.	E5	52
Lezhë, Alb.	C13	24
Lezhi, China	F1	42
Lezíria, Bela.	E13	10
L'gov, Russia	D5	32
Lhasa, China	D13	54
Lhasa, stm., China	D13	54
Lhazê, China	D11	54
Lhokhnga, Indon.	J2	48
Lhokseumawe, Indon.	J3	48
Lhoksukon, Indon.	J3	48
Lhorong, China	E4	36
L'Hospitalet de Llobregat, Spain	C13	20
Lhuntsi Dzong, Bhu.	E13	54
Li, Thai.	D4	48
Li, stm., China	G4	42
Li, stm., Thai.	D4	48
Liamuiga, Mount, vol., St. K./N.	c2	105a
Lian, stm., China	I5	42
Liancheng, China	I7	42
Lianga, Phil.	F6	52
Liangbuaya, Indon.	C10	50
Liangdang, China	E1	42
Lianghekou, China	G3	42
Liangpran, China	F2	42
Liangyuan, China	F9	42
Liangzi Hu, l., China	F6	42
Lianhua, China	H6	42
Lianhua Shan, mts., China	J6	42
Lianjiang, China	K4	42
Lianjiang, China	H8	42
Liannan, China	I5	42
Lianshui, China	E8	42
Lianxian, China	I5	42
Lianyuan, China	H4	42
Lianyungang, China	D8	42
Liao, stm., China	D5	38
Liaocheng, China	C7	42
Liaodong Bandao (Liaotung Peninsula), pen., China	D5	38
Liaodong Wan (Liaotung, Gulf of), b., China	A9	42
Liaoning, state, China	D5	38
Liaotung, Gulf of see Liaodong Wan, b., China	A9	42
Liaotung Peninsula see Liaodong Bandao, pen., China	D5	38
Liaoyang, China	D5	38
Liaoyuan, China	C6	38
Liaozhong, China	D5	38
Liard, stm., Can.	C6	106
Liat, Pulau, i., Indon.	E5	50
Libagon, Phil.	E5	52
Libano, Col.	E4	86
Libby, Mt., U.S.	B11	136
Libby Dam, dam, Mt., U.S.	B11	136
Libenge, D.R.C.	D3	66
Liberal, Ks., U.S.	D7	128
Liberal, Mo., U.S.	G3	120
Liberec, Czech Rep.	F11	16
Liberia, C.R.	G5	102
Liberia, ctry., Afr.	H3	64
Liberta, Antig.	f4	105b
Libertad, Ven.	C7	86
Libertador General Bernardo O'Higgins, state, Chile	G2	92
Liberty, Mo., U.S.	E3	120
Liberty, N.Y., U.S.	C11	114
Liberty, N.C., U.S.	I6	114
Liberty, S.C., U.S.	B3	116
Liberty, Tx., U.S.	G4	122
Libertyville, Il., U.S.	B9	120
Libo, China	G3	42
Libobo, Tanjung, c., Indon.	F8	44
Libode, S. Afr.	G9	70
Libon, Phil.	D4	52
Libourne, Fr.	E5	18
Libramont, Bel.	E14	14
Libreville, Gabon	D1	66
Liburang, Indon.	F12	50
Libya, ctry., Afr.	B3	62
Libyan Desert, des., Afr.	C5	62
Libyan Plateau, plat., Afr.	A4	62
Licancábur, Volcán, vol., S.A.	D3	90
Licantén, Chile	G1	92
Licata, Italy	G7	24
Lich, Ger.	F4	16
Licheng, China	C5	42
Lichfield, Eng., U.K.	I11	12
Lichinga, Moz.	C6	68
Lichtenau, Ger.	E5	16
Lichtenburg, S. Afr.	E7	70
Lichtenfels, Ger.	F7	16
Lichuan, China	H7	42
Lichuan, China	F3	42
Licking, stm., Ky., U.S.	F1	114
Lički Osik, Cro.	F12	22
Ličko Polje, val., Cro.	F12	22
Lida, Bela.	G8	10
Liddon Gulf, b., N.T., Can.	B17	140
Liden, Swe.	E7	8
Lidgerwood, N.D., U.S.	E1	118
Lidköping, Swe.	G5	8
Lido di Ostia, Italy	I9	22
Lidzbark, Pol.	C15	16
Lidzbark Warmiński, Pol.	B16	16
Liebenbergsvlei, stm., S. Afr.	E9	70
Liebig, Mount, mtn., Austl.	D6	74
Liechtenstein, ctry., Eur.	C6	22
Liège (Luik), Bel.	D14	14
Lielais Liepu kalns, hill, Lat.	D10	10
Lielvārde, Lat.	D7	10
Lienchou see Hepu, China	D9	22
Lienz, Aus.	D9	22
Liepāja, Lat.	D3	10
Liepājas ezers, l., Lat.	D4	10
Lier, Bel.	C13	14
Lierre see Lier, Bel.	C13	14
Liestal, Switz.	C4	22
Liești, Rom.	D14	26
Liévin, Fr.	D11	14
Lièvre, stm., Qc., Can.	C14	112
Liezen, Aus.	C11	22
Liffey, stm., Ire.	H6	12
Lifford, Ire.	G5	12
Lifou, i., N. Cal.	m16	79d
Ligatne, Lat.	C7	10
Lighthouse Point, pt., Fl., U.S.	J5	116
Lighthouse Point, c., Fl., U.S.	H14	122
Lighthouse Point, c., Mi., U.S.	C4	112
Lightning Creek, stm., Wy., U.S.	D7	126
Lightning Ridge, Austl.	G6	76
Lignite, N.D., U.S.	F11	124
Ligny-en-Barrois, Fr.	F14	14
Ligonha, stm., Moz.	D6	68
Ligonier, In., U.S.	G4	112
Ligonier, Pa., U.S.	D6	114
Liguria, state, Italy	F5	22
Ligurian Sea, s., Eur.	G5	22
Lihir Island, i., Pap. N. Gui.	a5	79a
Lihou Reefs and Cays, rf., Austl.	A8	76
Lihue, Hi., U.S.	b2	78a
Lihuel Calel, Parque Nacional, p.o.i., Arg.	H5	92
Lihula, Est.	B6	10
Lijiang, China	F5	36
Lik, stm., Laos	C6	48
Likasi (Jadotville), D.R.C.	G5	66
Likati, D.R.C.	D4	66
Likely, B.C., Can.	D9	138
Lik, Indon.	D2	50
Likino-Dulevo, Russia	E21	10
Lilbourn, Mo., U.S.	H8	120
Lilienfeld, Aus.	B12	22
Lilienthal, Ger.	C4	16
Lille, Fr.	D12	14
Lillebælt, strt., Den.	I3	8
Lillebonne, Fr.	E9	14
Lillehammer, Nor.	F3	8
Lillers, Fr.	D11	14
Lillestrøm, Nor.	F4	8
Lillhärdal, Swe.	F6	8
Lillington, N.C., U.S.	A7	116
Lillooet, B.C., Can.	F9	138
Lillooet, stm., B.C., Can.	G8	138
Lillooet Lake, l., B.C., Can.	F8	138
Lilongwe, Mwi.	C5	68
Liloy, Phil.	F4	52
Lim, stm., Eur.	F6	26
Lima, Para.	A9	92
Lima, Mt., U.S.	E14	136
Lima, N.Y., U.S.	B8	114
Lima, Oh., U.S.	D1	114
Lima (Limia), stm., Eur.	C2	20
Limanowa, Pol.	G16	16
Limari, stm., Chile	E2	92
Limas, Indon.	D4	50
Limassol see Lemesos, Cyp.	D4	58
Limavady, N. Ire., U.K.	F6	12
Limay, stm., Arg.	G3	90
Limay Mahuida, Arg.	H4	92
Limbang, Malay.	A9	50
Limbara, Monte, mtn., Italy	D3	24
Limbaži, Lat.	C7	10
Limbdi, India	G4	54
Limbe, Cam.	D1	66
Limbé, Haiti	C11	102
Limbunan see Pio V. Corpuz, Phil.	F5	52
Limburg an der Lahn, Ger.	F4	16
Limeira, Braz.	L2	88
Limerick, Sk., Can.	E7	124
Limerick (Luimneach), Ire.	I4	12
Limerick, state, Ire.	I4	12
Limestone, Me., U.S.	C9	110
Limestone, Lake, res., Tx., U.S.	F2	122
Limfjorden, l., Den.	H3	8
Limia (Lima), stm., Eur.	E1	20
Limingen, l., Nor.	D5	8
Limmared, Swe.	H5	8
Limmen Bight, b., Austl.	C7	74
Limmen Bight, stm., Austl.	B7	74
Limnos, i., Grc.	D8	28
Limoeiro, Braz.	D8	88
Limoeiro do Norte, Braz.	C6	88
Limoges, Fr.	D7	18
Limón, Hond.	E5	102
Limon, Co., U.S.	B4	128
Limone Piemonte, Italy	F4	22
Limoux, Fr.	F8	18
Limpopo, Parque Nacional do, p.o.i., Moz.	C10	70
Limpopo, stm., Afr.	D10	70
Linahamari, Russia	B14	8
Lin'an, China	F8	42
Linapacan Island, i., Phil.	E1	52
Linares, Chile	G2	92
Linares, Mex.	C9	100
Linares, Spain	F7	20
Linares, state, Chile	H2	92
Lincang, China	G5	36
Linch'ing see Linqing, China	C7	42
Lincoln, Arg.	G7	92
Lincoln, Eng., U.K.	H12	12
Lincoln, Ca., U.S.	E4	134
Lincoln, Il., U.S.	D8	120
Lincoln, Ks., U.S.	B10	128
Lincoln, Me., U.S.	E8	110
Lincoln, Mo., U.S.	F4	120
Lincoln, N.H., U.S.	F5	110
Lincoln, Ne., U.S.	K2	118
Lincoln, Mount, mtn., Co., U.S.	B2	128
Lincoln City, Or., U.S.	F2	136
Lincoln Creek, stm., Ne., U.S.	F15	126
Lincoln Park, Co., U.S.	C3	128
Lincoln Park, Mi., U.S.	B2	114
Lincoln Sea, s., N.A.	A13	141
Lincolnton, N.C., U.S.	A4	116
Lincoln Village, Ca., U.S.	F4	134
Lindale, Ga., U.S.	C13	122
Lindale, Tx., U.S.	E3	122
Lindau, Ger.	I5	16
Linde, stm., Russia	C13	34
Linden, Guy.	B6	84
Linden, Al., U.S.	E11	122
Linden, In., U.S.	H3	112
Linden, Mi., U.S.	B2	114
Linden, Tn., U.S.	B11	122
Lindesnes, c., Nor.	H2	8
Lindi, Tan.	F7	66
Lindi, stm., D.R.C.	D5	66
Lindos, sci., Grc.	G10	28
Lindsay, On., Can.	D11	112
Lindsay, Ca., U.S.	G6	134
Lindsay, Ne., U.S.	F15	126
Lindsay, Ok., U.S.	G11	128
Line Islands, is., Oc.	D11	72
Linesville, Pa., U.S.	C5	114
Lineville, Al., U.S.	D13	122
Lineville, Ia., U.S.	D4	120
Linfen, China	C4	42
Linganamakki Reservoir, res., India	D2	53
Lingao, China	L3	42
Lingayen, Phil.	B3	52
Lingayen Gulf, b., Phil.	B3	52
Lingbi, China	E7	42
Lingbo, Swe.	F7	8
Lingchuan, China	D5	42
Lingen, Ger.	D3	16
Lingfengwei, China	I6	42
Lingga, Kepulauan, is., Indon.	C4	50
Lingga, Pulau, i., Indon.	C4	50
Lingomo II, D.R.C.	D4	66
Lingqiu, China	B6	42
Lingshan, China	J3	42
Lingshi, China	C4	42
Lingshui, China	L4	42
Linguère, Sen.	F2	64
Lingwu, China	C2	42
Lingxian, China	H5	42
Lingyuan, China	A8	42
Linh, Ngoc, mtn., Viet.	E9	48
Linhai, China	G9	42
Linhares, Braz.	J5	88
Linhe, China	A2	42
Linhsia see Linxia, China	D5	36
Linjiang, China	D7	38
Linköping, Swe.	G7	8
Linli, China	G4	42
Linn, Ks., U.S.	B11	128
Linn, Mo., U.S.	F6	120
Linnansaari kansallispuisto, p.o.i., Fin.	E13	8
Linnhe, Loch, b., Scot., U.K.	E7	12
Linqing, China	C6	42
Linqu, China	C8	42
Linquan, China	E6	42
Linru, China	D5	42
Lins, Braz.	K1	88
Linstead, Jam.	i13	104d
Lintan, China	D5	36
Linton, In., U.S.	E10	112
Linton, N.D., U.S.	A12	126
Lintong, China	D3	42
Linwu, China	I5	42
Linxi, China	C8	36
Linxi, China	C3	38
Linxia, China	D5	36
Linxian, China	C4	42
Linyi, China	D8	42
Linyi, China	C7	42
Linyü see Shanhaiguan, China	A8	42
Linz, Aus.	B11	22
Lio Matoh, Malay.	B9	50
Lion, Golfe du, b., Fr.	G10	18
Lion, Golfe du, b., Fr.	G10	18
Lionel Town, Jam.	j13	104d
Liouesso, Congo	D3	66
Lipa, Phil.	D3	52
Lipan, Tx., U.S.	B9	130
Lipari, Italy	F9	24
Lipari, Isola, i., Italy	F9	24
Lipari, Isole see Eolie, Isole, is., Italy	F8	24
Lipcani, Mol.	A13	26
Lipeck, Russia	D6	32
Lípez, Cerro, mtn., Bol.	D3	90
Liping, China	H3	42
Lipin Bor, Russia	G20	10
Lipljan, Serb.	G8	26
Lipno, Pol.	D15	16
Lipno, údolní nádrž, res., Czech Rep.	H10	16
Lipova, Rom.	C8	26
Lipovcy, Russia	B9	38
Lippe, stm., Ger.	E3	16
Lippstadt, Ger.	E4	16
Lipscomb, Tx., U.S.	E8	128
Liptovský Mikuláš, Slov.	G15	16
Liptrap, Cape, c., Austl.	L5	76
Lira, Ug.	D6	66
Liri, stm., Italy	C7	24
Liria see Llíria, Spain	E10	20
Liro, Vanuatu	k17	79d
Lisala, D.R.C.	D4	66
Lisboa (Lisbon), Port.	F1	20
Lisboa, state, Port.	E1	20
Lisbon see Lisboa, Port.	F1	20
Lisbon, N.D., U.S.	A15	126
Lisbon, Oh., U.S.	D5	114
Lisburn, N. Ire., U.K.	G6	12
Lisburne, Cape, c., Ak., U.S.	C6	140
Lishe, China	G5	36
Lishi, China	C4	42
Lishu, China	C6	38
Lishui, China	G8	42
Lisichansk see Lysychans'k, Ukr.	E5	32
Lisieux, Fr.	E9	14
Liski, Russia	D5	32
L'Isle-Jourdain, Fr.	E10	12
Lisman, Al., U.S.	E10	122
Lismore, Austl.	G9	76
Lismore, N.S., Can.	E14	110
Lismore, Ire.	I5	12
Listowel, On., Can.	E9	112
Listowel, Ire.	I3	12
Litang, China	J3	42
Litang, China	E5	36
Litang, stm., China	F5	36
Litani, stm., S.A.	C7	84
Litchfield, Ct., U.S.	C12	114
Litchfield, Il., U.S.	E8	120
Litchfield, Mn., U.S.	F4	118
Litchfield, Ne., U.S.	F13	126
Litchville, N.D., U.S.	A14	126
Lithgow, Austl.	I8	76
Lithino, Akra, c., Grc.	I7	28
Lithonia, Ga., U.S.	D14	122
Lithuania, ctry., Eur.	E7	10
Litija, Slvn.	D11	22
Litoměřice, Czech Rep.	F10	16
Litomyšl, Czech Rep.	G12	16
Litovko, Russia	G16	34
Little, stm., U.S.	C3	116
Little, stm., Ok., U.S.	D11	130
Little, stm., U.S.	B9	130
Little, stm., U.S.	D11	130
Little, stm., U.S.	B8	122

Name	Map Ref.	Page
Little, stm., U.S.	D5	122
Little, Mountain Fork, stm., U.S.	C4	122
Little Abaco, i., Bah.	B9	96
Little Andaman, i., India	F7	46
Little Arkansas, stm., Ks., U.S.	C11	128
Little Beaver Creek, stm., U.S.	B7	128
Little Beaver Creek, stm., U.S.	A8	126
Little Belt see Lillebælt, strt., Den.	I3	8
Little Belt Mountains, mts., Mt., U.S.	D16	136
Little Bighorn, stm., U.S.	B5	126
Little Bighorn Battlefield National Monument, p.o.i., Mt., U.S.	B5	126
Little Blue, stm., U.S.	G15	126
Little Buffalo, stm., Can.	C8	106
Little Carpathians see Malé Karpaty, mts., Slov.	H13	16
Little Cayman, i., Cay. Is.	C7	102
Little Chute, Wi., U.S.	D1	112
Little Colorado, stm., Az., U.S.	H5	132
Little Current, On., Can.	C8	112
Little Current, stm., On., Can.	A12	118
Little Deep Creek, stm., N.D., U.S.	F12	124
Little Deschutes, stm., Or., U.S.	G5	136
Little Desert, des., Austl.	K3	76
Little Desert National Park, p.o.i., Austl.	K3	76
Little Dry Creek, stm., Mt., U.S.	G7	124
Little Falls, Mn., U.S.	E4	118
Little Falls, N.Y., U.S.	E15	112
Littlefork, Mn., U.S.	C5	118
Little Fork, stm., Mn., U.S.	C5	118
Little Hurricane Creek, stm., La., U.S.	E3	116
Little Inagua, i., Bah.	B11	102
Little Kanawha, stm., W.V., U.S.	E4	114
Little Karroo (Klein Karroo), plat., S. Afr.	H5	70
Little Lake, l., La., U.S.	H8	122
Little London, Jam.	i12	104d
Little Lost, stm., Id., U.S.	F13	136
Little Mexico, Tx., U.S.	D4	130
Little Missouri, stm., Ar., U.S.	D5	122
Little Missouri, stm., U.S.	B7	108
Little Namaqualand (Klein Namaland), hist. reg., S. Afr.	F3	70
Little Nicobar, i., India	G7	46
Little Osage, stm., U.S.	G3	120
Little Pee Dee, stm., S.C., U.S.	B6	116
Little Pic, stm., On., Can.	C12	118
Little Powder, stm., U.S.	B7	126
Little Quill Lake, l., Sk., Can.	C10	124
Little Rann of Kachchh, reg., India	G3	54
Little Red, stm., Ar., U.S.	B7	122
Little Red, Middle Fork, stm., Ar., U.S.	B6	122
Little Red Deer, stm., Ab., Can.	E16	138
Little River, stm., U.S.	C10	128
Little Rock, Ar., U.S.	C6	122
Little Rock, stm., U.S.	H2	118
Little Sable Point, c., Mi., U.S.	E3	112
Little Saint Bernard Pass, p., Eur.	D12	18
Little Sandy Creek, stm., Wy., U.S.	E3	126
Little Sioux, stm., U.S.	J3	118
Little Sioux, West Fork, stm., Ia., U.S.	B2	120
Little Smoky, stm., Ab., Can.	A14	138
Little Snake, stm., U.S.	C8	132
Littlestown, Pa., U.S.	E8	114
Little Tallapoosa, stm., U.S.	D13	122
Little Tennessee, stm., U.S.	A1	116
Little Tobago, i., Trin.	r13	105f
Littleton, Co., U.S.	B3	128
Littleton, N.H., U.S.	F5	110
Littleton, W.V., U.S.	E5	114
Little Valley, N.Y., U.S.	B7	114
Little Wabash, stm., Il., U.S.	F9	120
Little White, stm., S.D., U.S.	D12	126
Little Wood, stm., Id., U.S.	G12	136
Litvínov, Czech Rep.	F9	16
Liu, China	C6	38
Liu, stm., China	C5	38
Liu, stm., China	I3	42
Liuanua see Ontong Java, at., Sol. Is.	D7	72
Liuba, China	E2	42
Liuboml', Ukr.	E20	16
Liuchen, China	J4	42
Liucheng, China	I3	42
Liuchow see Liuzhou, China	I3	42
Liucura, Chile	I2	92
Liufang, China	H7	42
Liuhe, China	C6	38
Liuheng Dao, i., China	G10	42
Liujiazi, China	A9	42
Liupan Shan, mts., China	D2	42
Liushuquan, China	F16	32
Liuxi, stm., China	J5	42
Liuyang, China	G5	42
Liuyang, stm., China	G5	42
Liuzhou, China	I3	42
Livada, Rom.	B10	26
Livadija, Russia	C10	38
Livanjsko Polje, val., Bos.	F3	26
Lively, On., Can.	B8	112
Lively Island, i., Falk. Is.	J5	90
Live Oak, Ca., U.S.	D4	134
Live Oak, Fl., U.S.	F2	116
Livermore, Austl.	C4	74
Livermore, Ca., U.S.	F4	134
Livermore, Ia., U.S.	B3	120
Livermore, Ky., U.S.	G10	120
Livermore, Mount, mtn., Tx., U.S.	D3	130
Livermore Falls, Me., U.S.	F6	110
Liverpool, N.S., Can.	F12	110
Liverpool, Eng., U.K.	H10	12
Liverpool, Cape, c., Nu., Can.	C10	141
Liverpool Bay, b., N.T., Can.	A5	106
Liverpool Bay, b., Eng., U.K.	H9	12
Livingston, Guat.	E3	102
Livingston, Al., U.S.	E10	122
Livingston, Il., U.S.	F8	120
Livingston, La., U.S.	G8	122
Livingston, Mt., U.S.	E16	136
Livingston, Tn., U.S.	H12	120
Livingston, Tx., U.S.	G4	122
Livingston, Wi., U.S.	B7	120
Livingston, Lake, res., Tx., U.S.	G3	122
Livingstone, Zam.	D4	68
Livingstone Falls, wtfl., Afr.	A1	68
Livingstonia, Mwi.	C5	68
Livingston Manor, N.Y., U.S.	C11	114
Livno, Bos.	F4	26
Livny, Russia	H20	10
Livonia, La., U.S.	G7	122
Livonia, Mi., U.S.	B2	114
Livonia, N.Y., U.S.	B8	114
Livorno (Leghorn), Italy	G7	22
Livramento do Brumado, Braz.	G5	88
Liwale, Tan.	F7	66
Lixi, China	G6	42
Lixian, China	G4	42
Lixian, China	D1	42
Lixian see Black, stm., Asia	D9	56
Lixin, China	E7	42
Lixouri, Grc.	E3	28
Liyang, China	F8	42
Lizarda, Braz.	E2	88
Lizard Point, c., Eng., U.K.	L7	12
Lizarra see Estella, Spain	B8	20
Ljady, Bela.	F14	10
Ljahavičy, Bela.	G9	10
Ljahovskie ostrova, is., Russia	B17	34
Ljamca, Russia	D17	8
Ljaskavičy, Bela.	H11	10
Ljasnaja, Bela.	H10	10
Ljuban', Bela.	H10	10
Ljuban', Russia	A14	10
Ljubercy, Russia	E20	10
Ljubim, Blg.	H12	26
Ljubljana, Slvn.	D11	22
Ljubnica, Russia	C15	10
Ljubohna, Russia	G17	10
Ljubuški, Bos.	F4	26
Ljudinovo, Russia	G17	10
Ljudkovo, Russia	F17	10
Ljungan, stm., Swe.	E6	8
Ljungby, Swe.	H5	8
Ljusdal, Swe.	F7	8
Ljusina, Bela.	H9	10
Ljusnan, stm., Swe.	F6	8
Llancanelo, Laguna, l., Arg.	G3	92
Llandeilo, Wales, U.K.	J8	12
Llandrindod Wells, Wales, U.K.	I9	12
Llandudno, Wales, U.K.	H9	12
Llanelli, Wales, U.K.	J8	12
Llangefni, Wales, U.K.	H8	12
Llanidloes, Wales, U.K.	I9	12
Llano, stm., Tx., U.S.	D8	130
Llano Colorado, Mex.	L9	134
Llanos, pl., S.A.	E7	86
Llanquihue, Lago, l., Chile	H2	90
Lleida, Spain	C11	20
Lleida, co., Spain	B12	20
Llera de Canales, Mex.	D9	100
Llerena, Spain	F4	20
Lleulleu, Lago, l., Chile	I1	92
Llico, Chile	G1	92
Lliria, Spain	E10	20
Llívia, Spain	B12	20
Llobregat, stm., Spain	C12	20
Lloydminster, Sk., Can.	E9	106
Llucena, Spain	D10	20
Lluchmayor see Llucmajor, Spain	E13	20
Llucmajor, Spain	E13	20
Llullaillaco, Volcán, vol., S.A.	B3	92
Lo (Panlong), stm., Asia	A7	48
Loa, Ut., U.S.	E5	132
Loa, stm., Chile	D3	90
Loanda, Braz.	D6	90
Loange (Luange), stm., Afr.	F3	66
Lobamba, Swaz.	E10	70
Lobanovo, Russia	G21	10
Lobatse, Bots.	D7	70
Löbau, Ger.	E10	16
Lobaye, stm., C.A.R.	D3	66
Lobelville, Tn., U.S.	B11	122
Loberia, Arg.	I8	92
Lobnja, Russia	D20	10
Lobos, Arg.	G8	92
Lobos, Cayo, i., Mex.	A9	102
Lobos, Isla, i., Mex.	B3	100
Lobskoe, Russia	E16	8
Łobżenica, Pol.	C13	16
Locarno, Switz.	D5	22
Loches, Fr.	G10	14
Loch Garman see Wexford, Ire.	I6	12
Lochinver, Scot., U.K.	C7	12
Lochsa, stm., Id., U.S.	D12	136
Lock, Austl.	F7	74
Lockeport, N.S., Can.	G11	110
Lockerbie, Scot., U.K.	F9	12
Lockesburg, Ar., U.S.	D4	122
Lockhart, Austl.	J6	76
Lock Haven, Pa., U.S.	C8	114
Lockney, Tx., U.S.	G7	128
Lockport, Il., U.S.	C9	120
Lockport, La., U.S.	H8	122
Lockport, N.Y., U.S.	E11	112
Lockwood, Mo., U.S.	G4	120
Locminé, Fr.	G6	14
Loc Ninh, Viet.	G8	48
Locust Creek, stm., U.S.	D4	120
Locust Fork, stm., Al., U.S.	D11	122
Locust Grove, Ok., U.S.	H2	120
Lod (Lydda), Isr.	G5	58
Lodalskåpa, mtn., Nor.	F2	8
Lodejnoe Pole, Russia	F15	8
Lodève, Fr.	F9	18
Lodge Creek, stm., N.A.	F4	124
Lodge Grass, Mt., U.S.	B5	126
Lodgepole, Ab., Can.	C15	138
Lodgepole, Ne., U.S.	F10	126
Lodgepole Creek, stm., U.S.	D3	54
Lodhran, Pak.	D3	54
Lodi, Italy	E6	22
Lodi, Ca., U.S.	E4	134
Lodi, Wi., U.S.	H9	118
Lodja, D.R.C.	E4	66
Lodwar, Kenya	D7	66
Łódź, Pol.	E15	16
Łódź, state, Pol.	E15	16
Loei, Thai.	D5	48
Loei, stm., Thai.	D5	48
Loeriesfontein, S. Afr.	G4	70
Lofer, Aus.	C9	22
Lofoten, is., Nor.	C5	8
Lofoten Basin, unds.	A14	144
Loga, Niger	G5	64
Logan, Ia., U.S.	C2	120
Logan, Ks., U.S.	B9	128
Logan, N.M., U.S.	E13	114
Logan, Ut., U.S.	B5	132
Logan, W.V., U.S.	G4	114
Logan, Mount, mtn., Yk., Can.	C2	106
Logan Creek, stm., Ne., U.S.	E15	126
Logan Island, i., On., Can.	A10	118
Logan Martin Lake, res., Al., U.S.	D12	122
Logan Mountains, mts., Yk., Can.	C5	106
Logan Pass, p., Mt., U.S.	B13	136
Logansport, In., U.S.	H3	112
Logansport, La., U.S.	F5	122
Loganville, Ga., U.S.	C2	116
Logroño, Spain	B8	20
Løgstør, Den.	H3	8
Logudoro, reg., Italy	D2	24
Lohārdaga, India	G10	54
Lohiniva, Fin.	C11	8
Lohne, Ger.	D4	16
Loho see Luohe, China	E6	42
Lohrville, Ia., U.S.	B3	120
Loi, Phang, mtn., Laos	B6	48
Loi-kaw, Mya.	C3	48
Loi Mwe, Mya.	B4	48
Loing, stm., Fr.	F11	14
Loing, Canal du, can., Fr.	F11	14
Loir, stm., Fr.	G8	14
Loire, state, Fr.	D10	18
Loire, stm., Fr.	B4	18
Loire, Canal latéral à la, can., Fr.	C9	18
Loire-Atlantique, state, Fr.	G7	14
Loiret, state, Fr.	F11	14
Loir-et-Cher, state, Fr.	G10	14
Loja, Ec.	D2	84
Loja, Spain	G6	20
Loja, co., Spain	G6	20
Lokan Reservoir see Lokan tekojärvi, res., Fin.	C12	8
Lokan tekojärvi, res., Fin.	C12	8
Lokeren, Bel.	C13	14
Loket, Czech Rep.	F8	16
Lokichar, Kenya	D7	66
Lokichokio, Kenya	D6	66
Loknja, Russia	D13	10
Lokoja, Nig.	H6	64
Lokolama, D.R.C.	E3	66
Lokot', Russia	H17	10
Loksa, Est.	A8	10
Loks Land, i., Nu., Can.	E13	141
Lola, Gui.	H3	64
Loleta, Ca., U.S.	C1	134
Loliondo, Tan.	E7	66
Lolita, Tx., U.S.	F11	130
Lolland, i., Den.	I4	8
Lolo, Ms., U.S.	D12	136
Lolodorf, Cam.	D2	66
Lolo Pass, p., U.S.	D12	136
Lolowai, Vanuatu	j16	79d
Loltong, Vanuatu	j16	79d
Lolvavana, Passage, strt., Vanuatu	j16	79d
Lom, Blg.	F10	26
Lom, Nor.	F3	8
Lom, stm., Afr.	F2	62
Lomami, stm., D.R.C.	D4	66
Lomas de Zamora, Arg.	G8	92
Lomax, Il., U.S.	D6	120
Lop Buri, Thai.	E5	48
Lombardia, state, Italy	E6	22
Lombardy see Lombardia, state, Italy	E6	22
Lomblen, Pulau, i., Indon.	G7	44
Lombok, Indon.	H10	50
Lombok, i., Indon.	H10	50
Lombok, Selat, strt., Indon.	H9	50
Lomé, Togo	H5	64
Lomela, D.R.C.	E4	66
Lomela, stm., D.R.C.	E4	66
Lometa, Tx., U.S.	C9	130
Lomié, Cam.	D2	66
Lomira, Wi., U.S.	H10	118
Lommel, Bel.	C14	14
Lomond, Loch, l., Scot., U.K.	E8	12
Lomonosov, Russia	A12	10
Lomonosovka, Kaz.	D11	32
Lomovoe, Russia	D19	8
Lompobatang, Gunung, mtn., Indon.	F11	50
Lompoc, Ca., U.S.	I5	134
Lom Sak, Thai.	D5	48
Łomża, Pol.	C18	16
Łomża, state, Pol.	C18	16
Lonaconing, Md., U.S.	E7	114
Lonāvale, India	B1	53
Loncoche, Chile	G2	90
Loncopué, Arg.	G2	90
London, On., Can.	F8	112
London, Eng., U.K.	J12	12
London, Ar., U.S.	B5	122
London, Ky., U.S.	G1	114
London, Tx., U.S.	D8	130
Londonderry, N.S., Can.	E13	110
Londonderry (Derry), N. Ire., U.K.	F6	12
Londonderry, Cape, c., Austl.	B5	74
Londonderry, Isla, i., Chile	K2	90
Londrina, Braz.	D6	90
Lone Grove, Ok., U.S.	G11	128
Lone Oak, Ky., U.S.	G9	120
Lone Pine, Ca., U.S.	G7	134
Lone Rock, Wi., U.S.	A7	120
Lone Tree, Ia., U.S.	C6	120
Lone Wolf, Ok., U.S.	G9	128
Long, stm., China	I3	42
Longa, Ang.	C2	68
Longá, stm., Braz.	B5	88
Longa, proliv, strt., Russia	B24	34
Long Akah, Malay.	B9	50
Longana, Vanuatu	j17	79d
Longarone, Italy	D9	22
Longavi, Chile	G2	92
Longbangun, Indon.	C9	50
Long Bay, b., U.S.	C7	116
Long Beach, Ca., U.S.	J7	134
Long Beach, Ms., U.S.	G9	122
Long Beach, N.Y., U.S.	D12	114
Long Beach, Wa., U.S.	D2	136
Long Beach, i., N.J., U.S.	E11	114
Longboat Key, Fl., U.S.	I3	116
Long Branch, N.J., U.S.	D12	114
Long Cay, i., Bah.	m18	104f
Longchang, China	G1	42
Longchuan, China	I6	42
Long Creek, stm., N.A.	E10	124
Longde, China	D2	42
Long Eaton, Eng., U.K.	I11	12
Longford, Austl.	L6	76
Longford, Ire.	H5	12
Longford, state, Ire.	H5	12
Long Hu, l., China	F6	42
Longhua, China	A7	42
Longhui, China	H4	42
Longiram, Indon.	C9	50
Long Island, i., Ang.	f4	105b
Long Island, i., Austl.	D7	76
Long Island, i., Bah.	A10	102
Long Island, i., N.S., Can.	F10	110
Long Island, i., Nu., Can.	E14	106
Long Island, i., N.Y., U.S.	D12	114
Long Island Sound, strt., U.S.	D12	114
Longitudinal, Valle, val., Chile	H1	92
Longjiang, China	B9	36
Longkou, China	C9	42
Long Lake, N.Y., U.S.	G2	110
Long Lake, l., On., U.S.	B11	118
Longleaf, La., U.S.	F6	122
Long Leaf Park, N.C., U.S.	B8	116
Longli, China	H2	42
Longlin, China	G6	36
Longling, China	G4	36
Longmeadow, Ma., U.S.	B13	114
Longmont, Co., U.S.	A3	128
Long Mountain, mtn., Mo., U.S.	H5	120
Longnan, China	I6	42
Longnawan, Indon.	C9	50
Long Pine, Ne., U.S.	E13	126
Long Point, c., Bah.	n18	104f
Long Point, c., On., Can.	F14	112
Long Point, pen., Mb., Can.	A15	124
Long Point, pen., On., Can.	F9	112
Longquan, China	G8	42
Long Range Mountains, mts., Nf., Can.	j22	107a
Longreach, Austl.	D5	76
Longsegah, Indon.	B10	50
Longshan, China	G3	42
Longsheng, China	I4	42
Longs Peak, mtn., Co., U.S.	A3	128
Long Swamp, Br. Vir. Is.	e8	104b
Long Thanh, Viet.	G8	48
Longton, Ks., U.S.	G12	128
Longtown, Eng., U.K.	F10	12
Longueuil, Qc., Can.	E3	110
Longuyon, Fr.	E14	14
Longview, Ab., Can.	F16	138
Long View, N.C., U.S.	A4	116
Longview, Tx., U.S.	E4	122
Longview, Wa., U.S.	D4	136
Longwai, Indon.	C10	50
Longwy, Fr.	E14	14
Longxi, China	E5	36
Longxian, China	D2	42
Long Xuyen, Viet.	G7	48
Longyan, China	I7	42
Longyou, China	G8	42
Longzhen, China	B10	36
Longzhou, China	J2	42
Lonigo, Italy	E8	22
Löningen, Ger.	D3	16
Lonoke, Ar., U.S.	C7	122
Lonquimay, Volcán, vol., Chile	I2	92
Lons-le-Saunier, Fr.	H14	14
Lontra, stm., Braz.	D1	88
Loogootee, In., U.S.	F11	120
Lookout, Cape, c., N.C., U.S.	B9	116
Lookout Mountain, mts., U.S.	C13	122
Lookout Pass, p., U.S.	C11	136
Lookout Ridge, mts., Ak., U.S.	C8	140
Loolmalassie, vol., Tan.	E7	66
Loomis, Ne., U.S.	G13	126
Loomis, Wa., U.S.	B7	136
Loop Head, c., Ire.	I2	12
Lop, China	A5	46
Lop, stm., Viet.	F8	48
Lopatina, gora, mtn., Russia	F17	34
Lopatka, mys, c., Russia	F20	34
Lopatovo, Russia	D12	10
Lopburi see Lop Buri, Thai.	E5	48
Lopévi, i., Vanuatu	k17	79d
Lopez, Cap, c., Gabon	E1	66
Lop Nur, l., China	C3	36
Loptjuga, Russia	E22	8
Lora, Hámún-i-, l., Asia	D9	56
Lora del Rio, Spain	G5	20
Lorain, Oh., U.S.	C3	114
Loraine, Tx., U.S.	B7	130
Loralai, Pak.	C2	54
Lorca, Spain	G9	20
Lord Howe Island, i., Austl.	G6	72
Lord Howe Rise, unds.	L19	142
Lord Mayor Bay, b., Nu., Can.	B12	106
Lordsburg, N.M., U.S.	K8	132
Loreauville, La., U.S.	G7	122
Loreley, misc. cult., Ger.	F3	16
Lorena, Braz.	L3	88
Lorengau, Pap. N. Gui.	a4	79a
Lorenzo, Tx., U.S.	H7	128
Lorenzo Geyres, Ur.	F9	92
Loreto, Arg.	C9	92
Loreto, Mex.	D8	100
Loreto, Mex.	B3	100
Loreto, state, Peru	H4	86
Loreto, Italy	G10	22
Loretto, Ky., U.S.	G12	120
Loretto, Tn., U.S.	B11	122
Lorica, Col.	C4	86
Lorient, Fr.	G5	14
Lorimor, Ia., U.S.	C3	120
Loriol-sur-Drôme, Fr.	E10	18
Loris, S.C., U.S.	B7	116
Lorman, Ms., U.S.	F7	122
Lorn, Firth of, b., Scot., U.K.	E7	12
Lorne, Austl.	L5	76
Lorne, N.B., Can.	C10	110
Lorraine, hist. reg., Fr.	F14	14
Lorraine, state, Fr.	E14	14
Los, Îles de, is., Gui.	H2	64
Losada, stm., Col.	F4	86
Los Alamos, N.M., U.S.	F2	128
Los Aldamas, Mex.	B9	100
Los Andes, Chile	F2	92
Los Angeles, Chile	H1	92
Los Angeles, Ca., U.S.	I7	134
Los Angeles Aqueduct, aq., Ca., U.S.	H7	134
Los Antiguos, Arg.	I2	90
Los Banos, Ca., U.S.	F5	134
Los Blancos, Arg.	D4	90
Los Bolones, Cerro, mtn., Mex.	G12	100
Los Cerrillos, Arg.	E5	92
Los Conquistadores, Arg.	E8	92
Los Fresnos, Tx., U.S.	H10	130
Los Garza, Mex.	H8	130
Los Gatos, Ca., U.S.	F4	134
Loshan see Leshan, China	F5	36
Los Hermanos, Islas, is., Ven.	B9	86
Los Juries, Arg.	D6	92
Los Lagos, Chile	G2	90
Los Llanos, P.R.	B3	104a
Los López, Mex.	H8	130
Los Lunas, N.M., U.S.	I10	132
Los Mochis, Mex.	C4	100
Los Nogales, Mex.	F5	98
Los Palacios, Cuba	A6	102
Los Palacios y Villafranca, Spain	G4	20
Los Picachos, Parque Nacional, p.o.i., Col.	F4	86
Los Ríos, state, Ec.	H2	86
Los Roques, Islas, is., Ven.	B8	86
Los Sauces, Chile	H1	92
Lossiemouth, Scot., U.K.	D9	12
Lost, stm., U.S.	A4	134
Los Taques, Ven.	B6	86
Los Teques, Ven.	B8	86
Los Testigos, Islas, is., Ven.	B10	86
Lost Hills, Ca., U.S.	H6	134
Lost Nation, Ia., U.S.	C7	120
Lost River Range, mts., Id., U.S.	F13	136
Lost Trails Pass, p., U.S.	E13	136
Losua, Pap. N. Gui.	b5	79a
Los Vidrios, Mex.	F6	98
Los Vilos, Chile	E2	92
Los Yébenes, Spain	E7	20
Lot, stm., Fr.	E7	18
Lot, state, Fr.	E7	18
Lot-et-Garonne, state, Fr.	E6	18
Lothair, S. Afr.	E10	70
Lotošino, Russia	D18	10
Lotsane, stm., Bots.	C8	70
Lotta, stm., Eur.	B13	8
Lotukei, Jabal, mtn., Sudan	G6	62
Lotung, Tai.	I9	42
Louang Namtha, Laos	B5	48
Louangphrabang, Laos	C5	48
Louangphrabang, Laos	C6	48
Loudéac, Fr.	F6	14
Loudon, Tn., U.S.	A1	116
Loudonville, Oh., U.S.	D3	114
Loudun, Fr.	G9	14
Loue, stm., Fr.	G15	14
Louga, Sen.	F1	64
Loughborough, Eng., U.K.	I11	12
Loughrea, Ire.	H4	12
Louhans, Fr.	H14	14
Louin, Ms., U.S.	E9	122
Louisa, Ky., U.S.	F3	114
Louisbourg, N.S., Can.	E16	110
Louisburg, N.C., U.S.	H7	114
Louisdale, N.S., Can.	E15	110
Louise, Lake, l., Ak., U.S.	D10	140
Louiseville, Qc., Can.	D3	110
Louisiade Archipelago, is., Pap. N. Gui.	B10	74
Louisiana, Mn., U.S.	E6	120
Louisiana, state, U.S.	F6	122
Louis Trichardt, S. Afr.	C9	70
Louisville, Al., U.S.	F13	122
Louisville, Ga., U.S.	C3	116
Louisville, Ky., U.S.	F12	120
Louisville, Ne., U.S.	D1	120
Louisville, Oh., U.S.	D4	114
Louisville Ridge, unds.	M22	142
Louis-XIV, Pointe, c., Qc., Can.	E14	106
Loulé, Port.	G2	20
Loum, Cam.	D1	66
Louny, Czech Rep.	F9	16
Loup, stm., Ne., U.S.	F14	126
Loup City, Ne., U.S.	F14	126
Loups Marins, Lacs des, l., Qc., Can.	D16	106
Lourdes, Fr.	F5	18
Lourenço Marques see Maputo, Moz.	D11	70
Lourinhã, Port.	E1	20
Lousã, Port.	D2	20
Louth, Austl.	H5	76
Louth, Eng., U.K.	H12	12
Louth, Ire.	H6	12
Louth, state, Ire.	H6	12
Loutrá Aidipsoú, Grc.	E6	28
Louvain see Leuven, Bel.	D13	14
Louviers, Fr.	E10	14
Lovat', stm., Russia	B14	10
Loveč, Blg.	F11	26
Loveč, state, Blg.	F11	26
Loveland, Co., U.S.	G7	126
Lovell, Wy., U.S.	C4	126
Lovell Village, St. Vin.	p11	105e
Lovelock, Nv., U.S.	C7	134
Lovely, Ky., U.S.	G3	114
Lovere, Italy	E6	22
Lovington, Va., U.S.	G7	114
Lovington, N.M., U.S.	B4	130
Lovosice, Czech Rep.	F9	16
Lovozero, Russia	D13	8
Lovozero, ozero, l., Russia	C16	8
Lovua, Ang.	C3	68
Low, Qc., Can.	C14	112
Low, Cape, c., Nu., Can.	C13	106
Lowa, D.R.C.	E5	66
Lowa, stm., D.R.C.	E5	66
Lowden, Ia., U.S.	C7	120
Lowell, Ar., U.S.	H3	120
Lowell, In., U.S.	G2	112
Lowell, Ma., U.S.	B14	114
Lowell, Mi., U.S.	F4	112
Lowell, Oh., U.S.	E4	114
Lowell, Or., U.S.	G4	136
Lowell, Lake, res., Id., U.S.	G10	136
Löwenberg, Ger.	D8	16
Lower Arrow Lake, res., B.C., Can.	G12	138
Lower Austria see Niederösterreich, state, Aus.	B12	22
Lower California see Baja California, pen., Mex.	B2	96
Lower Egypt see Misr el-Bahri, hist. reg., Egypt	G2	58
Lower Glenelg National Park, p.o.i., Austl.	L3	76
Lower Hutt, N.Z.	E6	80
Lower Lake, l., U.S.	B5	134
Lower Manitou Lake, l., On., Can.	B6	118
Lower Post, B.C., Can.	D5	106
Lower Red Lake, l., Mn., U.S.	D3	118
Lower Saxony see Niedersachsen, state, Ger.	D4	16
Lower Trajan's Wall, misc. cult., Eur.	D15	26
Lower West End Point, c., Anguilla	A1	105a
Lower Woods Harbour, N.S., Can.	G10	110
Lowestoft, Eng., U.K.	I14	12
Lowgar, state, Afg.	A2	54
Łowicz, Pol.	D15	16
Lowman, Id., U.S.	F11	136
Lowmoor, Va., U.S.	G6	114
Lowry City, Mo., U.S.	F4	120
Lowville, N.Y., U.S.	E14	112
Loxton, Austl.	J3	76
Loyal, Wi., U.S.	G8	118
Loyalty Islands see Loyauté, Îles, is., N. Cal.	m16	79d
Loyauté, Îles (Loyalty Islands), is., N. Cal.	m16	79d
Loyoro, Ug.	D6	66
Lozère, state, Fr.	E9	18
Loznica, Serb.	E6	26
Lualaba, stm., D.R.C.	F5	66
Luama, stm., D.R.C.	E5	66
Lu'an, China	F7	42
Luancheng, China	J3	42
Luanco, Spain	A5	20
Luanda, Ang.	B1	68
Luando, stm., Ang.	C2	68
Luang, Khao (Mao Taung), mtn., Asia	H4	48
Luang, Thale, l., Thai.	I5	48
Luang Dang Dao, Doi, mtn., Thai.	C4	48
Luang Prabang see Louangphrabang, Laos	C6	48
Luanguinga (Loangue), stm., Afr.	F3	66
Luangwa, stm., Afr.	C5	68
Luanping, China	A7	42
Luan Toro, Arg.	H5	92
Luanxian, China	B8	42
Luapula, stm., Afr.	C5	68
Luar, Danau, l., Indon.	C7	50
Luarca, Spain	A4	20
Luba, Eq. Gui.	I6	64
Lubaantun, sci., Belize	D3	102
Lubāna, Lat.	D9	10
Lubang Islands, is., Phil.	D2	52
Lubango, Ang.	D1	68
Lubans, l., Lat.	D9	10
Lubao, D.R.C.	E4	66
Lubartów, Pol.	E18	16
Lubawa, Pol.	C15	16
Lübben, Ger.	E9	16
Lübbenau, Ger.	E9	16
Lübeck, Ger.	C6	16
Lubefu, D.R.C.	E4	66
Lubei, China	C8	42
Lubero, D.R.C.	D5	66
Lubień Kujawski, Pol.	D15	16
Lubilash, D.R.C.	F4	66
Lubin, Pol.	E12	16
Lublin, Pol.	E18	16
Lublin, state, Pol.	E18	16
Lubliniec, Pol.	F14	16
Lubny, Ukr.	D4	32
Lubok Antu, Malay.	C7	50
Lubsko, Pol.	E10	16
Lubudi, D.R.C.	F5	66
Lubuagan, Phil.	B3	52
Lubudi, stm., D.R.C.	F5	66
Lubuklinggau, Indon.	E3	50
Lubukpakam, Indon.	B1	50
Lubuksikaping, Indon.	C1	50
Lubumbashi (Elisabethville), D.R.C.	G5	66
Lubutu, D.R.C.	E5	66
Lübz, Ger.	C7	16
Lucala, stm., Ang.	B2	68
Lucania, hist. reg., Italy	D10	24
Lucania, Mount, mtn., Yk., Can.	C3	106
Lucapa, Ang.	B3	68
Lucas, Ia., U.S.	C4	120
Lucas, Ks., U.S.	B10	128
Lucban, Phil.	C3	52
Lucca, Italy	G7	22
Luce, Bay of, b., Scot., U.K.	G8	12
Lucedale, Ms., U.S.	G10	122
Lucena, Phil.	D3	52
Lucena, Spain	G6	20
Lucena del Cid see Llucena, Spain	D10	20
Lučenec, Slov.	H15	16
Lucera, Italy	C9	24
Lucerne see Luzern, Switz.	C5	22
Lucerne, La., U.S.	D3	134
Lucerne, Lake of see Vierwaldstätter See, l., Switz.	D5	22
Luchou see Luzhou, China	G1	42
Luchow see Luzhou, China	G1	42
Luckau, Ger.	E9	16
Luckenwalde, Ger.	D9	16
Luckhoff, S. Afr.	F7	70
Luck Lake, l., Sk., Can.	C6	124
Lucknow, India	E8	54
Lucknow, On., Can.	E8	112
Lucky Lake, Sk., Can.	C6	124
Luçon, Fr.	C4	18
Lucusse, Ang.	C3	68
Luda Kamčija, stm., Blg.	G14	26
Ludao, China	C8	38
Lüdenscheid, Ger.	E3	16
Lüderitz, Nmb.	E2	70
Ludhiāna, India	C5	54
Ludian, China	F5	36
Ludington, Mi., U.S.	E3	112
Ludlow, Eng., U.K.	I10	12
Ludlow, Ca., U.S.	H9	134
Ludogorie, reg., Blg.	F13	26
Ludowici, Ga., U.S.	E4	116
Ludvika, Swe.	F6	8
Ludwigsburg, Ger.	H5	16
Ludwigsfelde, Ger.	D9	16
Ludwigshafen am Rhein, Ger.	G4	16
Ludwigslust, Ger.	C7	16
Ludza, Lat.	D10	10
Luena, Ang.	C3	68
Luena, D.R.C.	F5	66
Luena, stm., Ang.	C3	68
Luepa, Ven.	E11	86
Lueyang, China	E2	42
Lufeng, China	J5	42
Lufira, stm., D.R.C.	F5	66
Lufkin, Tx., U.S.	F4	122
Luga, Russia	B12	10
Luga, stm., Russia	A11	10
Lugano, Switz.	D5	22
Lugano, Lago di, l., Eur.	D5	22
Luganville, Vanuatu	j16	79d
Lugenda, stm., Moz.	C6	68
Luggarus see Locarno, Switz.	D5	22
Lugnaquillia Mountain, mtn., Ire.	I6	12
Lugo, Italy	F8	22
Lugo, Spain	A3	20
Lugo, co., Spain	B3	20
Lugoj, Rom.	D8	26
Lugovskij, Russia	E11	34
Luhans'k, Ukr.	E5	32
Luhe, China	E8	42
Luhovicy, Russia	F21	10
Luhsien see Luzhou, China	G1	42
Luido, Moz.	B12	70
Luik see Liège, Bel.	D14	14
Luimneach see Limerick, Ire.	I4	12
Luino, Italy	D5	22
Luis L. León, Presa, res., Mex.	F2	130
Luís Muñoz Marín, Aeropuerto Internacional, P.R.	B3	104a
Luitpold Coast, cst., Ant.	C1	81
Luiza, D.R.C.	F4	66
Luján, Arg.	F4	92
Luján de Cuyo, Arg.	F3	92
Lujiang, China	F7	42
Lukang, Tai.	I9	42
Lukenie, stm., D.R.C.	E3	66
Lukeville, Az., U.S.	L4	132
Lukojanov, Russia	I21	8
Lukolela, D.R.C.	E3	66
Lukovit, Blg.	F11	26
Lukov, Pol.	E18	16
Łuków, Pol.	E18	16
Lukuga, stm., D.R.C.	F5	66
Lukula, D.R.C.	F2	66
Lukulu, Zam.	C3	68
Lukulu, stm., D.R.C.	F6	66
Luleå, Swe.	D10	8
Luleälven, stm., Swe.	C8	8
Lüleburgaz, Tur.	C10	28
Luliang, China	G5	36
Lüliang Shan, mts., China	C4	42
Luling, Tx., U.S.	E10	130
Lulong, China	B8	42
Lulua, stm., D.R.C.	F4	66
Luluabourg see Kananga, D.R.C.	F4	66
Lumajang, Indon.	H8	50
Lumajangdong Co, l., China	B8	54
Lumaku, Gunong, mtn., Malay.	A9	50
Lumana, D.R.C.	E5	66
Lumbala Kaquengue, Ang.	C4	68
Lumbala N'guimbo, Ang.	C3	68
Lumber, stm., U.S.	B6	116
Lumber City, Ga., U.S.	E3	116
Lumberton, N.C., U.S.	B7	116
Lumberton, W.V., U.S.	E5	114
Lumbis, Indon.	A10	50
Lumbrales, Spain	D4	20
Lumby, B.C., Can.	F11	138
Lumding, India	E14	54
Lumphat, Camb.	F8	48
Lumpkin, Ga., U.S.	E14	122
Lumsden, N.Z.	G3	80
Lumut, Malay.	J5	48
Lumut, Tanjung, c., Indon.	E4	50
Luna Pier, Mi., U.S.	C2	114
Lund, Swe.	I5	8
Lund, B.C., Can.	G6	138
Lund, Nv., U.S.	E2	132
Lundazi, Zam.	C5	68
Lundu, Malay.	C6	50
Lundy, i., Eng., U.K.	J8	12
Lüneburg, Ger.	C6	16
Lüneburger Heide, reg., Ger.	D6	16
Lunel, Fr.	F10	18
Lünen, Ger.	E3	16
Lunenburg, N.S., Can.	F12	110
Lunenburg, Va., U.S.	H7	114
Lunéville, Fr.	F15	14
Lunga, stm., Zam.	C4	68
Lungchi see Zhangzhou, China	I7	42
Lungch'üan see Longquan, China	G8	42
Lungleh, India	G14	54
Lungnak'o, China	C10	54
Lungtsin see Longzhou, China	J2	42
Lungué-Bungo (Lungwebungu), stm., Afr.	C3	68

Name	Map Ref.	Page

Lungwebungu (Lungué-Bungo), stm., Afr. C3 68
Lûni, India E4 54
Lûni, stm., India F4 54
Luninec, Bela. H9 10
Luninets see Luninec, Bela. H9 10
Lünkaransar, India D4 54
Luntai, China F14 32
Luo, stm., China D4 42
Luo, stm., China D4 42
Luobei, China B11 36
Luobu, China I3 42
Lucheng, China I3 42
Luoding, China J4 42
Luofu, D.R.C. E5 66
Luohe, China E6 42
Luoji, China E7 42
Luonan, China D4 42
Luoning, China D4 42
Luoqi, China G2 42
Luotian, China F6 42
Luowenba, China F2 42
Luoxiao Shan, mts., China .. H6 42
Luoyang, China D5 42
Luoyuan, China H8 42
Luozi, D.R.C. F2 66
Lupanshui, China F5 36
Lupar, stm., Malay. C7 50
Lupawa, Pol. B13 16
Lupeni, Rom. D10 26
Lupin see Manzhouli, China. B8 36
Luputa, D.R.C. F4 66
Luqiao, China E7 42
Luqiao, China G9 42
Luqu, China E5 36
Luque, Spain G6 20
Luquillo, P.R. B4 104a
Lure, Fr. G15 14
Luremo, Ang. B2 68
Lurgan, N. Ire., U.K. G6 12
Luribay, Bol. C3 90
Lurin, Peru F2 84
Lúrio, Moz. C7 68
Lúrio, stm., Moz. C6 68
Lusaka, Zam. D4 68
Lusambo, D.R.C. E4 66
Lusanga, D.R.C. E3 66
Lusangi, D.R.C. E5 66
Luscar, Ab., Can. C13 138
Luseland, Sk., Can. B4 124
Lushan, China E5 42
Lu Shan, mtn., China. G6 42
Lushnja see Lushnjë, Alb... D13 24
Lushnjë, Alb. D13 24
Lushoto, Tan. E7 66
Lüshun (Port Arthur), China . E4 38
Lusk, Wy., U.S. E8 126
Lussac-les-Châteaux, Fr.... C6 18
Lüt, Dasht-e, des., Iran C8 56
Lu-ta see Dalian, China E4 38
Lü Tao, i., Tai. J9 42
Lutembo, Ang. C3 68
Lutesville, Mo., U.S. G7 120
Luther, Ok., U.S. D4 112
Luther, Ok., U.S. F11 128
Lutherstadt Eisleben, Ger... E7 16
Lutherstadt Wittenberg, Ger. E8 16
Luti, Sol. Is. d7 79b
Luton, Eng., U.K. J12 12
Lutong, Malay. A8 50
ŀutselk'e, N.T., Can. C8 106
Lutz, Fl., U.S. H3 116
Lützow, Ger. C7 16
Lützow-Holm Bay, b., Ant. ... B8 81
Luuq, Som. D8 66
Luverne, Al., U.S. F12 122
Lu Verne, Ia., U.S. I4 118
Luverne, Mn., U.S. H2 118
Luvua, stm., D.R.C. F5 66
Luvuvhu, stm., S. Afr. C10 70
Luwegu, stm., Tan. F7 66
Luwingu, Zam. C4 68
Luwuk, Indon. F7 44
Luxapallila Creek, stm., U.S. . D11 122
Luxembourg, Lux. E14 14
Luxembourg, ctry., Eur. E15 14
Luxemburg, Wi., U.S. D2 112
Luxeuil-les-Bains, Fr. G15 14
Luxi, China C4 36
Luxor see El-Uqsor, Egypt ... B6 62
Luz, Braz. J3 88
Luza, Braz. F22 8
Luza, Russia A14 10
Luzern (Lucerne), Switz.... C5 22
Luzhai, China I3 42
Luzhou, China G1 42
Luziânia, Braz. I2 88
Luzilândia, Braz. B4 88
Lužki, Bela. E10 10
Luźnice, stm., Eur. G10 16
Luzon, i., Phil. B3 52
Luzon Strait, strt., Asia G16 30
L'viv, Ukr. F13 6
L'viv, co., Ukr. G19 16
L'vovskij, Russia E20 10
Lwówek, Pol. D12 16
Lyallpur see Faisalabad, Pak. .. C4 54
Lyckovo, Russia C15 10
Lycksele, Swe. D8 8
Lydenburg, S. Afr. D10 70
Lydia Mills, S.C., U.S. B3 116
Lyell, Mount, mtn., Can.... E13 138
Lyerly, Ga., U.S. C13 122
Lyford, Tx., U.S. H10 130
Lykošino, Russia B16 10
Lyle, Mn., U.S. H6 118
Lyman, Ne., U.S. F1 126
Lyman, S.C., U.S. B3 116
Lymans'ke, Ukr. C17 26
Lyme Bay, b., Eng., U.K.... K9 12
ŀyna (Lava), stm., Eur..... B16 16
Lynch, Ne., U.S. E14 126
Lynchburg, Oh., U.S. E2 114
Lynchburg, S.C., U.S. B5 116
Lynchburg, Tn., U.S. B12 122
Lynchburg, Va., U.S. G6 114
Lynd, stm., Austl. A4 76
Lynden, Wa., U.S. B4 136
Lyndhurst, Austl. B5 76
Lyndon, Ks., U.S. F2 120
Lyndon, Ky., U.S. F12 120
Lyndon, stm., Austl. D2 74
Lyndon B. Johnson, Lake, res., Tx., U.S. D9 130
Lyndon B. Johnson Space Center, sci., Tx., U.S. H3 122
Lyngen, b., Nor. B9 8
Lyngseidet, Nor. B9 8
Lynn, Al., U.S. C11 122
Lynn, Ma., U.S. B14 114
Lynndyl, Ut., U.S. D4 132
Lynn Haven, Fl., U.S. G13 122
Lynn Lake, Mb., U.S. D10 106
Lyntupy, Bela. E9 10
Lynx Lake, l., N.T., Can..... C9 106
Lyon, Fr. D10 18
Lyon Inlet, b., Nu., Can..... B14 106
Lyon Mountain, N.Y., U.S. .. F2 110
Lyonnais, hist. reg., Fr..... D10 18
Lyons, In., U.S. F10 120
Lyons, Ks., U.S. C10 128
Lyons, Mi., U.S. F5 112
Lyons, Ne., U.S. C1 120
Lyons, N.Y., U.S. E13 112
Lyons, stm., Austl. D3 74
Lysa Hora, Ukr. A18 26
Łysica, mtn., Pol. F16 16
Lyskovo, Russia H21 8
Lys'va, Russia C9 32
Lysychans'k, Ukr. E5 32
Lytham Saint Anne's, Eng., U.K. H9 12
Lytle, Tx., U.S. E9 130

M

Ma, stm., Asia C7 48
Ma'ān, Jord. H6 58
Ma'ān, state, Jord. H7 58
Ma'anshan, China F8 42
Maardu, Est. G11 8
Maarianhamina see Mariehamn, Fin. F9 8
Ma'arrat an-Nu'mān, Syria ... C7 58
Maas (Meuse), stm., Eur..... D14 14
Maasin, Phil. E5 52
Maastricht, Neth. D14 14
Mabalane, Moz. C11 70
Mabank, Tx., U.S. E2 122
Mabaruma, Guy. C12 86
Mabel Lake, l., B.C., Can. ... F12 138
Maben, Ms., U.S. D9 122
Mablethorpe, Eng., U.K..... H13 12
Mableton, Ga., U.S. D14 122
Mabton, Wa., U.S. D6 136
Mabuasehube Game Reserve, Bots. D6 70
Maca, Russia E12 34
Maca, Cerro, vol., Chile H2 90
Macachín, Arg. H6 92
Macaé, Braz. L5 88
Macaíba, Braz. C8 88
Macajuba, Braz. G5 88
Macalister, B.C., Can. D8 138
Macalister, stm., Austl. K6 76
Macalister, Mount, mtn., Austl. J7 76
MacAlpine Lake, l., Nu., Can. B10 106
Macan, Kepulauan, is., Indon. G12 50
Macapá, Braz. C7 84
Macará, Ec. D2 84
Macareo, Caño, stm., Ven... C11 86
MacArthur, Phil. E5 52
Macas, Ec. I2 86
Macau, Braz. C7 88
Macau see Aomen, China ... J5 42
Macaúbas, Braz. G4 88
McClenny, Fl., U.S. F3 116
Macclesfield, Eng., U.K..... H10 12
Macdhui, Ben, mtn., Afr. G9 70
MacDonald Lake, l., Austl.... D5 74
MacDonald Pass, p., Mt., U.S. D14 136
MacDonnell Ranges, mts., Austl. D6 74
Macdui, Ben, mtn., Scot., U.K. D9 12
Macedonia, ctry., Eur. B4 28
Macedonia, hist. reg., Eur.... H10 26
Maceió, Braz. E8 88
Macenta, Gui. H3 64
Maceo, Col. D4 86
Macerata, Italy G10 22
MacFarlane, stm., Sk., Can. . D9 106
Macgillycuddy's Reeks, mts., Ire. J3 12
McGregor, Mb., Can. D15 124
Machado, Braz. K3 88
Machado, stm., Braz. F5 84
Machagai, Arg. C7 92
Machaila, Moz. C11 70
Machakos, Kenya E7 66
Machala, Ec. D2 84
Machalí, Chile G2 92
Machalilla, Parque Nacional, p.o.i., Ec. H1 86
Machanga, Moz. B12 70
Machaquilá, stm., Guat..... D3 102
Machattie, Lake, l., Austl..... E2 76
Machaze, Moz. B11 70
Macheng, China F6 42
Macherla, India C4 53
Machias, Me., U.S. F9 110
Machilipatnam (Bandar), India C5 53
Machiques, Ven. B5 86
Machkund, res., India B6 53
Macho, Arroyo del, stm., N.M., U.S. H4 128
Machu Picchu, sci., Peru F3 84
Machupicchu, sci., Peru F3 84
Macía, Arg. F8 92
Macia, Moz. D11 70
Măcin, Rom. D15 26
Macintyre, stm., Austl. G7 76
Mackay, Austl. C7 76
Mackay, Id., U.S. G13 136
Mackay, Lake, l., Austl..... D5 74
MacKay Lake, l., N.T., Can. . C8 106
Mackenzie, stm., Austl..... D7 76
Mackenzie, stm., N.T., Can. . B4 106
Mackenzie Bay, b., Can..... C12 140
Mackenzie King Island, i., Can. B3 141
Mackenzie Mountains, mts., Can. C4 106
Mackinac, Straits of, strt., Mi., U.S. C4 112
Mackinac Bridge, Mi., U.S. .. C5 112
Mackinac Island, Mi., U.S. .. C5 112
Mackinaw, stm., Il., U.S. D9 120
Mackinaw City, Mi., U.S. C5 112
Macklin, Sk., Can. B4 124
Macksville, Austl. H9 76
Macksville, Ks., U.S. C9 128
Maclean, Austl. G9 76
Maclear, S. Afr. G9 70
Macleay, stm., Austl. H9 76
Macleod, Lake, l., Austl..... D2 74
Macmillan, stm., Yk., Can. .. C4 106
Macomb, Il., U.S. D7 120
Macomer, Italy D2 24
Mâcon, Fr. C10 18
Macon, Ga., U.S. D2 116
Macon, Il., U.S. E9 120
Macon, Mo., U.S. E5 120
Macon, Ms., U.S. D10 122
Macon, Bayou, stm., U.S. ... E7 122
Macoris, Cabo, c., Dom. Rep. C12 102
Macoupin Creek, stm., Il., U.S. E8 120
Macovane, Moz. B12 70
Macquarie, stm., Austl. H6 76
Macquarie, Lake, l., Austl.... I8 76
Macquarie Harbour, b., Austl. o12 77a
Macquarie Island, i., Austl... A20 81
Macquarie Marshes, sw., Austl. H6 76
Macquarie Ridge, unds. I18 142
Mac. Robertson Land, reg., Ant. B10 81
Macucuaui, stm., Braz. H11 86
Macugnaga, Italy E4 22
Macumba, stm., Austl. E7 76
Macuro, Ven. B10 86
Macusani, Peru F3 84
Macuspana, Mex. G12 100
Mad, stm., Ca., U.S. C2 134
Madaba, Jord. G6 58
Madadi, Chad D4 62
Madagascar, ctry., Afr..... D8 68
Madagascar Basin, unds.... L8 142
Madagascar Plateau, unds... M7 142
Madan, Blg. H11 26
Madanapalle, India E4 53
Madang, Pap. N. Gui. b4 79a
Madaoua, Niger G6 64
Mādārīpur, Bngl. G13 54
Madawaska, Me., U.S. C8 110

Madawaska, stm., On., Can. . C13 112
Madawaska Highlands, plat., On., Can. C12 112
Maduale Lake, l., Nu., Can. .. C12 106
Madaya, Mya. A3 48
Maddalena, Isola, i., Italy C3 24
Maddaloni, Italy C8 24
Maddock, N.D., U.S. G14 124
Madeira, i., Port. C1 64
Madeira, stm., S.A. E5 84
Madeira, Arquipélago de (Madeira Islands), is., Port. . C1 64
Madeira Islands see Madeira, Arquipélago da, is., Port. C1 64
Mädelegabel, mtn., Eur..... I6 16
Madeleine Range, mts., India . C2 53
Madeleine, Îles de la, is., Qc., Can. C15 110
Madeleine-Centre, Qc., Can. . A11 110
Madeline Island, i., Wi., U.S. . E8 118
Madera, Mex. A4 100
Madera, Ca., U.S. G5 134
Madera see Madeira, stm., S.A. E5 84
Madgaon, India D1 53
Madhepura, India F11 54
Madhubani, India E10 54
Madhugiri, India E3 53
Madhupur, India F11 54
Madhya Pradesh, state, India D4 46
Madibogo, S. Afr. E7 70
Madida, China C9 38
Madidi, stm., Bol. B3 90
Madill, Ok., U.S. C2 122
Madimba, D.R.C. E3 66
Madinat ash-Sha'b, Yemen .. G5 56
Madingo-Kayes, Congo E2 66
Madingou, Congo E2 66
Madirovalo, Madag. D8 68
Madison, Al., U.S. C12 122
Madison, Fl., U.S. F2 116
Madison, Ga., U.S. C2 116
Madison, In., U.S. F12 120
Madison, Me., U.S. F6 110
Madison, Mn., U.S. F2 118
Madison, N.C., U.S. H5 114
Madison, Ne., U.S. F15 126
Madison, S.D., U.S. C15 126
Madison, Wi., U.S. A8 120
Madison, W.V., U.S. F4 114
Madison Heights, Va., U.S. ... G6 114
Madison Range, mts., Mt., U.S. E15 136
Madisonville, Ky., U.S. G10 120
Madisonville, La., U.S. G8 122
Madisonville, Tn., U.S. A1 116
Madisonville, Tx., U.S. G2 122
Madiun, Indon. G7 50
Madiyi, China G4 42
Mado Gashi, Kenya D7 66
Madoi, China E4 36
Madona, Lat. D9 10
Madras see Chennai, India ... E5 53
Madras, Or., U.S. F5 136
Madre, Laguna, b., Mex..... C10 100
Madre, Laguna, b., Tx., U.S. . H10 130
Madre, Sierra, mts., Phil..... B3 52
Madre de Chiapas, Sierra, mts., N.A. G12 100
Madre de Dios, Isla, i., Chile J1 90
Madre del Sur, Sierra, mts., Mex. G9 100
Madre Occidental, Sierra, mts., Mex. B3 96
Madre Oriental, Sierra, mts., Mex. C8 100
Madrid, Spain D7 20
Madrid, Al., U.S. F13 122
Madrid, Ne., U.S. G11 126
Madrid, state, Spain D7 20
Madridejos, Spain E7 20
Madura, i., Indon. G8 50
Madura, Selat, strt., Indon. .. G8 50
Madurāntakam, India E4 53
Madurai, India G4 53
Mae Hong Son, Thai. C3 48
Mae Klong, stm., Thai. E4 48
Mae Ping Mae Hat Mae Kor National Park, p.o.i., Thai. .. D4 48
Mae Ramat, Thai. D3 48
Mae Sariang, Thai. C3 48
Maeser, Ut., U.S. C7 132
Mae Sot, Thai. D4 48
Maestra, Sierra, mts., Cuba B9 102
Maesteg, Spain B8 20
Mae Tha, Thai. C4 48
Maevatanana, Madag. D8 68
Maéwo, i., Vanuatu j17 79d
Mafeking, Mb., Can. B12 124
Mafeking see Mafikeng, S. Afr. D7 70
Mafeteng, Leso. F8 70
Maffra, Austl. K6 76
Mafia Island, i., Tan. F8 66
Mafikeng, S. Afr. D7 70
Mafra, Braz. C13 92
Magadan, Russia E19 34
Magadi, Kenya E7 66
Magaguadavic Lake, l., N.B., Can. E9 110
Magalhães de Almeida, Braz. B4 88
Magangué, Col. C4 86
Magaria, Niger G6 64
Magazine Mountain, mtn., Ar., U.S. B5 122
Magdagači, Russia F14 34
Magdalena, Arg. G9 92
Magdalena, Bol. B4 90
Magdalena, Mex. E7 100
Magdalena, N.M., U.S. I9 132
Magdalena, state, Col. B4 86
Magdalena, stm., Mex. F7 98
Magdalena, Bahía, b., Mex... C2 100
Magdalena, Isla, i., Chile.... H2 90
Magdalena, Punta, c., Col. ... E3 86
Magdalena de Kino, Mex..... F7 98
Magdeburg, Ger. D7 16
Magee, Ms., U.S. F9 122
Magelang, Indon. G7 50
Magellan, Strait of, strt., S.A. J2 90
Magenta, Italy E5 22
Magetan, Indon. G7 50
Maggiore, Lago, l., Eur...... C14 18
Maghāgha, Egypt J1 58
Maghama, Maur. F2 64
Maghâgha, mtn., Spain G5 20
Maglaj, Bos. E5 26
Maglie, Italy D12 24
Magnet, N.D., U.S. C14 124
Magnetawan, stm., On., Can. C10 112
Magnetic Island, i., Austl. ... B6 76
Magnitogorsk, Russia D9 32
Magnolia, Ar., U.S. D5 122
Magnolia, Ms., U.S. F8 122
Magod, stm., India F5 54
Mago, i., Fiji p20 79e
Mago, Qc., Can. E4 110
Magozal, Mex. E10 100
Magrath, Ab., Can. G18 138
Maguari, Cabo, c., Braz..... D8 84

Magumeri, Nig. G7 64
Māgura, Bngl. G12 54
Maguse Lake, l., Nu., Can. ... C12 106
Magway, Mya. B2 48
Magway, state, Mya. B2 48
Makoua, Congo E3 66
Mahabaleshwar, India C1 53
Mahabe, Madag. D8 68
Mahābhārat Lek, mts., Nepal. E11 54
Mahābhārat Range see Mahābhārat Lek, mts., Nepal. E11 54
Mahabo, Madag. E7 68
Mahačkala, Russia F7 32
Mahād, India B1 53
Mahādeo Range, mts., India . C2 53
Mahagi, D.R.C. D6 66
Mahajamba, stm., Madag. .. D8 68
Mahājan, India D4 54
Mahajanga, Madag. D8 68
Mahākālī (Sārda), stm., Asia . D8 54
Makakam, stm., Indon. D9 50
Mahalapye, Bots. E4 68
Maham, India D6 54
Mahānadi, stm., India H10 54
Mahanoy City, Pa., U.S. D9 114
Maharagama, Sri L. H4 53
Mahārājganj, India E10 54
Mahārājpur, India F7 54
Mahārāshtra, state, India E4 46
Mahasamund, India H9 54
Maha Sarakham, Thai. D6 48
Mahaut, Dom. j6 105c
Mahaweli, stm., Sri L. H5 53
Mahaxai, Laos D7 48
Mahbūbābād, India C4 53
Mahbūbnagar, India C4 53
Mahd adh-Dhahab, Sau. Ar... E5 56
Mahdia, Guy. E12 86
Mahdia, Tun. C7 62
Mahé, i., Sey. j13 69b
Mahébourg, Mrts. i10 69a
Mahendra Giri, mtn., India ... B7 53
Mahendranagar, Nepal E7 54
Mahenge, Tan. F7 66
Mahesāna, India G4 54
Maheshwar, India G5 54
Mahi, stm., India G4 54
Mahia Peninsula, pen., N.Z. .. D7 80
Mahilëŭ, Bela. G13 10
Mahilëŭ, state, Bela. G13 10
Mahina, Fr. Poly. u21 78h
Mahlabatini, S. Afr. F10 70
Mahmūdābād, India E8 54
Mahmudiye, Tur. D14 28
Mahnomen, Mn., U.S. D3 118
Mahogany Mountain, mtn., Or., U.S. G9 136
Mahogany Tree, Anguilla A1 105a
Mahomet, Il., U.S. D9 120
Mahon see Maó, Spain E15 20
Mahone Bay, N.S., Can..... F12 110
Mahone Bay, b., N.S., Can. .. F12 110
Mahood Lake, l., B.C., Can. .. E10 138
Mahora, Spain E9 20
Mahrāt, Jabal, plat., Yemen .. F7 56
Mahrauni, India F7 54
Mahuva, India H3 54
Maiaky, Ukr. C17 26
Maicao, Col. B5 86
Maichen, China K3 42
Maicuru, stm., Braz. D7 84
Maidenhead, Eng., U.K..... J12 12
Maidstone, Sk., Can. A4 124
Maidstone, Eng., U.K. J13 12
Maiduguri, Nig. G7 64
Maihar, India F8 54
Maijoma, Mex. F3 130
Maikala Range, mts., India .. G8 54
Maiko, stm., D.R.C. E5 66
Maília, Braz. D6 90
Maimbung, Phil. H3 52
Main, stm., Ger. G5 16
Main Channel, strt., On., Can. C8 112
Mai-Ndombe, Lac, l., D.R.C. . E3 66
Maine, state, U.S. E7 110
Maine, hist. reg., Fr. G8 110
Maine, Gulf of, b., N.A. G8 110
Maine-et-Loire, state, Fr..... G8 14
Maine-Soroa, Niger G5 64
Mainhardt, Ger. G5 16
Mainland, i., Scot., U.K. B9 12
Mainland, i., Scot., U.K. n18 12a
Mainling, China D14 54
Maintirano, Madag. D7 68
Mainz, Ger. G4 16
Maio, i., C.V. k10 65a
Maipo, stm., Chile G3 92
Maipó, Volcán, vol., S.A. G3 92
Maipú, Arg. H8 92
Maipú, Arg. H9 92
Maiquetía, Ven. B8 86
Maiqihanmin, China C2 38
Mairabari, India E14 54
Mairi, Braz. F6 88
Maisí, Punta, c., Cuba B10 102
Maiskhāl Island, i., Bngl..... H13 54
Maitembge, Bots. B9 70
Maitland, Austl. I8 76
Maitland, stm., On., Can. ... E8 112
Maiz, Islas del, is., Nic. F6 102
Maizuru, Japan D8 40
Maja, stm., Russia E15 34
Maja, stm., Braz. F11 86
Majene, Indon. E11 50
Maji, Eth. F7 62
Majiahe, China A7 48
Majiang, China I2 42
Majiang, China H2 42
Majja, Russia D15 34
Majkain see Mayqayyng, Kaz. D13 32
Majkop, Russia F6 32
Major, Puig, mtn., Spain E13 20
Majorca see Mallorca, Spain E13 20
Majskij, Russia F14 34
Majuro, atoll, Marsh. Is. C8 72
Maka, Sen. G2 64
Makabana, Congo E2 66
Makale, Indon. E11 50
Makamba, Bdi. E5 66
Makapu'u Head, c., Hi., U.S. . b4 78a
Makarakomburu, Mount, mtn., Sol. Is. e8 79b
Makarov, Russia G17 34
Makarska Strait see Makassar, Selat, strt., Indon. D11 50
Makasar, Selat, strt., Indon. D11 50
Makawao, Hi., U.S. c5 78a
Makgadikgadi, Bots. E4 68
Makgadikgadi Pans Game Reserve, Bots. B7 70
Makeni, S.L. H2 64
Malo, i., Vanuatu j16 79d
Makhado see Mayak Skuratovo, Russia G19 10
Makham, Thai. F5 48
Makiivka, Ukr. E5 32
Makin, i., Kir. C8 72
Makindu, Kenya E7 66
Makinsk, Kaz. D11 32
Makira, state, Sol. Is. f10 79b
Makira Harbour, b., Sol. Is. .. f9 79b

Makkah (Mekka), Sau. Ar..... E4 56
Makkovik, Nf., Can. D19 106
Makó, Hung. C7 26
Makokou, Gabon D2 66
Makongolosi, Tan. F6 66
Makran Coast, cst., Asia..... D9 56
Makrāna, India E5 54
Maksatiha, Russia C18 10
Maksimkin Jar, Russia. C15 32
Maktar, Tun. I3 24
Malabo, D.R.C. F4 66
Malabar Coast, cst., India ... F2 53
Malacacheta, Braz. I4 88
Malacca see Melaka, Malay. K6 48
Malacca, Strait of, strt., Asia . B2 50
Malacky, Slov. H13 16
Malad City, Id., U.S. A4 132
Malad City, Id., U.S. A4 132
Maladzečna, Bela. F9 10
Málaga, Col. D5 86
Málaga, Spain H6 20
Málaga, co., Spain H6 20
Malagasy Republic see Madagascar, ctry., Afr. D8 68
Malagón, Spain E7 20
Malaimbandy, Madag. E8 68
Malaita, state, Sol. Is. d9 79b
Malaita, i., Sol. Is. e9 79b
Malaja Kuril'skaja Grjada (Habomai-shotō), is., Russia C17 38
Malaja Višera, Russia B15 10
Malaka, Sempitan, strt., Indon. J2 48
Malakāl, Sudan F6 62
Malakand, Pak. A3 54
Malakoff, Tx., U.S. E2 122
Malakula, state, Vanuatu ... k16 79d
Malakula, i., Vanuatu k16 79d
Malambo, Col. B4 86
Malang, Indon. H8 50
Malangali, Tan. F6 66
Malanje, Ang. B2 68
Malanville, Benin G5 64
Malanzán, Arg. E4 92
Mala Panewa, stm., Pol..... F14 16
Mālāren, l., Swe. G7 8
Malargüe, Arg. G3 92
Malartic, Qc., Can. F15 106
Malaryta, Bela. H6 10
Malaspina, Arg. H3 90
Malaspina Glacier, ice, Ak., U.S. E11 140
Malatya, Tur. B4 56
Malaut, Tur. j16 79d
Malawi, ctry., Afr. C5 68
Malawi, Lake see Nyasa, Lake, l., Afr. C5 68
Malaya see Semenanjung Malaysia, hist. reg., Malay. . K6 48
Malaybalay, Phil. F5 52
Malayer, Iran C6 56
Malay Peninsula, pen., Asia .. J5 48
Malay Reef, rf., Austl. B7 76
Malaysia, ctry., Asia J3 44
Malbon, Austl. C3 76
Malbork, Pol. B15 16
Malbrán, Arg. D6 92
Malchin, Ger. C8 16
Malcolm, Austl. E4 74
Malcolm Island, i., B.C., Can. . C5 120
Malczyce, Pol. E12 16
Malden, i., Kir. D11 72
Maddalena, Isola di, i., Italy E2 24
Maldives, ctry., Asia I11 30
Maldonado, Ur. G10 92
Male, Mya. A2 48
Male', Mald. i12 46a
Maléas, Ákra, c., Grc. F6 28
Male' Atoll, at. Mald. i11 46a
Malegaon, India H5 54
Male Karpaty (Little Carpathians), mts., Slov. ... H13 16
Malema, Moz. C6 68
Malente, Ger. B6 16
Malesherbes, Fr. F11 14
Maleti, Maj., rgh., Chile H2 90
Malhanskij, Swe. D6 8
Malhanskij range, mts., Russia F10 34
Malheur, stm., Or., U.S. F9 136
Malheur, South Fork, stm., Or., U.S. G8 136
Malheur Lake, l., Or., U.S. ... G8 136
Mali, ctry., Afr. F4 64
Mali, stm., Mya. C8 46
Mali, i., Fiji p18 79e
Malik, Sudan F6 62
Malik Wādī al-, val., Sudan .. D5 62
Malili, Indon. E12 50
Malin see Malyn, Ukr. G15 10
Malin, Or., U.S. A4 134
Malindi, Kenya E8 66
Malinau, Indon. B10 50
Malines see Mechelen, Bel. .. C13 14
Malingping, Indon. G5 50
Malin Head, c., Ire. F5 12
Malino, Bukit, mtn., Indon. .. C12 50
Malinovka, stm., Russia..... B9 38
Malita, Phil. G5 52
Malizhen, China A7 48
Malkāpur, India H5 54
Malkara, Tur. C10 28
Mal'kavičy, Bela. H8 10
Malkīnia, N.M., U.S. E18 16
Malka, Russia E7 68
Mallacoota, Austl. K7 76
Mallacoota Inlet, b., Austl. .. K7 76
Mallaig, Scot., U.K. D7 12
Mallawī, Egypt K1 58
Mallery Lake, l., Nu., Can. ... C11 106
Mallet, Braz. B12 92
Malligasta, Arg. D4 92
Mallorca (Majorca), i., Spain E13 20
Mallow, Ire. I4 12
Malm, Nor. D4 8
Malmberget, Swe. C9 8
Malmbyburg, S. Afr. H4 70
Malmö, Swe. I5 8
Malmok, i., Neth. Ant. p23 104g
Malo, i., Vanuatu j16 79d
Maloelap, at., Marsh. Is. C8 72
Maloja, Switz. D6 22
Malojaroslavec, Russia E19 10
Malolos, Phil. C3 52
Malombe, Lake, l., Mwi. C6 68
Malone, N.Y., U.S. F2 110
Malonga, D.R.C. C4 68
Małopolska, reg., Pol. F17 16
Maloŝuika, Russia D20 8
Maloyaroslavets, Russia E17 10
Malott, Wa., U.S. B7 136

Małowice, Pol. E11 16
Måløy, Nor. E1 8
Malozemel'skaja Tundra, reg., Russia C24 8
Malpas, Austl. J3 76
Malpe, India D2 53
Malpeque Bay, b., P.E., Can. D13 110
Malprabha, stm., India D2 53
Malpura, India E5 54
Malta, Braz. D7 88
Malta, Lat. D10 10
Malta, Mt., U.S. F6 124
Malta, i., Malta I8 24
Malta, i., Malta H8 24
Malta Channel, strt., Eur. ... I8 24
Maltahöhe, Nmb. D3 70
Maluku (Moluccas), is., Indon. F8 44
Maluku, Laut (Molucca Sea), s., Indon. E7 44
Ma'lūlā, Syria E7 58
Malu Mare, Rom. E10 26
Malunda, Indon. E11 50
Mālvan, India C1 53
Malvern, Ar., U.S. C6 122
Malvern, Ia., U.S. K3 118
Malvern, Oh., U.S. D4 114
Malvérnia, Moz. C10 70
Malvinas Sur, Arg. D8 92
Malý Dunaj, stm., Slov. H13 16
Malya Haradziejčiky, Bela. .. H11 10
Malyj Anjuj, stm., Russia.... C21 34
Malyj Enisej, stm., Russia ... F8 34
Malyj Tajmyr, ostrov, i., Russia A10 34
Mama, Russia E11 34
Mamala, Rom. E15 26
Mamanguape, Braz. D8 88
Mamasa, Indon. E11 50
Mamasa, stm., Indon. E11 50
Mambajao, Phil. F5 52
Mambasa, D.R.C. D5 66
Mamberamo, stm., Indon. ... F10 44
Mambova, Phil. D3 52
Mamehakteko, Indon. C9 50
Mameigwess Lake, l., On., Can. B6 118
Mamfe, Cam. C1 66
Mamlyutka, Kaz. D11 32
Mammoth, Az., U.S. K6 132
Mammoth Cave National Park, p.o.i., Ky., U.S. G11 120
Mammoth Lakes, Ca., U.S. .. F7 134
Mammoth Spring, Ar., U.S. .. H6 120
Mamonovo, Russia F2 10
Mamoré, stm., S.A. F4 84
Mamou, Gui. G2 64
Mampikony, Madag. D8 68
Mamry, Jezioro, l., Pol. B17 16
Mamuju, Indon. E11 50
Mamuno, Bots. C5 70
Man, C. h. H3 64
Man, W.V., U.S. G4 114
Man, Isle of see Isle of Man, dep., Eur. G8 12
Mana, Hi., U.S. a2 78a
Manabí, state, Ec. H2 86
Manacacías, stm., Col. F5 86
Manacapuru, stm., Braz. ... I11 86
Manacapuru, stm., Braz. D5 84
Manacor, Spain E14 20
Manado (Menado), Indon. ... E7 44
Manaenki, Russia G19 10
Managua, Nic. F4 102
Managua, Lago de, l., Nic. ... F4 102
Manakara, Madag. E8 68
Manam Island, i., Pap. N. Gui. a4 79a
Mánamo, Caño, stm., Ven. .. C10 86
Manana Avaratra, Madag. ... D8 68
Mananjary, Madag. E8 68
Manantenina, Madag. E8 68
Manapire, stm., Ven. D8 86
Manapparai, India G4 53
Manar, stm., India B3 53
Manas, China C2 36
Manas, stm., Asia E13 54
Manasarovar see Mapam Yumco, l., China C8 54
Manas Hu, l., China D10 54
Manāslu, mtn., Nepal D10 54
Manasquan, N.J., U.S. D11 114
Manassas, Va., U.S. F8 114
Manastirea, Rom. E13 26
Manatee, Bela. B4 86
Manati, P.R. B3 104a
Manatuto, E. Timor G8 44
Manaus, Braz. D1 84
Manawa, Wi., U.S. G10 118
Manawoka, Pulau, i., Indon.. F9 44
Manay, Phil. G6 52
Manbij, Syria B8 58
Mancelona, Mi., U.S. D4 112
Mancha Real, Spain G7 20
Manche, state, Fr. E7 14
Manchegol, Bel., U.S. B6 42
Mancheral, India B4 53
Manchester, Eng., U.K. H10 12
Manchester, Ct., U.S. C13 114
Manchester, Ga., U.S. E14 122
Manchester, Ia., U.S. B6 120
Manchester, Ky., U.S. G2 114
Manchester, N.H., U.S. H5 110
Manchester, Oh., U.S. F2 114
Manchester, Tn., U.S. B12 122
Manchester, Vt., U.S. G3 110
Manchioneal, Jam. i14 104d
Manchouli see Manzhouli, China B8 36
Manchuria see Dong San Shen, hist. reg., China ...
Manciano, Italy H8 22
Mancos, Co., U.S. F8 132
Mancos, stm., N.A. G9 144
Mand, stm., Iran D7 56
Manda, Tan. G6 66
Manda, Jabal, mtn., Sudan .. F4 62
Mandabe, Madag. E7 68
Mandaguari, Braz. A12 92
Manda Island, i., Kenya E8 66
Mandal, Mong. B6 36
Mandalay, Mya. A2 48
Mandalay, state, Mya. B2 48
Mandan, N.D., U.S. A11 126
Mandar, Teluk, b., Indon. ... E11 50
Mandara Mountains (Mandara, Monts), mts., Afr. G7 64
Mandas, Italy E3 24
Mandaue, Phil. E4 52
Mandeb, Bab el, strt., Afr. .. E8 56
Mandera, Kenya D8 66
Manderson, Wy., U.S. C5 126
Mandeville, Jam. i13 104d
Mandi, India C6 54
Mandi Būrewāla, Pak. C4 54
Mandi Dabwāli, India D5 54
Mandiana, Gui. G3 64
Mandimba, Moz. C6 68
Mandioli, Pulau, i., Indon. ... F8 44
Mandioré, Lagoa, l., S.A. G6 84

Mandioré – Mawson I • 35

Name Map Ref. Page

Mandioré, Laguna see Mandioré, Lagoa, l., S.A. G6 84
Mandla, India G8 54
Mandlakazi, Moz. D11 70
Mandora, Austl. C4 74
Mandra, Pak. B4 54
Mandritsara, Madag. D8 68
Mandsaur, India F5 54
Mandun, China A4 48
Manduria, Italy D11 24
Māndvi, India H4 54
Māndvi, India G2 54
Mandya, India E3 53
Manendragarh, India G9 54
Manfalût, Egypt K1 58
Manfredonia, Italy I12 22
Manfredonia, Golfo di, b., Italy C10 24
Manga, Braz. H3 88
Manga, reg., Niger F7 64
Mangabeiras, Chapada das, hills, Braz. E2 88
Mangagoy, Phil. F6 52
Mangai, D.R.C. E3 66
Mangalagiri, India C5 53
Mangaldai, India E14 54
Mangalia, Rom. F15 26
Mangalore, India E2 53
Mangalvedha, India C2 53
Mangchang, China I2 42
Mange, China B9 54
Mangela, Mount see Nanggala Hill, mtn., Sol. Is. e7 79b
Manggar, Indon. E6 50
Mangham, La., U.S. E7 122
Mangin Range, mts., Mya. C8 46
Mangkalihat, Tanjung, c., Indon. C11 50
Manglares, Cabo, c., Col. G2 86
Mangla Reservoir, res., Pak. B4 54
Mangnai, China G16 32
Mangochi, Mwi. C6 68
Mangoky, stm., Madag. E7 68
Mangole, Pulau, i., Indon. F8 44
Mangrol, India H2 54
Mangrūl Pīr, India H6 54
Mangsang, Indon. E4 50
Mangshi see Luxi, China G4 36
Mangueira, Lagoa, b., Braz. F11 92
Mangueirinha, Braz. B11 92
Mangum, Ok., U.S. G9 128
Mangya, China D3 36
Manhattan, Ks., U.S. B12 128
Manhattan, Mt., U.S. E15 136
Manhiça, Moz. D11 70
Mān Hpāng, Mya. A4 48
Manhuaçu, Braz. K4 88
Manhuaçu, stm., Braz. J5 88
Manhumirim, Braz. K4 88
Maniago, Italy D9 22
Manica, Moz. D5 68
Manica, state, Moz. B11 70
Manicaland, state, Zimb. B11 70
Manic Deux, Réservoir, res., Qc., Can. A8 110
Manicoré, Braz. E5 84
Manicouagan, stm., Qc., Can. E17 106
Manicouagan, Réservoir, res., Qc., Can. E17 106
Maniganggo, China E4 36
Manigotagan, Mb., Can. C17 124
Manigotagan, stm., Can. C17 124
Manihiki, at., Cook Is. E10 72
Maniitsoq see Sukkertoppen, Grnld. D15 141
Mānikganj, Bngl. G13 54
Mānikpur, India F8 54
Manila, Phil. C3 52
Manila, Ar., U.S. I7 120
Manila, Ut., U.S. C7 132
Manila Bay, b., Phil. C3 52
Manilla, Austl. H8 76
Manily, Russia D22 34
Maningrida, Austl. B6 74
Maninjau, Danau, l., Indon. D1 50
Manipa, Selat, strt., Indon. F8 44
Manipur, state, India C7 46
Manipur, stm., Asia A1 48
Manisa, Tur. E10 28
Manisa, state, Tur. E11 28
Manistee, Mi., U.S. D3 112
Manistee, stm., Mi., U.S. D3 112
Manistique, Mi., U.S. C3 112
Manistique Lake, l., Mi., U.S. B4 112
Manito, Il., U.S. K9 118
Manitoba, state, Can. D11 106
Manitoba, Lake, l., Mb., Can. D15 124
Manitou, stm., On., Can. B5 118
Manitou, Lake, l., On., Can. C7 112
Manitou Beach, Sk., Can. C8 124
Manitou Lake, l., Sk., Can. B4 124
Manitoulin Island, i., On., Can. C7 112
Manitou Springs, Co., U.S. C3 128
Manitowaning, On., Can. C8 112
Manitowoc, Wi., U.S. D2 112
Maniwaki, Qc., Can. B13 112
Manizales, Col. E4 86
Manja, Madag. E7 68
Manjakandriana, Madag. D8 68
Manjeri, India F3 53
Mānjra, stm., India B3 53
Mankanza, D.R.C. D3 66
Mankato, Ks., U.S. B10 128
Mankato, Mn., U.S. G4 118
Mankera, Pak. C3 54
Mankota, Sk., Can. E6 124
Manley Hot Springs, Ak., U.S. D9 140
Manlleu, Spain B13 20
Manmād, India H5 54
Manna, Indon. F3 50
Mannahill, Austl. I3 76
Mannar, Sri L. G4 53
Mannar, Gulf of, b., Asia G4 53
Mannārgudi, India F4 53
Mannford, Ok., U.S. A2 122
Mannheim, Ger. G4 16
Manning, N.D., U.S. G11 124
Manning, S.C., U.S. C5 116
Manning Strait, strt., Sol. Is. d7 79b
Mannum, Austl. J2 76
Mannville, Ab., Can. C19 138
Manoharpur, India G10 54
Manokwari, Indon. F9 44
Manombo Atsimo, Madag. E7 68
Manono, D.R.C. F5 66
Manor, Sk., Can. E11 124
Manor, Tx., U.S. D10 130
Manosque, Fr. F11 18
Manouane, Lac, l., Qc., Can. C2 110
Manouane, Lac, res., Qc., Can. E16 106
Manp'o, Kor., N. D7 38
Mānpur, India H8 54
Manra, at., Kir. D9 72
Manresa, Spain C12 20
Mānsa, India C5 54
Mansa, Zam. C4 68
Mansafīs, Egypt J1 58
Mānsehra, Pak. A4 54
Mansel Island, i., Nu., Can. C14 106
Mansfield, Eng., U.K. H11 12
Mansfield, Ga., U.S. C2 116
Mansfield, Il., U.S. D9 120
Mansfield, La., U.S. E5 122
Mansfield, Mo., U.S. G5 120
Mansfield, Oh., U.S. D3 114
Mansfield, Pa., U.S. C8 114
Mansfield, Tx., U.S. B10 130
Mansfield, Mount, mtn., Vt., U.S. F4 110
Mansion, St. K./N. C2 105a
Mansôa, Gui.-B. G1 64
Manson, Ia., U.S. B3 120
Mansucum, Pan. H9 102
Mansura, La., U.S. F6 122
Manta, Ec. H1 86
Manta, Bahía de, b., Ec. H1 86
Mantagao, stm., Mb., Can. C16 124
Mantalingajan, Mount, mtn., Phil. F1 52
Mantanani Besar, Pulau, i., Malay. G1 52
Manteca, Ca., U.S. F4 134
Mantecal, Ven. D7 86
Mantena, Braz. J5 88
Manteo, N.C., U.S. I10 114
Mantes-la-Jolie, Fr. F10 14
Manti, Ut., U.S. D5 132
Mantiqueira, Serra da, mts., Braz. L3 88
Manton, Mi., U.S. D4 112
Mántova, Italy E7 22
Mantua, Cuba A5 102
Mantua see Mántova, Italy E7 22
Mantua, Oh., U.S. C4 114
Manturovo, Russia G21 8
Mäntyharju, Fin. F12 8
Manu, Peru F3 84
Manuae, at., Cook Is. E11 72
Manuae, at., Fr. Poly. E11 72
Manua Islands, is., Am. Sam. h13 79c
Manuel, Mex. D9 100
Manuel Alves, stm., Braz. F2 88
Manuel Alves Grande, stm., Braz. D2 88
Manuel Benavides, Mex. A6 100
Manuel F. Mantilla see Pedro R. Fernández, Arg. D8 92
Manuguru, India B5 53
Manui, Pulau, i., Indon. F7 44
Manukau, N.Z. C6 80
Manukau Harbour, b., N.Z. C6 80
Manus Island, i., Pap. N. Gui. a4 79a
Mānwat, India B3 53
Many, La., U.S. F5 122
Manyara, Lake, l., Tan. E7 66
Manyberries, Ab., Can. E3 124
Many Island Lake, l., Can. D3 124
Manyoni, Tan. F6 66
Many Peaks, Austl. E8 76
Manza, D.R.C. F5 66
Manzala, Bahra el-, l., Egypt G3 58
Manzanares, Spain E7 20
Manzanilla Point, c., Trin. s13 105f
Manzanillo, Cuba B9 102
Manzanillo, Mex. F6 100
Manzanillo Bay, b., N.A. C11 102
Manzano, N.M., U.S. G2 128
Manzano Peak, mtn., N.M., U.S. G2 128
Manzhouli, China B8 36
Manzini, Swaz. E10 70
Mao, Chad E3 62
Mao, Dom. Rep. C12 102
Maó, Spain E15 20
Maoba, China F3 42
Maoke, Pegunungan, mts., Indon. a2 79a
Maolin, China C5 38
Maoming, China K4 42
Mapaga, Indon. D11 50
Mapam Yumco, l., China C8 54
Mapane, Indon. D12 50
Mapari, stm., Braz. I8 86
Mapastepec, Mex. H12 100
Mapi, Indon. G10 44
Mapimí, Mex. C6 100
Mapimí, Bolsón de, des., Mex. B6 100
Mapire, Ven. D9 86
Mapiri, Bol. C3 90
Mapixari, Ilha, i., Braz. I9 86
Maple, stm., Ia., U.S. B2 120
Maple, stm., Mi., U.S. E5 112
Maple, stm., N.D., U.S. H16 124
Maple Creek, Sk., Can. E4 124
Maple Lake, Mn., U.S. F4 118
Maple Mount, Ky., U.S. G10 120
Maple Ridge, B.C., Can. G8 138
Mapleton, Ia., U.S. B2 120
Mapleton, Or., U.S. F3 136
Mapleton, Ut., U.S. C5 132
Mapuera, stm., Braz. C6 84
Maputo, Moz. D11 70
Maputo, state, Moz. D11 70
Maputo, stm., Afr. E11 70
Maqanshy, Kaz. E14 32
Maqat, Kaz. E8 32
Maqên Gangri, mtn., China E4 36
Maqna, Sau. Ar. J5 58
Maquan, stm., China D10 54
Maquela do Zombo, Ang. B2 68
Maquereau, Pointe au, c., Qc., Can. B12 110
Maquinchao, Arg. H3 90
Maquoketa, Ia., U.S. B7 120
Maquoketa, stm., Ia., U.S. B7 120
Maquoketa, North Fork, stm., Ia., U.S. B7 120
Mar, Serra do, mts., Braz. B13 92
Mara, stm., Afr. E7 66
Maraã, Braz. H9 86
Maraa, Fr. Poly. v21 78h
Marabá, Braz. C1 88
Marabahan, Indon. E9 50
Maraboon, Lake, res., Austl. D6 76
Maracá, Ilha de, i., Braz. F11 86
Maracá, Ilha de, i., Braz. C7 84
Maracaçumé, stm., Braz. A3 88
Maracaibo, Ven. B5 86
Maracaibo, Lago de, l., Ven. C6 86
Maracaju, Braz. D5 90
Maracanaú, Braz. B6 88
Maracás, Braz. G5 88
Maracay, Ven. B8 86
Marādah, Libya B3 62
Maradi, Niger G6 64
Marāghah, Sabkhat al-, l., Syria C8 58
Marāgheh, Iran B6 56
Maragogipe, Braz. G6 88
Maragoji, Braz. E8 88
Marahuaca, Cerro, mtn., Ven. F9 86
Maraial, Braz. E8 88
Marais des Cygnes, stm., U.S. F3 120
Marajó, Baía de, b., Braz. D8 84
Marajó, Ilha de, i., Braz. D8 84
Maralal, Kenya D7 66
Marali, C.A.R. C3 66
Maralinga, Austl. F6 74
Marambio, sci., Ant. B35 81
Marampa, S.L. H2 64
Maramsilli Reservoir, res., India H8 54
Maramureș, state, Rom. B10 26
Maran, Malay. K6 48
Marana, Az., U.S. K5 132
Marand, Iran B6 56
Marang, Malay. J6 48
Marangas, Phil. F1 52
Maranguape, Braz. B6 88
Maranhão, state, Braz. C3 88
Maranhão, stm., Braz. D9 84
Marano, Laguna di, b., Italy E10 22
Maranoa, stm., Austl. F7 76
Marañón, stm., Peru D2 84
Marasende, Pulau, i., Indon. F10 50
Mărășești, Rom. D14 26
Maratasã, stm., Braz. C4 88
Marathon, Austl. C4 76
Marathon, On., Can. C12 118
Marathon, Tx., U.S. D4 130
Marathon, Wi., U.S. G9 118
Marathónas, Grc. E6 28
Maratua, Pulau, i., Indon. B11 50
Marau, Braz. D11 92
Maraú, Braz. H6 88
Marauiá, stm., Braz. H9 86
Maravilha, Braz. C11 92
Maravillas, Mex. B6 100
Maravillas Creek, stm., Tx., U.S. E4 130
Marav Lake, l., Pak. D2 54
Maravovo, Sol. Is. e8 79b
Marawi, Phil. F5 52
Marawwah, i., U.A.E. E7 56
Marayes, Arg. E4 92
Marbella, Spain H6 20
Marble, N.C., U.S. A2 116
Marble Bar, Austl. D3 74
Marble Canyon, p., Az., U.S. G5 132
Marble Falls, Tx., U.S. D9 130
Marble Hall, S. Afr. D9 70
Marble Hill, Mo., U.S. G8 120
Marblemount, Wa., U.S. B5 136
Marble Rock, Ia., U.S. I6 118
Marburg, Ger. F4 16
Marburg, S. Afr. G10 70
Marca, Ponta da, c., Ang. D1 68
Marcal, stm., Hung. B4 26
Marcelin, Sk., Can. B7 124
Marceline, Mo., U.S. E5 120
March, Eng., U.K. I12 12
March (Morava), stm., Eur. H12 16
Marche, state, Italy G10 22
Marche, hist. reg., Fr. C8 18
Marche-en-Famenne, Bel. D14 14
Marchena, Spain G5 20
Marches see Marche, state, Italy G10 22
Mar Chiquita, Laguna, b., Arg. H9 92
Mar Chiquita, Laguna, l., Arg. E6 92
Marcigny, Fr. C10 18
Marco, Braz. B5 88
Marcos Juárez, Arg. F6 92
Marcus, Ia., U.S. B2 120
Marcus Baker, Mount, mtn., Ak., U.S. D10 140
Marcus Island see Minami-Tori-shima, i., Japan G19 30
Marcy, Mount, mtn., N.Y., U.S. F2 110
Mardān, Pak. A4 54
Mardarivka, Ukr. B16 26
Mar del Plata, Arg. H9 92
Mardin, Tur. B5 56
Maré, i., N. Cal. m17 79d
Mare a Brăilei, Insula, i., Rom. D14 26
Marea de Portillo, Cuba C9 102
Marechal Cândido Rondon, Braz. B10 92
Marechal Deodoro, Braz. E8 88
Maree, Loch, l., Scot., U.K. D7 12
Mareeba, Austl. A5 76
Maremma, reg., Italy H8 22
Marengo, Ia., U.S. C5 120
Marengo, Il., U.S. B9 120
Marenisco, Mi., U.S. E9 118
Marennes, Fr. D4 18
Marettimo, Isola, i., Italy G5 24
Marfa, Tx., U.S. D3 130
Margai Caka, l., China A6 46
Margaree Harbour, N.S., Can. D15 110
Margaret, stm., Austl. C5 74
Margaret Bay, B.C., Can. E3 138
Margaret River, Austl. F2 74
Margaretville, N.Y., U.S. B11 114
Margarita, Isla de, i., Ven. B9 86
Margate, S. Afr. G10 70
Margate, Eng., U.K. J14 12
Margate, Fl., U.S. J5 116
Margecany, Slov. H16 16
Margelan see Margilan, Uzb. F12 32
Margherita di Savoia, Italy C10 24
Margherita Peak, mtn., Afr. D5 66
Margilan, Uzb. F12 32
Margonin, Pol. D13 16
Margosatubig, Phil. G4 52
Māṛgow, Dasht-e, des., Afg. C9 56
Marha, Russia D13 34
Marha, stm., Russia C12 34
Maria, Îles, is., Fr. Poly. F11 72
María Cleofas, Isla, i., Mex. E5 100
María Elena, Chile D3 90
María Grande, Arg. E8 92
María Ignacia, Arg. H8 92
Maria Island, i., Austl. B7 74
Maria Island National Park, p.o.i., Austl. o14 77a
Mariakani, Kenya E7 66
María Madre, Isla, i., Mex. E5 100
María Magdalena, Isla, i., Mex. E5 100
Mariana, Braz. K4 88
Mariana Islands, is., Oc. B5 72
Mariana Ridge, unds. H17 142
Mariana Trench, unds. H17 142
Marian Lake, l., N.T., Can. C7 106
Marianna, Ar., U.S. C8 122
Marianna, Fl., U.S. G13 122
Mariano I. Loza, Arg. D8 92
Mariánské Lázně, Czech Rep. G8 16
Marias, stm., Mt., U.S. B16 136
Marias Pass, p., Mt., U.S. B13 136
María Teresa, Arg. G6 92
Mariato, Punta, c., Pan. I7 102
Maribo, Den. B7 16
Maribor, Slvn. D12 22
Maricao, P.R. B2 104a
Marico, stm., Afr. D8 70
Maricopa, Az., U.S. J4 132
Maricunga, Salar de, pl., Chile C3 92
Marié, stm., Braz. H8 86
Marie Byrd Land, reg., Ant. C29 81
Marie-Galante, i., Guad. i6 105c
Mariehamn, Fin. F9 8
Mariental, Nmb. D4 70
Marienville, Pa., U.S. C6 114
Mariestad, Swe. G5 8
Marieta, stm., Ven. E8 86
Marietta, Ga., U.S. D14 122
Marietta, Mn., U.S. G2 118
Marietta, Oh., U.S. E4 114
Marieville, Qc., Can. E3 110
Marignane, Fr. F11 18
Marigot, Dom. i6 105c
Marigot, Guad. A1 105a
Mariinsk, Russia C15 32
Mariinskoe, Russia F17 34
Marijampolė, Lith. F6 10
Marij El, state, Russia C7 32
Marília, Braz. D7 90
Marimba, Ang. B2 68
Marín, Mex. I7 130
Marín, Spain B2 20
Marina di Ravenna, Italy F9 22
Marina Fall, wtfl., Guy. E12 86
Mar''ina Horka, Bela. G11 10
Marinduque, i., Phil. D3 52
Marine City, Mi., U.S. B3 114
Marinette, Wi., U.S. C2 112
Maringá, Braz. D6 90
Marino, Vanuatu j16 79d
Marintu, Indon. C6 50
Marion, Al., U.S. E11 122
Marion, Ar., U.S. B8 122
Marion, Ia., U.S. B6 120
Marion, Il., U.S. G9 120
Marion, In., U.S. H4 112
Marion, Ks., U.S. C12 128
Marion, Ky., U.S. G9 120
Marion, La., U.S. E6 122
Marion, Ms., U.S. E10 122
Marion, N.C., U.S. I4 114
Marion, N.D., U.S. A14 126
Marion, Oh., U.S. D2 114
Marion, S.C., U.S. B6 116
Marion, Va., U.S. H4 114
Marion, Lake, res., S.C., U.S. C5 116
Marion Bay, b., Austl. o13 77a
Marion County Lake, res., Ks., U.S. C11 128
Marion Downs, Austl. D2 76
Marion Junction, Al., U.S. E11 122
Marion Reef, rf., Austl. B9 76
Marionville, Mo., U.S. G4 120
Maripa, Ven. D9 86
Mariposa, Ca., U.S. F5 134
Mariquita, Col. E4 86
Mariscal Estigarribia, Para. D4 90
Maritime Alps, mts., Eur. E12 18
Maritsa (Évros) (Marica) (Meriç), stm., Eur. C9 28
Mariupol', Ukr. E5 32
Mariusa, Caño, stm., Ven. C11 86
Mariveles, Phil. C3 52
Mariyampole see Marijampolė, Lith. F6 10
Marjanovka, Russia D12 32
Marka, Som. D8 66
Mārkāpur, India D4 53
Markaryd, Swe. H5 8
Markdale, On., Can. D9 112
Marked Tree, Ar., U.S. B8 122
Markesan, Wi., U.S. H10 118
Market Harborough, Eng., U.K. I12 12
Markham, On., Can. E10 112
Markham, Tx., U.S. F11 130
Markham Bay, b., Nu., Can. C16 106
Markit, China B12 56
Markle, In., U.S. H4 112
Markleeville, Ca., U.S. E6 134
Markovo, Russia D23 34
Marks, Russia D7 32
Marks, Ms., U.S. C8 122
Marktheidenfeld, Ger. G5 16
Marktoberdorf, Ger. I6 16
Marktredwitz, Ger. G8 16
Mark Twain Lake, res., Mo., U.S. E6 120
Marlboro, Ab., Can. C14 138
Marlboro, N.Y., U.S. C11 114
Marlborough, Austl. D7 76
Marlborough, Guy. B6 84
Marlborough, Ma., U.S. B14 114
Marlette, Mi., U.S. E6 112
Marlinton, W.V., U.S. F5 114
Marlow, Ok., U.S. G11 128
Marmaduke, Ar., U.S. H7 120
Marmande, Fr. E6 18
Marmara, Sea of see Marmara Denizi, s., Tur. C11 28
Marmara Adası, i., Tur. C10 28
Marmara Denizi (Marmara, Sea of), s., Tur. C11 28
Marmara Ereğlisi, Tur. C10 28
Marmara Gölü, l., Tur. E10 28
Marmaris, Tur. G11 28
Marmaton, stm., U.S. G3 120
Marmelos, stm., Braz. E5 84
Marmet, W.V., U.S. F4 114
Marmion Lake, l., On., Can. C7 118
Marmolada, mtn., Italy D8 22
Marmora, On., Can. D12 112
Marnay, Fr. G14 14
Marne, Ger. C4 16
Marne, Mi., U.S. E4 112
Marne, state, Fr. E13 14
Marne, stm., Fr. E11 14
Marne à la Saône, Canal de la, can., Fr. F14 14
Maroa, Ven. F8 86
Maroantsetra, Madag. D8 68
Maromandia, Madag. C8 68
Maromme, Fr. E10 14
Maromokotro, mtn., Madag. C8 68
Marondera, Zimb. D5 68
Maroni (Marowijne), stm., S.A. C7 84
Maros, Indon. F11 50
Maros (Mureș), stm., Eur. C7 26
Maroua, Cam. B2 66
Marovoay, Madag. D8 68
Marowijne (Maroni), stm., S.A. C7 84
Marqaköl köli, l., Kaz. E15 32
Marquand, Mo., U.S. G7 120
Marquard, S. Afr. F8 70
Marquesas Islands see Marquises, Îles, is., Fr. Poly. D12 72
Marquesas Keys, is., Fl., U.S. L3 116
Marquette, Ks., U.S. C11 128
Marquette, Mi., U.S. B2 112
Marquis, Gren. q10 105e
Marquises, Îles, is., Fr. Poly. D12 72
Marradi, Italy F8 22
Marrah, Jabal, hill, Sudan E4 62
Marrakech, Mor. C3 64
Marrakesh see Marrakech, Mor. C3 64
Marrawah, Austl. n12 77a
Marree, Austl. E7 74
Marrero, La., U.S. H8 122
Marromeu, Moz. D6 68
Marrupa, Moz. C6 68
Marsá al-Burayqah, Libya A3 62
Marsabit, Kenya D7 66
Marsala, Italy G6 24
Marsciano, Italy H9 22
Marseille, Fr. F11 18
Marseilles, Il., U.S. C9 120
Marsfjället, mtn., Swe. D6 8
Marshall, Lib. H2 64
Marshall, Ak., U.S. D7 140
Marshall, Ar., U.S. I5 120
Marshall, Mi., U.S. B1 114
Marshall, Mn., U.S. G3 118
Marshall, Mo., U.S. E4 120
Marshall, N.C., U.S. I3 114
Marshall, Tx., U.S. E4 122
Marshall, Va., U.S. F8 114
Marshall, stm., Austl. D7 74
Marshallberg, N.C., U.S. B9 116
Marshall Islands, ctry., Oc. H19 142
Marshall Islands, is., Marsh. Is. B7 72
Marshalltown, Ia., U.S. B5 120
Marshfield, Mo., U.S. G4 120
Marshfield, Wi., U.S. G8 118
Mars Hill, Me., U.S. D9 110
Mars Hill, N.C., U.S. I3 114
Marsh Island, i., La., U.S. H7 122
Marshville, N.C., U.S. A5 116
Marsing, Id., U.S. G10 136
Märsta, Swe. G7 8
Marstal, Den. B6 16
Martaban, Gulf of, b., Mya. D3 48
Martapura, Indon. E9 50
Martapura, Indon. F4 50
Marte R. Gómez, Presa, res., Mex. H9 130
Marthaguy Creek, stm., Austl. H6 76
Martha's Vineyard, i., Ma., U.S. C15 114
Martí, Cuba B9 102
Martigny, Switz. D4 22
Martigues, Fr. F11 18
Martin, Slov. G14 16
Martin, Ky., U.S. G3 114
Martin, Mi., U.S. F4 112
Martin, N.D., U.S. G13 124
Martin, Tn., U.S. H9 120
Martín, stm., Spain C10 20
Martina Franca, Italy D11 24
Martindale, Tx., U.S. E10 130
Mărtinești, Rom. D14 26
Martinez, Ca., U.S. E3 134
Martinez, Ga., U.S. C3 116
Martínez de la Torre, Mex. E10 100
Martinho Campos, Braz. J3 88
Martinique, dep., N.A. i15 96a
Martinique Passage, strt., N.A. k6 105c
Martin Lake, res., Al., U.S. E12 122
Martinópole, Braz. B5 88
Martinsberg, Aus. B12 22
Martinsburg, W.V., U.S. E7 114
Martins Ferry, Oh., U.S. D5 114
Martinsville, Il., U.S. E10 120
Martinsville, In., U.S. E11 120
Martinsville, Va., U.S. H5 114
Martin Vaz, Ilhas, is., Braz. H12 82
Martos, Spain G7 20
Martre, Lac la, l., N.T., Can. C7 106
Martti, Fin. C13 8
Marudi, Malay. A9 50
Marudu, Telukan, b., Malay. G1 52
Marugame, Japan E6 40
Maruim, Braz. F7 88
Maruoka, Japan C9 40
Marutea, at., Fr. Poly. E12 72
Marv Dasht, Iran D7 56
Marvine, Mount, mtn., Ut., U.S. E5 132
Mārwār, India F4 54
Mary, Turkmen. B9 56
Mary, stm., Austl. E9 76
Maryborough, Austl. E9 76
Maryborough, Austl. K4 76
Marydale, S. Afr. F5 70
Maryfield, Sk., Can. E12 124
Mary Kathleen, Austl. C2 76
Maryland, state, U.S. E8 114
Maryneal, Tx., U.S. B7 130
Maryport, Eng., U.K. G9 12
Marysvale, Ut., U.S. E4 132
Marysville, N.B., Can. D10 110
Marysville, Ca., U.S. D4 134
Marysville, Ks., U.S. L2 118
Marysville, Mi., U.S. B3 114
Marysville, Oh., U.S. D2 114
Marysville, Wa., U.S. B4 136
Maryville, Mo., U.S. D3 120
Maryville, Tn., U.S. I2 114
Marzagão, Braz. I1 88
Marzo, Punta, c., Col. D3 86
Masada see Meẕada, Ḥorvot, sci., Isr. G6 58
Masai Mara Game Reserve, Kenya E7 66
Masai Steppe, plat., Tan. E7 66
Masaka, Ug. E6 66
Masalembu Besar, Pulau, i., Indon. F9 50
Masamba, Indon. E12 50
Masan, Kor., S. D1 40
Masasi, Tan. G7 66
Masatepe, Nic. G4 102
Masaya, Nic. G4 102
Masbate, Phil. D4 52
Masbate, i., Phil. E4 52
Mascarene Basin, unds. K8 142
Mascarene Islands, is., Afr. i10 69a
Mascarene Plateau, unds. J8 142
Mascot, Tn., U.S. H2 114
Mascota, Mex. E6 100
Mascoutah, Il., U.S. F8 120
Maseru, Leso. F8 70
Mashan, China J3 42
Mashava, Zimb. D5 68
Mashhad, Iran B8 56
Mashi, China G6 42
Mashiko, Japan C13 40
Mashra'ar Raqq, Sudan F5 62
Masi-Manimba, D.R.C. E3 66
Masindi, Ug. D6 66
Masira, Gulf of see Maṣīrah, Khalīj, b., Oman F8 56
Maṣīrah, i., Oman E8 56
Maṣīrah, Khalīj, b., Oman F8 56
Masisea, Peru E3 84
Masjed-e Soleymān, Iran C6 56
Mask, Lough, l., Ire. H3 12
Maskanah, Syria B8 58
Masljanino, Russia D14 32
Mason, Mi., U.S. F5 112
Mason, Oh., U.S. E1 114
Mason, Tx., U.S. D8 130
Mason, W.V., U.S. E3 114
Mason City, Ia., U.S. A4 120
Mason City, Il., U.S. D8 120
Mason City, Ne., U.S. F13 126
Masqaṭ (Muscat), Oman E8 56
Massa, Italy F7 22
Massachusetts, state, U.S. B14 114
Massachusetts Bay, b., Ma., U.S. B15 114
Massafra, Italy D11 24
Massaguet, Chad E3 62
Massa Marittima, Italy G7 22
Massangena, Moz. B11 70
Massawa (Mitsiwa), Erit. D7 62
Massena, Ia., U.S. C3 120
Massena, N.Y., U.S. F2 110
Massenya, Chad E3 62
Massey, On., Can. B7 112
Massey Sound, strt., Nu., Can. B7 141
Massiac, Fr. D9 18
Massillon, Oh., U.S. D4 114
Massina, reg., Mali G4 64
Massinga, Moz. C12 70
Massingir, Moz. C11 70
Massive, Mount, mtn., Co., U.S. D10 132
Masson Island, i., Ant. B14 81
Mastābah, Sau. Ar. E4 56
Masterson, Tx., U.S. F6 128
Masterton, N.Z. E6 80
Mastic Point, Bah. K8 116
Mastung, Pak. D10 56
Masty, Bela. G7 10
Masuda, Japan E4 40
Masurai, Gunung, mtn., Indon. E2 50
Masuria see Mazury, reg., Pol. C16 16
Masvingo, Zimb. E5 68
Masvingo, state, Zimb. B10 70
Maṣyāf, Syria C7 58
Mata Amarilla, Arg. I2 90
Matabeleland North, state, Zimb. A9 70
Matabeleland South, state, Zimb. B9 70
Matabuena, Spain C7 20
Matacuni, stm., Ven. F9 86
Mata de São João, Braz. G6 88
Matadi, D.R.C. F2 66
Matagalpa, Nic. F5 102
Matagami, Qc., Can. F15 106
Matagorda, Tx., U.S. F12 130
Matagorda Island, i., Tx., U.S. F11 130
Matagorda Peninsula, pen., Tx., U.S. F11 130
Matahiae, Pointe, c., Fr. Poly. w22 78h
Matâi, Egypt J1 58
Mataiea, Fr. Poly. w22 78h
Mataiva, at., Fr. Poly. E12 72
Matak, Pulau, i., Indon. B5 50
Matakana, Austl. I5 76
Matale, Sri L. H5 53
Matam, Sen. F2 64
Matamoros, Mex. C10 100
Matamoros, Mex. C7 100
Matan, Indon. D7 50
Matandu, stm., Tan. F7 66
Matane, Qc., Can. B9 110
Matanni, Pak. B3 54
Matanzas, Cuba A7 102
Matanzas, Mex. E8 100
Matapan, Cape see Taínaro, Ákra, c., Grc. G5 28
Matape, stm., Mex. A3 100
Matapédia, Qc., Can. C9 110
Matapédia, Lac, l., Qc., Can. B9 110
Mataquito, stm., Chile G2 92
Matara, Sri L. I5 53
Mataram, Indon. H9 50
Mataranka, Austl. B6 74
Mataró, Spain C13 20
Matasiri, Pulau, i., Indon. F9 50
Matatiele, S. Afr. G9 70
Matatula, Cape, c., Am. Sam. h12 79c
Matâ'utu, Wal./F. E9 72
Matavera, Cook Is. a27 78j
Mataveri, Chile e29 78l
Mataveri, Aeropuerto, Chile f29 78l
Mataveri Airstrip see Mataveri, Aeropuerto, Chile f29 78l
Matehuala, Mex. D8 100
Mateke Hills, hills, Zimb. B10 70
Matera, Italy D10 24
Mateur, Tun. G3 24
Matha, Fr. D5 18
Mather, Mb., Can. E14 124
Mather, Pa., U.S. E5 114
Matheson, On., Can. F14 106
Mathews, Va., U.S. G9 114
Mathis, Tx., U.S. F10 130
Mathura (Muttra), India E6 54
Matias Barbosa, Braz. K4 88
Matías Romero, Mex. G11 100
Matícora, stm., Ven. B6 86
Matinha, Braz. B3 88
Matipó, Braz. K4 88
Matiyure, stm., Ven. D7 86
Mātli, Pak. F2 54
Mato, Cerro, mtn., Ven. D9 86
Mato Grosso, state, Braz. F6 84
Mato Grosso, Planalto do, plat., Braz. B5 90
Mato Grosso, Plateau of see Mato Grosso, Planalto do, plat., Braz. B5 90
Mato Grosso do Sul, state, Braz. C6 90
Matola Rio, Moz. D11 70
Matopos, Zimb. B9 70
Matosinhos, Port. C2 20
Matouying, China B8 42
Matozinhos, Braz. J3 88
Maṭraḥ, Oman E8 56
Matsudo, Japan D12 40
Matsue, Japan D6 40
Matsumoto, Japan C10 40
Matsusaka, Japan E9 40
Matsu Tao, i., Tai. H8 42
Matsutō, Japan C9 40
Matsuura, Japan F2 40
Matsuyama, Japan F5 40
Mattagami, stm., On., Can. F14 106
Mattamuskeet, Lake, l., N.C., U.S. A9 116
Mattaponi, stm., Va., U.S. G8 114
Mattawa, On., Can. B11 112
Mattawa, Wa., U.S. D7 136
Mattawamkeag, stm., Me., U.S. E8 110
Matterhorn, mtn., Eur. D13 18
Matterhorn, mtn., Nv., U.S. B1 132
Matthews Mountain, hill, Mo., U.S. G7 120
Matthew Town, Bah. C10 96
Mattighofen, Aus. B10 22
Mattoon, Il., U.S. E9 120
Mattoon, Wi., U.S. F9 118
Mattydale, N.Y., U.S. E13 112
Matua, Indon. E7 50
Matudo see Matsudo, Japan D12 40
Matue see Matsue, Japan D6 40
Matuku, i., Fiji q19 79e
Matumoto see Matsumoto, Japan C10 40
Maturín, Ven. C10 86
Matutina, Braz. J2 88
Matuzaka see Matsusaka, Japan E9 40
Maú (Ireng), stm., S.A. F12 86
Maúa, Moz. C6 68
Mau Aimma, India F8 54
Maubeuge, Fr. D12 14
Maud, Tx., U.S. D4 122
Maudaha, India F7 54
Maude, Austl. J5 76
Maués, Braz. D6 84
Maués, stm., Braz. D6 84
Mauganj, India F8 54
Maui, i., Hi., U.S. c5 78a
Mauk, Indon. F5 50
Mauldin, S.C., U.S. B3 116
Maule, state, Chile G2 92
Maule, stm., Chile G1 92
Maule, Laguna del, l., Chile G2 92
Mauléon-Licharre, Fr. F5 18
Maumee, Oh., U.S. G6 112
Maumee, stm., U.S. G6 112
Maumelle, Lake, res., Ar., U.S. C6 122
Maumere, Indon. G7 44
Maun, Bots. D3 68
Maunabo, P.R. B4 104a
Mauna Kea, vol., Hi., U.S. d6 78a
Maunaloa, Hi., U.S. b4 78a
Mauna Loa, vol., Hi., U.S. d6 78a
Maunath Bhanjan, India F9 54
Maungdaw, Mya. H14 54
Maungmagan, Mya. E3 48
Maunoir, Lac, l., N.T., Can. B6 106
Maupihaa, at., Fr. Poly. E11 72
Mau Rānīpur, India F7 54
Maurepas, Lake, l., La., U.S. G8 122
Maurice, Lake, l., Austl. E6 74
Mauricie, Parc national de la, p.o.i., Qc., Can. D3 110
Mauritania, ctry., Afr. F2 64
Mauritanie see Mauritania, ctry., Afr. F2 64
Mauritius, ctry., Afr. h10 69a
Mauron, Fr. F6 14
Mauston, Wi., U.S. H8 118
Mautau, c., Fr. Poly. r19 78g
Mauterndorf, Aus. C10 22
Mauthen, Aus. D9 22
Mauvais Coulee, stm., N.D., U.S. F14 124
Mava, Pap. N. Gui. b3 79a
Maverick, Az., U.S. J7 132
Mavinga, Ang. D3 68
Mavrovo Nacionalni Park, p.o.i., Mac. B3 28
Mavuradonha Mountains, mts., Zimb. D5 68
Mawchi, Mya. C3 48
Mawlaik, Mya. D7 46
Mawlamyine (Moulmein), Mya. D3 48
Mawson, sci., Ant. B11 81

Name	Map Ref.	Page
Maw Taung (Luang, Khao), mtn., Asia	G4	48
Max, N.D., U.S.	G12	124
Maxaranguape, Braz.	C8	88
Maxcanú, Mex.	B3	102
Maxixe, Moz.	C12	70
Maxville, On., Can.	E2	110
Maxwell, Ca., U.S.	D3	134
Maxwell, Ne., U.S.	F12	126
Maxwell, N.M., U.S.	E4	128
May, Tx., U.S.	B9	130
May, Cape, pen., N.J., U.S.	F11	114
May, Mount, mtn., Ab., Can.	B11	138
Maya, Pulau, i., Indon.	D6	50
Mayaguana, i., Bah.	A11	102
Mayaguana Passage, strt., Bah.	B1	104a
Mayagüez, P.R.	B1	104a
Mayang, China	H3	42
Mayarí, Cuba	B10	102
Maybole, Scot., U.K.	F8	12
Maydena, Austl.	o13	77a
Maydh, Som.	B9	66
Mayen, Ger.	F3	16
Mayenne, Fr.	F8	14
Mayenne, state, Fr.	F8	14
Mayenne, stm., Fr.	F8	14
Mayer, Az., U.S.	I4	132
Mayerthorpe, Ab., Can.	C15	138
Mayfield, Ky., U.S.	H9	120
Mayfield, Ut., U.S.	D5	132
Mayflower, Ar., U.S.	C6	122
Māyir, Syria	B8	58
Maykain see Mayqayyng, Kaz.		
Maymyo, Mya.	A3	48
Maynard, Ia., U.S.	B6	120
Maynardville, Tn., U.S.	H2	114
Mayne, stm., Austl.	D3	76
Mayo, Yk., Can.	C3	106
Mayo, Fl., U.S.	F2	116
Mayo, state, Ire.	H3	12
Mayo, stm., Arg.	I3	90
Mayo, stm., Mex.	B4	100
Mayon Volcano, vol., Phil.	D4	52
Mayor Buratovich, Arg.	G4	90
Mayotte, dep., Afr.	C8	68
Mayoyoque, Col.	G4	86
May Pen, Jam.	j13	104d
Mayqayyng, Kaz.	D13	32
Mayreau, i., St. Vin.	p11	105e
Mayskoe, Kaz.	D13	32
Mays Landing, N.J., U.S.	E11	114
Maysville, Ky., U.S.	F2	114
Maysville, Mo., U.S.	E3	120
Maysville, N.C., U.S.	B8	116
Maysville, Ok., U.S.	G11	128
Mayumba, Gabon	E2	66
Māyūram, India	F4	53
Mayville, Mi., U.S.	E6	112
Mayville, N.D., U.S.	G16	124
Mayville, N.Y., U.S.	B6	114
Maywood, Ne., U.S.	G12	126
Maza, Arg.	H6	92
Mazabuka, Zam.	D4	68
Mazagão, Braz.	D7	84
Mazamet, Fr.	F8	18
Mazán, stm., Peru	I4	86
Mazara, Val di, reg., Italy	G7	24
Mazara del Vallo, Italy	G6	24
Mazār-e Sharīf, Afg.	B10	56
Mazarrón, Golfo de, b., Spain	G9	20
Mazaruni, stm., Guy.	D11	86
Mazatenango, Guat.	E2	102
Mazatlán, Mex.	D5	100
Mažeikiai, Lith.	D5	10
Mazenod, Sk., Can.	E7	124
Mazinga, mtn., Neth. Ant.	C2	105a
Mazirbe, Lat.	C5	10
Mazon, Il., U.S.	C9	120
Mazowe, stm., Afr.	D5	68
Mazury (Masuria), reg., Pol.	C16	16
Mazyr, Bela.	D3	32
Mbabane, Swaz.	E10	70
M'bahiakro, C. Iv.	H4	64
Mbaïki, C.A.R.	D3	66
Mbake, Sen.	G1	64
Mbala, Zam.	B5	68
Mbalabala, Zimb.	B9	70
Mbale, Ug.	D6	66
Mbalmayo, Cam.	D2	66
Mbamba Bay, Tan.	G7	66
Mbandaka (Coquilhatville), D.R.C.	D3	66
Mbanga, Cam.	D1	66
Mbanika Island, i., Sol. Is.	e8	79b
M'banza Congo, Ang.	B1	68
Mbanza-Ngungu, D.R.C.	F3	66
Mbarara, Ug.	C6	66
Mbashe, stm., S. Afr.	H9	70
Mbava Island, i., Sol. Is.	d7	79b
Mbé, Cam.	C2	66
Mberengwa, Zimb.	B9	70
Mbeya, Tan.	F6	66
Mbigou, Gabon	E2	66
Mbinda, Congo	E2	66
Mbini, Eq. Gui.	I6	64
Mboi, D.R.C.	F4	66
Mboki, C.A.R.	C5	66
Mbola, Sol. Is.	e9	79b
Mborokua, i., Sol. Is.	e8	79b
Mborong, Indon.	H12	50
Mbouda, Cam.	C2	66
Mbour, Sen.	G1	64
Mbout, Maur.	F2	64
Mbuji-Mayi (Bakwanga), D.R.C.	F4	66
Mbuluzi, stm., Swaz.	E10	70
Mbwemkuru, stm., Tan.	F7	66
McAdam, N.B., Can.	E9	110
McAdoo, Pa., U.S.	D9	114
McAlester, Ok., U.S.	C3	122
McAllen, Tx., U.S.	H9	130
McArthur, Oh., U.S.	E3	114
McArthur, stm., Austl.	C7	74
McArthur River, Austl.	C7	74
McBain, Mi., U.S.	D4	112
McBee, S.C., U.S.	B5	116
McBeth Fjord, b., Nu., Can.	B17	106
McBride, B.C., Can.	C10	138
McCall Creek, Ms., U.S.	F8	122
McCamey, Tx., U.S.	C5	130
McCammon, Id., U.S.	H14	136
McCauley Island, i., B.C., Can.	E4	106
McCleary, Wa., U.S.	C3	136
McClellan Creek, stm., Tx., U.S.	F8	128
McClellanville, S.C., U.S.	C6	116
McClintock, Mount, mtn., Ant.	D21	81
McCloud, Ca., U.S.	B3	134
McCloud, stm., Ca., U.S.	B3	134
McClure, Il., U.S.	G8	120
McClusky, N.D., U.S.	G13	124
McColl, S.C., U.S.	B6	116
McComb, Ms., U.S.	F8	122
McConaughy, Lake, res., Ne., U.S.	F11	126
McConnellsburg, Pa., U.S.	E7	114
McConnelsville, Oh., U.S.	E4	114
McCook, Ne., U.S.	A8	128
McCormick, S.C., U.S.	C3	116
McCreary, Mb., Can.	D14	124
McCullough Mountain, mtn., Nv., U.S.	H1	132
McCune, Ks., U.S.	G2	120
McCurtain, Ok., U.S.	B4	122
McDade, Tx., U.S.	D10	130
McDermitt, Nv., U.S.	B8	134
McDermott, Oh., U.S.	F2	114

McDonald, Ks., U.S.	B7	128
McDonald, Lake, l., Mt., U.S.	B12	136
McDowell Peak, mtn., Az., U.S.	J4	132
Mcensk, Russia	G19	10
McEwen, Tn., U.S.	H10	120
McFadden, Wy., U.S.	B10	132
McFarland, Ca., U.S.	H6	134
McGehee, Ar., U.S.	D7	122
McGill, Nv., U.S.	D2	132
McGrath, Ak., U.S.	D8	140
McGraw, N.Y., U.S.	B9	114
McGregor, Tx., U.S.	C10	130
McGregor, stm., B.C., Can.	B9	138
McGregor Lake, l., Ab., Can.	F18	138
McHenry, Il., U.S.	B9	120
McHenry, Ms., U.S.	G9	122
McInji, Mwi.	C5	68
McIntosh, Al., U.S.	F10	122
McIntosh, Mn., U.S.	D3	118
McIntyre Bay, b., On., Can.	B10	118
McKean, stm., Nu., Can.	C17	106
McKee, Ky., U.S.	G2	114
McKeesport, Pa., U.S.	D6	114
McKenzie, Tn., U.S.	H9	120
McKenzie, stm., Or., U.S.	F4	136
McKenzie Bridge, Or., U.S.	F4	136
McKenzie Island, On., Can.	E12	106
McKinlay, Austl.	C3	76
McKinlay, stm., Austl.	C3	76
McKinley, Mount, mtn., Ak., U.S.	D9	140
McKinleyville, Ca., U.S.	C1	134
McKinney, Tx., U.S.	D2	122
McKittrick Summit, mtn., Ca., U.S.	H6	134
McLain, Ms., U.S.	F10	122
McLaurin, Ms., U.S.	F9	122
McLean, Il., U.S.	D8	120
McLean, Tx., U.S.	F8	128
McLeansboro, Il., U.S.	F9	120
McLennan, Ab., Can.	D7	106
McLeod, stm., Ab., Can.	C15	138
McLeod Bay, b., N.T., Can.	C8	106
McLeod Lake, B.C., Can.	B7	138
M'Clintock Channel, strt., Nu., Can.	A10	106
McLoughlin, Mount, mtn., Or., U.S.	A3	134
McLouth, Ks., U.S.	E2	120
M'Clure Strait, strt., N.T., Can.	B16	140
McMahon, Sk., Can.	D6	124
McMinnville, Or., U.S.	E3	136
McMinnville, Tn., U.S.	B13	122
McMurdo, sci., Ant.	C22	81
McMurdo Sound, strt., Ant.	C22	81
McNary, Az., U.S.	I7	132
McNeil, Ar., U.S.	D5	122
McPherson, Ks., U.S.	C11	128
McQueeney, Tx., U.S.	E9	130
McRae, Ar., U.S.	B7	122
McRae, Ga., U.S.	K6	116
McVeigh, Ky., U.S.	C3	114
McVille, N.D., U.S.	G15	124
McWilliams, Al., U.S.	F11	122
Mdantsane, S. Afr.	H8	70
M'drak, Viet.	F9	48
Mead, U.S.	C1	120
Mead, Lake, res., U.S.	G2	132
Meade, Ks., U.S.	D8	128
Meaden Peak, mtn., Co., U.S.	C9	132
Meadow, Ut., U.S.	E4	132
Meadow Lake, Sk., Can.	E9	106
Meadow Valley Wash, stm., Nv., U.S.	F2	132
Meadowview, Va., U.S.	H3	114
Meadville, Mo., U.S.	E4	120
Meadville, Ms., U.S.	F7	122
Meadville, Pa., U.S.	C5	114
Meaford, On., Can.	D9	112
Mealhada, Port.	D2	20
Meandarra, Austl.	F7	76
Meander River, Ab., Can.	D7	106
Mearim, stm., Braz.	B3	88
Meath, state, Ire.	H6	12
Meath, hist. reg., Ire.	H6	12
Meaux, Fr.	F11	14
Mecaya, stm., Col.	G4	86
Mecca see Makkah, Sau. Ar.	E4	56
Mechanicsburg, Oh., U.S.	D2	114
Mechanicsville, Ia., U.S.	C6	120
Mechanicsville, Va., U.S.	G8	114
Mechelen (Malines), Bel.	C13	14
Mecklenburg, hist. reg., Ger.	C7	16
Mecklenburger Bucht, b., Ger.	B7	16
Mecklenburg-Vorpommern, state, Ger.	C8	16
Mecubúri, Moz.	C6	68
Mecula, Moz.	C6	68
Meda, Port.	D3	20
Medak, India	B4	53
Medan, Indon.	B1	50
Medanosa, Punta, c., Arg.	I3	90
Mede, Italy	E5	22
Medeiros Neto, Braz.	I5	88
Medellín, Col.	D4	86
Médenine, Tun.	C6	64
Mederdra, Maur.	F1	64
Medford, Ok., U.S.	A2	134
Medford, Or., U.S.	A2	134
Medford, Wi., U.S.	F8	118
Medgidia, Rom.	E15	26
Mediapolis, Ia., U.S.	C6	120
Medias, Rom.	C11	26
Medicine Bow, Wy., U.S.	B10	132
Medicine Bow, stm., Wy., U.S.	A10	132
Medicine Bow Mountains, mts., U.S.	F6	126
Medicine Creek, stm., Mo., U.S.	E4	120
Medicine Hat, Ab., Can.	D3	124
Medicine Lake, Mt., U.S.	F9	124
Medicine Lodge, Ks., U.S.	D10	128
Medicine Lodge, stm., U.S.	I5	88
Medina see Al-Madīnah, Sau. Ar.	E4	56
Medina, N.Y., U.S.	E11	112
Medina, Oh., U.S.	C4	114
Medina, Tx., U.S.	E8	130
Medina, stm., Tx., U.S.	E9	130
Medinaceli, Spain	C8	20
Medina del Campo, Spain	C6	20
Medina, Punta, c., Chile	C2	92
Medina-Sidonia, Spain	H5	20
Medinipur, India	G11	54
Mediterranean Sea, s.	A4	62
Medje, D.R.C.	D5	66
Medjez el Bab, Tun.	H3	24
Medkovec, Blg.	F10	26
Médoc, reg., Fr.	D4	18
Médouneu, Gabon	D2	66
Meductic, N.B., Can.	E9	110
Medveda, Serb.	G8	26
Medvedica, stm., Russia	C19	10
Medvégalis, hill, Lith.	E5	10
Medvežjegorsk, Russia	E15	8
Medvežji ostrova, is., Russia	B21	34
Medyn', Russia	F18	10
Meekatharra, Austl.	E3	74
Meeker, Co., U.S.	C9	132
Meeks Bay, Ca., U.S.	D5	134
Meeladeen, Som.	B9	66

Meerane, Ger.	F8	16
Meersburg, Ger.	I5	16
Meerut, India	D6	54
Mega, Eth.	G7	62
Mega, Pulau, i., Indon.	E2	50
Megalópoli, Grc.	F4	28
Mégantic, Lac l., Qc., Can.	E5	110
Megara, Grc.	E6	28
Megargel, Tx., U.S.	H9	128
Meghālaya, state, India	F13	54
Meghna, stm., Bngl.	G13	54
Megisti, i., Grc.	G12	28
Megra, Russia	C19	8
Mehakit, Indon.	E9	50
Meharry, Mount, mtn., Austl.	D3	74
Mehedinți, state, Rom.	E10	26
Mehekar, India	H6	54
Meherrin, stm., U.S.	H7	114
Mehidpur, India	G5	54
Mehikoorma, Est.	B10	10
Mehndāwal, India	E9	54
Mehren'ga, Russia	F19	8
Mehrenga, stm., Russia	F19	8
Mehtar Lām, Afg.	C11	56
Mehun-sur-Yèvre, Fr.	G11	14
Mei, stm., China	H7	42
Mei, stm., China	I7	42
Meia Meia, Tan.	F7	66
Meia Ponte, stm., Braz.	I1	88
Meichuan, China	F6	42
Meiganga, Cam.	C2	66
Meighen Island, i., Nu., Can.	A5	141
Meigs, Ga., U.S.	E1	116
Meihekou, China	C6	38
Meihsien see Meizhou, China	I7	42
Meikeng, China	J6	42
Meiktila, Mya.	B2	48
Meiners Oaks, Ca., U.S.	I6	134
Meiningen, Ger.	F6	16
Meishan, China	E5	36
Meissen, Ger.	E9	16
Meitan, China	H2	42
Meizhou, China	I7	42
Mejillones, Chile	D2	90
Mejillones, Peninsula, pen., Chile	A2	92
Mejnypil'gyno, Russia	D24	34
Mékambo, Gabon	D2	66
Mek'elē, Eth.	E7	62
Mékhé, Sen.	F1	64
Mekhtar, Pak.	C2	54
Mekka see Makkah, Sau. Ar.	E4	56
Meknès, Mor.	C3	64
Mekong (Mékôngk) (Khong) (Lancang), stm., Asia	F9	46
Mekongga, Gunung, mtn., Indon.	F7	44
Mékôngk see Mekong, stm., Asia	F10	46
Melado, stm., Chile	H2	92
Melaka, Malay.	K6	48
Melaka, state, Malay.	K6	48
Melanesia, is., Oc.	D7	72
Melawi, stm., Indon.	D8	50
Melbourne, Austl.	K5	76
Melbourne, Ar., U.S.	H6	120
Melbourne, Fl., U.S.	H5	116
Melbourne, Ia., U.S.	J5	118
Melbourne Island, i., Nu., Can.	B10	106
Melcher, Ia., U.S.	C4	120
Melchor, Isla, i., Chile	I2	90
Melchor Múzquiz, Mex.	B8	100
Meldorf, Ger.	B4	16
Meldrum Bay, On., Can.	C6	112
Meldrum Creek, B.C., Can.	D8	138
Mélé, Baie, b., Vanuatu	k17	79d
Melekeok, Palau	g8	78b
Melenki, Russia	I19	8
Meleuz, Russia	D9	32
Mélèzes, stm., Qc., Can.	D16	106
Melfi, Chad	E3	62
Melfi, Italy	C9	24
Melfort, Sk., Can.	B9	124
Meliane, Oued, stm., Tun.	H4	24
Melide, Spain	B3	20
Melilla, Sp. N. Afr.	B4	64
Melimoyu, Cerro, vol., Chile.	H2	90
Melincué, Arg.	F7	92
Melita, Mb., Can.	E12	124
Melitopol', Ukr.	E5	32
Mellansel, Swe.	E8	8
Mellen, Wi., U.S.	E8	118
Mellerud, Swe.	G5	8
Mellish Reef, at., Austl.	C11	74
Mellit, Sudan	E5	62
Mělník, Czech Rep.	F10	16
Melo, Ur.	F10	92
Melolo, Indon.	H12	50
Melos see Mílos, i., Grc.	G7	28
Melrhir, Chott, l., Alg.	C6	64
Melrose, Austl.	E4	74
Melrose, Mn., U.S.	I6	76
Melrose, N.M., U.S.	F4	118
Melrose, Wi., U.S.	G5	128
Melsungen, Ger.	G8	118
Meltaus, Fin.	E5	16
Melton Mowbray, Eng., U.K.	C11	8
Melür, India	I12	12
Melvern Lake, res., Ks., U.S.	F4	53
Melville, Sk., Can.	F2	120
Melville, La., U.S.	D11	124
Melville, Cape, c., Austl.	G7	122
Melville Bugt, b., Grnld.	B9	74
Melville Hall Airport, Dom.	B12	141
Melville Hills, hills, Can.	i6	105c
Melville Island, i., Austl.	B7	106
Melville Island, i., Can.	B6	74
Melville Peninsula, pen., Nu., Can.	A17	140
Melvin, Il., U.S.	B14	106
Melvin, Tx., U.S.	D8	120
Melyana, Alg.	C8	130
Mélykút, Hung.	H13	20
Mēmar Co, l., China	C6	26
Memba, Moz.	A9	54
Membalong, Indon.	C7	68
Memboro, Indon.	E5	50
Memel see Klaipėda, Lith.	H11	50
Mēmele (Nemunėlis), stm., Eur.	E9	10
Memmingen, Ger.	D7	10
Mempawah, Indon.	I5	16
Memphis, Fl., U.S.	C7	52
Memphis, Mo., U.S.	I3	116
Memphis, Tn., U.S.	B8	120
Memphis, Tx., U.S.	B8	122
Memphrémagog, Lac (Memphrémagog Lake), l., N.A.	G8	128
Memphrémagog, Lake (Memphrémagog, Lac), res., N.A.	E4	110
Mena, Ar., U.S.	C4	122
Menado see Manado, Indon.	E7	44
Mēnaka, Mali	F5	64
Menan, Id., U.S.	G15	136
Menard, Tx., U.S.	D8	130
Menasha, Wi., U.S.	G10	118
Mende, Fr.	E9	18
Mendawai, Indon.	E8	50
Mendebo, mts., Eth.	F7	62
Mendenhall, Ms., U.S.	F9	122

Mendí, Eth.	F7	62
Mendi, Pap. N. Gui.	b3	79a
Mendocino, Ca., U.S.	D2	134
Mendocino, Cape, c., Ca., U.S.	C1	134
Mendocino Fracture Zone, unds.	E24	142
Mendon, Il., U.S.	D6	120
Mendota, Ca., U.S.	G5	134
Mendota, Il., U.S.	C9	120
Mendoza, Arg.	F3	92
Mendoza, state, Arg.	G3	92
Mendoza, stm., Arg.	F3	92
Mene de Mauroa, Ven.	B6	86
Mene Grande, Ven.	C6	86
Menemen, Tur.	E9	28
Menen, Bel.	D12	14
Menfi, Italy	G6	24
Mengban, China	A5	48
Mengcheng, China	E7	42
Mengdingjie, China	G4	36
Mengenlang, Palau	f8	78b
Menggala, Indon.	E4	50
Menggudai, China	B2	42
Menghai, China	B5	48
Mengjiawan, China	B3	42
Mengla, China	B5	48
Menglian, China	A4	48
Mengxian, China	D5	42
Mengyin, China	D7	42
Mengzi, China	A6	48
Menihek Lakes, l., Nf., Can.	E17	106
Menin see Menen, Bel.	D12	14
Menindee, Austl.	I4	76
Menjușa, Russia	B13	10
Menlo Park, Ca., U.S.	F3	134
Menno, S.D., U.S.	D15	126
Meno, Ok., U.S.	E10	128
Menomonee, Mi., U.S.	C2	112
Menominee, stm., U.S.	C1	112
Menomonee Falls, Wi., U.S.	A9	120
Menomonie, Wi., U.S.	G7	118
Menongue, Ang.	C2	68
Menor, Mar, b., Spain	G10	20
Menorca (Minorca), i., Spain	D15	20
Mentasta Lake, Ak., U.S.	D11	140
Mentawai, Kepulauan, is., Indon.	E1	50
Mentawai, Selat, strt., Indon.	D2	50
Menton, Fr.	F13	18
Mentor, Oh., U.S.	C4	114
Menyapa, Gunung, mtn., Indon.	C9	50
Menzel Bourguiba, Tun.	G3	24
Menzel Bou Zelfa, Tun.	H4	24
Menzelinsk, Russia	D8	32
Menzel Temime, Tun.	H5	24
Menzies, Austl.	E4	74
Menzies, Mount, mtn., Ant.	C10	81
Meobbaai, b., Nmb.	D2	70
Meoqui, Mex.	A6	100
Meota, Sk., Can.	A5	124
Meppel, Neth.	B15	14
Meppen, Ger.	D3	16
Meqerghane, Sebkha, pl., Alg.	D5	64
Mequinenza, Embalse de, res., Spain	C10	20
Mequon, Wi., U.S.	E2	112
Meramec, stm., Mo., U.S.	F7	120
Meran (Merano), Italy	D8	22
Merano (Meran), Italy	D8	22
Meratus, Pegunungan, mts., Indon.	E9	50
Merauke, Indon.	G11	44
Merbau, Indon.	C3	50
Merbein, Austl.	I4	76
Mercaderes, Col.	G3	86
Mercāra, India	E2	53
Merced, Ca., U.S.	F5	134
Merced, stm., Ca., U.S.	F5	134
Mercedario, Cerro, mtn., Arg.	E2	92
Mercedes, Arg.	G8	92
Mercedes, Arg.	G8	92
Mercedes, Arg.	F8	92
Mercedes, Tx., U.S.	H10	130
Mercer, Mo., U.S.	D4	120
Mercer, Pa., U.S.	C5	114
Mercersburg, Pa., U.S.	E7	114
Merchants Bay, b., Nu., Can.	D13	141
Mercoal, Ab., Can.	C13	138
Mercury, Nv., U.S.	G10	134
Mercury Islands, is., N.Z.	C6	80
Mercy, Cape, c., Nu., Can.	E13	141
Mercy Bay, b., N.T., Can.	B16	140
Meredith, N.H., U.S.	C7	128
Meredosia, Il., U.S.	E7	120
Meredith, Lake, res., Tx., U.S.	F7	128
Méré Lava, i., Vanuatu	j17	79d
Merevari, stm., Ven.	D9	86
Mereža, Russia	A19	10
Mergui, Mya.	F4	48
Mergui Archipelago, is., Mya.	G3	48
Meribah, Austl.	J3	76
Mérida, Mex.	B3	102
Mérida, Spain	F4	20
Mérida, Ven.	C6	86
Mérida, state, Ven.	C6	86
Mérida, Cordillera de, mts., Ven.	C6	86
Meridian, Ms., U.S.	E10	122
Meridian, Tx., U.S.	C10	130
Meridianville, Al., U.S.	C12	122
Mérignac, Fr.	E5	18
Merigold, Ms., U.S.	D8	122
Merikarvia, Fin.	F9	8
Merimbula, Austl.	K7	76
Merin, Laguna (Mirim, Lagoa), b., S.A.	F11	92
Merízalde, Col.	F3	86
Mezőkövesd, Hung.	B7	26
Merkinė, Lith.	F7	10
Merkys, stm., Lith.	F7	10
Merlin, Or., U.S.	H3	136
Meron, Har (Meron, Mount), mtn., Isr.	F13	126
Meron, Mount see Meron, Har, mtn., Isr.	E6	58
Merouane, Chott, l., Alg.	C6	64
Merredin, Austl.	F3	74
Merrill, mtn., Scot., U.K.	B1	120
Merrill, Ia., U.S.	H4	118
Merrill, Or., U.S.	H5	136
Merrill, Wi., U.S.	G9	118
Merrillan, Wi., U.S.	G8	118
Merrillville, In., U.S.	H5	110
Merriman, Ne., U.S.	H10	126
Merritt, B.C., Can.	F10	138
Merritt Island, Fl., U.S.	K5	116
Merriwa, Austl.	I8	76
Mer Rouge, La., U.S.	E7	122
Merrygoen, Austl.	H7	76
Merryville, La., U.S.	G5	122
Mersa Matruh, Egypt.	A5	62
Merseburg, Ger.	E7	16
Mersey, stm., Austl.	n13	77a
Mersey, stm., Eng., U.K.	H10	12
Mersing, Malay.	K6	48
Mērsrags, Lat.	C6	10
Merta, India	E5	54
Merthyr Tydfil, Wales, U.K.	J9	12
Mértola, Port.	G3	20

Mertz Glacier Tongue, ice, Ant.	B19	81
Méru, Fr.	E11	14
Meru, Kenya	D7	66
Merweville, S. Afr.	H5	70
Merzifon, Tur.	A4	56
Merzig, Ger.	G2	16
Mesa, Az., U.S.	J5	132
Mesabi Range, hills, Mn., U.S.	D6	118
Mesagne, Italy	D11	24
Mescalero, N.M., U.S.	H3	128
Meščerino, Russia	G20	10
Meschede, Ger.	E4	16
Mesewa see Massawa, Erit.	D7	62
Mesgouez, Lac, l., Qc., Can.	E16	106
Mesick, Mi., U.S.	D4	112
Mesilla, N.M., U.S.	K10	132
Meškuičiai, Lith.	D6	10
Mesolóngi, Grc.	E4	28
Mesopotamia, hist. reg., Asia	C5	56
Mesquite, Tx., U.S.	E2	122
Messalo, stm., Moz.	C6	68
Messina, Italy	F9	24
Messina, S. Afr.	C9	70
Messina, Gulf of see Messiniakós Kólpos, b., Grc.	G5	28
Messina, Stretto di, strt., Italy	F9	24
Messíni, Grc.	F4	28
Messíni, sci., Grc.	G5	28
Messiniakós Kólpos, b., Grc.	G5	28
Messix Peak, mtn., Ut., U.S.	B4	132
Messkirch, Ger.	H5	16
Messojaha, stm., Russia	C4	34
Mesta (Néstos), stm., Eur.	B6	28
Mestghanem, Alg.	B4	64
Mestre, ngh., Italy	E9	22
Mesuji, stm., Indon.	E4	50
Meta, state, Col.	F5	86
Meta, stm., S.A.	D7	86
Métabetchouan, Qc., Can.	B5	110
Métabetchouane, stm., Qc., Can.	B4	110
Meta Incognita Peninsula, pen., Nu., Can.	C17	106
Metairie, La., U.S.	H8	122
Metaline Falls, Wa., U.S.	B9	136
Metamora, Il., U.S.	D8	120
Metán, Arg.	B5	92
Metangula, Moz.	C5	68
Metapán, El Sal.	D3	102
Metaponto, sci., Italy	D10	24
Metaponto, sci., Italy	D10	24
Meteor Crater, crat., Az., U.S.	I6	132
Metharana, Mya.	D4	48
Methow, Wa., U.S.	B7	136
Methow, stm., Wa., U.S.	B6	136
Methven, N.Z.	F4	80
Metica, stm., Col.	E5	86
Metiskow, Ab., Can.	D3	124
Metlakatla, Ak., U.S.	E13	140
Metolius, stm., Or., U.S.	E12	22
Metropolis, Il., U.S.	G9	120
Metropolis, Il., U.S.	C2	112
Metter, Ga., U.S.	D3	116
Mettuppālaiyam, India	F3	53
Mettūr, India	F4	53
Metzingen, Ger.	H5	16
Meu, stm., Fr.	F7	14
Meulaboh, Indon.	J2	48
Meureudu, Indon.	J3	48
Meurthe, stm., Fr.	F15	14
Meurthe-et-Moselle, state, Fr.	F15	14
Meuse, state, Fr.	E14	14
Meuse (Maas), stm., Eur.	D14	14
Meuselwitz, Ger.	E8	16
Mexcala, stm., Mex.	G9	100
Mexia, Tx., U.S.	F2	122
Mexiana, Ilha, i., Braz.	C8	84
Mexicali, Mex.	K10	134
Mexican Hat, Ut., U.S.	F7	132
México see Ciudad de México, Mex.	F9	100
Mexico, Me., U.S.	F6	110
Mexico, Mo., U.S.	E6	120
Mexico, N.Y., U.S.	E13	112
México, city, N.A.	C4	96
México, state, Mex.	F9	100
Mexico, Gulf of, b., N.A.	B6	96
Mexico Basin, unds.	B5	144
Mexico Bay, b., N.Y., U.S.	E13	112
Meyādīn, Syria	B6	58
Meycauayan, Phil.	C3	52
Meyersdale, Pa., U.S.	B6	114
Meymaneh, Afg.	B9	56
Meyronne, Sk., Can.	E7	124
Meyungs, Palau	g7	78b
Mezada, Horvot (Masada), sci., Isr.	G6	58
Mezcalapa, stm., Mex.	G12	100
Mézene, Fr.	E14	116
Mēžciems, Lat.	C10	32
Mezen', Russia	D22	8
Mezen', stm., Russia	D21	8
Mezenskaja guba, b., Russia	C20	8
Mezőberény, Hung.	B7	26
Mezőcsát, Hung.	B7	26
Mezőkövesd, Hung.	B7	26
Mezőtúr, Hung.	B7	26
Mfangano Island, i., Kenya	E6	66
M'Goun, Irhil, mtn., Mor.	C3	64
M'hai, B'nom, mtn., Viet.	G8	48
Mhasvād, India	C2	53
Mhow, India	G5	54
Mi, stm., China	H5	42
Mia, Oued, stm., Alg.	D5	64
Miahuatlán de Porfirio Díaz, Mex.	G10	100
Miajadas, Spain	E5	20
Miami, Az., U.S.	J6	132
Miami, Fl., U.S.	K5	116
Miami, Mb., Can.	E15	124
Miami, Ok., U.S.	H3	120
Miami, Tx., U.S.	F8	128
Miami, stm., Oh., U.S.	E1	114
Miami Beach, Fl., U.S.	K5	116
Miami Canal, can., Fl., U.S.	J5	116
Miamisburg, Oh., U.S.	E1	114
Miami Springs, Fl., U.S.	K5	116
Mian Channún, Pak.	C4	54
Miandowāb, Iran	B6	56
Miandrivazo, Madag.	D8	68
Mianduhe, China	B9	36
Mianeh, Iran	B6	56
Miang, Phu, mtn., Thai.	D5	48
Mianhu, China	J6	42
Mianning, China	F5	36
Miānwāli, Pak.	B4	54
Mianxian, China	E2	42
Mianyang, China	E1	42
Mianzhu, China	E5	36
Miaodao Qundao, is., China	C8	38
Miaoli, Tai.	I9	42
Miao Ling, mts., China	H2	42

Miass, Russia	C10	32
Miass, stm., Russia	C10	32
Miastko, Pol.	B12	16
Micang Shan, mts., China	E2	42
Michałowce, Slov.	H17	16
Michaud, Point, c., N.S., Can.	E16	110
Micheal Peak, mtn., B.C., Can.	C4	138
Michel, B.C., Can.	G16	138
Miches, Dom. Rep.	C13	102
Michigan, In., U.S.	F15	124
Michigan, Lake, l., U.S.	E2	112
Michigan City, In., U.S.	G3	112
Michigan, state, U.S.	C10	108
Michigan, stm., Co., U.S.	G6	126
Michipicoten Island, i., On., Can.	F13	106
Michoacán, state, Mex.	F8	100
Micoud, St. Luc.	m7	105c
Micronesia, is., Oc.	B6	72
Micronesia, Federated States of, ctry., Oc.	D6	32
Mičurinsk, Russia	I21	8
Midai, Pulau, i., Indon.	B5	50
Midale, Sk., Can.	E10	124
Mid-Atlantic Ridge, unds.	F9	144
Middelburg, Neth.	C12	14
Middelburg, S. Afr.	D7	70
Middelburg, S. Afr.	G7	70
Middle, stm., B.C., Can.	B5	138
Middle, stm., Mn., U.S.	C3	120
Middle Alkali Lake, l., Ca., U.S.	B5	134
Middle America Trench, unds.	H29	142
Middle Andaman, i., India	F7	46
Middleborough, Ma., U.S.	C15	114
Middlebourne, W.V., U.S.	E5	114
Middleburg, N.Y., U.S.	B11	114
Middleburg, Pa., U.S.	D8	114
Middleburg, Vt., U.S.	F2	110
Middle Caicos, i., T./C. Is.	B12	102
Middle Fabius, stm., Mo., U.S.	D5	120
Middlefield, Oh., U.S.	C4	114
Middlegate, Norf. I.	y25	78i
Middle Loup, stm., Ne., U.S.	F14	126
Middlemount, Austl.	D7	76
Middle Musquodoboit, N.S., Can.	E13	110
Middleport, Oh., U.S.	E3	114
Middle Raccoon, stm., Ia., U.S.	J4	118
Middlesbrough, Eng., U.K.	G11	12
Middlesex, Belize	D3	102
Middle Stewiacke, N.S., Can.	E13	110
Middleton, N.S., Can.	F11	110
Middleton, Wi., U.S.	A8	120
Middleton Island, i., Ak., U.S.	E10	140
Middletown, Ca., U.S.	E3	134
Middletown, Ct., U.S.	C13	114
Middletown, De., U.S.	E10	114
Middletown, In., U.S.	H4	112
Middletown, Ky., U.S.	F12	120
Middletown, N.Y., U.S.	C11	114
Middletown, Oh., U.S.	E1	114
Middletown, Pa., U.S.	D9	114
Middletown, R.I., U.S.	C14	114
Middleville, Mi., U.S.	F4	112
Midi, Canal du, can., Fr.	F9	18
Midi de Bigorre, Pic du, mtn., Fr.	G6	18
Mid-Indian Basin, unds.	J10	142
Mid-Indian Ridge, unds.	J9	142
Midland, On., Can.	D10	112
Midland, Ca., U.S.	J2	132
Midland, Mi., U.S.	E5	112
Midland, Tx., U.S.	C5	130
Midlands, state, Zimb.	B10	70
Midlothian, Tx., U.S.	B11	130
Midongy Atsimo, Madag.	E8	68
Mid-Pacific Mountains, unds.	G19	142
Midsayap, Phil.	G5	52
Midville, Ga., U.S.	D3	116
Midway, B.C., Can.	G12	138
Midway, Ky., U.S.	F13	120
Midway, Ut., U.S.	C5	132
Midway Islands, dep., Oc.	G22	30
Midwest, Wy., U.S.	B8	116
Midwest, reg., Sau. Ar.	E2	108
Midwest City, Ok., U.S.	F11	128
Miechów, Pol.	F15	16
Miedzybórz, Pol.	E13	16
Międzylesie, Pol.	F12	16
Międzyrzec Podlaski, Pol.	D18	16
Międzyrzecz, Pol.	D11	16
Miedźna, Pol.	F15	16
Mielec, Pol.	F17	16
Mier, Mex.	B9	100
Miercurea-Ciuc, Rom.	C12	26
Mieres, Spain	A5	20
Mieroszów, Pol.	F12	16
Mîeru y Noriega, Mex.	I7	16
Mi'eso, Eth.	F8	62
Mieszkowice, Pol.	D10	16
Mifflinburg, Pa., U.S.	H12	112
Miguel Alemán (Presa, res., Mex.	F10	100
Miguel Alves, Braz.	B4	88
Miguel Auza, Mex.	C7	100
Miguel Calmon, Braz.	F5	88
Miguel Hidalgo, Presa, res., Mex.	B4	100
Miguel Riglos, Arg.	H6	92
Mihaești, Rom.	D9	26
Mihajlovka, Russia	D6	32
Mihajlovsk, Russia	D10	38
Mihajlovskij, Russia	D21	8
Mihanavičy, Bela.	G10	10
Mihara-yama, vol., Japan	E12	40
Mihinnskaja, Russia	F21	8
Mikame, Japan	F5	40
Mikasa, Japan	C15	38a
Mikašēvičy, Bela.	H9	10
Mikhrot Timna' (King Solomon's Mines), hist., Isr.	I5	58
Mikindani, Tan.	G7	66
Mikkeli (Sankt Michel), Fin.	F12	8
Mikołajki, Pol.	C17	16
Mikołów, Pol.	F14	16
Mikonui, stm., N.Z.	F3	80
Mikrá Préspa, Limni, l., Eur.	D15	24
Mikulov, Czech Rep.	H12	16
Mikumi, Tan.	F7	66
Mikun', Russia	B8	32
Mikuni, Japan	C9	40
Miladummadulu Atoll, at., Mald.	h12	46a
Milagro, Arg.	E5	92
Milagros, Phil.	D4	52
Milan see Milano, Italy	E5	22
Milan, Ga., U.S.	D2	116
Milan, In., U.S.	E12	120

Milan – Moose Jaw I • 37

Name	Map Ref.	Page
Milan, Mi., U.S.	B2	114
Milan, Mn., U.S.	F3	118
Milan, Mo., U.S.	D4	120
Milan, N.M., U.S.	H8	132
Milang, Austl.	J2	76
Milange, Moz.	D6	68
Milano (Milan), Italy	E6	22
Milâs, Tur.	F10	28
Milavidy, Bela.	H8	10
Milazzo, Italy	F9	24
Milazzo, Golfo di, b., Italy	F9	24
Milbank, S.D., U.S.	F2	118
Milburn, Ok., U.S.	C2	122
Milden, Sk., Can.	C6	124
Mildmay, On., Can.	D8	112
Mildura, Austl.	J4	76
Mile, China	G5	36
Miles, Austl.	F8	76
Miles, Tx., U.S.	C7	130
Miles City, Mt., U.S.	A7	126
Milestone, Sk., Can.	E9	124
Milet, sci., Tur.	F10	28
Milford, De., U.S.	F10	114
Milford, Ia., U.S.	H3	118
Milford, Ma., U.S.	B14	114
Milford, Me., U.S.	F8	110
Milford, Mi., U.S.	B2	114
Milford, N.H., U.S.	B14	114
Milford, Pa., U.S.	C11	114
Milford, Ut., U.S.	E4	132
Milford Center, Oh., U.S.	D2	114
Milford Haven, Wales, U.K.	J7	12
Milford Lake, res., Ks., U.S.	B11	128
Milford Sound, strt., N.Z.	G2	80
Mili, at., Marsh. Is.	C8	72
Milian, stm., Malay.	A10	50
Milicz, Pol.	E13	16
Miljatino, Russia	F17	10
Milk, stm., N.A.	B6	108
Milk, North Fork (North Milk), stm., N.A.	B13	136
Mil'kovo, Russia	F20	34
Milk River, Ab., Can.	G18	138
Millard, Ne., U.S.	C1	120
Millau, Fr.	E9	18
Millboro, Va., U.S.	F6	114
Millbrook, N.Y., U.S.	C12	114
Mill City, Or., U.S.	F4	136
Millcreek, Pa., U.S.	B5	114
Millcreek, Ut., U.S.	C5	132
Mill Creek, W.V., U.S.	F5	114
Milledgeville, Ga., U.S.	C2	116
Milledgeville, Il., U.S.	C8	120
Mille Lacs, Lac des, l., On., Can.	C8	118
Mille Lacs Lake, l., Mn., U.S.	E5	118
Millen, Ga., U.S.	D4	116
Miller, Mo., U.S.	G4	120
Miller, S.D., U.S.	C14	126
Miller Mountain, mtn., Nv., U.S.	E7	134
Millerovo, Russia	E6	32
Millersburg, Ky., U.S.	F1	114
Millersburg, Mi., U.S.	C5	112
Millersburg, Oh., U.S.	D4	114
Millersport, Oh., U.S.	I7	112
Millerton, N.Y., U.S.	C12	114
Millet, Ab., Can.	C17	138
Millevaches, Plateau de, plat., Fr.	D7	18
Millicent, Austl.	K3	76
Milligan, Fl., U.S.	G12	122
Milligan, Ne., U.S.	G15	126
Millington, Mi., U.S.	E6	112
Millington, Tn., U.S.	B9	122
Millinocket, Me., U.S.	E8	110
Mill Island, i., Ant.	B15	81
Mill Island, i., Nu., Can.	C15	106
Millry, Al., U.S.	F10	122
Mills, Wy., U.S.	E6	126
Mills Creek, stm., Austl.	D4	76
Mills Lake, l., N.T., Can.	C7	106
Millstream, Austl.	D3	74
Milltown, Mt., U.S.	D13	136
Milltown, Wi., U.S.	F6	118
Milltown Malbay, Ire.	I3	12
Mill Valley, Ca., U.S.	F3	134
Millville, N.J., U.S.	E10	114
Millwood, Va., U.S.	E7	114
Millwood Lake, res., Ar., U.S.	D4	122
Milne Land, i., Grnld.	C20	141
Milnor, N.D., U.S.	A15	126
Milo, Ab., Can.	F18	138
Mílos, i., Grc.	G7	28
Miłosław, Pol.	D13	16
Milparinka, Austl.	G3	76
Milroy, In., U.S.	E12	120
Milroy, Pa., U.S.	D8	114
Miltenberg, Ger.	G5	16
Milton, On., Can.	E10	112
Milton, N.Z.	H4	80
Milton, Fl., U.S.	G11	122
Milton, Ia., U.S.	D5	120
Milton, Pa., U.S.	G13	112
Milton, Wi., U.S.	B9	120
Milton-Freewater, Or., U.S.	E8	136
Milton Keynes, Eng., U.K.	I12	12
Miltonvale, Ks., U.S.	B11	128
Miltou, Chad	E3	62
Miluo, stm., China	G5	42
Milwaukee, Wi., U.S.	E2	112
Milwaukee, stm., Wi., U.S.	H11	118
Milwaukie, Or., U.S.	E4	136
Mimbres, stm., N.M., U.S.	K9	132
Mimizan-les-Bains, Fr.	E4	18
Mimoň, Czech Rep.	F10	16
Mimoso do Sul, Braz.	K5	88
Mims, Fl., U.S.	H5	116
Min, stm., China	F5	36
Min, stm., China	I8	42
Mina, Mex.	H7	130
Mina, Nv., U.S.	E7	134
Mīnā' al-Aḥmadī, Kuw.	D6	56
Mīnāb, Iran	D8	56
Minahasa, pen., Indon.	E7	44
Minakuchi, Japan	E9	40
Minamata, Japan	G3	40
Minami-Alps-kokuritsu-kōen, p.o.i., Japan	D11	40
Minami-Tori-shima, i., Japan	G19	30
Minas, Cuba	B9	102
Minas, Indon.	C2	50
Minas, Ur.	G10	92
Minas Basin, b., N.S., Can.	E12	110
Minas de Barroterán, Mex.	B8	100
Minas de Corrales, Ur.	E10	92
Minas de Matahambre, Cuba	A5	102
Minas Gerais, state, Braz.	C8	90
Minas Novas, Braz.	I4	88
Minatare, Ne., U.S.	F9	126
Minatitlán, Mex.	F11	100
Minbu, Mya.	B2	48
Minbya, Mya.	B1	48
Minbyin, Mya.	C1	48
Mincio, stm., Italy	E7	22
Minco, Ok., U.S.	F10	128
Minčol, mtn., Slov.	G17	16
Mindanao, i., Phil.	G5	52
Mindanao, stm., Phil.	G5	52
Mindelheim, Ger.	H6	16
Mindelo, C.V.	k10	65a
Mindemoya, On., Can.	C7	112
Minden, On., Can.	D11	112
Minden, Ger.	D4	16
Minden, La., U.S.	E5	122
Minden, Ne., U.S.	G14	126
Minden, Nv., U.S.	E6	134
Minden City, Mi., U.S.	E7	112
Mindoro, i., Phil.	D3	52
Mindoro Strait, strt., Phil.	D3	52
Mine, Japan	E4	40
Mine Centre, On., Can.	C6	118
Minehead, Eng., U.K.	J9	12
Mineiros, Braz.	G7	84
Mineola, Tx., U.S.	E3	122
Mineral, Wa., U.S.	D4	136
Mineral Point, Wi., U.S.	B7	120
Mineral Springs, Ar., U.S.	D5	122
Mineral Wells, Tx., U.S.	B9	130
Minersville, Pa., U.S.	H13	112
Minerva, Oh., U.S.	D4	114
Minervino Murge, Italy	C9	24
Mineville, N.Y., U.S.	F3	110
Minfeng, China	A5	46
Minga, D.R.C.	G5	66
Mingäçevir, Azer.	A6	56
Mingāora, Pak.	C11	56
Mingary, Austl.	I3	76
Mingene, Austl.	E3	74
Mingin, Mya.	A2	48
Minglanilla, Spain	E9	20
Mingo Junction, Oh., U.S.	D5	114
Mingo Lake, l., Nu., Can.	C16	106
Mingshui, China	B10	36
Mingulay, i., Scot., U.K.	E5	12
Mingyuegou, China	C8	38
Minhang, China	F9	42
Minh Hai, Viet.	H7	48
Minhla, Mya.	B2	48
Minhla, Mya.	C2	48
Minho, hist. reg., Port.	C2	20
Minho (Miño), stm., Eur.	B2	20
Minićevo, Serb.	F9	26
Minicoy Island, i., India	G3	46
Minigwal, Lake, l., Austl.	E4	74
Minija, stm., Lith.	E4	10
Minilya, Austl.	D2	74
Minilya, stm., Austl.	D2	74
Miniota, Mb., Can.	D12	124
Minitonas, Mb., Can.	B12	124
Minle, China	D5	36
Minna, Nig.	H6	64
Minneapolis, Ks., U.S.	B11	128
Minneapolis, Mn., U.S.	G5	118
Minnedosa, Mb., Can.	D13	124
Minneola, Ks., U.S.	D8	128
Minneota, Mn., U.S.	G2	118
Minnesota, state, U.S.	E4	118
Minnesota, stm., Mn., U.S.	G5	118
Minnesota Lake, Mn., U.S.	H5	118
Minnewanka, Lake, res., Ab., Can.	E15	138
Minnitaki Lake, l., On., Can.	B6	118
Mino, Japan	D9	40
Miño (Minho), stm., Eur.	B2	20
Minocqua, Wi., U.S.	F9	118
Minong, Wi., U.S.	E7	118
Minonk, Il., U.S.	D8	120
Minorca see Menorca, i., Spain	D15	20
Minot, N.D., U.S.	F12	124
Minqing, China	H8	42
Minquan, China	D6	42
Minquiers, Plateau des, is., Jersey	E6	14
Min Shan, mts., China	E5	36
Minsk, Bela.	G10	10
Minsk, state, Bela.	G10	10
Minskae uzvyšša, plat., Bela.	G10	10
Mińsk Mazowiecki, Pol.	D17	16
Minta, Cam.	D2	66
Minto, Mb., Can.	E13	124
Minto, Yk., Can.	C3	106
Minto, N.D., U.S.	C1	118
Minto, Lac, l., Qc., Can.	D16	106
Minto, Mount, mtn., Ant.	C22	81
Minto Inlet, b., N.T., Can.	A7	106
Minton, Sk., Can.	E9	124
Minturn, Co., U.S.	D10	132
Minûf, Egypt	H1	58
Minusinsk, Russia	D16	32
Minvoul, Gabon	D2	66
Minxian, China	E5	36
Minya *see* El-Minya, Egypt	J1	58
Minya el-Qamh, Egypt	H2	58
Mio, Mi., U.S.	D5	112
Miquan, China	F15	32
Mir, Bela.	G9	10
Mira, stm., Col.	G2	86
Mīrābād, Afg.	C9	56
Mirabella, Gulf of see Mirampéllou, Kólpos, b., Grc.	H8	28
Miracema do Tocantins, Braz.	E1	88
Mirador, Braz.	D3	88
Miradouro, Braz.	K4	88
Miraflores, Col.	G5	86
Miraflores, Col.	E5	86
Miraj, India	C2	53
Miramar, Arg.	I9	92
Miramar, Moz.	C12	70
Miramas, Fr.	F10	18
Miramichi Bay, b., N.B., Can.	C11	110
Mirampéllou, Kólpos, b., Grc.	H8	28
Mīrān, Pak.	C3	54
Miranda, Braz.	D5	90
Miranda, Col.	F3	86
Miranda, state, Ven.	B8	86
Miranda, stm., Braz.	D5	90
Miranda de Ebro, Spain	B7	20
Mirande, Fr.	F6	18
Mirando City, Tx., U.S.	G8	130
Mirandola, Italy	F8	22
Mira Táglio, Italy	E9	22
Miravalles, Volcán, vol., C.R.	G5	102
Miravete, Puerto de, p., Spain	E5	20
Mirbāṭ, Oman	F7	56
Mirecourt, Fr.	F14	14
Miri, Malay.	A9	50
Miria, Niger	G6	64
Miriam Vale, Austl.	E8	76
Mirim, Lagoa (Merín, Laguna), b., S.A.	F11	92
Miriñay, stm., Arg.	D9	92
Miritiparaná, stm., Col.	H6	86
Miriyama, Pap. N. Gui.	a3	79a
Mirnoe Ozero, Russia	C13	32
Mirny, sci., Ant.	B14	81
Mirnyj, Russia	D11	34
Mirnyy, sci., Ant.	B14	81
Miroslav, Czech Rep.	H12	16
Mirow, Ger.	C8	16
Mīrpur, Bngl.	G13	54
Mīrpur, Pak.	B4	54
Mīrpur Batoro, Pak.	F2	54
Mīrpur Khās, Pak.	F2	54
Mirror, Ab., Can.	D17	138
Miryang, Kor., S.	D1	40
Mirzāpur, India	F9	54
Misantla, Mex.	F10	100
Misawa, Japan	D14	38
Miscou Centre, N.B., Can.	C12	110
Miscou Island, i., N.B., Can.	C12	110
Miscou Point, c., N.B., Can.	B12	110
Mishan, China	B9	38
Mishawaka, In., U.S.	G3	112
Mishicot, Wi., U.S.	D2	112
Misima Island, i., Pap. N. Gui.	B10	74
Misiones, state, Arg.	C10	92
Misiones, state, Para.	C9	92
Misión Santa Rosa, Para.	D4	90
Misión San Vicente, Mex.	F4	98
Miskitos, Cayos, is., Nic.	E6	102
Miskolc, Hung.	A7	26
Mišnëvo, Russia	G19	10
Misool, Pulau, i., Indon.	F9	44
Miṣrātah, Libya	A3	62
Misr el-Bahrî (Lower Egypt), hist. reg., Egypt	G2	58
Misrikh, India	E8	54
Missinaibi, stm., On., Can.	E14	106
Missinaibi Lake, l., On., Can.	F14	106
Mission, B.C., Can.	G8	138
Mission, S.D., U.S.	D12	126
Mission, Tx., U.S.	H9	130
Mission Mountain, hill, Ok., U.S.	H3	120
Mission Viejo, Ca., U.S.	J8	134
Mississagi, stm., On., Can.	B6	112
Mississauga, On., Can.	E10	112
Mississinewa, stm., U.S.	H4	112
Mississippi, state, U.S.	D9	122
Mississippi, stm., On., Can.	C13	112
Mississippi, stm., U.S.	E9	108
Mississippi Lake, l., On., Can.	C13	112
Mississippi River Delta, La., U.S.	H9	122
Mississippi Sound, strt., U.S.	G10	122
Mississippi State, Ms., U.S.	D10	122
Missoula, Mt., U.S.	D12	136
Missouri, state, U.S.	F5	120
Missouri, stm., U.S.	D9	108
Missouri City, Tx., U.S.	H3	122
Mistake Creek, stm., Austl.	D6	76
Mistassibi, stm., Qc., Can.	A4	110
Mistassini, Qc., Can.	E16	106
Mistassini, Qc., Can.	B4	110
Mistassini, stm., Qc., Can.	B4	110
Mistassini, Lac, l., Qc., Can.	E16	106
Mistatim, Sk., Can.	B10	124
Mistelbach an der Zaya, Aus.	B13	22
Misterbianco, Italy	G9	24
Misti, Volcán, vol., Peru	G3	84
Misumi, Japan	E4	40
Mišutino, Russia	A19	10
Mita, Punta de, c., Mex.	E6	100
Mitchell, Austl.	F6	76
Mitchell, On., Can.	E8	112
Mitchell, In., U.S.	F11	120
Mitchell, Or., U.S.	F6	136
Mitchell, S.D., U.S.	D14	126
Mitchell, stm., Austl.	K6	76
Mitchell, stm., Austl.	C8	74
Mitchell, Mount, mtn., N.C., U.S.	I3	114
Mitchinamecus, stm., Qc., Can.	C2	110
Mitchinamecus, Réservoir, res., Qc., Can.	C1	110
Mît Ghamr, Egypt	H2	58
Mithapur, India	G2	54
Mithi, Pak.	F2	54
Mitidja, Plaine de la, pl., Alg.	H14	20
Mitiškovo, Russia	F16	10
Mitla, sci., Mex.	G10	100
Mito, Japan	C13	40
Mitsio, Nosy, i., Madag.	C8	68
Mitsukaidō, Japan	C13	40
Mitsuke, Japan	B11	40
Mittellandkanal, can., Ger.	D5	16
Mittenwald, Ger.	I7	16
Mittersill, Aus.	C9	22
Mittimatalik (Pond Inlet), Nu., Can.	A15	106
Mittweida, Ger.	E9	16
Mitú, Col.	G6	86
Mitumba, Monts, mts., D.R.C.	F5	66
Mitwaba, D.R.C.	F5	66
Mitzic, Gabon	D2	66
Miura, Japan	D12	40
Miura-hantō, pen., Japan	D12	40
Mixian, China	D5	42
Miyagi, state, Japan	A13	40
Miyake-jima, i., Japan	E12	40
Miyako, Japan	E14	38
Miyako-jima, i., Japan	G10	36
Miyakonojō, Japan	H4	40
Miyama, Japan	E9	40
Miyanojō, Japan	H3	40
Miyazaki, Japan	H4	40
Miyazaki, state, Japan	G4	40
Miyazu, Japan	D8	40
Miyoshi, Japan	E5	40
Miyun, China	A7	42
Miyun Shuiku, res., China	A7	42
Mīzan Teferī, Eth.	F7	62
Mizdah, Libya	A2	62
Mize, Ms., U.S.	F9	122
Mizen Head, c., Ire.	J3	12
Mizen Head, c., Ire.	I6	12
Mizhhir'ia, Ukr.	A10	26
Mizhi, China	C4	42
Mizil, Rom.	E13	26
Mizoram, state, India	G14	54
Mizpah Creek, stm., Mt., U.S.	A7	126
Mizque, Bol.	C3	90
Mizukaidō *see* Mitsukaidō, Japan	C13	40
Mizusawa, Japan	E14	38
Mjadzel, Bela.	F9	10
Mjakit, Russia	D19	34
Mjaksa, Russia	B21	10
Mjölby, Swe.	G6	8
Mjøsa, l., Nor.	F4	8
Mkalama, Tan.	E6	66
Mkhondvo, stm., Afr.	E10	70
Mkokotoni, Tan.	F7	66
Mkomazi, stm., S. Afr.	G10	70
Mkulwe, Tan.	F6	66
Mkuze, S. Afr.	E10	70
Mkuze, stm., S. Afr.	E11	70
Mkuze Game Reserve, S. Afr.	E11	70
Mladá Boleslav, Czech Rep.	F11	16
Mladenovac, Serb.	E7	26
Mlava, stm., Serb.	E8	26
Mława, Pol.	C16	16
Mljet, Otok, i., Cro.	H14	22
Mljet Nacionalni Park, p.o.i., Cro.	H14	22
Mmabatho, S. Afr.	D7	70
Mmadinare, Bots.	B8	70
Moa, stm., Afr.	H2	64
Moab, Ut., U.S.	E7	132
Moala, i., Fiji	q18	79e
Moama, Austl.	K5	76
Moamba, Moz.	D11	70
Moanda, Gabon	E2	66
Moar Lake, l., Can.	C18	124
Moate, Ire.	H5	12
Moba, D.R.C.	F5	66
Mobara, Japan	D13	40
Mobaye, C.A.R.	D4	66
Mobeetie, Tx., U.S.	F8	128
Moberly, Mo., U.S.	E5	120
Mobile, Al., U.S.	G10	122
Mobile, Az., U.S.	J4	132
Mobile, stm., Al., U.S.	G11	122
Mobile Bay, b., Al., U.S.	G10	122
Mobridge, S.D., U.S.	B12	126
Moca, Dom. Rep.	C12	102
Mocajuba, Braz.	B1	88
Mo Cay, Viet.	G8	48
Mocha *see* Al-Mukhā, Yemen	G5	56
Mochudi, Bots.	D8	70
Mocksville, N.C., U.S.	I5	114
Moclips, Wa., U.S.	C2	136
Môco, Morro de, mtn., Ang.	C2	68
Mocoa, Col.	G3	86
Mococa, Braz.	K2	88
Mocodoene, Moz.	C12	70
Mocoretá, Arg.	E8	92
Moctezuma, Mex.	G8	98
Moctezuma, stm., Mex.	E9	100
Moctezuma, stm., Mex.	G8	98
Mocuba, Moz.	D6	68
Modane, Fr.	D12	18
Modāsa, India	G4	54
Modder, stm., S. Afr.	F7	70
Módena, Italy	F7	22
Modeste, Mount, mtn., B.C., Can.	H6	138
Modesto, Ca., U.S.	F4	134
Modica, Italy	H8	24
Mödling, Aus.	B13	22
Modowi, Indon.	F9	44
Modra, Slov.	H13	16
Moe, Austl.	L6	76
Moeda, Braz.	K3	88
Moei (Thaungyin), stm., Asia	D3	48
Moema, Braz.	J3	88
Moengo, Sur.	B7	84
Moen-jo-Daro, sci., Pak.	D10	56
Moenkopi, Az., U.S.	G5	132
Moenkopi Wash, stm., Az., U.S.	G6	132
Moeris, Lake see Qârûn, Birket, l., Egypt	I1	58
Moeskroen *see* Mouscron, Bel.	D12	14
Moffat, Scot., U.K.	F9	12
Moga, India	C5	54
Mogadiscio *see* Muqdisho, Som.	D9	66
Mogadishu *see* Muqdisho, Som.	D9	66
Mogalakwena, stm., S. Afr.	C9	70
Mogami, stm., Japan	A13	40
Mogaung, Mya.	C8	46
Mogdy, Russia	F15	34
Mogilno, Pol.	D13	16
Mogincual, Moz.	D7	68
Mogoča, Russia	F12	34
Mogočin, Russia	C14	32
Mogogh, Sudan	F6	62
Mogok, Mya.	A3	48
Mogollon Rim, clf., Az., U.S.	I6	132
Mogor, Afg.	B1	54
Mogotes, Col.	D5	86
Mogotón, mtn., N.A.	F4	102
Moguer, Spain	G4	20
Mogzon, Russia	F11	34
Mohács, Hung.	C5	26
Mohall, N.D., U.S.	F12	124
Mohammed, Râs, c., Egypt	K5	58
Mohammedia, Mor.	C3	64
Mohania, India	F9	54
Mohawk, Mi., U.S.	D10	118
Mohawk, stm., N.Y., U.S.	B11	114
Mohe, China	F13	34
Mohéli see Mwali, i., Com.	C7	68
Mohnyin, Mya.	D8	46
Mohokare (Caledon), stm., Afr.	F8	70
Mohyliv-Podil's'kyi, Ukr.	A14	26
Moi, Nor.	G2	8
Moinești, Rom.	C13	26
Moira, stm., On., Can.	D12	112
Moiraba, Braz.	B1	88
Mo i Rana, Nor.	C5	8
Moiseevka, Russia	C13	32
Moisés Ville, Arg.	E7	92
Moisie, Qc., Can.	E17	106
Moisie, stm., Qc., Can.	E17	106
Moitaco, Ven.	C9	86
Mojácar, Spain	G9	20
Mojave, Ca., U.S.	H7	134
Mojave, stm., Ca., U.S.	H9	134
Mojave Desert, des., Ca., U.S.	D4	98
Mojero, stm., Russia	C9	34
Mojiguaçu, stm., Braz.	K2	88
Mojikit Lake, res., On., Can.	A10	118
Moji-Mirim, Braz.	L2	88
Mojo, Eth.	F7	62
Moju, Braz.	A1	88
Moju, stm., Braz.	D8	84
Mōka, Japan	C12	40
Mokāma, India	F10	54
Mōkapu Peninsula, pen., Hi., U.S.	b4	78a
Mokau, stm., N.Z.	D6	80
Mokelumne, stm., Ca., U.S.	E5	134
Moknine, Tun.	B7	64
Mokochu, Khao, mtn., Thai.	E4	48
Mokokchūng, India	C7	46
Mokolo, Cam.	B2	66
Mokolo, stm., S. Afr.	C8	70
Mokpalin, Mya.	D3	48
Mokp'o, Kor., S.	G7	38
Mokša, stm., Russia	D6	32
Mokwa, Nig.	H5	64
Mol, Bel.	C14	14
Mola di Bari, Italy	C11	24
Molat, Otok, i., Cro.	F11	22
Moldau see Vltava, stm., Czech Rep.	F10	16
Moldavia, hist. reg., Rom.	C13	26
Molde, Nor.	E2	8
Moldova, ctry., Eur.	B15	26
Moldova, stm., Rom.	C13	26
Moldoveanu, Vârful, mtn., Rom.	D11	26
Môle, Cap du, c., Haiti	C11	102
Mole Creek, Austl.	n13	77a
Molega Lake, l., N.S., Can.	F12	110
Molène, Île de, i., Fr.	F3	14
Molepolole, Bots.	D7	70
Molėtai, Lith.	E8	10
Molfetta, Italy	C10	24
Molina, Chile	G2	92
Molina de Aragón, Spain	D9	20
Molina de Segura, Spain	F9	20
Moline, Il., U.S.	C7	120
Moline, Ks., U.S.	D12	128
Molino, Fl., U.S.	G11	122
Molino de Valdo de Piedras, Mex.	E3	130
Molinos, Arg.	B4	92
Molise, state, Italy	C8	24
Mollendo, Peru	G3	84
Mölln, Ger.	C6	16
Mölndal, Swe.	H4	8
Molodežnaja, sci., Ant.	B9	81
Molodogvardeyskoe, Kaz.	D11	32
Mologa, stm., Russia	B19	10
Moloka'i, i., Hi., U.S.	b5	78a
Molokai Fracture Zone, unds.	G24	142
Molokovo, Russia	B19	10
Molong, Austl.	I7	76
Molopo, stm., Afr.	E5	70
Moloundou, Cam.	D3	66
Molson Lake, l., Mb., Can.	E11	106
Molu, Pulau, i., Indon.	G9	44
Moluccas see Maluku, is., Indon.	F8	44
Molucca Sea see Maluku, Laut, s., Indon.	F8	44
Molvoticy, Russia	C15	10
Moma, Moz.	D6	68
Moma, stm., Russia	C17	34
Mombaça, Braz.	C6	88
Mombasa, Kenya	E7	66
Mombetsu, Japan	B15	38
Momčilgrad, Blg.	H12	26
Momi, Fiji	p18	79e
Momotombo, Volcán, vol., Nic.	F4	102
Mompono, D.R.C.	D4	66
Mompós, Col.	C4	86
Momskij hrebet, mts., Russia	C18	34
Mon, state, Mya.	E3	48
Møn, i., Den.	I5	8
Mona, Ut., U.S.	D5	132
Mona, Isla de, i., P.R.	h14	96a
Mona, Punta, c., C.R.	H6	102
Monaca, Pa., U.S.	D5	114
Monach Islands, is., Scot., U.K.	D5	12
Monaco, Mon.	G4	22
Monaco, ctry., Eur.	F13	18
Monadnock Mountain, mtn., N.H., U.S.	B13	114
Monagas, state, Ven.	C10	86
Monaghan, Ire.	G6	12
Monaghan, state, Ire.	G6	12
Monahans, Tx., U.S.	C5	130
Monakino, Russia	C10	38
Mona Passage, strt., N.A.	C13	102
Monapo, Moz.	C7	68
Monarch, S.C., U.S.	B4	116
Monarch Mountain, mtn., B.C., Can.	E5	138
Monarch Pass, p., Co., U.S.	E10	132
Monashee Mountains, mts., B.C., Can.	F12	138
Monastir, Tun.	I4	24
Moncalieri, Italy	F4	22
Moncalvo, Italy	E5	22
Monção, Braz.	B3	88
Mončegorsk, Russia	B15	8
Mönchengladbach, Ger.	E2	16
Monchique, Port.	G2	20
Moncks Corner, S.C., U.S.	C5	116
Monclova, Mex.	B8	100
Moncton, N.B., Can.	D12	110
Monday, stm., Para.	B10	92
Mondego, stm., Port.	D3	20
Mondjamboli, D.R.C.	D4	66
Mondoubleau, Fr.	F9	14
Mondovi, Wi., U.S.	G7	118
Mondragone, Italy	C7	24
Monemvasía, Grc.	G6	28
Monessen, Pa., U.S.	D5	114
Monesterio, Spain	F4	20
Monett, Mo., U.S.	H4	120
Monette, Ar., U.S.	I7	120
Monfalcone, Italy	E10	22
Monferrato, hist. reg., Italy	F5	22
Monforte de Lemos, Spain	B3	20
Monga, D.R.C.	D4	66
Mongaguá, Braz.	B14	92
Mongalla, Sudan	F6	62
Mongers Lake, l., Austl.	E3	74
Monggon Qulu, China	B8	36
Möng Hai, Mya.	B4	48
Möng Hsat, Mya.	B4	48
Mongibello see Etna, Monte, vol., Italy	G8	24
Möng Küng, Mya.	B3	48
Möng Ma, Mya.	B4	48
Möng Nai, Mya.	B3	48
Mongo, Chad	E3	62
Mongol Altayn nuruu, mts., Asia	E16	32
Mongolia, ctry., Asia	E14	30
Mongonu, Nig.	G7	64
Möng Pai, Mya.	C3	48
Möng Pawn, Mya.	B3	48
Mongu, Zam.	D3	68
Möng Yai, Mya.	A4	48
Monico, Wi., U.S.	F9	118
Monida Pass, p., U.S.	F14	136
Monino, Russia	E21	10
Moniquirá, Col.	E5	86
Mõniste, Est.	H12	8
Monitor Valley, val., Nv., U.S.	E9	134
Mońki, Pol.	C18	16
Monkira, Austl.	E3	76
Monmouth, Wales, U.K.	J10	12
Monmouth, Or., U.S.	F3	136
Monmouth Mountain, mtn., B.C., Can.	E7	138
Mono, stm., Afr.	H5	64
Mono, Caño, stm., Col.	E7	86
Mono Island, i., Sol. Is.	d6	79b
Mono Lake, l., Ca., U.S.	E7	134
Monon, In., U.S.	H3	112
Monona, Ia., U.S.	H7	118
Monona, Wi., U.S.	A8	120
Monongahela, stm., U.S.	E6	114
Monopoli, Italy	D11	24
Monor, Hung.	B6	26
Monreal del Campo, Spain	D9	20
Monreale, Italy	F7	24
Monroe, La., U.S.	E6	122
Monroe, Mi., U.S.	C2	114
Monroe, N.C., U.S.	B5	116
Monroe, N.Y., U.S.	C11	114
Monroe, Or., U.S.	F3	136
Monroe, Ut., U.S.	E4	132
Monroe, Va., U.S.	G6	114
Monroe, Wa., U.S.	C4	136
Monroe, Wi., U.S.	B8	120
Monroe City, In., U.S.	F10	120
Monroe Lake, res., In., U.S.	E11	120
Monroeville, Al., U.S.	F11	122
Monroeville, In., U.S.	D1	114
Monroeville, Oh., U.S.	C3	114
Monroeville, Pa., U.S.	D6	114
Monrovia, Lib.	H2	64
Mons, Bel.	D12	14
Monsefú, Peru	E2	84
Monselice, Italy	E8	22
Monsenhor Hipólito, Braz.	D5	88
Monsenhor Tabosa, Braz.	C5	88
Mönsterås, Swe.	H7	8
Montabaur, Ger.	F3	16
Montagne, Neth. Ant.	p23	104g
Montagu, S. Afr.	H5	70
Montague, P.E., Can.	D14	110
Montague, Mi., U.S.	E3	112
Montague, Tx., U.S.	H11	128
Montague, Isla, i., Mex.	F5	98
Montague Island, i., Ak., U.S.	E10	140
Montagu Island, i., S. Geor.	K12	82
Montaigu, Fr.	H7	14
Montalbano Ionico, Italy	D10	24
Montalegre, Port.	C3	20
Montana, Blg.	F10	26
Montana, state, Blg.	F10	26
Montana, state, U.S.	B6	108
Montaña de Covadonga, Parque Nacional de la, p.o.i., Spain	A5	20
Montánchez, Spain	E4	20
Montanha, Braz.	J5	88
Montargis, Fr.	G11	14
Montauban, Fr.	E7	18
Montauk Point, c., N.Y., U.S.	C14	114
Montbard, Fr.	G13	14
Montbéliard, Fr.	G15	14
Mont Belvieu, Tx., U.S.	H3	122
Montblanc, Spain	C11	20
Montblanch *see* Montblanc, Spain	C11	20
Montbrison, Fr.	D9	18
Montbron, Fr.	D6	18
Montceau-les-Mines, Fr.	H13	14
Montclair, Ca., U.S.	I8	134
Mont-de-Marsan, Fr.	F5	18
Montdidier, Fr.	E11	14
Monte, Laguna del, l., Arg.	H6	92
Monteagudo, Bol.	C4	90
Monte Albán, sci., Mex.	G10	100
Monte Alegre, Braz.	D7	84
Monte Alegre de Goiás, Braz.	G2	88
Monte Alegre de Minas, Braz.	J1	88
Monte Alegre de Sergipe, Braz.	F7	88
Monte Azul, Braz.	H4	88
Montebello, Qc., Can.	C14	112
Montebello, P.R.	B2	104a
Montecarlo, Arg.	C10	92
Monte Carmelo, Braz.	J2	88
Monte Caseros, Arg.	E8	92
Montecassino, Abbazia di, rel., Italy	C7	24
Montecatini Terme, Italy	G7	22
Montecito, Ca., U.S.	I6	134
Monte Comán, Arg.	G4	92
Monte Creek, B.C., Can.	F11	138
Monte Cristi, Dom. Rep.	C12	102
Monte Cristo, Bol.	B4	90
Montecristo, Isola di, i., Italy	H7	22
Monte do Carmo, Braz.	F1	88
Monte Escobedo, Mex.	D7	100
Montefalco, Italy	H9	22
Montefiascone, Italy	H8	22
Montego Bay, Jam.	i12	104d
Monteiro, Braz.	D7	88
Montejicar, Spain	G7	20
Montejinni, Austl.	C6	74
Montelíbano, Col.	C4	86
Montélimar, Fr.	E10	18
Monte Lindo, stm., Para.	A9	92
Montellano, Spain	H5	20
Montello, Nv., U.S.	B2	132
Montello, Wi., U.S.	H9	118
Monte Maíz, Arg.	F6	92
Montemayor, Meseta de, plat., Arg.	H3	90
Montemorelos, Mex.	C9	100
Montemor-o-Velho, Port.	D2	20
Montemuro, mtn., Port.	C2	20
Montenegro, Braz.	D12	92
Montenegro see Crna Gora, state, Serb.	G6	26
Monte Pascoal, Parque Nacional de, p.o.i., Braz.	I5	88
Monte Patria, Chile	E2	92
Montepuez, Moz.	C6	68
Montepulciano, Italy	G8	22
Monte Quemado, Arg.	B6	92
Montereau-Faut-Yonne, Fr.	F11	14
Monterey, Ca., U.S.	G3	134
Monterey, Va., U.S.	F6	114
Monterey Bay, b., Ca., U.S.	G3	134
Montería, Col.	C3	86
Monteros, Arg.	C5	92
Monterotondo, Italy	H9	22
Monterrey, Mex.	C8	100
Montesano, Wa., U.S.	C3	136
Monte Sant'Angelo, Italy	I12	22
Monte Santu, Capo di, c., Italy	D3	24
Montes Claros, Braz.	I3	88
Montesilvano Marina, Italy	H11	22
Montevallo, Al., U.S.	D12	122
Montevarchi, Italy	G8	22
Montevideo, Ur.	G9	92
Montevideo, Mn., U.S.	G3	118
Monte Vista, Co., U.S.	D2	128
Montezuma, Ga., U.S.	D1	116
Montezuma, In., U.S.	I2	112
Montezuma, Ks., U.S.	D8	128
Montezuma Castle National Monument, p.o.i., Az., U.S.	I4	132
Montgenèvre, Col de, p., Fr.	E12	18
Montgomery, Al., U.S.	E12	122
Montgomery, La., U.S.	F6	122
Montgomery, Mn., U.S.	G5	118
Montgomery, Pa., U.S.	C8	114
Montgomery, Tx., U.S.	G3	122
Montgomery City, Mo., U.S.	E6	120
Montguyon, Fr.	D5	18
Monthey, Switz.	D3	22
Monticello, Ar., U.S.	D7	122
Monticello, Fl., U.S.	F2	116
Monticello, Il., U.S.	D9	120
Monticello, In., U.S.	H3	112
Monticello, Ky., U.S.	H13	120
Monticello, Mn., U.S.	F5	118
Monticello, Mo., U.S.	D6	120
Monticello, Ms., U.S.	F8	122
Monticello, N.Y., U.S.	C11	114
Monticello, Ut., U.S.	F7	132
Monticello, hist., Va., U.S.	G7	114
Montigny-le-Roi, Fr.	G14	14
Montigny-lès-Metz, Fr.	E15	14
Montijo, Pan.	I7	102
Montijo, Port.	F2	20
Montijo, Spain	F4	20
Montijo, Golfo de, b., Pan.	I7	102
Montilla, Spain	G6	20
Montivilliers, Fr.	E9	14
Mont-Joli, Qc., Can.	B8	110
Mont-Laurier, Qc., Can.	B14	112
Montluçon, Fr.	C8	18
Montmagny, Qc., Can.	D6	110
Montmédy, Fr.	E14	14
Montmorillon, Fr.	C6	18
Monto, Austl.	E8	76
Montoro, Spain	F6	20
Montour Falls, N.Y., U.S.	B9	114
Montpelier, Jam.	i13	104d
Montpelier, Id., U.S.	H15	136
Montpelier, In., U.S.	H4	112
Montpelier, Oh., U.S.	C1	114
Montpelier, Vt., U.S.	F4	110
Montpellier, Fr.	F9	18
Montréal, Qc., Can.	E3	110
Montreal, Wi., U.S.	E8	118
Montreal, stm., On., Can.	A10	112
Montreal Lake, l., Sk., Can.	E9	106
Montreuil-sur-Mer, Fr.	D10	14
Montreux, Switz.	D3	22
Montrose, Scot., U.K.	E10	12
Montrose, Co., U.S.	E9	132
Montrose, Mi., U.S.	E6	112
Montrose, Pa., U.S.	C9	114
Montrose, S.D., U.S.	D15	126
Montross, Va., U.S.	F9	114
Monts, Pointe des, c., Qc., Can.	A9	110
Mont-Saint-Michel, Qc., Can.	D1	110
Mont-Saint-Michel, Baie du, b., Fr.	F7	14
Mont-Saint-Michel, Le, rel., Fr.	F7	14
Montserrat, dep., N.A.	h15	96a
Mont-Tremblant, Parc de récréation du, p.o.i., Qc., Can.	D2	110
Monument, Or., U.S.	F7	136
Monument Draw, stm., U.S.	B5	130
Monument Peak, mtn., Co., U.S.	D9	132
Monument Valley, val., U.S.	F6	132
Monviso, mtn., Italy	F4	22
Monyo, Mya.	C2	48
Monywa, Mya.	A2	48
Monza, Italy	E6	22
Monze, Zam.	D4	68
Monzen, Japan	B9	40
Monzón, Spain	C11	20
Mooi, stm., S. Afr.	F10	70
Moolawatana, Austl.	G2	76
Moon, Mountains of the see Ruwenzori, mts., Afr.	D6	66
Moonie, Austl.	F8	76
Moonie, stm., Austl.	G7	76
Moora, Austl.	F3	74
Moorcroft, Wy., U.S.	C8	126
Moore, Id., U.S.	G13	136
Moore, Ok., U.S.	F11	128
Moore, Tx., U.S.	E8	130
Moore, Lake, l., Austl.	E3	74
Moorea, i., Fr. Poly.	v20	78h
Moorefield, W.V., U.S.	E7	114
Moore Haven, Fl., U.S.	J4	116
Mooreland, Ok., U.S.	E9	128
Mooresville, N.C., U.S.	A5	116
Moorhead, Mn., U.S.	E2	118
Moorhead, Ms., U.S.	D8	122
Mooringsport, La., U.S.	E5	122
Moornanyah Lake, l., Austl.	I4	76
Moorreesburg, S. Afr.	H4	70
Moosburg an der Isar, Ger.	H7	16
Moosehead Lake, l., Me., U.S.	E7	110
Moose Island, i., Mb., Can.	C16	124
Moose Jaw, Sk., Can.	D8	124

I·38 Moose Jaw – Mwenezi

Name	Map Ref.	Page
Moose Jaw, stm., Sk., Can.	D8	124
Moose Lake, Mn., U.S.	E6	118
Moose Lake, l., Ab., Can.	B19	138
Mooselookmeguntic Lake, l., Me., U.S.	F5	110
Moose Mountain, mtn., Sk., Can.	E11	124
Moose Mountain Creek, stm., Sk., Can.	E11	124
Moose Pass, Ak., U.S.	D10	140
Moosomin, Sk., Can.	D12	124
Moosonee, On., Can.	E14	106
Mootwingee National Park, p.o.i., Austl.	H4	76
Mopane, S. Afr.	C9	70
Mopipi, Bots.	B7	70
Moppo see Mokp'o, Kor., S.	G7	38
Mopti, Mali	G4	64
Moquegua, Peru	G3	84
Mór, Hung.	B5	26
Mòr, Glen, val., Scot., U.K.	D8	12
Mora, Cam.	B2	66
Mora, Port.	F2	20
Mora, Swe.	F6	8
Mora, Mn., U.S.	F5	118
Mora, stm., N.M., U.S.	F4	128
Morač, stm., Bela.	H10	10
Morādābād, India	D7	54
Morada Nova, Braz.	C6	88
Morada Nova de Minas, Braz.	J3	88
Morąg, Pol.	C15	16
Moral de Calatrava, Spain	F7	20
Moraleda, Canal, strt., Chile	H2	90
Morales, Laguna de, b., Mex.	D10	100
Moramanga, Madag.	D8	68
Moran, Ks., U.S.	G2	120
Moran, Mi., U.S.	B5	112
Moran, Tx., U.S.	B8	130
Morant Bay, Jam.	j14	104d
Morant Cays, is., Jam.	D10	102
Morant Point, c., Jam.	j14	104d
Morar, Loch, l., Scot., U.K.	E7	12
Moratalla, Spain	F9	20
Moratuwa, Sri L.	H4	53
Morava, hist. reg., Czech Rep.	G13	16
Morava (March), stm., Eur.	H12	16
Moravia, N.Y., U.S.	B9	114
Moravské Budějovice, Czech Rep.	G11	16
Morawa, Austl.	E3	74
Morawhanna, Guy.	C12	86
Moray Firth, b., Scot., U.K.	D9	12
Morbi, India	G3	54
Morbihan, state, Fr.	G6	14
Morcenx, Fr.	E5	18
Morden, Mb., Can.	E15	124
Mordovia see Mordovija, state, Russia	D6	32
Mordovija, state, Russia	D6	32
Mordves, Russia	F21	10
Mordvinia see Mordovija, state, Russia	D6	32
Mordy, Pol.	D18	16
More, Ben, mtn., Scot., U.K.	E7	12
Moreau, stm., S.D., U.S.	B12	126
Moreau, North Fork, stm., S.D., U.S.	B9	126
Moreau, South Fork, stm., S.D., U.S.	B9	126
Moreau Peak, mtn., S.D., U.S.	B9	126
Moreauville, La., U.S.	F7	122
Morecambe, Eng., U.K.	G9	12
Morecambe Bay, b., Eng., U.K.	H9	12
Moree, Austl.	G7	76
Morehead, Ky., U.S.	F2	114
Morehead City, N.C., U.S.	B9	116
Moreland, Ga., U.S.	D14	122
Moreland, Ky., U.S.	G13	120
Morelia, Mex.	F8	100
Morell, P.E., Can.	D14	110
Morella, Austl.	D4	76
Morelos, Mex.	I2	130
Morelos, Mex.	B5	100
Morelos, state, Mex.	F9	100
Morena, India	E6	54
Morena, Sierra, mts., Spain	F5	20
Morenci, Az., U.S.	J7	132
Moreni, Rom.	D12	26
Moreno, Bahía, b., Chile	A2	92
Møre og Romsdal, state, Nor.	E2	8
Moresby Island, i., B.C., Can.	E4	106
Moreton, Austl.	B8	74
Moreton Island, i., Austl.	F9	76
Moreuil, Fr.	E11	14
Morez, Fr.	H14	14
Morgan, Mn., U.S.	G3	118
Morgan, Mt., U.S.	F6	124
Morgan, Tx., U.S.	B10	130
Morgan, Ut., U.S.	B5	132
Morgan City, Al., U.S.	C12	122
Morgan City, La., U.S.	H7	122
Morganfield, Ky., U.S.	G10	120
Morgan Hill, Ca., U.S.	F4	134
Morganito, Ven.	E8	86
Morganton, N.C., U.S.	I4	114
Morgantown, In., U.S.	E11	120
Morgantown, Ms., U.S.	F8	122
Morgantown, Ms., U.S.	F7	122
Morgantown, W.V., U.S.	E6	114
Morgenzon, S. Afr.	E9	70
Morghāb (Murgab), stm., Asia	B9	56
Moriah, Mount, mtn., Nv., U.S.	D2	132
Moriarty, N.M., U.S.	G2	128
Morice, stm., B.C., Can.	B4	138
Morice Lake, l., B.C., Can.	B3	138
Morichal Largo, stm., Ven.	C10	86
Moricsala rezervāts, Lat.	C5	10
Moriki, Nig.	G6	64
Morino, Russia	C13	10
Morinville, Ab., Can.	C17	138
Morioka, Japan	E14	38
Morīri, Tso, l., India	B6	54
Morisset, Austl.	I8	76
Morjakovskij Zaton, Russia	C14	32
Morkoka, stm., Russia	D11	34
Morlaix, Fr.	F5	14
Morley, Mi., U.S.	E4	112
Mormal', Bela.	H12	10
Mormugao, India	D1	53
Morne-à-l'Eau, Guad.	h5	105c
Morne du Vitet, hill, Guad.	B2	105a
Morne Trois Pitons National Park, p.o.i., Dom.	j6	105c
Morney, Austl.	E3	76
Morning Sun, Ia., U.S.	C6	120
Mornington, Austl.	L5	76
Mornington, Isla, i., Chile	I1	90
Mornington Island, i., Austl.	C7	74
Morobe, Pap. N. Gui.	b4	79a
Morocco, In., U.S.	H2	112
Morocco, ctry., Afr.	C3	64
Moro Creek, stm., Ar., U.S.	D6	122
Morogoro, Tan.	F7	66
Moro Gulf, b., Phil.	G4	52
Moroleón, Mex.	E8	100
Morombe, Madag.	E7	68
Morón, Arg.	G8	92
Morón, Cuba	A8	102
Mörön, Mong.	B5	36
Morón, Ven.	B7	86
Morona, stm., S.A.	I3	86
Morona Santiago, state, Ec.	I3	86
Morondava, Madag.	E7	68
Morón de Almazán, Spain	C8	20
Morón de la Frontera, Spain	G5	20
Moroni, Com.	C7	68
Moroni, Ut., U.S.	D5	132
Moron Us, stm., China	E3	36
Morošečnoe, Russia	E20	34
Morotai, i., Indon.	E8	44
Moroto, Ug.	D6	66
Moroto, mtn., Ug.	D6	66
Morovis, P.R.	B3	104a
Morozovsk, Russia	E6	32
Morpeth, Eng., U.K.	F11	12
Morrilton, Ar., U.S.	B6	122
Morrin, Ab., Can.	E18	138
Morrinhos, Braz.	I1	88
Morrinhos, Braz.	B5	88
Morrinsville, N.Z.	C6	80
Morris, Mb., Can.	E16	124
Morris, Il., U.S.	C9	120
Morris, Mn., U.S.	F2	118
Morrisburg, On., Can.	D14	112
Morris Jesup, Kap, c., Grnld.	A19	141
Morrison, Arg.	F6	92
Morrison, Il., U.S.	C8	120
Morrisonville, Il., U.S.	E8	120
Morristown, Az., U.S.	J4	132
Morristown, In., U.S.	E12	120
Morristown, S.D., U.S.	B11	126
Morristown, Tn., U.S.	H2	114
Morrisville, Pa., U.S.	H15	112
Morro, Punta, c., Mex.	C2	102
Morro Bay, Ca., U.S.	H5	134
Morro do Chapéu, Braz.	F5	88
Morros, Braz.	B3	88
Morrosquillo, Golfo de, b., Col.	C3	86
Morrow, La., U.S.	G6	122
Morrumbala, Moz.	D6	68
Morrumbene, Moz.	C12	70
Morse, La., U.S.	G6	122
Morse, Tx., U.S.	E7	128
Morsi, India	H6	54
Mörskom see Myrskylä, Fin.	F11	8
Morson, On., Can.	B4	118
Mortagne-sur-Sèvre, Fr.	H8	14
Mortara, Italy	E5	22
Morteau, Fr.	G15	14
Morteros, Arg.	E6	92
Mortes, stm., Braz.	F7	84
Mortlach, Sk., Can.	D7	124
Mortlock Islands, is., Micron.	C6	72
Morton, Il., U.S.	D8	120
Morton, Mn., U.S.	G4	118
Morton, Tx., U.S.	H6	128
Morton, Wa., U.S.	D4	136
Morton National Park, p.o.i., Austl.	J7	76
Morua, Vanuatu	k17	79d
Moruya, Austl.	J7	76
Morvan, mts., Fr.	G13	14
Morvant, Trin.	s12	105f
Morven, Austl.	F6	76
Morven, Ga., U.S.	F2	116
Morven, N.C., U.S.	B5	116
Morwell, Austl.	L6	76
Moryń, Pol.	D10	16
Moržovec, ostrov, i., Russia	C20	8
Mosal'sk, Russia	F17	10
Mosbach, Ger.	G5	16
Moscos Islands, is., Mya.	E3	48
Moscow see Moskva, Russia	E20	10
Moscow, Id., U.S.	D10	136
Moscow see Moskva, stm., Russia	E21	10
Mosel (Moselle), stm., Eur.	G2	16
Moselebe, stm., Bots.	D7	70
Moselle, Ms., U.S.	F9	122
Moselle, state, Fr.	F15	14
Moselle (Mosel), stm., Eur.	G2	16
Moses Lake, Wa., U.S.	C7	136
Moses Point, Ak., U.S.	D7	140
Moshaweng, stm., S. Afr.	E6	70
Mosheim, Tn., U.S.	H3	114
Moshi, Tan.	E7	66
Mosinee, Wi., U.S.	G9	118
Mosjøen, Nor.	D5	8
Moskalvo, Russia	F17	34
Moskenesøya, i., Nor.	C5	8
Moskovskaja oblast', co., Russia	D19	10
Moskovskaja vozvyšennost', plat., Russia	E19	10
Moskva (Moscow), Russia	E20	10
Moskva, stm., Russia	E21	10
Moskvy, kanal imeni, can., Russia	D20	10
Mosomane, Bots.	C8	70
Mosonmagyaróvár, Hung.	B4	26
Mosopa, Bots.	D7	70
Mosqueiro, Braz.	D8	84
Mosquera, Col.	F2	86
Mosquito Coast see Mosquitos, Costa de, hist. reg., Nic.	F6	102
Mosquitos, Costa de, hist. reg., Nic.	F6	102
Mosquitos, Golfo de los, b., Pan.	H7	102
Moss, Nor.	G4	8
Mossaka, Congo	E3	66
Mossbank, Sk., Can.	E7	124
Mossburn, N.Z.	G2	80
Mosselbaai (Mossel Bay), S. Afr.	I6	70
Mossel Bay see Mosselbaai, S. Afr.	I6	70
Mossleigh, Ab., Can.	F17	138
Mossman, Austl.	C9	74
Moss Mountain, mtn., Ar., U.S.	C6	122
Mossoró, Braz.	C7	88
Moss Point, Ms., U.S.	G10	122
Moss Vale, Austl.	J8	76
Mossy, stm., Mb., Can.	C13	124
Most, Czech Rep.	F9	16
Mostar, Bos.	F4	26
Mostardas, Braz.	E12	92
Møsting, Kap, c., Grnld.	E17	141
Mostovaja, Russia	D16	10
Mostyn, Malay.	A11	50
Mosul see Al-Mawṣil, Iraq	B5	56
Møsvatnet, l., Nor.	G2	8
Mot'a, Eth.	E7	62
Mota del Cuervo, Spain	E8	20
Mota del Marqués, Spain	C5	20
Motagua, stm., N.A.	E3	102
Motal', Bela.	H8	10
Motala, Swe.	G6	8
Mota Lava, i., Vanuatu	i16	79d
Motaze, Moz.	D11	70
Moteve, Cap, c., Fr. Poly.	s18	78g
Motherwell, Scot., U.K.	F9	12
Motihāri, India	E10	54
Motloutse, stm., Bots.	B9	70
Motopu, Fr. Poly.	s18	78g
Motozintla de Mendoza, Mex.	H12	100
Motril, Spain	H7	20
Motru, Rom.	E10	26
Mott, N.D., U.S.	A10	126
Motu, stm., N.Z.	C7	80
Motueka, N.Z.	E5	80
Motul de Felipe Carrillo Puerto, Mex.	B3	102
Motutapu, i., Cook Is.	a27	78j
Motygino, Russia	C17	32
Motyklejka, Russia	E18	34
Mouaskar, Alg.	B5	64
Mouchoir Passage, strt., N.A.	B12	102
Moudjéria, Maur.	F2	64
Moúdros, Grc.	D8	28
Mouila, Gabon	E2	66
Mould Bay, N.T., Can.	A16	140
Moule à Chique, Cap, c., St. Luc.	m7	105c
Moulins, Fr.	H12	14
Moulmein see Mawlamyine, Mya.	D3	48
Moulmeingyun, Mya.	D2	48
Moulouya, Oued, stm., Mor.	C4	64
Moulton, Al., U.S.	C11	122
Moulton, Ia., U.S.	D5	120
Moulton, Tx., U.S.	E10	130
Moultrie, Ga., U.S.	E2	116
Moultrie, Lake, res., S.C., U.S.	C5	116
Mouly, N. Cal.	m16	79d
Mounana, Gabon	E2	66
Mound City, Ks., U.S.	F3	120
Mound City, Mo., U.S.	D2	120
Mound City, S.D., U.S.	B12	126
Moundou, Chad	F3	62
Moundridge, Ks., U.S.	C11	128
Mounds, Ok., U.S.	B2	122
Moundsville, W.V., U.S.	E5	114
Moundville, Al., U.S.	E11	122
Mounlapamôk, Laos	E7	48
Mountain, Wi., U.S.	C1	112
Mountain, stm., N.T., Can.	C5	106
Mountainair, N.M., U.S.	G2	128
Mountainaire, Az., U.S.	H5	132
Mountain Brook, Al., U.S.	D12	122
Mountain City, Ga., U.S.	B2	116
Mountain City, Nv., U.S.	B1	132
Mountain Creek, Al., U.S.	E12	122
Mountain Grove, Mo., U.S.	G5	120
Mountain Home, Ar., U.S.	H5	120
Mountain Home, Id., U.S.	G11	136
Mountain Iron, Mn., U.S.	D6	118
Mountain Lake, Mn., U.S.	H3	118
Mountain Nile, stm., Afr.	F6	62
Mountain Park, Ab., Can.	D13	138
Mountain Pine, Ar., U.S.	C5	122
Mountain View, Ar., U.S.	I5	120
Mountain View, Ca., U.S.	F3	134
Mountain View, Ok., U.S.	F10	128
Mountain View, Wy., U.S.	E6	126
Mountain Village, Ak., U.S.	D7	140
Mountain Zebra National Park, p.o.i., S. Afr.	H7	70
Mount Airy, N.C., U.S.	H5	114
Mount Alida, S. Afr.	F10	70
Mount Angel, Or., U.S.	E4	136
Mount Aspiring National Park, p.o.i., N.Z.	G3	80
Mount Athos see Ágio Óros, state, Grc.	C7	28
Mount Ayliff, S. Afr.	G9	70
Mount Ayr, Ia., U.S.	D3	120
Mount Barker, Austl.	F3	74
Mount Barker, Austl.	J2	76
Mount Berry, Ga., U.S.	C13	122
Mount Buffalo National Park, p.o.i., Austl.	K5	76
Mount Calm, Tx., U.S.	C11	130
Mount Carmel, Il., U.S.	F10	120
Mount Carmel, Pa., U.S.	D9	114
Mount Carroll, Il., U.S.	B7	120
Mount Clemens, Mi., U.S.	B3	114
Mount Cook National Park, p.o.i., N.Z.	F4	80
Mount Dora, Fl., U.S.	H4	116
Mount Enterprise, Tx., U.S.	F4	122
Mount Field National Park, p.o.i., Austl.	o13	77a
Mount Forest, On., Can.	D9	112
Mount Frere, S. Afr.	G9	70
Mount Gambier, Austl.	K3	76
Mount Garnet, Austl.	A5	76
Mount Gay, W.V., U.S.	G3	114
Mount Hagen, Pap. N. Gui.	b3	79a
Mount Holly, N.C., U.S.	A4	116
Mount Holly Springs, Pa., U.S.	H12	112
Mount Hope, Austl.	F7	74
Mount Hope, Ks., U.S.	D11	128
Mount Horeb, Wi., U.S.	B8	120
Mount Ida, Ar., U.S.	C5	122
Mount Isa, Austl.	C2	76
Mount Jackson, Va., U.S.	F7	114
Mount Juliet, Tn., U.S.	H11	120
Mount Kaputar National Park, p.o.i., Austl.	H8	76
Mount Lebanon, Pa., U.S.	D6	114
Mount Lofty Ranges, mts., Austl.	I2	76
Mount Magnet, Austl.	E3	74
Mount Manara, Austl.	I4	76
Mount Margaret, Austl.	F4	76
Mount Morgan, Austl.	D8	76
Mount Morris, Il., U.S.	I9	118
Mount Morris, Mi., U.S.	E6	112
Mount Olive, Il., U.S.	E8	120
Mount Olive, Ms., U.S.	F9	122
Mount Olive, N.C., U.S.	A7	116
Mount Orab, Oh., U.S.	E2	114
Mount Perry, Austl.	E8	76
Mount Pleasant, On., Can.	E9	112
Mount Pleasant, Ia., U.S.	D6	120
Mount Pleasant, Mi., U.S.	E5	112
Mount Pleasant, Pa., U.S.	D6	114
Mount Pleasant, S.C., U.S.	D6	116
Mount Pleasant, Tn., U.S.	B11	122
Mount Pleasant, Tx., U.S.	D4	122
Mount Pleasant, Ut., U.S.	D5	132
Mount Pulaski, Il., U.S.	D8	120
Mount Rainier National Park, p.o.i., Wa., U.S.	D5	136
Mount Revelstoke National Park, p.o.i., B.C., Can.	E12	138
Mount Riddock, Austl.	D6	74
Mount Saint Helens National Volcanic Monument, p.o.i., Wa., U.S.	D5	136
Mount Selinda, Zimb.	B11	70
Mount Somers, N.Z.	F4	80
Mount Sterling, Il., U.S.	E7	120
Mount Sterling, Ky., U.S.	F2	114
Mount Sterling, Oh., U.S.	E2	114
Mount Uniacke, N.S., Can.	F12	110
Mount Union, Pa., U.S.	D8	114
Mount Vernon, Austl.	D3	74
Mount Vernon, Al., U.S.	F10	122
Mount Vernon, Ga., U.S.	D3	116
Mount Vernon, Ia., U.S.	C6	120
Mount Vernon, Il., U.S.	F8	120
Mount Vernon, Ky., U.S.	G1	114
Mount Vernon, Mo., U.S.	G4	120
Mount Vernon, Oh., U.S.	D3	114
Mount Vernon, Or., U.S.	F7	136
Mount Vernon, S.D., U.S.	D14	126
Mount Vernon, Wa., U.S.	B4	136
Mount Vernon, hist., Va., U.S.	F8	114
Mount William National Park, p.o.i., Austl.	n13	77a
Mount Willoughby, Austl.	E6	74
Mount Wolf, Pa., U.S.	H13	112
Moura, Braz.	H11	86
Moura, Port.	F3	20
Mourdi, Dépression du, depr., Chad	D4	62
Mourdiah, Mali	G3	64
Mourne Mountains, mts., N. Ire., U.K.	G6	12
Mouscron, Bel.	D12	14
Moussa 'Ali, mtn., Afr.	B8	66
Moussoro, Chad	E3	62
Moutier, Switz.	C4	22
Moutong, Indon.	E7	44
Mouzáki, Grc.	D4	28
Movenda, D.R.C.	D4	66
Moweaqua, Il., U.S.	E8	120
Moxotó, stm., Braz.	E7	88
Moyahua, Mex.	E7	100
Moyale, Kenya	D7	66
Moyamba, S.L.	H2	64
Moyen Atlas, mts., Mor.	C4	64
Moyeuvre-Grande, Fr.	E14	14
Moyie, B.C., Can.	G15	138
Moyie, stm., N.A.	H14	138
Moyo, Pulau, i., Indon.	H10	50
Moyobamba, Peru	E2	84
Moyu, China	A4	46
M'oža (Měža), stm., Eur.	E14	10
Možajsk, Russia	E18	10
Mozambique, ctry., Afr.	D5	68
Mozambique Channel, strt., Afr.	D7	68
Mozambique Plateau, unds.	M6	142
Mozdok, Russia	F6	32
Mozolevo, Russia	A16	10
Mpala, D.R.C.	F5	66
Mpanda, Tan.	F6	66
Mphoengs, Zimb.	B8	70
Mpika, Zam.	C5	68
Mporokoso, Zam.	B5	68
Mpui, Tan.	F6	66
Mpumalanga, state, S. Afr.	E9	70
Mpwapwa, Tan.	F7	66
Mqanduli, S. Afr.	G9	70
Mrągowo, Pol.	C17	16
Mrkonjić Grad, Bos.	E3	26
M'Saken, Tun.	I4	24
Mscislau, Bela.	F14	10
Msciž, Bela.	F11	10
Msta, Russia	C17	10
Msta, stm., Russia	B15	10
Mszczonów, Pol.	E16	16
Mtama, Tan.	G7	66
Mtamvuna, stm., S. Afr.	G9	70
Mtwara, Tan.	G8	66
Mu, N. Cal.	m16	79d
Mu, stm., Mya.	A2	48
Mu, Cerro, mtn., S.A.	C5	86
Mu'a, Tonga	n14	78e
Mualang, Indon.	C7	50
Muanda, D.R.C.	F2	66
Muang Hay, Laos	B5	48
Muang Hôngsa, Laos	C5	48
Muang Hounxianghoung, Laos	B6	48
Muang Khammouan, Laos	D7	48
Muang Khao, Laos	C6	48
Muang Không, Laos	E7	48
Muang Khôngxédôn, Laos	E7	48
Muang La, Laos	B6	48
Muang Long, Laos	B5	48
Muang Ngoy, Laos	B6	48
Muang Nong, Laos	D8	48
Muang Ou Tai, Laos	A5	48
Muang Pak-Lay, Laos	C5	48
Muang Paktha, Laos	B5	48
Muang Pakxan, Laos	C6	48
Muang Phalan, Laos	D7	48
Muang Phônthong, Laos	E7	48
Muang Sam Sip, Thai.	E7	48
Muang Sing, Laos	B5	48
Muang Souvannakhili, Laos	E7	48
Muang Sung, Laos	B6	48
Muang Thatèng, Laos	E8	48
Muang Va, Laos	B6	48
Muang Vangviang, Laos	C6	48
Muang Xaignabouri, Laos	C5	48
Muang Xamtong, Laos	C6	48
Muang Xépôn, Laos	D7	48
Muang Yo, Laos	B5	48
Muar, Malay.	L6	48
Muar, stm., Malay.	K6	48
Muara, Bru.	A9	50
Muaraancalung, Indon.	C10	50
Muarabenangin, Indon.	D9	50
Muarabungo, Indon.	D2	50
Muaradua, Indon.	F4	50
Muaraenim, Indon.	E3	50
Muarajuloi, Indon.	D8	50
Muarakelingi, Indon.	E3	50
Muaralabuh, Indon.	D2	50
Muaralakitan, Indon.	E3	50
Muaralembu, Indon.	D2	50
Muarapangean, Indon.	B10	50
Muarapayang, Indon.	D9	50
Muarasabak, Indon.	D3	50
Muarasiberut, Indon.	D1	50
Muaratebo, Indon.	D3	50
Muarateladang, Indon.	E4	50
Muaratembesi, Indon.	D3	50
Muaratewe, Indon.	D9	50
Muaratunan, Indon.	D10	50
Mubārakpur, India	E9	54
Mubende, Ug.	D6	66
Mubi, Nig.	G7	64
Mubur, Pulau, i., Indon.	B4	50
Mucaitá, stm., Braz.	D4	88
Mucajaí, stm., Braz.	F11	86
Muchinga Escarpment, clf., Zam.	C4	68
Muchinga Mountains, mts., Zam.	C5	68
Muckadilla, Austl.	F7	76
Mučkas, Russia	D23	8
Mucojo, Moz.	C7	68
Muconda, Ang.	C3	68
Mucujê, Braz.	G5	88
Muçum, Braz.	D11	92
Mucuri, Braz.	J6	88
Mucuri, stm., Braz.	J6	88
Muda, stm., Malay.	J5	48
Mudan, stm., China	B10	36
Mudanjiang, China	B8	38
Mudanya, Tur.	C11	28
Mud Creek, stm., Ne., U.S.	F13	126
Mud Creek, stm., Tx., U.S.	E3	122
Muddus Nationalpark, p.o.i., Swe.	C9	8
Muddy, stm., Nv., U.S.	G2	132
Muddy Boggy Creek, stm., Ok., U.S.	C3	122
Muddy Creek, stm., Ut., U.S.	E6	132
Mudgee, Austl.	I7	76
Mudhol, India	C2	53
Mudjuga, Russia	E18	8
Mud Lake, l., Nv., U.S.	F8	134
Mudon, Mya.	D3	48
Mudurnu, Tur.	C14	28
Muelle de los Bueyes, Nic.	G5	102
Muenster, Tx., U.S.	H11	128
Muerto, Mar, l., Mex.	G11	100
Mufulira, Zam.	C4	68
Mufu Shan, mtn., China	G5	42
Mufu Shan, mts., China	G6	42
Mughal Sarāi, India	F9	54
Mugi, Japan	F7	40
Mu Gia, Deo, p., Asia	D7	48
Muğla, Tur.	F11	28
Muğla, state, Tur.	F11	28
Muḥammad Qawl, Sudan	C7	62
Muhanovo, Russia	D21	10
Muhavec, stm., Bela.	H7	10
Muhino, Russia	F14	34
Mühlacker, Ger.	H4	16
Mühldorf am Inn, Ger.	H8	16
Mühlhausen, Ger.	E6	16
Muhlig-Hofmann Mountains, mts., Ant.	C5	81
Mühlviertel, reg., Aus.	B11	22
Muḥradah, Syria	C7	58
Muhu, i., Est.	G10	8
Muié, Ang.	C3	68
Mui Hopohoponga Point, c., Tonga	n14	78e
Muineachán see Monaghan, Ire.	G6	12
Muine Bheag, Ire.	I6	12
Muite, Moz.	C6	68
Muja, Russia	E12	34
Mujnak, Uzb.	F9	32
Mukah, Malay.	B8	50
Mukalla see Al-Mukallā, Yemen	G6	56
Mukatsjeve, Ukr.	A9	26
Mukāwir, sci., Jord.	G6	58
Mukdahan, Thai.	D7	48
Mukden see Shenyang, China	D5	38
Mukeriān, India	C5	54
Mukharram al-Fawqānī, Syria	D7	58
Mukilteo, Wa., U.S.	C4	136
Mukinbudin, Austl.	F3	74
Mukomuko, Indon.	E2	50
Mukry, Turkmen.	B10	56
Muktsar, India	C5	54
Mūl, India	A4	53
Mula, China	F5	36
Mula, Spain	F9	20
Mula, stm., India	B1	53
Mula, stm., India	B2	53
Mulaku Atoll, at., Mald.	i12	46a
Mulan, China	B10	36
Mulas, Punta de, c., Cuba	B10	102
Mulatos, Mex.	A4	100
Mulbāgal, India	E4	53
Mulberry, Ar., U.S.	B4	122
Mulberry, Fl., U.S.	I4	116
Mulberry Fork, stm., Al., U.S.	D12	122
Mulberry Mountain, mtn., Ar., U.S.	I5	120
Mulchatna, stm., Ak., U.S.	D8	140
Mulchén, Chile	H1	92
Mulde, stm., Ger.	E8	16
Muldoon, Tx., U.S.	E10	130
Muldraugh, Ky., U.S.	G12	120
Muldrow, Ok., U.S.	B4	122
Muleshoe, Tx., U.S.	G6	128
Mulgowie, Austl.	F9	76
Mulgrave, N.S., Can.	E15	110
Mulhacén, mtn., Spain	G7	20
Mulhall, Ok., U.S.	E11	128
Mulhouse, Fr.	G16	14
Muling, China	B9	38
Muling, China	B9	38
Muling, stm., China	B9	38
Mulinu'u, Cape, c., Samoa	g11	79c
Mūlki, India	E2	53
Mull, Island of, i., Scot., U.K.	E6	12
Mullengudgery, Austl.	H6	76
Muller, Pegunungan, mts., Indon.	C8	50
Mullet Peninsula, pen., Ire.	G2	12
Mullet Pond Bay, Neth. Ant.	A1	105a
Mullett Lake, l., Mi., U.S.	C5	112
Mullewa, Austl.	E3	74
Müllheim, Ger.	I3	16
Mullin, Tx., U.S.	C9	130
Mullingar, Ire.	H5	12
Mullins, S.C., U.S.	B6	116
Mulobezi, Zam.	D4	68
Mulongo, D.R.C.	F5	66
Mulshi Lake, res., India	B1	53
Multai, India	H7	54
Multān, Pak.	C3	54
Multé, Mex.	D2	102
Mulumbe, Monts, mts., D.R.C.	F5	66
Mulvane, Ks., U.S.	D11	128
Mumbai (Bombay), India	B1	53
Mumbwa, Zam.	D4	68
Mumen, China	E2	42
Mumeng, Pap. N. Gui.	b4	79a
Mumford, Tx., U.S.	G2	122
Mun, stm., Thai.	E7	48
Muna, stm., Russia	C13	34
Muna, Pulau, i., Indon.	F7	44
Muncar, Indon.	H9	50
Münchberg, Ger.	F7	16
München (Munich), Ger.	H7	16
Munchique, Cerro, mtn., Col.	F3	86
Munchique, Parque Nacional, p.o.i., Col.	F3	86
Muncie, In., U.S.	H4	112
Muncy, Pa., U.S.	C9	114
Mundare, Ab., Can.	C18	138
Munday, Tx., U.S.	H9	128
Mundelein, Il., U.S.	B9	120
Münden, Ger.	E5	16
Mundra, India	G2	54
Mundrabilla, Austl.	F5	74
Mundubbera, Austl.	E8	76
Munfordville, Ky., U.S.	G12	120
Mungallala Creek, stm., Austl.	F6	76
Mungana, Austl.	C8	74
Mungar Junction, Austl.	E9	76
Mungbere, D.R.C.	D5	66
Mungeli, India	G8	54
Munger, India	F11	54
Mungindi, Austl.	G7	76
Mungo, Ang.	C2	68
Mungo National Park, p.o.i., Austl.	I4	76
Munhango, Ang.	C2	68
Munich see München, Ger.	H7	16
Muniesa, Spain	C10	20
Munim, stm., Braz.	B3	88
Munising, Mi., U.S.	B3	112
Muniz Freire, Braz.	K5	88
Munku-Sardyk, gora, mtn., Asia	D17	32
Münsingen, Ger.	H5	16
Munson, Ab., Can.	E18	138
Münster, Ger.	D3	16
Munster, Ger.	C6	16
Munster, hist. reg., Ire.	I3	12
Munte, Indon.	C11	50
Muntok, Indon.	E4	50
Munuscong Lake, l., N.A.	B5	112
Muong Hinh, Viet.	C7	48
Muong Saiapoun, Laos	C5	48
Muonio, Fin.	C10	8
Muping, China	C9	42
Muqdisho (Mogadiscio), Som.	D9	66
Muqui, Braz.	K5	88
Mur (Mura), stm., Eur.	D12	22
Mura (Mur), stm., Eur.	D12	22
Murajá, Braz.	D8	84
Murakami, Japan	A12	40
Murana, Indon.	F9	44
Muraši, Russia	C7	32
Murat, Fr.	D8	18
Murat, stm., Tur.	H17	6
Murat Dağı, mtn., Tur.	E12	28
Muratlı, Tur.	B10	28
Muravera, Italy	E3	24
Murayama, Japan	A13	40
Murça, Port.	C3	20
Murchison, Tx., U.S.	E3	122
Murchison, stm., Austl.	E2	74
Murchison, Mount, mtn., N.Z.	F4	80
Murcia, Spain	G9	20
Murcia, state, Spain	G9	20
Mur-de-Barrez, Fr.	E8	18
Murdo, S.D., U.S.	D12	126
Mürefte, Tur.	C10	28
Mureș, state, Rom.	C11	26
Mureș (Maros), stm., Eur.	C8	26
Muret, Fr.	F7	18
Murewa, Zimb.	D5	68
Murfreesboro, Ar., U.S.	C5	122
Murfreesboro, Tn., U.S.	I11	120
Murgab, Taj.	B11	56
Murgab (Morghāb), stm., Asia	B9	56
Murgha Kibzai, Pak.	C2	54
Murgon, Austl.	F8	76
Muri, Cook Is.	a27	78j
Muriaé, Braz.	K4	88
Muriaé, stm., Braz.	K5	88
Muribeca dos Guararapes, Braz.	E8	88
Murici, Braz.	E8	88
Muricizal, stm., Braz.	D1	88
Murīdke, Pak.	C5	54
Muriege, Ang.	C3	68
Müritz, l., Ger.	C8	16
Murmansk, Russia	B15	8
Murmanskaja oblast', co., Russia	C16	8
Murnau, Ger.	I7	16
Muro Lucano, Italy	D9	24
Murom, Russia	I19	8
Muromcevo, Russia	C13	32
Muroran, Japan	C14	38
Muroto, Japan	F7	40
Muroto-zaki, c., Japan	F7	40
Murowana Goślina, Pol.	D13	16
Murphy, Id., U.S.	G10	136
Murphy, N.C., U.S.	A1	116
Murphys, Ca., U.S.	E5	134
Murra Murra, Austl.	G6	76
Murrat el-Kubra, Buheirat (Great Bitter Lake), l., Egypt	H3	58
Murray, Ia., U.S.	C3	120
Murray, Ky., U.S.	H9	120
Murray, Ut., U.S.	C5	132
Murray, stm., Austl.	J2	76
Murray, stm., B.C., Can.	B9	138
Murray, Lake, l., Pap. N. Gui.	b3	79a
Murray, Lake, res., S.C., U.S.	B4	116
Murray Bridge, Austl.	J2	76
Murray Fracture Zone, unds.	F24	142
Murray Harbour, P.E., Can.	E14	110
Murray Maxwell Bay, b., Nu., Can.	A14	106
Murray River, P.E., Can.	D14	110
Murraysburg, S. Afr.	G6	70
Murree, Pak.	B4	54
Murrhardt, Ger.	H5	16
Murrumbidgee, stm., Austl.	J4	76
Murrumburrah, Austl.	J7	76
Murrupula, Moz.	D6	68
Mursala, Pulau, i., Indon.	L4	48
Murshidābād, India	F12	54
Murska Sobota, Slvn.	D13	22
Murtajāpur, India	H6	54
Murtee, Austl.	H4	76
Murter, Otok, i., Cro.	G12	22
Murtle Lake, l., B.C., Can.	D11	138
Murtoa, Austl.	K4	76
Murtosa, Port.	D2	20
Muru, Capu di, c., Fr.	H14	18
Murud, India	B1	53
Murud, Gunong, mtn., Malay.	B9	50
Murukta, Russia	C9	34
Murung, stm., Indon.	C9	50
Mururoa, at., Fr. Poly.	F13	72
Murwāra (Katni), India	G8	54
Murwillumbah, Austl.	G9	76
Murzuq, Libya	B2	62
Murzūq, Idhān, des., Libya	C2	62
Mürzzuschlag, Aus.	C12	22
Muş, Tur.	B5	56
Mūša (Mūsa), stm., Eur.	D6	10
Mūsa (Mūša), stm., Eur.	D6	10
Mûsa, Gebel (Sinai, Mount), mtn., Egypt	J5	58
Musadi, D.R.C.	E4	66
Musā'id, Libya	A4	62
Musala, mtn., Blg.	G10	26
Musan-ŭp, Kor., N.	C8	38
Muscat see Masqaṭ, Oman	E8	56
Muscat and Oman see Oman, ctry., Asia	F8	56
Muscatine, Ia., U.S.	C6	120
Muscle Shoals, Al., U.S.	C11	122
Musclow, Mount, mtn., B.C., Can.	C3	138
Muscoda, Wi., U.S.	A7	120
Musgrave, Austl.	B8	74
Mus-Haja, gora, mtn., Russia	D17	34
Mushie, D.R.C.	E3	66
Mushin, Nig.	H5	64
Mūsi, stm., India	C4	53
Musi, stm., Indon.	E4	50
Musicians Seamounts, unds.	F22	142
Muskegon, Mi., U.S.	E3	112
Muskegon, stm., Mi., U.S.	E4	112
Muskingum, stm., Oh., U.S.	E4	114
Muskogee, Ok., U.S.	I2	120
Muskoka, Lake, l., On., Can.	D10	112
Musoma, Tan.	E6	66
Musquodoboit Harbour, N.S., Can.	F13	110
Mussau Island, i., Pap. N. Gui.	a4	79a
Musselshell, stm., Mt., U.S.	G6	124
Mussende, Ang.	C2	68
Mussidan, Fr.	D6	18
Mussomeli, Italy	G7	24
Mussuma, Ang.	C3	68
Mustafakemalpaşa, Tur.	C11	28
Mustafa Kemal Paşa, stm., Tur.	D11	28
Mustahīl, Eth.	F8	62
Mustāng, Nepal	D9	54
Mustang Draw, stm., Tx., U.S.	B5	130
Mustang Island, i., Tx., U.S.	G10	130
Musters, Lago, l., Arg.	I3	90
Mustla, Est.	B8	10
Mustvee, Est.	B9	10
Muswellbrook, Austl.	I8	76
Mût, Egypt	B5	62
Mut, Tur.	B4	58
Mutá, Ponta do, c., Braz.	G6	88
Mutanchiang see Mudanjiang, China	B8	38
Mutankiang see Mudanjiang, China	B8	38
Mutare, Zimb.	D5	68
Mutlu (Rezovska), stm., Eur.	G14	26
Mutoko, Zimb.	D5	68
Mutoraj, Russia	B17	32
Mutsamudu, Com.	C7	68
Mutshatsha, D.R.C.	G4	66
Mutsu, Japan	D14	38
Mutsu-wan, b., Japan	D14	38
Mutton Bay, Qc., Can.	i22	107a
Mutuípe, Braz.	G6	88
Mutum, Braz.	J5	88
Mu Us Shamo (Ordos Desert), des., China	B3	42
Mūvattupula, India	F3	53
Muxima, Ang.	B1	68
Muyinga, Bdi.	E6	66
Muyumba, D.R.C.	F5	66
Muzaffarābād, Pak.	A4	54
Muzaffargarh, Pak.	C3	54
Muzaffarnagar, India	D6	54
Muzaffarpur, India	E10	54
Muzat, stm., China	C2	36
Muži, Russia	A10	32
Muzillac, Fr.	G6	14
Muztag, mtn., China	A5	46
Muztag, mtn., China	D2	36
Mvolo, Sudan	F6	62
Mvoti, stm., S. Afr.	F10	70
Mvuma, Zimb.	D5	68
Mwadui, Tan.	E6	66
Mwali, i., Com.	C7	68
Mwanza, Tan.	E6	66
Mweelrea, mtn., Ire.	H3	12
Mweka, D.R.C.	E4	66
Mwene-Ditu, D.R.C.	F4	66
Mwenezi, Zimb.	B10	70

Mwenezi – Nevada I • 39

Name — Map Ref. — Page

Mwenezi, stm., Afr. B10 70
Mweru, Lake, l., Afr. B4 68
Mweru Wantipa, Lake, l., Zam. B4 68
Mwilitau Islands (Purdy Islands), is., Pap. N. Gui. a4 79a
Mwinilunga, Zam. C3 68
Myājlār, India E3 54
Myall Lakes National Park, p.o.i., Austl. I9 76
Myanaung, Mya. C2 48
Myanmar (Burma), ctry., Asia D8 46
Myaungmya, Mya. D2 48
Mycenae see Mykínes, sci., Grc. F5 28
Myebon, Mya. B1 48
Myingyan, Mya. B2 48
Myitkyinā, Mya. C8 46
Myitnge, stm., Mya. B3 48
Myitta, Mya. E4 48
Myittha, Mya. B2 48
Myittha, stm., Mya. B2 48
Myjava, Slov. H13 16
Mykines, i., Far. Is. m34 8b
Mykínes, sci., Grc. F5 28
Mykolaïv, Ukr. F15 6
Mykolaïv, co., Ukr. B17 26
Mykolaïvka, Ukr. C16 26
Mýkonos, i., Grc. F8 28
Myla, Russia D24 8
Mymensingh (Nasirābād), Bngl. F13 54
Mynaral, Kaz. E12 32
Mynfontein, S. Afr. G6 70
Myohaung, Mya. B1 48
Myohyang-san, mtn., Kor., N. D7 38
Myōkō-san, vol., Japan C11 40
Myra, sci., Tur. G12 28
Mýrdalsjökull, ice, Ice. I30 8a
Myrskylä, Fin. F11 8
Myrtle Beach, S.C., U.S. C7 116
Myrtle Creek, Or., U.S. G3 136
Myrtle Grove, Fl., U.S. G11 122
Myrtle Point, Or., U.S. G2 136
Myrtletowne, Ca., U.S. C1 134
Myrtóön Pélagos, s., Grc. G6 28
Myškino, Russia C21 10
Myślenice, Pol. G15 16
Myślibórz, Pol. D10 16
Mysłowice, Pol. F15 16
Mysore, India E3 53
Mysore see Karnātaka, state, India F4 46
Mystic, Ct., U.S. C14 114
Mystrás, sci., Grc. F5 28
Mys Vhodnoj, Russia B6 34
Myszków, Pol. F15 16
Myt, Russia H20 8
My Tho, Viet. G8 48
Mytilíni, Grc. D9 28
Mytišči, Russia E20 10
Myton, Ut., U.S. C6 132
Mývatn, l., Ice. k31 8a
Mzimba, Mwi. C5 68
Mzimvubu, stm., S. Afr. G9 70
Mzintlava, stm., S. Afr. G9 70
Mzuzu, Mwi. C5 68

N

Na (Tengtiao), stm., Asia A6 48
Naab, stm., Ger. G7 16
Nā'ālehu, Hi., U.S. d6 78a
Naas, Ire. H6 12
Nababeep, S. Afr. F3 70
Nabari, Japan E9 40
Nabberu, Lake, l., Austl. E4 74
Nabburg, Ger. G8 16
Naberežnye Čelny, Russia C8 32
Nabeul, Tun. H4 24
Nābha, India C6 54
Nabire, Indon. F10 44
Nabī Shu'ayb, Jabal an-, mtn., Yemen F5 56
Nabouwalu, Fiji p19 79e
Nabq, Egypt J5 58
Nabula, China C7 54
Nābulus, W.B. F6 58
Nacala-a-Velha, Moz. C7 68
Nachingwea, Tan. G7 66
Nāchna, India E3 54
Náchod, Czech Rep. F12 16
Nachvak Fiord, b., Nf., Can. F13 141
Nacimiento, Chile H1 92
Nacimiento, Lake, res., Ca., U.S. H5 134
Naco, Mex. F8 98
Naco, Az., U.S. L6 132
Nacogdoches, Tx., U.S. F4 122
Nácori Chico, Mex. G8 98
Nacozari de García, Mex. F8 98
Ñacunday, Para. B10 92
Nadarivatu, Fiji p18 79e
Nadela, Spain B3 20
Nadiād, India G4 54
Nadi Bay, b., Fiji p18 79e
Nădlac, Rom. C7 26
Naduri, Fiji p19 79e
Nadvoicy, Russia E16 8
Nadym, Russia A12 32
Nadym, stm., Russia A12 32
Naenwa, India F5 54
Nærbø, Nor. G1 8
Næstved, Den. I4 8
Nafada, Nig. G7 64
Nafī, Sau. Ar. D5 56
Náfpaktos, Grc. E4 28
Náfplio, Grc. F5 28
Nafūsah, Jabal, hills, Libya A2 62
Naga, Phil. D4 52
Nagahama, Japan D9 40
Nagahama, Japan F5 40
Naga Hills, mts., Asia C7 46
Nagai, Japan A12 40
Nagai Island, i., Ak., U.S. F7 140
Nāgāland, state, India C7 46
Nagano, Japan C11 40
Nagano, state, Japan C11 40
Nagaoka, Japan B11 40
Nagaon, India E14 54
Nāgappattinam, India F4 53
Nagara, stm., Japan D9 40
Nagarhole Tiger Reserve, India E2 53
Nāgārjuna Sāgar, res., India C4 53
Nagarote, Nic. F4 102
Nagasaki, Japan G2 40
Nagasaki, state, Japan G2 40
Nagato, Japan E4 40
Nāgaur, India E4 54
Nāgāvali, stm., India B6 53
Nagda, India G5 54
Nāgercoil, India G3 53
Nagīna, India D7 54
Nagłowice, Pol. F15 16
Nago, Japan I19 39a
Nagold, Ger. H4 16
Nagornyj, Russia E13 34
Nagoya, Japan D9 40
Nāgpur, India H7 54
Nagqu, China C14 54
Nagua, Dom. Rep. C12 102
Naguabo, P.R. B4 104a
Nagyatád, Hung. C4 26
Nagybánya *see* Baia Mare, Rom. B10 26
Nagyecsed, Hung. B9 26
Nagykanizsa, Hung. C4 26
Nagykáta, Hung. B6 26
Nagykőrös, Hung. B6 26
Naha, Japan I18 39a
Nahabuan, Indon. C9 50
Nāhan, India C6 54
Nahanni Butte, N.T., Can. C6 106
Nahariyya, Isr. E5 58
Nahāvand, Iran C6 56
Nahe, China B9 36
Nahe, stm., Ger. G3 16
Nahma, Mi., U.S. C3 112
Nahodka, Russia C10 38
Nahodka, Russia A13 32
Nahoe, Fr. Poly. r19 78g
Nahoï, Cap, c., Vanuatu j16 79d
Nahuel Huapi, Lago, l., Arg. H2 90
Nahuel Niyeu, Arg. H3 90
Naica, Mex. B6 100
Naicam, Sk., Can. B9 124
Naila, Ger. F7 16
Naiman Qi, China C4 38
Nā'īn, Iran C7 56
Naini Tāl, India D7 54
Nainpur, India G8 54
Nairai, i., Fiji p19 79e
Nairn, La., U.S. H9 122
Nairobi, Kenya E7 66
Naitauba, i., Fiji p20 79e
Naivasha, Kenya E7 66
Naizishan, China C7 38
Najac, Fr. E8 18
Najafābād, Iran C7 56
Najasa, stm., Cuba B9 102
Najd (Nejd), hist. reg., Sau. Ar. D5 56
Najībābād, India D7 54
Najin, Kor., N. C9 38
Naka, stm., Japan C13 40
Nakajō, Japan A12 40
Nakama, Japan F3 40
Nakaminato, Japan C13 40
Nakamura, Japan G5 40
Nakano, Japan C11 40
Nakano-shima, i., Japan k19 39a
Nakasongola, Ug. D6 66
Nakatsu, Japan F4 40
Nakatsugawa, Japan D10 40
Nakhl, Egypt I4 58
Nakhon Nayok, Thai. E5 48
Nakhon Pathom, Thai. F5 48
Nakhon Phanom, Thai. D7 48
Nakhon Ratchasima, Thai. E6 48
Nakhon Sawan, Thai. E4 48
Nakhon Si Thammarat, Thai. H5 48
Nakhon Thai, Thai. D5 48
Nakina, On., Can. A12 118
Nakło nad Notecią, Pol. C13 16
Nakodar, India C5 54
Nakonde, Zam. B5 68
Nakskov, Den. I4 8
Naktong-gang, stm., Kor., S. C1 40
Nakuru, Kenya E7 66
Nakusp, B.C., Can. F13 138
Nālanda, India F10 54
Nalayh, Mong. B6 36
Nalbāri, India E13 54
Nal'čik, Russia F6 32
Nałęczów, Pol. E18 16
Nalgonda, India C4 53
Nallamalla Hills, mts., India D4 53
Nallıhan, Tur. C14 28
Nalón, stm., Spain A5 20
Nalong, China J2 42
Nālūt, Libya A2 62
Nam (Nan'a), stm., Asia B4 48
Namaacha, Moz. D10 70
Namacurra, Moz. D6 68
Namadgi National Park, p.o.i., Austl. J7 76
Namak, Daryācheh-ye, l., Iran C7 56
Namakan Lake, l., N.A. C6 118
Nāmakkal, India F4 53
Namangan, Uzb. F12 32
Namanyere, Tan. F6 66
Namapa, Moz. C6 68
Namarrói, Moz. D6 68
Namatanai, Pap. N. Gui. a5 79a
Nambour, Austl. F9 76
Nam Co, l., China C13 54
Nam Dinh, Viet. B7 48
Nam Du, Quan Dao, is., Viet. H6 48
Nameh, Indon. B10 50
Namen *see* Namur, Bel. D13 14
Namerikawa, Japan C10 40
Nametil, Moz. D6 68
Nam-gang, stm., Kor., N. E7 38
Namhae-do, i., Kor., S. G8 38
Namhan-gang, stm., Kor., S. F7 38
Namhkam, Mya. D8 46
Namib Desert, des., Nmb. E1 68
Namibe, Ang. D1 68
Namibia, ctry., Afr. E2 68
Namib Naukluft Park, p.o.i., Nmb. D2 70
Namie, Japan B14 40
Namies, S. Afr. F4 70
Namji-ri, Kor., S. D1 40
Namlea, Indon. F8 44
Namling, China D12 54
Nam Nao National Park, p.o.i., Thai. D5 48
Nam Ngum Reservoir, res., Laos C6 48
Namnoi, Khao, mtn., Mya. G4 48
Namoi, stm., Austl. H7 76
Nampa, Id., U.S. G10 136
Nampala, Mali F3 64
Nam Pat, Thai. D5 48
Nampawng, Mya. A3 48
Nam Phan (Cochin China), hist. reg., Viet. G8 48
Namp'o, Kor., N. E6 38
Nampula, Moz. D6 68
Namsang, Mya. B3 48
Namsen, stm., Nor. D5 8
Namsos, Nor. D4 8
Nam Tok, Thai. E4 48
Nam Tok Mae Surin National Park, p.o.i., Thai. C4 48
Namtu, Mya. A3 48
Namu, B.C., Can. E3 138
Namuka-I-Lau, i., Fiji q20 79e
Namúli, Serra, mts., Moz. D6 68
Namur (Namen), Bel. D13 14
Namutoni, Nmb. D2 68
Namwala, Zam. D4 68
Namwŏn, Kor., S. G7 38
Namysłów, Pol. E13 16
Nan, Thai. C5 48
Nan, stm., Thai. D5 48
Nan'a (Nam), stm., Asia B4 48
Nanaimo, B.C., Can. G6 138
Nanam, Kor., N. D8 38
Nan'an, China I8 42
Nanango, Austl. F8 76
Nanao, Japan B9 40
Nanatsu-jima, is., Japan B9 40
Nanbu, China F1 42
Nancha, China B10 36
Nanchang, China G6 42
Nancheng, China H7 42
Nancheng *see* Hanzhong, China E2 42
Nanching *see* Nanjing, China E8 42
Nanchong, China F2 42
Nanchuan, China G2 42
Nanch'ung *see* Nanchong, China F2 42
Nancowry Island, i., India G7 46
Nancy, Fr. F15 14
Nanda Devi, mtn., India C8 54
Nandaime, Nic. G4 102
Nandan, Japan E7 40
Nānded, India B3 53
Nāndgaon, India H5 54
Nandi Drug, mtn., India E3 53
Nandikotkūr, India D4 53
Nandu, China F8 42
Nandu, stm., China L4 42
Nāndūra, India H6 54
Nandurbār, India H4 54
Nandyāl, India D4 53
Nanfen, China D5 38
Nanfeng, China H7 42
Nanga-Eboko, Cam. D2 66
Nangakelawit, Indon. C8 50
Nangamau, Indon. D7 50
Nangaobat, Indon. C8 50
Nanga Parbat, mtn., Pak. B11 56
Nangapinoh, Indon. D7 50
Nangarhār, state, Afg. A3 54
Nangatayap, Indon. D7 50
Nanggala Hill, mtn., Sol. Is. e7 79b
Nangin, Mya. G4 48
Nangnim-ŭp, Kor., N. D7 38
Nangong, China C6 42
Nang Rong, Thai. E6 48
Nanguan, China C5 42
Nanhua, China F5 36
Nan Hulsan Hu, l., China D4 36
Nanika Lake, l., B.C., Can. C3 138
Nanjangūd, India E3 53
Nanjiang, China E2 42
Nanjing, China I7 42
Nanjing (Nanking), China E8 42
Nankang, China I6 42
Nanking *see* Nanjing, China E8 42
Nankoku, Japan F6 40
Nankye, Mya. E3 48
Nanle, China C6 42
Nanlei (Loi), stm., Asia A4 48
Nanling, China F8 42
Nan Ling, mts., China I5 42
Nanliu, stm., China J3 42
Nanlou Shan, mtn., China C7 38
Nannine, Austl. E3 74
Nanning, China J3 42
Na Noi, Thai. C5 48
Nanortalik, Grnld. E16 141
Nanpan, stm., China G5 36
Nānpāra, India E8 54
Nanpiao, China A9 42
Nanping, China H8 42
Nanping, China E5 36
Nansei, Japan E9 40
Nansei-shotō (Ryukyu Islands), is., Japan k19 39a
Nan Shan see Qilian Shan, mts., China D4 36
Nanshan Island, i., Asia C6 44
Nantais, Lac, l., Qc., Can. C16 106
Nantai-zan, vol., Japan C12 40
Nanterre, Fr. F11 14
Nantes, Fr. G7 14
Nantes à Brest, Canal de, can., Fr. F5 14
Nanticoke, Pa., U.S. C9 114
Nanto, Japan E9 40
Nanton, Ab., Can. F17 138
Nantong, China E9 42
Nant'ou, Tai. J9 42
Nantucket, Ma., U.S. C15 114
Nantucket Island, i., Ma., U.S. C15 114
Nantucket Sound, strt., Ma., U.S. C15 114
Nantulo, Moz. C6 68
Nantung *see* Nantong, China. E9 42
Nanty Glo, Pa., U.S. H11 112
Nanu, Pap. N. Gui. b3 79a
Nanuku Passage, strt., Fiji p20 79e
Nanumea, at., Tuvalu D8 72
Nanuque, Braz. I5 88
Nanusa, Kepulauan, is., Indon. E8 44
Nanxi, China G1 42
Nanxian, China G5 42
Nanxiang, China F9 42
Nanxiong, China I6 42
Nanyang, China E5 42
Nanyang Hu, l., China D7 42
Nanyi Hu, l., China F8 42
Nan-yō, Japan A13 40
Nanyuki, Kenya D7 66
Nanzamu, China C6 38
Nanzhao, China E5 42
Nao, Cabo de la see Nau, Cap de la, c., Spain F11 20
Naococane, Lac, l., Qc., Can. E16 106
Naogaon, Bngl. F12 54
Naokot, Pak. F2 54
Náousa, Grc. C5 28
Napa, Ca., U.S. E3 134
Napa, stm., Ca., U.S. E3 134
Napaku, Indon. B9 50
Napalkovo, Russia C3 34
Napanee, On., Can. D12 112
Napassoq, Grnld. D15 141
Naperville, Il., U.S. C9 120
Napido, Indon. F10 44
Napier, N.Z. D7 80
Napier, Mount, hill, Austl. C5 74
Napier Mountains, mts., Ant. B10 81
Naples *see* Napoli, Italy D8 24
Naples, Fl., U.S. J4 116
Naples, Id., U.S. B10 136
Naples, N.Y., U.S. B8 114
Naples, Tx., U.S. D4 122
Napo, state, Ec. H3 86
Napo, stm., S.A. D3 84
Napoleon, N.D., U.S. A13 126
Napoleonville, La., U.S. H7 122
Napoli (Naples), Italy D8 24
Napoli, Golfo di, b., Italy D8 24
Nappamerrie, Austl. F3 76
Nappanee, In., U.S. G4 112
Napu, Indon. H11 50
Nara, Japan E8 40
Nara, Mali F3 64
Nara, state, Japan E8 40
Nāra, stm., Pak. F2 54
Nara, stm., Russia E20 10
Narač, vozero, l., Bela. F9 10
Naracoorte, Austl. K3 76
Naradhan, Austl. I6 76
Naraini, India F8 54
Naramata, B.C., Can. G11 138
Naranjal, Ec. I2 86
Naranjito, P.R. B3 104a
Narasannapeta, India B7 53
Narasapur, India C5 53
Narasaraopet, India C4 53
Narasun, Russia A7 36
Narathiwat, Thai. I5 48
Narau (Narew), stm., Eur. D17 16
Nārāyanganj, Bngl. G13 54
Nārāyani (Gandak), stm., Asia E10 54
Nārāyanpet, India C3 53
Narbonne, Fr. F8 18
Nardò, Italy D11 24
Nares Strait, strt., N.A. B11 141
Narew (Narau), stm., Eur. D17 16
Nargund, India D2 53
Nariño, state, Col. G3 86
Narita, Japan D13 40
Nariva Swamp, sw., Trin. s12 105f
Nar'jan-Mar, Russia C25 8
Narkatiāganj, India E10 54
Narlı, Tur. A8 58
Narmada, stm., India H4 54
Nārnaul, India D6 54
Narodnaja, gora, mtn., Russia B10 32
Narodnaya, Mount see Narodnaja, gora, mtn., Russia B10 32
Naro-Fominsk, Russia E19 10
Narol, Pol. F19 16
Narooma, Austl. K8 76
Nārowāl, Pak. B5 54
Narrabri, Austl. H7 76
Narran, stm., Austl. G7 76
Narrandera, Austl. J6 76
Narraway, stm., Can. B11 138
Narrogin, Austl. F3 74
Narromine, Austl. I6 76
Narsaq *see* Narssaq, Grnld. E16 141
Narsimhapur, India G7 54
Narsinghgarh, India G6 54
Narsīpatnam, India C6 53
Narssaq, Grnld. E16 141
Naru, Japan G1 40
Naruto, Japan E7 40
Narva, Est. G13 8
Narva, Russia C16 32
Narva, stm., Eur. A11 10
Narvik, Nor. B7 8
Narvskij zaliv, b., Eur. A10 10
Narvskoe vodohranilišče, l., Eur. A10 10
Narwāna, India D6 54
Narwietooma, Austl. D6 74
Narym, Russia C14 32
Naryn, Kyrg. F13 32
Naryn, stm., Asia F13 32
Narynkol, Kaz. F13 32
Näsåker, Swe. E7 8
Na San, Thai. H4 48
Nasawa, Vanuatu j17 79d
Nasbinals, Fr. E9 18
Nasca, Peru F2 84
Nase *see* Naze, Japan k19 39a
Nash, Tx., U.S. D4 122
Nāshik, India H4 54
Nashua, Ia., U.S. B5 120
Nashua, N.H., U.S. B14 114
Nashville, Ar., U.S. D5 122
Nashville, Il., U.S. F8 120
Nashville, In., U.S. E11 120
Nashville, Mi., U.S. F4 112
Nashville, N.C., U.S. I8 114
Nashville, Tn., U.S. H11 120
Nashwaak, stm., N.B., Can. D10 110
Nashwauk, Mn., U.S. D5 118
Nasielsk, Pol. D16 16
Näsijärvi, l., Fin. F10 8
Nāṣir, Sudan F6 62
Nâsir, Buheirat see Nasser, Lake, res., Afr. C6 62
Nasīrābād, India E5 54
Nasr, Egypt H1 58
Nass, stm., B.C., Can. E5 106
Nassarawa, Nig. H6 64
Nassau, Bah. m18 104f
Nassau, N.Y., U.S. B12 114
Nassau International Airport, Bah. m18 104f
Nassau Island, i., Cook Is. E10 72
Nassawadox, Va., U.S. G10 114
Nasser, Lake (Nâsir, Buheirat), res., Afr. C6 62
Nässjö, Swe. H6 8
Nastapoka Islands, is., Nu., Can. D15 106
Nasu, Japan B13 40
Nasu-dake, vol., Japan B12 40
Nasukoin Mountain, mtn., Mt., U.S. B12 136
Nasva, Russia D13 10
Nata, Bots. E4 68
Nata, stm., Afr. B8 70
Natal, Braz. C8 88
Natal, B.C., Can. G16 138
Natal, Indon. C1 50
Natal see KwaZulu-Natal, state, S. Afr. F10 70
Natalia, Tx., U.S. E9 130
Natalkuz Lake, res., B.C., Can. C5 138
Natanes Plateau, plat., Az., U.S. J6 132
Natashquan, stm., Can. i21 107a
Natchez, Ms., U.S. F7 122
Natchez Trace Parkway, p.o.i., U.S. E9 122
Natchitoches, La., U.S. F5 122
Natewa Bay, b., Fiji p19 79e
Nāthdwāra, India F4 54
Natimuk, Austl. K3 76
Nation, stm., B.C., Can. A7 138
National City, Ca., U.S. K8 134
Natitingou, Benin G5 64
Native Bay, b., Nu., Can. C14 106
Natividade, Braz. F2 88
Natkyizin, Mya. E3 48
Natoma, Ks., U.S. B9 128
Nator, Bngl. F12 54
Natori, Japan A13 40
Natron, Lake, l., Afr. E7 66
Natrûn, Wadi el-, val., Egypt H1 58
Nattaung, mtn., Mya. C3 48
Natuna Besar, i., Indon. A6 50
Natuna Besar, Kepulauan, is., Indon. A5 50
Natuna Selatan, Kepulauan, is., Indon. B6 50
Natural Bridge, misc. cult., Va., U.S. G6 114
Natural Bridges National Monument, p.o.i., Ut., U.S. F6 132
Naturaliste, Cape, c., Austl. F2 74
Naturno, Italy D7 22
Nau, Cap de la, c., Spain F11 20
Naucelle, Fr. E8 18
Naucratis, hist., Egypt H1 58
Nauen, Ger. D8 16
Naugatuck, Ct., U.S. C12 114
Naughton, On., Can. B8 112
Naujaat (Repulse Bay), Nu., Can. B13 106
Naujamiestis, Lith. E6 10
Naujan, Lake, l., Phil. D3 52
Naujoji Akmenė, Lith. D5 10
Naumburg, Ger. E7 16
Naunglon, Mya. D3 48
Nā'ūr, Jord. G6 58
Nauru, state, Oc. p17 78f
Nauru International Airport, Nauru q17 78f
Nauški, Russia F10 34
Nausori, Fiji p19 79e
Nauta, Peru D3 84
Nautanwa, India E9 54
Nautla, Mex. E10 100
Nauvoo, Il., U.S. D6 120
Nava, Mex. A8 100
Navadwip, India G12 54
Navael'nja, Bela. G8 10
Navahrudak, Bela. G8 10
Navajo, N.M., U.S. H7 132
Navajo Mountain, mtn., Ut., U.S. F6 132
Navajo National Monument, p.o.i., Az., U.S. G6 132
Navajo Reservoir, res., U.S. G9 132
Naval, Phil. C7 44
Navalmoral de la Mata, Spain E5 20
Navan, Ire. H6 12
Navapolack, Bela. E11 10
Navāpur, India H4 54
Navarin, mys, c., Russia D24 34
Navarino, Isla, i., Chile K3 90
Navarra, state, Spain B9 20
Navarro Mills Lake, res., Tx., U.S. F2 122
Navasëlki, Bela. H7 10
Navasota, Tx., U.S. G2 122
Navasota, stm., Tx., U.S. D11 130
Navassa, N.C., U.S. B7 116
Navassa Island, i., N.A. C10 102
Navesnoe, Russia H20 10
Navia, Arg. G4 92
Navia, stm., Spain A4 20
Navidad, Chile F1 92
Navidad, stm., Tx., U.S. E11 130
Navio, Riacho do, stm., Braz. E6 88
Naviti, i., Fiji p18 79e
Navlja, Russia H17 10
Năvodari, Rom. E15 26
Navoi, Uzb. F11 32
Navojoa, Mex. B4 100
Navolato, Mex. C5 100
Navsāri, India H4 54
Nawa *see* Naha, Japan I18 39a
Nawābganj, Bngl. F12 54
Nawābganj, India E8 54
Nawābshāh, Pak. E2 54
Nawāda, India F10 54
Nāwah, Afg. B1 54
Nawalgarh, India E5 54
Nawāpāra, India H8 54
Naxçıvan, Azer. B6 56
Naxi, China G1 42
Náxos, i., Grc. F8 28
Nayāgarh, India H10 54
Nayarit, state, Mex. E6 100
Nāy Band, Kūh-e, mtn., Iran C8 56
Naylor, Mo., U.S. H7 120
Nayoro, Japan B15 38
Nazaré, Braz. D2 88
Nazaré, Port. E1 20
Nazaré da Mata, Braz. D8 88
Nazaré do Piauí, Braz. D4 88
Nazareth *see* Nazerat, Isr. F6 58
Nazarovo, Russia C16 32
Nazas, Mex. C6 100
Nazas, stm., Mex. C6 100
Nazca Ridge, unds. K5 144
Naze, Japan k19 39a
Naze, The see Lindesnes, c., Nor. H2 8
Nazerat (Nazareth), Isr. F6 58
Nazerat 'Illit, Isr. F6 58
Nazija, Russia A14 10
Nazilli, Tur. F11 28
Nazina, Russia B13 32
Nazko, stm., B.C., Can. D7 138
Nazlet el-'Amûdein, Egypt J1 58
Nazran', Russia F7 32
Nazrēt, Eth. F7 62
Nazwá, Oman E8 56
Nazyvaevsk, Russia C12 32
N'dalatando, Ang. B1 68
Ndali, Benin H5 64
Ndélé, C.A.R. C4 66
Ndendé, Gabon E2 66
N'Djamena (Fort-Lamy), Chad E3 62
Ndjolé, Gabon E2 66
Ndogo, Lagune, l., Gabon E2 66
Ndola, Zam. C4 68
Ndumu Game Reserve, S. Afr. E11 70
Neabul Creek, stm., Austl. F6 76
Neagh, Lough, l., N. Ire., U.K. G6 12
Neah Bay, Wa., U.S. B2 136
Neale, Lake, l., Austl. D6 74
Neamt, state, Rom. B13 26
Néa Páfos (Paphos), Cyp. D3 58
Neápoli, Grc. G6 28
Near Islands, is., Ak., U.S. g21 140a
Neath, Wales, U.K. J9 12
Nebine Creek, stm., Austl. G6 76
Nebitdag, Turkmen. B7 56
Neblina, Cerro de la see Neblina, Pico da, mtn., S.A. G9 86
Neblina, Pico da, mtn., S.A. G9 86
Nebo, Il., U.S. E7 120
Nebo, Mount, mtn., Ut., U.S. D5 132
Nebolči, Russia A16 10
Nebraska, state, U.S. C7 108
Nebraska City, Ne., U.S. D1 120
Necedah, Wi., U.S. G8 118
Nechako, stm., B.C., Can. C7 138
Nechako Reservoir, res., B.C., Can. C5 138
Neches, Tx., U.S. F3 122
Neches, stm., Tx., U.S. G4 122
Nechí, Col. C4 86
Nechí, stm., Col. D4 86
Nechranice, vodní nádrž, res., Czech Rep. F9 16
Neckarsulm, Ger. G5 16
Necker Island, i., Br. Vir. Is. d9 104b
Necochea, Arg. I8 92
Nederland, Tx., U.S. H4 122
Nêdong, China D13 54
Needhams Point, c., Barb. n8 105d
Needle Mountain, mtn., Wy., U.S. F17 136
Needles, Ca., U.S. I2 132
Needville, Tx., U.S. H3 122
Neegro, Qooriga, b., Som. C10 66
Ñeembucú, state, Para. C8 92
Neenah, Wi., U.S. G10 118
Neepawa, Mb., Can. D14 124
Nefëdovo, Russia C12 32
Nefta, Tun. C6 64
Neftçala, Azer. B6 56
Neftejugansk, Russia B12 32
Nefza, Tun. H3 24
Negage, Ang. B2 68
Negara, Indon. H9 50
Negara, stm., Indon. E9 50
Negaunee, Mi., U.S. B2 112
Negēlē, Eth. F7 62
Negeribatin, Indon. F4 50
Negeri Sembilan, state, Malay. K6 48
Negev Desert see HaNegev, reg., Isr. H5 58
Negombo, Sri L. H4 53
Negra, Laguna, l., Ur. G11 92
Negreira, Spain B2 20
Nègres, Pointe des, c., Mart. k6 105c
Negrești-Oaș, Rom. B10 26
Negritos, Peru D1 84
Negro, stm., Arg. H4 90
Negro, stm., Braz. C13 92
Negro, stm., Col. E4 86
Negro, stm., Para. B9 92
Negro, stm., S.A. I11 86
Negro, stm., S.A. F9 92
Negros, i., Phil. F4 52
Nehalem, stm., Or., U.S. E3 136
Neharèlae, Bela. G9 10
Nehawka, Ne., U.S. D1 120
Nehbandān, Iran C8 56
Nehe *see* Nahe, China B9 36
Néhoué, Baie de, b., N. Cal. m14 79d
Neiba, Dom. Rep. C12 102
Neichiang *see* Neijiang, China G1 42
Neidpath, Sk., Can. D6 124
Neiges, Piton des, mtn., Reu. i10 69a
Neijiang, China G1 42
Neikiang *see* Neijiang, China G1 42
Neilburg, Sk., Can. B4 124
Neillsville, Wi., U.S. G8 118
Nei Mongol, state, China C7 36
Nei Mongol see Nei Monggol, state, China C7 36
Neiqiu, China C6 42
Neira, Col. E4 86
Neisse see Lausitzer Neisse, stm., Eur. F10 16
Neisse see Nysa Łużycka, stm., Eur. E10 16
Neiva, Col. F4 86
Neixiang, China E4 42
Neja, Russia G20 8
Nejapa de Madero, Mex. G11 100
Nejd see Najd, hist. reg., Sau. Ar. D5 56
Nejdek, Czech Rep. F8 16
Nek'emtē, Eth. F7 62
Nelichu, mtn., Sudan F6 62
Nelidovo, Russia D15 10
Neligh, Ne., U.S. E14 126
Neljaty, Russia E12 34
Nel'kan, Russia E16 34
Nellikuppam, India F4 53
Nellore, India D4 53
Nel'ma, Russia G16 34
Nelson, B.C., Can. G13 138
Nelson, N.Z. E5 80
Nelson, Ne., U.S. A10 128
Nelson, stm., Mb., Can. D12 106
Nelson, Cape, c., Austl. L3 76
Nelson, Estrecho, strt., Chile J2 90
Nelson Lakes National Park, p.o.i., N.Z. E5 80
Nelson's Dockyard, hist., Antig. f4 105b
Nelsonville, Oh., U.S. E3 114
Nelspoort, S. Afr. H6 70
Nelspruit, S. Afr. D10 70
Néma, Maur. F3 64
Nemadji, stm., U.S. E6 118
Neman, Russia E4 10
Neman (Nemunas), stm., Eur. E4 10
Nembe, Nig. I6 64
Nemenčinė, Lith. F8 10
Nemeriči, Russia G16 10
Nemours, Fr. F11 14
Nemunas (Neman), stm., Eur. E4 10
Nemunėlis (Mēmele), stm., Eur. D7 10
Nemuro, Japan C16 38
Nemuro Strait, strt., Asia C16 38
Nen, stm., China B9 36
Nenagh, Ire. I4 12
Nenana, Ak., U.S. D10 140
Nenana, stm., Ak., U.S. D10 140
Nendo, i., Sol. Is. E7 72
Nene, stm., Eng., U.K. I13 12
Neneckij avtonomnyj okrug, Russia C23 8
Nenets see Neneckij avtonomnyj okrug, Russia C23 8
Nenetsia see Neneckij avtonomnyj okrug, Russia C23 8
Nenggiri, stm., Malay. J5 48
Neodesha, Ks., U.S. G2 120
Neoga, Il., U.S. E9 120
Néo Karlovási, Grc. F9 28
Neola, Ut., U.S. C6 132
Neopit, Wi., U.S. G10 118
Neosho, Mo., U.S. H3 120
Neosho, stm., U.S. H2 120
Nepa, stm., Russia C19 32
Nepal, ctry., Asia E9 54
Nepālgañj, Nepal D8 54
Nepa Nagar, India H6 54
Nepeña, Peru E2 84
Nephin, mtn., Ire. G3 12
Nepisiguit, stm., N.B., Can. C10 110
Nepisiguit Bay, b., N.B., Can. C11 110
Neptune, N.J., U.S. D11 114
Neptune Beach, Fl., U.S. F4 116
Nérac, Fr. E6 18
Nerča, stm., Russia F12 34
Nerčinsk, Russia F12 34
Nerčinskij Zavod, Russia F12 34
Nerehta, Russia H19 8
Neretva, stm., Eur. G15 22
Neriquinha, Ang. D3 68
Neris (Vilija), stm., Eur. F6 10
Nerja, Spain H7 20
Nerjungri, Russia E13 34
Nerl', Russia C20 10
Nerl', stm., Russia D22 10
Nerópolis, Braz. I1 88
Nerussa, stm., Russia H16 10
Nerva, Spain G4 20
Nes, Neth. C1 16
Nesbyen, Nor. F3 8
Neščarda, vozero, l., Bela. E12 10
Neskaupstaður, Ice. k32 8a
Nesna, Nor. C5 8
Nespelem, Wa., U.S. B7 136
Ness, Loch, l., Scot., U.K. D8 12
Ness City, Ks., U.S. C8 128
Nesselrode, Mount, mtn., N.A. D4 106
Nesterkovo, Russia A13 10
Nestoïta, Ukr. B16 26
Netanya, Isr. F5 58
Netherdale, Austl. C7 76
Netherlands, ctry., Eur. B14 14
Netherlands Antilles, dep., N.A. i14 96a
Netherlands Guiana see Surinam, ctry., S.A. C6 84
Netrakona, Bngl. F13 54
Nettilling Fiord, b., Nu., Can. B17 106
Nettilling Lake, l., Nu., Can. B17 106
Nett Lake, l., Mn., U.S. C5 118
Nettuno, Italy C6 24
Neubrandenburg, Ger. C9 16
Neuburg an der Donau, Ger. H7 16
Neuchâtel, Switz. D3 22
Neuchâtel, Lac de, l., Switz. D3 22
Neudorf, Sk., Can. D11 124
Neuenburg *see* Neuchâtel, Switz. D3 22
Neuenhagen, Ger. D9 16
Neuerburg, Ger. F2 16
Neufchâteau, Fr. F14 14
Neufchâtel-en-Bray, Fr. E10 14
Neu-Isenburg, Ger. F4 16
Neumarkt in der Oberpfalz, Ger. G7 16
Neumünster, Ger. B6 16
Neun, stm., Laos C6 48
Neunkirchen, Aus. C13 22
Neuquén, Arg. G3 90
Neuquén, state, Arg. G2 90
Neuquén, stm., Arg. G3 90
Neurara, Chile B3 92
Neuruppin, Ger. D8 16
Neuse, stm., N.C., U.S. A8 116
Neusiedl am See, Aus. C13 22
Neuss, Ger. E2 16
Neustadt, Ger. F7 16
Neustadt an der Aisch, Ger. G6 16
Neustadt an der Weinstrasse, Ger. G3 16
Neustadt bei Coburg, Ger. F6 16
Neustadt in Holstein, Ger. B6 16
Neustrelitz, Ger. C9 16
Neutral Hills, hills, Ab., Can. B3 124
Neu-Ulm, Ger. H6 16
Neuvic, Fr. D8 18
Neuwied, Ger. F3 16
Neva, stm., Russia A13 10
Nevada, Ia., U.S. B4 120
Nevada, Mo., U.S. G3 120
Nevada, state, U.S. D4 108

Name	Map Ref.	Page

Nevada, Sierra, mts., Spain .. G7 20
Nevada, Sierra, mts., Ca., U.S. .. F6 134
Nevada City, Ca., U.S. .. D4 134
Nevado, Cerro, mtn., Arg. .. G3 92
Nevado, Cerro, mtn., Col. .. E4 86
Nevado de Colima, Parque Nacional del, p.o.i., Mex. .. F7 100
Nevado de Toluca, Parque Nacional, p.o.i., Mex. .. F8 100
Neve, Serra da, mts., Ang. .. C1 68
Nevel', Russia .. D12 10
Nevel'sk, Russia .. G17 34
Nevel'skogo, proliv, strt., Russia .. F17 34
Never, Russia .. F13 34
Nevers, Fr. .. G12 14
Nevesinje, Bos. .. F5 26
Nevinnomyssk, Russia .. F6 32
Nevis, i., St. K./N. .. C2 105a
Nevis, Ben, mtn., Scot., U.K. .. E7 12
Nevis Peak, vol., St. K./N. .. C2 105a
Nevjansk, Russia .. C10 32
Nevşehir, Tur. .. B3 56
New, stm., Belize .. D3 102
New, stm., Guy. .. C6 84
New, stm., S.C., U.S. .. D4 116
New, stm., U.S. .. F4 114
Newala, Tan. .. G7 66
New Albany, In., U.S. .. F12 120
New Albany, Ms., U.S. .. C9 122
New Amsterdam, Guy. .. B6 84
New Angledool, Austl. .. G6 76
Newark, Ar., U.S. .. B7 122
Newark, De., U.S. .. E10 114
Newark, N.J., U.S. .. D11 114
Newark, N.Y., U.S. .. A8 114
Newark, Oh., U.S. .. D3 114
Newark-on-Trent, Eng., U.K. .. H12 12
Newark Valley, N.Y., U.S. .. B9 114
New Athens, Il., U.S. .. F8 120
New Baden, Il., U.S. .. F8 120
New Bedford, Ma., U.S. .. C15 114
Newberg, Or., U.S. .. E4 136
New Berlin, Il., U.S. .. E7 120
New Berlin, N.Y., U.S. .. B10 114
New Berlin, Wi., U.S. .. F1 112
Newbern, Al., U.S. .. E11 122
New Bern, N.C., U.S. .. A8 116
Newbern, Tn., U.S. .. H8 120
Newberry, Fl., U.S. .. G3 116
Newberry, S.C., U.S. .. B4 116
Newberry National Volcanic Monument, p.o.i., Or., U.S. .. G5 136
New Bethlehem, Pa., U.S. .. D6 114
New Bloomfield, Pa., U.S. .. H12 112
New Boston, Oh., U.S. .. F3 114
New Boston, Tx., U.S. .. D4 122
New Braunfels, Tx., U.S. .. E9 130
New Britain, Ct., U.S. .. C13 114
New Britain, i., Pap. N. Gui. .. b5 79a
New Brockton, Al., U.S. .. F12 122
Newbrook, Ab., Can. .. B17 138
New Brunswick, N.J., U.S. .. D11 114
New Brunswick, state, Can. .. D10 110
Newburg, Mo., U.S. .. G6 120
Newburgh, In., U.S. .. G10 120
Newburgh, N.Y., U.S. .. C11 114
Newburn, Eng., U.K. .. J11 12
Newburyport, Ma., U.S. .. B15 114
New Caledonia, dep., Oc. .. F7 72
New Caledonia see Nouvelle-Calédonie, i., N. Cal. .. m15 79d
New Caledonia Basin, unds. .. L19 142
New Carlisle, Qc., Can. .. B11 110
New Carlisle, Oh., U.S. .. E2 114
New Castile see Castilla la Nueva, hist. reg., Spain .. E7 20
Newcastle, Austl. .. I8 76
Newcastle, N.B., Can. .. C11 110
Newcastle, S. Afr. .. E9 70
Newcastle, St. K./N. .. C2 105a
Newcastle, In. Ire., U.K. .. G7 12
New Castle, Co., U.S. .. D9 132
New Castle, De., U.S. .. E10 114
New Castle, In., U.S. .. I4 112
Newcastle, Ne., U.S. .. I2 118
New Castle, Ok., U.S. .. F11 128
New Castle, Pa., U.S. .. D5 114
New Castle, Tx., U.S. .. A9 130
New Castle, Va., U.S. .. G5 114
Newcastle, Wy., U.S. .. D8 126
Newcastle Bay, b., Austl. .. B8 74
Newcastle-under-Lyme, Eng., U.K. .. I10 12
Newcastle upon Tyne, Eng., U.K. .. G10 12
Newcastle Waters, Austl. .. C6 74
Newcastle West, Ire. .. I3 12
New City, N.Y., U.S. .. C11 114
Newcomerstown, Oh., U.S. .. D4 114
New Concord, Oh., U.S. .. D4 114
New Cumberland, W.V., U.S. .. D5 114
Newdegate, Austl. .. F3 74
New Delhi, India .. D6 54
New Denver, B.C., Can. .. F13 138
New Edinburg, Ar., U.S. .. D6 122
New Effington, S.D., U.S. .. F1 118
Newell, Ia., U.S. .. B2 120
Newell, W.V., U.S. .. D5 114
Newell, Lake, l., Ab., Can. .. F19 138
New Ellenton, S.C., U.S. .. C4 116
Newellton, La., U.S. .. E7 122
New England, N.D., U.S. .. A10 126
New England National Park, p.o.i., Austl. .. H9 76
Newfane, N.Y., U.S. .. E11 112
Newfane, Vt., U.S. .. A13 114
New Florence, Pa., U.S. .. D6 114
Newfound Gap, p., U.S. .. I2 114
Newfoundland, i., Nf., Can. .. j22 107a
Newfoundland and Labrador, state, Can. .. i23 107a
Newfoundland Basin, unds. .. D9 144
New Franklin, Mo., U.S. .. E5 120
New Freedom, Pa., U.S. .. E9 114
New Galloway, Scot., U.K. .. F8 12
Newgate, B.C., Can. .. G15 138
New Georgia, i., Sol. Is. .. e7 79b
New Georgia Group, is., Sol. Is. .. d7 79b
New Georgia Sound, strt., Sol. Is. .. e8 79b
New Germany, N.S., Can. .. F12 110
New Glasgow, N.S., Can. .. E14 110
New Guinea, i. .. b3 79a
Newhalem, Wa., U.S. .. B5 136
New Hamburg, On., Can. .. E9 112
New Hebrides, is., Vanuatu .. k16 79d
New Hampshire, state, U.S. .. G5 110
New Hanover, i., S. Afr. .. F10 70
New Hanover, i., Pap. N. Gui. .. a4 79a
New Harmony, In., U.S. .. F10 120
New Hartford, Ia., U.S. .. I6 118
Newhaven, Eng., U.K. .. K13 12
New Haven, Ct., U.S. .. C13 114
New Haven, Il., U.S. .. G9 120
New Haven, Ky., U.S. .. G12 120
New Haven, Mo., U.S. .. F6 120
New Hazelton, B.C., Can. .. A3 138
New Hebrides see Vanuatu, ctry., Oc. .. k16 79d
New Hebrides, is., Vanuatu .. k16 79d
New Hebrides Trench, unds. .. L20 142
Newhebron, Ms., U.S. .. F9 122
New Holland, Il., U.S. .. K8 118
New Holland, Pa., U.S. .. D9 114
New Holstein, Wi., U.S. .. E1 112
New Hope, Al., U.S. .. C12 122

New Iberia, La., U.S. .. G7 122
New Ireland, i., Pap. N. Gui. .. a5 79a
New Jersey, state, U.S. .. D11 114
New Johnsonville, Tn., U.S. .. H10 120
New Kensington, Pa., U.S. .. D6 114
New Kent, Va., U.S. .. G8 114
New Kowloon see Xinjiulong, China .. J6 42
Newlands, Austl. .. C6 76
New Lexington, Oh., U.S. .. E3 114
New Lisbon, Wi., U.S. .. H8 118
New Liskeard, On., Can. .. F5 112
New Llano, La., U.S. .. F5 122
New London, Ct., U.S. .. C13 114
New London, Mo., U.S. .. E6 120
New London, N.H., U.S. .. G5 110
New London, Oh., U.S. .. C3 114
New London, Tx., U.S. .. E4 122
New London, Wi., U.S. .. G10 118
New Madrid, Mo., U.S. .. H8 120
Newman, Austl. .. D3 74
Newman, Ca., U.S. .. F4 134
Newman Grove, Ne., U.S. .. F15 126
Newmarket, On., Can. .. D10 112
New Market, Eng., U.K. .. I13 12
New Market, Al., U.S. .. C12 122
New Market, Ia., U.S. .. D3 120
Newmarket, N.H., U.S. .. G5 110
New Market, Va., U.S. .. F8 114
New Martinsville, W.V., U.S. .. E4 114
New Mexico, state, U.S. .. D9 98
New Milford, Ct., U.S. .. C12 114
New Milford, Pa., U.S. .. C10 114
Newnan, Ga., U.S. .. D14 122
New Norfolk, Austl. .. o13 77a
New Norway, Ab., Can. .. D18 138
New Orleans, La., U.S. .. G8 122
New Paris, Oh., U.S. .. I5 112
New Philadelphia, Oh., U.S. .. D4 114
New Pine Creek, Or., U.S. .. A5 134
New Plymouth, N.Z. .. D5 80
New Plymouth, Id., U.S. .. G10 136
Newport, Eng., U.K. .. K11 12
Newport, Wales, U.K. .. J10 12
Newport, Ar., U.S. .. B7 122
Newport, Ky., U.S. .. E1 114
Newport, Me., U.S. .. F7 110
Newport, N.C., U.S. .. B8 116
Newport, N.H., U.S. .. G4 110
Newport, Or., U.S. .. F2 136
Newport, Pa., U.S. .. D8 114
Newport, R.I., U.S. .. C14 114
Newport, Tn., U.S. .. I3 114
Newport, Vt., U.S. .. F4 110
Newport Beach, Ca., U.S. .. J7 134
Newport News, Va., U.S. .. G9 114
New Port Richey, Fl., U.S. .. H3 116
New Providence, i., Bah. .. C9 96
Newquay, Eng., U.K. .. K7 12
New Richland, Mn., U.S. .. H5 118
New Richmond, Qc., Can. .. B10 110
New Richmond, Wi., U.S. .. F6 118
New River, St. K./N. .. C2 105a
New Road, N.S., Can. .. F13 110
New Roads, La., U.S. .. G7 122
New Rochelle, N.Y., U.S. .. D12 114
New Ross, N.S., Can. .. F12 110
New Ross, Ire. .. I6 12
Newry, N. Ire., U.K. .. G6 12
Newry, S.C., U.S. .. B3 116
New Salem, N.D., U.S. .. A11 126
New Schwabenland, reg., Ant. .. C5 81
New Sharon, Ia., U.S. .. C5 120
New Siberian Islands see Novosibirskie ostrova, is., Russia .. A18 34
New Smyrna Beach, Fl., U.S. .. G5 116
New South Wales, state, Austl. .. I6 76
New Tazewell, Tn., U.S. .. H2 114
New Tecumseth, On., Can. .. D9 112
Newton, Ia., U.S. .. C4 120
Newton, Il., U.S. .. F9 120
Newton, Ks., U.S. .. C11 128
Newton, Ma., U.S. .. B14 114
Newton, Ms., U.S. .. E9 122
Newton, N.J., U.S. .. C11 114
Newton, N.C., U.S. .. A4 116
Newton, Tx., U.S. .. G5 122
Newton Falls, N.Y., U.S. .. F2 110
Newton Stewart, Scot., U.K. .. G8 12
New Town, N.D., U.S. .. F11 124
Newtownabbey, N. Ire., U.K. .. G6 12
Newtownards, N. Ire., U.K. .. G7 12
New Ulm, Mn., U.S. .. G4 118
New Ulm, Tx., U.S. .. H2 122
New Washington, Oh., U.S. .. D3 114
New Waterford, N.S., Can. .. D16 110
New Waverly, Tx., U.S. .. G3 122
New Westminster, B.C., Can. .. G8 138
New Whiteland, In., U.S. .. E11 120
New York, N.Y., U.S. .. D12 114
New York Mills, Mn., U.S. .. E3 118
New York State Barge Canal, can., N.Y., U.S. .. E12 112
New Zealand, ctry., Oc. .. D4 80
Neyrīz, Iran .. D7 56
Neyshābūr, Iran .. B8 56
Neyyāttinkara, India .. G3 53
Nezahualcóyotl, Presa, res., Mex. .. G12 100
Nezperce, Id., U.S. .. D10 136
Ngabang, Indon. .. C6 50
Ngabé, Congo .. E3 66
Ngambé, Cam. .. D2 66
Ngami, Lake, l., Bots. .. B6 70
Ngamiland, state, Bots. .. B6 70
Ngan-chou see Anhui, state, China .. F7 42
Nganglong Kangri, mts., China .. B9 54
Nganjuk, Indon. .. G7 50
Ngangla Ringco, l., China .. C9 54
Ngangzê Co, l., China .. C11 54
Ngao, Thai. .. C4 48
Ngaoui, Mont, mtn., Afr. .. C2 66
Ngaoundéré, Cam. .. C2 66
Ngape, Mya. .. B2 48
Ngaputaw, Mya. .. D2 48
Ngara, Tan. .. E6 66
Ngatangiia, Cook Is. .. a27 78j
Ngatangiia Harbour, b., Cook Is. .. a27 78j

Ngulu, at., Micron. .. C4 72
Ngum, stm., Laos .. C6 48
Nguna, Île, i., Vanuatu .. k17 79d
Nguru, Nig. .. G7 64
Nhacoongo, Moz. .. D12 70
Nhamundá, stm., Braz. .. D7 84
Nha Trang, Viet. .. F9 48
Nhill, Austl. .. K3 76
Nhoma, stm., Afr. .. D2 68
Niafounké, Mali .. F4 64
Niagara, Wi., U.S. .. C1 112
Niagara Falls, On., Can. .. E10 112
Niagara Falls, N.Y., U.S. .. A6 114
Niagara-on-the-Lake, On., Can. .. E10 112
Niagassola, Gui. .. G3 64
Niah, Malay. .. B8 50
Niamey, Niger .. G5 64
Niangara, D.R.C. .. D5 66
Niangay, Lac, l., Mali .. F4 64
Niangoloko, Burkina .. G4 64
Nianguá, stm., Mo., U.S. .. G5 120
Nia-Nia, D.R.C. .. D5 66
Niantic, Il., U.S. .. E8 120
Nianyushan, China .. G7 42
Nianzishan, China .. B9 36
Niari, stm., Congo .. E2 66
Nias, Pulau, i., Indon. .. L3 48
Nicaragua, ctry., N.A. .. F5 102
Nicaragua, Lago de, l., Nic. .. G5 102
Nicaragua, Lake see Nicaragua, Lago de, l., Nic. .. G5 102
Nicastro, Italy .. F10 24
Nice, Fr. .. F13 18
Niceville, Fl., U.S. .. G12 122
Nichinan, Japan .. H4 40
Nicholas Channel (San Nicolás, Canal de), strt., N.A. .. G11 108
Nicholasville, Ky., U.S. .. G13 120
Nicholls, Ga., U.S. .. E3 116
Nicholl's Town, Bah. .. B9 96
Nicholson, Pa., U.S. .. C10 114
Nickel Centre, On., Can. .. B8 112
Nicobar Islands, is., India .. G7 46
Nicola, B.C., Can. .. F10 138
Nicola, stm., B.C., Can. .. F9 138
Nicolae Bălcescu, Rom. .. B13 26
Nicolet, Qc., Can. .. D4 110
Nicolet, Lake, l., Mi., U.S. .. B5 112
Nicolet Sud-Ouest, stm., Qc., Can. .. E5 110
Nicollet, Mn., U.S. .. G4 118
Nicosia (Levkosía), Cyp. .. C4 58
Nicosia, Italy .. G8 24
Nicoya, Golfo de, b., C.R. .. H5 102
Nicoya, Península de, pen., C.R. .. H5 102
Nida, Lith. .. E3 10
Nida, stm., Pol. .. F16 16
Nidadavole, India .. C5 53
Nidzica, Pol. .. C16 16
Niebüll, Ger. .. B4 16
Niedere Tauern, mts., Aus. .. C10 22
Niederösterreich, state, Aus. .. B12 22
Niedersachsen, state, Ger. .. D4 16
Niekerkshoop, S. Afr. .. F6 70
Niemba, D.R.C. .. F5 66
Niemodlin, Pol. .. F13 16
Nienburg, Ger. .. D5 16
Niers, stm., Eur. .. C15 14
Niesky, Ger. .. E10 16
Nieszawa, Pol. .. D15 16
Nieu-Bethesda, S. Afr. .. G7 70
Nieuport see Nieuwpoort, Bel. .. C11 14
Nieuw Amsterdam, Sur. .. B6 84
Nieuw Nickerie, Sur. .. B6 84
Nieuwpoort, Bel. .. C11 14
Nieuwpoort, Neth. Ant. .. p22 104g
Nièvre, state, Fr. .. G12 14
Nifisha, Egypt .. H3 58
Niğde, Tur. .. A5 58
Niğde, state, Tur. .. A5 58
Nigel, S. Afr. .. E9 70
Niger, ctry., Afr. .. F6 64
Niger, stm., Afr. .. H6 64
Niger, Mouths of the, mth., Nig. .. I6 64
Nigeria, ctry., Afr. .. G6 64
Nighthawk, Wa., U.S. .. B7 136
Nigríta, Grc. .. C6 28
Niheïdät el-Súd, Gebel el-, mtn., Egypt .. J3 58
Nihommatsu, Japan .. B13 40
Nihuil, Embalse del, res., Arg. .. G3 92
Niigata, Japan .. B11 40
Niigata, state, Japan .. B11 40
Niihama, Japan .. F6 40
Ni'ihau, i., Hi., U.S. .. b1 78a
Nii-jima, i., Japan .. E12 40
Niitsu, Japan .. B12 40
Nijil, Jord.? Niitui?
Nijmegen, Neth. .. C14 14
Nijvel see Nivelles, Bel. .. D13 14
Nikel', Russia .. B10 56
Nikiski, Ak., U.S. .. D9 140
Nikki, Benin .. H5 64
Nikkō, Japan .. C12 40
Nikkō-kokuritsu-kōen, p.o.i., Japan .. B12 40
Nikolaevo, Russia .. B12 10
Nikolaevsk-na-Amure, Russia .. F17 34
Nikolaevskiy, Russia .. C6 32
Nikol'sk, Russia .. G21 8
Nikol'sk, Russia .. C8 32
Nikolski, Ak., U.S. .. F6 140
Nikol'skij, Russia .. F15 8
Nikol'skoe, Russia .. E22 34
Nikol'skoe, Russia .. H19 10
Nikopol', Ukr. .. E4 32
Nīkshahr, Iran .. D9 56
Nikšić, Serb. .. G5 26
Nikumaroro, at., Kir. .. D9 72
Nikunau, i., Kir. .. D8 72
Nil, Bahr el- see Nile, stm., Afr. .. D6 62
Nil, Nahr an- see Nile, stm., Afr. .. D6 62
Nila, Pulau, i., Indon. .. G9 44
Nilakka, l., Fin. .. E12 8
Nīmach, India .. F5 54
Nimba, Mount, mtn., Afr. .. H3 64
Nimbāhera, India .. F5 54
Nîmes, Fr. .. F10 18
Nimmitabel, Austl. .. K7 76
Nimrod Lake, res., Ar., U.S. .. C6 122
Nimule, Sudan .. G6 62
Ninda, Ang. .. C3 68
Nindigully, Austl. .. G7 76
Nine Degree Channel, strt., India .. G3 46
Nine Mile Beach, cst. .. L6 76

Ningdu, China .. H6 42
Ningguo, China .. F8 42
Ningguta see Ning'an, China .. D6 36
Ninghai, China .. H7 42
Ning-hia see Ningxia, state, China .. D6 36
Ninghua, China .. G6 64
Ningi, Nig. .. G6 64
Ningjing Shan, mts., China .. F4 36
Ningming, China .. J2 42
Ningming, China .. J2 42
Ningpo see Ningbo, China .. G9 42
Ningqiang, China .. E2 42
Ningshan, China .. E3 42
Ningsia see Yinchuan, China .. B2 42
Ningsia Hui see Ningxia, state, China .. D6 36
Ningsia Hui Autonomous Region see Ningxia, state, China .. D6 36
Ningwu, China .. B4 42
Ningxia, state, China .. D6 36
Ningxiang, China .. G5 42
Ningyuan, China .. I4 42
Ninh Binh, Viet. .. B7 48
Ninh Hoa, Viet. .. F9 48
Ninhue, Chile .. H1 92
Ninigo Group, is., Pap. N. Gui. .. a3 79a
Ninnescah, North Fork, stm., Ks., U.S. .. D10 128
Ninnescah, South Fork, stm., Ks., U.S. .. D10 128
Ninohe, Japan .. D14 38
Nioaque, Braz. .. D5 90
Niobrara, stm., U.S. .. E14 126
Nioghalvfjerdsfjorden, ice, Grnld. .. B22 141
Nioki, D.R.C. .. E3 66
Niono, Mali .. G3 64
Nioro, Mali .. F3 64
Niort, Fr. .. C5 18
Niota, Tn., U.S. .. B14 122
Nipāni, India .. C2 53
Nipawin, Sk., Can. .. E10 106
Nipe, Bahía de, b., Cuba .. B10 102
Nipigon, On., Can. .. C10 118
Nipigon, Lake, res., On., Can. .. B10 118
Nipigon Bay, b., On., Can. .. C10 118
Nipissing, Lake, l., On., Can. .. B10 112
Nipomo, Ca., U.S. .. H5 134
Niquelândia, Braz. .. H1 88
Niquero, Cuba .. B9 102
Niquivil, Arg. .. E3 92
Nira, stm., India .. B2 53
Nirasaki, Japan .. D11 40
Nirgua, Ven. .. B7 86
Nirmal, India .. B4 53
Nirmali, India .. E11 54
Niš, Serb. .. F8 26
Niṣāb, Yemen .. G6 56
Niṣāva, stm., Eur. .. F9 26
Niscemi, Italy .. G8 24
Nishio, Japan .. E10 40
Nishiwaki, Japan .. E7 40
Nisporeni, Mol. .. B15 26
Nisqually, stm., Wa., U.S. .. D4 136
Nísyros, i., Grc. .. G10 28
Nisser, l., Nor. .. G2 8
Nisswa, Mn., U.S. .. E4 118
Nitaure, Lat. .. C7 10
Niterói, Braz. .. L4 88
Nith, stm., On., Can. .. E9 112
Nitinat Lake, l., B.C., Can. .. H6 138
Nitra, Slov. .. H14 16
Nitra, stm., Slov. .. H14 16
Niuafo'ou, i., Tonga .. E9 72
Niuatoputapu, i., Tonga .. E9 72
Niue, dep., Oc. .. E10 72
Niulakita, i., Tuvalu .. E8 72
Niut, Gunung, mtn., Indon. .. C6 50
Niutao, i., Tuvalu .. D8 72
Niuzhuang, China .. A10 42
Nive, stm., Austl. .. E6 76
Nivelles, Bel. .. D13 14
Nivernais, hist. reg., Fr. .. G12 14
Niverville, Mb., Can. .. E16 124
Nixa, Mo., U.S. .. G4 120
Nixon, Nv., U.S. .. D6 134
Nizāmābād, India .. B4 53
Nizām Sāgar, res., India .. C3 53
Nižegorodskaja oblast', co., Russia .. H21 8
Nizip, Tur. .. A8 58
Nízke Tatry, Narodny Park, p.o.i., Slov. .. H15 16
Nizneangarsk, Russia .. E10 34
Nižnee Kujto, ozero, l., Russia .. D14 8
Nižneilimsk, Russia .. C18 32
Nižnekamsk, Russia .. C8 32
Nižnekamskoe vodohranilišče, res., Russia .. C8 32
Nižneudinsk, Russia .. D17 32
Nižnevartovsk, Russia .. B13 32
Nižnij Casučej, Russia .. F12 34
Nižnij Kuranah, Russia .. E14 34
Nižnij Novgorod (Gorky), Russia .. H21 8
Nižnij Tagil, Russia .. C10 32
Nižnjaja Peša, Russia .. C22 8
Nižnjaja Pojma, Russia .. C17 32
Nižnjaja Tavda, Russia .. C11 32
Nižnjaja Tunguska, Russia .. B16 32
Nizza Monferrato, Italy .. F5 22
Njandoma, Russia .. F19 8
Njazidja, i., Com. .. C7 68
Njombe, stm., Tan. .. F7 66
Njuhča, Russia .. E22 8
Njuja, stm., Russia .. D12 34
Njuk, ozero, l., Russia .. D14 8
Njuksenica, Russia .. F21 8
Njurba, Russia .. D12 34
Njuvčim, Russia .. B8 32
Nkambe, Cam. .. C2 66
Nkawkaw, Ghana .. H4 64
Nkhata Bay, Mwi. .. C5 68
Nkhotakota, Mwi. .. C5 68
Nkomi, Lagune, l., Gabon .. E1 66
Nkongsamba, Cam. .. D1 66
Nkwalini, S. Afr. .. F10 70
Nmai, stm., Mya. .. C8 46
Noakhali, Bngl. .. G13 54
Noatak, Ak., U.S. .. C7 140
Noatak, stm., Ak., U.S. .. C8 140
Nobeoka, Japan .. G4 40
Noble, Il., U.S. .. F9 120
Noblesville, In., U.S. .. H3 112
Nobres, Braz. .. F6 84
Nocatee, Fl., U.S. .. I4 116
Nocera Inferiore, Italy .. D8 24
Nockatunga, Austl. .. F4 76
Nocona, Tx., U.S. .. H11 128
Noetinger, Arg. .. F6 92
Nogales, Mex. .. F7 98
Nogales, Az., U.S. .. L5 132
Nogent-le-Rotrou, Fr. .. F9 14
Nogent-sur-Seine, Fr. .. F12 14
Noginsk, Russia .. E21 10
Nogliki, Russia .. F17 34
Nogoa, stm., Austl. .. E6 76
Nogoyá, Arg. .. F7 92
Nógrád, state, Hung. .. B6 26
Noguera Pallaresa, stm., Spain .. B12 20

Noguera Ribagorçana, stm., Spain .. B11 20
Nohar, India .. D5 54
Noia, Spain .. B2 20
Noir, Causse, plat., Fr. .. E9 18
Noir, Isla, i., Chile .. J2 90
Noire, stm., Qc., Can. .. B13 112
Noirmoutier, Île de, i., Fr. .. H6 14
Noirmoutier-en-l'Île, Fr. .. H6 14
Nojima-zaki, c., Japan .. E12 40
Nokha Mandi, India .. E4 54
Nokia, Fin. .. F10 8
Nokomis, Sk., Can. .. C8 124
Nokomis, Fl., U.S. .. I3 116
Nokomis, Il., U.S. .. E8 120
Nokou, Chad .. E2 62
Nokuku, Vanuatu .. j16 79d
Nola, C.A.R. .. D3 66
Nola, Italy .. D8 24
Nolichucky, stm., U.S. .. H2 114
Nolin, stm., Ky., U.S. .. G11 120
Nolin Lake, res., Ky., U.S. .. G11 120
Nolinsk, Russia .. C8 32
Nólsoy, i., Far. Is. .. n34 8b
Nombre de Dios, Pan. .. H8 102
Nome, Ak., U.S. .. D6 140
Nomozaki, Japan .. G2 40
Nomtsas, Nmb. .. D3 70
Nonacho Lake, l., N.T., Can. .. C8 106
Nonburg, Russia .. D24 8
Nondalton, Ak., U.S. .. D8 140
Nong'an, China .. B6 38
Nong Han, Thai. .. D6 48
Nong Khai, Thai. .. D6 48
Nongoma, S. Afr. .. E10 70
Nongpoh, India .. F13 54
Nongstoin, India .. F13 54
Nonoava, Mex. .. B5 100
Nonogasta, Arg. .. D4 92
Nonouti, at., Kir. .. D8 72
Nonsuch Bay, b., Antig. .. f4 105b
Nonthaburi, Thai. .. F5 48
Noonamah, Austl. .. B6 74
Noonan, N.D., U.S. .. F10 124
Noonkanbah, Austl. .. C4 74
Noordoostpolder, reg., Neth. .. B14 14
Noordpunt, c., Neth. Ant. .. p21 104g
Noordwijk aan Zee, Neth. .. B13 14
Noorvik, Ak., U.S. .. C7 140
Nootka Island, i., B.C., Can. .. G4 138
Nóqui, Ang. .. B1 68
Nora Islands see Norah, is., Erit. .. D7 62
Noralee, B.C., Can. .. B4 138
Noranda see Rouyn-Noranda, Qc., Can. .. F15 106
Nora Springs, Ia., U.S. .. A5 120
Norcatur, Ks., U.S. .. B8 128
Norcia, Italy .. H10 22
Norcross, Ga., U.S. .. D14 122
Nord, Grnld. .. A22 141
Nord, state, Fr. .. D12 14
Nord, Canal du, can., Fr. .. D12 14
Nordaustlandet, i., Nor. .. B29 141
Nordborg, Den. .. A5 16
Nordegg, Ab., Can. .. D14 138
Nordegg, stm., Ab., Can. .. D15 138
Norden, Ger. .. C3 16
Nordenšel'da, arhipelag, is., Russia .. A8 34
Nordenskjold Archipelago see Nordenšel'da, arhipelag, is., Russia .. A8 34
Norderney, i., Ger. .. C3 16
Norderstedt, Ger. .. C6 16
Nordfjord, b., Nor. .. F1 8
Nordfjordeid, Nor. .. F1 8
Nordhausen, Ger. .. E6 16
Nordhorn, Ger. .. D2 16
Nordjylland, state, Den. .. H4 8
Nordkapp (North Cape), c., Nor. .. A11 8
Nordkinnhalvøya, pen., Nor. .. A12 8
Nordland, state, Nor. .. C6 8
Nördlingen, Ger. .. H6 16
Nordmaling, Swe. .. E8 8
Nordostrundingen, c., Grnld. .. A23 141
Nord-Ostsee-Kanal (Kiel Canal), can., Ger. .. B5 16
Nordrhein-Westfalen, state, Ger. .. E4 16
Nordstrand, i., Ger. .. B4 16
Nord-Trøndelag, state, Nor. .. D5 8
Nordvik, Russia .. B11 34
Norfolk, Ne., U.S. .. E15 126
Norfolk, Va., U.S. .. H9 114
Norfolk Island, dep., Norf. I. .. x25 78i
Norfolk Island National Park, p.o.i., Norf. I. .. y25 78i
Norfolk Ridge, unds. .. L19 142
Norfork Lake, res., U.S. .. H5 120
Norikura-dake, vol., Japan .. C10 40
Noril'sk, Russia .. C6 34
Norlina, N.C., U.S. .. H7 114
Norland, On., Can. .. D11 112
Norman, Ar., U.S. .. C5 122
Norman, Ok., U.S. .. F11 128
Norman, stm., Austl. .. B3 76
Norman, Lake, res., N.C., U.S. .. A4 116
Normanby Island, i., Pap. N. Gui. .. c5 79a
Normandes, Îles see Channel Islands, is., Eur. .. L10 12
Normandie, hist. reg., Fr. .. F8 14
Normandie, Collines de, hills, Fr. .. F8 14
Normandin, Qc., Can. .. B4 110
Normandy see Normandie, hist. reg., Fr. .. F8 14
Normandy, Hills of see Normandie, Collines de, hills, Fr. .. F8 14
Normangee, Tx., U.S. .. F2 122
Norman Island, i., Br. Vir. Is. .. e8 104b
Normanton, Austl. .. A4 76
Norman Wells, N.T., Can. .. B5 106
Noroquay, Mex. .. C11 124
Norquay, Sk., Can. .. C11 124
Norra Storfjället, mtn., Swe. .. D6 8
Norris, Tn., U.S. .. H1 114
Norris Lake, res., Tn., U.S. .. H2 114
Norristown, Pa., U.S. .. D10 114
Norrköping, Swe. .. G7 8
Norrtälje, Swe. .. G8 8
Norseman, Austl. .. F4 74
Norsjö, Swe. .. D8 8
Norte, Cabo, c., Braz. .. C7 84
Norte, Serra do, plat., Braz. .. F6 84
Norte de Santander, state, Col. .. C5 86
Nortelândia, Braz. .. F6 84
North, S.C., U.S. .. C4 116
North, Cape, c., N.S., Can. .. D16 110
North Adams, Ma., U.S. .. B12 114
Northallerton, Eng., U.K. .. G11 12
Northam, Austl. .. F3 74

Northampton, Austl. .. E2 74
Northampton, Eng., U.K. .. I12 12
Northampton, Ma., U.S. .. B13 114
North Andaman, i., India .. F7 46
North Atlanta, Ga., U.S. .. C1 116
North Augusta, S.C., U.S. .. C4 116
North Aulatsivik Island, i., Nf., Can. .. F13 141
North Australian Basin, unds. .. K14 142
North Baltimore, Oh., U.S. .. C2 114
North Battleford, Sk., Can. .. B5 124
North Bay, On., Can. .. B10 112
North Bend, B.C., Can. .. G9 138
North Bend, Ne., U.S. .. J2 118
North Bend, Or., U.S. .. G2 136
North Bennington, Vt., U.S. .. B12 114
North Berwick, Scot., U.K. .. E10 12
North Berwick, Me., U.S. .. G6 110
North Borneo see Sabah, state, Malay. .. H1 52
North Bourke, Austl. .. H5 76
North Branch, Mi., U.S. .. E6 112
North Caicos, i., T./C. Is. .. B11 102
North Canadian, stm., Ok., U.S. .. F12 128
North Canton, Ga., U.S. .. C14 122
North Canton, Oh., U.S. .. D4 114
North Cape see Nordkapp, c., Nor. .. A11 8
North Cape, c., N.Z. .. B5 80
North Caribou Lake, l., On., Can. .. E12 106
North Carolina, state, U.S. .. D11 108
North Cascades National Park, p.o.i., Wa., U.S. .. B5 136
North Channel, strt., Eur. .. B7 12
North Channel, strt., U.K. .. F7 12
North Charleston, S.C., U.S. .. D5 116
North Chicago, Il., U.S. .. F2 112
North Chungcheong see Ch'ungch'ŏng-bukto, state, Kor., S. .. B1 40
Northcliffe, Austl. .. F3 74
North College Hill, Oh., U.S. .. C12 120
North Collins, N.Y., U.S. .. F11 112
North Concho, stm., Tx., U.S. .. C7 130
North Conway, N.H., U.S. .. F5 110
North Crossett, Ar., U.S. .. D6 122
North Cyprus see Cyprus, North, ctry., Asia .. C4 58
North Dakota, state, U.S. .. G13 124
North Downs, hills, Eng., U.K. .. J13 12
North Eagle Butte, S.D., U.S. .. B11 126
North East, Pa., U.S. .. E9 114
North-East, state, Bots. .. B8 70
Northeast Cape, Ak., U.S. .. D6 140
Northeast Cape Fear, stm., N.C., U.S. .. B8 116
Northeast Providence Channel, strt., Bah. .. B9 96
Northeim, Ger. .. E5 16
North English, Ia., U.S. .. C5 120
Northern see HaŻafon, state, Isr. .. F6 58
Northern Cape, state, S. Afr. .. G5 70
Northern Cook Islands, is., Cook Is. .. E10 72
Northern Division, state, Fiji. .. p20 79e
Northern Donets see Severskij Donec, stm., Eur. .. F16 9
Northern Dvina see Severnaja Dvina, stm., Russia .. E19 8
Northern Ireland, state, U.K. .. G6 12
Northern Mariana Islands, dep., Oc. .. B6 72
Northern Province, state, S. Afr. .. C9 70
Northern Sporades see Vóreioi Sporades, is., Grc. .. D6 28
Northern Territory, state, Austl. .. D6 74
North Fabius, stm., U.S. .. D6 120
Northfield, Mn., U.S. .. B13 114
Northfield, Vt., U.S. .. G5 110
North Fiji Basin, unds. .. K20 142
North Flinders Range, mts., Austl. .. H2 76
North Fond du Lac, Wi., U.S. .. H10 118
North Foreland, c., Eng., U.K. .. J14 12
North Fork, stm., U.S. .. H5 120
North Fort Myers, Fl., U.S. .. J4 116
North Frisian Islands, is., Eur. .. B3 16
Northglenn, Co., U.S. .. B4 128
North Gulfport, Ms., U.S. .. G9 122
North Gyeongsang see Kyŏngsang-bukto, state, Kor., S. .. C1 40
North Henik Lake, l., Nu., Can. .. C11 106
North Hero, Vt., U.S. .. F3 110
North Highlands, Ca., U.S. .. E4 134
North Horr, Kenya .. D7 66
North Island, i., N.Z. .. C5 80
North Judson, In., U.S. .. G3 112
North Kent Island, i., Nu., Can. .. B7 141
North Kingsville, Oh., U.S. .. C5 114
North Knife Lake, l., Mb., Can. .. D11 106
North Korea see Korea, North, ctry., Asia .. B7 38
North Lakhimpur, India .. C7 38
North Las Vegas, Nv., U.S. .. G1 132
North La Veta Pass, p., Co., U.S. .. D3 128
North Little Rock, Ar., U.S. .. C6 122
North Llano, stm., Tx., U.S. .. D8 130
North Logan, Ut., U.S. .. B5 132
North Loup, Ne., U.S. .. F14 126
North Loup, stm., Ne., U.S. .. F14 126
North Magnetic Pole, misc. cult. .. A3 141
North Mamm Peak, mtn., Co., U.S. .. D9 132
North Manchester, In., U.S. .. H4 112
North Manitou Island, i., Mi., U.S. .. C3 112
North Mankato, Mn., U.S. .. G4 118
North Miami, Fl., U.S. .. K5 116
North Miami Beach, Fl., U.S. .. K5 116
North Milk, stm., North Fork, stm. .. B13 136
North Myrtle Beach, S.C., U.S. .. C7 116
North New River Canal, can., Fl., U.S. .. J5 116
North Newton, Ks., U.S. .. C11 128
North Ossetia see Severnaja Osetija, state, Russia .. F6 32
North Palisade, mtn., Ca., U.S. .. F7 134
North Palm Beach, Fl., U.S. .. J5 116
North Park, Il., U.S. .. B9 120
North Peninsula, pen. .. A10 118
North Plains, pl., N.M., U.S. .. I8 132
North Platte, Ne., U.S. .. F12 126
North Point, c., Barb. .. n8 105d
North Pole, misc. cult. .. A4 94
Northport, Al., U.S. .. D11 122

Name	Map Ref.	Page
Northport, Mi., U.S.	C4	112
Northport, Wa., U.S.	B9	136
North Portal, Sk., Can.	E11	124
North Raccoon, stm., Ia., U.S.	C3	120
North Rhine-Westphalia see Nordrhein-Westfalen, state, Ger.	E4	16
North Richland Hills, Tx., U.S.	B10	130
North Rim, Az., U.S.	G4	132
North Ronaldsay, i., Scot., U.K.	B10	12
North Rustico, P.E., Can.	D13	110
North Salt Lake, Ut., U.S.	C5	132
North Saskatchewan, stm., Can.	E9	106
North Sea, s., Eur.	D9	6
North Shoal Lake, l., Mb., Can.	D16	124
North Shore City, N.Z.	C6	80
North Shoshone Peak, mtn., Nv., U.S.	D8	134
North Siberain Lowland see Severo-Sibirskaja nizmennost', pl., Russia	B6	34
North Skunk, stm., Ia., U.S.	C5	120
North Solitary Island, i., Austl.	G9	76
North Solomons, state, Pap. N. Gui.	d7	79b
North Spicer Island, i., Nu., Can.	B15	106
North Stradbroke Island, i., Austl.	F9	76
North Sumatra see Sumatera Utara, state, Indon.	K4	48
North Sydney, N.S., Can.	D16	110
North Taranaki Bight, b., N.Z.	D5	80
North Terre Haute, In., U.S.	E10	120
North Thompson, stm., B.C., Can.	F10	138
North Troy, Vt., U.S.	F4	110
North Tunica, Ms., U.S.	C8	122
North Uist, i., Scot., U.K.	D5	12
Northumberland Isles, is., Austl.	C7	76
Northumberland National Park, p.o.i., Eng., U.K.	F10	12
Northumberland Strait, strt., Can.	D12	110
North Umpqua, stm., Or., U.S.	G4	136
North Vancouver, B.C., Can.	G7	138
North Vietnam see Vietnam, ctry., Asia.	E9	48
Northville, N.Y., U.S.	G2	110
North-West, state, S. Afr.	E7	70
North West Bluff, c., Monts.	D3	105a
North West Cape, c., Austl.	D2	74
North-West Frontier, state, Pak.	A4	54
Northwest Miramichi, stm., N.B., Can.	C10	110
Northwest Pacific Basin, unds.	F18	142
Northwest Providence Channel, strt., Bah.	m17	104f
Northwest Territories, state, Can.	C6	106
North Wichita, stm., Tx., U.S.	H9	128
North Wilkesboro, N.C., U.S.	H4	114
North Windham, Me., U.S.	G6	110
Northwood, Ia., U.S.	H5	118
Northwood, N.D., U.S.	G16	124
North York, mph., On., Can.	E10	112
North York Moors National Park, p.o.i., Eng., U.K.	G12	12
North Zulch, Tx., U.S.	G2	122
Norton, Ks., U.S.	B9	128
Norton, Va., U.S.	H3	114
Norton Shores, Mi., U.S.	E3	112
Norton Sound, strt., Ak., U.S.	D6	140
Nortonville, Ks., U.S.	E2	120
Norvegia, Cape, c., Ant.	C3	81
Norwalk, Ct., U.S.	C12	114
Norwalk, Ia., U.S.	C4	120
Norwalk, Oh., U.S.	C3	114
Norway, Ia., U.S.	C6	120
Norway, Me., U.S.	F6	110
Norway, ctry., Eur.	E3	8
Norway Bay, b., Nu., Can.	A10	106
Norwegian Basin, unds.	B13	144
Norwegian Sea, s., Eur.	C3	30
Norwich, On., Can.	E9	112
Norwich, Eng., U.K.	I14	12
Norwich, Ct., U.S.	C13	114
Norwich, N.Y., U.S.	B10	114
Norwood, On., Can.	D11	112
Norwood, Co., U.S.	E8	132
Norwood, Ma., U.S.	B14	114
Norwood, N.C., U.S.	A5	116
Norwood, Oh., U.S.	E1	114
Noshiro, Japan	D13	38
Nosop (Nossob), stm., Afr.	D5	70
Nosovaja, Russia	B26	8
Nosovščina, Russia	E17	8
Nossa Senhora das Dores, Braz.	F7	88
Nossob (Nossob), stm., Afr.	D5	70
Nosy-Varika, Madag.	E8	68
Notasulga, Al., U.S.	E13	122
Notch Hill, B.C., Can.	F11	138
Noteč, stm., Pol.	D11	16
Nótio Aigaío, state, Grc.	G9	28
Noto, Italy	H9	24
Noto, Japan	B10	40
Noto, Golfo di, b., Italy	H9	24
Noto-hantō, pen., Japan	B10	40
Notozero, ozero, l., Russia	C14	8
Notre-Dame, N.B., Can.	D11	110
Notre-Dame, Monts, mts., Qc., Can.	B9	110
Notre-Dame-du-Laus, Qc., Can.	B14	112
Notrees, Tx., U.S.	C5	130
Nottawasaga, stm., On., Can.	D10	112
Nottawasaga Bay, b., On., Can.	D9	112
Nottaway, stm., Qc., Can.	E15	106
Nottingham, Eng., U.K.	I11	12
Nottingham Island, i., Nu., Can.	C15	106
Nottoway, stm., Va., U.S.	H8	114
Notukeu Creek, stm., Sk., Can.	E6	124
Notwane, stm., Afr.	D8	70
Nouadhibou, Maur.	E1	64
Nouâdhibou, Râs, c., Afr.	E1	64
Nouakchott, Maur.	F1	64
Nouâmghâr, Maur.	F1	64
Nouméa, N. Cal.	n16	79d
Nouoport, S. Afr.	G7	70
Nouveau-Québec, Cratère du, crat., Qc., Can.	C16	106
Nouvelle, Qc., Can.	B10	110
Nouvelle-Calédonie (New Caledonia), i., N. Cal.	m15	79d
Nouvelle-Écosse see Nova Scotia, state, Can.	G18	106
Nouvelle-France, Cap de, c., Qc., Can.	C16	106
Nova Andradina, Braz.	D6	90
Nová Baňa, Slov.	H14	16
Nova Caipemba, Ang.	B1	68
Nova Era, Braz.	J4	88
Nova Friburgo, Braz.	L4	88
Nova Gorica, Slvn.	D10	22
Nova Gradiška, Cro.	E14	22
Nova Granada, Braz.	K1	88
Nova Iguaçu, Braz.	L4	88
Novaja Ladoga, Russia	F14	8
Nova Maluksa, Russia	A14	10
Novaja Sibir', ostrov, i., Russia	B19	34
Novaja Zemlja, is., Russia	B8	30
Nova Kakhovka, Ukr.	E4	32
Nova Lamego, Gui.-B.	G2	64
Nova Lima, Braz.	K4	88
Novalukoml', Bela.	F11	10
Nova Mambone, Moz.	B12	70
Nova Olinda, Braz.	D6	88
Nová Paka, Czech Rep.	F11	16
Nova Ponte, Braz.	J2	88
Nova Prata, Braz.	D12	92
Novara, Italy	E5	22
Nova Roma, Braz.	G2	88
Nova Russas, Braz.	C5	88
Nova Scotia, state, Can.	G18	106
Nova Soure, Braz.	F6	88
Novato, Ca., U.S.	E3	134
Nova Venécia, Braz.	J5	88
Nova Vida, Braz.	F5	84
Nova Kazanka, Kaz.	E7	32
Novaya Zemlya see Novaya Zemlja, is., Russia	B8	30
Nova Zagora, Blg.	G13	26
Nové Hrady, Czech Rep.	H10	16
Novelda, Spain	F10	20
Nové Město nad Váhom, Slov.	H13	16
Nové Město na Morave, Czech Rep.	G12	16
Nové Zámky, Slov.	I14	16
Novgorod, Russia	B14	10
Novgorodskaja oblast', co., Russia	B15	10
Novi Bečej, Serb.	D7	26
Novi Beograd, Serb.	E7	26
Novice, Tx., U.S.	C8	130
Novigrad, Cro.	E10	22
Novikovo, Russia	G17	34
Novi Ligure, Italy	F5	22
Novinger, Mo., U.S.	D5	120
Novi Pazar, Blg.	F14	26
Novi Pazar, Serb.	F7	26
Novi Sad, Serb.	D6	26
Novo, Lago, l., Braz.	C7	84
Novo Airão, Braz.	H11	86
Novoaltajsk, Russia	D14	32
Novo Aripuanã, Braz.	E5	84
Novočerkassk, Russia	E6	32
Novodvinsk, Russia	D19	8
Novoe, Russia	C11	32
Novoenisejsk, Russia	C16	32
Novo Hamburgo, Braz.	D12	92
Novo Horizonte, Braz.	K1	88
Novoizborsk, Russia	C10	10
Novokačalinsk, Russia	B10	38
Novokašisk, Russia	F21	10
Novokazalinsk see Zhangaqazaly, Kaz.	E10	32
Novokujbyševsk, Russia	D7	32
Novokuzneck, Russia	D15	32
Novolazarevskaja, sci., Ant.	C6	81
Novo Mesto, Slvn.	E12	22
Novomoskovsk (Stalinogorsk), Russia	F21	10
Novo Oriente, Braz.	C5	88
Novopetrovskoe, Russia	E19	10
Novorossijsk, Russia	F5	32
Novorybnoe, Russia	B10	34
Novoržev, Russia	C12	10
Novošahtinsk, Russia	E6	32
Novoselovo, Russia	E7	34
Novoselytsia, Ukr.	A13	26
Novosergievka, Russia	D8	32
Novosibirsk, Russia	C14	32
Novosibirskie ostrova, is., Russia	A18	34
Novosibirskoe vodohranilišče, res., Russia	D14	32
Novosil's'ke, Ukr.	D15	26
Novosokol'niki, Russia	D12	10
Novotroick, Russia	D9	32
Novouzensk, Russia	D7	32
Novovjatsk, Russia	C7	32
Novozavidovskij, Russia	D19	10
Novozybkov, Russia	H14	10
Novska, Cro.	E13	22
Nový Bor, Czech Rep.	F10	16
Novyja Valosavičy, Bela.	G12	10
Novyj Jičín, Czech Rep.	G13	16
Novyj Nekouz, Russia	C20	10
Novyj Port, Russia	A12	32
Novyj Uzen' see Zhangaözen, Kaz.	F8	32
Novyj Vasjugan, Russia	C13	32
Novyj Port, Bela.	F10	10
Nowa Ruda, Pol.	F12	16
Nowa Sól, Pol.	E11	16
Nowe, Pol.	C14	16
Nowe Miasto nad Pilicą, Pol.	E16	16
Nowendoc, Austl.	H8	76
Nowgong, India	F7	54
Nowitna, stm., Ak., U.S.	D9	140
Nowogard, Pol.	C11	16
Nowogrodziec, Pol.	E11	16
Nowra, Austl.	J8	76
Nowrangapur, India	B6	53
Nowshāk, mtn., Asia	B11	56
Nowshera, Pak.	A4	54
Nowy Dwór Mazowiecki, Pol.	D16	16
Nowy Sącz, Pol.	G16	16
Nowy Staw, Pol.	B15	16
Nowy Targ, Pol.	G15	16
Noxapater, Ms., U.S.	E9	122
Noxen, Pa., U.S.	C9	114
Noxon, Mt., U.S.	B11	136
Noxubee, stm., U.S.	D10	122
Noy, stm., Laos	D7	48
Noya see Noia, Spain	B2	20
Noyon, Fr.	E11	14
Nsanje, Mwi.	D6	68
Nsawam, Ghana	H4	64
Nsok, Eq. Gui.	I7	64
Nsukka, Nig.	H6	64
Nsuta, Ghana	H4	64
Ntwetwe Pan, pl., Bots.	B7	70
Nu see Salween, stm., Asia.	C8	46
Nûbah, Jibāl an-, mts., Sudan.	E6	62
Nubian Desert, des., Sudan.	C6	62
Ñuble, stm., Chile	H2	92
Nucet, Rom.	C9	26
Nudol'-Šarino, Russia	D19	10
Nueces, stm., Tx., U.S.	G10	130
Nueces Plains, pl., Tx., U.S.	F8	130
Nueltin Lake, l., Can.	C11	106
Nuestra Señora de Talavera, Arg.	B6	92
Nueva, Isla, i., Chile	K3	90
Nueva Antioquia, Col.	D7	86
Nueva Ciudad Guerrero, Mex.	B9	100
Nueva Esparta, state, Ven.	B9	86
Nueva Galia, Arg.	G5	92
Nueva Germania, Para.	A9	92
Nueva Gerona, Cuba	B6	102
Nueva Imperial, Chile	G2	90
Nueva Italia de Ruiz, Mex.	F7	100
Nueva Loja, Ec.	G3	86
Nueva Palmira, Ur.	F8	92
Nueva Rosita, Mex.	A8	100
Nueva San Salvador, El Sal.	F3	102
Nueva Toltén, Chile	G2	90
Nueve, Canal Numero, can., Arg.	H8	92
Nuevitas, Cuba	B9	102
Nuevo, Bajo, unds., Col.	I5	86
Nuevo, Cayo, i., Mex.	E12	100
Nuevo, Golfo, b., Arg.	H4	90
Nuevo Camarón, Mex.	G8	130
Nuevo Casas Grandes, Mex.	F9	98
Nuevo Delicias, Mex.	B7	100
Nuevo Laredo, Mex.	B9	100
Nuevo León, state, Mex.	B8	100
Nuevo Primero de Mayo, Mex.	H9	130
Nuevo Progreso, Mex.	F12	100
Nuevo Rocafuerte, Ec.	H4	86
Nuevo San Lucas, Mex.	F2	130
Nûgssuaq, pen., Grnld.	C15	141
Nugu, res., India	F3	53
Nui, at., Tuvalu	D8	72
Nuku'alofa, Tonga	n14	78e
Nukuhu, Pap. N. Gui.	b4	79a
Nukus, Uzb.	F9	32
Nul, Vanuatu	k17	79d
Nulato, Ak., U.S.	D8	140
Nullagine, Austl.	D4	74
Nullarbor, Austl.	F6	74
Nullarbor Plain, pl., Austl.	F5	74
Numan, Nig.	H7	64
Numancia (Numantia), sci., Spain.	C8	20
Numantia see Numancia, sci., Spain.	C8	20
Numata, Japan	C12	40
Numazu, Japan	D11	40
Numfoor, Pulau, i., Indon.	F10	44
Numto, Russia	B12	32
Nunavut, state, Can.	B12	106
Nunda, N.Y., U.S.	B7	114
Nuneaton, Eng., U.K.	I11	12
Nuñez, Cape, c., S. Geor.	J9	90
Nunkun Island, i., Ak., U.S.	D6	140
Nunjiang, China	B10	36
Nunkun, mtn., India	A6	54
Nunnelly, Tn., U.S.	I10	120
Nuomin, stm., China	B10	36
Nuoro, Italy	D3	24
Nuqui, Col.	E3	86
Nura, Kaz.	E12	32
Nura, stm., Kaz.	E12	32
Nur Dağları, mts., Tur.	B7	58
Nuremberg see Nürnberg, Ger.	G6	16
Nuremburg see Nürnberg, Ger.	G6	16
Nuriootpa, Austl.	J2	76
Nürnberg (Nuremberg), Ger.	G6	16
Nürpur, India	B5	54
Nürtingen, Ger.	H5	16
Nusa Tenggara Barat, state, Indon.	G10	50
Nusa Tenggara Timur, state, Indon.	H12	50
Nusayriyah, Jabal an-, mts., Syria	C7	58
Nu Shan, mts., China	F4	36
Nūshan Hu, l., China	E8	42
Nushki, Pak.	D10	56
Nutrioso, Az., U.S.	J7	132
Nutter Fort, W.V., U.S.	E5	114
Nuuk see Godthåb, Grnld.	E15	141
Nuwerus, S. Afr.	G4	70
Nuwuveldberge, mts., S. Afr.	H5	70
Nüzvīd, India	C5	53
Nyabéssan, Cam.	D2	66
Nyabing, Austl.	F3	74
Nyack, N.Y., U.S.	C12	114
Nyahanga, Tan.	E6	66
Nyainqêntanglha Feng, mtn., China	C13	54
Nyainqêntanglha Shan, mts., China	C6	46
Nyainrong, China	B14	54
Nyakanazi, Tan.	E6	66
Nyala, Sudan	E5	62
Nyalam, China	D10	54
Nyamlell, Sudan	F5	62
Nyamtumbo, Tan.	G7	66
Nyanga, stm., Afr.	J7	64
Nyasa, Lake, l., Afr.	C5	68
Nyaunglebin, Mya.	C3	48
Nyboe Land, reg., Grnld.	A14	141
Nyborg, Den.	I4	8
Nybro, Swe.	H6	8
Nyêmo, China	A12	32
Nyeri, Kenya.	E7	66
Nyerol, Sudan	F6	62
Nyíma, Zam.	C5	68
Nyingchi, China	F3	36
Nyírbátor, Hung.	B9	26
Nyíregyháza, Hung.	B8	26
Nykøbing, Den.	B8	8
Nyköping, Swe.	G7	8
Nylstroom, S. Afr.	D9	70
Nymboida, stm., Austl.	G9	76
Nymburk, Czech Rep.	F11	16
Nynäshamn, Swe.	G7	8
Nyngan, Austl.	H6	76
Nyons, Fr.	E11	18
Nýrsko, Czech Rep.	G9	16
Nyš, Russia	F17	34
Nysa, Pol.	F13	16
Nysa Kłodzka, stm., Pol.	F12	16
Nysa Łużycka (Lausitzer Neisse), stm., Eur.	E10	16
Nyslott see Savonlinna, Fin.	F13	8
Nysted, Den.	B7	16
Nyunzu, D.R.C.	F5	66
Nyūzen, Japan	C10	40
Nyvrovo, Russia	F17	34
Nzébéla, Gui.	H3	64
Nzérékoré, Gui.	H3	64
N'zeto, Ang.	B1	68
Nzwani, i., Com.	C7	68

O

Name	Map Ref.	Page
Oahe, Lake, res., U.S.	A12	126
Oahe Dam, dam, S.D., U.S.	C12	126
O'ahu, i., Hi., U.S.	b4	78a
Oakbank, Austl.	I3	76
Oak Bay, B.C., Can.	H7	138
Oak Bluffs, Ma., U.S.	C15	114
Oak City, Ut., U.S.	D4	132
Oak City, N.C., U.S.	I8	114
Oakdale, Ca., U.S.	F5	134
Oakdale, La., U.S.	G6	122
Oakdale, Ne., U.S.	E14	126
Oakes, N.D., U.S.	A14	126
Oakfield, Me., U.S.	D8	110
Oakfield, Wi., U.S.	H10	118
Oak Grove, La., U.S.	E7	122
Oak Harbor, Wa., U.S.	B4	136
Oak Hill, Fl., U.S.	H5	116
Oak Hill, Oh., U.S.	F3	114
Oak Hill, W.V., U.S.	F6	114
Oak Knolls, Ca., U.S.	I8	134
Oak Lake, Mb., Can.	E13	124
Oak Lake, l., Mb., Can.	E13	124
Oak Lake, l., On., Can.	A5	118
Oakland, Ca., U.S.	F3	134
Oakland, Ia., U.S.	C2	120
Oakland, Md., U.S.	E6	114
Oakland, Me., U.S.	F7	110
Oakland, Ms., U.S.	C9	122
Oakland, Ne., U.S.	C1	120
Oakland, Or., U.S.	G3	136
Oakland City, In., U.S.	F10	120
Oakland Park, Fl., U.S.	J5	116
Oak Lawn, Il., U.S.	G2	112
Oakley, Id., U.S.	H13	136
Oakley, Ks., U.S.	B8	128
Oakman, Al., U.S.	D11	122
Oakohay Creek, stm., Ms., U.S.	F9	122
Oakover, stm., Austl.	D4	74
Oak Park, Il., U.S.	G2	112
Oak Ridge, Tn., U.S.	H1	114
Oak Ridge National Laboratory, sci., Tn., U.S.	H1	114
Oaktown, In., U.S.	F10	120
Oak View, Ca., U.S.	I6	134
Oakville, Mb., Can.	E15	124
Oakville, On., Can.	E10	112
Oakwood, Oh., U.S.	C1	114
Oamaru, N.Z.	G4	80
Oancea, Rom.	D15	26
Õarai, Japan	C13	40
Oatman, Az., U.S.	H2	132
Oaxaca, state, Mex.	G10	100
Oaxaca de Juárez, Mex.	G10	100
Ob', stm., Russia	B12	32
Obabika Lake, l., On., Can.	A9	112
Obaghan, stm., Kaz.	D10	32
Obama, Japan	D8	40
Obama, Japan	G3	40
Oban, Scot., U.K.	E7	12
Oban, Austl.	A13	40
Obanazawa, Japan	A13	40
O Barco de Valdeorras, Spain	B3	20
Ob Bay see Obskaja guba, b., Russia	A12	32
Obed, Ab., Can.	C13	138
Obeliai, Lith.	E8	10
Oberá, Arg.	C10	92
Oberhausen, Ger.	E2	16
Oberlin, La., U.S.	G6	122
Oberlin, Oh., U.S.	C3	114
Oberösterreich, state, Aus.	B10	22
Oberpullendorf, Aus.	C13	22
Oberursel, Ger.	F4	16
Oberviechtach, Ger.	G8	16
Ob Gulf see Obskaja guba, b., Russia	A12	32
Obi, Kepulauan, is., Indon.	F8	44
Obi, Pulau, i., Indon.	F8	44
Obi, Selat, strt., Indon.	F8	44
Óbidos, Braz.	D6	84
Obihiro, Japan	C15	38
Obi Islands see Obi, Kepulauan, is., Indon.	F8	44
Obion, Tn., U.S.	H8	120
Obion, stm., Tn., U.S.	H8	120
Obion, Middle Fork, stm., Tn., U.S.	H9	120
Oblačnaja, gora, mtn., Russia	C11	38
Oblong, Il., U.S.	F9	120
Obluč'e, Russia	G15	34
Obludé, Russia	E19	10
Obninsk, Russia	E19	10
Obnova, Blg.	F12	26
Obo, C.A.R.	C5	66
Obock, Dji.	E8	62
Obokote, D.R.C.	E5	66
Obozërskij, Russia	E19	8
O'Brien, Or., U.S.	A2	134
Obrovac, Cro.	F12	22
Obša, stm., Russia	E16	10
Obščij syrt, mts., Eur.	D8	32
Obskaja guba, b., Russia	A12	32
Obuasi, Ghana	H4	64
Obudu, Nig.	H6	64
Ocala, Fl., U.S.	G3	116
Ocamo, stm., Ven.	F9	86
Ocampo, Mex.	B8	100
Ocaña, Col.	C5	86
Ocaña, Spain	E7	20
Occhito, Lago di, res., Italy	C8	24
Occidental, Cordillera, mts., Col.	E3	86
Oceana, W.V., U.S.	G4	114
Ocean City, Md., U.S.	F10	114
Ocean City, N.J., U.S.	E11	114
Ocean Falls, B.C., Can.	D3	138
Ocean Island see Banaba, i., Kir.	D7	72
Ocean Park, Wa., U.S.	D2	136
Oceanside, Ca., U.S.	J8	134
Ocean Springs, Ms., U.S.	G10	122
Ocheyedan, Ia., U.S.	H3	118
Õchi, Japan	E7	40
Ochlockonee, stm., U.S.	F1	116
Ocho Rios, Jam.	i13	104d
Ochsenfurt, Ger.	G5	16
Ocilla, Ga., U.S.	E2	116
Ockelbo, Swe.	F7	8
Ocmulgee National Monument, p.o.i., Ga., U.S.	D2	116
Ocnița, Mol.	A14	26
Ocoa, Bahía de, b., Dom. Rep.	C12	102
Ocoee, Fl., U.S.	H4	116
Ocoña, stm., Peru	G3	84
Oconee, Lake, res., Ga., U.S.	C2	116
Oconomowoc, Wi., U.S.	A9	120
Oconto, Wi., U.S.	D2	112
Oconto Falls, Wi., U.S.	G10	118
Ocosingo, Mex.	G12	100
Ocotal, Nic.	F4	102
Ocotal, stm., Mex.	E7	100
Ocotlán, Mex.	E7	100
Ocotlán de Morelos, Mex.	G10	100
Ocozocuautla, Mex.	G12	100
Ocracoke Island, i., N.C., U.S.	A10	116
Ocumare del Tuy, Ven.	B8	86
Oda, Ghana	H4	64
Ōda, Japan	D5	40
Ōda, Jabal, mtn., Sudan.	C7	62
Odate, Japan	D14	38
Odawara, Japan	D12	40
Odda, Nor.	F2	8
Odebolt, Ia., U.S.	B2	120
Odell, Il., U.S.	C9	120
Odell, Tx., U.S.	G9	128
Odem, Tx., U.S.	G10	130
Odemira, Port.	G2	20
Ödemiş, Tur.	E10	28
Odendaalsrus, S. Afr.	E8	70
Odense, Den.	I3	8
Odenwald, mts., Ger.	G4	16
Oder (Odra), stm., Eur.	D10	16
Oderzo, Italy	E9	22
Odesa, Ukr.	C17	26
Odesa, co., Ukr.	C16	26
Odesskoe, Russia	D12	32
Odessa see Odesa, Ukr.	C17	26
Odessa, Tx., U.S.	C5	130
Odessa, Wa., U.S.	C8	136
Odienné, C. Iv.	H3	64
Odin, Mount, mtn., B.C., Can.	F12	138
Odincovo, Russia	E20	10
Odobești, Rom.	D14	26
Odolanów, Pol.	E13	16
Odorheiu Secuiesc, Rom.	C12	26
Odra (Oder), stm., Eur.	D10	16
Održywół, Pol.	E16	16
Odum, Ga., U.S.	E3	116
Odžaci, Serb.	D6	26
Oebisfelde, Ger.	D6	16
Oeiras, Braz.	D4	88
Oelsnitz, Ger.	F8	16
Oelwein, Ia., U.S.	B6	120
Oenpelli, Austl.	B6	74
Oetz, Aus.	C7	22
O'Fallon, Mo., U.S.	F7	120
Ofanto, stm., Italy	D9	24
Ofaqim, Isr.	G5	58
Offa, Nig.	H5	64
Offaly, state, Ire.	H5	12
Offenbach am Main, Ger.	F4	16
Offenburg, Ger.	H3	16
Ofu, i., Am. Sam.	h13	79c
Ogaden, reg., Afr.	F8	62
Ōgaki, Japan	D9	40
Ogallala, Ne., U.S.	F11	126
Ogan, stm., Indon.	E4	50
Ogasawara-guntō, is., Japan	G18	30
Ogatsu, Japan	A14	40
Ogawa, Japan	G3	40
Ogbomosho, Nig.	H5	64
Ogden, Ks., U.S.	B12	128
Ogden, Ut., U.S.	B5	132
Ogdensburg, N.Y., U.S.	D14	112
Ogeechee, stm., Ga., U.S.	D4	116
Ogema, Sk., Can.	E8	124
Ōgi, Japan	A11	40
Ōgidaki Mountain, hill, On., Can.	A6	112
Ogilvie, Mn., U.S.	F5	118
Ogilvie Mountains, mts., Yk., Can.	C3	106
Oglesby, Il., U.S.	C8	120
Oglethorpe, Ga., U.S.	D1	116
Ogliastra, reg., Italy	E3	24
Oglio, stm., Italy	E7	22
Ogmore, Austl.	D7	76
Ognon, stm., Fr.	G15	14
Ogoja, Nig.	H6	64
Ogoki, stm., On., Can.	E13	106
Ogooué, stm., Afr.	I7	64
Ogōri, Japan	E4	40
Ogosta, stm., Blg.	F10	26
Ogre, Lat.	D7	10
Ogre, stm., Lat.	D8	10
O Grove, Spain	B2	20
Ogulin, Cro.	E12	22
Ogunquit, Me., U.S.	G6	110
Ogurdžaly, ostrov, i., Turkmen.	B7	56
Oguzeli, Tur.	B8	58
Oha, Russia	F17	34
Ohanet, Alg.	D6	64
Ōhata, Japan	D14	38
Ohio, state, U.S.	C9	120
Ohio, stm., U.S.	G9	120
Ohio Peak, mtn., Co., U.S.	E9	132
'Ohonua, Tonga	o15	78e
Ohoopee, stm., Ga., U.S.	D3	116
Ohota, stm., Russia	E17	34
Ohotsk, Russia	E17	34
Ohře, stm., Eur.	F9	16
Ohrid, Mac.	B3	28
Ohrid, Lake, l., Eur.	D14	24
Ohrigstad, S. Afr.	D10	70
Öhringen, Ger.	G5	16
Ohura, Bahía de, l., Mex.	C4	100
Oi, stm., Japan	E11	40
Oiapoque, Braz.	C7	84
Oiapoque (Oyapok), stm., S.A.	C7	84
Oies, Île aux, i., Qc., Can.	C6	110
Oil Center, N.M., U.S.	B4	130
Oil City, La., U.S.	E4	122
Oil City, Pa., U.S.	C6	114
Oildale, Ca., U.S.	H7	134
Oilton, Ok., U.S.	A2	122
Oilton, Tx., U.S.	G9	130
Oil Trough, Ar., U.S.	B7	122
Oise, state, Fr.	E11	14
Oise, stm., Fr.	E11	14
Oistins, Barb.	n8	105d
Õita, Japan	F4	40
Õita, state, Japan	F4	40
Oituz, Pasul, p., Rom.	C13	26
Ōjat', stm., Russia	F15	8
Ojima, Japan	A6	100
Ojiya, Japan	B11	40
Ojmjakon, Russia	D17	34
Ojocaliente, Mex.	D7	100
Ojo de la Casa, Mex.	A9	100
Ojo del Carrizo, Mex.	E2	130
Ojo de Liebre, Laguna, b., Mex.	B1	100
Ojos del Salado, Nevado, mtn., S.A.	C3	92
Ojos Negros, Mex.	L9	134
Oka, Japan	D6	32
Oka, stm., Russia	D18	32
Okaba, Indon.	G10	44
Okahandja, Nmb.	B3	70
Okaihau, N.Z.	B5	80
Okak Islands, is., Nf., Can.	F13	141
Okanagan (Okanogan), stm., N.A.	G11	138
Okanagan Falls, B.C., Can.	G11	138
Okanagan Lake, l., B.C., Can.	G10	138
Okanagan Landing, B.C., Can.	F11	138
Okanogan, Wa., U.S.	B7	136
Okanogan (Okanagan), stm., N.A.	G11	138
Okanogan Range, mts., N.A.	A6	136
Ōkara, Pak.	C4	54
Okaukuejo, Nmb.	D2	68
Okavango (Cubango), stm., Afr.	D2	68
Okavango Delta, Bots.	D3	68
Okawa, Japan	F3	40
Okawville, Il., U.S.	F8	120
Okaya, Japan	C11	40
Okayama, Japan	E6	40
Okayama, state, Japan	E6	40
Okazaki, Japan	E10	40
Okeechobee, Fl., U.S.	I5	116
Okeechobee, Lake, l., Fl., U.S.	J5	116
Okeene, Ok., U.S.	E10	128
Okefenokee Swamp, sw., Ga., U.S.	F3	116
Okemos, Mi., U.S.	B1	114
Okene, Nig.	H6	64
Okha, India	H3	54
Okhaldhungā, Nepal	E11	54
Okhotsk, Sea of, s., Asia	D17	142
Okhtyrka, Ukr.	D4	32
Okiep, S. Afr.	F3	70
Okinawa, i., Japan	I19	39a
Okinawa-jima, i., Japan	I19	39a
Okinawa-shotō, is., Japan	I18	39a
Okino-Erabu-shima, i., Japan	I18	39a
Oki-shotō, is., Japan	C6	40
Oklahoma, state, U.S.	F11	128
Oklahoma City, Ok., U.S.	F11	128
Oklawaha, Fl., U.S.	G3	116
Oklee, Mn., U.S.	D3	118
Okmulgee, Ok., U.S.	B2	122
Okolo, Ug.	D6	66
Okolona, Ar., U.S.	D5	122
Okolona, Ky., U.S.	F12	120
Okondja, Gabon	E2	66
Okonek, Pol.	C12	16
Okotoks, Ab., Can.	F16	138
Okoyo, Congo	E2	66
Oktjabr', Russia	C20	10
Oktjabr'skij, Russia	D8	32
Oktjabr'skij, Russia	F14	34
Oktjabr'skij, Russia	G21	8
Oktjabr'skij, Russia	F20	8
Oktjabr'skoe, Russia	B10	32
Oktjabr'sk, Kaz.	E9	32
Oktyabr'sk see Oktjabr'sk, Kaz.	E9	32
Oktyabr'skoe, Kaz.	D11	32
Okuchi, Japan	G3	40
Okulovka, Russia	B16	10
Okunëv Nos, Russia	C25	8
Okushiri-tō, i., Japan	C13	38
Okuta, Nig.	H5	64
Okwa, stm., Afr.	C6	70
Ola, Ar., U.S.	B5	122
Ólafsfjörður, Ice.	j30	8a
Olancha, Ca., U.S.	G8	134
Olancha Peak, mtn., Ca., U.S.	G7	134
Olanchito, Hond.	E4	102
Öland, i., Swe.	H7	8
Olanta, S.C., U.S.	C6	116
Olary, Austl.	I3	76
Olathe, Co., U.S.	E8	132
Olathe, Ks., U.S.	F3	120
Olavarría, Arg.	H7	92
Oława (Ohlau), Pol.	F13	16
Olbia, Italy	D3	24
Olcott, N.Y., U.S.	E11	112
Old Castile see Castilla la Vieja, hist. reg., Spain	C7	20
Old Cork, Austl.	D3	76
Old Crow, Yk., Can.	C12	140
Old Crow, stm., N.A.	C11	140
Olden, Tx., U.S.	B9	130
Oldenburg, Ger.	C3	16
Oldenburg, hist. reg., Ger.	C3	16
Oldenburg in Holstein, Ger.	B6	16
Oldenzaal, Neth.	B15	14
Old Faithful Geyser, gysr., Wy., U.S.	F16	136
Old Forge, Pa., U.S.	C10	114
Old Fort Bay see Vieux-Fort, Qc., Can.	i22	107a
Oldham, Eng., U.K.	H10	12
Oldham, S.D., U.S.	C15	126
Old Harbor, Ak., U.S.	E9	140
Old Harbour, Jam.	j13	104d
Old Hickory Lake, res., Tn., U.S.	H11	120
Oldman, stm., Ab., Can.	G19	138
Old Mkushi, Zam.	C4	68
Old Norwood, Monts.	D3	105a
Old Road, Antig.	f4	105b
Old Road Bluff, c., Antig.	f4	105b
Old Road Town, St. K./N.	C2	105a
Olds, Ab., Can.	E16	138
Old Saybrook, Ct., U.S.	C13	114
Old Speck Mountain, mtn., Me., U.S.	F5	110
Old Tate, Bots.	B9	70
Old Town, Me., U.S.	F8	110
Olduvai Gorge, val., Tan.	E7	66
Old Wives Lake, l., Sk., Can.	D8	124
Olean, N.Y., U.S.	B7	114
O'Leary, P.E., Can.	D12	110
Olecko, Pol.	B18	16
Ölekma, stm., Russia	E13	34
Olëkminsk, Russia	D13	34
Olëkminskij Stanovik, mts., Russia	F12	34
Ølen, Nor.	G1	8
Olenegorsk, Russia	B15	8
Olenëk, Russia	C11	34
Olenëk, stm., Russia	C12	34
Olenëkskij zaliv, b., Russia	B13	34
Olenij, ostrov, i., Russia	B4	34
Oléron, Île d', i., Fr.	D4	18
Oleśnica, Pol.	E13	16
Ol'ga, Russia	C11	38
Olga, Mount, mtn., Austl.	D6	74
Olgastretet, strt., Nor.	B30	141
Ölgij, Mong.	E16	32
Olho, Port.	F5	8
Olho d'Água das Flores, Braz.	E7	88
Ol'hon, ostrov, i., Russia	F10	34
Olib, Otok, i., Cro.	F11	22
Olifants (Elefantes), stm., Afr.	D10	70
Olifants, stm., S. Afr.	H6	70
Olifants, stm., S. Afr.	H4	70
Olifantshoek, S. Afr.	E6	70
Olimbos (Olympus), mtn., Cyp.	D3	58
Olimpia, Braz.	K1	88
Olin, Ia., U.S.	B6	120
Olinda, Braz.	D8	88
Olite, Spain	B9	20
Oliva, Arg.	F6	92
Oliva, Spain	F10	20
Oliva de la Frontera, Spain	F3	20
Olivares, Cerro de, mtn., S.A.	E2	92
Olive Branch, Ms., U.S.	C9	122
Olive Hill, Ky., U.S.	F2	114
Olivehurst, Ca., U.S.	D4	134
Oliveira, Braz.	K3	88
Oliveira dos Brejinhos, Braz.	G4	88
Olivenza, Spain	F3	20
Oliver Springs, Tn., U.S.	H13	120
Olivet, Mi., U.S.	B1	114
Olivet, S.D., U.S.	D15	126
Olivia, Mn., U.S.	G4	118
Olivos, Arg.	F8	92
Oljutorskij, mys, c., Russia	E23	34
Oljutorskij zaliv, b., Russia	D22	34
Ollach, India	F6	122
Ollagüe, Chile	D3	90
Ollei, Palau	D3	78b
Olmedo, Spain	C6	20
Olmos, Peru	E2	84
Olney, Mt., U.S.	B12	136
Olney, Il., U.S.	F9	120
Olney, Tx., U.S.	H10	128
Oloj, stm., Russia	C21	34
Olomouc, Czech Rep.	G13	16
Olonec, Russia	F15	8
Olongapo, Phil.	C2	52
Oloron-Sainte-Marie, Fr.	F5	18
Olot, Spain	B13	20
Oloví, stm., Russia	E22	34
Olovjannaja, Russia	F12	34
Olpe, Ger.	E3	16
Olpe, Ks., U.S.	F1	120
Olsberg, Ger.	E4	16
Olszówka, Russia	E6	122
Olsztyn, Pol.	C16	16
Olsztynek, Pol.	C16	16
Olt, state, Rom.	E11	26
Olt, stm., Rom.	F11	26
Olten, Switz.	C4	22
Oltenița, Rom.	E13	26
Oltet, stm., Rom.	E11	26
Oltu, Tur.	A5	56
Oluan Pi, c., Tai.	K9	42
Olustee, Ok., U.S.	G9	128
Olutanga Island, i., Phil.	G4	52
Olvera, Spain	H5	20
Olymbos (Olympus), mtn., Cyp.	C4	58
Olympia, Braz.	K1	88
Olympia, Wa., U.S.	C4	136
Olympia see Olympía, Grc.	F4	28
Olympic Mountains, mts., Wa., U.S.	C3	136

Name	Map Ref.	Page

Olympic National Park, p.o.i., Wa., U.S. ... C3 136
Ólympos (Olympus, Mount), mtn., Grc. ... C5 28
Olympus see Olimbos, mtn., Cyp. ... C3 58
Olympus, Mount see Ólympos, mtn., Grc. ... C5 28
Olympus, Mount, mtn., Wa., U.S. ... C3 136
Om', stm., Russia ... D13 32
Ōmachi, Japan ... C10 40
Omae-zaki, c., Japan ... E11 40
Ōmagari, Japan ... E14 38
Omagh, N. Ire., U.K. ... G5 12
Omaha, Ne., U.S. ... C2 120
Omaha, Tx., U.S. ... D4 122
Omaheke, state, Nmb. ... C4 70
Omak, Wa., U.S. ... B7 136
Oman, ctry., Asia ... F8 56
Oman, Gulf of, b., Asia ... E8 56
Omaruru, Nmb. ... B3 70
Omaruru, stm., Nmb. ... B2 70
Omatako, mtn., Nmb. ... B3 70
Omatako, stm., Nmb. ... B3 70
Omate, Peru ... G3 84
Omboué, Gabon ... E1 66
Ombrone, stm., Italy ... H8 22
Omčak, Russia ... D18 34
Omdurman see Umm Durmān, Sudan ... D6 62
Ōme, Japan ... D12 40
Omega, Ga., U.S. ... E2 116
Omegna, Italy ... E5 22
Omemee, On., Can. ... D11 112
Omeo, Austl. ... K6 76
Ōmerköy, Tur. ... D10 28
Ömerli Baraji, res., Tur. ... C12 28
Ometepe, Isla de, i., Nic. ... G5 102
Ometepec, Mex. ... G9 100
Ōmi-hachiman, Japan ... D8 40
Omineca, stm., B.C., Can. ... D6 106
Omineca Mountains, mts., B.C., Can. ... D5 106
Ōmiya, Japan ... D12 40
Ommaney, Cape, c., Ak., U.S. ... E13 140
Ommanney Bay, b., Nu., Can. ... A10 106
Omo, stm., Afr. ... F7 62
Omoloj, stm., Russia ... B15 34
Omolon, stm., Russia ... C20 34
Omsk, Russia ... C12 32
Omsukčan, Russia ... D20 34
Omul, Vârful, mtn., Rom. ... D12 26
Ōmura, Japan ... G2 40
Omurtag, Blg. ... F13 26
Ōmuta, Japan ... F3 40
Omutinskij, Russia ... C11 32
Omutninsk, Russia ... C8 32
Onabas, Mex. ... A4 100
Onaga, Ks., U.S. ... E1 120
Onaman Lake, l., On., Can. ... A11 118
Onamia, Wi., U.S. ... E5 118
Onangué, Lac, l., Gabon ... E1 66
Onaping Lake, l., On., Can. ... A8 112
Onarga, Il., U.S. ... D10 120
Onatchiway, Lac res., Qc., Can. ... A5 110
Onawa, Ia., U.S. ... B1 120
Onaway, Mi., U.S. ... C5 112
Oncativo, Arg. ... E6 92
Once, Canal Numero, can., Arg. ... H8 92
Oncócua, Ang. ... D1 68
Onda, Spain ... E10 20
Ondangwa, Nmb. ... D2 68
Ondas, stm., Braz. ... G3 88
Ondava, stm., Slov. ... H17 16
Ondjiva, Ang. ... D2 68
Ondo, Japan ... E5 40
Ondo, Nig. ... H5 64
Öndörhaan, Mong. ... B7 36
Ondozero, ozero, l., Russia ... E15 8
Oneco, Fl., U.S. ... I3 116
Onega, Russia ... E17 8
Onega, stm., Russia ... E18 8
Onega, Lake see Onežskoe ozero, l., Russia ... F16 8
Onega Bay see Onežskaja guba, b., Russia ... D17 8
One Hundred and Two, stm., Mo., U.S. ... D3 120
One Hundred Fifty Mile House, B.C., Can. ... D9 138
One Hundred Mile House, B.C., Can. ... E9 138
Oneida, Il., U.S. ... C7 120
Oneida, N.Y., U.S. ... E14 112
Oneida, Tn., U.S. ... H13 120
Oneida Lake, l., N.Y., U.S. ... E14 112
O'Neill, Ne., U.S. ... E14 126
Onekama, Mi., U.S. ... D3 112
Onekotan, ostrov, i., Russia ... G20 34
Oneonta, Al., U.S. ... D12 122
Oneonta, N.Y., U.S. ... B10 114
Onești, Rom. ... C13 26
Onevai, i., Tonga ... n14 78e
Ongjin-ŭp, Kor., N. ... F6 38
Ongniud Qi, China ... C3 38
Ongole, India ... D5 53
Onilahy, stm., Madag. ... F7 68
Onion Creek, stm., Tx., U.S. ... D10 130
Onitsha, Nig. ... H6 64
Ōno, Japan ... D9 40
Onoda, Japan ... F4 40
Onomichi, Japan ... E6 40
Onon, Mong. ... B7 36
Onon, stm., Asia ... C9 36
Onoto, Ven. ... C9 86
Onotoa, at., Kir. ... D8 72
Onoway, Ab., Can. ... C16 138
Ons, Illa de, i., Spain ... B1 20
Onset, Ma., U.S. ... C15 114
Onslow, Austl. ... D3 74
Onslow Bay, b., N.C., U.S. ... B8 116
On-take, vol., Japan ... H3 40
Ontake-san, vol., Japan ... D10 40
Ontario, Ca., U.S. ... I8 134
Ontario, Or., U.S. ... F10 136
Ontario, state, Can. ... E13 106
Ontario Lake, l., N.A. ... E11 112
Ontinyent, Spain ... F10 20
Ontojärvi, l., Fin. ... D13 8
Ontonagon, Mi., U.S. ... D7 72
Onverwacht, Sur. ... B6 84
Oodnadatta, Austl. ... E7 74
Ooldea, Austl. ... F6 74
Oologah, Ok., U.S. ... H2 120
Oologah Lake, res., Ok., U.S. ... H2 120
Oorlogskloof, stm., S. Afr. ... G4 70
Oos-Londen see East London, S. Afr. ... H8 70
Oostburg, Wi., U.S. ... E2 112
Oostelijk Flevoland, reg., Neth. ... B14 14
Oostende, Bel. ... C11 14
Oosterhout, Neth. ... C13 14
Oosterschelde, est., Neth. ... C12 14
Ootsa Lake, B.C., Can. ... C4 138
Ootsa Lake, res., B.C., Can. ... C4 138
Opaka, Blg. ... F13 26
Opala, D.R.C. ... E4 66
Oparino, Russia ... G22 8
Opatija, Cro. ... E11 22

Opava, Czech Rep. ... G13 16
Opawica, stm., Qc., Can. ... A2 110
Opećenskij Posad, Russia ... B17 10
Opelika, Al., U.S. ... E13 122
Opelousas, La., U.S. ... G6 122
Opeongo, stm., On., Can. ... C12 112
Opeongo Lake, l., On., Can. ... C11 112
Ophir, Ak., U.S. ... D8 140
Ophir, Or., U.S. ... H2 136
Opihikao, Hi., U.S. ... d7 78a
Opinaca, stm., Qc., Can. ... E15 106
Opiscotéo, Lac, l., Qc., Can. ... E17 106
Opobo, Nig. ... I6 64
Opočka, Russia ... D11 10
Opoczno, Pol. ... E16 16
Opole, Pol. ... F13 16
Opole, state, Pol. ... F13 16
Opotiki, N.Z. ... D7 80
Oppdal, Nor. ... E3 8
Oppland, state, Nor. ... F3 8
Opportunity, Mt., U.S. ... D14 136
Opportunity, Wa., U.S. ... C9 136
Optima Lake, res., Ok., U.S. ... E7 128
Opua, N.Z. ... B6 80
Opunake, N.Z. ... D5 80
Opuwo, Nmb. ... D1 68
Oqsuqtooq (Gjoa Haven), Nu., Can. ... B11 106
Oquawka, Il., U.S. ... K7 118
Or, Côte d', mts., Fr. ... G13 14
Oracle, Az., U.S. ... K6 132
Oradea, Rom. ... B8 26
Öræfajökull, ice, Ice. ... k31 8a
Orahovica, Cro. ... E14 22
Orai, India ... F7 54
Oraibi Wash, stm., Az., U.S. ... H6 132
Oral, Kaz. ... D8 32
Oran see Wahran, Alg. ... B4 64
Orange, Austl. ... I7 76
Orange, Fr. ... E10 18
Orange, Ma., U.S. ... B13 114
Orange, Tx., U.S. ... G5 122
Orange, Va., U.S. ... F7 114
Orange (Oranje) (Senqu), stm., Afr. ... F3 70
Orange, Cabo c., Braz. ... C7 84
Orangeburg, S.C., U.S. ... C4 116
Orange City, Ia., U.S. ... A1 120
Orange Cove, Ca., U.S. ... G6 134
Orange Free State see Free State, state, S. Afr. ... F8 70
Orange Grove, Tx., U.S. ... G9 130
Orange Lake, Fl., U.S. ... G3 116
Orange Lake, l., Fl., U.S. ... G3 116
Orangeville, On., Can. ... E9 112
Orangeville, Ut., U.S. ... D5 132
Orange Walk, Belize ... C3 102
Orango, Ilha de, i., Gui.-B. ... G1 64
Orani, Phil. ... C3 52
Oranienburg, Ger. ... D8 16
Oranje see Orange, stm., Afr. ... F3 70
Oranje Gebergte, mts., Sur. ... C6 84
Oranjemund, Nmb. ... F3 70
Oranjestad, Aruba ... o19 104g
Oranje Vrijstaat see Free State, state, S. Afr. ... F8 70
Orăștie, Rom. ... D10 26
Orba Co, l., China ... A8 54
Orbetello, Italy ... H8 22
Órbigo, stm., Spain ... B5 20
Orbisonia, Pa., U.S. ... D8 114
Orbost, Austl. ... K7 76
Örbyhus, Swe. ... F7 8
Orcadas, sci., Ant. ... B36 81
Orchard City, Co., U.S. ... E8 132
Orchard Homes, Mt., U.S. ... D12 136
Orchard Mesa, Co., U.S. ... E8 132
Orchard Park, N.Y., U.S. ... B7 114
Ord, Ne., U.S. ... F14 126
Ord, stm., Austl. ... C5 74
Ord, Mount, mtn., Austl. ... C5 74
Ordenes see Ordes, Spain ... A2 20
Orderville, Ut., U.S. ... F4 132
Ordes, Spain ... A2 20
Ordesa y Monte Perdido, Parque Nacional de, p.o.i., Spain ... B10 20
Ord Mountain, mtn., Ca., U.S. ... I9 134
Ordos Desert see Mu Us Shamo, des., China ... B3 42
Ord River, Austl. ... C5 74
Ordu, Tur. ... A4 56
Ordway, Co., U.S. ... C5 128
Ordžonikidzeabad, Taj. ... B10 56
Örebro, Swe. ... G6 8
Örebro, state, Swe. ... G6 8
Oredež, Russia ... B13 10
Oredež, stm., Russia ... B13 10
Oregon, Il., U.S. ... B8 120
Oregon, Mo., U.S. ... D2 120
Oregon, Oh., U.S. ... C2 114
Oregon, state, U.S. ... G6 136
Oregon Caves National Monument, p.o.i., Or., U.S. ... A2 134
Oregon City, Or., U.S. ... E4 136
Oregon Dunes National Recreation Area, p.o.i., Or., U.S. ... G2 136
Orehovo-Zuevo, Russia ... E21 10
Orel, Russia ... G18 10
Orel', ozero, l., Russia ... F16 34
Orellana, Peru ... E2 84
Orellana, state, Ec. ... H3 86
Orellana, Embalse de, res., Spain ... E5 20
Orem, Ut., U.S. ... C5 132
Ore Mountains, mts., Eur. ... F8 16
Orenburg, Russia ... D8 32
Orencik, Tur. ... D12 28
Orense, Arg. ... I8 92
Orense see Ourense, Spain ... B3 20
Orense see Ourense, co., Spain ... B3 20
Oreor, i., Palau ... g8 78b
Orestes Pereyra, Mex. ... B6 100
Orestiáda, Grc. ... B9 28
Orford Ness, c., Eng., U.K. ... I14 12
Organ Pipe Cactus National Monument, p.o.i., Az., U.S. ... K4 132
Orgelet, Fr. ... H14 14
Orgosolo, Italy ... D3 24
Orgun, Afg. ... C10 56
Orhangazi, Tur. ... C12 28
Orhei, Mol. ... B15 26
Orhon, stm., Mong. ... B5 36
Orichuna, stm., Ven. ... D7 86
Orick, Ca., U.S. ... B1 134
Orient, Ia., U.S. ... C3 120
Orient, Wa., U.S. ... B8 136
Oriental, Cordillera, mts., Col. ... E5 86
Oriental, Cordillera, mts., Peru ... F3 84
Orientos, Austl. ... G3 76
Orihuela see Oriola, Spain ... F10 20
Orillia, On., Can. ... D10 112
Orimattila, Fin. ... F11 8
Orinduik, Guy. ... E11 86
Orinoco, stm., S.A. ... C10 86
Orinoco, Delta del, Ven. ... C11 86
Oriola, Spain ... F10 20
Orion, Il., U.S. ... C7 120
Oriskany, N.Y., U.S. ... E14 112
Orissa, state, India ... D5 46
Oristano, Italy ... E2 24
Oristano, Golfo di, b., Italy ... E2 24
Orituco, stm., Ven. ... C8 86

Orivesi, l., Fin. ... E13 8
Oriximiná, Braz. ... D6 84
Orizaba, Mex. ... F10 100
Orjahovo, Blg. ... F10 26
Orjen, mtn., Serb. ... G5 26
Orkney, Sk., Can. ... E5 124
Orkney, S. Afr. ... E8 70
Orkney Islands, is., Scot., U.K. ... C10 12
Orlândia, Braz. ... K1 88
Orlando, Fl., U.S. ... H4 116
Orléanais, hist. reg., Fr. ... F11 14
Orleans, On., Can. ... C14 112
Orléans, Fr. ... G10 14
Orleans, Ca., U.S. ... B2 134
Orleans, Ma., U.S. ... C15 114
Orleans, Ne., U.S. ... A9 128
Orleans, Vt., U.S. ... F4 110
Orléans, Canal d', can., Fr. ... G11 14
Orléans, Île d', i., Qc., Can. ... D6 110
Orlik, Russia ... G18 34
Orlovskaja oblast', co., Russia ... H19 10
Orly, Fr. ... F11 14
Ormara, Pak. ... D9 56
Ormiston, Sk., Can. ... E8 124
Ormoc, Phil. ... E5 52
Ormond Beach, Fl., U.S. ... G4 116
Ornain, stm., Fr. ... F14 14
Ornans, Fr. ... G15 14
Orne, state, Fr. ... F8 14
Orne, stm., Fr. ... F8 14
Orne, stm., Fr. ... E14 14
Ørnö, i., Swe. ... G8 8
Örnsköldsvik, Swe. ... E8 8
Oročen, Russia ... E14 34
Orocovis, P.R. ... B3 104a
Orocué, Col. ... E6 86
Orofino, Id., U.S. ... D10 136
Orog nuur, l., Mong. ... B5 36
Orohena, Mont, mtn., Fr. Poly. ... v22 78h
Oroluk, at., Micron. ... C6 72
Oromocto, N.B., Can. ... E10 110
Oromocto Lake, l., N.B., Can. ... E10 110
Oron, Nig. ... I6 64
Orona, at., Kir. ... D9 72
Orono, Me., U.S. ... F8 110
Orontes (Asi), stm., Asia ... B7 58
Oroquieta, Phil. ... F4 52
Orós, Braz. ... D6 88
Orós, Açude, res., Braz. ... D6 88
Orosei, Italy ... D3 24
Orosei, Golfo di, b., Italy ... D3 24
Oroshaza, Hung. ... C7 26
Oroszlány, Hung. ... B5 26
Orote Peninsula, pen., Guam ... j9 78c
Oroville, Ca., U.S. ... D4 134
Oroville, Lake, res., Ca., U.S. ... D4 134
Orpheus Island, i., Austl. ... B6 76
Orrick, Mo., U.S. ... E3 120
Orrin, N.D., U.S. ... F13 124
Orororo, Austl. ... I2 76
Orrs Island, Me., U.S. ... G7 110
Orša, Bela. ... F13 10
Orsk, Russia ... D9 32
Orsova, Rom. ... E9 26
Ortaca, Tur. ... G11 28
Ortakent, Tur. ... F10 28
Ortaklar, Tur. ... F10 28
Orta Nova, Italy ... C9 24
Ortega, Col. ... F4 86
Ortegal, Cabo, c., Spain ... A2 20
Orteguaza, stm., Col. ... G4 86
Orthon, stm., Bol. ... B3 90
Ortigueira, Spain ... A3 20
Ortigueira, Braz. ... B13 92
Ortiz, Mex. ... A3 100
Ortiz, Ven. ... C8 86
Ortona, Italy ... H11 22
Ortonville, Mn., U.S. ... F2 118
Orūmīyeh, Iran ... B6 56
Orūmīyeh, Daryācheh-ye (Urmia, Lake), l., Iran ... B6 56
Orust, i., Swe. ... G4 8
Orvieto, Italy ... H9 22
Orwell, Oh., U.S. ... C5 114
Orxon, stm., China ... B8 36
Orzinuovi, Italy ... E6 22
Orzyc, stm., Pol. ... D17 16
Orzysz, Pol. ... C17 16
Os, Nor. ... E4 8
Osa, Península de, pen., C.R. ... H6 102
Osage, Ia., U.S. ... H6 118
Osage, Wy., U.S. ... D8 126
Osage, stm., Mo., U.S. ... F5 120
Osage Beach, Mo., U.S. ... F5 120
Osage City, Ks., U.S. ... F2 120
Ōsaka, Japan ... E8 40
Ōsaka, state, Japan ... E8 40
Ōsaka-wan, b., Japan ... E8 40
Osakarovka, Kaz. ... D12 32
Ōsām, stm., Blg. ... F11 26
Osawatomie, Ks., U.S. ... F3 120
Osborne, Ks., U.S. ... B10 128
Osburn, Id., U.S. ... C11 136
Osceola, Ar., U.S. ... B8 122
Osceola, Ia., U.S. ... C4 120
Osceola, Mo., U.S. ... F4 120
Osceola, Wi., U.S. ... F6 118
Osceola Mills, Pa., U.S. ... D7 114
Oschatz, Ger. ... E9 16
Oschersleben, Ger. ... D7 16
Osečina, Serb. ... E6 26
Osër, stm., Russia ... F21 10
Osetrovo, Russia ... E10 34
Osgood, In., U.S. ... E12 120
Oshawa, On., Can. ... E11 112
Oshika, Japan ... A14 40
Oshika-hantō, pen., Japan ... A14 40
Ō-shima, i., Japan ... E12 40
Oshima-hantō, pen., Japan ... C14 38
Oshkosh, Ne., U.S. ... F10 126
Oshkosh, Wi., U.S. ... G10 118
Oshogbo, Nig. ... H5 64
Oshwe, D.R.C. ... E3 66
Osica de Jos, Rom. ... E11 26
Osijek, Cro. ... E15 22
Osilo, Italy ... D2 24
Osimo, Italy ... G10 22
Osinki, Russia ... D15 32
Osipovo Selo, Russia ... D13 10
Osire Süd, Nmb. ... B3 70
Oskaloosa, Ia., U.S. ... C5 120
Oskaloosa, Ks., U.S. ... E2 120
Oskarshamn, Swe. ... H7 8
Öskemen, Kaz. ... E14 32
Oskolkovo, Russia ... B26 8
Oslo, Nor. ... G4 8
Oslofjorden, b., Nor. ... G4 8
Osmānābād, India ... B3 53
Osmaneli, Tur. ... C12 28
Osmino, Russia ... A11 10
Osmussaar, i., Est. ... A6 10
Osnabrück, Ger. ... D4 16
Osorno, Chile ... H2 90
Osorno, Spain ... B6 20
Osoyoos, B.C., Can. ... G11 138
Oss, Neth. ... C14 14
Ossa, Mount, mtn., Austl. ... n13 77a
Ossabaw Island, i., Ga., U.S. ... E4 116
Osseo, Wi., U.S. ... G7 118
Ossian, In., U.S. ... H4 112
Ossining, N.Y., U.S. ... C12 114
Ossipee, N.H., U.S. ... G5 110
Ossjøen, l., Nor. ... F4 8
Ossóra, Russia ... E21 34

Ostaškov, Russia ... C16 10
Ostašovo, Russia ... E18 10
Oste, stm., Ger. ... C5 16
Ostende see Oostende, Bel. ... C11 14
Ostër (Ascir), stm., Eur. ... G15 10
Osterburg, Ger. ... D7 16
Osterholz-Scharmbeck, Ger. ... C4 16
Osterode am Harz, Ger. ... E6 16
Osterøyni, i., Nor. ... F1 8
Östersund, Swe. ... E6 8
Osterwieck, Ger. ... E6 16
Østfold, state, Nor. ... G4 8
Ostfriesische Inseln (East Frisian Islands), is., Ger. ... C3 16
Ostfriesland, hist. reg., Ger. ... C3 16
Östhammar, Swe. ... F8 8
Ostpreussen, hist. reg., Eur. ... F4 10
Ostrava, Czech Rep. ... G14 16
Ostróda, Pol. ... C15 16
Ostrogožsk, Russia ... D5 32
Ostrołęka, Pol. ... C17 16
Ostrołęka, state, Pol. ... D17 16
Ostrorog, Pol. ... D12 16
Ostrov, Czech Rep. ... F8 16
Ostrov, Russia ... C11 10
Ostrov, i., Slov. ... I13 16
Ostrov-Zalit, Russia ... B11 10
Ostrowiec Świętokrzyski, Pol. ... F17 16
Ostrów Mazowiecka, Pol. ... D17 16
Ostrów Wielkopolski, Pol. ... E13 16
Ostrzeszów, Pol. ... E13 16
Ostuni, Italy ... D11 24
O'Sullivan Lake, l., On., Can. ... A11 118
Osum, stm., Alb. ... D14 24
Ōsumi-hantō, pen., Japan ... H3 40
Osuna, Spain ... G5 20
Oswego, Il., U.S. ... C9 120
Oswego, Ks., U.S. ... G2 120
Oswego, N.Y., U.S. ... E13 112
Oswestry, Eng., U.K. ... I9 12
Oświęcim (Auschwitz), Pol. ... F15 16
Osyka, Ms., U.S. ... F8 122
Ōta, Japan ... C12 40
Otaci, Mol. ... A14 26
Ōtake, Japan ... E5 40
Otaki, N.Z. ... E6 80
Otaru, Japan ... C14 38
Otautau, N.Z. ... H2 80
Otava, Fin. ... F12 8
Otava, stm., Czech Rep. ... G9 16
Otavalo, Ec. ... G2 86
Otavi, Nmb. ... D2 68
Ōtawara, Japan ... C12 40
Otego Creek, stm., N.Y., U.S. ... B10 114
Oteotea, Sol. Is. ... e9 79b
Oteros, stm., Mex. ... B4 100
Otinapa, Mex. ... C6 100
Otis, Co., U.S. ... A6 128
Otis, Ks., U.S. ... C9 128
Otish, Monts, mts., Qc., Can. ... E16 106
Otjimbingwe, Nmb. ... C2 70
Otjinene, Nmb. ... B4 70
Otjiwarongo, Nmb. ... B3 70
Otjozondjou, stm., Nmb. ... B5 70
Otjozondjupa, state, Nmb. ... B3 70
Otočac, Cro. ... F12 22
Otoskwin, stm., On., Can. ... E13 106
Otra, stm., Nor. ... G2 8
Otradnyj, Russia ... D8 32
Ōtranto, Italy ... D12 24
Otranto, Strait of, strt., Eur. ... D12 24
Otrokovice, Czech Rep. ... G13 16
Otroya, i., Nor. ... E2 8
Ōtscher, mtn., Aus. ... C12 22
Ōtsu, Japan ... D8 40
Otta, Nor. ... F3 8
Ottawa, On., Can. ... C14 112
Ottawa, Il., U.S. ... C9 120
Ottawa, Ks., U.S. ... F2 120
Ottawa, Oh., U.S. ... C1 114
Ottawa (Outaouais), stm., Can. ... C15 112
Ottawa Islands, is., Nu., Can. ... D14 106
Otterburne, Mb., Can. ... E16 124
Otter Creek, Fl., U.S. ... G3 116
Otter Creek, stm., Vt., U.S. ... F3 110
Otter Lake, Mi., U.S. ... E6 112
Otter Tail, stm., Mn., U.S. ... E2 118
Otter Tail Lake, l., Mn., U.S. ... E2 118
Otterville, Mo., U.S. ... F5 120
Ottosdal, S. Afr. ... E7 70
Ottoshoop, S. Afr. ... D7 70
Ottoville, Oh., U.S. ... D1 114
Ottumwa, Ia., U.S. ... C5 120
Ottweiler, Ger. ... G3 16
Otway, Cape, c., Austl. ... L4 76
Otwock, Pol. ... D17 16
Ötztaler Alpen (Venoste, Alpi), mts., Eur. ... D7 22
Ou, stm., China ... I5 42
Ou, stm., China ... I8 42
Ou, stm., Laos ... B6 48
Ouacha, Niger ... G6 64
Ouachita, stm., U.S. ... F7 122
Ouachita, Lake, res., Ar., U.S. ... C5 122
Ouachita Mountains, mts., U.S. ... C4 122
Ouaco, N. Cal. ... m15 79d
Ouadda, C.A.R. ... C4 66
Ouagadougou, Burkina ... G4 64
Ouahigouya, Burkina ... G4 64
Ouahran see Wahran, Alg. ... B4 64
Ouaka, stm., C.A.R. ... C4 66
Oualâta, Maur. ... F3 64
Ouallene, Alg. ... F5 64
Ouanary, Fr. Gu. ... C7 84
Ouanda Djallé, C.A.R. ... C4 66
Ouango, C.A.R. ... D4 66
Ouangolodougou, C. Iv. ... H3 64
Ouarâne, reg., Maur. ... E3 64
Ouarkziz, Jbel, mts., Afr. ... D3 64
Ouarzazate, Mor. ... C3 64
Ouasiemsca, stm., Qc., Can. ... A4 110
Oubangui (Ubangi), stm., Afr. ... E3 66
Oudenaarde, Bel. ... D12 14
Oudtshoorn, S. Afr. ... H6 70
Oued Fodda, Alg. ... H12 20
Oued-Zem, Mor. ... C3 64
Ouémé, stm., Benin ... H5 64
Ouen, Île, i., N. Cal. ... n16 79d
Ouessant, Île d' (Ushant), i., Fr. ... F4 14
Ouésso, Congo ... D3 66
Ouezzane, Mor. ... C3 64
Ouidah, Benin ... H5 64
Ouimet Canyon, misc. cult., On., U.S. ... C10 118
Ouistreham, Fr. ... E8 14
Oujda, Mor. ... C4 64
Oulangan kansallispuisto, p.o.i., Fin. ... C13 8
Oulu (Uleåborg), Fin. ... D11 8
Oulu, state, Fin. ... D12 8
Oulujärvi, l., Fin. ... D12 8
Oulujoki, stm., Fin. ... D12 8
Oum-Chalouba, Chad ... D4 62
Oum-Hadjer, Chad ... E3 62
Oumiaou, China ... G5 42
Ounianga Kébir, Chad ... D3 62
Ourém, Braz. ... A2 88
Ourense, Spain ... B3 20
Ourense, co., Spain ... B3 20

Ouricuri, Braz. ... D5 88
Ourinhos, Braz. ... D7 90
Ouro Branco, Braz. ... D7 88
Ouro Fino, Braz. ... L2 88
Ouro Preto, Braz. ... K4 88
Ours, Grande chute à l', wtfl., Qc., Can. ... B4 110
Ourthe, stm., Bel. ... D14 14
Ōu-sammyaku, mts., Japan ... E14 38
Oust, can., Fr. ... F6 14
Outaouais (Ottawa), stm., Can. ... C15 112
Outardes, stm., Qc., Can. ... E17 106
Outer Hebrides, is., Scot., U.K. ... D5 12
Outer Island, i., Wi., U.S. ... D8 118
Outer Santa Barbara Passage, strt., Ca., U.S. ... J7 134
Outjo, Nmb. ... B3 70
Outlook, Sk., Can. ... C6 124
Outlook, Mt., U.S. ... F9 124
Out Skerries, is., Scot., U.K. ... n18 12a
Ovacık, Tur. ... B15 28
Ovada, Italy ... F5 22
Ovalle, Chile ... E2 92
Ovana, Cerro, mtn., Ven. ... E8 86
Ovar, Port. ... D2 20
Ovejas, Col. ... C4 86
Overbrook, Ks., U.S. ... F2 120
Overflowing, stm., Can. ... A12 124
Overland Park, Ks., U.S. ... F3 120
Overton, Ne., U.S. ... G13 126
Overton, Tx., U.S. ... E4 122
Overton Arm, b., Nv., U.S. ... G2 132
Övertorneå, Swe. ... C10 8
Ovett, Ms., U.S. ... F9 122
Ovid, Mi., U.S. ... B9 114
Ovidiopol', Ukr. ... C17 26
Oviedo, Spain ... A5 20
Ovinišče, Russia ... B20 10
Ovišu, Lat. ... C4 10
Ovoot, Mong. ... B7 36
Øvre Anárjohka Nasjonalpark, p.o.i., Nor. ... B13 8
Øvre Dividal Nasjonalpark, p.o.i., Nor. ... B8 8
Ovstug, Russia ... G16 10
Owando, Congo ... E3 66
Owase, Japan ... E9 40
Owasso, Ok., U.S. ... H2 120
Owatonna, Mn., U.S. ... G5 118
Owbi, Afg. ... C9 56
Owego, N.Y., U.S. ... B9 114
Owen, Wi., U.S. ... G8 118
Owendo, Gabon ... D1 66
Owens, stm., Ca., U.S. ... F7 134
Owensboro, Ky., U.S. ... G10 120
Owens Lake, l., Ca., U.S. ... G8 134
Owen Sound, On., Can. ... D8 112
Owen Stanley Range, mts., Pap. N. Gui. ... b4 79a
Owensville, In., U.S. ... F10 120
Owensville, Mo., U.S. ... F6 120
Owerri, Nig. ... H6 64
Owikeno Lake, l., B.C., Can. ... E3 138
Owingsville, Ky., U.S. ... F2 114
Owl, stm., Ab., Can. ... A19 138
Owl, stm., Mb., Can. ... D12 106
Owo, Nig. ... H6 64
Owosso, Mi., U.S. ... E5 112
Owyhee, Nv., U.S. ... B9 134
Owyhee, stm., U.S. ... G9 136
Owyhee, Lake, res., Or., U.S. ... G9 136
Owyhee, South Fork, stm., U.S. ... H10 136
Oxarfjördur, b., Ice. ... j31 8a
Oxbow, Sk., Can. ... E11 124
Oxelösund, Swe. ... G7 8
Oxford, N.Z. ... F5 80
Oxford, Eng., U.K. ... J11 12
Oxford, Al., U.S. ... D13 122
Oxford, In., U.S. ... H2 112
Oxford, Ks., U.S. ... D11 128
Oxford, Md., U.S. ... F9 114
Oxford, Me., U.S. ... F6 110
Oxford, Ms., U.S. ... C9 122
Oxford, N.C., U.S. ... H7 114
Oxford, N.Y., U.S. ... B10 114
Oxford, Oh., U.S. ... E13 120
Oxford, Pa., U.S. ... E9 114
Oxford Junction, Ia., U.S. ... J8 118
Oxford Lake, l., Mb., Can. ... E11 106
Oxford Peak, mtn., Id., U.S. ... H14 136
Oxkutzcab, Mex. ... B3 102
Oxley Downs, Austl. ... J4 76
Oxley Wild Rivers National Park, p.o.i., Austl. ... H8 76
Oxnard, Ca., U.S. ... I6 134
Oxus see Amu Darya, stm., Asia ... F10 32
Oya, stm., Malay. ... B8 50
Oyabe, Japan ... C9 40
Oyano, Japan ... G3 40
Oyapok (Oiapoque), stm., S.A. ... C7 84
Oyem, Gabon ... D2 66
Oyen, Ab., Can. ... C3 124
Oyo, Nig. ... H5 64
Oyonnax, Fr. ... C10 18
Oyyl, Kaz. ... E8 32
Ozamis, Phil. ... F4 52
Ozark, Al., U.S. ... F13 122
Ozark, Ar., U.S. ... B5 122
Ozark, Mo., U.S. ... G5 120
Ozark Plateau, plat., U.S. ... H4 120
Ozarks, Lake of the, res., Mo., U.S. ... F5 120
Ózd, Hung. ... A7 26
Ozerele, Russia ... F21 10
Ozernovskij, Russia ... F20 34
Ozërnyj, Russia ... D10 32
Ozery, Russia ... F21 10
Ozette Lake, l., Wa., U.S. ... B2 136
Ozieri, Italy ... D3 24
Ozinki, Russia ... D7 32
Ozona, Tx., U.S. ... D7 130
Ozorków, Pol. ... E15 16
Ōzu, Japan ... F5 40
Ozuluama, Mex. ... E9 100
Ozurgeti, Geor. ... F6 32

P

Paagoumène, N. Cal. ... m14 79d
Paama, i., Vanuatu ... k17 79d
Paamiut see Frederikshåb, Grnld. ... E15 141
Pa'auilo, Hi., U.S. ... c6 78a
Pabbay, i., Scot., U.K. ... D5 12
Pabbiring, Kepulauan, is., Indon. ... F11 50
Pabellón, Ensenada del, b., Mex. ... C5 100
Pabianice, Pol. ... E15 16
Pablo, Mt., U.S. ... C12 136
Pâbna, Bngl. ... G12 54
Pabradė, Lith. ... F8 10
Pacaás Novos, Serra dos, mts., Braz. ... E5 84
Pacajus, Braz. ... C6 88
Pacasmayo, Peru ... E2 84
Pacatuba, Braz. ... C6 88
Pachino, Italy ... H9 24
Pachitea, stm., Peru ... E3 84
Pachmarhi, India ... G7 54
Pāchora, India ... H5 54
Pachuca de Soto, Mex. ... E9 100
Pacific, B.C., Can. ... B2 138
Pacific, Mo., U.S. ... F7 120
Pacifica, Ca., U.S. ... F3 134
Pacific-Antarctic Ridge, unds. ... P22 142
Pacific Grove, Ca., U.S. ... G3 134
Pacific Ocean ... F20 142
Pacific Ranges, mts., B.C., Can. ... E5 138
Pacific Rim National Park, p.o.i., B.C., Can. ... H5 138
Paciran, Indon. ... G8 50
Pacitan, Indon. ... H7 50
Pacora, Pan. ... C2 86
Pacov, Czech Rep. ... G11 16
Pacui, stm., Braz. ... I3 88
Padada, Phil. ... G5 52
Padamo, stm., Ven. ... F9 86
Padampur, India ... H9 54
Padang, Indon. ... D2 50
Padang, Indon. ... G12 50
Padang, Indon. ... D6 50
Padang, Pulau, i., Indon. ... C3 50
Padang Endau, Malay. ... K6 48
Padangpanjang, Indon. ... C1 50
Padangsidempuan, Indon. ... C1 50
Padany, Russia ... E15 8
Padas, stm., Malay. ... A9 50
Padauari, stm., Braz. ... G9 86
Paddle, stm., Ab., Can. ... B16 138
Paddle Prairie, Ab., Can. ... D7 106
Paderborn, Ger. ... E4 16
Padjelanta Nationalpark, p.o.i., Swe. ... C7 8
Padloping Island, i., Nu., Can. ... D13 141
Padma see Ganges, stm., Asia ... G13 54
Pádova (Padua), Italy ... E8 22
Padra, India ... G4 54
Padrauna, India ... E9 54
Padre Bernardo, Braz. ... H1 88
Padre Island, i., Tx., U.S. ... G10 130
Padre Island National Seashore, p.o.i., Tx., U.S. ... G10 130
Padre Paraíso, Braz. ... I5 88
Padstow, Eng., U.K. ... K8 12
Padua see Pádova, Italy ... E8 22
Paducah, Ky., U.S. ... G9 120
Paducah, Tx., U.S. ... G8 128
Paea, Fr. Poly. ... v21 78h
Paeden, Kor., S. ... D1 40
Paektu-san, mtn., Asia ... C10 36
Paestum, sci., Italy ... D8 24
Páez, stm., Col. ... F4 86
Pafúri, Moz. ... C10 70
Pag, Otok, i., Cro. ... F11 22
Pagadenbaru, Indon. ... G5 50
Pagadian, Phil. ... G4 52
Pagai Selatan, Pulau, i., Indon. ... E2 50
Pagai Utara, Pulau, i., Indon. ... E2 50
Pagan, Mya. ... B2 48
Pagan, i., N. Mar. Is. ... B5 72
Pagaralam, Indon. ... E3 50
Pagastikós Kólpos, b., Grc. ... D5 28
Page, Az., U.S. ... G5 132
Page, N.D., U.S. ... G16 124
Pagégiai, Lith. ... E4 10
Pagerdewa, Indon. ... E4 50
Paget, Mount, mtn., S. Geor. ... J9 90
Pagoda Peak, mtn., Co., U.S. ... C9 132
Pagoda Point, c., Mya. ... E2 48
Pagon, Bukit, mtn., Asia ... A9 50
Pago Pago, Am. Sam. ... h12 79c
Pagosa Springs, Co., U.S. ... F9 132
Paguate, N.M., U.S. ... H9 132
Pagudpud, Phil. ... A3 52
Pāhala, Hi., U.S. ... d6 78a
Pahang, state, Malay. ... K6 48
Pahang, stm., Malay. ... K6 48
Pahokee, Fl., U.S. ... J5 116
Pahost, Bela. ... G12 10
Pahrump, Nv., U.S. ... G10 134
Pai, Thai. ... C4 48
Pai, stm., Asia ... C4 48
Paico, Peru ... F3 84
Paide, Est. ... B8 10
Paige, Tx., U.S. ... D10 130
Paignton, Eng., U.K. ... K9 12
Paiguano, Chile ... E2 92
Päijänne, l., Fin. ... F11 8
Paiko Co, l., China ... D10 54
Pailolo Channel, strt., Hi., U.S. ... b5 78a
Paimpol, Fr. ... F5 14
Painan, Indon. ... D2 50
Painesdale, Mi., U.S. ... D10 118
Painesville, Oh., U.S. ... C4 114
Paint, stm., Mi., U.S. ... B1 112
Paint Creek, stm., Oh., U.S. ... E14 120
Painted Desert, des., Az., U.S. ... H5 132
Painted Rock Reservoir, res., Az., U.S. ... K3 132
Paintsville, Ky., U.S. ... G3 114
Paisley, Scot., U.K. ... F8 12
Paisley, Or., U.S. ... H6 136
Paita, Peru ... E1 84
Paita, N. Cal. ... m15 79d
Paitan, Telukan, b., Malay. ... G1 52
Paiton, Indon. ... G8 50
Pajala, Swe. ... C10 8
Pajares, Puerto de, p., Spain ... B5 20
Pajaros Point, c., Br. Vir. Is. ... d9 104b
Pajer, gora, Russia ... C1 34
Paj-Hoj, hills, Russia ... A10 32
Paka, Malay. ... J6 48
Pākala, India ... E4 53
Pakanbaru, Indon. ... C2 50
Pakaraima Mountains, mts., S.A. ... E11 86
Pākaur, India ... F11 54
Pakch'ŏn, Kor., N. ... E6 38
Pakistan, ctry., Asia ... C2 46
Paklenica Nacionalni Park, p.o.i., Cro. ... F12 22
Pakokku, Mya. ... B2 48
Pakowki Lake, l., Ab., Can. ... E2 124
Pakpattan, Pak. ... C4 54
Pak Phanang, Thai. ... H5 48
Pak Phayun, Thai. ... I5 48
Pak Phraek, Thai. ... H4 48
Pakrac, Cro. ... E14 22
Paks, Hung. ... C5 26
Paktīā, state, Afg. ... B2 54
Paktīkā, state, Afg. ... C2 54
Pakwash Lake, l., On., Can. ... A5 118
Pakxé, Laos ... E7 48
Pala, Chad ... F2 62
Pala, Mya. ... F4 48
Palacios, Tx., U.S. ... F11 130
Palagruža, Otoči, is., Cro. ... H13 22
Palaia, India ... E4 53
Palaiochóra, Grc. ... H6 28
Pālakkodu, India ... E4 53
Palamós, Spain ... C14 20

Name	Map Ref.	Page
Pālampur, India	B6	54
Palamu National Park, p.o.i., India	G10	54
Palamut, Tur.	D10	28
Palana, Russia	E20	34
Palanan Bay, b., Phil.	B4	52
Palangkaraya, Indon.	E8	50
Palani, India	F3	53
Pālanpur, India	F4	54
Palaoa Point, c., Hi., U.S.	c4	78a
Palapye, Bots.	C8	70
Pālār, stm., India	E4	53
Palas de Rei, Spain	B3	20
Palatka, Russia	D19	34
Palatka, Fl., U.S.	G4	116
Palau, Italy	C3	24
Palau, ctry., Oc.	g8	78b
Palau Islands, is., Palau	D10	44
Palauk, Mya.	F4	48
Palaw, Mya.	F4	48
Palawan, i., Phil.	F2	52
Palawan Passage, strt., Phil.	F1	52
Palayan, Phil.	C3	52
Pālayankottai, India	G3	53
Palembang, Indon.	E3	50
Palena, Italy	I11	22
Palena, stm., S.A.	H2	90
Palencia, Spain	B6	20
Palencia, co., Spain	B6	20
Palen Lake, l., Ca., U.S.	J1	132
Palenque, Mex.	G13	100
Palenque, sci., Mex.	G12	100
Palermo, Col.	F4	86
Palermo, Italy	F7	24
Palermo, Ur.	F10	92
Palestina, Mex.	E6	130
Palestine, Ar., U.S.	B7	122
Palestine, Il., U.S.	E10	120
Palestine, Tx., U.S.	F3	122
Palestine, hist. reg., Asia	G6	58
Palestine, Lake, res., Tx., U.S.	E3	122
Palestrina, Italy	I9	22
Paletwa, Mya.	D7	46
Pālghāt, India	F3	53
Palgrave Point, c., Nmb.	E1	68
Palhano, stm., Braz.	C6	88
Pāli, India	F4	54
Palikir, Micron.	m11	78d
Palima, Indon.	F12	50
Palinuro, Capo, c., Italy	D9	24
Palisade, Ne., U.S.	A7	128
Palisades, Id., U.S.	G15	136
Palisades Reservoir, res., U.S.	G15	136
Pālītāna, India	H3	54
Palivere, Est.	A6	10
Palizada, Mex.	F12	100
Palk Bay, b., Asia	G5	53
Palkino, Russia	G20	8
Pālkonda, India	B6	53
Pālkonda Range, mts., India	D4	53
Palk Strait, strt., Asia	G4	53
Pallasturturi, mtn., Fin.	B11	8
Palliser, Cape, c., N.Z.	E6	80
Palma, Braz.	K4	88
Palma, Moz.	C7	68
Palma, stm., Braz.	G2	88
Palma, Badia de, b., Spain	E13	20
Palma del Rio, Spain	C6	68
Palma del Rio, Spain	G5	20
Palma de Mallorca, Spain	E13	20
Palma di Montechiaro, Italy	G7	24
Palmar, stm., Ven.	B6	86
Palmar, Lago Artificial del, res., Ur.	F9	92
Palmar Camp, Belize	D3	102
Palmarejo, P.R.	B1	104a
Palmares, Braz.	E8	88
Palmarito, Ven.	D6	86
Palmarola, Isola, i., Italy	D6	24
Palmas, Braz.	F1	88
Palmas, Braz.	C12	92
Palmas Bellas, Pan.	H7	102
Palmas de Monte Alto, Braz.	H4	88
Palma Soriano, Cuba	B9	102
Palm Bay, Fl., U.S.	H5	116
Palm Beach, Fl., U.S.	J5	116
Palmdale, Ca., U.S.	I7	134
Palm Desert, Ca., U.S.	J9	134
Palmeira, Braz.	B13	92
Palmeira das Missões, Braz.	C11	92
Palmeira dos Índios, Braz.	E7	88
Palmeiras, stm., Braz.	F2	88
Palmeirinhas, Ponta das, c., Ang.	B1	68
Palmelo, Braz.	I1	88
Palmer, P.R.	B4	104a
Palmer, Ak., U.S.	D10	140
Palmer, Ma., U.S.	B13	114
Palmer, Ne., U.S.	F14	126
Palmer, Tn., U.S.	B13	122
Palmer, sci., Ant.	B34	81
Palmer Lake, Co., U.S.	B3	128
Palmer Land, reg., Ant.	C34	81
Palmerston, at., Cook Is.	E10	72
Palmerston, Cape, c., Austl.	C7	76
Palmerston North, N.Z.	E6	80
Palmerton, Pa., U.S.	D10	114
Palmetto, Ga., U.S.	D14	122
Palmetto, La., U.S.	G6	122
Palmetto Point, c., Antig.	e4	105b
Palmi, Italy	F9	24
Palmira, Col.	F3	86
Palmira, Cuba	A7	102
Palmira, Ec.	I2	86
Palmitas, Ur.	F9	92
Palm Springs, Ca., U.S.	J9	134
Palmyra see Tudmur, Syria	D9	58
Palmyra, Il., U.S.	E7	120
Palmyra, Mo., U.S.	E6	120
Palmyra, N.Y., U.S.	A8	114
Palmyra, Va., U.S.	G7	114
Palmyra, sci., Syria	D9	58
Palmyra Atoll, at., Oc.	C10	72
Palo Alto, Mex.	H8	130
Palo Alto, Ca., U.S.	F3	134
Palo Blanco, P.R.	B2	104a
Palo Flechado Pass, p., N.M., U.S.	E3	128
Paloh, Malay.	B7	50
Paloich, Sudan	E6	62
Palojoensuu, Fin.	B10	8
Palomar Mountain, mtn., Ca., U.S.	J9	134
Palomas, Mex.	F4	130
Palo Pinto, Tx., U.S.	B9	130
Palopo, Indon.	E12	50
Palos, Cabo de, c., Spain	G10	20
Palo Santo, Arg.	B8	92
Palos Verdes Point, c., Ca., U.S.	J7	134
Palouse, stm., U.S.	D8	136
Palo Verde, Ca., U.S.	J2	132
Palpa, Peru	F2	84
Palpalá, Arg.	B5	92
Palu, Indon.	D11	50
Palu, Teluk, b., Indon.	D11	50
Paluga, Russia	D21	8
Palwal, India	D6	54
Pama, Burkina	G5	64
Pamanukan, Indon.	G5	50
Pâmban Channel, strt., India	G4	53
Pamban Island, i., India	G4	53
Pamekasan, Indon.	G8	50
Pamenang, Indon.	E3	50
Pameungpeuk, Indon.	G5	50
Pamiers, Fr.	F7	18
Pamir, mts., Asia	B11	56
Pamlico Sound, strt., N.C., U.S.	A10	116
Pampa, Tx., U.S.	F8	128
Pampa, stm., Braz.	I5	88
Pampa (Pampas), reg., Arg.	G4	90
Pampa Almirón, Arg.	C8	92
Pampa del Chañar, Arg.	E3	92
Pampa del Indio, Arg.	B7	92
Pampanga, stm., Phil.	C3	52
Pampanua, Indon.	F12	50
Pampas, Peru	F3	84
Pampas, stm., Peru	F3	84
Pampas see Pampa, reg., Arg.	F4	90
Pamplico, S.C., U.S.	B6	116
Pamplona, Col.	D5	86
Pamplona, Spain	B9	20
Pamukkale (Hierapolis), sci., Tur.	F12	28
Pamukova, Tur.	C13	28
Pana, Il., U.S.	E8	120
Panabá, Mex.	B3	102
Panabo, Phil.	G5	52
Panacea, Fl., U.S.	G14	122
Panadura, Sri L.	H4	53
Panagjurište, Blg.	G11	26
Panaitan, Pulau, i., Indon.	G4	50
Panaji, India	D1	53
Panamá, Pan.	H8	102
Panama, Ok., U.S.	B4	122
Panama, ctry., N.A.	F9	96
Panamá, Bahía de, b., Pan.	H8	102
Panamá, Canal de (Panama Canal), can., Pan.	H8	102
Panamá, Golfo de, b., Pan.	D2	86
Panama, Gulf of see Panamá, Golfo de, b., Pan.	D2	86
Panama, Isthmus of see Panamá, Istmo de, Pan.	H8	102
Panamá, Istmo de (Panama, Isthmus of), isth., Pan.	H8	102
Panama Basin, unds.	H5	144
Panama Canal see Panamá, Canal de, can., Pan.	H8	102
Panama City, Fl., U.S.	G13	122
Panamint Range, mts., Ca., U.S.	G8	134
Panamint Valley, val., Ca., U.S.	G8	134
Panao, Peru	E2	84
Panarea, Isola, i., Italy	F9	24
Panaro, stm., Italy	F8	22
Panay, i., Phil.	E4	52
Panay Gulf, b., Phil.	E4	52
Pancevo, Serb.	E7	26
Panciu, Rom.	D14	26
Panda, Moz.	D12	70
Pandaria, India	G8	54
Pan de Azúcar, Ur.	G10	92
Pandėlys, Lith.	D8	10
Pandharkawada, India	A4	53
Pandharpur, India	C2	53
Pāndhurna, India	H7	54
Pando, Ur.	G10	92
Panevėžys, Lith.	E7	10
Panga, D.R.C.	B4	48
Pangala, Congo	E2	66
Pangani, Indon.	E6	66
Pangani, Tan.	F7	66
Pangani, stm., Tan.	E7	66
Pangburn, Ar., U.S.	B7	122
Pangfou see Bengbu, China	F7	42
Panghkam, Mya.	D8	46
Pangi, D.R.C.	E5	66
Pangkajene, Indon.	F11	50
Pangkalanbrandan, Indon.	J4	48
Pangkalanbuun, Indon.	E7	50
Pangkalpinang, Indon.	E5	50
Pango Aluquem, Ang.	B1	68
Pangójin, Kor., S.	D2	40
Pangong Tso, l., Asia	B7	54
Panguitch, Ut., U.S.	F4	132
Panguna, Pap. N. Gui.	d6	79a
Pangutaran Group, is., Phil.	G3	52
Pangutaran Island, i., Phil.	G3	52
Pāni'au, mtn., Hi., U.S.	b1	78a
Panié, Mont, mtn., N. Cal.	m15	79d
Panipāt, India	D6	54
Panitan, Phil.	E4	52
Panj (Pjandž), stm., Asia	B11	56
Panjang, Selat, strt., Indon.	C3	50
Pankshin, Nig.	H6	64
Panlong (Lo), stm., Asia	A7	48
Panna, India	F8	54
Panna National Park, p.o.i., India	F7	54
Pannawonica, Austl.	D3	74
Pannirtuuq, Nu., Can.	B17	106
Panola, Tx., U.S.	E10	122
Páno Lévkara, Cyp.	D4	58
Panopah, Indon.	D7	50
Panovo, Russia	C18	32
Panruti, India	F4	53
Panshan, China	D4	38
Pantanal, reg., S.A.	C5	90
Pantanaw, Mya.	D2	48
Pantar, Pulau, i., Indon.	G7	44
Pantelleria, Isola di, i., Italy	H6	24
Pantonlabu, Indon.	J3	48
Pánuco, Mex.	E10	100
Pánuco, stm., Mex.	E9	100
Panxian, China	F5	36
Panyam, Nig.	H6	64
Panzós, Guat.	E3	102
Pao, stm., Thai.	D6	48
Pao, stm., Ven.	C8	86
Paochi see Baoji, China	D2	42
Paoki see Baoji, China	D2	42
Paola, Italy	E9	24
Paola, Ks., U.S.	F3	120
Paoli, In., U.S.	F11	120
Paopao, Fr. Poly.	v20	78h
Paoting see Baoding, China	B6	42
Paotow see Baotou, China	A4	42
Pápa, Hung.	B4	26
Papagaio, stm., Braz.	I10	86
Papagaios, Braz.	D3	88
Papagayo, Golfo de, b., C.R.	G4	102
Papa'ikou, Hi., U.S.	d6	78a
Papantla de Olarte, Mex.	E10	100
Papara, Fr. Poly.	v22	78h
Papa Stour, i., Scot., U.K.	n18	12a
Papeari, Fr. Poly.	w22	78h
Papeete, Fr. Poly.	v21	78h
Papenburg, Ger.	C3	16
Papetoai, Fr. Poly.	v20	78h
Paphos see Néa Páfos, Cyp.	D3	58
Papilė, Lith.	D5	10
Papillion, Ne., U.S.	C1	120
Papoose, Braz.	B2	90
Papua, Gulf of, b., Pap. N. Gui.	D5	72
Papua New Guinea, ctry., Oc.	b4	79a
Papulovo, Russia	F23	8
Papun, Mya.	D3	48
Papunaua, stm., Col.	G6	86
Papuri (Papurí), stm., S.A.	G6	86
Papuri (Papurí), stm., S.A.	G6	86
Pará, state, Braz.	D7	84
Pará, stm., Braz.	A1	88
Pará, stm., Braz.	J3	88
Parabel', Russia	C14	32
Paraburdoo, Austl.	D3	74
Paracatu, Braz.	I2	88
Paracatu, stm., Braz.	I3	88
Paracel Islands see Xisha Qundao, is., China	B5	50
Pārachinār, Pak.	B3	54
Paracho de Verduzco, Mex.	F7	100
Parachute, Co., U.S.	D8	132
Paracin, Serb.	E8	26
Paracuru, Braz.	B6	88
Parada, Punta, c., Peru	G2	84
Paradise, Ca., U.S.	D4	134
Paradise, Mt., U.S.	C12	136
Paradise, Nv., U.S.	G1	132
Paradise Island, i., Bah.	m18	104f
Paradise Valley, Nv., U.S.	B8	134
Pāradwīp, India	H11	54
Paragominas, Braz.	A1	88
Paragould, Ar., U.S.	H7	120
Paraguá, stm., Bol.	B4	90
Paraguá, stm., Ven.	D10	86
Paraguaçu, stm., Braz.	G6	88
Paraguai (Paraguay), stm., S.A.	D5	90
Paraguaipoa, Ven.	B6	86
Paraguaná, Península de, pen., Ven.	A6	86
Paraguari, Para.	B9	92
Paraguari, state, Para.	C9	92
Paraguay, ctry., S.A.	D5	90
Paraguay (Paraguai), stm., S.A.	E5	90
Paraíba, state, Braz.	D7	88
Paraíba do Sul, stm., Braz.	K5	88
Paraibano, Braz.	D3	88
Parainen, Fin.	F9	8
Paraiso, Mex.	F12	100
Paraiso, Pan.	H8	102
Parakou, Benin	H5	64
Paramakkudi, India	G4	53
Paramaribo, Sur.	B6	84
Parambu, Braz.	D5	88
Paramillo, Parque Nacional, p.o.i., Col.	D3	86
Paramirim, Braz.	G4	88
Paramirim, stm., Braz.	F4	88
Páramo de Masa, Puerto de, p., Spain	B7	20
Paramušir, ostrov, i., Russia	F20	34
Paramythiá, Grc.	D3	28
Paran, Nahal (Girafi, Wadi), stm.	I5	58
Paraná, Arg.	E7	92
Paraná, Braz.	G1	88
Paraná, state, Braz.	D6	90
Paraná, stm., Braz.	G1	88
Paraná, stm., S.A.	F5	90
Paranaguá, Braz.	B13	92
Paranaguá, Baía de, b., Braz.	B13	92
Paranaíba, Braz.	C6	90
Paranaíba, stm., Braz.	C6	90
Paranaidji, Braz.	D2	88
Paranapanema, stm., Braz.	D6	90
Paranapiacaba, Serra do, mts., Braz.	B13	92
Paranavaí, Braz.	D6	90
Parang, Phil.	G5	52
Parang, Pulau, i., Indon.	F7	50
Parângu Mare, Vârful, mtn., Rom.	D10	26
Paranhos, Braz.	A10	92
Paranoá, Lago do, res., Braz.	H2	88
Parapeti, stm., Bol.	C4	90
Paratinga, Braz.	G4	88
Paratoo, Austl.	I2	76
Paray-le-Monial, Fr.	C9	18
Pārbati, stm., India	F6	54
Pārbatipur, Bngl.	F12	54
Parbhani, India	B3	53
Parchim, Ger.	C7	16
Pardeeville, Wi., U.S.	H9	118
Pārdi, India	H4	54
Parding, China	B12	54
Pardo, stm., Braz.	D6	90
Pardo, stm., Braz.	H6	88
Pardo, stm., Braz.	L1	88
Pardo, stm., Braz.	D11	92
Pardo, stm., Braz.	K1	88
Pardubice, Czech Rep.	F11	16
Paredón, Mex.	C8	100
Parelhas, Braz.	D7	88
Paren', Russia	D21	34
Paren', stm., Russia	D21	34
Parent, Qc., Can.	C2	110
Parentis-en-Born, Fr.	E4	18
Parepare, Indon.	F11	50
Parera, Arg.	G5	92
Parfen'evo, Russia	F20	8
Parga, Grc.	D3	28
Parham, Antig.	f4	105b
Paria, Gulf of, b.	B10	86
Paria, Península de, pen., Ven.	B10	86
Pariaguán, Ven.	C9	86
Pariaman, Indon.	D1	50
Paricutín, vol., Mex.	F7	100
Parigi, Indon.	D12	50
Parika, Guy.	B6	84
Parikkala, Fin.	F13	8
Parima, stm., Braz.	F10	86
Parima, Serra (Parima, Sierra), mts., S.A.	F9	86
Parima, Sierra (Parima, Serra), mts., S.A.	F9	86
Parintins, Braz.	D6	84
Paris, On., Can.	E9	112
Paris, Fr.	F11	14
Paris, Ar., U.S.	B5	122
Paris, Id., U.S.	A5	132
Paris, Ky., U.S.	F1	114
Paris, Mo., U.S.	E5	120
Paris, Tn., U.S.	H9	120
Paris, Tx., U.S.	D3	122
Parisienne, Île, i., On., Can.	B5	112
Parita, Bahía de, b., Pan.	H7	102
Parit Buntar, Malay.	J5	48
Parkano, Fin.	E10	8
Park City, Mt., U.S.	B3	126
Park City, Ut., U.S.	C5	132
Parkdale, Or., U.S.	E5	136
Parker, Az., U.S.	I2	132
Parker, Co., U.S.	B4	128
Parker, Fl., U.S.	G13	122
Parker, Cape, c., Nu., Can.	B10	141
Parker Dam, Ca., U.S.	I2	132
Parker Dam, dam, U.S.	I2	132
Parkersburg, Il., U.S.	F9	120
Parkersburg, W.V., U.S.	E4	114
Park Falls, Wi., U.S.	F8	118
Park Forest, Il., U.S.	G2	112
Parkhill, On., Can.	E8	112
Parkland, Wa., U.S.	C4	136
Park Range, mts., Co., U.S.	C10	132
Park Rapids, Mn., U.S.	E3	118
Parkrose, Or., U.S.	E4	136
Parksley, Va., U.S.	G10	114
Parkston, S.D., U.S.	D15	126
Parksville, B.C., Can.	G6	138
Parkville, Md., U.S.	E9	114
Parkville, Mo., U.S.	E3	120
Parla, Spain	D7	20
Parlākimidi, India	B7	53
Parli, India	B3	53
Parma, Italy	F7	22
Parma, Mo., U.S.	H8	120
Parma, Oh., U.S.	C4	114
Parnaguá, Braz.	F3	88
Parnaíba, Braz.	B5	88
Parnaíba, stm., Braz.	B5	88
Parnaíbinha, stm., Braz.	E2	88
Parnamirim, Braz.	D7	88
Parnassós, mtn., Grc.	E6	28
Párnitha, mtn., Grc.	E6	28
Pärnu, Est.	G11	8
Pärnu, stm., Est.	G11	8
Pärnu laht, b., Est.	G11	8
Pārola, India	H5	54
Paromaj, Russia	F17	34
Paroo, stm., Austl.	G5	76
Páros, i., Grc.	F8	28
Parowan, Ut., U.S.	F4	132
Parque Nacional da Chapada da Diamantina, p.o.i., Braz.	G4	88
Parral, Chile	H2	92
Parral, stm., Mex.	B6	100
Parramatta, Austl.	I8	76
Parras de la Fuente, Mex.	C7	100
Parrish, Fl., U.S.	I3	116
Parrsboro, N.S., Can.	E12	110
Parry, Cape, c., N.T., Can.	A6	106
Parry Bay, b., Nu., Can.	B14	106
Parry Island, i., On., Can.	C9	112
Parry Peninsula, pen., N.T., Can.	B6	106
Parry Sound, On., Can.	C9	112
Parsberg, Ger.	G7	16
Parseta, stm., Pol.	B11	16
Parshall, N.D., U.S.	G11	124
Paršino, Russia	C20	32
Parsnip, stm., B.C., Can.	A8	138
Parsons, Ks., U.S.	G2	120
Parsons, Tn., U.S.	B10	122
Pärsti, Est.	B8	10
Partanna, Italy	G6	24
Parthenay, Fr.	H8	14
Partinico, Italy	F7	24
Partizansk, Russia	C10	38
Partizánske, Slov.	H14	16
Parú, stm., Ven.	E9	86
Paru de Oeste, stm., Braz.	C6	84
Pārvatipuram, India	B6	53
Paryang, China	C9	54
Parys, S. Afr.	E8	70
Pasadena, Ca., U.S.	I7	134
Pasadena, Tx., U.S.	H3	122
Pa Sak, stm., Thai.	E5	48
Paşakõy, N. Cyp.	C4	58
Pasarbantal, Indon.	E2	50
Pasawng, Mya.	C3	48
Pascagoula, Ms., U.S.	G10	122
Pascagoula, stm., Ms., U.S.	G10	122
Pașcani, Rom.	B13	26
Pasco, Wa., U.S.	D7	136
Pascoag, R.I., U.S.	C14	114
Pascua, Isla de (Easter Island) (Rapa Nui), i., Chile	f30	78l
Pas-de-Calais, state, Fr.	D11	14
Pasewalk, Ger.	C10	16
Pasir Mas, Malay.	J6	48
Pasirpengarayan, Indon.	C2	50
Pasir Puteh, Malay.	J6	48
Paškovo, Russia	G15	34
Pasłęka, stm., Pol.	C16	16
Pasley Bay, b., Nu., Can.	A11	106
Pasman, Otok, i., Cro.	G12	22
Pasmore, stm., Austl.	H2	76
Pasni, Pak.	D9	56
Paso de Indios, Arg.	H3	90
Paso del Cerro, Ur.	E9	92
Paso de los Libres, Arg.	D9	92
Paso de los Toros, Ur.	F9	92
Paso de Patria, Para.	B9	92
Paso de San Antonio, Mex.	E3	130
Paso Hondo, Mex.	H13	100
Paso Robles, Ca., U.S.	H5	134
Pasquia Hills, hills, Sk., Can.	A11	124
Pasrūr, Pak.	B5	54
Passadumkeag, Me., U.S.	E8	110
Passadumkeag Mountain, hill, Me., U.S.	E8	110
Passage Point, c., N.T., Can.	B16	140
Passaic, N.J., U.S.	H15	112
Passamaquoddy Bay, b., N.A.	E10	110
Passau, Ger.	H9	16
Passero, Capo, c., Italy	H9	24
Passo Fundo, Braz.	D11	92
Passo Real, Represa do, res., Braz.	D11	92
Passos, Braz.	K2	88
Pastavy, Bela.	E9	10
Pastaza, state, Ec.	H3	86
Pastaza, stm., S.A.	D2	84
Pastillo, P.R.	B3	104a
Pasto, Col.	G3	86
Pastos Bons, Braz.	D3	88
Pasuruan, Indon.	G8	50
Pasvalys, Lith.	D7	10
Pásztó, Hung.	B6	26
Patacamaya, Bol.	C3	90
Patadkal, sci., India	C3	53
Patagonia, Az., U.S.	L6	132
Patagonia, reg., Arg.	I2	90
Pātan, India	G3	54
Pathogue, N.Y., U.S.	D13	114
Patea, N.Z.	D6	80
Pategi, Nig.	H6	64
Pate Island, i., Kenya	E8	66
Patensie, S. Afr.	H7	70
Paternion, Aus.	D10	22
Paternò, Italy	G8	24
Pateros, Wa., U.S.	B7	136
Pathānkot, India	B5	54
Pathfinder Reservoir, res., Wy., U.S.	E6	126
Pathiu, Thai.	G4	48
Pathum Thani, Thai.	E5	48
Pati, Indon.	G7	50
Patía, stm., Col.	G3	86
Patiāla, India	C6	54
Patillas, P.R.	B3	104a
Pati Point, c., Guam	i10	78c
Pativilca, Peru	F2	84
Pātkai Range, mts., Asia	F4	36
Pat Mayse Lake, res., Tx., U.S.	D3	122
Pátmos, i., Grc.	F9	28
Patna, India	F11	54
Patnanongan Island, i., Phil.	C4	52
Patoka, Il., U.S.	F8	120
Patoka, stm., In., U.S.	F10	120
Patoka Lake, res., In., U.S.	F11	120
Patomskoe nagor'e, plat., Russia	E12	34
Patonga, Ug.	D6	66
Patos, Braz.	D7	88
Patos, stm., Arg.	F2	92
Patos, Lagoa dos, b., Braz.	E11	92
Patos de Minas, Braz.	J2	88
Patquía, Arg.	E3	92
Patrai, Gulf of see Patraïkós Kólpos, b., Grc.	E4	28
Patraïkós Kólpos, b., Grc.	E4	28
Patricio Lynch, Isla, i., Chile	I1	90
Patrocínio, Braz.	J2	88
Pattani, Thai.	I5	48
Pattaya, Thai.	F5	48
Patten, Me., U.S.	D8	110
Patterson, Ca., U.S.	F4	134
Patterson, Ga., U.S.	E3	116
Patterson, Mount, mtn., Yk., Can.	C4	106
Patti, Golfo di, b., Italy	F9	24
Pattison, Ms., U.S.	F8	122
Pattoki, Pak.	C4	54
Pattonsburg, Mo., U.S.	D3	120
Pattukkottai, India	F4	53
Pattullo, Mount, mtn., B.C., Can.	D3	106
Patuākhāli, Bngl.	G13	54
Patuca, stm., Hond.	E5	102
Pátzcuaro, Mex.	F8	100
Pau, Fr.	F5	18
Pau, Gave de, stm., Fr.	F5	18
Pau Brasil, Braz.	H6	88
Pau dos Ferros, Braz.	D6	88
Pauh, Indon.	E3	50
Pauini, stm., Braz.	E4	84
Pauini, stm., Braz.	H10	86
Pauk, Mya.	B2	48
Pauksa Taung, mtn., Mya.	C2	48
Paul, Id., U.S.	H13	136
Paulden, Az., U.S.	I4	132
Paulding, Ms., U.S.	E9	122
Paulicéia, Braz.	D6	90
Paulina Peak, mtn., Or., U.S.	G5	136
Pauline, Mount, mtn., Can.	C11	138
Paulino Neves, Braz.	B4	88
Paulistana, Braz.	E5	88
Paulistas, Braz.	J4	88
Paullina, Ia., U.S.	B2	120
Paulo Afonso, Braz.	E6	88
Paulo Afonso, Cachoeira de, wtfl., Braz.	E6	88
Paulpietersburg, S. Afr.	E10	70
Pauls Valley, Ok., U.S.	G11	128
Pauma, Mya.	D3	48
Paungde, Mya.	C2	48
Pauri, India	C7	54
Pauto, stm., Col.	E6	86
Pavia, Italy	E6	22
Pavilion, B.C., Can.	F9	138
Pavilosta, Lat.	D4	10
Pavlikeni, Blg.	F12	26
Pavlodar, Kaz.	D13	32
Pavlof Volcano, vol., Ak., U.S.	E7	140
Pavlovo, Russia	I20	8
Pavlovsk, Russia	A13	10
Pavlovsk, Russia	D14	32
Pavlovskij Posad, Russia	E21	10
Pavullo nel Frignano, Italy	F7	22
Pavuvu Island, i., Sol. Is.	e8	79b
Pawan, stm., Indon.	D7	50
Pawhuska, Ok., U.S.	E12	128
Pawn, stm., Mya.	C3	48
Pawnee, Il., U.S.	E8	120
Pawnee, Ok., U.S.	A2	122
Pawnee, stm., Ks., U.S.	C9	128
Pawnee Rock, Ks., U.S.	C9	128
Pawni, India	H7	54
Pawota, Mya.	D3	48
Paw Paw, Mi., U.S.	F4	112
Pawtucket, R.I., U.S.	C14	114
Paxoí, i., Grc.	D3	28
Paxson, Ak., U.S.	D10	140
Paxton, Ne., U.S.	F11	126
Paxton, Il., U.S.	E9	120
Payakumbuh, Indon.	D2	50
Payamli, Tur.	A9	58
Payerne, Switz.	D3	22
Payette, Id., U.S.	F10	136
Payette, stm., Id., U.S.	G10	136
Payette, North Fork, stm., Id., U.S.	F11	136
Payette, South Fork, stm., Id., U.S.	F11	136
Payne, Oh., U.S.	C1	114
Payne, Lac, l., Qc., Can.	D16	106
Paynes Find, Austl.	E3	74
Paynton, Sk., Can.	A5	124
Paysandú, Ur.	F8	92
Payson, Az., U.S.	I5	132
Payson, Il., U.S.	E6	120
Payson, Ut., U.S.	C5	132
Pazar, Tur.	A5	58
Pazarbaşı Burnu, c., Tur.	B13	28
Pazarcık, Tur.	A8	58
Pazardžik, Blg.	G11	26
Pazaryeri, Tur.	D12	28
Pčevža, Russia	A15	10
Pe, Mya.	F4	48
Pea, stm., U.S.	F12	122
Peabody, Ks., U.S.	C11	128
Peabody, Ma., U.S.	B14	114
Peace, stm., Fl., U.S.	I4	116
Peace, stm., Can.	D8	106
Peace River, Ab., Can.	D7	106
Peach Orchard, Ar., U.S.	C3	116
Peach Springs, Az., U.S.	H3	132
Peak District National Park, p.o.i., Eng., U.K.	H11	12
Peak Downs, Austl.	D7	76
Peak Hill, Austl.	E3	74
Peak Hill, Austl.	I7	76
Peãldoajvi, mtn., Fin.	B12	8
Peale, Mount, mtn., Ut., U.S.	E7	132
Pearisburg, Va., U.S.	G5	114
Pearl, Il., U.S.	E7	120
Pearl, stm., U.S.	F9	122
Pearland, Tx., U.S.	H3	122
Pearl Harbor, b., Hi., U.S.	b3	78a
Pearl Peak, mtn., Nv., U.S.	C1	132
Pearl River, La., U.S.	G9	122
Pearsall, Tx., U.S.	E8	130
Pearson, Ga., U.S.	E3	116
Peary Land, reg., Grnld.	A18	141
Pebane, Moz.	D6	68
Pebas, Peru	D3	84
Pebble Island, i., Falk. Is.	J5	90
Pecan Gap, Tx., U.S.	D2	122
Peçanha, Braz.	J4	88
Peças, Ilha das, i., Braz.	B13	92
Pecatonica, Il., U.S.	B8	120
Pecatonica, stm., U.S.	B7	120
Pečenga, Russia	B14	8
Pechora see Pečora, Russia	A8	32
Pechora Bay see Pečorskaja guba, b., Russia	A8	32
Pečora (Pechora), stm., Russia	A8	32
Pecoraro, Monte, mtn., Italy	F10	24
Pečorskaja guba, b., Russia	A8	32
Pečory, Russia	C10	10
Pecos, stm., U.S.	F12	98
Pecos National Monument, p.o.i., N.M., U.S.	F3	128
Pécs, Hung.	C5	26
Pedana, India	C5	53
Pedasi, Pan.	I7	102
Pedder, Lake, res., Austl.	o12	77a
Peddie, S. Afr.	H8	70
Pededze, stm., Eur.	C10	10
Pedernales, Dom. Rep.	C12	102
Pedernales, Ven.	C10	86
Pedernales, stm., Tx., U.S.	D9	130
Pedernales, Salar de, pl., Chile	C3	92
Pedra Azul, Braz.	I5	88
Pedra Branca, Braz.	C6	88
Pedra Lume, C.V.	k10	65a
Pedras de Fogo, Braz.	D8	88
Pedras Salgadas, Port.	C3	20
Pedraza, Col.	B4	86
Pedregal, Ven.	B6	86
Pedro, Point, c., Sri L.	G5	53
Pedro Afonso, Braz.	E1	88
Pedro Avelino, Braz.	C7	88
Pedro Cays, is., Jam.	D9	102
Pedro Gomes, Braz.	G7	84
Pedro II, Braz.	C5	88
Pedro II, Ilha, i., S.A.	G8	86
Pedro Juan Caballero, Braz.	D5	90
Pedro Leopoldo, Braz.	J3	88
Pedro Osório, Braz.	E11	92
Pedro R. Fernández, Arg.	D8	92
Pedro Velho, Braz.	D8	88
Peebles, Scot., U.K.	F9	12
Peebles, Oh., U.S.	F2	114
Pee Dee, stm., U.S.	A6	116
Peekskill, N.Y., U.S.	C12	114
Peel, I. of Man.	G8	12
Peel, stm., Can.	B4	106
Peel Point, c., N.T., Can.	B17	140
Peel Sound, strt., Nu., Can.	A11	106
Peene, stm., Ger.	C9	16
Peerless, Mt., U.S.	F8	124
Peesane, Sk., Can.	B10	124
Pegasus Bay, b., N.Z.	F5	80
Pegnitz, Ger.	G7	16
Pegu, Mya.	D3	48
Pegu Yoma, mts., Mya.	C2	48
Pegyš, Russia	E24	8
Pehlivanköy, Tur.	B9	28
Pehuajó, Arg.	G7	92
Peian see Bei'an, China	B10	36
Peiching see Beijing, China	B7	42
Peihai see Beihai, China	K3	42
Peikang, Tai.	J9	42
Peine, Ger.	D6	16
Peine, Pointe à, c., Dom.	j6	105c
Peinnechaung, i., Mya.	I14	54
Peiping see Beijing, China	B7	42
Peipus, Lake, l., Eur.	B10	10
Peiraiás (Piraeus), Grc.	F6	28
Peissenberg, Ger.	I7	16
Peixe, Braz.	G1	88
Peixian, China	D7	42
Peixoto, Represa de, res., Braz.	K2	88
Pekalongan, Indon.	G6	50
Pekan, Malay.	K6	48
Pekanbaru, Indon.	C2	50
Pekin, Il., U.S.	D8	120
Pekin, In., U.S.	F11	120
Peking see Beijing, China	B7	42
Pekul'nej, hrebet, mts., Russia	C24	34
Pelabohan Klang, Malay.	K5	48
Pelabuhanratu, Indon.	G5	50
Pelagie, Isole, is., Italy	I6	24
Pelaihari, Indon.	E9	50
Pelalawan, Indon.	C2	50
Pelczyce, Pol.	C11	16
Peleduj, Russia	C20	32
Pelée, Montagne, vol., Mart.	k6	105c
Pelee, Point, c., On., Can.	G7	112
Pelee Island, i., On., Can.	G7	112
Pelega, Vârful, mtn., Rom.	D9	26
Peleliu see Beliliou, i., Palau	D9	44
Peleng, Pulau, i., Indon.	F7	44
Pelham, Al., U.S.	D12	122
Pelham, Ga., U.S.	E1	116
Pelhřimov, Czech Rep.	G11	16
Pelican, Ak., U.S.	E12	140
Pelican Bay, b., Mb., Can.	B13	124
Pelican Lake, Wi., U.S.	F9	118
Pelican Lake, l., Mb., Can.	E14	124
Pelican Lake, l., Mb., Can.	C5	118
Pelican Lake, l., Mb., Can.	B13	124
Pelican Rapids, Mb., Can.	B13	124
Pelican Rapids, Mn., U.S.	E2	118
Pelister, Nacionalni Park, p.o.i., Mac.	B4	28
Peljekaise Nationalpark see Pieljekaise Nationalpark, p.o.i., Swe.	C6	8
Pelješac, Poluotok, pen., Cro.	H14	22
Pelješina, Russia	B15	10
Pella, Ia., U.S.	C5	120
Pella, sci., Grc.	C5	28
Pell City, Al., U.S.	D12	122
Pellegrini, Arg.	H6	92
Pellegrini, Lago, l., Arg.	I4	92
Pello, Fin.	C11	8
Pellworm, i., Ger.	B4	16
Pelly, Sk., Can.	C12	124
Pelly, stm., Yk., Can.	C4	106
Pelly Bay, b., Nu., Can.	B12	106
Pelly Crossing, Yk., Can.	C3	106
Pelly Lake, l., Nu., Can.	B10	106
Pelly Mountains, mts., Yk., Can.	C4	106
Pelón de Ñado, mtn., Mex.	C4	100
Peloponnese see Pelopónnisos, pen., Grc.	F5	28
Pelopónnisos, state, Grc.	F5	28
Pelopónnisos (Peloponnesus), pen., Grc.	F5	28
Pelotas, Braz.	E11	92
Pelotas, stm., Braz.	C12	92
Pelusium Bay see Tina, Khalîg el-, b., Egypt	G3	58
Pemadumcook Lake, l., Me., U.S.	E7	110
Pemalang, Indon.	G6	50
Pemangkat, Indon.	C6	50
Pematangsiantar, Indon.	B1	50
Pemba, Moz.	C7	68
Pemba, Zam.	D4	68
Pemba Island, i., Tan.	F7	66
Pemberton, Austl.	F3	74
Pemberton, B.C., Can.	F8	138
Pembina, N.D., U.S.	C1	124
Pembina, stm., N.A.	C16	124
Pembina Hills, hills, N.A.	E15	124
Pembroke, On., Can.	C12	112
Pembroke, Wales, U.K.	J8	12
Pembroke, Ga., U.S.	D4	116
Pembroke, Ky., U.S.	H10	120
Pembroke, Me., U.S.	E9	110
Pembroke, N.C., U.S.	B6	116
Pembroke, Cape, c., Nu., Can.	C14	106
Pembroke Pines, Fl., U.S.	K5	116
Pembrooke National Park, p.o.i., Wales, U.K.	J7	12
Pembuang, Indon.	D8	50

Name	Map Ref.	Page

Pemigewasset, stm., N.H., U.S. ... G5 110
Pemuco, Chile ... H1 92
Peñafiel, Port. ... C2 20
Peñalara, Pico de, mtn., Spain ... D6 20
Penalva, Braz. ... B3 88
Penang see George Town, Malay. ... J4 48
Peñaranda de Bracamonte, Spain ... D5 20
Pen Argyl, Pa., U.S. ... D10 114
Peñarroya-Pueblonuevo, Spain ... F5 20
Peñas, Cabo de, c., Spain ... A5 20
Penas, Golfo de, b., Chile ... I2 90
Penasco, N.M., U.S. ... E3 128
Pench National Park, p.o.i., India ... H7 54
Pendembu, S.L. ... H2 64
Pendembu, S.L. ... H2 64
Pendências, Braz. ... C7 88
Pendleton, In., U.S. ... H4 112
Pendleton, Or., U.S. ... E8 136
Pendleton, S.C., U.S. ... B3 116
Pendolo, Indon. ... E12 50
Pend Oreille, stm., N.A. ... B9 136
Pend Oreille, Lake, l., Id., U.S. ... B10 136
Pendžikent, Taj. ... B10 56
Penebel, Indon. ... H9 50
Penedo, Braz. ... F7 88
Penetanguishene, On., Can. ... D9 112
Peneus see Pineiós, stm., Grc. ... D5 28
Penfield, Pa., U.S. ... C7 114
Penganga, stm., India ... H6 54
Penghu, China ... I8 42
P'enghu Ch'üntao (Pescadores), is., Tai. ... J8 42
P'enghu Shuitao, strt., Tai. ... J8 42
Pengkou, China ... I7 42
Penglai, China ... C9 42
Pengpu see Bengbu, China E7 42
Pengshui, China ... G2 42
Pengwaluote Shan, mtn., China ... B11 54
Pengxi, China ... F1 42
Pengxian, China ... E5 36
Pengze, China ... G7 42
Penha, Braz. ... C13 92
Penhsi see Benxi, China ... D5 38
Penibética, Cordillera, mts., Spain ... G8 20
Peniche, Port. ... E1 20
Penicuik, Scot., U.K. ... F9 12
Penida, Nusa, i., Indon. ... H9 50
Peninsular Malaysia see Semenanjung Malaysia, hist. reg., Malay. ... K6 48
Peniscola, Spain ... D11 20
Penki see Benxi, China ... D5 38
Pennant Station, Sk., Can. ... D5 124
Penne, Italy ... H10 22
Penneru, stm., India ... D4 53
Penn Hills, Pa., U.S. ... H10 112
Pennine Alps, mts., Eur. ... C13 18
Pennines, mts., Eng., U.K. ... G10 12
Pennington Gap, Va., U.S. ... H2 114
Pennsboro, W.V., U.S. ... E4 114
Pennsylvania, state, U.S. ... C8 114
Penn Yan, N.Y., U.S. ... B8 114
Penny Ice Cap, ice, Nu., Can. ... B17 106
Penny Strait, strt., Nu., Can. ... B6 141
Peno, Russia ... D15 10
Penobscot, stm., Me., U.S. ... F8 110
Penobscot, East Branch, stm., Me., U.S. ... D8 110
Penobscot, West Branch, stm., Me., U.S. ... D7 110
Penobscot Bay, b., Me., U.S. ... F7 110
Penola, Austl. ... K3 76
Peñón de Ifac see Penyal d'Ifac, misc. cult., Spain. ... F11 20
Penong, Austl. ... F6 74
Penonomé, Pan. ... H7 102
Penrhyn, at., Cook Is. ... D11 72
Penrith, Austl. ... I8 76
Penrith, Eng., U.K. ... G10 12
Pensacola, Fl., U.S. ... G11 122
Pensacola Bay, b., Fl., U.S. ... G11 122
Pensacola Mountains, mts., Ant. ... D36 81
Pense, Sk., Can. ... D9 124
Pensilvania, Col. ... E4 86
Pentagon Mountain, mtn., Mt., U.S. ... C13 136
Pentecostes, Braz. ... B6 88
Pentecost Island see Pentecôte, i., Vanuatu j17 79d
Pentecote, state, Vanuatu j17 79d
Pentecôte (Pentecost Island), i., Vanuatu ... j17 79d
Penticton, B.C., Can. ... G11 138
Pentland, Austl. ... C5 76
Pentland Firth, strt., Scot., U.K. ... C9 12
Pentwater, Mi., U.S. ... E3 112
Penuba, Indon. ... D4 50
Peñuelas, P.R. ... B2 104a
Penuguan, Indon. ... E4 50
Penukonda, India ... D3 53
Penyal d'Ifac, misc. cult., Spain ... F11 20
Penza, Russia ... D7 32
Penzance, Eng., U.K. ... K7 12
Penzberg, Ger. ... I7 16
Penžina, stm., Russia. ... D22 34
Penžinskaja guba, b., Russia D21 34
Penžinskij hrebet, mts., Russia ... D22 34
Peoples Creek, stm., Mt., U.S. ... F5 124
People's Democratic Republic of Korea see Korea, North, ctry., Asia ... D7 38
Peoria, Az., U.S. ... J4 132
Peoria, Il., U.S. ... D8 120
Peoria Heights, Il., U.S. ... K9 118
Peotone, Il., U.S. ... C9 120
Pepel, S.L. ... H2 64
Pepin, Wi., U.S. ... G6 118
Pepin, Lake, l., U.S. ... G7 118
Peqin, Alb. ... C13 24
Perabumulih, Indon. ... E4 50
Perak, state, Malay. ... J5 48
Perak, stm., Malay. ... J5 48
Perak, Kuala, b., Malay. ... J5 48
Perales de Alfambra, Spain D9 20
Peralillo, Chile ... G2 92
Peralta, N.M., U.S. ... I10 132
Perambalur, India ... F4 53
Percé, Qc., Can. ... B12 110
Perchas, P.R. ... B2 104a
Perche, Collines du, hills, Fr. ... F9 14
Percival Lakes, l., Austl. ... D4 74
Percy Isles, is., Austl. ... C8 76
Perdida, stm., Braz. ... E2 88
Perdido, stm., U.S. ... G11 122
Perdido, Monte, mtn., Spain. ... B10 20
Perdizes, Braz. ... J2 88
Perdue, Sk., Can. ... B6 124
Perechyn, Ukr. ... H18 16
Perené, stm., Peru ... F2 84
Pereira, Col. ... E4 86
Perelazy, Russia ... G14 10
Peremyšl', Russia ... F18 10
Pereslavl'-Zalesskij, Russia D21 10
Pérez, Arg. ... F7 92
Pergamino, Arg. ... F7 92
Pergamum, sci., Tur. ... D10 28
Pergine Valsugana, Italy. ... D8 22
Perham, Mn., U.S. ... E3 118
Péribonka, Qc., Can. ... B4 110
Péribonka, stm., Qc., Can. ... B5 110
Péribonka, Lac, l., Qc., Can. ... E16 106
Perico, Arg. ... B5 92
Pericumã, stm., Braz. ... B3 88
Peridot, Az., U.S. ... J6 132
Perigirása, Indon. ... D3 50
Périgord, hist. reg., Fr. ... D6 18
Périgueux, Fr. ... D6 18
Perijá, Serranía de, mts., S.A. C5 86
Perim see Barīm, i., Yemen G5 56
Peri-Mirim, Braz. ... B3 88
Perito Moreno, Arg. ... I2 90
Peritoró, Braz. ... C3 88
Periyār, stm., India ... F3 53
Periyar Tiger Reserve, India ... G3 53
Perkasie, Pa., U.S. ... D10 114
Perkins, Ok., U.S. ... A2 122
Perlas, Archipiélago de las, is., Pan. ... H8 102
Perlas, Laguna de, b., Nic. ... F6 102
Perleberg, Ger. ... C7 16
Perlis, state, Malay. ... I5 48
Perm', Russia. ... C9 32
Pernambuco, state, Braz. ... D14 24
Pernambuco, state, Braz. ... E6 88
Pernik, Blg. ... G10 26
Péronne, Fr. ... E11 14
Perote, Mex. ... F10 100
Perow, B.C., Can. ... B4 138
Perpignan, Fr. ... G8 18
Perrault Falls, On., Can. ... A5 118
Perrin, Tx., U.S. ... A9 130
Perrine, Fl., U.S. ... K5 116
Perris, Ca., U.S. ... J8 134
Perro, Laguna del, l., N.M., U.S. ... G3 128
Perro, Punta del, c., Spain ... H4 20
Perros, Bahía de, strt., Cuba ... A8 102
Perros-Guirec, Fr. ... F5 14
Perry, Fl., U.S. ... F2 116
Perry, Ga., U.S. ... D2 116
Perry, Ia., U.S. ... C3 120
Perry, Ks., U.S. ... E2 120
Perry, Mi., U.S. ... B1 114
Perry, Mo., U.S. ... E6 120
Perry, N.Y., U.S. ... B7 114
Perry, Kap, c., Grnld. ... B11 141
Perry Lake, res., Ks., U.S. ... E2 120
Perrysburg, Oh., U.S. ... C2 114
Perry's Victory and International Peace Memorial, hist., Oh., U.S. ... C2 114
Perrysville, Oh., U.S. ... D3 114
Perryton, Tx., U.S. ... E8 128
Perryville, Ak., U.S. ... E8 140
Perryville, Ar., U.S. ... B6 122
Perryville, Ky., U.S. ... G12 120
Perseverancia, Bol. ... B4 90
Persia, Ia., U.S. ... C2 120
Persia see Iran, ctry., Asia ... C7 56
Persian Gulf, b., Asia ... D7 56
Perth, Austl. ... F3 74
Perth, On., Can. ... D13 112
Perth, Scot., U.K. ... E9 12
Perth Amboy, N.J., U.S. ... D11 114
Perth Basin, unds. ... L13 142
Pertominsk, Russia ... D18 8
Peru, Il., U.S. ... C8 120
Peru, In., U.S. ... H3 112
Peru, Ne., U.S. ... D2 120
Peru, N.Y., U.S. ... F3 110
Peru, ctry., S.A. ... E2 84
Peru Basin, unds. ... J5 144
Perućac, Jezero, res., Eur. ... G16 22
Peru-Chile Trench, unds. ... K6 144
Perugia, Italy. ... G9 22
Perugorría, Arg. ... D8 92
Peruíbe, Braz. ... B14 92
Perušić, Cro. ... F12 22
Pervomais'k, Ukr. ... A17 26
Pervomaisk, Russia ... I20 8
Pervomajskij, Russia ... F15 10
Pervoural'sk, Russia ... C9 32
Pervyj Kuril'skij proliv, strt., Russia. ... F20 34
Pesʼ, Russia ... B17 10
Pesaro, Italy. ... G9 22
Pescadores see P'enghu Ch'üntao, is., Tai. ... J8 42
Pescadores Channel see P'enghu Shuitao, strt., Tai. J8 42
Pescara, Italy ... H11 22
Pescara, stm., Italy ... H11 22
Pescasseroli, Italy ... C7 24
Pescia, Italy ... G7 22
Pesé, Pan. ... D1 86
Peshāwar, Pak. ... B3 54
Peshkopi, Alb. ... C14 24
Peshkopija see Peshkopi, Alb. ... C14 24
Peshtigo, Wi., U.S. ... C2 112
Peshtigo, stm., Wi., U.S. ... F10 118
Peski, Bela. ... G7 10
Pesočnoe, Russia ... B22 10
Peso da Régua, Port. ... C3 20
Pesqueria, stm., Mex. ... I8 130
Pessac, Fr. ... E5 18
Pest, state, Hung. ... B6 26
Pêstera, Blg. ... G11 26
Pestovo, Russia ... B18 10
Pêstraja Dresva, Russia ... D20 34
Petacalco, Bahía, b., Mex. ... G7 100
Petah Tiqwa, Isr. ... F5 58
Petal, Ms., U.S. ... F9 122
Petalcingo, Mex. ... G12 100
Petalión, Kólpos, b., Grc. ... F7 28
Petaluma, Ca., U.S. ... E3 134
Petare, Ven. ... B8 86
Petatlán, Mex. ... G8 100
Petawawa, On., Can. ... C12 112
Petén Itzá, Lago, l., Guat. ... D2 102
Petenwell Lake, res., Wi., U.S. ... G8 118
Peterborough, Austl. ... I2 76
Peterborough, On., Can. ... D11 112
Peterborough, Eng., U.K. ... I12 12
Peterhead, Scot., U.K. ... D11 12
Peter Island, i., Br. Vir. Is. ... e8 104b
Peter Isøy, i., Ant. ... B31 81
Peter Lake, l., Nu., Can. ... C12 106
Peterlee, Eng., U.K. ... G11 12
Peter Pond Lake, l., Sk., Can. ... D9 106
Petersburg, Ak., U.S. ... E13 140
Petersburg, In., U.S. ... K9 118
Petersburg, In., U.S. ... F10 120
Petersburg, Tx., U.S. ... B12 122
Petersburg, Tx., U.S. ... H7 128
Petersburg, Va., U.S. ... G8 114
Petersburg, W.V., U.S. ... F6 114
Petershagen, Ger. ... J12 12
Peterson, Ia., U.S. ... B2 120
Peter the Great Bay see Petra Velikogo, zaliv, b., Russia ... C9 38
Petilia Policastro, Italy. ... E10 24
Petit-Bourg, Guad. ... h5 105c
Petit-Canal, N.B., Can. ... E11 110
Petite Rivière Noire, Piton de la, mtn., Mrts. ... i10 69a
Petites-Anses, Guad. ... i5 105c
Petit Jean, stm., Ar., U.S. ... B5 122
Petitot, stm., Can. ... D6 106
Petit Piton, vol., St. Luc. ... m6 105c

Petitsikapau Lake, l., Nf., Can. ... E17 106
Petlād, India ... G4 54
Peto, Mex. ... B3 102
Petoskey, Mi., U.S. ... C5 112
Petra see Al-Baṭrāʾ, sci., Jord. ... H6 58
Petra Velikogo, zaliv, b. (Peter the Great Bay), b., Russia. ... C9 38
Petre, Point, c., On., Can. ... E12 112
Petrić, Blg. ... H10 26
Petrified Forest National Park, p.o.i., Az., U.S. ... I7 132
Petrila, Rom. ... D10 26
Petrinja, Cro. ... E13 22
Petriščevo, Russia ... E19 10
Petrodvorec, Russia ... A12 10
Petrolândia, Braz. ... E6 88
Petrólea, Col. ... C5 86
Petrolia, Tx., U.S. ... G10 128
Petrolina, Braz. ... E5 88
Petrolina de Goiás, Braz. ... I1 88
Petrona, Punta, c., P.R. ... C3 104a
Petropavl see Petropavlovsk, Kaz. ... D11 32
Petropavlovka, Russia ... F10 34
Petropavlovsk, Kaz. ... D11 32
Petropavlovsk-Kamčatskij, Russia ... F20 34
Petrópolis, Braz. ... L4 88
Petros, Tn., U.S. ... H13 120
Petroşani, Rom. ... D10 26
Petrovac, Serb. ... D6 32
Petrovsk, Russia ... D7 32
Petrovskij, Russia ... H18 8
Petrovsk-Zabajkal'skij, Russia ... F10 34
Petrozavodsk, Russia ... F15 8
Petrusburg, S. Afr. ... F7 70
Petrusville, S. Afr. ... G7 70
Petrykau, Bela. ... H11 10
Pettus, Tx., U.S. ... F10 130
Petuhovo, Russia ... C11 32
Peuetsagoe, Gunung, vol., Indon. ... J3 48
Peureulak, Indon. ... J3 48
Peusangan, stm., Indon. ... J3 48
Pevek, Russia ... C23 34
Peza, stm., Russia ... D23 8
Pezawa Taung, mtn., Mya. ... C2 48
Pézenas, Fr. ... F9 18
Pezinok, Slvk. ... H13 16
Pfarrkirchen, Ger. ... H8 16
Pforzheim, Ger. ... H4 16
Pfronten, Ger. ... I6 16
Pfunds, Aus. ... D7 22
Pfungstadt, Ger. ... G4 16
Pha-an, Mya. ... D3 48
Phagwara, India ... C5 54
Phalaborwa, S. Afr. ... C10 70
Phalodi, India ... E4 54
Phaltan, India ... C2 53
Phan, Thai. ... C4 48
Phanat Nikhom, Thai. ... F5 48
Phangan, Ko, i., Thai. ... H5 48
Phangnga, Thai. ... H4 48
Phaniang, stm., Thai. ... D6 48
Phanom Dongrak Range (Dângrêk, Chuŏr Phnum), mts., Asia ... C3 44
Phan Rang, Viet. ... G9 48
Phan Thiet, Viet. ... G9 48
Phan Thong, Thai. ... F5 48
Pharenda, India ... E9 54
Pharr, Tx., U.S. ... H9 130
Phat Diem, Viet. ... B8 48
Phatthalung, Thai. ... I5 48
Phayao, Thai. ... C4 48
Phelps, N.Y., U.S. ... B8 114
Phelps, Wi., U.S. ... E9 118
Phelps Lake, l., N.C., U.S. ... I9 114
Phenix City, Al., U.S. ... E13 122
Phepane, stm., S. Afr. ... E6 70
Phet Buri, Thai. ... F4 48
Phetchabun, Thai. ... D5 48
Phetchabun, Thiu Khao, mts., Thai. ... D5 48
Phetchaburi, Thai. ... F4 48
Phibun Mangsahan, Thai. ... E7 48
Phichai, Thai. ... D5 48
Phichit, Thai. ... D5 48
Philadelphia, Ms., U.S. ... E9 122
Philadelphia, N.Y., U.S. ... D14 112
Philadelphia, Pa., U.S. ... E10 114
Phil Campbell, Al., U.S. ... C11 122
Philip, S.D., U.S. ... C11 126
Philippeville see Skikda, Alg. ... B6 64
Philippeville, Bel. ... D13 14
Philippi, W.V., U.S. ... E5 114
Philippine see Filippoi, sci., Grc. ... B7 28
Philippi, Lake, l., Austl. ... E2 76
Philippine Basin, unds. ... H15 142
Philippines, ctry., Asia ... C4 52
Philippine Sea, s., Asia ... H15 142
Philippine Trench, unds. ... H15 142
Philippolis, S. Afr. ... F7 70
Philipsburg, Mt., U.S. ... D13 136
Philipsburg, Pa., U.S. ... D7 114
Philip Smith Mountains, mts., Ak., U.S. ... C10 140
Philipstown, S. Afr. ... G7 70
Phillaur, India ... C5 54
Phillip Island, i., Austl. ... L5 76
Phillips, Me., U.S. ... F6 110
Phillips, Tx., U.S. ... F7 128
Phillips, Wi., U.S. ... F8 118
Phillipsburg, Ga., U.S. ... E2 116
Phillipsburg, N.J., U.S. ... D10 114
Philo, Il., U.S. ... E9 120
Philo, Oh., U.S. ... E4 114
Philpots Island, i., Nu., Can. ... C10 141
Phimai, Thai. ... E6 48
Phitsanulok, Thai. ... D5 48
Phnom Penh see Phnum Pénh, Camb. ... G7 48
Phnum Pénh (Phnom Penh), Camb. ... G7 48
Phoenix, Az., U.S. ... J4 132
Phoenix, N.Y., U.S. ... E13 112
Phoenix, Or., U.S. ... A3 134
Phoenix Islands, is., Kir. ... D9 72
Phoenixville, Pa., U.S. ... D10 114
Phofung (Sources, Mont-aux-), mtn., Afr. ... F9 70
Phon, Thai. ... E6 48
Phong, stm., Thai. ... D6 48
Phôngsali, Laos ... B6 48
Phon Phisai, Thai. ... D6 48
Phitsanulok, Thai. ... D5 48
Phra Chedi Sam Ong, p., Asia ... E4 48
Phrae, Thai. ... C5 48
Phra Nakhon Si Ayutthaya, Thai. ... E5 48
Phran Kratai, Thai. ... D4 48
Phrom Phiram, Thai. ... D5 48
Phu Cat, Viet. ... E9 48
Phuket, Thai. ... I4 48
Phuket, Ko, i., Thai. ... I4 48
Phu Ly, Viet. ... B7 48
Phum Duang, stm., Thai. ... H4 48
Phumĭ Bâ Khăm, Camb. ... F8 48
Phumĭ Bĕng, Camb. ... F7 48
Phumĭ Chămbák, Camb. ... G7 48
Phumĭ Chŭŏy Sĕng, Camb. ... F8 48
Phumĭ Kâmpóng Srâlau, Camb. ... E7 48
Phumĭ Kâmpóng Trâbêk, Camb. ... F7 48
Phumĭ Kaôh Kêt, Camb. ... F7 48
Phumĭ Khpôb, Camb. ... F7 48

Phumĭ Lvéa Kraôm, Camb.... F6 48
Phumĭ Narŭng, Camb. ... F7 48
Phumĭ Prêk Kák, Camb. ... F7 48
Phumĭ Puŏk Chăs, Camb. ... F6 48
Phumĭ Sâmraông, Camb. ... E6 48
Phumĭ Srê Kôkir, Camb. ... F8 48
Phumĭ Tbêng, Camb. ... F7 48
Phumĭ Thmâ Pôk, Camb. ... F6 48
Phumĭ Tœk Chŏu, Camb. ... F6 48
Phu My, Russia. ... E9 48
Phuoc Long, Viet. ... G8 48
Phuoc Long, Viet. ... E16 16
Phu Pan National Park, p.o.i., Thai. ... D6 48
Phu Quoc, Dao, i., Viet. ... G6 48
Phu Tho, Viet. ... B7 48
Phu Vang, Viet. ... D8 48
Pi, stm., China ... F7 42
Piaçabuçu, Braz. ... F7 88
Piacenza, Italy ... F6 22
Piákia, Austl. ... E9 76
Piancó, Braz. ... D7 88
Pianosa, Isola, i., Italy ... H6 22
Pianosa, Isola, i., Italy ... H12 22
Piapot, Sk., Can. ... E4 124
Piasecznio, Pol. ... D16 16
Piaski, Pol. ... E18 16
Piatã, Braz. ... G5 88
Piatra-Neamţ, Rom. ... B13 26
Piauí, state, Braz. ... D4 88
Piauí, stm., Braz. ... D4 88
Piauí, Morro do, mtn., Braz.. ... H2 88
Piave, stm., Italy ... E9 22
Piaxtla, stm., Mex. ... D5 100
Piazza Armerina, Italy ... G8 24
Pibor Post, Sudan ... F6 62
Pibor, stm., Sudan ... B12 118
Picacho, Az., U.S. ... K5 132
Picardie, hist. reg., Fr. ... E11 14
Picardy see Picardie, hist. reg., Fr. ... E11 14
Picayune, Ms., U.S. ... G9 122
Pichanal, Arg. ... D4 90
Picher, Ok., U.S. ... H3 120
Pichilemu, Chile ... G1 92
Pichilingue, Mex. ... C3 100
Pichis, stm., Peru ... I5 92
Pichincha, state, Ec. ... H2 86
Pichucalco, Mex. ... G12 100
Pickardville, Ab., Can. ... B16 138
Pickens, Ms., U.S. ... E9 122
Pickens, S.C., U.S. ... B3 116
Pickerel, stm., On., Can. ... D10 122
Pickerel Lake, l., Mb., Can. ... B14 124
Pickering, Eng., U.K. ... G12 12
Pickle Lake, On., Can. ... E12 106
Pickstown, S.D., U.S. ... D14 126
Pickton, Tx., U.S. ... D3 122
Pickwick Lake, res., U.S. ... B10 122
Pico, mtn., C.V. ... I10 65a
Pico, i., Port. ... C3 60
Pico da Neblina, Parque Nacional, p.o.i., Braz. ... G9 86
Pico de Orizaba, Parque Nacional, p.o.i., Mex. ... F10 100
Pico de Orizaba, Volcán (Citlaltépetl, Volcán), vol., Mex. ... F10 100
Picos, Braz. ... D5 88
Picquigny, Fr. ... E11 14
Picton, On., Can. ... D12 112
Picton, N.Z. ... E6 80
Picton, Isla, i., Chile ... K3 90
Pictou, N.S., Can. ... E14 110
Pictou Island, i., N.S., Can. ... E14 110
Picture Butte, Ab., Can. ... G18 138
Pictured Rocks National Lakeshore, p.o.i., Mi., U.S. ... B3 112
Picuí, Braz. ... D7 88
Picún Leufú, Arg. ... G3 90
Pidálion, Akrotírion, c., Cyp. ... D5 58
Pidhorodna, Ukr. ... A17 26
Piduratalagala, mtn., Sri L. ... H5 53
Piedecuesta, Col. ... D5 86
Piedmont see Piemonte, state, Italy ... C8 24
Piedmont, Al., U.S. ... D13 122
Piedmont, Mo., U.S. ... G7 120
Piedmont see Piemonte, state, Italy ... F5 22
Piedra, stm., Co., U.S. ... F9 132
Piedra, Cerro, mtn., Chile ... H1 92
Piedra del Águila, Arg. ... H3 90
Piedrafita, Puerto de, p., Spain ... B3 20
Piedrahita, Spain ... D5 20
Piedras, Punta, c., Arg. ... G9 92
Piedras, Punta, c., Ven. ... B11 86
Piedras Blancas, Arg. ... E8 92
Piedras Negras, Guat. ... D2 102
Piedras Negras, Mex. ... A8 100
Pieksämäki, Fin. ... E12 8
Pielinen, l., Fin. ... E13 8
Pieljekaise Nationalpark, p.o.i., Swe. ... C6 8
Piemonte, state, Italy ... F5 22
Pienaarsrivier, S. Afr. ... D8 70
Pienięzno, Pol. ... B16 16
Pieniński Park Narodowy, p.o.i., Pol. ... G16 16
Pienza, Italy ... G8 22
Pierce, Co., U.S. ... G8 126
Pierce, Id., U.S. ... D11 136
Pierce City, Mo., U.S. ... E14 120
Pierpont, S.D., U.S. ... B15 126
Pierre, S.D., U.S. ... C12 126
Pierre, Bayou, stm., La., U.S. ... F5 122
Pierre, Bayou, stm., Ms., U.S. ... F8 122
Pierre Part, La., U.S. ... G7 122
Pierreville, Trin. ... s13 105f
Pierz, Mn., U.S. ... F4 118
Piešt'any, Slov. ... H13 16
Pietarsaari, Fin. ... E10 8
Pietermaritzburg, S. Afr. ... F10 70
Pietersburg, S. Afr. ... C9 70
Pietrasanta, Italy ... G7 22
Piet Retief, S. Afr. ... E10 70
Pietrosu, Vârful, mtn., Rom. ... B12 26
Pigeon, Mi., U.S. ... E7 112
Pigeon, stm., Mb., Can. ... B17 124
Pigeon Forge, Tn., U.S. ... I2 114
Pigeon Lake, l., Ab., Can. ... C16 138
Pigeon River, stm., U.S. ... D10 112
Piggs Peak, Swaz. ... E10 70
Pigüé, Arg. ... H6 92
Pihāri, India ... E8 54
Pihlajavesi, l., Fin. ... F13 8
Pihtipudas, Fin. ... E11 8
Pihíljajjapan, Mex. ... H12 100
Pikalëvo, Russia ... A17 10
Pikangikum, On., Can. ... E12 106
Pikes Peak, mtn., Co., U.S. ... C3 128
Pikeville, Ky., U.S. ... G3 114
Pikeville, S. Afr. ... H4 70
Piketon, Oh., U.S. ... E2 114
Pikou, China ... B10 42
Pikounda, Congo ... D3 66
Pila, Pol. ... C12 16
Pila, state, Pol. ... C12 16
Pilanesberg Game Reserve, p.o.i., S. Afr. ... D8 70
Pilão Arcado, Braz. ... E4 88
Pilar, Arg. ... H4 92
Pilar, Para. ... B8 92
Pilar de Goiás, Braz. ... H2 88
Pilar do Sul, Braz. ... A14 92
Pilares, Mex. ... F7 98
Pilas Group, is., Phil. ... G4 52
Pilawa, Pol. ... D17 16

Pilcomayo, stm., S.A. ... D4 90
Pilcomayo, Brazo Norte, stm., Para. ... B8 92
Pilcomayo, Brazo Sur del, stm., S.A. ... B8 92
Pilcomayo, parque Nacional, p.o.i., Arg. ... B8 92
Pilger, Ne., U.S. ... E15 126
Pilgrim's Rest, S. Afr. ... D10 70
Pili, Phil. ... D4 52
Pilibhīt, India ... D7 54
Pilica, stm., Pol. ... E16 16
Pilliga, Austl. ... H7 76
Pilot, The, mtn., Austl. ... K7 76
Pilot Butte, Sk., Can. ... D9 124
Pilot Knob, Mo., U.S. ... G7 120
Pilot Knob, mtn., Id., U.S. ... E11 136
Pilot Mound, Mb., Can. ... E15 124
Pilot Mountain, N.C., U.S. ... H5 114
Pilot Peak, mtn., Nv., U.S. ... E8 134
Pilot Point, mtn., Wy., U.S. ... F16 136
Pilot Rock, Or., U.S. ... E8 136
Pilottown, La., U.S. ... H9 122
Pilsen see Plzeň, Czech Rep. ... G9 16
Pilu, stm., Mya. ... B3 48
Pilzno, Pol. ... G17 16
Pima, Az., U.S. ... K7 132
Pimba, Austl. ... F7 74
Pimenta, Braz. ... F4 88
Pimenta Bueno, stm., Braz. ... B3 88
Pimental, Braz. ... B3 88
Pinang, Pulau, i., Malay. ... J4 48
Pınarbaşı, Tur. ... B16 28
Pinar del Río, Cuba ... A5 102
Pinarello, Fr. ... H15 18
Pınarhisar, Tur. ... B10 28
Pinas, Arg. ... E5 92
Pinatubo, Mount, vol., Phil. ... C3 52
Pincher Creek, Ab., Can. ... G17 138
Pinchi Lake, l., B.C., Can. ... B6 138
Pinckneyville, Il., U.S. ... F8 120
Pinconning, Mi., U.S. ... E5 112
Pindale, Mya. ... B3 48
Pindamonhangaba, Braz. ... L3 88
Pindaré, stm., Braz. ... B3 88
Pindaré-Mirim, Braz. ... B3 88
Pindi Gheb, Pak. ... B4 54
Pindobaçu, Braz. ... F5 88
Pindos Óros (Pindus Mountains), mts., Grc. ... D4 28
Pindus Mountains see Pindos Óros, mts., Grc. ... D4 28
Pine, stm., Mi., U.S. ... E5 112
Pine Apple, Al., U.S. ... F11 122
Pine Barrens, reg., N.J., U.S. ... E11 114
Pine Bluff, Ar., U.S. ... C7 122
Pine Bush, N.Y., U.S. ... C11 114
Pine Castle, Fl., U.S. ... H4 116
Pine City, Mn., U.S. ... F6 118
Pine Creek, Austl. ... B6 74
Pine Creek, stm., Nv., U.S. ... C9 134
Pine Creek, stm., Pa., U.S. ... C8 114
Pine Falls, Mb., Can. ... D17 124
Pinega, Russia ... D20 8
Pinega, stm., Russia ... D20 8
Pine Grove, W.V., U.S. ... E5 114
Pine Hill, Austl. ... D6 76
Pine Hill, Al., U.S. ... F11 122
Pine Hills, Fl., U.S. ... H4 116
Pinehouse Lake, l., Sk., Can. ... D9 106
Pinehurst, Ga., U.S. ... D2 116
Pinehurst, Id., U.S. ... E10 136
Pinehurst, N.C., U.S. ... A6 116
Pinehurst Lake, l., Ab., Can. ... B19 138
Píndos (Peneus), stm., Grc. ... D5 28
Pine Island, Mn., U.S. ... G6 118
Pine Island, i., Fl., U.S. ... J3 116
Pine Island Bay, b., Ant. ... C30 81
Pinellas Park, Fl., U.S. ... I3 116
Pine Mountain, mtn., Ca., U.S. ... H4 134
Pineora, Ga., U.S. ... A8 138
Pine Point, N.T., Can. ... C8 106
Pine Ridge, S.D., U.S. ... D10 126
Pine River, Mb., Can. ... C13 124
Pine River, Mn., U.S. ... E4 118
Pinerolo, Italy ... F4 22
Piñeros, Isla, i., P.R. ... B4 104a
Pines, Isle of see Juventud, Isla de la, i., Cuba ... B6 102
Pines, Lake O' The, res., Tx., U.S. ... E4 122
Pine Swamp Knob, mtn., W.V., U.S. ... E6 114
Pinetop-Lakeside, Az., U.S. ... I6 132
Pinetops, N.C., U.S. ... I8 114
Pinetown, S. Afr. ... F10 70
Pine Valley, val., Ut., U.S. ... F3 132
Pineville, Ky., U.S. ... H2 114
Pineville, La., U.S. ... F6 122
Pineville, Mo., U.S. ... H3 120
Pineville, W.V., U.S. ... G4 114
Pinewood, S.C., U.S. ... C5 116
Ping, stm., Thai. ... D4 48
Pingaring, Austl. ... F3 74
Pingba, China ... H1 42
Pingchang, China ... F2 42
Pingding, China ... C5 42
Pingdingshan, China ... D5 42
Pingdu, China ... C8 42
Pingelly, Austl. ... F3 74
Pingguo, China ... J2 42
Pinghu, China ... F9 42
Pingjiang, China ... G5 42
Pingli, China ... E3 42
Pingliang, China ... D2 42
Pingluo, China ... B2 42
Pingnan, China ... H7 42
Pingnan, China ... J4 42
Pingshan, China ... B5 42
Pingshi, China ... I5 42
Pingtan, China ... I8 42
P'ingtung, Tai. ... J9 42
Pingtang, China ... I1 42
Pingtingshan, China ... E5 42
Pingwu, China ... E5 36
Pingxi, China ... H5 42
Pingxiang, China ... H5 42
Pingxiang, China ... J2 42
Pingyang, China ... H9 42
Pingyao, China ... C5 42
Pingyi, China ... D7 42
Pingyin, China ... C7 42
Pingyuan, China ... C6 42
Pinhão, Braz. ... B12 92
Pinheiro, Braz. ... B3 88
Pinheiros, Braz. ... J5 88
Piní, Pulau, i., Indon. ... C4 50
Pinjarra, Austl. ... F3 74
Pinjug, Russia ... F22 8
Pinkiang see Harbin, China ... B7 38
Pink Mountain, B.C., Can. ... D6 106
Pinnacle Buttes, mtn., Wy., U.S. ... G17 136
Pinnacles National Monument, p.o.i., Ca., U.S. ... G4 134
Pinnaroo, Austl. ... J3 76
Pinneberg, Ger. ... C5 16
Pinos, Mex. ... D8 100
Pinos, Isla de see Juventud, Isla de la, i., Cuba. ... B6 102
Pinos Puente, Spain ... G7 20
Pinrang, Indon. ... E11 50
Pins, Île des, i., N. Cal. ... n17 79d
Pins, Pointe aux, c., On., Can. ... F8 112
Pinsk, Bela. ... H9 10

Pinsk Marshes see Pripet Marshes, reg., Eur. ... H12 10
Pinson, Al., U.S. ... D12 122
Pinta, Isla, i., Ec. ... h11 84a
Pintada Arroyo, stm., N.M., U.S. ... G3 128
Pintados, Chile ... D3 90
Pintasan, Malay. ... A10 50
Pinto Butte, mtn., Sk., Can. ... E6 124
Pintoyacu, stm., Ec. ... H3 86
Pin Valley National Park, p.o.i., India ... C6 54
Pioche, Nv., U.S. ... F2 132
Piombino, Italy ... H7 22
Pioneer Mine, B.C., Can. ... F8 138
Pionerskij, Russia ... F3 10
Pionki, Pol. ... E17 16
Piorini, stm., Braz. ... D5 84
Piorini, Lago, l., Braz. ... D5 84
Piotrków Trybunalski, Pol. ... E15 16
Pio V. Corpuz, Phil. ... E5 52
Piotrkow, state, Pol. ... E15 16
Piove di Sacco, Italy. ... E8 22
Pio XII, Braz. ... B3 88
Pipanaco, Salar de, pl., Arg. ... D4 92
Pipar, India ... E4 54
Piparia, India ... G7 54
Pipar Road, India ... E4 54
Pipe Spring National Monument, p.o.i., Az., U.S. ... G4 132
Pipestem Creek, stm., N.D., U.S. ... G14 124
Pipestone, Mn., U.S. ... H2 118
Pipestone, stm., On., Can. ... E12 106
Pipestone Creek, stm., Can. ... E12 124
Pipestone National Monument, p.o.i., Mn., U.S. ... G2 118
Pipinas, Arg. ... G9 92
Piplán, Pak. ... B3 54
Pipmuacan, Réservoir, res., Qc., Can. ... A6 110
Piqua, Oh., U.S. ... D1 114
Piquet Carneiro, Braz. ... C6 88
Piquiri, stm., Braz. ... B11 92
Piracanjuba, Braz. ... I1 88
Piracanjuba, stm., Braz. ... I1 88
Piracicaba, Braz. ... L2 88
Piracicaba, stm., Braz. ... L2 88
Piracuruca, Braz. ... B3 88
Pirae, Fr. Poly. ... v21 78h
Piraeus see Peiraiás, Grc. ... F6 28
Piraí do Sul, Braz. ... B12 92
Piraju, Braz. ... L1 88
Pirajuí, Braz. ... L1 88
Piram Island, i., India ... H4 54
Piran, Slvn. ... E10 22
Pirané, Arg. ... B8 92
Piranga, Braz. ... K4 88
Piranhas, Braz. ... G7 84
Piranhas, stm., Braz. ... E1 88
Piranhas, stm., Braz. ... C7 88
Piranji, stm., Braz. ... C6 88
Pirapemas, Braz. ... B3 88
Pirapora, Braz. ... I3 88
Pirapozinho, Braz. ... D6 90
Piraquara, Braz. ... B13 92
Pirassununga, Braz. ... K2 88
Pirata, Monte, hill, P.R. ... B4 104a
Piratinga, stm., Braz. ... H2 88
Piratini, Braz. ... E11 92
Piratini, stm., Braz. ... D10 92
Piratuba, Braz. ... C11 92
Piráyú, Braz. ... B9 92
Pire, Port. ... L1 88
Piribebuy, Braz. ... B9 92
Pirin, Parcul Naţionalowe, p.o.i., Blg. ... H10 26
Piripiri, Braz. ... C5 88
Piritu, Ven. ... C7 86
Pirmasens, Ger. ... G3 16
Pirna, Ger. ... F9 16
Pirojpur, Bngl. ... G12 54
Pirot, Serb. ... F9 26
Pirovano, Arg. ... H7 92
Pirovskoe, Russia ... C16 32
Pir Panjāl Range, mts., Asia ... B5 54
Pirtleville, Az., U.S. ... L7 132
Pirttikylä, Fin. ... E9 8
Piru, Indon. ... F8 44
Piru, Ca., U.S. ... I7 134
Pisa, Italy ... G7 22
Pisagua, Chile ... D2 90
Pisco, Peru ... F2 84
Piscolt, Rom. ... B9 26
Písek, Czech Rep. ... G10 16
Pishan, China ... A4 46
Pishchanka, Ukr. ... A15 26
Pisinemo, Az., U.S. ... K4 132
Pismo Beach, Ca., U.S. ... H5 134
Pisticci, Italy ... D10 24
Pistoia, Italy ... G7 22
Pisuerga, stm., Spain ... C6 20
Pit, stm., Ca., U.S. ... B4 134
Pit, North Fork, stm., Ca., U.S. ... B5 134
Pita, Gui. ... G2 64
Pitalito, Col. ... G4 86
Pitanga, Braz. ... B12 92
Pitangui, Braz. ... J3 88
Pitcairn, dep., Pit. ... c28 78k
Piteå, Swe. ... D9 8
Piteälven, stm., Swe. ... D7 8
Piteşti, Rom. ... E11 26
Pithapuram, India ... C6 53
Pithiviers, Fr. ... F11 14
Pithorāgarh, India ... D8 54
Pitinga, stm., Braz. ... H12 86
Pitiquito, Mex. ... F6 98
Pitkjaranta, Russia ... F14 8
Pitljar, Russia ... A11 32
Pitomača, Cro. ... D14 22
Pitrufquén, Chile ... G2 90
Pitt Island, i., B.C., Can. ... C2 138
Pitt Lake, l., B.C., Can. ... G8 138
Pittsboro, N.C., U.S. ... I6 114
Pittsburg, Ks., U.S. ... G3 120
Pittsburg, Tx., U.S. ... E4 122
Pittsburgh, Pa., U.S. ... D6 114
Pittsfield, Il., U.S. ... E7 120
Pittsfield, Ma., U.S. ... B12 114
Pittsfield, Me., U.S. ... F7 110
Pittsfield, N.H., U.S. ... G5 110
Pittston, Pa., U.S. ... C10 114
Pittsview, Al., U.S. ... E13 122
Pittsworth, Austl. ... F8 76
Pituil, Arg. ... D4 92
Pium, Braz. ... F1 88
Piura, Peru ... E1 84
Piute Peak, mtn., Ca., U.S. ... H7 134
Piuxi, Russia ... ...
Pivdennyj Buh, stm., Ukr. ... A17 26
Pizarro, Col. ... E3 86
Pizzo, Italy. ... F10 24
Pjakupur, stm., Russia ... C13 32
Pjalica, Russia ... C18 8
Pjalma, Russia ... E16 8
Pjana, stm., Russia ... H21 8
Pjandž (Panj), stm., Asia ... B11 56
Pjaozero, ozero, l., Russia ... C14 8
Pjasina, stm., Russia ... B6 34
Pjasinskij zaliv, b., Russia ... B5 34
Pjatigorsk, Russia ... F6 32
Pjažieva Sel'ga, Russia ... F16 8
Placentia, Nf., Can. ... j23 107a
Placerville, Ca., U.S. ... E5 134
Placetas, Cuba ... A8 102
Plácido Rosas, Ur. ... F11 92
Plai Mat, stm., Thai. ... E6 48
Plain City, Ut., U.S. ... B4 132
Plain Dealing, La., U.S. ... E5 122
Plainfield, Ct., U.S. ... C13 114
Plainfield, In., U.S. ... I3 112
Plainfield, N.J., U.S. ... D11 114

Plains – Prince of Wales Island I • 45

Name	Map Ref.	Page
Plains, Ga., U.S.	E14	122
Plains, Ks., U.S.	D8	128
Plains, Mt., U.S.	C12	136
Plainview, Mn., U.S.	G6	118
Plainview, Ne., U.S.	E15	126
Plainview, Tx., U.S.	G7	128
Plainville, In., U.S.	F10	120
Plainwell, Mi., U.S.	F4	112
Plakhtiïvka, Ukr.	C16	26
Plamondon, Ab., Can.	B18	138
Plampang, Indon.	H10	50
Planá, Czech Rep.	G8	16
Plana, L'Illa, i., Spain	F10	20
Planada, Ca., U.S.	F5	134
Planalto, Braz.	C11	92
Planchón, Cerro del (El Planchón, Volcán), vol., S.A.	G2	92
Planeta Rica, Col.	C4	86
Plano, Il., U.S.	C9	120
Plano, Tx., U.S.	D2	122
Plantagenet, On., Can.	E2	110
Plantation, Fl., U.S.	J5	116
Plant City, Fl., U.S.	I3	116
Plantersville, Ms., U.S.	C10	122
Plantsite, Az., U.S.	J7	132
Plaquemine, La., U.S.	G7	122
Plasencia, Spain	D4	20
Plaster Rock, N.B., Can.	D9	110
Plasy, Czech Rep.	G9	16
Plata, Isla de la, i., Ec.	H1	86
Plata, Río de la, est., S.A.	G9	92
Plato, Col.	C4	86
Platte, stm., Ne., U.S.	C7	108
Platte, stm., U.S.	E3	120
Platte, Île, i., Sey.	k13	69b
Platte Center, Ne., U.S.	F15	126
Platte City, Mo., U.S.	E3	120
Platteville, Co., U.S.	A4	128
Platteville, Wi., U.S.	B7	120
Plattsburgh, N.Y., U.S.	F3	110
Plattsmouth, Ne., U.S.	D2	120
Plau, Ger.	C8	16
Plauen, Ger.	F8	16
Plav, Serb.	G6	26
Plavsk, Russia	G20	10
Playa Azul, Mex.	G7	100
Playa de Fajardo, P.R.	B4	104a
Playa de Guayanilla, P.R.	B2	104a
Playa de Naguabo, P.R.	B4	104a
Playa de Ponce, P.R.	C2	104a
Playa Noriega, Laguna, l., Mex.	A3	100
Playa Vicente, Mex.	G11	100
Playgreen Lake, l., Mb., Can.	E11	106
Play Ku, Viet.	F8	48
Plaza, N.D., U.S.	F12	124
Pleasant, Mount, hill, N.B., Can.	E9	110
Pleasant Bay, N.S., Can.	D16	110
Pleasantdale, Sk., Can.	B9	124
Pleasant Grove, Ut., U.S.	C5	132
Pleasant Hill, Il., U.S.	E7	120
Pleasant Hill, La., U.S.	F5	122
Pleasant Hill, Mo., U.S.	F3	120
Pleasanton, Ks., U.S.	F3	120
Pleasanton, Tx., U.S.	F9	130
Pleasantville, N.J., U.S.	E11	114
Pleasantville, Pa., U.S.	C6	114
Pleaux, Fr.	D8	18
Plehanovo, Russia	F20	10
Plenty, Sk., Can.	C5	124
Plenty, Bay of, b., N.Z.	C7	80
Plentywood, Mt., U.S.	F9	124
Pleščeevo, ozero, l., Russia	D21	10
Pleseck, Russia	E19	8
Plessisville, Qc., Can.	D5	110
Pleszew, Pol.	E13	16
Plétipi, Lac, l., Qc., Can.	E16	106
Plettenbergbaai, S. Afr.	I6	70
Pleven, Blg.	F11	26
Plevna, Mt., U.S.	A8	126
Plitvička Jezera Nacionalni Park, p.o.i., Cro.	F12	22
Pljevlja, Serb.	F6	26
Pljuskovo, Russia	H16	10
Pljussa, stm., Russia	A11	10
Płock, Pol.	D15	16
Płock, state, Pol.	D15	16
Ploërmel, Fr.	G6	14
Ploiești, Rom.	E12	26
Plomb du Cantal, mtn., Fr.	D8	18
Plomer, Point, c., Austl.	H9	76
Plön, Ger.	B6	16
Płońsk, Pol.	D16	16
Ploskoe, Russia	H21	10
Plotnica, Bela.	H9	10
Ploudalmézeau, Fr.	F4	14
Plovdiv, Blg.	G11	26
Plovdiv, state, Blg.	G11	26
Plumerville, Ar., U.S.	B6	122
Plummer, Id., U.S.	C9	136
Plumridge Lakes, l., Austl.	E5	74
Plumtree, Zimb.	B8	70
Plungė, Lith.	E4	10
Plutarco Elías Calles, Presa, res., Mex.	G8	98
Plymouth, Monts.	D3	105a
Plymouth, Eng., U.K.	K8	12
Plymouth, Ca., U.S.	E5	134
Plymouth, Il., U.S.	D6	120
Plymouth, Ma., U.S.	C15	114
Plymouth, N.C., U.S.	I9	114
Plymouth, Ne., U.S.	A11	128
Plymouth, N.H., U.S.	G5	110
Plymouth, Oh., U.S.	C3	114
Plymouth, Pa., U.S.	C10	114
Plzeň, Czech Rep.	G9	16
Pô, Burkina	G4	64
Po, stm., Italy	F8	22
Po, Foci del, mth., Italy	F9	22
Po, Mouths of the see Po, Foci del, mth., Italy	F9	22
Poarta Orientală, Pasul, p., Rom.	D9	26
Pobè, Benin	H5	64
Pobeda, gora, mtn., Russia	C18	34
Pobedino, Russia	G17	34
Pobedy, pik, mtn., Asia	F14	32
Poblado Cerro Gordo, P.R.	A3	104a
Poblado Jacaguas, P.R.	B2	104a
Poblado Medianía Alta, P.R.	B4	104a
Poblado Santana, P.R.	B2	104a
Pobra de Trives, Spain	B3	20
Pocahontas, Ar., U.S.	H6	120
Pocahontas, Ia., U.S.	B3	120
Poção, Braz.	E7	88
Pocatello, Id., U.S.	H14	136
Počep, Russia	H16	10
Počinok, Russia	D4	32
Pocitos, Salar, pl., Arg.	B4	92
Poço da Cruz, Açude, res., Braz.	E7	88
Poções, Braz.	H5	88
Pocola, Ok., U.S.	B4	122
Pocomoke City, Md., U.S.	F10	114
Poconé, Braz.	G6	84
Pocono Mountains, hills, Pa., U.S.	C10	114
Pocono Summit, Pa., U.S.	C10	114
Poço Redondo, Braz.	E7	88
Poços de Caldas, Braz.	K2	88
Pocrane, Braz.	J5	88
Podbereze, Russia	D13	10
Podborove, Russia	A18	10
Poddębice, Pol.	E14	16
Poddore, Russia	C13	10
Poděbrady, Czech Rep.	F11	16
Podgorica (Titograd), Serb.	G6	26
Podjuga, Russia	F19	8
Podkamennaja Tunguska, Russia	B16	32
Podkamennaja Tunguska, stm., Russia	B16	32
Podlasie, reg., Pol.	D19	16
Podol'sk, Russia	E20	10
Podor, Sen.	F2	64
Podporože, Russia	F16	8
Podravina, reg., Cro.	E15	22
Podtësovo, Russia	C16	32
Podujevo, Serb.	G8	26
Poel, i., Ger.	B7	16
Poelela, Lagoa, l., Moz.	D12	70
Pofadder, S. Afr.	F4	70
Pogar, Russia	H16	10
Poggibonsi, Italy	G8	22
Pogoanele, Rom.	E13	26
Pogoreloe Gorodišče, Russia	D17	10
Pogradec, Alb.	D14	24
Pogradeci see Pogradec, Alb.	D14	24
Pograničnyj, Russia	B9	38
P'ohang, Kor., S.	C2	40
Pohjanmaa, reg., Fin.	D11	8
Pohnpei, i., Micron.	I11	78d
Pohri, India	F6	54
Pohvistnevo, Russia	D8	32
Pöide, Est.	B6	10
Poinsett, Cape, c., Ant.	B16	81
Poinsett, Lake, l., S.D., U.S.	C15	126
Point, Tx., U.S.	E3	122
Point Arena, Ca., U.S.	E2	134
Point Au Fer Island, i., La., U.S.	H7	122
Point Baker, Ak., U.S.	E13	140
Pointe-à-la-Garde, Qc., Can.	B10	110
Pointe a la Hache, La., U.S.	H9	122
Pointe-à-Pitre, Guad.	h5	105c
Pointe-à-Pitre-le Raizet, Aéroport de, Guad.	h5	105c
Pointe du Canonnier, c., Guad.	A1	105a
Point Edward, On., Can.	E7	112
Pointe-Noire, Congo	E2	66
Pointe-Noire, Guad.	h5	105c
Point Fortin, Trin.	s12	105f
Point Hope, Ak., U.S.	C6	140
Point Jupiter, c., St. Vin.	p11	105e
Point Lake, l., N.T., Can.	B8	106
Point Marion, Pa., U.S.	E5	114
Point Pelee National Park, p.o.i., On., Can.	G7	112
Point Pleasant, N.J., U.S.	D11	114
Point Reyes National Seashore, p.o.i., Ca., U.S.	E2	134
Point Roberts, Wa., U.S.	B3	136
Point Salines International Airport, Gren.	q10	105e
Point Sapin, N.B., Can.	D12	110
Poisson Blanc, Lac du, res., Qc., Can.	B14	112
Poissy, Fr.	F10	14
Poitiers, Fr.	H9	14
Poitou, hist. reg., Fr.	C5	18
Poivre Atoll, i., Sey.	k12	69b
Pojarkovo, Russia	G14	34
Pojoaque Valley, N.M., U.S.	F2	128
Pojuca, Braz.	G6	88
Pojuca, stm., Braz.	G6	88
Pokaran, India	E3	54
Pokataroo, Austl.	G7	76
Pokharā, Nepal	D10	54
Poko, D.R.C.	D5	66
Pokrovsk, Russia	D14	34
Pokrovskoe, Russia	H19	10
Pola, stm., Russia	C14	10
Polacca Wash, stm., Az., U.S.	H6	132
Polack, Bela.	E11	10
Pola de Lena, Spain	A5	20
Pola de Siero, Spain	A5	20
Poland, ctry., Eur.	D15	16
Polanów, Pol.	B12	16
Polatlı, Tur.	D15	28
Polcura, Chile	H2	92
Poldnevica, Russia	G22	8
Polebridge, Mt., U.S.	B12	136
Pol-e Khomrī, Afg.	B10	56
Polese see Pripet Marshes, reg., Eur.	H12	10
Polesine, reg., Italy	E8	22
Polewali, Indon.	E11	50
Polgár, Hung.	B8	26
Poli, Cam.	C2	66
Poli, China	D8	42
Policastro, Golfo di, b., Italy	E9	24
Police (Pölitz), Pol.	C10	16
Polička, Czech Rep.	G12	16
Polillo Island, i., Phil.	C3	52
Polillo Islands, is., Phil.	C4	52
Pólis, Cyp.	C3	58
Polist', stm., Russia	C14	10
Polistena, Italy	F10	24
Poljarnyj, Russia	C24	34
Poljarnyj, Russia	B15	8
Poljarnyj Ural, mts., Russia	A10	32
Polk, Ne., U.S.	F15	126
Polk, Pa., U.S.	C6	114
Pol'kino, Russia	B8	34
Pollāchi, India	F3	53
Pöllau, Aus.	C12	22
Pollino, Monte, mtn., Italy	E10	24
Pollock, La., U.S.	F6	122
Pollock, S.D., U.S.	B12	126
Polnovo-Seliger, Russia	C15	10
Polo, Il., U.S.	B8	120
Polomet', stm., Russia	C15	10
Polonnaruwa, Sri L.	H5	53
Polonnaruwa, sci., Sri L.	H5	53
Polotnjanyj, Russia	F19	10
Polotsk see Polack, Bela.	E11	10
Polski Trămbeš, Blg.	F12	26
Polson, Mt., U.S.	C12	136
Poltava, Ukr.	E4	32
Poltimore, Qc., Can.	C14	112
Põltsamaa, Est.	G12	8
Poluj, stm., Russia	A11	32
Polunočnoe, Russia	B10	32
Polur, India	E4	53
Polvijärvi, Fin.	E13	8
Políaigos, i., Grc.	G7	28
Polynesia, is., Oc.	J22	142
Polysajevo, Russia	F6	34
Pomarkku, Fin.	F9	8
Pombal, Braz.	D7	88
Pomerania, hist. reg., Eur.	C11	16
Pomeranian Bay, b., Eur.	B10	16
Pomerene, Az., U.S.	K6	132
Pomerode, Braz.	C13	92
Pomeroy, Ia., U.S.	B3	120
Pomeroy, Wa., U.S.	D9	136
Pomfret, S. Afr.	D6	70
Pomi, Rom.	B10	26
Pomme de Terre, stm., Mn., U.S.	F3	118
Pomme de Terre, stm., Mo., U.S.	G4	120
Pomme de Terre Lake, res., Mo., U.S.	G4	120
Pomona, Ca., U.S.	I8	134
Pomona, Ks., U.S.	F2	120
Pomona Lake, res., Ks., U.S.	F2	120
Pomorskij proliv, strt., Russia	B24	8
Pompano Beach, Fl., U.S.	J5	116
Pompei, sci., Italy	D8	24
Pompejevka, Russia	G15	34
Pompéu, Braz.	J3	88
Pomquet, N.S., Can.	E15	110
Ponass Lakes, l., Sk., Can.	B9	124
Ponazyrevo, Russia	G22	8
Ponca, Ne., U.S.	B1	120
Ponca City, Ok., U.S.	E11	128
Ponca Creek, stm., U.S.	E14	126
Ponce, P.R.	B2	104a
Ponce, Aeropuerto, P.R.	B2	104a
Ponce de Leon, Fl., U.S.	G12	122
Poncha Pass, p., Co., U.S.	C2	128
Pond Creek, Ok., U.S.	E11	128
Ponderay, Id., U.S.	B10	136
Pondicherry (Puducheri), India	F4	53
Pondicherry, state, India	E5	53
Pond Inlet see Mittimatalik, Nu., Can.	A15	106
Pond Inlet, b., Nu., Can.	A15	106
Pondosa, Ca., U.S.	B4	134
Ponente, Riviera di, cst., Italy	F5	22
Ponérihouen, N. Cal.	m15	79d
Ponferrada, Spain	B4	20
Pongolo, stm., S. Afr.	E10	70
Poniatowa, Pol.	E17	16
Ponizove, Russia	E14	10
Ponnaiyār, stm., India	E4	53
Ponnāni, India	F2	53
Ponnūru Nidubrolu, India	C5	53
Ponoj, Russia	C19	8
Ponoj, stm., Russia	C18	8
Ponoka, Ab., Can.	D17	138
Ponorogo, Indon.	G7	50
Pons, Fr.	D5	18
Ponta Delgada, Port.	C3	60
Ponta Grossa, Braz.	B12	92
Pontalina, Braz.	I1	88
Ponta Porã, Braz.	D5	90
Pontarlier, Fr.	H15	14
Pontas de Pedra, Braz.	D8	88
Pontassieve, Italy	G8	22
Pontchartrain, Lake, l., La., U.S.	G8	122
Pontchâteau, Fr.	G6	14
Pont-de-Vaux, Fr.	C10	18
Ponte Alta do Bom Jesus, Braz.	G2	88
Ponte-Caldelas, Spain	B2	20
Ponte de Lima, Port.	C2	20
Pontedera, Italy	G7	22
Pontedeume, Spain	A2	20
Ponte do Púngoè, Moz.	A12	70
Ponteix, Sk., Can.	E6	124
Ponte Nova, Braz.	K4	88
Ponte Serrada, Braz.	C12	92
Pontevedra, Spain	B2	20
Pontevedra, co., Spain	B2	20
Pontiac, Il., U.S.	D9	120
Pontiac, Mi., U.S.	B2	114
Pontianak, Indon.	C6	50
Pontine Islands see Ponziane, Isole, is., Italy	D6	24
Pontivy, Fr.	F5	14
Pontoise, Fr.	E11	14
Pontotoc, Ms., U.S.	C9	122
Pontotoc, Tx., U.S.	D9	130
Pontremoli, Italy	F6	22
Pontresina, Switz.	D6	22
Pont-Rouge, Qc., Can.	D5	110
Ponts, Spain	C12	20
Pont-sur-Yonne, Fr.	F12	14
Pontus Mountains see Doğu Karadeniz Dağları, mts., Tur.	A5	56
Pontypridd, Wales, U.K.	J9	12
Ponyri, Russia	H19	10
Ponziane, Isole (Pontine Islands), is., Italy	D6	24
Poole, Eng., U.K.	K11	12
Pooley Island, i., B.C., Can.	D2	138
Poolville, Tx., U.S.	B10	130
Pooncarie, Austl.	I4	76
Poopó, Bol.	C3	90
Poopó, Lago, l., Bol.	C3	90
Popayán, Col.	F3	86
Pope, Ms., U.S.	C8	122
Popești-Leordeni, Rom.	E13	26
Popham Bay, b., Nu., Can.	C17	106
Popigaj, Russia	B11	34
Popigaj, stm., Russia	B10	34
Popiltah Lake, l., Austl.	I3	76
Poplar, Mt., U.S.	F8	124
Poplar, stm., Can.	B16	124
Poplar, stm., N.A.	F8	124
Poplar, West Fork (West Poplar), stm., N.A.	F8	124
Poplar Bluff, Mo., U.S.	H7	120
Poplar Hill, On., Can.	E12	106
Poplar Point, Mb., Can.	D16	124
Poplarville, Ms., U.S.	G9	122
Popocatépetl, Volcán, vol., Mex.	F9	100
Popoh, Indon.	H7	50
Popokabaka, D.R.C.	F3	66
Popoli, Italy	H10	22
Popondetta, Pap. N. Gui.	b4	79a
Popovo, Blg.	F13	26
Poprad, Slov.	G16	16
Poprad, stm., Eur.	G16	16
Popricani, Rom.	B14	26
Pŏptong-ŭp, Kor., N.	E7	38
Poquoson, Va., U.S.	G9	114
Porangatu, Braz.	G1	88
Porbandar, India	H2	54
Porce, stm., Col.	D4	86
Porcher Island, i., B.C., Can.	E4	106
Porco, Bol.	C3	90
Porcos, stm., Braz.	G3	88
Porcuna, Spain	G6	20
Porcupine, stm., N.A.	B3	106
Pordenone, Italy	D9	22
Pordim, Blg.	F11	26
Poreče, Russia	E18	10
Poreče-Rybnoe, Russia	C22	10
Porhov, Russia	C12	10
Pori (Björneborg), Fin.	F9	8
Porjaguba, Russia	C15	8
Porlamar, Ven.	B10	86
Porog, Russia	E18	8
Poronajsk, Russia	G17	34
Poroshkove, Ukr.	H18	16
Porpoise Bay, b., Ant.	B17	81
Porrentruy, Switz.	C3	22
Porretta Terme, Italy	F7	22
Porsangen, b., Nor.	A11	8
Porsangerhalvøya, pen., Nor.	A11	8
Porsgrunn, Nor.	G3	8
Porsuk, stm., Tur.	D13	28
Portachuelo, Bol.	C4	90
Port Adelaide, Austl.	J2	76
Portadown, N. Ire., U.K.	G6	12
Portage, Mi., U.S.	F4	112
Portage, Ut., U.S.	B4	132
Portage Bay, b., Mb., Can.	C15	124
Portage Lake, l., Mi., U.S.	D10	118
Portage la Prairie, Mb., Can.	E15	124
Portageville, Mo., U.S.	H8	120
Portal, Ga., U.S.	D4	116
Portal, N.D., U.S.	F11	124
Port Alberni, B.C., Can.	G6	138
Portalegre, Port.	E3	20
Portalegre, state, Port.	E3	20
Portales, N.M., U.S.	G5	128
Port Alfred, S. Afr.	H8	70
Port Alice, B.C., Can.	F3	138
Port Allen, La., U.S.	G7	122
Port Alma, Austl.	D8	76
Port Angeles, Wa., U.S.	B3	136
Port Antonio, Jam.	i14	104d
Port Aransas, Tx., U.S.	G10	130
Portarlington, Ire.	H5	12
Port Arthur, Austl.	o13	77a
Port Arthur see Lüshun, China	E4	38
Port Arthur, Tx., U.S.	H4	122
Port Askaig, Scot., U.K.	F6	12
Port Augusta, Austl.	F7	74
Port au Port Peninsula, pen., Nf., Can.	B17	110
Port-au-Prince, Haiti	C11	102
Port-au-Prince, Baie de, b., Haiti	C11	102
Port Austin, Mi., U.S.	D6	112
Port Blair, India	F7	46
Port Borden, P.E., Can.	D13	110
Port Byron, Il., U.S.	J8	118
Port Canning, India	G12	54
Port-Cartier, Qc., Can.	E17	106
Port Chalmers, N.Z.	G4	80
Port Charlotte, Fl., U.S.	J3	116
Port Clinton, Oh., U.S.	C3	114
Port Clyde, Me., U.S.	G7	110
Port Colborne, On., Can.	F10	112
Port Coquitlam, B.C., Can.	G8	138
Port-de-Paix, Haiti	C11	102
Port Dickson, Malay.	K5	48
Porte Crayon, Mount, mtn., W.V., U.S.	F6	114
Port Edward see Weihai, China	C10	42
Port Edward, S. Afr.	G10	70
Port Edwards, Wi., U.S.	G9	118
Porteirinha, Braz.	H4	88
Portel, Braz.	D7	84
Port Elgin, N.B., Can.	D12	110
Port Elgin, On., Can.	D8	112
Port Elizabeth, S. Afr.	H7	70
Port-en-Bessin, Fr.	E8	14
Porter, Tx., U.S.	G3	122
Port Erin, I. of Man	G8	12
Porter Point, c., St. Vin.	o11	105e
Porterville, S. Afr.	H4	70
Porterville, Ca., U.S.	G7	134
Porterville, Ms., U.S.	E10	122
Portete, Bahía, b., Col.	A6	86
Port Fairy, Austl.	L4	76
Port Gamble, Wa., U.S.	C4	136
Port-Gentil, Gabon	E1	66
Port Gibson, Ms., U.S.	F8	122
Port Graham, Ak., U.S.	E9	140
Port-Harcourt, Nig.	I6	64
Port Hardy, B.C., Can.	F3	138
Port Hawkesbury, N.S., Can.	E15	110
Port Hedland, Austl.	D3	74
Port Heiden, Ak., U.S.	E8	140
Port Hill, P.E., Can.	D13	110
Porthmadog, Wales, U.K.	I8	12
Port Hood, N.S., Can.	D15	110
Port Hope, On., Can.	E11	112
Port Hope, Mi., U.S.	E7	112
Port Huron, Mi., U.S.	B3	114
Portimão, Port.	G2	20
Port Isabel, Tx., U.S.	H10	130
Port Jervis, N.Y., U.S.	C11	114
Port Kembla, Austl.	J8	76
Port Lairge see Waterford, Ire.	I5	12
Portland, Austl.	L3	76
Portland, Austl.	I7	76
Portland, Ar., U.S.	D7	122
Portland, In., U.S.	H5	112
Portland, Me., U.S.	G6	110
Portland, N.D., U.S.	G16	124
Portland, Or., U.S.	E4	136
Portland, Tn., U.S.	H11	120
Portland, Tx., U.S.	G10	130
Portland, Bill of, c., Eng., U.K.	K10	12
Portland, Cape, c., Austl.	n13	77a
Portland, Isle of, i., Eng., U.K.	K10	12
Portland Bay, b., Austl.	L3	76
Portland Bight, b., Jam.	j13	104d
Portland Point, c., Jam.	j13	104d
Portlaoise, Ire.	H5	12
Port Lavaca, Tx., U.S.	F11	130
Port Leyden, N.Y., U.S.	E14	112
Port Lincoln, Austl.	F7	74
Port Loko, S.L.	H2	64
Port-Louis, Guad.	h5	105c
Port Louis, Mrts.	h10	69a
Port-Lyautey see Kénitra, Mor.	C3	64
Port MacDonnell, Austl.	L3	76
Port Macquarie, Austl.	H9	76
Port Maria, Jam.	i14	104d
Port McNeill, B.C., Can.	F3	138
Port McNicoll, On., Can.	D10	112
Port Moller, Ak., U.S.	E7	140
Port Morant, Jam.	j14	104d
Portmore, Jam.	j13	104d
Port Moresby, Pap. N. Gui.	b4	79a
Port Morien, N.S., Can.	D17	110
Port Neches, Tx., U.S.	H4	122
Port Nelson, Mb., Can.	D12	106
Portneuf, stm., Qc., Can.	B7	110
Portneuf, stm., Id., U.S.	H14	136
Port Neville, B.C., Can.	F4	138
Port Nolloth, S. Afr.	F3	70
Port Norris, N.J., U.S.	E10	114
Porto, Port.	C2	20
Porto, state, Port.	C2	20
Porto Acre, Braz.	E4	84
Porto Alegre, Braz.	E12	92
Porto Alegre, S. Tom./P.	J6	64
Porto Amboim, Ang.	C1	68
Portobelo, Pan.	H8	102
Porto Calvo, Braz.	E8	88
Porto de Moz, Braz.	D7	84
Porto de Pedras, Braz.	E8	88
Porto dos Gaúchos, Braz.	F6	84
Porto Empedocle, Italy	G7	24
Porto Esperança, Braz.	C5	90
Porto Esperidião, Braz.	G6	84
Porto Feliz, Braz.	L2	88
Portoferraio, Italy	H7	22
Porto Ferreira, Braz.	K2	88
Port of Ness, Scot., U.K.	C6	12
Porto Franco, Braz.	D2	88
Port of Spain, Trin.	s12	105f
Portogruaro, Italy	E9	22
Portola, Ca., U.S.	D5	134
Portomaggiore, Italy	F8	22
Porto Mendes, Braz.	B10	92
Porto Murtinho, Braz.	D5	90
Porto Nacional, Braz.	F1	88
Porto-Novo, Benin	H5	64
Porto Novo, India	F4	53
Port Orange, Fl., U.S.	G5	116
Port Orchard, Wa., U.S.	C4	136
Port Orford, Or., U.S.	H2	136
Porto San Giorgio, Italy	G10	22
Porto Santana, Braz.	D7	84
Porto Santo, i., Port.	C1	64
Porto Santo Stefano, ngh., Italy	H7	22
Porto Seguro, Braz.	I6	88
Porto Tolle, Italy	F9	22
Porto Torres, Italy	D2	24
Porto União, Braz.	C12	92
Porto Válter, Braz.	E3	84
Porto-Vecchio, Fr.	H15	18
Porto Velho, Braz.	E5	84
Portoviejo, Ec.	H1	86
Port Patrick, Vanuatu	m17	79d
Port Perry, On., Can.	D11	112
Port Phillip Bay, b., Austl.	L5	76
Port Pirie, Austl.	F7	74
Portree, Scot., U.K.	D6	12
Port Renfrew, B.C., Can.	H6	138
Port Rowan, On., Can.	F9	112
Port Royal, Jam.	j14	104d
Port Royal, Pa., U.S.	D8	114
Port Royal, S.C., U.S.	D5	116
Port Said see Bûr Sa'îd, Egypt	G3	58
Port Saint Joe, Fl., U.S.	H13	122
Port Saint Johns, S. Afr.	G9	70
Port Saint Lucie, Fl., U.S.	I5	116
Port Sanilac, Mi., U.S.	E7	112
Port Saunders, Nf., Can.	i22	107a
Portsea, Austl.	L5	76
Portsmouth, Dom.	i6	105c
Portsmouth, Eng., U.K.	K11	12
Portsmouth, N.H., U.S.	G6	110
Portsmouth, Oh., U.S.	F2	114
Portsmouth, Va., U.S.	H9	114
Portsoy, Scot., U.K.	D10	12
Port Stanley, On., Can.	F8	112
Port Sudan see Būr Sūdān, Sudan	D7	62
Port Sulphur, La., U.S.	H9	122
Port Talbot, Wales, U.K.	J9	12
Porttipahdan tekojärvi, l., Fin.	B12	8
Port Townsend, Wa., U.S.	B4	136
Portugal, ctry., Eur.	D3	20
Portugalete, Spain	A7	20
Portuguesa, state, Ven.	C7	86
Portuguesa, stm., Ven.	C8	86
Portuguese Guinea see Guinea-Bissau, ctry., Afr.	G1	64
Port Vila, Vanuatu	k17	79d
Portville, N.Y., U.S.	B7	114
Port-Vladimir, Russia	B15	8
Port Wentworth, Ga., U.S.	D4	116
Port Wing, Wi., U.S.	E7	118
Porus, Jam.	i13	104d
Porvenir, Chile	J2	90
Porvoo, Fin.	F11	8
Porzuna, Spain	E6	20
Posadas, Arg.	C9	92
Posadas, Spain	G5	20
Posavina, val., Eur.	E14	22
Pošehon'e, Russia	B22	10
Poseidonos, Naós toy, sci., Grc.	F6	28
Posen, Mi., U.S.	C6	112
Poshan see Boshan, China	C7	42
Posio, Fin.	C12	8
Poso, Indon.	D12	50
Poso, Danau, l., Indon.	D12	50
Poso, Teluk, b., Indon.	D12	50
Pospeliha, Russia	D14	32
Posse, Braz.	H2	88
Possession Island, i., Nmb.	E2	70
Pössneck, Ger.	F7	16
Possum Kingdom Lake, res., Tx., U.S.	B9	130
Post, Tx., U.S.	A6	130
Posta de Jihuites, Mex.	I2	130
Postelle, Tn., U.S.	A1	116
Postmasburg, S. Afr.	F6	70
Postojna, Slvn.	E11	22
Postrervalle, Bol.	C4	90
Postville, Ia., U.S.	A6	120
Potaro, stm., Guy.	E12	86
Potaro-Siparuni, state, Guy.	E12	86
Potchefstroom, S. Afr.	E8	70
Poté, Braz.	I5	88
Poteau, Ok., U.S.	B4	122
Poteet, Tx., U.S.	E9	130
Potenza, Italy	D9	24
Potgietersrus, S. Afr.	D9	70
Poth, Tx., U.S.	E9	130
Potholes Reservoir, res., Wa., U.S.	D7	136
Poti, Geor.	F6	32
Poti, stm., Braz.	C4	88
Potiraguá, Braz.	H6	88
Potiskum, Nig.	G7	64
Potomac, Il., U.S.	H2	112
Potomac, stm., U.S.	F9	114
Potomac, North Fork South Branch, stm., U.S.	F6	114
Potomac, South Branch, stm., U.S.	E7	114
Potomac Heights, Md., U.S.	F8	114
Potosí, Bol.	C3	90
Potosi, Mo., U.S.	G7	120
Potrerillos, Chile	C3	92
Potro, Cerro del (El Potro, Cerro), mtn., S.A.	D3	92
Potsdam, Ger.	D9	16
Potsdam, N.Y., U.S.	F2	110
Pott, Île, i., N. Cal.	I14	79d
Potter, Ne., U.S.	F9	126
Potterville, Mi., U.S.	B1	114
Potts Camp, Ms., U.S.	C9	122
Pottstown, Pa., U.S.	D10	114
Pottsville, Pa., U.S.	D9	114
Pouancé, Fr.	G7	14
Poughkeepsie, N.Y., U.S.	C11	114
Poulan, Ga., U.S.	E2	116
Poulsbo, Wa., U.S.	C4	136
Poultney, Vt., U.S.	G3	110
Poum, N. Cal.	m14	79d
Pouso Alegre, Braz.	L3	88
Poŭthĭsăt, Camb.	F6	48
Poŭthĭsăt, stm., Camb.	F6	48
Poutini see Westland National Park, p.o.i., N.Z.	F3	80
Poutrincourt, Lac, l., Qc., Can.	A2	110
Považská Bystrica, Slov.	G14	16
Povenec, Russia	E16	8
Póvoa de Varzim, Port.	C2	20
Povorino, Russia	D6	32
Povorotnyj, mys, c., Russia	C10	38
Povungnituk, Qc., Can.	C15	106
Povungnituk, stm., Qc., Can.	C15	106
Powassan, On., Can.	B10	112
Poway, Ca., U.S.	K9	134
Powder, stm., Or., U.S.	F9	136
Powder, stm., U.S.	A7	126
Powder, South Fork, stm., Wy., U.S.	D6	126
Powderly, Tx., U.S.	D3	122
Powder River Pass, p., Wy., U.S.	C5	126
Powell, Wy., U.S.	C4	126
Powell, stm., U.S.	H2	114
Powell, Lake, res., U.S.	F5	132
Powell Creek, stm., Austl.	E5	76
Powellhurst, Or., U.S.	E4	136
Powell Lake, l., B.C., Can.	F6	138
Powell River, B.C., Can.	G6	138
Powers, Mi., U.S.	C2	112
Powers, Or., U.S.	H2	136
Powers Lake, N.D., U.S.	F11	124
Powhatan, Va., U.S.	G7	114
Powhatan Point, Oh., U.S.	E4	114
Poxoréu, Braz.	G7	84
Poya, N. Cal.	m15	79d
Poyang Hu, l., China	G7	42
Poyen, Ar., U.S.	C6	122
Poygan, Lake, l., Wi., U.S.	G9	118
Požarevac, Serb.	E8	26
Poza Rica de Hidalgo, Mex.	E10	100
Požega, Cro.	E14	22
Požega, Serb.	F7	26
Poznań, Pol.	D12	16
Poznań, state, Pol.	D12	16
Pozoblanco, Spain	F6	20
Pozo-Cañada, Spain	F9	20
Pozo del Molle, Arg.	F6	92
Pozo del Tigre, Arg.	B7	92
Pozuelos, Ven.	B9	86
Pozzallo, Italy	H8	24
Pozzuoli, Italy	D8	24
Prachatice, Czech Rep.	G10	16
Prachin Buri, Thai.	E5	48
Prachuap Khiri Khan, Thai.	G4	48
Pradera, Col.	F3	86
Prado, Braz.	I6	88
Prados, Braz.	K3	88
Præstø, Den.	A8	16
Prague see Praha, Czech Rep.	F10	16
Prague, Ne., U.S.	F16	126
Prague, Ok., U.S.	B2	122
Praha (Prague), Czech Rep.	F10	16
Praha, state, Czech Rep.	F10	16
Praha, mtn., Czech Rep.	G9	16
Prahova, state, Rom.	D13	26
Prahova, stm., Rom.	E13	26
Praia, C.V.	I10	65a
Praia Grande, Braz.	D13	92
Prainha Nova, Braz.	E5	84
Prairie, Austl.	C5	76
Prairie, stm., Mi., U.S.	G4	112
Prairie City, Ia., U.S.	C4	120
Prairie City, Il., U.S.	D7	120
Prairie Creek, stm., Ne., U.S.	F15	126
Prairie Dog Creek, stm., Ks., U.S.	B8	128
Prairie du Chien, Wi., U.S.	A6	120
Prairie du Sac, Wi., U.S.	H9	118
Prairie River, Sk., Can.	B11	124
Prairies, Coteau des, hills, U.S.	C16	126
Prairies, Lake of the, res., Can.	C12	124
Prairie View, Tx., U.S.	G3	122
Prairie Village, Ks., U.S.	B14	128
Pran Buri, Thai.	F4	48
Pran Buri, stm., Thai.	F4	48
Prānhita, stm., India	B5	53
Praslin, i., Sey.	j13	69b
Prasonísi, Ákra, c., Grc.	H10	28
Praszka, Pol.	E14	16
Prata, Braz.	J1	88
Prata, stm., Braz.	J1	88
Prata, stm., Braz.	I2	88
Pratāpgarh, India	F5	54
Pratápolis, Braz.	K2	88
Pratas Island see Tungsha Tao, i., Tai.	K7	42
Prat de Llobregat see El Prat de Llobregat, Spain	C12	20
Prato, Italy	G8	22
Pratt, Ks., U.S.	D10	128
Prattville, Al., U.S.	E12	122
Pratudão, stm., Braz.	H3	88
Pravdinskij, Russia	D20	10
Pravia, Spain	A4	20
Praya, Indon.	H10	50
Preajba, Rom.	E12	26
Prečistoe, Russia	G19	8
Predeal, Rom.	D12	26
Preeceville, Sk., Can.	C11	124
Preetz, Ger.	B6	16
Pregolja, stm., Russia	F3	10
Pregonero, Ven.	D6	86
Preguiças, stm., Braz.	B4	88
Preila, Lith.	E4	10
Prĕk Poŭthĭ, Camb.	G7	48
Prelate, Sk., Can.	D4	124
Premnitz, Ger.	D8	16
Premont, Tx., U.S.	G9	130
Premuda, Otok, i., Cro.	F11	22
Prenjasi see Prrenjas, Alb.	C14	24
Prentiss, Ms., U.S.	F9	122
Prenzlau, Ger.	C9	16
Preobraženie, Russia	C10	38
Preparis Island, i., Mya.	F7	46
Preparis North Channel, strt., Mya.	E7	46
Preparis South Channel, strt., Mya.	F7	46
Přerov, Czech Rep.	G13	16
Prescott, On., Can.	D14	112
Prescott, Ar., U.S.	D5	122
Prescott, Az., U.S.	I4	132
Prescott, Wi., U.S.	G6	118
Prescott Island, i., Nu., Can.	A11	106
Presidencia de la Plaza, Arg.	C7	92
Presidencia Roca, Arg.	C8	92
Presidencia Roque Sáenz Peña, Arg.	C7	92
Presidente Dutra, Braz.	C3	88
Presidente Epitácio, Braz.	D6	90
Presidente Hayes, state, Para.	B8	92
Presidente Prudente, Braz.	D6	90
Presidio, Tx., U.S.	E3	130
Presidio, stm., Mex.	D6	100
Presnogor'kovka, Kaz.	D11	32
Prešov, Slov.	H17	16
Prespa, Lake, l., Eur.	D14	24
Presque Isle, Me., U.S.	D8	110
Presque Isle, pen., Pa., U.S.	B5	114
Prestea, Ghana	H4	64
Preston, Eng., U.K.	H10	12
Preston, Ia., U.S.	B7	120
Preston, Id., U.S.	A5	132
Preston, Ks., U.S.	D10	128
Preston, Mn., U.S.	H6	118
Prestonsburg, Ky., U.S.	G3	114
Prestwick, Scot., U.K.	F8	12
Preto, stm., Braz.	I2	88
Preto, stm., Braz.	G1	88
Preto, stm., Braz.	B4	88
Preto, stm., Braz.	L4	88
Preto, stm., Braz.	K1	88
Preto, stm., Braz.	I9	86
Preto, stm., Braz.	F3	88
Preto do Igapó-açu, stm., Braz.	E5	84
Pretoria (Tshwane), S. Afr.	D9	70
Pretty Prairie, Ks., U.S.	D10	128
Préveza, Grc.	E3	28
Prey Lvéa, Camb.	G7	48
Prey Vêng, Camb.	G7	48
Pribilof Islands, is., Ak., U.S.	E5	140
Priboj, Serb.	F6	26
Příbram, Czech Rep.	G10	16
Price, Ut., U.S.	D6	132
Price, stm., Ut., U.S.	D6	132
Price Island, i., B.C., Can.	D2	138
Prichard, Al., U.S.	G10	122
Prickly Pear Cays, is., Anguilla	A1	105a
Priddy, Tx., U.S.	C9	130
Priego de Córdoba, Spain	G6	20
Priekule, Lat.	D4	10
Priekule, Lith.	E4	10
Prieska, S. Afr.	F6	70
Priest, stm., Id., U.S.	B10	136
Priest Lake, res., Id., U.S.	B9	136
Priest River, Id., U.S.	B10	136
Prieta, Peña, mtn., Spain	A6	20
Prieto Diaz, Phil.	D5	52
Prievidza, Slov.	H14	16
Prijedor, Bos.	E3	26
Prilep, Mac.	B4	28
Priluki, Russia	A22	10
Primeira Cruz, Braz.	B4	88
Primera, Tx., U.S.	H10	130
Primero, stm., Arg.	E6	92
Primghar, Ia., U.S.	A2	120
Primorsk, Russia	F13	8
Primorskij, Russia	C9	38
Primorskij hrebet, mts., Russia	F10	34
Primo Tapia, Mex.	K8	134
Primrose Lake, l., Can.	E9	106
Prince Albert, Sk., Can.	A8	124
Prince Albert, S. Afr.	H6	70
Prince Albert Sound, strt., N.T., Can.	A7	106
Prince Alfred, Cape, c., N.T., Can.	B15	140
Prince Charles Island, i., Nu., Can.	B15	106
Prince Charles Mountains, mts., Ant.	C11	81
Prince Edward Island, state, Can.	D13	110
Prince Edward Island, i., P.E., Can.	F18	106
Prince Edward Island National Park, p.o.i., P.E., Can.	D13	110
Prince Frederick, Md., U.S.	F9	114
Prince George, B.C., Can.	C8	138
Prince George, Va., U.S.	G8	114
Prince Gustaf Adolf Sea, s., Can.	B4	141
Prince of Wales Island, i., Austl.	B8	74
Prince of Wales Island, i., Nu., Can.	A11	106

Name	Map Ref.	Page
Prince of Wales Island, i., Ak., U.S.	E13	140
Prince of Wales Strait, strt., N.T., Can.	B15	140
Prince Olav Coast, cst., Ant..	B9	81
Prince Patrick Island, i., N.T., Can.	A16	140
Prince Regent Inlet, b., Nu., Can.	A12	106
Prince Rupert, B.C., Can.	E4	106
Prince Rupert Bluff Point, c., Dom.	i5	105c
Princes Islands see Kizil Adalar, is., Tur.	C11	28
Princess Anne, Md., U.S.	F10	114
Princess Astrid Coast, cst., Ant.	C6	81
Princess Charlotte Bay, b., Austl.	B8	74
Princess Martha Coast, cst., Ant.	C4	81
Princess Ragnhild Coast, cst., Ant.	C7	81
Princess Royal Island, i., B.C., Can.	C1	138
Princes Town, Trin.	s12	105f
Princeton, B.C., Can.	G10	138
Princeton, Ca., U.S.	D3	134
Princeton, Il., U.S.	F10	120
Princeton, Ky., U.S.	G9	120
Princeton, Me., U.S.	E9	110
Princeton, Mi., U.S.	B2	112
Princeton, N.C., U.S.	A7	116
Princeton, N.J., U.S.	D11	114
Princeton, Wi., U.S.	H9	118
Princeton, W.V., U.S.	G4	114
Princeville, Qc., Can.	C1	110
Princeville, Il., U.S.	D8	120
Prince William Sound, strt., Ak., U.S.	D10	140
Príncipe, i., S. Tom./P.	I6	64
Principe da Beira, Braz.	F5	84
Prineville, Or., U.S.	F6	136
Pringsewu, Indon.	F4	50
Prinsen Margaretkanaal, can., Neth.	A14	14
Prins Karls Forland, i., Nor.	B27	141
Prinzapolka, stm., Nic.	F5	102
Priozersk, Russia	F14	8
Pripet (Prypjac'), stm., Eur.	H10	10
Pripet Marshes, reg., Eur.	H12	10
Pripoljarnyj Ural, mts., Russia	A9	32
Priština, Serb.	G8	26
Pritchett, Co., U.S.	D6	128
Pritzwalk, Ger.	C8	16
Privas, Fr.	E10	18
Priverno, Italy	C7	24
Privodino, Russia	F22	8
Prizren, Serb.	G7	26
Prjaža, Russia	F15	8
Probolinggo, Indon.	G8	50
Probstzella, Ger.	F7	16
Procida, Isola di, i., Italy	D7	24
Procter, B.C., Can.	G13	138
Proctor, Mn., U.S.	E6	118
Proctor Lake, res., Tx., U.S.	C9	130
Proddatūr, India	D4	53
Proença-a-Nova, Port.	E2	20
Progreso, Mex.	B3	102
Progreso, Mex.	B8	100
Progreso, Mex.	K10	134
Progreso, Ur.	G9	92
Proḥladnyj, Russia	F6	32
Project City, Ca., U.S.	C3	134
Prokopevsk, Russia	D15	32
Prokuplje, Serb.	F8	26
Proletarskij, Russia	E20	10
Prome (Pyè), Mya.	C2	48
Pronja, stm., Bela.	G14	10
Pronja, stm., Russia	F21	10
Prony, Baie de, b., N. Cal.	n16	79d
Prophet, stm., B.C., Can.	D6	106
Prophetstown, Il., U.S.	C8	120
Propriá, Braz.	F7	88
Propriano, Fr.	H14	18
Proserpine, Austl.	C7	76
Prosna, stm., Pol.	E14	16
Prospect, Oh., U.S.	D2	114
Prosperidad, Phil.	F5	52
Prosser, Wa., U.S.	D7	136
Prostějov, Czech Rep.	G12	16
Prostki, Pol.	C18	16
Proston, Austl.	F8	76
Proszowice, Pol.	F16	16
Protection, Ks., U.S.	D9	128
Protem, S. Afr.	I5	70
Protva, stm., Russia	F20	10
Provadija, Blg.	F14	26
Prøven (Kangersuatsiaq), Grnld.	C14	141
Provence, hist. reg., Fr.	F12	18
Providence, Ky., U.S.	G10	120
Providence, R.I., U.S.	C14	114
Providence, Ut., U.S.	B5	132
Providence, Atoll de, i., Sey.	k12	69b
Providence, Cape, c., N.Z.	H2	80
Providencia, Mex.	G4	130
Providencia, Isla de, i., Col.	F7	102
Providenciales, i., T./C. Is.	B11	102
Providenija, Russia	D26	34
Provincetown, Ma., U.S.	B15	114
Provins, Fr.	F12	14
Provo, Ut., U.S.	C5	132
Provo, stm., Ut., U.S.	C5	132
Provost, Ab., Can.	B3	124
Prozor, Bos.	F14	24
Prudentópolis, Braz.	B12	92
Prudhoe Bay, Ak., U.S.	B10	140
Prudhoe Bay, i., Austl.	C7	76
Prudnik, Pol.	F13	16
Pruszków, Pol.	D16	16
Prut, stm., Eur.	D15	26
Pružany, Bela.	H7	10
Prydz Bay, b., Ant.	B12	81
Pryluky, Ukr.	D4	32
Pryor, Ok., U.S.	H2	120
Przasnysz, Pol.	D16	16
Przedbórz, Pol.	E15	16
Przemyśl, Pol.	G18	16
Przemyśl, state, Pol.	F18	16
Przeworsk, Pol.	F18	16
Psachná, Grc.	E6	28
Pskov, Russia	C11	10
Pskov, Lake, l., Eur.	B11	10
Pskovskaja oblast', co., Russia	C11	10
Pszczyna, Pol.	G14	16
Ptarmigan, Cape, c., N.T.	A7	106
Ptolemais, Grc.	C4	28
Ptuj, Slvn.	D12	22
Puakatike, Volcán, vol., Chile	e30	78l
Puán, Arg.	H6	92
Pucallpa, Peru	E3	84
Pucará, Bol.	D4	90
Pučeveem, stm., Russia	C23	34
Pučež, Russia	H20	8
Pucheng, China	H8	42
Pucheng, China	D3	42
Púchov, Slov.	G14	16
Pučišća, Cro.	G13	22
Pudasjärvi, Fin.	D12	8
Pudož, Russia	F17	8
Puduari, stm., Braz.	I11	86
Puducherry see Pondicherry, India	F4	53
Pudukkottai, India	F4	53
Puebla, state, Mex.	F10	100
Puebla de Don Fadrique, Spain	G8	20
Puebla de Sanabria, Spain	B4	20
Puebla de Zaragoza, Mex.	F9	100
Pueblito, Mex.	E2	130
Pueblito de Ponce, P.R.	B1	104a
Pueblo, Co., U.S.	C4	128
Pueblonuevo, Col.	C4	86
Pueblo Nuevo, Mex.	B2	104a
Pueblo Nuevo, Ven.	B7	86
Pueblo Viejo, Laguna, l., Mex.	D10	100
Pueblo Yaqui, Mex.	B4	100
Puente-Caldelas see Ponte-Caldelas, Spain	B2	20
Puente del Arzobispo, Spain	E5	20
Puentedeume see Pontedeume, Spain	A2	20
Puente Genil, Spain	G6	20
Puerca, Punta, c., P.R.	B4	104a
Puerco, stm., N.M., U.S.	I10	132
Puerco, stm., U.S.	I7	132
Puerto Acosta, Bol.	C3	90
Puerto Adela, Para.	B10	92
Puerto Aisén, Chile	I2	90
Puerto Alegre, Bol.	B4	90
Puerto Ángel, Mex.	H10	100
Puerto Arista, Mex.	H11	100
Puerto Armuelles, Pan.	H6	102
Puerto Asís, Col.	G3	86
Puerto Ayacucho, Ven.	E8	86
Puerto Baquerizo Moreno, Ec.	i12	84a
Puerto Barrios, Guat.	E3	102
Puerto Bermúdez, Peru	F3	84
Puerto Berrío, Col.	D4	86
Puerto Bolívar, Col.	A5	86
Puerto Boyacá, Col.	E4	86
Puerto Cabello, Ven.	B7	86
Puerto Cabezas, Nic.	F6	102
Puerto Carreño, Col.	D8	86
Puerto Chicama, Peru	E2	84
Puerto Colombia, Col.	B4	86
Puerto Cortés, Hond.	E3	102
Puerto Cumarebo, Ven.	B7	86
Puerto Deseado, Arg.	I3	90
Puerto Escondido, Mex.	H10	100
Puerto Escondido, c., Ven.	p20	104g
Puerto Esperanza, Arg.	B10	92
Puerto Fonciere, Para.	D5	90
Puerto Francisco de Orellana, Ec.	H3	86
Puerto Heath, Bol.	B3	90
Puerto Iguazú, Arg.	B10	92
Puerto Ingeniero Ibáñez, Chile	I2	90
Puerto Inírida, Col.	F7	86
Puerto Juárez, Mex.	B4	102
Puerto La Cruz, Ven.	B9	86
Puerto Leguízamo, Col.	H4	86
Puerto Libertad, Mex.	G6	98
Puerto Limón, Col.	F5	86
Puerto Limón, C.R.	G6	102
Puertollano, Spain	F6	20
Puerto Lobos, Arg.	H4	90
Puerto López, Col.	E5	86
Puerto Madero, Mex.	H12	100
Puerto Madryn, Arg.	H3	90
Puerto Maldonado, Peru	F4	84
Puerto Montt, Chile	H2	90
Puerto Morelos, Mex.	B4	102
Puerto Natales, Chile	J2	90
Puerto Padre, Cuba	B9	102
Puerto Páez, Ven.	D8	86
Puerto Palmer, Pico, mtn., Mex.	G6	130
Puerto Peñasco, Mex.	F6	98
Puerto Pinasco, Para.	D5	90
Puerto Pirámides, Arg.	H4	90
Puerto Piray, Arg.	C10	92
Puerto Pirítu, Ven.	B9	86
Puerto Plata, Dom. Rep.	C12	102
Puerto Princesa, Phil.	F2	52
Puerto Real, P.R.	B1	104a
Puerto Real, Spain	H4	20
Puerto Rico, Arg.	C10	92
Puerto Rico, Arg.	B3	90
Puerto Rico, Col.	G4	86
Puerto Rico, dep., N.A.	b3	104a
Puerto Rico Trench, unds.	G7	144
Puerto Rondón, Col.	D6	86
Puerto San José, Guat.	F2	102
Puerto San Julián, Arg.	I3	90
Puerto Santa Cruz, Arg.	J3	90
Puerto Sastre, Para.	D5	90
Puerto Suárez, Bol.	C5	90
Puerto Tejada, Col.	F3	86
Puerto Tolosa, Col.	H4	86
Puerto Umbría, Col.	G3	86
Puerto Vallarta, Mex.	E6	100
Puerto Varas, Chile	H2	90
Puerto Victoria, Arg.	C10	92
Puerto Viejo, C.R.	G5	102
Puerto Villamil, Ec.	i11	84a
Puerto Villamizar, Col.	C5	86
Puerto Wilches, Col.	D5	86
Puerto Yabapobó, Para.	D5	90
Pueyrredón, Lago (Cochrane, Lago), l., S.A.	I2	90
Pūgačov, Russia	D7	32
Puget Sound, strt., Wa., U.S.	C4	136
Puglia, state, Italy	C10	24
Pugö-ri, Kor., N.	D9	38
Puhi-waero see South West Cape, c., N.Z.	H2	80
Puhja, Est.	B9	10
Pui, India	C14	26
Puigcerdà, Spain	B12	20
Puigmal d' Err (Puigmal), mtn., Eur.	G8	18
Pujiang, China	G8	42
Pujiang, China	G8	42
Pujilí, Ec.	H2	86
Puka see Pukë, Alb.	B13	24
Pukaki, Lake, l., N.Z.	F4	80
Pukch'ŏng-up, Kor., N.	D8	38
Pukë, Alb.	B13	24
Pukekohe, N.Z.	C6	80
Pukhrāyān, India	E7	54
Puksoozero, Russia	E19	8
Pula, Cro.	F10	22
Pula, Italy	F3	24
Pulacayo, Bol.	D3	90
Pulantien see Xinjin, China	B9	42
Pulap, at., Micron.	C5	72
Púlar, Cerro, vol., Chile	B3	92
Pulaski, N.Y., U.S.	E13	112
Pulaski, Tn., U.S.	B11	122
Pulaski, Va., U.S.	G5	114
Pulaudok, Indon.	E3	50
Pulau Pinang, state, Malay.	J5	48
Puławy, Pol.	E18	16
Pulgaon, India	H7	54
Puli, Tai.	J9	42
Pulicat, India	E5	53
Pulicat Lake, l., India	E4	53
Puliyangudi, India	G3	53
Pullman, Wa., U.S.	D9	136
Pulog, Mount, mtn., Phil.	B3	52
Pulon'ga, Russia	C18	8
Pułtusk, Pol.	D16	16
Puma Yumco, l., China	D13	54
Pumei, China	A7	48
Pumpkin Buttes, mtn., Wy., U.S.	D7	126
Pumpkin Creek, stm., Mt., U.S.	B7	126
Pumpkin Creek, stm., Ne., U.S.	F10	126
Puná, Isla, i., Ec.	I1	86
Punaauia, Fr. Poly.	v21	78h
Punakha, Bhu.	E12	54
Punan, Indon.	B10	50
Punata, Bol.	C3	90
Pūnch, India	B5	54
Punchaw, B.C., Can.	C7	138
Pune (Poona), India	B1	53
Punganūru, India	E4	53
P'ungsan-ŭp, Kor., N.	D7	38
Pungué, stm., Afr.	A12	70
Punia, D.R.C.	E5	66
Punilla, Sierra de la, mts., Arg.	D3	92
Punitaqui, Chile	E2	92
Punjab, state, India	C5	54
Punjab, state, India	C4	54
Punnichy, Sk., Can.	C9	124
Puno, Peru	G3	84
Punta Alta, Arg.	I6	92
Punta Arenas, Chile	J2	90
Punta Banda, Cabo, c., Mex.	L9	134
Punta Cardón, Ven.	B6	86
Punta Colnett, Mex.	F4	98
Punta de Agua Creek (Tramperos Creek), stm., U.S.	E5	128
Punta del Díaz, Chile	C2	92
Punta del Cobre, Chile	C2	92
Punta del Este, Ur.	G10	92
Punta Delgada, Arg.	H4	90
Punta de los Llanos, Arg.	E4	92
Punta de Piedras, Ven.	B9	86
Punta Gorda, Nic.	G6	102
Punta Gorda, Fl., U.S.	J3	116
Punta Gorda, Bahía de, b., Nic.	G6	102
Punta Negra, Salar de, pl., Chile	B3	92
Punta Prieta, Mex.	A1	100
Puntarenas, C.R.	G5	102
Punta Santiago, P.R.	B4	104a
Punto Fijo, Ven.	B6	86
Punung, Indon.	H7	50
Puper, Indon.	F9	44
Puppy's Point, c., Norf. I.	y24	78i
Puqi, China	F5	42
Puqian, China	L4	42
Puquio, Peru	F3	84
Pur, stm., Russia	A13	32
Puracé, Volcán, vol., Col.	F3	86
Pūranpur, India	D7	54
Purcell, Ok., U.S.	F11	128
Purcell Mountains, mts., N.A.	F14	138
Purcellville, Va., U.S.	E8	114
Purdy, Mo., U.S.	H3	120
Puré (Purui), stm., S.A.	I6	86
Purgatoire, stm., Co., U.S.	D5	128
Puri, India	I10	54
Purificación, Col.	F4	86
Purísima, Mex.	E7	130
Purísima, stm., Mex.	C9	100
Purmerend, Neth.	B13	14
Pūrna, stm., India	H5	54
Pūrna, stm., India	H6	54
Pūrnia, India	F11	54
Puronga, Russia	F19	8
Puruí (Puré), stm., S.A.	I6	86
Purulia, India	G11	54
Puruni, stm., Guy.	D12	86
Purús, stm., S.A.	E4	84
Puruvesi, l., Fin.	F13	8
Purvis, Ms., U.S.	F9	122
Purwakarta, Indon.	G5	50
Purwodadi, Indon.	G6	50
Purwodadi, Indon.	G6	50
Purwokerto, Indon.	G6	50
Purworejo, Indon.	G6	50
Pusa, Malay.	C7	50
Pusad, India	B3	53
Pusan (Fusan), Kor., S.	D2	40
Pusan-jikhalsi, state, Kor., S.	D2	40
Pusat Gayo, Pegunungan, mts., Indon.	J3	48
Pushkar, India	E5	54
Puškin, Russia	A13	10
Puškino, Russia	D20	10
Püspökladány, Hung.	B8	26
Püssi, Est.	A10	10
Pustozersk, Russia	C25	8
Putaendo, Chile	F2	92
Putao, Mya.	C8	46
Putian, China	I8	42
Putian, China	I8	42
Putignano, Italy	D10	24
Puting, Tanjung, c., Indon.	E7	50
Putnam, Ct., U.S.	C14	114
Putney, Ga., U.S.	E1	116
Putney, Vt., U.S.	B13	114
Putorana, plato, plat., Russia	C7	34
Puttalam, Sri L.	G4	53
Puttalam Lagoon, b., Sri L.	G4	53
Puttūr, India	E4	53
Putú, Chile	G1	92
Putumayo, state, Col.	H3	86
Putumayo (Içá), stm., S.A.	H4	86
Putussibau, Indon.	C8	50
Putyla, Ukr.	B12	26
Puula, l., Fin.	F12	8
Puurmani, Est.	B9	10
Puyallup, Wa., U.S.	C4	136
Puyang, China	D6	42
Puy-de-Dôme, state, Fr.	D9	18
Puymorens, Col de, p., Fr.	G7	18
Puyo, Ec.	H3	86
Pweto, D.R.C.	F5	66
Pwinbyu, Mya.	B2	48
Pyalo, Mya.	C2	48
Pyapon, Mya.	D2	48
Pyawbwe, Mya.	B3	48
Pyhäjärvi, l., Fin.	E11	8
Pyhäjärvi, l., Fin.	F9	8
Pyhäjoki, Fin.	D10	8
Pyhäjoki, Fin.	D11	8
Pyhäselkä, l., Fin.	E13	8
Pyhäntunturi, mtn., Fin.	C12	8
Pyin Oo Lwin see Maymyo, Mya.	A3	48
Pýlos, Grc.	G4	28
Pymatuning Reservoir, res., U.S.	C5	114
Pyöktong-úp, Kor., N.	D6	38
P'yŏngch'ang, Kor., S.	B1	40
P'yŏnggang, Kor., N.	E7	38
P'yŏngyang, Kor., N.	E6	38
Pyote, Tx., U.S.	C4	130
Pyramid Lake, l., Nv., U.S.	D6	134
Pyramid Peak, mtn., Wy., U.S.	G16	136
Pyrenees, mts., Eur.	G6	18
Pyrénées-Atlantiques, state, Fr.	F5	18
Pyrénées Occident, Parc National de, p.o.i., Fr.	G5	18
Pyrénées-Orientales, state, Fr.	G8	18
Pýrgos, Grc.	F4	28
Pytalovo, Russia	C10	10
Pyu, Mya.	C3	48
Pyūthān, Nepal.	D9	54

Q

Name	Map Ref.	Page
Qaanaaq see Thule, Grnld.	B12	141
Qabbāsīn, Syria	B8	58
Qacentina (Constantine), Alg.	B6	64
Qā'en, Iran	C8	56
Qagan Moron, stm., China	C3	38
Qagan Nur, l., China	C7	36
Qahar Youyi Zhongqi, China	A5	42
Qaidam, stm., China	D4	36
Qaidam Pendi, bas., China	D3	36
Qaidanay, Kaz.	C10	32
Qal'at ash-Shaqif (Beaufort Castle), sci., Leb.	E6	58
Qal'at Bīshah, Sau. Ar.	E5	56
Qal'at Şāliḥ, Iraq	C6	56
Qal'at-ye Now, Afg.	C9	56
Qallābāt, Sudan	E7	62
Qalyūb, Egypt	H2	58
Qamani'tuaq (Baker Lake), Nu., Can.	C11	106
Qamar, Ghubbat al-, b., Yemen	F7	56
Qamdo, China	E4	36
Qamea, i., Fiji	p20	79e
Qāminis, Libya	A3	62
Qānā, Leb.	E6	58
Qandahār see Kandahār, Afg.	C10	56
Qandala, Som.	B9	66
Qapshaghay, Kaz.	F13	32
Qaqortoq see Julianehåb, Grnld.	E16	141
Qarabutaq, Grnld.	D10	32
Qārah, Syria	D7	58
Qaratal', stm., Kaz.	E13	32
Qarataū, Kaz.	F11	32
Qarataū zhotasy, mts., Kaz.	F11	32
Qaraton, Kaz.	E8	32
Qaraūyl, Kaz.	E13	32
Qarazhal, Kaz.	E12	32
Qardho, Som.	C9	66
Qarqan, stm., China	G15	32
Qaraqaraly, Kaz.	E13	32
Qarsaqbay, Kaz.	E11	32
Qārūn, Birket (Moeris, Lake), l., Egypt	I1	58
Qarwāw, Ra's, c., Oman	F8	56
Qasigiannguit see Christianshåb, Grnld.	D15	141
Qaşr al-Azraq, sci., Jord.	G7	58
Qaşr al-Kharānah, sci., Jord.	G7	58
Qaşr al-Mushattā, sci., Jord.	G7	58
Qaşr aţ-Ţūbah, sci., Jord.	G7	58
Qaşr Dab'ah, sci., Jord.	G7	58
Qaşr-e Shīrīn, Iran	C6	56
Qasr Farāfra, Egypt	B5	62
Qaţanā, Syria	E7	58
Qatar, ctry., Asia	D7	56
Qatrani, Gebel, hill, Egypt	I1	58
Qaţţāra, Munkhafad el- (Qattara Depression), depr., Egypt	B5	62
Qattara Depression see Qaţţāra, Munkhafad el-, depr., Egypt	B5	62
Qaţţīnah, Buhayrat, res., Syria	D7	58
Qausuittuq (Resolute), Nu., Can.	C7	141
Qayghy, Kaz.	D10	32
Qazaly, Kaz.	E10	32
Qazaqtyng usaqshoqylyghy (Kazakh Hills), hills, Kaz.	D12	32
Qāzigund, India	B5	54
Qazimámmád, Azer.	A6	56
Qazvin, Iran	B6	56
Qena, Egypt	B6	62
Qena (Qinā, Wādī), stm., Egypt	K3	58
Qeqertarsuaq see Godhavn, Grnld.	D15	141
Qeşari, Horbat (Caesarea), sci., Isr.	F5	58
Qeshm, Jazireh-ye, i., Iran.	D8	56
Qetura, Isr.	I5	58
Qezel Owzan, stm., Iran	B6	56
Qian, stm., China	J3	42
Qian Gorlos, China	B6	38
Qianjiang, China	F3	42
Qianning, China	E5	36
Qianshan, China	F7	42
Qianwei, China	F5	36
Qianxi, China	H1	42
Qianxinan, China	H2	42
Qiaolima, China	A8	54
Qiaowan, China	C4	36
Qidong, China	H5	42
Qiemo, China	G15	32
Qigong, China	F5	36
Qijiang, China	G2	42
Qila Saifullāh, Pak.	C2	54
Qilian Shan, mtn., China	D4	36
Qilian Shan, mts., China	D4	36
Qimen, China	G7	42
Qin, stm., China	D5	42
Qing, stm., China	F4	42
Qingcheng, China	C7	42
Qingdao (Tsingtao), China	C9	42
Qingfeng, China	D6	42
Qinggang, China	B10	38
Qinghai, state, China	D4	36
Qinghai Hu, l., China	D5	36
Qingjiang, China	F6	42
Qingjiang, China	F8	42
Qinglonggang, China	E9	42
Qingquan, China	F8	42
Qingshen, China	F5	36
Qingshui, China	D2	42
Qingshui, stm., China	H3	42
Qingshuihe, China	B4	42
Qingtang, China	I5	42
Qingtian, China	G8	42
Qingxu, China	C5	42
Qingyang, China	C2	42
Qingyang, China	F8	42
Qingyuan, China	H5	42
Qingyuan, China	C7	42
Qingyuan, China	B8	38
Qingzhen, China	H2	42
Qingzhou, China	C8	42
Qinhuangdao, China	B8	42
Qin Ling, mts., China	E3	42
Qinshihuang Mausoleum (Terra Cotta Army), sci., China	D3	42
Qinshui, China	D5	42
Qinxian, China	C5	42
Qinyang, China	D5	42
Qinyuan, China	C5	42
Qinzhou, China	K3	42
Qionghai, China	L4	42
Qionglaishan, mts., China	E5	36
Qiongzhong, China	L3	42
Qiongzhou Haixia, strt., China	K4	42
Qiqian, China	F13	34
Qiqihar, China	B9	36
Qiryat Ata, Isr.	F6	58
Qiryat Gat, Isr.	G5	58
Qiryat Shemona, Isr.	E6	58
Qishn, Yemen	F7	56
Qitai, China	C2	36
Qitaihe, China	B11	36
Qitamu, China	C10	38
Qixia, China	C9	42
Qixian, China	D6	42
Qiyang, China	H4	42
Qizhou, China	F6	42
Qizil Jilga, China	A7	54
Qom, Iran	C7	56
Qomsheh, Iran	C7	56
Qonggyai, China	D13	54
Qongyrat, Kaz.	E12	32
Qorghalzhyn, Kaz.	D12	32
Qórnoq, Grnld.	E15	141
Qosshaghyl, Kaz.	E8	32
Qostanay, Kaz.	D10	32
Qowowuyag (Chopu), mtn., Asia	D11	54
Qu, stm., China	F2	42
Qu, stm., China	G8	42
Quabbin Reservoir, res., Ma., U.S.	B13	114
Quadra Island, i., B.C., Can.	F5	138
Quadros, Lagoa dos, l., Braz.	D12	92
Quakenbrück, Ger.	D3	16
Qualicum Beach, B.C., Can.	G6	138
Quambatook, Austl.	J4	76
Quang Ngai, Viet.	E9	48
Quang Trach, Viet.	D8	48
Quantico, Va., U.S.	F8	114
Quanyang, China	C7	38
Quanzhou, China	I8	42
Qu'Appelle, Sk., Can.	D10	124
Qu'Appelle, stm., Can.	D12	124
Qu'Appelle Dam, dam, Sk., Can.	D7	124
Quaraí, Braz.	E9	92
Quaraí (Cuareim), stm., S.A.	E9	92
Quarles, Pegunungan, mts., Indon.	E11	50
Quarryville, Pa., U.S.	E9	114
Quartier d'Orléans, Guad.	A1	105a
Quartu Sant'Elena, Italy	E3	24
Quartz Lake, l., Nu., Can.	A14	106
Quartz Mountain, mtn., Or., U.S.	G4	136
Quartzsite, Az., U.S.	J2	132
Quchán, Iran	A8	56
Quchigïe, China	G4	42
Queanbeyan, Austl.	J7	76
Québec, Qc., Can.	D5	110
Québec, state, Can.	E16	106
Quebeck, Tn., U.S.	I12	120
Quebra-Anzol, stm., Braz.	J2	88
Quebracho, Ur.	E9	92
Quebrada Seca, P.R.	B4	104a
Quedal, Cabo, c., Chile	H2	90
Quedlinburg, Ger.	E7	16
Queen Charlotte Islands, is., B.C., Can.	E4	106
Queen Charlotte Sound, strt., B.C., Can.	E2	138
Queen Charlotte Strait, strt., B.C., Can.	F3	138
Queen City, Mo., U.S.	D5	120
Queen City, Tx., U.S.	D4	122
Queen Elizabeth Islands, is., Can.	B13	94
Queen Mary Coast, cst., Ant.	B14	81
Queen Maud Gulf, b., Nu., Can.	B10	106
Queen Maud Land, reg., Ant.	C4	81
Queen Maud Mountains, mts., Ant.	D23	81
Queenscliff, Austl.	L5	76
Queensland, state, Austl.	D6	74
Queensport, N.S., Can.	E15	110
Queenstown, Austl.	o12	77a
Queenstown, N.Z.	G3	80
Queenstown, S. Afr.	G8	70
Queguay Grande, stm., Ur.	F9	92
Queimada Nova, Braz.	E5	88
Queimadas, Braz.	F6	88
Queimadas, Braz.	E4	88
Quela, Ang.	B2	68
Quelelevu, i., Fiji	p20	79e
Quelimane, Moz.	D6	68
Quelpart Island see Cheju-do, i., Kor., S.	H7	38
Quemado, Tx., U.S.	F7	130
Quemado, Punta de, c., Cuba	B10	102
Quemoy see Chinmen Tao, i., Tai.	I8	42
Quemú Quemú, Arg.	H6	92
Quequén, Arg.	I8	92
Query, stm., Col.	G6	86
Quercy, hist. reg., Fr.	E7	18
Querétaro, Mex.	E8	100
Querétaro, state, Mex.	E7	98
Quesada, Spain	G7	20
Queshan, China	E6	42
Quesnel, B.C., Can.	D8	138
Quesnel, stm., B.C., Can.	D8	138
Quesnel Lake, l., B.C., Can.	D9	138
Que Son, Viet.	E9	48
Questa, N.M., U.S.	E3	128
Quetena, stm., l., On., Can.	C17	118
Quetta, Pak.	C10	56
Quetzaltenango, Guat.	E2	102
Quevedo, Ec.	H2	86
Quezon City, Phil.	C3	52
Qufu, China	D7	42
Quibala, Ang.	C1	68
Quibaxe, Ang.	B1	68
Quibdó, Col.	E3	86
Quiberon, Fr.	G5	14
Quibor, Ven.	C7	86
Quiculungo, Ang.	B2	68
Quila, Mex.	C5	100
Quilengues, Ang.	C1	68
Quilimarí, Chile	F2	92
Quillabamba, Peru	F3	84
Quillacollo, Bol.	C3	90
Quill Lake, Sk., Can.	B9	124
Quillota, Chile	F2	92
Quilon, India	G3	53
Quilpie, Austl.	F5	76
Quilpué, Chile	F2	92
Quimari, Alto de, mtn., Col.	C3	86
Quimaria, Ang.	B1	68
Quimby, Ia., U.S.	B2	120
Quimili, Arg.	C6	92
Quimper (Kemper), Fr.	F4	14
Quimperlé, Fr.	G5	14
Quinault, stm., Wa., U.S.	C3	136
Quince Mil, Peru	F3	84
Quincy, Ca., U.S.	D4	134
Quincy, Fl., U.S.	G14	122
Quincy, Il., U.S.	E6	120
Quincy, Ma., U.S.	B14	114
Quindío, state, Col.	E4	86
Quines, Arg.	F5	92
Quinhagak, Ak., U.S.	E7	140
Quinlan, Tx., U.S.	E2	122
Quinn, stm., Nv., U.S.	B7	134
Quintanar de la Orden, Spain	E7	20
Quintana Roo, state, Mex.	C3	102
Quinte, Bay of, b., On., Can.	D12	112
Quinto, Spain	C10	20
Quinto, stm., Arg.	G5	92
Quinton, Ok., U.S.	B3	122
Quipapá, Braz.	E7	88
Quiquil Mountain, mtn., Md., U.S.	E8	114
Quirigua, sci., Guat.	E3	102
Quirihue, Chile	H1	92
Quirindi, Austl.	H8	76
Quirinópolis, Braz.	C6	88
Quiroga, Mex.	F8	100
Quirós, Cap, c., Vanuatu	j16	79d
Quissanã, Moz.	C7	68
Quissico, Moz.	D12	70
Quitaque, Tx., U.S.	G7	128
Quitasueño, unds., Col.	E7	102
Quitasueño, Banco de see Quitasueño, unds., Col.	E7	102
Quita Sueño Bank see Quitasueño, unds., Col.	E7	102
Quiterajo, Moz.	C7	68
Quitilipi, Arg.	C7	92
Quitman, Ga., U.S.	F2	116
Quitman, Tx., U.S.	E3	122
Quito, Ec.	H2	86
Quixadá, Braz.	C6	88
Quixeramobim, Braz.	C6	88
Qujiadian, China	C5	38
Qujing, China	F5	36
Qujiu, China	J2	42
Qulin, Mo., U.S.	H7	120
Qumarlêb, China	E4	36
Qumrān, Khirbat, hist., W.B.	G6	58
Quoich, stm., Nu., Can.	C12	106
Quorn, Austl.	F7	74
Quoxo, stm., Bots.	C7	70
Qurdūd, Sudan	E5	62
Qus, Egypt	B6	62
Quseir, Egypt	B7	62
Qutdligssat, Grnld.	C15	141
Quthing, Leso.	G8	70
Quweisna, Egypt	H2	58
Quxian, China	F2	42
Qüxü, China	D13	54
Quyang, China	B6	42
Quyghan, Kaz.	E12	32
Quy Nhon, Viet.	F9	48
Quyon, Qc., Can.	C13	112
Quyquyó, Para.	C9	92
Quzhou, China	G8	42
Quzhou, China	C6	42
Qyzylorda, Kaz.	F11	32
Qyzyltū, Kaz.	D12	32

R

Name	Map Ref.	Page
Raab (Rába), stm., Eur.	D12	22
Raalte, Neth.	B15	14
Ra'ananna, Isr.	F5	58
Raas, Pulau, i., Indon.	G9	50
Raasay, i., Scot., U.K.	D6	12
Raasiku, Est.	A8	10
Rab, Otok, i., Cro.	F11	22
Rāba, Indon.	H11	50
Rába (Raab), stm., Eur.	D12	22
Rabade, Spain	A3	20
Rabak, Sudan	E6	62
Rabat, Malta	I8	24
Rabat, Malta	H8	24
Rabat, Mor.	C3	64
Rabaul, Pap. N. Gui.	a5	79a
Rabbit Creek, stm., S.D., U.S.	B10	126
Rabbit Ears Pass, p., Co., U.S.	C10	132
Rabi, i., Fiji.	p20	79e
Rābi', Ash-Shallāl ar- (Fourth Cataract), wtfl., Sudan	D6	62
Rābigh, Sau. Ar.	E4	56
Rabka, Pol.	G15	16
Rabkavi Banhatti, India	C2	53
Rābnita, Mol.	B16	26
Raboēčestrovsk, Russia	D16	8
Rabwāh, Pak.	C4	54
Rabyānah, Ramlat, des., Libya	C4	62
Raccoon, stm., Ia., U.S.	C3	120
Raccoon Creek, stm., Oh., U.S.	E15	120
Race, Cape, c., Nf., Can.	j23	107a
Race Point, c., Ma., U.S.	B15	114
Rach Gia, Viet.	G7	48
Rach Gia, Vinh, b., Viet.	H7	48
Raciąż, Pol.	D16	16
Racibórz, Pol.	F14	16
Racine, Wi., U.S.	F2	112
Radaškovičy, Bela.	F10	10
Rădăuți, Rom.	B12	26
Radcliff, Ky., U.S.	G12	120
Radeberg, Ger.	E9	16
Radebeul, Ger.	E9	16
Radford, Va., U.S.	G5	114
Rādhanpur, India	G3	54
Rădinești, Rom.	E10	26
Radisson, Sk., Can.	B6	124
Radium Hot Springs, B.C., Can.	F14	138
Radnice, Czech Rep.	G9	16
Radofinnikovo, Russia	A13	10
Radom, Pol.	E17	16
Radom, state, Pol.	E16	16
Radomsko, Pol.	E15	16
Radomyśl Wielki, Pol.	F17	16
Radoviš, Mac.	B5	28
Radstadt, Aus.	C10	22
Radutino, Russia	H17	10
Radviliškis, Lith.	E6	10
Radville, Sk., Can.	E9	124
Radymno, Pol.	G18	16
Radzyń Chełmiński, Pol.	C14	16
Rae, N.T., Can.	C7	106
Rae, stm., Nu., Can.	B7	106
Rāe Bareli, India	E8	54
Raeford, N.C., U.S.	B6	116
Rae Isthmus, isth., Nu., Can.	B13	106
Rae Strait, strt., Nu., Can.	B12	106
Raeside, Lake, l., Austl.	E4	74
Rafael Freyre, Cuba	B10	102
Rafah, Gaza	G5	58
Rafhā', Sau. Ar.	D5	56
Rafsanjān, Iran	C8	56
Raft, stm., U.S.	H13	136
Raga, Sudan	F5	62
Ragged Island, i., Bah.	A10	102
Ragged Island Range, is., Bah.	A10	102
Ragged Top Mountain, mtn., Wy., U.S.	F7	124
Ragland, Al., U.S.	D12	122
Rāghogarh, India	G6	54
Rahachow, Bela.	H14	10
Rahad al-Bardī, Sudan	E4	62
Rahatgarh, India	G7	54
Rahimatpur, India	C1	53
Rahīm Ki Bāzār, Pak.	F2	54
Rahīmyār Khān, Pak.	D3	54
Rāiganj, India	F12	54
Raigarh, India	H9	54
Railroad Valley, val., Nv., U.S.	E10	134
Railton, Austl.	n13	77a
Rainbow Bridge National Monument, p.o.i., Ut., U.S.	F6	132
Rainbow Falls, wtfl., B.C., Can.	D11	138
Rainelle, W.V., U.S.	G5	114
Rainier, Mount, vol., Wa., U.S.	D5	136
Rainy, stm., N.A.	C4	118
Rainy River, On., Can.	C4	118
Raipur Uplands, plat., India	H9	54
Raisen, India	G6	54
Raisin, stm., Mi., U.S.	C2	114
Raivavae, i., Fr. Poly.	F12	72
Rajapālaiyam, India	G3	53
Rājahmundry, India	C5	53
Rājaldesar, India	D5	54
Rājampet, India	D4	53
Rajang, stm., Malay.	B8	50
Rājapur, India	B1	53
Rajasthān, state, India	E4	54
Rājbāri, Bngl.	G12	54

Rajčihinsk – River Cess I • 47

Name | Map Ref. | Page

Rajčihinsk, Russia G14 34
Rāj Gangpur, India G10 54
Rājgarh, India E6 54
Rājgarh, India G6 54
Rājgarh, India D5 54
Rajik, Indon. E4 50
Rājkot, India G3 54
Rāj Nāndgaon, India H8 54
Rājpipla, India H4 54
Rājpur, India G5 54
Rājpura, India C6 54
Rājshāhi, Bngl. F12 54
Rājshāhi, state, Bngl. F12 54
Rājula, India H3 54
Raka, stm., China D11 54
Rakamaz, Hung. A8 26
Rakaposhi, mtn., Pak. B11 56
Rakata, Pulau (Krakatoa), i., Indon. G4 50
Rakhine, state, Mya. C1 48
Rakhiv, Ukr. A11 26
Rakitnoe, Russia B11 36
Rakiura see Stewart Island, i., N.Z. H3 80
Rakoniewice, Pol. D12 16
Rakops, Bots. B7 70
Rakovník, Czech Rep. F9 16
Råkvåg *see* Råkvågen, Nor. E4 8
Råkvågen, Nor. E4 8
Rakvere, Est. G12 8
Raleigh, Ms., U.S. E9 122
Raleigh, N.C., U.S. I7 114
Ralik Chain, is., Marsh. Is. C7 72
Ralls, Tx., U.S. H7 128
Ralston, Pa., U.S. C9 114
Ramah, N.M., U.S. H8 132
Rām Allāh, W.B. G6 58
Rāmanagaram, India E3 53
Rāmanāthapuram, India G4 53
Rāmānuj Ganj, India G9 54
Ramat Gan, Isr. F5 58
Ramat HaSharon, Isr. F5 58
Ramatlabama, Bots. D7 70
Rambervillers, Fr. F15 14
Rambouillet, Fr. F10 14
Rambutyo Island, i., Pap. N. Gui. a4 79a
Rām Dās, India B5 54
Rāmdurg, India C2 53
Ramea, Nf., Can. j22 107a
Ramene, Russia F20 8
Ramenskoe, Russia E21 10
Rāmeswaram, India G4 53
Rāmgarh, Bngl. G13 54
Rāmgarh, India E5 54
Rāmgarh, India G10 54
Ram Head, c., V.I.U.S. e8 104b
Rāmhormoz, Iran C6 56
Ramírez, Mex. I10 130
Ramírez, Mex. G7 130
Ramla, Isr. G5 58
Ramlu, mtn., Afr. E8 62
Ramm, Jabal, mtn., Jord. I6 58
Rāmnagar, India F9 54
Rāmnagar, India D7 54
Râmnicu Sărat, Rom. D14 26
Râmnicu Vâlcea, Rom. D11 26
Ramona, Ca., U.S. J9 134
Ramona, S.D., U.S. C15 126
Ramos, Mex. D8 100
Ramos, stm., Mex. C6 100
Ramotswa, Bots. D7 70
Rampart, Ak., U.S. C9 140
Ramparts, stm., N.T., Can. B4 106
Rāmpur, India D7 54
Rāmpur, India C6 54
Rāmpura, India F5 54
Rāmpur Hāt, India F11 54
Ramree Island, i., Mya. C1 48
Ramseur, N.C., U.S. I6 114
Ramsey, I. of Man G8 12
Ramsey Lake, l., On., Can. A7 112
Ramsgate, Eng., U.K. J14 12
Ramshorn Peak, mtn., Mt., U.S. E15 136
Rāmtek, India H7 54
Rāmu, Bngl. H14 54
Ramu, stm., Pap. N. Gui. a3 79a
Ramville, Îlet, i., Mart. k7 105c
Ramygala, Lith. E7 10
Rānāghāt, India G12 54
Rana Kao, Volcán, vol., Chile f29 78l
Rāna Pratāp Sāgar, res., India F5 54
Ranau, Malay. H1 52
Ranau, Danau, l., Indon. F3 50
Ranburne, Al., U.S. D13 122
Rancagua, Chile G2 92
Rancah, Indon. G6 50
Rancevo, Russia D16 10
Rancharia, Braz. D6 90
Ranchería, stm., Col. B5 86
Ranchester, Wy., U.S. C5 126
Rānchi, India G10 54
Ranchillos, Arg. C5 92
Ranch Lake, l., Sk., Can. B9 124
Rancho Cordova, Ca., U.S. E4 134
Rancho Nuevo, Mex. H7 130
Ranchos, Arg. G8 92
Ranco, Lago, l., Chile H2 90
Rancul, Arg. G5 92
Randazzo, Italy G8 24
Randers, Den. H4 8
Randleman, N.C., U.S. I6 114
Randlett, Ok., U.S. G10 128
Randolph, Az., U.S. K5 132
Randolph, Me., U.S. F7 110
Randolph, Ne., U.S. E15 126
Randolph, N.Y., U.S. B7 114
Randolph, Ut., U.S. B5 132
Random Lake, Wi., U.S. E2 112
Randsfjorden, l., Nor. F3 8
Ranfurly, N.Z. G4 80
Rāngāmāti, Bngl. G13 54
Rangantemiang, Indon. D8 50
Rangas, Tanjung, c., Indon. E11 50
Rangasa, Tanjung, c., Indon. E11 50
Rangaunu Bay, b., N.Z. B5 80
Rangeley, Me., U.S. E6 110
Ranger, Tx., U.S. B9 130
Rangia, India E13 54
Rangitaiki, stm., N.Z. D7 80
Rangitata, stm., N.Z. F4 80
Rangitikei, stm., N.Z. D7 80
Rangkasbitung, Indon. G4 50
Rangoon *see* Yangon, Mya. D2 48
Rangoon, stm., Mya. D3 48
Rangpur, Bngl. F12 54
Rangpur, Pak. C3 54
Rangsang, Pulau, i., Indon. C3 50
Rānībennur, India D2 53
Rānīganj, India G11 54
Rānikhet, India D7 54
Rankamhaeng National Park, p.o.i., Thai. D4 48
Ranken, stm., Austl. D7 74
Ranken Store, Austl. C7 74
Rankin, Il., U.S. H2 112
Rankin, Tx., U.S. C6 130
Rankin Inlet *see* Kangiqsliniq, Nu., Can. C12 106
Rankins Springs, Austl. I6 76
Rann of Kutch see Kutch, Rann of, reg., Asia D2 46
Ranong, Thai. H4 48
Ranongga Island, i., Sol. Is. e7 79b
Ranot, Thai. I5 48
Ransiki, Indon. F9 44
Ransom, Ks., U.S. C8 128
Ranson, W.V., U.S. E8 114
Rantabe, Madag. D8 68
Rantaukampar, Indon. C2 50
Rantaupanjang, Indon. D2 50
Rantauprapat, Indon. B1 50
Rantekombola, Bulu, mtn., Indon. E12 50
Rantepao, Indon. E11 50
Rantoul, Il., U.S. D9 120
Raohe, China B11 36
Raoping, China J7 42
Raoul, Ga., U.S. B2 116
Raoul-Blanchard, Mont, mtn., Qc., Can. C6 110
Raoul Island, i., N.Z. F9 72
Rapa, i., Fr. Poly. F12 72
Rapallo, Italy F6 22
Rapang, Indon. E11 50
Rapa Nui see Pascua, Isla de, i., Chile f30 78l
Rāpar, India G3 54
Rapel, stm., Chile F2 92
Rapel, Embalse, res., Chile G2 92
Rapelli, Arg. C5 92
Raper, Cape, c., Nu., Can. B17 106
Rapidan, stm., Va., U.S. F7 114
Rapid City, Mb., Can. D13 124
Rapid City, S.D., U.S. C9 126
Rapid Creek, stm., S.D., U.S. D9 126
Rapide-Blanc, Qc., Can. C4 110
Rapid River, Mi., U.S. C2 112
Räpina, Est. G12 8
Rappahannock, stm., Va., U.S. G9 114
Rāpti, stm., Asia E9 54
Rapu Rapu Island, i., Phil. D5 52
Raraka, at., Fr. Poly. E12 72
Rarotonga, i., Cook Is. a26 78j
Rarotonga International Airport, Cook Is. a26 78j
Rasa, Punta, c., Arg. H9 92
Ra's al-Khaymah, U.A.E. D8 56
Ra's Ba'labakk, Leb. D7 58
Râșcani, Mol. B14 26
Rașcov, Mol. B15 26
Ras Dashen Terara, mtn., Eth. E7 62
Ras Dejen see Ras Dashen Terara, mtn., Eth. E7 62
Ras Djebel, Tun. G4 24
Raseiniai, Lith. E5 10
Râs el-Barr, Egypt G2 58
Rashād, Sudan E6 62
Rashid (Rosetta), Egypt G1 58
Rashid, Masabb (Rosetta Mouth), mth., Egypt G1 58
Rasht, Iran B6 56
Raška, Serb. F7 26
Rās Koh, mtn., Pak. D10 56
Rasm al-Arwām, Sabkhat, l., Syria C8 58
Râșnov, Rom. D12 26
Rasra, India F9 54
Rassua, ostrov, i., Russia G19 34
Rast, Rom. F10 26
Rastatt, Ger. H4 16
Rastede, Ger. C4 16
Rastenburg *see* Kętrzyn, Pol. B17 16
Rásttigáisá, mtn., Nor. A12 8
Ratak Chain, is., Marsh. Is. C8 72
Ratamka, Bela. G10 10
Ratangarh, India D5 54
Rat Buri, Thai. F4 48
Rāth, India F7 54
Rathbun Lake, res., Ia., U.S. D4 120
Rathdrum, Id., U.S. C9 136
Rathenow, Ger. D8 16
Rathkeale, Ire. I3 12
Ráth Luirc, Ire. I4 12
Rathwell, Mb., Can. E15 124
Rat Island, i., Ak., U.S. g22 140a
Rat Islands, is., Ak., U.S. g22 140a
Ratlām, India G5 54
Ratmanova, ostrov, i., Russia C27 34
Ratnāgiri, India C1 53
Ratnapura, Sri L. H5 53
Raton, N.M., U.S. E4 128
Raton Pass, p., N.M., U.S. E4 128
Rats, stm., Qc., Can. A4 110
Rattanaburi, Thai. E6 48
Rattaphum, Thai. I5 48
Rattlesnake, Mt., U.S. D13 136
Rattlesnake Creek, stm., Ks., U.S. D10 128
Ratz, Mount, mtn., B.C., Can. D4 106
Ratzeburg, Ger. C6 16
Rau, Indon. C2 50
Raub, Malay. K5 48
Rauch, Arg. H8 92
Raul Soares, Braz. K4 88
Rauma, Fin. F9 8
Rauma, stm., Nor. E2 8
Rauna, Lat. C8 10
Raung, Gunung, vol., Indon. H9 50
Raurkela, India G10 54
Răut, stm., Mol. B14 26
Ravalgaon, India H5 54
Ravanusa, Italy G7 24
Ravena, N.Y., U.S. B12 114
Ravenna, Italy F9 22
Ravenna, Ky., U.S. G2 114
Ravenna, Ne., U.S. F13 126
Ravenna, Oh., U.S. G8 112
Ravensburg, Ger. I5 16
Ravenscrag, Sk., Can. E4 124
Ravenshoe, Austl. A5 76
Ravensthorpe, Austl. F4 74
Ravenswood, W.V., U.S. F4 114
Rāvi, stm., Asia C4 54
Ravnina, Turkmen. B9 56
Rāwah, Iraq C5 56
Rawaki, at., Kir. D9 72
Rāwalpindi, Pak. B4 54
Rawas, stm., Indon. E3 50
Rawdon, Qc., Can. D3 110
Rawicz, Pol. E12 16
Rawlinna, Austl. F4 74
Rawlins, Wy., U.S. B9 132
Rawson, Arg. H4 90
Rawson, Arg. G7 92
Raxāul, India E10 54
Ray, Cape, c., Nf., Can. C17 110
Raya, Indon. C11 50
Raya, Bukit, mtn., Indon. D8 50
Rāyachoti, India D4 53
Rāyadurg, India D3 53
Rāyagarha, India B6 53
Ray Hubbard, Lake, res., Tx., U.S. E2 122
Raymond, Ab., Can. G18 138
Raymond, Il., U.S. E8 120
Raymond, Mn., U.S. F3 118
Raymond, Wa., U.S. D3 136
Raymond Terrace, Austl. I8 76
Raymondville, Tx., U.S. H10 130
Raymore, Sk., Can. C9 124
Rayne, La., U.S. G6 122
Rayones, Mex. C8 100
Rayong, Thai. F5 48
Rayside-Balfour, On., Can. B8 112
Raytown, Mo., U.S. E3 120
Rayville, La., U.S. E7 122
Raz, Pointe du, c., Fr. F4 14
Războieni, Rom. B13 26
Razdolinsk, Russia C16 32
Răzeni, Mol. C15 26
Razgrad, Blg. F13 26
Razim, Lacul, l., Rom. E15 26
Rāznas ezers, l., Lat. D10 10
Razorback Mountain, mtn., B.C., Can. E6 138
Răzvani, Rom. E13 26
Ré, Île de, i., Fr. C4 18
Reading, Eng., U.K. J11 12
Reading, Mi., U.S. C1 114
Reading, Oh., U.S. E1 114
Reading, Pa., U.S. D9 114
Readlyn, Ia., U.S. B5 120
Readstown, Wi., U.S. H8 118
Real, stm., Braz. F6 88
Real, Cordillera, mts., S.A. G4 84
Real del Castillo, Mex. L9 134
Real del Padre, Arg. G4 92
Realicó, Arg. G5 92
Reardan, Wa., U.S. C8 136
Reata, Mex. B8 100
Reay, Scot., U.K. C9 12
Rebecca, Lake, l., Austl. F4 74
Rebiana Sand Sea see Rabyānah, Ramlat, des., Libya C4 62
Reboly, Russia E14 8
Rebouças, Braz. B12 92
Rebun-tō, i., Japan B14 38
Recanati, Italy G10 22
Recherche, Archipelago of the, is., Austl. F4 74
Recife, Braz. E8 88
Recinto, Chile H2 92
Recklinghausen, Ger. E2 16
Reconquista, Arg. D8 92
Recreio, Braz. K4 88
Recreo, Arg. D5 92
Rector, Ar., U.S. H7 120
Rèčyča, Bela. H13 10
Recz, Pol. C11 16
Red (Hong, Song) (Yuan), stm., Asia D9 46
Red, stm., N.A. A2 118
Red, stm., U.S. H10 120
Red, stm., U.S. E9 108
Red, Elm Fork, stm., U.S. F8 128
Red, North Fork, stm., U.S. G9 128
Red, Prairie Dog Town Fork, stm., U.S. H7 122
Red, Salt Fork, stm., U.S. G9 128
Redang, Pulau, i., Malay. J6 48
Red Bank, N.J., U.S. D11 114
Red Bank, Tn., U.S. B13 122
Red Bay, Nf., Can. i22 107a
Red Bay, Al., U.S. C10 122
Redbay, Fl., U.S. G12 122
Redberry Lake, l., Sk., Can. B6 124
Red Bluff, Ca., U.S. C3 134
Red Bluff Reservoir, res., U.S. C4 130
Red Boiling Springs, Tn., U.S. H12 120
Red Canyon, p., S.D., U.S. D9 126
Redcar, Eng., U.K. G11 12
Red Cedar, stm., Mi., U.S. F5 112
Red Cedar Lake, l., On., Can. B9 112
Redcliff, Ab., Can. D3 124
Red Cliff, Co., U.S. D10 132
Redcliff *see* Red Cliff, Co., U.S. D10 132
Redcliffe, Austl. F9 76
Redcliffe, Mount, mtn., Austl. E4 74
Red Cliffs, Austl. J3 76
Red Cloud, Ne., U.S. A10 128
Red Creek, stm., Ms., U.S. G10 122
Red Deer, Ab., Can. D17 138
Red Deer, stm., Can. F19 138
Red Deer, stm., Can. B12 124
Red Deer Lake, l., Mb., Can. B12 124
Reddersburg, S. Afr. F8 70
Red Devil, Ak., U.S. D8 140
Redding, Ca., U.S. C3 134
Redditch, Eng., U.K. I10 12
Redenção, Braz. C6 88
Redfield, S.D., U.S. C14 126
Redford, Tx., U.S. E3 130
Redhead, Trin. s13 105f
Redja, stm., Russia C14 10
Redkey, In., U.S. H4 112
Redkino, Russia D19 10
Red Lake, On., Can. E12 106
Red Lake, l., On., Can. E12 106
Red Lake, l., Az., U.S. H2 132
Red Lake, stm., Mn., U.S. D2 118
Red Lake Falls, Mn., U.S. D2 118
Red Lake Road, On., Can. B5 118
Redlands, Ca., U.S. I8 134
Redlands, Co., U.S. D8 132
Red Level, Al., U.S. F12 122
Red Lion, Pa., U.S. E9 114
Red Lodge, Mt., U.S. B3 126
Redmond, Or., U.S. F5 136
Redmond, Ut., U.S. D5 132
Redmond, Wa., U.S. C4 136
Red Mountain, mtn., Mt., U.S. C14 136
Red Mountain Pass, p., Co., U.S. F9 132
Red Oak, Ia., U.S. D2 120
Redon, Fr. G6 14
Redonda, Isla, i., Ven. t12 105f
Redonda Islands, is., B.C., Can. F6 138
Redondela, Spain B2 20
Redondo, Port. F3 20
Redondo Beach, Ca., U.S. J7 134
Redoubt Volcano, vol., Ak., U.S. D9 140
Red Pass, B.C., Can. D11 138
Red Rock, B.C., Can. C8 138
Red Rock, On., Can. C10 118
Red Rock, stm., Mt., U.S. F14 136
Red Rock, Lake, res., Ia., U.S. C4 120
Redruth, Eng., U.K. K7 12
Red Sea, s. C7 62
Redvers, Sk., Can. E12 124
Redwater, Ab., Can. C17 138
Redwater, stm., Mt., U.S. G8 124
Redwillow, stm., Can. A11 138
Red Willow Creek, stm., Ne., U.S. G12 126
Red Wing, Mn., U.S. G6 118
Redwood, stm., Mn., U.S. G3 118
Redwood Falls, Mn., U.S. G3 118
Redwood National Park, p.o.i., Ca., U.S. B1 134
Ree, Lough, l., Ire. H5 12
Reed City, Mi., U.S. E4 112
Reeder, N.D., U.S. A10 126
Reed Lake, l., Sk., Can. D6 124
Reedley, Ca., U.S. G6 134
Reedsburg, Wi., U.S. H8 118
Reedsville, Wi., U.S. D2 112
Reefton, N.Z. F4 80
Reelfoot Lake, l., Tn., U.S. H8 120
Rees, Ger. E2 16
Reese, Mi., U.S. E6 112
Reese, stm., Nv., U.S. C9 134
Reeseville, Wi., U.S. H10 118
Refuge Cove, B.C., Can. F6 138
Refugio, Tx., U.S. F10 130
Rega, stm., Pol. C11 16
Regência, Braz. J6 88
Regeneração, Braz. D4 88
Regensburg, Ger. H8 16
Regent, N.D., U.S. A10 126
Reggâne, Alg. D5 64
Reggio di Calabria, Italy F9 24
Reggio nell'Emilia, Italy F7 22
Reghin, Rom. C11 26
Regina, Sk., Can. D9 124
Región Metropolitana, state, Chile F2 92
Registan see Rīgestān, reg., Afg. C9 56
Registro, Braz. B14 92
Regozero, Russia D14 8
Rehau, Ger. F7 16
Rehoboth, Nmb. C3 70
Rehoboth Beach, De., U.S. F10 114
Reḥovot, Isr. G5 58
Reichenbach, Ger. F8 16
Reidsville, Ga., U.S. D3 116
Reidsville, N.C., U.S. H6 114
Reigate, Eng., U.K. J12 12
Reihoku, Japan G2 40
Reims (Rheims), Fr. E12 14
Rein Anteriur (Vorderrhein), stm., Switz. D6 22
Reinbeck, Ia., U.S. B5 120
Reindeer Lake, l., Can. D10 106
Reinga, Cape, c., N.Z. B5 80
Reinosa, Spain A6 20
Reisa Nasjonalpark, p.o.i., Nor. B10 8
Reisterstown, Md., U.S. E9 114
Reitz, S. Afr. E9 70
Reliance, N.T., Can. C9 106
Remada, Tun. C7 64
Remagen, Ger. F3 16
Remanso, Braz. E4 88
Rembang, Indon. G7 50
Remedios, Col. D4 86
Remedios, Pan. H7 102
Remedios, Punta, c., El Sal. F2 102
Remer, Mn., U.S. D5 118
Remington, Va., U.S. F8 114
Rémiré, Fr. Gu. C7 84
Remiremont, Fr. G15 14
Remoulins, Fr. F10 18
Rempang, Pulau, i., Indon. C3 50
Remscheid, Ger. E3 16
Remsen, Ia., U.S. B1 120
Remus, Mi., U.S. E4 112
Renaix *see* Ronse, Bel. D12 14
Renata, B.C., Can. G12 138
Rencēni, Lat. C8 10
Rende, Italy E10 24
Rend Lake, res., Il., U.S. F8 120
Rendova Island, i., Sol. Is. e7 79b
Rendsburg, Ger. B5 16
Renfrew, On., Can. C13 112
Rengat, Indon. D3 50
Rengel, Indon. G8 50
Rengo, Chile G2 92
Reng Tlāng, mtn., Asia H14 54
Renheji, China F6 42
Renhuai, China H2 42
Reni, Ukr. D15 26
Renland, reg., Grnld. C20 141
Renmark, Austl. J3 76
Rennell, i., Sol. Is. E7 72
Rennell, Islas, is., Chile J2 90
Rennell and Bellona, state, Sol. Is. f9 79b
Rennes, Fr. F7 14
Rennie, Mb., Can. E18 124
Reno, Nv., U.S. D6 134
Reno, stm., Italy F8 22
Reno Hill, mtn., Wy., U.S. E6 126
Renoster, stm., S. Afr. G5 70
Renous, N.B., Can. D11 110
Renovo, Pa., U.S. C8 114
Rensjön, Swe. B8 8
Rensselaer, In., U.S. H2 112
Rensselaer, N.Y., U.S. B12 114
Rentería, Spain A9 20
Renton, Wa., U.S. C4 136
Renville, Mn., U.S. G3 118
Renwick, Ia., U.S. B4 120
Reo, Indon. H12 50
Repetek, Turkmen. B9 56
Repton, Al., U.S. F11 122
Republic, Mi., U.S. B1 112
Republic, Mo., U.S. G4 120
Republic, Wa., U.S. B8 136
Republican, stm., U.S. B11 128
Republican, North Fork, stm., U.S. A6 128
Republican, South Fork, stm., U.S. B7 128
Republic of Korea see Korea, South, ctry., Asia G8 38
Repulse Bay *see* Naujaat, Nu., Can. B13 106
Repulse Bay, b., Austl. C7 76
Repvåg, Nor. A11 8
Requena, Spain E9 20
Reriutaba, Braz. C5 88
Reşadiye Yarımadası, pen., Tur. G10 28
Reschenpass (Resia, Passo di), p., Eur. C16 18
Reschenscheideck see Reschenpass, p., Eur. C16 18
Reschenscheideck see Resia, Passo di, p., Eur. C16 18
Resen, Mac. B4 28
Reserva, Braz. B12 92
Reserve, La., U.S. G8 122
Reserve, N.M., U.S. J8 132
Resia, Passo di (Reschenpass), p., Eur. C16 18
Resistencia, Arg. C8 92
Reşiţa, Rom. D8 26
Resko, Pol. C11 16
Resolute *see* Qausuittuq, Nu., Can. C7 141
Resolution Island, i., Nu., Can. E12 141
Resolution Island, i., N.Z. G2 80
Resplendor, Braz. J5 88
Restigouche, stm., Can. C9 110
Restinga Seca, Braz. D11 92
Reston, Mb., Can. E12 124
Retalhuleu, Guat. E2 102
Retamosa, Ur. F10 92
Retezat, Parcul Național, p.o.i., Rom. D9 26
Rethel, Fr. E13 14
Réthymno, Grc. H7 28
Rettihovka, Russia B10 38
Reunion, dep., Afr. I11 60
Reus, Spain C12 20
Reuss, stm., Switz. C5 22
Reuterstadt Stavenhagen, Ger. C8 16
Reutlingen, Ger. H5 16
Revda, Russia C16 8
Revelstoke, B.C., Can. F12 138
Revelstoke, Lake, res., B.C., Can. E12 138
Reventazón, Peru E1 84
Revilla del Campo, Spain B7 20
Revillagigedo, Islas, is., Mex. F2 100
Revillagigedo Island, i., Ak., U.S. E13 140
Revillagigedo Islands see Revillagigedo, Islas, is., Mex. F2 100
Revin, Fr. E13 14
Revolución, Mex. H2 130
Rewa, India F8 54
Rewāri, India D6 54
Rexburg, Id., U.S. G15 136
Rexford, Ks., U.S. B8 128
Rexford, Mt., U.S. B11 136
Rey, Isla del, i., Pan. H8 102
Rey, Laguna del, l., Mex. B7 100
Reyes, Bol. B3 90
Reyes, Point, c., Ca., U.S. F2 134
Reyhanlı, Tur. B7 58
Reykjanes Ridge, unds. C10 144
Reykjavík, Ice. k28 8a
Reyno, Ar., U.S. H7 120
Reynolds, Ga., U.S. D1 116
Reynolds, N.D., U.S. G16 124
Reynosa, Mex. B9 100
Rezé, Fr. G7 14
Rēzekne, Lat. D10 10
Rezina, Mol. B15 26
Rezovo, Blg. G15 26
Rezovska (Mutlu), stm., Eur. G14 26
Rhaetian Alps, mts., Eur. C15 18
Rhame, N.D., U.S. A9 126
Rheda-Wiedenbrück, Ger. E4 16
Rheims *see* Reims, Fr. E12 14
Rhein, Sk., Can. C11 124
Rhein see Rhine, stm., Eur. C15 14
Rheine, Ger. D3 16
Rheinland-Pfalz, state, Ger. G3 16
Rhine, Ga., U.S. E2 116
Rhine (Rhein) (Rhin), stm., Eur. C15 14
Rhinelander, Wi., U.S. F9 118
Rhineland-Palatinate see Rheinland-Pfalz, state, Ger. G3 16
Rhinns Point, c., Scot., U.K. F6 12
Rhir, Cap, c., Mor. C2 64
Rho, Italy E5 22
Rhode Island, state, U.S. C14 114
Rhode Island Sound, strt., U.S. C14 114
Rhodes *see* Ródos, Grc. G11 28
Rhodes see Ródos, i., Grc. G10 28
Rhodesia see Zimbabwe, ctry., Afr. D4 68
Rhodes Matopos National Park, p.o.i., Zimb. B8 70
Rhodes' Tomb, hist., Zimb. B9 70
Rhodope Mountains, mts., Eur. H11 26
Rhön, mts., Ger. F5 16
Rhondda, Wales, U.K. J9 12
Rhône, state, Fr. D10 18
Rhône, stm., Eur. F10 18
Rhyl, Wales, U.K. H9 12
Riachão, Braz. D2 88
Riachão do Jacuípe, Braz. F6 88
Riacho de Santana, Braz. G4 88
Riachos, Islas de los, is., Arg. H4 90
Riamkanan, Waduk, res., Indon. E9 50
Riaño, Spain A6 20
Riau, state, Indon. D2 50
Riau, Kepulauan, is., Indon. C4 50
Riaza, Spain C7 20
Ribadeo, Spain A3 20
Ribas do Rio Pardo, Braz. D6 90
Ribáuè, Moz. C6 68
Ribe, Den. I3 8
Ribe, state, Den. I3 8
Ribeira, Braz. B13 92
Ribeira do Pombal, Braz. F6 88
Ribeirão, Braz. E8 88
Ribeirão Preto, Braz. K2 88
Ribeirão Vermelho, Braz. K3 88
Ribeiro Gonçalves, Braz. D3 88
Ribera, Italy G7 24
Riberalta, Bol. B3 90
Rib Lake, Wi., U.S. F8 118
Ribnica, Slvn. E11 22
Ribnitz-Damgarten, Ger. B8 16
Ribstone Creek, stm., Ab., Can. D19 138
Ricardo Flores Magón, Mex. F9 98
Riccione, Italy F9 22
Rice, Tx., U.S. E2 122
Rice Lake, l., On., Can. D11 112
Riceville, Ia., U.S. H6 118
Riceville, Tn., U.S. B14 122
Richan, On., Can. B6 118
Richard B. Russell Lake, res., U.S. B3 116
Richard Collinson Inlet, b., N.T., Can. B17 140
Richards, Tx., U.S. G3 122
Richards Bay, S. Afr. F11 70
Richards Bay, b., S. Afr. F11 70
Richards Island, i., N.T., Can. C13 140
Richardson, Tx., U.S. E2 122
Richardson, Wa., U.S. B4 136
Richardson Mountains, mts., Can. B3 106
Richard Toll, Sen. F1 64
Riche, Pointe, c., Nf., Can. i22 107a
Richelieu, Fr. G9 14
Richelieu, stm., Qc., Can. E3 110
Richer, Mb., Can. E17 124
Richey, Mt., U.S. G8 124
Richfield, Mn., U.S. G5 118
Richfield, Pa., U.S. D8 114
Richfield, Ut., U.S. E4 132
Richfield Springs, N.Y., U.S. B11 114
Richford, Vt., U.S. F4 110
Rich Hill, Mo., U.S. F3 120
Richibucto, N.B., Can. D12 110
Richland, Ga., U.S. E14 122
Richland, Mi., U.S. F4 112
Richland, Mt., U.S. F7 124
Richland, Wa., U.S. D7 136
Richland Center, Wi., U.S. H8 118
Richland Creek, stm., Tx., U.S. C11 130
Richlands, Va., U.S. G4 114
Richland Springs, Tx., U.S. C9 130
Richmond, Austl. C4 76
Richmond, Austl. I8 76
Richmond, B.C., Can. G7 138
Richmond, On., Can. C14 112
Richmond, Qc., Can. E4 110
Richmond, N.Z. E5 80
Richmond, S. Afr. G6 70
Richmond, S. Afr. F10 70
Richmond, Eng., U.K. G11 12
Richmond, Ca., U.S. F3 134
Richmond, In., U.S. I5 112
Richmond, Ky., U.S. G1 114
Richmond, Me., U.S. F7 110
Richmond, Mi., U.S. B3 114
Richmond, Mn., U.S. F4 118
Richmond, Mo., U.S. E4 120
Richmond, Tx., U.S. H3 122
Richmond, Ut., U.S. B5 132
Richmond, Va., U.S. G8 114
Richmond Heights, Fl., U.S. K5 116
Richmond Highlands, Wa., U.S. C4 136
Richmond Hill, On., Can. E10 112
Richmond Hill, Ga., U.S. E4 116
Richmond Peak, mtn., St. Vin. o11 105e
Richton, Ms., U.S. F9 122
Richwood, Oh., U.S. D2 114
Richwood, W.V., U.S. F5 114
Ricobayo, Embalse de, res., Spain C4 20
Riddle, Or., U.S. H3 136
Rideau, stm., On., Can. C14 112
Ridgecrest, Ca., U.S. H8 134
Ridgedale, Sk., Can. A9 124
Ridgeland, Ms., U.S. E8 122
Ridgeland, S.C., U.S. D4 116
Ridgetown, On., Can. F8 112
Ridgeville, Mb., Can. E16 124
Ridgeville, S.C., U.S. C5 116
Ridgeway, Mo., U.S. D4 120
Ridgway, Co., U.S. E9 132
Ridgway, Il., U.S. G9 120
Ridgway, Pa., U.S. C7 114
Riding Mountain National Park, p.o.i., Mb., Can. D13 124
Riegelwood, N.C., U.S. B7 116
Riesa, Ger. E9 16
Riesco, Isla, i., Chile J2 90
Riesi, Italy G8 24
Riet, stm., S. Afr. F7 70
Riet, stm., S. Afr. H5 70
Rietavas, Lith. E4 10
Rietfontein (Buitsivango), stm., Afr. B4 70
Rieti, Italy H9 22
Rif, mts., Mor. C4 64
Riffe Lake, res., Wa., U.S. D4 136
Rifle, Co., U.S. D9 132
Rifstangi, c., Ice. j31 8a
Rift Valley, val., Afr. F7 62
Rīga, Lat. D7 10
Riga, Gulf of, b., Eur. C6 10
Rigaih, Indon. J2 48
Rigby, Id., U.S. G14 136
Rīgestān, reg., Afg. C9 56
Riggins, Id., U.S. E10 136
Rigi, mtn., Switz. C5 22
Rigo, Pap. N. Gui. b4 79a
Rig-Rig, Chad E2 62
Riihimäki, Fin. F11 8
Riiser-Larsen Peninsula, pen., Ant. B8 81
Riječki Zaljev, b., Cro. E11 22
Rijeka (Fiume), Cro. E11 22
Rijssen, Neth. D2 16
Rillito, Az., U.S. K5 132
Rimatara, i., Fr. Poly. F11 72
Rimavská Sobota, Slov. H15 16
Rimbey, Ab., Can. D16 138
Rimersburg, Pa., U.S. C6 114
Rimini, Italy F9 22
Rimouski, Qc., Can. B8 110
Rimouski, stm., Qc., Can. B8 110
Rinbung, China C7 46
Rinca, Pulau, i., Indon. H11 50
Rincon, Ga., U.S. D4 116
Rincon, N.M., U.S. K9 132
Rinconada, Arg. D3 90
Rincón del Bonete, Lago Artificial de, res., Ur. F9 92
Rincón de Romos, Mex. D7 100
Rīngas, India E5 54
Ringdove, Vanuatu k16 79d
Ringebu, Nor. F4 8
Ringgold, Ga., U.S. C13 122
Ringim, Nig. G6 64
Ringkøbing, Den. H2 8
Ringkøbing, state, Den. H3 8
Ringkøbing Fjord, b., Den. H2 8
Ringling, Ok., U.S. G11 128
Ringsted, Ia., U.S. H4 118
Ringvassøya, i., Nor. A8 8
Rinjani, Gunung, vol., Indon. H10 50
Rinteln, Ger. D5 16
Rio, Wi., U.S. H9 118
Riobamba, Ec. H2 86
Río Blanco, Chile F2 92
Rio Branco, Braz. E4 84
Río Branco, Ur. F11 92
Río Bravo, Mex. C9 100
Río Bravo, Parque Internacional del, p.o.i., Mex. F5 130
Rio Brilhante, Braz. D6 90
Río Bueno, Chile H2 90
Rio Casca, Braz. K4 88
Río Ceballos, Arg. E5 92
Río Chico, Ven. B9 86
Rio Claro, Braz. L2 88
Rio Claro, Trin. s12 105f
Río Colorado, Arg. I5 92
Río Cuarto, Arg. F5 92
Rio das Pedras, Moz. C12 70
Rio de Janeiro, Braz. L4 88
Rio de Janeiro, state, Braz. L4 88
Rio Dell, Ca., U.S. C1 134
Río de Oro, Col. C5 86
Rio do Sul, Braz. C13 92
Rio Espera, Braz. K4 88
Rio Felix, stm., N.M., U.S. H3 128
Río Gallegos, Arg. J3 90
Río Grande, Arg. J3 90
Rio Grande, Braz. F11 92
Río Grande, Mex. D7 100
Río Grande, Nic. F4 102
Río Grande, P.R. B4 104a
Rio Grande (Bravo), stm., N.A. H13 98
Rio Grande do Norte, state, Braz. C7 88
Rio Grande do Sul, state, Braz. D11 92
Ríohacha, Col. B5 86
Río Hato, Pan. H7 102
Rio Hondo, Tx., U.S. H10 130
Rio Hondo, stm., N.M., U.S. H3 128
Rio Hondo, Embalse, res., Arg. C5 92
Río Jueyes, P.R. B3 104a
Riolândia, Braz. D6 90
Rio Largo, Braz. E8 88
Riom, Fr. D9 18
Río Mayo, Arg. I2 90
Río Mulatos, Bol. C3 90
Riondel, B.C., Can. G14 138
Rio Negro, Braz. C13 92
Ríonegro, Col. D5 86
Río Negro, state, Arg. G3 90
Rio Negro, Pantanal do, sw., Braz. C5 90
Rionero in Vulture, Italy D9 24
Riópar, Spain F8 20
Rio Pardo, Braz. E11 92
Rio Pardo de Minas, Braz. H4 88
Río Piedras, P.R. B3 104a
Rio Piracicaba, Braz. J4 88
Rio Pomba, Braz. K4 88
Rio Preto, Braz. L3 88
Rio Rancho, N.M., U.S. H10 132
Rio Real, Braz. F6 88
Río Segundo, Arg. E5 92
Ríosucio, Col. E4 86
Río Tercero, Arg. F5 92
Rio Tinto, Braz. D8 88
Rio Verde, Braz. G7 84
Ríoverde, Mex. E8 100
Rio Verde de Mato Grosso, Braz. C6 90
Rio Vista, Ca., U.S. E4 134
Riozinho, stm., Braz. E3 88
Riozinho, stm., Braz. D4 84
Ripley, N.Y., U.S. B6 114
Ripley, Oh., U.S. F2 114
Ripley, Tn., U.S. B9 122
Ripoll, Spain B13 20
Ripon, Qc., Can. E1 110
Ripon, Eng., U.K. G11 12
Ripon, Ca., U.S. F4 134
Ripon, Wi., U.S. H10 118
Riposto, Italy G9 24
Risaralda, state, Col. E3 86
Risbäck, Swe. D6 8
Rishīkesh, India C7 54
Rishiri-suidō, strt., Japan B14 38
Rishiri-tō, i., Japan B14 38
Rishon LeẔiyyon, Isr. G5 58
Rising Star, Tx., U.S. B9 130
Rising Sun, In., U.S. F12 120
Rising Sun, Md., U.S. E9 114
Risle, stm., Fr. E9 14
Risnjak, mtn., Cro. E11 22
Risti, Est. A7 10
Ristna, Est. G9 8
Rita Blanca Creek, stm., Tx., U.S. F6 128
Ritchie, S. Afr. F7 70
Ritidian Point, c., Guam i10 78c
Ritter, Mount, mtn., Ca., U.S. F6 134
Rittman, Oh., U.S. D4 114
Ritzville, Wa., U.S. C8 136
Rivadavia, Arg. E3 92
Rivadavia, Arg. G6 92
Rivadavia, Chile D2 92
Riva del Garda, Italy E7 22
Rivas, Nic. G5 102
Rive-de-Gier, Fr. D10 18
Rivera, Arg. H6 92
Rivera, Ur. E10 92
River Cess, Lib. H3 64

Name	Map Ref.	Page
Riverdale, Ca., U.S.	G6	134
Riverdale, N.D., U.S.	G12	124
River Falls, Al., U.S.	F12	122
River Falls, Wi., U.S.	G6	118
Riverhead, N.Y., U.S.	D13	114
Riverhurst, Sk., Can.	D7	124
Riverina, reg., Austl.	J5	76
River John, N.S., Can.	E13	110
River Jordan, B.C., Can.	H6	138
River Road, Or., U.S.	F3	136
Rivers, Mb., Can.	D13	124
Riversdale, S. Afr.	I5	70
Riverside, Ca., U.S.	J8	134
Riverside, Ia., U.S.	C6	120
Riverside, Tx., U.S.	G3	122
Riverside, Wa., U.S.	B7	136
Rivers Inlet, B.C., Can.	E3	138
Riverleigh, Austl.	C7	74
Riverton, N.Z.	H2	80
Riverton, Il., U.S.	E8	120
Riverton, Ne., U.S.	A10	128
Riverton, Ut., U.S.	C4	132
Riverton, Wy., U.S.	F7	114
Riverton, Wy., U.S.	D4	126
Riverton Heights, Wa., U.S.	C4	136
River View, Al., U.S.	E13	122
Rives, Tn., U.S.	H8	120
Rivesville, W.V., U.S.	E5	114
Riviera, Tx., U.S.	G10	130
Riviera Beach, Fl., U.S.	J5	116
Rivière-à-Pierre, Qc., Can.	C5	110
Rivière-Bleue, Qc., Can.	C7	110
Rivière-de-la-Chaloupe, Qc., Can.	A14	110
Rivière-du-Loup, Qc., Can.	C7	110
Rivière-Matawin, Qc., Can.	D3	110
Rivière-Pilote, Mart.	I7	105c
Rivière-Salée, Mart.	k7	105c
Rivne, Ukr.	E14	6
Rivoli, Italy	E4	22
Rivoli Bay, b., Austl.	K2	76
Riyadh see Ar-Riyāḍ, Sau. Ar.	E6	56
Riyāq, Leb.	E7	58
Rize, Tur.	A5	56
Rizzuto, Capo, c., Italy	F11	24
Rjad, Russia	C18	10
Rjazan', Russia	D5	32
Rjazancevo, Russia	D22	10
Rjazanskaja oblast', co., Russia	I19	8
Rjažsk, Russia	D6	32
Rjukan, Nor.	G3	8
Ro, N. Cal.	m16	79d
Roachdale, In., U.S.	I3	112
Road Town, Br. Vir. Is.	e8	104b
Roan Mountain, Tn., U.S.	H3	114
Roanne, Fr.	C9	18
Roanoke, Al., U.S.	D13	122
Roanoke, Il., U.S.	D8	120
Roanoke, Va., U.S.	G6	114
Roanoke, Va., U.S.	H8	114
Roanoke Island, i., N.C., U.S.	I10	114
Roanoke Rapids, N.C., U.S.	H8	114
Roanoke Rapids Lake Dam, dam, N.C., U.S.	H8	114
Roan Plateau, plat., U.S.	D7	132
Roaring Spring, Pa., U.S.	D7	114
Roaring Springs, Tx., U.S.	H7	130
Roatán, Isla de, i., Hond.	D4	102
Robbins, N.C., U.S.	A6	116
Robbins, Tn., U.S.	H13	120
Robbins Island, i., Austl.	n12	77a
Robbinsville, N.C., U.S.	A2	116
Robe, Austl.	K2	76
Robe, Mount, hill, Austl.	H3	76
Robel, Ger.	C8	16
Robersonville, N.C., U.S.	I8	114
Roberta, Ga., U.S.	D1	116
Robert Lee, Tx., U.S.	C7	130
Roberts, Id., U.S.	G14	136
Roberts, Il., U.S.	B3	126
Robertsdale, Al., U.S.	G11	122
Robertsfors, Swe.	D9	8
Robert S. Kerr Lake, res., U.S.	B3	122
Robertson, S. Afr.	H4	70
Roberts Peak, mtn., B.C., Can.	D10	138
Roberts Port, Lib.	H2	64
Roberval, Qc., Can.	B4	110
Robinson, Il., U.S.	E10	120
Robinson, Tx., U.S.	C10	130
Róbinson Crusoe, Isla, i., Chile	I7	82
Robinvale, Austl.	J4	76
Robledo, Spain	F8	20
Roblin, Mb., Can.	C12	124
Roboré, Bol.	C5	90
Rob Roy Island, i., Sol. Is.	d7	79b
Robson, Mount, mtn., B.C., Can.	C11	138
Robstown, Tx., U.S.	G10	130
Roca, Cabo da, c., Port.	F1	20
Roçado, Braz.	D3	88
Rocafuerte, Ec.	H1	86
Roca Partida, Isla, i., Mex.	F2	100
Rocas, Atol das, at., Braz.	F11	82
Rocciamelone, mtn., Italy	E4	22
Rocha, Ur.	G10	92
Rochdale, Eng., U.K.	H10	12
Rochechouart, Fr.	D6	18
Rochefort, Fr.	D5	18
Rochelle, Ga., U.S.	E2	116
Rochelle, Il., U.S.	C8	120
Roche-Percée, Sk., Can.	E10	124
Rochester, Eng., U.K.	J13	12
Rochester, In., U.S.	B2	114
Rochester, Mi., U.S.	B2	114
Rochester, Mn., U.S.	G6	118
Rochester, N.H., U.S.	G5	110
Rochester, N.Y., U.S.	E12	112
Rochester, Tx., U.S.	H9	128
Rochlitz, Ger.	E8	16
Rock, stm., U.S.	J8	118
Rock, stm., U.S.	H2	118
Rockall, i., Scot., U.K.	D6	6
Rockall Rise, unds.	C12	144
Rock Bay, B.C., Can.	F5	138
Rock Creek, B.C., Can.	G11	138
Rock Creek, stm., N.A.		
Rock Creek, stm., Mt., U.S.	D13	136
Rock Creek, stm., Wa., U.S.	C9	134
Rock Creek Butte, mtn., Or., U.S.	F8	136
Rockdale, Il., U.S.	C9	120
Rockdale, Tx., U.S.	D11	130
Rockefeller Plateau, plat., Ant.	D27	81
Rockenhausen, Ger.	G3	16
Rock Falls, Il., U.S.	C8	120
Rockford, Al., U.S.	E12	122
Rockford, Il., U.S.	B8	120
Rockford, Oh., U.S.	D1	114
Rockford, Tn., U.S.	B15	122
Rockglen, Sk., Can.	E8	124
Rockhampton, Austl.	D8	76
Rockhampton Downs, Austl.	C7	74
Rock Hill, S.C., U.S.	B4	116
Rockingham, N.C., U.S.	B6	116
Rockingham Bay, b., Austl.	A5	76
Rock Island, Il., U.S.	C7	120
Rocklake, N.D., U.S.	F14	124
Rockland, On., Can.	C14	112
Rockland, Id., U.S.	H14	136
Rockland, Me., U.S.	B15	114
Rocklands Reservoir, l., Austl.	K3	76
Rockledge, Fl., U.S.	H5	116
Rocklin, Ca., U.S.	E4	134
Rockmart, Ga., U.S.	D13	122
Rockport, In., U.S.	G10	120
Rockport, Ky., U.S.	G11	120
Rockport, Ma., U.S.	B15	114
Rockport, Me., U.S.	F7	110
Rock Port, Mo., U.S.	D2	120
Rock Rapids, Ia., U.S.	H2	118
Rock Rwy., Wy., U.S.	F6	126
Rocksprings, Tx., U.S.	E7	130
Rock Springs, Wy., U.S.	B7	132
Rockstone, Guy.	B6	84
Rock Tombs see Speos, hist., Egypt	K1	58
Rock Valley, Ia., U.S.	H2	118
Rockville, In., U.S.	I2	112
Rockville, Md., U.S.	E8	114
Rockwall, Tx., U.S.	E2	122
Rockwell, Ia., U.S.	B4	120
Rockwell, N.C., U.S.	A5	116
Rockwood, Me., U.S.	E7	110
Rockwood, Pa., U.S.	I10	112
Rockwood, Tn., U.S.	I13	120
Rocky Cape National Park, p.o.i., Austl.	n12	77a
Rockyford, Ab., Can.	E17	138
Rocky Ford, Co., U.S.	C5	128
Rocky Mount, N.C., U.S.	I8	114
Rocky Mount, Va., U.S.	H5	114
Rocky Mountain, mtn., Mt., U.S.	C14	136
Rocky Mountain House, Ab., Can.	D16	138
Rocky Mountain National Park, p.o.i., Co., U.S.	G7	126
Rocky Mountains, mts., N.A.	D6	106
Rocky Mountain Trench, val., N.A.	G15	138
Rocky Point, c., Bah.	K8	116
Rodalben, Ger.	G3	16
Rodbār, Afg.	C9	56
Rødbyhavn, Den.	I4	8
Rodeo, Arg.	E3	92
Rodeo, Mex.	C6	100
Rodeo, N.M., U.S.	L7	132
Roderick Island, i., B.C., Can.	D2	138
Rodewisch, Ger.	F8	16
Rodez, Fr.	E8	18
Roding, Ger.	G8	16
Rodino, Russia	G21	8
Rodney, On., Can.	F8	112
Rodney, Cape, c., Ak., U.S.	D6	140
Rodniki, Russia	H19	8
Ródos (Rhodes), Grc.	G11	28
Ródos (Rhodes), i., Grc.	G10	28
Rodrigues, i., Mrts.	K9	142
Roebourne, Austl.	D3	74
Roebuck Bay, b., Austl.	C4	74
Roeland Park, Ks., U.S.	E3	120
Roermond, Neth.	C14	14
Roeselare, Bel.	D11	14
Roes Welcome Sound, strt., Nu., Can.	C13	106
Roff, Ok., U.S.	C2	122
Rogačevo, Russia	D20	10
Rogaguá, Laguna, l., Bol.	B3	90
Rogaguado, Laguna, l., Bol.	B3	90
Rogaland, state, Nor.	G2	8
Rogaška Slatina, Slvn.	D12	22
Rogers, Ar., U.S.	H3	120
Rogers, Tx., U.S.	D10	130
Rogers, Mount, mtn., Va., U.S.	H4	114
Rogers Lake, l., Ca., U.S.	I8	134
Rogers Pass, p., B.C., Can.	E13	138
Rogersville, Al., U.S.	C11	122
Rogersville, N.B., Can.	D11	110
Rogersville, Tn., U.S.	H3	114
Roggewein, Cabo, c., Chile	e30	78l
Rogliano, Fr.	G15	18
Rognedino, Russia	G16	10
Rogue, stm., Or., U.S.	H2	136
Rohri, Pak.	E2	54
Rohtak, India	D6	54
Roi Et, Thai.	E6	48
Roi Georges, Îles du, is., Fr. Poly.	E12	72
Roilianka, Ukr.	C16	26
Rojas, Arg.	G7	92
Rojo, Cabo, c., Mex.	E10	100
Rojo, Cabo, c., P.R.	C1	104a
Rokan, Indon.	C2	50
Rokan, stm., Indon.	C2	50
Rokel, stm., S.L.	H2	64
Rokiškis, Lith.	E8	10
Rokycany, Czech Rep.	G9	16
Roland, Ia., U.S.	E16	124
Roland, Ar., U.S.	C6	122
Rolândia, Braz.	D6	90
Roldanillo, Col.	E3	86
Rolfe, Ia., U.S.	B3	120
Roll, Az., U.S.	K2	132
Rolla, Mo., U.S.	G6	120
Rolla, N.D., U.S.	F14	124
Rolling Fork, Ms., U.S.	E8	122
Rolling Fork, stm., Ky., U.S.	G12	120
Rollingstone, Austl.	B6	76
Rollins, Mt., U.S.	C12	136
Rolvsøya, i., Nor.	A10	8
Roma, Austl.	F7	76
Roma (Rome), Italy	I9	22
Roma, Leso.	F9	70
Roma, Tx., U.S.	H8	130
Romagna, hist. reg., Italy	F9	22
Roman, Rom.	C13	26
Romanche Gap, unds.	I12	144
Romang, Pulau, i., Indon.	G8	44
Romania, ctry., Eur.	D11	26
Roman Nose Mountain, mtn., Or., U.S.	G3	136
Romano, Cape, c., Fl., U.S.	K4	116
Romano, Cayo, i., Cuba	A9	102
Romans-sur-Isère, Fr.	D10	18
Romanzof Mountains, mts., Ak., U.S.	C11	140
Romblon, Phil.	D4	52
Rome see Roma, Italy	I9	22
Rome, Ga., U.S.	C13	122
Rome, N.Y., U.S.	E14	112
Romilly-sur-Seine, Fr.	F12	14
Romney, W.V., U.S.	E7	114
Romny, Ukr.	D4	32
Romont, Switz.	D3	22
Romorantin-Lanthenay, Fr.	G10	14
Rompin, stm., Malay.	K6	48
Romsey, Eng., U.K.	J11	12
Ron, Mui, c., Viet.	C8	48
Rona, i., Scot., U.K.	D7	12
Rona, i., Scot., U.K.	B7	12
Ronan, Mt., U.S.	C12	136
Roncador, Banco see Roncador, Cayos de, unds., Col.	F7	102
Roncador, Cayos de, unds., Col.	F7	102
Roncador, Serra do, plat., Braz.	F7	84
Roncador Bank see Roncador, Cayos de, unds., Col.	F7	102
Ronda, Serranía de, mts., Spain	H5	20
Rondane Nasjonalpark, p.o.i., Nor.	F3	8
Ronde, Pointe, c., Dom.	i5	105c
Rondônia, state, Braz.	F5	84
Rondonópolis, Braz.	G7	84
Rong, stm., China	I3	42
Rong'an, China	I3	42
Rongcheng, China	C10	42
Ronge, Lac la, l., Sk., Can.	D10	106
Rongelap, at., Marsh. Is.	B7	72
Rongjiang, China	I3	42
Rongkop, Indon.	H7	50
Rongshui, China	I3	42
Rongxian, China	J4	42
Ronne, Den.	I6	8
Ronneby, Swe.	H6	8
Ronne Ice Shelf, ice, Ant.	C34	81
Ronse, Bel.	D12	14
Ronuro, stm., Braz.	F7	84
Roodhouse, Il., U.S.	E7	120
Roof Butte, mtn., Az., U.S.	G7	132
Rooiboklaagte, stm., Nmb.	B5	70
Roorkee, India	D6	54
Roosendaal, Neth.	C13	14
Roosevelt, Mn., U.S.	C3	118
Roosevelt, Ok., U.S.	G9	128
Roosevelt, Ut., U.S.	C6	132
Roosevelt, stm., Braz.	E5	84
Roosevelt Campobello Roosevelt International Park, p.o.i., N.B., Can.	F10	110
Roosevelt Island, i., Ant.	C24	81
Root, stm., U.S.	H7	118
Ropaži, Lat.	C7	10
Roper, N.C., U.S.	I9	114
Roper, stm., Austl.	B6	74
Roper Valley, Austl.	B6	74
Ropesville, Tx., U.S.	H6	128
Roque, Braz.	B3	88
Roquefort, Fr.	E5	18
Roraima, state, Braz.	C5	84
Roraima, Mount, mtn., S.A.	E11	86
Røros, Nor.	E4	8
Rosa, Lake, l., Bah.	B11	102
Rosales, Mex.	A6	100
Rosalia, Wa., U.S.	C9	136
Rosamond, Ca., U.S.	I7	134
Rosamond Lake, l., Ca., U.S.	I7	134
Rosario, Arg.	F7	92
Rosário, Braz.	B3	88
Rosario, Mex.	D5	100
Rosario, Mex.	B4	100
Rosario, Para.	B9	92
Rosario, Ur.	G9	92
Rosario, stm., Arg.	B5	92
Rosario, Bahía del, b., Mex.	G4	98
Rosario, Islas del, is., Col.	B4	86
Rosario de Arriba, Mex.	F4	98
Rosario de Lerma, Arg.	B5	92
Rosario del Tala, Arg.	F8	92
Rosário do Sul, Braz.	E10	92
Rosário Oeste, Braz.	F6	84
Rosarito, Mex.	K8	134
Rosarito, Mex.	A2	100
Rosarno, Italy	F9	24
Rosas, Mex.		
Roscoe, S.D., U.S.	B13	126
Roscoe, Tx., U.S.	B7	130
Roscommon, Ire.	H4	12
Roscommon, state, Ire.	H4	12
Roscrea, Ire.	I5	12
Rose, Mount, mtn., Nv., U.S.	D5	134
Roseau, Dom.	j6	105c
Roseau, Mn., U.S.	C2	118
Roseau, stm., N.A.	C2	118
Roseberth, Austl.	E2	76
Rosebery, Austl.	n12	77a
Roseboro, N.C., U.S.	B7	116
Rosebud, Mt., U.S.	A6	126
Rosebud, S.D., U.S.	D12	126
Rosebud, Tx., U.S.	C11	130
Rosebud, stm., Ab., Can.	E17	138
Rosebud Creek, stm., Mt., U.S.	A6	126
Roseburg, Or., U.S.	G3	136
Rosebush, Mi., U.S.	E5	112
Rose City, Mi., U.S.	D5	112
Rosedale, Austl.	E8	76
Rosedale, Ab., Can.	E18	138
Rosedale, La., U.S.	G7	122
Rosedale, Ms., U.S.	D7	122
Rose Hill, N.C., U.S.	B7	116
Rose Hill, Va., U.S.	H2	114
Rose Island, i., Bah.	K8	116
Rosemary, Ab., Can.	F18	138
Rosenberg, Tx., U.S.	H3	122
Rosenheim, Ger.	I8	16
Rosepine, La., U.S.	G5	122
Roses, Golfe de, b., Spain	B14	20
Roses, Golfo de see Roses, Golfe de, b., Spain	B14	20
Roseto degli Abruzzi, Italy	H11	22
Rosetown, Sk., Can.	C6	124
Rosetta see Rashid, Egypt.	G1	58
Rosetta Mouth see Rashid, Masabb, mth., Egypt	G1	58
Rose Valley, Sk., Can.	B10	124
Roseville, Il., U.S.	D7	120
Roseville, Mi., U.S.	B2	114
Rosholt, S.D., U.S.	F2	118
Rosholt, Wi., U.S.	G9	118
Rosica, stm., Blg.	F12	26
Rosiclare, Il., U.S.	G9	120
Rosignol, Guy.	B6	84
Roşiori de Vede, Rom.	E12	26
Roskilde, Den.	I4	8
Roskilde, state, Den.	I5	8
Roslavl', Russia	G16	10
Rosman, N.C., U.S.	A3	116
Rosmead, S. Afr.	G7	70
Ros Mhic Thriúin see New Ross, Ire.	I6	12
Ross, Austl.	o13	77a
Ross, stm., Yk., Can.	C4	106
Rossano, Italy	E10	24
Rossan Point, c., Ire.	G4	12
Rossburn, Mb., Can.	D13	124
Rosseau, Lake, l., On., Can.	C10	112
Rossel, Cap, c., N. Cal.	m16	79d
Rossell y Rius, Ur.	F10	92
Rossford, Oh., U.S.	C2	114
Ross Ice Shelf, ice, Ant.	D23	81
Rossignol, Lake, l., N.S., Can.	F11	110
Ross Island, i., Ant.	C22	81
Ross Lake, res., N.A.	B5	136
Rossland, B.C., Can.	G13	138
Rosslau, Ger.	E8	16
Rosso, Maur.	F1	64
Ross-on-Wye, Eng., U.K.	J10	12
Rossosh', Russia	D5	32
Ross R. Barnett Reservoir, res., Ms., U.S.	E9	122
Ross River, Yk., Can.	C4	106
Ross Sea, s., Ant.	C23	81
Røssvatnet, l., Nor.	D5	8
Rossville, Ga., U.S.	C13	122
Rossville, Il., U.S.	H2	112
Rossville, Ks., U.S.	E2	120
Rostāq, Afg.	B10	56
Rosthern, Sk., Can.	B7	124
Rostock, Ger.	B7	16
Rostov, Russia	C22	10
Rostov-na-Donu, Russia	E6	32
Rosvinskoe, Russia	C24	8
Roswell, Ga., U.S.	C1	116
Roswell, N.M., U.S.	H3	128
Rota, i., N. Mar. Is.	B5	72
Rotan, Tx., U.S.	B7	130
Rotenburg, Ger.	C5	16
Rothaargebirge, mts., Ger.	E4	16
Rothesay, Scot., U.K.	F7	12
Rothsay, Mn., U.S.	E2	118
Rothwell, N.B., Can.	D10	110
Roti, Pulau, i., Indon.	H7	44
Roto, Austl.	I5	76
Rotondella, Italy	D10	24
Rotorua, N.Z.	D7	80
Rottenburg am Neckar, Ger.	H4	16
Rotterdam, Neth.	C13	14
Rotterdam, N.Y., U.S.	B11	114
Rottweil, Ger.	H4	16
Rotuma, i., Fiji	E8	72
Roubaix, Fr.	D12	14
Roudnice nad Labem, Czech Rep.	F9	16
Rouen, Fr.	E10	14
Rouge, stm., Qc., Can.	E2	110
Rough, stm., Ky., U.S.	G11	120
Rough River Lake, res., U.S.	G11	120
Rouleau, Sk., Can.	D9	124
Roulers see Roeselare, Bel.	D11	14
Roulette, Pa., U.S.	C7	114
Round Hill Head, c., Austl.	E8	76
Round Lake, Mn., U.S.	H3	118
Round Lake, l., On., Can.	C12	112
Round Mound, hill, Ks., U.S.	C9	128
Round Mountain, Nv., U.S.	E8	134
Round Mountain, mtn., Austl.	H9	76
Round Rock, Tx., U.S.	D10	130
Roundup, Mt., U.S.	A4	126
Rousay, i., Scot., U.K.	B9	12
Rouses Point, N.Y., U.S.	E3	110
Roussillon, hist. reg., Fr.	G8	18
Routhierville, Qc., Can.	B9	110
Rouyn-Noranda, Qc., Can.	F15	106
Rovaniemi, Fin.	C11	8
Rovenskaja Slabada, Bela.	H13	10
Rovereto, Italy	E8	22
Roversi, Arg.	C6	92
Rovigo, Italy	E8	22
Rovuma (Ruvuma), stm., Afr.	C6	68
Rowan Lake, l., On., Can.	B5	118
Rowena, Austl.	G7	76
Rowland, N.C., U.S.	B6	116
Rowley, stm., Nu., Can.	A15	106
Rowley Island, i., Nu., Can.	B14	106
Roxas, Phil.	D4	52
Roxboro, N.C., U.S.	H7	114
Roxborough, Trin.	H13	105f
Roxburgh, N.Z.	G3	80
Roxton, Tx., U.S.	D3	122
Roy, N.M., U.S.	F4	128
Roy, Ut., U.S.	B4	132
Roy, Wa., U.S.	C4	136
Royal Bardīyā Wild Life Reserve, India	D8	54
Royal Canal, can., Ire.	H6	12
Royal Center, In., U.S.	H3	112
Royal Chitwan National Park, p.o.i., Nepal	E10	54
Royal City, Wa., U.S.	D7	136
Royale, Isle, i., Mi., U.S.	D10	118
Royal Gorge, p., Co., U.S.	C3	128
Royal Leamington Spa, Eng., U.K.	I11	12
Royal Natal National Park, p.o.i., S. Afr.	F9	70
Royal Oak, Mi., U.S.	B2	114
Royalton, Mn., U.S.	F4	118
Royal Tunbridge Wells, Eng., U.K.	J13	12
Royan, Fr.	D5	18
Roye, Fr.	E11	14
Royston, Eng., U.K.	I12	12
Royston, Ga., U.S.	B2	116
Rožan, Pol.	D17	16
Roždestveno, Russia	C20	10
Rozdil'na, Ukr.	C17	26
Rozewie, Przylądek, c., Pol.	B14	16
Rožňava, Slov.	H16	16
Roznov, Rom.	C13	26
Rožňov, Pol.	G16	16
Roztocze, hills, Eur.	F19	16
Roztoky, Czech Rep.	F10	16
Rrogozhina see Rrogozhinë, Alb.	C13	24
Rrogozhinë, Alb.	C13	24
Rtiščevo, Russia	D6	32
Ru, stm., China	E6	42
Ruacana Falls, wtfl., Afr.	D1	68
Ruahine Range, mts., N.Z.	D6	80
Ruapehu, Mount, vol., N.Z.	D6	80
Ruapuke Island, i., N.Z.	H3	80
Rubcovsk, Russia	D14	32
Rubi, stm., D.R.C.	D4	66
Rubio, Ven.	D5	86
Rubondo Island, i., Tan.	E6	66
Ruby, Ak., U.S.	D8	140
Ruby Dome, mtn., Nv., U.S.	C1	132
Ruby Lake, res., Nv., U.S.	C1	132
Ruby Mountains, mts., Nv., U.S.	C1	132
Ruby Valley, val., Nv., U.S.	C1	132
Rucheng, China	I5	42
Ruciane-Nida, Pol.	C17	16
Ruda Śląska, Pol.	F14	16
Rudall, India	E8	54
Rudersdorf, Ger.	D9	16
Rudkøbing, Den.	B6	16
Rudnaja Pristan', Russia	B11	38
Rudnja, Russia	F14	10
Rudnyj, Russia	B11	38
Rudnyj, Kaz.	D10	32
Rudo, Bos.	F6	26
Rudolf, Lake (Turkana), l., Afr.	D7	66
Rudolf Häyk' see Rudolf, Lake, l., Afr.	D7	66
Rudolstadt, Ger.	F7	16
Rudong, China	E9	42
Rudozem, Blg.	H11	26
Rudyard, Mi., U.S.	B5	112
Rue, Fr.	D10	14
Rufā'ah, Sudan	E6	62
Ruffin, S.C., U.S.	C5	116
Rufiji, stm., Tan.	F7	66
Rufino, Arg.	G6	92
Rufisque, Sen.	G1	64
Rufunsa, Zam.	D4	68
Rufus, Or., U.S.	E6	136
Rugāji, Lat.	D10	10
Rugao, China	E9	42
Rugby, Eng., U.K.	I11	12
Rugby, N.D., U.S.	F14	124
Rügen, i., Ger.	B9	16
Rugged Mountain, mtn., B.C., Can.	F4	138
Ruhengeri, Rw.	E5	66
Ruhnu, i., Est.	B6	10
Ruhpolding, Ger.	I8	16
Ruhr, stm., Ger.	E3	16
Ruhunu National Park, p.o.i., Sri L.	H5	53
Rui'an, China	H9	42
Ruidoso, N.M., U.S.	H3	128
Ruidoso, stm., N.M., U.S.	I3	128
Ruihong, China	G7	42
Ruijin, China	I6	42
Ruiz, Mex.	D6	100
Ruiz, Nevado del, vol., Col.	E4	86
Ruiz de Montoya, Arg.	C10	92
Ruki, stm., D.R.C.	E3	66
Rukwa, Lake, l., Tan.	F6	66
Ruleville, Ms., U.S.	D8	122
Rulo, Ne., U.S.	D2	120
Rûm, i., Scot., U.K.	D6	12
Rum, stm., Mn., U.S.	F5	118
Ruma, Serb.	D6	26
Rumbek, Sudan	F5	62
Rum Cay, i., Bah.	C10	96
Rumia, Pol.	B14	16
Rumigny, Fr.	E13	14
Rumoi, Japan	B14	38
Runan, China	E6	42
Runanga, N.Z.	F4	80
Runde, stm., Zimb.	B10	70
Rundéni, Lat.	D10	10
Rundu, Nmb.	D2	68
Rūng, Kaôh, i., Camb.	G6	48
Runge, Tx., U.S.	F10	130
Rungwa, Tan.	F6	66
Rungwa, stm., Tan.	F6	66
Running Water Draw, stm., U.S.	G6	128
Ruo, stm., China	C4	36
Ruoqiang, China	D2	36
Ruoxi, China	G6	42
Rupat, Pulau, i., Indon.	C2	50
Rupert, Id., U.S.	H13	136
Rupert, W.V., U.S.	G5	114
Rupert, stm., Qc., Can.	E15	106
Rupert Creek, stm., Austl.	C4	76
Rupnuni, stm., Guy.	F12	86
Rur, stm., Eur.	D15	14
Rural Retreat, Va., U.S.	H4	114
Rurrenabaque, Bol.	B3	90
Rurutu, i., Fr. Poly.	F11	72
Rusape, Zimb.	D5	68
Rusayris, Khazzan ar-,	E6	62
Ruse, Blg.	F12	26
Ruse, state, Blg.	F13	26
Rusera, India	F11	54
Rushan, China	C9	42
Rush Center, Ks., U.S.	C9	128
Rush City, Mn., U.S.	F5	118
Rush Creek, stm., Co., U.S.	C5	128
Rushford, Mn., U.S.	H7	118
Rushmore, Mn., U.S.	H3	118
Rushville, Il., U.S.	D7	120
Rushville, In., U.S.	E12	120
Rusinga Island, i., Kenya	E6	66
Rusizi, stm., Afr.	E5	66
Rusk, Tx., U.S.	F3	122
Rusné, Lith.	E4	10
Russas, Braz.	C6	88
Russell, Mb., Can.	D12	124
Russell, Ia., U.S.	D4	120
Russell, Ks., U.S.	C10	128
Russell, Ky., U.S.	F3	114
Russell, Cape, c., N.T., Can.	A16	140
Russell Cave National Monument, p.o.i., Al., U.S.	C13	122
Russell Islands, is., Sol. Is.	e8	79b
Russellkonda, India	I10	54
Russells Point, Oh., U.S.	D2	114
Russell Springs, Ky., U.S.	G12	120
Russellville, Al., U.S.	C11	122
Russellville, Ar., U.S.	B5	122
Russellville, Ky., U.S.	H11	120
Rüsselsheim, Ger.	G4	16
Russia, ctry., Eur.	B18	2
Russian, stm., Ca., U.S.	E2	134
Russiaville, In., U.S.	H3	112
Russkij, Russia	C9	38
Rustavi, Geor.	F7	32
Rustburg, Va., U.S.	G6	114
Rustenburg, S. Afr.	D8	70
Ruston, La., U.S.	E6	122
Rutana, Bdi.	E5	66
Rute, Spain	G6	20
Ruteng, Indon.	H12	50
Ruth, Nv., U.S.	D1	132
Rutherford, N.C., U.S.	A3	116
Rutherfordton, N.C., U.S.	A3	116
Ruthin, Wales, U.K.	H9	12
Ruthven, Ia., U.S.	H4	118
Rutland, B.C., Can.	G11	138
Rutland, N.D., U.S.	A15	126
Rutland, Vt., U.S.	G4	110
Rutledge, Ga., U.S.	C2	116
Rutog, China	B7	54
Rutshuru, D.R.C.	E5	66
Rutter, On., Can.	B9	112
Ruvuma (Rovuma), stm., Afr.	C6	68
Ruwenzori, mts., Afr.	D6	66
Ruwenzori Range see Ruwenzori, mts., Afr.	D6	66
Ruy Barbosa, Braz.	G5	88
Ruza, Russia	E19	10
Ruza, stm., Russia	E18	10
Ruzaevka, Russia	D7	32
Ružany, Bela.	H7	10
Ružomberok, Slov.	G15	16
Rwanda, ctry., Afr.	E5	66
Ryan, Ok., U.S.	G11	128
Ryan Peak, mtn., Id., U.S.	G12	136
Ryback, Kaz.	E14	32
Rybačij, poluostrov, pen., Russia	B15	8
Rybinsk, Russia	B21	10
Rybinskoe vodohranilišče (Rybinsk Reservoir), res., Russia	B21	10
Rybinsk Reservoir see Rybinskoe vodohranilišče, res., Russia	B21	10
Rybnik, Pol.	F14	16
Rybnoe, Russia	E7	34
Ryde, Eng., U.K.	K11	12
Ryderwood, Wa., U.S.	D3	136
Rydzyna, Pol.	E12	16
Ryegate, Mt., U.S.	A3	126
Rye Patch Reservoir, res., Nv., U.S.	C7	134
Ryfoss, Nor.	F3	8
Ryley, Ab., Can.	C18	138
Rylovići, Russia	H15	10
Ryl'sk, Russia	D4	32
Rymařov, Czech Rep.	G13	16
Ryōhaku-sanchi, mts., Japan	C9	40
Ryōtsu, Japan	A11	40
Rysy, mtn., Eur.	G15	16
Ryūgasaki, Japan	D13	40
Ryukyu Islands see Nansei-shotō, is., Japan	k19	39a
Ryukyu Trench, unds.	G15	142
Ržanica, Russia	G16	10
Rzeszów, Pol.	F18	16
Rzeszów, state, Pol.	F17	16
Ržev, Russia	D17	10

S

Sa, Thai.	C5	48
Saale, stm., Ger.	E7	16
Saalfeld, Ger.	F7	16
Saar see Saarland, state, Ger.	G2	16
Saarbrücken, Ger.	G2	16
Saarburg, Ger.	G2	16
Saaremaa, i., Est.	B5	10
Saarijärvi, Fin.	E11	8
Saaristomeren kansallispuisto, p.o.i., Fin.	G9	8
Saarland, state, Ger.	G2	16
Saarlouis, Ger.	G2	16
Saavedra, Arg.	H6	92
Šaba, i., Neth. Ant.	B1	105a
Šabac, Serb.	E6	26
Sabadell, Spain	C13	20
Sabae, Japan	D9	40
Sabah, state, Malay.	H1	52
Sabah, hist. reg., Malay.	D6	44
Sabak, Malay.	K5	48
Sabalana, Kepulauan, is., Indon.	G11	50
Sabana, Archipiélago de, is., Cuba	A7	102
Sabana de la Mar, Dom. Rep.	C13	102
Sabana de Mendoza, Ven.	C6	86
Sabanagrande, Hond.	F4	102
Sabana Grande, P.R.	B2	104a
Sabanalarga, Col.	B4	86
Sabana Llana, Col.	B3	104a
Sabang, Indon.	J2	48
Sabang, Indon.	C11	50
Sabarei, Kenya	D7	66
Sábar, stm., India	C5	53
Sābarmati, stm., India	G4	54
Sab'atayn, Ramlat as-, sand, Yemen	F6	56
Sabbioneta, Italy	E7	22
Sāberī, Hāmūn-e, l., Asia	C9	56
Sabetha, Ks., U.S.	E2	120
Sabhā, Libya	B2	62
Sabidana, Jabal, mtn.,	D7	62
Sabie, S. Afr.	D10	70
Sabiē, stm., Afr.	D10	70
Sabile, Lat.	C5	10
Sabina, Oh., U.S.	E2	114
Sabina, hist. reg., Italy	H9	22
Sabinal, Tx., U.S.	E8	130
Sabinal, stm., Tx., U.S.	E8	130
Sabinal, Cayo, i., Cuba	B9	102
Sabinas, Mex.	B8	100
Sabinas, stm., Mex.	B8	100
Sabinas Hidalgo, Mex.	B8	100
Sabine, stm., U.S.	G5	122
Sabine Bay, b., Can.	A17	140
Sabine Lake, l., U.S.	H5	122
Sabine Pass, strt., U.S.	H5	122
Sabinópolis, Braz.	J4	88
Sabiote, Spain	F7	20
Sabla, Blg.	F15	26
Sable, Cape, c., N.S., Can.	G11	110
Sable, Cape, pen., Fl., U.S.	K4	116
Sable Island, i., N.S., Can.	G16	110
Sablah, Shallāl as- (Sixth Cataract), wtfl., Sudan	D6	62
Šablykino, Russia	H18	10
Sabor, stm., Port.	C4	20
Sabou, Burkina	G4	64
Sabrina Coast, cst., Ant.	B16	81
Şabyā, Sau. Ar.	F5	56
Sabyin, Mya.	C2	48
Sabzevār, Iran	B8	56
Sac, stm., Mo., U.S.	G4	120
Sacaton, Az., U.S.	J5	132
Sac City, Ia., U.S.	B3	120
Sācele, Rom.	D12	26
Sachayoj, Arg.	C6	92
Sachsen (Saxony), hist. reg., Ger.	F9	16
Sachsen (Saxony), hist. reg., Ger.	D5	16
Sachsen-Anhalt, state, Ger.	D7	16
Sachs Harbour, N.T., Can.	B14	140
Šack, Bela.	G10	10
Sackets Harbor, N.Y., U.S.	E13	112
Sackville, N.B., Can.	E12	110
Saco, Me., U.S.	G6	110
Saco, Mt., U.S.	F6	126
Sacramento, Braz.	J2	88
Sacramento, Ca., U.S.	E4	134
Sacramento, stm., Ca., U.S.	E4	134
Sacramento Mountains, mts., N.M., U.S.	E10	98
Sacramento Valley, val., Ca., U.S.	D3	134
Sacramento Wash, stm., Az., U.S.	H2	132
Sacred Heart, Mn., U.S.	G3	118
Sádaba, Spain	B9	20
Şa'dah, Yemen	F5	56
Sadak Taung, mtn., Mya.	E4	48
Sada-misaki, c., Japan	F4	40
Sada-misaki-hantō, pen., Japan	F4	40
Sadang, stm., Indon.	E11	50
Sa Dao, Thai.	I5	48
Sadda, Pak.	B3	54
Saddle Mountain, mtn., Co., U.S.	C3	128
Saddle Mountain, mtn., Or., U.S.	E3	136
Saddle Peak, hill, India	F7	46
Sa Dec, Viet.	G7	48
Sādiqābād, Pak.	D3	54
Sadiya, India	C8	46
Sadlers, St. K./N.	C2	105a
Sado, i., Japan	A11	40
Sado, stm., Port.	F2	20
Sado-kaikyō, strt., Japan	B11	40
Sadowara, Japan	G4	40
Sādri, India	F4	54
Sadrinsk, Russia	C10	32
Sädvaluspen, Swe.	C7	8
Saegertown, Pa., U.S.	C5	114
Saerluojia Hu, l., China	B11	54
Šafárikovo, Slov.	H16	16
Saffle, Swe.	G5	8
Saffron Walden, Eng., U.K.	I13	12
Safi, Mor.	C3	64
Safid Koh, Selseleh-ye, mts., Afg.	C9	56
Safonovo, Russia	E16	10
Safonovo, Russia	D22	8
Saframbolu, Tur.	B15	28
Saga, China	D10	54
Saga, Japan	F3	40
Saga, state, Japan	F3	40
Sagae, Japan	A13	40
Sagaing, Mya.	B2	48
Sagaing, state, Mya.	A2	48
Sagamihara, Japan	D12	40
Saganaga Lake, l., N.A.	C7	118
Saganthit Kyun, i., Mya.	F4	48
Sāgar, India	G7	54
Sāgar, India	D2	53
Sagara, Japan	E11	40
Sagaranten, Indon.	G5	50
Sage, Mount, mtn., Br. Vir. Is.	e8	104b
Sage Creek, stm., Mt., U.S.	B16	136
Sagerton, Tx., U.S.	A8	130
Saginaw, Mi., U.S.	E6	112
Saginaw, stm., Mi., U.S.	E6	112
Saginaw Bay, b., Mi., U.S.	E6	112
Sagleipie, Lib.	H3	64
Saglek Bay, b., Nf., Can.	F13	141
Sagonar, Russia	D16	32
Şagu, Rom.	C8	26
Saguache, Co., U.S.	C2	128
Saguache Creek, stm., Co., U.S.	C2	128
Sagua de Tánamo, Cuba	B10	102
Sagua la Grande, Cuba	A7	102
Saguaro National Park, p.o.i., Az., U.S.	K5	132
Saguenay, stm., Qc., Can.	B7	110
Sagunt, Spain	E10	20
Sagunto see Sagunt, Spain	E10	20
Ságwāra, India	G5	54
Sa'gya, China	D12	54

Sahagún – San Buenaventura I • 49

Name — Map Ref. — Page

Sahagún, Col. C4 86
Sahagún, Spain. B5 20
Sahalin, ostrov, i., Russia F17 34
Sahalinskij zaliv, b., Russia F17 34
Sahara, des., Afr. E5 64
Sahāranpur, India C6 54
Saharsa, India F11 54
Sahel see Sudan, reg., Afr. E4 62
Sāhibganj, India F11 54
Sāhīwāl, Pak. C4 54
Sāhīwāl, Pak. C4 54
Šahovskaja, Russia D18 10
Šahrisabz, Uzb. G11 32
Šahtjorsk, Russia G17 34
Šahty, Russia E6 32
Sahuaripa, Mex. A4 100
Sahuarita, Az., U.S. L5 132
Sahuayo de José María Morelos, Mex. E7 100
Šahunja, Russia H22 8
Šahy, Slov. H14 16
Sai Buri, Thai. I5 48
Sai Buri, stm., Thai. I5 48
Saidor, Pap. N. Gui. b4 79a
Saidpur, Bngl. F12 54
Saidu, Pak. C11 56
Saigō, Japan C6 40
Saigon see Thanh Pho Ho Chi Minh, Viet. G8 48
Saijō, Japan F6 40
Saiki, Japan G4 40
Šaim, Russia B10 32
Saimaa, l., Fin. F13 8
Sainte Agathe, Mb., Can. E16 124
Sainte-Agathe-des-Monts, Qc., Can. D2 110
Saint-Agrève, Fr. D10 18
Saint Alban's, Nf., Can. j22 107a
Saint Albans, Eng., U.K. J12 12
Saint Albans, Vt., U.S. F3 110
Saint Albans, W.V., U.S. F4 114
Saint Albert, Ab., Can. C17 138
Saint Aldhelm's Head, c., Eng., U.K. K10 12
Saint-Alexis-des-Monts, Qc., Can. D3 110
Saint-Amand-Mont-Rond, Fr. H11 14
Saint-André-Avellin, Qc., Can. E1 110
Saint Andrew, Barb. n8 105d
Saint Andrew, Mount, mtn., St. Vin. o11 105e
Saint Andrews, N.B., Can. E9 110
Saint Andrews, Scot., U.K. E10 12
Saint Andrews, S.C., U.S. D5 116
Sainte-Anne, Guad. h6 105c
Sainte-Anne, Mart. I7 105c
Sainte Anne, Lac, l., Ab., Can. C16 138
Sainte-Anne-de-Beaupré, Qc., Can. C5 110
Sainte-Anne-de-Madawaska, N.B., Can. C8 110
Sainte-Anne-des-Monts, Qc., Can. A10 110
Sainte-Anne-du-Lac, Qc., Can. D1 110
Saint Ann's Bay, Jam. i13 104d
Saint-Anselme, Qc., Can. D6 110
Saint Ansgar, Ia., U.S. H5 118
Saint Anthony, Nf., Can. i22 107a
Saint Anthony, Id., U.S. G15 136
Saint Arnaud, Austl. K4 76
Saint Augustin, Qc., Can. i22 107a
Saint Augustine, Fl., U.S. G4 116
Saint Austell, Eng., U.K. K8 12
Saint-Avold, Fr. E15 14
Saint-Barthélemy, i., Guad. B2 105a
Saint-Basile, N.B., Can. C8 110
Saint Bathans, Mount, mtn., N.Z. G3 80
Saint Bees Head, c., Eng., U.K. G9 12
Saint-Boniface-de-Shawinigan, Qc., Can. D3 110
Saint-Bonnet, Fr. E11 18
Saint Brides Bay, b., Wales, U.K. J7 12
Saint-Brieuc, Fr. F6 14
Saint-Brieuc, Baie de, b., Fr. F6 14
Saint Catharines, On., Can. E10 112
Saint Catherine, Mount, vol., Gren. q10 105e
Saint Catherines Island, i., Ga., U.S. E4 116
Saint Catherine's Point, c., Eng., U.K. K11 12
Saint-Céré, Fr. E7 18
Saint-Chamond, Fr. D10 18
Saint Charles, Id., U.S. A5 132
Saint Charles, Il., U.S. C9 120
Saint Charles, Mi., U.S. E5 112
Saint Charles, Mn., U.S. H6 118
Saint Charles, Mo., U.S. F7 120
Saint Charles Mesa, Co., U.S. C4 128
Saint Christopher (Saint Kitts), i., St. K./N. C2 105a
Saint Christopher and Nevis see Saint Kitts and Nevis, ctry., N.A. C2 105a
Saint Clair, Mi., U.S. B3 114
Saint Clair, Mo., U.S. F6 120
Saint Clair, stm., N.A. B3 114
Saint Clair, Lake, l., N.A. B3 114
Saint Clair Shores, Mi., U.S. B3 114
Saint-Claud, Fr. D6 18
Saint Claude, Mb., Can. E15 124
Saint-Claude, Fr. C11 18
Saint-Claude, Guad. h5 105c
Saint Cloud, Fl., U.S. H4 116
Saint Cloud, Mn., U.S. F4 118
Sainte-Croix, Qc., Can. D5 110
Saint Croix, i., V.I.U.S. g10 104c
Saint Croix, stm., N.A. E9 110
Saint Croix, stm., U.S. G6 118
Saint Croix Falls, Wi., U.S. F6 118
Saint Croix Island National Monument, p.o.i., Me., U.S. E10 110
Saint-Cyr, stm., Qc., Can. A1 110
Saint David, Az., U.S. L6 132
Saint David's, Wales, U.K. J7 12
Saint David's Head, c., Wales, U.K. J7 12
Saint David's Island, i., Ber. k16 104e
Saint-Denis, Fr. E11 14
Saint-Denis, Reu. i10 69a
Saint-Dié, Fr. F15 14
Saint-Dizier, Fr. F13 14
Saint-Donat-de-Montcalm, Qc., Can. D2 110
Saint Edward, Ne., U.S. F15 126
Saint Elias, Cape, c., Ak., U.S. E11 140
Saint Elias, Mount, mtn., N.A. C2 106
Saint Elias Mountains, mts., N.A. D12 140
Saint-Élie, Fr. Gu. C7 84
Saint Elmo, Il., U.S. E9 120
Saint-Étienne, Fr. D10 18
Saint-Étienne-du-Rouvray, Fr. E10 14
Saint-Eugène, Qc., Can. B4 110
Saint-Eustache, Qc., Can. E2 110
Saint-Fabien, Qc., Can. B8 110
Saint-Félicien, Qc., Can. B4 110
Saint-Félix-de-Valois, Qc., Can. D3 110
Saint-Florent-sur-Cher, Fr. G11 14
Saint-Flour, Fr. D9 18
Sainte-Foy, ngh., Qc., Can. D5 110
Sainte-Foy-la-Grande, Fr. E6 18
Saint Francis, Ks., U.S. B7 128
Saint Francis, Wi., U.S. I11 118
Saint Francis, stm., N.A. C7 110
Saint Francis, stm., U.S. C8 122
Saint Francis, Cape, c., S. Afr. I7 70
Saint Francis Bay, b., S. Afr. I7 70
Saint Francisville, Il., U.S. F10 120
Saint Francisville, La., U.S. G7 122
Saint-François, Guad. h6 105c
Saint-François, stm., Qc., Can. D4 110
Saint-François, Lac, l., Can. E2 110
Saint-François, Lac, res., Qc., Can. E5 110
Saint-Gabriel, Can. B8 110
Saint-Gabriel-de-Gaspé, Qc., Can. B12 110
Saint-Gall see Sankt Gallen, Switz. C6 22
Saint-Gaudens, Fr. F6 18
Sainte Genevieve, Mo., U.S. G7 120
Saint George, Austl. G7 76
Saint George, Ber. k16 104e
Saint George, N.B., Can. E10 110
Saint George, On., Can. E9 112
Saint George, Ut., U.S. F3 132
Saint George, Cape, c., Fl., U.S. H13 122
Saint George, Point, c., Ca., U.S. B1 134
Saint George Island, i., Fl., U.S. H14 122
Saint-Georges, Qc., Can. D6 110
Saint-Georges, Qc., Can. D4 110
Saint-Georges, Fr. Gu. C7 84
Saint George's, Gren. q10 105e
Saint George's Bay, b., Nf., Can. j22 107a
Saint Georges Bay, b., N.S., Can. E15 110
Saint George's Channel, strt., Eur. J7 12
Saint George's Channel, strt., Pap. N. Gui. a5 79a
Saint-Gilles-Croix-de-Vie, Fr. H6 14
Saint Gotthard Pass see San Gottardo, Passo del, p., Switz. D5 22
Saint Helena, Ca., U.S. E3 134
Saint Helena, dep., Afr. H5 60
Saint Helena Bay see Sint Helenabaai, b., S. Afr. H3 70
Saint Helens, Eng., U.K. H10 12
Saint Helens, Or., U.S. E4 136
Saint Helens, Mount, vol., Wa., U.S. D4 136
Saint Helier, Jersey E6 14
Saint-Hilaire-du-Harcouët, Fr. F7 14
Saint-Hyacinthe, Qc., Can. E4 110
Saint Ignace Island, i., On., Can. C11 118
Saint Ignatius, Guy. F12 86
Saint Ignatius, Mt., U.S. C12 136
Saint-Isidore, N.B., Can. C11 110
Saint Ives, Eng., U.K. K7 12
Saint James, Mi., U.S. C4 112
Saint James, Mn., U.S. G4 118
Saint James, Mo., U.S. G6 120
Saint James, Cape, c., B.C., Can. E4 106
Saint James Islands, is., V.I.U.S. e7 104b
Saint-Jean, Guad. B2 105a
Saint-Jean, Lac, res., Qc., Can. B4 110
Saint Jean Baptiste, Mb., Can. E16 124
Saint-Jean-d'Angély, Fr. C5 18
Saint-Jean-de-Luz, Fr. F4 18
Saint-Jean-de-Maurienne, Fr. D12 18
Saint-Jean-du-Gard, Fr. E9 18
Saint-Jean-Port-Joli, Qc., Can. C6 110
Saint-Jean-sur-Richelieu, Qc., Can. E3 110
Saint-Jérôme, Qc., Can. E3 110
Saint Jo, Tx., U.S. H11 128
Saint Joe, stm., Id., U.S. C11 136
Saint John, N.B., Can. E10 110
Saint John, N.D., U.S. F14 124
Saint John, Wa., U.S. C9 136
Saint John, i., V.I.U.S. e8 104b
Saint John, stm., N.A. E10 110
Saint John, Cape, c., Nf., Can. E19 106
Saint John's, Antig. f4 105b
Saint John's, Nf., Can. j23 107a
Saint Johns, Az., U.S. I7 132
Saint Johns, Mi., U.S. E5 112
Saint Johns, stm., Fl., U.S. G4 116
Saint Johnsbury, Vt., U.S. F4 110
Saint Joseph, Dom. j6 105c
Saint Joseph, Il., U.S. D9 120
Saint Joseph, Mi., U.S. F3 112
Saint Joseph, Mn., U.S. F4 118
Saint Joseph, Mo., U.S. E3 120
Saint Joseph, stm., U.S. G5 112
Saint Joseph, stm., U.S. G3 112
Saint Joseph, Lake, l., On., Can. E12 106
Saint-Joseph-de-Beauce, Qc., Can. D6 110
Saint Joseph Island, i., On., Can. B6 112
Saint-Jovite, Qc., Can. D2 110
Saint-Julien-en-Born, Fr. E4 18
Sainte-Julienne, Qc., Can. E3 110
Saint-Junien, Fr. D6 18
Saint Just, P.R. B4 104a
Saint Kilda, i., Scot., U.K. D4 12
Saint Kitts see Saint Christopher, i., St. K./N. C2 105a
Saint Kitts and Nevis, ctry., N.A. C2 105a
Saint-Lambert, ngh., Qc., Can. E3 110
Saint Landry, La., U.S. G6 122
Saint Laurent, Mb., Can. D16 124
Saint-Laurent (Saint Lawrence), stm., N.A. B8 110
Saint-Laurent du Maroni, Fr. Gu. B7 84
Saint Lawrence, Austl. D7 76
Saint Lawrence (Saint-Laurent), stm., N.A. B8 110
Saint Lawrence, Gulf of, b., Can. F18 106
Saint Lawrence Island, i., Ak., U.S. D5 140
Saint-Léandre, Qc., Can. B9 110
Saint-Léonard, N.B., Can. C9 110
Saint-Lô, Fr. E7 14
Saint Louis, Sk., Can. B8 124
Saint-Louis, Guad. i6 105c
Saint-Louis, Sen. F1 64
Saint Louis, Mi., U.S. E5 112
Saint Louis, Mo., U.S. F7 120
Saint Louis, stm., U.S. E6 118
Saint-Louis, Lac, l., Qc., Can. E3 110
Saint-Louis de Kent, N.B., Can. D12 110
Saint Louis Park, Mn., U.S. G5 118
Saint-Loup-sur-Semouse, Fr. G14 14
Sainte-Luce, Mart. I7 105c
Saint Lucia, ctry., N.A. m6 105c
Saint Lucia, Cape, c., S. Afr. F11 70
Saint Lucia, Lake, l., S. Afr. E11 70
Saint Lucia Channel, strt., N.A. I6 105c
Saint Lucia Game Reserve, S. Afr. F11 70
Saint Lucie Canal, can., Fl., U.S. J5 116
Saint Magnus Bay, b., Scot., U.K. n18 12a
Saint-Malo, Fr. F7 14
Saint-Malo, Golfe de, b., Fr. F6 14
Saint-Marc, Haiti C11 102
Saint-Marc, Canal de, strt., Haiti C11 102
Saint-Marc-des-Carrières, Qc., Can. D4 110
Sainte-Marie, Mart. k7 105c
Sainte Marie, Nosy, i., Madag. D9 68
Saint Maries, Id., U.S. C10 136
Saint Marks, stm., Fl., U.S. F1 116
Saint-Martin (Sint Maarten), i., N.A. A1 105a
Saint-Martin, Cap, c., Mart. k6 105c
Saint Martin, Lake, l., Mb., Can. C15 124
Saint Martins, N.B., Can. E11 110
Saint Martinville, La., U.S. G7 122
Saint Mary, Mo., U.S. G8 120
Saint Mary, stm., N.A. G18 138
Saint Mary Peak, mtn., Austl. H2 76
Saint Mary Reservoir, res., Ab., Can. G17 138
Saint Marys, Austl. n14 77a
Saint Marys, Ak., U.S. D7 140
Saint Marys, Ga., U.S. F4 116
Saint Marys, Ks., U.S. E1 120
Saint Marys, Pa., U.S. C7 114
Saint Marys, W.V., U.S. E4 114
Saint Mary's, i., Eng., U.K. L6 12
Saint Marys, stm., U.S. H5 112
Saint Marys, stm., U.S. F4 116
Saint Mary's Bay, b., Nf., Can. j23 107a
Saint Marys Bay, b., N.S., Can. F10 110
Saint Marys City, Md., U.S. F9 114
Saint-Mathieu, Fr. D6 18
Saint Matthew Island, i., Ak., U.S. D5 140
Saint Matthews, Ky., U.S. F12 120
Saint-Maurice, stm., Qc., Can. D4 110
Sainte-Maxime, Fr. F12 18
Saint Meinrad, In., U.S. F11 120
Saint Michael, Ak., U.S. D7 140
Saint Michaels, Md., U.S. F9 114
Saint-Michel-des-Saints, Qc., Can. D2 110
Saint-Mihiel, Fr. F14 14
Saint Moritz see Sankt Moritz, Switz. D6 22
Saint-Nazaire, Fr. G6 14
Saint-Nicolas see Sint-Niklaas, Bel. C12 14
Saint-Omer, Fr. D11 14
Saintonge, hist. reg., Fr. D5 18
Saint-Pacôme, Qc., Can. C7 110
Saint-Pamphile, Qc., Can. D7 110
Saint Paris, Oh., U.S. D2 114
Saint-Patrice, Lac, l., Qc., Can. B12 112
Saint Paul, Ab., Can. B19 138
Saint-Paul, Reu. i10 69a
Saint Paul, In., U.S. E12 120
Saint Paul, Ks., U.S. G2 120
Saint Paul, Mn., U.S. G5 118
Saint Paul, Va., U.S. H3 114
Saint Paul, stm., Lib. H2 64
Saint-Paul, Île, i., Afr. M10 142
Saint Paul Island, i., Ak., U.S. E6 140
Saint Paul's, St. K./N. C2 105a
Saint Pauls, N.C., U.S. B7 116
Saint Paul's Point, c., Pit. c28 78k
Saint Peter, Mn., U.S. G4 118
Saint Peter Port, Guern. E6 14
Saint Peters, N.S., Can. E16 110
Saint Peters Bay, P.E., Can. D14 110
Saint Petersburg see Sankt-Peterburg, Russia A13 10
Saint Petersburg, Fl., U.S. I3 116
Saint-Pierre, Mart. k6 105c
Saint-Pierre, Reu. i10 69a
Saint-Pierre, St. P./M. j22 107a
Saint Pierre, i., Sey. k12 69b
Saint-Pierre, Lac, l., Qc., Can. D3 110
Saint Pierre and Miquelon, dep., N.A. j22 107a
Saint Pierre-Jolys, Mb., Can. E16 124
Saint-Pierre-sur-Dives, Fr. E8 14
Saint-Pol-sur-Ternoise, Fr. D11 14
Saint-Pons-de-Thomères, Fr. F8 18
Saint-Prime, Qc., Can. B4 110
Saint-Prosper-de-Dorchester, Qc., Can. D6 110
Saint-Quentin, N.B., Can. C9 110
Saint-Quentin, Fr. E12 14
Saint-Raphaël, Fr. F12 18
Saint-Raymond, Qc., Can. D5 110
Saint Regis Falls, N.Y., U.S. F2 110
Saint-Rémy-de-Provence, Fr. F10 18
Saint Robert, Mo., U.S. G5 120
Saint-Roch-de-Mékinac, Qc., Can. D3 110
Saint-Romuald, Qc., Can. D5 110
Sainte-Rose-du-dégelis see Dégelis, Can. C8 110
Sainte Rose du Lac, Mb., Can. C14 124
Saintes, Fr. D5 18
Saint-Savin, Fr. H9 14
Saint-Siméon, Qc., Can. C6 110
Saint Simons Island, Ga., U.S. E4 116
Saint Simons Island, i., Ga., U.S. E4 116
Saintes-Maries-de-la-Mer, Fr. F10 18
Saint Stephen, S.C., U.S. C6 116
Sainte-Thérèse-de-Blainville, Qc., Can. E3 110
Saint Thomas, On., Can. F8 112
Saint Thomas, N.D., U.S. F16 124
Saint Thomas, i., V.I.U.S. e7 104b
Saint-Tite, Qc., Can. D4 110
Saint-Trond see Sint-Truiden, Bel. D14 14
Saint-Tropez, Fr. F12 18
Saint-Ubalde, Qc., Can. D4 110
Saint-Urbain-de-Charlevoix, Qc., Can. C6 110
Saint-Valéry-en-Caux, Fr. E9 14
Saint-Vallier, Fr. D10 18
Sainte-Véronique, Qc., Can. D2 110
Saint Vincent, Mn., U.S. C1 118
Saint Vincent, i., St. Vin. o11 105e
Saint-Vincent, Baie de, b., N. Cal. n15 79d
Saint Vincent, Gulf, b., Austl. J2 76
Saint Vincent and the Grenadines, ctry., N.A. p10 105e
Saint Vincent Passage, strt., N.A. m7 105c
Saint-Vith, Bel. D14 14
Saint Walburg, Sk., Can. E9 106
Saint-Yrieix-la-Perche, Fr. D7 18
Saint-Yvon, Qc., Can. A12 110
Saipan, i., N. Mar. Is. B5 72
Saiqi, China H8 42
Saitama, state, Japan C12 40
Saito, Japan G4 40
Sai Yok National Park, p.o.i., Thai. E4 48
Sajama, Nevado, mtn., Bol. C3 90
Sajanogorsk, Russia D16 32
Sajat, Turkmen. B9 56
Šajman, Taj. B11 56
Sajószentpéter, Hung. A7 26
Sak, stm., S. Afr. G5 70
Sa Kaeo, Thai. F6 48
Sakai, Japan E8 40
Sakaide, Japan E6 40
Sakaiminato, Japan D6 40
Sakakawea, Lake, res., N.D., U.S. G12 124
Sakala, Pulau, i., Indon. G10 50
Sakami, stm., Qc., Can. E15 106
Sakami, Lac, l., Qc., Can. E15 106
Sakania, D.R.C. G5 66
Sakaraha, Madag. E7 68
Sakarya, Tur. C13 28
Sakarya, state, Tur. C13 28
Sakarya (Sangarius), stm., Tur. B13 28
Sakata, Japan A12 40
Sakawa, Japan F6 40
Sakchu-ŭp, Kor., N. D6 38
Sakété, Benin H5 64
Sakhalin see Sahalin, ostrov, i., Russia F17 34
Sakhnin, Isr. F6 58
Şakht Sar, Iran B7 56
Šakiai, Lith. E6 10
Sakiet Sidi Youssef, Tun. H2 24
Sakishima-shotō, is., Japan G9 36
Sakon Nakhon, Thai. D6 48
Sakrand, Pak. E2 54
Saks, Al., U.S. D13 122
Sakti, India H9 54
Saku, Japan C11 40
Sakuma, Japan D10 40
Sakurai, Japan E8 40
Sal, i., C.V. k10 65a
Šal'a, Slov. H13 16
Sala, Swe. F7 8
Salaberry-de-Valleyfield, Qc., Can. E2 110
Salacgrīva, Lat. C7 10
Sala Consilina, Italy D9 24
Salada, Laguna, l., Mex. F5 98
Saladas, Arg. D8 92
Saladillo, Arg. G8 92
Saladillo, stm., Arg. D6 92
Saladillo Dulce, Arroyo, stm., Arg. E7 92
Salado, stm., Arg. D4 92
Salado, stm., Arg. G9 92
Salado, stm., Arg. E7 92
Salado, stm., Arg. I5 92
Salado, stm., Cuba B9 102
Salado, stm., Mex. B9 100
Salado, stm., N.M., U.S. I9 132
Salaga, Ghana H4 64
Salairskij krjaž, mts., Russia D14 32
Sălaj, state, Rom. B10 26
Šalakuša, Russia E19 8
Salal, Chad E3 62
Şalālah, Oman F7 56
Salālah, Sudan C7 62
Salamanca, Chile E2 92
Salamanca, Mex. E8 100
Salamanca, Spain D5 20
Salamanca, N.Y., U.S. F11 112
Salamanca, co., Spain D4 20
Salamanga, Moz. E11 70
Salamat, Bahr, stm., Chad F3 62
Salamina, Col. E4 86
Salamína, Grc. F6 28
Salamína, i., Grc. F6 28
Salamis, sci., N. Cyp. C4 58
Salamīyah, Syria C8 58
Salamonie, stm., In., U.S. H4 112
Salantai, Lith. D4 10
Salaquí, Col. D3 86
Salaquí, stm., Col. D3 86
Salas, Peru E2 84
Salas de los Infantes, Spain B7 20
Salatiga, Indon. G7 50
Salavat, Russia D9 32
Salaverry, Peru E2 84
Salawati, i., Indon. F9 44
Salāya, India G2 54
Sala y Gómez, Isla, i., Chile L28 142
Sala y Gomez Ridge, unds. L29 142
Şalbani, India G11 54
Šalčininkai, Lith. F8 10
Salcombe, Eng., U.K. K9 12
Saldaña, Spain B6 20
Saldaña, stm., Col. F4 86
Saldanha, S. Afr. H3 70
Saldungaray, Arg. I7 92
Saldus, Lat. D5 10
Sale, Austl. L6 76
Salé, Mor. C3 64
Sale Creek, Tn., U.S. B13 122
Saleh, Teluk, b., Indon. H10 50
Salehard, Russia A11 32
Salem, India F4 53
Salem, Monts. D3 105a
Salem, Ar., U.S. H6 120
Salem, Ia., U.S. D6 120
Salem, Il., U.S. F9 120
Salem, Ma., U.S. B15 114
Salem, Mo., U.S. G6 120
Salem, N.H., U.S. B14 114
Salem, N.J., U.S. E10 114
Salem, N.Y., U.S. G3 110
Salem, Oh., U.S. D5 114
Salem, Or., U.S. F3 136
Salem, S.D., U.S. D15 126
Salem, Va., U.S. G5 114
Salem, W.V., U.S. E5 114
Salemi, Italy G6 24
Salem Upland, plat., Mo., U.S. G6 120
Salentina, Penisola, pen., Italy D12 24
Salerno, Italy D8 24
Salerno, Golfo di, b., Italy D8 24
Salers, Fr. D8 18
Salgar, Col. D4 86
Salgótarján, Hung. A6 26
Salgueiro, Braz. E6 88
Salher, mtn., India H4 54
Sali, Cro. G12 22
Salida, Co., U.S. C3 128
Salihli, Tur. E11 28
Salihorsk, Bela. H10 10
Salima, Mwi. C5 68
Salimbatu, Indon. B10 50
Salin, Mya. B2 48
Salina, Ks., U.S. C11 128
Salina, Ut., U.S. E5 132
Salina Cruz, Mex. G11 100
Salina Point, c., Bah. A10 102
Salinas, Braz. I4 88
Salinas, Ec. I1 86
Salinas, Mex. G5 130
Salinas, P.R. C3 104a
Salinas, Ca., U.S. G4 134
Salinas, stm., Braz. I4 88
Salinas, stm., N.A. D2 102
Salinas, stm., Ca., U.S. G4 134
Salinas, Pampa de las, pl., Arg. E4 92
Salinas de Hidalgo, Mex. D8 100
Salinas Pueblo Missions National Monument, p.o.i., N.M., U.S. G2 128
Salinas Victoria, Mex. I7 130
Saline, Mi., U.S. B2 114
Saline, stm., Ar., U.S. D6 122
Saline, stm., Ar., U.S. C4 122
Saline, stm., Ks., U.S. C11 128
Saline Bayou, stm., La., U.S. E6 122
Saline Lake, l., La., U.S. F6 122
Salines, Cap de ses, c., Spain E14 20
Salines, Point, c., Gren. r10 105e
Salines, Pointe des, c., Mart. I7 105c
Salinópolis, Braz. D8 84
Salipolo, Indon. E11 50
Salisbury, Austl. J2 76
Salisbury, Eng., U.K. J11 12
Salisbury, Md., U.S. F10 114
Salisbury, Mo., U.S. E5 120
Salisbury, N.C., U.S. I5 114
Salisbury, Pa., U.S. E6 114
Salisbury see Harare, Zimb. D5 68
Salisbury Island, i., Nu., Can. C15 106
Salisbury Plain, pl., Eng., U.K. J11 12
Salish Mountains, mts., Mt., U.S. B12 136
Salitpa, Al., U.S. F10 122
Salitre, stm., Braz. E5 88
Şalkhad, Syria F7 58
Salles-Curan, Fr. E8 18
Salliq (Coral Harbour), Nu., Can. C14 106
Sallisaw, Ok., U.S. B4 122
Salluit, Qc., Can. C15 106
Salmi, Russia F14 8
Salmo, B.C., Can. G13 138
Salmon, stm., B.C., Can. B8 138
Salmon, stm., N.B., Can. D11 110
Salmon, stm., Id., U.S. E10 136
Salmon, Middle Fork, stm., Id., U.S. E12 136
Salmon, South Fork, stm., Id., U.S. E11 136
Salmon Arm, B.C., Can. F11 138
Salmon Falls Creek, stm., U.S. H12 136
Salmon Gums, Austl. F4 74
Salmon Peak, mtn., Tx., U.S. E7 130
Salmon River Mountains, mts., Id., U.S. F12 136
Salmon Valley, B.C., Can. B8 138
Salo, Fin. F10 8
Salò, Italy E7 22
Salome, Az., U.S. J3 132
Salomon, Cap, c., Mart. I6 105c
Salon-de-Provence, Fr. F11 18
Salonga, Parc National de la, p.o.i., D.R.C. E4 66
Salonika see Thessaloníki, Grc. C6 28
Salonika, Gulf of see Thermaïkós Kólpos, b., Grc. C6 28
Salonta, Rom. C8 26
Salor, stm., Spain E4 20
Salpausselʹkja, mts., Eur. B3 32
Sal Rei, C.V. k10 65a
Salsacate, Arg. E5 92
Salsipuedes, Canal, strt., Mex. A2 100
Sal'sk, Russia E6 32
Salsomaggiore Terme, Italy F6 22
Salt, stm., Az., U.S. J4 132
Salt, stm., Mo., U.S. E6 120
Salt, Middle Fork, stm., Mo., U.S. E5 120
Salt, North Fork, stm., Mo., U.S. E5 120
Salta, Arg. B5 92
Salta, state, Arg. D4 90
Saltanovka, Russia H17 10
Saltash, Eng., U.K. K8 12
Salt Basin, l., Tx., U.S. C2 130
Salt Cay, i., Bah. m18 104f
Saltcoats, Sk., Can. C11 124
Salt Creek, stm., Il., U.S. D8 120
Saltee Islands, is., Ire. I6 12
Saltfjellet Svartisen Nasjonalpark, p.o.i., Nor. C6 8
Saltillo, Mex. C8 100
Saltillo, Tn., U.S. B10 122
Salt Lake City, Ut., U.S. C4 132
Salto, Arg. G7 92
Salto, Ur. E9 92
Salto del Guairá, Para. A10 92
Salto Grande, Embalse, res., S.A. E8 92
Salton City, Ca., U.S. J9 134
Salton Sea, l., Ca., U.S. J10 134
Salto Santiago, Represa de, res., Braz. B11 92
Saltspring Island, i., B.C., Can. H7 138
Saltville, Va., U.S. H4 114
Saluda, Va., U.S. G9 114
Saluda, stm., S.C., U.S. B4 116
Salûm, Egypt A5 62
Sālūmbar, India F5 54
Sālūr, India B6 53
Saluzzo, Italy F4 22
Salvador, Braz. G6 88
Salvador, El see El Salvador, ctry., N.A. F3 102
Salvador, Lake, l., La., U.S. H8 122
Salvatierra, Mex. E8 100
Salviac, Fr. E7 18
Salween (Nu) (Khong) (Thanlwin), stm., Asia E8 46
Salyan, Azer. B6 56
Salyān, Nepal D9 54
Salyer, Ca., U.S. C2 134
Salyersville, Ky., U.S. G2 114
Salzach, stm., Eur. B9 22
Salzburg, Aus. C10 22
Salzburg, state, Aus. C10 22
Salzgitter, Ger. D6 16
Salzkammergut, reg., Aus. C10 22
Salzwedel, Ger. D7 16
Samacá, Col. E5 86
Samacèvičy, Bela. G14 10
Samagaltaj, Russia D16 32
Samah, Libya B3 62
Samales Group, is., Phil. G3 52
Samalga Pass, strt., Ak., U.S. g25 140a
Samal Island, i., Phil. G5 52
Sāmalkot, India C6 53
Samâlût, Egypt J1 58
Samaná, Dom. Rep. C13 102
Samāna, India C5 54
Samaná, Bahía de, b., Dom. Rep. C13 102
Samaná, Cabo, c., Dom. Rep. C13 102
Samana Cay, i., Bah. A11 102
Samandağı, Tur. B6 58
Samaniego, Col. G3 86
Samaqua, stm., Qc., Can. A4 110
Samar, i., Phil. E5 52
Samara, Russia D8 32
Samara, stm., Russia D8 32
Samarai, Pap. N. Gui. c5 79a
Samaria, Id., U.S. A4 132
Samaria Gorge see Samariás, Farángi, p., Grc. H6 28
Samariapo, Ven. E8 86
Samariás, Farángi (Samaria Gorge), p., Grc. H6 28
Samarinda, Indon. D10 50
Samarka, Russia B10 38
Samarkand, Uzb. G11 32
Sāmarrā', Iraq C5 56
Samastīpur, India F10 54
Samaúna, Braz. E5 84
Samba Caju, Ang. B2 68
Sambaíba, Braz. D3 88
Sambalpur, India H9 54
Sambar, Tanjung, c., Indon. E7 50
Sambas, Indon. C6 50
Sambava, Madag. C9 68
Şambayat, Tur. A9 58
Sambhal, India D7 54
Sāmbhar, India E5 54
Sāmbhar Lake, l., India E5 54
Sambir, Ukr. G19 16
Sambit, Pulau, i., Indon. C11 50
Sambito, stm., Braz. D5 88
Samboja, Indon. D10 50
Sâmbor, Camb. F7 48
Samborombón, stm., Arg. G9 92
Samborombón, Bahía, b., Arg. G9 92
Sambre, stm., Eur. D12 14
Sambre à l'Oise, Canal de la, can., Fr. E12 14
Sambriāl, Pak. B5 54
Samch'ŏk, Kor., S. B2 40
Sam Chom, Khao, mtn., Thai. H4 48
Same, Tan. E7 66
Sam Ford Fiord, b., Nu., Can. A16 106
Samfya, Zam. C4 68
Samka, Mya. B3 48
Samnangjin, Kor., S. D1 40
Sam Ngao, Thai. D4 48
Samoa, ctry., Oc. g12 79c
Samoa Islands, is., Oc. h12 79c
Samo Alto, Chile E2 92
Samobor, Cro. E12 22
Samoded, Russia E19 8
Samokov, Blg. G10 26
Sámos, i., Grc. F9 28
Samoset, Fl., U.S. I3 116
Samosir, Pulau, i., Indon. B1 50
Samothrace see Samothráki, i., Grc. C8 28
Samothráki, Grc. C8 28
Samothráki (Samothrace), i., Grc. C8 28
Sampacho, Arg. F5 92
Sampanahan, Indon. E10 50
Sampang, Indon. G8 50
Sampit, Indon. E8 50
Sampit, stm., Indon. E8 50
Sampit, Teluk, b., Indon. E8 50
Sampwe, D.R.C. F5 66
Sam Rayburn Reservoir, res., Tx., U.S. F4 122
Samro, ozero, l., Russia B11 10
Sam Son, Viet. C7 48
Samsun, Tur. A4 56
Samsu-ŭp, Kor., N. D7 38
Samtown, La., U.S. F6 122
Samuhú, Arg. C7 92
Samui, Ko, i., Thai. H5 48
Samundri, Pak. C4 54
Samut Prakan, Thai. F5 48
Samut Sakhon, Thai. F5 48
Samut Songkhram, Thai. F5 48
San, Mali G3 64
San (Xan), stm., Asia F8 48
San, stm., China E8 42
San (Syan), stm., Eur. F18 16
Saña, Peru E2 84
Şan'ā', Yemen F5 56
Sana, stm., Bos. E3 26
Sanaa see Şan'ā', Yemen F5 56
Sanabu, Egypt K1 58
Sanaga, stm., Cam. D2 66
San Agustín, Arg. E5 92
San Agustín, Arg. I8 92
San Agustín, Mex. C1 130
San Agustin, Cape, c., Phil. G6 52
Sanak Islands, is., Ak., U.S. F7 140
San Alberto, Mex. G6 130
San Ambrosio, Isla, i., Chile H7 82
Sanana, Pulau, i., Indon. F8 44
Sānand, India G4 54
Sanandaj, Iran B6 56
San Andreas, Ca., U.S. E5 134
San Andrés, Col. F7 102
San Andrés, Isla de, i., Col. F7 102
San Andres Mountains, mts., N.M., U.S. H2 128
San Andrés Sajcabajá, Guat. E2 102
San Andrés Tuxtla, Mex. F11 100
San Andrés y Providencia, state, Col. F7 102
Sananduva, Braz. C12 92
San Angelo, Tx., U.S. C7 130
San Antero, Col. C4 86
San Antonio, Arg. D5 92
San Antonio, Chile F2 92
San Antonio, Col. F4 86
San Antonio, Ur. E9 92
San Antonio, N.M., U.S. J9 132
San Antonio, N.M., U.S. F2 128
San Antonio, Tx., U.S. E9 130
San Antonio, stm., Tx., U.S. F10 130
San Antonio, Cabo, pen., Arg. H9 92
San Antonio, Cabo de, c., Cuba B5 102
San Antonio, Lake, res., Ca., U.S. H4 134
San Antonio, Mount, mtn., Ca., U.S. I8 134
San Antonio, Punta, c., Mex. B3 100
San Antonio Abad see Sant Antoni de Portmany, Spain F12 20
San Antonio Bay, b., Tx., U.S. F11 130
San Antonio de Bravo, Mex. D3 130
San Antonio de La Paz see San Antonio, Arg. D5 92
San Antonio de los Baños, Cuba A6 102
San Antonio de los Cobres, Arg. B4 92
San Antonio del Táchira, Ven. D5 86
San Antonio de Tamanaco, Ven. C8 86
San Antonio el Grande, Mex. F2 130
San Antonio Mountain, mtn., N.M., U.S. E2 128
San Antonio Oeste, Arg. H4 90
Sanatorium, Ms., U.S. F9 122
San Augustine, Tx., U.S. F4 122
San Augustin Pass, p., N.M., U.S. K10 132
Sanāw, Yemen F7 56
Sanāwad, India G6 54
San Bartolomeo in Galdo, Italy C9 24
San Benedetto del Tronto, Italy H10 22
San Benedetto Po, Italy E7 22
San Benedicto, Isla, i., Mex. F3 100
San Benito, Tx., U.S. H10 130
San Benito, stm., Ca., U.S. G4 134
San Benito Mountain, mtn., Ca., U.S. G5 134
San Bernard, stm., Tx., U.S. E12 130
San Bernardino, Ca., U.S. I8 134
San Bernardino Mountains, mts., Ca., U.S. I9 134
San Bernardino Strait, strt., Phil. D5 52
San Bernardo, Chile F2 92
San Bernardo, Islas de, is., Col. C3 86
San Bernardo del Viento, Col. C3 86
Sanbe-yama, vol., Japan D5 40
San Blas, Mex. E6 100
San Blas, Mex. B4 100
San Blas, Cape, c., Fl., U.S. H13 122
San Blas, Golfo de, b., Pan. H8 102
San Blas, Serranía de, mts., Pan. H8 102
San Borja, Bol. B3 90
Sanborn, Ia., U.S. H3 118
Sanborn, N.D., U.S. H15 124
San Bruno, Ca., U.S. F3 134
San Buenaventura, Bol. B3 90
San Buenaventura, Mex. B8 100

I·50 San Buenaventura – São Domingos

Name	Map Ref.	Page
San Buenaventura *see* Ventura, Ca., U.S.	I6	134
San Carlos, Chile	H2	92
San Carlos, Mex.	C9	100
San Carlos, Mex.	A8	100
San Carlos, Nic.	G5	102
San Carlos, Phil.	E4	52
San Carlos, Phil.	C3	52
San Carlos, Ur.	G10	92
San Carlos, Az., U.S.	J6	132
San Carlos, Ca., U.S.	F3	134
San Carlos, Ven.	C7	86
San Carlos, stm., C.R.	G5	102
San Carlos, stm., Ven.	C7	86
San Carlos Centro, Arg.	E7	92
San Carlos de Bariloche, Arg.	H2	90
San Carlos de Bolívar, Arg.	H7	92
San Carlos de Guaroa, Col.	F5	86
San Carlos del Zulia, Ven.	C5	86
San Carlos de Río Negro, Ven.	G8	86
San Carlos Reservoir, res., Az., U.S.	J6	132
San Cataldo, Italy	G7	24
San Cayetano, Arg.	I8	92
Sancha, stm., China	H1	42
Sanchahe, China	B7	38
Sanchenglong, China	B4	38
San Ciro de Acosta, Mex.	E9	100
San Clemente, Spain	E8	20
San Clemente, Ca., U.S.	J8	134
San Clemente Island, i., Ca., U.S.	K7	134
San Cristóbal, Arg.	E7	92
San Cristóbal, Dom. Rep.	C12	102
San Cristóbal, Ven.	D5	86
San Cristobal, i., Sol. Is.	f9	79b
San Cristóbal, Bahía, b., Mex.	B1	100
San Cristóbal, Isla, i., Ec.	i12	84a
San Cristóbal, Volcán, vol., Nic.	F4	102
San Cristóbal de las Casas, Mex.	G12	100
Sancti Spíritus, Cuba	A8	102
Sancy, Puy de, mtn., Fr.	D8	18
Sand, Nor.	G2	8
Sand, stm., Ab., Can.	B19	138
Sand, stm., S. Afr.	F8	70
Sand, stm., S. Afr.	C9	70
Sandai, Indon.	D7	50
Sandakan, Malay.	H2	52
Sândăn, Camb.	F8	48
Sandaré, Mali	G2	64
Sand Arroyo, stm., U.S.	D7	128
Sanday, i., Scot., U.K.	B10	12
Sandefjord, Nor.	G4	8
Sanderson, Tx., U.S.	D5	130
Sandersville, Ga., U.S.	D3	116
Sandersville, Ms., U.S.	F9	122
Sand Fork, W.V., U.S.	F5	114
Sand Hill, stm., Mn., U.S.	D2	118
Sand Hills, hills, Ne., U.S.	F11	126
Sāndi, India	E8	54
Sandia, Peru	F4	84
San Diego, Ca., U.S.	K8	134
San Diego, Tx., U.S.	G9	130
San Diego, Cabo, c., Arg.	J3	90
San Diego Aqueduct, aq., Ca., U.S.	J8	134
Sandıklı, Tur.	E13	28
Sandīla, India	E8	54
Sandilands Village, Bah.	m18	104f
Sand Key, i., Fl., U.S.	I3	116
Sand Lake, l., On., Can.	A4	118
Sandnes, Nor.	G1	8
Sandoa, D.R.C.	F4	66
Sandomierz, Pol.	F17	16
Sandoná, Col.	G3	86
San Donà di Piave, Italy	E9	22
Sandovo, Russia	B19	10
Sandoway, Mya.	C2	48
Sandown, Eng., U.K.	K11	12
Sand Point, Ak., U.S.	E7	140
Sandpoint, Id., U.S.	B10	136
Sandringham, Austl.	E2	76
Sandspit, B.C., Can.	E4	106
Sand Springs, Ok., U.S.	A2	122
Sand Springs, Tx., U.S.	B6	130
Sandstone, Austl.	E3	74
Sandstone, Mn., U.S.	E5	118
Sandu Ao, b., China	H8	42
Sandusky, Mi., U.S.	E7	112
Sandusky, Oh., U.S.	C3	114
Sandvika, Nor.	G4	8
Sandviken, Swe.	F7	8
Sandwich, Eng., U.K.	J14	12
Sandwich Bay, b., Nmb.	C2	70
Sandwick, B.C., Can.	G5	138
Sandwīp Island, i., Bngl.	G13	54
Sandy, Or., U.S.	E4	136
Sandy, Ut., U.S.	C5	132
Sandy Bay Mountain, mtn., Me., U.S.	E6	110
Sandy Cape, c., Austl.	E9	76
Sandy Cape, c., Austl.	n12	77a
Sandy Creek, stm., Austl.	I5	76
Sandy Hook, Ky., U.S.	F2	114
Sandy Hook, spit, N.J., U.S.	D12	114
Sandykači, Turkmen.	B9	56
Sandy Lake, l., On., Can.	E12	106
Sandy Point, c., Trin.	r13	105f
Sandy Point Town, St. K./N.	C2	105a
Sandy Springs, Ga., U.S.	C1	116
Sandžak, reg., Serb.	F6	26
San Elizario, Tx., U.S.	C1	130
San Enrique, Arg.	G7	92
San Estanislao, Para.	B9	92
San Esteban, Isla, i., Mex.	A2	100
San Esteban de Gormaz, Spain	C7	20
San Felipe, Chile	F2	92
San Felipe, Col.	G8	86
San Felipe, Mex.	E8	100
San Felipe, Mex.	F5	98
San Felipe, Ven.	B7	86
San Felipe, Cayos de, is., Cuba	B6	102
San Felipe Nuevo Mercurio, Mex.	C7	100
San Felipe Pueblo, N.M., U.S.	F2	128
San Felíu de Guixols *see* Sant Feliu de Guíxols, Spain	C14	20
San Félix, Isla, i., Chile	H6	82
San Fernando, Chile	G2	92
San Fernando, Mex.	C9	100
San Fernando, Mex.	F6	130
San Fernando, Phil.	B2	52
San Fernando, Phil.	C3	52
San Fernando, Spain	H4	20
San Fernando, Trin.	s12	105f
San Fernando, Ca., U.S.	I7	134
San Fernando de Apure, Ven.	D8	86
San Fernando de Atabapo, Ven.	E8	86
San Fernando del Valle de Catamarca, Arg.	D4	92
Sånfjällets Nationalpark, p.o.i., Swe.	E5	8
Sanford, Co., U.S.	D2	128
Sanford, Fl., U.S.	H4	116
Sanford, Me., U.S.	G6	110
Sanford, N.C., U.S.	A6	116
Sanford, Tx., U.S.	F7	128
Sanford, stm., Austl.	E3	74
Sanford, Mount, vol., Ak., U.S.	D11	140
San Francisco, Arg.	E6	92
San Francisco, El Sal.	F3	102
San Francisco, Ca., U.S.	F3	134
San Francisco, stm., Arg.	B5	92
San Francisco, stm., U.S.	J8	132
San Francisco, Paso de, p., S.A.	C3	92
San Francisco Bay, b., Ca., U.S.	F3	134
San Francisco Creek, stm., Tx., U.S.	E5	130
San Francisco de Borja, Mex.	B5	100
San Francisco de Horizonte, Mex.	I4	130
San Francisco del Chañar, Arg.	D5	92
San Francisco del Oro, Mex.	B5	100
San Francisco del Rincón, Mex.	E7	100
San Francisco de Macorís, Dom. Rep.	C12	102
San Francisco de Mostazal, Chile	F2	92
San Gabriel, Ec.	G3	86
San Gabriel Chilac, Mex.	F10	100
San Gabriel Mountains, mts., Ca., U.S.	I8	134
Sangamankanda Point, c., Sri L.	H5	53
Sangamner, India	B1	53
Sangamon, stm., Il., U.S.	D7	120
Sangar, Russia	D14	34
Sangasanga-dalam, Indon.	D10	50
San Gavino Monreale, Italy	E2	24
Sangay, vol., Ec.	I2	86
Sangay, Parque Nacional, p.o.i., Ec.	H3	86
Sange, D.R.C.	F5	66
Sangeang, Pulau, i., Indon.	H11	50
Sanger, Ca., U.S.	G6	134
Sanger, Tx., U.S.	H11	128
Sângera, Mol.	B15	26
Sangerhausen, Ger.	E7	16
San Germán, P.R.	B1	104a
Sangerville, Me., U.S.	E7	110
Sanggan, stm., China	A6	42
Sanggau, Indon.	C7	50
Sangha, stm., Afr.	E3	66
Sanghar, Pak.	E2	54
Sangihe, Kepulauan, is., Indon.	E7	44
Sangihe, Pulau, i., Indon.	E8	44
San Gil, Col.	D5	86
Sangilen, hrebet, mts., Russia	D17	32
San Gimignano, Italy	G7	22
San Giovanni in Fiore, Italy	E10	24
San Giovanni in Persiceto, Italy	F8	22
San Giovanni Rotondo, Italy	C9	24
San Giovanni Valdarno, Italy	G8	22
Sangiyn Dalay nuur, l., Mong.	B4	36
Sangju, Kor., S.	F8	38
Sangkapura, Indon.	F8	50
Sângkê, stm., Camb.	F6	48
Sangkulirang, Indon.	C10	50
Sāngli, India	C2	53
Sangmélima, Cam.	D2	66
Sāngole, India	C2	53
Sangolquí, Ec.	H2	86
San Gorgonio Mountain, mtn., Ca., U.S.	I9	134
San Gottardo, Passo del, p., Switz.	D5	22
Sangre de Cristo Mountains, mts., U.S.	E3	128
San Gregorio, Arg.	G6	92
Sangre Grande, Trin.	s12	105f
Sangro, stm., Italy	H11	22
Sangrūr, India	C5	54
Sangsang, China	D11	54
Sangue, stm., Braz.	F6	84
Sangutane, stm., Moz.	C11	70
Sangya, China	C13	54
San Hipólito, Punta, c., Mex.	B1	100
Sanhu, China	H6	42
Sânhûr, Egypt	I1	58
Sanibel Island, i., Fl., U.S.	J3	116
San Ignacio, Arg.	C10	92
San Ignacio, Mex.	B2	100
San Ignacio, Mex.	D8	100
San Ignacio, Para.	C9	92
San Ignacio, Isla, i., Mex.	C4	100
San Ignacio, Laguna, b., Mex.	B2	100
San Ignacio de Moxo, Bol.	B3	90
San Ignacio de Velasco, Bol.	C4	90
San Isidro, Arg.	D5	92
San Isidro, Arg.	G8	92
San Isidro del General, C.R.	H5	102
San Jacinto, Col.	C4	86
San Jacinto, Ca., U.S.	J9	134
San Jacinto Peak, mtn., Ca., U.S.	J9	134
San Jaime, Arg.	E8	92
San Javier, Arg.	E8	92
San Javier, Arg.	C10	92
San Javier, Bol.	C4	90
San Javier, Chile	G2	92
San Javier, Mex.	H8	130
San Javier, Ur.	F8	92
San Javier, stm., Arg.	E8	92
Sanjay National Park, p.o.i., India	G8	54
San Jerónimo, Guat.	E2	102
Sanjiang, China	I3	42
Sanjō, Japan	B11	40
San Joaquín, Bol.	B4	90
San Joaquín, stm., Bol.	B4	90
San Joaquin, stm., Ca., U.S.	E4	134
San Joaquín de Omaguas, Peru	D3	84
San Joaquin Valley, val., Ca., U.S.	G5	134
San Jorge, Arg.	E6	92
San Jorge, stm., Col.	C4	86
San Jorge, Bahía de, b., Mex.	F6	98
San Jorge, Golfo, b., Arg.	I3	90
San Jorge Island, i., Sol. Is.	e8	79b
San José, C.R.	H5	102
San José, Mex.	F7	130
San Jose, Phil.	E3	52
San Jose, Ca., U.S.	F4	134
San Jose, Il., U.S.	D8	120
San Jose, N.M., U.S.	F3	128
San José, Ven.	q19	104g
San Jose, stm., N.M., U.S.	I9	132
San José, Cerro, mtn., Mex.	H2	130
San José, Isla, i., Mex.	C3	100
San José, Isla, i., Pan.	H8	102
San José, Laguna, b., P.R.	B3	104a
San José de Bácum, Mex.	B3	100
San José de Batuc, Mex.	A3	100
San José de Chiquitos, Bol.	C4	90
San José de Feliciano, Arg.	E8	92
San José de Guanipa, Ven.	C9	86
San José de Jáchal, Arg.	E3	92
San José de la Popa, Mex.	H7	130
San José de las Lajas, Cuba	A6	102
San José del Cabo, Mex.	D4	100
San José del Guaviare, Col.	F5	86
San José de Mayo, Ur.	G9	92
San José de Ocuné, Col.	E6	86
San José de Tiznados, Ven.	C8	86
San Jose Island, i., Tx., U.S.	G11	130
San Juan, Arg.	E3	92
San Juan, Mex.	E3	130
San Juan, P.R.	B3	104a
San Juan, state, Arg.	E3	92
San Juan, stm., Arg.	F4	92
San Juan, stm., Col.	E3	86
San Juan, stm., Mex.	H8	130
San Juan, stm., N.A.	G5	102
San Juan, stm., U.S.	F6	132
San Juan, stm., Ven.	B10	86
San Juan, Cabezas de, c., P.R.	B4	104a
San Juan, Cabo, c., Arg.	J4	90
San Juan Basin, bas., N.M., U.S.	G8	132
San Juan Bautista, Mex.	H6	130
San Juan Bautista, Para.	C9	92
San Juan Bautista *see* Sant Joan de Labritja, Spain	E12	20
San Juan Bautista, Ca., U.S.	G4	134
San Juan Creek, stm., Ca., U.S.	H5	134
San Juan de Colón, Ven.	C5	86
San Juan de Guadalupe, Mex.	C7	100
San Juan de la Maguana, Dom. Rep.	C12	102
San Juan del Norte, Nic.	G6	102
San Juan de los Cayos, Ven.	B7	86
San Juan de los Morros, Ven.	C8	86
San Juan del Río, Mex.	E8	100
San Juan del Río, Mex.	C6	100
San Juan del Sur, Nic.	G4	102
San Juan de Micay, stm., Col.	F3	86
San Juan de Payara, Ven.	D8	86
San Juan de Sabinas, Mex.	G6	130
San Juanico, Mex.	B2	100
San Juan Islands, is., Wa., U.S.	B3	136
San Juanito, Isla, i., Mex.	E5	100
San Juan Mountains, mts., Co., U.S.	C9	98
San Juan Nepomuceno, Col.	C4	86
San Juan Nepomuceno, Para.	C9	92
San Justo, Arg.	E7	92
Sankarani, stm., Afr.	G3	64
Sankeshwar, India	C2	53
Sankh, stm., India	G10	54
Sankheda, India	G4	54
Sankosh, stm., Asia	E13	54
Sankt Anton am Arlberg, Aus.	C7	22
Sankt Gallen, Switz.	C6	22
Sankt Goarshausen, Ger.	F3	16
Sankt Ingbert, Ger.	G3	16
Sankt Michel *see* Mikkeli, Fin.	F12	8
Sankt Moritz, Switz.	D6	22
Sankt-Peterburg (Saint Petersburg), Russia	A13	10
Sankt Peter-Ording, Ger.	B4	16
Sankt Pölten, Aus.	B12	22
Sankt Veit an der Glan, Aus.	D11	22
Sankt-Vith *see* Saint-Vith, Bel.	D14	14
Sankt Wendel, Ger.	G3	16
Sankuru, stm., D.R.C.	E4	66
San Lázaro, Cabo, c., Mex.	C2	100
San Leandro, Ca., U.S.	F3	134
San Leonardo, Mex.	G3	130
Şanlıurfa (Urfa), Tur.	A9	58
Şanlıurfa, state, Tur.	A9	58
San Lorenzo, Arg.	F7	92
San Lorenzo, Arg.	D8	92
San Lorenzo, Bol.	D4	90
San Lorenzo, Ec.	G2	86
San Lorenzo, Mex.	C7	100
San Lorenzo, P.R.	B4	104a
San Lorenzo, stm., Mex.	C5	100
San Lorenzo, Cabo, c., Ec.	H1	86
San Lorenzo, Isla, i., Mex.	A2	100
San Lorenzo, Monte (Cochrane, Cerro), mtn., S.A.	I2	90
San Lorenzo de la Parrilla, Spain	E8	20
Sanlúcar de Barrameda, Spain	H4	20
San Lucas, Bol.	D3	90
San Lucas, Mex.	D3	100
San Lucas, Cabo, c., Mex.	D4	100
San Luis, Arg.	F4	92
San Luis, Cuba	B10	102
San Luis, Guat.	D3	102
San Luis, Co., U.S.	D3	128
San Luis, Ven.	B7	86
San Luis, state, Arg.	F5	92
San Luís, Laguna, l., Bol.	B4	90
San Luis, Sierra de, mts., Arg.	F5	92
San Luis Creek, stm., Co., U.S.	C3	128
San Luis de la Paz, Mex.	E8	100
San Luis Gonzaga, Mex.	C3	100
San Luis Gonzaga, Bahía, b., Mex.	G5	98
San Luis Jilotepeque, Guat.	E3	102
San Luis Obispo, Ca., U.S.	H5	134
San Luis Potosí, Mex.	D8	100
San Luis Potosí, state, Mex.	D8	100
San Luis Reservoir, res., Ca., U.S.	F4	134
San Luis Río Colorado, Mex.	E5	98
San Luis Valley, val., Co., U.S.	D3	128
San Manuel, Arg.	H8	92
San Manuel, Az., U.S.	K6	132
San Marcial, stm., Mex.	A3	100
San Marcos, Col.	C4	86
San Marcos, Mex.	G9	100
San Marcos, Tx., U.S.	E9	130
San Marcos, Isla, i., Mex.	B2	100
San Marino, S. Mar.	G9	22
San Marino, ctry., Eur.	G9	22
San Martín, Arg.	F3	92
San Martín, Arg.	D5	92
San Martín, Col.	F5	86
San Martín, stm., Bol.	B4	90
San Martin, sci., Ant.	B34	81
San Martín, Lago (O'Higgins, Lago), l., S.A.	I2	90
San Martín de los Andes, Arg.	H2	90
San Martino di Castrozza, ngh., Italy	D8	22
San Mateo, Mex.	G1	130
San Mateo *see* Sant Mateu del Maestrat, Spain	D10	20
San Mateo, Ca., U.S.	F3	134
San Mateo, Fl., U.S.	G4	116
San Mateo, N.M., U.S.	H9	132
San Matías, Bol.	C5	90
San Matías, Golfo, b., Arg.	H4	90
Sanmen, China	G9	42
Sanmenhsia *see* Sanmenxia, China	D4	42
Sanmenxia, China	D4	42
San Miguel, Ec.	H2	86
San Miguel, El Sal.	F3	102
San Miguel, Mex.	A8	100
San Miguel, Pan.	H8	102
San Miguel, stm., Bol.	B4	90
San Miguel, stm., S.A.	G3	86
San Miguel, stm., Co., U.S.	E8	132
San Miguel, Golfo de, b., Pan.	H8	102
San Miguel de Allende, Mex.	E8	100
San Miguel de Cruces, Mex.	C6	100
San Miguel del Monte, Arg.	G8	92
San Miguel de Salcedo, Ec.	H2	86
San Miguel de Tucumán, Arg.	C4	92
San Miguel Island, i., Ca., U.S.	I5	134
Sanming, China	H7	42
San Miniato, Italy	G7	22
Sannār, Sudan	E6	62
Sannicandro Garganico, Italy	I12	22
San Nicolás, Peru	G2	84
San Nicolas, Phil.	A3	52
San Nicolás de los Arroyos, Arg.	F7	92
San Nicolás de los Garza, Mex.	C8	100
San Nicolas Island, i., Ca., U.S.	J6	134
Sânnicolau Mare, Rom.	C7	26
Sannieshof, S. Afr.	E7	70
Sannikova, proliv, strt., Russia	B16	34
Sano, Japan	C12	40
Sanok, Pol.	G18	16
Sânon, stm., Fr.	F15	14
San Pablo, Phil.	C3	52
San Pablo Bay, b., Ca., U.S.	E3	134
San Pasqual, Punta, c., Mex.	C3	100
San Pedro, Arg.	B5	92
San Pedro, Arg.	F8	92
San Pedro, Arg.	C5	92
San Pedro, Chile	F2	92
San-Pédro, C. Iv.	I3	64
San Pedro, Col.	C4	86
San Pedro, Neth. Ant.	A1	105a
San Pedro, state, Para.	B9	92
San Pedro, stm., Mex.	F8	98
San Pedro, stm., Mex.	G2	130
San Pedro, stm., N.A.	K6	132
San Pedro, stm., N.A.	D2	102
San Pedro, Punta, c., Chile	B2	92
San Pedro, Volcán, vol., Chile	D3	90
San Pedro Carchá, Guat.	E2	102
San Pedro de Jujuy *see* San Pedro, Arg.	B5	92
San Pedro de las Colonias, Mex.	C7	100
San Pedro del Gallo, Mex.	C6	100
San Pedro del Paraná, Para.	C9	92
San Pedro de Macorís, Dom. Rep.	C13	102
San Pedro de Ycuamandiyú, Para.	B9	92
San Pedro Peaks, mtn., N.M., U.S.	G10	132
San Pedro Sula, Hond.	E3	102
San Pedro Tabasco, Mex.	D2	102
San Pellegrino Terme, Italy	E6	22
San Pietro, Isola di, i., Italy	E2	24
San Pitch, stm., Ut., U.S.	D5	132
Sanquhar, Scot., U.K.	F9	12
Sanquianga, Parque Nacional, p.o.i., Col.	F2	86
San Quintín, Cabo, c., Mex.	F4	98
San Rafael, Arg.	G3	92
San Rafael, Chile	G2	92
San Rafael, Mex.	C8	100
San Rafael, Ca., U.S.	E3	134
San Rafael, N.M., U.S.	H8	132
San Rafael, Ven.	B6	86
San Rafael, stm., Mex.	F5	98
San Rafael, stm., Ut., U.S.	E6	132
San Rafael del Norte, Nic.	F4	102
San Rafael Swell, plat., Ut., U.S.	E6	132
San Ramón, Arg.	C5	92
San Ramón, Bol.	B4	90
San Ramón de la Nueva Orán, Arg.	D4	90
San Remo, Italy	G4	22
San Rodrigo, stm., Mex.	F6	130
San Roque, Arg.	D8	92
San Roque, Punta, c., Mex.	B1	100
San Saba, Tx., U.S.	C9	130
San Saba, stm., Tx., U.S.	C9	130
San Salvador, Arg.	E8	92
San Salvador, El Sal.	F3	102
San Salvador, i., Bah.	C10	96
San Salvador de Jujuy, Arg.	A5	92
Sansanné-Mango, Togo	G5	64
San Sebastián, P.R.	B1	104a
San Sebastián *see* Donostia-San Sebastián, Spain	A9	20
San Sebastián, Bahía, b., Arg.	J3	90
Sansepolcro, Italy	G9	22
San Severo, Italy	I12	22
Sansha, China	H9	42
San Simon, Az., U.S.	K7	132
San Simon, stm., Az., U.S.	K7	132
San Simon Wash, stm., Az., U.S.	K4	132
Sanski Most, Bos.	E3	26
San Solano, Arg.	E4	92
Sans-Souci, sci., Haiti	C11	102
Santa, stm., Peru	E2	84
Santa Adélia, Braz.	K1	88
Santa Amalia, Spain	E4	20
Santa Ana, Bol.	B3	90
Santa Ana, Ec.	H1	86
Santa Ana, El Sal.	E3	102
Santa Ana, Mex.	F7	98
Santa Ana, Mex.	C8	100
Santa Ana, Ca., U.S.	J8	134
Santa Ana, Ven.	C9	86
Santa Ana del Alto Beni, Bol.	C3	90
Santa Anna, Tx., U.S.	C8	130
Santa Bárbara, Chile	H2	92
Santa Barbara, Col.	E4	86
Santa Bárbara, Hond.	E3	102
Santa Bárbara, Mex.	B6	100
Santa Barbara, Ca., U.S.	I6	134
Santa Bárbara, Ven.	D6	86
Santa Barbara Channel, strt., Ca., U.S.	I6	134
Santa Barbara Island, i., Ca., U.S.	J7	134
Santa Catalina, Gulf of, b., Ca., U.S.	J7	134
Santa Catalina, Isla, i., Mex.	C3	100
Santa Catalina Island, i., Ca., U.S.	J7	134
Santa Catarina, Mex.	C8	100
Santa Catarina, Mex.	L10	134
Santa Catarina, state, Braz.	C12	92
Santa Catarina, Ilha de, i., Braz.	C13	92
Santa Cecília, Braz.	C12	92
Santa Clara, Col.	I7	86
Santa Clara, Cuba	A7	102
Santa Clara, Ca., U.S.	F3	134
Santa Clara, Ut., U.S.	F3	132
Santa Clara, stm., Ca., U.S.	I7	134
Santa Clarita, Ca., U.S.	I7	134
Santa Clotilde, Peru	D3	84
Santa Coloma de Farners, Spain	C13	20
Santa Coloma de Farnés *see* Santa Coloma de Farners, Spain	C13	20
Santa Comba, Spain	A2	20
Santa Cruz, Braz.	D8	88
Santa Cruz, Braz.	J5	88
Santa Cruz, C.R.	G5	102
Santa Cruz, Phil.	D4	52
Santa Cruz, Phil.	C3	52
Santa Cruz, Phil.	C2	52
Santa Cruz, Ca., U.S.	G3	134
Santa Cruz, state, Arg.	I2	90
Santa Cruz, stm., Arg.	J3	90
Santa Cruz, stm., N.A.	J4	132
Santa Cruz, Isla, i., Ec.	i11	84a
Santa Cruz Cabrália, Braz.	I6	88
Santa Cruz de la Sierra, Bol.	C4	90
Santa Cruz del Quiché, Guat.	E2	102
Santa Cruz del Sur, Cuba	B9	102
Santa Cruz de Mudela, Spain	F7	20
Santa Cruz do Capibaribe, Braz.	D7	88
Santa Cruz do Piauí, Braz.	D5	88
Santa Cruz do Rio Pardo, Braz.	L1	88
Santa Cruz do Sul, Braz.	D11	92
Santa Cruz Island, i., Ca., U.S.	J6	134
Santa Cruz Islands, is., Sol. Is.	E7	72
Santa Elena, Arg.	E8	92
Santa Elena, Ec.	I1	86
Santa Elena, Mex.	B7	100
Santa Elena, Bahía de, b., Ec.	H1	86
Santa Elena, Cabo, c., C.R.	G4	102
Santa Eufemia, Spain	F6	20
Santa Eulalia, Spain	D9	20
Santa Eulalia del Río *see* Santa Eulària del Riu, Spain	E12	20
Santa Eulària del Riu, Spain	E12	20
Santa Fe, Arg.	E7	92
Santa Fe, Spain	G7	20
Santa Fe, N.M., U.S.	F3	128
Santa Fe, state, Arg.	D7	92
Santa Fe, stm., Fl., U.S.	G3	116
Santa Fe Baldy, mtn., N.M., U.S.	F3	128
Santa Fe de Bogotá *see* Bogotá, Col.	E4	86
Santa Fe de Minas, Braz.	I3	88
Santa Fé do Sul, Braz.	D6	90
Santa Filomena, Braz.	E3	88
Sant'Agata di Militello, Italy	F8	24
Santa Gertrudis, Mex.	G2	130
Santa Helena, Braz.	B3	88
Santa Helena de Goiás, Braz.	G7	84
Santai, China	F1	42
Santa Inês, Braz.	G5	88
Santa Inés, Bahía, b., Mex.	B3	100
Santa Inés, Isla, i., Chile	J2	90
Santa Isabel, Arg.	H4	92
Santa Isabel, P.R.	C3	104a
Santa Isabel, i., Sol. Is.	e8	79b
Santa Isabel, stm., Mex.	F1	130
Santa Isabel, Pico de, mtn., Eq. Gui.	I6	64
Santa Isabel Creek, stm., Tx., U.S.	G8	130
Santa Juliana, Braz.	J2	88
Santal, Baie du, b., N. Cal.	m16	79d
Santa Lucía, Arg.	D8	92
Santa Lucía, Ur.	G9	92
Santa Lucia Range, mts., Ca., U.S.	G4	134
Santaluz, Braz.	F6	88
Santa Luzia, Braz.	D7	88
Santa Magdalena, Arg.	G6	92
Santa Magdalena, Isla, i., Mex.	C2	100
Santa Margarita, Ca., U.S.	H5	134
Santa Margarita, Isla, i., Mex.	C2	100
Santa Margherita Ligure, Italy	F6	22
Santa María, Arg.	C4	92
Santa Maria, Braz.	D10	92
Santa María, Mex.	F6	130
Santa Maria, Ca., U.S.	I5	134
Santa Maria, i., Vanuatu	j16	79d
Santa Maria, stm., Braz.	E10	92
Santa María, stm., Mex.	F9	98
Santa María, stm., Mex.	E8	100
Santa Maria, stm., Az., U.S.	I3	132
Santa María, Bahía, b., Mex.	C4	100
Santa María, Cabo, c., Ur.	G10	92
Santa Maria, Cabo de, c., Ang.	C1	68
Santa Maria, Cabo de, c., Port.	H3	20
Santa María, Isla, i., Chile	H1	92
Santa María, Isla, i., Ec.	i11	84a
Santa María, Laguna de, l., Mex.	F9	98
Santa María Asunción Tlaxiaco, Mex.	G10	100
Santa Maria Capua Vetere, Italy	C7	24
Santa María Colotepec, Mex.	H10	100
Santa Maria da Boa Vista, Braz.	E5	88
Santa Maria da Vitória, Braz.	G3	88
Santa Maria de Itabira, Braz.	J4	88
Santa María del Oro, Mex.	C6	100
Santa María del Río, Mex.	E8	100
Santa Maria di Leuca, Capo, c., Italy	E12	24
Santa Maria do Suaçuí, Braz.	J4	88
Santa María la Real de Nieva, Spain	C6	20
Santa Marinella, Italy	H8	22
Santa Marta, Col.	B4	86
Santa Marta, Cabo de, c., Ang.	C1	68
Santa Marta, Ciénaga Grande, b., Col.	B4	86
Santa Mónica, Mex.	F7	130
Santa Monica, Ca., U.S.	I7	134
Santa Monica Bay, b., Ca., U.S.	J7	134
Santan, Indon.	D10	50
Santana, Braz.	G3	88
Santana, Coxilha de (Santa Ana, Cuchilla de), hills, S.A.	E10	92
Santana, Ilha de, i., Braz.	B4	88
Santana da Boa Vista, Braz.	E11	92
Santana do Ipanema, Braz.	E7	88
Santana do Livramento, Braz.	E9	92
Santander, Col.	F3	86
Santander, Phil.	F4	52
Santander, Spain	A7	20
Santander, state, Col.	D5	86
Santander Jiménez, Mex.	C9	100
Sant'Andrea, Isola, i., Italy	D11	24
Santanghu, China	C3	36
Santanilla, Islas, is., Hond.	D6	102
Sant'Antine, Nuraghe, hist., Italy	D2	24
Sant'Antioco, Italy	E2	24
Sant'Antioco, Isola di, i., Italy	E2	24
Sant Antoni de Portmany, Spain	F12	20
Santanyí, Spain	E14	20
Santa Paula, Ca., U.S.	I6	134
Santaquin, Ut., U.S.	D5	132
Santa Quitéria, Braz.	C5	88
Santa Quitéria do Maranhão, Braz.	B4	88
Santarcangelo di Romagna, Italy	F9	22
Santarém, Braz.	D7	84
Santarém, Port.	E2	20
Santarém, state, Port.	E2	20
Santaren Channel, strt., Bah.	C9	96
Santa Rita, Braz.	D8	88
Santa Rita, Col.	G5	86
Santa Rita, Hond.	E3	102
Santa Rita, Mex.	G7	130
Santa Rita, Mt., U.S.	B14	136
Santa Rita, Ven.	B6	86
Santa Rosa, Arg.	H5	92
Santa Rosa, Braz.	C10	92
Santa Rosa, Braz.	H2	88
Santa Rosa, Col.	F7	86
Santa Rosa, Ec.	D2	84
Santa Rosa, Ca., U.S.	E3	134
Santa Rosa, Tx., U.S.	H10	130
Santa Rosa, Ven.	C7	86
Santa Rosa, Ven.	D7	86
Santa Rosa, Mount, hill, Guam	i10	78c
Santa Rosa Beach, Fl., U.S.	G12	122
Santa Rosa de Copán, Hond.	E3	102
Santa Rosa del Conlara, Arg.	F5	92
Santa Rosa de Leales, Arg.	C5	92
Santa Rosa de Osos, Col.	D4	86
Santa Rosa de Sucumbíos, Ec.	G3	86
Santa Rosa de Viterbo, Col.	E5	86
Santa Rosa Island, i., Ca., U.S.	J5	134
Santa Rosalía, Mex.	B2	100
Santa Rosalía, Mex.	H9	130
Santa Rosalía, Ven.	C7	86
Santa Rosa Wash, stm., Az., U.S.	K5	132
Šantarskie ostrova, is., Russia	E16	34
Santa Sylvina, Arg.	C7	92
Santa Teresa, Braz.	J5	88
Santa Teresa, Mex.	C9	100
Santa Teresa, stm., Braz.	G1	88
Santa Teresa, Embalse de, res., Spain	D5	20
Santa Teresa, Fortaleza de, hist., Ur.	F11	92
Santa Uxía, Spain	B1	20
Santa Vitória do Palmar, Braz.	F11	92
Santee, Ca., U.S.	K8	134
Santee, stm., S.C., U.S.	C6	116
Santee Dam, dam, S.C., U.S.	C5	116
Sant'Eufemia, Golfo di, b., Italy	F9	24
Sant Feliu de Guíxols, Spain	C14	20
Santhià, Italy	E5	22
Santiago, Braz.	D10	92
Santiago, Chile	F2	92
Santiago, Mex.	D4	100
Santiago, Pan.	H7	102
Santiago, Para.	C9	92
Santiago, i., C.V.	l10	65a
Santiago, stm., Mex.	C6	100
Santiago, stm., S.A.	D2	84
Santiago, Isla, i., Ec.	i11	84a
Santiago de Compostela, Spain	B2	20
Santiago de Cuba, Cuba	C9	102
Santiago del Estero, Arg.	C5	92
Santiago del Estero, state, Arg.	C5	92
Santiago de los Caballeros, Dom. Rep.	C12	102
Santiago Island, i., Phil.	B2	52
Santiago Ixcuintla, Mex.	E6	100
Santiago Jamiltepec, Mex.	G10	100
Santiago Larre, Arg.	G8	92
Santiago Papasquiaro, Mex.	C6	100
Santiago Peak, mtn., Ca., U.S.	J8	134
Santiago Peak, mtn., Tx., U.S.	E4	130
Santiaguillo, Laguna, l., Mex.	C6	100
Santiam Pass, p., Or., U.S.	F5	136
Säntis, mtn., Switz.	C6	22
Santisteban del Puerto, Spain	F7	20
Sant Joan de Labritja, Spain	E12	20
Sant Jordi, Golf de, b., Spain	D11	20
Sant Mateu del Maestrat, Spain	D10	20
Santo Amaro, Braz.	G6	88
Santo Amaro, Braz.	B4	88
Santo André, Braz.	L2	88
Santo Ângelo, Braz.	D10	92
Santo Antão, i., C.V.	k10	65a
Santo Antônio, Braz.	D8	88
Santo António, S. Tom./P.	I6	64
Santo Antônio, stm., Braz.	I3	88
Santo Antônio, stm., Braz.	F1	88
Santo Antônio da Patrulha, Braz.	D12	92
Santo Antônio de Jesus, Braz.	G6	88
Santo Antônio de Pádua, Braz.	K4	88
Santo Antônio do Amparo, Braz.	K3	88
Santo Antônio do Içá, Braz.	D4	84
Santo Augusto, Braz.	C11	92
Santo Domingo, Dom. Rep.	C13	102
Santo Domingo, Mex.	I3	130
Santo Domingo, Mex.	D8	100
Santo Domingo, Mex.	C2	100
Santo Domingo, Ven.	D5	86
Santo Domingo de la Calzada, Spain	B7	20
Santo Domingo de los Colorados, Ec.	H1	86
Santo Domingo Pueblo, N.M., U.S.	F2	128
Santo Domingo Tehuantepec, Mex.	G11	100
Santo Domingo Zanatepec, Mex.	G11	100
Santo Estêvão, Braz.	G6	88
Santo / Malo, state, Vanuatu	j16	79d
San Tomé, Ven.	C9	86
Santo Onofre, stm., Braz.	G4	88
Santorini see Thíra, i., Grc.	G8	28
Santos, Braz.	L2	88
Santos Dumont, Braz.	K4	88
Santo Tirso, Port.	C2	20
Santo Tomás, Mex.	L9	134
Santo Tomás, Punta, c., Mex.	L9	134
Santo Tomé, Arg.	E7	92
Santo Tomé, Arg.	D9	92
San Vicente de Alcántara, Spain	E3	20
San Vicente de Baracaldo *see* Barakaldo, Spain	A8	20
San Vicente del Caguán, Col.	F4	86
San Vincente, Arg.	D5	92
San Vincenzo, Italy	G7	22
San Vito, Capo, c., Italy	F6	24
Sanya, China	L3	42
Sanyati, stm., Zimb.	D4	68
Sanyō, Japan	E4	40
Sanyuan, China	D3	42
Sanzao Dao, i., China	K5	42
Sanza Pombo, Ang.	B2	68
São Benedito, Braz.	C5	88
São Benedito do Rio Preto, Braz.	B3	88
São Bento, Braz.	B3	88
São Bento do Norte, Braz.	C7	88
São Bento do Sul, Braz.	C13	92
São Bento do Una, Braz.	E7	88
São Borja, Braz.	D10	92
São Caetano do Sul, Braz.	L2	88
São Carlos, Braz.	L2	88
São Cristóvão, Braz.	F7	88
São Domingos, Braz.	G2	88
São Domingos, Braz.	C11	92
São Domingos, Gui.-B.	G1	64

São Domingos do Maranhão – Seonāth I • 51

Name	Map Ref.	Page
São Domingos do Maranhão, Braz.	C3	88
São Felipe, Braz.	H5	88
São Félix de Balsas, Braz.	D3	88
São Francisco, Braz.	H3	88
São Francisco, stm., Braz.	H5	88
São Francisco, stm., Braz.	E6	88
São Francisco, Baía de, b., Braz.	C13	92
São Francisco, Ilha de, i., Braz.	C13	92
São Francisco de Assis, Braz.	D10	92
São Francisco de Goiás, Braz.	H1	88
São Francisco de Paula, Braz.	D12	92
São Francisco do Maranhão, Braz.	D4	88
São Francisco do Sul, Braz.	C13	92
São Gabriel, Braz.	E10	92
São Gabriel, Braz.	F5	88
São Gabriel da Palha, Braz.	J5	88
São Gabriel de Goiás, Braz.	H2	88
São Gonçalo do Sapucaí, Braz.	K3	88
São Gonçalo dos Campos, Braz.	G6	88
Sao Hill, Tan.	F7	66
São Jerônimo, Braz.	E12	92
São Jerônimo da Serra, Braz.	A12	92
São João da Aliança, Braz.	H2	88
São João da Barra, Braz.	K5	88
São João da Boa Vista, Braz.	L2	88
São João de Cortês, Braz.	B3	88
São João Del Rei, Braz.	K3	88
São João do Araguaia, Braz.	C1	88
São João do Jaguaribe, Braz.	C6	88
São João do Piauí, Braz.	E4	88
São João dos Patos, Braz.	D4	88
São Joaquim, Braz.	D12	92
São Joaquim, Parque Nacional de, p.o.i., Braz.	D13	92
São Joaquim da Barra, Braz.	K1	88
São José, Braz.	C13	92
São José, stm., Braz.	J5	88
São José da Laje, Braz.	E7	88
São José das Piranhas, Braz.	D6	88
São José de Anauá, Braz.	G11	86
São José do Cedro, Braz.	C11	92
São José do Egito, Braz.	D7	88
São José do Gurupi, Braz.	A2	88
São José do Mipibu, Braz.	D8	88
São José do Peixe, Braz.	D4	88
São José do Rio Preto, Braz.	K1	88
São José dos Campos, Braz.	L3	88
São José dos Pinhais, Braz.	B13	92
São Leopoldo, Braz.	D12	92
São Lourenço, Braz.	L3	88
São Lourenço, Pantanal de, sw., Braz.	C5	90
São Lourenço do Sul, Braz.	E12	92
São Luís, Braz.	B3	88
São Luís do Curu, Braz.	B6	88
São Luís do Quitunde, Braz.	E8	88
São Luís Gonzaga, Braz.	D10	92
São Manuel, Braz.	L1	88
São Manuel, stm., Braz.	E6	84
São Marcos, stm., Braz.	I2	88
São Marcos, Baía de, b., Braz.	B3	88
São Mateus, Braz.	J6	88
São Mateus, Braço Norte, stm., Braz.	J5	88
São Mateus do Sul, Braz.	B12	92
São Miguel, Braz.	D6	88
São Miguel, i., Port.	C3	60
São Miguel do Araguaia, Braz.	F7	84
São Miguel d'Oeste, Braz.	C11	92
São Miguel do Guamá, Braz.	A2	88
São Miguel dos Campos, Braz.	E7	88
São Miguel do Tapuio, Braz.	C5	88
Saona, Isla, i., Dom. Rep.	C13	102
Saône, stm., Fr.	C10	18
Saône-et-Loire, state, Fr.	C10	18
Saoner, India	H7	54
São Nicolau, i., C.V.	k10	65a
São Nicolau, stm., Braz.	C5	88
São Paulo, Braz.	L2	88
São Paulo, state, Braz.	D7	90
São Paulo de Olivença, Braz.	D4	84
São Paulo do Potengi, Braz.	C7	88
São Pedro do Piauí, Braz.	C4	88
São Pedro do Sul, Port.	D2	20
São Raimundo das Mangabeiras, Braz.	D3	88
São Raimundo Nonato, Braz.	E4	88
São Romão, Braz.	I3	88
São Roque, Braz.	L2	88
São Roque, Cabo de, c., Braz.	C8	88
São Sebastião, Braz.	L3	88
São Sebastião, Ilha de, i., Braz.	L3	88
São Sebastião, Ponta, c., Moz.	C12	70
São Sebastião do Paraíso, Braz.	K2	88
São Sepé, Braz.	E11	92
São Simão, Braz.	K2	88
São Simão, Represa de, res., Braz.	C7	90
São Timóteo, Braz.	G4	88
São Tomé, Braz.	C7	88
São Tomé, S. Tom./P.	I6	64
São Tomé, i., S. Tom./P.	I6	64
São Tomé, Cabo de, c., Braz.	L5	88
São Tomé, Pico de, mtn., S. Tom./P.	I6	64
Sao Tome and Principe, ctry., Afr.	I6	64
Saoura, Oued, stm., Alg.	D4	64
São Valério, stm., Braz.	F1	88
São Vicente, Braz.	M2	88
São Vicente, i., C.V.	k9	65a
São Vicente, Cabo de, c., Port.	H1	20
Sapanca, Tur.	C13	28
Sape, Selat, strt., Indon.	H11	50
Sapele, Nig.	H6	64
Sapelo Island, i., Ga., U.S.	E4	116
Sápes, Grc.	B8	28
Sapitwa, mtn., Mwi.	D6	68
Šapki, Russia	A14	10
Šapkina, stm., Russia	C26	8
Sapockin, Bela.	G6	10
Sappa Creek, stm., U.S.	A9	128
Sappa Creek, South Fork, stm., Ks., U.S.	B8	128
Sappho, Wa., U.S.	B2	136
Sapporo, Japan	C14	38
Sap Songkhla, Thale, l., Thai.	I5	48
Saptakosī, stm., Nepal	E11	54
Sapudi, Pulau, i., Indon.	G9	50
Sapulpa, Ok., U.S.	A2	122
Sapwe, D.R.C.	G5	66
Saqqâra, Egypt	I2	58
Saqqâra, Pyramides de (Step Pyramid), hist., Egypt	I1	58
Saqqez, Iran	B6	56
Saraana, Baie, b., Qc., Can.	B1	110
Sarāb, Iran	B6	56
Saraburi, Thai.	E5	48
Saracura, stm., Braz.	G5	88
Saraféré, Mali	F4	64
Saragosa, Tx., U.S.	C4	130
Saragossa see Zaragoza, Spain	C10	20
Sarāi Naurang, Pak.	B3	54
Saraipāli, India	H9	54
Sarajevo, Bos.	F5	26
Saraji, Austl.	D7	76
Sarakhs, Iran	B9	56
Saraktaš, Russia	D9	32
Saraland, Al., U.S.	G10	122
Saran', Kaz.	E12	32
Saran, Gunung, mtn., Indon.	D7	50
Saranac, Mi., U.S.	F4	112
Saranac, stm., N.Y., U.S.	F3	110
Saranda see Sarandë, Alb.	E13	24
Sarandë, Alb.	E13	24
Sarandi, Braz.	C11	92
Sarandí del Yi, Ur.	F10	92
Sarandí Grande, Ur.	F9	92
Sarangani Bay, b., Phil.	H5	52
Sarangani Islands, is., Phil.	H5	52
Sarangani Strait, strt., Phil.	H5	52
Sārangarh, India	H9	54
Sārangpur, India	G6	54
Saranpaul', Russia	B10	32
Saransk, Russia	D6	32
Saraphi, Thai.	C4	48
Sarapul, Russia	C8	32
Sarāqib, Syria	C7	58
Sarare, stm., Ven.	D6	86
Sarasota, Fl., U.S.	I3	116
Sarata, Ukr.	C16	26
Saratoga, Ca., U.S.	F3	134
Saratoga, Tx., U.S.	G4	122
Saratoga, Wy., U.S.	B10	132
Saratoga Springs, N.Y., U.S.	G2	110
Saratov, Russia	D7	32
Saratov Reservoir see Saratovskoe vodohranilišče, res., Russia	D7	32
Saratovskoe vodohranilišče, res., Russia	D7	32
Sarāvān, Iran	D9	56
Saravan, Laos	E8	48
Saravena, Col.	D5	86
Sarawak, state, Malay.	B8	50
Sarawak, hist. reg., Malay.	E5	44
Saray, Tur.	B10	28
Saraya, Gui.	G2	64
Sarayevo see Sarajevo, Bos.	F5	26
Sarayköy, Tur.	F11	28
Sarayönü, Tur.	E15	28
Sarbāz, Iran	D9	56
Sarcelle, Passe de la, strt., N. Cal.	n16	79d
Sarcidano, reg., Italy	E3	24
Sarcoxie, Mo., U.S.	G3	120
Sārda (Mahākālī), stm., Asia	D8	54
Sardah, Bngl.	F12	54
Sardārpur, India	G5	54
Sardārshahr, India	D5	54
Sardegna, state, Italy	D4	24
Sardegna (Sardinia), i., Italy	D3	24
Sardinata, Col.	H11	102
Sardinia see Sardegna, state, Italy	D4	24
Sardinia see Sardegna, i., Italy	D3	24
Sardis, Al., U.S.	E12	122
Sardis, Ga., U.S.	D4	116
Sardis, Tn., U.S.	B10	122
Sardis, sci., Tur.	E10	28
Sardis Lake, res., Ms., U.S.	C9	122
Sardis Lake, res., Ok., U.S.	C3	122
Šardonem', Russia	E21	8
Sarek, mtn., Swe.	C7	8
Sareks Nationalpark, p.o.i., Swe.	C7	8
Sar-e Pol, Afg.	B10	56
Sarepta, La., U.S.	E5	122
Sargent, Ga., U.S.	D14	122
Sargent, Ne., U.S.	F13	126
Sargodha, Pak.	B4	54
Sarh, Chad	F3	62
Sārī, Iran	B7	56
Saría, i., Grc.	H10	28
Sarıgöl, Tur.	E11	28
Sarıkaya, Tur.	E15	28
Sarikei, Malay.	B7	50
Sarina, Austl.	C7	76
Sariñena, Spain	C10	20
Sariska Tiger Reserve, India	E6	54
Sarita, Tx., U.S.	G10	130
Sariwŏn, Kor., N.	E6	38
Sarıyar Barajı, res., Tur.	D14	28
Šarja, Russia	G21	8
Sark, i., Guern.	E6	14
Šarkaŭščyna, Bela.	E10	10
Şarkikaraağaç, Tur.	E14	28
Şarköy, Tur.	C10	28
Šarles, N.D., U.S.	F15	124
Šarlyk, Russia	D9	32
Sarmi, Indon.	F10	44
Sarmiento, Arg.	I3	90
Särna, Swe.	F5	8
Sarnia, On., Can.	F7	112
Sarno, Italy	D8	24
Sarolangun, Indon.	E3	50
Saronic Gulf see Saronikós Kólpos, b., Grc.	F6	28
Saronikós Kólpos, b., Grc.	F6	28
Saronno, Italy	E6	22
Saros Körfezi, b., Tur.	C9	28
Sárospatak, Hung.	A8	26
Sarowbī, Afg.	C10	56
Sarpsborg, Nor.	G4	8
Sarqan, Kaz.	E13	32
Sarralbe, Fr.	E15	14
Sarre (Saar), stm., Eur.	E15	14
Sarrebourg, Fr.	F16	14
Sarreguemines, Fr.	E16	14
Šarscin, Bela.	H14	10
Sartang, stm., Russia	C15	34
Sartell, Mn., U.S.	F4	118
Sartène, Fr.	H14	18
Sarthe, state, Fr.	G9	14
Sarthe, stm., Fr.	G8	14
Saruhanlı, Tur.	E10	28
Sárvár, Hung.	B3	26
Sárvíz, can., Hung.	C5	26
Saryg-Sep, Russia	D17	32
Sarykamyšskoe ozero, l., Asia	A8	56
Saryözek, Kaz.	F13	32
Šarypovo, Russia	C15	32
Saryqopa köli, l., Kaz.	E10	32
Sarysū, stm., Kaz.	E11	32
Sary-Taš, Kyrg.	G12	32
Sarzana, Italy	F6	22
Sasabeneh, Eth.	F8	62
Sasaginnigak Lake, l., Mb., Can.	C17	124
Sasakwa, Ok., U.S.	C2	122
Sasamungga, Sol. Is.	d7	79b
Sāsarām, India	F9	54
Sasayama, Japan	D8	40
Sásd, Hung.	C5	26
Sasebo, Japan	F2	40
Saseginaga, Lac, l., Qc., Can.	A11	112
Saskatchewan, state, Can.	E9	106
Saskatchewan, stm., Can.	E10	106
Saskatoon, Sk., Can.	B7	124
Saskylah, Russia	B11	34
Sasolburg, S. Afr.	E8	70
Sasovo, Russia	D6	32
Saspamco, Tx., U.S.	E9	130
Sassafras, Ky., U.S.	G2	114
Sassafras Mountain, mtn., U.S.	A3	116
Sassandra, C. Iv.	I3	64
Sassandra, stm., C. Iv.	I3	64
Sassari, Italy	D2	24
Sassnitz, Ger.	B9	16
Sasso Marconi, Italy	F8	22
Sassuolo, Italy	F7	22
Sasyk, ozero, l., Ukr.	D16	26
Sasyqqöl köli, l., Kaz.	E14	32
Satadougou, Mali	G2	64
Satah Mountain, vol., B.C., Can.	D6	138
Sata-misaki, c., Japan	H3	40
Satāna, India	H5	54
Sátão, Port.	D3	20
Sātāra, India	C1	53
Satara Ruskamp, S. Afr.	D10	70
Satélite, Mex.	C1	130
Satellite Beach, Fl., U.S.	H5	116
Satengar, Pulau, i., Indon.	G10	50
Satevó, Mex.	G1	130
Satevó, stm., Mex.	G1	130
Satilla, stm., Ga., U.S.	E4	116
Sátiro Dias, Braz.	F6	88
Satīt (Tekezē), stm., Afr.	E7	62
Šatki, Russia	I20	8
Satluj see Sutlej, stm., Asia	C5	54
Satna, India	F8	54
Sátoraljaújhely, Hung.	A8	26
Sātpura Range, mts., India	H6	54
Satsuma-hantō, pen., Japan	H3	40
Satsunan-shotō, is., Japan	k19	39a
Sattahip, Thai.	F5	48
Satui, Indon.	E9	50
Satu Mare, Rom.	B9	26
Satu Mare, state, Rom.	B10	26
Satun, Thai.	I4	48
Šatura, Russia	I18	8
Saturnino M. Laspiur, Arg.	E6	92
Satyamangalam, India	F3	53
Sauce, Arg.	E8	92
Sauce Corto, Arroyo, stm., Arg.	H7	92
Saucier, Ms., U.S.	G9	122
Saucillo, Mex.	A6	100
Sauđárkrókur, Ice.	k30	8a
Saudi Arabia, ctry., Asia	E5	56
Sauerland, reg., Ger.	E4	16
Saueruiná, stm., Braz.	F6	84
Saugatuck, Mi., U.S.	F3	112
Saugeen, stm., On., Can.	D8	112
Saugerties, N.Y., U.S.	B12	114
Saugstad, Mount, mtn., B.C., Can.	D4	138
Saujil, Arg.	D4	92
Sauk, stm., Mn., U.S.	F4	118
Sauk Centre, Mn., U.S.	F3	118
Sauk City, Wi., U.S.	H9	118
Sauk Rapids, Mn., U.S.	F4	118
Saukville, Wi., U.S.	E1	112
Saül, Fr. Gu.	C7	84
Sauldre, Canal de la, can., Fr.	B8	18
Saulgau, Ger.	I5	16
Saulieu, Fr.	G13	14
Sault aux Cochons, stm., Qc., Can.	A7	110
Sault-de-Vaucluse, Fr.	E11	18
Saulteaux, stm., Ab., Can.	B16	138
Sault Sainte Marie, On., Can.	B5	112
Sault Sainte Marie, Mi., U.S.	B5	112
Saumarez Reef, rf., Austl.	C9	76
Saumlaki, Indon.	G9	44
Saumur, Fr.	G8	14
Saunders Island, i., Falk. Is.	J4	90
Saunders Island, i., S. Geor.	K12	82
Sauquoit, N.Y., U.S.	B10	114
Saurimo, Ang.	B3	68
Sausar, India	H7	54
Sausu, Indon.	D12	50
Sautar, Ang.	C2	68
Sauteurs, Gren.	q10	105e
Sauveterre-de-Guyenne, Fr.	E5	18
Sauwald, for., Aus.	B10	22
Sauzal, Mex.	C1	130
Sava, stm., Eur.	F16	22
Savai'i, i., Samoa	g11	79c
Savalou, Benin	H5	64
Savanna, Il., U.S.	B7	120
Savanna, Ok., U.S.	C3	122
Savannah, Ga., U.S.	D4	116
Savannah, Tn., U.S.	B10	122
Savannah, stm., U.S.	D4	116
Savannah River Plant, sci., S.C., U.S.	C4	116
Savannah Sound, Bah.	K9	116
Savannakhét, Laos	D7	48
Savanna-la-Mar, Jam.	i12	104d
Savant Lake, On., Can.	A8	118
Savant Lake, l., On., Can.	A8	118
Sāvantvādi, India	D1	53
Savanūr, India	D2	53
Savaştepe, Tur.	D10	28
Savè, Benin	H5	64
Save (Sabi), stm., Afr.	E5	68
Sāveh, Iran	B7	56
Savelugu, Ghana	H4	64
Savenay, Fr.	G7	14
Saverdun, Fr.	F7	18
Savigliano, Italy	F4	22
Savino-Borisovskaja, Russia	E21	8
Savinskij, Russia	E19	8
Savissik, Grnld.	B13	141
Šavnik, Serb.	G6	26
Savoie, state, Fr.	D12	18
Savoie, hist. reg., Fr.	D12	18
Savo Island, i., Sol. Is.	e8	79b
Savona, B.C., Can.	F10	138
Savona, Italy	F5	22
Savonlinna, Fin.	F13	8
Savoy, Tx., U.S.	D2	122
Savoy see Savoie, hist. reg., Fr.	D12	18
Savran', Ukr.	A17	26
Savusavu Bay, b., Fiji	p19	79e
Savu Sea see Sawu, Laut, s., Indon.	G7	44
Sawah, Indon.	B9	50
Sawahlunto, Indon.	D2	50
Sawāi Mādhopur, India	E6	54
Sawākin, Sudan	D7	62
Sawankhalok, Thai.	D4	48
Sawara, Japan	D13	40
Sawata, Japan	A11	40
Sawatch Range, mts., Co., U.S.	B2	128
Sawdā', Jabal, mtn., Sau. Ar.	F5	56
Sawdā', Jabal as-, hills, Libya	A4	62
Sawdā', Qurnat as-, mtn., Leb.	D7	58
Sawdirī, Sudan	E5	62
Şawqirah, Oman	F8	56
Şawqirah, Dawḩat, b., Oman	F8	56
Sawtooth National Recreation Area, p.o.i., Id., U.S.	F12	136
Sawu, Laut (Savu Sea), s., Indon.	G7	44
Sawu, Pulau, i., Indon.	H7	44
Sawyer, Mi., U.S.	G3	112
Sawyer, N.D., U.S.	F12	124
Saxby, stm., Austl.	B3	76
Saxon, Wi., U.S.	E8	118
Saxony see Sachsen, state, Ger.	F9	16
Saxony see Sachsen, hist. reg., Ger.	D5	16
Saxony-Anhalt see Sachsen-Anhalt, state, Ger.	D7	16
Saxton, Pa., U.S.	D7	114
Say, Niger	G5	64
Sayan Mountains, mts., Asia	D17	32
Sayaxché, Guat.	D2	102
Şaydā (Sidon), Leb.	E6	58
Şaydā, state, Leb.	E6	58
Sayḩūt, Yemen	F7	56
Sayil, sci., Mex.	B3	102
Saylac, Som.	B8	66
Saylūn, Khirbat (Shiloh), hist., W.B.	F6	58
Sayram Hu, l., China	F14	32
Sayre, Ok., U.S.	F9	128
Sayre, Pa., U.S.	C9	114
Sayreville, N.J., U.S.	D11	114
Sayward, B.C., Can.	F5	138
Saywūn, Yemen	F6	56
Saza, Japan	F2	40
Sazan, i., Alb.	D13	24
Sba, Alg.	D4	64
Ščadryn, Bela.	H12	10
Scafell Pike, mtn., Eng., U.K.	G9	12
Scalea, Italy	E9	24
Scammon Bay, Ak., U.S.	D6	140
Scandia, Ks., U.S.	B11	128
Scanlon, Mn., U.S.	E6	118
Scapa Flow, b., Scot., U.K.	C9	12
Scapegoat Mountain, mtn., Mt., U.S.	C14	136
Ščapino, Russia	E20	34
Scappoose, Or., U.S.	E3	136
Ščara, stm., Bela.	G8	10
Scarborough, St. K./N.	C2	105a
Scarborough, Trin.	r13	105f
Scarborough, Eng., U.K.	G12	12
Scarborough, ngh., On., Can.	E10	112
Scărişoara, Rom.	F11	26
Scarp, i., Scot., U.K.	C5	12
Scawfell Island, i., Austl.	C7	76
Šćedro, Otok, i., Cro.	G13	22
Ščekino, Russia	F20	10
Ščelkovo, Russia	E20	10
Sceptre, Sk., Can.	D4	124
Ščerbakovo, Russia	C21	34
Ščerbinka, Russia	E20	10
Schaffhausen, Switz.	C5	22
Schaffhouse see Schaffhausen, Switz.	C5	22
Schärding, Aus.	B10	22
Schefferville, Qc., Can.	E17	106
Scheinfeld, Ger.	G6	16
Schelde, stm., Eur.	C13	14
Schell Creek Range, mts., Nv., U.S.	D2	132
Schenectady, N.Y., U.S.	B11	114
Schenevus Creek, stm., N.Y., U.S.	B11	114
Schertz, Tx., U.S.	E9	130
Schiedam, Neth.	C13	14
Schiermonnikoog, i., Neth.	C2	16
Schiltigheim, Fr.	F16	14
Schio, Italy	E8	22
Schkeuditz, Ger.	E8	16
Schladming, Aus.	C10	22
Schlater, Ms., U.S.	D8	122
Schleiden, Ger.	F2	16
Schleswig, Ger.	B5	16
Schleswig, Ia., U.S.	B2	120
Schleswig-Holstein, state, Ger.	B6	16
Schlitz, Ger.	F5	16
Schlüchtern, Ger.	F5	16
Schmölln, Ger.	F8	16
Schneeberg, Ger.	F8	16
Schneeberg, mtn., Ger.	F7	16
Schneverdingen, Ger.	C5	16
Schœlcher, Mart.	k6	105c
Schofield, Wi., U.S.	G9	118
Schoharie, N.Y., U.S.	B11	114
Schoharie Creek, stm., N.Y., U.S.	B11	114
Schönebeck, Ger.	D7	16
Schongau, Ger.	I6	16
Schopfheim, Ger.	I3	16
Schorndorf, Ger.	H5	16
Schouten, Kepulauan, is., Indon.	F10	44
Schouten Island, i., Austl.	o14	77a
Schouten Islands, is., Pap. N. Gui.	a3	79a
Schramberg, Ger.	H4	16
Schreiber, On., Can.	C11	118
Schriever, La., U.S.	H8	122
Schrobenhausen, Ger.	H7	16
Schulenburg, Tx., U.S.	E11	130
Schultz Lake, l., Nu., Can.	C11	106
Schuyler, Va., U.S.	G7	114
Schuylkill, stm., Pa., U.S.	D10	114
Schuylkill Haven, Pa., U.S.	D9	114
Schwabach, Ger.	G7	16
Schwaben, hist. reg., Ger.	H5	16
Schwäbische Alb, mts., Ger.	H5	16
Schwäbisch Gmünd, Ger.	H5	16
Schwäbisch Hall, Ger.	G5	16
Schwabmünchen, Ger.	H6	16
Schwandorf in Bayern, Ger.	G7	16
Schwaner, Pegunungan, mts., Indon.	D8	50
Schwarzach im Pongau, Aus.	C10	22
Schwarzwald (Black Forest), mts., Ger.	H4	16
Schwatka Mountains, mts., Ak., U.S.	C8	140
Schwaz, Aus.	C8	22
Schwechat, Aus.	B13	22
Schwedt, Ger.	C10	16
Schweinfurt, Ger.	F5	16
Schweizer Nationalpark, p.o.i., Switz.	D7	22
Schweizer-Reineke, S. Afr.	E7	70
Schwerin, Ger.	C7	16
Schweriner See, l., Ger.	C7	16
Schwyz, Switz.	C5	22
Sciacca, Italy	G6	24
Scicli, Italy	H8	24
Scilly, Isles of, is., Eng., U.K.	L6	12
Scio, Oh., U.S.	D4	114
Scio, Or., U.S.	F4	136
Scioto, stm., Oh., U.S.	E3	114
Šćit, mtn., Bos.	E4	26
Scobey, Mt., U.S.	F8	124
Scone, Austl.	I8	76
Scooba, Ms., U.S.	E10	122
Scordia, Italy	G8	24
Scoresby Land, reg., Grnld.	C21	141
Scoresbysund (Ittoqqortoormiit), Grnld.	C21	141
Scoresby Sund, strt., Grnld.	C21	141
Scotia, N.Y., U.S.	B12	114
Scotia Ridge, unds.	N8	144
Scotia Sea, s.	K10	82
Scotland, On., Can.	E9	112
Scotland, S.D., U.S.	D15	126
Scotland, Tx., U.S.	H10	128
Scotland, state, U.K.	E8	12
Scotlandville, La., U.S.	G7	122
Scotsburn, N.S., Can.	E14	110
Scott, Sk., Can.	B5	124
Scott, Ms., U.S.	D7	122
Scott, stm., Ca., U.S.	B3	134
Scott, Cape, c., B.C., Can.	F2	138
Scott, Mount, mtn., Or., U.S.	H4	136
Scott Base, sci., Ant.	C22	81
Scott City, Mo., U.S.	G8	120
Scott Coast, cst., Ant.	C20	81
Scottdale, Pa., U.S.	D6	114
Scott Island, i., Ant.	B23	81
Scott Islands, is., B.C., Can.	F2	138
Scott Peak, mtn., Id., U.S.	F14	136
Scott Reef, rf., Austl.	B4	74
Scottsbluff, Ne., U.S.	F9	126
Scotts Bluff National Monument, p.o.i., Ne., U.S.	F9	126
Scottsboro, Al., U.S.	C12	122
Scottsdale, Austl.	n13	77a
Scottsdale, Az., U.S.	J5	132
Scotts Head, c., Dom.	j6	105c
Scotts Hill, Tn., U.S.	B10	122
Scottsville, Ky., U.S.	H11	120
Scottville, Mi., U.S.	E3	112
Scourie, Scot., U.K.	C7	12
Scout Lake, Sk., Can.	E8	124
Scranton, N.D., U.S.	A9	126
Scranton, Pa., U.S.	C10	114
Screven, Ga., U.S.	E3	116
Scribner, Ne., U.S.	J2	118
Scrub Island, i., Anguilla	A2	105a
Ščuče, Russia	C10	32
Ščučinsk see Shchūchīnsk, Kaz.	D12	32
Ščučyn, Bela.	G7	10
Scugog, Lake, l., On., Can.	D11	112
Scunthorpe, Eng., U.K.	H12	12
Scutari, Lake, l., Eur.	H16	22
Ščytkavičy, Bela.	G10	10
Seabrook, Lake, l., Austl.	F3	74
Seaford, De., U.S.	F10	114
Seaforth, On., Can.	E8	112
Seahorse Point, c., Nu., Can.	C15	106
Sea Islands, is., U.S.	E5	116
Sea Isle City, N.J., U.S.	E11	114
Seal, stm., Mb., Can.	D11	106
Seal, Cape, c., S. Afr.	I6	70
Sea Lake, Austl.	J4	76
Sealark Channel, strt., Sol. Is.	e9	79b
Seal Cays, is., T./C. Is.	B12	102
Seale, Al., U.S.	E13	122
Sealevel, N.C., U.S.	B9	116
Seal Island, i., N.S., Can.	G10	110
Sealy, Tx., U.S.	H2	122
Seara, Braz.	C11	92
Searcy, Ar., U.S.	B7	122
Searles Lake, l., Ca., U.S.	H8	134
Searsport, Me., U.S.	F7	110
Seaside, Ca., U.S.	G4	134
Seaside, Or., U.S.	D3	136
Seaside Park, N.J., U.S.	E11	114
Seattle, Wa., U.S.	C4	136
Sebago Lake, l., Me., U.S.	G6	110
Se Bai, stm., Thai.	E7	48
Sebakung, Indon.	D10	50
Sebangan, Teluk, b., Indon.	E8	50
Sebangka, Pulau, i., Indon.	C4	50
Sebastian, Tx., U.S.	H10	130
Sebastian, Cape, c., Or., U.S.	A1	134
Sebastián Vizcaíno, Bahía, b., Mex.	A1	100
Sebastopol, Ca., U.S.	E3	134
Sebastopol, Ms., U.S.	E9	122
Sebec Lake, l., Me., U.S.	E7	110
Šebekino, Russia	D5	32
Seben, Tur.	C14	28
Sebeş, Rom.	D10	26
Sebes Körös (Crişul Repede), stm., Eur.	B8	26
Sebewaing, Mi., U.S.	E6	112
Sebež, Russia	D11	10
Sebino see Iseo, Lago d', l., Italy	E6	22
Sebnitz, Ger.	F10	16
Sebree, Ky., U.S.	G10	120
Sebring, Fl., U.S.	I4	116
Sebuku, Indon.	A10	50
Sebuku, Teluk, b., Indon.	A11	50
Sebuyau, Malay.	C7	50
Secchia, stm., Italy	F7	22
Sechura, Peru	E1	84
Sechura, Desierto de, des., Peru	E1	84
Seclantás, Arg.	B4	92
Sečovská Polianka, Slov.	H17	16
Section, Al., U.S.	C13	122
Security, Co., U.S.	C4	128
Seda, China	E5	36
Seda, Lith.	D5	10
Sedah, Indon.	B4	74
Sedalia, Ab., Can.	C3	124
Sedalia, Mo., U.S.	F4	120
Sedan, Fr.	E13	14
Sedanovo, Russia	C18	32
Sedayu, Indon.	G8	50
Seddon, Kap, c., Grnld.	B14	141
Sedel'nikovo, Russia	C13	32
Séderon, Fr.	E11	18
Sedgewick, Ab., Can.	D19	138
Sedgwick, Co., U.S.	G10	126
Sedgwick, Ks., U.S.	D11	128
Sédhiou, Sen.	G1	64
Sedlčany, Czech Rep.	G10	16
Sedom (Sodom), hist., Isr.	G6	58
Sedro Woolley, Wa., U.S.	B4	136
Šeduva, Lith.	E6	10
Seehausen, Ger.	D7	16
Seeheim, Nmb.	E3	70
Seeis, Nmb.	C3	70
Seekoei, stm., S. Afr.	G7	70
Seeley Lake, Mt., U.S.	C13	136
Seelyville, In., U.S.	E10	120
Sées, Fr.	F9	14
Seesen, Ger.	E6	16
Sefadu, S.L.	H2	64
Seferihisar, Tur.	E9	28
Segama, stm., Malay.	A11	50
Segamat, Malay.	K6	48
Ségbana, Benin	G5	64
Segeri, Indon.	F11	50
Segesta, sci., Italy	G6	24
Segeža, Russia	E15	8
Segorbe, Spain	E10	20
Ségou, Mali	G3	64
Šegovary, Russia	E20	8
Segovia, Spain	D6	20
Segovia, co., Spain	C6	20
Segozero, ozero, l., Russia	E15	8
Segre, stm., Eur.	H6	18
Seguam Island, i., Ak., U.S.	g24	140a
Séguédine, Niger	E7	64
Séguéla, C. Iv.	H3	64
Seguí, Arg.	E7	92
Seguin, Tx., U.S.	E10	130
Segundo, stm., Arg.	E6	92
Seguntur, Indon.	C10	50
Segura, stm., Spain	F10	20
Segura, Sierra de, mts., Spain	G8	20
Sehithwa, Bots.	B6	70
Sehore, India	G6	54
Sehwān, Pak.	D10	56
Seibert, Co., U.S.	B6	128
Seikpyu, Mya.	B2	48
Seiland, i., Nor.	A10	8
Seiling, Ok., U.S.	E9	128
Seim, stm., Eur.	D4	32
Seinäjoki, Fin.	E10	8
Seine, stm., Mb., Can.	E17	124
Seine, stm., On., Can.	C6	118
Seine, stm., Fr.	E9	14
Seine, Baie de la, b., Fr.	E8	14
Seine, Bay of the see Seine, Baie de la, b., Fr.	E8	14
Seine-et-Marne, state, Fr.	F12	14
Seine-Maritime, state, Fr.	E9	14
Seixal, Port.	F1	20
Seixas, Ponta do, c., Braz.	D8	88
Sejmčan, Russia	D19	34
Sejny, Pol.	B19	16
Sekayam, stm., Indon.	C7	50
Sekayu, Indon.	E3	50
Sekeladi, Indon.	E3	50
Şeki, Azer.	A6	56
Šeki, Japan	D9	40
Sekiu, Wa., U.S.	B2	136
Sekoma, Bots.	D6	70
Sekondi, Ghana	I4	64
Šeksna, Russia	A21	10
Šelagskij, mys, c., Russia	B23	34
Selama, Malay.	J5	48
Selangor, state, Malay.	K5	48
Selaru, Pulau, i., Indon.	G9	44
Selatan, Tanjung, c., Indon.	F9	50
Selatpanjang, Indon.	C3	50
Selawik, Ak., U.S.	C8	140
Selawik Lake, l., Ak., U.S.	C7	140
Selayar, Pulau, i., Indon.	G12	50
Selayar, Selat, strt., Indon.	F12	50
Selb, Ger.	F8	16
Selbusjøen, l., Nor.	E4	8
Selby, Eng., U.K.	H11	12
Selby, S.D., U.S.	B12	126
Selbyville, De., U.S.	F10	114
Sel'co, Russia	G17	10
Sel'co, Russia	E19	8
Selçuk, Tur.	F10	28
Seldovia, Ak., U.S.	E9	140
Selebi-Phikwe, Bots.	C9	70
Šelečnja, Russia	H17	10
Šelehov, Russia	D18	32
Selemdža, stm., Russia	F14	34
Selemdžinsk, Russia	F15	34
Selenduma, Russia	F10	34
Selenge, D.R.C.	E3	66
Selenge, stm., Asia	G9	34
Selenicë, Alb.	D13	24
Selennjah, stm., Russia	C16	34
Sélestat, Fr.	F16	14
Seleznëvo, Russia	F13	8
Selfoss, Ice.	I29	8a
Selfridge, N.D., U.S.	A11	126
Sel'gon, Russia	G16	34
Sélibabi, Maur.	F2	64
Seliger, ozero, l., Russia	C15	10
Seligman, Az., U.S.	H4	132
Šelihova, zaliv, b., Russia	D20	34
Selimbau, Indon.	C8	50
Selinsgrove, Pa., U.S.	D8	114
Selinunte, sci., Italy	G6	24
Selišče, Russia	D16	10
Seližarovo, Russia	D16	10
Selkirk, Mb., Can.	D17	124
Selkirk, Scot., U.K.	F10	12
Selkirk Mountains, mts., N.A.	F13	138
Sellers, S.C., U.S.	B6	116
Sellersburg, In., U.S.	F12	120
Selles-sur-Cher, Fr.	G10	14
Selm, Ger.	E3	16
Selma, Al., U.S.	E11	122
Selma, Ca., U.S.	G6	134
Selma, N.C., U.S.	A7	116
Selmer, Tn., U.S.	B10	122
Selmont, Al., U.S.	E11	122
Šelon', stm., Russia	B13	10
Selong, Indon.	H10	50
Selva, Arg.	D6	92
Selvagens, Ilhas, is., Port.	C1	64
Selvas, for., Braz.	F8	82
Selway, stm., Id., U.S.	D11	136
Selwyn, Austl.	C3	76
Selwyn, Passage, strt., Vanuatu	k16	79d
Selwyn Lake, l., Can.	D10	106
Selwyn Mountains, mts., Can.	C4	106
Selwyn Range, mts., Austl.	C3	76
Seman, stm., Alb.	D13	24
Semangka, Teluk, b., Indon.	F4	50
Semara, W. Sah.	D2	64
Semarang, Indon.	G7	50
Semayang, Kenohan, l., Indon.	D10	50
Sembakung, stm., Indon.	B10	50
Semcy, Russia	H16	10
Semenanjung Malaysia, hist. reg., Malay.	K6	48
Semenov, Russia	H21	8
Semeru, Gunung, vol., Indon.	H8	50
Semey (Semipalatinsk), Kaz.	D13	32
Semežava, Bela.	H10	10
Semichi Islands, is., Ak., U.S.	g21	140a
Semiluki, Russia	D5	32
Semily, Czech Rep.	F11	16
Seminary, Ms., U.S.	F9	122
Seminoe Reservoir, res., Wy., U.S.	A9	132
Seminole, Ok., U.S.	B2	122
Seminole, Tx., U.S.	B5	130
Seminole, Lake, res., U.S.	G14	122
Seminole Draw, stm., U.S.	B5	130
Semīozernoe, Kaz.	D10	32
Semipalatinsk see Semey, Kaz.	D13	32
Semitau, Indon.	C7	50
Semizbughy, Kaz.	D13	32
Semliki, stm., Afr.	D6	66
Semnān, Iran	B7	56
Semois, stm., Eur.	E13	14
Semporna, Malay.	A11	50
Semuda, Indon.	E8	50
Semža, Russia	C21	8
Sên, stm., Camb.	F7	48
Sena, Bol.	B3	90
Senador Canedo, Braz.	I1	88
Senador Pompeu, Braz.	C6	88
Senaki, Geor.	F6	32
Sena Madureira, Braz.	E4	84
Senanayake Samudra, res., Sri L.	H5	53
Senanga, Zam.	D3	68
Senath, Mo., U.S.	H7	120
Senatobia, Ms., U.S.	C8	122
Sendai, Japan	H3	40
Sendai, Japan	A13	40
Sendelingsdrif, Nmb.	F3	70
Sendhwa, India	H5	54
Sendurjana, India	H7	54
Senduruhan, Indon.	D7	50
Senebui, Tanjung, c., Indon.	B2	50
Seneca, Il., U.S.	C9	120
Seneca, Ks., U.S.	E1	120
Seneca, Mo., U.S.	H3	120
Seneca, S.C., U.S.	B3	116
Seneca, Mount, mtn., N.Y., U.S.	B7	114
Seneca Falls, N.Y., U.S.	B9	114
Seneca Lake, l., N.Y., U.S.	B8	114
Senegal, ctry., Afr.	G2	64
Sénégal, stm., Afr.	F2	64
Senekal, S. Afr.	F8	70
Senetosa, Capu di (Senetosa, Punta di), c., Fr.	H14	18
Senetosa, Punta di see Senetosa, Capu di, c., Fr.	H14	18
Senftenberg, Ger.	E10	16
Sengés, Braz.	B13	92
Sênggê, stm., China	B8	54
Senhor do Bonfim, Braz.	F5	88
Senica, Slov.	H13	16
Senigallia, Italy	G10	22
Senirkent, Tur.	E13	28
Senise, Italy	D10	24
Senja, i., Nor.	B7	8
Senkaku-shotō, is., Japan	F9	36
Şenköy, Tur.	B7	58
Šenkursk, Russia	E20	8
Senlis, Fr.	E11	14
Senmonorom, Camb.	F8	48
Senneterre, Qc., Can.	F15	106
Senoia, Ga., U.S.	D14	122
Şenpazar, Tur.	B16	28
Šens, Fr.	F12	14
Senta, Serb.	D7	26
Sentarum, Danau, l., Indon.	C7	50
Sentinel, Ok., U.S.	F9	128
Sentinel Butte, mtn., N.D., U.S.	A8	126
Senyavin Islands, is., Micron.	C6	72
Seo de Urgel see La Seu d'Urgell, Spain	B12	20
Seonāth, stm., India	H8	54

Name   Map   Page
                                      Ref.

Seoni, India................. G7   54
Seoni Mālwa, India.......... G6   54
Seoul see Sŏul, Kor., S...... F7   38
Sepanjang, Pulau, i., Indon.. G9   50
Sepasu, Indon............... C10   50
Sepetiba, Baía de b., Braz... L4   88
Sepi, Sol. Is................ e8   79b
Sepik, stm., Pap. N. Gui..... a3   79a
Sẹpopol, Pol................ B17   16
Sept-Îles, Qc., Can......... E17   106
Sepúlveda, Spain............ C7   20
Seputih, stm., Indon......... F4   50
Sequatchie, stm., Tn., U.S.. B13   122
Sequillo, stm., Spain........ C5   20
Sequim, Wa., U.S............ B3   136
Sequoia National Park,
  p.o.i., Ca., U.S........... G7   134
Serabad, Uzb............... B10   56
Serafimovič, Russia......... E6   32
Seraing, Bel................ D14   14
Seram (Ceram), i., Indon.... F8   44
Seram, Laut (Ceram Sea),
  s., Indon.................. F8   44
Serang, Indon.............. G5   50
Serasan, Pulau, i., Indon.... B6   50
Serasan, Selat, strt., Indon.. B6   50
Sarajevo see Sarajevo, Bos.. F5   26
Serbeulangit,
  Pegunungan, mts., Indon... K3   48
Serbia see Srbija, state,
  Serb...................... E7   26
Serbia and Montenegro
  (Yugoslavia), ctry., Eur... F6   26
Serdo, Eth................. E8   62
Serdobsk, Russia........... D6   32
Séré'ama, Mont, mtn.,
  Vanuatu.................. i16   79d
Serebrjanye Prudy, Russia .. F21   10
Serebrjansk, Russia......... E14   32
Sered', Slov............... H13   16
Seredejskij, Russia......... F18   10
Serëdka, Russia............ B11   10
Seremban, Malay............ K5   48
Serengeti National Park,
  p.o.i., Tan............... E6   66
Serengeti Plain, pl., Tan.... E6   66
Serengka, Indon............ D7   50
Serenje, Zam............... C5   68
Seret (Siret), stm., Eur..... A12   26
Sergač, Russia............. D11   32
Sergeevka, Russia.......... C10   38
Sergeja Kirova, ostrova,
  is., Russia................ A6   34
Sergen, Tur................ B10   28
Sergiev Posad, Russia....... D21   10
Serginskij, Russia........... B10   32
Sergipe, state, Braz........ F7   88
Sergozero, ozero, l.,
  Russia.................... C17   8
Seria, Bru................. A9   50
Serian, Malay.............. C7   50
Seribudolok, Indon......... B1   50
Seridó, stm., Braz.......... D7   88
Sérifos, i., Grc............ F7   28
Serik, Tur................. G14   28
Serinyol, Tur............... B7   58
Serio, stm., Italy........... E6   22
Serkovo, Russia............ A15   32
Šerlovaja Gora, Russia...... F12   34
Serov, Russia.............. C10   32
Serowe, Bots............... C8   70
Serpejsk, Russia............ F17   10
Serpentine Lakes, l.,
  Austl..................... E5   74
Serpents Mouth, strt........ C11   86
Serpuhov, Russia........... F20   10
Serra, Braz................ K5   88
Serra Branca, Braz......... D7   88
Serra da Canastra, Parque
  Nacional da, p.o.i., Braz... K2   88
Serra da Capivara, Parque
  Nacional da, p.o.i., Braz... E4   88
Serra do Outes, Spain...... B1   20
Serra do Navio, Braz........ C7   84
Serra do Salitre, Braz....... J2   88
Serra dos Órgãos, Parque
  Nacional da, p.o.i., Braz... L4   88
Serrana, Braz.............. K2   88
Serrana, Cayo de, unds.,
  Col...................... E7   102
Serrana Bank see Serrana,
  Cayo de, unds., Col....... E7   102
Serrania, Braz.............. K2   88
Serranía de la Neblina,
  Parque Nacional,
  p.o.i., Ven............... G8   86
Serranilla, Banco see
  Serranilla, Cayo de,
  unds., Col................ E8   102
Serranilla, Cayo de,
  unds., Col................ E8   102
Serranilla Bank see
  Serranilla, Cayo de,
  unds., Col................ E8   102
Serrano, Banco see
  Serrana, Cayo de,
  unds., Col................ E7   102
Serra Talhada, Braz........ E6   88
Serres, Fr.................. E11   18
Sérres, Grc................ B6   28
Serrezuela, Arg............ E5   92
Serrinha, Braz.............. F6   88
Serrita, Braz............... D6   88
Sertânia, Braz.............. E7   88
Sertãozinho, Braz.......... K1   88
Serui, Indon................ F10   44
Serule, Bots............... B8   70
Serutu, Pulau, i., Indon..... D6   50
Seruwai, Indon............. J4   48
Sêrxü, China.............. E4   36
Seryševo, Russia........... F14   34
Sesayap, stm., Indon....... B10   50
Sesayap Lama, Indon....... B10   50
Seseganaga Lake, l.,
  On., Can................. A8   118
Sese Islands, is., Ug....... E6   66
Sesfontein, Nmb............ D1   68
Sesheke, Zam.............. D3   68
Sesia, stm., Italy........... E5   22
Sesibu, Indon.............. A10   50
Sessa Aurunca, Italy........ C7   24
Sestao, Spain.............. A7   20
Sestri Levante, Italy........ F6   22
Sestroreck, Russia.......... F14   8
Sešupė, stm., Eur.......... F5   10
Šeta, Lith................. E7   10
Sète, Fr................... F9   18
Sete Barras, Braz........... B13   92
Sete Cidades, Parque
  Nacional da, p.o.i., Braz... C5   88
Sete Lagoas, Braz.......... J3   88
Sete Quedas, Parque
  Nacional da, p.o.i., Braz... A11   92
Sete Quedas, Salto das
  (Guaíra, Salto del),
  wtfl., S.A................. B10   92
Seth Ward, Tx., U.S........ G7   128
Seto, Japan............... D10   40
Seto-naikai (Inland Sea),
  s., Japan................. E5   40
Seton Portage, B.C., Can.... F8   138
Settat, Mor................ C3   64
Setté Cama, Gabon......... E1   66
Sette-Daban, hrebet,
  mts., Russia.............. D16   34
Settlers, S. Afr............. D9   70
Setúbal, Port.............. F1   20
Setúbal, state, Port........ F2   20
Setúbal, Baía de b., Port.... F2   20
Seul, Lac, l., On., Can...... A6   118
Seul Choix Point, c., Mi., U.S. C4   112
Seulimeum, Indon.......... J2   48

Sevan, Lake see Sevana
  Lich, l., Arm.............. A6   56
Sevana Lich, l., Arm........ A6   56
Sevastopol', Ukr............ G15   6
Ševelevskaja, Russia........ F20   8
Seven Persons, Ab., Can.... E3   124
Seven Sisters Peaks,
  mtn., B.C., Can........... B2   138
Seventy Mile House,
  B.C., Can................ E9   138
Severn, stm., On., Can...... E12   106
Severn, stm., U.K........... J10   12
Severnaja Dvina
  (Northern Dvina), stm.,
  Russia................... E19   8
Severnaja Osetija,
  state, Russia............. F6   32
Severnaja Sos'va,
  stm., Russia.............. B10   32
Severnaja Zemlja, is.,
  Russia................... B12   30
Severna Park, Md., U.S...... C13   32
Severnoe, Russia........... F6   32
Severnye uvaly, hills,
  Russia................... C7   32
Severnyj Ural, mts.,
  Russia................... B9   32
Severočeský,
  state, Czech Rep.......... F10   16
Severodvinsk
  (Molotovsk), Russia....... D18   8
Severo-Enisejskij, Russia.... B16   32
Severo-Kuril'sk, Russia...... F20   34
Severomoravský,
  state, Czech Rep.......... G13   16
Severomorsk, Russia........ B15   8
Severo-Sibirskaja
  nizmennost' (North
  Siberian Lowland),
  pl., Russia................ B6   34
Severoural'sk
  (Severouralsk), Russia..... B9   32
Severo-Zadonsk, Russia..... F21   10
Severy, Ks., U.S............ D12   128
Sevettijärvi, Fin............ B13   8
Sevier, stm., Ut., U.S....... D4   132
Sevier, East Fork, stm.,
  Ut., U.S.................. F5   132
Sevier Desert, des.,
  Ut., U.S.................. D4   132
Sevier Lake, l., Ut., U.S..... B6   98
Sevierville, Tn., U.S........ I2   114
Sevilla, Col................ E4   86
Sevilla (Seville), Spain...... G5   20
Sevilla, co., Spain.......... G5   20
Seville see Sevilla, Spain.... G5   20
Seville, Fl., U.S............ G4   116
Sevlievo, Blg............... F12   26
Sewäni, India.............. D5   54
Seward, Ak., U.S............ D10   140
Seward, Ne., U.S........... G15   126
Seward, Pa., U.S............ D7   114
Seward Peninsula, pen.,
  Ak., U.S.................. C7   140
Sexsmith Ab., Can.......... A12   138
Sextín, stm., Mex........... B6   100
Seybaplaya, Mex........... C2   102
Seychelles, ctry., Afr....... k12   69b
Seychelles, is., Sey........ k13   69b
Seydişehir, Tur............. F14   28
Seyðisfjördur, Ice.......... k32   8a
Seyhan, stm., Tur.......... B6   58
Seyhan Baraji, res., Tur..... A6   58
Seymour, Austl............. K5   76
Seymour, S. Afr............ H8   70
Seymour, Ct., U.S.......... C12   114
Seymour, In., U.S........... F12   120
Seymour, Mo., U.S......... G5   120
Seymour, Tx., U.S.......... H9   128
Seymour, Wi., U.S.......... D1   112
Sézanne, Fr................ E10   22
Sézanne, Fr................ F12   14
Sfákia, Grc................ H7   28
Sfântu Gheorghe, Rom..... D12   26
Sfântu Gheorghe,
  Bratul, stm., Rom........ E16   26
Sfântu Gheorghe,
  Ostroul, i., Rom.......... D16   26
Sfax, Tun.................. C7   64
's-Gravenhage (The
  Hague), Neth............. B13   14
Sha, stm., China........... H7   42
Sha, stm., China........... E6   42
Shaanxi, state, China....... E3   42
Shabeelle (Shebelė
  Wenz, Wabē), stm., Afr.... D8   66
Shabunda, D.R.C........... E5   66
Shabwah, Yemen.......... F6   56
Shache (Yarkant), China.... B12   56
Shackleton Ice Shelf,
  ice, Ant.................. B14   81
Shackleton Range, mts.,
  Ant...................... D2   81
Shady Cove, Or., U.S....... A3   134
Shady Grove, Fl., U.S....... F2   116
Shadyside, Oh., U.S........ E5   114
Shag Rocks, r., S. Geor..... J8   90
Shāhābād, India........... H6   54
Shāhābād, India........... C6   54
Shāhābād, India........... E7   54
Shāhāda, India............ H5   54
Shah Alam, Malay.......... K5   48
Shāhdādpur, Pak.......... F2   54
Shahdol, India............. G8   54
Shahe, China.............. J3   42
Shahezhen, China......... A7   42
Shāhjahānpur, India....... E7   54
Shāh Kot, Pak............. C4   54
Shāhpur, India............ C3   53
Shāhpur, Pak.............. D2   54
Shāhpura, India........... E5   54
Shāhpura, India........... G8   54
Shāhpura, India........... F5   54
Shahr-e Kord, Iran......... C7   56
Shāighālu, Pak............ C2   54
Shājāpur, India............ G6   54
Shakawe, Bots............. B3   68
Shaker Heights, Oh., U.S... G8   112
Shakespeare Island, i.,
  On., Can................. B10   118
Shakhtinsk, Kaz........... E12   32
Shaki, Nig................. H5   64
Shakopee, Mn., U.S........ G5   118
Shakotan-hantō,
  pen., Japan............... C14   38
Shaktoolik, Ak., U.S........ D7   140
Shala, Lake see Shala
  Hāyk', l., Eth............ F7   62
Shala Hāyk', l., Eth........ F7   62
Shalalth, B.C., Can......... F8   138
Shaler Mountains, mts.,
  Can...................... A8   106
Shallowater, Tx., U.S....... H6   128
Shalqar, Kaz............... E9   32
Shaluli Shan, mts., China... E4   36
Shām, Jabal ash-,
  mtn., Oman.............. E8   56
Shamattawa, Mb., Can..... D12   106
Shamban, Sudan.......... F6   62
Shambu, Eth............... F7   62
Shāmli, India.............. D6   54
Shamokin, Pa., U.S......... D9   114
Shamrock, Fl., U.S......... G2   116
Shamrock, Tx., U.S......... D5   106
Shamva, Zimb.............. D5   68
Shan, state, Mya.......... B4   48
Shancheng, China......... C2   42
Shandi, Sudan............. D6   62
Shandong, state, China.... C7   42
Shandong Bandao
  (Shantung Peninsula),
  pen., China.............. C9   42

Shand uul, mtn., Mong..... C5   36
Shangani, Zimb............ A9   70
Shangani, stm., Zimb....... D4   68
Shangbahe, China......... F6   42
Shangbahe, China......... F6   42
Shangch'iu see
  Shangqiu, China.......... D6   42
Shangchuan Dao, i., China.. K5   42
Shanghai, China........... C7   36
Shanghai, China........... F9   42
Shanghai, state, China..... F9   42
Shanghai Shih see
  Shanghai, state, China.... I4   38
Shanghang, China......... I7   42
Shanghe, China............ C7   42
Shangjao see Shangrao,
  China.................... G7   42
Shangjin, China............ E4   42
Shangjin, China............ J3   42
Shangqing, China.......... I8   42
Shangqiu, China........... D6   42
Shangqiu, China........... D6   42
Shangrao, China........... G7   42
Shangshui, China.......... E6   42
Shangsi, China............. J2   42
Shangsian, China.......... E3   42
Shangyi, China............ A6   42
Shangying, China.......... B7   38
Shangyou Shuiku, res.,
  China.................... I6   42
Shangyu, China............ F9   42
Shangzhi, China........... B8   38
Shantou, China............ A8   42
Shanhaiguan, China....... A8   42
Shanhetun, China......... B7   38
Shankou, China............ K3   42
Shannon, Il., U.S........... C10   122
Shannon, Ms., U.S......... D10   122
Shannon, Ire............... I3   12
Shannon Ø, i., Grnld....... B22   141
Shannontown, S.C., U.S.... C5   116
Shanshan, China.......... C3   36
Shansi see Shanxi,
  state, China............. B5   42
Shantar Islands see
  Šantarskie ostrova,
  is., Russia................ E16   34
Shantipur, India........... G12   54
Shantou, China............ J7   42
Shantung see Shandong,
  state, China............. C7   42
Shantung Peninsula see
  Shandong Bandao,
  pen., China.............. C9   42
Shanwei, China............ J6   42
Shanxi, state, China........ B5   42
Shanxian, China........... D7   42
Shanyang, China........... E3   42
Shanyin, China............ B5   42
Shaoguan, China.......... I5   42
Shaohing see Shaoxing,
  China.................... G9   42
Shaoshan see Shaoguan,
  China.................... G9   42
Shaokuan see Shaoguan,
  China.................... I5   42
Shaolong, stm., China..... C3   38
Shaowu, China............ H7   42
Shaoxing, China........... G9   42
Shaoyang, China.......... H4   42
Shaqqā, Syria............. F7   58
Shaqrā', Sau. Ar.......... D6   56
Shaqrā', Yemen........... G6   56
Shar, Kaz.................. E14   32
Shara, gora, mtn., Asia..... A5   56
Sharbaqty, Kaz............ D13   32
Shardara, Kaz............. F11   32
Shardara bögeni,
  res., Asia................ A10   56
Sharga, stm., Mong....... C16   38
Sharin Gol, Mong.......... B6   36
Sharjah see
  Ash-Shāriqah, U.A.E...... D8   56
Shark Bay, b., Austl......... E2   74
Sharktooth Mountain,
  mtn., B.C., Can........... D5   106
Sharm el-Sheikh, Egypt..... K5   58
Sharon, Ct., U.S........... C12   114
Sharon, Pa., U.S........... C5   114
Sharon, Tn., U.S........... H9   120
Sharon, Wi., U.S........... B9   120
Sharpe, Lake, res.,
  S.D., U.S................. C12   126
Sharpes, Mn. Afr.......... B9   70
Shashemene, Eth.......... F7   62
Shashi, China.............. F5   42
Shasi see Shashi, China.... F5   42
Shasta, Ca., U.S........... C3   134
Shasta, Mount, vol.,
  Ca., U.S................. B3   134
Shasta Lake, res., Ca., U.S.. C3   134
Shāti', Wādi ash-
  stm., Libya............... B2   62
Shats'k, Ukr............... E19   16
Shetland Islands, is.,
  Scot., U.K................ n17   12a
Shetrunji, stm., India....... H3   54
Shexian, China............ G8   42
Sheyang, China............ C9   42
Sheyenne, N.D., U.S....... G14   124
Sheyenne, stm., N.D., U.S... H16   124
Sheykhābād, Afg.......... A2   54
Shiant Islands, is.,
  Scot., U.K................ D6   12
Shibām, Yemen............ F6   56
Shibata, Japan............ B11   40
Shibīn el-Kôm, Egypt...... H1   58
Shibukawa, Japan......... C12   40
Shicheng, China........... H7   42
Shickley, Ne., U.S.......... G15   126
Shidao, China............. C10   42
Shidler, Ok., U.S........... E12   128
Shieli, Kaz................. F11   32
She, stm., China........... F6   42
Shiga, state, Japan........ D9   40
Shigezhuang, China....... H8   42
Shigouyi, China........... C2   42
Shiguaigou, China......... A4   42
Shihch'i see Zhongshan,
  China.................... J5   42
Shihchiachuang see
  Shijiazhuang, China...... C6   42
Shihkiachwang see
  Shijiazhuang, China...... C6   42
Shijiazhuang, China....... C6   42
Shijiazhuang, China....... C6   42
Shijiu Hu, l., China......... F8   42
Shikārpur, India........... D2   53
Shikārpur, Pak............ E2   54
Shikohābād, India......... E7   54
Shikoku, i., Japan......... F6   40
Shikoku-sanchi, mts.,
  Japan.................... F6   40
Shikotsu-ko, l., Japan...... C14   38
Shilbottle, Eng., U.K........ F11   12
Shildon, Eng., U.K......... G11   12
Shillelagh, Ire............. I6   12
Shillington, Pa., U.S........ H13   112
Shillong, India............. F13   54
Shiloh see Saylūn,
  Khirbat, hist., W.B........ F6   58
Shilong, China............. J5   42
Shimabara, Japan......... F3   40
Shimabara, Japan......... E11   40
Shiman, state, Som........ B9   66
Shimane, state, Japan..... D5   40
Shimian, China............ F5   36
Shimizu, Japan............ D11   40
Shimla, India.............. C6   54
Shimminato, Japan........ C10   40
Shimoda, Japan........... E11   40

Shelby, Ne., U.S........... F15   126
Shelbyville, Il., U.S......... E9   120
Shelbyville, In., U.S........ E12   120
Shelbyville, Mo., U.S....... E5   120
Shelbyville, Tn., U.S........ B12   122
Shelby, Lake, res.,
  Il., U.S.................. E8   120
Sheldon, Il., U.S........... H3   118
Sheldon, Mo., U.S......... G3   120
Shelek, Kaz............... F13   32
Shelekhov, Gulf of see
  Šelihova, zaliv, b., Russia.. E9   140
Shelikof Strait, strt.,
  Ak., U.S.................. E9   140
Shell, stm., Mb., Can....... C12   124
Shellbrook, Sk., Can........ A7   124
Shell Creek, stm., Ne., U.S.. C8   138
Shelley, B.C., Can.......... C8   138
Shellharbour, Austl........ J8   76
Shell Lake, Wi., U.S........ F7   118
Shellman, Ga., U.S......... F14   122
Shellmouth Dam, dam,
  Mb., Can................ D12   124
Shell Rock, Ia., U.S......... B5   120
Shell Rock, stm., Ia., U.S.... I6   118
Shellsburg, Ia., U.S......... B5   120
Shelton, Ct., U.S........... C12   114
Shelton, Ne., U.S.......... G14   126
Shelton, Wa., U.S.......... C3   136
Shemogue, N.B., Can...... D12   110
Shemonaîkha, Kaz........ D14   32
Shemonaîkha see
  Šemonaihaa, Kaz........ D14   32
Shenandoah, Ia., U.S...... D2   120
Shenandoah, Pa., U.S...... F7   114
Shenandoah, stm., U.S..... E8   114
Shenandoah, North Fork,
  stm., Va., U.S............ F7   114
Shenandoah, South Fork,
  stm., Va., U.S............ F7   114
Shenandoah National
  Park, p.o.i., Va., U.S...... F7   114
Shenber, Kaz.............. E11   32
Shenchi, China............ B4   42
Shencottah, India......... G3   53
Shendam, Nig............. H6   64
Shenge, S.L................ H2   64
Shengsi Liedao, is., China .. I5   38
Shengxian, China.......... G9   42
Shenhabaref, Pak., U.S.... C6   140
Shenjing, China........... J5   42
Shenmu, China............ B4   42
Shenqiu, China............ E6   42
Shenshi see Shaanxi,
  state, China............. E3   42
Shenton, Mount, mtn.,
  Austl.................... E4   74
Shenxian, China........... C6   42
Shenyang (Mukden), China.. D5   38
Shenzhen, China........... J6   42
Sheoganj, India........... F4   54
Sheopur, India............. F6   54
Shepard, Ab., Can......... E17   138
Shepherd, Mi., U.S......... E5   112
Shepherd, state, Vanuatu.. k17   79d
Shepherd, Îles,
  is., Vanuatu.............. k17   79d
Shepherdstown, W.V., U.S.. E7   114
Shepherdsville, Ky., U.S.... F12   120
Shepparton, Austl......... K5   76
Sheppey, Isle of, i.,
  Eng., U.K................ J13   12
Sherard, Cape, c., Nu., Can. C10   141
Sherard Osburn Fjord,
  b., Grnld................. A14   141
Sherborne, Eng., U.K....... K10   12
Sherbro Island, i., S.L...... H2   64
Sherbrooke, N.S., Can..... E14   110
Sherbrooke, Qc., Can...... E15   110
Sherburn, Mn., U.S......... H4   118
Sherburne, N.Y., U.S....... B10   114
Sheridan, Ar., U.S.......... C6   122
Sheridan, In., U.S.......... H3   112
Sheridan, Or., U.S.......... E3   136
Sheridan, Tx., U.S.......... E11   130
Sheridan, Wy., U.S......... C6   136
Sherman, N.Y., U.S......... B6   114
Sherman, Tx., U.S.......... D2   122
Sherman Mills, Me., U.S.... E8   110
Sherman Mountain, mtn.,
  Ar., U.S.................. I4   120
Sherman Station, Me., U.S.. E8   110
Sherpur, Bngl.............. F12   54
Sherpur, Bngl.............. F13   54
Sherridon, Mb., Can....... E10   106
Sherrill, N.Y., U.S.......... E14   112
Shertallai, India........... G3   53
's-Hertogenbosch, Neth.... C14   14
Sherwood, Ar., U.S......... C6   122
Sherwood, Oh., U.S........ C1   114
Sherwood, Tn., U.S......... B12   122
Sherwood Park, Ab., Can... C17   138
Sherwood Shores, Tx., U.S.. D9   130
Shesh Gav, Afr............ C8   56
Shoshka, Ukr.............. C8   70
Shouchang, China......... G8   42
Shouguang, China......... H8   42
Shouning, China........... H8   42
Shouxian, China........... E6   42
Show Low, Az., U.S......... I6   132

Shimodate, Japan......... C13   40
Shimoga, India............ E2   53
Shimonoseki, Japan....... F3   40
Shimono-shima, i., Japan .. E2   40
Shin, stm., Japan.......... B11   40
Shin, Loch, l., Scot., U.K.... C8   12
Shinano, stm., Japan...... B11   40
Shindand, Afg............. C9   56
Shingbwiyang, Mya........ C8   46
Shingū, Japan............. F9   40
Shingū, Japan............. E7   40
Shingwidzi, S. Afr.......... C10   70
Shingwidzi (Singuédeze),
  stm., S. Afr.............. C10   70
Shinji-ko, l., Japan......... D5   40
Shinjo, Japan.............. A13   40
Shinyanga, Tan............ E6   66
Shiocton, Wi., U.S.......... G10   118
Shiogama, Japan.......... A14   40
Shiojiri, Japan............. C10   40
Shiono-misaki, c., Japan ... F8   40
Shioya-zaki, c., Japan...... C13   40
Shiping, China............. G2   42
Shiping, China............. G2   42
Shipki Pass see
  Sípčenski Prohod, p., Blg.. G12   26
Shipman, Va., U.S.......... G7   114
Shippegan, N.B., Can...... C12   110
Shippensburg, Pa., U.S..... D8   114
Shiprock, N.M., U.S......... G8   132
Shipshaw, stm., Qc., Can... B6   110
Shipu, China............... G9   42
Shiquan, China............ E3   42
Shiquanhe see
  Shiquanhe, China........ B8   54
Shiqma, stm., Isr.......... G5   58
Shira, stm., Indon.......... E6   50
Shírāz, Iran............... D7   56
Shirbīn, Egypt............. G2   58
Shiretoko-misaki, c., Japan.. B16   38
Shir Kūh, mtn., Iran........ C7   56
Shirley, In., U.S............ I4   112
Shīrīnāb, Iran............. A13   40
Shirone, Japan............ B11   40
Shirpur, India............. H5   54
Shírvān, Iran.............. B8   56
Shishaldin Volcano,
  vol., Ak., U.S............. F7   140
Shishi, China.............. I8   42
Shisui, Japan.............. C13   40
Shitang, China............. H9   42
Shiv, India................ F4   54
Shively, Ky., U.S........... F12   120
Shivpuri, India............ F6   54
Shivta, Horvot
  (Subeita), sci., Isr........ H5   58
Shiwwts Plateau, plat.,
  Az., U.S.................. G3   132
Shixing, China............. I6   42
Shiyan, China.............. E4   42
Shizhu, China.............. F3   42
Shizugawa, Japan......... A14   40
Shizui, China.............. C2   42
Shizunai, Japan........... C15   38
Shizuoka, Japan........... E11   40
Shizuoka, state, Japan..... E10   40
Shkodër, Alb.............. B13   24
Shkodra see Shkodër, Alb... B13   24
Shkumbin, stm., Alb........ C14   24
Shö, stm., Japan........... C10   40
Shoal, stm., Fl., U.S........ G12   122
Shoal Creek, stm., Mo., U.S.. E4   120
Shoal Creek, stm., Mo., U.S.. H3   120
Shoalhaven, stm., Austl..... J8   76
Shoal Lake, l., Can......... B3   118
Shoals, In., U.S............ F11   120
Shoalwater Bay, b., Austl... D8   76
Shōbara, China............ E6   40
Shōdo-shima, i., Japan..... E7   40
Sholapur, India............ B3   53
Sholaqqorghan, Kaz....... F11   32
Sholaqqorghan, Kaz....... F11   32
Shonzhy, Kaz.............. F13   32
Shoqpar, Kaz.............. F12   32
Shorāpur, India............ C3   53
Shoreacres, B.C., Can...... G13   138
Shorewood, Wi., U.S....... C2   112
Shorkot, Pak.............. C3   54
Shortandy, Kaz............ D12   32
Shortland Island, i., Sol. Is.. d6   79b
Shortland Islands, is., Sol. Is. d6   79b
Shoshone, Id., U.S......... H12   136
Shoshone, stm., Wy., U.S... C4   126
Shoshone, South Fork,
  stm., Wy., U.S............ G17   136
Shoshone Lake, l., Wy.,
  U.S...................... F15   136
Shoshone Mountains,
  mts., Nv., U.S............ E8   134
Shoshone Peak, mtn.,
  Nv., U.S................. G9   134
Shoshone Range, mts.,
  Nv., U.S................. C8   134
Shoshong, Bots............ C8   70
Shuwak, Sudan............ E7   62

Shuyak Island, i., Ak., U.S... E9   140
Shuyang, China............ D8   42
Shwangliao see Liaoyuan,
  China.................... C6   38
Shwebo, Mya.............. A2   48
Shwegun, Mya............. D3   48
Shwegyin, Mya............ D3   48
Shyghys-Qongyrat, Kaz.... E12   32
Shymkent, Kaz............ F11   32
Shyok, India............... A7   54
Shyok, stm., Asia.......... B4   46
Si, stm., China............. D7   42
Sia, Indon................. G9   44
Siāhān Range, mts., Pak... D9   56
Siak, stm., Indon........... C2   50
Siak Sri Indrapura, Indon... C3   50
Siam see Thailand,
  ctry., Asia................ E5   48
Siam, Gulf of see
  Thailand, Gulf of, b., Asia.. G5   48
Sian see Xi'an, China....... D3   42
Siangtan see Xiangtan,
  China.................... H5   42
Sianów, Pol............... B12   16
Siantan, Pulau, i., Indon.... B4   50
Siapa, stm., Ven........... G9   86
Siargao Island, i., Phil...... F6   52
Siasconset, Ma., U.S....... C15   114
Siasi, Phil................. H3   52
Siasi Island, i., Phil........ H3   52
Šiaškotan, ostrov, i., Russia . G19   34
Siauliai, Lith.............. E6   10
Siauliai, Lith.............. E6   10
Sibaj, Russia.............. D9   32
Sibayi, Lake, l., S. Afr....... E11   70
Šibenik, Cro............... G12   22
Siberia see Sibir', reg.,
  Russia................... C12   34
Sibi, Pak.................. D10   56
Sibigo, Indon.............. K2   48
Sibir', reg., Russia......... C12   34
Sibircevo, Russia.......... B10   38
Sibirjakova, ostrov, i.,
  Russia................... B4   34
Sibiti, Congo.............. E2   66
Sibiu, Rom................ D11   26
Sibiu, state, Rom.......... D11   26
Sibley, Ia., U.S............ H3   118
Sibley, La., U.S............ E5   122
Sibley, Ms., U.S........... F7   122
Sibley Peninsula, pen.,
  On., Can................ C10   118
Siblag, Indon.............. C1   50
Sibsāgar, India........... B7   50
Sibu, Malay............... B7   50
Sibuguey Bay, b., Phil...... G4   52
Sibut, C.A.R.............. C3   66
Sibutu Island, i., Phil...... H2   52
Sibutu Passage, strt., Asia .. H2   52
Sibuyan Island, i., Phil...... D4   52
Sibuyan Sea, s., Phil....... D4   52
Sicamous, B.C., Can....... F11   138
Sicapoo, Mount, mtn., Phil.. B3   52
Siccus, stm., Austl......... H2   76
Sichang see Xichang, China. F5   36
Si Chon, Thai.............. H4   48
Sichuan, state, China...... E5   36
Sichuan Pendi, bas., China.. F1   42
Sicié, Cap, c., Fr........... F11   18
Sicilia (Sicily), i., Italy...... G7   24
Sicilia (Sicily), i., Italy...... G7   24
Sicily see Sicilia, state, Italy . F8   24
Sicily see Sicilia, i., Italy.... G8   24
Sicily, Strait of, strt.,
  Mediterranean........... G5   24
Sicily Island, La., U.S....... F7   122
Sicuani, Peru.............. F3   84
Sid, Serb................. D6   26
Sidari, see Sayada, Leb.... E7   58
Sidi Barrani, Egypt........ A5   62
Sidi bel Abbès, Alg......... B5   64
Sidi-Ifni, Mor.............. D2   64
Siding Spring Mountain,
  mtn., Austl............... H7   76
Sidirókastro, Grc.......... B6   28
Sidi Sālim, Egypt.......... G1   58
Sidlaghatta, India......... E3   53
Sidley, Mount, mtn., Ant.... K9   12
Sidmouth, Eng., U.K....... K9   12
Sidnaw, Mt., U.S.......... D10   118
Sidney, B.C., Can.......... H7   138
Sidney, Il., U.S............ G9   134
Sidney, Ia., U.S............ J8   118
Sidney, Mt., U.S........... G9   124
Sidney, N.Y., U.S.......... F10   126
Sidney, Ne., U.S........... B10   114
Sidney, Oh., U.S........... D1   114
Sidney Lanier Lake,
  res., Ga., U.S............ B2   116
Sidon see Şaydā, Leb....... E7   58
Sidon, Ms., U.S............ D8   122
Sidorovsk, Russia......... A14   32
Sidra, Gulf of see Surt,
  Khalīj, b., Libya.......... A3   62
Siedlce, Pol............... D6   16
Siedlikowo, Braz........... D18   16
Siedlce, state, Pol......... D17   16
Siegburg, Ger............. E16   16
Siegen, Ger............... F5   16
Siemianowice Śląskie, Pol.. F15   16
Siĕmpang, Camb........... E8   48
Siĕmréab, Camb........... F6   48
Siena, Italy................ G8   22
Sienyang see Xianyang,
  China.................... D3   42
Sieradz, Pol............... E14   16
Sieradz, state, Pol......... E14   16
Sieraków, Pol.............. D12   16
Sierpc, Pol................ D15   16
Sierra Blanca, Tx., U.S..... C2   130
Sierra Blanca Peak,
  mtn., N.M., U.S........... H3   128
Sierra Chica, Arg.......... H3   90
Sierra Gorda, Chile........ A3   90
Sierra Leone, ctry., Afr..... H2   64
Sierra Mojada, Mex........ G4   130
Sierra Nevada see Nevada,
  Sierra, mts., Spain....... G6   20
Sierra Nevada, Parque
  Nacional, p.o.i., Ven...... C6   86
Sierra Vista, Az., U.S....... L6   132
Sierre, Switz.............. D4   22
Siesta Key, Fl., U.S......... F7   116
Sifnos, i., Grc............. G7   28
Sifón Villanueva, Mex...... G10   100
Siga, Indon................ D1   50
Sigatoka, Fiji.............. q18   79e
Sighetu Marmaţiei, Rom... B10   26
Sighişoara, Rom........... C11   26
Sigli, Indon............... E19   34
Siglijik, Russia............ C12   26
Siglufjördur, Ice........... j30   8a
Sigmaringen, Ger......... H5   16
Signal Mountain, Tn., U.S... B13   122
Signal Mountain, mtn.,
  Vt., U.S.................. F4   110
Signy, sci., Ant............ B36   81
Sigourney, Ia., U.S......... C5   120
Sigsig, Ec................. D2   84
Siguanea, Ensenada de
  la, b., Cuba.............. B6   102
Siguatepeque, Hond....... E3   102
Sigüenza, Spain........... C8   20
Siguiri, Gui................ G3   64
Sigulda, Lat............... C7   10

Name	Map Ref.	Page
Sigurd, Ut., U.S.	E5	132
Siguri Falls, wtfl., Tan.	F7	66
Sihabuhabu, Dolok, mtn., Indon.	B1	50
Sihanoukville see Kâmpóng Saôm, Camb.	G6	48
Sihor, India	H3	54
Sihora, India	G8	54
Sihote-Alin', mts., Russia	E17	30
Šihtovo, Russia	E15	10
Sihui, China	J5	42
Siirt, Tur.	B5	56
Sija, Russia	E19	8
Sijunjung, Indon.	D2	50
Sikandarābād, India	D6	54
Sikanni Chief, stm., B.C., Can.	D6	106
Sikao, Thai.	I4	48
Sikar, India	E5	54
Sikasso, Mali	G3	64
Sikeston, Mo., U.S.	H8	120
Sikhote-Alin Mountains see Sihote-Alin', mts., Russia	E17	30
Sikiang see Xi, stm., China	J5	42
Siking see Xi'an, China	D3	42
Síkinos, i., Grc.	G8	28
Sikkim, state, India	E12	54
Sikonge, Tan.	F6	66
Šikotan, ostrov (Shikotan-tō), i., Russia	C17	38
Siktjah, Russia	B13	34
Sikuati, Malay.	G1	52
Síkyōn, sci., Grc.	F5	28
Šil, stm., Spain	B3	20
Šila, Russia	E7	34
Šilalė Lith.	E5	10
Silao, Mex.	E8	100
Silas, Al., U.S.	F10	122
Silaut, Indon.	E2	50
Šilay, Phil.	E4	52
Silchar, India	F14	54
Šile, Tur.	B12	28
Siler City, N.C., U.S.	I6	114
Sileru, stm., India	C5	53
Silesia, hist. reg., Eur.	F13	16
Siletitengiz köli, l., Kaz.	D12	32
Siletz, Or., U.S.	F3	136
Siletz, stm., Or., U.S.	F3	136
Silgaḍhi, Nepal	D8	54
Silghāt, India	E14	54
Silhouette, i., Sey.	j13	69b
Siliana, Tun.	H3	24
Siliana, Oued, stm., Tun.	I3	24
Silifke, Tur.	B4	58
Siling Co, l., China	C12	54
Silistra, Blg.	E14	26
Šiliuti, Tur.	B11	28
Šiljan, l., Swe.	F6	8
Šilka, Russia	F12	34
Šilka, stm., Russia	F12	34
Silkeborg, Den.	H3	8
Sillamäe, Est.	A10	10
Sillem Island, i., Nu., Can.	A16	106
Sillian, Aus.	D9	22
Sillon de Talbert, pen., Fr.	F5	14
Šilovici, Russia	E15	10
Silsbee, Tx., U.S.	G4	122
Silton, Sk., Can.	D9	124
Šiluas, Indon.	C6	50
Šilutė Lith.	E4	10
Silvânia, Braz.	I1	88
Silvassa, India	H4	54
Silver, Tx., U.S.	B7	130
Silver Bank Passage, strt., N.A.	B12	102
Silver Bell, Az., U.S.	K5	132
Silver City, N.C., U.S.	B6	116
Silver City, N.M., U.S.	K8	132
Silver Creek, Ms., U.S.	F9	122
Silver Creek, stm., U.S.	F15	126
Silver Creek, stm., Az., U.S.	I6	132
Silver Creek, stm., Or., U.S.	G7	136
Silverdale, Wa., U.S.	C4	136
Silver Lake, U.S.	E2	120
Silver Lake, Mn., U.S.	G4	118
Silver Lake, Wi., U.S.	F1	112
Silver Lake, l., Or., U.S.	G7	136
Silver Lake, l., Or., U.S.	G5	136
Silver Spring, Md., U.S.	E8	114
Silver Star Mountain, mtn., Wa., U.S.	B6	136
Silverthrone Mountain, vol., B.C., Can.	E4	138
Silverton, Austl.	H3	76
Silverton, B.C., Can.	G13	138
Silverton, Co., U.S.	F9	132
Silverton, Tx., U.S.	G7	128
Silvi, Italy	H11	22
Silvia, Col.	F3	86
Silvies, stm., Or., U.S.	G7	136
Šimanovsk, Russia	F14	34
Simao, China	A5	48
Simão Dias, Braz.	F6	88
Simav, Tur.	D11	28
Simav, stm., Tur.	C11	28
Simbach, Ger.	H8	16
Simbo Island, i., Sol. Is.	e7	79b
Simcoe, On., Can.	F9	112
Simcoe, Lake, l., On., Can.	D10	112
Simdega, India	G10	54
Simeria, Rom.	D10	26
Simeulue, Pulau, i., Indon.	K2	48
Simferopol', Ukr.	G15	6
Simikot, Nepal	C8	54
Similkameen, stm., N.A.	G10	138
Simití, Col.	D4	86
Simi Valley, Ca., U.S.	I7	134
Simizu see Shimizu, Japan	D11	40
Simla, Co., U.S.	B4	128
Simmern, Ger.	G3	16
Simmie, Sk., Can.	E5	124
Simms, Mt., U.S.	C15	136
Simnas, Lith.	F6	10
Simoca, Arg.	C5	92
Simões, Braz.	D5	88
Simojärvi, l., Fin.	C12	8
Simojovel, Mex.	G12	100
Simon, Lac, l., Qc, Can.	E1	100
Simonette, stm., Ab., Can.	A12	138
Simonoseki see Shimonoseki, Japan	F3	40
Simonstad see Simon's Town, S. Afr.	I4	70
Simon's Town, S. Afr.	I4	70
Simoom Sound, B.C., Can.	F4	138
Simpang, Indon.	D3	50
Simpang-kiri, stm., Indon.	K3	48
Simplon Pass, p., Switz.	D4	22
Simpson Desert, Austl.	D7	74
Simpson Island, i., On., Can.	C11	118
Simpson Peninsula, pen., Nu., Can.	B13	106
Simpson Strait, strt., Nu., Can.	B11	106
Simpsonville, S.C., U.S.	B3	116
Simrishamn, Swe.	I6	8
Simsonbaai, Neth. Ant.	A1	105a
Simunjan, Malay.	C7	50
Simušír, ostrov, i., Russia	G19	34
Sina, stm., India	B2	53
Sinabang, Indon.	K3	48
Sinabung, Gunung, vol., Indon.	K4	48
Sinai (Sinai Peninsula), pen., Egypt	J4	58
Sinai, Mount see Mūsā, Gebel, mtn., Egypt.	J5	58
Sinai, Mount, vol., Gren.	q10	105e
Sinai, Rom.	D12	26
Sinai Peninsula see Sinai, pen., Egypt	J4	58
Sinajana, Guam	j10	78c
Sinaloa, state, Mex.	C5	100
Sinaloa, stm., Mex.	C5	100
Sinamaica, Ven.	B6	86
Sinan, China.	H3	42
Sinanpaşa, Tur.	E13	28
Sinäwin, Libya	A2	62
Sincan, Tur.	D15	28
Sincé, Col.	B2	84
Sincelejo, Col.	C4	86
Sinch'ang-ŭp, Kor., N.	D8	38
Sin-ch'on, Kor., N.	E6	38
Sinclair, Wy., U.S.	B9	132
Sinclair, Lake, res., Ga., U.S.	C2	116
Sinclair Mills, B.C., Can.	B9	138
Sind, state, Pak.	F2	54
Sind, stm., India	F7	54
Sindaṅgan, Phil.	F4	52
Sindangbarang, Indon.	G5	50
Sindara, Gabon	E2	66
Sindari, India	F3	54
Sindelfingen, Ger.	H4	16
Sindhnūr, India	D3	53
Sindhulī Māḍi, Nepal	E10	54
Sindingale, India	C2	48
Sindor, Russia.	B8	32
Sines, Port.	G2	20
Sinfra, C. Iv.	H3	64
Singalamwe, Nmb.	D3	68
Singapore, Sing.	C3	50
Singapore, ctry., Asia	L6	48
Singapore, Strait of, strt., Asia.	C4	50
Singaraja, Indon.	H9	50
Sing Buri, Thai.	E5	48
Singen, Ger.	I4	16
Singida, Tan.	E6	66
Singitic Gulf see Agíou Órous, Kólpos, b., Grc.	C6	28
Singkaling Hkámti, Mya.	C8	46
Singkang, Indon.	F11	50
Singkawang, Indon.	C6	50
Singkep, Pulau, i., Indon.	D4	50
Singkil, Indon.	K3	48
Singkuang, Indon.	C1	50
Singleton, Austl.	I8	76
Singleton, Mount, mtn., Austl.	E3	74
Singuédeze (Shingwidzi), stm., Afr.	C10	70
Sining see Xining, China	D5	36
Sinj, Cro.	G13	22
Sinjah, Sudan	E6	62
Sinjai, Indon.	F12	50
Sinjaja, stm., Eur.	D11	10
Sinjaja, stm., Russia	D14	34
Sinjuga, Russia.	E12	34
Sinkat, Sudan	D7	62
Sinkiang see Xinjiang, state, China	A5	46
Sinnamahoning, Pa., U.S.	C7	114
Sinnamary, Fr. Gu.	B7	84
Sinnar, India.	B2	53
Sinnūris, Egypt	I1	58
Sinnyŏng, Kor., S.	C1	40
Sinoie, Lacul, l., Rom.	E15	26
Sinop, Tur.	A4	56
Sinsheim, Ger.	G4	16
Sinsiang see Xinxiang, China	D5	42
Sinskoe, Russia	D14	34
Sintang, Indon.	C7	50
Sint Christoffelberg, hill, Neth. Ant.	p21	104g
Sint Eustatius, i., Neth. Ant.	B1	105a
Sint Helenabaai, b., S. Afr.	H3	70
Sint Kruis, Neth. Ant.	p21	104g
Sint Maarten (Saint-Martin), i., N.A.	A1	105a
Sint Nicolaas, Aruba	p20	104g
Sint-Niklaas, Bel.	C12	14
Sintra, Port.	F1	20
Sint-Truiden, Bel.	D14	14
Sinú, stm., Col.	C4	86
Sinūiju, Kor., N.	D6	38
Sint, stm., Hung.	C5	26
Siocon, Phil.	G4	52
Siófok, Hung.	C5	26
Sion, Switz.	D4	22
Siorapaluk, Grnld.	B12	141
Sioux Center, Ia., U.S.	H2	118
Sioux City, Ia., U.S.	B1	120
Sioux Falls, S.D., U.S.	D1	118
Sioux Lookout, On., Can.	A6	118
Sioux Narrows, On., Can.	B4	118
Sioux Rapids, Ia., U.S.	B2	120
Sipalay, Phil.	F4	52
Sipan, Otok, i., Cro.	H14	22
Sipapo, stm., Ven.	E8	86
Siparia, Trin.	s12	105f
Šipčenski Prohod (Shipka Pass), p., Blg.	G12	26
Sipicyno, Russia	F22	8
Siping, China	C6	38
Sipiwesk Lake, l., Mb., Can.	D11	106
Siple, Mount, mtn., Ant.	C28	81
Siple Island, i., Ant.	C28	81
Si Prachan, Thai.	E4	48
Sipsey, stm., Al., U.S.	D10	122
Sipunskij, mys, c., Russia	F21	34
Sipura, Pulau, i., Indon.	E1	50
Siqueira Campos, Braz.	A12	92
Siquia, stm., Nic.	F5	102
Siquijor, Phil.	F4	52
Siquijor Island, i., Phil.	F4	52
Siquirres, C.R.	G6	102
Šira, India	E3	53
Šira, stm., Nor.	G2	8
Si Racha, Thai.	F5	48
Siracusa, Italy.	G9	24
Sirāhā, Nepal.	E11	54
Sīrājganj, Bngl.	F12	54
Sir Bani Yās, i., U.A.E.	E7	56
Sirdar, B.C., Can.	G14	138
Sir Douglas, Mount, mtn., Can.	F15	138
Sir Edward Pellew Group, is., Austl.	C7	74
Siret, Rom.	B12	26
Siret (Seret), stm., Eur.	A12	26
Sirhān, Wādī as-, val., Sau. Ar.	H8	58
Sirik, Tanjong, c., Malay.	B7	50
Sirikit Reservoir, res., Thai.	D5	48
Sirino, Monte, mtn., Italy	D9	24
Sir James MacBrien, Mount, mtn., N.T., Can.	C4	106
Sīrjān, Iran	D8	56
Sirkeli, Tur.	E12	10
Sirocina, Bela.	E12	10
Širohi, India	F4	54
Širokovo, Russia	C17	32
Širokovskij, Russia	C9	32
Sirpsindiği, Tur.	B9	28
Širri, Jazīreh-ye, i., Iran	D7	56
Sirsa, India	D5	54
Sirsi, India	D2	53
Sirsilla, India	B4	53
Sirte, Gulf of see Surt, Khalīj, b., Libya	A3	62
Sir Timothy's Hill, hill, St. K./N.	C2	105a
Širupa, stm., Mex.	G8	98
Širvintos, Lith.	E7	10
Sir Wilfrid Laurier, Mount, mtn., B.C., Can.	D11	138
Sisak, Cro., Jap. N.A.	F6	66
Si Sa Ket, Thai.	E7	48
Sishen, S. Afr.	E6	70
Sishilije, China	G7	42
Sishui, China	D7	42
Sisib Lake, l., Mb., Can.	B14	124
Sisimiut see Holsteinsborg, Grnld.	D15	141
Siskiyou Pass, p., Or., U.S.	A3	134
Sisseton, S.D., U.S.	F1	118
Sīstān, reg., Asia	C9	56
Sister Bay, Wi., U.S.	C2	112
Sisteron, Fr.	E11	18
Sisters, Or., U.S.	F5	136
Sistersville, W.V., U.S.	E5	114
Sit', stm., Russia	B20	10
Sītāmarhi, India	E10	54
Sītāpur, India	E8	54
Siteia, Grc.	H9	28
Siteki, Swaz.	E10	70
Si Thep, sci., Thai.	E5	48
Sithonía, pen., Grc.	C6	28
Sítio d'Abadia, Braz.	H2	88
Sitka, Ak., U.S.	E12	140
Sitkalidak Island, i., Ak., U.S.	E9	140
Sittard, Neth.	C14	14
Sitten see Sion, Switz.	D4	22
Sittoung, stm., Mya.	C3	48
Sittwe, Mya.	D7	46
Siuna, Nic.	F5	102
Siuslaw, stm., Or., U.S.	G3	136
Sivaganga, India	G4	53
Sivakāsi, India	G3	53
Sivang, Russia	F14	34
Sivas, Tur.	B4	56
Šiveluč, vulkan, vol., Russia	E21	34
Siverek, Tur.	B4	56
Siverskij, Russia	A12	10
Sivrihisar, Tur.	D14	28
Siwa, Egypt	B5	62
Siwalik Range, mts., India	C6	54
Siwān, India	E10	54
Siyang, China	E8	42
Sizuoka see Shizuoka, Japan	E11	40
Sjælland, i., Den.	I4	8
Sjalec, Bela.	G13	10
Sjamža, Russia	F19	8
Sjarheevičy, Bela.	G10	10
Sjas'stroj, Russia	A15	10
Sjas'stroj, Russia	F15	8
Sjenica, Serb.	F7	26
Sjuzikozero, Russia	F18	8
Skærfjorden, b., Grnld.	B22	141
Skaftafell Nasjonalpark, p.o.i., Ice.	k31	8a
Skagafjörður b., Ice.	j31	8a
Skagen, Den.	H4	8
Skagerrak, strt., Eur.	H3	8
Skagit, stm., N.A.	H8	138
Skagway, Ak., U.S.	E12	140
Skaistkalne, Lat.	D7	10
Skalbmierz, Pol.	F16	16
Skalino, Russia	G18	8
Skalistyj Golec, gora, mtn., Russia	E12	34
Skalka, l., Swe.	C8	8
Skåne, state, Swe.	H5	8
Skärdu, Pak.	B12	56
Skarszewy, Pol.	B14	16
Skarżysko-Kamienna, Pol.	E16	16
Skaudvilė Lith.	E5	10
Skawina, Pol.	F15	16
Skeena, stm., B.C., Can.	B1	138
Skeena Crossing, B.C., Can.	A3	138
Skeena Mountains, mts., B.C., Can.	D5	106
Skegness, Eng., U.K.	H13	12
Skei, Nor.	F2	8
Skeleton Coast, cst., Nmb.	B1	70
Skellefteå, Swe.	D9	8
Skellefteälven, stm., Swe.	D8	8
Skellytown, Tx., U.S.	F7	128
Skerryvore, r., Scot., U.K.	E5	12
Ski, Nor.	G4	8
Skiatook, Ok., U.S.	H1	120
Skibbereen, Ire.	J3	12
Skidal', Bela.	G7	10
Skiddaw, mtn., Eng., U.K.	G9	12
Skidmore, Tx., U.S.	F10	130
Skien, Nor.	G3	8
Skierniewice, Pol.	D16	16
Skierniewice, state, Pol.	E16	16
Skikda, Alg.	B6	64
Skilak Lake, l., Ak., U.S.	D9	140
Skillet Fork, stm., Il., U.S.	F9	120
Skinnastaðir, Ice.	j31	8a
Skipton, Austl.	K4	76
Skipton, Eng., U.K.	H10	12
Skive, Den.	H3	8
Skjálfandafljót, stm., Ice.	k31	8a
Sklad, Russia	B13	34
Šklou, Bela.	F13	10
Skofja Loka, Slvn.	D11	22
Skoganvarre, Nor.	B11	8
Skoganvarri see Skoganvarre, Nor.	B11	8
Skokie, Il., U.S.	F2	112
Skón, Camb.	F7	48
Skópelos, i., Grc.	D6	28
Skopin, Russia	D5	32
Skopje, Mac.	A4	28
Skopje see Skopje, Mac.	A4	28
Skórcz, Pol.	C14	16
Skövde, Swe.	G5	8
Skowhegan, Me., U.S.	F7	110
Skownan, Mb., Can.	C14	124
Skriplivka, Russia	C13	10
Skrudaliena, Lat.	E9	10
Skudeneshavn, Nor.	G1	8
Skukuza, S. Afr.	D10	70
Skull Valley, Az., U.S.	I4	132
Skuna, stm., Ms., U.S.	D9	122
Skunk, stm., Ia., U.S.	D6	120
Skuodas, Lith.	D4	10
Skuratovskij, Russia	F20	10
Skwierzyna, Pol.	D11	16
Skye, Island of, i., Scot., U.K.	D6	12
Skyland, N.C., U.S.	A3	116
Skyring, Peninsula, pen., Chile	I1	90
Skyring, Seno, strt., Chile	J2	90
Skýros, i., Grc.	E7	28
Slabada, Bela.	G11	10
Slagelse, Den.	I4	8
Slagnäs, Swe.	D8	8
Slamet, Gunung, vol., Indon.	G6	50
Slancy, Russia	A11	10
Slaney, stm., Ire.	H6	12
Slănic, Rom.	D12	26
Slano, Cro.	H14	22
Slaný, Czech Rep.	F10	16
Slater, Ia., U.S.	C4	120
Slater, Mo., U.S.	E4	120
Slatina, Cro.	E14	22
Slatina, Rom.	E11	26
Slaughter, La., U.S.	G7	122
Slaunae, Bela.	F12	10
Slautnoe, Russia	D23	34
Slave, stm., Can.	D8	106
Slave Coast, cst., Afr.	H5	64
Slave Lake, Ab., Can.	A16	138
Slavgorod, Russia	D13	32
Slavjanka, Russia	C9	38
Slavjansk-na-Kubani, Russia	E5	32
Slavkoviči, Russia	C12	10
Slavonia see Slavonija, hist. reg., Cro.	E14	22
Slavonija, hist. reg., Cro.	E14	22
Slavonski Brod, Cro.	E15	22
Slavsk, Russia	E3	10
Sławno, Pol.	B12	16
Slayton, Mn., U.S.	G3	118
Sleaford, Eng., U.K.	H12	12
Sledge, Ms., U.S.	C8	122
Sledzjuki, Bela.	G13	10
Sleeper Islands, is., Nu., Can.	D14	106
Sleeping Bear Dunes National Lakeshore, p.o.i., Mi., U.S.	D3	112
Sleepy Eye, Mn., U.S.	G4	118
Slesin, Pol.	D14	16
Slidell, La., U.S.	G9	122
Slide Mountain, mtn., N.Y., U.S.	B11	114
Sliema, Malta	I8	24
Slievekimalta, mtn., Ire.	I4	12
Sligeach see Sligo, Ire.	G4	12
Sligo, Ire.	G4	12
Sligo, state, Ire.	G4	12
Sligo Bay, b., Ire.	G4	12
Slino, ozero, l., Russia	C16	10
Slippery Rock, Pa., U.S.	C5	114
Sliven, Blg.	G13	26
Sljudjanka, Russia	D18	32
Sloan, Nv., U.S.	H1	132
Slobidka, Ukr.	B16	26
Slobodskoj, Russia	C8	32
Slobozia, India	F14	34
Slobozia, Mol.	C16	26
Slobozia, Rom.	E14	26
Slocan, B.C., Can.	G13	138
Slocan Lake, l., B.C., Can.	G13	138
Slocomb, Al., U.S.	F13	122
Słomniki, Pol.	F15	16
Slonim, Bela.	G8	10
Slough, Eng., U.K.	J12	12
Slovakia, ctry., Eur.	H14	16
Slovenia, ctry., Eur.	E11	22
Slovenia see Slovenia, ctry., Eur.	E11	22
Slovenské rudohorie, mts., Slov.	H15	16
Slov'ians'k, Ukr.	E5	32
Slovinka, Russia	G20	8
Słowiński Park Narodowy, p.o.i., Pol.	B13	16
Słubice, Pol.	D10	16
Slučaj, stm., Bela.	H10	10
Sluck, Bela.	G10	10
Sluknov, Czech Rep.	E10	16
Słupca, Pol.	D13	16
Słupia, stm., Pol.	B13	16
Słupsk (Stolp), Pol.	B13	16
Slussfors see Sluck, Bela.	G10	10
Smalandsfarvandet, b., Den.	I4	8
Smalininkai, Lith.	E5	10
Smaljavičy, Bela.	F10	10
Smallwood Reservoir, res., Nf., Can.	E18	106
Smalouka, Bela.	E13	10
Smederevo, Serb.	E7	26
Smeralda, Costa, cst., Italy	C3	24
Smethport, Pa., U.S.	C7	114
Šmidovič, Russia	G15	34
Smila, Ukr.	E4	32
Smiley, Sk., Can.	C4	124
Smiley, Tx., U.S.	E10	130
Smiltene, Lat.	C8	10
Smith, Ab., Can.	A16	138
Smith, stm., U.S.	B2	134
Smith, stm., Mt., U.S.	C15	136
Smith, stm., U.S.	F3	136
Smith, stm., U.S.	H5	114
Smith Arm, b., N.T., Can.	B6	106
Smith Bay, b., Ak., U.S.	B9	140
Smith Canyon, p., Co., U.S.	D5	128
Smithers, B.C., Can.	B3	138
Smithfield, mtn., Eng., U.K.	G8	70
Smithfield, N.C., U.S.	A7	116
Smithfield, Va., U.S.	G9	114
Smith Island, i., Sumisu-jima, i., Japan	E13	36
Smith Island, i., N.C., U.S.	C8	116
Smithland, Ky., U.S.	G9	120
Smith Mountain Lake, res., Va., U.S.	G6	114
Smith Point, c., Va., U.S.	E13	110
Smith River, Ca., U.S.	B1	134
Smiths, Al., U.S.	E13	122
Smiths Falls, On., Can.	D13	112
Smiths Grove, Ky., U.S.	G11	120
Smithton, Austl.	n12	77a
Smithville, Ga., U.S.	E14	122
Smithville, Ms., U.S.	C10	122
Smithville, Tn., U.S.	I12	120
Smithville, Tx., U.S.	D10	130
Smithville Lake, res., Mo., U.S.	E3	120
Smoke Creek Desert, des., Nv., U.S.	C6	134
Smokey, Cape, c., N.S., Can.	D16	110
Smoky, stm., Ab., Can.	A12	138
Smoky Cape, c., Austl.	H9	76
Smoky Dome, mtn., Id., U.S.	G12	136
Smoky Hill, stm., U.S.	B12	128
Smoky Hill, North Fork, stm., U.S.	B7	128
Smoky Lake, Ab., Can.	B18	138
Smoky Mountains, mts., U.S.	G13	136
Smøla, i., Nor.	E2	8
Smolensk, Russia	F15	10
Smolenskaja-Moskovskaja vozvyšennost', plat., Eur.	F16	10
Smolenskaja oblast', co., Russia	F15	10
Smoljan, Blg.	H11	26
Smoot, Wy., U.S.	H16	136
Smoothrock Lake, l., On., Can.	A9	118
Smorodovka, Russia	C12	10
Smyrna, De., U.S.	E10	114
Smyrna see İzmir, Tur.	E10	28
Smyrna, Ga., U.S.	D14	122
Smyrna, Tn., U.S.	I11	120
Smythe, Mount, mtn., B.C., Can.	D6	106
Snæfell, mtn., Ice.	k32	8a
Snaefell, mtn., I. of Man	G8	12
Snæfellsnes, pen., Ice.	k28	8a
Snag, Yk., Can.	C3	106
Snake, stm., Yk., Can.	B4	106
Snake, stm., U.S.	F7	136
Snake River Plain, pl., Id., U.S.	G13	136
Snake Valley, val., U.S.	D3	132
Snares Islands, is., N.Z.	D4	80
Snåsavatnet, l., Nor.	D4	8
Sneads, Fl., U.S.	G14	122
Sneedville, Tn., U.S.	H2	114
Sneek, Neth.	A14	14
Snežka, mtn., Czech Rep.	F11	16
Sniardwy, Jezioro, l., Pol.	C17	16
Sniatyn, Ukr.	A12	26
Snina, Slov.	H18	16
Snipe Lake, l., Ab., Can.	A14	138
Sniježnik, mtn., Slvn.	H11	10
Snøhetta, mtn., Nor.	E3	8
Snohomish, Wa., U.S.	C4	136
Snoqualmie Pass, p., Wa., U.S.	C5	136
Snøtinden, mtn., Nor.	C5	8
Snov, stm., Eur.	H15	10
Snowbird Lake, l., N.T., Can.	C10	106
Snowdon, mtn., Wales, U.K.	H8	12
Snowdonia National Park, p.o.i., Wales, U.K.	I8	12
Snowflake, Az., U.S.	I6	132
Snow Hill, Md., U.S.	F10	114
Snow Hill, N.C., U.S.	A8	116
Snow Lake, Mb., Can.	E10	106
Snowmass Mountain, mtn., Co., U.S.	D9	132
Snow Mountain, mtn., Ca., U.S.	D3	134
Snowtown, Austl.	I2	76
Snowy, stm., Austl.	K7	76
Snowy Mountain, mtn., N.Y., U.S.	G2	110
Snowy Mountains, mts., Austl.	K7	76
Snuöl, Camb.	F8	48
Snyder, Ok., U.S.	G10	128
Snyder, Tx., U.S.	B7	130
Soacha, Col.	E4	86
Soalala, Madag.	D8	68
Soap Lake, Wa., U.S.	C7	136
Soavinandriana, Madag.	D8	68
Sobaek-sanmaek, mts., Kor., S.	C1	40
Soběslav, Czech Rep.	G10	16
Sobinka, Russia	I19	8
Sobradinho, Braz.	D11	92
Sobradinho, Represa de, res., Braz.	E5	88
Sobral, Braz.	B5	88
Sobrance, Slov.	H18	16
Socha, Col.	D5	86
Sochaczew, Pol.	D16	16
Soch'e see Shache, China.	B12	56
Société, Archipel de la (Society Islands), is., Fr. Poly.	E11	72
Society Hill, S.C., U.S.	B6	116
Society Islands see Société, Archipel de la, is., Fr. Poly.	E11	72
Soco, stm., Dom. Rep.	C13	102
Socompa, Paso (Socompa, Portezuelo de), p., S.A.	B3	92
Socompa, Portezuelo de (Socompa, Paso), p., S.A.	B3	92
Soconusco, Sierra de see Madre de Chiapas, Sierra, mts., N.A.	G12	100
Socorro, Col.	D5	86
Socorro, N.M., U.S.	I10	132
Socorro, Tx., U.S.	C1	130
Socorro, Isla, i., Mex.	F3	100
Socotra see Suquṭrá, i., Yemen	G7	56
Soc Trang, Viet.	H8	48
Socuéllamos, Spain	E8	20
Soda Creek, B.C., Can.	D8	138
Soda Lake, l., Ca., U.S.	H9	134
Sodankylä, Fin.	C12	8
Soda Springs, Id., U.S.	H15	136
Söderhamn, Swe.	F7	8
Södermanland, state, Swe.	G7	8
Södertälje, Swe.	G7	8
Sodo, Eth.	F7	62
Sodom see Sedom, hist., Isr.	G6	58
Sodus, N.Y., U.S.	E12	112
Sodwana Bay National Park, p.o.i., S. Afr.	E11	70
Soekmekaar, S. Afr.	C9	70
Soest, Ger.	E4	16
Soest, Neth.	B14	14
Sofala, Moz.	B12	70
Sofala, state, Moz.	B12	70
Sofia see Sofija, Blg.	G10	26
Sofija (Sofia), Blg.	G10	26
Sofija, state, Blg.	G10	26
Sofijsk, Russia	F16	34
Sofporog, Russia	D14	8
Sofronovo, Russia	D20	10
Sogamoso, Col.	E5	86
Sogamoso, stm., Col.	D5	86
Sogcho see Sokch'o, Kor., S.	A1	40
Sogda, Russia	F15	34
Sognefjorden, b., Nor.	F1	8
Sogn og Fjordane, state, Nor.	F2	8
Sogod, Phil.	E5	52
Sogo Nur, l., China	B5	36
Sogoza, stm., Russia	B22	10
Soguksu Milli Parkı, p.o.i., Tur.	C15	28
Söğüt Gölü, l., Tur.	F12	28
Sog Xian, China	B14	54
Sohâgpur, India	G6	54
Sohano, Pap. N. Guin.	d7	79b
Sohar see Şuḥār, Oman	E8	56
Sohng, Nig.	H7	64
Soignies, Bel.	D12	14
Sointula, B.C., Can.	F4	138
Soira, mtn., Erit.	E7	62
Soissons, Fr.	E12	14
Sojana, Russia	D20	8
Sojat, India	F4	54
Sŏjosŏn-man, b., Kor., N.	E6	38
Sok, stm., Russia	D8	32
Sôk'ch'o, Kor., S.	A1	40
Söke, Tur.	F10	28
Sokele, D.R.C.	F4	66
Sokodé, Togo	H5	64
Sokol, Russia	G19	8
Sokolka, Pol.	C19	16
Sokolo, Mali	G3	64
Sokółów Małopolski, Pol.	F18	16
Sokone, Sen.	G1	64
Sokoto, Nig.	G6	64
Sokoto, stm., Nig.	G5	64
Sokyriany, Ukr.	A14	26
Sol, Costa del, cst., Spain	H6	20
Sola, Vanuatu	j16	79d
Solacolu, Rom.	E13	26
Solana Beach, Ca., U.S.	J8	134
Solânea, Braz.	D8	88
Solano, Phil.	B3	52
Solāpur, India	C2	53
Solca, Rom.	B12	26
Soldiers Grove, Wi., U.S.	H8	118
Soldotna, Ak., U.S.	D9	140
Soledad, Col.	B4	86
Soledad, Ca., U.S.	G4	134
Soledad, Ven.	C10	86
Soledad Díez Gutiérrez, Mex.	D8	100
Soledade, Braz.	D11	92
Soledad Pass, p., Ca., U.S.	I7	134
Solen, N.D., U.S.	A12	126
Solenzara, Fr.	H15	18
Soleure see Solothurn, Switz.	C4	22
Solihull, Eng., U.K.	I11	12
Solikamsk, Russia	C9	32
Solila, Madag.	E8	68
Soľ-Ilec'k, Russia	D9	32
Solimões, stm. see Amazon, stm., S.A.	D7	84
Solingen, Ger.	E3	16
Solís de Mataojo, Ur.	G10	92
Sollefteå, Swe.	E7	8
Sollentuna, Swe.	G7	8
Soller, Spain	E13	20
Solnečnogorsk, Russia	D19	10
Sologne, reg., Fr.	G10	14
Sologoncy, Russia	C11	34
Solok, Indon.	D2	50
Solomennoe, Russia	—	—
Solomon, Az., U.S.	K7	132
Solomon, stm., U.S.	B11	128
Solomon, North Fork, stm., Ks., U.S.	B10	128
Solomon, South Fork, stm., Ks., U.S.	B10	128
Solomon Basin, unds.	J18	142
Solomon Islands, ctry., Oc.	D7	72
Solomon Sea, s., Oc.	d7	79b
Solomon's Pools see Sulaymān, Birak, sci., W.B.	G5	58
Solon, China	B9	36
Solon, Ia., U.S.	C6	120
Solon, Me., U.S.	F7	110
Solothurn, Switz.	C4	22
Soloveckie ostrova, is., Russia	D16	8
Solov'evka, Russia	F12	34
Solov'evsk, Russia	F13	34
Solsona, Spain	C12	20
Šolta, Otok, i., Cro.	G13	22
Soltānābād, Iran	B8	56
Soltau, Ger.	C5	16
Solvang, Ca., U.S.	I5	134
Solway, N.Y., U.S.	A9	114
Sol'vyčegodsk, Russia	F22	8
Solway Firth, b., U.K.	G9	12
Solwezi, Zam.	C4	68
Soma, Russia	D18	8
Sōma, Japan	B13	40
Soma, Tur.	D10	28
Somabhula, Zimb.	D4	68
Somalia, ctry., Afr.	D9	66
Somali Basin, unds.	I8	142
Somaliland see Somalia, ctry., Afr.	D9	66
Somali Republic see Somalia, ctry., Afr.	D9	66
Sombo, Ang.	B3	68
Sombor, Serb.	D6	26
Sombrerete, Mex.	D7	100
Sombrero Channel, strt., India	G7	46
Sombrio, Lagoa do, l., Braz.	D13	92
Somdari, India.	F4	54
Somerset, Austl.	n12	77a
Somerset, Co., U.S.	E9	132
Somerset, Ky., U.S.	G13	120
Somerset, Oh., U.S.	E3	114
Somerset, Tx., U.S.	E9	130
Somerset East, S. Afr.	H7	70
Somerset Island, i., Nu., Can.	A12	106
Somers Point, N.J., U.S.	E11	114
Somersworth, N.H., U.S.	G5	110
Somerton, Az., U.S.	K2	132
Somerville, N.J., U.S.	D11	114
Somerville, Tn., U.S.	B9	122
Somerville, Tx., U.S.	G2	122
Somerville Lake, res., Tx., U.S.	D11	130
Someş (Szamos), stm., Eur.	B9	26
Somino, Russia	A17	10
Somme, state, Fr.	D11	14
Somme, stm., Fr.	E11	14
Somme, Baie de la, b., Fr.	D10	14
Sommen, l., Swe.	H6	8
Sommerda, Ger.	E7	16
Somogy, state, Hung.	C4	26
Somosierra, Puerto de, p., Spain	C7	20
Somosomo, Fiji	p20	79e
Somosomo Strait, strt., Fiji	p19	79e
Somovo, Russia	H17	10
Somport, Col du (Somport, Puerto de), p., Eur.	G5	18
Somport, Puerto de (Somport, Col du), p., Eur.	G5	18
Sompuis, Fr.	F13	14
Sonamarg, India	A5	54
Sonamukhi, India	G11	54
Sönch'ŏn-ŭp, Kor., N.	E6	38
Sønderborg, Den.	I3	8
Sønderjylland, state, Den.	I3	8
Søndre Strømfjord, Grnld.	D15	141
Sondrio, Italy	D6	22
Soneput, India	H9	54
Song, Nig.	H7	64
Song Bay Hap, Cua, b., Viet.	H7	48
Song Cau, Viet.	F9	48
Song Da see Black, stm.	D9	46
Songea, Tan.	G7	66
Song Hong see Red, stm., Asia	D9	46
Songhua, stm., China	B7	38
Songhua Hu, res., China	C7	38
Songjiang, China	F9	42
Songjŏng, Kor., S.	G7	38
Sŏngju, Kor., S.	D1	40
Songkhla, Thai.	I5	48
Songkhram, stm., Thai.	D6	48
Songlinba, China	F5	36
Söngnam, Kor., S.	F7	38
Songnim, Kor., N.	E6	38
Songxi, China	H8	42
Songxian, China	D5	42
Song Youqi, China	D7	36
Sonid Zuoqi, China	C7	36
Sonīpat, India	D6	54
Sonkovo, Russia	C20	10
Sonmiani, Pak.	D10	56
Sonmiani Bay, b., Pak.	D10	56
Sonneberg, Ger.	F7	16
Sonningdale, Sk., Can.	B6	124
Sono, stm., Braz.	E3	88
Sono, stm., Braz.	I3	88
Sonora, Ca., U.S.	F5	134
Sonora, Tx., U.S.	D7	130
Sonora, state, Mex.	F7	98
Sonora, stm., Mex.	G7	98
Sonora, Desierto de, des., N.A.	F6	98
Sonoqor, Iran	C6	56
Sonsón, Col.	E4	86
Sonsonate, El Sal.	F3	102
Sonsorol Islands, is., Palau	D9	44
Sonstraal, S. Afr.	E6	70
Son Tay, Viet.	B7	48
Sonthofen, Ger.	I6	16
Soochow see Suzhou, China	F9	42
Sooke, B.C., Can.	H7	138
Sooner Lake, res., Ok., U.S.	A1	122
Sopchoppy, Fl., U.S.	G14	122
Soperton, Ga., U.S.	D3	116
Sopki, Russia	C13	10
Sopot, Pol.	B14	16

Name	Map Ref.	Page
Sop Pong, Laos	A6	48
Sopron, Hung.	B3	26
Sopur, India	A5	54
Sora, Italy	I10	22
Sorada, India	I10	54
Sorata, Bol.	C3	90
Sorbhog, India	E13	54
Sorel, Qc., Can.	D3	110
Sorell, Cape, c., Austl.	o12	77a
Sorfold, Nor.	C6	8
Sorgues, Fr.	E10	18
Soria, Spain	C8	20
Soria, co., Spain	C8	20
Soriano, Ur.	F8	92
Sørli, Nor.	D5	8
Sørø, Den.	I4	8
Soro, India	H11	54
Soro, Monte, mtn., Italy	G8	24
Soroca, Mol.	A15	26
Sorocaba, Braz.	L2	88
Soročinsk, Russia	D8	32
Soroco, P.R.	B4	104a
Sorol, at., Micron.	C5	72
Soron, India	E7	54
Sorong, Indon.	F9	44
Sororó, stm., Braz.	C1	88
Sorot', stm., Russia	C12	10
Soroti, Ug.	D6	66
Sørøya, i., Nor.	A10	8
Sorrento, Italy	D8	24
Sorrento, La., U.S.	G8	122
Sorris-Sorris, Nmb.	B2	70
Sor Rondane Mountains, mts., Ant.	C7	81
Sorsk, Russia	D16	32
Sorso, Italy	D2	24
Sorsogon, Phil.	D4	52
Sort, Spain	B12	20
Sortavala, Russia	F14	8
Sør-Trøndelag, state, Nor.	E4	8
Sõrve neem, c., Est.	C4	10
Sosa, stm., Russia	D18	10
Sos del Rey Católico, Spain	B9	20
Soskovo, Russia	H18	10
Sosna, stm., Russia	H21	10
Sosneado, Cerro, mtn., Arg.	G3	92
Sosnogorsk, Russia	B8	32
Sosnovec, Russia	D15	8
Sosnovka, Kaz.	D13	32
Sosnovka, Russia	C19	8
Sosnovo-Ozërskoe, Russia	F11	34
Sosnovskoe, Russia	I20	8
Sosnovyj Bor, Russia	A11	10
Sosnowiec, Pol.	F15	16
Soso, Ms., U.S.	F9	122
Sos'va, Russia	B10	32
Sotkamo, Fin.	D13	8
Soto, Mex.	F1	130
Soto la Marina, Mex.	D9	100
Soto la Marina, Barra, i., Mex.	C10	100
Sotra see Store Sotra, i., Nor.	F1	8
Sotteville-lès-Rouen, Fr.	E9	14
Souanké, Congo	D2	66
Soubré, C. Iv.	H3	64
Soudan, Pa., U.S.	D10	114
Soufrière, St. Luc.	m6	105c
Soufrière, vol., Guad.	h5	105c
Soufrière, vol., St. Vin.	o11	105e
Soufrière Hills, vol., Monts.	d3	105a
Souillac, Fr.	E7	18
Sŏul (Seoul), Kor., S.	F7	38
Soulac-sur-Mer, Fr.	D4	18
Sound, The, strt., Eur.	I5	8
Sounding Creek, stm., Ab., Can.	E19	138
Sounding Lake, l., Ab., Can.	B3	124
Sources, Mont-aux- (Phofung), mtn., Afr.	F9	70
Soure, Braz.	D8	84
Sour el Ghozlane, Alg.	H14	20
Souris, Mb., Can.	E13	124
Souris, stm., N.A.	E13	124
Sourlake, Tx., U.S.	G4	122
Sourland Mountain, hill, N.J., U.S.	D11	114
Sousa, Braz.	D6	88
Sousel, Port.	F3	20
Sousse, Tun.	I4	24
Sout, stm., S. Afr.	H6	70
South, stm., N.C., U.S.	B7	116
South Africa, ctry., Afr.	F7	70
South America, cont.	G9	4
Southampton, On., Can.	D8	112
Southampton, Eng., U.K.	K11	12
Southampton, N.Y., U.S.	D13	114
Southampton, Cape, c., Nu., Can.	C13	106
Southampton Island, i., Nu., Can.	C14	106
South Andaman, i., India	F7	46
South Anna, stm., Va., U.S.	G8	114
South Antler Creek see Antler, stm., N.A.	E12	124
South Australia, state, Austl.	E6	74
South Australian Basin, unds.	M15	142
Southaven, Ms., U.S.	B8	122
South Baldy, mtn., N.M., U.S.	J9	132
Southbank, B.C., Can.	B5	138
South Bay, Fl., U.S.	J5	116
South Bay, b., Nu., Can.	C14	106
South Bay, b., On., Can.	C8	112
South Baymouth, On., Can.	C7	112
South Bend, In., U.S.	G3	112
South Bend, Wa., U.S.	D3	136
South Bohemia see Jihočeský kraj, state, Czech Rep.	G10	16
South Borneo see Kalimantan Selatan, state, Indon.	E9	50
South Boston, Va., U.S.	H6	114
Southbridge, N.Z.	F5	80
Southbridge, Ma., U.S.	B13	114
South Brookfield, N.S., Can.	F11	110
South Bruny Island, i., Austl.	o13	77a
South Burlington, Vt., U.S.	F3	110
South Carolina, state, U.S.	C5	116
South Celebes see Sulawesi Selatan, state, Indon.	E11	50
South Charleston, W.V., U.S.	F4	114
South China Basin, unds.	H14	142
South China Sea, s., Asia	H15	30
South Dakota, state, U.S.	C12	126
South Downs, hills, Eng., U.K.	K12	12
South East, state, Bots.	D7	70
South East Cape, c., Austl.	o13	77a
Southeast Indian Ridge, unds.	N12	142
Southeast Pacific Basin, unds.	P25	142
South East Point, c., Austl.	L6	76
Southend-on-Sea, Eng., U.K.	J13	12
Southern, state, Bots.	D7	70
Southern see HaDarom, state, Israel	H5	58
Southern Alps, mts., N.Z.	F4	80
Southern Bug see Pivdennyy Buh, stm., Ukr.	A17	26
Southern Cook Islands, is., Cook Is.	E10	72
Southern Cross, Austl.	F3	74
Southern Ghāts, mts., India	G3	53
Southern Indian Lake, l., Mb., Can.	D10	106
Southern Ocean	N13	142
Southern Pines, N.C., U.S.	A6	116
South Esk, stm., Austl.	n13	77a
South Fabius, stm., Mo., U.S.	E6	120
South Fallsburg, N.Y., U.S.	C11	114
Southfield, Mi., U.S.	B2	114
South Fiji Basin, unds.	L20	142
South Foreland, c., Eng., U.K.	J14	12
South Fork, Co., U.S.	F10	132
South Fulton, Tn., U.S.	H8	120
Southgate, Mi., U.S.	B2	114
South Georgia, i., S. Geor.	J9	90
South Georgia and the South Sandwich Islands, dep., S.A.	K11	82
South Grand, stm., Mo., U.S.	F3	120
South Hātia Island, i., Bngl.	G13	54
South Haven, Mi., U.S.	F3	112
South Henderson, N.C., U.S.	H7	114
South Henik Lake, l., Nu., Can.	C11	106
South Hero, Vt., U.S.	F3	110
South Hill Village, Anguilla	A1	105a
South Holston Lake, res., U.S.	H3	114
South Honshu Ridge, unds.	G16	142
South Houston, Tx., U.S.	H3	122
South Indian Basin, unds.	O12	142
South Indian Lake, Mb., Can.	D11	106
South International Falls, Mn., U.S.	C5	118
South Island, i., N.Z.	G5	80
South Konkan Hills, hills, India	C1	53
South Korea see Korea, South, ctry., Asia	G8	38
South Lake Tahoe, Ca., U.S.	E5	134
Southland, Tn., U.S.	H7	128
Southlawn, Il., U.S.	E8	120
South Llano, stm., Tx., U.S.	D8	130
South Loup, stm., Ne., U.S.	F13	126
South Lyon, Mi., U.S.	F6	112
South Magnetic Pole, misc. cult.	B18	81
South Manitou Island, i., Mi., U.S.	C3	112
South Miami, Fl., U.S.	K5	116
South Milwaukee, Wi., U.S.	F2	112
South Moravia see Jihomoravský kraj, state, Czech Rep.	G12	16
South Nahanni, stm., N.T., Can.	C5	106
South Nation, stm., On., Can.	C14	112
South Negril Point, c., Jam.	i12	104d
South Ogden, Ut., U.S.	B5	132
South Orkney Islands, is., Ant.	B36	81
South Paris, Me., U.S.	F6	110
South Pass, p., Wy., U.S.	E4	126
South Pekin, Il., U.S.	D8	120
South Pittsburg, Tn., U.S.	B13	122
South Platte, stm., U.S.	F11	126
South Point, c., Barb.	n8	105d
South Pole, misc. cult., Ant.	D1	81
Southport (Gold Coast), Austl.	F9	76
Southport, N.C., U.S.	o13	77a
Southport, Eng., U.K.	H9	12
Southport, In., U.S.	E11	120
Southport, N.C., U.S.	C7	116
South Portland, Me., U.S.	G6	110
South Range, Mi., U.S.	D10	118
South River, On., Can.	C10	112
South Ronaldsay, i., Scot., U.K.	C10	12
South Sandwich Islands, is., S. Geor.	K11	82
South Sandwich Trench, unds.	N11	144
South Saskatchewan, stm., Can.	A8	124
South Shetland Islands, is., Ant.	B35	81
South Sioux City, Ne., U.S.	I2	118
South Skunk, stm., Ia., U.S.	C5	120
South Slocan, B.C., Can.	G13	138
South Sound, b., Br. Vir. Is.	e9	104b
South Spicer Island, i., Nu., Can.	B15	106
South Sulphur, stm., Tx., U.S.	D3	122
South Sumatra see Sumatera Selatan, state, Indon.	E4	50
South Taranaki Bight, b., N.Z.	D5	80
South Thompson, stm., B.C., Can.	F11	138
South Torrington, Wy., U.S.	E8	126
South Uist, i., Scot., U.K.	D5	12
South Umpqua, stm., Or., U.S.	G3	136
South Ventana Cone, mtn., Ca., U.S.	G4	134
South Vietnam see Vietnam, ctry., Asia	E9	48
South West Africa see Namibia, ctry., Afr.	E2	68
South West Cape, c., Austl.	o12	77a
South West Cape, c., N.Z.	H2	80
South West City, Mo., U.S.	H3	120
Southwest Harbor, Me., U.S.	F8	110
Southwest Indian Ridge, unds.	M8	142
Southwest Miramichi, stm., N.B., Can.	D10	110
Southwest National Park, p.o.i., Austl.	o12	77a
Southwest Pacific Basin, unds.	M23	142
Southwest Point, c., Bah.	K8	116
South Whitley, In., U.S.	G4	112
South Wichita, stm., Tx., U.S.	H9	128
South Windham, Me., U.S.	G6	110
Southwold, Eng., U.K.	I14	12
Sovata, Rom.	C11	26
Sovetsk, Russia	G20	10
Sovetsk, Russia	E4	10
Sovetsk, Russia	C7	32
Sovetskaja Gavan', Russia	G17	34
Sovetskij, Russia	F13	8
Sovpole, Russia	D20	8
Sowa Pan, pl., Bots.	B7	70
Soweto, S. Afr.	E8	70
Sōya-misaki, c., Japan	B14	38
Soyang-chŏsuji, res., Kor., S.	F7	38
Soyo, Ang.	B1	68
Sož, stm., Eur.	H13	10
Sozaq, Kaz.	F11	32
Sozimskij, Russia	C8	32
Sozopol, Blg.	G14	26
Spa, Bel.	D14	14
Spain, ctry., Eur.	E7	20
Spalding, Sk., Can.	B9	124
Spalding, Eng., U.K.	I12	12
Spanish, On., Can.	B7	112
Spanish, stm., On., Can.	B8	112
Spanish Fork, Ut., U.S.	C5	132
Spanish Point, c., Ber.	k15	104e
Spanish Sahara see Western Sahara, dep., Afr.	E2	64
Spanish Town, Br. Vir. Is.	e9	104b
Spanish Town, Jam.	i13	104d
Sparks, N.v., U.S.	D6	134
Sparland, Il., U.S.	C8	120
Sparlingville, Mi., U.S.	F7	112
Sparrows Point, Md., U.S.	E9	114
Sparta see Spárti, Grc.	F5	28
Sparta, Ga., U.S.	C3	116
Sparta, Il., U.S.	F8	120
Sparta, Ky., U.S.	F13	120
Sparta, Mi., U.S.	E5	112
Sparta, N.C., U.S.	H4	114
Sparta, N.J., U.S.	C11	114
Sparta, Tn., U.S.	I12	120
Sparta, Wi., U.S.	H8	118
Spartanburg, S.C., U.S.	B4	116
Spárti, Grc.	F5	28
Spartivento, Capo, c., Italy	G10	24
Spartivento, Capo, c., Italy	I19	8
Spas-Klepiki, Russia	I19	8
Spassk-Dal'nij, Russia	B10	38
Spearfish, S.D., U.S.	C8	126
Spearville, Ks., U.S.	D9	128
Spednic Lake, l., N.A.	E9	110
Speedway, In., U.S.	I3	112
Speightstown, Barb.	n8	105d
Speke Gulf, b., Tan.	E6	66
Spencer, In., U.S.	E11	120
Spencer, Ia., U.S.	H3	118
Spencer, Ne., U.S.	E14	126
Spencer, Wi., U.S.	G8	118
Spencer, W.V., U.S.	F4	114
Spencer, Cape, c., Austl.	G7	74
Spencer, Cape, c., N.B., Can.	E11	110
Spencer Gulf, b., Austl.	F7	74
Spencerville, Oh., U.S.	D1	114
Spences Bridge, B.C., Can.	F9	138
Speos (Rock Tombs), hist., Egypt	K1	58
Sperryville, Va., U.S.	F7	114
Spétses, i., Grc.	F6	28
Spey, stm., Scot., U.K.	D9	12
Speyer, Ger.	G4	16
Spezia see La Spezia, Italy	F6	22
Spezzano Albanese, Italy	E10	24
Sphinx see Abū el-Hul, hist., Egypt	I1	58
Spickard, Mo., U.S.	D4	120
Spilimbergo, Italy	D9	22
Spillville, Ia., U.S.	A5	120
Spinazzola, Italy	D10	24
Spindale, N.C., U.S.	A4	116
Spires see Speyer, Ger.	G4	16
Spirit Lake, Ia., U.S.	H3	118
Spirit River, Ab., Can.	D7	106
Spiro, Ok., U.S.	B4	122
Spišská Nová Ves, Slov.	H16	16
Spitsbergen, i., Nor.	A4	30
Spitsbergen Bank, unds.	B5	142
Spittal an der Drau, Aus.	D10	22
Split, Cro.	G13	22
Split Lake, res., Mb., Can.	D11	106
Spogi, Lat.	D9	10
Spokane, Wa., U.S.	C9	136
Spokane, stm., U.S.	C9	136
Spoleto, Italy	H9	22
Spoon, stm., Il., U.S.	D7	120
Spooner, Wi., U.S.	F7	118
Sporava, Bela.	H8	10
Spornoe, Russia	D19	34
Spotsylvania, Va., U.S.	F8	114
Sprague, Wa., U.S.	C9	136
Spratly Islands, is., Asia	D5	44
Spray, stm., Or., U.S.	F7	136
Spree, stm., Ger.	E10	16
Spremberg, Ger.	E10	16
Spring, stm., Ar., U.S.	H6	120
Spring, stm., U.S.	H3	120
Spring, South Fork, stm., U.S.	H6	120
Springbok, S. Afr.	F3	70
Spring City, Tn., U.S.	B14	122
Spring City, Ut., U.S.	D5	132
Spring Creek, stm., Austl.	D3	76
Spring Creek, stm., S.D., U.S.	C8	134
Springdale, Nf., Can.	j22	107a
Springdale, Ar., U.S.	H3	120
Springdale, Ut., U.S.	F4	132
Springdale, Wa., U.S.	B9	136
Springe, Ger.	D5	16
Springerville, Az., U.S.	I7	132
Springfield, N.S., Can.	F12	110
Springfield, Co., U.S.	D6	128
Springfield, Fl., U.S.	G13	122
Springfield, Ga., U.S.	D4	116
Springfield, Id., U.S.	G14	136
Springfield, Il., U.S.	E8	120
Springfield, Ma., U.S.	B13	114
Springfield, Mn., U.S.	G4	118
Springfield, Mo., U.S.	G4	120
Springfield, Oh., U.S.	E2	114
Springfield, Or., U.S.	F3	136
Springfield, S.C., U.S.	C4	116
Springfield, S.D., U.S.	E14	126
Springfield, Tn., U.S.	H10	120
Springfield, Vt., U.S.	G4	110
Springfontein, S. Afr.	G7	70
Spring Glen, Ut., U.S.	D5	132
Spring Green, Wi., U.S.	A7	120
Spring Grove, Mn., U.S.	H7	118
Springhill, N.S., Can.	E12	110
Springhill, La., U.S.	D5	122
Spring Hope, N.C., U.S.	I7	114
Springhouse, B.C., Can.	E8	138
Spring Lake, N.C., U.S.	A7	116
Springs, S. Afr.	E9	70
Springsure, Austl.	D7	76
Springvale, Me., U.S.	G6	110
Springvale, Austl.	H2	80
Springville, Al., U.S.	D12	122
Springville, Ut., U.S.	G7	134
Springville, N.Y., U.S.	B7	114
Sproat Lake, l., B.C., Can.	G5	138
Spruce Grove, Ab., Can.	C17	138
Spruce Knob, mtn., W.V., U.S.	F6	114
Spruce Mountain, mtn., Az., U.S.	I4	132
Spruce Pine, N.C., U.S.	I4	114
Spulico, Capo, c., Italy	E10	24
Spurgeon, Tx., U.S.	G4	122
Spurn Head, c., Eng., U.K.	H13	12
Spuzzum, B.C., Can.	G9	138
Squamish, B.C., Can.	G7	138
Square Lake, l., N.H., U.S.	G1	8
Square Lake, l., Me., U.S.	G8	104
Squatec, Qc., Can.	k15	104e
Squaw Cap Mountain, mtn., N.B., Can.	C10	110
Squaw Peak, mtn., Mt., U.S.	C12	136
Squilax, B.C., Can.	F11	138
Squillace, Golfo di, b., Italy	F10	24
Squinzano, Italy	D12	24
Sragen, Indon.	G7	50
Srbija (Serbia), state, Serb.	E7	26
Srbobran, Serb.	D6	26
Srê Âmbêl, Camb.	G6	48
Sredinnyj hrebet, mts., Russia	E20	34
Sredna Gora, mts., Blg.	G11	26
Srednee Kujto, ozero, l., Russia	D14	8
Srednekolymsk, Russia	C19	34
Srednerusskaja vozvyšennost', plat., Russia	D5	32
Srednesibirskoe ploskogor'e (Central Siberian Uplands), plat., Russia	C10	34
Srednij Ural, mts., Russia	C9	32
Srednij Vasjugan, Russia	C13	32
Srednjaja Olëkma, Russia	E13	34
Śrem, Pol.	D13	16
Sremska Kamenica, Serb.	D7	26
Sremska Mitrovica, Serb.	E6	26
Sremski Karlovci, Serb.	D7	26
Srêng, stm., Camb.	F6	48
Srêpôk, stm., Camb.	F8	48
Sri Aman, Malay.	C7	50
Sri Jayewardenepura Kotte, Sri L.	H4	53
Srīkākulam, India	B6	53
Sri Kālahasti, India	E4	53
Sri Lanka, ctry., Asia	G5	53
Srinagar, India	A5	54
Srīrampur, India	B2	53
Srirangam, India	F4	53
Srivardhan, India	B1	53
Srīvilliputtūr, India	G3	53
Šroda Śląska, Pol.	E12	16
Šroda Wielkopolska, Pol.	D13	16
Sseu-tch'ouan see Sichuan, state, China	E5	36
Ssup'ing see Siping, China	C6	38
Staaten, stm., Austl.	C8	74
Stade, Ger.	C5	16
Stadlandet, pen., Nor.	E1	8
Stadl-Paura, Aus.	B10	22
Stadskanaal, Neth.	A16	14
Stadtallendorf, Ger.	F5	16
Stadtoldendorf, Ger.	E5	16
Stafford, Eng., U.K.	I10	12
Stafford, Ks., U.S.	C10	128
Stafford Springs, Ct., U.S.	C13	114
Staffordsville, Ky., U.S.	G14	120
Stagen, Indon.	E10	50
Staines, Eng., U.K.	J12	12
Staked Plain see Estacado, Llano, pl., U.S.	H6	128
Stakhanov, Ukr.	E5	32
Stalać, Serb.	F8	26
Stalowa Wola, Pol.	F18	16
Stamford, Austl.	C4	76
Stamford, Eng., U.K.	I12	12
Stamford, Ct., U.S.	C12	114
Stamford, N.Y., U.S.	B11	114
Stamford, Tx., U.S.	B8	130
Stamford, Lake, res., Tx., U.S.	A8	130
Stamps, Ar., U.S.	D5	122
Stanaford, W.V., U.S.	G4	114
Stanberry, Mo., U.S.	D3	120
Stancionno-Ojašinskij, Russia	C14	32
Standard, Ab., Can.	E18	138
Standerton, S. Afr.	E9	70
Standish, Mi., U.S.	E6	112
Stanfield, Or., U.S.	E7	136
Stanford, Ky., U.S.	G13	120
Stanford, Mt., U.S.	C16	136
Stanger, S. Afr.	F10	70
Stanislaus, stm., Ca., U.S.	F5	134
Stanley, Austl.	n12	77a
Stanley, N.B., Can.	D10	110
Stanley, Falk. Is.	J5	90
Stanley, N.C., U.S.	A4	116
Stanley, N.D., U.S.	F11	124
Stanley, Wi., U.S.	G7	118
Stanley Falls, wtfl., D.R.C.	D4	66
Stanley Reservoir, res., India	F3	53
Stanleyville see Kisangani, D.R.C.	D5	66
Stanovoe nagor'e, mts., Russia	E11	34
Stanovoj hrebet, mts., Russia	E14	34
Stanovoy Mountains see Stanovoj nagor'e, mts., Russia	E11	34
Stanthorpe, Austl.	G8	76
Stanton, Ky., U.S.	G2	114
Stanton, Mi., U.S.	E4	112
Stanton, N.D., U.S.	G12	124
Stanton, Ne., U.S.	F15	126
Stanton, Tn., U.S.	B9	122
Stantonsburg, N.C., U.S.	A8	116
Stanwood, Wa., U.S.	B4	136
Staples, Mn., U.S.	E4	118
Stapleton, Al., U.S.	G11	122
Stąporków, Pol.	E16	16
Star, Ms., U.S.	E8	122
Star, N.C., U.S.	A6	116
Starachowice, Pol.	E17	16
Staraja Rudnja, Bela.	H13	10
Staraja Russa, Russia	B14	10
Stara Pazova, Serb.	D7	26
Stara Zagora, Blg.	G12	26
Starbuck, Mb., Can.	E16	124
Starbuck, Wa., U.S.	D8	136
Starbuck, i., Kir.	D11	72
Star City, Ar., U.S.	D7	122
Star City, Sk., Can.	B9	124
Star City, W.V., U.S.	E6	114
Stargard Szczeciński, Pol.	C11	16
Stargo, Az., U.S.	J7	132
Star Harbour, b., Sol. Is.	f10	79b
Stari Grad, Cro.	G13	22
Starij Rjad, Russia	B17	10
Stari Vlah, reg., Serb.	F7	26
Starke, Fl., U.S.	G3	116
Starkville, Ms., U.S.	D10	122
Starnberg, Ger.	H7	16
Starnberger See, l., Ger.	I7	16
Staroaltajskoe, Russia	D14	32
Starobil's'k, Ukr.	E5	32
Starodub, Russia	H15	10
Starogard Gdański, Pol.	C14	16
Starokozache, Ukr.	C16	26
Starominskaja, Russia	E5	32
Staroščerbinovskaja, Russia	C7	34
Star Peak, mtn., Nv., U.S.	C7	134
Start Point, c., Eng., U.K.	K9	12
Staryja Darohi, Bela.	G11	10
Staryj Oskol, Russia	D5	32
Stassfurt, Ger.	E7	16
State College, Pa., U.S.	D7	114
State Line, Ms., U.S.	F10	122
Stateline, Nv., U.S.	E5	134
Staten Island see Estados, Isla de los, i., Arg.	J4	90
Statesboro, Ga., U.S.	D4	116
Statesville, N.C., U.S.	I4	114
Staunton, Il., U.S.	E8	120
Staunton, Va., U.S.	F6	114
Staunton see Roanoke, stm., U.S.	H8	114
Stavanger, Nor.	G1	8
Stavely, Ab., Can.	F17	138
Stavne, stm., N.B., Can.	C10	110
Stavne, Nor.	E4	8
Stavropol', Russia	F6	32
Stawell, stm., Austl.	C5	76
Stawell, Austl.	K4	76
Stawiszyn, Pol.	E14	16
Steamboat Springs, Co., U.S.	C10	132
Stearns, Ky., U.S.	H13	120
Stębark, Pol.	C16	16
Steele, Mo., U.S.	H8	120
Steele, N.D., U.S.	H14	124
Steele, Mount, mtn., Wy., U.S.	B9	132
Steels Point, c., Norf. I.	y25	78i
Steelville, Mo., U.S.	G6	120
Steensby Inlet, b., Nu., Can.	A15	106
Steenwijk, Neth.	B15	14
Steep Rock, Mb., Can.	C15	124
Stefanie, Lake, l., Afr.	G7	62
Stefansson Island, i., Nu., Can.	A9	106
Ştefan Vodă, Rom.	E14	26
Stege, Den.	B8	16
Stehekin, Wa., U.S.	B6	136
Steiermark, state, Aus.	C11	22
Steinbach, Mb., Can.	E17	124
Steinfurt, Ger.	D3	16
Steinhausen, Nmb.	B4	70
Steinkjer, Nor.	D4	8
Stekljanka, Russia	G19	8
Stella, S. Afr.	E7	70
Stellarton, N.S., Can.	E14	110
Stellenbosch, S. Afr.	H4	70
Stelvio, Parco Nazionale dello, p.o.i., Italy	D7	22
Stelvio, Passo dello, p., Italy	D7	22
Stendal, Ger.	D7	16
Stende, Lat.	C5	10
Stephen, Mn., U.S.	C2	118
Stephens, Ar., U.S.	D5	122
Stephens, Port, b., Austl.	I9	76
Stephens City, Va., U.S.	E7	114
Stephens Creek, Austl.	H3	76
Stephens Lake, res., Mb., Can.	D11	106
Stephenville, Nf., Can.	j22	107a
Stephenville, Tx., U.S.	B9	130
Stepnjak, Kaz.	D12	32
Stepovak Bay, b., Ak., U.S.	E8	140
Steptoe Valley, val., Nv., U.S.	D2	132
Stepurino, Russia	D18	10
Sterëa Elláda, state, Grc.	E5	28
Sterkstroom, S. Afr.	G8	70
Sterling, Co., U.S.	A5	128
Sterling, Il., U.S.	C8	120
Sterling, Ks., U.S.	C10	128
Sterling, Mi., U.S.	D5	112
Sterling, Ne., U.S.	A12	128
Sterling City, Tx., U.S.	C7	130
Sterlington, La., U.S.	E6	122
Sterlitamak, Russia	D9	32
Šternberk, Czech Rep.	G13	16
Sterzing see Vipiteno, Italy	D8	22
Stettin see Szczecin, Pol.	C10	16
Stettler, Ab., Can.	D18	138
Steubenville, Oh., U.S.	D5	114
Stevenage, Eng., U.K.	J12	12
Stevenson, Al., U.S.	C13	122
Stevenson Entrance, strt., Ak., U.S.	E9	140
Stevens Pass, p., Wa., U.S.	C5	136
Stevens Peak, mtn., Id., U.S.	C11	136
Stevens Point, Wi., U.S.	G9	118
Stevensville, Mi., U.S.	F3	112
Stevensville, Mt., U.S.	D12	136
Stewardson, Il., U.S.	E9	120
Stewart, B.C., Can.	D4	106
Stewart, stm., Yk., Can.	C3	106
Stewart, Isla, i., Chile	J2	90
Stewart Island, i., N.Z.	H3	80
Stewartstown, Pa., U.S.	E9	114
Stewart Valley, Sk., Can.	D6	124
Stewartville, Mn., U.S.	H6	118
Stewiacke, N.S., Can.	E13	110
Steynsburg, S. Afr.	G8	70
Steyr, Aus.	B11	22
Steytlerville, S. Afr.	H7	70
Stickney, S.D., U.S.	D14	126
Stiene, Lat.	C7	10
Stif, Alg.	B6	64
Stigler, Ok., U.S.	B3	122
Stih, hora, mtn., Ukr.	A10	26
Stikine, stm., N.A.	D4	106
Stikine Ranges, mts., B.C., Can.	D4	106
Stilbaai, S. Afr.	I5	70
Stilfontein, S. Afr.	E8	70
Stillhouse Hollow Lake, res., Tx., U.S.	D10	130
Stillwater, B.C., Can.	G6	138
Stillwater, Mn., U.S.	F6	118
Stillwater, Ok., U.S.	A11	122
Stillwell, Ok., U.S.	I3	120
Stînca-Costești, Lacul, res., Eur.	B14	26
Stine Mountain, mtn., Mt., U.S.	E13	136
Stinking Water Creek, stm., Ne., U.S.	G11	126
Stinnett, Tx., U.S.	F7	128
Štip, Mac.	B5	28
Stirling, Austl.	F3	74
Stirling, Scot., U.K.	E8	12
Stirling City, Ca., U.S.	D4	134
Stirling Range, mts., Austl.	F3	74
Stjørdalshalsen, Nor.	E4	8
Stjernøya, i., Nor.	A10	8
Stobi, sci., Mac.	B4	28
Stockach, Ger.	I5	16
Stockbridge, Ga., U.S.	C1	116
Stockbridge, Mi., U.S.	B1	114
Stockdale, Tx., U.S.	E10	130
Stockerau, Aus.	B13	22
Stockholm, Swe.	G8	8
Stockholm, state, Swe.	G8	8
Stockport, Eng., U.K.	H10	12
Stockton, Al., U.S.	G11	122
Stockton, Ca., U.S.	F4	134
Stockton, Il., U.S.	B8	120
Stockton, Ks., U.S.	B9	128
Stockton-on-Tees, Eng., U.K.	G11	12
Stockton Plateau, plat., Tx., U.S.	D5	130
Stockton Reservoir, res., Mo., U.S.	G4	120
Stockton Springs, Me., U.S.	F8	110
Stoczek Łukowski, Pol.	E17	16
Stœng Trêng, Camb.	F8	48
Stoke-on-Trent, Eng., U.K.	I11	12
Stokes Point, c., Austl.	n11	77a
Stolberg, Ger.	F2	16
Stolbovoj, ostrov, i., Russia	B16	34
Stoneboro, Pa., U.S.	C5	114
Stonehaven, Scot., U.K.	E10	12
Stonehenge, hist., Eng., U.K.	J11	12
Stone Mountain, Ga., U.S.	C1	116
Stone Mountain, mtn., Vt., U.S.	F5	110
Stoneville, N.C., U.S.	H6	114
Stonewall, Mb., Can.	D16	124
Stonewall, Ms., U.S.	E10	122
Stonington, Il., U.S.	E8	120
Stonington, Me., U.S.	F8	110
Stony Creek, stm., Ca., U.S.	D3	134
Stony Lake, l., Mb., Can.	D11	106
Stony Plain, Ab., Can.	C16	138
Stony Point, N.C., U.S.	I4	114
Stony Rapids, Sk., Can.	D9	106
Stony River, Ak., U.S.	D8	140
Stopnica, Pol.	F16	16
Stora Lulevatten, l., Swe.	C8	8
Storavan, l., Swe.	D8	8
Stord, i., Nor.	G1	8
Storebælt, strt., Den.	I4	8
Store Koldewey, i., Grnld.	B22	141
Storen, Nor.	E4	8
Store Sotra, i., Nor.	F1	8
Storkerson Bay, b., N.T., Can.	B14	140
Storkerson Peninsula, pen., Nu., Can.	A9	106
Storlien, Swe.	E5	8
Storm Bay, b., Austl.	o13	77a
Storm Lake, Ia., U.S.	B2	120
Stornoway, Scot., U.K.	C6	12
Storozhynets', Ukr.	A12	26
Storrs, Ct., U.S.	C13	114
Storsjøen, l., Nor.	F4	8
Storsjön, l., Swe.	E5	8
Storstrøm, state, Den.	I5	8
Storthoaks, Sk., Can.	E12	124
Stortoman, Swe.	D7	8
Storuman, l., Swe.	D6	8
Storvik, l., Swe.	D7	8
Storvreta, Swe.	F7	8
Story City, Ia., U.S.	B4	120
Stosch, Isla, i., Chile	I1	90
Stoubcy, Bela.	G9	10
Stoughton, Sk., Can.	E10	124
Stoughton, Ma., U.S.	B14	114
Stoughton, Wi., U.S.	B8	120
Stoŭng, stm., Camb.	F7	48
Stow, Oh., U.S.	C4	114
Stowe, Vt., U.S.	F4	110
Stowell, Tx., U.S.	H4	122
Stowmarket, Eng., U.K.	I14	12
Stoyoma Mountain, mtn., B.C., Can.	G9	138
Stradella, Italy	E6	22
Stradzečy, Bela.	I6	10
Strahan, Austl.	o12	77a
Strakonice, Czech Rep.	G9	16
Stralsund, Ger.	B9	16
Strand, S. Afr.	H4	70
Stranraer, Scot., U.K.	G8	12
Strasbourg, Sk., Can.	C9	124
Strasbourg, Fr.	F16	14
Strasburg, N.D., U.S.	A12	126
Strasburg, Oh., U.S.	D4	114
Strasburg, Pa., U.S.	D9	114
Strășeni, Mol.	B15	26
Stratford, N.Z.	D6	80
Stratford, Ca., U.S.	G6	134
Stratford, Ct., U.S.	C12	114
Stratford, Ia., U.S.	B4	120
Stratford, Ok., U.S.	C2	122
Stratford, Wi., U.S.	G8	118
Stratford-upon-Avon, Eng., U.K.	I11	12
Strathalbyn, Austl.	J2	76
Strathclair, Mb., Can.	D13	124
Strathgordon, Austl.	o12	77a
Strathlorne, N.S., Can.	D15	110
Strathmore, Ab., Can.	E17	138
Strathmore, val., Scot., U.K.	E9	12
Strathroy, On., Can.	F8	112
Strathy Point, c., Scot., U.K.	B6	128?
Stratton, Co., U.S.	B6	128
Stratton, Me., U.S.	E6	110
Stratton, Ne., U.S.	A7	128
Straubing, Ger.	H8	16
Strausberg, Ger.	D9	16
Strawberry, stm., Ar., U.S.	H6	120
Strawberry Mountain, mtn., Or., U.S.	F8	136
Strawberry Reservoir, res., Ut., U.S.	C5	132
Strawn, Tx., U.S.	B9	130
Streaky Bay, b., Austl.	F6	74
Streatham, B.C., Can.	C4	138
Streator, Il., U.S.	C9	120
Stredoslovenský Kraj, state, Slov.	H15	16
Streeter, N.D., U.S.	A13	126
Streetsboro, Oh., U.S.	C4	114
Streetsville, On., Can.	E10	112
Strehaia, Rom.	E10	26
Strelka-Čunja, Russia	B18	32
Strel'na, stm., Russia	C18	8
Strel'skaja, Russia	G22	8
Strenči, Lat.	C8	10
Strešyn, Bela.	H13	10
Strickland, stm., Pap. N. Gui.	b3	79a
Strimon, Gulf of see Strymonikós Kólpos, b., Grc.	C6	28
Strjama, stm., Blg.	G11	26
Stroeder, Arg.	H4	90
Strofades, is., Grc.	F3	28
Stromboli, Isola, i., Italy	F9	24
Strome, Ab., Can.	D18	138
Stromeferry, Scot., U.K.	D7	12
Stromsburg, Ne., U.S.	F15	126
Strömstad, Swe.	G4	8
Strömsund, Swe.	E6	8
Strong, stm., Ms., U.S.	E9	122
Stronghurst, Il., U.S.	D7	120
Stronsay, i., Scot., U.K.	B10	12
Stroud, Austl.	I8	76
Stroud, Eng., U.K.	J10	12
Stroud, Ok., U.S.	B2	122
Stroudsburg, Pa., U.S.	D10	114
Struga, Mac.	B3	28
Struma, stm., Eur.	H10	26
Strumble Head, c., Wales, U.K.	I7	12
Strunino, Russia	D21	10
Struthers, Oh., U.S.	C5	114
Stryj, stm., Ukr.	H19	16
Stryker, Oh., U.S.	C1	114
Strymonikós Kólpos, (Strimon, Gulf of), b., Grc.	C6	28
Strzegom, Pol.	F12	16
Strzelce Krajeńskie, Pol.	D11	16
Strzelce Opolskie, Pol.	F14	16
Strzelecki Creek, stm., Austl.	G3	76
Strzelecki Desert, des., Austl.	G3	76
Strzelin, Pol.	F13	16
Strzyżów, Pol.	G17	16
Stuart, Fl., U.S.	I5	116
Stuart, Ia., U.S.	C3	120
Stuart, Va., U.S.	H5	114
Stuart, i., Ak., U.S.	D7	140
Stuart Island, i., Ak., U.S.	D7	140
Stuart's Draft, Va., U.S.	G6	114
Studen Kladenec, Jazovir, res., Blg.	H12	26
Stuie, B.C., Can.	D4	138
Stung Treng see Stœng Trêng, Camb.	F8	48
Stupino, Russia	F20	10
Stura di Demonte, stm., Italy	F3	22
Sturge Island, i., Ant.	B21	81
Sturgeon, stm., On., Can.	A9	112
Sturgeon Bay, Wi., U.S.	D2	112
Sturgeon Bay, b., Mb., Can.	B15	124

Sturgeon Falls – Talaud Islands I • 55

Name Map Ref. Page

Sturgeon Falls, On., Can. B10 112
Sturgeon Lake, l., Ab., Can. A13 138
Sturgeon Lake, l., On., Can. A7 118
Sturgeon Lake, l., On., Can. D11 112
Sturgis, Sk., Can. C11 124
Sturgis, Ky., U.S. G10 120
Sturgis, Mi., U.S. G4 112
Sturgis, S.D., U.S. C9 126
Štúrovo, Slov. I10 16
Sturt, Mount, mtn., Austl. G3 76
Sturtevant, Wi., U.S. F2 112
Sturt National Park, p.o.i., Austl. G3 76
Sturt Stony Desert, des., Austl. G3 76
Stutterheim, S. Afr. H8 70
Stuttgart, Ger. H5 16
Stuttgart, Ar., U.S. C7 122
Stylis, Grc. E5 28
Styr, stm., Eur. H9 10
Styria see Steiermark, state, Aus. C11 22
Su see Shū, Kaz. F12 32
Suaçuí Grande, stm., Braz. J4 88
Suai, Malay. B8 50
Suaita, Col. D5 86
Suapure, stm., Ven. D8 86
Suaqui Grande, Mex. A4 100
Subah, Indon. G6 50
Subang, Indon. G5 50
Subansiri, stm., Asia D14 54
Subarnarekha, stm., India G11 54
Šūbāṭ, stm., Sudan F6 62
Subate, Lat. D8 10
Subei, China D3 36
Subeita see Shivta, Horvot, sci., Isr. H5 58
Subiaco, Italy I10 22
Sublette, Ks., U.S. D8 128
Sublett Range, mts., Id., U.S. H14 136
Subotica, Serb. C6 26
Sucarnoochee, stm., U.S. E10 122
Succotah, hist., Egypt H3 58
Suceava, Rom. B13 26
Suceava, state, Rom. B12 26
Suchań, Pol. C11 16
Suchou see Suzhou, China F9 42
Süchow see Xuzhou, China D7 42
Sucio, stm., Col. D3 86
Sucre, Bol. C3 90
Sucre, Col. C4 86
Sucre, state, Col. C4 86
Sucre, state, Ven. B10 86
Sucuaro, Col. E7 86
Sucumbíos, state, Ec. H3 86
Sucuriju, Braz. C8 84
Sucuriú, stm., Braz. C6 90
Sud, state, N. Cal. m16 79d
Sud, Canal du, strt., Haiti C11 102
Suda, Russia A20 10
Suda, stm., Russia A20 10
Sudan, Tx., U.S. G6 128
Sudan, ctry., Afr. E5 62
Sudan, reg., Afr. E4 62
Sudišči, Russia H20 10
Sudbury, On., Can. B8 112
Sudbury, Eng., U.K. I13 12
Sudd see As-Sudd, reg., Sudan F6 62
Sudetes, mts., Eur. F11 16
Sudogda, Russia H19 8
Sudomskaja vozvyšennosť, plat., Russia C12 10
Sudosť, stm., Eur. H16 10
Südtirol see Trentino-Alto Adige, state, Italy D8 22
Suðuroy, i., Far. Is. n34 8b
Sue, stm., Sudan F5 62
Sueca, Spain E10 20
Suez see El-Suweis, Egypt I3 58
Suez, Gulf of see Suweis, Khalîg el-, b., Egypt J4 58
Suez Canal see Suweis, Qanâ el-, can., Egypt H3 58
Suffield, Ab., Can. D2 124
Suffolk, Va., U.S. H9 114
Sufu see Kashi, China B12 56
Sugar City, Id., U.S. G15 136
Sugar Hill, Ga., U.S. B1 116
Sugar Island, i., Mi., U.S. B5 112
Sugar Land, Tx., U.S. H3 122
Sugarloaf, hill, Oh., U.S. C4 114
Sugarloaf Mountain, mtn., Me., U.S. E6 110
Sugarloaf Point, c., Austl. I9 76
Suğla Gölü, l., Tur. F14 28
Sugoj, stm., Russia D20 34
Sugut, stm., Malay. G1 52
Suhag, Egypt B6 62
Suhai Hu, l., China G16 32
Suhana, Russia C12 34
Şuhār, Oman E8 56
Sühbaatar, Mong. A6 36
Suhindol, Blg. F12 26
Suhiniči, Russia F18 10
Suhl, Ger. F6 16
Suhodol'skij, Russia G21 10
Suhona, stm., Russia F22 8
Suhoverkovo, Russia D18 10
Suhumi, Geor. F6 32
Şuhut, Tur. E13 28
Suiá-Miçu, stm., Braz. F7 84
Suichuan, China H6 42
Suide, China C4 42
Suifu see Yibin, China F5 36
Suihua, China B10 36
Suijiang, China F5 36
Suileng, China B10 36
Suining, China E7 42
Suining, China F1 42
Suipacha, Arg. G8 92
Suiping, China E5 42
Suippes, Fr. E13 14
Suir, stm., Ire. I5 12
Suixi, China E7 42
Suiyang, China H2 42
Suiyang, China B9 38
Suiyangdian, China E5 42
Suizhong, China A9 42
Suizhou, China F5 42
Šuja, Russia H19 8
Šuja, stm., Russia E15 8
Sujāngarh, India E5 54
Sujāwal, Pak. F2 54
Sukabumi, Indon. G5 50
Sukadana, Indon. D6 50
Sukadana, Indon. F4 50
Sukadana, Teluk, b., Indon. D6 50
Sukagawa, Japan B13 40
Sukamara, Indon. E7 50
Sukaraja, Indon. E7 50
Sukau, Malay. A11 50
Sukhothai, Thai. D4 48
Sukhumi see Suhumi, Geor. F6 32
Sukkertoppen (Maniitsoq), Grnld. D15 141
Sukkozero, Russia E14 8
Sukkur, Pak. E2 54
Sukoharjo, Indon. G7 50
Sukromlja, Russia D17 10
Sukses, Nmb. B3 70
Sukumo, Japan G5 40
Sukunka, stm., B.C., Can. A9 138
Sul, Baía, b., Braz. C13 92
Sula, i., Nor. F1 8
Sula, stm., Russia C23 8
Sula, Kepulauan (Sula Islands), is., Indon. F8 44
Sulaiman Range, mts., Pak. C3 54
Sula Islands see Sula, Kepulauan, is., Indon. F8 44
Sulawesi (Celebes), i., Indon. F7 44
Sulawesi Selatan, state, Indon. E11 50
Sulawesi Tengah, state, Indon. D12 50
Sulawesi Tenggara, state, Indon. E12 50
Sulaymān, Birak (Solomon's Pools), sci., W.B. G5 58
Sulcis, reg., Italy E2 24
Sulechów, Pol. D11 16
Sulęcin, Pol. D11 16
Sulejówek, Pol. D17 16
Sulen, Mount, mtn., Pap. N. Gui. a3 79a
Sulina, Rom. D16 26
Sulina, Braţul, stm., Rom. D16 26
Sulingen, Ger. D4 16
Sulitelma, mtn., Eur. C7 8
Sullana, Peru D1 84
Sulligent, Al., U.S. D10 122
Sullivan, Il., U.S. E9 120
Sullivan, In., U.S. E10 120
Sullivan Lake, l., Ab., Can. E18 138
Sulmona, Italy H10 22
Sulphur, La., U.S. G5 122
Sulphur, Ok., U.S. C2 122
Sulphur, stm., U.S. D5 122
Sulphur Springs, Tx., U.S. D3 122
Sulphur Springs Draw, stm., U.S. H6 128
Sulphur Springs Valley, val., Az., U.S. L7 132
Sultan, Wa., U.S. C5 136
Sultan Alonto, Lake, l., Phil. G5 52
Sultandağı, Tur. E14 28
Sultanhisar, Tur. F11 28
Sultan Kudarat, Phil. G4 52
Sultānpur, India E8 54
Sulu Archipelago, is., Phil. H3 52
Sulu Chi, l., China C11 54
Sulūq, Libya A4 62
Sulu Sea, s., Asia F2 52
Sulzbach-Rosenberg, Ger. G7 16
Šum, Russia A14 10
Šumadija, reg., Serb. E7 26
Sumangat, Tanjong, c., Malay. G1 52
Sumatera (Sumatra), i., Indon. E3 44
Sumatera Barat, state, Indon. D2 50
Sumatera Selatan, state, Indon. E4 50
Sumatera Utara, state, Indon. K4 48
Sumatra see Sumatera, i., Indon. E3 44
Sumba, Far. Is. n34 8b
Sumba, i., Indon. H11 50
Sumba, Selat, strt., Indon. H11 50
Sumbawa, i., Indon. H10 50
Sumbawa Besar, Indon. H10 50
Sumbawanga, Tan. F6 66
Sumbe, Ang. C1 68
Sumburgh Head, c., Scot., U.K. o18 12a
Sumé, Braz. D7 88
Sumedang, Indon. G5 50
Sümeg, Hung. B4 26
Šumen, Blg. F13 26
Sumenep, Indon. G8 50
Šumerlja, Russia C7 32
Sumisu-jima (Smith Island), i., Japan E13 36
Šumjači, Russia G15 10
Summerfield, Fl., U.S. G3 116
Summerfield, N.C., U.S. H6 114
Summer Lake, l., Or., U.S. H6 136
Summerland, B.C., Can. G11 138
Summerside, P.E., Can. D13 110
Summersville, Mo., U.S. G6 120
Summerton, S.C., U.S. C5 116
Summerville, Ga., U.S. C13 122
Summerville, S.C., U.S. C5 116
Summit, S.D., U.S. F1 118
Summit Lake, B.C., Can. B8 138
Summit Mountain, mtn., Nv., U.S. D9 134
Sumner, Ia., U.S. B5 120
Sumner, Ms., U.S. D8 122
Sumner, Wa., U.S. C4 136
Sumoto, Japan E7 40
Šumpangbinangae, Indon. F11 50
Šumperk, Czech Rep. G13 16
Sumpiuh, Indon. G6 50
Sumqayıt, Azer. A6 56
Šumšu, ostrov, i., Russia F20 34
Sumter, S.C., U.S. C5 116
Šumusta el-Waqf, Egypt J1 58
Sumy, Ukr. D4 32
Sumzom, China F4 36
Sun, stm., Mt., U.S. C14 136
Sunāmganj, Bngl. F13 54
Sunbright, Tn., U.S. H13 120
Sunburst, Mt., U.S. B14 136
Sunbury, Austl. K5 76
Sunbury, Oh., U.S. D3 114
Sunbury, Pa., U.S. D9 114
Sunchales, Arg. E7 92
Suncho Corral, Arg. G6 92
Sunch'ŏn, Kor., N. E6 38
Sunch'ŏn-ŭp, Kor., N. G7 38
Sun City, Az., U.S. J4 132
Suncook, N.H., U.S. G5 110
Sunda, Selat (Sunda Strait), strt., Indon. G4 50
Sundance, Wy., U.S. C8 126
Sundarbans, reg., Asia H12 54
Sundargarh, India G9 54
Sunda Shelf, unds. I13 142
Sunda Strait see Sunda, Selat, strt., Indon. G4 50
Sundays, stm., S. Afr. H7 70
Sunde, Nor. G1 8
Sunderland, Eng., U.K. G11 12
Sundown, Tx., U.S. H6 128
Sundridge, On., Can. C10 112
Sundsvall, Swe. E7 8
Sunflower, Ms., U.S. D8 122
Sunflower, Mount, mtn., Ks., U.S. B7 128
Sungaianyar, Indon. E10 50
Sungaibuntu, Indon. F5 50
Sungaidareh, Indon. D2 50
Sungaiguntung, Indon. C3 50
Sungai Kolok, Thai. I5 48
Sungailiat, Indon. E5 50
Sungailangsat, Indon. D2 50
Sungailimau, Indon. D1 50
Sungaipenuh, Indon. E2 50
Sungai Petani, Malay. J5 48
Sungaipinang, Indon. D8 50
Sungairotan, Indon. E4 50
Sungaiselan, Indon. E5 50
Sungari see Songhua, stm., China B11 36
Sungari Reservoir see Songhua Hu, res., China C7 38
Sungchiang see Songjiang, China F9 42
Sungguminasa, Indon. F11 50
Sungsang, Indon. E4 50
Sunland Park, N.M., U.S. L10 132
Sunne, Swe. G5 8
Sunnynook, Ab., Can. E19 138
Sunnyside, Ut., U.S. D6 132
Sunnyside, Wa., U.S. D7 136
Sunnyslope, Ab., Can. E17 138
Sunnyvale, Ca., U.S. F3 134
Sun Prairie, Wi., U.S. A8 120
Sunrise, Fl., U.S. J5 116
Sunrise, Wy., U.S. E8 126
Sunrise Manor, Nv., U.S. G1 132
Sunset, La., U.S. G6 122
Sunset, Tx., U.S. H11 128
Sunset Country, reg., Austl. J3 76
Sunset Crater National Monument, p.o.i., Az., U.S. H5 132
Sunshine, Austl. K5 76
Suntar, Russia D12 34
Suntar-Hajata, hrebet, mts., Russia D17 34
Sun Valley, Id., U.S. G12 136
Sunwu, China B10 36
Sunwui see Jiangmen, China J5 42
Sunyani, Ghana H4 64
Suojarvi, Russia E15 8
Suomussalmi, Fin. D13 8
Suō-nada, s., Japan F4 40
Suordah, Russia C15 34
Supamo, stm., Ven. D10 86
Supaul, India E11 54
Superí see La Merced, Arg. D5 92
Superior, Az., U.S. J5 132
Superior, Mt., U.S. C12 136
Superior, Wi., U.S. E6 118
Superior, Wy., U.S. B7 132
Superior, Laguna, b., Mex. G11 100
Superior, Lake, l., N.A. B10 108
Supetar, Cro. G13 22
Suphan Buri, Thai. E4 48
Suphan Buri, stm., Thai. E5 48
Suponevo, Russia G17 10
Supung Reservoir, res., Asia D6 38
Suqian, China E8 42
Sūq Suwayq, Sau. Ar. E4 56
Suquṭrā (Socotra), i., Yemen G7 56
Şūr (Tyre), Leb. E6 58
Şūr, Oman E8 56
Sur, Point, c., Ca., U.S. G4 134
Sura, stm., Russia C7 32
Surabaya, Indon. G8 50
Surakarta, Indon. G7 50
Şūrān, Syria C7 58
Šurany, Slov. H14 16
Surat, Austl. F7 76
Sūrat, India H4 54
Sūratgarh, India D4 54
Surat Thani, Thai. H4 48
Suraž, Bela. E13 10
Suraž, Russia G15 10
Surendranagar, India G3 54
Surf City, N.J., U.S. E11 114
Surfers Paradise, Austl. G9 76
Surgères, Fr. C5 18
Surgoinsville, Tn., U.S. H3 114
Surgut, Russia B12 32
Suriāpet, India C4 53
Surigao, Phil. F5 52
Surin, Thai. E6 48
Surinam, ctry., S.A. C6 84
Suring, Wi., U.S. D1 112
Surprise Valley, val., U.S. B5 134
Surrency, Ga., U.S. E3 116
Surrey, N.D., U.S. F12 124
Surry, Va., U.S. G9 114
Sursee, Switz. C5 22
Surt, Libya A3 62
Surt, Khalīj (Sidra, Gulf of), b., Libya A3 62
Surtanāhu, Pak. E2 54
Surtsey, i., Ice. l29 8a
Suru, Pap. N. Gui. b3 79a
Sürüç, Tur. A9 58
Suruga-wan, b., Japan E11 40
Surulangun, Indon. E3 50
Surumu, stm., Braz. F11 86
Šuryškary, Russia A10 32
Susa, Italy E4 22
Sušac, Otok, i., Cro. H13 22
Sūsah, Libya A4 62
Susaki, Japan F6 40
Susanino, Russia F17 34
Susanino, Russia G19 8
Susanville, Ca., U.S. C5 134
Šušenskoe, Russia D16 32
Susitna, stm., Ak., U.S. D9 140
Susleni, Mol. B15 26
Susoh, Indon. K3 48
Susong, China F7 42
Suspiro del Moro, Puerto, p., Spain G7 20
Susquehanna, Pa., U.S. C10 114
Susquehanna, stm., U.S. E9 114
Susquehanna, West Branch, stm., Pa., U.S. C8 114
Susques, Arg. D3 90
Sussex, N.B., Can. E11 110
Sussex, N.J., U.S. C11 114
Sussex, Va., U.S. H8 114
Susuman, Russia D18 34
Susurluk, Tur. D11 28
Susuzmüsellim, Tur. B9 28
Šušvė, stm., Lith. E6 10
Sutak, India B6 54
Sutherland, S. Afr. H5 70
Sutherland, Ia., U.S. A2 120
Sutherlin, Or., U.S. G3 136
Sutjeska Nacionalni Park, p.o.i., Bos. F5 26
Sutlej (Langqên) (Satluj), stm., Asia D3 54
Sutter, Ca., U.S. D4 134
Sutter Buttes, mtn., Ca., U.S. D4 134
Sutter Creek, Ca., U.S. E5 134
Sutton, Ak., U.S. D10 140
Sutton, W.V., U.S. F5 114
Sutton, Monts see Green Mountains, mts., N.A. G4 110
Sutton in Ashfield, Eng., U.K. H11 12
Sutton West, On., Can. D10 112
Suttor, stm., Austl. C6 76
Sutwik Island, i., Ak., U.S. E8 140
Suure-Jaani, Est. B8 10
Suur Munamägi, hill, Est. C9 10
Suur Pakri, i., Est. A6 10
Suva, Fiji q19 79e
Suvadiva Atoll, at., Mald. i12 46a
Suvarlı, Tur. A8 58
Suvasvesi, l., Fin. E12 8
Suvorov, Russia F19 10
Suwa, Japan C11 40
Suwałki, Pol. B18 16
Suwałki, state, Pol. C18 16
Suwannaphum, Thai. E6 48
Suwannee, stm., U.S. G2 116
Suwanose-jima, i., Japan k19 39a
Suwarrow, at., Cook Is. E10 72
Suweis, Khalîg el- (Suez, Gulf of), b., Egypt J4 58
Suweis, Qanâ el- (Suez Canal), can., Egypt H3 58
Suwŏn, Kor., S. F7 38
Suzaka, Japan C11 40
Suzdal', Russia H19 8
Suzhou, China F9 42
Suzhou, China E7 42
Suzigou, China A10 42
Suzuka, Japan E9 40
Suzuka-sammyaku, mts., Japan D9 40
Suzu-misaki, c., Japan B10 40
Suzun, Russia D14 32
Suzzara, Italy F7 22
Svalbard, dep., Eur. B6 30
Svaliava, Ukr. A10 26
Svapa, stm., Russia H18 10
Svappavaara, Swe. C9 8
Svärdsjö, Swe. F6 8
Svartenhuk, pen., Grnld. C15 141
Svartisen, ice, Nor. C5 8
Svataj, Russia C19 34
Svay Riĕng, Camb. G7 48
Svėdasai, Lith. E8 10
Svegssjön, l., Swe. E5 8
Švėkšna, Lith. E4 10
Svelvik, Nor. G4 8
Švenčionėliai, Lith. E8 10
Švenčionys, Lith. E9 10
Svendborg, Den. A6 16
Šventoji, Lith. D3 10
Šventoji, stm., Lith. E7 10
Sverdlovsk see Ekaterinburg, Russia C10 32
Sverdrup, ostrov, i., Russia B4 34
Sverdrup Channel, strt., Nu., Can. A6 141
Sverdrup Islands, is., Nu., Can. B5 141
Sveti Nikole, Mac. B4 28
Svetlahorsk, Bela. H12 10
Svetlaja, Russia B12 36
Svetlogorsk, Russia F2 10
Svetlograd, Russia E6 32
Svetlyj, Russia D10 32
Svetlyj, Russia F3 10
Svetlyj, Russia E12 34
Svetogorsk, Russia F13 8
Svetozarevo, Serb. F8 26
Svidník, Slov. G17 16
Svilengrad, Blg. H13 26
Svínoy, i., Far. Is. m34 8b
Svir, Bela. F9 10
Svir', stm., Russia F16 8
Svirica, Russia F15 8
Svirsk, Russia D18 32
Svislač, stm., Bela. G11 10
Svištov, Blg. F12 26
Svit, Slov. G16 16
Svitavy, Czech Rep. G12 16
Svjacilavičy, Bela. H14 10
Svjatoj Nos, mys, c., Russia B18 8
Svjatoj Nos, mys, c., Russia B17 34
Svobodnyj, Russia F14 34
Svolvær, Nor. B6 8
Svratka, stm., Czech Rep. G12 16
Swabia see Schwaben, hist. reg., Ger. H5 16
Swain Reefs, rf., Austl. C9 76
Swainsboro, Ga., U.S. D3 116
Swains Island, at., Am. Sam. E9 72
Swakop, stm., Nmb. C2 70
Swakopmund, Nmb. C2 70
Swale, stm., Eng., U.K. G11 12
Swan, stm., Ab., Can. A15 138
Swan, stm., Can. B13 124
Swan, stm., Mt., U.S. C13 136
Swanage, Eng., U.K. K11 12
Swanee see Suwannee, stm., U.S. G2 116
Swan Hill, Austl. J4 76
Swan Hills, Ab., Can. B15 138
Swan Islands see Santanilla, Islas, is., Hond. D6 102
Swan Lake, Mb., Can. E15 124
Swan Lake, l., Mb., Can. B13 124
Swan Lake, l., Mn., U.S. G4 118
Swannanoa, N.C., U.S. I3 114
Swan Peak, mtn., Mt., U.S. C13 136
Swanquarter, N.C., U.S. A9 116
Swan Range, mts., Mt., U.S. C13 136
Swan Reach, Austl. J2 76
Swan River, Mb., Can. B12 124
Swansboro, N.C., U.S. B8 116
Swansea, Austl. o13 77a
Swansea, Wales, U.K. J8 12
Swanton, Vt., U.S. F3 110
Swanville, Mn., U.S. F4 118
Swart-Mfolozi, stm., S. Afr. F10 70
Swartz Creek, Mi., U.S. F6 112
Swarzędz, Pol. D13 16
Swāt, stm., Pak. A3 54
Swatow see Shantou, China J7 42
Swaziland, ctry., Afr. E10 70
Sweden, ctry., Eur. E6 8
Swedish Knoll, mtn., Ut., U.S. D5 132
Swedru, Ghana H4 64
Sweeny, Tx., U.S. E12 130
Sweet Briar, Va., U.S. G6 114
Sweetgrass, Mt., U.S. A15 136
Sweet Grass Hills, hills, Mt., U.S. B15 136
Sweet Home, Tx., U.S. E10 130
Sweet Springs, Mo., U.S. F4 120
Sweetwater, Tn., U.S. A1 116
Sweetwater, Tx., U.S. B7 130
Sweetwater, stm., Wy., U.S. E5 126
Swellendam, S. Afr. H5 70
Świdnica, Pol. F12 16
Świdnik, Pol. E18 16
Świdwin, Pol. C11 16
Świebodzice, Pol. F12 16
Świebodzin, Pol. D11 16
Świecie, Pol. C14 16
Świerzawa, Pol. E11 16
Świętokrzyski Park Narodowy, p.o.i., Pol. F16 16
Swift Current, Sk., Can. D6 124
Swift Current Creek, stm., Sk., Can. D6 124
Swinburne, Cape, c., Nu., Can. A11 106
Swindle Island, i., B.C., Can. D2 138
Swindon, Eng., U.K. J11 12
Swinford, Ire. H4 12
Świnoujście (Swinemünde), Pol. C9 16
Switzerland, ctry., Eur. C14 18
Swords, Ire. H6 12
Syalah, Russia C13 34
Syan (San), stm., Eur. F18 16
Sycamore, Ga., U.S. E2 116
Sycamore, Il., U.S. C9 120
Sycamore, Oh., U.S. D2 114
Syčovka, Russia E17 10
Sydenham, stm., On., Can. F7 112
Sydney, Austl. I8 76
Sydney, N.S., Can. D16 110
Sydney Bay, b., Norf. I. y25 78i
Sydney Lake, l., On., Can. A4 118
Sydney Mines, N.S., Can. D16 110
Šyičy, Bela. H12 10
Syke, Ger. D4 16
Sykesville, Pa., U.S. C7 114
Syktyvkar, Russia B8 32
Sylacauga, Al., U.S. D12 122
Sylhet, Bngl. F13 54
Syloga, Russia E20 8
Sylt, i., Ger. B4 16
Sylva, N.C., U.S. A2 116
Sylvan Grove, Ks., U.S. C10 128
Sylvania, Ga., U.S. D4 116
Sylvania, Oh., U.S. C2 114
Sylvan Lake, Ab., Can. D16 138
Sylvan Lake, l., Ab., Can. D16 138
Sylvan Pass, p., Wy., U.S. F16 136
Sylvester, Ga., U.S. E2 116
Sylvester, Tx., U.S. B7 130
Sym, Russia B15 32
Syme see Sými, i., Grc. G10 28
Sými, i., Grc. G10 28
Šymkent see Shymkent, Kaz. F11 32
Synevir, Ukr. A10 26
Syowa, sci., Ant. C9 81
Syracuse, In., U.S. G4 112
Syracuse, Ks., U.S. C7 128
Syracuse, Ne., U.S. D1 120
Syracuse, N.Y., U.S. A9 114
Syrdarīya see Syr Darya, stm., Asia F11 32
Syrdarja, Uzb. A10 56
Syr Darya (Syrdarīya), stm., Asia F11 32
Syria, ctry., Asia B4 56
Syriam, Mya. D3 48
Syrian Desert (Shām, Bādiyat ash-), des., Asia C4 56
Sýrna, i., Grc. G9 28
Sýros, i., Grc. F7 28
Sysmä, Fin. F11 8
Sysola, stm., Russia B8 32
Syt'kovo, Russia D16 10
Syväri, l., Fin. E13 8
Syzran', Russia D7 32
Szabolcs-Szatmár-Bereg, state, Hung. A9 26
Szamos (Someș), stm., Eur. B9 26
Szamotuły, Pol. D12 16
Szarvas, Hung. C7 26
Szczawnica, Pol. G16 16
Szczecin (Stettin), Pol. C10 16
Szczecin, state, Pol. C11 16
Szczecinek, Pol. C12 16
Szczuczyn, Pol. C18 16
Szczytno, Pol. C17 16
Szechwan see Sichuan, state, China E5 36
Szechwan Basin see Sichuan Pendi, bas., China F1 42
Szeged, Hung. C7 26
Szeghalom, Hung. B8 26
Székesfehérvár, Hung. B5 26
Szekszárd, Hung. C5 26
Szentendre, Hung. B5 26
Szentes, Hung. C7 26
Szeping see Siping, China C6 38
Szerencs, Hung. A8 26
Szob, Hung. B5 26
Szolnok, Hung. B7 26
Szombathely, Hung. B3 26
Szprotawa, Pol. E11 16
Szubin, Pol. C13 16
Szypliszki, Pol. B19 16

T

Taal, Lake, l., Phil. D3 52
Tábara, Spain C5 20
Tabar Islands, is., Pap. N. Gui. a5 79a
Tabarka, Tun. H2 24
Tabasco, state, Mex. D6 96
Tabelbala, Alg. D4 64
Taber, Ab., Can. G18 138
Tabernes de Valldigna see Tavernes de la Valldigna, Spain E10 20
Tabira, Braz. D7 88
Tablas de Daimiel, Parque Nacional de las, p.o.i., Spain E7 20
Tablas Island, i., Phil. D4 52
Tablas Strait, strt., Phil. D3 52
Tablat, Alg. H14 20
Table Mountain, mtn., Az., U.S. K6 132
Table Rock, Ne., U.S. D1 120
Table Rock Lake, res., U.S. H4 120
Table Top, mtn., Az., U.S. K4 132
Tablones, P.R. B4 104a
Taboi, Mount, hill, St. Vin. p11 105e
Tábor, Czech Rep. G10 16
Tabor, Russia B19 34
Tabor, Ia., U.S. D2 120
Tabora, Tan. E6 66
Tabor City, N.C., U.S. B7 116
Tabou, C. Iv. I3 64
Tabrīz, Iran B6 56
Tabuaeran, at., Kir. C11 72
Tabu-dong, Kor., S. C1 40
Tabuk, Phil. B3 52
Tabūk, Sau. Ar. J7 58
Tabuleiro do Norte, Braz. C6 88
Tabwémasana, Mont, mtn., Vanuatu j16 79d
Tacámbaro de Codallos, Mex. F8 100
Tacaná, Volcán, vol., N.A. H12 100
Tacañitas, Arg. D6 92
Taché, Lac, l., N.T., Can. C7 106
Tacheng, China B1 36
Tachia, stm., Tai. I9 42
Tachichitlte, Isla de, i., Mex. C4 100
Tachie, stm., B.C., Can. B6 138
Táchira, state, Ven. D6 86
Tachoshui, Tai. I9 42
Tacima, Braz. D8 88
Tacloban, Phil. E5 52
Taclobo, Phil. D4 52
Tacna, Peru G3 84
Tacna, Az., U.S. K3 132
Tacoma, Wa., U.S. C4 136
Taconic Range, mts., U.S. B12 114
Taco Pozo, Arg. B6 92
Tacuarembó, Ur. E9 92
Tacuarembó, stm., Ur. E10 92
Tacuarí, stm., Ur. F10 92
Tacutu (Takutu), stm., S.A. F11 86
Tademaït, Plateau du, plat., Alg. D5 64
Tādepallegūdem, India C5 53
Tadjemout, Alg. D5 64
Tadjerouine, Tun. I2 24
Tadjoura, Dji. E8 62
Tadotsu, Japan E6 40
Tadoule Lake, l., Mb., Can. D11 106
Tadoussac, Qc., Can. B7 110
Tādpatri, India D4 53
T'aean, Kor., S. F7 38
T'aebaek-sanmaek, mts., Asia F8 38
Taech'ŏn, Kor., S. F7 38
Taedong-gang, stm., Kor., N. E6 38
Taegu, Kor., S. D1 40
Taejin, Kor., S. C2 40
Taejŏn, Kor., S. F7 38
Taeng, stm., Thai. C4 48
Tafahi, i., Tonga E9 72
Tafalla, Spain B9 20
Tafanlieh, Tai. J9 42
Tafassâsset, Oued, stm., Afr. E6 64
Tafassasset, Ténéré du, des., Niger E7 64
Taféa, state, Vanuatu l17 79d
Tafelberg, hill, Neth. Ant. p22 104g
Tafí Viejo, Arg. C5 92
Tafo, Ghana H4 64
Taft, Ca., U.S. H6 134
Taft, Tx., U.S. F10 130
Taftān, Kūh-e, vol., Iran D9 56
Taga, Samoa g11 79c
Tagajō, Japan A14 40
Taganrog, Russia E5 32
Tagânt, reg., Maur. F2 64
Tagawa, Japan F3 40
Tagaytay, Phil. C3 52
Tagbilaran, Phil. F4 52
Tage, Pap. N. Gui. b3 79a
Tagish Lake, l., Can. C3 106
Tagliamento, stm., Italy E9 22
Taglio di Po, Italy E9 22
Taguatinga, Braz. G2 88
Taguke, China B10 54
Tagula Island, i., Pap. N. Gui. B10 74
Tagum, Phil. G5 52
Tagus (Tajo) (Tejo), stm., Eur. E2 20
Tahakopa, N.Z. H3 80
Tahan, Gunong, mtn., Malay. J6 48
Tahat, mtn., Alg. E6 64
Tahiataš, Uzb. F9 32
Tahifet, Alg. E6 64
Tahiryuak Lake, l., N.T., Can. A8 106
Tahiti, i., Fr. Poly. v23 78h
Tahiti-Faaa, Aéroport International de, Fr. Poly. v21 78h
Tahkuna nina, c., Est. A5 10
Tahlequah, Ok., U.S. I3 120
Tahoe, Lake, l., U.S. E5 134
Tahoe City, Ca., U.S. D5 134
Tahoe Lake, l., Nu., Can. A8 106
Tahoka, Tx., U.S. A6 130
Tahoua, Niger F5 64
Tahquamenon, stm., Mi., U.S. B4 112
Tahta, Egypt L2 58
Tahta, Russia E6 32
Tahta-Bazar, Turkmen. B9 56
Tahtaköprü, Tur. D12 28
Tahtamygda, Russia F13 34
Tahtsa Lake, res., B.C., Can. C3 138
Tahtsa Peak, mtn., B.C., Can. C3 138
Tahuata, i., Fr. Poly. s18 78g
Tahulandang, Pulau, i., Indon. E7 44
Tahuna, Indon. E8 44
Tai'an, China C7 42
Taiarapu, Presqu'île de, pen., Fr. Poly. w22 78h
Taibai Shan, mtn., China E2 42
Taibilla, Sierra de, mts., Spain F8 20
Taibus Qi, China C8 36
Taicang, China F9 42
T'aichou see Taizhou, China E8 42
T'aichung, Tai. I9 42
Taieri, stm., N.Z. G4 80
Taigu, China C5 42
Taihang Shan, mts., China C5 42
Taihape, N.Z. D6 80
Taihe, China H6 42
Taihe, China E6 42
Taihezhen, China B5 38
T'aihsien see Taizhou, China E8 42
Taihu, China F7 42
Tai Hu, l., China F9 42
Taikang, China D6 42
Taikou, China F4 42
Tailai, China B9 36
Tai Lake see Tai Hu, l., China F9 42
Tailem Bend, Austl. J2 76
Taimba, Russia B17 32
T'ainan, Tai. J8 42
Taínaro, Ákra, c., Grc. G5 28
Taining, China H7 42
Taiobeiras, Braz. H4 88
T'aipei, Tai. I9 42
T'aipeihsien, Tai. I9 42
Taiping, China J2 42
Taiping, Malay. J5 48
Taipingdian, China E4 42
Taipu, Braz. C8 88
Tais, Indon. F3 50
Taisha, Japan D5 40
Taishan, China J5 42
Tai Shan see Yuhuang Ding, mtn., China C9 42
Taishun, China H8 42
Taitao, Península de, pen., Chile I2 90
T'aitung, Tai. J9 42
Taivalkoski, Fin. D12 8
Taiwan, ctry., Asia J9 42
Taiwan Strait, strt., Asia I8 42
Taixian, China E9 42
Taixing, China E9 42
Ṭaiyiba, Isr. F6 58
Taiyuan, China C5 42
Taizhao, China D14 54
Taizhou, China E8 42
Taizi, stm., China D5 38
Tajbola, Russia B15 8
Tajga, Russia C15 32
Tajgonos, mys, c., Russia D21 34
Tajgonos, poluostrov, pen., Russia D21 34
Tajikistan, ctry., Asia B11 56
Tajima, Japan B12 40
Tajimi, Japan D10 40
Tajique, N.M., U.S. G2 128
Tajitos, Mex. F6 98
Tāj Mahal, hist., India E7 54
Tajmura, stm., Russia B18 32
Tajmyr, ozero, l., Russia B9 34
Tajmyr, poluostrov, pen., Russia B7 34
Tajšet, Russia C17 32
Tajumulco, Volcán, vol., Guat. E2 102
Tajuña, stm., Spain D7 20
Tak, Thai. D4 48
Takachu, Bots. C5 70
Takahagi, Japan C13 40
Takahashi, Japan E6 40
Takahe, Mount, mtn., Ant. C29 81
Takaka, N.Z. E5 80
Takakkaw Falls, wtfl., B.C., Can. E14 138
Takalar, Indon. F11 50
Takamatsu, Japan E7 40
Takanabe, Japan G4 40
Takaoka, Japan C9 40
Takasago, Japan E7 40
Takasaki, Japan C11 40
Takatsuki, Japan E8 40
Ta-kaw, Mya. B4 48
Takayama, Japan C10 40
Takefu, Japan D9 40
Takenake, China A8 54
Takengon, Indon. J3 48
Takeo, Japan F3 40
Take-shima, is., Asia B4 40
Taketa, Japan G4 40
Takêv, Camb. G7 48
Takhatpur, India G8 54
Takhli, Thai. E5 48
Takhta-Bazar see Tahta-Bazar, Turkmen. B9 56
Takijuq Lake, l., Nu., Can. B8 106
Takikawa, Japan C14 38
Takla Lake, l., B.C., Can. A5 138
Takla Landing, B.C., Can. D5 106
Takla Makan Desert see Taklimakan Shamo, des., China G14 32
Taklimakan Shamo (Takla Makan Desert), des., China G14 32
Takolekaju, Pegunungan, mts., Indon. E11 50
Taksimo, Russia F10 34
Taku, Japan F3 40
Takuan, Mount, vol., Pap. N. Gui. d6 79b
Takum, Nig. H7 64
Takutea, i., Cook Is. E11 72
Takutu (Tacutu), stm., S.A. F11 86
Talačyn, Bela. F12 10
Talagang, Pak. B4 54
Talagante, Chile F2 92
Talaimannar, Sri L. G4 53
Talāja, India H4 54
Talak, reg., Niger F6 64
Tālāla, India H3 54
Talang, Gunung, vol., Indon. D2 50
Talangbetutu, Indon. E4 50
Talangpadang, Indon. F4 50
Talangrimbo, Indon. E4 50
Talara, Peru D1 84
Talas, Kyrg. F12 32
Talasea, Pap. N. Gui. b4 79a
Tal'at al-Jamā'ah, Rujm, mtn., Jord. H6 58
Talata Mafara, Nig. G6 64
Talaud, Kepulauan (Talaud Islands), is., Indon. E8 44
Talaud Islands see Talaud, Kepulauan, is., Indon. E8 44

I·56 Talavera de la Reina – Tervola

Name	Map Ref.	Page
Talavera de la Reina, Spain	D5	20
Talawanta, Austl.	B3	76
Talawdī, Sudan	E6	62
Talayan, Phil.	G5	52
Talbotton, Ga., U.S.	E14	122
Talbragar, stm., Austl.	I7	76
Talca, Chile	G2	92
Talcahuano, Chile	H1	92
Tālcher, India	H10	54
Talco, Tx., U.S.	D3	122
Taldom, Russia	D20	10
Taldykorgan *see* Taldyqorghan , Kaz.	F13	32
Taldyqorghan, Kaz.	F13	32
Talence, Fr.	E5	18
Talent, Or., U.S.	A3	134
Talgar *see* Talghar, Kaz.	F13	32
Talghar, Kaz.	F13	32
Talhār, Pak.	F2	54
Taliabu, Pulau, i., Indon.	F7	44
Talibon, Phil.	E5	52
Talibong, Ko, i., Thai.	I4	48
Talica, Russia	C10	32
Talien *see* Dalian, China	B9	42
Tālīkota, India	C3	53
Taliparamba, India	E2	53
Talisay, Phil.	E4	52
Taliwang, Indon.	H10	50
Talkeetna, Ak., U.S.	D9	140
Talkeetna Mountains, mts., Ak., U.S.	D10	140
Talla, Egypt	J1	58
Talladega, Al., U.S.	D12	122
Tallahala Creek, stm., Ms., U.S.	F9	122
Tallahassee, Fl., U.S.	F1	116
Tallahatchie, stm., Ms., U.S.	D8	122
Tallangatta, Austl.	K6	76
Tallapoosa, Ga., U.S.	D13	122
Tallapoosa, stm., U.S.	E12	122
Tallard, Fr.	E11	18
Tallassee, Al., U.S.	E12	122
Tall as-Sulṭān, sci., Gaza	G6	58
Tall Bīsah, Syria	D7	58
Tallinn, Est.	G11	8
Tallmadge, Oh., U.S.	C4	114
Tall Rif'at, Syria	B8	58
Tallulah, La., U.S.	E7	122
Talmage, Ca., U.S.	D2	134
Talmage, Ne., U.S.	K2	118
Tal'menka, Russia	D14	32
Talnah, Russia	C6	34
Taloda, India	H5	54
Taloga, Ok., U.S.	E10	128
Talok, Indon.	C11	50
Tāloqān, Afg.	B10	56
Talovka, Russia	F7	32
Talquin, Lake, res., Fl., U.S.	G14	122
Talsi, Lat.	C5	10
Taltal, Chile	B2	92
Taltson, stm., N.T., Can.	C8	106
Talu, Indon.	C1	50
Taluk, Indon.	D2	50
Talumphuk, Laem, c., Thai.	H5	48
Talurqjuak, Nu., Can.	B12	106
Talvikjulja, Russia	B13	8
Talwood, Austl.	G7	76
Tama, Arg.	E4	92
Tama, Ia., U.S.	C5	120
Tamalameque, Col.	C5	86
Tamale, Ghana	H4	64
Tamalea, Indon.	E11	50
Tamalpais, Mount, mtn., Ca., U.S.	F3	134
Tamana, Japan	G3	40
Tamana, Mount, hill, Trin.	s12	105f
Tamanaco, stm., Ven.	C9	86
Tamaniquá, Braz.	I9	86
Taman Negara, p.o.i., Malay.	J6	48
Tamano, Japan	E6	40
Tamanquaré, Ilha, i., Braz.	H9	86
Tamapatz, Mex.	E9	100
Tamar, stm., Austl.	n13	77a
Tamarac, stm., Mn., U.S.	C2	118
Tamaroa, Il., U.S.	F8	120
Tamási, Hung.	C5	26
Tamaulipas, state, Mex.	C9	100
Tamazulapan del Progreso, Mex.	G9	100
Tamazunchale, Mex.	E9	100
Tambacounda, Sen.	G2	64
Tambakboyo, Indon.	G7	50
Tamba-kōchi, plat., Japan	D8	40
Tambangsawah, Indon.	E3	50
Tambara, Moz.	D5	68
Tāmbaram, India	E5	53
Tambej, Russia	B3	34
Tambelan, Kepulauan, is., Indon.	C5	50
Tamberías, Arg.	E3	92
Tambo, stm., Austl.	K6	76
Tambohorano, Madag.	D7	68
Tambolongang, Pulau, i., Indon.	G12	50
Tambora, Gunung, vol., Indon.	H10	50
Tamboril, Braz.	C5	88
Tamboryacu, stm., Peru	H4	86
Tambov, Russia	D6	32
Tambre, stm., Spain	B2	20
Tambu, Teluk, b., Indon.	C11	50
Tambunan, Malay.	H1	52
Tambura, Sudan	F5	62
Tâmchekkeṭ, Maur.	F2	64
Tame, Col.	D6	86
Tameapa, Mex.	C5	100
Tâmega, stm., Port.	C3	20
Tamel Aike, Arg.	I2	90
Tamenghest, Alg.	E6	64
Tamenghest, Oued, stm., Alg.	E5	64
Tamga, Russia	B10	38
Tamgak, Adrar, mtn., Niger	F6	64
Tamiahua, Mex.	E10	100
Tamiahua, Laguna de, l., Mex.	E10	100
Tamiami Canal, can., Fl., U.S.	K4	116
Tamil Nādu, state, India	F4	53
Tamiš (Timiș), stm., Eur.	D7	26
Tâmîya, Egypt	I1	58
Tamkūhi, India	E10	54
Tam Ky, Viet.	E9	48
Tammerfors *see* Tampere, Fin.	F10	8
Tammisaari, Fin.	G10	8
Tamms, Il., U.S.	G8	120
Tampa, Fl., U.S.	I3	116
Tampa Bay, b., Fl., U.S.	I3	116
Tampang, Indon.	F4	50
Tampaon, stm., Mex.	E9	100
Tampere (Tammerfors), Fin.	F10	8
Tampico, Mex.	D10	100
Tampico, Il., U.S.	C8	120
Tampin, Malay.	K6	48
Tamsagbulag, Mong.	B8	36
Tamshiyacu, Peru	D3	84
Tamsweg, Aus.	C10	22
Tamu, Mya.	D7	46
Tamuning, Guam	i10	78c
Tamworth, Austl.	H8	76
Tamworth, Eng., U.K.	I11	12
Tana (Teno), stm., Eur.	B12	8
Tana, stm., Kenya	D8	66
Tana, Lake see T'ana Häyk', l., Eth.	E7	62
Tanabe, Japan	F8	40
Tanabi, Braz.	K1	88
Tana bru, Nor.	A12	8
Tanacross, Ak., U.S.	D11	140
Tanafjorden, b., Nor.	A13	8
Tanaga Island, i., Ak., U.S.	g23	140a
T'ana Häyk', l., Eth.	E7	62
Tanahbala, Pulau, i., Indon.	F2	44
Tanahgrogot, Indon.	D10	50
Tanahjampea, Pulau, i., Indon.	G12	50
Tanahmasa, Pulau, i., Indon.	F2	44
Tanahmerah, Indon.	G10	44
Tanah Merah, Malay.	J6	48
Tanahputih, Indon.	C2	50
Tanakeke, Pulau, i., Indon.	F11	50
Tanakpur, India	D7	54
Tanami Desert, des., Austl.	C5	74
Tan An, Viet.	G8	48
Tanana, Ak., U.S.	C9	140
Tanana, stm., Ak., U.S.	D10	140
Tananarive *see* Antananarivo, Madag.	D8	68
Tanbar, Austl.	E3	76
Tan Chau, Viet.	G7	48
Tanch'ŏn-ŭp, Kor., N.	D8	38
Tancítaro, Pico de, mtn., Mex.	F7	100
Tanda, Egypt	K1	58
Tānda, India	E9	54
Tānda, India	C5	54
Tandag, Phil.	F6	52
Tandaltī, Sudan	E6	62
Ţăndărei, Rom.	E14	26
Tandil, Arg.	H8	92
Tando Ādam, Pak.	F2	54
Tando Allāhyār, Pak.	F2	54
Tandou Lake, l., Austl.	I3	76
Tandula Tank, res., India	H8	54
Tandun, Indon.	C2	50
Tāndūr, India	C3	53
Tanega-shima, i., Japan	I9	38
Tanezrouft, des., Afr.	E4	64
Tang, stm., China	E7	42
Tang, stm., China	E5	42
Tang, stm., China	B6	42
Tanga, Russia	F11	34
Tanga, Tan.	F7	66
Tangail, Bngl.	F12	54
Tanga Islands, is., Pap. N. Gui.	a5	79a
Tanga Langua, c., Gren.	q10	105e
Tanganyika see Tanzania, ctry., Afr.	F6	66
Tanganyika, Lake, l., Afr.	F6	66
Tangarana, stm., Peru	I4	86
Tangarare, Sol. Is.	e8	79b
Tanger (Tangier), Mor.	B3	64
Tangerang, Indon.	G5	50
Tangerhütte, Ger.	D7	16
Tangermünde, Ger.	D7	16
Tanggu, China	B7	42
Tanggulashan, China	A14	54
Tanggula Shan, mts., China	E3	36
Tanggula Shankou, p., China	B13	54
Tanghe, China	E5	42
Tangi, Pak.	A3	54
Tangier, N.S., Can.	F14	110
Tangier *see* Tanger, Mor.	B3	64
Tangier, Va., U.S.	G10	114
Tangipahoa, stm., U.S.	G8	122
Tangjiagou, China	F7	42
Tangkou, China	F8	42
Tangmai, China	E4	36
Tango-hantō, pen., Japan	D8	40
Tangra Yumco, l., China	C11	54
Tangshan, China	B8	42
Tangtou, China	D8	42
Tangyan, Mya.	A4	48
Tangyin, China	D6	42
Tangyuan, China	B10	36
Tanhoj, Russia	F10	34
Taniantaweng Shan, mts., China	F4	36
Tanigawa-dake, mtn., Japan	C11	40
Tanimbar, Kepulauan, is., Indon.	G9	44
Tanintharyi, state, Mya.	F3	48
Tanis, hist., Egypt	H2	58
Tanjay, Phil.	F4	52
Tanjung, Indon.	H10	50
Tanjung, Indon.	E9	50
Tanjungbalai, Indon.	B1	50
Tanjungbatu, Indon.	C3	50
Tanjungbatu, Indon.	B11	50
Tanjungkarang-Telukbetung *see* Bandar Lampung, Indon.	F4	50
Tanjunglabu, Indon.	E5	50
Tanjungpandan, Indon.	E5	50
Tanjungpinang, Indon.	C4	50
Tanjungpura, Indon.	K4	48
Tanjungraja, Indon.	E4	50
Tanjungredep, Indon.	B10	50
Tanjungselor, Indon.	B10	50
Tanjunguban, Indon.	C4	50
Tānk, Pak.	B3	54
Tankwa, stm., S. Afr.	H5	70
Tanna, i., Vanuatu	I17	79d
Tannenberg *see* Stębark, Pol.	C16	16
Tanner, Mount, mtn., B.C., Can.	G12	138
Tannu-Ola, hrebet, mts., Asia	D16	32
Tannūrah, Ra's, c., Sau. Ar.	D7	56
Tanon Strait, strt., Phil.	E4	52
Tanout, Niger	F6	64
Tanquinho, Braz.	G6	88
Tanshui, Tai.	I9	42
Tanta, Egypt	H2	58
Tan-Tan, Mor.	D2	64
Tantoyuca, Mex.	E9	100
Tanuku, India	C5	53
Tanvald, Czech Rep.	F11	16
Tanyang, Kor., S.	C1	40
Tanzania, ctry., Afr.	F6	66
Tao'er, stm., China	B5	38
Taohuazhen, China	A6	42
Taole, China	B2	42
Taonan, China	B5	38
Taongi, at., Marsh. Is.	B7	72
Taormina, Italy	G9	24
Taos, Mo., U.S.	F5	120
Taos, N.M., U.S.	E3	128
Taos Pueblo, N.M., U.S.	E3	128
Taoudenni, Mali	E4	64
Taounate, Mor.	C4	64
Taourirt, Mor.	C4	64
Taoyuan, China	G4	42
Taoyüan, Tai.	I9	42
Tapa, Est.	G11	8
Tapachula, Mex.	H12	100
Tapaga, Cape, c., Samoa	h12	79c
Tapah, Malay.	J5	48
Tapajós, stm., Braz.	D6	84
Tapaktuan, Indon.	K3	48
Tapalqué, Arg.	H7	92
Tapauá, stm., Braz.	E4	84
Tapejara, Braz.	D12	92
Taperoá, Braz.	D7	88
Tapes, Braz.	E12	92
Tapeta, Lib.	H3	64
Taphan Hin, Thai.	D5	48
Taphoen, stm., Thai.	E4	48
Tāpi, stm., India	H4	54
Ta Pi, stm., Thai.	H4	48
Tapiche, stm., Peru	E3	84
Tapini, Pap. N. Gui.	b4	79a
Taplan National Park, p.o.i., Thai.	E6	48
Tāplejungg, Nepal	E11	54
Tappen, N.D., U.S.	H14	124
Tapuae-o-Uenuku, mtn., N.Z.	E5	80
Tapuio, stm., Braz.	C3	88
Tapul Group, is., Phil.	H3	52
Tapun, Mya.	C2	48
Tapuruquara, Braz.	H9	86
Taqāṭu' Hayyā, Sudan	D7	62
Taquara, Braz.	D12	92
Taquaras, Ponta das, c., Braz.	C13	92
Taquari, stm., Braz.	D12	92
Taquari Novo, stm., Braz.	C5	90
Taquaritinga, Braz.	K1	88
Tar, stm., N.C., U.S.	I8	114
Tara, Austl.	F8	76
Tara, Russia	C12	32
Tara, stm., Eur.	G16	22
Tara, stm., Russia	C13	32
Taraba, stm., Nig.	H7	64
Tarabuco, Bol.	C3	90
Ţarābulus (Tripoli), Leb.	D6	58
Ţarābulus (Tripoli), Libya	A2	62
Ţarābulus (Tripolitania), hist. reg., Libya	A2	62
Taraclia, Mol.	D15	26
Tarago, Austl.	J7	76
Taraira (Traíra), stm., S.A.	H7	86
Taraju, Indon.	G6	50
Tarakan, Indon.	B10	50
Tarakan, Pulau, i., Indon.	B10	50
Taralga, Austl.	J7	76
Tara Nacionalni Park, p.o.i., Serb.	F6	26
Tārānagar, India	D5	54
Taranaki, Mount (Egmont, Mount), vol., N.Z.	D6	80
Tarancón, Spain	D8	20
Taranto, Italy	D11	24
Taranto, Golfo di, b., Italy	E10	24
Tarapoto, Peru	E2	84
Taraquá, Braz.	G7	86
Tarare, Fr.	D10	18
Tarariras, Ur.	G9	92
Tarāsa Dwīp, i., India	G7	46
Tarascon, Fr.	F10	18
Tarascon-sur-Ariège, Fr.	G7	18
Tarasovo, Russia	C19	32
Tarat, Alg.	D6	64
Tarata, Bol.	C3	90
Taratakbuluh, Indon.	C2	50
Tarauacá, stm., Braz.	E3	84
Taravao, Isthme de, isth., Fr. Poly.	v22	78h
Tarawa, at., Kir.	C8	72
Tarawera, N.Z.	D7	80
Taraz (Žambyl), Kaz.	F12	32
Tarazona, Spain	C9	20
Tarbagataj, hrebet see Tarbagatay, khrebet, mts., Asia	E14	32
Tarbagatay, khrebet, mts., Asia	E14	32
Tarbagatay Shan see Tarbagatay, khrebet, mts., Asia	E14	32
Tarbela Reservoir, res., Pak.	A4	54
Tarbert, Scot., U.K.	D6	12
Tarbes, Fr.	F6	18
Tarboro, N.C., U.S.	I8	114
Tarbū, Libya	B3	62
Tarcoola, Austl.	F6	74
Tardoki-Jani, gora, mtn., Russia	G16	34
Taree, Austl.	H9	76
Tareja, Russia	B7	34
Tärendö, Swe.	C10	8
Tarentum, Pa., U.S.	D6	114
Tarfa, Wadi el-, stm., Egypt	J2	58
Tarfaya, Mor.	D2	64
Targhee Pass, p., U.S.	F15	136
Tărgovište, Blg.	F13	26
Târgoviște, Rom.	E12	26
Târgu Bujor, Rom.	D14	26
Târgu Frumos, Rom.	B14	26
Târgu Jiu, Rom.	D10	26
Târgu Mureș, Rom.	C11	26
Târgu-Neamț, Rom.	B13	26
Târgu Ocna, Rom.	C13	26
Târgu Secuiesc, Rom.	D12	26
Tarifa, Spain	H5	20
Tarifa, Punta de, c., Spain	H5	20
Tarija, Bol.	D4	90
Tarikere, India	E2	53
Tarim, stm., China	F14	32
Tarim Pendi, bas., China	F12	30
Taritatu, stm., Indon.	F10	44
Tarkastad, S. Afr.	G8	70
Tarkio, Mo., U.S.	D2	120
Tarkio, stm., U.S.	D2	120
Tarko-Sale, Russia	B13	32
Tarkwa, Ghana	H4	64
Tarlac, Phil.	C3	52
Tarm, Den.	I3	8
Tarma, Peru	F2	84
Tarn, state, Fr.	F8	18
Tarn, stm., Fr.	F7	18
Tärnaby, Swe.	D6	8
Tarnak, stm., Afg.	B1	54
Târnava Mare, stm., Rom.	C11	26
Târnăveni, Rom.	C11	26
Tarn-et-Garonne, state, Fr.	F7	18
Tarnobrzeg, Pol.	F17	16
Tarnobrzeg, state, Pol.	F17	16
Tarnogród, Pol.	F18	16
Târnova, Mol.	A14	26
Tarnów, Pol.	G16	16
Tarnów, state, Pol.	G16	16
Tarnowskie Góry, Pol.	F14	16
Taro, Sol. Is.	d7	79b
Taro, stm., Italy	F7	22
Taron, Pap. N. Gui.	a5	79a
Tarong, Austl.	F8	76
Taroom, Austl.	E7	76
Taroudannt, Mor.	C3	64
Ta Roun, Co, mtn., Viet.	D8	48
Tarpon Springs, Fl., U.S.	H3	116
Tarquinia, Italy	H8	22
Tarra, stm., S.A.	C5	86
Tarrafal, C.V.	k10	65a
Tarragona, Spain	C12	20
Tarragona, co., Spain	D11	20
Tarraleah, Austl.	o13	77a
Tarrasa *see* Terrassa, Spain	C13	20
Tàrrega, Spain	C12	20
Tárrega *see* Tàrrega, Spain	C12	20
Tarsus, Tur.	B5	58
Tartagal, Arg.	D4	90
Tartu, Est.	G12	8
Ţarţūs, Syria	D6	58
Ţarţūs, state, Syria	D7	58
Tarum, stm., Indon.	G5	50
Tarumirim, Braz.	J5	88
Tarumizu, Japan	H3	40
Tarutao, Ko, i., Thai.	I4	48
Tarutao National Park, p.o.i., Thai.	I4	48
Tarutino, Russia	E19	10
Tarutung, Indon.	B1	50
Tarvisio, Italy	D10	22
Tarzan, Tx., U.S.	B6	130
Taşağıl, Tur.	B2	58
Tasāwah, Libya	B2	62
Tasböget, Kaz.	F11	32
Taseeva, stm., Russia	C16	32
Taseevo, Russia	C17	32
Taseko Lakes, l., B.C., Can.	E7	138
Taseko Mountain, mtn., B.C., Can.	E7	138
Tāsgaon, India	C2	53
Tashi Gang Dzong, Bhu.	E13	54
Ţashk, Daryācheh-ye, l., Iran	D7	56
Tasikmalaya, Indon.	G5	50
Tåsinge, i., Den.	B6	16
Taškent, Uzb.	F11	32
Taškepri, Turkmen.	B9	56
Taš-Kumyr, Kyrg.	F12	32
Tasman Basin, unds.	N18	142
Tasman Bay, b., N.Z.	E5	80
Tasmania, state, Austl.	n13	77a
Tasmania, i., Austl.	o13	77a
Tasman Peninsula, pen., Austl.	o13	77a
Tasman Sea, s., Oc.	G7	72
Tășnad, Rom.	B9	26
Tassialouc, Lac, l., Qc., Can.	D16	106
Taštagol, Russia	D15	32
Tastiota, Mex.	A3	100
Tata, Hung.	B5	26
Tata, Mor.	D3	64
Tatabánya, Hung.	B5	26
Tatarbunary, Ukr.	D16	26
Tatarija, state, Russia	C8	32
Tatarinka, Russia	E16	10
Tatarsk, Russia	C13	32
Tatarskij proliv, strt., Russia	G17	34
Tatarskoe-Maklakovo, Russia	I21	8
Tatarstan see Tatarija, state, Russia	C8	32
Tatar Strait see Tatarskij proliv, strt., Russia	G17	34
Tate, Ga., U.S.	B1	116
Tate, stm., Austl.	A4	76
Tateyama, Japan	E12	40
Tate-yama, vol., Japan	C10	40
Tathlina Lake, l., N.T., Can.	C7	106
Tatlayoko Lake, B.C., Can.	E6	138
Tatlayoko Lake, l., B.C., Can.	E6	138
Tatlow, Mount, mtn., B.C., Can.	E7	138
Tatnam, Cape, c., Mb., Can.	D12	106
Tatranský Narodny Park, p.o.i., Slov.	G15	16
Tatrzański Park Narodowy, p.o.i., Pol.	G15	16
Tatsuno, Japan	E7	40
Tatsuno, Japan	D10	40
Tatuí, Braz.	L1	88
Tatum, N.M., U.S.	H5	128
Tatum, Tx., U.S.	E4	122
Tat'ung *see* Datong, China	A5	42
Tatvan, Tur.	B5	56
Tau, Am. Sam.	h13	79c
Tau, Nor.	G1	8
Tau, i., Am. Sam.	h13	79c
Tauá, Braz.	C5	88
Taubaté, Braz.	L3	88
Tauberbischofsheim, Ger.	G5	16
Taujskaja guba, b., Russia	E18	34
Taumarunui, N.Z.	D6	80
Taumaturgo, Braz.	E3	84
Taum Sauk Mountain, mtn., Mo., U.S.	G7	120
Taungbon, Mya.	E3	48
Taungdwingyi, Mya.	B2	48
Taunggyi, Mya.	B3	48
Taungnyo Range, mts., Mya.	E3	48
Taungup, Mya.	C2	48
Taungup Pass, p., Mya.	C2	48
Taunsa, Pak.	C3	54
Taunton, Eng., U.K.	J9	12
Taunton, Ma., U.S.	C14	114
Taupo, N.Z.	D6	80
Taupo, Lake, l., N.Z.	D7	80
Tauragė, Lith.	E5	10
Tauranga, N.Z.	C7	80
Taurianova, Italy	F9	24
Taurisano, Italy	E12	24
Tauroa Point, c., N.Z.	B5	80
Taurus Mountains see Toros Dağları, mts., Tur.	A3	58
Taūshyq, Kaz.	F8	32
Tautira, Fr. Poly.	v23	78h
Tavares, Braz.	D7	88
Tavas, Tur.	F12	28
Tavastehus *see* Hämeenlinna, Fin.	F10	8
Tavda, Russia	C11	32
Tavda, stm., Russia	C11	32
Tavernes de la Valldigna, Spain	E10	20
Tavernier, Fl., U.S.	K5	116
Taveuni, i., Fiji	p20	79e
Taviano, Italy	E11	24
Tavira, Port.	G3	20
Tavistock, On., Can.	E9	112
Tavistock, Eng., U.K.	K8	12
Tavolara, Isola, i., Italy	D3	24
Tavoliere, reg., Italy	C9	24
Tavor, Har, mtn., Isr.	F6	58
Tavoy Point, c., Mya.	F3	48
Tavşanlı, Tur.	D12	28
Tavua, Fiji	p18	79e
Tawaeli, Indon.	D11	50
Tawakoni, Lake, res., Tx., U.S.	E2	122
Tawas City, Mi., U.S.	D6	112
Tawau, Malay.	A10	50
Tawîla, Gezira, is., Egypt	K4	58
Tawitawi Group, is., Phil.	H3	52
Tawitawi Island, i., Phil.	H2	52
Ţawkar, Sudan	D7	62
Taxco de Alarcón, Mex.	F8	100
Taxkorgan Tajik Zizhixian, China	B12	56
Tay, stm., Scot., U.K.	E9	12
Tay, Firth of, b., Scot., U.K.	E9	12
Tay, Loch, l., Scot., U.K.	E8	12
Tayabamba, Peru	E2	84
Tayabas Bay, b., Phil.	D3	52
Tayan, Indon.	C7	50
Taylor, Az., U.S.	I6	132
Taylor, Ne., U.S.	F13	126
Taylor, Tx., U.S.	D10	130
Taylor, Mount, mtn., N.M., U.S.	H9	132
Taylors, S.C., U.S.	B3	116
Taylorsville, Ky., U.S.	F12	120
Taylorsville, Ms., U.S.	F9	122
Taylorsville, N.C., U.S.	I4	114
Taylorville, Il., U.S.	E8	120
Taymā', Sau. Ar.	K9	58
Taymouth, N.B., Can.	D10	110
Taymyr Peninsula see Tajmyr, poluostrov, pen., Russia	B7	34
Tay Ninh, Viet.	G8	48
Taytay, Phil.	E2	52
Tayu, Indon.	G7	50
Taz, stm., Russia	A14	32
Taza, Mor.	C4	64
Tazewell, Tn., U.S.	H2	114
Tazewell, Va., U.S.	G4	114
Tazin, stm., Can.	C8	106
Tazin Lake, l., Sk., Can.	D9	106
Tazovskaja guba, b., Russia	A13	32
Tazovskij, Russia	A13	32
Tazovskij poluostrov, pen., Russia	C4	34
Tbessa, Alg.	B6	64
Tbilisi, Geor.	F6	32
Tchaourou, Benin	H5	64
Tchentlo Lake, l., B.C., Can.	A5	138
Tchesinkut Lake, l., B.C., Can.	B5	138
Tchibanga, Gabon	E2	66
Tcho-kiang see Zhejiang, state, China	G8	42
Tchollíré, Cam.	C2	66
Tchula, Ms., U.S.	D8	122
Tczew, Pol.	B14	16
Té, stm., Camb.	F8	48
Teá, stm., Braz.	H9	86
Teaca, Rom.	C11	26
Teaehoa, c., Fr. Poly.	s18	78g
Teague, Tx., U.S.	F2	122
Teahupoo, Fr. Poly.	w22	78h
Te Anau, Lake, l., N.Z.	G2	80
Teapa, Mex.	G12	100
Te Awamutu, N.Z.	C6	80
Teba, Spain	H5	20
Tebakang, Malay.	C7	50
Tebicuary, stm., Para.	C9	92
Tebicuary-mí, stm., Para.	C9	92
Tebingtinggi, Indon.	B1	50
Tebingtinggi, Indon.	E3	50
Tebingtinggi, Pulau, i., Indon.	C3	50
Tébourba, Tun.	H3	24
Téboursouk, Tun.	H3	24
Tecalitlán, Mex.	F7	100
Tecate, Mex.	K9	134
Techirghiol, Rom.	E15	26
Techlé, W. Sah.	E2	64
Techou *see* Dezhou, China	C7	42
Tecka, Arg.	H2	90
Tecka, stm., Arg.	H2	90
Tecomán, Mex.	F7	100
Tecopa, Ca., U.S.	H9	134
Tecpan de Galeana, Mex.	G8	100
Tecuala, Mex.	D6	100
Tecuci, Rom.	D14	26
Tecumseh, Ok., U.S.	B2	122
Tedžen, Turkmen.	B9	56
Tedžen (Harīrūd), stm., Asia	B9	56
Teec Nos Pos, Az., U.S.	G7	132
Teeli, Russia	D16	32
Tees, stm., Eng., U.K.	G11	12
Teeswater, On., Can.	D8	112
Tefé, Braz.	D5	84
Tefé, stm., Braz.	D4	84
Tefenni, Tur.	F12	28
Tegal, Indon.	G6	50
Tégama, reg., Niger	F6	64
Tegéa, sci., Grc.	F5	28
Tegineneng, Indon.	F4	50
Tegucigalpa, Hond.	E4	102
Tegul'det, Russia	C15	32
Tehachapi, Ca., U.S.	H7	134
Tehachapi Pass, p., Ca., U.S.	H7	134
Tehek Lake, l., Nu., Can.	C12	106
Tehrān (Teheran), Iran	B7	56
Tehrathum, Nepal	E11	54
Tehuacán, Mex.	F10	100
Tehuantepec, Golfo de, b., Mex.	H11	100
Tehuantepec, Gulf of see Tehuantepec, Golfo de, b., Mex.	H11	100
Tehuantepec, Isthmus of see Tehuantepec, Istmo de, isth., Mex.	G11	100
Tehuantepec, Istmo de, isth., Mex.	G11	100
Teignmouth, Eng., U.K.	K9	12
Teixeira, Braz.	D7	88
Teixeira Pinto, Gui.-B.	G1	64
Tejakula, Indon.	H9	50
Tejkovo, Russia	H19	8
Tejon Pass, p., Ca., U.S.	I7	134
Tejupilco de Hidalgo, Mex.	F8	100
Tekamah, Ne., U.S.	C1	120
Tekapo, Lake, l., N.Z.	F4	80
Tekax, Mex.	B3	102
Teke, Tur.	B12	28
Teke Burnu, c., Tur.	E9	28
Tekeli, Kaz.	F13	32
Tekezē (Satīt), stm., Afr.	E7	62
Tekirdağ, Tur.	C10	28
Tekirdağ, state, Tur.	B10	28
Tekkali, India	B7	53
Tekoa, Wa., U.S.	C9	136
Tekonsha, Mi., U.S.	B1	114
Te Kuiti, N.Z.	D6	80
Tel, stm., India	A6	53
Tela, Hond.	E4	102
Telaopengsha Shan, mtn., China	C11	54
Telavi, Geor.	F7	32
Tel Aviv-Jaffa *see* Tel Aviv-Yafo, Isr.	F5	58
Tel Aviv-Yafo, Isr.	F5	58
Telč, Czech Rep.	G11	16
Teleckoe, ozero, l., Russia	D15	32
Telefomin, Pap. N. Gui.	b3	79a
Telegraph Creek, B.C., Can.	D4	106
Telêmaco Borba, Braz.	B12	92
Telemark, state, Nor.	G3	8
Telembí, stm., Col.	G2	86
Telén, Arg.	H5	92
Telen, stm., Indon.	C10	50
Telenești, Mol.	B15	26
Teleno, mtn., Spain	B4	20
Teleorman, state, Rom.	E12	26
Teleorman, stm., Rom.	E12	26
Telescope Point, c., Gren.	q10	105e
Telese, Italy	C8	24
Telford, Eng., U.K.	I10	12
Télimélé, Gui.	G2	64
Telire, stm., C.R.	H6	102
Teljo, Jabal, mtn., Sudan	E5	62
Telkwa, B.C., Can.	B3	138
Tell Basta, hist., Egypt	H2	58
Tell City, In., U.S.	G11	120
Tell El-Amarna, hist., Egypt	K1	58
Tellel Rub, hist., Egypt	H2	58
Teller, Ak., U.S.	C6	140
Tellicherry, India	F2	53
Tellier, Arg.	I3	90
Tello, Col.	F4	86
Telluride, Co., U.S.	F9	132
Tel Megiddo, sci., Isr.	F6	58
Telmen nuur, l., Mong.	B4	36
Teloloapan, Mex.	F8	100
Telos see Tílos, i., Grc.	G10	28
Telsen, Arg.	H3	90
Telšiai, Lith.	E5	10
Teltow, Ger.	D9	16
Telukbayur, Indon.	D2	50
Telukbayur, Indon.	B10	50
Telukdalem, Indon.	L3	48
Teluk Intan, Malay.	K5	48
Tema, Ghana	H5	64
Temagami, Lake, l., On., Can.	A9	112
Temaju, Pulau, i., Indon.	C6	50
Te Manga, mtn., Cook Is.	a26	78j
Temangga, Indon.	C7	50
Tematangi, at., Fr. Poly.	F12	72
Temax, Mex.	B3	102
Tembeling, stm., Malay.	J6	48
Tembenči, stm., Russia	A17	32
Tembesi, stm., Indon.	D3	50
Tembilahan, Indon.	D3	50
Temblador, Ven.	C10	86
Temblor Range, mts., Ca., U.S.	H6	134
Teme, stm., Eng., U.K.	I10	12
Temecula, Ca., U.S.	J8	134
Temelli, Tur.	D15	28
Temengor, Tasik, res., Malay.	J5	48
Temetiu, mtn., Fr. Poly.	s18	78g
Temir, Kaz.	E9	32
Temirtau, Kaz.	D12	32
Témiscaming, Qc., Can.	B10	112
Témiscamingue, Lac (Timiskaming, Lake), res., Can.	B10	112
Témiscouata, Lac, l., Qc., Can.	C7	110
Tëmkino, Russia	E17	10
Temora, Austl.	J6	76
Temosachic, Mex.	A5	100
Tempe, Az., U.S.	J5	132
Tempe, Danau, l., Indon.	F12	50
Tempino, Indon.	D3	50
Tempio Pausania, Italy	D2	24
Temple, Tx., U.S.	C10	130
Templi, Valle dei, sci., Italy	G7	24
Templin, Ger.	C9	16
Tempoal, stm., Mex.	E9	100
Tempoal de Sánchez, Mex.	E9	100
Tempy, Russia	D20	10
Temuco, Chile	G2	90
Temwen, i., Micron.	m12	78d
Tena, Ec.	H3	86
Tenabo, Mex.	B2	102
Tenaha, Tx., U.S.	F4	122
Tena Kourou, mtn., Burkina	G4	64
Tenāli, India	C5	53
Tenasserim, Mya.	F4	48
Tendaho, Eth.	E8	62
Tende, Col de, p., Eur.	E13	18
Ten Degree Channel, strt., India	G7	46
Tendō, Japan	A13	40
Ténenkou, Mali	G3	64
Ténéré, des., Niger	F7	64
Ténès, Alg.	H12	20
Ténès, Cap, c., Alg.	H12	20
Teng, stm., Mya.	B3	48
Tengah, Kepulauan, is., Indon.	G10	50
Tengchong, China	G4	36
Tenggara, Nusa (Lesser Sunda Islands), is., Indon.	G6	44
Tenggara Celebes see Sulawesi Tenggara, state, Indon.	E12	50
Tenggarong, Indon.	D10	50
Tengger Shamo, des., China	D5	36
Tenghilan, Malay.	G1	52
Tengiz köli, l., Kaz.	D11	32
Tengréla, C. Iv.	G3	64
Tengtiao (Na), stm., Asia	A6	48
Tengxian, China	J4	42
Tengxian, China	D7	42
Tenkāsi, India	G3	53
Tenke, D.R.C.	G5	66
Tenkeli, Russia	B17	34
Tenkiller Ferry Lake, res., Ok., U.S.	B4	122
Tenkodogo, Burkina	G4	64
Tennant Creek, Austl.	C6	74
Tennessee, state, U.S.	D10	108
Tennessee, stm., U.S.	A11	122
Tennille, Ga., U.S.	D3	116
Teno, Chile	G2	92
Teno (Tana), stm., Eur.	B12	8
Tenom, Malay.	A9	50
Tenos *see* Tínos, Grc.	F8	28
Tenos see Tínos, i., Grc.	F8	28
Tenosique, Mex.	D2	102
Tenryū, Japan	E10	40
Tenryū, stm., Japan	E10	40
Tensas, stm., La., U.S.	F7	122
Tensed, Id., U.S.	C10	136
Ten Sleep, Wy., U.S.	C5	126
Tenterfield, Austl.	G8	76
Ten Thousand Islands, is., Fl., U.S.	K4	116
Tentolomatinan, Gunung, mtn., Indon.	E7	44
Teocaltiche, Mex.	E7	100
Teodelina, Arg.	G7	92
Teófilo Otoni, Braz.	I5	88
Teo Lakes, l., Sk., Can.	C4	124
Teotihuacán, sci., Mex.	F9	100
Tepa, Indon.	G8	44
Tepalcatepec, Mex.	F7	100
Tepebaşı, Tur.	B3	58
Tepehuanes, Mex.	C6	100
Tepehuanes, stm., Mex.	C6	100
Tepeji de Ocampo, Mex.	F9	100
Tepelenë, Alb.	D13	24
Tepic, Mex.	E6	100
Teplice, Czech Rep.	F9	16
Tepoca, Bahía de, b., Mex.	F6	98
Tepoca, Punta, c., Mex.	G6	98
Ter, stm., Spain	B14	20
Téra, Niger	G5	64
Tera, stm., Spain	C4	20
Teradomari, Japan	B11	40
Teraina, i., Kir.	C11	72
Teramo, Italy	H10	22
Terbuny, Russia	H21	10
Terceira, i., Port.	C3	60
Tercero, stm., Arg.	F6	92
Terdal, India	C2	53
Terek, stm., Russia	G18	6
Terempa, Indon.	B5	50
Terengganu, state, Malay.	J6	48
Terengganu, stm., Malay.	J6	48
Terenos, Braz.	D6	90
Teresina, Braz.	C4	88
Teresópolis, Braz.	L4	88
Terespol, Pol.	D19	16
Terevaka, Cerro, mtn., Chile	e29	78l
Tergüün Bogd uul, mtn., Mong.	C5	36
Teriang, stm., Malay.	K6	48
Teriberka, Russia	B16	8
Terihi, i., Fr. Poly.	t19	78g
Terlingua, Tx., U.S.	E4	130
Terlingua Creek, stm., Tx., U.S.	E4	130
Termas del Arapey, Ur.	E9	92
Termas de Río Hondo, Arg.	C5	92
Termez, Uzb.	B10	56
Termini Imerese, Italy	G7	24
Termini Imerese, Golfo di, b., Italy	F7	24
Terminillo, Monte, mtn., Italy	H9	22
Términos, Laguna de, b., Mex.	C2	102
Termoli, Italy	H11	22
Termonde *see* Dendermonde, Bel.	C12	14
Ternej, Russia	B12	38
Terneuzen, Neth.	C12	14
Terni, Italy	H9	22
Ternitz, Aus.	C12	22
Ternopil', Ukr.	F14	6
Terpenija, mys, c., Russia	G17	34
Terpenija, zaliv, b., Russia	G17	34
Terra Alta, W.V., U.S.	E6	114
Terra Bella, Ca., U.S.	H6	134
Terrace, B.C., Can.	B2	138
Terracina, Italy	C7	24
Terra Cotta Army (Qinshihuang Mausoleum), sci., China	D3	42
Terral, Ok., U.S.	H11	128
Terralba, Italy	E2	24
Terra Santa, Braz.	D6	84
Terrassa, Spain	C13	20
Terrebonne Bay, b., La., U.S.	H8	122
Terre-de-Bas, Guad.	i5	105c
Terre-de-Haut, Guad.	i5	105c
Terre-de-Haut, i., Guad.	i5	105c
Terre Haute, In., U.S.	E10	120
Terrell, Tx., U.S.	E2	122
Terre-Neuve see Newfoundland and Labrador, state, Can.	i23	107a
Territoire du Yukon see Yukon, state, Can.	B3	106
Territoires du Nord-Ouest see Northwest Territories, state, Can.	C6	106
Terry, Ms., U.S.	E8	122
Terry, Mt., U.S.	A7	126
Terschelling, i., Neth.	A14	14
Terskej-Alatau, hrebet, mts., Kyrg.	F13	32
Teruel, Col.	F4	86
Teruel, Spain	D9	20
Teruel, co., Spain	D10	20
Terujak, Indon.	J3	48
Tervola, Fin.	C11	8

Terzaghi Dam – Torna I • 57

Name	Map Ref.	Page
Terzaghi Dam, dam, B.C., Can.	F8	138
Tes, stm., Asia	D16	32
Tescott, Ks., U.S.	B11	128
Teseney, Erit.	D7	62
Teshekpuk Lake, l., Ak., U.S.	B9	140
Teshio, Japan	B14	38
Teshio, stm., Japan	B15	38
Teslin, Yk., Can.	C4	106
Teslin, stm., Can.	C4	106
Teslin Lake, l., Can.	C4	106
Tësovo, Russia	E17	10
Tësovo-Netyl'skij, Russia	B13	10
Tësovskij, Russia	B13	10
Tessalit, Mali	E5	64
Tessaoua, Niger	G6	64
Testa, Capo, c., Italy	C3	24
Testour, Tun.	H3	24
Tetachuck Lake, res., B.C., Can.	C4	138
Tete, Moz.	D5	68
Tête Jaune Cache, B.C., Can.	D11	138
Tetepare Island, i., Sol. Is.	e7	79b
Teterow, Ger.	C8	16
Tetica, mtn., Spain	G8	20
Teton, Id., U.S.	G15	136
Teton, stm., Id., U.S.	G15	136
Teton, stm., Mt., U.S.	C15	136
Tetonia, Id., U.S.	G15	136
Teton Range, mts., Wy., U.S.	G16	136
Tetouan, Mor.	B4	64
Tetovo, Mac.	A4	28
Tetufera, Mont, mtn., Fr. Poly.	v22	78h
Teuco, stm., Arg.	D4	90
Teulada, Italy	F2	24
Teulada, Capo, c., Italy	F2	24
Teulon, Mb., Can.	D16	124
Teutoburger Wald, hills, Ger.	D4	16
Teuva, Fin.	E9	8
Tevere (Tiber), stm., Italy	H9	22
Teverya, Isr.	F6	58
Te Waewae Bay, b., N.Z.	H2	80
Tewah, Indon.	D8	50
Tewantin-Noosa, Austl.	F9	76
Tewkesbury, Eng., U.K.	I11	12
Texada Island, i., B.C., Can.	G6	138
Texana, Lake, res., Tx., U.S.	F11	130
Texarkana, Ar., U.S.	D4	122
Texarkana, Tx., U.S.	D4	122
Texas, Austl.	G8	76
Texas, state, U.S.	E8	108
Texas City, Tx., U.S.	H4	122
Texel, i., Neth.	A13	14
Texhoma, Ok., U.S.	E7	128
Texico, N.M., U.S.	G5	128
Texoma, Lake, res., U.S.	H11	128
Teyateyaneng, Leso.	F8	70
Teyvareh, Afg.	C9	56
Teziutlán, Mex.	F10	100
Tezpur, India	E14	54
Tezzeron Lake, l., B.C., Can.	B6	138
Tha, stm., Laos	B5	48
Tha-anne, stm., Nu., Can.	C11	106
Thabana-Ntlenyana, mtn., Leso.	F9	70
Thabaung, Mya.	D2	48
Thabazimbi, S. Afr.	D8	70
Thabyu, Mya.	E4	48
Thagyettaw, Mya.	F3	48
Thai Binh, Viet.	B8	48
Thailand, ctry., Asia	E5	48
Thailand, Gulf of, b., Asia	G5	48
Thai Nguyen, Viet.	B7	48
Thak, Pak.	C3	54
Thal, Pak.	B3	54
Thala, Tun.	I2	24
Thal Desert, des., Pak.	C3	54
Thalfang, Ger.	G2	16
Tha Li, Thai.	D5	48
Thalia, Tx., U.S.	H9	128
Thālith, Ash-Shallāl ath- (Third Cataract), wtfl., Sudan	D6	62
Thalwil, Switz.	C5	22
Thames, N.Z.	C6	80
Thames, stm., On., Can.	F8	112
Thames, stm., Eng., U.K.	J13	12
Thames, Firth of, b., N.Z.	C6	80
Thamesford, On., Can.	E8	112
Thamesville, On., Can.	F7	112
Thāna, India	B1	53
Thandaung, Mya.	C3	48
Thangoo, Austl.	C4	74
Thangool, Austl.	E8	76
Thanh Hoa, Viet.	C7	48
Thanh Pho Ho Chi Minh (Saigon), Viet.	G8	48
Thanjāvūr, India	F4	53
Thann, Fr.	B12	18
Thap Than, stm., Thai.	E6	48
Tharabwin West, Mya.	F4	48
Tharād, India	F3	54
Thar Desert (Great Indian Desert), des., Asia	D3	54
Thargomindah, Austl.	F5	76
Tharrawaddy, Mya.	D2	48
Tha Sala, Thai.	H4	48
Thásos, Grc.	C7	28
Thásos, i., Grc.	C7	28
Thásos, sci., Grc.	C7	28
Thaton, Mya.	D3	48
Tha Tum, Thai.	E6	48
Thau, Bassin de, l., Fr.	F9	18
Thaungyin (Moei), stm., Asia	D3	48
Thaya (Dyje), stm., Eur.	H12	16
Thayawthadangyi Kyun, i., Mya.	F3	48
Thayer, Ks., U.S.	G2	120
Thayer, Mo., U.S.	H6	120
Thayetchaung, Mya.	F4	48
Thayetmyo, Mya.	C2	48
Thazi, Mya.	B3	48
Thebes see Thíva, Grc.	E6	28
The Bottom, Neth. Ant.	B1	105a
The Cheviot, mtn., Eng., U.K.	F10	12
The Dalles, Or., U.S.	E5	136
Thedford, Ne., U.S.	E12	126
The Father see Ulawun, Mount, vol., Pap. N. Gui.	b5	79a
The Fens, reg., Eng., U.K.	I12	12
The Fishing Lakes, l., Sk., Can.	D10	124
The Granites, hill, Austl.	D6	74
The Hague see 's-Gravenhage, Neth.	B12	14
The Heads, c., Or., U.S.	H2	136
Theinkun, Mya.	G4	48
The Lakes National Park, p.o.i., Austl.	L6	76
The Little Minch, strt., Scot., U.K.	D6	12
Thelon, stm., Can.	C11	106
The Lynd, Austl.	B5	76
The Minch, strt., Scot., U.K.	D6	12
Thenia, Alg.	H14	20
Theodore, Austl.	E8	76
Theodore, Sk., Can.	C10	124
Theodore, Al., U.S.	G10	122
Theodore Roosevelt National Park North Unit, p.o.i., N.D., U.S.	G10	124
Theodore Roosevelt National Park South Unit, p.o.i., N.D., U.S.	G10	124
The Pas, Mb., Can.	E10	106
Thepha, Thai.	I5	48
The Pinnacle, hill, Mo., U.S.	E6	120
The Rand see Witwatersrand, mts., S. Afr.	D8	70
Theresa Creek, stm., Austl.	D6	76
The Rhins, pen., Scot., U.K.	G7	12
Thermaïkós Kólpos (Salonika, Gulf of), b., Grc.	C6	28
Thermopolis, Wy., U.S.	D4	126
Thermopylae see Thermopýles, hist., Grc.	E5	28
Thermopýles (Thermopylae), hist., Grc.	E5	28
The Rock, Austl.	J6	76
The Rockies, mtn., Wa., U.S.	D4	136
The Rope, clf., Pit.	c28	78k
Thesiger Bay, b., N.T., Can.	B15	140
The Slot see New Georgia Sound, strt., Sol. Is.	e8	79b
Thessalía, state, Grc.	D5	28
Thessalía, hist. reg., Grc.	D5	28
Thessalon, On., Can.	B6	112
Thessaloníki (Salonika), Grc.	C6	28
Thessaly see Thessalía, hist. reg., Grc.	D5	28
Thetford, Eng., U.K.	I13	12
Thetford Mines, Qc., Can.	D5	110
Theunissen, S. Afr.	F8	70
The Valley, Anguilla	A1	105a
The Village, Ok., U.S.	F11	128
The Wash, b., Eng., U.K.	I13	12
The Weald, reg., Eng., U.K.	J13	12
Thibodaux, La., U.S.	H8	122
Thief Lake, l., Mn., U.S.	C3	118
Thief River Falls, Mn., U.S.	C2	118
Thiene, Italy	E8	22
Thiers, Fr.	D9	18
Thiès, Sen.	G1	64
Thika, Kenya	E7	66
Thimphu, Bhu.	E12	54
Thingvallavatn, l., Ice.	k29	8a
Thingvellir, Ice.	k29	8a
Thingvellir Nasjonalpark, p.o.i., Ice.	k29	8a
Thio, N. Cal.	m16	79d
Thionville, Fr.	E15	14
Thíra, Grc.	G8	28
Thíra (Santorini), i., Grc.	G8	28
Third Cataract see Thālith, Ash-Shallāl ath-, wtfl., Sudan	D6	62
Thiruvananthapuram (Trivandrum), India	G3	53
Thiruvārūr, India	F4	53
Thistilfjörđur, b., Ice.	j32	8a
Thíva, Grc.	E6	28
Thiviers, Fr.	D6	18
Thjórsá, stm., Ice.	k30	8a
Thohoyandou, S. Afr.	C10	70
Thoi Binh, Viet.	H7	48
Thomas, Ok., U.S.	F10	128
Thomas, W.V., U.S.	E6	114
Thomaston, Al., U.S.	E11	122
Thomaston, Ga., U.S.	D1	116
Thomaston, Me., U.S.	F7	110
Thomasville, Ga., U.S.	F2	116
Thomasville, N.C., U.S.	I5	114
Thompson, Mb., Can.	D11	106
Thompson, Ia., U.S.	H5	118
Thompson, N.D., U.S.	D1	118
Thompson, stm., B.C., Can.	F9	138
Thompson, stm., U.S.	E4	120
Thompson Falls, Mt., U.S.	C11	136
Thompson Peak, mtn., Ca., U.S.	B3	134
Thomsen, stm., N.T., Can.	B16	140
Thomson, Ga., U.S.	C3	116
Thomson, Il., U.S.	C7	120
Thomson, stm., Austl.	E4	76
Thongwa, Mya.	D3	48
Thonon-les-Bains, Fr.	C12	18
Thonotosassa, Fl., U.S.	H3	116
Thonze, Mya.	D2	48
Thorhild, Ab., Can.	B17	138
Thórisvatn, l., Ice.	k30	8a
Thorlákshöfn, Ice.	l29	8a
Thornaby-on-Tees, Eng., U.K.	G11	12
Thornbury, On., Can.	D9	112
Thorndale, Tx., U.S.	D10	130
Thornton, Co., U.S.	B4	128
Thornton, Tx., U.S.	F2	122
Thorntonville, Tx., U.S.	C4	130
Thorp, Wi., U.S.	G8	118
Thorsby, Ab., Can.	C16	138
Thorshavn see Tórshavn, Far. Is.	n34	8b
Thórshöfn, Ice.	j32	8a
Thouars, Fr.	H8	14
Thoune see Thun, Switz.	D4	22
Thousand Lake Mountain, mtn., Ut., U.S.	E5	132
Thousand Oaks, Ca., U.S.	I7	134
Thousand Ships Bay, b., Sol. Is.	e8	79b
Thousand Springs Creek, stm., U.S.	B2	132
Thrace, hist. reg., Eur.	H13	26
Thrakikó Pélagos, s., Grc.	C8	28
Three Forks, Mt., U.S.	E15	136
Three Gorges Dam, dam, China	F4	42
Three Hills, Ab., Can.	E17	138
Three Hummock Island, i., Austl.	n12	77a
Three Kings Islands, is., N.Z.	B5	80
Three Mile Plains, N.S., Can.	F12	110
Three Points, Cape, c., Ghana	I4	64
Three Rivers, Mi., U.S.	G4	112
Three Rivers, Tx., U.S.	F9	130
Three Sisters, mtn., Or., U.S.	F5	136
Three Sisters Islands, is., Sol. Is.	f10	79b
Three Springs, Austl.	E3	74
Thrissur see Trichūr, India	F3	53
Throssel, Lake, l., Austl.	E4	74
Thu, Cu Lao, i., Viet.	G9	48
Thuan Chau, Viet.	B6	48
Thu Dau Mot, Viet.	G8	48
Thuin, Bel.	D13	14
Thule (Qaanaaq), Grnld.	B12	141
Thun, Switz.	D4	22
Thun Chang, Thai.	C5	48
Thunder Bay, On., Can.	C9	118
Thunder Bay, b., On., Can.	C9	118
Thunderbird, Lake, res., Ok., U.S.	F11	128
Thunderbolt, Ga., U.S.	D4	116
Thunder Butte Creek, stm., S.D., U.S.	B10	126
Thunder Creek, stm., Sk., Can.	D7	124
Thuner See, l., Switz.	D4	22
Thung Salaeng Luang National Park, p.o.i., Thai.	D5	48
Thung Wa, Thai.	I4	48
Thüringen, state, Ger.	F7	16
Thüringer Wald, mts., Ger.	F6	16
Thuringia see Thüringen, state, Ger.	F7	16
Thurles, Ire.	I5	12
Thurmont, Md., U.S.	E8	114
Thursday Island, Austl.	B8	74
Thurso, Scot., U.K.	C9	12
Thurston Island, i., Ant.	C31	81
Thusis, Switz.	D6	22
Thylungra, Austl.	F4	76
Thyolo, Mwi.	D5	68
Thysville see Mbanza-Ngungu, D.R.C.	F3	66
Tiachiv, Ukr.	A10	26
Tianchang, China	E8	42
Tiandeng, China	J2	42
Tiandong, China	J2	42
Tian'e, China	I2	42
Tiangang, China	C7	38
Tianguá, Braz.	B5	88
Tianjin (Tientsin), China	B7	42
Tianjin, state, China	B7	42
Tianjun, China	D4	36
Tianlin, China	I2	42
Tian Ling, mtn., China	B8	38
Tianmen, China	F5	42
Tianqiaoling, China	C8	38
Tianshifu, China	D6	38
Tianshui, China	D1	42
Tiantai, China	G9	42
Tiantang, China	J4	42
Tianwangsi, China	F8	42
Tianyang, China	J2	42
Tianzhen, China	A6	42
Tianzhu, China	D5	36
Tianzhu, China	H3	42
Tiarei, Fr. Poly.	v22	78h
Tiaro, Austl.	E9	76
Tiassalé, C. Iv.	H4	64
Ti'avea, Samoa	g12	79c
Tibaji, stm., Braz.	A12	92
Tibal-og, Phil.	G5	52
Tibasti, Sarīr, des., Libya	C3	62
Tibati, Cam.	C2	66
Tibbie, Al., U.S.	F10	122
Tiber see Tevere, stm., Italy	H9	22
Tiberias, Lake see Kinneret, Yam, l., Isr.	F6	58
Tibesti, mts., Afr.	C3	62
Tibet see Xizang, state, China	B5	46
Tibet, Plateau of see Qing Zang Gaoyuan, plat., China	B6	46
Tiblawan, Phil.	G6	52
Tibnīn, Leb.	E6	58
Tibooburra, Austl.	G4	76
Tiburón, Cabo, c.	C3	86
Tiburón, Isla, i., Mex.	G6	98
Tiča, Jazovir, res., Blg.	F13	26
Ticao Island, i., Phil.	D4	52
Tîchît, Maur.	F3	64
Ticino, stm., Eur.	D14	18
Tickfaw, stm., U.S.	G8	122
Ticonderoga, N.Y., U.S.	G3	110
Ticul, Mex.	B3	102
Tidioute, Pa., U.S.	C6	114
Tidiquin, Jbel, mtn., Mor.	C4	64
Tidjikja, Maur.	F2	64
Tiébissou, C. Iv.	H3	64
T'iehling see Tieling, China	C5	38
Tiel, Neth.	C14	14
Tieli, China	B10	36
Tieling, China	C5	38
Tielt, Bel.	C12	14
Tiémé, C. Iv.	H3	64
T'ienching see Tianjin, China	B7	42
Tien Giang see Mekong, stm., Asia	F9	46
Tien Shan, mts., Asia	F13	32
T'ienshui see Tianshui, China	D1	42
Tientsin see Tianjin, China	B7	42
Tientsin see Tianjin, state, China	B7	42
Tien Yen, Viet.	B8	48
Tie Plant, Ms., U.S.	D9	122
Tierp, Swe.	F7	8
Tierra Amarilla, Chile	C2	92
Tierra Blanca, Mex.	F10	100
Tierra Blanca, Mex.	G3	130
Tierra Blanca Creek, stm., U.S.	G6	128
Tierra de Campos, reg., Spain	C5	20
Tierra del Fuego, state, Arg.	J3	90
Tierra del Fuego, i., S.A.	J3	90
Tiétar, stm., Spain	E5	20
Tietê, Braz.	L2	88
Tietê, stm., Braz.	D6	90
Tiéti, N. Cal.	m15	79d
Tiffany Mountain, mtn., Wa., U.S.	B7	136
Tiffin, Oh., U.S.	C2	114
Tifton, Ga., U.S.	E2	116
Tiga, Île, i., N. Cal.	m16	79d
Tigalda Island, i., Ak., U.S.	F7	140
Tigapuluh, Pegunungan, mts., Indon.	D3	50
Tighina, Mol.	C16	26
Tigil', Russia	E20	34
Tignall, Ga., U.S.	C3	116
Tignish, P.E., Can.	D12	110
Tigoda, stm., Russia	A14	10
Tigre, Col.	F7	86
Tigre, stm., Peru	D2	84
Tigre, stm., Ven.	C10	86
Tigris (Dicle) (Dijlah), stm., Asia	C5	56
Tiguentourine, Alg.	D6	64
Tihany, hist., Hung.	C4	26
Tihert, Alg.	B5	64
Tihon, Russia	G22	8
Tihookeanskij, Russia	C10	38
Tihoreck, Russia	E6	32
Tihua see Ürümqi, China	C2	36
Tihuatlán, Mex.	E10	100
Tihvin, Russia	A16	10
Tijuana, Mex.	K8	134
Tijuana, stm., N.A.	K9	134
Tijucas, Braz.	C13	92
Tijucas do Sul, Braz.	B13	92
Tijuco, stm., Braz.	J1	88
Tikal, sci., Guat.	D3	102
Tikal, Parque Nacional, p.o.i., Guat.	D3	102
Tikrīt, Iraq	C5	56
Tikša, Russia	D15	8
Tikšeozero, ozero, l., Russia	C14	8
Tiksi, Russia	B14	34
Tiladummati Atoll, at., Mald.	h12	46a
Tilburg, Neth.	C14	14
Tilbury, On., Can.	F7	112
Tilcha, Austl.	G3	76
Tilden, Il., U.S.	F8	120
Tilden, Ne., U.S.	E15	126
Tilden, Tx., U.S.	F9	130
Tilhar, India	D7	54
Tilimsen, Alg.	C4	64
Tilin, Mya.	B2	48
Tillabéri, Niger	G5	64
Tilley, Ab., Can.	F19	138
Tillia, Niger	F5	64
Tillmans Corner, Al., U.S.	G10	122
Tillson, N.Y., U.S.	C11	114
Tillsonburg, On., Can.	F9	112
Tílos, i., Grc.	G10	28
Tilpa, Austl.	H5	76
Tilton, N.H., U.S.	G5	110
Tiltonsville, Oh., U.S.	D5	114
Tima, Egypt	L2	58
Timaná, Col.	G3	86
Timanskij krjaž, hills, Russia	B8	32
Timaru, N.Z.	G4	80
Timbalier Bay, b., La., U.S.	H8	122
Timbaúba, Braz.	D8	88
Timbavati Game Reserve, S. Afr.	D10	70
Timbedgha, Maur.	F3	64
Timber Lake, S.D., U.S.	B11	126
Timbiras, Braz.	C4	88
Timbó, Braz.	C13	92
Timbo, Lib.	H3	64
Timbuktu see Tombouctou, Mali	F4	64
Timétrine, Mali	F4	64
Timétrine, mts., Mali	F4	64
Timimoun, Alg.	D5	64
Timirist, Râs, c., Maur.	F1	64
Timirjazevo, Russia	E4	10
Timiș, state, Rom.	D8	26
Timiș (Tamiš), stm., Eur.	D7	26
Timiskaming, Lake (Témiscamingue, Lac), res., Can.	B10	112
Timișoara, Rom.	D8	26
Timmendorfer Strand, Ger.	B7	16
Timmins, On., Can.	F14	106
Timmonsville, S.C., U.S.	B6	116
Timms Hill, mtn., Wi., U.S.	F8	118
Timna'see Mikhrot Timna', hist., Isr.	I5	58
Timok, stm., Eur.	E9	26
Timon, Braz.	C4	88
Timor, i., Asia	G8	44
Timor Sea, s.	K15	142
Timošino, Russia	H21	8
Timotes, Ven.	C6	86
Timpanogos Cave National Monument, p.o.i., Ut., U.S.	C5	132
Timpton, stm., Russia	E14	34
Timšer, Russia	B9	32
Tims Ford Lake, res., Tn., U.S.	B12	122
Tina, stm., S. Afr.	G9	70
Tîna, Khalîg el- (Pelusium Bay), b., Egypt	G3	58
Tinaca Point, c., Phil.	H5	52
Tinambung, Indon.	E11	50
Tinapagee, Austl.	G5	76
Tinaquillo, Ven.	C7	86
Tindivanam, India	E4	53
Tindouf, Alg.	D3	64
Tineba, Pegunungan, mts., Indon.	D12	50
Tineg, stm., Phil.	B3	52
Ting, stm., China	I7	42
Tinggi, Pulau, i., Malay.	K7	48
Tingha, Austl.	G8	76
Tinghert, Ḥamādat (Tinghert, Plateau du), plat., Afr.	D7	64
Tinghert, Plateau du (Tinghert, Ḥamādat), plat., Afr.	D6	64
Tinghsien see Dingxian, China	B6	42
Tinglev, Den.	B5	16
Tingo María, Peru	E2	84
Tingri, China	D11	54
Tingri see Dinggyê, China	D11	54
Tinguiririca, Volcán, vol., Chile	G2	92
Tinharé, Ilha de, i., Braz.	G6	88
Tinh Bien, Viet.	G7	48
Tinian, i., N. Mar. Is.	B5	72
Tinjar, stm., Malay.	B9	50
Tínos, Grc.	F8	28
Tínos, i., Grc.	F8	28
Tinsley, Ms., U.S.	E8	122
Tinsukia, India	C8	46
Tintagel, B.C., Can.	B5	138
Tintina, Arg.	C6	92
Tintinara, Austl.	J3	76
Tio, Erit.	E8	62
Tiobrad Árann see Tipperary, Ire.	I4	12
Tioga, N.D., U.S.	F11	124
Tiojala, Fin.	F10	8
Tioman, Pulau, i., Malay.	K7	48
Tionesta, Pa., U.S.	C6	114
Tipasa, Alg.	H13	20
Tipitapa, Nic.	F4	102
Tippecanoe, stm., In., U.S.	H3	112
Tipperary, Ire.	I4	12
Tipperary, state, Ire.	I5	12
Tipton, Ca., U.S.	G6	134
Tipton, Ia., U.S.	C6	120
Tipton, Mo., U.S.	F5	120
Tipton, Ok., U.S.	G9	128
Tipton, Mount, mtn., Az., U.S.	H2	132
Tiptonville, Tn., U.S.	H8	120
Tip Top Mountain, mtn., On., Can.	F13	106
Tiptūr, India	E3	53
Tiputini, stm., Ec.	H4	86
Tira, Isr.	F5	58
Tīrān, i., Sau. Ar.	K5	58
Tiran, Strait of, strt.	K5	58
Tirana see Tiranë, Alb.	C13	24
Tiranë, Alb.	C13	24
Tirano, Italy	D7	22
Tiraspol, Mol.	C16	26
Tire, Tur.	E10	28
Tiree, i., Scot., U.K.	E6	12
Tirich Mīr, mtn., Pak.	B11	56
Tirna, stm., India	B3	53
Tirodi, India	H7	54
Tirol, state, Aus.	C8	22
Tiros, Braz.	J3	88
Tirso, stm., Italy	E2	24
Tīrthahalli, India	E2	53
Tiruchchirāppalli, India	F4	53
Tiruchengodu, India	F3	53
Tirukkalukkunram, India	E5	53
Tirukkovilūr, India	F4	53
Tiruliai, Lith.	E6	10
Tirunelveli, India	G3	53
Tirupati, India	E4	53
Tiruppattūr, India	E4	53
Tiruppur, India	F3	53
Tirūr, India	F2	53
Tirutturaippūndi, India	F4	53
Tiruvalla, India	G3	53
Tiruvannāmalai, India	E4	53
Tirūvottiyūr, India	E5	53
Tiruvur, India	C5	53
Tisa (Tisza) (Tysa), stm., Eur.	D7	26
Tisaiyanvilai, India	G3	53
Tisdale, Sk., Can.	B9	124
Tishomingo, Ok., U.S.	C2	122
Ṭisīyah, Syria	F7	58
Tiskilwa, Il., U.S.	C8	120
Tisovec, Slov.	H15	16
Tīsta, stm., Asia	F12	54
Tisza (Tisa) (Tysa), stm., Eur.	C7	26
Tiszaföldvár, Hung.	C7	26
Tiszaújváros, Hung.	B7	26
Tiszavasvári, Hung.	A8	26
Titaf, Alg.	D4	64
Tit-Ary, Russia	B14	34
Titicaca, Lake, l., S.A.	G4	84
Titilāgarh, India	H9	54
Titonka, Ia., U.S.	H4	118
Titov Veles, Mac.	B4	28
Titran, Nor.	E2	8
Tittabawassee, stm., Mi., U.S.	E5	112
Tittmoning, Ger.	H8	16
Titule, D.R.C.	D5	66
Titusville, Fl., U.S.	H5	116
Titusville, Pa., U.S.	C6	114
Tiuni, India	C6	54
Tivaouane, Sen.	F1	64
Tiverton, Eng., U.K.	K9	12
Tivoli, Italy	I9	22
Tivoli, Tx., U.S.	F11	130
Tiyās, Syria	D8	58
Tizimín, Mex.	B3	102
Tizi-Ouzou, Alg.	B5	64
Tizmant el-Zawâya, Egypt	I1	58
Tiznados, stm., Ven.	C8	86
Tiznit, Mor.	D3	64
Tjörn, i., Swe.	G4	8
Tjukalinsk, Russia	C12	32
Tjul'gan, Russia	D9	32
Tjumen', Russia	C10	32
Tjung, stm., Russia	D13	34
Tjuva-Guba, Russia	B15	8
Tlacotalpan, Mex.	F11	100
Tlacotepec, Mex.	G9	100
Tlahualilo de Zaragoza, Mex.	B7	100
Tlalnepantla, Mex.	F9	100
Tlaltenango de Sánchez Román, Mex.	E7	100
Tlapaneco, stm., Mex.	G9	100
Tlaquepaque, Mex.	E7	100
Tlaxcala, state, Mex.	F9	100
Tlaxcala de Xicohténcatl, Mex.	F9	100
Tłuszcz, Pol.	D17	16
Tmassah, Libya	B3	62
Tnâot, stm., Camb.	G7	48
Toa Alta, P.R.	B3	104a
Toa Baja, P.R.	B3	104a
Toachi, stm., Ec.	H2	86
Toahayana, Mex.	B5	100
Toamasina, Madag.	D8	68
Toba, Japan	E9	40
Toba, Danau, l., Indon.	K4	48
Tobago, i., Trin.	r13	105f
Toba Inlet, b., B.C., Can.	F6	138
Toba Kākar Range, mts., Pak.	C10	56
Tobarra, Spain	F9	20
Tobas, Arg.	D6	92
Toba Tek Singh, Pak.	C4	54
Tobejuba, Isla, i., Ven.	C11	86
Tobermorey, Austl.	D7	74
Tobermory, On., Can.	C8	112
Tobermory, Scot., U.K.	E6	12
Tobias, Ne., U.S.	G15	126
Tobias Barreto, Braz.	F6	88
Tobin, Mount, mtn., Nv., U.S.	C8	134
Tobique, stm., N.B., Can.	C9	110
Toboali, Indon.	E5	50
Tobol (Tobyl), stm., Asia	C11	32
Toboli, Indon.	D12	50
Tobol'sk, Russia	C11	32
Toboso, Phil.	E4	52
Tobruk see Ṭubruq, Libya	A4	62
Tobseda, Russia	B25	8
Tobyhanna, Pa., U.S.	C10	114
Tobyl, Kaz.	D10	32
Tobyl (Tobol), stm., Asia	D10	32
Tobylzhan, Kaz.	D13	32
Tobyš, stm., Russia	C24	8
Tocantínia, Braz.	E1	88
Tocantinópolis, Braz.	D2	88
Tocantins, state, Braz.	F8	84
Tocantins, stm., Braz.	D8	84
Tocantins, stm., Braz.	F1	88
Tocantinzinho, stm., Braz.	H1	88
Tochcha Lake, l., B.C., Can.	B5	138
Tochigi, Japan	C12	40
Tochigi, state, Japan	C12	40
Tochio, Japan	B12	40
Toco, Trin.	s13	105f
Tocoa, Hond.	E5	102
Toconao, Chile	D3	90
Tocopilla, Chile	D2	90
Tocuco, stm., Ven.	C5	86
Tocumwal, Austl.	J5	76
Tocuyo, stm., Ven.	B7	86
Tocuyo de la Costa, Ven.	B7	86
Toda Rāisingh, India	E5	54
Todi, Italy	H9	22
Todos os Santos, Baia de, b., Braz.	G6	88
Todos Santos, Bol.	C3	90
Todos Santos, Mex.	D3	100
Todos Santos, Bahía de, b., Mex.	L8	134
Tofino, B.C., Can.	G5	138
Toga, i., Vanuatu	i16	79d
Togi, Japan	B9	40
Togiak, Ak., U.S.	E7	140
Togian, Kepulauan, is., Indon.	F7	44
Togo, ctry., Afr.	H5	64
Togtoh, China	A4	42
Togučin, Russia	C14	32
Togur, Russia	C14	32
Togwotee Pass, p., Wy., U.S.	G15	136
Tōhaku, Japan	D6	40
Tohiea, Mont, mtn., Fr. Poly.	v20	78h
Tohopekaliga, Lake, l., Fl., U.S.	H4	116
Tohtamyš, Taj.	B11	56
Toi-misaki, c., Japan	H4	40
Toiyabe Range, mts., Nv., U.S.	D8	134
Tōjō, Japan	E6	40
Tojtepa, Uzb.	F11	32
Tok, Ak., U.S.	D11	140
Tokachi, stm., Japan	C15	38
Tokachi-dake, vol., Japan	C15	38
Tokaj, Hung.	A8	26
Tōkamachi, Japan	B11	40
Tokara-kaikyō, strt., Japan	j19	39a
Tokara-rettō, is., Japan	k19	39a
Tokat, Tur.	A4	56
Tŏkchŏk-kundo, is., Kor., S.	F6	38
Tokelau, dep., Oc.	D9	72
Tokko, Russia	D12	34
Tokma, Russia	C19	32
Tokmak, Kyrg.	F13	32
Tokoro, stm., Japan	C15	38
Tokoroa, N.Z.	D6	80
Tok-to, is., Asia	B4	40
Toktogul, Kyrg.	F12	32
Tokuno-shima, i., Japan	I19	39a
Tokur, Russia	F15	34
Tokushima, Japan	E7	40
Tokushima, state, Japan	F7	40
Tokuyama, Japan	E4	40
Tokwe, stm., Zimb.	B10	70
Tōkyō, Japan	D12	40
Tōkyō, state, Japan	D12	40
Tokyo Bay see Tōkyō-wan, b., Japan	D12	40
Tōkyō-daigaku-uchūkūkan-kenkyūsho, sci., Japan	H4	40
Tōkyō-wan, b., Japan	D12	40
Tôlañaro, Madag.	F8	68
Tolbo, Mong.	B3	36
Töle bī, Kaz.	F12	32
Toledo, Braz.	B11	92
Toledo, Col.	D5	86
Toledo, Phil.	E4	52
Toledo, Spain	E6	20
Toledo, Il., U.S.	E9	120
Toledo, Oh., U.S.	C2	114
Toledo, Or., U.S.	F3	136
Toledo, co., Spain	E6	20
Toledo, Montes de, mts., Spain	E6	20
Toledo Bend Reservoir, res., U.S.	F4	122
Tolentino, Italy	G10	22
Toli, China	B1	36
Toliara, Madag.	E7	68
Tolima, state, Col.	E4	86
Tolima, Nevado del, vol., Col.	E4	86
Tolitoli, Indon.	C12	50
Toljatti, Russia	D7	32
Tol'ka, Russia	B14	32
Tolleson, Az., U.S.	J4	132
Tolloche, Arg.	B6	92
Tolmači, Russia	C18	10
Tolmezzo, Italy	D10	22
Tolmin, Slvn.	D10	22
Tolna, state, Hung.	C5	26
Tolo, Teluk, b., Indon.	F7	44
Tolosa, Spain	A8	20
Tolstoj, mys, c., Russia	E20	34
Tolti, Pak.	A6	54
Tolú, Col.	C4	86
Toluca, Il., U.S.	D8	120
Toluca, Nevado de, vol., Mex.	F9	100
Toluca de Lerdo, Mex.	F9	100
Tom', stm., Russia	C14	32
Tomah, Wi., U.S.	H8	118
Tomahawk, Wi., U.S.	F9	118
Tomakomai, Japan	C14	38
Tomanivi, mtn., Fiji	p19	79e
Tomar, Port.	E2	20
Tomari, Russia	G17	34
Tomás Gomensoro, Ur.	E9	92
Tomasine, stm., Qc., Can.	B13	112
Tomaszów Lubelski, Pol.	F19	16
Tomaszów Mazowiecki, Pol.	E15	16
Tombador, Serra do, plat., Braz.	F6	84
Tomball, Tx., U.S.	G3	122
Tombigbee, stm., U.S.	F10	122
Tombos, Braz.	K5	88
Tombouctou (Timbuktu), Mali	F4	64
Tombstone, Az., U.S.	L6	132
Tombstone Mountain, mtn., Yk., Can.	C3	106
Tombua, Ang.	D1	68
Tom Burke, S. Afr.	C9	70
Tomé, Chile	H1	92
Tomé-Açu, Braz.	B1	88
Tomelilla, Swe.	I5	8
Tomelloso, Spain	E8	20
Tomichi Creek, stm., Co., U.S.	C2	128
Tomini, Indon.	C12	50
Tomini, Teluk, b., Indon.	F7	44
Tomioka, Japan	C11	40
Tommot, Russia	E14	34
Tomo, stm., Col.	E7	86
Tompkins, Sk., Can.	D5	124
Tompkinsville, Ky., U.S.	H12	120
Tompo, Indon.	C12	50
Tom Price, Austl.	D3	74
Tomptokan, Russia	E15	34
Tomsk, Russia	C15	32
Toms River, N.J., U.S.	E11	114
Tonalá, Mex.	G12	100
Tonami, Japan	C9	40
Tonantins, Braz.	I7	86
Tonantins, stm., Braz.	I7	86
Tonasket, Wa., U.S.	B7	136
Tonawanda, N.Y., U.S.	B6	114
Tonbo, Mya.	C2	48
Tonbridge, Eng., U.K.	J13	12
Tondano, Indon.	E8	44
Tønder, Den.	B4	16
Tondi, India	G4	53
Tone, stm., Japan	D13	40
Tonekābon, Iran	B7	56
Tonga, ctry., Oc.	E9	72
Tongaat, S. Afr.	F10	70
Tong'an, China	I7	42
Tonganoxie, Ks., U.S.	E2	120
Tonga Ridge, unds.	K21	142
Tongariro National Park, p.o.i., N.Z.	D6	80
Tongatapu, state, Tonga	o14	78e
Tongatapu, i., Tonga	n13	78e
Tonga Trench, unds.	L21	142
Tongbai, China	E5	42
Tongbai Shan, mts., China	E5	42
Tongbei, China	B10	36
Tongcheng, China	F7	42
Tongchuan, China	D3	42
Tongde, China	D5	36
Tongeren, Bel.	D14	14
Tongguan, China	G5	42
Tongguan, China	D3	42
Tonghai, China	G5	36
Tonghe, China	B10	36
Tonghua, China	D6	38
Tongjiang, China	B11	36
Tongjiang, China	F2	42
Tongjosŏn-man, b., Kor., N.	E7	38
Tongliang, China	G1	42
Tongliao, China	C4	38
Tongling, China	F7	42
Tongling, China	J3	42
Tonglu, China	G8	42
Tongnae, Kor., S.	D2	40
Tongnan, China	F1	42
Tongo, Austl.	H4	76
Tongoa, i., Vanuatu	k17	79d
Tongoy, Chile	E2	92
Tongren, China	H3	42
Tongren, China	D5	36
Tongres see Tongeren, Bel.	D14	14
Tongsa Dzong, Bhu.	E13	54
Tongtian, stm., China	E4	36
Tongue, Scot., U.K.	C8	12
Tongue, stm., U.S.	A7	126
Tongue of the Ocean, unds.	C9	96
Tongwei, China	D1	42
Tongxian, China	B7	42
Tongxin, China	C1	42
Tongxu, China	D6	42
Tongyu, China	B5	38
Tongzi, China	G2	42
Tonj, Sudan	F5	62
Tonk, India	E5	54
Tonkawa, Ok., U.S.	E11	128
Tonkin see Bac Phan, hist. reg., Viet.	A7	48
Tonkin, Gulf of, b., Asia	C8	48
Tônlé Sab, Bœng, l., Camb.	F6	48
Tonle Sap see Tônlé Sab, Bœng, l., Camb.	F6	48
Tonneins, Fr.	E6	18
Tonopah, Nv., U.S.	E8	134
Tonoshō, Japan	E7	40
Tonosí, Pan.	D1	86
Tonotha, Bots.	B8	70
Tons, stm., India	F8	54
Tønsberg, Nor.	G4	8
Tonstad, Nor.	G2	8
Tonto Creek, stm., Az., U.S.	I5	132
Tonto National Monument, p.o.i., Az., U.S.	J5	132
Toodyay, Austl.	F3	74
Tooele, Ut., U.S.	C4	132
Toogoolawah, Austl.	F9	76
Toomsboro, Ga., U.S.	D2	116
Toora-Hem, Russia	D17	32
Toowoomba, Austl.	F8	76
Topeka, Ks., U.S.	E2	120
Top Hill, hill, Gren.	q11	105e
Topia, Mex.	C5	100
Topki, Russia	C15	32
Topko, gora, mtn., Russia	E16	34
Topley, B.C., Can.	B4	138
Toplița, Rom.	C12	26
Topocalma, Punta, c., Chile	G1	92
Topol'čany, Slov.	H14	16
Topolobampo, Mex.	C4	100
Topolovățu Mare, Rom.	D8	26
Toporok, Russia	B16	10
Topozero, ozero, l., Russia	D14	8
Toppenish, Wa., U.S.	D6	136
Topsa, Russia	E20	8
Top Springs, Austl.	C6	74
Tor, Eth.	F6	62
Torbalı, Tur.	E10	28
Torbat-e Ḥeydarīyeh, Iran	B8	56
Torbat-e Jām, Iran	B9	56
Torbrook, N.S., Can.	F12	110
Torch Lake, l., Mi., U.S.	C4	112
Tordesillas, Spain	C5	20
Töre, Swe.	C10	8
Torgau, Ger.	E8	16
Torghay, Kaz.	E10	32
Torghay, stm., Kaz.	E10	32
Torghay üstirti, plat., Kaz.	D10	32
Torghay zhylgh, reg., Kaz.	D10	32
Torhout, Bel.	C12	14
Toribulu, Indon.	D11	50
Torino (Turin), Italy	E4	22
Torit, Sudan	G6	62
Tormes, stm., Spain	C5	20
Torna, Russia	B20	8
Torna, mtn., India	B1	53

Name　　　　　　Map　Page
　　　　　　　　Ref.

Torneälven
　(Tornionjoki), stm., Eur..... C10　8
Torneträsk, l., Swe.......... B8　8
Torngat Mountains, mts.,
　Can..................... F13　141
Tornillo, Tx., U.S........... C1　130
Tornionjoki
　(Torneälven), stm., Eur..... C10　8
Tornquist, Arg.............. I6　92
Toro, Spain................ C5　20
Toro, mtn., Mex............ F6　100
Toro, Lago del, l., Chile...... J2　90
Toro, Punta, c., Chile....... F1　92
Törökszentmiklós, Hung. ... B7　26
Torom, Russia.............. F16　34
Toronto, On., Can.......... E10　112
Toronto, Ks., U.S........... G1　120
Toronto, S.D., U.S.......... G2　118
Toropec, Russia............ D14　10
Tororo, Ug................. D6　66
Toros Dağları (Taurus
　Mountains), mts., Tur. .... A3　58
Torosozero, Russia......... E18　8
Toroume, hill, Cook Is. ..... b26　78j
Torquay, Sk., Can.......... E10　124
Torquay (Torbay), Eng., U.K.. K9　12
Torrance, Ca., U.S.......... J7　134
Torrão, Port............... F2　20
Torreblanca, Spain.......... D11　20
Torre del Greco, Italy....... D8　24
Torredonjimeno, Spain...... G6　20
Torrejoncillo, Spain........ E4　20
Torrejón de Ardoz, Spain.... D7　20
Torrejón-Tiétar, Embalse
　de, res., Spain............ E5　20
Torrelavega, Spain.......... A6　20
Torremolinos, Spain........ H6　20
Torrens, Lake, l., Austl...... F7　74
Torrens Creek, Austl........ C5　76
Torrens Creek, stm., Austl.... D5　76
Torrent, Arg............... D9　92
Torrent, Spain............. E10　20
Torrente see Torrent, Spain... E10　20
Torrenueva, Spain.......... F7　20
Torreón, Mex.............. C7　100
Torre Pellice, Italy......... F4　22
Torreperojil, Spain.......... F7　20
Torres, Braz............... D13　92
Torres, Îles, is., Vanuatu .... i16　79d
Torres Islands see
　Torres, Îles, is., Vanuatu ... i16　79d
Torres Strait, strt., Oc....... b3　79a
Torres Vedras, Port......... E1　20
Torrevella, Spain........... G10　20
Torrevieja see Torrevella,
　Spain.................... G10　20
Torridon, Scot., U.K........ D7　12
Torrijos, Spain............. D6　20
Torrington, Ct., U.S........ C12　114
Torrington, Wy., U.S........ E8　126
Torröjen, l., Swe........... E5　8
Torsa (Amo), stm., Asia..... E12　54
Torsby, Swe............... F5　8
Torshavn (Thorshavn),
　Far. Is.................. n34　8b
Tortola, i., Br. Vir. Is........ e8　104b
Tórtolas, Cerro de las (Las
　Tórtolas, Cerro), mtn., S.A.. D2　92
Tortona, Italy.............. F5　22
Tortorici, Italy............. F8　24
Tortosa, Spain............. D11　20
Tortosa, Cap de, c., Spain.... D11　20
Tortue, Île de la,
　i., Haiti.................. B11　102
Tortuga Island see
　Tortue, Île de la, i., Haiti ... B11　102
Tortuguero, Laguna, b.,
　P.R..................... B2　104a
Toruń, Pol................ B2　16
Toruń, state, Pol........... C15　16
Torup, Swe................ H5　8
Toržok, Russia............. C17　10
Torzym, Pol............... D11　16
Tosa, Japan............... F6　40
Tosa-shimizu, Japan........ G5　40
Tosa-wan, b., Japan........ F6　40
Tosca, S. Afr.............. D6　70
Toscana, state, Italy........ G8　22
Toses, Collada de, p.,
　Spain.................... B12　20
Tosno, Russia............. A13　10
Toson Hu, l., China......... D4　36
Tosontsengel, Mong........ B4　36
Tostado, Arg.............. D7　92
Tostamaa, Est............. G10　8
Tosu, Japan............... F3　40
Totana, Spain............. G9　20
Toteng, Bots.............. B6　70
Totiyas, Som.............. D8　66
Tot'ma, Russia............ F20　8
Totness, Sur.............. B6　84
Totoya, i., Fiji............. q20　79e
Tottenham, Austl........... I6　76
Tottenham, On., Can....... D10　112
Tottori, Japan............. D7　40
Tottori, state, Japan........ D6　40
Touba, C. Iv............... H3　64
Toubkal, Jebel, mtn., Mor.... C3　64
Touchet, stm., Wa., U.S..... D8　136
Touchwood Lake, l., Ab.,
　Austl.................... C5　76
Towla, Mount, mtn., Zimb.... B9　70
Town and Country, Wa.,
　U.S..................... C9　136
Town Hill, hill, Ber......... k16　104e
Townsend, Mt., U.S........ D15　136
Townshend Island, i.,
　Austl.................... D8　76
Townsville, Austl........... B6　76
Towson, Md., U.S.......... E9　114
Towuti, Danau, l., Indon..... F7　44
Toyah, Tx., U.S............ C4　130
Toyah Creek, stm., Tx., U.S... D4　130
Toyama, Japan............. C10　40
Toyama, state, Japan....... C10　40
Toyama-wan, b., Japan...... C10　40
Tōyō, Japan............... F6　40

Tōyō, Japan............... F7　40
Toyohashi, Japan........... E10　40
Toyokawa, Japan........... E10　40
Toyonaka, Japan........... E8　40
Toyooka, Japan............ D7　40
Toyosaka, Japan........... B12　40
Toyota, Japan............. D10　40
Toyotomi, Japan........... E3　40
Tozeur, Tun............... C6　64
Trabzon, Tur.............. A4　56
Tracadie, N.B., Can........ C12　110
Tracy, Qc., Can............ E3　110
Tracy, Ca., U.S............ F4　134
Tracy City, Tn., U.S........ B13　122
Tradewater, stm., Ky., U.S... G10　120
Traer, Ia., U.S............. B5　120
Trafalgar, Cabo, c., Spain.... H4　20
Traid, Spain............... D9　20
Tráighlí see Tralee, Ire....... I3　12
Traiguén, Chile............ I1　92
Traill, B.C., Can........... G13　138
Traill Ø, i., Grnld.......... C21　141
Traipu, Braz............... E8　88
Traira (Taraira), stm., S.A.... H7　86
Trairi, Braz............... B6　88
Trakai, Lith............... F7　10
Tralee, Ire................ I3　12
Trá Lí see Tralee, Ire........ I3　12
Trammel, Va., U.S.......... G3　114
Tramperos Creek (Punta
　de Agua Creek), stm., U.S.. E5　128
Tramping Lake, l., Sk., Can... B5　124
Tra My, Viet.............. E9　48
Trân, Blg................. G9　26
Tranås, Swe............... G6　8
Trancas, Arg.............. C5　92
Tranco de Beas, Embalse
　de, res., Spain............ F8　20
Trang, Thai................ I4　48
Trangan, Pulau, i., Indon..... G9　44
Trang Dinh, Viet........... A8　48
Trani, Italy................ C10　24
Tran Ninh see Xiangkhoang,
　Plateau de, plat., Laos...... C6　48
Tranqueras, Ur............. E9　92
Transantarctic
　Mountains, mts., Ant...... D30　81
Transkei, hist. reg., S. Afr.... G8　70
Transylvania, hist.
　reg., Rom................ C10　26
Transylvanian Alps see
　Carpaţii Meridionali,
　mts., Rom................ D11　26
Trapani, Italy.............. F6　24
Trapper Peak, mtn., Mt.,
　U.S..................... E12　136
Traralgon, Austl............ L6　76
TĀrza, reg., Maur.......... F1　64
Trasimeno, Lago, l., Italy.... G9　22
Trás-os-Montes, hist. reg.,
　Port..................... C3　20
Trat, Thai................ F6　48
Traun, stm., Aus........... B11　22
Traun, mtn., Aus........... B11　22
Traunstein, Ger............ I8　16
Travellers Lake, l., Austl..... I4　76
Traverse, Lake, res., U.S..... F2　118
Traverse City, Mi., U.S...... D4　112
Tra Vinh, Viet............. H8　48
Travis, Lake, l., Tx., U.S..... D10　130
Travnik, Bos.............. E4　26
Trayning, Austl............ F3　74
Trbovlje, Slvn............. D12　22
Třebíč, Czech Rep......... F11　16
Trebinje, Bos.............. G5　26
Trebišov, Slov............. H17　16
Trebbinka, Pol............. D18　16
Trece Martires, Phil......... C3　52
Tregosse Islets, is., Austl..... A8　76
Tregubovo, Russia.......... B14　10
Treinta y Tres, Ur.......... F10　92
Trélazé, Fr................ G8　14
Trelew, Arg............... H3　90
Trelleborg, Swe............ I5　8
Tremadoc Bay, b., Wales,
　U.K..................... I8　12
Tremblant, Mont, mtn.,
　Qc., Can................ D2　110
Trembleur Lake, l.,
　B.C., Can................ B5　138
Tremiti, Isole, is., Italy...... H12　22
Tremont, Il., U.S........... K9　118
Tremonton, Ut., U.S........ B4　132
Tremp, Spain.............. B11　20
Tempealava, Wi., U.S....... G7　118
Trenche, stm., Qc., Can..... B4　110
Trenčín, Slov.............. H14　16
Trenel, Arg............... G5　92
Trèng, Cam................ F6　48
Trenggalek, Indon.......... H7　50
Trenque Lauquen, Arg....... G6　92
Trent, stm., On., Can....... D12　112
Trent, stm., Eng., U.K....... I12　12
Trente et Un Milles, Lac
　des, l., Qc., Can.......... B13　112
Trentino-Alto Adige,
　state, Italy............... D8　22
Trento (Trent), Italy........ D7　22
Trenton, On., Can.......... E14　110
Trenton, On., Can.......... D12　112
Trenton, Fl., U.S........... G3　116
Trenton, Ga., U.S.......... C13　122
Trenton, Mo., U.S.......... D4　120
Trenton, N.C., U.S.......... A8　116
Trenton, Ne., U.S.......... A8　128
Trenton, N.J., U.S.......... D11　114
Trentwood, Wa., U.S........ C9　136
Trepassey, Nf., Can......... j23　107a
Tres Algarrobos, Arg........ G6　92
Tres Arroyos, Arg.......... I7　92
Três Corações, Braz......... K3　88
Tres Coroas, Braz.......... D12　92
Três de Maio, Braz......... C10　92
Três Esquinas, Col.......... D6　90
Três Lagos, Arg............ J2　90
Tres Lomas, Arg........... H6　92
Três Marias, Braz.......... J3　88
Três Marias, Islas, is., Mex... E5　100
Três Marias,
　Represa de, res., Braz..... J3　88
Tres Montes,
　Península, pen., Chile...... I1　90
Tres Montosas, mtn.,
　N.M., U.S............... I9　132
Tres Palos, Laguna, l., Mex... G9　100
Três Passos, Braz.......... C11　92
Três Picos, Cerro, mtn., Arg... K3　88
Três Pontas, Braz.......... K3　88
Três Puntas, Cabo, c., Arg... L4　90
Três Rios, Braz............ L4　92
Três Virgenes, Volcán de
　las, vol., Mex............ B2　100
Tres Zapotes, sci., Mex...... F11　100
Tretten, Nor.............. G4　8
Treuchtlingen, Ger......... H6　16
Treuenbrietzen, Ger......... C8　16
Treviglio, Italy............ E6　22
Treviso, Italy.............. E7　22
Trevorton, Pa., U.S......... D9　114
Trgovište, Serb............ G9　26
Triadruna, Austl............ o13　77a
Triberg, Ger.............. H4　16
Tribugá, Ensenada
　de, b., Col............... E3　86
Tribune, Ks., Can.......... C7　128
Tricarico, Italy............ D10　24
Tricase, Italy.............. E12　24
Trichinópoly, Limni, l., Grc... E4　28
Trichūr, India............. F3　53
Tri County Supply Canal,
　can., Ne., U.S............ G12　126
Trida, Austl............... I5　76

Trident Peak, mtn., Nv., U.S.. B7　134
Trier, Ger................. G2　16
Trieste (Trst), Italy........ E10　22
Trieste, Gulf of, b., Eur...... E10　22
Triglav, mtn., Slvn.......... D10　22
Triguero, Spain............ G4　20
Trikala, Grc............... D4　28
Trikora, Puncak, mtn.,
　Indon.................... F10　44
Trilby, Fl., U.S............. H3　116
Triman, Pak............... D2　54
Trincheras, Mex............ F7　98
Trincomalee, Sri L.......... G5　53
Trindade, Braz............. I1　88
Trindade, i., Braz........... H12　82
Třinec, Czech Rep.......... G14　16
Trinidad, Bol.............. B3　90
Trinidad, Col.............. E6　86
Trinidad, Cuba............ B8　102
Trinidad, Ur............... F9　92
Trinidad, Co., U.S.......... D4　128
Trinidad, Tx., U.S.......... E2　122
Trinidad, i., Trin........... s13　105f
Trinidad, Isla, i., Arg....... I7　92
Trinidad and Tobago,
　ctry., N.A................ s13　105f
Trinity, Tx., U.S............ G3　122
Trinity, stm., Ca., U.S....... C2　134
Trinity, stm., Tx., U.S....... D13　130
Trinity Peak, stm.,
　Tx., U.S................. H11　128
Trinity, South Fork,
　stm., Ca., U.S............ C2　134
Trinity, West Fork,
　stm., Tx., U.S............ H11　128
Trinity Bay, b., Nf., Can..... j23　107a
Trinity Bay, b., Tx., U.S..... H4　122
Trinity Islands, is., Ak., U.S... E9　140
Trinity Peak, mtn., Nv., U.S.. C7　134
Trinity Site, hist., N.M., U.S.. H2　128
Trino, Italy............... E5　22
Tripa, stm., Indon.......... J3　48
Tripoli, Grc............... F5　28
Tripoli see Tarābulus, Leb.... D6　58
Tripoli see Tarābulus, Libya... A2　62
Tripoli, Ia., U.S............ I6　118
Tripolis, sci., Tur........... F12　28
Tripolitania see Tarābulus,
　hist. reg., Libya........... A2　62
Tripp, S.D., U.S............ D15　126
Tripura, state, India........ G13　54
Tristan da Cunha Group,
　is., St. Hel............... J4　60
Tristao, Îles, is., Gui........ G2　64
Triste, Golfo, b., Ven....... B7　86
Triste, Spain.............. B10　20
Triumph, La., U.S.......... H9　122
Trivandrum see
　Thiruvananthapuram, India G3　53
Trnava, Slov.............. H13　16
Troandie Islands, is.,
　Pap. N. Gui.............. b5　79a
Trogir, Cro................ G13　22
Troia, Italy............... C9　24
Troick, Russia............. D10　32
Troickoe, Russia........... D15　32
Troickoe, Russia........... G16　34
Troicko-Pečorsk, Russia..... B9　32
Troina, Italy.............. G8　24
Troisdorf, Ger............. F2　16
Trois-Pistoles, Qc., Can..... B7　110
Trois Pitons, Morne,
　vol., Dom................ j6　105c
Trois-Rivières, Qc., Can..... D5　110
Trois-Rivières, Guad....... i5　105c
Trojan, Blg................ G11　26
Trojanova Tabla, hist.,
　Serb..................... E9　26
Trollhättan, Swe........... G5　8
Trombetas, stm., Braz....... C6　84
Troms, state, Nor.......... B8　8
Tromsø, Nor.............. B8　8
Trona, Ca., U.S............ H8　134
Tronador, Cerro, mtn., S.A... H2　90
Trondheim, Nor............ E4　8
Trondheimsfjorden, b., Nor... E4　8
Troödos, Cyp............. D3　58
Troödos Mountains, mts.,
　Cyp..................... D3　58
Troon, Scot., U.K.......... F8　12
Trophy Mountain, vol.,
　B.C., Can................ E11　138
Tropic, Ut., U.S............ F4　132
Tropojë, Alb.............. B14　24
Troškūnai, Lith............ E7　10
Trosna, Russia............ H18　10
Trotus, stm., Rom.......... C13　26
Trout, Tx., U.S............ C3　122
Trout, La., U.S............ F6　122
Trout, stm., N.T., Can....... L5　132
Trout Creek, Mi., U.S....... E9　118
Trout Creek Pass, p.,
　Co., U.S................ C3　128
Trout Lake, l., N.T., Can..... D5　106
Trout Lake, l., On., Can..... C12　106
Troutville, Va., U.S......... G6　114
Troutville-sur-Mer, Fr....... E7　14
Trowbridge, Eng., U.K....... J10　12
Troy, Al., U.S............. F13　122
Troy, Id., U.S............. D10　136
Troy, Ks., U.S............. B7　122
Troy, Mo., U.S............ A6　116
Troy, N.H., U.S............ B13　114
Troy, N.Y., U.S............ B12　114
Troy, Oh., U.S............. D1　114
Troy, Pa., U.S............. C9　114
Troy, Tn., U.S............. H8　120
Troy, Tx., U.S............. C10　130
Troyan see Truva, sci., Tur... D9　28
Troyes, Fr................ F13　14
Troy Peak, mtn., Nv., U.S.... E10　132
Trst see Trieste, Italy....... E10　22
Trstená, Slov.............. G15　16
Truax, Sk., Can............ E8　124
Trubčevsk, Russia.......... H16　10
Trudfront, Russia.......... E7　32
Trujillo, Col.............. E4　86
Trujillo, Hond............. E5　102
Trujillo, Peru.............. E2　84
Trujillo, Spain............ E5　20
Trujillo, Ven.............. C6　86
Trujillo Alto, P.R........... B4　104a
Truk Islands see Chuuk,
　is., Micron............... C6　72
Tukituki, stm., N.Z......... D7　80
Tulare, Ca., U.S........... G6　134
Tulare Lake Bed, reg.,
　Ca., U.S................. G6　134

Truyère, stm., Fr........... E8　18
Tryon, N.C., U.S........... A3　116
Tryon, Ne., U.S............ F12　126
Trzcianka, Pol............. C12　16
Trzciel, Pol............... D11　16
Trzebiatów, Pol............ B11　16
Trzebinia, Pol............. F15　16
Trzebnica, Pol............ E13　16
Tsagaannuur, Mong......... E15　32
Tsaidam Basin see Qaidam
　Pendi, bas., China......... D3　36
Tsala Apopka Lake, l.,
　Fl., U.S................. H3　116
Tsamkong see Zhanjiang,
　China................... K4　42
Ts'anghsien see
　Cangzhou, China.......... B7　42
T'sangwu see Wuzhou, China J4　42
Tsaratanana, Madag........ D8　68
Tsaratanana, mts., Madag.... C8　68
Tsau, Bots................ C7　68
Tsavo, Kenya.............. E7　66
Tsavo National Park, mtn.,
　B.C., Can................ C4　138
Tsebrykove, Ukr........... B17　26
Tses, Nmb................ D4　70
Tsetserleg, Mong.......... B5　36
Tsévié, Togo.............. H5　64
Tshabong, Bots............ D6　70
Tshane, Bots.............. D5　70
Tshela, D.R.C.............. E2　66
Tshibala, D.R.C............ E4　66
Tshidilamolomo, S. Afr...... D7　70
Tshikapa, D.R.C............ F4　66
Tshofa, D.R.C............. F5　66
Tshuapa, stm., D.R.C........ E4　66
Tshumbe (Chiumbe), stm.,
　Afr..................... B3　68
Tshwane see Pretoria,
　S. Afr................... D9　70
Tsiafajavona, vol., Madag.... D8　68
Tsiigehtchic, N.T., Can...... B4　106
Tsimlyansk Reservoir see
　Cimljanskoe vodohranilišče,
　res., Russia.............. E6　32
Tsinan see Jinan, China...... C7　42
Tsineng, S. Afr............ E6　70
Tsinghai see Qinghai,
　state, China.............. D4　36
Tsingkiang see
　Qingjiang, China.......... E8　42
Tsingtao see Qingdao, China . C9　42
Tsingyuan see Baoding,
　China................... B6　42
Ts'in-hai see Qinghai,
　state, China.............. D4　36
Tsining see Jining, China..... D7　42
Tsining Shan see Qin
　Ling, mts., China.......... E3　42
Tsintsabis, Nmb........... C3　68
Tsiombe, Madag........... F8　68
Tsipa see Cipa, stm., Russia .. F11　34
Tsirisbihina, stm., Madag..... D7　68
Tsiroanomandidy, Madag.... D8　68
Tsitsihar see Qiqihar, China . B9　36
Tsna see Cna, stm., Russia ... D6　32
Tsomo, stm., S. Afr......... H8　70
Tsomog, Mong............ B6　36
Tsu, Japan................ E8　40
Tsubame, Japan........... B11　40
Tsubata, Japan............ C9　40
Tsuchiura, Japan........... C13　40
Tsugaru-kaikyō, strt., Japan.. D14　38
Tsukumi, Japan............ F4　40
Tsukushi-sanchi, mts.,
　Japan................... F3　40
Tsumeb, Nmb............. D2　53
Tsumis, Sudan............. E6　62
T'ungchou see Tongxian,
　China................... B7　42
T'ungch'uan see
　Tongchuan, China......... D3　42
Tung Hai see East China
　Sea, s., Asia.............. F9　36
Tsushima-kaikyō (Eastern
　Channel), strt., Japan...... F2　40
Tsushima, is., Japan........ D7　40
Tsuyama, Japan............ D7　40
Tswaane, Bots............. C6　70
T'ung'an see
　Huangshan, China......... G8　42
Tunduru, Tan.............. G7　66
Tundža, stm., Eur.......... G12　26
Tunga, stm., India.......... D3　53
Tungabhadra, stm., India .... D3　53
Tungabhadra Reservoir,
　res., India............... D2　53
Tungchang, China.......... D2　53
Tunggal, stm., Indon........ D3　50
Tungkal, stm., Indon........ D3　50
Tungla, Nic............... F5　102
Tungliao see Tongliao,
　China................... C4　38
Tungsha Tao (Pratas Island),
　i., Tai................... K7　42
Tungshih, Tai............. J7　42
Tungsten, N.T., Can........ C5　106
Tunguragua, state, Ec....... H2　86
Tunguragua, vol., Ec........ H2　86
Tuni, India................ C6　53
Tunia, stm., Col............ F4　86
Tunis, Tun................ A6　64
Tunis, Golfe de, b., Tun..... G4　24
Tunisia, ctry., Afr.......... C6　64
Tunisie see Tunisia,
　ctry., Afr................ C6　64
Tunja, Col................ E5　86
Tunkhannock, Pa., U.S...... C9　114
Tunuyán, Ar., U.S.......... C5　92
Tunuyán, stm., Arg......... F3　92
Tunxi, China.............. G8　42
Tuo, stm., China........... E2　42
Tuobuluage, China......... C12　42
Tuojiang, Russia........... D13　34
Tuoj-Haja, Russia.......... B20　32
Tuokusidawan Ling, mtn.,
　China................... A6　46
Tuolumne, can., Ca., U.S.... F5　134
Tupá, Braz................ D1　92
Tupaciguara, Braz.......... J1　88
Tupanciretã, Braz.......... D10　92
Tuparro, stm., Col......... F6　86
Tuparro, stm., Col......... C10　122
Tupelo, Ms., U.S........... C10　122
Tupelo, Ms., U.S........... D2　122
Tupinambarana, Ilha, i.,
　Braz.................... D6　84
Tupirasabá, Braz........... H1　88
Tupiza, Bol............... A3　92
Tupper Lake, N.Y., U.S...... F2　110

Tulare Lake Canal, can.,
　Ca., U.S................. G6　134
Tularosa, N.M., U.S......... H2　128
Tularosa Valley, bas.,
　N.M., U.S............... E9　98
Tulbagh, S. Afr............ H4　70
Tulcea, Rom............... G3　86
Tulcea, Rom.............. D15　26
Tulelake, Ca., U.S.......... B4　134
Tulcea, state, Rom......... D15　26
Tule Lake, l., Ca., U.S....... B4　134
Tulemalu Lake, l., Nu., Can... C11　106
Tule Valley, val., Ut., U.S..... D3　132
Tuli, Zimb................ B9　70
Tuliszków, Pol............. D14　16
Tulia, Tx., U.S............. C5　106
Túlkarm, W.B.............. F6　58
Tullahoma, Tn., U.S........ B12　122
Tullamore, Ire............. H5　12
Tulle, Fr.................. D7　18
Tulln, Aus................ B13　22
Tulln, Aus................ B10　86
Tulsa, Ok., U.S............ B18　138
Tulsequah, B.C., Can....... D4　106
Tul'skaja oblast', co., Russia .. G20　10
Tuluá, Col................ E4　86
Tulum, Mex............... B4　102
Tulum, sci., Mex........... B4　102
Tulun, Russia.............. D18　32
Tuma, stm., Nic............ F5　102
Tumacacori National
　Historical Park, p.o.i.,
　Az., U.S................. L5　132
Tumaco, Col.............. G2　86
Tumaco, Rada de, b., Col..... G2　86
Tuman-gang (Tumen),
　stm., Asia............... C8　38
Tumanskij, Russia.......... D24　34
Tumany, Russia............ D20　34
Tumbarumba, Austl......... J6　76
Tumbes, Peru............. D1　84
Tumbes, Punta, c., Chile..... H1　92
Tumber Ridge, B.C., Can.... A10　138
Tumen, China............. C8　38
Tumen (Tuman-gang),
　stm., Asia............... C8　38
Tumeremo, Ven............ D11　86
Tumiritinga, Braz.......... J5　88
Tumkūr, India............. E3　53
Tumotegi, China........... A4　42
Tumpat, Malay............ I6　48
Tumsar, India............. H7　54
Tumtum, Wa., U.S......... C9　136
Tumu, Ghana.............. G4　64
Tumuc-Humac Mountains,
　mts., S.A................ C6　84
Tumut, Austl.............. J7　76
Tumwater, Wa., U.S........ D4　136
Tun, stm., Thai............ D4　48
Tunapuna, Trin............ s12　105f
Tunari, Cerro, mtn., Bol..... C3　90
Tunas de Zaza, Cuba....... B2　102
Tunchang, China........... L3　42
Turfan Depression see
　Turpan Pendi, depr.,
　China................... C2　36
Turgaj see Torghay,
　stm., Kaz................ E10　32
Turgajskaja ložbina
　see Torghay zhyigh,
　reg., Kaz................ D10　32
Turgajskoe plato see
　Torghay üstirti, plat., Kaz... D10　32
Turgay see Torghay,
　stm., Kaz................ E10　32
Turginovo, Russia.......... D18　10
Turgoš, Russia............ A18　10
Turgutlu, Tur.............. E10　28
Túri, Est................. B8　10
Turia (Túria), stm., Spain.... D9　20
Túria (Turia), stm., Spain.... D9　20
Turiaçu, stm., Braz......... A3　88
Turiaçu, stm., Braz......... B3　88
Turimiquire, Cerro,
　mtn., Ven................ B10　86
Turin, Ab., Can............ F18　138
Turin see Torino, Italy....... E4　22
Turinsk, Russia............ C10　32
Turka, Ukr................ G19　16
Turkana, Lake see
　Rudolf, Lake, l., Afr....... D7　66
Turkestanskij hrebet,
　mts., Asia................ B10　56
Türkeve, Hung............ B7　26
Turkey, ctry., Asia.......... B3　56
Turkey Creek, stm., Ne., U.S.. K2　118
Turkish Republic of
　Northern Cyprus see
　Cyprus, North, ctry., Asia .. C4　58
Türkistan, Kaz............. F11　32
Turkmenistan, ctry., Asia.... B8　56
Turkmenistan, ctry., Asia.... B8　56
Türkoğlu, Tur.............. A7　58
Turks and Caicos
　Islands, dep., N.A......... A12　102
Turks Island Passage,
　strt., T./C. Is............. B12　102
Turks Islands, is., T./C. Is.... B12　102
Turku (Åbo), Fin.......... F9　8
Turkwel, stm., Kenya....... D7　66
Turley, Ok., U.S........... H2　120
Turlock, Ca., U.S.......... F5　134
Turmalina, Braz........... I4　88
Turmantas, Lith........... E9　10
Turnagain, stm., B.C., Can... D5　106
Turneffe Islands, is., Belize... B3　102
Turner, Mt., U.S........... F15　124
Turner, Or., U.S........... F4　136
Turners Falls, Ma., U.S...... B13　114
Turnhout, Bel............. C13　14
Turnov, Czech Rep......... F11　16
Turnu Măgurele, Rom....... F11　16
Turnu Roşu, Pasul, p., Rom.. D11　26
Turočak, Russia........... D15　32
Turon, Ks., U.S............ D10　128
Turpan, China............. C2　36
Turpan Pendi (Turfan
　Depression), depr., China .. C2　36
Turquino, Pico, mtn., Cuba .. C9　102
Turrell, Ar., U.S............ B8　122
Turret Peak, mtn., Az., U.S... I5　132
Turtle, stm., Mb., Can....... D14　124
Turtle-Flambeau Flowage,
　res., Wi., U.S............. E8　118
Turtle Islands, is., S.L....... H2　64
Turtle Lake, N.D., U.S....... G13　124
Turtle Lake, Wi., U.S........ F6　118
Turu, stm., Russia.......... B18　32
Turuhansk, Russia.......... C6　34
Turvo, Braz............... D13　92
Turvo, stm., Braz........... K1　88
Turwi, stm., Zimb.......... B10　70
Turzovka, Slov............. G14　16
Tuscaloosa, Al., U.S........ D11　122
Tuscaloosa, Lake, res.,
　Al., U.S................. D11　122
Tuscany see Toscana,
　state, Italy............... G8　22
Tuscarora Mountain,
　mts., Pa., U.S............ D8　114
Tuscola, Tx., U.S.......... B8　130
Tuscola, Mo., U.S.......... C11　122
Tuscumbia, Mo., U.S........ F5　120
Tuscumbia, Al., U.S........ C13　122
Tuskegee, Al., U.S......... D9　140
Tutayev, Russia........... C22　10
Tuticorin, India........... G4　53
Tutin, Serb............... B4　26
Tutóia, Braz.............. B4　88
Tutoko, Mount, mtn., N.Z... G3　80
Tutrakan, Blg............. E13　26
Turtle Creek Lake, res.,
　Ks., U.S................ B12　128
Tutuala, E. Timor.......... G8　44
Tutuila, i., Am. Sam........ h12　79c
Tutupaca, Volcán,
　vol., Peru................ G3　84
Tutwiler, Ms., U.S.......... C8　122
Tützing, Ger.............. I7　16
Tuul, stm., Mong.......... B6　36
Tuva, state, Russia......... D16　32
Tuvalu, ctry., Oc.......... D8　72
Tuvuca, i., Fiji............. p20　79e
Tuwayq, Jabal,
　mts., Sau. Ar............. E6　56
Tuxford, Sk., Can.......... D8　124
Túxpan de Rodríguez
　Cano, Mex............... E10　100
Tuxtepec, Mex............ F10　100
Tuxtla Gutiérrez, Mex...... G12　100
Túy, stm., Ven............ B8　86
Túy see Tui, Spain.......... B2　20
Tuy Hòa, Viet............. F9　48
Tuyen Quang, Viet......... B7　48
Tuy Hoa, Viet............. F9　48
Tüyün see Duyun, China .... H2　42
Tüyür, Burj at-, hill, Sudan... C5　62
Tuz, Iraq................. C5　56
Tuz Gölü, l., Tur........... B3　56
Tuzigoot National
　Monument, p.o.i., Az., U.S. I4　132
Tuzla, Bos................ E6　26
Tuzlu, Ukr................ D17　26
Tvardiţa, Mol............. C15　26
Tver' (Kalinin), Russia....... D18　10
Tverca, stm., Russia........ C18　10
Tverskaja oblast', co., Russia . D17　10
Tweed, On., Can........... D12　112
Tweed, stm., U.K.......... F10　12
Tweed Heads, Austl......... F9　76
Twee Riviere, S. Afr........ H6　70
Twelve Mile Lake, l.,
　Sk., Can................. E7　124
Twentehkanaal, can., Neth... B15　14
Twentynine Palms, Ca., U.S.. I9　134
Twin Buttes Reservoir, res.,
　Tx., U.S................. C7　130
Twin City, Ga., U.S......... D3　116
Twin Falls, Id., U.S......... H12　136
Twin Falls, Id., U.S......... H4　53
Twin Lakes, Wi., U.S........ B9　120
Twinsburg, Oh., U.S........ C4　114
Twisp, Wa., U.S........... B6　136
Twitchell Reservoir,
　res., Ca., U.S............ H5　134
Two Butte Creek, stm.,
　Co., U.S................ D6　128
Twofold Bay, b., Austl....... K7　76
Two Harbors, Mn., U.S...... D7　118

Two Medicine – Várzea da Palma I • 59

Name	Map Ref.	Page
Two Medicine, stm., Mt., U.S.	B14	136
Two Rivers, Wi., U.S.	D2	112
Tybee Island, Ga., U.S.	D5	116
Tychy, Pol.	F14	16
Tyczyn, Pol.	G18	16
Tye, Tx., U.S.	B8	130
Tygda, Russia	F14	34
Tyler, Mn., U.S.	G2	118
Tyler, Tx., U.S.	E3	122
Tylertown, Ms., U.S.	F8	122
Tylihul, stm., Ukr.	B17	26
Tylihul's'kyi lyman, l., Ukr.	B17	26
Tym, stm., Russia	C14	32
Tymovskoe, Russia	F17	34
Tynda, Russia	E13	34
Tyndall, S.D., U.S.	D15	126
Tyndaris, sci., Italy	F8	24
Tynemouth, Eng., U.K.	F11	12
Tynset, Nor.	E4	8
Tyre see Şūr, Leb.	E6	58
Tyrifjorden, l., Nor.	F3	8
Tyrma, Russia	F15	34
Tyrma, stm., Russia	F15	34
Tyrnavos, Grc.	D5	28
Tyrone, Ok., U.S.	E7	128
Tyrrell, Lake, l., Austl.	J4	76
Tyrrhenian Sea, s., Eur.	G11	6
Tysa (Tisa) (Tisza), stm., Eur.	A10	26
Tysnesøya, i., Nor.	F1	8
Tysse, Nor.	F1	8
Tytuvėnai, Lith.	E6	10
Ty Ty, Ga., U.S.	E2	116
Tyva see Tuva, state, Russia	D16	32
Tzaneen, S. Afr.	C9	70
Tzekung see Zigong, China	F5	36
Tzeliutsing see Zigong, China	F5	36
Tzucacab, Mex.	B3	102
Tzukung see Zigong, China	F5	36
Tzupo see Boshan, China	C7	42
Tzupo see Zibo, China	C8	42
U		
Uatumã, stm., Braz.	D6	84
Uauá, Braz.	E6	88
Uaupés, Braz.	H8	86
Uaupés (Vaupés), stm., S.A.	G7	86
Uaxactún, sci., Guat.	D3	102
Ubá, Braz.	K4	88
Ubaidullaganj, India	G6	54
Ubaitaba, Braz.	H6	88
Ubajara, Parque Nacional de, p.o.i., Braz.	B5	88
Ubangi (Oubangui), stm., Afr.	E3	66
Ubatã, Braz.	H6	88
Ubaté, Col.	E5	86
Ubatuba, Braz.	L3	88
Ube, Japan	F4	40
Úbeda, Spain	F7	20
Uberaba, Braz.	J2	88
Uberlândia, Braz.	J1	88
Überlingen, Ger.	I5	16
Ubiña, Peña, mtn., Spain	B4	20
Ubl'a, Slov.	H18	16
Ubly, Mi., U.S.	E7	112
Ubombo, S. Afr.	E11	70
Ubon Ratchathani, Thai.	E7	48
Ubrique, Spain	H5	20
Ubundu, D.R.C.	E5	66
Učaly, Russia	D9	32
Učami, Russia	B17	32
Ucayali, stm., Peru	D3	84
Uchinoura, Japan	H4	40
Uchiura-wan, b., Japan	C14	38
Uchiza, Peru	E2	84
Uchoa, Braz.	K1	88
Uckermark, reg., Ger.	C9	16
Ucon, Id., U.S.	G15	136
Učur, stm., Russia	E15	34
Uda, stm., Russia	F15	34
Uda, stm., Russia	C17	32
Udagamandalam, India	F3	53
Udaipur, India	F4	54
Udalguri, India	E13	54
Udall, Ks., U.S.	D11	128
Udamalpet, India	F3	53
Udankudi, India	G4	53
Udaquiola, Arg.	H8	92
Udaypur, Nepal	E11	54
Uddevalla, Swe.	G4	8
Uddjaur, l., Swe.	D8	8
Udgīr, India	B3	53
Udhampur, India	B5	54
Udimskij, Russia	F21	8
Udine, Italy	D10	22
Udmurtia see Udmurtija, state, Russia	C8	32
Udmurtija, state, Russia	C8	32
Udokan, hrebet, mts., Russia	E12	34
Udomlja, Russia	C17	10
Udon Thani, Thai.	D6	48
Udskaja guba, b., Russia	F16	34
Udskoe, Russia	F15	34
Udupi, India	E2	53
Udža, Russia	B12	34
Ueckermünde, Ger.	C10	16
Ueda, Japan	C11	40
Uele, stm., D.R.C.	D4	66
Uelen, Russia	C26	34
Uel'kal', Russia	C25	34
Uelzen, Ger.	C6	16
Ueno, Japan	E9	40
Uere, stm., D.R.C.	D5	66
Uetersen, Ger.	C5	16
Ufa, Russia	D9	32
Ufa, stm., Russia	C9	32
Uffenheim, Ger.	G6	16
Ugab, stm., Nmb.	E2	68
Uganda, ctry., Afr.	D6	66
Ugărčin, Blg.	F11	26
Ugarit, sci., Syria	C6	58
Ugashik, Ak., U.S.	E8	140
Uglegorsk, Russia	G17	34
Uglekamensk, Russia	C10	38
Uglič, Russia	C21	10
Ugljan, Otok, i., Cro.	F12	22
Ugodiči, Russia	C22	10
Ugodskij Zavod, Russia	E19	10
Ugra, stm., Russia	F18	10
Uherské Hradiště, Czech Rep.	G13	16
Uherský Brod, Czech Rep.	H13	16
Uhlenhorst, Nmb.	C3	70
Uhra, stm., Russia	B22	10
Uhta, Russia	B8	32
Uhta, Russia	F18	8
Uíge, Ang.	B1	68
Uinebona, stm., Ven.	E10	86
Uinta Mountains, mts., Ut., U.S.	C6	132
Uiraúna, Braz.	D6	88
Ŭisŏng, Kor., S.	C1	40
Uitenhage, S. Afr.	H7	70
Uithuizermeeden, Neth.	A15	14
Uj, stm., Asia	D10	32
Ujandina, stm., Russia	C17	34
Ujar, Russia	C16	32
Ujelang, at., Marsh. Is.	C7	72
Újfehértó, Hung.	B8	26
Ujhāni, India	D7	54
Uji, Japan	E8	40
Uji-guntō, is., Japan	H2	40
Ujiji, Tan.	E5	66
Ujjain, India	G5	54
Ujung, Indon.	G12	50
Ujunggenteng, Indon.	G5	50
Ujungkulon National Park, p.o.i., Indon.	G4	50
Ujungpandang (Makasar), Indon.	F11	50
Uk, Russia	C17	32
Uka, Russia	E21	34
Ukara Island, i., Tan.	E6	66
Ukerewe Island, i., Tan.	E6	66
Ukiah, Ca., U.S.	D2	134
Uki Ni Masi Island, i., Sol. Is.	f9	79b
Ukmergė, Lith.	E7	10
Ukraine, ctry., Eur.	F15	6
Ukui, Indon.	D3	50
Ukyr, Russia	G10	34
Ula, Bela.	E12	10
Ulaanbaatar, Mong.	B6	36
Ulaangom, Mong.	G7	34
Ulan, Austl.	I7	76
Ulan Bator see Ulaanbaatar, Mong.	B6	36
Ulan Buh Shamo, des., China	A2	42
Ulan-Burgasy, hrebet, mts., Russia	F10	34
Ulanhot, China	B9	36
Ulanów, Pol.	F18	16
Ulansuhai Nur, l., China	A3	42
Ulan-Ude, Russia	F10	34
Ulawa Island, i., Sol. Is.	e9	79b
Ulawun, Mount (The Father), vol., Pap. N. Gui.	b5	79a
Ulchin, Kor., S.	B2	40
Ulcinj, Serb.	H6	26
Ulco, S. Afr.	F7	70
Uldz, stm., Asia	B8	36
Uleåborg see Oulu, Fin.	D11	8
Ulen, Mn., U.S.	D2	118
Ulety, Russia	F11	34
Ulëz, Alb.	C13	24
Ulhāsnagar, India	B1	53
Ul'ianovka, Ukr.	A17	26
Uliastay, Mong.	B4	36
Ulindi, stm., D.R.C.	E5	66
Ulja, Russia	E17	34
Uljanovo, Russia	G18	10
Uljanovsk, Russia	D7	32
Ul'kan, Russia	C19	32
Ulla, stm., Spain	B2	20
Ulladulla, Austl.	J8	76
Ullin, Il., U.S.	G8	120
Ullŭng-do, i., Kor., S.	B3	40
Ulm, Ger.	H5	16
Ulm, Mt., U.S.	C15	136
Ulmarra, Austl.	G9	76
Ulmeni, Rom.	D13	26
Ulónguè, Moz.	C5	68
Ulsan, Kor., S.	D2	40
Ulster, hist. reg., Eur.	G5	12
Ulster Canal, can., Eur.	G5	12
Ulu, Indon.	E8	44
Ulu, Russia	D14	34
Ulúa, stm., Hond.	E3	102
Ulubat Gölü, l., Tur.	C11	28
Uluborlu, Tur.	E13	28
Uluçınar, Tur.	B6	58
Uludağ, mtn., Tur.	C12	28
Uludağ Yarımdası Milli Parkı, p.o.i., Tur.	C12	28
Ulukışla, Tur.	A5	58
Ulul, i., Micron.	C5	72
Ulungur, stm., China	B2	36
Ulungur Hu, l., China	B2	36
Ulunhan, Russia	F11	34
Uluru (Ayers Rock), mtn., Austl.	E6	74
Ulverston, Eng., U.K.	G9	12
Ulverstone, Austl.	n12	77a
Ulysses, Ks., U.S.	D7	128
Ulytaū zhotasy, mts., Kaz.	E11	32
Uma, China	F13	34
Umán, Mex.	B3	102
Umanak, Grnld.	C15	141
Umanak Fjord, b., Grnld.	C15	141
Umargāon, India	H4	54
Umaria, India	G8	54
Umarizal, Braz.	D7	88
Umarkot, Pak.	F2	54
Umatac, Guam	j9	78c
Umatilla, Fl., U.S.	H4	116
Umatilla, Or., U.S.	E7	136
Umatilla, stm., Or., U.S.	E7	136
Umatilla, Lake, res., U.S.	E4	136
Umba, Russia	C16	8
Umbertide, Italy	G9	22
Umboi Island, i., Pap. N. Gui.	b4	79a
Umbria, state, Italy	G9	22
Umbukul, Pap. N. Gui.	a4	79a
Umbuzero, ozero, l., Russia	C16	8
Umeå, Swe.	E9	8
Umeälven, stm., Swe.	D8	8
Umfolozi Game Reserve, S. Afr.	F10	70
Umfors, Swe.	C6	8
Umfreville Lake, res., On., Can.	A3	118
Umkomaas, S. Afr.	G10	70
Umm al-Arānib, Libya	B2	62
Umm al-Jimāl, Khirbat, sci., Jord.	F7	58
Umm al-Qaywayn, U.A.E.	D8	56
Umm as-Sa'd, sci., Syria	E7	58
Umm Bel, Sudan	E5	62
Umm Durmān (Omdurman), Sudan	D6	62
Umm el Faḥm, Isr.	F6	58
Umm Lajj, Sau. Ar.	D4	56
Umm Mitmam, sand, Egypt	H3	58
Umm Omeiyid, Râs, mtn., Egypt	K3	58
Umm Ruwābah, Sudan	E6	62
Umm Sayyālah, Sudan	E6	62
Umnak Island, i., Ak., U.S.	g25	140a
Umpqua, stm., Or., U.S.	G3	136
Umpulo, Ang.	C2	68
'Umrān, Yemen	F5	56
Umraniye, Tur.	D14	28
Umred, India	H7	54
Umreth, India	G4	54
Umtata, S. Afr.	G9	70
Umuarama, Braz.	A11	92
Umzingwani, stm., Zimb.	B9	70
Umzinto, S. Afr.	G10	70
Una, Braz.	H6	88
Una, India	H3	54
Una, stm., Eur.	E13	22
Unac, stm., Bos.	E3	26
Unadilla, Ga., U.S.	D2	116
Unadilla, N.Y., U.S.	B10	114
Unaí, Braz.	I2	88
Unalakleet, Ak., U.S.	D7	140
Unalaska, Ak., U.S.	F6	140
Unalaska Island, i., Ak., U.S.	F6	140
Unare, stm., Ven.	C9	86
'Unayzah, Sau. Ar.	D5	56
Uncia, Bol.	C3	90
Uncompahgre Peak, mtn., Co., U.S.	E9	132
Uncompahgre Plateau, plat., Co., U.S.	E8	132
Unden, l., Swe.	G5	8
Underberg, S. Afr.	F9	70
Undva nina, c., Est.	B4	10
Uneča, Russia	H15	10
Uneiuxi, stm., Braz.	H9	86
Unga Island, i., Ak., U.S.	E7	140
Ungava, Péninsule d', pen., Qc., Can.	D16	106
Ungava Bay, b., Can.	D17	106
Ungava Peninsula see Ungava, Péninsule d', pen., Qc., Can.	D16	106
Ungch'ŏn, Kor., S.	D1	40
Unggi-ŭp, Kor., N.	C9	38
Ungheni, Mol.	B14	26
União, Braz.	C4	88
União dos Palmares, Braz.	E7	88
Unicoi, Tn., U.S.	H3	114
Uniejów, Pol.	D14	16
Unimak Island, i., Ak., U.S.	F7	140
Unimak Pass, strt., Ak., U.S.	F6	140
Unini, stm., Braz.	H11	86
Unión, Arg.	G5	92
Unión, Para.	B9	92
Union, Ia., U.S.	B4	120
Union, La., U.S.	G8	122
Union, N.J., U.S.	D11	114
Union, Or., U.S.	E9	136
Union, S.C., U.S.	B4	116
Union, Wa., U.S.	C3	136
Union, W.V., U.S.	G5	114
Union Bay, B.C., Can.	G6	138
Union City, Ga., U.S.	D14	122
Union City, Mi., U.S.	F4	112
Union City, Oh., U.S.	D1	114
Union City, Pa., U.S.	C6	114
Union City, Tn., U.S.	H8	120
Unión de Reyes, Cuba	A7	102
Unión de Tula, Mex.	E7	100
Union Flat Creek, stm., U.S.	D9	136
Union Grove, Wi., U.S.	F1	112
Union Island, i., St. Vin.	p10	105e
Union Point, Ga., U.S.	C2	116
Union Springs, Al., U.S.	E13	122
Uniontown, Al., U.S.	E11	122
Uniontown, Ky., U.S.	G10	120
Uniontown, Pa., U.S.	E6	114
Unionville, Mi., U.S.	E6	112
United, Pa., U.S.	D6	114
United Arab Emirates, ctry., Asia	E7	56
United Arab Republic see Egypt, ctry., Afr.	B5	62
United Kingdom, ctry., Eur.	D8	6
United States, ctry., N.A.	C10	102
Unity, Sk., Can.	B4	124
Universal City, Tx., U.S.	E9	130
University, Ms., U.S.	C9	122
University City, Mo., U.S.	F7	120
University Park, N.M., U.S.	K10	132
University Park, Tx., U.S.	E2	122
Unjha, India	G4	54
Unnão, India	E8	54
Uno, Canal Numero, can., Arg.	H9	92
Unquillo, Arg.	E5	92
Unst, i., Scot., U.K.	n19	12a
Unstrut, stm., Ger.	E7	16
Unža, stm., Russia	G21	8
Unzen-dake, vol., Japan	G3	40
Uong Bi, Viet.	B8	48
Uozu, Japan	C10	40
Upa, stm., Russia	G20	10
Upanema, Braz.	C7	88
Upata, Ven.	C10	86
Upemba, Lac, l., D.R.C.	F5	66
Upernavik, Grnld.	C14	141
Upía, stm., Col.	E5	86
Upington, S. Afr.	F5	70
Upland, Ne., U.S.	A10	128
Upleta, India	H3	54
Upolu, i., Samoa	h11	79c
Upolu Point, c., Hi., U.S.	c6	78a
Upper Arlington, Oh., U.S.	D2	114
Upper Arrow Lake, l., B.C., Can.	F13	138
Upper Austria see Oberösterreich, state, Aus.	B10	22
Upper Blackville, N.B., Can.	D10	110
Upper Darby, Pa., U.S.	E10	114
Upper Egypt see El-Sa'îd, hist. reg., Egypt	J2	58
Upper Fraser, B.C., Can.	B8	138
Upper Ganga Canal (Upper Ganges Canal), can., India	D6	54
Upper Iowa, stm., U.S.	H7	118
Upper Kapuas Mountains, mts., Asia	C8	50
Upper Klamath Lake, l., Or., U.S.	H5	136
Upper Lake, Ca., U.S.	D3	134
Upper Lake, l., Ca., U.S.	B5	134
Upper Manitou Lake, l., On., Can.	B5	118
Upper Musquodoboit, N.S., Can.	E14	110
Upper Red Lake, l., Mn., U.S.	C4	118
Upper Sandusky, Oh., U.S.	D2	114
Upper Takutu-Upper Essequibo, state, Guy.	F12	86
Upper Trajan's Wall, misc. cult., Mol.	C15	26
Upper Volta see Burkina Faso, ctry., Afr.	G4	64
Uppsala, Swe.	G7	8
Uppsala, state, Swe.	F7	8
Upshi, India	B6	54
Upton, Ky., U.S.	G12	120
Urabá, Golfo de, b., Col.	C3	86
Uracoa, Ven.	C10	86
Uraj, Russia	B10	32
Urakawa, Japan	C15	38
Ural, stm.	E8	32
Ural Mountains see Ural'skie gory, mts., Russia	C9	32
Ural'sk see Oral, Kaz.	D8	32
Ural'skie gory (Ural Mountains), mts., Russia	C9	32
Urana, Austl.	J6	76
Urandangi, Austl.	D7	74
Urangan, Austl.	E9	76
Urania, La., U.S.	F6	122
Uranium City, Sk., Can.	D9	106
Uraricaá, stm., Braz.	F10	86
Uraricoera, Braz.	F11	86
Uraricoera, stm., Braz.	F11	86
Ura-Tjube, Taj.	B10	56
Uravakonda, India	D3	53
Uravan, Co., U.S.	E8	132
Urawa, Japan	D12	40
Urbana, Ar., U.S.	D6	122
Urbana, Il., U.S.	D9	120
Urbana, Oh., U.S.	D2	114
Urbandale, Ia., U.S.	C4	120
Urbania, Italy	G9	22
Urbino, Italy	G9	22
Urcos, Peru	F3	84
Urdinarrain, Arg.	F8	92
Ure, stm., Eng., U.K.	G11	12
Urèčča, Bela.	H10	10
Uren', Russia	H21	8
Ureña, Ven.	D5	86
Ures, Mex.	G7	98
Ureshino, Japan	F2	40
Urewera National Park, p.o.i., N.Z.	D7	80
Urgenč, Uzb.	F10	32
Urho Kekkosen kansallispuisto, p.o.i., Fin.	B12	8
Uriah, Al., U.S.	F11	122
Uriah, Mount, mtn., N.Z.	E4	80
Uribante, stm., Ven.	D6	86
Uribe, Col.	F4	86
Uribia, Col.	B5	86
Urich, Mo., U.S.	F4	120
Urique, stm., Mex.	B5	100
Ūritskīy, Kaz.	D11	32
Urjung-Haja, Russia	B11	34
Urjupinsk, Russia	D6	32
Urla, Tur.	E9	28
Urlaţi, Rom.	D13	26
Urlings, Antig.	f4	105b
Urmia see Orūmīyeh, Iran	B6	56
Urmia, Lake see Orūmīyeh, Daryācheh-ye, l., Iran	B6	56
Uromi, Nig.	H6	64
Uroševac, Serb.	G8	26
Urrao, Col.	D3	86
Ursa, Il., U.S.	D6	120
Uruaçu, Braz.	H1	88
Uruapan, Mex.	L9	134
Uruapan del Progreso, Mex.	F7	100
Urubamba, Peru	F3	84
Urubamba, stm., Peru	F3	84
Urubaxi, stm., Braz.	H9	86
Urubu, stm., Braz.	D6	84
Urubu, stm., Braz.	F1	88
Uruburetama, Braz.	B6	88
Urucará, Braz.	D6	84
Urucu, stm., Braz.	D5	84
Uruçuca, Braz.	H6	88
Uruçuí, Serra da, hills, Braz.	E3	88
Urucuia, stm., Braz.	I3	88
Uruçuí-preto, stm., Braz.	E3	88
Uruguai (Uruguay), stm., S.A.	F8	92
Uruguaiana, Braz.	D9	92
Uruguay, ctry., S.A.	F10	92
Uruguay (Uruguai), stm., S.A.	F8	92
Urumchi see Ürümqi, China	C2	36
Ürümqi, China	C2	36
Urup, ostrov, i., Russia	G19	34
Urupês, Braz.	K1	88
Urutaí, Braz.	I1	88
Uruwira, Tan.	F6	66
Ürzhar, Kaz.	E14	32
Urziceni, Rom.	E13	26
Uržum, Russia	C7	32
Usa, Japan	F4	40
Usa, stm., Russia	A9	32
Uşak, Tur.	E12	28
Uşak, state, Tur.	E12	28
Ušaki, Russia	A13	10
Usakos, Nmb.	B2	70
Usborne, Mount, mtn., Falk. Is.	J5	90
Uščerpe, Russia	H14	10
U.S. Department of Energy Hanford Site, sci., Wa., U.S.	D7	136
Usedom, i., Eur.	B10	16
Ushant see Ouessant, Île d', i., Fr.	F3	14
Üsharal, Kaz.	E14	32
Ushashi, Tan.	E6	66
Üshtöbe, Kaz.	E13	32
Ushuaia, Arg.	J3	90
Usingen, Ger.	F4	16
Usinsk, Russia	A9	32
Usk, Wa., U.S.	B9	136
Usk, stm., Wales, U.K.	J9	12
Uslar, Ger.	E5	16
Usmas ezers, l., Lat.	C4	10
Usole, Russia	C9	32
Usole-Sibirskoe, Russia	D18	32
Uspallata, Arg.	F3	92
Uspanapa, stm., Mex.	G11	100
Ussuri (Wusuli), stm., Asia	C11	36
Ussurijsk, Russia	C10	38
Ust'-Barguzin, Russia	F10	34
Ust'-Belaja, Russia	C23	34
Ust'-Bolšereck, Russia	F20	34
Ust'-Čaun, Russia	C23	34
Ust'-Chorna, Ukr.	A10	26
Ust'-Cil'ma, Russia	D25	8
Uste, Russia	G18	8
Uster, Switz.	C5	22
Ustica, Isola di, i., Italy	F7	24
Ust'-Ilimsk, Russia	C18	32
Ust'-Ilimskoe vodohranilišče, res., Russia	C18	32
Ústí nad Labem, Czech Rep.	F10	16
Ústí nad Orlicí, Czech Rep.	G12	16
Ust'-Išim, Russia	C12	32
Ustja, stm., Russia	F21	8
Ust'-Javron'ga, Russia	E21	8
Ustjuckoe, Russia	B18	10
Ustjužna, Russia	B19	10
Ustka, Pol.	B12	16
Ust'-Kamčatsk, Russia	E21	34
Ust'-Kamenogorsk see Öskemen, Kaz.	E14	32
Ust'-Koksa, Russia	D15	32
Ust'-Kujda, Russia	B16	34
Ust'-Kulom, Russia	B8	32
Ust'-Kut, Russia	C19	32
Ust'-Lyža, Russia	A9	32
Ust'-Maja, Russia	D15	34
Ust'-Man'ja, Russia	B10	32
Ust'-Nera, Russia	D17	34
Ust'-Njukža, Russia	E13	34
Uštobe see Üshtöbe, Kaz.	E13	32
Ust'-Omčug, Russia	D18	34
Ust'-Ordynskij, Russia	D18	32
Ust'-Ozërnoe, Russia	C15	32
Ust'-Pinega, Russia	D19	8
Ust'-Reki, Russia	E22	8
Ustroń, Pol.	G14	16
Ust'-Sumy, Russia	D14	32
Ust'-Ulagan, Russia	D15	32
Ust'-Urgal, Russia	F15	34
Ust-Urt Plateau, plat., Asia	F9	32
Ust-Vyjskaja, Russia	E22	8
Usu, China	C1	36
Usuki, Japan	F4	40
Usulután, El Sal.	F3	102
Usumacinta, stm., N.A.	D2	102
Usumbura see Bujumbura, Bdi.	E5	66
Ušumun, Russia	F14	34
Usvjaty, Russia	E13	10
Utah, state, U.S.	D5	132
Utah Lake, l., Ut., U.S.	C5	132
Utata, Russia	D18	32
Ute, Ia., U.S.	B2	120
Ute Creek, stm., N.M., U.S.	F5	128
Utegi, Tan.	E6	66
Utena, Lith.	E8	10
Utete, Tan.	F7	66
Uthai Thani, Thai.	E4	48
Uthal, Pak.	D10	56
U Thong, Thai.	E4	48
Utiariti, Braz.	F6	84
Utica, Ks., U.S.	C8	128
Utica, Mi., U.S.	F6	112
Utica, Ms., U.S.	E8	122
Utica, N.Y., U.S.	E14	112
Utica, Oh., U.S.	D3	114
Utica see Utique, sci., Tun.	G3	24
Utiel, Spain	E9	20
Utila, Isla de, i., Hond.	D4	102
Utinga, stm., Braz.	G5	88
Utique (Utica), sci., Tun.	G3	24
Uto, Japan	G3	40
Utopia, Tx., U.S.	E8	130
Utorgoš, Russia	B13	10
Utraula, India	E9	54
Utrecht, Neth.	B14	14
Utrecht, S. Afr.	E10	70
Utrera, Spain	G5	20
Utrik, at., Marsh. Is.	B7	72
Utroja, stm., Eur.	D10	10
Utsunomiya, Japan	C12	40
Uttamapālaiyam, India	G3	53
Uttaradit, Thai.	D4	48
Uttaranchal, state, India	C7	54
Uttarkāshi, India	C7	54
Uttar Pradesh, state, India	E7	54
Utuado, P.R.	B2	104a
Utukok, stm., Ak., U.S.	C7	140
Utupua, i., Sol. Is.	E7	72
Uulu, Est.	B7	10
Uvá, stm., Col.	F7	86
Uvalda, Ga., U.S.	D3	116
Uvalde, Tx., U.S.	E8	130
Uvaravičy, Bela.	H13	10
Uvarovo, Russia	D6	32
Uvdal, Nor.	F3	8
Uvinza, Tan.	F6	66
Uvira, D.R.C.	E5	66
Uvs Lake see Uvsu-Nur, ozero, l., Asia	F7	34
Uvsu-Nur, ozero, l., Asia	F7	34
Uvworé, c., Vanuatu	I17	79d
Uwa, Japan	F5	40
Uwajima, Japan	F5	40
Uwayl, Sudan	F5	62
Uxbridge, On., Can.	D10	112
Uxmal, sci., Mex.	B3	102
Uyo, Nig.	H6	64
Uyuni, Bol.	D3	90
Uyuni, Salar de, pl., Bol.	D3	90
Uzbekistan, ctry., Asia	E10	30
Uzda, Bela.	G10	10
Uzerche, Fr.	D7	18
Uzgen, Kyrg.	F12	32
Uzhhorod, Ukr.	A9	26
Užice, Serb.	F6	26
Uzlovaja, Russia	F20	10
Üzümlü, Tur.	G12	28
Uzun Ada, i., Tur.	E9	28
Uzunköprü, Tur.	B9	28
Uzunkuduk, Uzb.	F11	32
Užur, Russia	C16	32
Užventis, Lith.	E5	10
V		
Vaal, stm., S. Afr.	F7	70
Vaaldam, res., S. Afr.	E8	70
Vaalwater, S. Afr.	D8	70
Vaasa (Vasa), Fin.	E9	8
Vabalninkas, Lith.	D7	10
Vác, Hung.	B6	26
Vacacaí, stm., Braz.	E11	92
Vacaria, Braz.	D12	92
Vacaria, stm., Braz.	I4	88
Vacaville, Ca., U.S.	E4	134
Vaccarès, Étang de, l., Fr.	F10	18
Vache, Île à, i., Haiti	C11	102
Vad, Russia	I21	8
Vadakara see Badagara, India	F2	53
Vădeni, Rom.	D14	26
Vadnagar, India	G4	54
Vado, N.M., U.S.	K10	132
Vadodara (Baroda), India	G4	54
Vado Ligure, Italy	F5	22
Vadsø, Nor.	A13	8
Vaduz, Liech.	C6	22
Vaga, stm., Russia	F20	8
Vågåmo, Nor.	F3	8
Vágar, i., Far. Is.	m34	8b
Vaghena Island, i., Sol. Is.	d7	79b
Vah, stm., Russia	B13	32
Váh, stm., Slov.	H13	16
Vahsel, Cape, c., S. Geor.	J9	90
Vaiden, Ms., U.S.	D9	122
Vaigai, stm., India	G4	53
Vaigat, strt., Grnld.	C15	141
Vaijāpur, India	B2	53
Vaikam, India	G3	53
Väike-Maarja, Est.	A9	10
Vail, Co., U.S.	D10	132
Vail, Ia., U.S.	B2	120
Vaimali, Vanuatu	k17	79d
Vaippār, stm., India	G4	53
Vaison-la-Romaine, Fr.	E11	18
Vaitahu, Fr. Poly.	s18	78g
Vākhān, hist. reg., Afg.	B11	56
Valaam, Russia	F14	8
Valadeces, Mex.	H9	130
Valandovo, Mac.	B5	28
Valašské Meziříčí, Czech Rep.	G13	16
Valatie, N.Y., U.S.	B12	114
Vâlcea, state, Rom.	E11	26
Vălčedrăm, Blg.	F10	26
Valcheta, Arg.	H3	90
Valdagno, Italy	E8	22
Valdai Hills see Valdajskaja vozvyšennost', hills, Russia	C15	10
Valdaj, Russia	B16	10
Valdaj, Russia	E16	8
Valdajskaja vozvyšennost' (Valdai Hills), hills, Russia	C15	10
Valdarno, val., Italy	G8	22
Val-de-Cães, Braz.	A1	88
Valdecañas, Embalse de, res., Spain	E5	20
Valdemarsvik, Swe.	G7	8
Valdepeñas, Spain	F7	20
Valderaduey, stm., Spain	C5	20
Valdés, Península, pen., Arg.	H4	90
Val-des-Bois, Qc., Can.	C14	112
Valdez, Ak., U.S.	D10	140
Valdivia, Chile	G2	90
Valdivia, Col.	D4	86
Valdobbiadene, Italy	E8	22
Val-d'Oise, state, Fr.	E10	14
Val-d'Or, Qc., Can.	F15	106
Valdosta, Ga., U.S.	F2	116
Valdoviño see Aviño, Spain	A2	20
Vale, Or., U.S.	G9	136
Valemount, B.C., Can.	D11	138
Valença, Braz.	L4	88
Valença, Braz.	G6	88
Valença, Port.	B2	20
Valença do Piauí, Braz.	D4	88
Valence, Fr.	E10	18
Valencia, Phil.	F5	52
València, Spain	E10	20
Valencia, Ven.	B7	86
València, state, Spain	E10	20
València, co., Spain	E10	20
València, Golf de, b., Spain	E10	20
Valencia, Golfo de see València, Golf de, b., Spain	E10	20
Valencia, Gulf of see València, Golf de, b., Spain	E10	20
Valencia, Lago de, l., Ven.	B8	86
Valencia de Alcántara, Spain	E3	20
Valencia de Don Juan, Spain	B5	20
Valencia Island, i., Ire.	J2	12
Valenciennes, Fr.	D12	14
Valente, Braz.	F6	88
Valentin, Russia	C11	38
Valentine, Ne., U.S.	E12	126
Valentine, Tx., U.S.	D3	130
Valenza, Italy	F5	22
Valera, Ven.	C6	86
Valga, Est.	H12	8
Valiente, Península, pen., Pan.	H7	102
Valili, mtn., Fiji	p19	79e
Valjevo, Serb.	E6	26
Valkeakoski, Fin.	F11	8
Valkenswaard, Neth.	C14	14
Valkininkas, Lith.	F7	10
Valladares, Mex.	H7	130
Valladolid, Mex.	B3	102
Valladolid, Spain	C6	20
Valladolid, co., Spain	C6	20
Vall de Uxó see La Vall d'Uixó, Spain	E10	20
Valle, Lat.	D7	10
Vallecillo, Mex.	H7	130
Valle d'Aosta, state, Italy	E4	22
Valle de Allende, Mex.	H2	130
Valle de la Pascua, Ven.	C8	86
Valle del Cauca, state, Col.	F3	86
Valle del Rosario, Mex.	G1	130
Valle de Olivos, Mex.	B5	100
Valle de Santiago, Mex.	E8	100
Valledupar, Col.	B5	86
Vallée d'Aoste see Valle d'Aosta, state, Italy	E4	22
Valle Edén, Ur.	E9	92
Vallegrande, Bol.	C4	90
Valle Hermoso, Mex.	C10	100
Vallejo, Ca., U.S.	E3	134
Vallenar, Chile	D2	92
Valle Redondo, Mex.	K9	134
Valletta, Malta	I8	24
Valley, Al., U.S.	E13	122
Valley, Ne., U.S.	C1	120
Valley, Wa., U.S.	B9	136
Valley, stm., Mb., Can.	C13	124
Valley Bend, W.V., U.S.	F6	114
Valley City, N.D., U.S.	H16	124
Valley East, On., Can.	B8	112
Valley Falls, Ks., U.S.	E2	120
Valley Farms, Az., U.S.	K5	132
Valley Head, Al., U.S.	C13	122
Valley Mills, Tx., U.S.	C10	130
Valley of the Kings, sci., Egypt	B6	62
Valley Springs, S.D., U.S.	H2	118
Valley Station, Ky., U.S.	F12	120
Valleyview, Ab., Can.	A13	138
Valley View, Tx., U.S.	H11	128
Vallimanca, Arroyo, stm., Arg.	H7	92
Vallorbe, Switz.	D3	22
Valls, Spain	C12	20
Valmeyer, Il., U.S.	F7	120
Valmiera, Lat.	C8	10
Valoria la Buena, Spain	C6	20
Valožyn, Bela.	F9	10
Vālpārai, India	F3	53
Valparaíso, Chile	F2	92
Valparaíso, Mex.	D7	100
Valparaiso, Fl., U.S.	G12	122
Valparaiso, In., U.S.	G2	112
Valparaiso, Ne., U.S.	F16	126
Valparaíso, state, Chile	F2	92
Valréas, Fr.	E10	18
Vals, stm., S. Afr.	E8	70
Vals, Tanjung, c., Indon.	G10	44
Valsbaai see False Bay, b., S. Afr.	I4	70
Valtimo, Fin.	E13	8
Valujki, Russia	D5	32
Valverde del Camino, Spain	G4	20
Valyncy, Bela.	E11	10
Vamori Wash, stm., Az., U.S.	L5	132
Van, Tur.	B5	56
Van, Lake see Van Gölü, l., Tur.	B5	56
Vanadzor, Arm.	A5	56
Vanajavesi, l., Fin.	F10	8
Van Alstyne, Tx., U.S.	D2	122
Vananda, B.C., Can.	G6	138
Vanavara, Russia	B18	32
Van Bruyssel, Qc., Can.	C4	110
Van Buren, Ar., U.S.	B4	122
Van Buren, Me., U.S.	C8	110
Vanceboro, Me., U.S.	E9	110
Vanceburg, Ky., U.S.	F2	114
Vancouver, B.C., Can.	G7	138
Vancouver, Wa., U.S.	E4	136
Vancouver Island, i., B.C., Can.	G4	138
Vancouver Island Ranges, mts., B.C., Can.	G5	138
Vandalia, Il., U.S.	F8	120
Vandalia, Mo., U.S.	E6	120
Vandalia, Oh., U.S.	E1	114
Vandavāsi, India	E4	53
Vanderbijlpark, S. Afr.	E8	70
Vanderbilt, Tx., U.S.	F11	130
Vanderhoof, B.C., Can.	B6	138
Vanderkloof Dam, res., S. Afr.	F7	70
Vanderlin Island, i., Austl.	C7	74
Vandervoort, Ar., U.S.	C4	122
Van Diemen Gulf, b., Austl.	B6	74
Vandry, Qc., Can.	C3	110
Vandžiogala, Lith.	E6	10
Vanegas, Mex.	D8	100
Vänern, l., Swe.	G5	8
Vänersborg, Swe.	G5	8
Vangaindrano, Madag.	E8	68
Van Gölü, l., Tur.	B5	56
Vangunu Island, i., Sol. Is.	e8	79b
Van Horn, Tx., U.S.	C3	130
Van Horne, Ia., U.S.	B5	120
Vanier, ngh., On., Can.	C14	112
Vanikolo, i., Sol. Is.	E7	72
Vanimo, Pap. N. Gui.	a3	79a
Vanino, Russia	G17	34
Vānīvilāsa Sāgara, res., India	E3	53
Vāniyambādi, India	E4	53
Vankarem, Russia	C25	34
Vankleek Hill, On., Can.	E2	110
Van Lear, Ky., U.S.	G3	114
Vanna, i., Nor.	A8	8
Vännäs, Swe.	E8	8
Vanndale, Ar., U.S.	B8	122
Vannes, Fr.	G6	14
Van Ninh, Viet.	F9	48
Van Phong, Vung, b., Viet.	F9	48
Van Phong Bay see Van Phong, Vung, b., Viet.	F9	48
Van Reenen, S. Afr.	F9	70
Van Rees, Pegunungan, mts., Indon.	F10	44
Vanrhynsdorp, S. Afr.	G4	70
Vansant, Va., U.S.	G3	114
Vansittart Island, i., Nu., Can.	B14	106
Vanskoe, Russia	B19	10
Vanthali, India	H3	54
Vanua Balavu, i., Fiji	p20	79e
Vanua Lava, i., Vanuatu	i16	79d
Vanua Levu, i., Fiji	p19	79e
Vanuatu (New Hebrides), ctry., Oc.	k16	79d
Van Wert, Oh., U.S.	D1	114
Van Wyksdorp, S. Afr.	H5	70
Van Zylsrus, S. Afr.	E6	70
Vao, N. Cal.	n16	79d
Var, state, Fr.	F12	18
Var, stm., Fr.	F13	18
Varada, stm., India	D2	53
Varallo, Italy	E5	22
Vārānasi (Benares), India	F9	54
Varandej, Russia	A9	32
Varangerfjorden, b., Nor.	A14	8
Varangerhalvøya, pen., Nor.	A13	8
Varano, Lago di, l., Italy	I12	22
Varaždin, Cro.	D13	22
Varazze, Italy	F5	22
Varberg, Swe.	H5	8
Vardak, state, Afg.	A2	54
Vardar (Axiós), stm., Eur.	B5	28
Varde, Den.	I3	8
Vardø, Nor.	A14	8
Varel, Ger.	C4	16
Varela, Arg.	G4	92
Varėna, Lith.	F7	10
Varennes-sur-Allier, Fr.	C9	18
Varese, Italy	E5	22
Vârfurile, Rom.	C9	26
Vargem, Riacho da, stm., Braz.	E6	88
Vargem Grande, Braz.	B3	88
Varginha, Braz.	K3	88
Varkallai, India	G3	53
Varkaus, Fin.	E12	8
Värmeln, l., Swe.	G5	8
Värmland, state, Swe.	G5	8
Varna, Blg.	F14	26
Varna, Russia	D10	32
Varna, state, Blg.	F14	26
Värnamo, Swe.	H6	8
Varniai, Lith.	E5	10
Varnjany, Bela.	F9	10
Varnsdorf, Czech Rep.	F10	16
Varnville, S.C., U.S.	D4	116
Várpalota, Hung.	B5	26
Värska, Est.	C10	10
Varvarin, Serb.	F8	26
Várzea, stm., Braz.	C11	92
Várzea Alegre, Braz.	D6	88
Várzea da Palma, Braz.	I3	88

Name	Map Ref.	Page
Várzea Grande, Braz.	G6	84
Varzino, Russia	B17	8
Vas, state, Hung.	B3	26
Vasa see Vaasa, Fin.	E9	8
Vasai, India	E3	46
Vasalemma, Est.	A7	10
Vasco, País see Euskal Herriko, state, Spain	A8	20
Vashkivtsi, Ukr.	A14	26
Vashkivtsi, Ukr.	A12	26
Vashon Island, i., Wa., U.S.	C4	136
Vasilevičy, Bela.	H12	10
Vasilevskij Moh, Russia	C18	10
Vasilika, Grc.	C6	28
Vasjugan, stm., Russia	C13	32
Vaška, stm., Russia	D21	8
Vaskelovo, Russia	F14	8
Vaslui, Rom.	C14	26
Vaslui, state, Rom.	C14	26
Vass, N.C., U.S.	A6	116
Vassar, Mi., U.S.	E6	112
Västerås, Swe.	G7	8
Västerbotten, state, Swe.	D8	8
Västernorrland, state, Swe.	E7	8
Västervik, Swe.	H7	8
Västmanland, state, Swe.	G7	8
Vasto, Italy	H11	22
Västra Götaland, state, Swe.	G4	8
Vasvár, Hung.	B3	26
Vatan, Fr.	G10	14
Vatican see Vatican City, ctry., Eur.	I9	22
Vatican City, ctry., Eur.	I9	22
Vaticano, Capo, c., Italy	F9	24
Vatnajökull, ice, Ice.	k31	8a
Vatomandry, Madag.	D8	68
Vatra Dornei, Rom.	B12	26
Vättern, l., Swe.	G6	8
Vatu-i-ra Channel, strt., Fiji	p19	79e
Vatukoula, Fiji	p18	79e
Vauclin, Montagne du, mtn., Mart.	k7	105c
Vaucluse, state, Fr.	F11	18
Vaucouleurs, Fr.	F14	14
Vaughan, On., Can.	E10	112
Vaughn, N.M., U.S.	G3	128
Vaukavysk, Bela.	G7	10
Vaupés, state, Col.	G6	86
Vaupés (Uaupés), stm., S.A.	G7	86
Vava'u, i., Tonga	E9	72
Vavoua, C. Iv.	H3	64
Vavuniya, Sri L.	G5	53
Växjö, Swe.	H6	8
Vaza-barris, stm., Braz.	E6	88
Vazante, Braz.	J2	88
Vazuza, stm., Russia	E17	10
Vazuzskoe vodohranilišče, res., Russia	E16	10
Veazie, Me., U.S.	F8	110
Veblen, S.D., U.S.	B15	126
Vecht (Vechte), stm., Eur.	B15	14
Vechta, Ger.	D4	16
Vechte (Vecht), stm., Eur.	B15	14
Vecpiebalga, Lat.	C8	10
Vecsés, Hung.	B6	26
Veddige, Swe.	H4	8
Vedea, stm., Rom.	F12	26
Vedia, Arg.	G7	92
Vednoe, Russia	C19	10
Veedersburg, In., U.S.	H2	112
Veendam, Neth.	A15	14
Veenendaal, Neth.	C14	14
Vega, i., Nor.	D4	8
Vega Alta, P.R.	B3	104a
Vega Baja, P.R.	B3	104a
Vegreville, Ab., Can.	C18	138
Veguita, N.M., U.S.	I10	132
Veinticinco de Mayo, Arg.	G7	92
Veiros, Braz.	D7	84
Veisiejai, Lith.	F6	10
Vejle, Den.	I3	8
Vejle, state, Den.	I3	8
Vela Luka, Cro.	H13	22
Velas, Cabo, c., C.R.	G4	102
Velázquez, Ur.	G10	92
Velden, Ger.	H8	16
Veleka, stm.	G14	26
Veleušcina, Bela.	F11	10
Vélez, Col.	D5	86
Vélez-Málaga, Spain	H6	20
Vel'gija, Russia	B17	10
Velhas, stm., Braz.	J3	88
Velika, stm., Russia	C11	10
Velikaja, stm., Russia	D23	34
Velikaja Kema, Russia	B12	38
Velika Morava, stm., Serb.	E8	26
Velikie Luki, Russia	D13	10
Veliki Ustjug, Russia	F21	8
Veliki Vítorog, mtn., Bos.	E4	26
Velikoe, Russia	G17	8
Velikoe, ozero, l., Russia	C19	10
Velikonda Hills, hills, India	D4	53
Veliko Tárnovo, Blg.	F12	26
Velikovisočnoe, Russia	C25	8
Veli Lošinj, Cro.	F11	22
Velingara, Sen.	G2	64
Veliž, Russia	E14	10
Velké Kapušany, Slov.	H18	16
Velké Meziříčí, Czech Rep.	G12	16
Vella Gulf, strt., Sol. Is.	d7	79b
Vella Lavella, i., Sol. Is.	d7	79b
Vellār, stm., India	F4	53
Velletri, Italy	I9	22
Vellore, India	E4	53
Velma, Ok., U.S.	G11	128
Vel'sk, Russia	F20	8
Velten, Ger.	D9	16
Velva, N.D., U.S.	F13	124
Velyka Mykhailivka, Ukr.	B16	26
Velykodolyns'ke, Ukr.	C17	26
Velykopolis'ke, Ukr.	C16	26
Velykyi Bychkiv, Ukr.	B11	26
Velykyi Kuialnyk, stm., Ukr.	B17	26
Venadillo, Col.	E4	86
Venado Tuerto, Arg.	F6	92
Venafro, Fr.	C8	24
Venâncio Aires, Braz.	D11	92
Vence, Fr.	F13	18
Venda, hist. reg., S. Afr.	C10	70
Vendas Novas, Port.	F2	20
Vendée, state, Fr.	C4	18
Vendéen, Bocage, reg., Fr.	C4	18
Vendôme, Fr.	G10	14
Vendrell see El Vendrell, Spain	C12	20
Veneta, Laguna, b., Italy	E9	22
Venetie, Ak., U.S.	C11	140
Veneto, state	E8	22
Venev, Russia	F21	10
Venézia (Venice), Italy	E9	22
Venezuela, ctry., S.A.	B4	84
Venezuela, Golfo de b., S.A.	A3	84
Venezuela, Gulf of see Venezuela, Golfo de, b., S.A.	A3	84
Venezuelan Basin, unds.	G7	144
Vengerovo, Russia	C14	32
Vengurla, India	D1	53
Veniaminof, Mount, vol., Ak., U.S.	E8	140
Venice see Venézia, Italy	E9	22
Venice, Fl., U.S.	I3	116
Venice, La., U.S.	H9	122
Venice, Gulf of b., Eur.	E9	22
Vénissieux, Fr.	D10	18
Venkatagiri, India	E4	53
Venlo, Neth.	C15	14
Venosa, Italy	D9	24
Venoste, Alpi (Ötztaler Alpen), mts., Eur.	D7	22
Venray, Neth.	C15	14
Venta, stm., Eur.	C4	10
Ventanas, Ec.	H2	86
Ventersdorp, S. Afr.	E8	70
Venterstad, S. Afr.	G7	70
Veurne, Bel.	C11	14
Ventimiglia, Italy	G4	22
Ventotene, Isola, i., Italy	D7	24
Ventspils, Lat.	C4	10
Ventuari, stm., Ven.	E8	86
Ventura, Ca., U.S.	I6	134
Venturia, N.D., U.S.	B13	126
Venustiano Carranza, Mex.	G12	100
Venustiano Carranza, Presa, res., Mex.	B8	100
Vera, Arg.	D7	92
Vera, Spain	G9	20
Vera, Cape, c., Nu., Can.	B8	141
Veracruz, Mex.	F10	100
Veracruz, state, Mex.	F10	100
Veranópolis, Braz.	D12	92
Verāval, India	H3	54
Verbania, Italy	E5	22
Verbano see Maggiore, Lago, l., Eur.	C14	18
Verbeek, Pegunungan, mts., Indon.	E12	50
Verbilki, Russia	D20	10
Vercelli, Italy	E5	22
Vercors, reg., Fr.	E11	18
Verde, stm., Braz.	D4	90
Verde, stm., Braz.	F4	88
Verde, stm., Braz.	H1	88
Verde, stm., Braz.	J1	88
Verde, stm., Braz.	F6	84
Verde, stm., Mex.	E7	100
Verde, stm., Az., U.S.	J5	132
Verde, Cape, c., Bah.	A10	102
Verde Grande, stm., Braz.	H4	88
Verden, Ger.	D5	16
Verden, Ok., U.S.	F10	128
Verde Pequeno, stm., Braz.	H4	88
Verdi, stm., Braz.	D5	134
Verdigre, Ne., U.S.	E14	126
Verdigris, stm., U.S.	E13	128
Verdon, stm., Fr.	F12	18
Verdon, ngh., Qc., Can.	E3	110
Verdun-sur-Garonne, Fr.	F7	18
Verdun-sur-Meuse, Fr.	E14	14
Vereeniging, S. Afr.	E9	70
Veregin, Sk., Can.	C11	124
Vereja, Russia	E19	10
Vereščagino, Russia	B15	32
Vergennes, Vt., U.S.	F3	110
Verhnedneprovskij, Russia	E16	10
Verhneimbatsk, Russia	B15	32
Verhnemulomskoe vodohranilišče, res., Russia	B14	8
Verhneural'sk, Russia	D9	32
Verhnevilujsk, Russia	D13	34
Verhnij Baskunčak, Russia	E7	32
Verhnij Most, Russia	C11	10
Verhnij Ufalej, Russia	C10	32
Verhnjaja Amga, Russia	E14	34
Verhnjaja Angara, stm., Russia	E11	34
Verhnjaja Inta, Russia	A10	32
Verhnjaja Salda, Russia	C10	32
Verhnjaja Tajmyra, stm., Russia	B8	34
Verhnjaja Tojma, Russia	E21	8
Verhnjaja Tura, Russia	C15	34
Verhojanskij hrebet (Verhoyansk Mountains), mts., Russia	C14	34
Verhopuja, Russia	F19	8
Verhove, Russia	H20	10
Verigin see Veregin, Sk., Can.	C11	124
Verín, Spain	C3	20
Veríssimo, Braz.	J1	88
Verkhovyna, Ukr.	A11	26
Verkhoyansk Mountains see Verhojanskij hrebet, mts., Russia	C14	34
Vermelho, stm., Braz.	E2	88
Vermilion, Oh., U.S.	C3	114
Vermilion, stm., Ab., Can.	C19	138
Vermilion, stm., On., Can.	B8	112
Vermilion, stm., Il., U.S.	C6	118
Vermilion Bay, b., La., U.S.	H6	122
Vermilion Lake, l., On., Can.	A6	118
Vermilion Lake, l., Mn., U.S.	D5	118
Vermilion Pass, p., Can.	E14	138
Vermillion, S.D., U.S.	E16	126
Vermillion, stm., S.D., U.S.	E15	126
Vermillion, East Fork, stm., S.D., U.S.	D15	126
Vermilion, stm., Qc., Can.	C3	110
Vermont, Il., U.S.	D7	120
Vermont, state, U.S.	F3	110
Vernal, Ut., U.S.	C7	132
Verndale, Mn., U.S.	E3	118
Verneuil, Fr.	F9	14
Vernon, B.C., Can.	F11	138
Vernon, Al., U.S.	D10	122
Vernon, Ct., U.S.	C13	114
Vernon, In., U.S.	F12	120
Vernon, Tx., U.S.	G9	128
Vernon, Ut., U.S.	C4	132
Vernonia, Or., U.S.	E3	136
Vernon Lake, res., La., U.S.	F5	122
Vernon River, P.E., Can.	D13	110
Vero Beach, Fl., U.S.	I5	116
Verona, On., Can.	C5	28
Verona, On., Can.	D13	112
Verona, Italy	E8	22
Verona, Ms., U.S.	C10	122
Verónica, Arg.	G9	92
Versailles, Fr.	F11	14
Versailles, II., U.S.	E7	120
Versailles, Ky., U.S.	F13	120
Versailles, Mo., U.S.	F5	120
Versailles, Oh., U.S.	D1	114
Veršino-Darasunskij, Russia	F12	34
Veršino-Šahtaminskij, Russia	F12	34
Verterdero, P.R.	B3	104a
Vertientes, Cuba	B8	102
Verulam, S. Afr.	F10	70
Verviers, Bel.	D14	14
Verwoerd Reservoir see Gariep Dam, res., S. Afr.	G7	70
Vescovato, Fr.	G15	18
Veselí nad Lužnicí, Czech Rep.	G10	16
Veselyj Jar, Russia	C11	38
Vesole, Monte, mtn., Italy	D9	24
Vespasiano, Braz.	J4	88
Vesta, C.R.	H6	102
Vest-Agder, state, Nor.	G2	8
Vestavia Hills, Al., U.S.	D12	122
Vesterålen, i., Nor.	B6	8
Vestfjorden, b., Nor.	C6	8
Vestfold, state, Nor.	G4	8
Vestmannaeyjar, Ice.	I29	8a
Vestsjælland, state, Den.	I4	8
Vestvågøya, i., Nor.	B5	8
Vesuvio (Vesuvius), vol., Italy	D8	24
Vesuvius see Vesuvio, vol., Italy	D8	24
Veszprém, Hung.	B4	26
Veszprém, state, Hung.	B4	26
Vésztő, Hung.	C8	26
Vet, stm., Italy	F8	70
Vetapālem, India	D5	53
Vetju, Russia	E24	8
Vetlanda, Swe.	H6	8
Vetluga, Russia	H21	8
Vetluga, stm., Russia	C7	32
Vetluzskij, Russia	G21	8
Vetlužskij, Russia	H21	8
Vetrişoaia, Rom.	C15	26
Vetschau, Ger.	E9	16
Veurne, Bel.	C11	14
Vevay, Switz.	D3	22
Veynes, Fr.	E11	18
Vézère, stm., Fr.	D7	18
Viacha, Bol.	C3	90
Viadana, Italy	F7	22
Viale, Arg.	E8	92
Viamão, Braz.	E12	92
Viamonte, Arg.	F6	92
Vian, Ok., U.S.	B4	122
Viana, Braz.	B3	88
Viana do Bolo, Spain	B3	20
Viana do Castelo, Port.	C1	20
Viana do Castelo, state, Port.	C2	20
Viani, Lat.	D9	10
Viangchan (Vientiane), Laos	D6	48
Viaregio, Italy	G7	22
Vibank, Sk., Can.	D10	124
Viborg, Den.	H3	8
Viborg, S.D., U.S.	D15	126
Viborg, state, Den.	H3	8
Vibo Valentia, Italy	F10	24
Vic, Spain	C13	20
Vicam, Mex.	B3	100
Vicebsk, Bela.	E13	10
Vicebsk, state, Bela.	E11	10
Vicente Guerrero, Mex.	D6	100
Vicente Guerrero, Presa, res., Mex.	D9	100
Vicenza, Italy	E8	22
Viceroy, Sk., Can.	E8	124
Vichada, state, Col.	E7	86
Vichada, stm., Col.	E7	86
Vichadero, Ur.	E10	92
Vichra, stm., Eur.	F14	10
Vichuquén, Chile	G1	92
Vichy, Fr.	C9	18
Vici, Ok., U.S.	E9	128
Vicksburg, Ms., U.S.	E8	122
Victor, Ia., U.S.	C5	120
Victor, Id., U.S.	G15	136
Victor, Mt., U.S.	D12	136
Victor Harbor, Austl.	J2	76
Victoria, B.C., Can.	H7	138
Victoria, P.E., Can.	D13	110
Victoria, Sey.	I11	92
Victoria see Labuan, Malay.	A9	50
Victoria see Rabat, Malta	H8	24
Victoria, Sey.	j13	69b
Victoria, Ks., U.S.	C11	10
Victoria, Tx., U.S.	E10	130
Victoria, Va., U.S.	G7	114
Victoria, state, Austl.	K4	76
Victoria, stm., Austl.	C6	74
Victoria, Chutes see Victoria Falls, wtfl., Afr.	D4	68
Victoria, Lake, l., Afr.	E6	66
Victoria, Lake, l., Austl.	I3	76
Victoria, Mount, mtn., Mya.	B1	48
Victoria, Mount, mtn., Pap. N. Gui.	b4	79a
Victoria Falls, wtfl., Afr.	D4	68
Victoria Fjord, b., Grnld.	A16	141
Victoria Harbour, On., Can.	D10	112
Victoria Island, i., Can.	A8	106
Victoria Land, reg., Ant.	C20	81
Victoria Nile, stm., Afr.	D6	66
Victoria Peak, mtn., Belize	D3	102
Victoria Peak, mtn., B.C., Can.	F4	138
Victoria River Downs, Austl.	C6	74
Victorias, Phil.	E4	52
Victoria Strait, strt., Nu., Can.	B10	106
Victoria The Village see The Village, Ok., U.S.	F11	128
Victoriaville, Qc., Can.	D4	110
Victoria West, S. Afr.	G6	70
Victorica, Arg.	H5	92
Victorino, Ven.	F8	86
Victorville, Ca., U.S.	I8	134
Vičuga, Russia	H19	8
Vicuña, Chile	E2	92
Vicuña Mackenna, Arg.	F5	92
Vidalia, Ga., U.S.	D3	116
Vidalia, La., U.S.	F7	122
Vidal Ramos, Braz.	C13	92
Videira, Braz.	C12	92
Vidigueira, Port.	F3	20
Vidin, Blg.	F9	26
Vidisha, India	G6	54
Vidor, Tx., U.S.	G4	122
Vidoy, i., Far. Is.	m34	8b
Vidra, Rom.	E13	26
Vidsel, Swe.	D9	8
Vidzeme, hist. reg., Lat.	C8	10
Viechtach, Ger.	G8	16
Viedma, Arg.	H4	90
Viedma, Lago, l., Arg.	I2	90
Vieille Case, Dom.	i6	105c
Viejo, Cerro, mtn., Peru	F5	84
Viella, Spain	B11	20
Vienna see Wien, Aus.	B13	22
Vienna, Ga., U.S.	D2	116
Vienna, Il., U.S.	G9	120
Vienna, Mo., U.S.	F5	120
Vienna, W.V., U.S.	E4	114
Vienna see Wien, state, Aus.	B13	22
Vienna Woods see Wienerwald, mts., Aus.	B13	22
Vienne, Fr.	D10	18
Vienne, state, Fr.	C6	18
Vienne, stm., Fr.	C6	18
Vientiane see Viangchan, Laos	D6	48
Vieques, P.R.	B5	104a
Vieques, Aeropuerto, P.R.	B5	104a
Vieques, Isla de, i., P.R.	B5	104a
Vierge, Pointe du, c., Guad.	i5	105c
Vieux-Habitants, Guad.	h5	105c
Vievis, Lith.	F7	10
Vigala, Est.	B7	10
Vigan, Phil.	B3	52
Vigevano, Italy	E5	22
Vígia, Braz.	A1	88
Vigie Airport, St. Luc.	m7	105c
Vignola, Italy	F7	22
Vigo, Spain	B1	20
Vigo, Ría de, est., Spain	B1	20
Vihāri, Pak.	D4	54
Vihowa, Pak.	C3	54
Vihren, mtn., Blg.	H10	26
Viinijärvi, Fin.	E13	8
Vijayapura, Ind.	C3	53
Vijapur, India	G4	54
Vijayawāda, India	C5	53
Vikārābād, India	C3	53
Viking, Ab., Can.	C19	138
Vikna, Nor.	D4	8
Vikna, i., Nor.	D4	8
Vikramasingapuram, India	G3	53
Vikulovo, Russia	C12	32
Vila da Ribeira Brava, C.V.	k10	65a
Vila de Sena, Moz.	D5	68
Vila do Bispo, Port.	G1	20
Vila do Conde, Port.	C2	20
Vila Fontes, Moz.	D6	68
Vilafranca del Panadès see Vilafranca del Penedès, Spain	C12	20
Vilafranca del Penedès, Spain	C12	20
Vila Franca de Xira, Port.	F2	20
Vila Gamito, Moz.	C5	68
Vilagarcía de Arousa, Spain	B1	20
Vilaine, stm., Fr.	G7	14
Vilaka, Lat.	C10	10
Vilalba, Spain	A3	20
Vilanandro, Tanjona, c., Madag.	D7	68
Vilāni, Lat.	D9	10
Vilankulo, Moz.	B12	70
Vila Nova de Famalicão, Port.	C2	20
Vila Nova de Gaia, Port.	C2	20
Vilanova i la Geltrú, Spain	C12	20
Vila Real, Port.	C3	20
Vila Real, Spain	E10	20
Vila Real, state, Port.	C3	20
Vila Velha, Braz.	K5	88
Vilar Formoso, Port.	C2	20
Vilcabamba, Cordillera de, mts., Peru	F3	84
Vilejka, Bela.	F9	10
Vilelas, Arg.	C6	92
Vilhelmina, Swe.	D7	8
Vilhena, Braz.	F5	84
Vilija (Neris), stm., Eur.	F6	10
Viljandi, Est.	C8	10
Vilju, stm., Russia	D13	34
Viljujsk, Russia	D13	34
Viljujskoe vodohranilišče, res., Russia	B20	32
Vilkaviškis, Lith.	F6	10
Vil'kickogo, ostrov, i., Russia.	A19	34
Vil'kickogo, proliv, strt., Russia	A9	34
Vilkija, Lith.	E6	10
Villa Abecia, Bol.	D3	90
Villa Ana, Arg.	D8	92
Villa Ángela, Arg.	C7	92
Villa Atamisqui, Arg.	D6	92
Villa Bella, Bol.	B3	90
Villa Berthet, Arg.	C7	92
Villablino, Spain	A4	20
Villa Bruzual, Ven.	C7	86
Villa Cañás, Arg.	G7	92
Villa Carlos Paz, Arg.	E5	92
Villacarrillo, Spain	F7	20
Villacastín, Spain	D6	20
Villach, Aus.	D10	22
Villacidro, Italy	E2	24
Villa Concepción del Tío, Arg.	E6	92
Villa Constitución, Arg.	F7	92
Villa de Arista, Mex.	D8	100
Villa de Cos, Mex.	D7	100
Villa de Cura, Ven.	B8	86
Villa del Carmen, Arg.	F5	92
Villa del Río, Spain	G6	20
Villa del Rosario, Arg.	E6	92
Villa del Rosario, Ven.	B5	86
Villa de Soto, Arg.	E5	92
Villadiego, Spain	B7	20
Villa Dolores, Arg.	F5	92
Villa Flores, Mex.	G12	100
Villa Florida, Para.	C9	92
Villafranca de los Barros, Spain	F4	20
Villafranca di Verona, Italy	E7	22
Villagarcía de Arosa see Vilagarcía de Arousa, Spain	B1	20
Villa General Roca, Arg.	H9	92
Villa Gesell, Arg.	H9	92
Villagrán, Mex.	C9	100
Villa Grove, Il., U.S.	E9	120
Villaguay, Arg.	E8	92
Villa Guerrero, Mex.	F9	100
Villa Hayes, Para.	B9	92
Villahermosa, Mex.	G12	100
Villa Hidalgo, Mex.	H3	130
Villa Huidobro, Arg.	G5	92
Villa Insurgentes, Mex.	C3	100
Villa Iris, Arg.	I6	92
Villajoyosa see La Vila Joiosa, Spain	F10	20
Villa Juárez, Mex.	B8	100
Villa Krause, Arg.	E3	92
Villalba, P.R.	B3	104a
Villaldama, Mex.	B8	100
Villalón, Phil.	E5	52
Villalonga, Arg.	I7	92
Villalpando, Spain	C5	20
Villa Mainero, Mex.	C9	100
Villa María, Arg.	F6	92
Villamartín, Spain	H5	20
Villa Mazán, Arg.	D4	92
Villa Media Agua, Arg.	E3	92
Villa Mercedes, Arg.	F5	92
Villa Montes, Bol.	D4	90
Villa Nueva, Arg.	B5	86
Villanueva, N.M., U.S.	F3	128
Villanueva de Córdoba, Spain	F6	20
Villanueva de la Serena, Spain	F5	20
Villanueva de la Sierra, Spain	D4	20
Villanueva de los Infantes, Spain	F8	20
Villanueva del Río y Minas, Spain	G4	20
Villanova y Geltrú see Vilanova i la Geltrú, Spain	C12	20
Villa Ocampo, Arg.	D8	92
Villa Ocampo, Mex.	H2	130
Villa Oliva, Para.	B8	92
Villa Pérez, P.R.	B2	104a
Villapinzón, Col.	E5	86
Villarcayo, Spain	B7	20
Villa Regina, Arg.	G3	90
Villa Reynolds, Arg.	F5	92
Villa Rica, Ga., U.S.	D14	122
Villa-Real see Vila-Real, Port.	E10	20
Villarrica, Para.	B9	92
Villarrobledo, Spain	E8	20
Villarrubia de los Ojos, Spain	E7	20
Villa Santa Rita de Catuna, Arg.	E4	92
Villa Serrano, Bol.	C4	90
Villa Unión, Arg.	D6	92
Villa Unión, Mex.	D5	100
Villaverde, Ven.	C7	86
Villavicencio, Col.	E5	86
Villaviciosa de Córdoba, Spain	F5	20
Villazón, Bol.	D3	90
Villefranche-de-Rouergue, Fr.	E8	18
Villefranche-sur-Saône, Fr.	C10	18
Villena, Spain	F10	20
Villeneuve-sur-Lot, Fr.	E6	18
Villeneuve-sur-Yonne, Fr.	F12	14
Ville Platte, La., U.S.	G6	122
Villers-Cotterêts, Fr.	E12	14
Villerupt, Fr.	E14	14
Villeta, Col.	E4	86
Villeurbanne, Fr.	D10	18
Villiers, S. Afr.	E9	70
Villingen-Schwenningen, Ger.	H4	16
Villisca, Ia., U.S.	D3	120
Vilnius, Lith.	F8	10
Vilsbiburg, Ger.	H8	16
Vil'shanka, Ukr.	A17	26
Vilshofen, Ger.	H9	16
Viluppuram, India	F4	53
Vilvoorde, Bel.	D13	14
Vilvorde see Vilvoorde, Bel.	D13	14
Vimmerby, Swe.	H6	8
Vimperk, Czech Rep.	G9	16
Vina, stm., Cam.	D3	134
Viña del Mar, Chile	F2	92
Vinalhaven, Me., U.S.	F8	110
Vinalhaven Island, i., Me., U.S.	F8	110
Vinarós, Spain	D11	20
Vincennes, In., U.S.	F10	120
Vincennes Bay, b., Ant.	B15	81
Vincent, Al., U.S.	D12	122
Vinces, Ec.	H2	86
Vindelälven, stm., Swe.	D8	8
Vindhya Range, mts., India	G6	54
Vinegar Hill, mtn., Or., U.S.	F8	136
Vineland, N.J., U.S.	E10	114
Vinemont, Al., U.S.	C12	122
Vineyard Haven, Ma., U.S.	C15	114
Vineyard Sound, strt., Ma., U.S.	C15	114
Ving Nghe Tinh, state, Viet.	C7	48
Vinh, Viet.	C7	48
Vinhais, Port.	C3	20
Vinh Long, Viet.	G8	48
Vinh Yen, Viet.	B7	48
Vinita, Ok., U.S.	H2	120
Vinkovci, Cro.	E15	22
Vinnytsia, Ukr.	A16	26
Vinson Massif, mtn., Ant.	C32	81
Vintilă Vodă, Rom.	D13	26
Vinton, Ia., U.S.	B5	120
Vinton, Va., U.S.	G6	114
Viola, Il., U.S.	C7	120
Viooslsdrif, S. Afr.	F3	70
Vipiteno, Italy	D8	22
Vir, Otok, i., Cro.	F11	22
Virac, Phil.	D5	52
Viramgām, India	G3	54
Virandrapet, India	F4	53
Virbalis, Lith.	F5	10
Virden, Mb., Can.	E13	124
Virden, Il., U.S.	E8	120
Virden, N.M., U.S.	K8	132
Vire, Fr.	F8	14
Virgem da Lapa, Braz.	I4	88
Vírgenes, Cabo, c., S.A.	J3	90
Virgil, Ks., U.S.	C13	128
Virgin, stm., U.S.	H2	132
Virgin Gorda, i., Br. Vir. Is.	e9	104b
Virginia, S. Afr.	F8	70
Virginia, Il., U.S.	E7	120
Virginia, Mn., U.S.	D6	118
Virginia, state, U.S.	G7	114
Virginia Beach, Va., U.S.	H10	114
Virginia City, Mt., U.S.	E14	136
Virginia City, Nv., U.S.	D6	134
Virginia Falls, wtfl., N.T., Can.	C5	106
Virginia Peak, mtn., Nv., U.S.	D6	134
Virgin Islands, dep., N.A.	h14	96a
Virgin Islands, is., N.A.	e7	104b
Virgin Islands National Park, p.o.i., V.I.U.S.	e7	104b
Virgin Passage, strt., N.A.	B5	104a
Virihaure, l., Swe.	C7	8
Virje, Cro.	D13	22
Virojoki, Fin.	F12	8
Viroqua, Wi., U.S.	H7	118
Virovitica, Cro.	E14	22
Virrat, Fin.	E10	8
Virtaniemi, Fin.	B13	8
Virtsu, Est.	B7	10
Viru, Peru	E2	84
Virudunagar, India	G3	53
Viru-Nigula, Est.	A9	10
Virvytė, stm., Lith.	D5	10
Vis, Otok, i., Cro.	G12	22
Visale, Sol. Is.	e8	79b
Visalia, Ca., U.S.	G6	134
Visayan Islands, is., Phil.	E4	52
Visayan Sea, s., Phil.	E4	52
Visby, Swe.	H8	8
Viscount, Sk., Can.	C7	124
Viscount Melville Sound, strt., Can.	B11	94
Višegrad, Bos.	F6	26
Viseu, Braz.	A1	88
Viseu, Port.	D3	20
Viseu, state, Port.	D3	20
Vishākhapatnam, India	C6	53
Vişina, Rom.	F12	26
Viškovo, Bela.	E5	26
Visoko, Bos.	F5	26
Visoki Decani, i., S. Geor.	K12	82
Visp, Switz.	D4	22
Visrivier, stm., Nmb.	D3	70
Vista, Ca., U.S.	J8	134
Vistula see Wisła, stm., Pol.	C15	16
Vitasaya, Spain	A11	10
Vita Lagoon, b., Eur.	B16	16
Vita, Mb., Can.	E17	124
Vitarte, Peru	F2	84
Vitebsk see Vicebsk, Bela.	E13	10
Viterbo, Italy	H8	22
Vitez, Bos.	E4	26
Viti Levu, i., Fiji	p19	79e
Vitim, stm., Russia	E11	34
Vitimsko ploskogor'e, plat., Russia	F11	34
Vitkov, Czech Rep.	G13	16
Vitória, Braz.	K5	88
Vitória da Conquista, Braz.	H5	88
Vitória de Santo Antão, Braz.	E8	88
Vitória do Mearim, Braz.	B3	88
Vitorino Freire, Braz.	C3	88
Vitoria see Gasteiz, Spain	B8	20
Vitré, Fr.	F7	14
Vitry-le-François, Fr.	F13	14
Vittel, Fr.	F13	14
Vittoria, Italy	H8	24
Vittório Veneto, Italy	E9	22
Viveiro, Spain	A3	20
Vivero see Viveiro, Spain	A3	20
Vivi, stm., Russia	B20	34
Vivian, La., U.S.	E4	122
Vizcaíno, Desierto de, des., Mex.	B2	100
Vizcaya see Bizkaiko, co., Spain	A8	20
Vize, Tur.	B10	28
Vizhas, stm., Russia	D22	8
Vizianagaram, India	B6	53
Vizille, Fr.	E13	14
Vizinga, Russia	B7	32
Vjalikaja Maščanica, Bela.	G12	10
Vjalikaja Radvaničy, Bela.	H7	10
Vjaseja, Bela.	G10	10
Vjatka, stm., Russia	C8	32
Vjatskie Poljany, Russia	C8	32
Vjazemskij, Russia	G15	34
Vjaz'ma, Russia	E17	10
Vjazniki, Russia	H20	8
Vjazovie, Russia	F10	10
Vosés (Ad<ç>, stm., Eur.	D13	24
Vlaardingen, Neth.	C13	14
Vlădeasa, Vârful, mtn., Rom.	C9	26
Vladičin Han, Serb.	G8	26
Vladikavkaz, Russia	F6	32
Vladimir, Russia	H18	8
Vladimirskaja oblast', co., Russia	I19	8
Vladislav, Russia	E16	10
Vladivostok, Russia	C9	38
Vlasenica, Bos.	E5	26
Vlasotince, Serb.	G9	26
Vlasovo, Russia	B16	34
Vlieland, i., Neth.	A13	14
Vlissingen, Neth.	C12	14
Vlora see Vlorë, Alb.	D13	24
Vlorë, Alb.	D13	24
Vltava (Moldau), stm., Czech Rep.	F10	16
Vnukovo, Russia	E20	10
Vöcklabruck, Aus.	C10	22
Vo Dat, Viet.	G8	48
Vodla, stm., Russia	F17	8
Vodlozero, ozero, l., Russia	E16	8
Vodosalma, Russia	D14	8
Voel, stm., S. Afr.	H7	70
Voghera, Italy	F6	22
Vohimena, Tanjona, c., Madag.	F8	68
Vohipeno, Madag.	E8	68
Võhma, Est.	G11	8
Voi, Kenya	E7	66
Voinești, Rom.	B14	26
Voinjama, Lib.	H3	64
Voiron, Fr.	D11	18
Voitsberg, Aus.	C12	22
Vojmsjön, l., Swe.	D6	8
Vojnica, Russia	D14	8
Vojvodina, co., Serb.	D7	26
Vokhma, Russia	H6	102
Volcano, Hi., U.S.	d6	78a
Volcano Islands see Kazan-rettō, is., Japan	G18	30
Volčiha, Russia	D14	32
Volda, Nor.	E1	8
Volga, stm., Russia	C6	32
Volga, S.D., U.S.	G2	118
Volga-Baltic Canal see Volgo-Baltijskij kanal, can., Russia	G17	8
Volgino, Russia	B16	10
Volgo-Baltijskij kanal, can., Russia	G17	8
Volgodonsk, Russia	E6	32
Volgograd, Russia	E6	32
Volgograd Reservoir see Volgogradskoe vodohranilišče, res., Russia	E7	32
Volgogradskoe vodohranilišče, res., Russia	D7	32
Volhov, Russia	A15	10
Volhov, stm., Russia	B14	10
Volíssos, Grc.	D8	28
Völkermarkt, Aus.	D11	22
Volklingen, Ger.	G2	16
Volkovysk see Vaukavysk, Bela.	G7	10
Volochanka, Russia	B7	34
Volodarskoe, Kaz.	D11	32
Vologda, Russia	A22	10
Vologodskaja oblast', co., Russia	G19	8
Volokolamsk, Russia	D18	10
Volonga, Russia	C22	8
Volos, Grc.	D5	28
Volos, Gulf of see Pagasitikós Kólpos, b., Grc.	D5	28
Volosovo, Russia	A12	10
Volot, Russia	C13	10
Volovo, Russia	G21	10
Vol'sk, Russia	D7	32
Volta, stm., Ghana	H5	64
Volta Blanche (White Volta), stm., Afr.	G4	64
Volta Noire (Black Volta) (Mouhoun), stm., Afr.	G4	64
Volta Redonda, Braz.	L3	88
Volterra, Italy	G7	22
Vol'teva, Russia	D21	8
Voltri, ngh., Italy	F5	22
Volturno, stm., Italy	C8	24
Volvi, Límni, l., Grc.	C6	28
Volyn', co., Ukr.	A15	26
Volžsk, Russia	C7	32
Volžskij, Russia	E6	32
Vonavona Island, i., Sol. Is.	e7	79b
Vonda, Sk., Can.	B7	124
Vondanka, Russia	G22	8
Vondrozo, Madag.	E8	68
Von Frank Mountain, mtn., Ak., U.S.	D8	140
Vónnafjörður, Ice.	k32	8a
Vopnafjörður, b., Eur.	k32	8a
Vorarlberg, state, Aus.	C6	22
Vorarlberg, Ger.	I4	8
Vórdenrhein see Rein Anterur, stm., Switz.	D6	22
Vordingborg, Den.	I4	8
Vóreio Aigaío, state, Grc.	D8	28
Vóreioi Sporádes, is., Grc.	D6	28
Vóreios Evvoïkós, b., Grc.	D5	28
Vorkuta, Russia	A10	32
Vormsi, i., Est.	G10	8
Vorob'evo, Russia	B7	34
Voronco, Mol.	C15	10
Voronezh, Russia	D5	32
Voronja, stm., Russia	H21	10
Voronok, Russia	B16	10
Voronov, Russia	H15	10
Voronovo, Russia	E5	34
Vórøterneset, hist. reg., Ger.	C9	16
Vorsma, Russia	H20	8
Vørtekanna Nunatak, mtn., Ant.	C8	81
Võrtsjärv, l., Est.	C9	10
Võru, Est.	H12	8
Vosges, state, Fr.	F15	14
Vosges, mts., Fr.	E16	14
Voskresensk, Russia	E21	10
Voskresenskoe, Russia	C20	10
Voskresenskoe, Russia	H21	8
Voss, Nor.	F2	8
Vostočno-Sibirskoe more, s., Russia	B20	34
Vostočnyj Sajan, mts., Russia	D17	32
Vostok, i., Kir.	E11	72
Vostok, sci., Ant.	C15	81
Votice, Czech Rep.	G10	16
Votkinsk, Russia	C8	32
Votuporanga, Braz.	D7	90
Vouga, stm., Port.	D2	20
Vouziers, Fr.	E13	14
Voyageurs National Park, p.o.i., Mn., U.S.	C6	118

Name	Map Ref.	Page
Voyeykov Ice Shelf, ice, Ant.	B17	81
Vože, ozero, l., Russia	F18	8
Vožega, Russia	F19	8
Voznesene, Russia	F16	8
Vozroždenija, ostrov, i., Asia	E9	32
Vraca, Blg.	F10	26
Vradyivka, Ukr.	F10	26
Vrancea, state, Rom.	D13	26
Vrangelja, ostrov (Wrangel Island), i., Russia	B24	34
Vranje, Serb.	G8	26
Vratsa see Vraca, Blg.	F10	26
Vrbas, Serb.	D6	26
Vrbas, stm., Bos.	E4	26
Vrbovec, Cro.	E13	22
Vrchlabí, Czech Rep.	F11	16
Vrede, S. Afr.	E9	70
Vredenburg, S. Afr.	H3	70
Vredenburgh, Al., U.S.	F11	122
Vredenburg-Saldanha see Vredenburg, S. Afr.	H3	70
Vredendal, S. Afr.	G4	70
Vriddhāchalam, India	F4	53
Vrindāvan, India	E6	54
Vršac, Serb.	D8	26
Vrútky, Slov.	G14	16
Vryburg, S. Afr.	E7	70
Vryheid, S. Afr.	E10	70
Vselug, ozero, l., Russia	C14	10
Vsetín, Czech Rep.	G13	16
Vsevidof, Mount, mtn., Ak., U.S.	F6	140
Vučitrn, Serb.	G7	26
Vukovar, Cro.	E16	22
Vulcan, Ab., Can.	F17	138
Vulcan, Rom.	D10	26
Vulcănești, Mol.	D15	26
Vulcano, Isola, i., Italy	F8	24
Vuisino see Bolsena, Lago di, l., Italy	H9	22
Vung Tau, Viet.	G8	48
Vunakis, Pap. N. Gui.	b5	79a
Vunisea, Fiji	p19	79e
Vunisea, Fiji	q18	79e
Vuohijärvi, l., Fin.	F11	8
Vuyyūru, India	C5	53
Vyāra, India	H4	54
Vyborg (Viipuri), Russia	F13	8
Vyčegda, stm., Russia	B7	32
Vyčegodskij, Russia	F22	8
Východočeský, state, Czech Rep.	F11	16
Východoslovenský Kraj, state, Slov.	H17	16
Vygoniči, Russia	G16	10
Vygozero, ozero, l., Russia	E16	8
Vyksa, Russia	I20	8
Vylkove, Ukr.	D16	26
Vynohradiv, Ukr.	A10	26
Vypolzovo, Russia	C16	10
Vyrica, Russia	A13	10
Vyšgorodok, Russia	C11	10
Vyškod', Russia	C13	10
Vyškov, Czech Rep.	G12	16
Vyšneol'šanoe, Russia	H20	10
Vyšnevolockoe vodohranilišče, res., Russia	C16	10
Vyšnij Voločok, Russia	C17	10
Vysoké Mýto, Czech Rep.	G12	16
Vysokiníči, Russia	F19	10
Vysokoe, Russia	D17	10
Vysokogornyj, Russia	G16	34
Vysokovsk, Russia	D19	10
Vytebet', stm., Russia	G18	10
Vytegra, Russia	F17	8
Vyzhnytsia, Ukr.	A12	26

W

Name	Map Ref.	Page
Wa, Ghana	G4	64
Waal, stm., Neth.	C14	14
Waalwijk, Neth.	C14	14
Wabag, Pap. N. Gui.	b3	79a
Wabakimi Lake, l., On., Can.	A8	118
Wabamun, Ab., Can.	B15	138
Wabamun Lake, l., Ab., Can.	C15	138
Wabana, Nf., Can.	j23	107a
Wabasca, stm., Ab., Can.	D7	106
Wabasca-Desmarais, Ab., Can.	D8	106
Wabash, In., U.S.	H4	112
Wabash, stm., U.S.	F9	120
Wabasha, Mn., U.S.	G6	118
Wabasso, Mn., U.S.	F10	118
Wabera, Eth.	F8	62
Wabowden, Mb., Can.	E11	106
Wąbrzeźno, Pol.	C14	16
Wabu Hu, l., China	E7	42
Waccamaw, stm., U.S.	C7	116
Waccamaw, Lake, l., N.C., U.S.	B7	116
Wachapreague, Va., U.S.	G10	114
Wachau, reg., Aus.	B12	22
Wacissa, Fl., U.S.	F2	116
Waco, Tx., U.S.	C10	130
Waco Lake, res., Tx., U.S.	C10	130
Waconda Lake, res., Ks., U.S.	B10	128
Wadayama, Japan	D7	40
Wad Bandah, Sudan	E5	62
Wadbilliga National Park, p.o.i., Austl.	K7	76
Waddenzee, strt., Neth.	A14	14
Waddington, N.Y., U.S.	D14	112
Waddington, Mount, mtn., B.C., Can.	E5	138
Wadena, Sk., Can.	C10	124
Wadena, Mn., U.S.	E3	118
Wadesboro, N.C., U.S.	B5	116
Wādī as-Sīr, Jord.	G6	58
Wadley, Al., U.S.	D13	122
Wadley, Ga., U.S.	D3	116
Wad Madanī, Sudan	E6	62
Wadowice, Pol.	G15	16
Wadsworth, Nv., U.S.	D6	134
Wadsworth, Oh., U.S.	C4	114
Wafangdian, China	B9	42
Wageningen, Neth.	C14	14
Wager Bay, b., Nu., Can.	B13	106
Wagga Wagga, Austl.	J6	76
Wagin, Austl.	F3	74
Waging am See, Ger.	I8	16
Wagner, S.D., U.S.	D14	126
Wagon Mound, N.M., U.S.	F4	128
Wagontire Mountain, mtn., Or., U.S.	G7	136
Wagrien, reg., Ger.	B6	16
Wągrowiec, Pol.	D13	16
Waha, Libya	B4	62
Wahai, Indon.	F8	44
Wāh Cantonment, Pak.	B3	54
Wahiawā, Hi., U.S.	b3	78a
Wahpeton, N.D., U.S.	E2	118
Wahran (Oran), Alg.	B4	64
Wai, India	B1	53
Waialua, Hi., U.S.	b3	78a
Wai'anae, Hi., U.S.	b3	78a
Waiau, N.Z.	F5	80
Waiau, stm., N.Z.	G2	80
Waiau, stm., N.Z.	F5	80
Waiblingen, Ger.	H5	16
Waidhofen an der Thaya, Aus.	B12	22
Waidhofen an der Ybbs, Aus.	C11	22
Waigeo, Pulau, i., Indon.	F9	44
Waiheke Island, i., N.Z.	C6	80
Waikabubak, Indon.	H11	50
Waikato, stm., N.Z.	C6	80
Waikelo, Indon.	H11	50
Waikerie, Austl.	J2	76
Wailuku, Hi., U.S.	c5	78a
Waimate, N.Z.	G4	80
Waimea, Hi., U.S.	a2	78a
Wainganga, stm., India	H7	54
Waingapu, Indon.	H12	50
Waini, stm., Guy.	D12	86
Wainunu Bay, b., Fiji	p19	79e
Wainwright, Ab., Can.	B3	124
Wainwright, Ak., U.S.	B7	140
Waipukurau, N.Z.	E7	80
Wairarapa, Lake, l., N.Z.	E6	80
Wairau, stm., N.Z.	E5	80
Wairoa, N.Z.	D7	80
Wairoa, stm., N.Z.	D6	80
Waisisi, Vanuatu	l17	79d
Waitaki, stm., N.Z.	G4	80
Waitara, N.Z.	D6	80
Waitemata, N.Z.	C6	80
Waite Park, Mn., U.S.	F4	118
Waitotara, N.Z.	D6	80
Waitsburg, Wa., U.S.	D8	136
Waiwo, Indon.	F9	44
Wajima, Japan	B9	40
Wajir, Kenya	D8	66
Waka, D.R.C.	D4	66
Waka, Eth.	F7	62
Wakarusa, In., U.S.	G3	112
Wakasa-wan, b., Japan	D8	40
Wakatipu, Lake, l., N.Z.	G3	80
Wakaw, Sk., Can.	B8	124
Wakayama, Japan	E8	40
Wakayama, state, Japan	F8	40
WaKeeney, Ks., U.S.	B9	128
Wakefield, Eng., U.K.	H11	12
Wakefield, Ma., U.S.	B14	114
Wakefield, Mi., U.S.	E15	126
Wakefield, Va., U.S.	H8	114
Wake Forest, N.C., U.S.	I7	114
Wake Island, dep., Oc.	E12	54
Wake Island, at., Wake I.	H19	142
Wakema, Mya.	D2	48
Waki, Japan	E7	40
Wakkanai, Japan	B14	38
Wakita, Ok., U.S.	E10	128
Wakomata Lake, l., On., Can.	B6	112
Wakonda, S.D., U.S.	E15	126
Waku Kungo, Ang.	C2	68
Walachia, hist. reg., Rom.	E11	26
Walanae, stm., Indon.	F12	50
Walawe, stm., Sri L.	H5	53
Walbrzych, Pol.	F12	16
Wałbrzych, state, Pol.	F12	16
Walcha, Austl.	H8	76
Walcott, Ia., U.S.	C7	120
Walcott, N.D., U.S.	E1	118
Walcott, Lake, res., Id., U.S.	H13	136
Walcz, Pol.	C12	16
Waldbröl, Ger.	F3	16
Walden, On., Can.	B8	112
Walden, Co., U.S.	C10	132
Waldheim, Sk., Can.	B7	124
Waldkirchen, Ger.	H9	16
Waldmünchen, Ger.	G8	16
Waldo, B.C., Can.	G15	138
Waldoboro, Me., U.S.	F7	110
Waldorf, Md., U.S.	F9	114
Waldport, Or., U.S.	F2	136
Waldron, Sk., Can.	D11	124
Waldron, Ar., U.S.	C4	122
Waldron, In., U.S.	E12	120
Waldshut-Tiengen, Ger.	I4	16
Waldviertel, reg., Aus.	B12	22
Wales, state, U.K.	I9	12
Wales Island, i., Nu., Can.	B13	106
Walewale, Ghana	G4	64
Walgett, Austl.	G6	76
Walgreen Coast, cst., Ant.	C30	81
Walhachin, B.C., Can.	F10	138
Walhalla, N.D., U.S.	F15	124
Walhalla, S.C., U.S.	B2	116
Walhalla, hist., Ger.	G8	16
Walker, Ia., U.S.	B6	120
Walker, stm., Nv., U.S.	D7	134
Walker Bay, b., S. Afr.	I4	70
Walker Lake, l., Nv., U.S.	E7	134
Walkerton, On., Can.	D8	112
Walkerton, In., U.S.	G3	112
Walkertown, N.C., U.S.	H5	114
Walkerville, Mt., U.S.	D14	136
Wall, S.D., U.S.	D10	126
Wallace, Id., U.S.	C11	136
Wallace, N.C., U.S.	B7	116
Wallace, Ne., U.S.	G11	126
Wallaceburg, On., Can.	F7	112
Wallal Downs, Austl.	C4	74
Wallam Creek, stm., Austl.	G6	76
Wallangarra, Austl.	G8	76
Wallaroo, Austl.	F7	74
Wallasey, Eng., U.K.	H9	12
Walla Walla, Wa., U.S.	D8	136
Wallingford, Ct., U.S.	C13	114
Wallingford, Vt., U.S.	G4	110
Wallis, Tx., U.S.	H2	122
Wallis, Îles, is., Wal.lF.	E9	72
Wallis and Futuna, dep., Oc.	E9	72
Wallisville Lake, res., Tx., U.S.	H4	122
Wall Lake, Ia., U.S.	I3	118
Wallowa, Or., U.S.	E9	136
Wallowa, stm., Or., U.S.	E9	136
Walls of Jericho National Park, p.o.i., Austl.	n13	77a
Walnut, Il., U.S.	C2	120
Walnut, Il., U.S.	C8	120
Walnut, Ms., U.S.	C10	122
Walnut, N.C., U.S.	I3	114
Walnut, stm., Ks., U.S.	D11	128
Walnut Canyon National Monument, p.o.i., Az., U.S.	H5	132
Walnut Cove, N.C., U.S.	H5	114
Walnut Creek, stm., Ks., U.S.	C9	128
Walnut Grove, Ms., U.S.	E9	122
Walnut Ridge, Ar., U.S.	H7	120
Walnut Springs, Tx., U.S.	B10	130
Walpole, Austl.	G3	74
Walpole, N.H., U.S.	G4	110
Walsall, Eng., U.K.	I11	12
Walsenburg, Co., U.S.	D4	128
Walsh, Ab., Can.	E3	124
Walsh, stm., Austl.	A5	76
Walsrode, Ger.	D5	16
Walterboro, S.C., U.S.	D5	116
Walters, Ok., U.S.	G10	128
Waltershausen, Ger.	F6	16
Walthall, Ms., U.S.	D9	122
Walton, N.S., Can.	E13	110
Walton, In., U.S.	H3	112
Walton, N.Y., U.S.	B10	114
Walvisbaai see Walvis Bay, Nmb.	C2	70
Walvis Bay (Walvisbaai), Nmb.	C2	70
Walvis Bay, b., Nmb.	C2	70
Walvis Ridge, unds.	K14	144
Walworth, Wi., U.S.	B9	120
Wamba, D.R.C.	D5	66
Wamba, Nig.	H6	64
Wamba (Uamba), stm., Afr.	F3	66
Wampsville, N.Y., U.S.	A10	114
Wampú, Hond.	E5	102
Wampú, stm., Hond.	E5	102
Wamsutter, Wy., U.S.	B9	132
Wanaaka, l., N.Z.	G3	80
Wanaka, Lake, l., N.Z.	G3	80
Wan'an, China	H6	42
Wanapitei Lake, l., On., Can.	B9	112
Wanapitei Lake, l., On., Can.	B8	112
Wanbaoshan, China	B6	38
Wanbi, Austl.	J3	76
Wanblee, S.D., U.S.	D11	126
Wanchese, N.C., U.S.	I10	114
Wandel Hav, s., Grnld.	A22	141
Wandering, stm., Ab., Can.	A18	138
Wanfoxia, China	C4	36
Wang, stm., Thai.	D4	48
Wanganui, N.Z.	D6	80
Wanganui, stm., N.Z.	D6	80
Wangaratta, Austl.	K6	76
Wangcun, China	C7	42
Wangdu Phodrang, Bhu.	E12	54
Wangiwangi, Pulau, i., Indon.	G7	44
Wang Noi, Thai.	E5	48
Wangpan Yang, b., China	F9	42
Wangqing, China	C8	38
Wangtai, China	H7	42
Wangyehmiao see Ulanhot, China	B9	36
Wanhedian, China	E5	42
Wanhsien see Wanxian, China	F3	42
Wani, India	A4	53
Wanie-Rukula, D.R.C.	D5	66
Wanigela, Pap. N. Gui.	b4	79a
Wanipigow, stm., Can.	C18	124
Wänkäner, India	F4	54
Wanneroo, Austl.	F3	74
Wannian, China	G7	42
Wanning, China	L4	42
Wanparti, India	C4	53
Wantan, China	F4	42
Wanxian, China	F3	42
Wanyuan, China	F2	42
Wanzai, China	G6	42
Wanzleben, Ger.	D7	16
Wapakoneta, Oh., U.S.	D1	114
Wapanucka, Ok., U.S.	C2	122
Wapato, Wa., U.S.	D6	136
Wapello, Ia., U.S.	C6	120
Wāpi, India	H4	54
Wapiti, stm., Can.	A12	138
Wappingers Falls, N.Y., U.S.	C12	114
Wapsipinicon, stm., U.S.	J8	118
War, W.V., U.S.	G4	114
Warangal, India	B4	53
Wārāseoni, India	H7	54
Waratah, Austl.	n12	77a
Waratah Bay, b., Austl.	L5	76
Warburg, Ger.	E4	16
Warburton, Austl.	K5	76
Ward, stm., Austl.	E6	76
Warden, S. Afr.	E9	70
Wardha, India	H7	54
Wardha, stm., India	H7	54
Ward Hill, hill, Scot., U.K.	C9	12
Wardlow, Ab., Can.	F19	138
Wardner, B.C., Can.	G15	138
Wardsville Draw, stm., U.S.	B5	130
Waremme, Bel.	D14	14
Waren, Ger.	C8	16
Waren, Indon.	F10	44
Warenai, stm., Indon.	F10	44
Warenda, Austl.	D3	76
Warendorf, Ger.	E3	16
Wargla, Alg.	C6	64
Warialda, Austl.	G8	76
Warin Chamrap, Thai.	E7	48
Warkworth, On., Can.	D11	112
Warman, Sk., Can.	B7	124
Warmandi, Indon.	F9	44
Warmbad, Nmb.	F4	70
Warmbad, S. Afr.	D9	70
Warm Baths see Warmbad, S. Afr.	D9	70
Warminster, Eng., U.K.	J10	12
Warminster, Pa., U.S.	D10	114
Warm Springs, Ga., U.S.	E14	122
Warm Springs, Mt., U.S.	D14	136
Warm Springs, Or., U.S.	F5	136
Warnemünde, ngh., Ger.	B7	16
Warner, Ab., Can.	G18	138
Warner, N.H., U.S.	G5	110
Warner Lakes, l., Or., U.S.	H6	136
Warner Mountains, mts., U.S.	B5	134
Warner Peak, mtn., Or., U.S.	A6	134
Warner Robins, Ga., U.S.	D2	116
Warnow, stm., Ger.	B8	16
Warra, Austl.	F8	76
Warracknabeal, Austl.	K4	76
Warragul, Austl.	L5	76
Warrawagine, Austl.	D4	74
Warrego, stm., Austl.	G5	76
Warren, Ar., U.S.	D6	122
Warren, In., U.S.	H4	112
Warren, Mi., U.S.	B2	114
Warren, Mn., U.S.	C2	118
Warren, Oh., U.S.	C5	114
Warren, Pa., U.S.	C6	114
Warrens, Wi., U.S.	G8	118
Warrensburg, Mo., U.S.	F4	120
Warrensburg, N.Y., U.S.	G3	110
Warrenton, S. Afr.	F7	70
Warrenton, Mo., U.S.	F6	120
Warrenton, N.C., U.S.	H7	114
Warrenton, Or., U.S.	D2	136
Warri, Nig.	H6	64
Warrington, Eng., U.K.	H10	12
Warrington, Fl., U.S.	G11	122
Warrior, Al., U.S.	D12	122
Warrnambool, Austl.	L4	76
Warroad, Mn., U.S.	C3	118
Warrumbungle National Park, p.o.i., Austl.	H7	76
Warsaw see Warszawa, Pol.	D16	16
Warsaw, Il., U.S.	D6	120
Warsaw, In., U.S.	G4	112
Warsaw, Ky., U.S.	F13	120
Warsaw, Mo., U.S.	F4	120
Warsaw, N.Y., U.S.	A7	114
Warsaw, N.Y., U.S.	B7	114
Warspite, Ab., Can.	B18	138
Warszawa (Warsaw), Pol.	D16	16
Warszawa, state, Pol.	D16	16
Warta, Pol.	D11	16
Warta, stm., Pol.	D11	16
Wartburg, Tn., U.S.	H13	120
Wartrace, Tn., U.S.	B12	122
Warud, India	H7	54
Warwick, Austl.	G9	76
Warwick, Eng., U.K.	I11	12
Warwick, N.Y., U.S.	C11	114
Warwick, R.I., U.S.	C14	114
Warwick Channel, strt., Austl.	B7	74
Wasaga Beach, On., Can.	D10	112
Wasagu, Nig.	G6	64
Wasatch Range, mts., Ut., U.S.	C5	132
Wasbank, S. Afr.	F10	70
Wascana Creek, stm., Sk., Can.	D9	124
Wasco, Ca., U.S.	H6	134
Wasco, Or., U.S.	E6	136
Waseca, Mn., U.S.	G5	118
Wasgomuwa National Park, p.o.i., Sri L.	H5	53
Washademoak Lake, l., N.B., Can.	E11	110
Washburn, Il., U.S.	D8	120
Washburn, N.D., U.S.	G12	124
Washburn, Wi., U.S.	E7	118
Washburn, Mount, mtn., Wy., U.S.	F16	136
Washburn Lake, l., Nu., Can.	A9	106
Wāshīm, India	H6	54
Washington, D.C., U.S.	F8	114
Washington, Ga., U.S.	C3	116
Washington, Ia., U.S.	C6	120
Washington, Il., U.S.	D8	120
Washington, In., U.S.	F10	120
Washington, La., U.S.	G6	122
Washington, Mo., U.S.	F6	120
Washington, N.J., U.S.	D11	114
Washington, N.C., U.S.	D5	114
Washington, Pa., U.S.	D5	114
Washington, Ut., U.S.	F3	132
Washington, Va., U.S.	F7	114
Washington, state, U.S.	C5	136
Washington, Mount, mtn., N.H., U.S.	F5	110
Washington Court House, Oh., U.S.	E2	114
Washington Island, i., Wi., U.S.	C3	112
Washington Land, reg., Grnld.	A12	141
Washington Terrace, Ut., U.S.	B5	132
Washita, stm., U.S.	G12	128
Washow Bay, b., Mb., Can.	C17	124
Washpool National Park, p.o.i., Austl.	G9	76
Washtucna, Wa., U.S.	D8	136
Wasian, Indon.	F9	44
Wasilków, Pol.	C19	16
Wasior, Indon.	F9	44
Waskada, Mb., Can.	E13	124
Waskaganish, Qc., Can.	E15	106
Waskahigan, stm., Ab., Can.	B13	138
Waskom, Tx., U.S.	E4	122
Waspam, Nic.	E5	102
Wassenaar, Neth.	B13	14
Wasseralfingen, Ger.	H6	16
Wassy, Fr.	F13	14
Watampone, Indon.	F12	50
Watamsopeng, Indon.	F11	50
Watatic, Mount, mtn., Ma., U.S.	B14	114
Waterberge, mts., S. Afr.	D8	70
Waterbury, Ct., U.S.	C12	114
Wateree Lake, res., S.C., U.S.	B5	116
Waterford (Port Láirge), Ire.	I5	12
Waterford, Pa., U.S.	C6	114
Waterford, Pa., U.S.	B9	120
Waterford, Wi., U.S.	I5	12
Waterhen Lake, l., Mb., Can.	B14	124
Water Island, i., V.I.U.S.	e7	104b
Waterloo, Austl.	C4	74
Waterloo, Bel.	D13	14
Waterloo, On., Can.	E9	112
Waterloo, Qc., Can.	E4	110
Waterloo, Al., U.S.	C10	122
Waterloo, Il., U.S.	F7	120
Waterloo, N.Y., U.S.	B8	114
Waterloo, Wi., U.S.	A9	120
Waterman, Il., U.S.	C9	120
Waterproof, La., U.S.	F7	122
Watersmeet, Mi., U.S.	E9	118
Waterton-Glacier International Peace Park, p.o.i., N.A.	B13	136
Waterton Lakes National Park, p.o.i., Ab., Can.	G16	138
Watertown, N.Y., U.S.	E14	112
Watertown, S.D., U.S.	C15	126
Watertown, Wi., U.S.	A9	120
Waterval Boven, S. Afr.	D10	70
Water Valley, Ms., U.S.	C9	122
Waterville, N.S., Can.	E12	110
Waterville, Ks., U.S.	B12	128
Waterville, Me., U.S.	F7	110
Waterville, Oh., U.S.	C1	114
Waterville, Wa., U.S.	C6	136
Watervliet, N.Y., U.S.	B12	114
Watford, Eng., U.K.	J12	12
Watford City, N.D., U.S.	G10	124
Watkins Glen, N.Y., U.S.	B9	114
Watkinsville, Ga., U.S.	C2	116
Watling Island see San Salvador, i., Bah.	C10	96
Watonga, Ok., U.S.	F10	128
Watrous, Sk., Can.	C8	124
Watsa, D.R.C.	D5	66
Watseka, Il., U.S.	H2	112
Watsikengo, D.R.C.	E4	66
Watson, Sk., Can.	B9	124
Watson Lake, Yk., Can.	C5	106
Watsonville, Ca., U.S.	G4	134
Watt Mountain, vol., Dom.	j6	105c
Watts Bar Lake, res., Tn., U.S.	B14	122
Wattsburg, Pa., U.S.	B6	114
Wattwil, Switz.	C5	22
Watubela, Kepulauan, is., Indon.	F9	44
Watzmann, mtn., Ger.	I8	16
Waubay Lake, l., S.D., U.S.	B15	126
Wauchope, Austl.	D6	74
Wauchula, Fl., U.S.	I4	116
Waucoma, Ia., U.S.	B6	120
Wauconda, Wa., U.S.	B7	136
Waugh, Mb., Can.	B3	118
Waukara, Bukit, mtn., Indon.	D11	50
Waukarlycarly, Lake, l., Austl.	D4	74
Waukegan, Il., U.S.	F2	112
Waukesha, Wi., U.S.	A9	120
Waukon, Ia., U.S.	H7	118
Waunakee, Wi., U.S.	A8	120
Wauneta, Ne., U.S.	G11	126
Waupaca, Wi., U.S.	H10	118
Waupun, Wi., U.S.	H10	118
Waurika, Ok., U.S.	G11	128
Waurika Lake, res., Ok., U.S.	G10	128
Wausa, Ne., U.S.	E15	126
Wausau, Wi., U.S.	G9	118
Wauseon, Oh., U.S.	C1	114
Wautoma, Wi., U.S.	G9	118
Wauwatosa, Wi., U.S.	E1	112
Wauzeka, Wi., U.S.	A7	120
Wave Hill, Austl.	C6	74
Waveland, Ms., U.S.	G9	122
Waverley, N.S., Can.	E13	110
Waverly, Ia., U.S.	B5	120
Waverly, Mo., U.S.	E4	120
Waverly, Ne., U.S.	D1	120
Waverly, N.Y., U.S.	B9	114
Waverly, Oh., U.S.	E2	114
Waverly, Tn., U.S.	H10	120
Waverly, Va., U.S.	G8	114
Waverly Hall, Ga., U.S.	E14	122
Wāw, Sudan	F5	62
Wawa, On., Can.	F14	106
Wawa, Nig.	H5	64
Wawa, stm., Nic.	E5	102
Wāw al-Kabīr, Libya	B3	62
Wawanesa, Mb., Can.	E14	124
Waxahachie, Tx., U.S.	B11	130
Way, Lake, l., Austl.	E4	74
Waya, i., Fiji	p18	79e
Waycross, Ga., U.S.	E3	116
Wayland, Ia., U.S.	C6	120
Wayland, Ky., U.S.	G3	114
Wayland, Mi., U.S.	F4	112
Waylyn, S.C., U.S.	D6	116
Wayne, Ab., Can.	E17	138
Wayne, Mi., U.S.	B2	114
Wayne, Ne., U.S.	E15	126
Wayne, N.J., U.S.	D11	114
Wayne, W.V., U.S.	F3	114
Wayne City, Il., U.S.	F9	120
Waynesboro, Ga., U.S.	C3	116
Waynesboro, Ms., U.S.	F10	122
Waynesboro, Tn., U.S.	B11	122
Waynesboro, Va., U.S.	F6	114
Waynesburg, Pa., U.S.	D8	120
Waynesville, N.C., U.S.	A3	116
Waynoka, Ok., U.S.	E10	128
Wāzah Khwāh, Afg.	B2	54
Wazirābād, Pak.	B5	54
Wda, stm., Pol.	C14	16
We, Kuta, l., Indon.	J2	48
Weatherford, Ok., U.S.	F10	128
Weatherford, Tx., U.S.	B10	130
Weatherly, Pa., U.S.	D10	114
Weaubleau, Mo., U.S.	G4	120
Weaver Lake, l., Mb., Can.	B17	124
Weaverville, Ca., U.S.	C3	134
Weaverville, N.C., U.S.	I3	114
Webb, Ms., U.S.	D8	122
Webb, Sk., Can.	D8	124
Webbwood, On., Can.	B7	112
Weber, stm., Ut., U.S.	B5	132
Weber City, Va., U.S.	H3	114
Webster, Ab., Can.	A12	138
Webster, Fl., U.S.	H3	116
Webster, Ma., U.S.	B14	114
Webster, Wi., U.S.	F6	118
Webster City, Ia., U.S.	B4	120
Weda, Indon.	E8	44
Weddell Island, i., Falk. Is.	J4	90
Weddell Sea, s., Ant.	B36	81
Wedderburn, Austl.	K4	76
Wedgeport, N.S., Can.	G11	110
Wedowee, Al., U.S.	D13	122
Wedza, Zimb.	D5	68
Weedsport, N.Y., U.S.	B9	114
Weed, Ca., U.S.	B4	134
Weems, Va., U.S.	G9	114
Weenen, S. Afr.	F10	70
Weeping Water, Ne., U.S.	D1	120
Weert, Neth.	C14	14
Wee Waa, Austl.	H7	76
Wegorzewo, Pol.	B17	16
Węgrów, Pol.	D17	16
Wei, stm., China	C6	42
Wei, stm., China	D3	42
Wei, stm., China	D3	42
Weichang, China	C2	38
Weichuan, China	D6	42
Weida, Ger.	F8	16
Weiden in der Oberpfalz, Ger.	G7	16
Weifang, China	C8	42
Weihai, China	C10	42
Weihaiwei see Weihai, China	C10	42
Weihe, China	B8	38
Weilburg, Ger.	F4	16
Weilheim, Ger.	I7	16
Weimar, Ger.	E7	16
Weimar, Tx., U.S.	E11	130
Weinan, China	D3	42
Weinheim, Ger.	G4	16
Weipa, Austl.	B8	74
Weippe, Id., U.S.	D11	136
Weir, Ks., U.S.	D14	128
Weir, Ms., U.S.	D9	122
Weir, stm., Austl.	G8	76
Weirton, W.V., U.S.	D5	114
Weisburd, Arg.	C6	92
Weiser, Id., U.S.	F10	136
Weiser, stm., Id., U.S.	F10	136
Weishan Hu, l., China	D7	42
Weishi, China	D6	42
Weissenburg in Bayern, Ger.	G7	16
Weissenfels, Ger.	E7	16
Weiss Lake, res., U.S.	C13	122
Weisswasser, Ger.	E10	16
Weitra, Aus.	B11	22
Weixi, China	F4	36
Weixian, China	C6	42
Weiyuan, stm., China	A5	48
Weiz, Aus.	C12	22
Wejherowo, Pol.	B14	16
Wekoewa Punt, c., Neth. Ant.	p23	104g
Welaka, Fl., U.S.	G4	116
Welch, Ok., U.S.	H2	120
Welch, Tx., U.S.	B5	130
Welch, W.V., U.S.	G4	114
Welcome, Mn., U.S.	H4	118
Weldiya, Arg.	E7	62
Weldon, Sk., Can.	A8	124
Weldon, N.C., U.S.	H8	114
Weldon, stm., U.S.	D4	120
Weleetka, Ok., U.S.	B2	122
Welk'īt'ē, Eth.	F7	62
Welkom, S. Afr.	E8	70
Welland, stm., Eng., U.K.	I12	12
Wellborn, Fl., U.S.	F3	116
Wellborn, Tx., U.S.	G2	122
Wellesley Islands, is., Austl.	C8	74
Wellingborough, Eng., U.K.	I12	12
Wellington, Austl.	I7	76
Wellington, On., Can.	E12	112
Wellington, S. Afr.	H4	70
Wellington, N.Z.	E6	80
Wellington, Co., U.S.	G7	126
Wellington, Ks., U.S.	D11	128
Wellington, Mo., U.S.	E4	120
Wellington, Oh., U.S.	C3	114
Wellington, Tx., U.S.	G8	128
Wellington, Isla, i., Chile	I2	90
Wellington Bay, b., Nu., Can.	B9	106
Wellington Channel, strt., Nu., Can.	B7	141
Wellman, Ia., U.S.	C6	120
Wellman, Tx., U.S.	A5	130
Wells, Eng., U.K.	J10	12
Wells, Mn., U.S.	H5	118
Wells, N.Y., U.S.	G2	110
Wells, Lake, l., Austl.	E4	74
Wells, Mount, hill, Austl.	C5	74
Wellsboro, Pa., U.S.	C8	114
Wellsburg, Ia., U.S.	B5	120
Wellsburg, W.V., U.S.	D5	114
Wells-next-the-Sea, Eng., U.K.	I13	12
Wellston, Oh., U.S.	E3	114
Wellsville, Ks., U.S.	C13	128
Wellsville, Mo., U.S.	E6	120
Wellsville, N.Y., U.S.	B8	114
Wellsville, Oh., U.S.	D5	114
Wellsville, Ut., U.S.	B5	132
Wellton, Az., U.S.	K2	132
Wels, Aus.	B10	22
Welshpool, Wales, U.K.	I9	12
Welwyn Garden City, Eng., U.K.	J12	12
Wembley, Eng., U.K.	A11	138
Wena, D.R.C.	E4	66
Wenatchee, Wa., U.S.	C6	136
Wenatchee Mountains, mts., Wa., U.S.	C6	136
Wenceslau Braz, Braz.	L1	88
Wenchang, China	L4	42
Wencheng, China	H8	42
Wenchi, Ghana	H4	64
Wenchou see Wenzhou, China	F9	36
Wendeng, China	C10	42
Wenden, Az., U.S.	J3	132
Wendeng, China	C10	42
Wendover, Ut., U.S.	C2	132
Weng, stm., China	I6	42
Weng'an, China	H2	42
Wengyuan, China	I6	42
Wenlin, China	G8	42
Wenlock, stm., Austl.	B8	74
Wenquan, China	E14	32
Wenshan, China	A7	48
Wenshang, China	D7	42
Wenshui, China	C4	42
Wenshui, China	C4	42
Wensleydale, val., Eng., U.K.	G11	12
Wentworth, Austl.	J3	76
Wentworth, S.D., U.S.	D4	42
Wenxi, China	D4	42
Wenxian, China	D5	42
Wenzhou, China	F9	36
Wepener, S. Afr.	F8	70
Werda, Bots.	D6	70
Werdau, Ger.	F8	16
Werder, Ger.	D8	16
Werder, Ger.	D8	16
Werdohl, Ger.	E3	16
Wernigerode, Ger.	E6	16
Werra, stm., Ger.	E5	16
Werrikimbe National Park, p.o.i., Austl.	H9	76
Werris Creek, Austl.	H8	76
Wertheim, Ger.	G5	16
Wesel, Ger.	E2	16
Weser, stm., Ger.	C4	16
Weskan, Ks., U.S.	C7	128
Weslaco, Tx., U.S.	H10	130
Weslemkoon Lake, l., On., Can.	C12	112
Wesley, Dom.	i6	105c
Wesleyville, Pa., U.S.	B5	114
Wessel, Cape, c., Austl.	B7	74
Wessel Islands, is., Austl.	B7	74
Wessington, S.D., U.S.	C14	126
Wessington Springs, S.D., U.S.	C14	126
West, Ms., U.S.	D9	122
West, Tx., U.S.	C10	130
West Allis, Wi., U.S.	E1	112
West Antarctica, reg., Ant.	D30	81
West Bank, dep., Asia	F6	58
West Bay, N.S., Can.	E15	110
West Bay, b., Tx., U.S.	E12	130
West Bend, Ia., U.S.	B3	120
West Bend, Wi., U.S.	E1	112
West Bengal, state, India	G11	54
West Blocton, Al., U.S.	D11	122
West Bohemia see Západočeský kraj, state, Czech Rep.	G9	16
West Borneo see Kalimantan Barat, state, Indon.	D7	50
West Branch, Ia., U.S.	C6	120
Westbridge, B.C., Can.	G11	138
West Bromwich, Eng., U.K.	I11	12
Westbrook, Mn., U.S.	G3	118
Westbrook, Tx., U.S.	B6	130
West Burlington, Ia., U.S.	D6	120
West Burra, i., Scot., U.K.	n18	12a
Westby, Austl.	J6	76
West Caicos, i., T./C. Is.	B11	102
West Cape, c., N.Z.	G2	80
West Cape Howe, c., Austl.	G3	74
West Carlisle, Oh., U.S.	H6	128
West Caroline Basin, unds.	I16	142
West Chester, Pa., U.S.	E10	114
Westchester Station, N.S., Can.	E13	110
Westcliffe, Co., U.S.	C3	128
West Columbia, S.C., U.S.	B4	116
West Columbia, Tx., U.S.	H3	122
West Cote Blanche Bay, b., La., U.S.	H7	122
West Des Moines, Ia., U.S.	C4	120
West Dolores, stm., Co., U.S.	F8	132
West Elk Peak, mtn., Co., U.S.	E9	132
West End, Ar., U.S.	C5	122
West End, N.C., U.S.	A6	116
Westerland, Ger.	B4	16
Westerly, R.I., U.S.	C14	114
Western, state, Sol. Is.	e7	79b
Western, stm., Austl.	D4	76
Western Australia, state, Austl.	D4	74
Western Cape, state, S. Afr.	H5	70
Western Channel, strt., Asia	E2	40
Western Desert, des., Egypt	B5	62
Western Division, state, Fiji	p18	79e
Western Dvina (Daugava) (Zapadnaja Dzvina), stm., Eur.	D7	10
Western Ghāts, mts., India	E3	46
Westernport, Md., U.S.	E6	114
Western Sahara, dep., Afr.	E2	64
Western Samoa see Samoa, ctry., Oc.	g12	79c
Western Sayans see Zapadnyj Sajan, mts., Russia	D16	32
Western Shore, N.S., Can.	F12	110
Westerschelde, est., Neth.	C12	14
Westerstede, Ger.	C3	16
Westerville, Oh., U.S.	D3	114
Westerwald, mts., Ger.	F3	16
West European Basin, unds.	D12	144
West Falkland, i., Falk. Is.	J4	90
West Fargo, N.D., U.S.	E1	118
Westfield, Il., U.S.	H3	112
Westfield, In., U.S.	H3	112
Westfield, Ma., U.S.	B13	114
Westfield, N.J., U.S.	D11	114
Westfield, N.Y., U.S.	B6	114
Westfield, Wi., U.S.	H9	118
West Fork, Ar., U.S.	I3	120
West Frankfort, Il., U.S.	G9	120
West Friese Eilanden, is., Neth.	A14	14
West Frisian Islands see West Friese Eilanden, is., Neth.	A14	14
Westgate, Austl.	F6	76
West Grand Lake, res., Me., U.S.	E8	110
West Hamlin, W.V., U.S.	F3	114
West Hartford, Ct., U.S.	C13	114
West Haven, Ct., U.S.	C13	114
West Helena, Ar., U.S.	C8	122
Westhoff, Tx., U.S.	E10	130
West Hope, N.D., U.S.	F12	124
West Indies, is.	C7	82
West Java see Jawa Barat, state, Indon.	G5	50
West Jefferson, N.C., U.S.	H4	114
West Jordan, Ut., U.S.	C4	132
West Kingston, R.I., U.S.	C14	114
West Lafayette, In., U.S.	H2	112
West Lake, La., U.S.	G5	122
Westland National Park, p.o.i., N.Z.	F3	80
West Liberty, Ia., U.S.	C6	120
West Liberty, Ky., U.S.	G2	114
West Liberty, Oh., U.S.	D2	114
Westlock, Ab., Can.	B16	138
West Lorne, On., Can.	F8	112
Westmeath, state, Ire.	H5	12
West Memphis, Ar., U.S.	B8	122
Westminster, Co., U.S.	B3	128

Name	Map Ref.	Page

Westminster, Md., U.S. E9 114
West Monroe, La., U.S. E6 122
Westmoreland, Ks., U.S. B12 128
Westmoreland, Tn., U.S. H11 120
Westmorland, can., Fl., U.S. . . . J10 134
West Nicholson, Zimb. B9 70
West Nishnabotna, stm.,
  Ia., U.S. C2 120
West Nueces, stm., Tx.,
  U.S. E7 130
West Nusa Tenggara see
  Nusa Tenggara Barat,
  state, Indon. G10 50
Weston, Id., U.S. A4 132
Weston, Mo., U.S. E3 120
Weston, Oh., U.S. C2 114
Weston, Or., U.S. E8 136
Weston, W.V., U.S. E5 114
Weston-super-Mare, Eng.,
  U.K. J9 12
West Orange, Tx., U.S. G5 122
Westover, Tn., U.S. B10 122
West Palm Beach, Fl., U.S. . . . J5 116
West Palm Beach Canal,
  can., Fl., U.S. J5 116
West Pensacola, Fl., U.S. G11 122
Westphalia, Ks., U.S. F2 120
West Plains, Mo., U.S. H6 120
West Point, Ga., U.S. E13 122
West Point, Ia., U.S. D6 120
West Point, Ky., U.S. F11 120
West Point, Ms., U.S. D10 122
West Point, Ne., U.S. J2 118
West Point, N.Y., U.S. C11 114
West Point Lake, res., U.S. . . . G9 114
West Point Lake, res., U.S. . . . D13 122
West Poplar (Poplar
  West Fork), stm., N.A. F8 124
Westport, N.S., Can. F10 110
Westport, On., Can. D13 112
Westport, Ire. H3 12
Westport, Ct., U.S. C12 114
Westport, In., U.S. E12 120
Westport, Or., U.S. D3 136
Westpunt, c., Aruba o19 104g
West Quoddy Head, c.,
  Me., U.S. F10 110
Westray, i., Scot., U.K. B9 12
West Richland, Wa., U.S. D7 136
West Road, stm., B.C., Can. . . C7 138
West Rutland, Vt., U.S. G3 110
West Salem, Il., U.S. F9 120
West Salem, Oh., U.S. D3 114
West Shoal Lake, l.,
  Mb., Can. D16 124
West Siberian Plain see
  Zapadno-Sibirskaja
  ravnina, pl., Russia B12 32
West Slovakia see
  Zapadoslovenský Kraj,
  state, Slov. H14 16
West Spanish Peak, mtn.,
  Co., U.S. D4 128
West Sumatra see
  Sumatera Barat, state,
  Indon. D2 50
West Terre Haute, In., U.S. . . . E10 120
West Union, Ia., U.S. B6 120
West Union, Oh., U.S. F2 114
West Unity, Oh., U.S. C1 114
West Valley City, Ut., U.S. . . . C4 132
West Vancouver, B.C., Can. . . G7 138
Westville, N.S., Can. E14 110
Westville, In., U.S. G3 112
West Virginia, state, U.S. F5 114
West Walker, stm., U.S. E4 132
West Warwick, R.I., U.S. C14 114
West Webster, N.Y., U.S. E12 112
Westwold, B.C., Can. F11 138
Westwood, Ca., U.S. C5 134
Westwood Lakes, Fl., U.S. . . . K5 116
West Wyalong, Austl. I6 76
West Yellowstone, Mt., U.S. . . F15 136
Wetar, Pulau, i., Indon. G8 44
Wetar, Selat, strt., Asia G8 44
Wetaskiwin, Ab., Can. C17 138
Wete, Tan. E7 66
Wethersfield, Ct., U.S. C13 114
Wetmore, Ks., U.S. E2 120
Wetumpka, Al., U.S. E12 122
Wetzlar, Ger. F4 16
Wewahitchka, Fl., U.S. G13 122
Wewak, Pap. N. Gui. a3 79a
Wewoka, Ok., U.S. B2 122
Wexford, Ire. I6 12
Wexford, state, Ire. I6 12
Weyburn, Sk., Can. D10 124
Weymontachie, Qc., Can. C3 110
Weymouth, Eng., U.K. F10 110
Weymouth, Eng., U.K. K10 12
Weymouth, Ma., U.S. B15 114
Whakatane, N.Z. C7 80
Whangarei, N.Z. B6 80
Whapmagoostui, Qc., Can. . . . D15 106
Wharfe, stm., Eng., U.K. H11 12
Wharton, W.V., U.S. G4 114
Wharton Basin, unds. K12 142
Wharton Lake, l., Nu., Can. . . C10 106
Whataroa, N.Z. F4 80
What Cheer, Ia., U.S. C5 120
Whatley, Al., U.S. F11 122
Wheatland, Ca., U.S. D4 134
Wheatland, La., U.S. C7 120
Wheatley, On., Can. F7 112
Wheatley, Ar., U.S. C7 122
Wheaton, Il., U.S. C9 120
Wheaton, Md., U.S. E8 114
Wheat Ridge, Co., U.S. B3 128
Wheeler, Ms., U.S. C10 122
Wheeler, Tx., U.S. F8 128
Wheeler, Stm., Qc., Can. D17 106
Wheeler Lake, res., Al., U.S. . C11 122
Wheeler Peak, mtn.,
  N.M., U.S. E3 128
Wheeler Peak, mtn., Nv.,
  U.S. D2 132
Wheeling, W.V., U.S. D5 114
Wheelwright, Arg. F7 92
Wheelwright, Ky., U.S. G3 114
Whidbey Island, i., Wa., U.S. . B4 136
Whiskey Peak, mtn., Wy.,
  U.S. E5 126
Whistler, B.C., Can. F8 138
Whitakers, N.C., U.S. H8 114
Whitby, On., Can. E11 112
Whitby, Eng., U.K. H10 12
Whitchurch-Stouffville,
  On., Can. E10 112
White, Ga., U.S. C14 122
White, stm., N.A. C2 106
White, stm., Az., U.S. J6 132
White, stm., In., U.S. F11 120
White, stm., Nv., U.S. F1 132
White, stm., S.D., U.S. H11 124
White, stm., Vt., U.S. C5 136
White, stm., Wa., U.S. C7 132
White, stm., U.S. D13 126
White, stm., U.S. C7 122
White, East Fork, stm.,
  In., U.S. F10 120
White, Lake, l., Austl. D5 74
White Bay, b., Nf., Can. j22 107a
White Bear Lake, Mn., U.S. . . F6 118
White Bluff, Tn., U.S. H10 120
White Butte, mtn., N.D., U.S. . A9 126
White Castle, La., U.S. G7 122
White City, Ks., U.S. C12 128
White Cliffs, Austl. H4 76
White Deer, Tx., U.S. F7 128
Whiteface, stm., Mn., U.S. . . . D6 118
Whiteface Mountain,
  mtn., N.Y., U.S. F3 110

Whitefield, N.H., U.S. F5 110
Whitefish, Mt., U.S. B12 136
Whitefish Bay, Wi., U.S. A10 120
Whitefish Bay, b., On., Can. . . B4 118
Whitefish Bay, b., N.A. B5 118
Whitefish Lake, l., Ab.,
  Can. B18 138
Whitefish Lake, l.,
  N.T., Can. C9 106
Whitefish Point, Mi., U.S. B4 112
Whitefish Point, c., Mi., U.S. . B4 112
White Hall, Al., U.S. C6 122
White Hall, Il., U.S. E7 120
Whitehouse, Tx., U.S. E3 122
Whitehall, Mi., U.S. E3 112
Whitehall, N.Y., U.S. G3 110
Whitehall, Wi., U.S. G7 118
Whitehaven, Eng., U.K. G9 12
Whitehorse, Yk., Can. C4 106
White House, Tn., U.S. H11 120
Whitehouse, Tx., U.S. E3 122
White Island, i., N.A. B13 106
White Island, i., N.Z. C7 80
White Lake, S.D., U.S. D14 126
White Lake, Wi., U.S. F10 118
White Lake, l., On., Can. C13 112
White Lake, l., La., U.S. H6 122
Whitemark, Austl. n13 77a
White Mountain Peak,
  mtn., Ca., U.S. F7 134
White Mountains, mts.,
  N.H., U.S. F5 110
Whitemouth, stm., Mb.,
  Can. E18 124
Whitemouth Lake, l.,
  Mb., Can. E18 124
Whitemud, stm., Mb., Can. . . D15 124
White Nile (Abyad,
  Al-Bahr al-), stm., Afr. E6 62
White Oak, Tx., U.S. E4 122
White Oak Creek, stm.,
  Tx., U.S. D3 122
White Otter Lake, l.,
  On., Can. B6 118
White Pigeon, Mi., U.S. G4 112
Whitepine, Mt., U.S. C11 136
White Pine, Tn., U.S. H2 114
White Plains, N.C., U.S. H5 114
White Plains, N.Y., U.S. C12 114
Whiteriver, Az., U.S. J6 132
White River, S.D., U.S. D12 126
White River Junction,
  Vt., U.S. G4 110
White Rock, B.C., Can. G8 138
White Russia see
  Belarus, ctry., Eur. E14 6
Whitesail Lake, res.,
  B.C., Can. C3 138
Whitesand, stm., Sk., Can. . . . C11 124
White Sands National
  Monument, p.o.i.,
  N.M., U.S. B1 130
Whitesboro, Tx., U.S. D2 122
White Sea see Beloe
  more, s., Russia D18 8
White Settlement, Tx., U.S. . . B10 130
White Springs, Fl., U.S. F3 116
White Sulphur Springs,
  Mt., U.S. D16 136
White Sulphur Springs,
  W.V., U.S. G5 114
Whitesville, Ky., U.S. G11 120
Whiteville, N.C., U.S. B7 116
Whiteville, Tn., U.S. B9 122
White Volta (Volta
  Blanche), stm., Afr. G4 64
Whitewater, Wi., U.S. F6 124
Whitewater, Mi., U.S. B9 120
Whitewater, stm., U.S. E13 120
Whitewater Baldy, mtn.,
  N.M., U.S. J8 132
Whitewater Creek, stm.,
  N.A. F6 124
Whitewater Lake, l.,
  Mb., Can. E13 124
White Woman Creek, stm.,
  U.S. C7 128
Whitewood, Austl. C4 76
Whitewood, Sk., Can. D11 124
Whitewood, S.D., U.S. C9 126
Whithorn, Jam. i12 104d
Whithorn, Scot., U.K. G8 12
Whiting, Ia., U.S. B1 120
Whiting, Ks., U.S. E2 120
Whitley City, Ky., U.S. H13 120
Whitman, Ma., U.S. B15 114
Whitmire, S.C., U.S. B4 116
Whitmore Mountains,
  mts., Ant. D31 81
Whitney, On., Can. C11 112
Whitney, Lake, res.,
  Tx., U.S. C10 130
Whitney, Mount, mtn.,
  Ca., U.S. G7 134
Whitney Point, N.Y., U.S. B9 114
Whitsunday Island, i.,
  Austl. C7 76
Whittemore, Ia., U.S. A3 120
Whittemore, Mi., U.S. D6 112
Whittle, Cap, c., Qc., Can. . . . i22 107a
Whittlesea, Austl. K5 76
Whittlesey, Mount, hill,
  Wi., U.S. E8 118
Whitwell, In., U.S. B13 122
Wholdaia Lake, l., N.T.,
  Can. C9 106
Whyalla, Austl. F7 74
Whycocomagh, N.S., Can. . . . E15 110
Wiang Phan, Thai. B4 48
Wiarton, On., Can. D8 112
Wichian Buri, Thai. E5 48
Wichita, Ks., U.S. D11 128
Wichita, stm., Tx., U.S. G10 128
Wichita Falls, Tx., U.S. H10 128
Wick, Scot., U.K. C9 12
Wickenburg, Az., U.S. J4 132
Wickepin, Austl. F3 74
Wickett, Tx., U.S. C5 130
Wickham, Austl. D3 74
Wickiup Reservoir, res.,
  Or., U.S. G5 136
Wickliffe, Ky., U.S. H8 120
Wicklow, Ire. H6 12
Wicklow, state, Ire. H7 12
Wicklow Head, c., Ire. I7 12
Wicklow Mountains, mts.,
  Ire. H6 12
Widgeegoara Creek, stm.,
  Austl. F6 76
Wiecbork, Pol. C13 16
Wieleń, Pol. D12 16
Wieliczka, Pol. F15 16
Wielkopolska, reg., Pol. E13 16
Wielkopolski Park
  Narodowy, p.o.i., Pol. D12 16
Wieluń, Pol. E14 16
Wien (Vienna), Aus. B13 22
Wien, state, Aus. B13 22
Wiener Neustadt, Aus. C13 22
Wienerwald, mts., Aus. B13 22
Wieprz, stm., Pol. E17 16
Wieprza, stm., Pol. B12 16
Wieprz-Krzna,
  Kanał, can., Pol. E19 16
Wierden, Neth. B15 14
Wiergate, Tx., U.S. F5 122
Wieruszów, Pol. E14 16
Wierzyca, stm., Pol. B14 16
Wiesbaden, Ger. F4 16
Wiesloch, Ger. G4 16
Wigan, Eng., U.K. H10 12
Wiggins, Co., U.S. A4 128
Wiggins, Ms., U.S. G9 122
Wight, Isle of, i., Eng., U.K. . . K11 12
Wigtown, Scot., U.K. G8 12

Wilbur, Wa., U.S. C8 136
Wilburton, Ok., U.S. C3 122
Wilcannia, Austl. H4 76
Wilcox, Sk., Can. D9 124
Wilcox, Ne., U.S. A9 128
Wildcat Creek, stm., In., U.S. . H3 112
Wildcat Hill, mtn., Sk., Can. . A11 124
Wild Coast, cst., S. Afr. H9 70
Wilder, Id., U.S. G9 136
Wilderness of Judaea
  (Midbar Yehuda), des., Asia . G6 58
Wildhay, stm., Ab., Can. C13 138
Wildhorse Creek, stm., U.S. . . G10 126
Wild Horse Lake, l.,
  Mt., U.S. B17 136
Wild Rice, stm., Mn., U.S. . . . D2 118
Wild Rice, stm., N.D., U.S. . . . H17 124
Wildrose, N.D., U.S. F10 124
Wild Rose, Wi., U.S. G9 118
Wildwood, Ab., Can. C15 138
Wildwood, N.J., U.S. F11 114
Wilge, stm., S. Afr. E9 70
Wilhelm, Mount, mtn.,
  Pap. N. Gui. b3 79a
Wilhelmina Gebergte,
  mts., Sur. C6 84
Wilhelmshaven, Ger. B3 70
Wilkerson Pass, p., Co., U.S. . B3 128
Wilkes-Barre, Pa., U.S. C10 114
Wilkesboro, N.C., U.S. H4 114
Wilkes Land, reg., Ant. C16 81
Wilkie, Sk., Can. B5 124
Willacoochee, Ga., U.S. E2 116
Willamette, stm., Or., U.S. . . . E3 136
Willamette, Middle Fork,
  stm., Or., U.S. G4 136
Willamina, Or., U.S. E3 136
Willandra Billabong
  Creek, stm., Austl. I5 76
Willandra National Park,
  p.o.i., Austl. I5 76
Willapa Bay, b., Wa., U.S. . . . D2 136
Willard, Mo., U.S. G4 120
Willard, Oh., U.S. C3 114
Willard, Ut., U.S. B4 132
Willard, Punta, c., Mex. A2 100
Willcox, Az., U.S. K7 132
Willcox Playa, l., Az., U.S. . . . K7 132
Willemstad, Neth. Ant. p22 104g
Willeroo, Austl. C6 74
William, Mount, mtn., Austl. . . K4 76
William "Bill" Dannelly
  Reservoir, res., Al., U.S. . . . E11 122
Williams, Az., U.S. H4 132
Williams, Ia., U.S. I5 118
Williams, Mn., U.S. C3 118
Williams, Austl. C3 76
Williamsburg, Ia., U.S. C5 120
Williamsburg, Ky., U.S. H1 114
Williamsburg, Va., U.S. G9 114
Williams Lake, B.C., Can. D8 138
Williamson, N.Y., U.S. E12 112
Williamson, W.V., U.S. G3 114
Williamson, stm., Or., U.S. . . . H5 136
Williamson, Mount, mtn.,
  Ca., U.S. G7 134
Williamsport, Pa., U.S. C8 114
Williamston, Mi., U.S. F5 112
Williamston, S.C., U.S. B3 116
Williamstown, Ky., U.S. F1 114
Williamstown, N.J., U.S. E11 114
Williamstown, W.V., U.S. E4 114
Williamsville, Il., U.S. L9 118
Willikies, Antig. f4 105b
Willimantic, Ct., U.S. C13 114
Willingboro, N.J., U.S. D10 114
Willis, Tx., U.S. G3 122
Willis Group, is., Austl. C10 74
Williston, Fl., U.S. G3 116
Williston, N.D., U.S. F10 124
Williston, S.C., U.S. C4 116
Williston Lake, res., B.C.,
  Can. D6 106
Willits, Ca., U.S. D2 134
Willmar, Mn., U.S. F3 118
Willoughby, Oh., U.S. C4 114
Willoughby Bay, b., Antig. . . . f4 105b
Willow, Ak., U.S. D10 140
Willow, stm., B.C., Can. C8 138
Willowbrook, Sk., Can. C10 124
Willow Bunch, Sk., Can. E8 124
Willow Bunch Lake, l.,
  Sk., Can. E8 124
Willow Creek, Ca., U.S. C2 134
Willow Creek, Mt., U.S. E15 136
Willow Creek, stm., Ab.,
  Can. F17 138
Willow Creek, stm., Or.,
  U.S. F9 136
Willow Lake, S.D., U.S. C15 126
Willow Lake, l., N.T.,
  Can. C7 106
Willowmore, S. Afr. H6 70
Willowra, Austl. D6 74
Willow Reservoir, res.,
  Wi., U.S. F9 118
Willows, Ca., U.S. D3 134
Willow Springs, Mo., U.S. . . . H6 120
Willowvale, S. Afr. H9 70
Wills Creek, stm., Austl. C3 76
Wills Point, Tx., U.S. E2 122
Wilmar, Ar., U.S. D6 122
Wilmer, Al., U.S. G10 122
Wilmer, Tx., U.S. E2 122
Wilmette, Il., U.S. F2 112
Wilmington, De., U.S. E10 114
Wilmington, N.C., U.S. B7 116
Wilmington, Oh., U.S. E2 114
Wilmington, Vt., U.S. H4 110
Wilmore, Ky., U.S. G13 120
Wilmot, S.D., U.S. F2 118
Wilpattu National Park,
  p.o.i., Sri L. G4 53
Wilsall, Mt., U.S. D16 136
Wilson, Austl. H2 76
Wilson, Ar., U.S. B8 122
Wilson, Ks., U.S. C10 128
Wilson, N.C., U.S. I8 114
Wilson, N.Y., U.S. E11 112
Wilson, Ok., U.S. G11 128
Wilson, stm., Austl. F4 76
Wilson, Cape, c., Nu., Can. . . B14 106
Wilson, Mount, mtn., Az.,
  U.S. H2 132
Wilson, Mount, mtn., Co.,
  U.S. F8 132
Wilson Lake, res., Al.,
  U.S. C11 122
Wilson Lake, res., Ks.,
  U.S. C10 128
Wilsons Promontory,
  pen., Austl. L6 76
Wilsons Promontory
  National Park, p.o.i., Austl. . L6 76
Wilsonville, Ne., U.S. A8 128
Wilton, Me., U.S. F6 110
Wilton, N.H., U.S. B14 114
Wilton, Wi., U.S. H8 118
Wilton, stm., Austl. B6 74
Wiluna, Austl. E4 74
Wimauma, Fl., U.S. I3 116
Wimberley, Tx., U.S. D9 130
Winamac, In., U.S. G3 112
Winburg, S. Afr. F8 70
Winchendon, Ma., U.S. B13 114
Winchester, Eng., U.K. J11 12

Winchester, Il., U.S. E7 120
Winchester, In., U.S. H5 112
Winchester, Ky., U.S. G14 114
Winchester, Tn., U.S. B12 122
Winchester, Va., U.S. E7 114
Wind, stm., Yk., Can. B3 106
Wind, stm., Wy., U.S. D4 126
Wind Cave National Park,
  p.o.i., S.D., U.S. D9 126
Winder, Ga., U.S. B2 116
Windermere, B.C., Can. F15 138
Windermere, Eng., U.K. G10 12
Windfall, Ab., Can. B14 138
Windhoek, Nmb. C3 70
Windigo, stm., Qc., Can. C3 110
Windom, Mn., U.S. H3 118
Windorah, Austl. E4 76
Window Rock, Az., U.S. H7 132
Wind River Peak, mtn.,
  Wy., U.S. E3 126
Wind River Range, mts.,
  Wy., U.S. D3 126
Windsor, Austl. I8 76
Windsor, N.S., Can. E12 110
Windsor, On., Can. F6 112
Windsor, Qc., Can. E5 110
Windsor, Eng., U.K. J12 12
Windsor, Ct., U.S. E13 114
Windsor, Co., U.S. C13 114
Windsor, Il., U.S. E9 120
Windsor, Mo., U.S. F4 120
Windsor, N.C., U.S. I9 114
Windsor, Va., U.S. H9 114
Windsor Forest, Ga., U.S. E4 116
Windsor Locks, Ct., U.S. C13 114
Windthorst, Tx., U.S. H10 128
Windward, Gren. p11 105e
Windward Islands, is., N.A. . . k6 105c
Windward Passage, strt.,
  N.A. C11 102
Windy Peak, mtn., Co., U.S. . . C2 128
Winfield, Al., U.S. D11 122
Winfield, Ks., U.S. D12 128
Winfield, Mo., U.S. F7 120
Winfield, W.V., U.S. F4 114
Wing, N.D., U.S. G13 124
Wingate, N.C., U.S. B5 116
Wingham, Austl. H9 76
Wingham, On., Can. E8 112
Winifreda, Arg. I7 16
Winisk, stm., On., Can. D13 106
Winisk, On., Can. E13 106
Winisk Lake, l., On., Can. E13 106
Wink, Tx., U.S. C4 130
Winkana, Mya. E4 48
Winkelman, Az., U.S. K6 132
Winkler, Mb., Can. E16 124
Winlock, Wa., U.S. D3 136
Winneba, Ghana. H4 64
Winnebago, Mn., U.S. H5 118
Winnebago, stm., Ia., U.S. . . . H5 118
Winnebago, Lake, l.,
  Wi., U.S. G10 118
Winneconne, Wi., U.S. G10 118
Winnemucca, Nv., U.S. B8 134
Winnemucca Lake, l.,
  Nv., U.S. C6 134
Winner, S.D., U.S. D13 126
Winnetka, Il., U.S. F2 112
Winnett, Mt., U.S. H5 124
Winnibigoshish, Lake,
  res., Mn., U.S. D4 118
Winnie, Tx., U.S. H4 122
Winning, Austl. D2 74
Winnipeg, Mb., Can. E16 124
Winnipeg, stm., Can. E11 106
Winnipeg, Lake, l., Mb.,
  Can. E11 106
Winnipeg Beach, Mb., Can. . . D17 124
Winnipegosis, Mb., Can. C13 124
Winnipegosis, Lake, l.,
  Can. B13 124
Winnipesaukee, Lake, l.,
  N.H., U.S. G5 110
Winnsboro, La., U.S. E7 122
Winnsboro, S.C., U.S. B4 116
Winnsboro, Tx., U.S. E3 122
Winnsboro Mills, S.C., U.S. . . B4 116
Winona, Ks., U.S. B7 128
Winona, Mn., U.S. G7 118
Winona, Mo., U.S. G6 120
Winona, Ms., U.S. D9 122
Winooski, stm., Vt., U.S. F4 110
Winschoten, Neth. A15 14
Winschoterdiep, can.,
  Neth. A15 14
Winsen, Ger. C6 16
Winslow, Az., U.S. H6 132
Winslow, In., U.S. F10 120
Winslow, Me., U.S. F7 110
Winsted, Ct., U.S. G4 118
Winston, Fl., U.S. H3 116
Winston, Or., U.S. G3 136
Winston-Salem, N.C., U.S. . . . H5 114
Winter, Wi., U.S. F8 118
Winter Garden, Fl., U.S. H4 116
Winter Harbor, Me., U.S. F8 110
Winter Harbour, B.C., Can. . . . F2 138
Winterhaven, Ca., U.S. K2 132
Winter Haven, Fl., U.S. I4 116
Winters, Ca., U.S. E3 134
Winterset, Ia., U.S. C4 120
Winterswijk, Neth. B15 14
Winterthur, Switz. C5 22
Winterville, Ms., U.S. D7 122
Winterville, N.C., U.S. A8 116
Winthrop, Wa., U.S. B6 136
Winthrop Harbor, Il., U.S. . . . F2 112
Wintinna, Austl. E6 74
Winton, N.C., U.S. H8 114
Winton, N.Z. H3 80
Winton, Austl. D4 76
Wiseman, Ak., U.S. C9 140
Wishek, N.D., U.S. A13 126
Wisła, Pol. G14 16
Wisła (Vistula), Pol. B14 16
Wiślany, Mierzeja, spit, Eur. . B15 16
Wisłok, stm., Pol. F17 16
Wisłoka, stm., Pol. F17 16
Wisner, La., U.S. E7 122
Wisner, Ne., U.S. I8 118
Wister, Ok., U.S. C4 122
Wisznice, Pol. E18 16
Witbank, S. Afr. D9 70
Witham, Eng., U.K. H12 12
Witham, stm., Eng., U.K. H12 12
Withlacoochee, stm., U.S. . . . F2 116
Witkowo, Pol. D13 16
Wit-Mfolozi, stm., S. Afr. F10 70
Witney, Eng., U.K. J11 12
Witnossob, stm., Nmb. D4 70
Witsand, S. Afr. I5 70
Witt, Il., U.S. E8 120
Wittenberg, Wi., U.S. G9 118
Wittenberge, Ger. C7 16
Wittenburg, Ger. C6 16
Wittenoom, Austl. D3 74
Wittingen, Ger. D6 16

Wittlich, Ger. G2 16
Wittmund, Ger. C3 16
Wittstock, Ger. C8 16
Witu Islands, is., Pap.
  N. Gui. a5 79a
Witvlei, Nmb. C4 70
Witwatersrand, mts., S. Afr. . . D8 70
Witzenhausen, Ger. E5 16
Wiżajny, Pol. B18 16
Wkra, stm., Pol. C15 16
Włdawa, Pol. E11 16
Włocławek, Pol. D15 16
Włocławek, state, Pol. D14 16
Włoszczowa, Pol. F15 16
Woburn, Ma., U.S. B14 114
Wodonga, Austl. K6 76
Wodzisław Śląski, Pol. G14 16
Wokam, Pulau, i., Indon. G10 44
Woking, On., Can. J12 12
Wokingham Creek, stm.,
  Austl. C4 76
Wolbrom, Pol. F15 16
Wolcott, In., U.S. D10 120
Wolcott, N.Y., U.S. E13 112
Wolcottville, In., U.S. G4 112
Woleai, at., Micron. C5 72
Wolf, stm., Ms., U.S. G9 122
Wolf, stm., Wi., U.S. G10 118
Wolf, stm., U.S. B9 122
Wolf, Volcán, vol., Ec. h11 84a
Wolfach, Ger. H4 16
Wolf Creek, Or., U.S. H3 136
Wolf Creek, stm., Mt., U.S. . . C17 136
Wolf Creek, stm., U.S. E9 128
Wolf Creek Pass, p., Co., U.S. . F10 132
Wolf Creek Reservoir,
  res., Ks., U.S. F2 120
Wolfeboro, N.H., U.S. G5 110
Wolfe Island, i., On., Can. . . . D13 112
Wolfen, Ger. E8 16
Wolfenbüttel, Ger. D6 16
Wolfforth, Tx., U.S. H6 128
Wolfhagen, Ger. E4 16
Wolf Lake, l., Ab., Can. B20 138
Wolf Point, Mt., U.S. F8 124
Wolfratshausen, Ger. I7 16
Wolf Rock, r., Eng., U.K. L7 12
Wolfsberg, Aus. D11 22
Wolfsburg, Ger. D6 16
Wolfville, N.S., Can. E12 110
Wolgast, Ger. B9 16
Woliński Park
  Narodowy, p.o.i., Pol. C10 16
Wollaston Lake, l., Sk., Can. . D10 106
Wollaston Peninsula,
  pen., Can. B7 106
Wollongong, Austl. J8 76
Wołomin, Pol. D17 16
Wolseley, Sk., Can. D10 124
Wolsey, S.D., U.S. C14 126
Wolverhampton, Eng., U.K. . . I11 12
Wolverton, Eng., U.K. I12 12
Wonarah, Austl. C7 74
Wonder Lake, Il., U.S. F8 76
Wondai, Austl. F8 76
Wonderland, Ca., U.S. C4 134
Wondinong, Austl. E3 74
Wonewoc, Wi., U.S. H8 118
Wŏnju, Kor., S. F7 38
Wonogiri, Indon. G7 50
Wonosari, Indon. G7 50
Wonosobo, Indon. G6 50
Wŏnsan, Kor., N. E7 38
Wonthaggi, Austl. L5 76
Wood, S.D., U.S. D12 126
Wood, stm., Ne., U.S. G13 126
Wood, Mount, mtn., Mt.,
  U.S. E17 136
Woodall Mountain, hill,
  Ms., U.S. C10 122
Woodbine, Ga., U.S. F4 116
Woodbine, Ia., U.S. C2 120
Woodbridge, Eng., U.K. I14 12
Woodbridge, Va., U.S. F8 114
Woodburn, Or., U.S. E4 136
Woodbury, N.J., U.S. E10 114
Woodbury, Tn., U.S. I11 120
Woodhull, Il., U.S. C7 120
Woodlake, Ca., U.S. G6 134
Woodland, Ca., U.S. E4 134
Woodland, Me., U.S. E9 110
Woodland, Pa., U.S. D7 114
Woodland Park, Co., U.S. C3 128
Woodridge, Mb., Can. E17 124
Wood River, Ne., U.S. G14 126
Woodroffe, Mount, mtn.,
  Austl. E6 74
Woodruff, Az., U.S. I6 132
Woodruff, S.C., U.S. B3 116
Woodruff, Wi., U.S. F9 118
Woods, Lake, l., Austl. C6 74
Woods, Lake of the, l., N.A. . . B3 118
Woodsboro, Tx., U.S. F10 130
Woodsfield, Oh., U.S. C15 114
Woodside, Austl. L6 76
Woodstock, Austl. A8 130
Woodstock, N.B., Can. D9 110
Woodstock, On., Can. E9 112
Woodstock, Eng., U.K. J11 12
Woodstock, Il., U.S. B9 120
Woodstock, N.Y., U.S. B11 114
Woodstock, Va., U.S. F7 114
Woodsville, N.H., U.S. F4 110
Woodville, Ms., U.S. F7 122
Woodville, N.Z. E6 80
Woodville, Al., U.S. C12 122
Woodville, Fl., U.S. F2 116
Woodville, Ms., U.S. F7 122
Woodville, Oh., U.S. G6 112
Woodville, Tx., U.S. G5 122
Woodward, Ok., U.S. B12 128
Woody, stm., Mb., Can. B12 124
Woody Head, c., Austl. G9 76
Woolmarket, Ms., U.S. G9 122
Woomera, Austl. F7 74
Woonsocket, R.I., U.S. B14 114
Woonsocket, S.D., U.S. C14 126
Woorabinda, Austl. E7 76
Wooramel, Austl. E2 74
Wooramel, stm., Austl. D2 74
Wooster, Oh., U.S. D3 114
Worcester, S. Afr. H4 70
Worcester, Eng., U.K. I10 12
Worcester, Ma., U.S. B14 114
Worden, Mt., U.S. A4 128
Wörgl, Aus. C9 22
Workington, Eng., U.K. G9 12
Worksop, Eng., U.K. H11 12
Worland, Wy., U.S. C5 126
Worms, Ger. G4 16
Worthing, Eng., U.K. K12 12
Worthington, In., U.S. E11 120
Worthington, Mn., U.S. H3 118
Worthington, Oh., U.S. D3 114
Worthington Peak, mtn.,
  Nv., U.S. E1 132
Wotje, at., Marsh. Is. B7 72
Wotu, Indon. E12 50
Wouhta, Nic. F6 102
Wounded Knee, S.D., U.S. . . . D10 126
Wounded Knee Creek,
  stm., S.D., U.S. D10 126
Wowan, Austl. E8 76
Wowoni, Pulau, i., Indon. F7 44
Woy Woy, Austl. I8 76

Wrangel Island see
  Vrangelja, ostrov, i., Russia . B24 34
Wrangell, Ak., U.S. E13 140
Wrangell, Cape, c., Ak., U.S. . g21 140a
Wrangell Mountains,
  mts., Ak., U.S. D11 140
Wrath, Cape, c., Scot., U.K. . . C8 12
Wrens, Ga., U.S. C3 116
Wrentham, Ab., Can. G18 138
Wrexham, Wales, U.K. H10 12
Wright, Mount, mtn.,
  B.C., Can. B14 136
Wright City, Mo., U.S. F6 120
Wright Patman Lake,
  res., Tx., U.S. D4 122
Wrightson, Mount, mtn.,
  Az., U.S. L6 132
Wrightstown, Wi., U.S. D1 112
Wrightsville, Ga., U.S. D3 116
Wrightsville Beach,
  N.C., U.S. B8 116
Wrigley, N.T., Can. C6 106
Wrigley, On., Can. I10 120
Wrocław (Breslau), Pol. E13 16
Wrocław, state, Pol. E13 16
Wrong Lake, l., Mb., Can. . . . B17 124
Wrottesley, Cape, c.,
  N.T., Can. B15 140
Wroxton, Sk., Can. C12 124
Września, Pol. D13 16
Wschowa, Pol. E12 16
Wu, stm., China. H3 42
Wu, stm., China. G7 42
Wu, stm., China. G2 42
Wu, stm., China. I5 42
Wu, stm., China. H4 42
Wubu, China. C4 42
Wuchang, China B7 38
Wuchang Hu, l., China. F7 42
Wuchin see Changzhou,
  China. F8 42
Wuchou see Wuzhou, China . . J4 42
Wuchow see Wuzhou, China . . J4 42
Wuchuan, China. K4 42
Wuchuan, China. A4 42
Wuchung see Wuzhong,
  China C2 42
Wuda, China. B2 42
Wudaoliang, China. D3 36
Wudi, China. C7 42
Wuding, China. F5 36
Wuding, stm., China. C4 42
Wufeng, China. F4 42
Wugang, China. H4 42
Wugong, China. D2 42
Wugong Shan, mts., China . . . H5 42
Wuhai, China. B2 42
Wuhan (Hankow), China. F6 42
Wuhsi see Wuxi, China. F9 42
Wuhsing see Huzhou, China. . F9 42
Wuhu, China. F8 42
Wuhua, China. J6 42
Wuhuanchi, China. C4 38
Wüjang, China. B7 54
Wujia, stm., China. A3 42
Wujiang, China. H2 42
Wukang, China. F8 42
Wukari, Nig. H6 64
Wukeshu, China. B7 38
Wulateqianqi, China. A3 42
Wuliang Shan, mts., China . . . G5 36
Wulong, China. G2 42
Wuluhan, Indon. H8 50
Wulumuch'i see
  Ürümqi, China C2 36
Wuluo, China. H3 42
Wuming, China. J3 42
Wundwin, Mya. B2 48
Wunnummin Lake, l., On.,
  Can. E13 106
Wunstorf, Ger. D5 16
Wupatki National
  Monument, p.o.i., Az., U.S. . H5 132
Wuppertal, Ger. E3 16
Wuppertal, S. Afr. H4 70
Wuqi, China. C3 42
Wuqia, China. B12 56
Wuqiang, China. B6 42
Wurno, Nig. G6 64
Würzburg, Ger. G5 16
Wurzen, Ger. E8 16
Wushan, China. F3 42
Wushenqi, China. B3 42
Wushi, China. F4 42
Wush'ee West, China. F9 42
Wusuli (Ussuri), stm., Asia . . . B11 36
Wutai, China. B5 42
Wutai Shan, mtn., China B5 42
Wutong, China. I3 42
Wutongqiao, China. F5 36
Wutsin see Changzhou,
  China. F8 42
Wuwei, China. D5 36
Wuwei, China. F7 42
Wuxi, China. F3 42
Wuxi, China. F9 42
Wuxiang, China. C5 42
Wuyang, China. H4 42
Wuyi, China. G8 42
Wuyishan, China. H7 42
Wuyuan, China. A3 42
Wuyuan, China. G7 42
Wuzhai, China. B4 42
Wuzhi Shan (Wuzhi Peak),
  mtn., China. L3 42
Wuzhong, China. C2 42
Wuzhou, China. J4 42
Wyaconda, stm., Mo., U.S. . . D6 120
Wyandotte, Mi., U.S. B2 114
Wyandra, Austl. F5 76
Wyangala, Lake, res.,
  Austl. J7 76
Wyatt, In., U.S. H3 112
Wycheproof, Austl. K4 76
Wye, stm., U.K. J10 12
Wyeville, Wi., U.S. G8 118
Wykoff, Mn., U.S. H6 118
Wymark, Sk., Can. D6 124
Wymondham, Eng., U.K. I13 12
Wymore, Ne., U.S. K2 118
Wyndham, Austl. C5 74
Wyndmere, N.D., U.S. B8 118
Wynne, Ar., U.S. B8 122
Wynniatt Bay, b., Can. A8 106
Wynne, Tx., U.S. E12 128
Wynot, Ne., U.S. H1 118
Wynyard, Austl. n12 77a
Wynyard, Sk., Can. C8 124
Wyodak, Wy., U.S. C7 126
Wyoming, On., Can. F7 112
Wyoming, Ia., U.S. B6 120
Wyoming, Mi., U.S. F4 112
Wyoming, state, U.S. E5 126
Wyoming Peak, mtn., Wy.,
  U.S. H16 136
Wyong, Austl. I8 76
Wyperfeld National
  Park, p.o.i., Austl. J3 76
Wysokie Mazowieckie, Pol. . . D18 16
Wyszków, Pol. D17 16
Wytheville, Va., U.S. H4 114

Name	Map Ref.	Page
X		
Xaafuun, Raas, c., Som.	B10	66
Xàbia, Spain	F11	20
Xaidulla, China	A4	46
Xainza, China	C12	54
Xai-Xai, Moz.	D11	70
Xalapa (Jalapa), Mex.	F10	100
Xalin, Som.	C9	66
Xam (Chu), stm., Asia	B7	48
Xambioá, Braz.	D1	88
Xambrê, stm., Braz.	A11	92
Xam Nua, Laos	B7	48
Xa-Muteba, Ang.	B2	68
Xan (San), stm., Asia	A9	48
Xangongo, Ang.	D2	68
Xankändi, Azer.	B6	56
Xánthi, Grc.	B7	28
Xanxerê, Braz.	C11	92
Xapecó, stm., Braz.	C11	92
Xapuri, Braz.	F4	84
Xaª Moron, stm., China.	C3	38
Xàtiva, Spain	F10	20
Xau, Lake, pl., Bots.	B7	70
Xavantina, Braz.	D6	90
Xaxim, Braz.	C11	92
Xcalak, Mex.	C4	102
X-Can, Mex.	B4	102
Xelva, Spain.	E9	20
Xenia, Oh., U.S.	E2	114
Xepenehe, N. Cal.	m16	79d
Xhumo, Bots.	B7	70
Xi, stm., China	J5	42
Xiachuan Dao, i., China	K5	42
Xiagaixin, China	A5	48
Xiamen (Amoy), China	I7	42
Xi'an (Sian), China	D3	42
Xianfeng, China	G3	42
Xiang, stm., China	G5	42
Xiangcheng, China	E5	42
Xiangfan, China	F4	42
Xianggang (Hong Kong), China.	J6	42
Xiangkhoang, Laos	C6	48
Xiangkhoang, Plateau de (Tran Ninh), plat., Laos	C6	48
Xiangning, China	D4	36
Xiangride, China	D4	36
Xiangshan, China	G9	42
Xiangtan, China	H5	42
Xiangxiang, China	H5	42
Xiangyin, China	G5	42
Xiangyuan, China	C5	42
Xiangzhou, China	G3	42
Xianju, China	G9	42
Xianshui, stm., China	B9	46
Xiantao, China	D3	42
Xianyang, China	G8	42
Xianyou, China	I8	42
Xiao, stm., China	G8	42
Xiaochengzi, China	C5	38
Xiaogan, China	F5	42
Xiaoguai, China	B1	36
Xiao Hinggan Ling (Lesser Khingan Range), mts., China.	B10	36
Xiaojin, China	E5	36
Xiaolan, China	B7	38
Xiaoluxi, stm., China	D2	38
Xiaopingyang, China	J3	42
Xiaoshan, China	F9	42
Xiaoxian, China	D7	42
Xiaoyi, China	C4	42
Xiapu, China	H9	42
Xiawa, China	C4	38
Xiaxian, China	D4	42
Xibo, stm., China	D3	38
Xichang, China	F5	36
Xichong, China	F1	42
Xicoténcatl, Mex.	D9	100
Xié, stm., Braz.	G8	86
Xifei, stm., China	E7	42
Xifeng, China	H2	42
Xifeng, China	C6	38
Xigazê, China	D12	54
Xihan, stm., China	F5	42
Xihe, China	F5	42
Xiheying, China	B6	42
Xihua, China	D1	42
Xiji, China	D1	42
Xiliao, stm., China	C5	38
Xilin, China	D11	54
Xilinhot, China	C2	38
Ximakou, China	E8	42
Ximalin, China	A6	42
Ximiao, China	C5	36
Xin, stm., China	G7	42
Xin'an, China	E4	42
Xin'anjiang Shuiku, res., China.	G8	42
Xinavane, Moz.	D11	70
Xin Barag Youqi, China	B8	36
Xin Barag Zuoqi, China	B8	36
Xinbin, China	D6	38
Xincai, China	E6	42
Xinchang, China	G9	42
Xincheng, China	B6	42
Xincheng, China	C3	42
Xindu, China	I4	42
Xinfeng, China	I6	42
Xinfeng Shuiku, res., China.	J6	42
Xing'an, China	A9	42
Xingcheng, China	H6	42
Xingguo, China	I6	42
Xinghai, China	D4	36
Xinghe, China	A5	42
Xinghua, China	E8	42
Xinglong, China	D1	42
Xingren, China	F6	36
Xingrenbu, China	C1	42
Xingtai, China	C6	42
Xingtang, China	B6	42
Xingu, stm., Braz.	D7	84
Xingxian, China	C4	42
Xingyi, China	F5	36
Xinhe, China	C6	42
Xinhua, China	H4	42
Xinhui, China	J5	42
Xining, China	D5	36
Xinji, China	D4	42
Xinjiang, China	D4	42
Xinjiang, state, China	A5	46
Xinjin, China	E5	36
Xinjin, China	B9	42
Xinjiulong (New Kowloon), China.	J6	42
Xinkai, stm., China	C5	38
Xinli, China	B7	38
Xinlitun, China	D5	38
Xinmin, China	C5	38
Xinning, China	H4	42
Xinshao, China	H4	42
Xintian, China	I5	42
Xinwen, China	D7	42
Xinxian, China	B5	42
Xinxian, China	F6	42
Xinxiang, China	D5	42
Xinxing, China	C8	38
Xinyang, China	E6	42
Xinye, China	E5	42
Xinyi, China	D4	42
Xinzhou, China	L3	42
Xinzhou, China	H6	42
Xiongyuecheng, China	A9	42
Xiping, China	E6	42
Xiping, China	G8	42
Xiqing Shan, mts., China	D4	36
Xique-Xique, Braz.	F4	88
Xirdalan, Azer.	B6	56
Xishanqiao, China	I7	42
Xisha Qundao (Paracel Islands), is., China	B5	50
Xishui, China	F6	42
Xiti, China	B9	54
Xiu, stm., China	G6	42
Xi Ujimqin Qi, China	B2	38
Xiushui, China	G6	42
Xiuyan, China	A10	42
Xiva, Spain	E10	20
Xixabangma Feng, mtn., China.	D10	54
Xixi, China	H8	42
Xixian, China	E6	42
Xixiang, China	E2	42
Xixona, Spain	F10	20
Xiyang, China	C5	42
Xizang (Tibet), state, China	B5	46
Xizi, China	D3	38
Xochicalco, sci., Mex.	F9	100
Xochistlahuaca, Mex.	G9	100
Xu, stm., China	H7	42
Xuancheng, China	F8	42
Xuan'en, China	F3	42
Xuang, stm., Laos	B6	48
Xuanhua, China	F2	42
Xuanhua, China	A6	42
Xuanwei, China	F5	36
Xuchang, China	D5	42
Xun, stm., China	J4	42
Xungru, China	D10	54
Xunwu, China	I6	42
Xuyong, China	H4	42
Xúquer see Júcar, stm., Spain.	E10	20
Xuwen, China	K4	42
Xuyi, China	E8	42
Xuyong, China	G1	42
Xuzhou, China	D7	42
Xylókastro, Grc.	E5	28
Y		
Yaak, Mt., U.S.	B11	136
Yaan, China	E5	36
Yaapeet, Austl.	J3	76
Yablonovy Range see Jablonovyj hrebet, mts., Russia.	F11	34
Yabluniv, Ukr.	A12	26
Yabrīn, Sau. Ar.	E6	56
Yabucoa, P.R.	B4	104a
Yabuli, China	B8	38
Yacambú, Parque Nacional, p.o.i., Ven.	C7	86
Yacata, i., Fiji	p20	79e
Yacheng, China	L3	42
Yachi, stm., China	H2	42
Yaco see Iaco, stm., S.A.	F4	84
Yacuiba, Bol.	D4	90
Yacuma, stm., Bol.	C3	90
Yadgir, India	C3	53
Yadkin, stm., N.C., U.S.	H4	114
Yadkinville, N.C., U.S.	H5	114
Yadong, China.	E12	54
Yafran, Libya	A2	62
Yagasa Cluster, i., Fiji	q20	79e
Yagoua, Cam.	B3	66
Yagradagzê Shan, mtn., China.	D4	36
Yaguajay, Cuba	A8	102
Yaguarón (Jaguarão), stm., S.A.	F11	92
Yaguas, stm., S.A.	I6	86
Yahe, China	B9	38
Yahk, B.C., Can.	G14	138
Yahualica, Mex.	E7	100
Yai, Khao, mtn., Thai.	I4	48
Yainax Butte, mtn., Or., U.S.	A4	134
Yaita, Japan	C12	40
Yaitopya see Ethiopia, ctry., Afr.	F7	62
Yaizu, Japan	E11	40
Yajiang, China	E5	36
Yakacik, Tur.	B7	58
Yakeshi, China	B9	36
Yakima, Wa., U.S.	D6	136
Yakima, stm., Wa., U.S.	D7	136
Yakmach, Pak.	D9	56
Yako, Burkina	G4	64
Yakoma, D.R.C.	D4	66
Yakumo, Japan	C14	38
Yaku-shima, i., Japan	I9	38
Yakutat Bay, b., Ak., U.S.	E11	140
Yakutia see Jakutija, state, Russia	D14	34
Yala, Thai.	I5	48
Yalahau, Laguna de, b., Mex.	B4	102
Yale, B.C., Can.	G9	138
Yale, Mi., U.S.	E7	112
Yale, Ok., U.S.	A2	122
Yale, Mount, mtn., Co., U.S.	C2	128
Yalgoo, Austl.	E3	74
Yalinga, C.A.R.	C4	66
Yalobusha, stm., Ms., U.S.	D9	122
Yalong, stm., China	E5	36
Yalova, Tur.	C12	28
Yalpuh, ozero, l., Ukr.	D15	26
Yalu (Amnok-kang), stm., Asia.	D7	38
Yalu, stm., China	D6	38
Yalvaç, Tur.	E14	28
Yamaga, Japan	F3	40
Yamagata, Japan	A13	40
Yamagata, state, Japan	A13	40
Yamaguchi, Japan	E4	40
Yamaguchi, state, Japan	E4	40
Yamal Peninsula see Jamal, poluostrov, pen., Russia.	B2	34
Yamanaka, Japan	C9	40
Yamanashi, state, Japan	D11	40
Yamasaki, Japan	D7	40
Yamaska, stm., Qc., Can.	E4	110
Yamatengwumulu, China	D4	36
Yamba, Austl.	G9	76
Yambio, Sudan	G5	62
Yamdena, Pulau, i., Indon.	G9	44
Yame, Japan	F3	40
Ya Men, b., China	J5	42
Yamethin, Mya.	B3	48
Yamma Yamma, Lake, l., Austl.	F3	76
Yamoussoukro, C. Iv.	H4	64
Yampa, stm., Co., U.S.	C8	132
Yampil', Ukr.	A15	26
Yamsay Mountain, mtn., Or., U.S.	H5	136
Yamuna, stm., India	F8	54
Yamzho Yumco, l., China	D13	54
Yan, stm., China	C4	42
Yan, stm., Sri L.	G5	53
Yanac, Austl.	K3	76
Yanagawa, Japan	F3	40
Yanai, Japan	F4	40
Yanam, India	C6	53
Yan'an, China	C4	42
Yanbu' al-Bahr, Sau. Ar.	E4	56
Yanceyville, N.C., U.S.	H6	114
Yanchang, China	C4	42
Yanchi, China	C2	42
Yanco Creek, stm., Austl.	J5	76
Yanda Creek, stm., Austl.	H5	76
Yandama Creek, stm., Austl.	G3	76
Yandé, Île, i., N. Cal.	m14	79d
Yandina, Sol. Is.	e8	79b
Yandoon, Mya.	D2	48
Yanfolila, Mali	G3	64
Yang, stm., Thai.	D7	48
Yangambi, D.R.C.	D4	66
Yang, stm., China	I7	42
Yangbajain, China	C13	54
Yangcheng, China	D5	42
Yangchiang see Yangjiang, China.	K4	42
Yangchou see Yangzhou, China.	E8	42
Yangchow see Yangzhou, China	E8	42
Yangch'üan see Yangquan, China	C5	42
Yangchun, China	J4	42
Yangdachengzi, China	B6	38
Yanggao, China	A5	42
Yanghexi, China	G3	42
Yangjiang, China	K4	42
Yangkü see Taiyuan, China	C5	42
Yangliuqing, China	B7	42
Yangon (Rangoon), Mya.	D2	48
Yangon, state, Mya.	D3	48
Yangpingguan, China	E1	42
Yangquan, China	C5	42
Yangriwan, China	F4	42
Yangsan, Kor., S.	D2	40
Yangshan, China	I5	42
Yangshuo, China	I4	42
Yangtze see Chang, stm., China.	F8	36
Yangtze see Jinsha, stm., China	F5	36
Yangxian, China	E2	42
Yangxin, China	G6	42
Yangyang, Kor., S.	A1	40
Yangyuan, China	A5	42
Yangzhou, China	E8	42
Yanhe, China	G3	42
Yanji, China	C8	38
Yanji, China	C8	38
Yanjiadian, China	B9	42
Yankeetown, Fl., U.S.	G3	116
Yankton, S.D., U.S.	E15	126
Yanqi, China	C2	36
Yanqing, China	A6	42
Yanshou, China	B8	38
Yantabulla, Austl.	G5	76
Yantai, China	C9	42
Yantan, China	G9	42
Yanting, China	F1	42
Yantongshan, China	C6	38
Yanzhou, China	D7	42
Yao, Chad	E3	62
Yaoundé, Cam.	D2	66
Yaoxian, China	D3	42
Yao Yai, Ko, i., Thai.	I4	48
Yap, i., Micron.	C4	72
Yapacana, Parque Nacional, p.o.i., Ven.	F8	86
Yapacani, Bol.	C4	90
Yapen, Pulau, i., Indon.	F10	44
Yapen, Selat, strt., Indon.	F10	44
Yappar, stm., Austl.	B4	76
Yaque del Norte, stm., Dom. Rep.	C12	102
Yaqui, stm., Mex.	G8	98
Yaquina, stm., Or., U.S.	F3	136
Yaracuy, state, Ven.	B7	86
Yaraka, Austl.	D5	76
Yardımcı, Tur.	A10	58
Yardımcı Burnu, c., Tur.	G13	28
Yari, stm., Col.	H5	86
Yariga-take, mtn., Japan	C10	40
Yarīm, Yemen	G5	56
Yaring, Thai.	I5	48
Yaritagua, Ven.	B7	86
Yarkand see Shache, China	B12	56
Yarkand see Yarkant, stm., China.	G13	32
Yarkant see Shache, China	B12	56
Yarkant, stm., China	G13	32
Yarloop, Austl.	F3	74
Yarmouth, N.S., Can.	G10	110
Yarmouth, Me., U.S.	G6	110
Yarmu, Pap. N. Gui.	a3	79a
Yarram, Austl.	L6	76
Yarraman, Austl.	F9	76
Yarrawonga, Austl.	K5	76
Yarumal, Col.	D4	86
Yasawa Group, is., Fiji	p18	79e
Yashiro-jima, i., Japan	F5	40
Yasinia, Ukr.	A11	26
Yasothon, Thai.	E6	48
Yass, Austl.	J7	76
Yasugi, Japan	D6	40
Yasuní, stm., Ec.	H3	86
Yasuni, Parque Nacional, p.o.i., Ec.	H4	86
Yata, stm., Bol.	B3	90
Yatağan, Tur.	F11	28
Yatê, N. Cal.	n16	79d
Yates City, Il., U.S.	D7	120
Yathkyed Lake, l., Nu., Can.	C11	106
Yating, China	I2	42
Yatsuga-take, mtn., Japan	D11	40
Yatsuo, Japan	C10	40
Yatsushiro, Japan	G3	40
Yatsushiro-kai, b., Japan	G3	40
Yatuá, stm., Ven.	G8	86
Yauca, Peru	G3	84
Yauco, P.R.	B2	104a
Yautepec, Mex.	F9	100
Yavari (Javari), stm., S.A.	D3	84
Yavaros, Mex.	B4	100
Yavatmāl, India	H7	54
Yaví, Cerro, mtn., Ven.	E9	86
Yavita, Ven.	F8	86
Yaviza, Pan.	H9	102
Yavoriv, Ukr.	G19	16
Yavuzeli, Tur.	A8	58
Yaw, stm., Mya.	B2	48
Yawatahama, Japan	F5	40
Yaxchilan, sci., Mex.	D2	102
Yayladağı, Tur.	C7	58
Yayuan, China	D7	38
Yazd, Iran	C7	56
Yazoo, stm., Ms., U.S.	E8	122
Yazoo City, Ms., U.S.	E8	122
Ybbs an der Donau, Aus.	B12	22
Yding Skovhøj, hill, Den.	I3	8
Ydra (Hydra), i., Grc.	F6	28
Ydra, i., Grc.	E6	28
Ye, Mya.	D3	48
Yebyu, Mya.	D3	48
Yecheng, China	B12	56
Yech'ŏn, Kor., S.	C1	40
Yecla, Spain	F9	20
Yedashe, Mya.	C3	48
Yedi Göller Milli Parkı, p.o.i., Tur.	B14	28
Yederan, stm., Nig.	G7	64
Yeeda, Austl.	C4	74
Yeghegnadzor, Arm.	B6	56
Yei, Sudan	G6	62
Yeji, China	F6	42
Yela Island, i., Pap. N. Gui.	B10	74
Yelarbon, Austl.	G8	76
Yell, i., Scot., U.K.	n18	12a
Yellandu, India	C5	53
Yellow see Huang, stm., China.	D8	36
Yellow, stm., Wi., U.S.	F7	118
Yellow, stm., Wi., U.S.	G8	118
Yellow Grass, Sk., Can.	E9	124
Yellowhead Pass, p., Can.	D12	138
Yellow House Draw, stm., Tx., U.S.	H3	122
Yellowknife, N.T., Can.	C8	106
Yellowknife, stm., N.T., Can.	C8	106
Yellow Sea, s., Asia	B7	108
Yellowstone, stm., U.S.	B7	108
Yellowstone, Clarks Fork, stm., U.S.	B3	126
Yellowstone Falls, wtfl., Wy., U.S.	F16	136
Yellowstone Lake, l., Wy., U.S.	F16	136
Yellowstone National Park, Wy., U.S.	F16	136
Yellowstone National Park, p.o.i., U.S.	F16	136
Yellowtail Dam, dam, Mt., U.S.	B4	126
Yellville, Ar., U.S.	H5	120
Yelverton Bay, b., Nu., Can.	A9	141
Yemen, ctry., Asia	F6	56
Yenagoa, Nig.	H6	64
Yenangyaung, Mya.	B2	48
Yenanma, Mya.	C2	48
Yen Bai, Viet.	B7	48
Yench'eng see Yancheng, China.	E9	42
Yenchi see Yanji, China	C8	38
Yenda, Austl.	J6	76
Yenderé, Burkina	G4	64
Yendi, Ghana	H4	64
Ye-ngan, Mya.	B3	48
Yengisar, China	B12	56
Yengo National Park, p.o.i., Austl.	I8	76
Yenice, Tur.	A6	58
Yenice, stm., Tur.	B15	28
Yenicekale, Tur.	A7	58
Yenierenköy, N. Cyp.	C5	58
Yenimehmetli, Tur.	D15	28
Yenipazar, Tur.	C13	28
Yenişehir, Tur.	C12	28
Yenisey see Enisej, stm., Russia.	C6	34
Yenshuichen, Tai.	J9	42
Yentai see Yantai, China	C9	42
Yeola, India	H5	54
Yeo Lake, l., Austl.	E4	74
Yeovil, Eng., U.K.	K10	12
Yepachic, Mex.	A4	100
Yeppoon, Austl.	D8	76
Yerevan (Erivan), Arm.	A5	56
Yerington, Nv., U.S.	E7	134
Yerlisu, Tur.	C9	28
Yermo, Ca., U.S.	I9	134
Yerupajá, Nevado, mtn., Peru	F2	84
Yerushalayim (Jerusalem), Isr.	G6	58
Yesa, Embalse de, res., Spain.	B9	20
Yeşildere, Tur.	A4	58
Yeşilköy, Tur.	C11	28
Yeşiltepe, Tur.	A3	58
Yeso, N.M., U.S.	G4	128
Yetman, Austl.	G8	76
Yetti, reg., Afr.	D3	64
Ye-u, Mya.	A2	48
Yeu, Île d', i., Fr.	H6	14
Yevlax, Azer.	A6	56
Yexian, China	E5	42
Yexian, China	C8	42
Yeywa, Mya.	B3	48
Ygatimí, Para.	B10	92
Yguazú, stm., Para.	B10	92
Yhú, Para.	B10	92
Yi'an, China	B10	36
Yibin, China	F5	36
Yibug Caka, l., China	B11	54
Yichang, China	F4	42
Yicheng, China	F4	42
Yicheng, China	C5	42
Yichuan, China	D5	42
Yichuan, China	C3	42
Yichuan see Yinchuan, China	B2	42
Yichun, China	B10	36
Yichun, China	H6	42
Yidie, China	C4	42
Yidu, China	F4	42
Yidu, China	C8	42
Yifeng, China	G6	42
Yığılca, Tur.	C14	28
Yilan, China	B10	36
Yilaxi, China	C7	38
Yiliang, China	F5	36
Yilong, China	F2	42
Yin, stm., Mya.	A2	48
Yinbaing, Mya.	D3	48
Yinchuan, China	B2	42
Ying, stm., China	E6	42
Yingcheng, China	F5	42
Yingcheng see Yingchengzi, China.	B6	38
Yingchengzi, China	B6	38
Yingde, China	I5	42
Yingjing, stm., China	C3	38
Yingkou, China	A10	42
Yingpan, China	I2	42
Yingpan, China	G4	42
Yingshan, China	F5	42
Yingshouyingzi, China	A7	42
Yingtan, China	G7	42
Yingxian, China	B5	42
Yining, China	F14	32
Yinjiang, China	G3	42
Yinmabin, Mya.	A2	48
Yinmatu, stm., China	D2	38
Yinnyein, Mya.	D3	48
Yin Shan, mts., China	C6	36
Yi'ong, stm., China	E3	36
Yirga 'Alem, Eth.	F7	62
Yirol, Sudan	F6	62
Yishan, China	I3	42
Yishui, China	D8	42
Yitong, China	C6	38
Yitulihe, China	A9	36
Yiwu, China	F3	36
Yiwu, China	G8	42
Yixian, China	A8	42
Yixing, China	F8	42
Yixun, stm., China	A7	42
Yiyang, China	G5	42
Yiyang, China	C5	42
Yiyang, China	C8	42
Yizhang, China	I5	42
Ylä-Kitka, l., Fin.	C13	8
Yli-li, Fin.	D11	8
Ylivieska, Fin.	D11	8
Ymer Ø, i., Grnld.	C21	141
Ynykčanskij, Russia	D16	34
Yoakum, Tx., U.S.	E10	130
Yocona, stm., Ms., U.S.	C9	122
Yog Point, c., Phil.	C5	52
Yogyakarta, Indon.	H7	50
Yoho National Park, p.o.i., B.C., Can.	E14	138
Yōka, Japan	D7	40
Yokadouma, Cam.	D2	66
Yōkaichi, Japan	D9	40
Yokkaichi, Japan	E9	40
Yoko, Cam.	C2	66
Yokohama, Japan	D12	40
Yokosuka, Japan	D12	40
Yokote, Japan	E14	38
Yola, Nig.	H7	64
Yolombó, D.R.C.	D4	66
Yom, stm., Thai.	D5	48
Yonago, Japan	D6	40
Yoncalla, Or., U.S.	G3	136
Yonezawa, Japan	B12	40
Yong'an, China	I7	42
Yongcheng, China	D7	42
Yǒngch'ǒn, Kor., S.	D1	40
Yongchuan, China	G1	42
Yongchun, China	I7	42
Yongdeng, China	D5	36
Yǒngdǒk, Kor., S.	C2	40
Yongding, stm., China	A6	42
Yǒngdong, Kor., S.	F7	38
Yongfeng, China	H6	42
Yonggi, Kor., S.	C1	40
Yōngil-man, b., Kor., S.	C2	40
Yŏngju, Kor., S.	C1	40
Yongkang, China	G9	42
Yongle, stm., China	H5	42
Yongning, China	J3	42
Yongning, China	B1	42
Yongqing, China	B6	42
Yongren, China	F5	36
Yongshan, China	F5	36
Yongshou, China	D2	42
Yongtai, China	I8	42
Yongxing, China	H5	42
Yongxing, China	B4	42
Yongxiu, China	G6	42
Yongzhou, China	H4	42
Yonibana, S.L.	H2	64
Yonkers, N.Y., U.S.	D12	114
Yonne, state, Fr.	G12	14
Yonne, stm., Fr.	F12	14
Yopal, Col.	E5	86
Yopurga, China	B12	56
York, Austl.	F3	74
York, Eng., U.K.	H11	12
York, Al., U.S.	E10	122
York, N.D., U.S.	F14	124
York, Pa., U.S.	E9	114
York, S.C., U.S.	A4	116
York, Cape, c., Austl.	B8	74
York, Kap, c., Grnld.	B12	141
Yorke Peninsula, pen., Austl.	F7	74
Yorketown, Austl.	G7	74
York Factory, Mb., Can.	D12	106
Yorkshire Dales National Park, p.o.i., Eng., U.K.	G10	12
York Sound, strt., Austl.	B4	74
Yorkton, Sk., Can.	C11	124
Yorktown, Tx., U.S.	E10	130
Yorktown, Va., U.S.	G9	114
Yorkville, Il., U.S.	J10	118
Yorkville, N.Y., U.S.	E14	112
Yoro, Hond.	E4	102
Yoron-jima, i., Japan	l19	39a
Yosemite National Park, p.o.i., Ca., U.S.	F6	134
Yosemite Village, Ca., U.S.	F6	134
Yoshii, stm., Japan	E7	40
Yōsōbulag see Altay, Mong.	B4	36
Yos Sudarso, Pulau, i., Indon.	G10	44
Yōsu, Kor., S.	G7	38
You, stm., China	G6	36
Youbou, B.C., Can.	H6	138
Youghal, Ire.	J5	12
Young, Austl.	J7	76
Young, Sk., Can.	C8	124
Young, Ur.	F9	92
Younghusband Peninsula, pen., Austl.	K2	76
Young Island, i., Ant.	B21	81
Youngs Rock, r., Pit.	c28	78k
Youngstown, Ab., Can.	C2	124
Youngstown, N.Y., U.S.	E10	112
Youngstown, Oh., U.S.	C5	114
Youngsville, La., U.S.	G6	122
Youngsville, N.C., U.S.	H7	114
Yountville, Ca., U.S.	E3	134
Youssoufia, Mor.	C3	64
Youxian, China	H5	42
Youyang, China	G3	42
Yōyang-ni, Kor., S.	B1	40
Yozgat, Tur.	B3	56
Ypres see Ieper, Bel.	D11	14
Ypsilanti, Mi., U.S.	B2	114
Yreka, Ca., U.S.	B3	134
Yrghyz, Kaz.	E10	32
Ysabel Channel, strt., Pap. N. Gui.	a4	79a
Ystad, Swe.	I5	8
Ystädeh-ye Moqor, Āb-e, l., Afg.	B2	54
Ytterhogdal, Swe.	E6	8
Yu, stm., China	J3	42
Yuam, stm., Thai.	C3	48
Yuan see Red, stm., Asia	D9	46
Yuan, stm., China	H6	42
Yuan, stm., China	G4	42
Yuanling, China	G4	42
Yuanmou, China	F5	36
Yuantan, China	J5	42
Yuanyang, China	D5	42
Yuasa, Japan	E8	40
Yuba City, Ca., U.S.	D4	134
Yūbari, Japan	C15	38
Yucaipa, Ca., U.S.	I8	134
Yucatán, state, Mex.	B3	102
Yucatán, Península de (Yucatan Peninsula), pen., N.A.	C2	102
Yucatan Channel, strt., N.A.	B4	102
Yucatan Peninsula see Yucatán, Península de, pen., N.A.	C2	102
Yucca, Az., U.S.	I2	132
Yucca Mountain, mtn., Nv., U.S.	G9	134
Yucca Valley, Ca., U.S.	I9	134
Yucheng, China	C7	42
Yuci, China	C5	42
Yudu, China	I6	42
Yuechi, China	F2	42
Yueqing, China	G9	42
Yueyang, China	G5	42
Yufa, China	B7	42
Yugan, China	G7	42
Yugoslavia see Serbia and Montenegro, ctry., Eur.	F6	26
Yuhebu, China	C3	42
Yuhuang Dao, i., China	C9	42
Yuhuang Ding, mtn., China.	C8	42
Yukon, Ok., U.S.	F11	128
Yukon, state, Can.	B3	106
Yukon, stm., N.A.	D7	140
Yukon Flats, sw., Ak., U.S.	C11	140
Yukuhashi, Japan	F3	40
Yuli, China	C2	36
Yüli, Tai.	J9	42
Yulin, China	B3	42
Yulin, China	L3	42
Yuma, Az., U.S.	K2	132
Yuma, Co., U.S.	A6	128
Yuma, Bahía de, b., Dom. Rep.	C13	102
Yumare, Ven.	B7	86
Yumbel, Chile	H1	92
Yumbo, Col.	F3	86
Yumen, China	D4	36
Yumenzhen, China	C8	36
Yumt uul, mtn., Mong.	B5	36
Yuna, stm., Dom. Rep.	C13	102
Yunak, Tur.	E14	28
Yuncheng, China	D4	42
Yuncheng, China	D6	42
Yungay, Chile	H2	92
Yungchi see Jilin, China	C7	38
Yungchia see Wenzhou, China.	G9	42
Yungning see Nanning, China.	J3	42
Yun Ling, mts., China	F4	36
Yun Ling, mts., China	E5	36
Yunnan, state, China	G5	36
Yunnanfu see Kunming, China.	F5	36
Yunta, Austl.	I2	76
Yunwu Shan, mtn., China	A7	42
Yunxi, China	E4	42
Yunxian, China	E4	42
Yunxiao, China	I7	42
Yunyang, China	F3	42
Yunyang see Yunxian, China.	E4	42
Yunzalin, stm., Mya.	D3	48
Yuping, China	H3	42
Yuqing, China	H2	42
Yurimaguas, Peru	E2	84
Yuriria, Laguna de, l., Mex.	E8	100
Yuruá see Juruá, stm., S.A.	D8	84
Yuruari, stm., Ven.	D11	86
Yurubi, Parque Nacional, p.o.i., Ven.	B7	86
Yurungkax, stm., China	A5	46
Yuscarán, Hond.	F4	102
Yūsef, Bahr (Yūsuf, Bahr), can., Egypt	K1	58
Yushan, China	G8	42
Yü Shan, mtn., Tai.	J9	42
Yushanzhen, China	G3	42
Yushu, China	E4	36
Yushu, China	B7	38
Yutai, China	D7	42
Yutian, China	B7	42
Yuty, Para.	C9	92
Yūtz'u see Yuci, China	C5	42
Yuxian, China	B6	42
Yuxian, China	C5	42
Yuxian, China	D5	42
Yuyao, China	F9	42
Yuzawa, Japan	E14	38
Z		
Zaandam see Zaanstad, Neth.	B13	14
Zaanstad, Neth.	B13	14
Zabalac', Bela.	G7	10
Zăbalţ, Rom.	C8	26
Zabīd, Yemen	F5	56
Zabinka, Bela.	H6	10
Zabkowice Śląskie, Pol.	F12	16
Žabljak, Serb.	F6	26
Żabno, Pol.	F16	16
Zābol, Iran	C9	56
Zābol, state, Afg.	C1	54
Zabolotiv, Ukr.	A12	26
Zabor'e, Bela.	E12	10
Zabore, Russia	F15	10
Zabory, Russia	F14	16
Zabrze, Pol.	F14	16
Zabyčanne, Bela.	G14	10
Zacapa, Guat.	E3	102
Zacapu, Mex.	F8	100
Zacatecas, Mex.	D7	100
Zacatecas, state, Mex.	D7	100
Zacatelco, Mex.	F10	100
Zacoalco de Torres, Mex.	E7	100
Zacualtipan, Mex.	E9	100
Zadar (Zara), Cro.	F12	22
Zadetkale Kyun, i., Mya.	G3	48
Zadetkyi Kyun, i., Mya.	H3	48
Zadoi, China	B8	46
Za'farāna, well, Egypt	I3	58
Zafer Burnu, c., N. Cyp.	C5	58
Zafirovo, Blg.	F13	26
Zafra, Spain	F4	20
Żagań, Pol.	E11	16
Zagare, Lith.	D6	10
Zagazig, Egypt	H2	58
Zaghouan, Tun.	H4	24
Zaghouan, Jebel, mtn., Tun.	H4	24
Zagora, Mor.	C3	64
Zagórz, Pol.	G18	16
Zagreb, Cro.	E12	22
Zagros, Kūhhā-ye, mts., Iran	C7	56
Zagros Mountains see Zāgros, Kūhhā-ye, mts., Iran	C7	56
Zāhedān, Iran	D9	56
Zahirābād, India	C3	53
Zahlah, Leb.	E6	58
Zahnitkiv, Ukr.	A15	26
Zahrebetnoe, Russia	B17	8
Zaire see Congo, Democratic Republic of the, ctry., Afr.	E4	66
Zaire see Congo, stm., Afr.	F2	66
Zajecar, Serb.	E9	26
Zajsan see Zaysam, Kaz.	E14	32
Zajsan, ozero see Zhaysang köli, l., Kaz.	E14	32
Zaka, Zimb.	B10	70
Zakamensk, Russia	F9	34
Zakarpattia, co., Ukr.	A10	26
Zakhidnyi Buh (Bug) (Buh), stm., Eur.	D17	16
Zakho, Iraq	B5	56
Zakliczyn, Pol.	G16	16
Zakopane, Pol.	G16	16
Zakouma, Chad	E3	62
Zakroczym, Pol.	D16	16
Zākros, sci., Grc.	H9	28
Zákynthos, i., Grc.	F3	28
Zala, state, Hung.	C4	26
Zalaegerszeg, Hung.	C4	26
Zalamea de la Serena, Spain.	F5	20
Zalantun, China	B9	36
Zalāri, Russia	D18	32
Zalău, Rom.	B10	26
Zalim, Sau. Ar.	E5	56
Zalingei, Sudan	E4	62
Zaludok, Bela.	G7	10
Zama, Ms., U.S.	E9	122
Zamakh, Yemen	F6	56
Zambeze (Zambezi), stm., Afr.	D5	68
Zambezi, stm., Afr.	D3	68
Zambezi Escarpment, clf., Zimb.	D4	68
Zambia, ctry., Afr.	C4	68
Zamboanga, Phil.	G3	52
Zamboanga Peninsula, pen., Phil.	G3	52
Zambrów, Pol.	C18	16
Zambyl see Taraz, Kaz.	F12	32
Zameņagša, Russia	D24	8
Zami, stm., Mya.	D4	48
Zamora, Ec.	D2	84
Zamora, Spain.	C5	20
Zamora, co., Spain.	C4	20
Zamora de Hidalgo, Mex.	F7	100
Zamość, Pol.	F19	16
Zamość, state, Pol.	F19	16
Zanaga, Congo	E2	66
Záncara, stm., Spain.	E8	20
Zanda, China	B6	54
Zanesville, Oh., U.S.	E4	114
Zangla, India	B6	54
Zanjān, Iran	B6	56
Zanjón, stm., Arg.	C5	92
Zante see Zákynthos, i., Grc.	F3	28
Zanthus, Austl.	F4	74
Zanzibar, Tan.	F7	66
Zanzibar Channel, strt., Tan.	F7	66
Zaostrove, Russia	F14	8
Zaō-zan, vol., Japan.	A13	40
Zaozërnyj, Russia	C16	32
Zaozhuang, China	D7	42
Zap, N.D., U.S.	G12	124
Zapadnaja Dvina, Russia	D15	10

Name	Map Ref.	Page
Zapadna Morava, stm., Serb.	F8	26
Zapadno-Sibirskaja ravnina (West Siberian Plain), pl., Russia.	B12	32
Zapadnyj hrebet, mts., Russia	F17	34
Zapadnyj Sajan, mts., Russia	D16	32
Západočeský kraj, state, Czech Rep.	G9	16
Západoslovenský Kraj, state, Slov.	H14	16
Zapala, Arg.	G2	90
Zapata, Tx., U.S.	H8	130
Zapata, Península de, pen., Cuba	A7	102
Zapatoca, Col.	D5	86
Zapatosa, Ciénaga de, l., Col.	C5	86
Zapljuse, Russia	B12	10
Zapole, Russia	B12	10
Zapoljarnyj, Russia	B14	8
Zapopan, Mex.	E7	100
Zaporizhzhia, Ukr.	E5	32
Zaprudnja, Russia	C10	38
Zaqatala, Azer.	A6	56
Zaragoza, Mex.	A8	100
Zaragoza, Mex.	C1	130
Zaragoza (Saragossa), Spain.	C10	20
Zaragoza, co., Spain	C9	20
Zarajsk, Russia	F21	10
Zaranj, Afg.	C9	56
Zarasai, Lith.	E9	10
Zárate, Arg.	G8	92
Zarautz, Spain	A8	20
Zarauz see Zarautz, Spain	A8	20
Zaraza, Ven.	C9	86
Zareče, Russia	C14	8
Zarečensk, Russia	C14	8
Zarghon Shahr, Afg.	C10	56
Zaria, Nig.	G6	64
Żarki, Pol.	F15	16
Žarma see Zharma, Kaz.	E14	32
Zărnești, Rom.	D12	26
Zarubino, Russia	C9	38
Zarumilla, Peru.	D1	84
Zary, Pol.	E11	16
Zarzaïtine, Alg.	D6	64
Zarzal, Col.	E4	86
Zasa, Lat.	D8	10
Zāskār, stm., India	B6	54
Zāskār Mountains, mts., Asia	B7	54
Zaslavje, Bela.	F10	10
Zastava, Russia	G22	8
Zasule, Russia	D22	8
Žatec, Czech Rep.	F9	16
Zatyshshya, Ukr.	B16	26
Zavalla, Tx., U.S.	F4	122
Zave, Zimb.	D5	68
Zavet, Blg.	F13	26
Zavodoukovsk, Russia.	C11	32
Zavodovski Island, i., S. Geor.	K12	81
Zavolžsk, Russia	H20	8
Zawadzkie, Pol.	F14	16
Zawiercie, Pol.	F15	16
Żawiyat al-Mukhaylá, Libya	A4	62
Zaysan, Kaz.	E14	32
Zaysan, Lake see Zhaysang köli, l., Kaz.	E14	32
Zayü, stm., China	C8	46
Zayzan see Zaysan, Kaz.	E14	32
Zaza, stm., Cuba	B8	102
Zaza, Presa, res., Cuba	B8	102
Zbąszynek, Pol.	D11	16
Zbraslav, Czech Rep.	G10	16
Žd'ár nad Sazavou, Czech Rep.	G11	16
Ždiar, Slov.	G16	16
Zduńska Wola, Pol.	E14	16
Zearing, Ia., U.S.	B4	120
Zeballos, B.C., Can.	G4	138
Zebedelia, S. Afr.	D9	70
Zebulon, Ga., U.S.	C1	116
Zedang, China	D13	54
Zeebrugge, Bel.	C11	14
Zeehan, Austl.	n12	77a
Zeeland, Mi., U.S.	F4	112
Zeeland, N.D., U.S.	B13	126
Zeerust, S. Afr.	D7	70
Žefat, Isr.	F6	58
Zehdenick, Ger.	D9	16
Zeil, Mount, mtn., Austl.	D6	74
Zeist, Neth.	B14	14
Zeitz, Ger.	E8	16
Zeja, Russia	F14	34
Zeja, stm., Russia	F14	34
Zejskoe vodohranilišče, res., Russia	F14	34
Zelee, Cape, c., Sol. Is.	e9	79b
Zelenoborskij, Russia.	C14	8
Zelenogorsk, Russia	F13	8
Zelenograd, Russia	D20	10
Zelenogradsk, Russia	F3	10
Zelenokumsk, Russia	F6	32
Železnodorožnyj, Russia	B8	32
Železnodorožnyj, Russia	F4	10
Železnogorsk, Russia	H18	10
Železnogorsk-Ilimskij, Russia	C18	32
Zelienople, Pa., U.S.	D5	114
Zella-Mehlis, Ger.	F6	16
Zell am See, Aus.	C9	22
Zell am Ziller, Aus.	C8	22
Žel'va, Bela.	G7	10
Želva, Lith.	E8	10
Žemaitijos nacionalnis parkas, p.o.i., Lith.	D4	10
Zembin, Bela.	F11	10
Zembra, Île, i., Tun.	G4	24
Zémio, C.A.R.	C4	66
Zempoala, sci., Mex.	F10	100
Zemun, Serb.	E7	26
Zeng, stm., China	J5	42
Zenica, Bos.	E4	26
Zenon Park, Sk., Can.	A10	124
Zentsūji, Japan	E6	40
Zenza do Itombe, Ang.	B1	68
Zephyr, Tx., U.S.	C9	130
Zephyrhills, Fl., U.S.	H3	116
Zepu, China	B12	56
Zeravšan, stm., Asia	B10	56
Zeravšanskij hrebet, mts., Asia	B10	56
Zerbst, Ger.	D8	16
Żerków, Pol.	D13	16
Zerqan, Alb.	C14	24
Žešart, Russia	E23	8
Zeulenroda, Ger.	F7	16
Zeven, Ger.	C5	16
Zevenaar, Neth.	E2	16
Zeydābād, Afg.	A2	54
Zeytinbağı, Tur.	C11	28
Zêzere, stm., Port.	E2	20
Zgierz, Pol.	E15	16
Zgorzelec, Pol.	E11	16
Zhabuchaka Hu, l., China	C9	54
Zhakou, China.	F5	42
Zhaltyr, Kaz.	D12	32
Zhambyl see Taraz, Kaz.	F12	32
Zhambyl, Kaz.	E12	32
Zhang, stm., China	I6	42
Zhang, stm., China	C5	42
Zhangaözen, Kaz.	F8	32
Zhanga Qalqotan, Kaz.	D11	32
Zhangaqazaly, Kaz.	E10	32
Zhangatas, Kaz.	F11	32
Zhangbei, China	A6	42
Zhangguangcai Ling, mts., China	B8	38
Zhanghuang, China	K3	42
Zhangjiakou, China	A6	42
Zhangping, China	I7	42
Zhangpu, China	I7	42
Zhangqiu, China	C7	42
Zhangshuping, China	F4	42
Zhangwu, China	C5	38
Zhangye, China	D5	36
Zhangzhou, China	I7	42
Zhānibek, Kaz.	E7	32
Zhanjiang, China	K4	42
Zhanyu, China	B5	38
Zhao'an, China	J7	42
Zhaodong, China	A7	38
Zhaojue, China	C9	46
Zhaoping, China	I4	42
Zhaoqing, China	J5	42
Zhaotong, China	F5	36
Zhaoxing, China	B11	36
Zhaoyuan, China	B10	36
Zharí Namco, l., China	C10	54
Zharkent, Kaz.	F13	32
Zharma, Kaz.	E14	32
Zharsuat, Kaz.	E12	32
Zhaxi Co, l., China	B10	54
Zhaxigang, China	B7	54
Zhaysang köli, l., Kaz.	E14	32
Zhayylma, Kaz.	D10	32
Zhayya see Ural, stm.	E8	32
Zhayyq see Ural, stm.	E8	32
Zhecheng, China	D6	42
Zhegu, China	D13	54
Zhejiang, state, China	G8	42
Zhelezinka, Kaz.	D13	32
Zhelin, China	F9	42
Zhem see Embi, stm., Kaz.	E9	32
Zhenbeikou, China	B2	42
Zheng'an, China	G2	42
Zhengding, China	B6	42
Zhenghe, China	H8	42
Zhenglan Qi, China	C8	36
Zhengning, China	D3	42
Zhengyang, China	E6	42
Zhengzhou, China	D5	42
Zhenhai, China	G9	42
Zhenjiang, China	E8	42
Zhenlai, China	B9	36
Zhenning, China	H1	42
Zhenping, China	E5	42
Zhentou, stm., China	E6	42
Zhenxiong, China	F5	36
Zhenyu, China	H9	42
Zhenyuan, China	H3	42
Zhenyuan, China	D2	42
Zherong, China	H8	42
Zhetiqara, Kaz.	D10	32
Zhezdi, Kaz.	E11	32
Zhezqazghan, Kaz.	E11	32
Zhijiang, China	H3	42
Zhixia, China	G8	42
Zhob, Pak.	C2	54
Zhob, stm., Pak.	C10	56
Zholymbet, Kaz.	D12	32
Zhongba, China	C5	46
Zhongdian, China	F4	36
Zhongning, China	C1	42
Zhongpingchang, China	F3	42
Zhongshan, China	J5	42
Zhongshan, China	I4	42
Zhongshan, sci., Ant.	B12	81
Zhongtiao Shan, mts., China	D4	42
Zhongwei, China	C1	42
Zhongxian, China	F3	42
Zhongxiang, China	F5	42
Zhongyaozhan, China	F14	34
Zhosaly, Kaz.	E10	32
Zhoucun, China	C7	42
Zhouning, China	H8	42
Zhoushan Dao, i., China	F9	42
Zhoushan Qundao, is., China	F10	42
Zhouzhi, China	D3	42
Zhuanghe, China	B10	42
Zhuanglang, China	D1	42
Zhucheng, China	C7	42
Zhuhe, China	G5	42
Zhuji, China	G9	42
Zhujia Jian, i., China	G10	42
Zhujiang Kou, est., Asia.	J5	42
Zhumadian, China	E5	42
Zhuolu, China	A6	42
Zhuozhou, China	B6	42
Zhuozi, China	A5	42
Zhushan, China	E4	42
Zhuxi, China	E3	42
Zhuzhou, China	H5	42
Zhympity, Kaz.	D8	32
Zhytomyr, Ukr.	E14	6
Zi, stm., China	C8	42
Zi, stm., China	G4	42
Ziārat, Pak.	C10	56
Zibo, China	C8	42
Zichang, China	C3	42
Ziębice, Pol.	F13	16
Zielona Góra, Pol.	E11	16
Zielona Góra, state, Pol.	D11	16
Zierikzee, Neth.	C12	14
Ziesar, Ger.	D8	16
Zifta, Egypt	H2	58
Žigalovo, Russia	D19	32
Žigansk, Russia	C13	34
Zigong, China	F5	36
Zigui, China	F4	42
Ziguinchor, Sen.	G1	64
Zihuatanejo, Mex.	G8	100
Ziiyang, China	E3	42
Zijin, China	J6	42
Zikhron Ya'aqov, Isr.	F5	58
Žilaja Tambica, Russia	E17	8
Žilino, Russia	F4	10
Zillah, Libya	B3	62
Zillertaler Alpen (Aurine, Alpi), mts., Eur.	C8	22
Zilupe, Lat.	D11	10
Zilwaukee, Mi., U.S.	E6	112
Zima, Russia	D18	32
Zimapán, Mex.	E9	100
Zimbabwe, ctry., Afr.	D4	68
Zimbabwe Ruins, sci., Zimb.	B10	70
Zimi, S.L.	H2	64
Zimnicea, Rom.	F12	26
Zimonino, Russia	G14	10
Zinder, Niger	G6	64
Zinga Mulike, Tan.	F7	66
Zion, Il., U.S.	F2	112
Zion National Park, p.o.i., Ut., U.S.	F4	132
Zionsville, In., U.S.	I3	112
Zipaquirá, Col.	E5	86
Zirbitzkogel, mtn., Aus.	C11	22
Žirjatino, Russia.	G16	10
Žirovnice, Czech Rep.	G11	16
Zitong, China	F1	42
Zittau, Ger.	F10	16
Ziway, Lake see Ziway Häyk', l., Eth.	F7	62
Ziway Häyk', l., Eth.	F7	62
Zixi, China	H6	42
Ziya, stm., China	B7	42
Ziyang, China	I4	42
Ziyuan, China	I4	42
Zizdra, stm., Russia	F19	10
Zizhou, China	C3	42
Žižica, Russia	D14	10
Žižickoe, ozero, l., Russia	D14	10
Zlaté Moravce, Slov.	H14	16
Zlatoust, Russia	C9	32
Zlatoustovsk, Russia	F15	34
Zlín, Czech Rep.	G13	16
Zlīţan, Libya	A2	62
Złobin, Bela.	H13	10
Złoczew, Pol.	E14	16
Złotoryja, Pol.	E11	16
Złotów, Pol.	C13	16
Zlynka, Russia	H14	10
Zmeinogorsk, Russia.	D14	32
Žmigród, Pol.	E12	16
Zmiïnyj, ostriv, i., Ukr.	D17	26
Znamenka, Russia	F17	10
Znamensk, Russia	F4	10
Znamenskoe, Russia	C12	32
Žnin, Pol.	D13	16
Znojmo, Czech Rep.	H12	16
Zoar, S. Afr.	H5	70
Žodzina, Bela.	F11	10
Zoétélé, Cam.	D2	66
Zogang, China	F4	36
Žohova, ostrov, i., Russia	A19	34
Zohreh, stm., Iran	C7	56
Zolotaja Gora, Russia	F14	34
Zomba, Mwi.	D6	68
Zonguldak, Tur.	B14	28
Zonguldak, state, Tur.	B15	28
Zonza, Fr.	H15	18
Zorita, Spain	E5	20
Zorra, Arroyo de la, stm., Mex.	E6	130
Zouar, Chad	C3	62
Zouérat, Maur.	E2	64
Zoug see Zug, Switz.	C5	22
Zouxian, China	D7	42
Zovka, Russia	B11	10
Zrenjanin, Serb.	D7	26
Zuata, stm., Ven.	C9	86
Zubaydīyah, Jabal az-, mtn., Syria	E8	58
Zubovo, Russia	F17	8
Zudáñez, Bol.	C4	90
Zuera, Spain	C10	20
Zufar (Dhofar), reg., Oman.	F7	56
Zug, Switz.	C5	22
Zugdidi, Geor.	F6	32
Zuger See, l., Switz.	C5	22
Zugspitze, mtn., Eur.	I6	16
Zújar, stm., Spain	F5	20
Žukopa, Russia	D15	10
Žukovka, Russia	G16	10
Žukovskij, Russia	E21	10
Zuli, stm., China	D1	42
Zulia, state, Ven.	C5	86
Zulia, stm., S.A.	C5	86
Zululand, hist. reg., S. Afr.	F10	70
Zumbo, Moz.	D5	68
Zumbrota, Mn., U.S.	G6	118
Zungeru, Nig.	H6	64
Zunhua, China	A7	42
Zuni, stm., U.S.	I7	132
Zuni Pueblo, N.M., U.S.	H8	132
Zunyi, China	H2	42
Zuo, stm., China	J2	42
Zuodeng, China	J2	42
Zuomuchedong Hu, l., China	D12	54
Zuoyun, China	A5	42
Žuravičy, Bela.	G13	10
Zürich (Zurigo), Switz.	C5	22
Zurich, Lake see Zürichsee, l., Switz.	C5	22
Zürichsee, l., Switz.	C5	22
Zurigo see Zürich, Switz.	C5	22
Zurmi, Nig.	G6	64
Zuša, stm., Russia	G19	10
Žut, Otok, i., Cro.	G12	22
Zutphen, Neth.	B15	14
Zuwārah, Libya	A2	62
Zuwayzā, Jord.	G6	58
Zvenigorod, Russia	E19	10
Zvezdec, Blg.	G14	26
Zvezdnyj, Russia.	C19	32
Zvishavane, Zimb.	B9	70
Zvolen, Slov.	H15	16
Zwedru, Lib.	H3	64
Zweibrücken, Ger.	G3	16
Zweisimmen, Switz.	D4	22
Zwickau, Ger.	F8	16
Zwierzyniec, Pol.	F18	16
Zwoleń, Pol.	E17	16
Zwolle, Neth.	B14	14
Zwolle, La., U.S.	F5	122
Żyrardów, Pol.	D16	16
Zyrjanka, Russia	C19	34
Zyrjanovsk see Zyryanovsk, Kaz.	E14	32
Zyrjanskoe, Russia	C15	32
Zyryan see Zyryanovsk, Kaz.	E14	32
Zyryanovsk, Kaz.	E14	32
Žytkavičy, Bela.	H10	10
Żywiec, Pol.	G15	16